Transformational Interventions for Business, Technology, and Healthcare

Darrell Norman Burrell
Marymount University, USA

IGI Global
PUBLISHER of TIMELY KNOWLEDGE

A volume in the Advances in Business Strategy and Competitive Advantage (ABSCA) Book Series

Published in the United States of America by
IGI Global
Business Science Reference (an imprint of IGI Global)
701 E. Chocolate Avenue
Hershey PA, USA 17033
Tel: 717-533-8845
Fax: 717-533-8661
E-mail: cust@igi-global.com
Web site: http://www.igi-global.com

Library of Congress Cataloging-in-Publication Data

Names: Burrell, Darrell Norman, 1966- editor.
Title: Transformational interventions for business, technology, and healthcare / edited by Darrell Burrell.
Description: Hershey, PA : Business Science Reference, [2024] | Includes bibliographical references and index. | Summary: "This book embarks on a profound exploration of the intricate and continually evolving terrain of diversity, equity, inclusion, and organizational development across the realms of Healthcare, Education, Business, and Technology"-- Provided by publisher.
Identifiers: LCCN 2023040273 (print) | LCCN 2023040274 (ebook) | ISBN 9798369316344 (hardcover) | ISBN 9798369316351 (ebook)
Subjects: LCSH: Organizational change. | Social responsibility of business. | Diversity in the workplace. | Personnel management--Technological innovations. | Medical care--Technological innovations. | Computer security.
Classification: LCC HD58.8 .T6973 2024 (print) | LCC HD58.8 (ebook) | DDC 352.3/67--dc23/eng/20231005
LC record available at https://lccn.loc.gov/2023040273
LC ebook record available at https://lccn.loc.gov/2023040274

This book is published in the IGI Global book series Advances in Business Strategy and Competitive Advantage (ABSCA) (ISSN: 2327-3429; eISSN: 2327-3437)

British Cataloguing in Publication Data
A Cataloguing in Publication record for this book is available from the British Library.

Advances in Business Strategy and Competitive Advantage (ABSCA) Book Series

Patricia Ordóñez de Pablos
Universidad de Oviedo, Spain

ISSN:2327-3429
EISSN:2327-3437

Mission

Business entities are constantly seeking new ways through which to gain advantage over their competitors and strengthen their position within the business environment. With competition at an all-time high due to technological advancements allowing for competition on a global scale, firms continue to seek new ways through which to improve and strengthen their business processes, procedures, and profitability.

The **Advances in Business Strategy and Competitive Advantage (ABSCA) Book Series** is a timely series responding to the high demand for state-of-the-art research on how business strategies are created, implemented and re-designed to meet the demands of globalized competitive markets. With a focus on local and global challenges, business opportunities and the needs of society, the **ABSCA** encourages scientific discourse on doing business and managing information technologies for the creation of sustainable competitive advantage.

Coverage

- Innovation Strategy
- Differentiation Strategy
- Value Chain
- Outsourcing
- Entrepreneurship & Innovation
- Balanced Scorecard
- Ethics and Business Strategy
- Strategy Performance Management
- Globalization
- Customer-Orientation Strategy

IGI Global is currently accepting manuscripts for publication within this series. To submit a proposal for a volume in this series, please contact our Acquisition Editors at Acquisitions@igi-global.com or visit: http://www.igi-global.com/publish/.

The Advances in Business Strategy and Competitive Advantage (ABSCA) Book Series (ISSN 2327-3429) is published by IGI Global, 701 E. Chocolate Avenue, Hershey, PA 17033-1240, USA, www.igi-global.com. This series is composed of titles available for purchase individually; each title is edited to be contextually exclusive from any other title within the series. For pricing and ordering information please visit http://www.igi-global.com/book-series/advances-business-strategy-competitive-advantage/73672. Postmaster: Send all address changes to above address.

Titles in this Series

For a list of additional titles in this series, please visit: http://www.igi-global.com/book-series/advances-business-strategy-competitive-advantage/73672

Handbook of Research on Designing Sustainable Strategies to Develop Entrepreneurial Intention
Ramakrishna Yanamandra (Skyline University College, UAE) and Logaiswari Indiran (Universiti Teknologi Malaysia, Malaysia)
Business Science Reference • © 2023 • 642pp • H/C (ISBN: 9781668487815) • US $295.00

Strategic Management and International Business Policies for Maintaining Competitive Advantage
Ailson J. De Moraes (Royal Holloway University of London, UK)
Business Science Reference • © 2023 • 411pp • H/C (ISBN: 9781668468456) • US $295.00

Digital Natives as a Disruptive Force in Asian Businesses and Societies
Omkar Dastane (UCSI Graduate Business School, UCSI University, Malaysia) Aini Aman (Universiti Kebangsaan Malaysia, Malaysia) and Nurhizam Safie Bin Mohd Satar (Universiti Kebangsaan Malaysia, Malaysia)
Business Science Reference • © 2023 • 322pp • H/C (ISBN: 9781668467824) • US $250.00

Handbook of Research on Sustainable Consumption and Production for Greener Economies
Richa Goel (Symbiosis International University, India) and Sukanta Kumar Baral (Indira Gandhi National Tribal University, India)
Business Science Reference • © 2023 • 481pp • H/C (ISBN: 9781668489697) • US $295.00

Cases on the Resurgence of Emerging Businesses
Shefali Saluja (Chitkara Business School, Chitkara University, India) Dhiresh Kulshrestha (Chitkara Business School, Chitkara University, India) and Sandhir Sharma (Chitkara Business School, Chitkara University, India)
Business Science Reference • © 2023 • 316pp • H/C (ISBN: 9781668484883) • US $265.00

Handbook of Research on Sustainability Challenges in the Wine Industry
Bartolomé Marco-Lajara (University of Alicante, Spain) Armand Gilinsky (Sonoma State University, USA) Javier Martínez-Falcó (University of Alicante, Spain & Stellenbosch University, South Africa) and Eduardo Sánchez-García (University of Alicante, Spain)
Business Science Reference • © 2023 • 435pp • H/C (ISBN: 9781668469422) • US $295.00

Opportunities and Challenges of Business 5.0 in Emerging Markets
Sumesh Dadwal (Northumbria University, UK) Pawan Kumar (Lovely Professional University, India) Rajesh Verma (Lovely Professional University, India) and Gursimranjit Singh (Lovely Professional University, India)
Business Science Reference • © 2023 • 357pp • H/C (ISBN: 9781668464038) • US $250.00

IGI Global
PUBLISHER of TIMELY KNOWLEDGE

701 East Chocolate Avenue, Hershey, PA 17033, USA
Tel: 717-533-8845 x100 • Fax: 717-533-8661
E-Mail: cust@igi-global.com • www.igi-global.com

Table of Contents

Detailed Table of Contents

Cybercrime costs an estimated $575 billion per year and healthcare continues to be the most targeted sector in the world. News headlines are rife with data leaks and data breach incidents. These breaches lead to the theft of personal, financial, and health information from users who are often only notified of the breach well after it occurred, and the damage has already been done. Insider threats can be loosely categorized as malicious or negligent, based on their intent (or lack thereof). This case study focuses on one such malicious incident where a ring of hospital employees was indicted for allegedly selling patient credit card and medical information online. The authors provide practitioners with a deeper understanding of how PII is misused, motivations for its theft, and recommendations to avoid such incidents in their own organizations.

Sustainability should encompass social and environmental bottom lines with the expectations of also securing financial stability in the context of business operations. With sustainability as a business, social, ecological, or environmental system, it is important to understand that each system has its unique challenges that require resolution. Approaches and solutions in response to these unique systems may differ, but the need for sustainability and corporate social responsibility (CSR) is a universal imperative for long-term success. The primary focus of this chapter examines themes relating to leadership and management dynamics that influence sustainability strategy development, analysis, and the future direction of corporate sustainability and CSR.

Cybersecurity criminals often use social engineering techniques to meet their objectives. The most egregious cybersecurity attacks may be designed to get an organization to override defenses, change standards, or convince governing bodies to change laws and regulations through political pressure, espionage, or litigation. By creating cultures of trust or mistrust, organizational leaders can be persuaded to declassify information or make changes that allow such adversaries to gain access to things that are unavailable to them. Through time and strategy, cybercriminals can weaken cybersecurity defense capabilities and awareness. Organizations people trust may use social engineering against consumers through online advertisements, cookies, and spyware to gather data, like IP addresses, location histories, and browsing preferences, for gain and profit. This study highlights areas where social engineering tools are designed into devices and activities to influence behavior in personal and professional settings.

Ultrasonic imaging has proven to be a valuable tool in kidney diagnosis, providing essential information about kidney size, shape, position, and function; and detecting structural abnormalities like cysts, stones, and infections. However, its effectiveness in kidney diagnostics is subject to operator expertise, leading to potential variations in image interpretation and diagnostic outcomes. It is crucial to explore automated approaches and computer-assisted diagnosis systems to address these challenges and enhance kidney diagnostics. Regrettably, the integration of such systems into kidney diagnostics has not been extensively investigated. Therefore, this study confirms the proposal of using a random forest classifier to detect kidney Nephrolithiasis. Notably, the classifier achieved an impressive accuracy of 96.33% compared to other machine learning classifiers, utilizing a test dataset of 100 kidney images.

This study aims to analyze some of the theoretical, conceptual, and methodological implications between organizational anthropology and ethnography. Departing from the assumption that ethnographic analysis and interpretive research on organizational anthropology has an emergent and symbolic role rooted in social processes and with no a priori assumptions, with explanations and categories defined by the organizational actors. The method employed is based on analytical and descriptive issues from the theoretical and empirical literature review leading to reflective analysis. It is concluded that ethnographic methodology is pertinent to be used in the analysis of its interactions, with organizational anthropology as a new specialty in organizational studies.

Research shows that 70-90% of mergers and acquisitions (M&As) fail due to culture clashes. The number of mergers and acquisitions in the healthcare industry has been increasing, driving the need for better change management practices. Hospital mergers and acquisitions are essential for financially struggling hospitals, especially rural hospitals. This chapter explores the value of management consulting interventions as tool to make mergers in healthcare more effective.

The cyberattack called SolarWinds carried out against the United States government has been characterized as a collective leadership failure. The United States Federal Government is confronted with the brutal reality of an understaffed or under-skilled cybersecurity workforce and a need for more competent leaders. The focus of federal organizations is increasingly shifting toward management and organizational efficiency. As a result, more and more of these companies are turning to executive coaching to strengthen the leadership abilities of government supervisors. Executive coaching has emerged as a prominent trend in recent years, becoming increasingly popular in pursuing organizational performance, business capacity, and leadership development. This study uses a qualitative research approach to explore the value and benefit of executive leadership coaching as a tool for developing technical managers.

Agent-based modeling (ABM) serves as a powerful and innovative tool to evaluate and address cybersecurity risks in the auto industry. With the increasing integration of advanced technologies in modern vehicles, the potential vulnerabilities and threats to cybersecurity have become a major concern. ABM allows cybersecurity experts to simulate complex interactions among autonomous agents representing various components of the automotive ecosystem, such as vehicles, manufacturers, suppliers, and hackers. ABM can effectively model real-world scenarios and assess how cyber threats propagate and spread throughout the system. It enables the identification of critical points of weakness and potential attack vectors, aiding in the development of proactive strategies to mitigate cybersecurity risks. Through iterative simulations and data-driven analysis, ABM empowers stakeholders in the auto industry to make informed decisions and implement robust security measures that safeguard against cyber-attacks, ensuring the safety and trustworthiness of connected and autonomous vehicles.

This chapter explores "violence against women" as a social justice and public health issue. Violence against women is a form of discrimination and inequality that violates human rights. It is a gross violation of a person's right to life, liberty, and security, and is one of the most pervasive human rights issues in the United States. It disproportionately affects women of color, LGBTQ+ individuals, and other marginalized communities, often in more extreme and dangerous forms. It is a public health issue, as it can cause physical and psychological harm to victims and lead to long-term health problems, such as depression and anxiety. It can cause economic hardship for victims, as domestic violence and sexual assault often result in job loss, missed work days, and decreased productivity. Violence against women is a safety issue, as it can lead to increased fear and insecurity in public spaces, making it difficult for women to access services, work, and participate in public life. This chapter explores the topic through a review of current and emerging literature.

Laborera is a fictional company. The company is a cloud-based software vendor that specializes in human capital management applications. Laborera is entangled in a class action discrimination suit for its artificial intelligence tools that allegedly prescreen and disqualify applicants in protected categories. Porter's five forces model and McKinsey's strategic horizons offer a framework for strategic review. Deal and Kennedy and the Denison organizational culture model are used to strengthen Laborera's organizational culture. The Bridges transition model and the McKinsey 7-S model enable transition and thoughtful organizational change management. Laborera improves ethical decision making, including decision processes involving a human-machine team, using the fairness/justice approach, and the common good approach. This case study demonstrates theoretical applications of risk management for software companies desiring to leverage artificial intelligence within innovative software applications.

Medical devices, from wearable health trackers to pacemakers and telehealth visits, have become increasingly prevalent. Addressing concerns about data privacy and risk management is essential with the amount of personal data collected through these devices rising. While the Health Insurance Portability and Accountability Act (HIPAA) has long been considered the primary regulation for patient personal health information data, the Food and Drug Administration (FDA) and the Healthcare Supply Chain Association (HSCA) have enacted new guidelines that aim to hold medical device manufacturers accountable for data privacy and risk management. The chapter concludes that these legal regulations individually touch upon essential aspects of patient data privacy and medical device safety; however, their combined influence provides a more substantial base to hold medical de-vice manufacturers responsible for risk management and data protection.

Cyber threats have become a major concern in today's world. As the United States Department of Defense (DoD) increasingly relies on the military supply chain systems to support the operations of their military forces, cyber threats have the potential to cause significant damage. These systems are responsible for the transportation, storage, and distribution of materials and equipment from the supplier to the end user, which includes both military personnel and civilian personnel. It is also responsible for the acquisition, maintenance, and disposal of materials and equipment. The purpose of this chapter is to examine the critical cyber threats posed to the DoD military supply chain systems and provide recommendations to address them.

and technology.

Generative artificial intelligence (GAI) has made outstanding strides in recent years, with a good-sized impact on software product management. Drawing on pertinent articles from 2016 to 2023, this systematic literature evaluation reveals generative AI's potential applications, benefits, and constraints in this area. The study shows that technology can assist in idea generation, market research, customer insights, product requirements engineering, and product development. It can help reduce development time and costs through automatic code generation, customer feedback analysis, and more. However, the technology's accuracy, reliability, and ethical consideration persist. Ultimately, generative AI's practical application can significantly improve software product management activities, leading to more efficient use of resources, better product outcomes, and improved end-user experiences.

The human brain plays a significant role in controlling the behavior of the human body with respect to sensory stimuli, external/internal motor stimuli, and so on. EEG signals are informative signals that contain knowledge about the condition of the brain. They are nonstationary and nonlinear in nature and so, it is hard to detect the subtle yet significant changes in the signals using just the human eye. This gives engineers the opportunity to apply numerous algorithms for the detection of such subtle yet significant changes in EEG signals. Various algorithms have been developed and are being used to extract the important features from EEG signals. It has been established through research that the nonlinear features of EEG mostly comprise the abrupt transitions and its chaotic and random behavior. In this chapter, the effect of EEG signals on diagnosing 6 brain disorders, namely, epilepsy, autism, Alzheimer's disease, Parkinson's disease, schizophrenia, and ischemic brain stroke, is discussed in detail.

This chapter examined the internal control procedures for an organization's purchasing card program. Utilizing the results of the company's most recent audit, it was found that inefficiencies existed in the company's internal control processes. The data provided also indicated that processes and procedures are not currently in place for the acceptable use of the company's credit card. This lack of policies and procedures led to the misappropriation of funds. Theoretical and practical implications were discussed in this chapter. This study reveals how a risk management plan can protect the institution and the employees.

This case study describes the experience of an organization in crisis. An audit conducted by the company's board of directors revealed that directors have been charging personal expenses to their company charge cards. The company is losing an average of $375,000 per year to this practice. The former chief financial officer has resigned after two years of bringing this to the attention of the chief operating officer and the chief executive officer. Now the organization has new management in these three positions, but they need to find a strategy to manage the situation, which remains the same. The application of strategy models, organizational culture theories, ethical decision-making theories, and leadership theories are recommended as solutions to correct the unwanted behavior. Finally, the implementation of an accountable plan is recommended along with policy and procedure surrounding expenses.

The complex and time-consuming nature of magnetic resonance imaging (MRI) may make it difficult to autonomously diagnose tumors in the brain, possibly leading to erroneous detection and classification. Identifying brain tumors is a complex process due primarily to relying on multiple modules for a comprehensive evaluation. In response, advances in deep learning have paved the way for automated medical image analysis and diagnostics. Convolutional neural networks (CNNs) are crucial for visual learning and image classification. The current investigation presents a novel approach for data augmentation that is integrated with state-of-the-art models, namely Efficient-NetB0, VGG16, ResNet50, InceptionV3, and MobileNetV2, to accurately classify various types of brain tumors, including glioma, meningioma, and pituitary tumors. The algorithm was subjected to testing utilizing benchmark data from existing literature.

This chapter discusses the future of the retail industry, driven by innovation, employee centricity, and digital transformation. The emerging trend of "phygital" marketing, blending physical and digital experiences for a seamless customer journey, is explored. Digitalization, digitization, and digital transformation are defined as methods for transforming the business model. Phygital marketing enhances customer engagement through interactive and immersive experiences. The impact of digitalization and innovation on various aspects of the business model is highlighted. The pandemic accelerated the shift towards phygital marketing, with social media and e-commerce playing a crucial role. By embracing phygital marketing, companies can engage with diverse customers and build lasting relationships.

The increasing prevalence of cybercrime poses significant challenges to small businesses, which often lack the resources and expertise to effectively manage their cybersecurity risk. This chapter investigates the potential of cybersecurity communities of practice (CoPs) as a viable solution to support small businesses in addressing these challenges and mitigating the risks associated with cybercrime. By participating in CoPs, small businesses can pool resources, share knowledge, and develop innovative strategies to tackle cybersecurity challenges. The collaborative nature of these communities enables small businesses to leverage collective knowledge and experiences, obtain unique insights from experts across diverse disciplines, and receive invaluable feedback from peers. In conclusion, the chapter argues that cybersecurity CoPs can play a vital role in enhancing the cybersecurity practices of small businesses, reducing cybercrime costs, and ultimately strengthening their overall cybersecurity risk management.

Humanity is currently experiencing an influx of threats against the global supply chain. Many of them have resulted in catastrophic outcomes. It has never been more critical for organizations and governments to tackle this vital issue. Developing nations amid digital transformation efforts are especially vulnerable. In this chapter, the researcher lays the foundation for a phenomenological qualitative study in Botswana. The author briefly provides background on supply chain cybersecurity and Industry 4.0. The methodology of an ongoing study in Botswana is presented, including its purpose, research design, data-gathering procedures, and protocol. The significance of the study, as well as limitations and delimitations, are described. The research questions aim to paint a holistic picture of the examined topic. The author includes some notable responses to offer a glance through the eyes of the participants on the investigated phenomenon. The researcher aims to continue with the analysis within a subsequent academic item.

Preface

Welcome to *Transformational Interventions for Business, Technology, and Healthcare*. Within the pages of this edited reference book, we embark on a profound exploration of the intricate and continually evolving terrain of diversity, equity, inclusion, and organizational development across the realms of Healthcare, Education, Business, and Technology. Our primary objective is to furnish an all-encompassing resource that offers tangible insights and innovative strategies for confronting the pressing challenges that modern organizations grapple with in today's intricate world.

The words of esteemed diversity expert Vernā Myers, who stated that "Diversity is being invited to the party; inclusion is being asked to dance," hold a profound resonance as we navigate the multifaceted issues shaping contemporary workplaces. The seismic shifts in the job market and impactful social movements, such as the #MeToo movement and Black Lives Matter protests, have brought about unprecedented transformation in organizational dynamics.

This convergence of events, coupled with the rapid stride of technological progress, presents both opportunities and obstacles. It is within this dynamic context that we jump into the core of this book, dissecting the intersections of diversity, inclusion, equity, and organizational efficacy. Through a multidisciplinary lens, we scrutinize how these themes intersect and exert influence across diverse sectors.

At the heart of our exploration stands Organizational Development (OD), a vehicle for effecting change. OD, which entails refining existing processes, crafting new paradigms, and devising solutions to intricate organizational conundrums, takes the spotlight. This book underscores the utmost importance of progress—a goal that assumes varied dimensions in differing contexts. Our intent is to elucidate the evolving concepts of equity, inclusiveness, collaboration, efficiency, and efficacy, and their ramifications throughout the lifecycle of organizations.

The focal point of this book is to offer a comprehensive, interdisciplinary academic approach that dissects the real-world consequences of multifaceted organizational challenges. Our goal is to present progressive, actionable solutions that tackle challenges head-on, rectify detrimental dynamics, and cultivate an environment that reveres rights, embraces diversity, and amplifies all voices.

Our audience is wide-ranging, encompassing university faculty, professionals in healthcare, education, technology, leadership, psychology, social science, and business, along with doctoral students, management consultants, corporate leaders, researchers, diversity and inclusion professionals, and policymakers. The covered topics are equally diverse, spanning from workplace dynamics and technological strides to healthcare disparities and the nuances of organizational metamorphosis.

Within the ensuing pages, distinguished scholars and practitioners contribute their insights, experiences, and expertise to illuminate these pivotal issues. The breadth and depth of topics aim to offer a holistic comprehension of the challenges at hand while presenting actionable strategies that drive constructive transformation.

In the following section, we delve into a comprehensive chapter overview that provides a glimpse into the wealth of knowledge and insights this book has to offer. Each chapter tackles a unique facet of the complex interplay between diversity, equity, inclusion, and organizational development in the domains of Healthcare, Education, Business, and Technology. From cybersecurity risk management in the biotechnology and healthcare sectors to the intricate dynamics of sustainability and environmental racism, the authors explore critical topics with depth and nuance. These chapters offer a roadmap to navigate the multifaceted challenges faced by organizations today and illuminate practical strategies that drive positive change.

In Chapter 1, the focus shifts to the realm of cybercrime, where the staggering $575 billion annual cost and healthcare sector vulnerability take center stage. Through a compelling case study, the malicious sale of patient information is dissected, highlighting the motives behind data breaches. The chapter offers practitioners insights into the misuse of Personally Identifiable Information (PII), delving into the motivations for its theft and furnishing recommendations to fortify organizations against such incidents.

Chapter 2 digs into the intricate world of sustainability within the domain of business. With a keen eye on leadership and management dynamics, the chapter unpacks the multifaceted challenges in devising sustainable strategies. Focused on Corporate Social Responsibility (CSR), this chapter evaluates the essence of sustainability across various business paradigms, unraveling the universal importance of embedding sustainability principles for long-term organizational success.

In Chapter 3, the spotlight shifts to the realm of cybersecurity, where the manipulative art of social engineering takes center stage. This chapter peels back the layers of sophisticated cyberattacks, revealing how adversaries manipulate trust and exploit vulnerabilities. The exploration illuminates the potential of these tactics to compromise personal and professional settings, underscoring the imperative for heightened awareness and defense mechanisms.

Turning to medical diagnostics, Chapter 4 uncovers the role of technology in revolutionizing kidney health assessment. Highlighting the importance of accuracy and consistency in diagnostic imaging, the chapter proposes a Random Forest classifier's efficacy in detecting kidney Nephrolithiasis. With a remarkable accuracy rate, the study underscores the potential of automated systems to enhance diagnostic precision and patient care.

Chapter 5 explores the realms of organizational anthropology and ethnography, exploring their interplay. This chapter examines how ethnographic analysis can unearth organizational dynamics, revealing a symbiotic relationship that influences insights into the social processes driving organizational behavior.

In the context of healthcare mergers, Chapter 6 introduces management consulting interventions as a vital tool to streamline the process. Analyzing the increasing prevalence of mergers, the chapter presents a framework for effective change management, highlighting how interventions can enhance the efficiency of merging healthcare entities.

Chapter 7 shifts focus to executive leadership coaching, particularly in government sectors. With cybersecurity vulnerabilities looming, the chapter explores how executive coaching can empower government supervisors to navigate the evolving landscape, equipping them with leadership skills crucial for maintaining organizational performance and efficiency.

Moving to the auto industry, Chapter 8 unleashes the potential of Agent-based Modeling (ABM) as a countermeasure against cyber threats. This chapter showcases how ABM can simulate cyber attacks' propagation, enabling stakeholders to identify vulnerabilities and strategize proactive cybersecurity measures, ultimately ensuring the safety of connected and autonomous vehicles.

Chapter 9 addresses the sobering issue of violence against women as a social justice and public health concern. With a focus on its wide-ranging impacts, from physical and psychological harm to economic hardship, the chapter delves into this pervasive issue through a review of current literature, emphasizing the need for comprehensive action.

Chapter 10 ventures into the realm of risk management for software companies. Through the lens of a fictional case, the chapter applies strategic models to address challenges arising from artificial intelligence integration. With insights into ethical decision-making and organizational culture, this case study offers a theoretical framework for managing AI-related risks.

In Chapter 11, the convergence of medical devices and data privacy takes center stage. Addressing the evolving landscape of patient data security, the chapter explores how legal regulations, including HIPAA, FDA, and HSCA guidelines, collectively shape medical device manufacturers' accountability for data protection and risk management.

Chapter 12 confronts cyber threats to the Department of Defense (DoD) military supply chain systems. Highlighting the potential vulnerabilities and their consequences, the chapter proposes recommendations to fortify these systems against cyber attacks, ensuring their functionality and integrity.

As technology penetrates daily life, Chapter 13 unveils a novel approach to malware detection and analysis. Harnessing the power of decision trees, the chapter introduces an effective method that outperforms existing solutions, achieving high precision and recall rates. The study opens new avenues in cybersecurity defense strategies.

Chapter 14 zooms in on the intersection of sports marketing and student athletes' name, image, and likeness (NIL) activities. With a backdrop of changing NCAA regulations, the chapter examines the historical context and implications of NIL on student-athlete compensation, shedding light on this evolving landscape.

Turning to risk management, Chapter 15 heralds the era of inclusive change management in organizational dynamics. By prioritizing human factors engineering and cybersecurity, this chapter underscores the critical role these elements play in mitigating risks and enhancing patient safety, advocating for a holistic approach to change management.

In the throes of the COVID-19 pandemic, Chapter 16 contemplates the synergy of generative artificial intelligence (GAI) and software product management. This systematic literature review inquires into GAI's applications, benefits, and constraints, revealing its potential to reshape software development processes and outcomes.

Chapter 17 investigates the realm of electroencephalography (EEG) signals and their diagnostic potential. By harnessing nonlinear features, the chapter explores their role in diagnosing brain disorders, illustrating how advanced algorithms can revolutionize EEG-based diagnostics.

The realms of finance and accountability take the stage in Chapter 18, as internal control procedures for purchasing card programs are scrutinized. This chapter highlights inefficiencies and misappropriation of funds, suggesting strategies to correct these behaviors and safeguard institutional resources.

In Chapter 19, cybersecurity communities of practice (CoPs) emerge as a potential solution for small businesses navigating cyber threats. Through collaboration and shared knowledge, CoPs empower small businesses to pool resources and devise strategies to enhance their cybersecurity practices, demonstrating the strength in collective defense.

Chapter 20 casts a spotlight on wearable biosensors, presenting a powerful tool for real-time health monitoring. Amid the promise of improved healthcare, the chapter also examines information security risks inherent in IoT integration, underscoring the need for balanced advancements.

Chapter 21 presents a strategic consulting approach to enhance workplace well-being within the New York City Department of Health and Mental Hygiene. By weaving together insights from the COVID-19 pandemic and system theory, the chapter proposes a transformational plan to elevate employee well-being.

With an emphasis on accuracy and efficiency, Chapter 22 navigates the challenges of diagnosing brain tumors through advanced technology. Leveraging deep learning models, the chapter unveils an innovative approach to classifying brain tumors, showcasing the potential to revolutionize diagnostic accuracy.

The future of retail is explored in Chapter 24, where digital transformation and "phygital" marketing take center stage. This chapter unpacks the impact of blending physical and digital experiences, shedding light on how these shifts reshape customer engagement and business models.

Chapter 25 explores the convergence of change management and cybersecurity, highlighting the importance of prioritizing human factors engineering. By weaving ethical considerations and organizational culture, the chapter advocates for a holistic approach to managing cybersecurity risks.

Chapter 26 peers into the intricate challenges of hospital cybersecurity during and beyond the COVID-19 pandemic. With a focus on ethics, organizational culture, and leadership, this chapter illuminates the multifaceted nature of safeguarding patient data and healthcare operations amidst global uncertainty.

The chapter 27 study explores the potential of cybersecurity communities of practice (CoPs) as a promising solution to aid small businesses in addressing these challenges and mitigating cybercrime-related risks. By engaging in CoPs, small businesses can combine their resources, exchange knowledge, and formulate innovative strategies to combat cybersecurity issues.

Chapter 28 addresses the pressing issue of global supply chain threats and their potentially catastrophic consequences, highlighting the urgency for both organizations and governments to address this challenge. Particularly, developing nations undergoing digital transformation are at heightened risk.

In essence, our aspiration is for this book to shine as a guiding beacon, directing organizations toward equitable, effective, and inclusive practices that not only elevate their internal cultures but also contribute positively to the broader societal tapestry. As editors, we extend our gratitude to all contributors who have participated in this venture. We invite readers to go on a journey of exploration, introspection, and profound transformation.

Darrell Norman Burrell
Marymount University, USA

Chapter 1
Cybercrime and Insider Threats in Healthcare Organizations: Motive, Prevention, and Mitigation

Michelle Denise Espinoza
https://orcid.org/0009-0009-5213-6974
Marymount University, USA

ABSTRACT

Cybercrime costs an estimated $575 billion per year and healthcare continues to be the most targeted sector in the world. News headlines are rife with data leaks and data breach incidents. These breaches lead to the theft of personal, financial, and health information from users who are often only notified of the breach well after it occurred, and the damage has already been done. Insider threats can be loosely categorized as malicious or negligent, based on their intent (or lack thereof). This case study focuses on one such malicious incident where a ring of hospital employees was indicted for allegedly selling patient credit card and medical information online. The authors provide practitioners with a deeper understanding of how PII is misused, motivations for its theft, and recommendations to avoid such incidents in their own organizations.

BACKGROUND

Cybercrime costs an estimated $575 billion per year and healthcare continues to be the most targeted sector in the world (Abulencia, 2021). News headlines are rife with data leak and data breach incidents. These breaches lead to the theft of personal, financial, and health information from users who are often only notified of the breach well after it occurred, and the damage has already been done. When the perpetrators are an organization's employees, the impact of lowered morale and trust levels among employees should also be factored into costs (Burrell et al., 2021).

Personal health information (PHI) breaches, an impermissible use or disclosure of protected personal health information, are extremely consequential for healthcare organizations, their patients, and their customers (Pool et al., 2019). In 2022, 588 breaches were reported to US Health and Human Services,

DOI: 10.4018/979-8-3693-1634-4.ch001

affecting 44.7 million patients in total (Office of Information Security, 2023). Perhaps due to the ease of accessibility to patient data, the number of people required to handle each patient's data, or due to relaxed cybersecurity policies, but in comparison to other industries, healthcare organizations are more vulnerable to data breaches (Gordon, 2017). Unauthorized access, theft, and hacking/IT incidents accounted for 98% of 2022 US healthcare data breaches (Office of Information Security, 2023).

Examples of such incidents include a 2019 breach in which 23,000 patient records at Critical Care Pulmonary & Sleep Associates were compromised when a hacker gained access to an employee's email account and sent out phishing emails to other employees, eventually exposing patient data (Davis, 2019). In 2021, a pharmaceutical company employee was charged with uploading more than 12,000 files containing trade secrets related to its COVID-19 vaccine, to a rival company using a corporate laptop over a three-day window (Office of Information Security, 2023). Also in 2021, a San Diego hospital employee was charged with stealing the identities of dying patients to file fraudulent COVID benefit claims (Brewster, 2021).

Insider threats figure prominently in healthcare data breaches, much more than other industries (Verizon, 2022). An insider threat is potentially a person within a healthcare organization or a contractor who has access to assets or inside information concerning the organization's security practices, data, and computer systems (Office of Information Security, 2023). Insider threats can be loosely categorized as malicious or negligent, based on their intent [or lack thereof] (Office Information Security, 2021).

This case study centers on one such malicious incident where a ring of hospital employees was indicted for allegedly selling patient credit card and medical information online. The study aims to provide insights that can assist organizations in preventing and mitigating similar incidents. To protect the privacy of the case study subject, they will hereafter be referred to as Hospital X.

PROBLEM STATEMENT

Healthcare organizations are the most vulnerable to cybersecurity incidents, yet few healthcare organizations implement adequate cybersecurity practices. The average cost per healthcare insider threat incident in 2022 was a staggering $10.10 million (Ponemon Institute, 2023). Employee theft is particularly harmful because in addition to the reputational risk and financial impact, internal theft incidents lead victimized organizations to experience high rates of employee turnover and lower levels of interpersonal and organizational trust (Payne & Gainey, 2004). Without effective implementation of corrective actions and a focus on cybersecurity culture, healthcare organizations will continue to bear the exorbitant costs of cybercrime. Therefore, it is crucial to provide practitioners with an understanding of how PII is misused, the motivations behind its theft, and actionable recommendations to prevent such incidents within their organizations.

LITERATURE REVIEW

Cybercrime

Cybercrime, or internet-based criminal activity, was once characterized as a reputation economy where bad actors were motivated to carry out malicious acts in pursuit of receiving 'street cred' among their hacker peers (Miller, 2007). Today, cybercrime is a cash economy where exploits and vulnerabilities are bought and sold by public companies and underground organizations alike (Miller, 2007). Unlike common street crimes, an instance of cybercrime may cut across multiple jurisdictions and geographies whose nexus is difficult to pinpoint (Paschal et al., 2021). An employee from Hospital X who sells a credit card number or medical record using a site hosted on a server in Ireland to a buyer in Thailand will have just committed a transnational crime, which jurisdiction should they be prosecuted in? If that same employee conspires to commit the crime using Discord with chat participants in Nigeria and Germany, which jurisdiction should they and their co-conspirators be prosecuted in? This example illustrates the challenges law enforcement face when investigating and prosecuting cybercrime.

Carding Shops

Carding shops and forums are online marketplaces to traffic stolen credit card information. One of the better-known carding shops, JokerStash, shuttered its doors in February 2021 making off with a reported $2.1 billion in Bitcoin after evading law enforcement for years (Winder, 2021). Stolen credit card information is often used to launder money (Winder, 2021). The price that a stolen credit card may fetch online through carding shops depends heavily on factors such as the issuing bank, country of origin, and whether the card can be used in person (Bulakh, 2017). Carding shops use various evasion techniques to facilitate this underground economy, including but not limited to, changing domain names, requiring CAPTCHAs and blocking HTTP requests not originating from a browser. Almost 70% of cards sold by carding shops are priced at or below the cost banks incur in re-issuing them. Carding shops can also serve as early indicators of a data breach (Ebrahimi et al., 2023).

Identity Theft

Identity theft is sometimes referred to as a 'gateway crime' in that it can lead to a series of much more serious crimes (Mohan & Kumar, 2020). Even with fragments of a person's identity information such as their social security number, identity thieves are often able to complete the person's identity by using secondary sources of information freely available online (Liu et al., 2020). Identity theft is a faceless fraud committed by fraudsters who are often located in territories with no extradition treaty, resulting in significant challenges for authorities to track down and bring them to justice (Compin, 2016). Medical records typically fetch a higher price on the dark web because unlike a credit card that can be instantly shut off and rendered useless, a person's identity information persists for years and can be used to file taxes, take out fraudulent loans, or to commit other crimes under the assumed identity such as identity theft's less talked-about cousin, medical identity theft (US Senate Intelligence Committee, 2022).

Medical Identity Theft

The World Health Organization went as far as referring to medical identity theft as the crime of information that will kill you (Labong, 2018). Medical identity theft and related fraud are negative effects of data breaches whereby a criminal could receive medical treatment by assuming the identity of another patient, or defraud a government program, insurance company, or even the patient themselves (Mancini, 2014). Medical identity theft can continue for years before being discovered by the patient who may be prompted to scrutinize their medical records after denial of benefits or inexplicable denial of coverage

(Mancini, 2014). Unlike the rights of identity theft victims to obtain, dispute, and correct their credit reporting histories, no such rights to remediation exist for medical identity theft victims (FTC).

Data Breach

Data breach, as defined by U.S. Code, means the loss or theft of, or other unauthorized access to, other than an unauthorized access incidental to the scope of employment, data containing sensitive personal information, in electronic or printed form, that results in the potential compromise of the confidentiality or integrity of the data. US Department of Health and Human Services defines five main known causes of breaches, namely, unauthorized access/disclosure, hacking/IT incident, improper disposal, loss, and theft that lead to a direct breach of PHI. The incident in this case study involves both unauthorized disclosure and theft. Data breaches generally happen because of negligence, human error, or other non-malicious behavior that created a security vulnerability (Katz, 2018). Data breaches can occur without exposing PHI. Disclosure requirements of data breaches are governed by various laws and regulations depending on where the breach occurred, and the type of information that may have been exposed.

Electronic Health Records

The HITECH Act of 2009 pushed all healthcare organizations to adopt an electronic health record system. The premise of the initiative was that electronic health records systems would reduce clinical errors, improve patient care coordination, and enhance patient privacy. However, organizations without commensurate cybersecurity policies inadvertently made it easier for thieves to take millions of records at once. In 2014 when the government launched the Electronic Health Record initiative, the government lost more than $14 billion to fraudulent practices (U.S. Government Accounting Office, 2016).

Causes of Fraud

Fraud Triangle Theory

Fraud Triangle Theory, a theoretical framework, is used to explain fraud committed at both the individual and organizational levels (Muhtar et al., 2018). The three factors comprising the triangle are opportunity, pressure, and rationalization. The opportunity arises for computer fraud when there is an absence of controls, ineffective controls, or the ability to override controls (Jiang, 2022). Without a real or perceived opportunity, fraud will not likely be committed (Abdullahi & Mansor, 2018). Pressure such as personal financial trouble, gambling debt, living beyond one's means, or a drug addiction can contribute to fraudulent actions (Abdullahi & Mansor, 2018). Lastly, when employees feel wronged in some way, they may justify or rationalize fraudulent actions (Lokanan, 2018). According to the theory, all three elements must be present for the perpetrator to commit fraud (Abdullahi & Mansor, 2018). Fraud Triangle Theory is the dominant fraud theory used in auditing and forensic accounting professional standards (Murphy & Free, 2016).

Routine Activity Theory

Routine Activity Theory suggests that the presence of a motivated offender (i.e., the employee), the availability of a suitable target (i.e., the employer's assets), and the absence of capable guardianship (i.e., lack of monitoring or oversight) could converge to increase the likelihood of theft (Korgaonkar, 2021). Like the Fraud Triangle Theory, the Routine Activity Theory says that fraud cannot be committed if any of these elements are not present (Mui & Mailley, 2015). Routine Action Theory assumes that people make a rational choice to commit crimes (Wang, et al., 2015). Organizational justice theory explains how perceptions of fairness or unfairness are created within an organizational context (Leventhal et al., 1980; Willison et al., 2018). Individuals who feel that their employer has been unfair will be more likely to engage in unethical conduct. One might argue that the rationalization to commit theft or fraud because a person feels wronged by the organization they work for, is tantamount to vigilantism.

Insider Threat and the Threat Kill Chain

Insider threats can be examined through what is referred to as the insider threat kill chain, this begins with the radicalization of the worker (a trigger point) wherein he becomes motivated to commit a malicious act. This is followed by searching for opportunities to engage in malicious insider behavior, and finally leads to the malicious act such as exfiltrating data when the opportunity arises (Colwill, 2009). Damage can be mitigated by organizations by intervening in the process at any point in the insider threat kill chain prior to data exfiltration.

One could argue that the Threat Kill Chain concept combines and simplifies the existing Fraud Triangle theory with Routine Activity theory in that a motivated offender has already rationalized their intentions, whether this rationalization stems from pressure or greed is irrelevant, and the motivated offender simply needs an opportunity to carry out their intention. Figure 1, Simplified Cause and Effect, summarizes this concept.

Figure 1. Simplified cause and effect

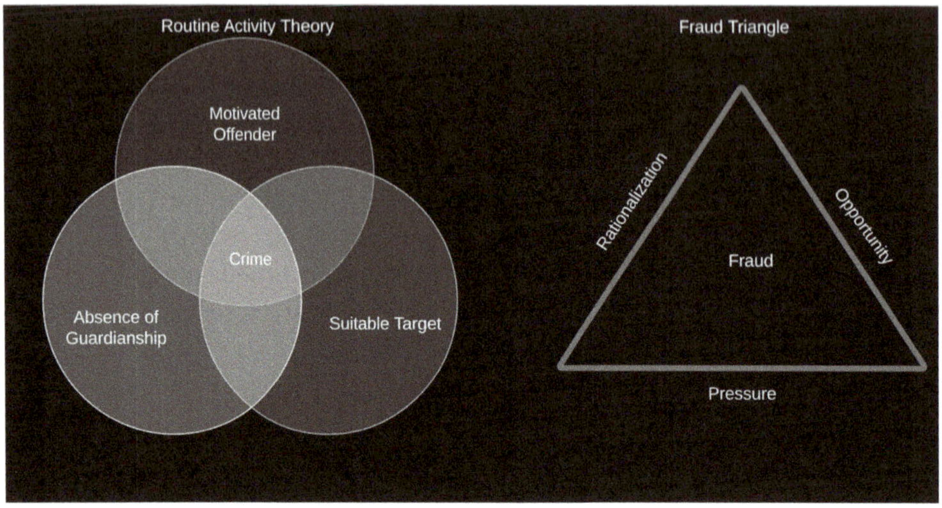

FIXING THE PROBLEM

Deterring, preventing, and detecting fraud or insider threats in an organization requires a multi-pronged approach. We recommend using Wilhelm's Fraud Management Life Cycle as the framework and examining the organizational culture, leadership, ethical, policy, and strategy theory subcomponents corresponding to each stage. Herein we assume a situationist perspective in that external factors, such as an organization's culture, play a crucial role in determining an employee's decision when presented with an ethical choice (Zimbardo, 2004).

WILHELM FRAUD MANAGEMENT LIFE CYCLE

No business is immune from fraud, and eliminating all fraud is not possible (Omar et al., 2016). The key to effective mitigation of the effects of fraud is to take preventative action through anti-fraud strategies (Mangala & Kumari, 2015). One such framework through which organizations can take steps to deter, detect, and protect against fraud is Wilhelm's Fraud Management Life Cycle which consists of eight stages, each of which requires a balance in the competing and complementary actions within the fraud management life cycle (Wilhelm, 2004). Figure 2 illustrates the eight stages of the life cycle.

Figure 2. Wilhelm Fraud management life cycle

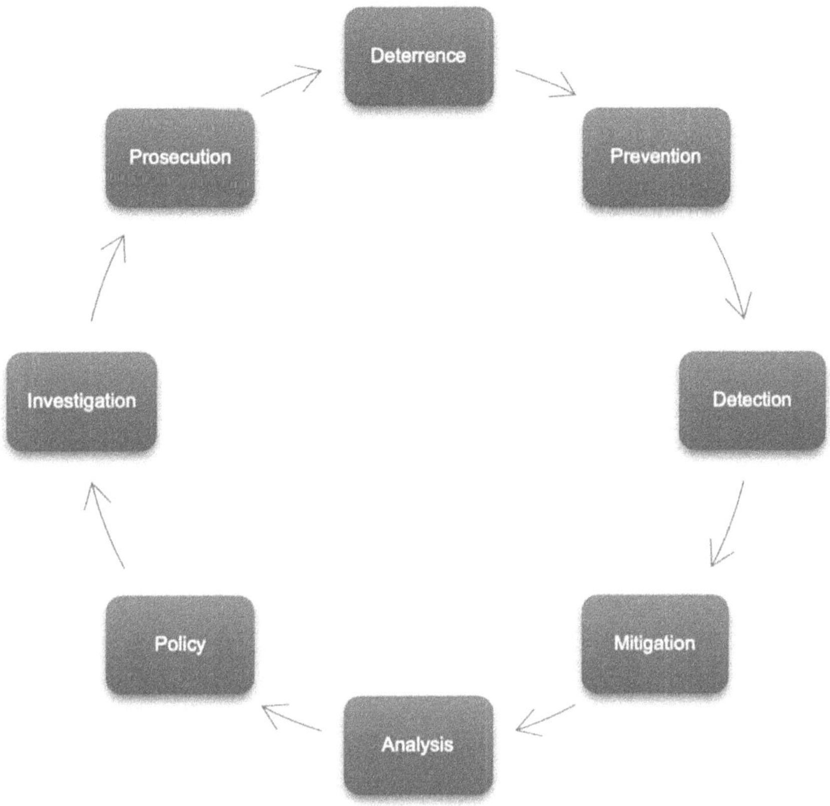

Stage One: Deterrence

Deterrence is characterized by actions and activities intended to stop or prevent fraud before it is attempted (Wilhelm 2004). COVID-19 increased the prevalence of remote work which reduced the likelihood of observant co-workers impeding or deterring the malevolent actions of insider threats (Burrell et al., 2022). With reduced defenses, organizations must lean more heavily into the deterrent effect achieved through fostering a strong ethical environment.

Organizational Culture

Much as canaries in coal mines warned miners when carbon monoxide levels posed an imminent danger to coal miners, incidents such as the employee theft that occurred at Hospital X should be viewed as symptoms of a deeper problem. Hall's (1976) cultural iceberg model suggests that 90% of an organization's culture is hidden beneath the surface or invisible to onlookers. To get to the crux of a problematic culture, an organization experiencing serious incidents of unethical conduct must take a deeper and objective look at how the ethical tone, organizational values, leadership, and security cultures might foster or even encourage unethical conduct (Burrell et al., 2021). Zimbardo (2004) argues that while a few bad apples might spoil the barrel, a vinegar barrel will always transform sweet cucumbers into sour pickles – regardless of the best intentions, resilience, and genetic nature of those cucumbers.

Cybersecurity and general stewardship of an organization should be a shared responsibility. Inculcating Hibbard's (2006) canoe theory into every employee requires unified messaging from the top. Canoe theory can be summarized as:

1. Think of your organization as a long canoe (1 team, in it together)
2. The canoe has a destination (shared goals)
3. Everyone in the canoe has a seat and paddle (equally equipped to contribute towards the goal)
4. Everyone is expected to paddle (shared responsibility)
5. Those who won't paddle have to get out of the canoe (no deadweight)
6. Those who prevent others from paddling have to adjust or get out of the canoe
7. There are no passengers in the canoe (hold each other accountable)
8. There is a coxswain (look to your leaders for direction)
9. No other crewmember has a title
10. Crewmembers are multi-talented
11. The canoe theory understands crisis
12. The canoe theory says you have the right to be happy

The canoe theory fosters an environment of shared accountability, shared duty to protect an organization, and makes it easier for employees to speak up when they witness a peer engaging in unethical conduct. Organizations that do not foster this mindset are prone to situations where employees turn a blind eye to unethical conduct.

Leadership

Leaders, or Coxswain as referenced in the Canoe Theory, set the ethical tone in an organization. Messaging from leadership can make or break an organization's culture. Transformational leaders are the most effective messengers, particularly in organizations where the ethical bar needs to be raised or reset (Johnson, 2020). Transformational leaders are driven by duty, not to be confused with the duty-based approach to ethical decision-making, and are guided by universal ethical principles (Johnson, 2020).

According to Bass and Avolio, transformational leadership is characterized by the following:

1. Idealized influence: transformational leaders put follower's needs above their own, act as role models, and are admired, respected, and trusted by their followers.
2. Inspirational motivation: transformational leaders provide meaning to their followers' tasks, are enthusiastic, and motivate followers to develop desirable visions for the future.
3. Intellectual stimulation: transformational leaders encourage creativity, encourage followers to question assumptions, reframe situations, solicit solutions from followers and frame mistakes as learning opportunities from which their followers can grow.
4. Individualized consideration: transformational leaders act as coaches who foster personal development. They foster a growth-oriented environment and focus on the needs of each individual under their charge.

If organizations do not have leaders who embrace/embody transformational leadership, then implementing leadership training and identifying candidates who subscribe to the virtue approach in ethical decision-making is another viable option. Individuals who rely on virtue ethics can be identified as growth-oriented, of high moral character, and who believe in a higher calling that transcends organizational rules and policies (Johnson, 2020). Their peers may describe them as idealists.

Stage Two: Prevention

Like stage 1, prevention involves actions and activities to prevent fraud from occurring (Wilhelm, 2004). Organizations should investigate the hiring standards and screening practices of any companies they subcontract with to ensure alignment with the organization's internal standards and to reduce the risk of insider threats among their subcontractors (Burrell et al., 2021). Organizations should ensure that employee incentives or compensation packages do not inadvertently create conflicting priorities with the cybersecurity policies that they wish to implement. Measuring employee performance on how quickly they process patient intakes may result in employees taking shortcuts that compromise data security. If billing departments accept payment over the phone, ensure that employees ask the caller to repeat their card number rather than the employee reading the card number back to the caller. Company-issued mobile devices coupled with mobile device management, for example, can provide organizations better control and monitoring of the applications used and data transmitted.

Office Layout

Ensure that computer monitors are angled so that information on the screen cannot easily be read by other patients standing at a check-in counter. Installing card access systems can enable organizations to monitor and audit employee movement and information access. Attention to acoustics and potentially investing in sound-dampening technology can reduce the likelihood of sensitive information being overheard by unauthorized individuals.

Awareness Training

A vital component of prevention is simply awareness. Doing everything within one's power to safeguard identification information as it flows through various information channels is the most effective strategy that individuals and organizations can take to prevent identity theft (Labong, 2019). Corresponding reporting and monitoring are also important aspects of the awareness program, but reporting is part of Stage III.

Stage Three: Detection

Detection is characterized by actions and activities intended to identify and locate fraud before, during, and after the completion of the fraudulent activity (Wilhelm, 2004). Detection encompasses three closely related activities in the fraud arena: fraud testing, fraud attempts, and fraud successes (Wilhelm, 2004).

Fraud is a primary source of organizational losses, amounting up to 5% of yearly revenue (Omair & Alturki, 2020). Investing in a forensic team to untangle fraudulent activity is unfeasible for most small and medium enterprises and this example speaks to the need for more robust prevention and detection methods that can be employed by smaller organizations; the goal of a fraud detection system may be to make optimal use of a company's limited inspection capacity (Baesens et al., 2015). A person's medical record fetches a higher price in the criminal world than a stolen credit card because, unlike a credit card number which can simply be deactivated by its issuer, the information in medical records is enduring and can be used for identity theft, falsifying prescriptions, insurance fraud, etc. Knowledge of guardianship and control mechanisms allows employee thieves to be more successful in their criminal acts (Clarke, 1997), and the ability to effectively avoid detection is a key reason why small business employee thieves can steal for long periods (Kennedy, 2014). We advise organizations to guard their detection methods from internal users to reduce the likelihood of employees successfully circumventing detection.

According to the 2022 Association of Certified Fraud Examiners report, organizations with fraud reporting hotlines reduced cut their median fraud loss by half (ACFE, 2022). Email and web-based fraud-reporting options increase the likelihood of employees reporting fraud sooner. Whistleblower hotlines should be considered another effective tool for organizations to include in their detection arsenal.

Stage Four: Mitigation

Mitigation focuses on fast actions that are intended to reduce the extent of the fraud, the amount of the associated fraud losses and the effort and expense required to recover or correct the impact of the fraudulent activity (Wilhelm, 2004). In theory, the faster that fraud activity is detected, and mitigation activities are initiated, the less time, effort and expense will have to be invested in correcting the consumer's credit report (Wilhelm, 2004). Some organizations are reluctant to press charges when theft is discovered. This reluctance could stem from concerns about reputational risk (i.e. what will people think if they find out?) or the reluctance may stem from not wanting to deal with the cost and inconvenience of legal proceedings (Wilhelm, 2004). The individual(s) committing the fraud typically move on to work in other organizations, who are unaware of their prior fraudulent acts, and the cycle repeats itself (Wilhelm, 2004).

Stage Five: Analysis

The analysis stage is characterized by activities to identify and understand losses that occurred despite the deterrence, detection, prevention, and mitigation stage activities (Wilhelm, 2004). The analysis could be viewed as the feedback stage during which organizations receive data regarding performance from each of the other stages (Wilhelm, 2004).

Stage Six: Policy

Policy activities create, evaluate, communicate, and assist in the deployment of fraud policies to reduce the incidence of fraud and the inconvenience to legitimate customers and to allocate the resources required to successfully combat fraud (Wilhelm, 2004). Policy development and implementation are typically done by an organization's leadership team (Wilhelm, 2004). An organization's leaders influence the actions and behaviors of lower-level employees and can make or break a successful cybersecurity policy (Abulencia, 2021). Nudge theory, or letting users believe that adherence to policies is their idea rather than letting them feel that the policy is being forced upon them is useful in deploying and enforcing policy (Johnson, 2020).

Stage Seven: Investigation

Investigation activities obtain enough evidence and information to stop fraudulent activity, to obtain recovery of assets or restitution, and to provide information and support for the successful prosecution and conviction of the fraudster(s) (Wilhelm, 2004). One of the most critical support components in the investigative function is the development of training on, and maintenance of, detailed investigative procedures (Wilhelm, 2004). Depending on the severity and extent of the fraud being investigated, some organizations may need to enlist the help of forensic auditors from outside consulting agencies.

Stage Eight: Prosecution or Redress

This stage is focused on prosecutorial and judicial authorities as well as with law enforcement (Wilhelm, 2004). For organizations that do not choose to press charges, this stage may consist of structuring restitution payments directly with the individual(s) involved. Wilhelm (2004) noted that some organizations refuse to prosecute thieves or share detection methods with industry peers because they view pushing the thievery to competitors as a competitive advantage. However, organizations that engage in this mindset should re-review the organizational culture suggestions in the deterrence stage, because knowingly harming industry peers is a red flag that your organization may be fostering an unethical climate.

Leadership

Situational leadership does not take a one size fits all approach, but rather prescribes that leaders adapt their leadership style or decision-making to each situation (Johnson, 2020). Some organizations choose to implement a zero-tolerance policy and prosecute incidents of employee theft to the full extent of the law. However, like California's three-strike law, a blanket prosecution policy could harm unintended individuals (The Three Strikes and You're Out Law, 'n.d'). We recommend using the Fairness/Justice approach instead, which weighs the merits of each case individually (Johnson, 2020).

Table 1. Wilhelm's Fraud management life cycle

Wilhelm's Fraud Management Life Cycle		
Stage #	Stage Name	Primary Objective
I	Deterrence	Stop or prevent before fraud is attempted
II	Prevention	Avoid occurrence
III	Detection	Identify and locate if fraud is occurring
IV	Mitigation	Minimize the damage
V	Analysis	Analyze the damage
VI	Policy	Update and evaluate policies
VII	Investigation	Investigate the incident
VIII	Prosecution	Restitution or remediation

CONCLUSION

Healthcare organizations face significant vulnerabilities to cybersecurity incidents, resulting in substantial financial losses, reputational damage, and compromised patient information. The prevalence of insider threats further exacerbates these risks, making it crucial for healthcare organizations to implement robust cybersecurity practices and to set the ethical tone in their organizations. This chapter explored various aspects of cybercrime, including the alarming costs associated with healthcare insider threat incidents, the motivations behind fraud and theft, and the detrimental impact of data breaches and identity theft. We provided a framework, summarized in Table 1, through which organizations can take steps to deter, detect, and protect against fraud.

The recommendations herein were by no means exhaustive, but we provide a starter blueprint for organizations to implement their fraud prevention programs and suggestions to repair or improve the ethical environment of their organizations. Healthcare organizations must acknowledge the shared responsibility of cybersecurity and prioritize the protection of patient data to avoid the dire consequences of cybercrime. Healthcare organizations weighing the prioritization of protecting their patients' healthcare data should also weigh their responsibility in upholding the Hippocratic Oath that their physicians took.

REFERENCES

Abdullahi, R., & Mansor, N. (2018). Fraud prevention initiatives in the Nigerian public sector: Understanding the relationship of fraud incidences and the elements of fraud triangle theory. *Journal of Financial Crime*, *25*(2), 527–544. doi:10.1108/JFC-02-2015-0008

Abulencia, J. (2021). The cost of cybercrime in the US healthcare sector. *Computer Fraud & Security*, *2021*(11), 8–13. doi:10.1016/S1361-3723(21)00117-2

Baesens, B., Van Vlasselaer, V., & Verbeke, W. (2015). *Fraud Analytics Using Descriptive, Predictive, and Social Network Techniques: A Guide to Data Science for Fraud Detection (Wiley and SAS Business Series)* (1st ed.). Wiley. doi:10.1002/9781119146841

Bevan, R. (2015). *The Changemaking Checklists: A Toolkit for Planning, Leading, and Sustaining Change*. ChangeStart Press.

Bulakh, V. (2017). *Online fraud economy: Characterization and defense* (M. Gupta, Ed.). Indiana University.

Burke, A., van Stel, A., & Thurik, R. (2010). Blue Ocean vs. Five Forces. *Harvard Business Review*. https://hbr.org/2010/05/blue-ocean-vs-five-forces

Burrell, D. N., Nobles, C., Cusak, A., & Omar, M. (2022). Cybercrime and the Nature of Insider Threat Complexities in Healthcare and Biotechnology Engineering Organizations. *Journal of Crime and Criminal Behavior.*

Compin, F. (2016). Do financial criminals commit perfect crimes? *Journal of Financial Crime*, *23*(3), 624–636. doi:10.1108/JFC-03-2015-0018

Cybersecurity is Patient Safety. (2022). US Senate Intelligence Committee. https://www.warner.senate.gov/public/_cache/files/f/5/f5020e27-d20f-49d1-b8f0-bac298f5da0b/0320658680B8F1D29C9A94895044DA31.cips-report.pdf

Daramola, O. E., Abu, J. M., Daramola, L. O., & Akande, T. M. (2019). Medical Identity Fraud in Health Insurance Schemes: Creating Awareness in Nigeria. *Asian Journal of Case Reports in Medicine and Health*, *2*(1), 1–6.

Davis, J. (2019a, January 31). Phishing hack breaches PHI of 23,000 Colorado patients for 3 months. *Health IT Security*. https://healthitsecurity.com/news/phishing-hack-breaches-phi-of- 23000-colorado-patients-for-3-months

Ebrahimi, M., Surdeanu, M., Samtani, S., & Chen, H. (2018). Detecting Cyber Threats in Non-English Dark Net Markets: A Cross-Lingual Transfer Learning Approach. *2018 IEEE International Conference on Intelligence and Security Informatics (ISI)*, 85–90. Federal Trade Commission. https://www.consumer.ftc.gov/articles/pdf-0009-taking-charge.pdf

Furlan, S., & Bajec, M. (2008). Holistic approach to fraud management in health insurance. *Journal of Information and Organizational Sciences*, *32*(2), 99–114.

Genes, R. (2016). Code cyber: Preventing breaches at hospitals and health care practices. *Journal of Health Care Compliance*, *18*(3), 13–18.

Harwell, D. (2023, April 15). The military loved Discord for Gen Z recruiting. Then the leaks began. *The Washington Post*. https://www.washingtonpost.com/technology/2023/04/15/discord-military-recruitment-pentagon-document-leaks/

Hibbard, D., Hibbard, M., & Stockman, J. (2006). The Canoe Theory: A Business Success Strategy for Leaders and Associates (0 ed.). iUniverse, Inc.

Jiang, R. (2022). Exploring Employees' Computer Fraud Behaviors using the Fraud Triangle Theory. *Pacific Asia Journal of the Association for Information Systems*, *14*(4), 4.

Johnson, C. E. (2020). *Meeting the Ethical Challenges of Leadership: Casting Light or Shadow* (7th ed.). SAGE Publications, Inc.

Katz, B. (2018). *Connecting care for patients: Interdisciplinary care transition and collaboration*. Jones & Bartlett Learning.

Kennedy, J. P. (2017). Functional redundancy as a response to employee theft within small businesses. *Security Journal; London*, *30*(1), 162–183.

Korgaonkar, P., Becerra, E. P., Mangleburg, T., & Bilgihan, A. (2021). Retail employee theft: When retail security alone is not enough. *Psychology and Marketing*, *38*(5), 721–734. doi:10.1002/mar.21460

Labong, R. C. (2019). Identity Theft Protection Strategies: A Literature Review. *Journal of Academic Research*, *4*(2), 1–12.

Liu, Y., Lin, F. Y., Ahmad-Post, Z., Ebrahimi, M., Zhang, N., Hu, J. L., Xin, J., Li, W., & Chen, H. (2020). Identifying, Collecting, and Monitoring Personally Identifiable Information: From the Dark Web to the Surface Web. *2020 IEEE International Conference on Intelligence and Security Informatics (ISI)*, (pp. 1–6). IEEE. 10.1109/ISI49825.2020.9280540

Lokanan, M. E. (2018). Informing the fraud triangle: Insights from differential association theory. *Journal of Theoretical Accounting Research*, *14*(1), 55–98.

Mancini, M. (2014). Medical identity theft in the emergency department: Awareness is crucial. *The Western Journal of Emergency Medicine*, *15*(7), 899–901. doi:10.5811/westjem.2014.8.22438 PMID:25493150

Mangala, D., & Kumari, P. (2015). Corporate fraud prevention and detection: Revisiting the literature. *Journal of Commerce and Accounting Research.*, *4*(1), 52–62. doi:10.21863/jcar/2015.4.1.006

Miller, C. (n.d.). *The legitimate vulnerability market: the secretive world of 0-day exploit sales.*

Mohan, G. C., & Kumar, D. (2020). Identity theft: A small step towards big financial crimes. *Journal of Financial Crime*, *27*(3), 897–910. doi:10.1108/JFC-01-2020-0014

Muhtar, S., Sutaryo, M., & Sriyanto, S. (2018). Corruption in Indonesian local government: Study on triangle fraud theory. *International Journal of Business and Society*, *19*, 536–552.

Mui, G., & Mailley, J. (2015). A tale of two triangles: Comparing the fraud triangle with criminology's crime triangle. *Accounting Research Journal*, *28*(1), 45–58. doi:10.1108/ARJ-10-2014-0092

Murphy, P. R., & Free, C. (2016). Broadening the fraud triangle: Instrumental climate and fraud. *Behavioral Research in Accounting*, *28*(1), 41–56. doi:10.2308/bria-51083

Nohria, N., & Beer, M. (2000). Cracking the Code of Change. *Harvard Business Review*. https://hbr.org/2000/05/cracking-the-code-of-change

Office of Information Security. (2023, March 9). *Data Exfiltration Trends in Healthcare*. Data Exfiltration Trends in Healthcare. https://www.hhs.gov/sites/default/files/data-exfiltration-in-healthcare-tlpclear.pdf

Omair, B., & Alturki, A. (2020). A Systematic Literature Review of Fraud Detection Metrics in Business Processes. *IEEE Access : Practical Innovations, Open Solutions*, *8*, 26893–26903. doi:10.1109/ACCESS.2020.2971604

Parker, G., Van Alstyne, M., & Choudary, S. (2016). *Platform revolution:How networked markets are transforming the economy and how to make them work for you*. Norton & Company, Inc.

Paschal, U., Nwankwo, W., Masajuwa, F. U., Imoisi, S., & Chinedu, P. U. (2021). Cybercrime detection and prevention efforts in the last decade: An overview of the possibilities of machine learning models. https://doi.org/ doi:10.48047/rigeo.11.07.92

Ponemon Institute. (2022). *Cost of a Data Breach*. Ponemon Institute. https://www.ibm.com/downloads/cas/3R8N1DZJ

Pool, J. K., Akhlaghpour, S., Fatehi, F., & Burton-Jones, A. (2019). *Causes and Impacts of Personal Health Information (PHI) Breaches: A Scoping Review and Thematic Analysis*. AISEL. https://aisel.aisnet.org/pacis2019/71/

Porter, M. E. (2001). Strategy and the Internet. *Harvard Business Review*. https://hbr.org/2001/03/strategy-and-the-internet

Quinn, R. E., Hildebrandt, H. W., Rogers, P. S., & Thompson, M. P. (1991). A Competing Values Framework for Analyzing Presentational Communication in Management Contexts. *Journal of Business Communication*, *28*(3), 213–232. doi:10.1177/002194369102800303

Sternstein, J. (2017). Healthcare security ailments and treatments the world needs to know. *ISSA Journal*, *15*(9), 25–30.

The Three Strikes and You're Out Law. (n.d.). LAO. https://lao.ca.gov/analysis_1995/3strikes.html

U.S. Government Accounting Office. (2013). GAO's 2013 high-risk update Medicare and Medicaid (*GAO Publication No. GAO-13-433T*). USGAO.

Van Alstyne, Parker, & Choudary. (2016). Pipelines, Platforms, and the New Rules of Strategy. *Harvard Business Review*, *94*(4), 54–62.

Verizon. (2022). *Data Breach Investigations Report*. Verizon. https://www.verizon.com/business/resources/T449/reports/dbir/2022-data-breach-investigations-report-dbir.pdf

Wang, J., Gupta, M., & Rao, H. R. (2015). Insider threats in a financial institution: Analysis of attack-proneness of information systems applications. *Management Information Systems Quarterly*, *39*(1), 91–112. doi:10.25300/MISQ/2015/39.1.05

Wilhelm, W. K. (2004). The fraud management lifecycle theory: A holistic approach to fraud management. *Journal of Economic Crime Management*, *2*(2), 1–38.

Winder, D. (2021, February 14). Cybercrime Joker Retires With A Reported $2.1 Billion In Bitcoin. *Forbes Magazine*. https://www.forbes.com/sites/daveywinder/2021/02/14/cybercrime-joker-retires-becomes-a-bitcoin-billionaire/

Zimbardo, P. G. (2004). A situationist perspective on the psychology of evil: Understanding how good people are transformed into perpetrators. In A. G. Miller (Ed.), The social psychology of good and evil, (pp (Vol. 498, pp. 21–50). The Guilford Press.

Chapter 2
Application and Analysis for Sustainability Strategy Development:
Research, Process, Models, Leadership, Management, and Technology

Emad Rahim
https://orcid.org/0000-0002-9391-747X
Bellevue University, USA

ABSTRACT

Sustainability should encompass social and environmental bottom lines with the expectations of also securing financial stability in the context of business operations. With sustainability as a business, social, ecological, or environmental system, it is important to understand that each system has its unique challenges that require resolution. Approaches and solutions in response to these unique systems may differ, but the need for sustainability and corporate social responsibility (CSR) is a universal imperative for long-term success. The primary focus of this chapter examines themes relating to leadership and management dynamics that influence sustainability strategy development, analysis, and the future direction of corporate sustainability and CSR.

INTRODUCTION

Analysis of the Field

The concept of sustainability leadership is based on the idea that the long-term success of businesses, organizations, and societies depends on their ability to identify and manage the interrelated economic, environmental, and social challenges. In recent years, the need for sustainable practices and strategies

DOI: 10.4018/979-8-3693-1634-4.ch002

has become increasingly apparent, and sustainability leadership has emerged as a way to help organizations and individuals address these issues (Beshears, et al., 2019).

One approach to sustainability leadership is the triple bottom line (TBL), which focuses on environmental, social, and economic performance (Beshears, et al., 2019). This approach has been adopted by many organizations, including governments, businesses, and nonprofits. It is based on the idea that an organization should strive to achieve its goals in a way that is socially, environmentally, and economically responsible (Beshears, et al., 2019). The TBL approach is often used to evaluate an organization's sustainability performance and to ensure that any changes made to improve sustainability are sustainable in the long-term (Beshears, et al., 2019).

Another approach to sustainability leadership is the eco-efficiency model, which emphasizes the use of resources efficiently and reducing waste. This model focuses on improving the efficiency of production processes and reducing the environmental impact of products and services (Beshears, et al., 2019). Eco-efficiency is a key component in sustainable production, and organizations that embrace this approach are better able to reduce their environmental impact (Beshears, et al., 2019).

A third approach to sustainability leadership is the stakeholder engagement approach, which is focused on engaging stakeholders in the development of sustainable strategies (Beshears, at el., 2019). This approach focuses on building relationships with stakeholders, understanding their needs and concerns, and working collaboratively to develop sustainable solutions. This approach is often used in the development of environmental policies, such as climate change initiatives, and is an important element of sustainability leadership (Beshears, et al., 2019). There are a number of challenges associated with sustainability leadership, including the need to prioritize sustainability goals, manage conflicting interests, and ensure that sustainability initiatives are implemented effectively. Additionally, sustainability leadership requires organizations to invest in training and development to ensure that employees have the skills and knowledge needed to effectively lead sustainable initiatives. Despite the challenges, there are a number of benefits associated with sustainability leadership. These include increased organizational efficiency, improved public image, increased customer loyalty, and reduced environmental impact. Additionally, sustainable practices can lead to increased profits, as organizations are better able to save money through reduced waste and improved efficiency (Beshears, et al., 2019). Organizations looking to develop and implement sustainability leadership can take a number of steps. These include establishing a sustainability strategy, investing in training and development, and engaging stakeholders. Additionally, organizations should develop metrics to evaluate their progress and ensure that their sustainability initiatives are being implemented effectively (Beshears, et al., 2019).

Over the last few decades, corporate operations and sustainability have become increasingly intertwined (Beshears, et al., 2019). As businesses become more aware of their environmental impacts, they have begun to create sustainable operations that allow them to remain profitable while also reducing their environmental footprint (Hansen, et al., 2019).

Corporate operations and sustainability is the practice of incorporating sustainable practices into a business' operations in order to reduce its environmental impact, while still remaining profitable (Hansen, et al., 2019). This can include changes to the way a business sources its materials, designs its products, and produces and distributes its goods and services. Sustainable practices can also include using renewable energy sources and reducing waste. By leveraging these strategies, businesses can reduce their environmental impact and remain competitive in today's market.

There are numerous benefits to incorporating sustainable practices into a business' operations. One of the most significant benefits is that it can help a business to reduce its environmental impact (Hansen, et al., 2019). This includes reducing its emissions of carbon dioxide and other greenhouse gases, as well as reducing the use of resources such as water and energy. Additionally, sustainable practices can help to reduce the amount of waste a business generates and the amount of pollution it creates (Murtaza, et al., 2020). In addition to reducing a business' environmental impact, sustainable operations can also improve its bottom line. By reducing its resource consumption and energy costs, a business can save money and remain competitive in today's market. Additionally, sustainable operations can provide a business with a competitive edge, as more and more consumers are looking to purchase products and services from businesses that have incorporated sustainable practices (Hansen, et al., 2019). Finally, sustainable operations can help to improve a business' public image. As consumers become more aware of a business' environmental impact, they are more likely to purchase from businesses that have adopted sustainable operations. This can help to increase brand loyalty and improve a business' reputation in the marketplace.

There are many different ways in which businesses are incorporating sustainable operations into their operations. One of the most common strategies is to use renewable energy sources. This can include using solar, wind, and geothermal energy to power a business' operations. Additionally, businesses can incorporate sustainable manufacturing practices such as reducing water and energy consumption and reducing waste. Another example of sustainable operations is the use of green building materials. This can include the use of recycled materials, as well as environmentally-friendly materials such as bamboo and cork. Additionally, businesses can also use green construction techniques such as energy efficient windows and insulation. Finally, businesses can also implement sustainable supply chain management practices. This can include sourcing raw materials from sustainable suppliers, as well as reducing the amount of energy and resources used in the production and distribution of goods and services (Hansen, et al., 2019).

Problem Statement

The global trend towards corporate sustainability has been driven by a variety of factors, including increased consumer demand, regulatory pressure, and the recognition of the long-term benefits of sustainable practices. According to the 2018 Global Corporate Sustainability Report by EY, global sustainability spending in 2017 increased by 17% from the previous year, reaching a total of €14.3 trillion (Metzger, 2018). This increase in sustainability spending has been driven by organizations of all sizes, from large multinational corporations to small and medium-sized enterprises (SMEs) (Metzger, 2018). In addition to increased investment in corporate sustainability, companies are also taking steps to improve their environmental performance. A study conducted by EY in 2017 found that 81% of companies had implemented environmental management systems (EMS) and 94% of companies had established environmental goals (Metzger, 2018). Furthermore, companies are increasingly reporting on their sustainability performance, with the number of sustainability reports increasing by more than 50% between 2017 and 2018 (Metzger, 2018). The Financial Impacts of Corporate Sustainability Companies' investments in sustainability practices can result in significant financial benefits. According to the 2018 Global Corporate Sustainability Report by EY, companies that implemented sustainability initiatives experienced an average return on investment of 12%, compared to 8% for companies that did not (Metzger, 2018). Furthermore, companies that have implemented sustainability practices have seen an average reduction in their costs of 5%, compared to 2% for companies that have not (Metzger, 2018).

In addition to the financial benefits of corporate sustainability, stakeholders, such as employees, customers, investors, and the local community, play an important role in driving sustainability initiatives.

According to the 2018 Global Corporate Sustainability Report, stakeholders are increasingly expecting companies to demonstrate their commitment to sustainability, with 87% of companies surveyed noting that their sustainability initiatives have been driven by stakeholder demand (Metzger, 2018). Furthermore, companies are increasingly recognizing the importance of engaging stakeholders in their sustainability initiatives, with the majority of companies surveyed indicating that they involve stakeholders in the development, implementation, and monitoring of their sustainability initiatives (Metzger, 2018). This paper explores the complexitics of sustainability from emerging and existing aspects from the literature with a focus on leadership interventions.

SIGNIFICANCE OF THE STUDY

Corporate sustainability is the concept of companies taking responsibility for their impacts on the environment and society, and taking measures to reduce their negative effects. Corporate sustainability strategies aim to create a balance between economic, environmental, and social benefits for all stakeholders.

The economic impacts of corporate sustainability strategies are significant. Studies have shown that companies with sustainability initiatives have higher stock returns than companies without them (Schwarz & Sattler, 2019). Additionally, companies with strong sustainability initiatives often attract more investors and partners, as investors and partners are increasingly drawn to companies that are committed to sustainability (Giovannini et al., 2019). Finally, sustainability initiatives often lead to increased efficiency, cost savings, and other economic benefits (Henderson et al., 2018).

The environmental impacts of corporate sustainability strategies are equally important. Studies have shown that sustainability initiatives can lead to reduced carbon emissions, water use, and energy consumption (Robins & Schaper, 2017). Additionally, sustainability initiatives help to reduce waste, conserve resources, and protect ecosystems (Robins & Schaper, 2017). Finally, sustainability strategies can lead to improved air and water quality, reduced environmental risks, and increased environmental resilience (Henderson et al., 2018).

Finally, the social impacts of corporate sustainability strategies are also significant. Studies have shown that companies with strong sustainability initiatives often have improved relationships with local communities, and that these initiatives often lead to increased job satisfaction and a sense of meaning and purpose among employees (Robins & Schaper, 2017). Additionally, these initiatives can help to reduce poverty, provide access to education, and promote social and economic equality (Henderson et al., 2018).

Identifying current and future costs and benefits for past and current operations, integration of these costs and benefits into decisions, and integrating assessments of social, political, and environmental risks, are ways to improve the capital investment decision-making process (Epstein & Buhovac, 2008). King (2008) found that political freedoms and entitlements, economic facilities, social opportunities, transparency guarantees, and protective security work together to facilitate both human and economic development. Identification of specific risks is essential to the overall management plan.

Organizational leadership plays an integral role in the development and implementation of corporate sustainability strategies. Corporate sustainability, which is defined as "the management of an organization's economic, environmental, and social impacts on society and the natural environment," (Kotler, & Lee, 2016, p. 2) has become an increasingly important issue for businesses of all sizes. Organizations are being held to higher standards of accountability for their actions and are being encouraged to make a positive impact on society and the environment. The success of corporate sustainability strategies is largely dependent on the actions of organizational leaders.

The Role of Organizational Leadership in Corporate Sustainability Strategies

Organizational leaders play a major role in the success of corporate sustainability strategies. Leaders have the ability to set the tone for the organization and create an environment in which sustainability is seen as an important part of the organization's mission. Leaders can also use their influence to ensure that sustainability strategies are implemented effectively and that the organization is held accountable for its actions. According to Humphreys and Boje (2013), "organizational leaders must be stewards of sustainability, setting the tone, developing the framework, and demonstrating their commitment to the organization's sustainability initiatives" (p. 10). Organizational leaders have the ability to influence the strategies used to achieve sustainability goals. Leaders can use their influence to ensure that sustainability strategies are based on scientific evidence and research, and that they are aligned with the organization's values and mission. They can also use their influence to ensure that sustainability strategies are implemented effectively and that the organization is held accountable for its actions. Humphreys and Boje (2013) note that "organizational leaders must be stewards of sustainability, setting the tone, developing the framework, and demonstrating their commitment to the organization's sustainability initiatives" (p. 10). Organizational leaders also have the ability to motivate employees to support sustainability initiatives. Leaders can use their influence to encourage employees to participate in sustainability initiatives and to ensure that sustainability goals are seen as an integral part of the organization's mission.

According to Ntounis and Gounaris (2018), "Successful implementation of a corporate sustainability program is contingent on the active participation of organizational members" (p. 88). Therefore, it is important for organizational leaders to create an environment in which employees feel motivated and empowered to support sustainability initiatives. Organizational leaders also have the ability to build relationships with external stakeholders to ensure that sustainability strategies are successful. Leaders can use their influence to engage stakeholders in meaningful dialogue and to ensure that sustainability strategies are implemented in a way that benefits both the organization and the broader community. According to O'Rourke (2015), "The key to successful sustainability engagement with external stakeholders is to recognize that, while corporate interests are important, they must be balanced against the interests of other stakeholders" (p. 16). Therefore, it is important for organizational leaders to ensure that sustainability strategies are implemented in a way that is beneficial to all stakeholders.

Senior management is obligated to develop an encompassing risk management plan. Management must identify strategic, operational, reporting, and compliance risks as part of measuring the overall impact of social and environmental risks (Epstein & Buhovac, 2008). Porter and Kramer (2006) introduced a framework to identify all of the positive and negative effects of corporate social responsibility (CSR) risks, determine which ones to address, and developed effective ways to address these effects. Scenario-based, fuzzy logic, and Monte Carlo simulation are methods used to measure social and environmental risks (Epstein & Buhovac, 2008). The management of these risks must be part of a concept of leadership that produces results.

The leadership drives sustainability strategy theme is supported by specific findings. The author found the integration of rewards and performance with sustainability goals and strategy will improve corporate decision-making and shareholder values (Epstein & Buhovac, 2008). Alignment of corporate and sustainability strategies with performance measures and rewards will improve sustainability, financial, and operational processes, performance, and overcome barriers (Correia, 2019; Epstein & Buhovac, 2008. Beinhocker (2006) suggested mutually reinforcing structure and processes along with norms and culture to create a coherent social architecture as a method used to overcome barriers. Leadership must also look beyond the human dimension and address the economic impact.

Findings supported the economic impact of leadership concepts introduced within the company. Improved economic sustainability needs to focus on human development, which includes the critical allocation of resources to the creation of human well-being in nonmarket segments (King, 2008). The adoption of cooperating, performing, and innovating norms will reduce hierarchy, increase autonomy, and encourage diversity (Beinhocker, 2006). Any system must include multiple analytic measures at multiple stages of the strategy; including financial and nonfinancial measures linked to the strategy and the decision-making process (Beinhocker, 2006). Leadership is key to any strategy develop, which is made better with the support of a revised culture.

Developing a widely accepted culture is the basis for the theme of new thinking, which is required to facilitate sustainability. Grinde and Khare (2008) argued that the world is composed of innumerable interdependent systems, biological, physical, economic, and social; those who consider components individually do so at their peril. Addressing social issues of shared value could support self-sustaining solutions (Beerannavar, 2020; Porter & Kramer, 2006). These concepts should provide a foundation to begin a discussion about the value of new thinking within the corporate leadership.

New thinking appears to be the foundation to develop new organizational and sustainment models. Barsh (2008) noted new organizational models are needed to engage in thinking-intensive work, support hierarchical decision-making, and enable self-directed professionals to collaborate. Durrance (1997) stated chaordic systems would facilitate order and structure along with a distinct life cycle pattern, where control is traded for dynamic possibility. Hock (2000) concluded that the most abundant, least expensive, and abused resource is human ingenuity, and chaordic leadership is a way to harness it. These innovations in thinking will provide insight into what trends will survive scrutiny.

Facilitating new thinking engenders buy-in from the stakeholders. A company must include in their sustainability strategy a risk profile that accounts for background risk sources, real versus perceived risk, and relevant social and political risk (Epstein & Buhovac, 2008). When integrating leadership concepts into corporate strategy, organizations should routinely account for market and nonmarket impacts, such as costs reductions from efficiencies, reduced future costs of environmental cleanup, internal control, ethic breaches, and personnel problems from social sensitivity (Armani et al., 2020; Epstein & Buhovac, 2008). General Electrics' Jack Welch argued that overcoming these CSR barriers requires a fundamental rethinking of an organization's social architecture (Beinhocker, 2006). These findings are illustrative of the various dilemmas indicative of researching the field of sustainability.

RESEARCH METHODS AND TOPICS

Under the heading of Findings, the role of stakeholders in achieving sustainability is mentioned as being critical to planning, developing, and implementing corporate sustainability by engaging stakeholders. Clifton and Amran (2011) posited the stakeholder approach (SHA) is consistent with sustainable world objectives, and SHA practices at the management level are likely to see progress in achieving sustainable world objectives. Garvare and Johansson (2010) described a conceptual model of stakeholder management that explains actual behavior of organizations and sustainability and expands upon the relationship between organizational sustainability and global sustainability. Concepts such as stakeholder analysis and managing leadership initiatives drive the leadership discussion for SHA.

Stakeholder Analysis

Stakeholder analysis is a technique that could enhance an organization's ability to enact change for the better. Managers should overcome complacency, articulate a clear vision, and get everyone engaged in the process in order to effect change (Lucey, 2008). Dee Hock the founder of VISA, used the chaordic system as a tool to help organizations resolve the impact of managing the paradox of chaos (Durrance, 1997). Chaordic leaders should recognize and modify conditions, articulate a sense of community, and communicate a vision as a norm, rather than because of change (Hock, 2000). Stebbins and Shani (2009) noted managers are responsible for collaboration and its outcomes, and is a preferred method for addressing complex system-wide change (McGuire, 2006). Several steps must be followed to ensure a thorough analysis.

The first step in this discussion is identifying stakeholders. Review of the articles found that primary stakeholders, such as shareholders, suppliers, public authorities, and financial partners, are distinguished from other stakeholders as having both the means of bringing attention to their needs and the ability to take action if those needs are not met (Garvare & Johansson, 2010). Sloan (2009) argued corporate engagement of stakeholders focused on managing risk is valuable, but not sufficient to achieve sustainability. Engagement oriented on collaborating with stakeholders can lead to learning, innovation, and fundamental corporate transformation (Sloan, 2009). The next step is assigning the appropriate position and management level responsible for communicating with the stakeholders.

In most cases, senior executives are responsible for managing stakeholders and sustaining lines of communication. Perrini and Tencati (2006) stated corporate sustainability is the capacity of a firm to continue operating over extended periods of time, and depends on the sustainability of its stakeholder relationships. To advance the integration of SHA, a company should address stakeholder interests and the meeting of corporate social responsibilities in terms of sustainable objectives (Clifton & Amran, 2011). Stakeholder relationships must be the guiding principle for the managerial decision-making process (Perrini & Tencati, 2006). Another step is identifying the needs and wants of the various stakeholders.

These needs and wants must be prioritized in accordance with the influence of the stakeholder and the corporate interests of the company. Of the three stakeholder attributes of interest, urgency, and legitimacy, interest appears the most problematic, because it is has the potential to focus management too much on achievement of corporate interests (Clifton & Amran, 2011; Correia, 2019). The SHA theory posited an organization that satisfies or exceeds the demands of its stakeholders would fall short of providing solutions to uncertainty (Garvare & Johansson, 2010). The results of prioritization lead to integration of the previous steps of stakeholder management analysis.

Integration of the results of stakeholder analysis is a critical final step in the process. Tenuta (2010) concluded businesses should integrate with different stakeholders' groups that represent the economic, social, and environmental impacts of organizational sustainability goals. The author concluded the findings of the RESPONSE project provides substantial evidence that stakeholders expect corporations to attend to their interests, make a positive contribution to society and stakeholder engagement, to become integrated into core business processes (Sloan, 2009). The sustainability evaluation and reporting system (SERS) structure is flexible enough to be used by businesses of different sizes operating in different sectors and countries (Perrini & Tencati, 2006). These facts support a direct relationship that the role of stakeholders has with the themes of the benefits of CSR, managing risk, and the leadership drives sustainability strategy, thus, assisting in the long-term survival of an organization (Armani et al., 2020).

With change as a backdrop, trends in leadership tend to be symbiotic to an overall sustainability strategy. Mirchandani and Ikerd (2008) posited sustainable leadership could create and maintain synergistic relations with key stakeholders. Gibbs (2009) stated sustainability entrepreneurs are seen as leading the effort to address fears over global warming and their associated negative environmental impacts. Makipere and Yip (2008) concluded that although industries are under pressure to achieve sustainability, it is possible for every company to become a leader in sustainability, but leaders should learn to manage sustainability drivers and barriers that impact their companies. These trends are favored as potential solutions, but present challenges to those companies who do not embrace leadership initiatives as a mean to achieve sustainability.

Managing Leadership Initiatives

There remains an ongoing challenge of managing leadership initiatives in sustainable organizations. Nirenberg and Romine (2000) noted that the leader's individual value orientation and the dominant collective value orientation of the group of decision makers are the actual drivers of decisions and change programs, and determine the success or failure of those efforts. An integrative challenge is suggested to devise incentive structures using compromises, exchanges, side payments, rules, or other compensation to secure the assistance of a sufficient number of actors to enact or implement a policy or program (Beerannavar, 2020; Page, 2010). Innovation can enhance the topic of sustainability in leadership through advocating new strategic and corporate decision-making.

At the core of any trend in leadership theory is the challenge of managing the human dimension. Companies will have to balance revolutionary thinking with practical experimentation in pursuit of new, innovative management models (Barsh, 2008). Beck et al. (2008) stated change processes are governed by deceleration; change inhibits further change and unobserved organization-specific change propensity has the potential to heavily bias the results obtained with standard models. Buchanan et al. (2005) noted sustaining any profound change process requires a fundamental shift in thinking in order to understand the forces and challenges that impede progress and to develop workable strategies for dealing with these challenges. Other factors beyond theory should be explored to identify how to make leaders more effective change agents.

Organizational practices and processes can be skewed or changed by the introduction of collaborative management concepts. Franken et al. (2009) posited the challenges to successful strategy execution are: 1). the relentless pressure from shareholders for greater profitability, requiring a redefinition of strategy more frequently; 2). the increased complexity of organizations affecting people, processes, structures, technologies, suppliers, and business partners; 3). balancing the demands of successfully executing complex change programs with the demands of managing current business performance; 4). low levels of involvement of a large number of managers across all functions at an early stage of strategy execution and; 5). the difficulty of securing the required resources to execute the strategy. No theory, issues, practices, or processes can be considered a panacea; therefore, future research is still needed to contribute to the larger body of knowledge of management.

RECOMMENDATION FOR FUTURE RESEARCH

Areas of further research should focus on aspects of sustaining leadership. It is logical to posit studies, and research will support the notion of direct and indirect relationships between leadership and the goal of sustainability. Coping strategies, models, standardized techniques, and the role of technology are some of the areas considered for further research.

Coping Strategies

First, coping strategies are focused on the need to look at resistance to change as it relates to effective collaborative management. Lüscher and Lewis (2008) stated managing change is recognized as the ultimate managerial responsibility, as firms continuously engage in some form of change from shifting organizational boundaries to altering firm structure to revising decision-making processes. One study found that resistance to change exists, but is generally not strong enough to affect the change process. Resistance seems to always be more powerful in strategic changes than in evolutionary ones, because a culture of entrenched values limits innovation and creative capability by not allowing the existence of dissident people. Additionally, fast and changing environments obstruct the adoption of appropriate decisions by departments (Del Val & Fuentes, 2003). The authors concluded that resistance to change is an essential factor in any change process, allowing an understanding of the phenomenon that hinders the process, resistance to change is generally higher in strategic changes than in evolutionary ones (Del Val & Fuentes, 2003). An understanding of the change process can form the basis for recognizing the relationship between resistance to change and collaborative management.

In addition, leaders must identify the impediments and consequences of trying to overcome resistance to change. A study found change processes are governed by deceleration; change inhibits further change, and unobserved organization-specific change propensity has the potential to heavily bias the results obtained with standard models (Beck et al., 2008). Herold et al. (2008) noted change commitment is a psychological alignment with, or attachment to, the change rather than just reflecting a favorable disposition toward it, such as being open to, or accepting of it. Coping strategies are the foundation for effective collaborative management.

Models for Collaboration

Developing new models for collaborative is the second area of further research. Koontz and Thomas (2006) stated there are benefits of collaborative environmental management, but very little evidence that these processes improve the environment. The Koontz and Thomas study revealed the following outcomes: 1). collaboration leads to better decisions and effective equitable solutions; 2). successful collaborative efforts lead to increased trust and social capital and perceptions of changes in environmental quality; 3). changes in biological diversity and 4). changes in environmental parameters appropriate to a specific resource. There is acceptance of collaboration as a standard component of public management that supplements established public management theory (McGuire, 2006). A model using these factors will support the development of a collaborative management strategy.

Public organizations provide an environment conducive to testing models as politics impede the full implementation of collaborative management. The use of collaborative public management has grown significantly over the past two decades, governments at all levels have increasingly turned to collaboration, it is lauded as a creative alternative to hierarchical outcomes, and is criticized over concerns about equity and decision quality (Koontz & Thomas, 2006). An integrative leadership framework can distinguish meaningful changes in key dimensions of collaborative governance (Page, 2010). Visser (2004) posited collaborative management of a metropolis using a jurisdiction-based management model stands out, because it combines a high degree of collaboration with the advancement by cities of their strategic interests in an environment of inter-jurisdictional interdependence. These potential models are useful in developing new techniques to implement collaborative management as part of a set of standardized techniques to train leaders.

Standardized Techniques for Leaders

The last area of further research is identifying standardized techniques for leaders to use in executing collaborative management. Some researchers concluded as change intensifies complexity, ambiguity, and equivocality, and tensions become increasingly pervasive in daily life, the ability to comprehend paradox is emerged as a critical managerial skill process (Lüscher & Lewis, 2008). The authors stated managerial sensemaking is a method for middle managers to interpret, communicate, and implement change processes (Lüscher & Lewis, 2008). Public managers should possess activation, framing, mobilizing, and synthesizing skills to organize the behaviors to apply the right people and resources needed to achieve program goals, and further research is needed to explore whether there is an identifiable cycle for development of public collaboration management (McGuire, 2006). To successfully enact change, managers must overcome their innate complacency, and then articulate a clear vision to engage everyone in the process (Lucey, 2008). Borowski and Pahl-Wostl (2008) suggested social learning in collaborative planning could overcome factors such as pressure to learn, openness, gains, and incentives. Such leadership techniques will require leaders to embrace emerging schools of thoughts in the field of management.

Specific tools have proven to be effective collaborative management techniques. Power tools, such as fiat, force, coercion, and threats, are used when there is little consensus on either dimension of agreement (Christensen et al., 2006). Management tools drive change when the agreement is focused on coordination and processes through the use of training, standard operating procedures, and measurement systems (Christensen et al., 2006). Leadership tools can elicit cooperation as long as there is a high level of consensus that a change is consistent with employee expectations (Christensen et al., 2006). Techniques, models, and understanding resistance to change are areas that could minimize the impact of collaborative management strategies and provide direction for the field of management.

In addition, impacts of implementing collaborative management strategies will require leaders to address internal organizational factors. Leaders who apply collaborative management must recognize that the effects of prior changes governed by organizational routines are skewed by deep-rooted cultural values in the organization (Beck et al., 2008; Del Val & Fuentes, 2003). The exact implications of these impacts are unknown, but the resulting leadership behaviors are directly related to the amount of commitment by employees and stakeholders (Armani et al., 2020; Herold et al., 2008). The future direction of research in the field of management should specifically address these impacts.

Role of Technology

Building the body of knowledge should look at how technology is viewed by corporations to prepare and train future leaders. IPCC (2007) posited governments have a crucial supportive role in providing policy, legal, and regulatory frameworks to facilitate investment and technology transfer, which is also supported by Beerannavar (2020) and Baumgartner and Ebner (2010). Baumgartner and Ebner (2010) identified the types of sustainability strategies as:

- Introverted – risk mitigation strategy that focuses on legal and other external standards concerning environmental and social aspects in order to avoid risks.
- Extroverted – legitimating strategy focusing on external relationships and license to operate.
- Conservative – efficiency strategy that focuses on eco-efficiency and cleaner production.
- Visionary – holistic sustainability strategy focused on sustainability issues within all business activities, which offer customers and stakeholders' unique advantages.

The increased complexity of organizations affecting people, processes, structures, technologies, suppliers, and business partners are challenges to successful strategy execution (Franken et al., 2009). The selection of a strategy to guide change agents should drive the development of future leadership training requirements.

In addition, corporations should view the role of technology as part of an overall corporate sustainability strategy. Policies are needed to create incentives for producers and consumers to invest in technologies (IPCC, 2007). Senge et al. (2009) suggested tech-savvy executives must embrace constant system evolution and identify what key assumptions of the business strategy and sustainment can be addressed by technology. Technology should be embraced as an integral part of implementing a sustainability plan.

CONCLUSION

Several conclusions reinforced the premise of the findings supporting the themes of managing risk, the leadership drives sustainability strategy, and new thinking is required to facilitate sustainability. The costs and benefits of sustainability strategies are cross dimensional throughout organizations and should take into account multiple stakeholder objectives (Epstein & Buhovac, 2008). Christensen et al. (2006), Jones et al. (2004), and Lucey (2008) support the value of using techniques such as ownership, change tools, and vision statements to create and maintain momentum for change initiatives. Kumar et al. (2007) and McGuire (2006) concluded it is a requirement that executives learn new managerial skills to support their execution strategy. As with any study, not every aspect of an issue, theory, or concept is adequately addressed, so gaps in the research are revealed.

Scholars will have a clear set of next steps to continue research in the field of sustainability. Theoretical foundations for sustainability will evolve in the direction of greater integration, while stakeholder expectations present significant opportunities for firms that develop and extend capabilities to ensure legitimacy and sustain these processes (Mirchandani & Ikerd, 2008). Although industries are under pressure to achieve sustainability, it is possible for every company to become a leader in sustainability, but leaders need to manage the sustainability drivers and barriers that impact their companies (Makipere & Yip, 2008). Further research can contribute to the overall body of knowledge in achieving sustainability as a primary focus of exploration.

In conclusion, more corporations and their business investors are recognizing the importance and benefits of incorporating sustainability as a strategic priority that involves significant business risks. Business and environmental sustainability strategy development requires a coordinated, cooperative, and iterative focused process of ideas and actions to achieve economic, environmental, and social objectives in a balanced and integrative manner (Beerannavar, 2020; Garvare & Johansson, 2010). The literature and research covered, along with the processes, tools, techniques, lessons learned, and best practices described in this article highlights the evolution of sustainability as both a corporate strategy and business opportunity.

REFERENCES

Armani, A. B., Petrini, M., & Santos, A. C. (2020). What are the attributes of sustainable leadership? *Revista Brasileira de Gestão de Negócios*, *22*(4), 820–835. doi:10.7819/rbgn.v22i4.4086

Barsh, J. (2008). Innovative management: A conversation with Gary Hamel and Lowell Bryan. (cover story). *The McKinsey Quarterly*, *1*, 24.

Baumgartner, R. J., & Ebner, D. (2010). Corporate sustainability strategies: Sustainability profiles and maturity levels. *Sustainable Development (Bradford)*, *18*(2), 76–89. doi:10.1002d.447

Beck, N., Brüderl, J., & Woywode, M. (2008). Momentum or deceleration? Theoretical and methodological reflections on the analysis of organizational change. *Academy of Management Journal*, *51*(3), 413–435. doi:10.5465/amj.2008.32625943

Beerannavar, C. R. (2020). The role of corporations in achieving ecological sustainability: Evaluating the environmental performance of corporations. In *Interdisciplinary Approaches to Public Policy and Sustainability* (pp. 228–247). IGI Global. https://www.igi-global.com/book/interdisciplinary-approaches-public-policy-sustainability/227626 doi:10.4018/978-1-7998-0315-7.ch011

Beinhocker, E. D. (2006). The adaptable corporation. *The McKinsey Quarterly*, *2*, 76.

Beshears, J., Gillingham, K., Groom, B., & Jotzo, F. (2019). The Benefits and Challenges of Sustainability Leadership. *Sustainability*, *11*(11), 3168. doi:10.3390u11113130

Bolton, M. (2022). A system leverage points approach to governance for sustainable development. *Sustainability Science*, *17*(6), 2427–2457. doi:10.100711625-022-01188-x

Borowski, I., & Pahl-Wostl, C. (2008). Where can social learning be improved in international river basin management in Europe? *European Environment*, *18*(4), 216–227. doi:10.1002/eet.479

Buchanan, D., Fitzgerald, L., Ketley, D., Gollop, R., Jones, J. L., Lamont, S. S., Neath, A., & Whitby, E. (2005). No going back: A review of the literature on sustaining organizational change. *International Journal of Management Reviews*, *7*(3), 189–205. doi:10.1111/j.1468-2370.2005.00111.x

Buhl, A., Schmidt-Keilich, M., Muster, V., Blazejewski, S., Schrader, U., Harrach, C., Schäfer, M., & Süßbauer, E. (2019). Design thinking for sustainability: Why and how design thinking can foster sustainability-oriented innovation development. *Journal of Cleaner Production*, *231*, 1248–1257. doi:10.1016/j.jclepro.2019.05.259

Christensen, C. M., Marx, M., & Stevenson, H. H. (2006). The tools of cooperation and change. *Harvard Business Review*, *84*(10), 73–80. PMID:17040041

Clifton, D., & Amran, A. (2011). The stakeholder approach: A sustainability perspective. *Journal of Business Ethics*, *98*(1), 121–136. doi:10.100710551-010-0538-6

Correia, M. S. (2019). Sustainability: An Overview of the Triple Bottom Line and Sustainability Implementation. [IJoSE]. *International Journal of Strategic Engineering*, *2*(1), 29–38. https://www.igi-global.com/article/sustainability/219322. doi:10.4018/IJoSE.2019010103

Del Val, M. P., & Fuentes, C. M. (2003). Resistance to change: A literature review and empirical study. *Management Decision*.

Duca, I., & Gherghina, R. (2018). CSR Initiatives: An opportunity for the business environment. In *Ethics and Decision-Making for Sustainable Business Practices* (pp. 187-202). IGI Global. https://www.igi-global.com/book/corporate-social-responsibility/197763

Durrance, B. (1997). The evolutionary vision of Dee Hock: From chaos to chaords. *Training and Development-Alexandria-American Society for Training and Development*, *51*(4), 24–31.

Epstein, M. J., & Buhovac, A. R. (2008). *Making sustainability work: Best practices in managing and measuring corporate social, environmental, and economic impacts*. Greenleaf.

Franken, A., Edwards, C., & Lambert, R. (2009). Executing strategic change: Understanding the critical management elements that lead to success. *California Management Review*, *51*(3), 49–73. doi:10.2307/41166493

Garvare, R., & Johansson, P. (2010). Management for sustainability–A stakeholder theory. *Total Quality Management & Business Excellence*, *21*(7), 737–744. doi:10.1080/14783363.2010.483095

Gibbs, D. (2009). Sustainability entrepreneurs, ecopreneurs and the development of a sustainable economy. *Greener Management International,* (55).

Giovannini, S., Zeppetella, G., & Lazzarotti, V. (2019). Sustainable development and corporate financial performance: Evidence from the panel data. *Management Decision*, *57*(4), 990–1009.

Grinde, J., & Khare, A. (2008). The ant, the grasshopper or Schrödinger's cat: An exploration of concepts of sustainability. *Journal of Environmental Assessment Policy and Management*, *10*(2), 115–141. doi:10.1142/S1464333208003007

Hansen, L. H., Møller, P., & Scholderer, J. (2019). Corporate responsibility and sustainability: An introduction. *International Journal of Management Reviews*, *21*(4), 1034–1052.

Henderson, E., Schaper, M. T., & Robins, A. (2018). Measuring value created through sustainability initiatives. *Sustainability*, *10*(2), 590.

Herold, D. M., Fedor, D. B., Caldwell, S., & Liu, Y. (2008). The effects of transformational and change leadership on employees' commitment to a change: A multilevel study. *The Journal of Applied Psychology*, *93*(2), 346–357. doi:10.1037/0021-9010.93.2.346 PMID:18361637

Hock, D. (2000). The art of chaordic leadership. *Leader to Leader*, *15*(Winter), 20–26.

Humphreys, J., & Boje, D. (2013). Organizational leadership for sustainability: Achieving a triple bottom line. *Business Strategy and the Environment*, *22*(1), 7–17.

Jepsen, A. L., & Eskerod, P. (2009). Stakeholder analysis in projects: Challenges in using current guidelines in the real world. *International Journal of Project Management, 27*(4), 335–343. doi:10.1016/j.ijproman.2008.04.002

Jones, J., Aguirre, D., & Calderone, M. (2004). 10 principles of change management. *Strategy & Business*, 35.

King, M. C. (2008). What sustainability should mean. *Challenge, 51*(2), 27–39. doi:10.2753/0577-5132510204

Koontz, T. M., & Thomas, C. W. (2006). What do we know and need to know about the environmental outcomes of collaborative management? *Public Administration Review, 66*(s1), 111–121. doi:10.1111/j.1540-6210.2006.00671.x

Kotler, P., & Lee, N. (2016). *Corporate social responsibility: Doing the most good for your company and your cause*. John Wiley & Sons.

Kumar, S., Kant, S., & Amburgey, T. L. (2007). Public agencies and collaborative management approaches: Examining resistance among administrative professionals. *Administration & Society, 39*(5), 569–611. doi:10.1177/0095399707303635

Lucey, J. (2008). Why is the failure rate for organization change so high? *Management Services: Journal of the Institute of Practitioners in Work Study. Organization and Methods, 52*(4), 10–19.

Lüscher, L. S., & Lewis, M. W. (2008). Organizational change and managerial sensemaking: Working through paradox. *Academy of Management Journal, 51*(2), 221–240. doi:10.5465/amj.2008.31767217

Makipere, K., & Yip, G. (2008). Sustainable leadership. *Business Strategy Review, 19*(1), 64–67. doi:10.1111/j.1467-8616.2008.00521.x

McGuire, M. (2006). Collaborative public management: Assessing what we know and how we know it. *Public Administration Review, 66*(s1), 33–43. doi:10.1111/j.1540-6210.2006.00664.x

Méndez, P. F., Clement, F., Palau-Salvador, G., Diaz-Delgado, R., & Villamayor-Tomas, S. (2022). Understanding the governance of sustainability pathways: Hydraulic megaprojects, social–ecological traps, and power in networks of action situations. *Sustainability Science*, 1–19. doi:10.100711625-022-01258-0

Metzger, M. J. (2018). *2018 Global Corporate Sustainability Report*. EY. https://www.ey.com/Publication/vwLUAssets/ey-global-corporate-sustainability-report-2018/$FILE/ey-global-corporate-sustainability-report-2018.pdf

Mirchandani, D., & Ikerd, J. (2008). Building and maintaining sustainable organizations. *Organizational Management Journal, 5*(1), 40–51. doi:10.1057/omj.2008.6

Murtaza, H., Rahman, M. M., & Jalil, M. A. (2020). Corporate Sustainability: An Overview. *Corporate Social Responsibility and Environmental Management, 27*(1), 64–73.

Nirenberg, J., & Romine, P. (2000). The crafting of leadership: Values, moral assumptions and organizational change. *OD Practitioner, 32*(2), 4–17.

Ntounis, N., & Gounaris, S. (2018). Employee engagement in corporate sustainability: The roles of sustainability leadership and corporate social responsibility. *Business Strategy and the Environment*, *27*(1), 86–99.

O'Rourke, D. (2015). Corporate sustainability engagement with external stakeholders: A strategic guide. *Business Strategy and the Environment*, *24*(1), 12–20.

Page, S. (2010). Integrative leadership for collaborative governance: Civic engagement in Seattle. *The Leadership Quarterly*, *21*(2), 246–263. doi:10.1016/j.leaqua.2010.01.005

Perrini, F., & Tencati, A. (2006). Sustainability and stakeholder management: The need for new corporate performance evaluation and reporting systems. *Business Strategy and the Environment*, *15*(5), 296–308. doi:10.1002/bse.538

Porter, M., & Kramer, M. (2006). Strategy and society: The link between competitive advantage and corporate social responsibility. *Harvard Business Review*, *84*(12), 78–92. PMID:17183795

Robins, A., & Schaper, M. T. (2017). *The sustainability advantage: Seven business case benefits of a triple bottom line*. Sage Publications.

Schwarz, J. M., & Sattler, H. (2019). Corporate sustainability and stock returns in the U.S. stock market. Sustainability Accounting. *Management and Policy Journal*, *10*(1), 111–144.

Senge, P., Smith, B., Kruschwitz, N., Laur, J., & Schley, S. (2009). The necessary revolution. *Leader to Leader*, *51*(51), 24–28. doi:10.1002/ltl.314

Sloan, P. (2009). Redefining stakeholder engagement: From control to collaboration. *Journal of Corporate Citizenship*, *36*(36), 25–40. doi:10.9774/GLEAF.4700.2009.wi.00005

Stebbins, M. W., & Shani, A. B. (2009). Clinical inquiry and reflective design in a secrecy-based organization. *The Journal of Applied Behavioral Science*, *45*(1), 59–89. doi:10.1177/0021886308327235

Tenuta, P. (2010). The measurement of sustainability. *Review of Business Research*, *10*(2), 163–171.

Chapter 3
How Emerging Technologies Spawn New Social Engineering Paradigms

Horace C. Mingo
https://orcid.org/0000-0002-2395-2990
University of North Carolina at Chapel Hill, USA

ABSTRACT

Cybersecurity criminals often use social engineering techniques to meet their objectives. The most egregious cybersecurity attacks may be designed to get an organization to override defenses, change standards, or convince governing bodies to change laws and regulations through political pressure, espionage, or litigation. By creating cultures of trust or mistrust, organizational leaders can be persuaded to declassify information or make changes that allow such adversaries to gain access to things that are unavailable to them. Through time and strategy, cybercriminals can weaken cybersecurity defense capabilities and awareness. Organizations people trust may use social engineering against consumers through online advertisements, cookies, and spyware to gather data, like IP addresses, location histories, and browsing preferences, for gain and profit. This study highlights areas where social engineering tools are designed into devices and activities to influence behavior in personal and professional settings.

INTRODUCTION

Research into new social engineering paradigms began with realizing the potential for executing social engineering attacks by gaining access to information from everyday objects and devices in our homes, offices, markets, and public environments called the Internet of Things (IoT). Social engineering is a common method used by hackers to circumvent security barriers by exploiting human weaknesses (Wang et al., 2021). Social engineering consists of four stages that may be repeated as many as required to achieve the goal:

1. Compile the essential background information on the victim.

DOI: 10.4018/979-8-3693-1634-4.ch003

2. Establish a trusting connection with the victim.
3. Make use of the available information and carry out the assault.
4. End the contact without leaving any traces.

The term Internet of Things refers to the general concept of things, particularly everyday objects, that are readable, recognizable, locatable, addressable, and/or controllable via the Internet, whether via RFID, wireless LAN, wide-area network, or other means (Harit et al., 2017). The number of IoT attack vectors seems limitless, and the lack of standardized security for such devices makes them the obvious target for gathering data to launch social engineering attacks as well as other attacks that benefit from interactive surveillance and data collection.

The Internet of Things (IoT) has the capacity to link billions of everyday objects. that we come into contact with daily, such as automobiles and other machines, as well as many things that we may not be aware of, such as food, clothing, boundaries, landmarks, commodities, infrastructure, and more (Harit et al., 2017). The overall footprint and complexity of disparate entities capable of interacting with IoT devices (Matyokurehwa et al., 2022) create a social engineering attack vector (Wang et al., 2021) fueled by a global array of supply chains (Omitola & Wills, 2018). This study looks at the various landscapes of threats and vulnerabilities targeted by modern cybersecurity attack vectors.

Attackers can use IoT and AI technologies to conduct social engineering attacks by exploiting vulnerabilities in the devices and systems that make up the Internet of Things (IoT) and by using AI-powered bots to mimic human behavior and manipulate individuals into divulging sensitive information or taking malicious actions. These vulnerabilities can be found in the devices and systems that make up the Internet of Things (IoT).

PROBLEM STATEMENT

According to Kostadinov (2021), the whole process of social engineering, enhanced by artificial intelligence (AI), machine learning (ML), and the Internet of Things (IoT), which can be used to gather information on people for the sole purpose of spear phishing them or to impersonate their voices can be highly targeted and automated at scale.

Nefarious entities design malicious software, advertisements, and devices to monetize data used to manipulate human behavior (Petropoulos, 2022) and control an increasing number of devices through emerging Internet and computer technologies (Matyokurehwa et al., 2022). With the growing use of the Internet in state institutions, it is possible to get illicit access to private and business information and state secrets and to conduct crimes such as espionage, treason, or the publication of state secrets via the Internet (Kotukh et al., 2021).

SIGNIFICANCE OF THE PROJECT

Lack of research makes state-of-the-art literature reviews invaluable tools to offer new perspectives on current issues and point out areas for further research to assess and develop knowledge within a research field (Grant & Booth, 2009; Snyder, 2019). When compared to other empirical research, literature reviews need to be more related to evolving technologies in the field of cybersecurity. Literature reviews of social engineering in cybersecurity need more transparent, systematic procedures to replicate research and trace the arguments and conclusions. This research aims to elaborate on the significance of literature reviews in assessing the influence of specific advancing technologies.

METHODOLOGY

The method employed in this project was a state-of-the-art literature review with content analysis of 55 articles published in peer-reviewed journals and news articles written in English between 2009 and 2022. Key search terms included: social engineering, adware, cybersecurity threats, cybercrime, digital privacy, supply chain threats, classified information, Internet of Things, malware, online advertising, data privacy, and literature review. The databases and their hosts (shown in parentheses) included ResearchGate, Academia.edu, Semantic Scholar, Google Scholar, ACM Digital Library, NIH National Library of Medicine, JSTOR, Mendeley, EBSCOhost, Open Access Library (oalib.com), and worldwidescience.org.

CHALLENGES BROUGHT BY CLOUD COMPUTING

Organizations moved toward artificial intelligence and cloud computing as the world adapted to the COVID-19 pandemic and global supply chain shortages (Zainuddin et al., 2022). Artificial Intelligence (AI) Innovations are helping retailers bring more automation into retail stores to provide automated customer service (Song & Kim, 2022; Haenlein & Kaplan, 2021; Murphy et al., 2019). Cloud computing is a model for delivering information technology services over the internet using a virtualized and scalable infrastructure. This model gives users the ability to gain access to shared resources in the form of a service that is customized to meet their requirements without requiring them to purchase, install, maintain, or otherwise manage the underlying computing resources themselves (Vareschi & Picoto, 2021; Garrison et al., 2015).

The global COVID-19 pandemic drove more businesses to the cloud due to the high levels of employee resignations that have already affected their ability to maintain critical IT infrastructures (Bardhan et al., 2022). The global expansion that started in the 1970s (Afesorgbor et al., 2021) sent many critical jobs in the United States overseas as organizations sought to lower costs amid an increasingly competitive environment. The aftermath of COVID-19 saw compromised supply chains and an inability to get critical resources like computer chips and other products from our significant global expansion (Mendoza, 2021).

Schwartz (2017) described how the years from 2016 to 2022 showed the world the contempt the American people increasingly had for American corporations. These corporations showed an unapologetic, blatant disregard for the welfare of the American worker and the American government, to whom they seem to hold no allegiance. The board of directors only seems to hold allegiance to the shareholders who made the monetary investment. Although the American workers who invest time and labor are equally responsible for the success and profit of the corporations, they are disregarded by the board of directors, arguably as the rule of law (Schwartz, 2017). Schwartz shows that the American corporation is a corporate citizen who, as a rule, shows no allegiance or patriotism and does not defend or honor the nation or its employees.

SOCIAL ENGINEERING THE INTERNET OF THINGS

The Internet of Things (IoT) is defined as an infrastructure of networked items, people, systems, and information resources, as well as intelligent services that enable them to process and respond to information from the real and virtual worlds (Omitola & Wills, 2018). Many of the devices we interact with daily, from cars and machines to many things we may not realize, such as food, clothing, boundaries, landmarks, commodities, infrastructure, and more (Harit et al., 2017), are designed to collect data. These devices can support social engineering campaigns by capturing information to socially engineer consumers for marketing and social influence. Collectively, IoT devices capture unimaginable volumes of information in the forms of location, date, time, history, preferences, video, voice, location, metadata, and more (Mugariri, 2022).

Many anticipate that an increasing number of gadgets and items will be connected in previously unheard-of ways. For instance, by 2020, it was anticipated that the number of connected devices would exceed connected humans by a ratio of 6:1 and that 26 billion gadgets would be linked (Omitola & Wills, 2018). Already there are billions of things connected to the Internet around us that make us vulnerable to cyber-attacks. IoT devices are capable of being remotely controlled by malicious actors, making them vulnerable to being weaponized and hijacked for Distributed Denial of Service (DDoS) assaults (Ali et al., 2022) and theft of resources via man-in-the-middle attacks while they are transferring data on a network (Kanade, 2018).

The Internet of Things (IoT) is vulnerable to attacks that target various things, including physical objects, protocols, data, and software. Physical objects include the physical components that the attackers may target. Protocols include communication methods used inside an organization that may be targeted by attackers (Matyokurehwa et al., 2022). Thalen (2021) reported that many IoT users were attacked on a massive scale in Texas through one of the numerous smart meters attached to their homes. Thalen further explained that modern households have smart meters for water, natural gas, and electricity that exchange information with one another and are connected to one or more central hubs that relay data to their respective utility provider.

The Internet of Things (IoT) is a technological trend that aims to integrate Internet communication into billions of everyday items and devices that we come into contact with on a daily basis, including machines and cars as well as numerous items that we might not realize, like food containers, clothing, boundaries, landmarks, commodities, infrastructure, and more (Harit et al., 2017). Most people do not realize the vulnerabilities imposed upon them by smart televisions with undetectable cameras or smart coffee machines at the coffee shop that may be able to access their smartphones (CISOMAG, 2020). We will likely see more devices deployed to greet customers, detect theft, manage inventory, help customers find things, and answer questions (Bogue, 2019). The Internet of Things (IoT) generates vast volumes of sensitive information about people and equipment and generates new attack channels and a larger surface (Wang et al., 2021).

Over time, IoT may replace the Internet user as the weakest link in cybersecurity. One example of how IoT devices could be used in a social engineering attack is through the use of compromised smart home devices such as security cameras or door locks. Attackers could exploit security vulnerabilities in these devices to gain unauthorized access to the home network, which could be used to steal sensitive information, monitor activity, or launch attacks against other targets. Similarly, AI-powered bots can be used to automate and scale social engineering attacks. By analyzing publicly available data and social media profiles, bots can create convincing fake personas that mimic the behavior and communication style of real people. These bots can then be used to send phishing emails, conduct spear-phishing attacks, or spread disinformation campaigns through social media. In addition to automated attacks, attackers can also use AI and IoT devices to create more convincing social engineering scenarios. For example, an attacker could use an AI-powered voice assistant to impersonate a victim's boss or colleague, tricking the victim into sharing sensitive information or transferring funds to a fraudulent account.

SOCIAL ENGINEERING AS A BUSINESS

Cybersecurity and privacy issues are linked to how the Internet of Things will influence business strategies (Donner & Steep, 2021). According to Algarni et al. (2013), the goal of information security is to secure the system's integrity, confidentiality, and availability. Although each piece can be broken, damaged, or harmed by exploiting the vulnerability of technology or individuals, it has been discovered that individuals are the security's weakest link. Algarni et al. explain that social engineering is the practice of misleading and manipulating others to assist attackers in achieving their objectives. This can be accomplished by persuading victims to divulge sensitive information or execute an action that benefits the attacker. Consequently, social engineering has become a contentious issue in information security due to its remarkable complexity and astonishing simplicity.

To exploit the user or weakest link, criminals use malicious advertisements for social engineering attacks to persuade users to share valuable information, buy fake offerings, or download undesirable software (Vadrevu & Perdisci, 2019). Vadrevu and Perdisci found that 24% or sixteen out of sixty-seven domains deployed by advertising networks offered malicious ads. Vadrevu and Perdisci showed how they found the URLs used to launch a social engineering attack on a Spanish streaming website.

A Business Model Built on Deception

Criminals, organizations, and governments use social engineering techniques to exploit people for profit and influence on a large scale (Vadrevu & Perdisci, 2019). Carnavalet and Mannan (2019) studied Wajam Internet Technologies, Inc., based in Montreal, Canada, because it was a business that succeeded by building its business model on adware capabilities. Wajam's product was a social media search engine supported by ad revenue, designed to improve search results of the various search engines by adding content pulled from the consumer's social media networks. Before the owners sold Wajam to China to avoid litigation from the Canadian government, their advertisement-supported social search engine had evolved into a malicious product with advanced capabilities designed for anti-virus evasion, browser injection, and web traffic interception.

The ads often link to content designed to exploit the reader in numerous ways. Szczepkowski and Szczepkowski (2021) demonstrate that through deception and technology, entities can monetize online traffic by publishing adware, malicious or deceptive advertising software constructed to produce revenue. The advertisers pay the website publisher when the consumers view the advertisements. The revenue incentive is much higher when the consumer clicks on the advertisement. The pay-per-click advertising model influences the publisher to find creative ways to coerce the viewer into clicking the advertisement cloaked under the guise of a sensational news story (Szczepkowski & Szczepkowski, 2021). Szczepkowski and Szczepkowski (2021) declared that beyond the bad information supplied by the advertisements, a malicious website publisher or an advertiser could track activities and use various means to commit acts of fraud and deception.

Tracking Your Behavior for Profit

It is difficult to substantiate the threat that adware poses to the user if the cybersecurity folks only see adware as software that automatically displays or downloads advertising material to online users, often in undesirable ways (Gao et al., 2019). Users trade their personal information for a free service in exchange for utilizing free services such as social media, mapping tools that provide directions, and platforms to discover goods, services, and housing. For example, when customers use social media, mapping tools that provide directions, the business that provided that tool captures information about the customers' preferences and discovers the types of material those customers should be exposed to (Donner & Steep, 2021).

Donner and Steep (2021) note that consumer insights make data-driven business models possible. For example, shops can tailor their advertising efforts; automobile manufacturers can collect data on driving habits to predict failures, and ridesharing services can determine prices by tracking congestion and demand patterns. However, Borgolte and Feamster (2020) found that the excessive data collection, behavioral stalking, and demographic targeting at the foundation of most online advertisements are so invasive that Target Corporation could accurately predict the delivery dates of its pregnant customers based on online shopping and browsing patterns. The Target Corporation used this information to send a targeted advertisement through the United States Postal Service that unintentionally revealed a daughter's pregnancy to her father (Feamster, 2020). Borgolte and Feamster posited that the increasingly egregious advertising practices of data collection and breaches led to the legislature by the European Union and the State of California in the form of the General Protection Data Act (GDPR) and the California Consumer Privacy Act (CCPA). Overwhelmingly, consumers are concerned about the proliferation of targeted online advertisements that contravene personal privacies and propagate malicious software (Cai et al., 2020).

SOCIAL ENGINEERING THE SUPPLY CHAIN

The supply chain is one of the most rapidly developing concepts in which popularity grew as a result of market globalization and the need to meet the ever more sophisticated needs of the customers. A supply chain is an advanced 21st-century network created by the demand from the customer and supply from suppliers, manufacturers, and wholesale traders, which feature rapid reaction times and practical cooperation in quality control and cost reduction (Wolnowska & Kasyk, 2021).

According to Glas (2021), many organizations use open-source software to reduce the high cost of software development operations. Ohm (2018) showed that open-source software is such a threat to the software supply chain that it was listed on the OWASP Top Ten security risks for 2021. Ohm cited Janaszek (2018), explaining that open-source software is an attractive target for software supply chain attacks because several thousand open-source projects may deploy one open-source package. These software supply chain attacks leverage the increasing use of open source during software development. In 2017, the NotPetya supply chain attack caused Ukraine and other global organizations billions of dollars in damages (Ohm, 2018). Open-source software supply chain attacks use techniques to evoke trust and avoid the detection of malicious code inserted into open-source software packages. These clandestine digital algorithms are designed to pass vulnerabilities to projects employing open-source software (Ohm et al., 2020).

In the first three months of 2021, there was a 42% increase in the number of cyber supply chain assaults reported by 137 businesses against 27 different third-party providers (Yeboah-Ofori et al., 2021). Traditional cybersecurity methods are inadequate to cover supply chain complexities that involve a disparity of criminals, stakeholders, software, networks, and components (Pal & Alam, 2017). Globalization adds to the supply chain complexity, and attack motives are spread across disparate globally competitive companies, individuals, and governments (Ohm et al., 2020). Previous studies failed to show how attacks on supply chains around the world may have been reinforced by cyber-attacks (Urciuoli et al., 2013). Cash, products, services, and data travel together through a supply chain pipeline to form a virtual matrix of decentralized organizations (Sarumi & Okunoye, 2021).

Urciuoli et al. (2013) demonstrated how cybercrime supports criminal activities in the supply chain by showing how social engineering plays a part in various criminal activities such as cargo crime, smuggling, counterfeiting with intimidation and blackmailing using the Internet as a critical communication component for sabotage.

SOCIAL ENGINEERING ATTACK VECTORS IN CRITICAL INFRASTRUCTURE

Social engineering attacks can pose a significant threat to critical infrastructure, which includes systems and networks that are essential for the functioning of society, such as power grids, transportation networks, and water treatment facilities. Attackers can use a variety of social engineering tactics to exploit vulnerabilities in critical infrastructure, including:

1. Phishing and Spear Phishing: Attackers can send emails or messages that appear to be from legitimate sources to trick employees into divulging sensitive information, downloading malware, or clicking on malicious links.
2. Baiting: Attackers can leave physical devices or media, such as USB drives or CDs, in public places or near critical infrastructure sites, hoping that someone will pick them up and plug them into a computer, inadvertently installing malware or other malicious software.
3. Impersonation: Attackers can impersonate legitimate employees or contractors to gain unauthorized access to critical infrastructure systems, either by physically entering a facility or through remote access.
4. Pretexting: Attackers can create a false pretext, such as claiming to be conducting a security audit or performing maintenance to gain access to critical infrastructure systems.
5. Social Media Engineering: Attackers can use social media to gather information about critical infrastructure employees, including their job titles, relationships, and hobbies, which can be used to craft more convincing phishing emails or to conduct targeted attacks.

Critical infrastructures are interconnected with many other systems and may inherit their vulnerabilities. The inability to identify the scope of vulnerability and threats is a constant challenge. Adopting COTS (Commercial-Off-The-Shelf) into critical infrastructure brings new threats and vulnerabilities. Ready-made commercial products help to reduce time and costs and improve performance needed to gain a competitive advantage. Further research will help reduce the risks (Hawkins & Gravier, 2019).

Industry 4.0 integration introduces a myriad of understudied threats and vulnerabilities into critical infrastructure around the world.

Critical infrastructures are moving toward cloud computing (Adelmeyer & Teuteberg, 2018), more so now as it grapples with the realities of the necessary remote workforces spawned by the pandemic (Bardhan et al., 2022). Industrial control systems that deliver vital manufacturing, communication, and energy services to critical infrastructure are no exception (Maglaras et al., 2018). Critical infrastructures interconnected through the Internet inherit all the cybersecurity threats and issues that the Internet brings. Inviting the entire world into a critical infrastructure environment requires a firm commitment to cybersecurity. Failure to do so may leave entire populations vulnerable to physical and economic harm.

Ginter (2016) detailed the National Institute of Standards and Technology (NIST) framework for strengthening the cybersecurity of critical infrastructure in the United States. The NIST framework organizes security controls into five categories: Identify, Protect, Detect, Respond, and Recover. The threats that IoT devices bring to utilities and critical infrastructures have not been widely recognized or understood by the public. Ginter cautions that gaining situational awareness of the dynamic states of interconnected networks on critical infrastructure systems can be extremely difficult to achieve and maintain.

Hawkins and Gravier (2019) conducted a literature review to identify the antecedents and consequences of COTS adoption from software engineering, supply chain, knowledge management, marketing, and Department of Defense system acquisition to show that commercial products help to reduce time, costs, and improve performance needed to gain competitive advantage (Hawkins & Gravier, 2019). There is a trend toward using more Commercial-off-the-Shelf (COTS) components in nuclear applications as the cost of developing custom components in nuclear facilities is becoming increasingly prohibitive (Guerra & Fletcher, 2021). Critical infrastructures that integrate COTS software and hardware into their systems are destined to inherit the integration, supply chain, external dependency, and cybersecurity threats and issues that COTS software and hardware bring with them.

The introduction of Internet-enabled devices into the manufacturing environment by employees and visitors carrying cell phones, connected wearables, tablet computers, and other devices creates a chaotic environment for manufacturing cybersecurity. Ani et al. (2017) posit that human behavior and misconduct are the biggest threat to industrial and manufacturing cybersecurity defense. More recent attack trends show a steep rise in activity from highly organized groups like the Black Vine, who collaborate with a network of partners to conduct cyber-based espionage campaigns against healthcare, energy, and aerospace industries that make use of industry 4.0. These groups target sensitive organizational data, intellectual property, and product secrets (Mullet et al., 2021).

CONCLUSION

The consumer's ability to trust companies, organizations, and governments is waning as data gets used more often to cause more harm to the public. Organizations with interests in politics, marketing, warfare, religion, and crime use social engineering against consumers under the guise of market intelligence to earn trust and build confidence in their offerings. The monetization of this trust can lead to many forms of manipulation and attack as information about the consumer's activities and behavior is sold and resold in the marketplace for consumer data. The vast amounts of data collected about consumers, devices, and the environment have enormous value and have the power to influence markets and affect the psychological well-being of demographic populations.

Petropoulos (2022) posits that massive amounts of data gathered for AI algorithmic systems can shape the framework and control the timing of marketing strategies that target users at the individual level with manipulative strategies that are far more effective and difficult to detect. Furthermore, manipulation can take many forms, including the use of AI algorithms to detect human biases, personalized addictive strategies for the consumption of goods, and exploiting individuals' emotionally vulnerable states to promote products and services that match well with their temporary emotions. Petropoulos noted that manipulation is frequently combined with clever design tactics, marketing strategies, predatory advertising, and pervasive behavioral price discrimination to steer users to inferior choices that can be easily monetized by firms that use AI algorithms. The article shows that these strategies all have one thing in common: they reduce the (economic) value users can derive from services to increase firm profitability.

Data collected by IoT devices throughout personal, corporate, or natural environments can be used for consumer manipulation, public compulsion, insider trading, espionage, and social engineering attacks against family interests, corporate leaders, and government employees. However, it is common practice for organizations accused of malfeasance to protect their institutional boundaries by pointing the finger of blame toward third parties and striving to socially engineer the victims, the public, and the courts to believe them. (Cherrier & Türe, 2022).

According to Donner and Steep (2021), the Internet of Things (IoT) revolution enables the collection of real-time data on the preferences and behaviors of consumers, contextualized geographically and temporally. Moreover, the rapid expansion of IoT is exemplified by the fact that 90 percent of the world's data was generated in the last two years and that the rate is still accelerating exponentially towards a data volume 40 times the size of 2017 by 2020. Donner and Steep posit that this is driven by appliances, automobiles, and cell phones rapidly becoming data-collecting devices.

According to Sehgal et al. (2022), IoT enables digital marketers to collect and gather customer behavior, purchasing patterns, location, and other information in unprecedented ways. IoT can collect so much data about a user that it is possible to track even when the customer is interested in purchasing their services and products. As discussed by Donner and Steep (2021), consumer profiling raises several regulatory issues, including those of fairness and transparency when people exchange personal information for services, increased risk of security breaches, and the effects of algorithmic bias as algorithms become more pervasive in determining crucial commercial and social aspects of life. Furthermore, we can reduce our vulnerabilities by maintaining the awareness that surveillance is built into devices like IoT designed to listen, watch, and track everyone and everything in its proximity. Donner and Steep (2021) posited that recent studies had highlighted the importance of further investigating the impact of the Internet of Things on society and industry.

Ani et al. (2017) posit that human behavior and misconduct are the biggest threat to industrial and manufacturing cybersecurity defense. More recent attack trends show a steep rise in activity from highly organized groups like the Black Vine, who collaborate with a network of partners to conduct cyber-based espionage campaigns against healthcare, energy, and aerospace industries using industry 4.0. These groups target sensitive organizational data, intellectual property, and product secrets (Mullet et al., 2021). Above and beyond the usual protection measures, Mullet et al. (2021) propose that the best countermeasures for manufacturing cybersecurity should include more focus on the encryption of stored data, communications, and data streams as well secure VPN, Wi-Fi, and Internet Protocols (IP) communications.

With the advancement of technology comes a rise in the number of attempts to breach cybersecurity. Hackers are employing a wide variety of social engineering strategies in addition to other highly sophisticated methods to take advantage of their victims (Hijji & Alam, 2021). Social engineering, supply chain vulnerabilities, the Internet of Things, and artificial intelligence offer substantial security risks to organizations. Cybercriminals utilize social engineering to deceive workers into disclosing sensitive information or gaining illegal access to networks, whereas supply chain assaults use vulnerabilities in the systems of third-party vendors to obtain sensitive information. Internet of Things and artificial intelligence vulnerabilities could be exploited to gain network access or to steal sensitive information. Organizations need to implement proactive measures to protect themselves against these risks.

To protect against social engineering attacks, organizations should train their employees to recognize phishing and other forms of social engineering attacks. Employees should be encouraged to report suspicious emails or messages and should never click on links or open attachments from unknown sources. Implementing multi-factor authentication and encryption can help mitigate the risk of social engineering attacks.

To protect against social engineering attacks that leverage IoT and AI, organizations should implement security best practices such as strong password policies, network segmentation, regular software updates, and employee training to recognize and report suspicious activity. Additionally, organizations should consider using AI-powered security solutions that can detect and mitigate threats in real time.

To protect critical infrastructure from social engineering attacks, organizations must implement robust security policies and practices, such as regular employee training and awareness programs, multi-factor authentication, access controls, and incident response plans. Organizations should also conduct regular security assessments and audits to identify and address critical infrastructure system vulnerabilities. Lastly, it is essential to establish a security culture that encourages employees to report suspicious activity and places a premium on security in every aspect of business operations.

Organizations should implement security measures to mitigate supply chain vulnerabilities, including vendor assessments, contract negotiations, and audits. The vendor's security policies and practices must align with the organization's security standards, and vendors should have a contingency plan in place in the event of a security breach. Additionally, organizations should limit access to sensitive information to only trusted third-party vendors.

IoT devices and AI systems must also be secured through proper configuration and management. It is recommended that Internet of Things (IoT) devices be physically separated from business networks and that frequent security patches be installed. Restrictions should be put in place to ensure that only authorized employees have access to artificial intelligence systems. These systems should be monitored for irregularities and suspicious activity.

In conclusion, organizations need to take a comprehensive strategy for cybersecurity by tackling weaknesses in social engineering, supply chains, the internet of things, and artificial intelligence. This may be accomplished by putting into place the most effective security policies, providing frequent training for employees, and conducting security audits. Organizations may reduce the likelihood of being targeted by cybercriminals and safeguard their sensitive data if they maintain a state of constant vigilance and proactivity.

REFERENCES

Abate, A. F., Bisogni, C., Cascone, L., Castiglione, A., Costabile, G., & Mercuri, I. (2020). Social robot interactions for social engineering: Opportunities and open issues. *2020 IEEE Intl Conf on Dependable, Autonomic and Secure Computing, Intl Conf on Pervasive Intelligence and Computing, Intl Conf on Cloud and Big Data Computing, Intl Conf on Cyber Science and Technology Congress (DASC/PiCom/CBDCom/CyberSciTech)*. IEEE. 10.1109/DASC-PICom-CBDCom-CyberSciTech49142.2020.00097

Adelmeyer, M., & Teuteberg, F. (2018). Cloud Computing Adoption in Critical Infrastructures-Status Quo and Elements of a Research Agenda. *Proceedings of the Multikonferenz Wirtschaftsinformatik, 2018*, 1345–1356.

Afesorgbor, S. K., van Bergeijk, P., & Demena, B. A. (2021). *Does COVID-19 threaten globalization?* International Institute of Social Studies (ISS). ISS working papers. General series No. 683

Algarni, A., Xu, Y., Chan, T., & Tian, G. (2013). *Toward understanding social engineering.*

Ali, M. H., Jaber, M. M., Abd, S. K., Rehman, A., Awan, M. J., Damaševičius, R., & Bahaj, S. A. (2022). Threat Analysis and Distributed Denial of Service (DDoS) Attack Recognition in the Internet of Things (IoT). *Electronics (Basel), 11*(3), 494. doi:10.3390/electronics11030494

Ani, U. P., He, H., & Tiwari, A. (2017). Review of cybersecurity issues in industrial critical infrastructure: Manufacturing in perspective. *Journal of Cyber Security Technology, 1*(1), 32–74. doi:10.1080/23742917.2016.1252211

Bardhan, R., Byrd, T., & Boyd, J. (2022). *Workforce Management during the Time of COVID-19—Lessons Learned and Future Measures*. COVID. doi:10.3390/covid3010001

Bogue, R. (2019). Strong prospects for robots in retail. *The Industrial Robot, 46*(3), 326–331. doi:10.1108/IR-01-2019-0023

Borgolte, K., & Feamster, N. (2020). *Understanding the Performance Costs and Benefits of Privacy-focused Browser Extensions. Proceedings of The Web Conference 2020*. Association for Computing Machinery. https://doi-org.proxymu.wrlc.org/10.1145/3366423.3380292

Cai, Y., Yee, G. O. M., Gu, Y. X., & Lung, C.-H. (2020). Threats to Online Advertising and Countermeasures: A Technical Survey. *Digital Threats: Research and Practice*. https://doi-org.proxymu.wrlc.org/10.1145/3374136

Carnavalet, X.D., & Mannan, M. (2019). Privacy and Security Risks of "Not-a-Virus" Bundled Adware: The Wajam Case. *ArXiv, abs/1905.05224.*

Chen, L., Chen, J., & Xia, C. (2022). Social network behavior and public opinion manipulation. *Journal of Information Security and Applications, 64*, 103060. doi:10.1016/j.jisa.2021.103060

Cherrier, H., & Türe, M. (2022). Blame work and the scapegoating mechanism in market status-quo. *Journal of Business Research, 144*, 1207–1217. doi:10.1016/j.jbusres.2022.02.061

CISOMAG. (2020, January 10). 10 IoT Security Incidents That Make You Feel Less Secure. *Cyber Security Magazine*. https://cisomag.com/10-iot-security-incidents-that-make-you-feel-less-secure/

Donner, H., & Steep, M. (2021). Monetizing the IoT Revolution. *Sustainability (Basel)*, *13*(4), 2195. doi:10.3390u13042195

Gao, J., Li, L., Kong, P., Bissyandé, T. F., & Klein, J. (2019). Should You Consider Adware as Malware in Your Study? *2019 IEEE 26th International Conference on Software Analysis, Evolution and Reengineering (SANER)* (pp. 604-608). IEEE.

Garrison, G., Wakefield, R. L., & Kim, S. (2015). The effects of IT capabilities and delivery model on cloud computing success and firm performance for cloud supported processes and operations. *International Journal of Information Management*, *35*(4), 377–393. doi:10.1016/j.ijinfomgt.2015.03.001

Ginter, A. (2016). *SCADA Security - What's broken and how to fix it*. Abterra Technologies, Inc.

Glas, B. (2021). *A08:2021 – Software and Data Integrity Failures*. A08 Software and Data Integrity Failures - OWASP Top 10:2021. https://owasp.org/Top10/A08_2021-Software_and_Data_Integrity_Failures/

Grant, M. J., & Booth, A. (2009). A typology of reviews: An analysis of 14 review types and associated methodologies. *Health Information and Libraries Journal*, *26*(2), 91–108. doi:10.1111/j.1471-1842.2009.00848.x PMID:19490148

Guerra, S., & Fletcher, G. (2021). Overview of Approaches to the Use and Licensing of COTS Digital Devices in Safety Critical Industries. *12th Nuclear Plant Instrumentation, Control and Human-Machine Interface Technologies (NPIC&HMIT 2021).*

Haenlein, M., & Kaplan, A. (2021). Artificial intelligence and robotics: Shaking up the business world and society at large. *Journal of Business Research*, *124*, 405–407. doi:10.1016/j.jbusres.2020.10.042

Harit, A., Ezzati, A., & Elharti, R. (2017, March). Internet of things security: challenges and perspectives. In *Proceedings of the Second International Conference on Internet of things, Data and Cloud Computing*, (pp. 1-8). ACM. 10.1145/3018896.3056784

Hawkins, T. G., & Gravier, M. J. (2019). Integrating COTS technology in defense systems: A knowledge-based framework for improved performance. *European Journal of Innovation Management*, *22*(3), 493–523. doi:10.1108/EJIM-08-2018-0177

Hijji, M., & Alam, G. (2021). A multivocal literature review on growing social engineering based cyber-attacks/Threats during the COVID-19 pandemic: Challenges and prospective solutions. *IEEE Access : Practical Innovations, Open Solutions*, *9*, 7152–7169. doi:10.1109/ACCESS.2020.3048839 PMID:34786300

Janaszek, M. (2018). State of package.json dependencies. *Medium*. https://medium.com/warsawjs/ state-of-package-json-dependencies-de99828b6c3f.

Kanade, D.M. (2018). Internet of Things Security: Challenges and Opportunities. *International Journal for Research in Applied Science and Engineering Technology*.

Kayan, H., Nunes, M., Rana, O. F., Burnap, P., & Perera, C. (2022). Cybersecurity of Industrial Cyber-Physical Systems: A Review. *ACM Computing Surveys*, *54*(11s), 1–35. doi:10.1145/3510410

Kostadinov, D. (2021, June 7). *Machine learning for social engineering*. Infosec Resources. https://resources.infosecinstitute.com/topic/machine-learning-for-social-engineering/

Kotukh, Y. V., Kislov, D., Yarovoi, T., Kotsiuba, R. O., & Bondarenko, O. H. (2021). *Cybercrime and subculture of cybercriminals*. Linguistics and Culture Review. doi:10.21744/lingcure.v5nS4.1769

Lynn, C. K. (2002). Private eyes are watching you: Consumer online privacy protection-lessons from home and abroad. *Texas International Law Journal*, *37*(2), 387–420.

Maglaras, L. A., Kim, K. H., Janicke, H., Ferrag, M. A., Rallis, S., Fragkou, P., Maglaras, A., & Cruz, T. J. (2018). Cyber security of critical infrastructures. *Ict Express*, *4*(1), 42–45. doi:10.1016/j.icte.2018.02.001

Matyokurehwa, K., Rudhumbu, N., Gombiro, C., & Chipfumbu-Kangara, C. (2022). Enhanced social engineering framework mitigating against social engineering attacks in higher education. *Security and Privacy*, *5*(5), e237. doi:10.1002py2.237

Mendoza, A. R. (2021). Disruptions in global value chains due to COVID-19: Stylized facts and policy lessons. *The Philippine Review of Economics*, *58*(1&2), 214–240. doi:10.37907/9ERP1202JD

Mugariri, P., Abdullah, H., García-Torres, M., Parameshchari, B. D., & Abdul Sattar, K. N. (2022). Promoting information privacy protection awareness for Internet of Things (IoT). *Mobile Information Systems*, *2022*, 1–11. Advance online publication. doi:10.1155/2022/4247651

Mullet, V., Sondi, P., & Ramat, É. (2021). A Review of Cybersecurity Guidelines for Manufacturing Factories in Industry 4.0. *IEEE Access : Practical Innovations, Open Solutions*, *9*, 23235–23263. doi:10.1109/ACCESS.2021.3056650

Murphy, J., Gretzel, U., & Pesonen, J. (2019). Marketing robot services in hospitality and tourism: The role of anthropomorphism. *Journal of Travel & Tourism Marketing*, *36*(7), 784–795. doi:10.1080/10548408.2019.1571983

Ohm, M., Plate, H., Sykosch, A., & Meier, M. (2020). Backstabber's Knife Collection: A Review of Open Source Software Supply Chain Attacks. *Lecture Notes in Computer Science*, *12223*, 23–43. doi:10.1007/978-3-030-52683-2_2

Omitola, T., & Wills, G. (2018). Towards mapping the security challenges of the Internet of Things (IoT) supply chain. *Procedia Computer Science, 126,* 441-450. doi:10.1016/j.procs.2018.07.278

Pal, O., Srivastava, V., & Alam, B. (2017). Cyber security risks and challenges in supply chain. *International Journal of Advanced Research in Computer Science*, *8*(5), 662–666. doi:10.26483/ijarcs.v8i5.3385

Petropoulos, G. (2022, February 2). *The dark side of artificial intelligence: Manipulation of human behaviour*. Bruegel. https://www.bruegel.org/blog-post/dark-side-artificial-intelligence-manipulation-human-behaviour

Sarumi, J.A., & Okunoye, A. (2021). A Review of Potential Threats in Supply Chain Cyber Security. *Advances in Multidisciplinary and scientific Research Journal Publication.*

Schwartz, Y. (2017). *Recovering corporate patriotism*. National Affairs. https://www.nationalaffairs.com/publications/detail/recovering-corporate-patriotism

Sehgal, P., Kumar, B., Sharma, M., Salameh, A. A., Kumar, S., & Asha, P. (2022). Role of IOT in Transformation of Marketing: A Quantitative Study of Opportunities and Challenges. *Webology, 19*(1).

Snyder, H. (2019). Literature review as a research methodology: An overview and guidelines. *Journal of Business Research, 104*, 333–339. doi:10.1016/j.jbusres.2019.07.039

Song, C. S., & Kim, Y. K. (2022). The role of the human-robot interaction in consumers' acceptance of humanoid retail service robots. *Journal of Business Research, 146*, 489–503. doi:10.1016/j.jbusres.2022.03.087

Szczepkowski, D., & Szczepkowski, P. (2021). *Adware as one form of disinformation*. Studia Administracji i Bezpieczeństwa. doi:10.5604/01.3001.0015.6253

Thalen, M. (2021, June 24). Exclusive: Hacker reveals smart meters are spilling secrets about the Texas snowstorm. *The Daily Dot*. https://www.dailydot.com/debug/hacker-smart-meter-texas-snowstorm/

Title 18 U.S. Code § 798 - Disclosure of classified information (2012, January 3). U.S. Government Publishing Office. https://www.govinfo.gov/app/details/USCODE-2011-title18/USCODE-2011-title18-partI-chap37-sec798&collectionCode=USCODE

Urciuoli, L., Männistö, T., Hintsa, J., & Khan, T. (2013). Supply Chain Cyber Security – Potential Threats. *Information & Security: An International Journal, 29*, 51–68.

Vadrevu, P., & Perdisci, R. (2019). What You See is NOT What You Get: Discovering and Tracking Social Engineering Attack Campaigns. In *Proceedings of the Internet Measurement Conference (IMC '19)* (pp.308-321). Association for Computing Machinery. https://doi-org.proxymu.wrlc.org/10.1145/3355369.3355600

Vareschi, R. D., & Picoto, W. N. (2021). The critical factors for cloud computing adoption during SARS-CoV-2 pandemic. [OJAKM]. *Online Journal of Applied Knowledge Management, 9*(2), 46–64. doi:10.36965/OJAKM.2021.9(2)46-64

Wang, Z., Zhu, H., & Sun, L. (2021). Social engineering in cybersecurity: Effect mechanisms, human vulnerabilities and attack methods. *IEEE Access : Practical Innovations, Open Solutions, 9*, 11895–11910. doi:10.1109/ACCESS.2021.3051633

Yeboah-Ofori, A., Ismail, U. M., Swidurski, T., & Opoku-Boateng, F. (2021). Cyberattack ontology: A knowledge representation for cyber supply chain security. *2021 International Conference on Computing, Computational Modelling and Applications (ICCMA)*. IEEE. 10.1109/ICCMA53594.2021.00019

Zainuddin, N., Deraman, N., Loh, V. V., & Hafsah, A. (2022). A systematic review on flexibility enablers in logistics survivability. *Quantum Journal of Social Sciences and Humanities, 3*(6), 116-131. https://www.qjssh.com/index.php/qjssh/article/view/200

Chapter 4
Analysis of Ultrasound Images in Kidney Failure Diagnosis Using Deep Learning

Naresh Tiwari
Capital Technology University, USA

Yazeed Ghadi
Al Ain University, UAE

Marwan Omar
Illinois Institute of Technology, USA

ABSTRACT

Ultrasonic imaging has proven to be a valuable tool in kidney diagnosis, providing essential information about kidney size, shape, position, and function; and detecting structural abnormalities like cysts, stones, and infections. However, its effectiveness in kidney diagnostics is subject to operator expertise, leading to potential variations in image interpretation and diagnostic outcomes. It is crucial to explore automated approaches and computer-assisted diagnosis systems to address these challenges and enhance kidney diagnostics. Regrettably, the integration of such systems into kidney diagnostics has not been extensively investigated. Therefore, this study confirms the proposal of using a random forest classifier to detect kidney Nephrolithiasis. Notably, the classifier achieved an impressive accuracy of 96.33% compared to other machine learning classifiers, utilizing a test dataset of 100 kidney images.

1. INTRODUCTION

The frequency of kidney stones has seen an increase in the past 40 years. However, the term "kidney stone" encompasses a variety of situations, from asymptomatic stones to frequent ureteral obstructions, even leading to kidney failure. This is because kidney stones can be caused by a multitude of factors. This leads us to our first problem statement:

DOI: 10.4018/979-8-3693-1634-4.ch004

1. Problem Statement 1 - Non-standardized Diagnostic Methods: There is a significant issue with the current state of kidney stone diagnostics, as the methods are not standardized, leading to varying results and treatment approaches.

As a part of the treatment process, kidney stone patients may benefit from a more focused approach on the classification of kidney stones, predictive tools for estimating the chance of recurrence, and personalized prevention strategies. Despite advances in recurrence prediction methods, there are still major hurdles.This leads us to our second problem statement:

2. Problem Statement 2 - Operator-dependent Variations in Image Interpretation and Diagnostic Outcomes:

One significant challenge is that the effectiveness of kidney diagnostics through ultrasound imaging is often tied to operator expertise, leading to potential variations in image interpretation and diagnostic outcomes.

In the studies focusing on the frequency of kidney stones, a wide range of results have been obtained. This variability is partly due to the absence of a standard procedure for categorizing stones. A classification system might aid our understanding of kidney stone formation and its clinical treatment (Thongprayoon et al.,2020). This leads us to our third problem statement:

3. Problem Statement 3 - Lack of Automated Approaches in Kidney Diagnostics:

Additionally, there is a scarcity of automated approaches and computer-assisted diagnosis systems in kidney diagnostics. Implementing such systems could improve accuracy and reduce reliance on individual operator skills.

These problems underline the importance of this study, which aims to explore the use of machine learning in improving kidney diagnostics. Our focus is specifically on the use of a Random Forest classifier for detecting kidney Nephrolithiasis, and we compare its performance with other machine learning classifiers.

People all across the world are increasingly having trouble with kidney stones. Up to 50% of people could get kidney stones again. Nephrolithiasis is related to chronic renal disease as well as kidney failure. People think their food plays a big role in whether or not they have kidney stones. There is strong evidence that dehydration is the primary cause of urolithiasis. There is still some debate over whether tap water, mineral water, fruit juices, soft drinks, tea, and coffee have different impacts, even though it has been shown that sufficient fluids is good. Kidney stone development is influenced by oxalate, calcium, sodium chloride, protein, and carbs. Sodium chloride is another food component that can change the urine's risk profile. Patients with kidney stones frequently need a particular diet and an assessment of nutritional risk factors as part of their treatment (Siener, 2021).

The author of (Salazar et al.,2022) said that Machine learning (ML) algorithms are becoming more important in the medical field since they may be used to identify various diseases, each with its unique set of symptoms. The authors of (Khamparia and Pandey,2020) used support vector machine analysis (SVM) to determine CKD. To make the data easier to understand, the authors used a variety of approaches, such as principal component analysis (P.C.A.). An SVM model using Gaussian radial basis selection beat its competitors in accuracy and precision based on their data. Several researchers investigated and contrasted kernel functions using random forest models. There aren't many articles that compare and contrast SVM with A.I. (computational intelligence) models. In additional research, four kinds of kidney disease were identified and categorized using support vector machine (SVM) and artificial neural network (ANN) techniques. The ANN was demonstrated to be the most accurate model when compared to the other models. Similarities between statistical and artificial intelligence models have also been extensively researched, and class-balanced order for dual classes with the non-uniform distribution (Salazar et al., 2020). The best diet strategy for CKD patients can be found by analyzing data using various classification techniques, such as multiple-class decision trees and decision forests, multiple-class logistic regression, and multiple-class ANN. The statistics showed that among the investigated models, multi-class decision trees had the highest accuracy (99.17%). Many different fields are currently using deep learning (DL) techniques. Examples include physiological inputs and medical imaging.

DL models have successfully classified data, separating lesions in medical pictures and identifying lesions (Yildirim et al., 2021). DL models have been developed using MRIs, CT images, and X-rays. The Covid-19, cardiac arrhythmia, prostate cancer, brain tumors, skin cancer, and breast cancer are just a few of the disorders these models have helped doctors diagnose.

Additionally, bladder and kidney stones can be independently located in urology using DL methods. Based on microcomputed tomography (Fitri et al., 2020) developed, a CNN-based classification system for urinary stones. 2,430 micro-CT slices were used for the measurement, and the accuracy was found to be 0.9959. A CNN model was created by (Jendeberg et al., 2021) to detect pelvic calcifications. They concluded that the CNN model was more precise than the advice of seven imaging specialists. A CNN model was given instructions (Längkvist et al., 2018) to find ureteral stones in sparse C.T. slices. Based on the facts we had, we were able to come to this conclusion.

This study aimed to create a model that reduces the likelihood that a doctor will err and avoids missing stones while using C.T. scan images. Most people with kidney stones would most likely present in the emergency room, but it is not always easy to get a radiologist there with the requisite training. Reporting CT scan results could take longer if there aren't enough doctors on staff. The likelihood of inaccuracy rises when imaging is carried out more quickly than usual (Parakh et al., 2019). Computer-assisted evaluation of the kidney for the early and precise diagnosis will also be a big improvement in the medical industry as it takes a lot of time to report computed tomography. This is due to how time-consuming it is to document C.T. scans. Figure 1 shows the automated kidney stone detection using C.T. images.

Figure 1. Automated kidney stone detection using C.T. images
Bennett, C. C. (2018).

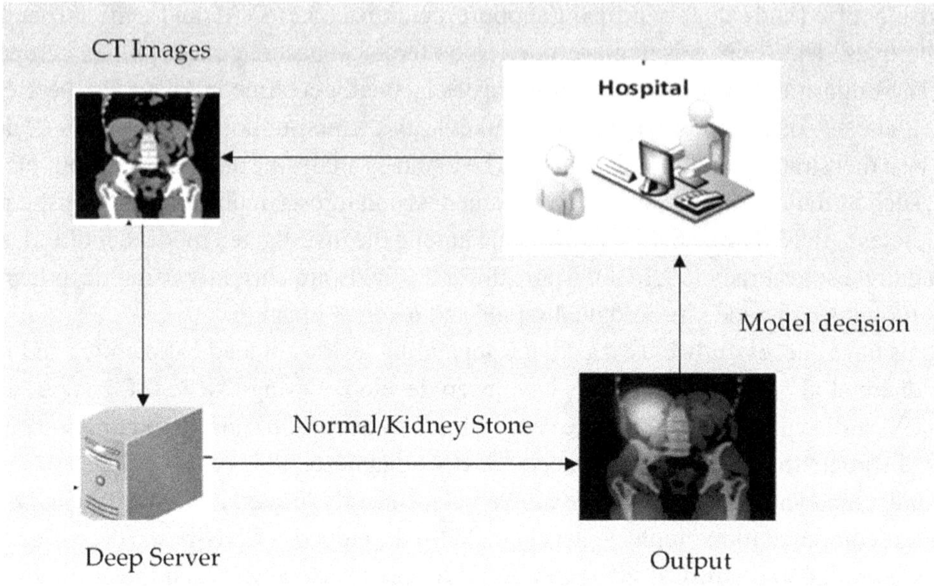

A person's digestive system separates the necessary nutrients from waste products when they eat. Particles may injure the body if they continue moving through the system. Small screens called nephrons are in charge of filtering blood in the kidneys. Because they eliminate dangerous compounds from circulation, the kidneys are essential.

The kidneys create vitamin D, control blood pressure, and assist in the creation of red blood cells in addition to maintaining the body's fluid and mineral balance. Urine from the kidneys passes through the ureters, emerges from them, and enters the bladder. It appears likely that kidneys are important for a person's general health and longevity. The body has difficulty controlling blood pressure and removing extra fluid from circulation when it has kidney disease. Diabetes, brought on by too much blood sugar, has several negative effects on a person's health. One of these techniques involves renal damage. Increased blood pressure on the vessel's walls is a symptom of hypertension (Linehan, 2012). Kidney failure is one of the main causes of untreated hypertension, while hypertension is one of the main causes of renal failure.

Early detection aims to reduce symptoms, stop the disease from worsening, and reverse any adverse effects. Depending on the patient's state, the medicine may also partially restore kidney function.

When abnormal tissue is present in one or both organs, kidney tumors can form. Both benign and malignant tumors exist. Renal cells are the only cells impacted by K.T. (kidney Transplant). Medical professionals say certain kidney cells have undergone a genetic change (or "mutation") that causes kidney tumors. A kidney cell's D.N.A. contains instructions on deciding whether it needs to develop and divide quickly. Cells can multiply and grow throughout the organism (Linehan, 2012). The cancer could have developed in the kidney from its origin, or moved there from another organ, such as the lung (Rizzo et al., 2023). Two of the many signs and indicators that K.T. can induce in patients are a failure to eat and unexplained weight loss. Both can make it difficult for them to lead normal lives (Wang et al., 2021).. Renal tumors comprise about 3.7% of all cancer cases in the U.S. About 62,000 Americans are given a kidney cancer diagnosis each year. The average population age raises the incidence of kidney cancer. The issue affects men more frequently than women (Gharaibeh et al, 2022). A contrast between a healthy kidney and a kidney with cancer is shown in Figure 2.

Figure 2. Illustration of healthy kidneys and kidneys with tumours
(Gharaibeh et al., 2022).

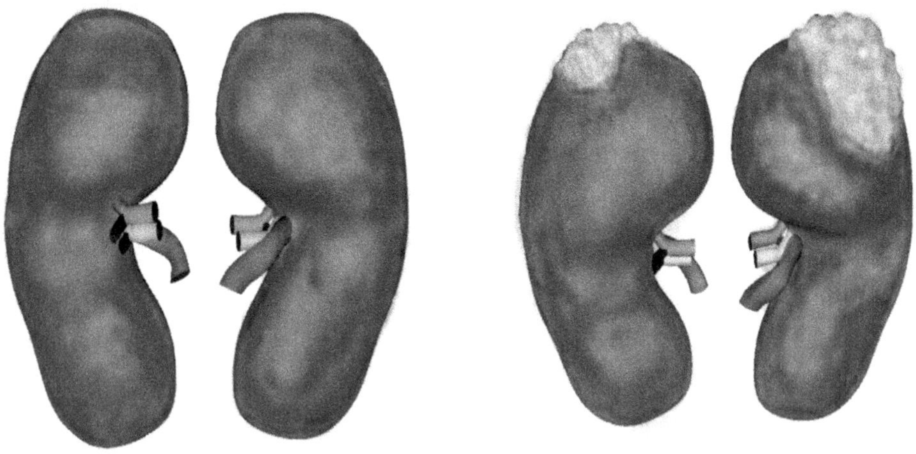

Significance of the study

Supervised classifiers have been used in the past to diagnose a number of diseases correctly. The CKD dataset was sorted by the authors of (Zhang et al., 2018) using the support vector machine (SVM) and k-nearest neighbor (K.N.N.) classifiers. A few metrics used to compare models' performance include precision, memory, precision, and the F1 score. The author of (Hsu et al., 2018) compared the effectiveness of machine learning (ML) and traditional regression models using artificial neural networks, decision trees, and logistic models. With a 93% success rate once all the data was analyzed, Recent studies show that ML models are frequently used in healthcare environments. ANN, backpropagation, and SVM were employed along with other ML techniques to categorize and forecast kidney stone sickness in patients (Iftikhar et al., 2023). The patient classification and outcome calculations were done using the formulae. The most effective machine learning algorithm used most commonly is backpropagation. Despite this, several academics have looked into how SVM and naïve Bayes (N.B.) models relate to one another. For instance, researchers in (Zhang et al., 2018) combined N.B. models with SVM to assess the precision of models for several categories of renal disease and to identify various diseases. As a result, the results show that SVM models are the best at categorizing data and are typically considered the most accurate classifiers. This study examined various ML models side by side to assess how well they could forecast CKD.

Nephrolithiasis, or kidney stone disease, has been associated with changes in urine solutes, particularly hypercalciuria. Nephrolithiasis, commonly called "kidney stone disease," is another name for this illness. Less than 15% of people with kidney stones have a condition that makes the stones form unexpectedly.

The amount is determined by how many people have visited treatment facilities for kidney stones. These conditions include primary hyperoxaluria, cystinuria, Bartter syndrome, renal tubular acidosis accompanying hearing loss, and others.

On the other hand, Nephrolithiasis may have various reasons, according to a study. Nephrolithiasis is more likely to be inherited than hypercalciuria by more than 45 percentage points. People have a significant genetic vulnerability to produce stones, even though the cause is unknown (Howles and Thakker, 2020).

Even though kidney stone disease is one of the conditions studied the longest, little is understood about how stones form and grow over time. Numerous ideas and methods for surgically removing kidney stones have been created and put into practice due to the quick advancement of medical technology over the past few decades. According to the authors' work and other groups' research, kidney stones can develop using at least five different processes. Too concentrated urine crystallizes, which is a common cause of intracranial crystal precipitation. Most experts agree that Randall's plaques are the primary cause of calcium oxalate stones. The development of innovative kidney stone-preventing medications may use sexual hormones as pharmacological targets since they may be crucial in developing Nephrolithiasis (Wang et al., 2021).

A vital part of the cell, mitochondria produce energy and control processes like apoptosis, oxidative stress, and calcium homeostasis. There is proof that kidney stone illness (Nephrolithiasis, urolithiasis) is brought on by oxidative stress, inflammation, and tissue damage. Calcium oxalate, in the form of CaOx, makes up the majority of kidney stones. Recent studies have linked Randall's plaque development, the retention and aggregation of CaOx crystals, and kidney stone formation to mitochondrial dysfunction (Chaiyarit and Thongboonkerd, 2020).

Obesity has many harmful impacts, and it is a widespread problem not just in the United States but around the globe. Their risk of suffering agonizing kidney stones rises along with the number of fat people. There are several pathophysiological mechanisms that connect fat to kidney stone development (Poore et al., 2020).

Urologists are constantly developing new surgical procedures for kidney stones, whether they are improved versions of existing techniques or creative uses for them. If these technologies are to continue to be as helpful as possible, they will need to be able to adapt to the growing demand for "mini" treatments (Terry et al., 2020).

Preventing repeated kidney stones is the most effective plan of practice, not only because of the pain they bring in the short term but also because of the risk they provide for the development of chronic renal disease in the long run (Uribarri, 2020).

Although kidney stones are more common in adults, they are also becoming more frequent in children. The most common reason for increasing medical costs and disease is kidney stones. Clinical symptoms and indicators can differ significantly. It is important to rule out primary hyperoxaluria if a young child has kidney stones and the disease. Kidney stones are more vulnerable to recurring in children because they are more likely to have metabolic problems. Minimally invasive surgery is now possible because of recent advances in medicine. A team of specialists from several disciplines is needed for complete management. When identifying kidney illnesses, including primary hyperoxaluria, Dent's disease, and renal tubular acidosis (R.T.A.), it is essential to maintain a high index of suspicion because these abnormalities might alter how the kidneys function and develop (Ang et al., 2020).. Figure 3 shows the human kidney stones.

Figure 3. Locations of kidney stones in the Human urinary system
(Alelign and Petros, 2018).

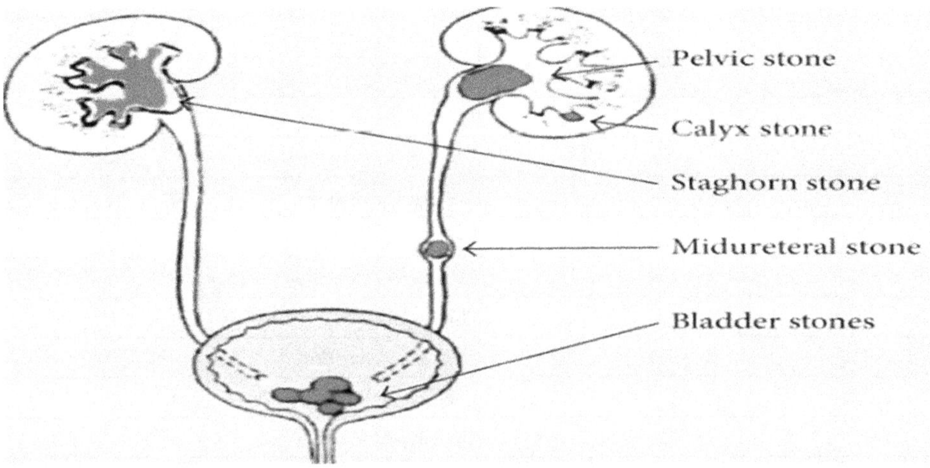

One of the ways kidney stones are diagnosed is through urine analysis. Other procedures include blood tests, abdominal X-rays, and C.T. imaging. Kidney stones are initially diagnosed using imaging, which is also essential in deciding which procedure to remove them (Brisbane et al., 2016).

Most machine learning algorithms can be classified as directed or unguided. Machine learning (ML) is increasingly used in software to enhance user experience. A type of unsupervised learning known as "decision trees" can be applied to classification and regression tasks. It is possible to use decision trees. The structure resembles a tree since it has a root node, branches, nodes inside the branches, and leaf nodes. Binary and multiclass classification issues can be separated using the Naive Bayes approach. The "random forest" approach to group learning can be utilized for regression, classification, and other tasks. It is necessary to build many decision trees during this method's training phase (Bell, 2022).

The remaining part of the paper is given as. Section 2 contains a literature review in which some previous studies are discussed. Section 3 methodology of paper is completely described and section 4 illustrates the results in detail. Section 5 concludes the conclusion and future work of the paper. Table 1 illustrates the list of observations.

Table 1. Shows the list of observations

Abbreviation	Full Form
SVM	Support Vector Machine
D.T.	Decision Tree
M.L.P.	Multi-Layer Perceptron
ANN	Artificial Neural Networks
L.R.	logistic Regression
ML	Machine learning
MCC	Matthews Correlation Coefficient
LDA	Linear Discriminant Analysis
M.A.E.	Mean Absolute Error
R.M.S.E.	Root Mean Squared Error
R.A.E.	Relative Absolute Error
R.R.S.E.	Root Relative Squared Error
P.C.A.	Principal Component Analysis
DL	Deep learning
KT	Kidney Transplant
CAD	Computer-Assisted Diagnosis
CT	Computed Tomography
H.M.A.N.N.	Heterogeneous Modified Artificial Neural Network

2. LITERATURE REVIEW

The authors go into great detail about how the information system was built and the way kidney stones are categorized. The best performance was achieved by the Inception v3 architecture (weighted precision, recall, and F1-score of 0.97, 0.98, and 0.97, respectively). Still, it was also shown that a shallow machine learning strategy (the X.G. Boost classifier) could come close to the effectiveness of the most promising deep-learning techniques. This study is the first to examine methods to get the most diagnostic information out of ureter scope images (Ochoa-Ruiz et al., 2022).

455 people received a C.T. scan between January 2016 and January 2020 to see if they had kidney stones. Among these patients, there were 50 excluded instances and 405 confirmed cases of kidney stones. According to the size of the kidney stones, patients were categorized into three groups: those with stones smaller than 1 centimeter, between 1 and 2 millimeters, and larger than 2 centimeters. Two doctors analyzed all 2,959 CT scans of the 455 patients from all three aircraft. After that, a deep learning system was used to analyze the C.T. scans. The model's sensitivity, specificity, and positive and negative predictive values, and accuracy were all examined and assessed (Caglayan et al., 2022).

Recent developments in artificial intelligence (A.I.) suggest that deep learning (DL) could autonomously assess whether a person has kidney stones or not using coronal computed tomography (C.T.) images. Individual cross-sectional C.T. scans were obtained using a process that involved 1799 pictures. In 96.82% of cases our newly created automatic model can identify kidney stones in C.T. scans. We have shown that our model can identify kidney stones of any size, even the smallest ones. Our recently created DL model, now accessible for clinical usage, outperformed expectations on a bigger dataset with 433 individuals. This study suggests that more difficult urological problems can be solved using DL approaches, which are becoming more popular (Yildirim et al., 2021).

To automatically detect and score kidney stones using the S.T.O.N.E. nephrolithometry system, this work aims to create and evaluate a deep learning and thresholding-based model. The method for finding stones worked perfectly. It has a positive predictive value of 98.7% (236/239) and a sensitivity of 95.9% (236/246). The hydronephrosis classification method's area under the curve (A.U.C.) was 0.97. The scoring model matched well with the radiologist's results for stone size, tract length, number of affected calyces, and essence grade (= 0.95, 95% confidence interval [CI]: 0.92 to 0.98; = 0.97, 95% CI: 0.95 to 1.00; and = 0.97, 95% CI: 0.94 to 1.00). For N.C.C.T. pictures to automatically locate and score stones, it was decided to develop a scoring model (Cui et al., 2021).

63 kidney stones had been removed in the stone lab. Each stone had at least two digital photos taken of it, one of the interior and one of the exterior. Microsoft's ResNet-101 algorithm divided each image into many groups using a deep convolutional neural network (CNN). Cross-validation with the leave-one-out method was used to test this model. The network's prediction recall was the main focus of the evaluation. Digital photographs of kidney stones can be analyzed using deep convolutional neural networks (CNNs) to determine their makeup. Future studies will be necessary to determine whether DL can be utilized for digital endoscopy to identify the makeup of stones. This technology may improve the effectiveness of surgery by enabling endoscopic and laser instruments to work together and automatically change laser settings depending on the type of stone identified (Black et al., 2020). Figure 4 illustrates a human kidney stretcher.

Figure 4. Anatomy of human kidney
(Abdelrahman and Viriri, 2022).

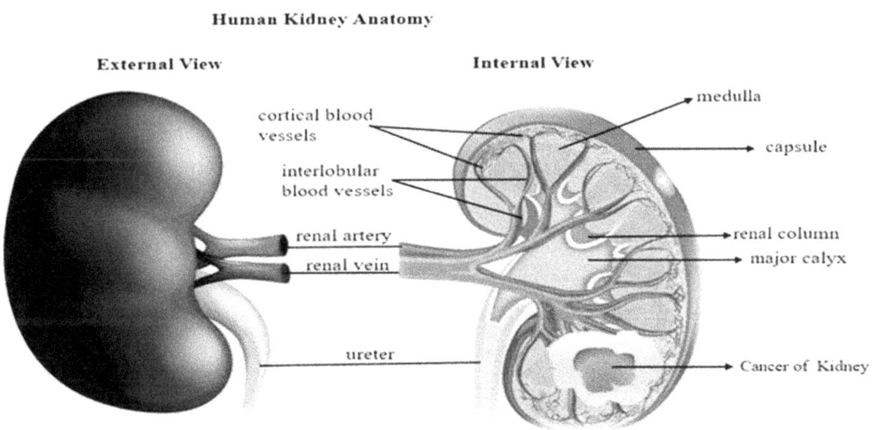

The study included 91 C.T. colonography (C.T.C.) scans that detected kidney stones and 89 C.T. colonography images that did not. Both image pairs were put together with skill. To compare the outcomes to accepted standards, the remaining 50% of the data was used for testing and training. An external validation set comprised 6185 CTC scans taken on individuals getting care at a different facility. Labels with the patients' names were attached to these photographs. The photos were cleaned using thresholding, region-growing, and gradient-based anisotropic de-noising after being split into kidney segments with a 3D U-Net model. The location of kidney stones was then determined using a 13-layer convolutional neural network predictor, along with the areas where the results were inaccurate. Our deep learning-based system outperformed a previous system that didn't employ deep learning on a specific validation set(Elton et al., 2022)

The authors created and tested an algorithm to assess whether an image has a nodule by contrasting and comparing several examples. By giving the radiologist more information, they can more rapidly assess whether the nodule is cancerous. Accuracy was just one of many variables that were strongly considered and weighted during the performance evaluation process. Sensitivity, precision, and accuracy scores for the final CNN algorithm are 90.64%, 90.47%, and 84.8%, respectively. These numbers are reasonably close together. One may argue that CNN's ability to lower the frequency of false positives is due to the significant continual training that its staff members get (Haq et al., 2022).

The patients' ages, genders, blood sugar levels, heart rates, and electrocardiograms were used to determine the results. They then assembled data from a variety of sources, including a hospital. The suggested professional approach for medical diagnosis can be used to identify a disease's cause and choose the most appropriate strategy of action for several diseases, including cardiac issues. The expert system is then updated with the calculated precise and soft values. The diagnostic evaluation at the hospital makes use of current expert systems. The inference engine compares the data's fuzzy analysis to the knowledge base's previously processed data. This stage is carried out after giving the expert system the precise information. The expert system used for defuzzification will initially act unnecessarily. It will convert the fuzzy set value into something people can understand. After completing the fuzzy sets value estimate, the expert physician system decides the type of heart condition a patient has. Following the diagnostic process, the expert system rated the risk of cardiovascular disease as "low," "high," or "risky." Following the conclusion of the diagnostic phase, the expert system will suggest a pharmaceutical dosage, and the doctor will decide on a treatment strategy and dosage based on that advice (Mazhar et al., 2022).

Researchers are examining how tissues are currently colored to distinguish between healthy and diseased regions in a study using grayscale M.R. images of the human brain. The study focuses on the processes that were used. The proposed method colorizes various non-typical locations using connected components and index-based colorization techniques. This automatic approach produces the most likely results after changing inputs like brightness and pixel grid values. A novel approach for coloring the R.O.I. areas can be developed after the regions have been separated. Using this technique, the region is divided into discrete sections, each given a unique color. The types of tissues present can be determined by processing data using the watershed-based area segmentation approach and the R.O.I. selection method based on morphological operation. Vectors of brightness and pixels are the best inputs for coloring after segmenting and choosing the region of interest (R.O.I.). The benefits of this painting method include improved contrast, P.S.N.R., and S.S.I.M. Compared to our suggested method, the conventional color transfer technique previously used in the industry is slow and necessitates more processing time (Haq et al., 2022).Table 2 shows different methods used for kidney stones and the results of these methods.

Table 2. Results of some previous methods

Ref.	Objective	Methods	Accuracy %
[36]	Kidney stones identification	Segmentation + ANN	86
[37]	Stones in the kidneys against phlebitis	Radionics + Ada Boost classifier	85
[38]	Removal of kidney stones, with a focus on the prediction of postoperative factors	ANN	94
39]	Determine when the patient will still have stones after the initial treatment.	Feature extraction + sequential forward selection + multiple classifier scheme	60
[40]	Stone-free prediction	Light gradient boosting method	87.9
[41]	Predict diabetic kidney disease	SVM radial	94
[40]	Predict diabetic kidney disease	Unbalanced random forest	83.5
[42]	Predict diabetic kidney disease	WEKA	83.5
[43]	Resolution image-based renal pathology	Convolutional neural network	>80
[44]	Differentiate between kidney chromophore renal cell carcinoma and oncocytoma.	Linear SVM	80
[45]	Classify papillary renal cell carcinoma stages	Feature extraction and random forest	88.5
[46]	Kidney and tumor segmentation	3D U-Net	Mean Kidney Tumor Dice 0.9168
[47]	Kidney and tumor segmentation	Cascade 3D U-Net	Mean Kidney Tumor Dice 0.9064
[48]	Kidney and tumor segmentation	Multi-resolution 3D V-Net	Mean Kidney Tumor Dice 0.8815

This study investigated the potential of deep learning for skin cancer detection. This made it possible for researchers to evaluate the effectiveness of various techniques. This work additionally defined the requirements for creating a skin cancer detection app. The main components of these requirements are segmenting the entire image and monitoring of lesions using deep learning algorithms. The methods used in this poll stand out when it comes to these two criteria. The many types of cancer are also divided into groups according to how they are identified (Mazhar et al., 2023).

Similarly, the researchers showed that pulmonary tuberculosis might be identified in symmetrical C.T. scan pictures using a reliable and precise machine vision technique. One lung or a piece of each lung may be damaged, as tuberculosis can progress in any direction. Images from C.T. scans of infected and uninfected lungs were preprocessed with selection and cropping, grayscale image conversion, and filtering to identify areas of interest (R.O.I.s) for study. However, only the six traits with the largest improvement were picked for the final optimization. Images of healthy and sick T.B. were distinguished using a variety of classifiers based on supervised learning. ANN: n class)-based predictor Multi-Layer Perceptron (M.L.P.) outperformed the others. It ran in less than a second and had a 99 percent accuracy rate. Following Bayes Net (96.83% accurate, 0.9 seconds) were Random Forest (98.83%), J48 (98.67%),

Log it Boost (98%), AdaBoostM1 (97.16%), and Random Forest (98.83%). Following M.L.P., Random Forest and J48 both reached 98% accuracy (Haq et al., 2022)

Despite their lack of precision, shallow approaches have been shown to be reliable and easy to understand. Deep learning-based approaches, on the other hand, are incredibly accurate but cannot be explained. But important choices require computer-assisted diagnosis (CAD), which may recommend an approach based on credible data rather than just demanding it. This study looked at different ways to learn component prototypes necessary for building models that make sense. Similar to the M.C.A. method, our approach offers a category for a picture of a kidney stone patch and explains why it belongs there (Flores-Araiza et al., 2022).

This work attempts to identify the principal component of single- and multi-component kidney stones using dual-energy computed tomography and machine learning. Wheelie measuring 80 grams, weddellite measuring 21 grams, calcium phosphate measuring 39 kilos, cysteine measuring 20 grams, struvite measuring 13 grams, uric acid measuring 18 grams, and xanthine measuring 9 grams were all found in the stones. The stones ranged in diameter from 3 to 18 millimeters. The principal component was correctly predicted for each cell in the N.D. testing dataset with an accuracy of 91.1%. The accuracy while gathering statistics on one's own varied between 87.1% and 90.4%. Dual-energy CT and machine learning can accurately identify the major component in even the most complicated stones, regardless of the administration technique (Große Hokamp et al., 2020).

The heterogeneous modified artificial neural network (H.M.A.N.N.) has been introduced as a solution for the early detection, segmentation, and diagnosis of chronic renal failure on the Internet of Medical Things platform. A Support Vector Machine and a Multilayer Perceptron (M.L.P.) that uses the "Back-propagation" technique are also included in the H.M.A.N.N. that is offered. The "preprocessing" stage of the proposed method uses an ultrasonic picture. Segmentation is utilized to amplify the target region in an ultrasound picture of the kidney. The kidney segmentation process using the H.M.A.N.N. approach is incredibly accurate and reduces the amount of time needed to describe the form (Ma et al., 2020).

3. METHODOLOGY

3.1 Data Analysis Techniques

The doctors at Bahawalpur Victoria Hospital in Bahawalpur and reliable online sources provided the study's data. Two distinct procedures were used to achieve this goal. The first is a series of photographs taken in the United States. It will be used to gather data from the U.S. and offer exact parameters for analysis using the WEKA and CV IP technologies. For this reason, programmers like WEKA and the CV IP tools have already been set up.

3.2 WEKA

Using visualization techniques, the narrative displays the four main WEKA letters—filters, classifiers, clusters, and N-type linkages. These tools make it possible to visualize datasets, classifier predictions, and groups in two dimensions. The suggested approach to completing the job is shown in figure 5.

Figure 5. The proposed method

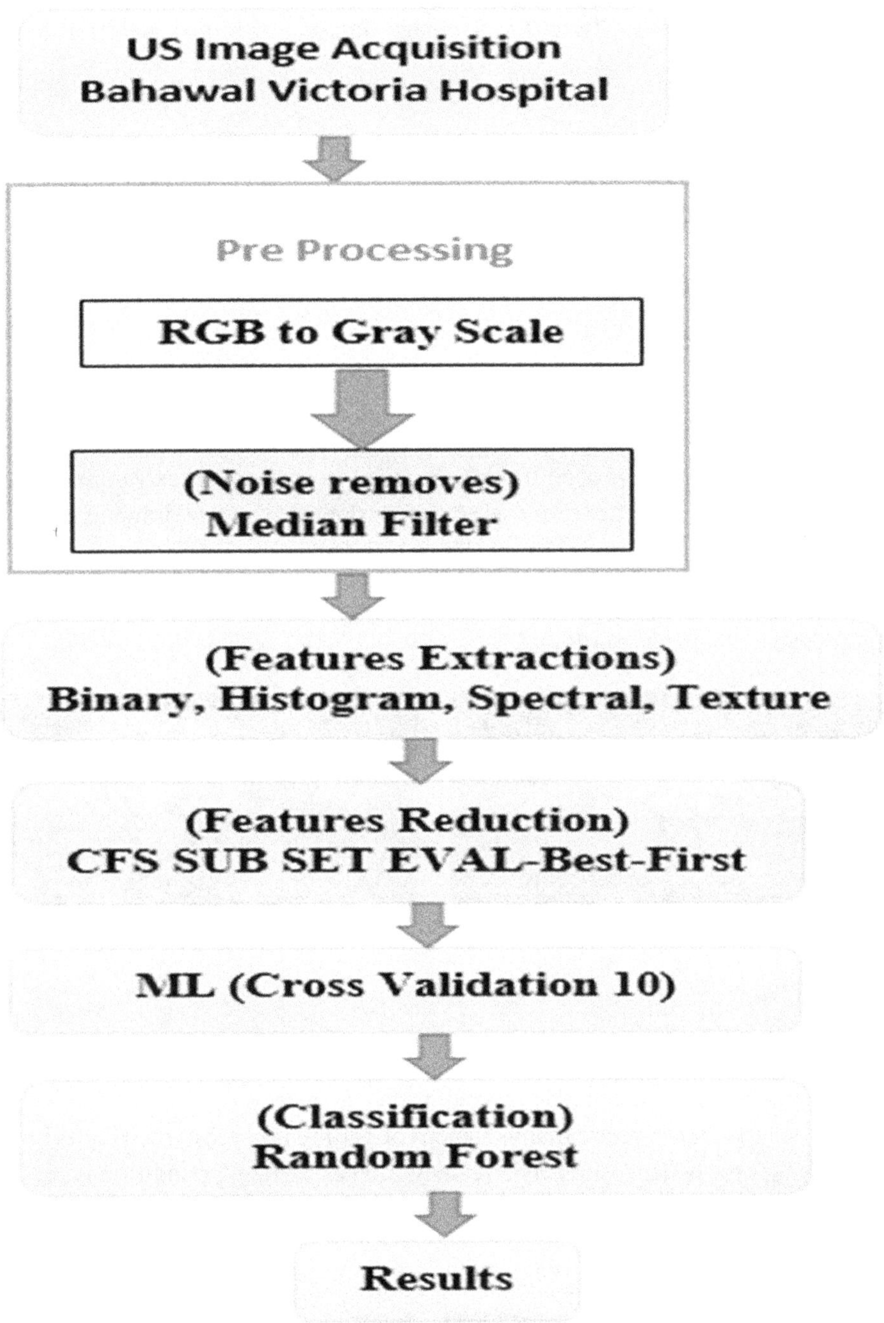

3.3 Image Database

The image database is a collection of U.S. images of kidney nephrolithiasis, pictures from different sources, and Bahawalpur Victoria Hospital (BVH) Bahawalpur, Pakistan. These images are gathered and arranged in a well-managed and disciplined way and used when necessary, and easily accessible when processing starts. Collected different U.S. image datasets of kidney nephrolithiasis for disease processing and early detection.

3.4 Image Pre-Processing

Pre-processing is a leading step in computer science, finding the precise direction to detect the reason for Nephrolithiasis. Most researchers prefer this method to diagnose Nephrolithiasis before going to any action. It enhances the image by using techniques like C.L.A.H.E. and wiener filtering for pre-processing, i.e., C.V.I.P. tools for U.S. images. I have collected pictures and done pre-processing on them.

3.5 Image Cropping

In cropping, the U.S. images are cropped to reduce noise. In cutting, an extra unnecessary portion is removed from the image; to get a better result, we can do cropping by using drawing tools, image viewer, paint tools, etc. The kidney image cropping condition is presented in Fig 6.

Figure 6. Kidney image cropping condition

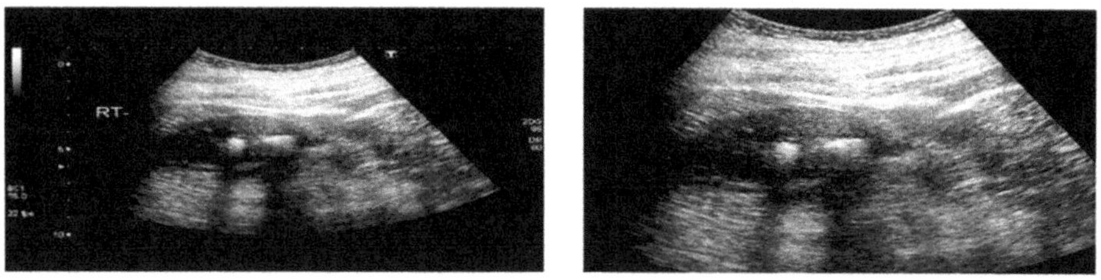

Kidney US Image before cropping   Kidney US Image after cropping

3.6 Image Resizing

The original image is large, so there are many chances of getting noisy. So, resizing is crucial to change all images to equal sizes for better results. The Kidney Images Resizing condition is presented in Fig 7.

Figure 7. Kidney Images resizing condition

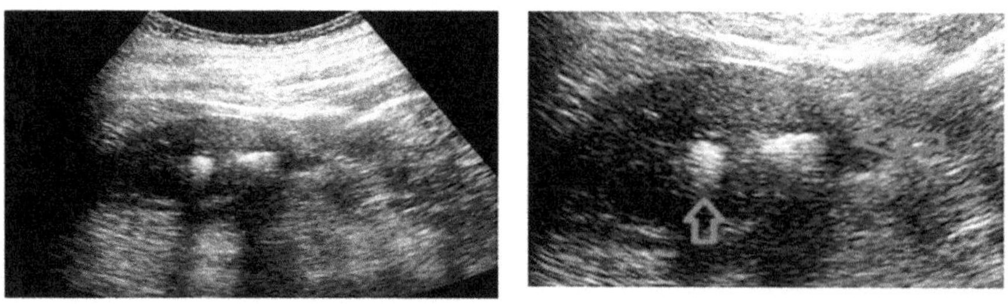

Kidney US Image before Resizing   Kidney US Image after Resizing

3.7 Features Extraction

Implementation features like as many images counting GIF, JPEG, B.M.P., and PNG, as well as the rare format, can be read by C.V.I.P. tools. C.V.I.P. toolchains have the standard shape for giving out functions. For example, representation compression, valid and geometric operation descriptions, sharping shape manipulation, framc discovcry, scgmcntation, and arithmetic transformation. The datasets and their features are presented in Table 1.

3.8. Histogram features

This type of graph consists of a rectangle whose width is proportional to the frequency of the researched variable and whose length is related to the class interval. To visually show the distribution of a set of numbers as a whole, histograms or a subset of them are widely used. In data analysis, histograms are used to summarize data from continuous or discontinuous interval scale readings (Awad and Hassaballah, 2016).

3.9. Texture Features

Texture features describe any object's exterior distinctiveness and appearance, showing the number of its essential parts. Generally, texture features disclose as soft or hard, horizontal otherwise irregular, rude before delicate, matt otherwise glossy, etc. These are experimental on top of non-natural or everyday objects, e.g., wood, plants, materials, and skin. Image quality gives us information concerning the spatial understanding of shade otherwise intensities within an image or selected area of an image. Image texture is a single technique to assist in segmentation otherwise organization of the picture. Image textures can be produced from a captured image that is artificial or found in the natural scene. Texture images in computer graphics can be analyzed using structured and static methods. A texture measure at every pixel gives values by segmenting the image into regions of similar textures. Texture and spectral features are explained. WEKA is a gathering of mechanism knowledge algorithms intended for the information drawing out tasks. The algorithm can be functional straight toward a dataset; otherwise, call from you possess Java code. WEKA contains the mechanism for the information pre-processing, classification, weakening cluster, relationship system, and idea.

3.10. Classification

The process is also used to separate damaged and normal cells from the results obtained from feature optimization. It is the last stage, so there is no chance of getting the wrong observation. For classification, K.N.N., SVM, and ANN are the most common methods (Phyu, 2009).

3.10.1. Supervised Classification

Based on the idea, a user can manually program some of the pixels in an image as test pixels and then inform the image processing software to utilize those test pixels as a reference when labeling the other pixels in the picture. One of several potential preparation locations is chosen based on the user's degree of skill. The user can set a minimum degree of similarity between the additional pixels that must be combined. The training area's dark nature is typically used to establish the region's boundaries, with reflection in a narrow spectral band a common requirement. The user can also choose the number of classes for each lesson. Absolute production analyses and map categorization by analysts typically combine supervised and unsupervised classification techniques (Berry et al., 2019) .

3.10.2. Unsupervised Classification

Unsupervised classification is analyzing an image by computer software without the aid of a human observer beside the person running the test. Photos can be grouped using the resulting "group of pixels by frequent uniqueness." Links are created between pixels by a computer system, which also arranges them in a pattern. If the user selects the algorithm and number of classes the software should use, that is not helpful for categorization. The computer's grouping of pixels based on how frequently they appear must match the actual qualities above the kidney (such as benign, cancer, etc.), and the user must protect the region's privacy (Berry et al., 2019) .

4. EXPERIMENTS AND RESULTS

Before running the most effective algorithm, preprocessing requires using a variety of ways to extract the fewest possible attributes from an image for optimal performance. The suggested technique is put into practice in the next section by gathering data using WEKA and CV IP tools version 5.6e. These programs are perfect for medical imaging because they are very good at obtaining findings and recognizing features. Using ultrasound technology, the initial cohort of 100 patients was photographed. Patients with kidney issues were investigated separately from those who underwent regular U.S. imaging. The same amount of pictures were included in each collection of 50 photos. The photo count of a dataset consists of 100 images of American objects. The next step is to add the photographs to CV IP tools after cropping and condensing them in an image editor. The tools turn photos that have been cropped into grayscale. Each image has undergone six different processing steps: the blur radius of the wand starts at 32*32, while the column and row's width and height start at 128*128. All of this is accomplished using the return on investment (R.O.I.) approach. Before being changed from color to black and white, each of the 100 images is cropped and shrunk similarly. After then, the pictures are arranged in a circle to find the best spot. Six R.O.I.s with the same dimensions (width, height, and radii) were created for each image. The row and column change when 16 values are added to each image.The binary, histogram, and texture properties safeguarded this R.O.I. There are 21 entries in total displayed on this page. A text file is completed and then transformed into a CSV file. Then, a raff file with various outcomes is created using the WEKA application.

Table 3. Collected image dataset

Normal Kidney	Nephrolithiasis Kidney
200	200

For pattern classification, use WEKA software version 3.8.2. Before being submitted to a range of classification algorithms, such as “Random Forest,” “M.L.P.,” “ISO,” “Legit Boost,” “Byes Nett,” and “J48,” the dataset is first put through a series of pre-processing and feature-optimization phases. The author contrasts the different classifications that the different systems generate. Patterns are categorized using WEKA v3.8.2. The author undertakes data pre-processing and feature optimization before applying various classification algorithms, such as “Random Forest,” “M.L.P.,” “ISO,” “Legit Boost,” “Byes Nett,” and “J48,” to the dataset and chooses the best approach for this study. Examples of training and evaluation datasets can be found in this chapter. The author also contrasts the different classifications that the different systems generate.

4.1 Random Forest Classifier

Time taken to build the model: 0.38 seconds

Test mode: Cross-validation 10

4.1.1 Summary of Random Forest Classifier

A Summary of the Random Forest Classifier is presented in Table 4.

Table 4. Summary of random forest classifier

“Instances”	299	
“Correct	282	95.3333%
“Incorrectly”	11	3.6667%
Kappa statistic	0.9267	
“MAE	0.0817	
“M.S.E.”	0.2015	
“R.A.A.”	16.3321%	
“R.R.S.E.”	40.2909%	

4.1.2 Detailed Accuracy by Class

The accuracy of the dataset using the Random Forest Classifier is presented in Fig 8. Random Forest Classifier Detailed Accuracy is shown in Table 5.

Table 5. Random forest classifier detailed accuracy

T.P.	F.P.	Precision	Recall	F Measure	MCC	ROC Area	Class
0.953	0.027	0.973	0.953	0.963	0.927	0.970	Normal
0.973	0.047	0.954	0.973	0.964	0.927	0.970	Nephrolithiasis
0.963	0.037	0.964	0.963	0.963	0.927	0.970	Weighted Average

Figure 8. Accuracy of dataset using random forest classifier

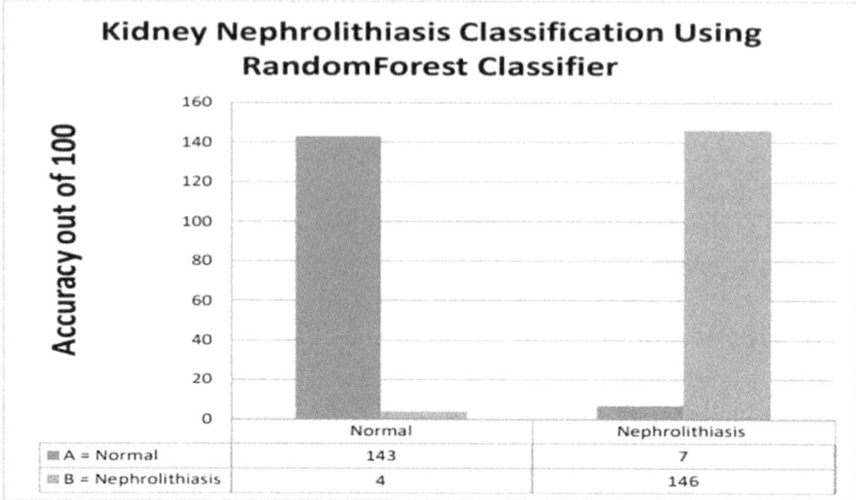

4.2 Multilayer Perceptron Classifier

- Time is taken to build the model: 1.16 seconds
- Test mode: Cross-validation

4.2.1 Summary of Multilayer Perceptron Classifier

A summary of the Multilayer Perceptron Classifier is presented in Table 6.

Table 6. Summary of multilayer perceptron classifier

" Instances"	290	
"Correctly	280	96.67%
"Incorrectly"	10	3.4%
Kappa statistic	0.9133	
"MAE	0.0563	
"M.S.E."	0.1906	
"R.A.A."	11.2592%	
"R.R.S.E."	38.1158%	

4.2.2 Detailed Accuracy by Class

The accuracy of the dataset using the M.L.P. Classifier is presented in Fig 9. Random Forest Classifier Detailed Accuracy is shown in Table 7.

Table 7. Random forest classifier detailed accuracy

T.P. Rate	F.P. Rate	Precision	Recall	F Measure	MCC	ROC Area	Class
0.947	0.033	0.966	0.947	0.956	0.914	0.979	Normal
0.967	0.053	0.948	0.967	0.957	0.914	0.979	Nephrolithiasis
0.957	0.043	0.957	0.957	0.957	0.14	0.979	Weighted Average

Figure 9. Accuracy of dataset using M.L.P. classifier

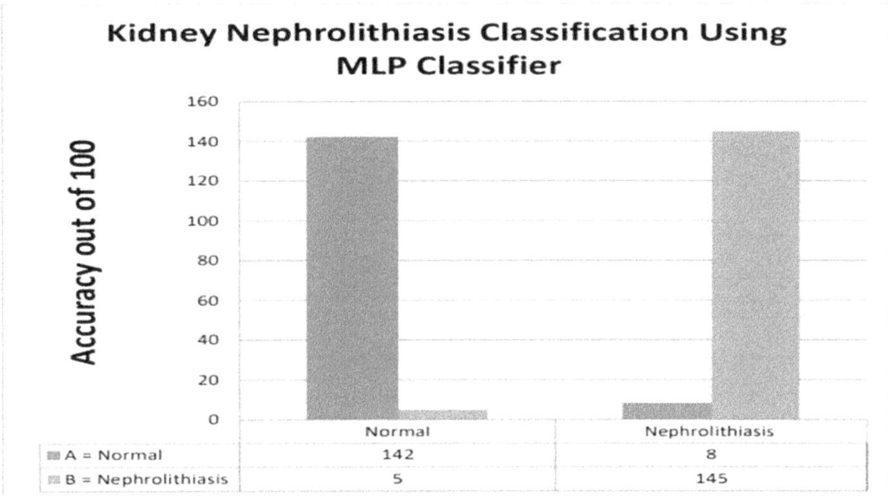

4.3 Logit Boost Classifier

Time is taken to build the model: 0.03 seconds
Test mode: Cross-validation.

4.3.1 Summary of Logit Boost Classifier

The logit Boost Classifier Summary is presented in Table 8.

Table 8. Logit boost classifier summary

" Instances"	300	
"Correctly	286	95.4%
"Incorrectly"	14	4.7%
Kappa statistic	0.91	
"MAE	0.085	
"M.S.E."	0.21	
"R.A.A."	16.9%	
"R.R.S.E."	41.6%	

4.3.2 Detailed Accuracy by Class

Logit Boost Classifier Accuracy by Class is presented in Table 9.

Table 9. Logit boost classifier accuracy by class

T.P. Rate	F.P. Rate	Precision	Recall	F Measure	MCC	ROC Area	Class
0.940	0.033	0.966	0.940	0.953	0.907	0.974	Normal
0.967	0.060	0.942	0.967	0.954	0.907	0.974	Nephrolithiasis
0.953	0.047	0.954	0.953	0.953	0.907	0.974	Weighted Average

The accuracy of the dataset using the Logit Boost Classifier is presented in Fig 10.

Figure 10. Accuracy of dataset using logit boost classifier

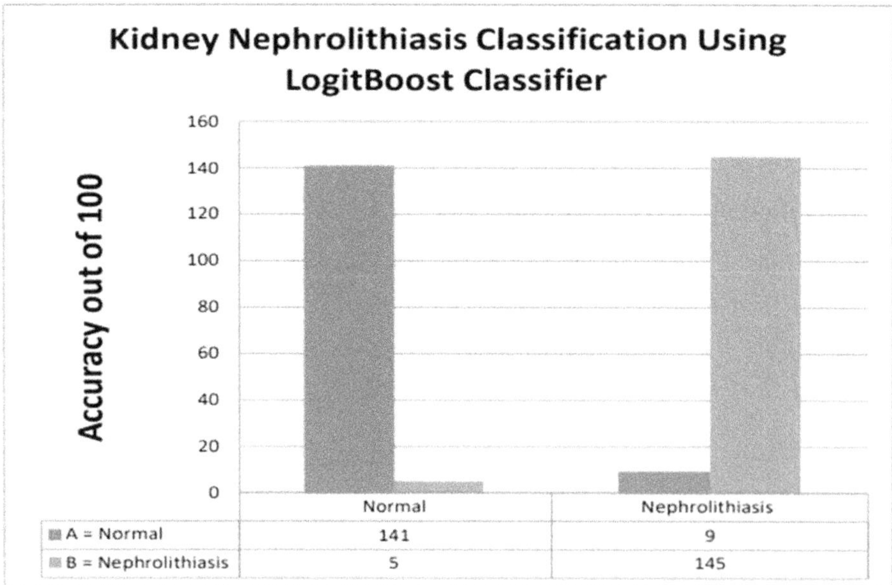

4.4 Iterative Classifier Optimizer

Time is taken to build the model: 0.55 seconds
Test mode: Cross-validation

4.4.1 Summary of Iterative Classifier Optimizer

An Iterative Classifier Summary is presented in Table 10.

Table 10. Iterative classifier summary

" Instances"	300	
"Correctly	289	95.4%
"Incorrectly"	11	4.7%
Kappa statistic	0.9267	
"MAE	0.0817	
"M.S.E."	0.2015	
"R.A.A."	16.3321%	
"R.R.S.E."	40.2909%	

4.4.2 Detailed Accuracy by Class

The accuracy of the dataset using an Iterative Classifier Optimizer Classifier is presented in Fig 11. And an iterative Classifier Accuracy by Class is shown in Table 10

Table 11. Iterative classifier accuracy by class

T.P. Rate	F.P. Rate	Precision	Recall	F Measure	MCC	ROC Area	Class
0.940	0.033	0.966	0.940	0.953	0.907	0.974	Normal
0.967	0.060	0.942	0.967	0.954	0.907	0.974	Nephrolithiasis
0.953	0.047	0.954	0.953	0.953	0.907	0.974	Weighted Average

Figure 11. Accuracy of dataset using iterative classifier optimizer classifier

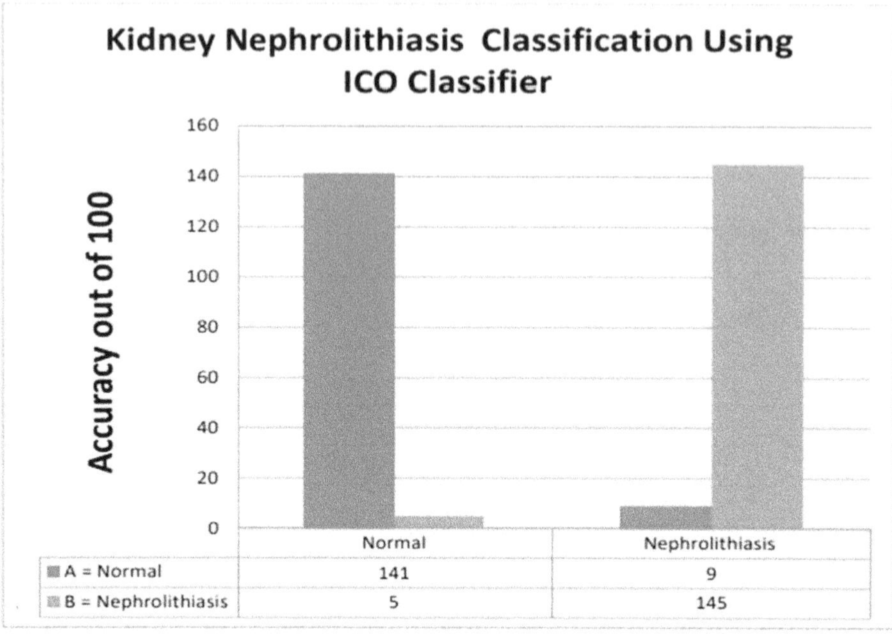

4.5 Bayes Net Classifier

Time is taken to build a model: 0.08 seconds
Test mode: Cross-validation

4.5.1 Bayes Net Classifier Summary

Bayes Net Classifier Summary is presented in Table 12.

Table 12. The Bayes Net classifier summary

" Instances"	**300**	
"Correctly	**284**	94.66%
"Incorrectly"	**16**	5.3333%
Kappa statistic	0.89	
"MAE	0.053	
"M.S.E."	0.2275	
"R.A.A."	10.59%	
"R.R.S.E."	45.50%	

4.5.2 Detailed Accuracy by Class

The accuracy of the dataset using the Bayes Net Classifier is presented in Figure 12. And Bayes Net Classifier Accuracy by Class is shown in Table 13.

Table 13. Bayes Net Classifier accuracy by class

T.P. Rate	F.P. Rate	Precision	Recall	F Measure	MCC	ROC Area	Class
0.953	0.060	0.941	0.953	0.947	0.893	0.974	Normal
0.940	0.047	0.953	0.940	0.946	0.893	0.977	Nephrolithiasis
0.947	0.053	0.947	0.947	0.947	0.893	0.975	Weighted Average

Figure 12. Accuracy of dataset using Bayes Net classifier

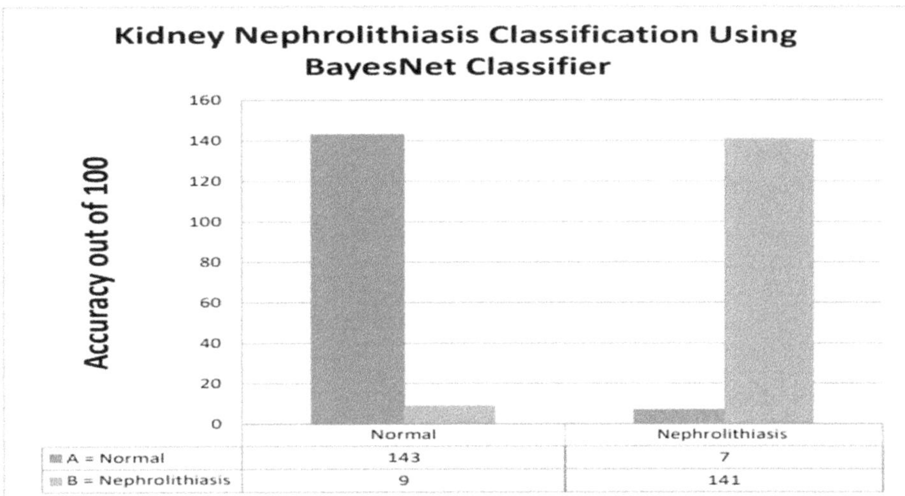

4.6 J48 Classifier

Time is taken to build the model: 0.03 seconds
Test mode: Cross-validation

4.6.1 Summary of J48 Classifier

J48 Classifier Summary is presented in Table 14.

Table 14. J48 Classifier summary

" Instances"	300	
"Correctly	283	94.3333%
"Incorrectly"	17	5.6666%
Kappa statistic	0.8867	
"MAE	0.0777	
"M.S.E."	0.2294	
"R.A.A."	15.5438%	
"R.R.S.E."	45.8745%	

4.6.2 Detailed Accuracy by Class

The accuracy of the dataset using the J48 classifier is presented in Figure 13. The detailed Accuracy by Class of the J48 Classifier is shown in Table 14.

Table 15. Detailed accuracy by class of J48 classifier

T.P. Rate	F.P. Rate	Precision	Recall	F Measure	MCC	ROC Area	Class
0.913	0.027	0.972	0.913	0.942	0.888	0.953	Normal
0.973	0.087	0.918	0.973	0.945	0.888	0.953	Nephrolithiasis
0.943	0.057	0.945	0.943	0.943	0.888	0.953	Weighted Average

Figure 13. Accuracy of dataset using J48 classifier

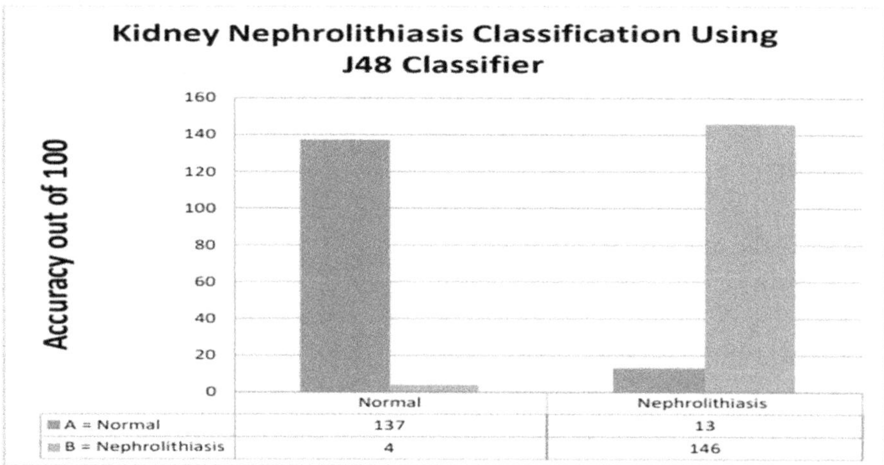

4.7 Comparatively Analysis of Applied Machine Learning Classifiers

In the end, a Random Forest classifier accurately detected kidney nephrolithiasis 96.33% of the time. The classification performance of several machine learning techniques is shown in the graph above, Figure 18

The classification Accuracy Graph among Different Machine Learning Classifiers is presented in Figure 14.

Figure 14. Classification accuracy graph among different machine learning classifiers

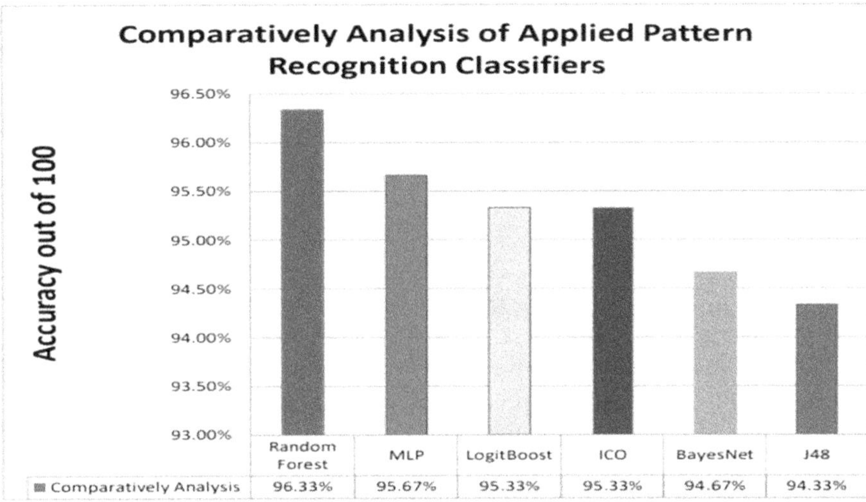

5. CONCLUSION

Addressing the significant issue of non-standardized diagnostic methods for kidney stones, this study has confirmed the proposal of using a Random Forest classifier to detect kidney Nephrolithiasis. The issue of "kidney Nephrolithiasis identification using machine learning" is crucial despite its difficulties. While some focus on Nephrolithiasis feature extraction and normal feature extraction, others try improving feature extraction methodologies. Machine learning methods like percentage split and cross-validation are used to include these novel properties. After data cleaning and training, we used top-tier classifiers to find measures of Nephrolithiasis and separate them from the other data. The Random Forest Tree approach yields a success rate of 96.33 percent, which is the greatest achievable. For separating Nephrolithiasis from common areas, some machine learning and machine vision approaches can increase the precision of 2D ultrasound data.

This finding underscores the potential of integrating machine learning algorithms into the current renal detection systems. Tackling the challenge of operator-dependent variations in image interpretation and diagnostic outcomes, this integration would significantly improve the accuracy of diagnoses while reducing reliance on individual operator skills and minimizing human interaction.

Moreover, responding to the lack of automated approaches in kidney diagnostics, embracing the advancements of machine learning can enhance the overall effectiveness of kidney diagnostics and elevate patient care.

6. FUTURE WORK

This research can be extended to using 3D ultrasound images. I take two classes, standard Nephrolithiasis, according to the scope of my research. But this research can be the extent to "kidney analysis" by taking 4 classes, white meter, grey meter, cerebrospinal fluids, and tumour, to identify the surface of the kidney. This would ensure better, faster, and more reliable diagnosis and treatment for patients suffering from kidney diseases

REFERENCES

Abdelrahman, A., & Viriri, S. (2022). Kidney Tumor Semantic Segmentation Using Deep Learning: A Survey of State-of-the-Art. *Journal of Imaging*, *8*(3), 55. doi:10.3390/jimaging8030055 PMID:35324610

Aminsharifi, A., Irani, D., Pooyesh, S., Parvin, H., Dehghani, S., Yousofi, K., Fazel, E., & Zibaie, F. (2017). Artificial neural network system to predict the postoperative outcome of percutaneous nephrolithotomy. *Journal of Endourology*, *31*(5), 461–467. doi:10.1089/end.2016.0791 PMID:28287830

Ang, A. J., Sharma, A. A., & Sharma, A. (2020). Nephrolithiasis: Approach to diagnosis and management. *Indian Journal of Pediatrics*, *87*(9), 716–725. doi:10.100712098-020-03424-7 PMID:32794099

Awad, A. I., & Hassaballah, M. (2016). *Image feature detectors and descriptors. Studies in Computational Intelligence*. Springer International Publishing. doi:10.1007/978-3-319-28854-3

Bell, J. (2022). What is machine learning? Machine Learning and the City: Applications in Architecture and Urban Design, 207-216.

Bennett, C. C. (2018). Artificial intelligence for diabetes case management: the intersection of physical and mental health. arXiv preprint arXiv:1810.03044.

Berry, M. W., Mohamed, A., & Yap, B. W. (2019). *Supervised and unsupervised learning for data science*. Springer.

Black, K. M., Law, H., Aldoukhi, A., Deng, J., & Ghani, K. R. (2020). Deep learning computer vision algorithm for detecting kidney stone composition. *BJU International*, *125*(6), 920–924. doi:10.1111/bju.15035 PMID:32045113

Brisbane, W., Bailey, M. R., & Sorensen, M. D. (2016). An overview of kidney stone imaging techniques. *Nature Reviews. Urology*, *13*(11), 654–662. doi:10.1038/nrurol.2016.154 PMID:27578040

Caglayan, A., Horsanali, M. O., Kocadurdu, K., Ismailoglu, E., & Guneyli, S. (2022). Deep learning model-assisted detection of kidney stones on computed tomography. *International Braz J Urol*, *48*(5), 830–839. doi:10.15901677-5538.ibju.2022.0132 PMID:35838509

Chaiyarit, S., & Thongboonkerd, V. (2020). Mitochondrial dysfunction and kidney stone disease. *Frontiers in Physiology*, *11*, 566506. doi:10.3389/fphys.2020.566506 PMID:33192563

Cui, Y., Sun, Z., Ma, S., Liu, W., Wang, X., Zhang, X., & Wang, X. (2021). Automatic detection and scoring of kidney stones on noncontrast C.T. images using STONE nephrolithometry: Combined deep learning and thresholding methods. *Molecular Imaging & Biology*, *23*(3), 436–445. doi:10.100711307-020-01554-0 PMID:33108801

De Perrot, T., Hofmeister, J., Burgermeister, S., Martin, S. P., Feutry, G., Klein, J., & Montet, X. (2019). Differentiating kidney stones from phleboliths in unenhanced low-dose computed tomography using radiomics and machine learning. *European Radiology*, *29*(9), 4776–4782. doi:10.100700330-019-6004-7 PMID:30747299

Elton, D. C., Turkbey, E. B., Pickhardt, P. J., & Summers, R. M. (2022). A deep learning system for automated kidney stone detection and volumetric segmentation on noncontrast C.T. scans. *Medical Physics*, *49*(4), 2545–2554. doi:10.1002/mp.15518 PMID:35156216

Fitri, L. A., Haryanto, F., Arimura, H., YunHao, C., Ninomiya, K., Nakano, R., Haekal, M., Warty, Y., & Fauzi, U. (2020). Automated classification of urinary stones based on microcomputed tomography images using convolutional neural network. *Physica Medica*, *78*, 201–208. doi:10.1016/j.ejmp.2020.09.007 PMID:33039971

Flores-Araiza, D., ... (2022). Interpretable deep learning classifier by detection of prototypical parts on kidney stones images. arXiv preprint arXiv:2206.00252.

Gharaibeh, M., Alzu'bi, D., Abdullah, M., Hmeidi, I., Al Nasar, M. R., Abualigah, L., & Gandomi, A. H. (2022). Radiology imaging scans for early diagnosis of kidney tumors: A review of data analytics-based machine learning and deep learning approaches. *Big Data and Cognitive Computing*, *6*(1), 29. doi:10.3390/bdcc6010029

Große Hokamp, N., Lennartz, S., Salem, J., Pinto dos Santos, D., Heidenreich, A., Maintz, D., & Haneder, S. (2020). Dose independent characterization of renal stones by means of dual energy computed tomography and machine learning: An ex-vivo study. *European Radiology*, *30*(3), 1397–1404. doi:10.100700330-019-06455-7 PMID:31773296

Haq, I., Mazhar, T., Malik, M. A., Kamal, M. M., Ullah, I., Kim, T., Hamdi, M., & Hamam, H. (2022). Lung Nodules Localization and Report Analysis from Computerized Tomography (C.T.) Scan Using a Novel Machine Learning Approach. *Applied Sciences (Basel, Switzerland)*, *12*(24), 12614. doi:10.3390/app122412614

Haq, I., Ullah, N., Mazhar, T., Malik, M. A., & Bano, I. (2022). A Novel Brain Tumor Detection and Coloring Technique from 2D M.R.I. Images. *Applied Sciences (Basel, Switzerland)*, *12*(11), 5744. doi:10.3390/app12115744

Hou, X., et al. (2019). Cascaded semantic segmentation for kidney and tumor.

Howles, S. A., & Thakker, R. V. (2020). Genetics of kidney stone disease. *Nature Reviews. Urology*, *17*(7), 407–421. doi:10.103841585-020-0332-x PMID:32533118

Iftikhar, H., Khan, M., Khan, Z., Khan, F., Alshanbari, H. M., & Ahmad, Z. (2023). A Comparative Analysis of Machine Learning Models: A Case Study in Predicting Chronic Kidney Disease. *Sustainability (Basel)*, *15*(3), 2754. doi:10.3390u15032754

Isensee, F., & Maier-Hein, K. H. (2019). An attempt at beating the 3D U-Net. arXiv preprint arXiv:1908.02182. doi:10.24926/548719.001

Jendeberg, J., Thunberg, P., & Lidén, M. (2021). Differentiation of distal ureteral stones and pelvic phleboliths using a convolutional neural network. *Urolithiasis*, *49*(1), 41–49. doi:10.100700240-020-01180-z PMID:32107579

Jeong, J., Chang, K., Lee, J., & Choi, J. (2022). A warning system for urolithiasis via retrograde intrarenal surgery using machine learning: An experimental study. *BMC Urology*, *22*(1), 80. doi:10.118612894-022-01032-5 PMID:35668401

Khamparia, A., & Pandey, B. (2020). A novel integrated principal component analysis and support vector machines-based diagnostic system for detection of chronic kidney disease. *International Journal of Data Analysis Techniques and Strategies*, *12*(2), 99–113. doi:10.1504/IJDATS.2020.106641

Längkvist, M., Jendeberg, J., Thunberg, P., Loutfi, A., & Lidén, M. (2018). Computer aided detection of ureteral stones in thin slice computed tomography volumes using Convolutional Neural Networks. *Computers in Biology and Medicine*, *97*, 153–160. doi:10.1016/j.compbiomed.2018.04.021 PMID:29730498

Linehan, W. M. (2012). Genetic basis of kidney cancer: Role of genomics for the development of disease-based therapeutics. *Genome Research*, *22*(11), 2089–2100. doi:10.1101/gr.131110.111 PMID:23038766

Ma, F., Sun, T., Liu, L., & Jing, H. (2020). Detection and diagnosis of chronic kidney disease using deep learning-based heterogeneous modified artificial neural network. *Future Generation Computer Systems*, *111*, 17–26. doi:10.1016/j.future.2020.04.036

Mazhar, T., & .... (2023). The role of machine learning and deep learning approaches for the detection of skin cancer. *Health Care*, *12*(3), 269. PMID:36766989

Mazhar, T., Nasir, Q., Haq, I., Kamal, M. M., Ullah, I., Kim, T., Mohamed, H. G., & Alwadai, N. (2022). A Novel Expert System for the Diagnosis and Treatment of Heart Disease. *Electronics (Basel)*, *11*(23), 3989. doi:10.3390/electronics11233989

Mu, G., et al. (2019). Segmentation of kidney tumor by multi-resolution vb-nets.

Ochoa-Ruiz, G., ... (2022). On the in vivo recognition of kidney stones using machine learning. arXiv preprint arXiv:2201.08865.

Parakh, A., Lee, H., Lee, J. H., Eisner, B. H., Sahani, D. V., & Do, S. (2019). Urinary stone detection on C.T. images using deep convolutional neural networks: Evaluation of model performance and generalization. *Radiology. Artificial Intelligence*, *1*(4), e180066. doi:10.1148/ryai.2019180066 PMID:33937795

Phyu, T. N. (2009). Survey of classification techniques in data mining. In *Proceedings of the international multiconference of engineers and computer scientists*.

Poore, W., & … . (2020). Obesity and its impact on kidney stone formation. *Reviews in Urology*, *22*(1), 17. PMID:32523467

Rizzo, A., Racca, M., Dall'Armellina, S., Rescigno, P., Banna, G. L., Albano, D., Dondi, F., Bertagna, F., Annunziata, S., & Treglia, G. (2023). The Emerging Role of PET/CT with PSMA-Targeting Radiopharmaceuticals in Clear Cell Renal Cancer: An Updated Systematic Review. *Cancers (Basel)*, *15*(2), 355. doi:10.3390/cancers15020355 PMID:36672305

Salazar, L. H., & … . (2020). Using different models of machine learning to predict attendance at medical appointments. *Journal of Information Systems Engineering & Management*, *5*(4), em0122. doi:10.29333/jisem/8430

Salazar, L. H. A., Leithardt, V. R. Q., Parreira, W. D., da Rocha Fernandes, A. M., Barbosa, J. L. V., & Correia, S. D. (2022). Application of machine learning techniques to predict a patient's no-show in the healthcare sector. *Future Internet*, *14*(1), 3. doi:10.3390/fi14010003

Schena, F. P., Anelli, V. W., Trotta, J., Di Noia, T., Manno, C., Tripepi, G., D'Arrigo, G., Chesnaye, N. C., Russo, M. L., Stangou, M., Papagianni, A., Zoccali, C., Tesar, V., Coppo, R., Tesar, V., Maixnerova, D., Lundberg, S., Gesualdo, L., Emma, F., … Cangemi, C. (2021). Development and testing of an artificial intelligence tool for predicting end-stage kidney disease in patients with immunoglobulin A nephropathy. *Kidney International*, *99*(5), 1179–1188. doi:10.1016/j.kint.2020.07.046 PMID:32889014

Shabaniyan, T., Parsaei, H., Aminsharifi, A., Movahedi, M. M., Jahromi, A. T., Pouyesh, S., & Parvin, H. (2019). An artificial intelligence-based clinical decision support system for large kidney stone treatment. *Australasian Physical & Engineering Sciences in Medicine*, *42*(3), 771–779. doi:10.100713246-019-00780-3 PMID:31332724

Siener, R. (2021). Nutrition and kidney stone disease. *Nutrients*, *13*(6), 1917. doi:10.3390/nu13061917 PMID:34204863

Singh, N. P., Bapi, R. S., & Vinod, P. (2018). Machine learning models to predict the progression from early to late stages of papillary renal cell carcinoma. *Computers in Biology and Medicine*, *100*, 92–99. doi:10.1016/j.compbiomed.2018.06.030 PMID:29990647

Terry, R. S., Whelan, P. S., & Lipkin, M. E. (2020). New devices for kidney stone management. *Current Opinion in Urology*, *30*(2), 144–148. doi:10.1097/MOU.0000000000000710 PMID:31895890

Thongprayoon, C., Krambeck, A. E., & Rule, A. D. (2020). Determining the true burden of kidney stone disease. *Nature Reviews. Nephrology*, *16*(12), 736–746. doi:10.103841581-020-0320-7 PMID:32753740

Uribarri, J. (2020). Chronic kidney disease and kidney stones. *Current Opinion in Nephrology and Hypertension*, *29*(2), 237–242. doi:10.1097/MNH.0000000000000582 PMID:31972597

Wang, Z., Zhang, Y., Zhang, J., Deng, Q., & Liang, H. (2021). Recent advances on the mechanisms of kidney stone formation. *International Journal of Molecular Medicine*, *48*(2), 1–10. doi:10.3892/ijmm.2021.4982 PMID:34132361

Yang, S. W., Hyon, Y. K., Na, H. S., Jin, L., Lee, J. G., Park, J. M., Lee, J. Y., Shin, J. H., Lim, J. S., Na, Y. G., Jeon, K., Ha, T., Kim, J., & Song, K. H. (2020). Machine learning prediction of stone-free success in patients with urinary stone after treatment of shock wave lithotripsy. *BMC Urology*, *20*(1), 1–8. doi:10.118612894-020-00662-x PMID:32620102

Yang, S. W., Hyon, Y. K., Na, H. S., Jin, L., Lee, J. G., Park, J. M., Lee, J. Y., Shin, J. H., Lim, J. S., Na, Y. G., Jeon, K., Ha, T., Kim, J., & Song, K. H. (2020). Machine learning prediction of stone-free success in patients with urinary stone after treatment of shock wave lithotripsy. *BMC Urology*, *20*(1), 1–8. doi:10.118612894-020-00662-x PMID:32620102

Yildirim, K., Bozdag, P. G., Talo, M., Yildirim, O., Karabatak, M., & Acharya, U. R. (2021). Deep learning model for automated kidney stone detection using coronal C.T. images. *Computers in Biology and Medicine*, *135*, 104569. doi:10.1016/j.compbiomed.2021.104569 PMID:34157470

Zhang, H. (2018). Chronic kidney disease survival prediction with artificial neural networks. In *2018 IEEE International Conference on Bioinformatics and Biomedicine (BIBM)* (pp. 1639-1642). 10.1109/BIBM.2018.8621294

Zhang, H. (2018). Chronic kidney disease survival prediction with artificial neural networks. In *2018 IEEE International Conference on Bioinformatics and Biomedicine (BIBM)* (pp. 1639-1642). 10.1109/BIBM.2018.8621294

Zhao, C. (2023). Development of a Convolutional Neural Network for Automated Detection of Kidney Stones on Computed Tomography Images. *Journal of Digital Imaging*, 1–9.

Zheng, S. (2020). Kidney stone detection on CT images using deep learning with convolutional neural network. *Journal of Medical Imaging and Health Informatics*, *10*(10), 2195–2201.

Chapter 5
Ethnography and Organizational Anthropology

José G. Vargas-Hernandez
Tecnològico Superior de Jalisco, Mexico

María F. Higuera-Cota
https://orcid.org/0000-0001-8285-1076
Universidad Autónoma de Sinaloa, Mexico

Omar C. Vargas-González
https://orcid.org/0000-0002-6089-956X
Tecnológico Nacional de México, Ciudad Guzmán, Mexico

ABSTRACT

This study aims to analyze some of the theoretical, conceptual, and methodological implications between organizational anthropology and ethnography. Departing from the assumption that ethnographic analysis and interpretive research on organizational anthropology has an emergent and symbolic role rooted in social processes and with no a priori assumptions, with explanations and categories defined by the organizational actors. The method employed is based on analytical and descriptive issues from the theoretical and empirical literature review leading to reflective analysis. It is concluded that ethnographic methodology is pertinent to be used in the analysis of its interactions, with organizational anthropology as a new specialty in organizational studies.

INTRODUCTION

Organizational anthropology and ethnography are two disciplines that share an interest in understanding social and cultural processes within the context of organizations. Although both disciplines have evolved separately, in recent decades there have been several points of convergence and a growing demand to apply ethnographic approaches in organizational anthropology research. The aim of this analysis is to examine the theoretical, conceptual, and methodological implications between organizational anthro-

DOI: 10.4018/979-8-3693-1634-4.ch005

pology and ethnography, in order to evaluate the emerging and symbolic role of interpretive research in organizational anthropology.

It is important to highlight that organizational anthropology is a discipline that has emerged from various situations, conditions, and anthropological perspectives, which has led to different perspectives and approaches. Organizations are considered legitimate research laboratories in fields such as organizational anthropology, psychology, and sociology, and are relevant to the organizational and administrative school of thought, complementing other disciplines such as sociology, psychology, biology, and history.

In a differentiated socioeconomic world, diverse contexts are demanding new anthropologically-oriented organizational forms as specific responses to survival and adaptability. The emic perspective of organization members is key to nourishing anthropology and organizational theory, according to Gonnet (2012).

In this context, the relevance of ethnography as a methodology for organizational anthropology research becomes evident. Ethnographic methodology is based on analytical and descriptive questions from theoretical and empirical literature review, which leads to reflective analysis. This allows for the analysis of the interactions between organizational anthropology and ethnography as a new specialty in organizational studies. In conclusion, it is concluded that ethnographic methodology is pertinent to be used in the analysis of the theoretical, conceptual, and methodological implications between organizational anthropology and ethnography, which will allow for the advancement in understanding social and cultural processes within the context of organizations.

PROBLEM STATEMENT

Organizational anthropology is an interdisciplinary field that seeks to understand the complex relationships between humans and organizations. This discipline is based on the collaboration of various fields, such as psychology, social anthropology, ethnology, sociology, among others. However, according to Fotaki *et al.* (2020), there is still a need for greater inclusion of the anthropological perspective in organizational studies.

Organizational anthropology has historically focused on researching organizational structures, work practices, corporate culture, and cultural diversity within organizations. Although the discipline has developed theoretical models and research methodologies in collaboration with other fields, such as industrial and organizational psychology, there are still knowledge gaps. For example, the discipline has tended to focus more on the description and analysis of organizational practices and less on the analysis of workers' subjective experience and the processes that influence their behavior.

On the other hand, ethnography and other anthropological approaches offer valuable tools for researching processes of signification, the social construction of reality, and subjective experience. These approaches can complement the more quantitative and structural approaches of organizational anthropology and enrich our understanding of behavioral problems in the workplace.

Therefore, this study aims to explore how the inclusion of the anthropological perspective can contribute to a solid theoretical framework for organizational psychology and how it can generate dialogue between disciplines to address behavioral problems in organizations. It is expected that this study will contribute to the consolidation of organizational anthropology as a discipline that integrates various theoretical and methodological perspectives to understand the complexity of contemporary organizations.

Next, we will address the section "Importance of the study," which considers various definitions and theoretical perspectives that have emerged in this field. It also highlights the need to approach the study of organizations from a multidisciplinary perspective, with anthropology, paleontology, historiography, and sociology as the main approaches.

IMPORTANCE OF STUDY

The definitions of organizational anthropology to define its field of study are based on the capitalist international division of intellectual labor. Instead of using anthropological metaphors such as "character," "tribe," or "clan," capitalist concepts such as performance and efficiency, based on the Toyota organizational paradigm, should be considered, according to Berg and Faucheux (1982) and Alvesson and Berg (1992).

According to Smirnova (2016), anthropology has evolved to include administrative, cultural, and social anthropology in physical and organizational contexts. Industrial, organizational, and business anthropology, according to Roca i Girona (2001), focuses on the organizational industrial business environment. Industrial anthropology differs from economic anthropology, according to Roca (1998), as it focuses on the economic activity of societies, while economic anthropology focuses on the economy of societies. Industrial anthropology refers to both industrial and non-industrial work, and its object of study is the industrial organization, shop, farm, craft workshops, whether in the formal or informal economy. Industrial anthropology is an anthropology of industrial society focused on historical problems related to industrialism and its social anthropology.

Applied anthropology in industrial societies can be defined in terms of its practical use in a historical context. According to Maestre Alfonso (1983), anthropology is interested in studying complex industrial societies and intervening in different areas of organizational studies influenced by ideological and material power in industrial organizations. In this way, the process of formation and development of organizational anthropology, under the approach of applied anthropology, is linked to the phenomena of industrialization of societies.

Organizational anthropology focuses on studying human organizations, and through empirical research, it is possible to explain the opportunities and limitations associated with the use of anthropological methods in management and organizations. However, organizational anthropological research must also take into account the context, history, and process centered on the actor, and must be distinguished from intervention in organizations.

García Canclini (1995) and Krambia-Kapardis and Zopiatis (2021) argue that multidisciplinary research on organizations involves disciplines such as sociology, psychology, anthropology, and communication studies. Therefore, the study of organizations should be approached in a multidisciplinary manner, from a micro perspective on human groups, with anthropology, paleontology, historiography, and sociology as main approaches, aiming towards an anthropology of organizations.

The proposed methodology for conducting a detailed study on the relationship between organizational anthropology and ethnographic research in organizational settings will be presented shortly. The comprehensive review of theoretical and empirical literature that will be conducted, and how descriptive and analytical questions will be integrated to achieve a deeper understanding of the theoretical, conceptual, and methodological implications of organizational anthropology and ethnography will also be described.

METHOD

The methodology proposed for this study involves a thorough review and analysis of the theoretical and empirical literature related to organizational anthropology and its relationship with ethnographic research in organizational settings. The analysis integrates descriptive and analytical questions to gain a deeper understanding of the theoretical, conceptual, and methodological implications of organizational anthropology and ethnography. Subsequently, critical reflection on the findings will help identify key ideas and implications for future research in the field. The proposed methodology contributes to a better understanding of the role and potential of ethnographic research in organizational settings, providing a valuable guide for future research in the area of organizational anthropology.

In the field of anthropology, there is a branch dedicated to the study of organizations and the social interactions that occur within them: organizational anthropology. This discipline focuses on examining the cultural and social aspects of organizations, including how organizational structures and practices influence human behavior. To analyze these issues, organizational anthropology uses a variety of methods, including ethnography, which focuses on detailed observation and analysis of behaviors in a specific social context. In the following sections, we will explore some of the theoretical, conceptual, and methodological implications that arise when using ethnography in the study of organizational anthropology.

ORGANIZATIONAL ANTHROPOLOGY

Anthropological organizational is considered an emerging field, which has emerged as a discipline in convergence with sociology and psychology, and the intersections between the local and the global to analyze the organizational components of complex societies, as well as their transformative effects on the cultural dynamics in traditional models of capitalist organization. The connection between anthropology and organizational studies in a discipline of anthropological organization accounts for the social diversity of human meanings. And these types of studies are applicable to all types of organizations regardless of their nature and identity.

Authors such as Corsín Jiménez (2007), Caulkins, & Ann (2013), Garsten, & Anette (2013), and Sapienza and Gupta (2022) mention that administrative and organizational anthropology, also known as anthropological organization, is a science that studies the interactions between objects and people in the management field. For Kottak (2011) and Limberg and Rodriguez (2020), anthropological organization studies the diversity of human conditions that involves adaptability in the space and time of organizations, biology, society, culture, language, etc.

Regarding the fundamental concepts of the theoretical framework of anthropological organization, these are oriented to analyze the reality of organizations as an object of study of anthropology, leading to processes of change in the professional programs of various disciplines aimed at applying anthropology in organizational studies of industrial societies.

Specifically, organizational anthropology provides support for human realities, such as social constructions, symbolic, cultural, and ideological aspects of organizations. The theories and methodologies of organizational anthropology should be compatible with the reality of organizations developed through processes of transformation and formation of societies and companies.

Likewise, organizational anthropology contributes to analyzing the perspectives of actors, providing the human side of organizations made up of human beings. Organizational anthropology is a means to provide background for the study of human beings in organizations that focuses on management and profitability, efficiency, and effectiveness. According to Richardson (1955) and Kostera (2018), anthropology in organizations supports the human relations approach in organizations, along with psychology and non-systematized knowledge.

Regarding the field of organizational anthropology, Roca (1998) and Yelvington and Fisher (2021) consider that it focuses on the research of human relationships, behaviors, and cultures among different processes of organizations, businesses, industries, enterprises, corporations, etc., as systems to provide knowledge, reveal their nature, and contribute to critique, change, improve, denounce, etc. It is worth noting that the production of knowledge in applied organizational anthropology focused on the diversity of organizations requires changes towards more collaborative efforts in professional work. The production of knowledge within the anthropological organization itself as a discipline with its various approaches requires collaboration with change and professional work in parallel.

In reference above, Chanlat (1994) and Metzgar and Orr (2020) highlight that the anthropology of organizations is a symbolic, ideological, cultural, sense, and identity aspect that creates and develops multiple realities. In other words, the anthropology of organizations is perceived through symbols that reveal internal relationships as unified elements for work, social culture, organizational and corporate culture, and subcultures within organization members. Thus, theoretical knowledge of organizational anthropology contributes objective tools to industrial psychology oriented towards understanding human problems and aspects in organizations.

The study of organizations from an anthropological perspective considers behavior, structure, group values, and other factors, which leads to an analysis of how organizations function (Jordan, 2013). Anthropological organizational studies, on the other hand, describe the sociopolitical relationships within organizational structures aimed at modifying and transforming forms of commitment, time and space, information technologies, and communication. It is worth noting that the dimensions of anthropological organizational studies have been modified by information technologies from the perspective of related disciplines interested in working within organizations.

Anthropological organizational studies examine human organizations. The anthropological dimension of human beings accounts for a more humanistic organization focused on social meaning and identity, which leads to the diversity of human groups. This, in turn, leads to the creation and development of predominantly human organizations.

In this section, we will explore the classical theory of anthropology and its relevance to organizational studies. We will examine the key concepts and principles that underpin this theory and their implications for understanding organizational behavior. We will also discuss how the classical theory of anthropology has influenced contemporary organizational research and practice.

THE CLASSICAL THEORY OF ANTHROPOLOGY: FROM AN ORGANIZATIONAL PERSPECTIVE

Anthropology emphasizes the specificities of human groups within organizations, differentiating itself from sociology by engaging with the people being studied. The classical theory of anthropology in organizations describes them as political entities in which various groups pursue their interests and objectives, analyzing the existence of competition between multiple cultural groups and forming a social structure destined to translate demands into culture.

Classical anthropology advocates for an anthropology of the current world with critical positions and methodological crossings in materialistic and idealistic versions of interpretivism, with a common core of familiarizing the exotic to construct otherness as a practical way of constructing knowledge for participatory practices, as proposed by the ethnomethodological approach (Menéndez, 2006). The above allows for building processes of reflection and questioning of classical anthropological theories and their role in society within the scientific framework of Marxism.

According to Baer (2014), the anthropological perspective of organizations provides insight that big data fails to fully analyze and interpret data related to various organizational stakeholders such as customers, as human sciences allow us to understand human subjectivity in deciphering the functions of technology used to create goods and services. The concept of business anthropology, supported by Jordan (2013), expands anthropological practice not only for the benefit of organizations in topics related to group behavior, work processes, organizational change, diversity, globalization, etc. In this regard, Caulkins & Jordan (2013) and Morales Inga & Morales Tristán (2018) point out that organizational anthropology is a dynamic field in organizational studies that, rather than a unified theory, is composed of multiple theoretical approaches with diverse methodologies developed and used in various contexts.

In line with the above, the methodology of organizational anthropology aims to collect and use primary information to design an experiential feedback workshop supported by classic tools such as SWOT analysis, group interviews, problem trees, etc., that lead to diagnosing problems and finding solutions. At the same time, the analytical tools of organizational anthropology are used to analyze hierarchies and relationships between and within groups and organizations (Lomnitz, 1975; Horst, Miller, & Sinanan, 2021). In addition, the quantitative methodology of organizational anthropology is the combination of techniques such as participant observation and psychometrics to achieve the necessary qualifications to obtain objective numerical data about participants and obtain comprehensive individual results.

From the perspective of organizational anthropology, imagination is the individual perception and beliefs that construct the process of social construction of reality generated by interactions between humans, enabling the organizational anthropological perspective created by humans in society of the symbolic world beyond reality (Cely-López & Gómez Niño, 2016). In this regard, Jaumier (2020) warns that anthropology plays a role in understanding alternative organizations and the acts of imagining new ones that lean towards the experiences and local meanings of organization members as a field of problematization rather than theory.

The role of organizational anthropology focuses more on human relationships than on production processes, indicating that the organization is a community oriented towards building and strengthening identity, which, supported by organizational culture, values, norms, rituals, myths, etc., develops a vision to generate value. Individuals and communities in organizational anthropology promote intervention practices to identify necessary community perceptions about program design processes to promote the development of community organizations.

Regarding the anthropology of organizations and history, according to Llobera (2009), they contribute to appreciating epistemic cycles, resulting in flexible epistemic refuges focused on constructing alterity supported by other disciplines that tend to question ethnocentric and relativistic rationalities that lead to the context of creative imagination.

For Czarniawska (2012) and Moeran and Béji-Bécheur (2021), organizational anthropology is positioned in business and managerial research programs, focusing on analyzing practices in co-evolution with market institutions. Organizational anthropology has reached a stage of maturity focused on analyzing organizational theories, based on the emergence of the discipline that provides historical characteristics in the development of traditional and innovative methodologies, and philosophical approaches to organizations and managerial research, according to Kunda (1986), Weeks (2004), and Marcus (2021), who affirm that anthropological journeys establish explicit connections between anthropology and the study of organizations.

Organizational anthropology is a relatively new field of study that focuses on understanding the cultural and social aspects of organizations. This discipline has gained increasing attention in recent years, as more and more organizations recognize the importance of understanding the social and cultural factors that influence their operations. Organizational anthropology provides valuable insights into the complex social dynamics that shape organizational behavior, as well as the cultural factors that underpin organizational practices and structures. In this section, we will explore the usefulness of organizational anthropology and its potential for informing organizational research and practice. We will examine the key contributions that organizational anthropology has made to our understanding of organizational behavior, and we will also discuss the challenges and limitations of this approach.

USEFULNESS OF ORGANIZATIONAL ANTHROPOLOGY

In this sense, Fotaki et al. (2020) affirm that the analysis of spirituality, symbolism, and narration in organization studies is explicitly committed to anthropology. Organizational anthropology prioritizes symbolic meanings over more rational thinking, makes the human side of the organization relevant, and contributes to a holistic perspective of human behavior in organizations (Páramo, 2018; Roca i Girona, 2001). Ultimately, anthropology...

Interpretive research in organizational anthropology has an emerging and symbolic role rooted in social processes and without a priori assumptions, with explanations and categories defined by organizational actors (Cely-López & Gómez-Niño, 2016). Symbolic magical meanings about human rationality lead to showing the human side of organizations. On the other hand, the lack of interest of symbolic anthropology in the organizational process is due to the technocracy obsessed with efficiency and effectiveness imposing organizational thinking (Chanlat, 1994).

Anthropology and sociology have in common the social aspect, but what differentiates them is that the anthropological approach makes each human group's concerns more specific, leading to better analysis of organizational phenomena such as organizational culture, which goes against the positive approach. Both anthropology and sociology study and analyze human and social issues and concerns in organizations that lead to the establishment of general and universal social laws. However, anthropology does not deal with the general laws that account for the diversity of human groups manifested in specific characteristics, analyzing social and cultural details, giving them identity and meaning.

The sociology and anthropology of organizations have in common the social aspect, although the latter gives meaning to the cultural and ideological identity specificities of the diverse groups that construct multiple realities (Chanlat, 1994; Beker and Dutton, 2021). Anthropological and sociological sensitivity analyzes human beings in contemporary organizations responsible for the future. Anthropology accounts for the social aspect of the diversity of individuals and human groups and studies, seeking hidden differences that lead to their meaning and characteristics, with an emphasis on specificities.

The specialties of organizational anthropology aim to study various aspects of human constitution. In other words, an organizational anthropology applied in organizational contexts deals with organized individuals, focusing on the horizon of organizational study through intervention and research processes to generate new knowledge with the aim of solving social problems. For Thomas Barfield (2000), applied anthropology focuses on solving practical problems, creating guidelines, providing information, and taking action in categories of applied research and intervention.

Therefore, applying the knowledge of organizational anthropology to the different fields of organizational action, focusing on the analysis of the development of organizational life within the sociocultural context, if researchers are involved, contributes to the creation of theoretical knowledge. On the other hand, both anthropology and sociology deal with the social aspect of the organization, the universal and general laws of the social considering the positivist aspect. For example, anthropology studies the social organization of societies, language, beliefs, etc., in organizations. Thus, the analysis of organizational anthropology contributes to the study of issues related to the company and entrepreneurs, tools, methods, categories, etc.

The pioneering analysis in organizational and business anthropology was in the analysis of simple societies to complex societies. Business anthropology studies as a social science aim to explain the behavior of elites by addressing theoretical and methodological challenges using anthropological methods and tools to analyze practices and references of positions of power whose subjects of study are marginal subordinates (Cerutti, 2003; Hernández, 2013). In other words, studies of entrepreneurship under organizational anthropology aimed to explain the behaviors of elites.

Socio-anthropological sensitivity moves management theory away from the linear causality of action-benefit (Muñoz, 2011) and provides the elements that reproduce the logic of organizational management that leads to the agency of financialization of the economy as the protagonist of social creation instead of considering it as a fatalism. Management is based on anthropology, sociology, psychology, etc. Administrative thinking includes socio-anthropological sensitivity that leads to sharpening the vision for a contextualized and modulated sustainable action of the public-private dialectic.

Organizational factors are analyzed in analytical theoretical approaches of organizational anthropology and administration and symbolic interactionism that deal with the categories of organizational environments and contexts that come from the information and confirmation emanating from semi-structured interviews, dimensions, and sub-dimensions (Cely-López, & Gómez-Niño, 2016).

In this regard, Cely-López & Gómez-Niño (2016) highlight that organizational anthropology contributes to the administrative process of planning, organization, integration, direction, and control; to social accounting that deals with issues related to employees, the social community, social responsibility, environmental and ethical issues, etc. For Baba (2012), organizational management structures rely on social and organizational anthropology to seek effectiveness in private companies and public organizations. In other words, public administration influenced by anthropology aims to humanize formation in organizations.

Anthropological and sociological sensitivity identifies the phenomena and objects of the complexity of human beings who lead collective organizational life. Studies such as that of Jamie Uys lead to theoretical and methodological accumulation of organizational anthropology and sociology. And although the interaction time to study groups in organizational sociology is shorter and sporadic than in organizational anthropology that is dedicated to an intimate study of the group for a longer period, institutional time management was able to fulfill positional functions with advantage to plan from an anthropological perspective of organizations.

Traditional and organizational anthropology links technology to broaden the organizational approach and apply knowledge that contributes to the generation of initiatives for the construction of local and indigenous meanings. It should be noted that technologies contribute to organizational systems in the creation and promotion of new companies, evaluation of technological intervention projects through the formulation of policies and strategies framed in organizational anthropology, contribute to the creation and capture of value in public-private partnerships, etc.

Regarding this, Roberts and Grabowski (1996) and Rakowski, Kossakowski, and Siemienska (2021) state that organizational anthropology analyzes different technologies with an emphasis on traditional technologies developed contextually with their own resources, and Western technologies classified as mechanical, human, and knowledge-based. Through theoretical study via documentary and bibliographic analysis, the aim is to explore the relationships between organizational anthropology and traditional technology as part of the organizational space.

The term anthropology was coined by François Auguste Péron, a French naturalist and explorer (1775-1810). It refers to the science born in the 19th century that studies man. Currently, research on the relationship between anthropology and organizational studies, introducing the theory and management of organizational anthropology, began in the mid-twentieth century, moving anthropology away from its traditional core object of study based on knowledge from pre-industrial and non-industrial communities towards a disciplinary interest in organizational concerns and problems (Marzal, 1996). It is worth noting that the development of organizational, labor, and industrial anthropology is interconnected. As a scientific discipline, anthropology becomes an applied science that proposes applied industrial anthropology to study problems of work anthropology and its functional relationship with society, such as the phenomenon of rural migration to urban areas (Esteva, 1984, 1955; Capel, 2009; Garsten and Nyqvist, 2022).

The history of organizational anthropology and business organizations in the academic field is complementary developments to theoretical knowledge in the development of organizational psychology applied to specific practices such as product and service diversification. In relation to this, Harvey (2004) and Fumagalli (2019) affirm that historical reality prompted science and technology to establish the Fordist production system that strengthened the bureaucratic organizational system to control production from the perspective of rationality characterized as instrumental by the critical perspective.

For authors such as Corsín Jiménez (2007), Caulkins, & Ann (2013), and North & Gita (2014), organizational studies require new concepts, approaches, and technologies such as organizational and management anthropology, creative and knowledge management, etc., conducive to personal and social development. A review of organization theory and organizational studies and their different approaches and relationships with anthropology highlights the anthropological perspective that leads to the humanistic aspect of organizations.

Organizational anthropology was established in 1927 with the Western Electric Company project in the industrial plants of Hawthorne, Chicago, as a scientific discipline directed by the sociologist and industrial psychologist Elton Mayo of the Harvard Business School. It is related to the management school called neo-human relations or human resources created and developed by the same psychologist with his research in the Hawthorne plants between 1927 and 1932 (Chanlat, 2019; Roca i Girona, 2001).

Mayo's interest was to study worker job satisfaction from a socio-psychological perspective. Authors such as Malinowski (1944), Radcliffe-Brown (1952), and Lloyd Warner (1952) participated in this project, laying the foundations for the theory of organizational anthropology. The latter is considered the father of organizational anthropology for the work carried out as an ethnologist and sociologist (Bélanger and LeBlanc, 2011; Moeran, 2020). The studies and analyses constructed from organizational anthropology contribute to clarifying the differences between the referents to support arguments and solve problems that arise between managers and workers. In addition, organizational anthropology includes issues related to the welfare of workers assumed as organizations of political development.

Based on experiments with the workforce and their productivity, Mayo developed industrial psychology to support the human dimension of organizations, which marked the beginning of organizational anthropology. Organizational anthropology demonstrated that job satisfaction and worker productivity are determined by their human relationships developed through the use of anthropological, ethnographic, and participant observation techniques (Richardson 1955; Scully, 2019). Given the concept of organizational anthropology, organizations internally train for productivity, motivation, and member training to create and develop an identity based on organizational capability.

Organizational anthropology began to gain relevance from the famous Hawthorne research project and later with the research of the Society for Applied Anthropology, giving rise to the Journal of Applied Anthropology, renamed Human Organization (Santibáñez, 1994). This emerged in the early 1950s as an expected priority in organizational research interrupted by the crisis in the school of human relations that led to the adoption of the managerial perspective. The first anthropological studies were conducted by Caudill (1958) in a psychiatric hospital.

Munizaga (1988) conducted the first organizational anthropology study. During the 1970s, organizational anthropology presented unfavorable academic and scientific production, struggled to institutionalize and implement programs to train organizational anthropologists to study organizational work dynamics, transculturation in organizational fields, social development, etc.

Organizational anthropology was established as a discipline of social sciences based on ethnographic research methodologies during the 1980s (Bate, 1997) with the aim of studying and analyzing the nature and functioning of public and private organizations. Some classics in the literature of business anthropology are Holzberg and Maureen (1981), Pérez-Lizaur (2010), Basaldúa (2005), and Urban and Koh (2013).

Subsequently, organizational anthropology evolved into a sub-discipline of managerial research with a focus on working conditions, workload and schedules, and the management of organizational processes. This shift towards managerial research led to new areas of interest for the development of organizational anthropology and management disciplines, such as knowledge management and creativity, which aim to promote personal development and foster skills and relationships within the socio-ecological system, encompassing both society and nature. As a result, organizational anthropology is now engaged in conducting organizational analysis to better understand and facilitate the development of organizational management.

The perspectives of organizational psychology in the analysis of organizational behavior are thought more as dysfunctional behaviors, fears and dilemmas, etc., to be addressed as problems and options to position oneself strategically consistently to deal with anthropology for management. While anthropology contributes to meeting the managerial needs and demands of organizations, giving rise to organizational anthropology from the managerial perspective, methods, tools, and instruments for management. In other words, organizational anthropology must contribute to designing and developing managerial tools and instruments for organization analysis.

The orientation of organizational anthropology towards the managerialist approach moves away from the humanistic approach that leads to practical application outside the tensions between work and capital, prioritizing the maximization of profits and profitability. The relationships between both disciplines, anthropology, and organizations, are a consequence of the interactions found in managing the boundaries of behavior to make potential contributions to learning and applying on topics of people's well-being aligned with capital and labor.

Organizational anthropology expands interactions between individuals and the complicated social environment exerting the impact of human formation, care, and respect for people. Therefore, the focus of organizational anthropology is complementary to the organizational focus in evaluating job competencies by producing different types of information and data that would not be available if only one were used.

Regarding the instrumental conception of the human being, Chanlat (1994) and Brand and Wissen (2020) describe it as manipulative, although other anthropologists argue that organizational behavior has been strengthened with the homo economicus as the dominant conception. It is precisely because of these differences that the categories of the economic model are validated to understand the characterization of symbolic, mythical, magical, normative, and religious phenomena of organizational life and family affairs that can coexist simultaneously. Where the focus of anthropological organization in personnel selection alleviates some of the problems.

In other words, an anthropological approach to organizations contributes to expanding and complementing knowledge in talent management. Therefore, practical organizational anthropology serves management in the management of knowledge of specific organizational problems from the theoretical and methodological frameworks of anthropology and anthropological techniques, which makes them necessary for organizational development.

Organizational anthropological facilitation is the professional external intervention aimed at improving institutional management practices of actors pursuing their own objectives based on the concepts and objects of study of organizational anthropology, such as the construction of alterity and reflexivity. It is assigned as a function of organizational management to urge higher education institutions to prepare knowledge.

From a perspective of organizational anthropology with a specific contribution to organizational facilitation through a reconversion of positioning forms towards problems, there is participatory action in social processes, collective actions with specific formal and informal purposes. Participatory and facilitation processes as transfer instruments are methodological challenges that arise as opportunities and difficulties to situate non-traditional actions as objects of organizational anthropology from different asymmetrical rationalities. These challenges must be addressed according to the anthropological contribution of the methodological principles of organizational facilitation and participation aimed at creating and changing organizational and management culture.

Reflections on management practices take the framework of organizational anthropology to the point of becoming a discipline in organizational studies. This alternative must be included in academic questions and concerns to strategically position themselves in the theoretical and practical deepening of an anthropology for management. The theoretical framework of organizational anthropology and the involved references have a place in the anthropology of practice. Indeed, the practice of anthropology in organizational dynamics confronts processes between managers and workers in order to change the methodological approach, affecting the entire human being enrolled in organizational behavior, demanding commitment and responsibility with oneself.

The main concepts and principles that are the foundation of social anthropology will be analyzed, and the evolution of this field of study will be discussed, including how it has integrated novel perspectives and methodologies over time.

SOCIAL ANTHROPOLOGY STUDIES SOCIAL RELATIONS AND STRUCTURES

The analysis from social anthropology of the family, the entrepreneur, and the company are linked actors. Studies on simple societies in anthropology analyze the kinship systems of society, such as the case of

Lebanese entrepreneurs in southeastern Mexico (Ramírez Carrillo, 1992), the determinants of the family pattern of entrepreneurs (Nader, 1972) in a comparative analysis. Practice for social agents applying anthropological imagination (Gravano, 1995) and the case method in organizational management in institutions, organizations, and movements.

Organizational anthropology studies in organizations, entrepreneurship, and family refer to the family-organization. The perspective of anthropology on family and business revolves around analyzing the interplay of the company and the work participation of family members and the relationships established among them, focusing on issues related to family members who are both workers and owners in organizations. A social anthropology analysis of the family business sees it as a domestic business unit that emphasizes the family's functions as a primary network. Organizational anthropology studies equate the family as a domestic unit of members who bring relationships, resources, practices, and so on.

The field of social management through the anthropology of organizations contributes to constructing options, including relevant methodological and ideological ones. Organizational anthropology seeks to describe and analyze the structuring of social relationships in work, presentation and corporate appearance, duration, forms of commitment, experiences, new spaces and times, and other elements in organizational management. Mexican anthropology, like the Manchester School of Anthropology, seeks to overcome the bias of the managerial approach of organizational anthropology. In this regard, the organizational crisis coincided with the emergence of the Manchester School in organizational anthropology, influenced by Gluckman (1940), on research carried out on industrial organizations, including participant observation that led to the contradiction of the harmony at work proposed by the School of Human Resources, where social situations fit within a wider structure. The link between two organizations, the economic unit, and the domestic unit, expands that family in the analysis of social networks characterized as a structure and represented by individuals or other networks from 1960 according to García and Oliveira.

Mexican anthropology has more recent origins, but it has achieved a high impact and scope in economic, social, political, and cultural achievements. Anthropological studies in Mexico originated with the colonization process in the sixteenth century, followed by social and cultural contradictions in the need to describe and interpret indigenous cultures. In independent Mexico in the nineteenth century, anthropology focused on issues and concerns related to the interpretation of existing social reality in search of a common identity, creating a stable and strong state, and the origin of the professionalization of anthropology.

In the early twentieth century, physical anthropology and ethnology began in Mexico. This led to the development of empirically applied organizational anthropology at the end of the same century, articulating niches of work, although professional practice is more related to management actions in academic institutions. In 1910, the National School of American Archeology and Ethnology was founded, introducing the paradigm of indigenous anthropology with Manuel Gamio, becoming one of the lasting currents of anthropological thought (González, 2003; Villanueva, Serrano & Vera, 1999; Matos, 1987). It developed topics such as the themes, problems, and concerns of applied anthropology in Mexico aimed at recovering national identity and local history that revolve around the analysis to understand what is specific.

In the 1920s and 1930s, the integrationist conception of anthropology was formed, called the New Anthropology committed to nationalist interests with the teaching of anthropology in the academic programs of the National Polytechnic Institute and the National School of Anthropology and History (Olive, 1987). Traditional limits of anthropology as a discipline focused on the study of social groups such as peasants, migrants, workers, etc., during the 1970s, complementing Mexican anthropology carried out by Esteban Krotz (1993) and García & Krotz (1988) with an emphasis on the cultural heritage of the national state.

Marxist theory and the critical perspective have a strong influence on the theoretical framework that supports the development of Mexican anthropology. While critical organizational studies are inspired by anthropology, it has not been credited that the contributions remain implicit and elusive, revealing an incomplete history (Mir & Fayard, 2021). However, anthropological criticality provides a focus on power dynamics and fronts, and its empirical focus on managerial practices in indigenous organizations and informal scenarios. In turn, the contributions of the organizational anthropological approach complement feminist economies by making visible unpaid domestic work (Domínguez Forgueras, 2019).

In correspondence with the above, Roca i Girona (2001) and Lashaw (2020) indicate that the study of anthropology in organizations is considered more complex for anthropologists because they are implicitly under criticism for being involved in a contractual relationship in exchange for a salary for work. However, despite the imperfections of organizational anthropology in organizational studies, which are characterized by the potential for cross-fertilization and academic scrutiny, this approach should focus on organizational sciences that can benefit from organizational anthropology and ethnography as a method (Bate, 1997).

Latin American organizations and work situations are a laboratory for organizational anthropology research, analysis, formulation, and application of policies in public and private formal structured organizations (Bermúdez, 2017). Organizational anthropological production in Latin America is at the beginning of a dialogue and discussion based on the differences between history, regions, ethnicities, and other specificities of methodologies, research practices, convergences, and differences detected.

Additionally, organizational anthropology is an interdisciplinary profession whose specificity begins to develop by focusing on designing a comprehensive model considering the neighborhood as a symbol and the semiotic mechanisms established in the construction of meaning. Therefore, organizational anthropology consulting requires a global and more objective tool capable of shortening the time to develop field research for comprehensive results with an emphasis on organizational analysis.

Gravano (1992) and Heckscher (2018) describe organizational anthropology as referring to the intervention and facilitation of organizational processes through the use of methodological tools that are not necessarily applied, while practical anthropology focuses on listening, interpreting, objectifying, and transferring the practices of participants to make decisions about actions to follow and achieve effectiveness. Likewise, Cely-López & Gómez-Niño (2016) affirm that organizational anthropology delves into the analysis of behaviors, values, beliefs, customs in all organizational practices and activities related to work life, lifestyles, human development, education, and training, etc. In other words, trends in educational disciplines are aimed at sharing knowledge about organizational anthropology assigned as a separate subject on administrative topics.

In summary, the agency of people and social movements in social structures is the new trend in anthropological studies to reveal dynamic changes with the commitment to explain integration processes through research.

Organizational ethnography is a research methodology that focuses on the detailed and systematic study of cultural and social practices in a specific organizational context. This discipline has become increasingly important in understanding the dynamics of organizations and how they affect human behavior. Organizational ethnography is based on participant observation, interviews, and document analysis, which allows researchers to acquire a deep and contextualized understanding of organizational practices and dynamics. In this section, we will explore organizational ethnography and its contribution to the study of organizations. We will analyze the key concepts and principles that underpin this research methodology, and discuss how it can be applied in specific organizational settings to obtain useful and relevant information. We will also address the challenges and limitations of organizational ethnography and its relationship with other research methodologies in the field of organizational anthropology.

ORGANIZATIONAL ETHNOGRAPHY

Organizational anthropology and organizational sociology are privileged within the referential framework of management by the methods of ethnography and ethnology to conduct research on their respective objects of study with the aim of acquiring a more useful anthropological and sociological sensitivity to organizational administration and management. Ethnography within the socio-cultural anthropology in organizational contexts supports problem-solving and provides theoretical-conceptual elements of organizational anthropology oriented towards the analysis of institutional behavior and relationships.

Anthropological organizational theory and practical tools are offered by organizational anthropology and ethnography to study and analyze organizational functions, practices, activities, processes, and relationships. According to Bate (1997), organizational anthropology is a discipline that uses ethnographic research methodologies aimed at analyzing the nature and functioning of organizations as a subject of study established since the 1980s. Ethnography, on the other hand, is the most representative anthropological and ethnographic research technique directed towards understanding and holistic observation of the system of organizational phenomena and behavior through the description of the interacting elements (Hammersley & Atkinson, 2007; Moeran & Garsten, 2015).

Therefore, organizational ethnography is the application of methodological techniques developed by anthropologists such as Malinowski and Radcliffe Brown. Hence, organizational anthropology and ethnography have become relevant in using methodological knowledge in organizational and management theory and research. However, organizational ethnography and anthropological studies have created the field of organizational behavior, leading to a separate field and losing touch with the essential qualities of anthropology. Anthropology remains the forgotten science in organizational studies (Bate, 1997).

There is a growing interest in the ethnographic methodology used in organizational anthropology to be formally and structurally applied in public and private organizations, policies, and structures such as associations, companies, and cooperatives. The anthropological reflexivity of organizations conceives ethnography to investigate and implement intervention processes capable of facilitating the understanding of behaviors and practices to record the voice of the voiceless.

The writing of anthropological ethnographies of organizations distinguishes itself from organizational science. Regarding this, Van Maanen (1987) indicates that the influence of research is reflected in organizational anthropology and organizational ethnography. Also, Turco (2016) and Anteby (2013) consider organizational ethnography fertile in anthropological research in organizational and management studies, using ethnographic methods as indicated by Barley (1986) and Orlikowski (2002), in sharing meanings in organizational communities (Bechky, 2003).

The Hawthorne studies demonstrate the anthropological approach to studying culture using the ethnological method applied by Warner under Mayo's direction to analyze the human side of the organization in a group of workers as a small society. It should be noted that Mayo's ethnographic work is a practical approach to studying human problems and behaviors in organizations, providing significant contributions to organizations such as objective observation, participatory method, social group, etc.

Organizational ethnographies contribute to theoretical development and improve organizations and businesses by resorting to anthropology to gather information that big data is unable to obtain to understand people's patterns of life (Lebeau, 2017). Regarding the ethnographic approach to organizational improvement, it was nurtured by a dialectical-institutional project towards a model of conflict theory centered on contradiction and negativity (Lourau, 1979).

Organizational anthropology studies began with tools and methodologies developed by traditional ethnography, which have been criticized by Roca i Girona (2001) as poorly defined and as a result of heresy or contradiction.

On the other hand, the new tools of ethnography and organizational anthropology currently form the foundation for theoretical empirical research in the economic environment, allowing for the analysis of patterns, perspectives, and rhythms of organizational life that are incorporated into dominant organizational research. Finally, the ethnographic study of gender policies in the global movement, such as the work published on para-ethnography in business organizations that implement gender equality policies by Fisher (2012a, b), remains an organizational research challenge.

CONCLUSION

Organizational anthropology and ethnography are two disciplines that have been studied together in recent decades due to their importance in understanding organizations and human behavior within them. This study has addressed the analysis of some of the theoretical, conceptual, and methodological implications between organizational anthropology and ethnography, based on the assumption that ethnographic analysis of organizations and interpretive research on organizational anthropology have an emerging and symbolic role rooted in social processes and without prior assumptions, with explanations and categories defined by organizational actors.

To achieve this objective, a method based on analytical and descriptive questions was used, based on the theoretical and empirical review of the literature that leads to reflective analysis. As a result, it has been found that ethnographic methodology is relevant to be used in the analysis of its interactions with organizational anthropology as a new specialty in organizational studies.

Ethnographic research allows us to understand the reality of organizations from a holistic and global perspective, encompassing both cultural and social, political, and economic aspects that influence organizational behavior. In addition, interpretive research in organizational anthropology allows us to understand the complexity of social processes in organizations and their interaction with the environment.

Reflective analysis of the literature has allowed us to identify some of the challenges and opportunities that arise when combining these two disciplines. One of the challenges is to achieve adequate integration of the concepts and methodologies of both disciplines, which implies a constant task of reflection and analysis. On the other hand, the opportunities offered by this combination are multiple, as it allows us to understand organizations from a more complete and detailed perspective and offers new possibilities for generating knowledge and innovation in organizational management.

In short, the combination of organizational anthropology and ethnography offers a broad and comprehensive perspective for the analysis of organizations, which is highly relevant in an increasingly globalized and complex world. This combination allows us to analyze the interactions between cultural, social, political, and economic aspects that influence organizational behavior and contributes to a more detailed understanding of social processes in organizations. In this sense, it can be concluded that ethnographic methodology is pertinent to be used in the analysis of the interactions between organizational anthropology and ethnography as new specialties in organizational studies.

RECOMMENDATIONS

Constructing a theoretical framework for organizational anthropology that supports the analysis of the phenomenon in depth. This framework should be based on methodological contributions that are widely used in organizational studies to provide meaning and context to the research.

To utilize anthropological components such as artifacts and processes that hold meaning in order to structure organizational transformations that promote the creation, transmission, and reproduction of knowledge. This approach will aid in the development of organizational anthropology as an ethnographic discipline that is centered on shared meanings and incorporates both spiritual and material aspects.

Institutions of higher education should promote the humanization of management by supporting new concepts, technologies, and approaches that foster self-development and social development. These new fields of knowledge, such as organizational anthropology, knowledge, and creative management, are crucial for the development of human beings, social relationships, and creative capabilities.

Finally, anthropology can contribute to the study of organizations by exploring and revealing the basic dimensions of human beings. By studying these dimensions, it is possible to gain a deeper understanding of human behavior in the context of organizational studies. For example, future research can focus on analyzing organizational anthropology related to traditional technology, providing a space for reflection to generate new insights and perspectives.

REFERENCES

Alvesson, M., & Berg, P. O. (1992). *Corporate culture and organizational symbolism: An overview*. Walter de Gruyter. doi:10.1515/9783110136074

Anteby, M. (2013). *Manufacturing morals: The values of silence in business school education*. University of Chicago Press. doi:10.7208/chicago/9780226092508.001.0001

Baba, M. (2012). Anthropology and Business: Influence and Interests. *Journal of Business Anthropology*, *1*(1), 20–71. doi:10.22439/jba.v1i1.3546

Baer, D. (2014). Here's why companies are desparate to hire anthrologists. *Business Insider.* https://www.businessinsider.com/heres-why-companies-aredesperatetohireanthropologists-2014-3

Baker, S. E., & Dutton, E. (2021). Sociology and anthropology of organizations: Overlapping histories, converging futures. *Annual Review of Sociology*, *47*, 17–36. doi:10.1146/annurev-soc-080220-024059

Barfield, T. (Ed.). (2000). *Diccionario de Antropología*. Siglo XXI Editores.

Barley, S. R. (1986). Technology as an occasion for structuring: Evidence from observations of CT scanners and the social order of radiology departments. *Administrative Science Quarterly*, *31*(1), 78–108. doi:10.2307/2392767 PMID:10281188

Basaldúa, M. (2005). Los empresarios de la compañía industrial cerillera de san Juan del Rio: Antropología de la industria cerillera. [Tesis de doctorado, Universidad Iberoamericana. México].

Bate, S. P. (1997). Whatever happened to organizational anthropology? A review of the field of organizational ethnography and anthropological studies. *Human Relations*, *50*(9), 1147–1175. doi:10.1177/001872679705000905

Bechky, B. A. (2003). Sharing meaning across occupational communities: The transformation of understanding on a production floor. *Organization Science*, *14*(3), 312–330. doi:10.1287/orsc.14.3.312.15162

Bélanger, A. et LeBlanc, M-N. (2011). *Socio-anthropologie de la culture populaire. Séminaire de Doctorat en sociologie. SOC 9004-40.* Montréal: Université du Québec à Montréal (UQÀM). [inédito].

Berg, P. O., & Faucheux, C. (1982). *The Symbolic Management of Company Cultures*. Unpublished book manuscript, INSEAD, Fontainebleau.

Bermúdez, H. L. (2017). Sociology and Anthropology in administrator training. In Forum Doctoral (pp. 27-27).

Brand, U., & Wissen, M. (2020). Homo economicus as a dangerous fetish: A plea for the social-ecological transformation of the economy. *Environmental Politics*, *29*(5), 836–855.

Caudill, W. (1958). Some Uses of Anthropology: Theoretical and Applied. *American Anthropologist New Series, 60*(4), 762-764.

Caulkins, D., & Jordan, A. T. (Eds.). (2013). *A Companion to Organizational Anthropology*. Wiley-Blackwell.

Caulkins, D. D., & Ann, J. (2013). *Companion to Organizational Anthropology*. Blackwell Publishing.

Cely-López, C. L., & Gómez-Niño, O. (2016). An anthropological perspective of organizations from sociocultural characterization, management, and social accounting. The case of a tertiary education institution. *Cuadernos de Contabilidad*, *17*(43).

Cerutti, M. (2003) Los estudios empresariales en América Latina ¿el debate interminable? *Boletín de Historia Económica*. https://www.audhe.org.uy/Boletin_Audhe/Boletin_2/Boletin_02_Cerutti.pdf

Chanlat, J. (1994). Hacia una antropología de la organización. En Gestión y política pública, 317-364, México.

Chanlat, J. F. (2019). Antropología de las organizaciones. *Revista del Centro de Estudios de Sociología del Trabajo*, (11), 17–39.

Corsín Jiménez, A. (2007). *The Anthropology of Organizations*. Ashgate Publishing Limited.

Czarniawska, B. (2012). Organization theory meets anthropology: A story of an encounter. *Journal of Business Anthropology*, *1*(1), 118–140. doi:10.22439/jba.v1i1.3549

Domínguez Folgueras, M. (2019). ¿Cuánto vale el trabajo doméstico en España? *Observatorio Social de La Caixa*. https://bit.ly/2Rmnhyg

Esteva Fabregat, C. (1955). *Caracter social y familia obrera en México*. [Tesis de Maestría en etnología, presentada en la Escuela de Antropología e Historia de México].

Esteva Frabegat, C. (1984). *[1973]. Antropología industrial*. Anthropos.

Fisher, M. (2012a). *Wall Street Women, Duke University Press*, Durham, North Carolina. Fisher, M. (2012b), Toward a feminist para-ethnography on gender equality policy making in business. *Collaborative Anthropologies*, *5*. doi:10.1353/cla.2012.0009

Fotaki, M., Altman, Y., & Koning, J. (2020). Spirituality, symbolism, and storytelling in twentyfirst-century organizations: Understanding and addressing the crisis of imagination. *Organization Studies*, *41*(1), 7–30. doi:10.1177/0170840619875782

Fumagalli, A. (2019). Fordism and Taylorism: Two Parallel Historical Trajectories or Two Sides of the Same Coin? *Journal of Economic Issues*, *53*(2), 411–418.

García Canclini, N. (1982). *Las Culturas Populares en el capitalismo*. Nueva Imagen.

García Mora, C., & Krotz, E. (1988). *La antropología en México: panorama histórico* (Vol. 9). Instituto Nacional de Antropología e Historia.

Garsten, Ch., & Anette, N. (2013). *Organizational Anthropology: Doing Ethnography in and Among Complex Organizations*. Pluto Press.

Garsten, C., & Nyqvist, A. (2022). Anthropological perspectives on the study of organizations: Historical trends and future directions. *Current Anthropology*, *63*(1), 1–17.

Gluckman, M. (1940). *Analysis of a Social Situation in Zululand*. Manchester University.

Gonnet, J. (2012). Cultura, organizaciones y antropología. Una revisión crítica. Avá. *Revista de Antropología* (21), 151-170. https://www.redalyc.org/articulo.oa?id=16903026800

Gonzàlez Gamio, A. (2003). *Manuel Gamio: una lucha sin final*. Universidad Nacional Autónoma de México.

Gravano, A. (1992). Antropología Práctica, muestra y posibilidades de la Antropología Organizacional. Publicar en Antropología y Ciencias Sociales, Buenos Aires.

Gravano, A. (1995). La imaginación antropológica; interpelaciones a la otredad construida y al método antropológico. *Publicar en Antropología y Ciencias Sociales.*, *5*, 71–91.

Hammersley, M., & Atkinson, P. (2007). *Ethnography*. Routledge.

Harvey, D. (2004). *La condición de la posmodernidad*. Amorrortu editores.

Heckscher, C. M. (2018). Anthropology and Organizational Development: An Ethnographic Approach to Organizational Change. *Journal of Business Anthropology*, *7*(1), 117–134.

Hernández, V. (2013) Genealogía de una elite rural: elucidación antropológica de una práctica de poder. *Mundo Agrario*, *13*(26). https://www.redalyc.org/pdf/845/84527468004.pdf

Holzberg, C., & Maureen, G. (1981). *Anthropology and Industry reappraisal and new directions. Ann. Review of Anthropology* (Vol. 10). Estados Unidos. doi:10.1146/annurev.an.10.100181.001533

Horst, H., Miller, D., & Sinanan, J. (2021). Anthropological perspectives on organizational hierarchy: A review and synthesis. *Current Opinion in Psychology*, *42*, 7–12. doi:10.1016/j.copsyc.2021.03.011

Jaumier, S. (2020). Why does the study of alternative organizations (so badly) need anthropology? In R. Mir & A.-L. Fayard (Eds.), *The Routledge Companion to Anthropology and Business* (pp. 414–432). Routledge. DO. doi:10.4324/9781003052456-22

Jordan, A. (2013). *Bussines Anthropology*. Waveland Press, Inc.

Kostera, M. (2018). *Anthropological Approach to Organizations: Understanding and Managing the Human Dimension*. Palgrave Macmillan.

Kottak, C. P. (2011). *Antropología cultural*. McGrawHill.

Krambia-Kapardis, M., & Zopiatis, A. (2021). *Contemporary Organization Theory: A Critical Review of the Field*. Palgrave Macmillan.

Krotz, E. (1993). Antropología y antropólogos en México: elementos de balance para construir perspectivas: (pp. 361-380). En: Balance de la Antropología en América Latina y el Caribe Universidad Nacional Autónoma de México. México.

Kunda, G. (1986). *Engineering culture: Control and commitment in a high-tech corporation*. Temple University Press.

Lashaw, A. (2020). The Complexities of Being a Practicing Anthropologist in Organizations: An Analysis of the Ethics of the AAA and EPIC Codes of Ethics. *Journal of Business Anthropology*, *9*(2), 200–220.

Lebeau, S. (2017). *Minnesota Business*. https://www.minnesotabusiness.com/anthropology-business

Limberg, H., & Rodriguez, L. (Eds.). (2020). *Handbook of Organizational Anthropology*. Routledge.

Llobera, J. (1975). *(Comp.): La antropología como ciencia*. Anagrama.

Lomnitz, L. (1975). Anthropology of scientific research at UNAM. In *Science and Development* (Vol. 6). CONACYT.

Lourau, R. (1979). *El análisis institucional*. Amorrortu.

Maestre Alfonso, J. (1983). *Introducción a la Antropología social*. Akla.

Malinowski, B. (1944). *A scientific theory of culture and other essays*. University of North Carolina Press.

Marcus, G. E. (2021). Anthropological engagements with organizational travel. *Anthropological Theory*, *21*(2-3), 332–346. doi:10.1177/1463499620977503

Marzal, M. M. (1996). *Historia de la anthropologìa. Volume I. Anthropologìa indìgena*. Ediciones Abya-Yala.

Matos Moctezuma, E. (1987). Román Piña Chan y la Escuela Nacional de Antropología e Historia: (pp. 81-90). En: Homenaje a Román Piña Chan Universidad Nacional Autónoma de México – Instituto de Investigaciones Antropológicas. México.

Menéndez, E. (1996). *Fundamentals of economics*.

Menéndez, E. (2006). Participación social en salud: las representaciones y las prácticas. In E. Menéndez (Ed.), *Spinelli, H.: Participación social ¿para qué?* (pp. 81–115). Lugar Editorial.

Metzgar, E., & Orr, S. (2020). Anthropology and organizational culture: An analysis of cultural change and resistance. *International Journal of Business and Social Science*, *11*(6).

Mills, W. (1961). *La imaginación sociológica*. Fondo de Cultura Económica.

Mir, R., & Fayard, A.-L. (2021). Anthropology and organizational studies: A symbiotic connection. In R. Mir & A.-L. Fayard (Eds.), *The Routledge Companion to Anthropology and Business* (pp. 1–13). Routledge.

Moeran, B. (2020). Lloyd Warner and the Emergence of Organizational Anthropology. *Journal of Organizational Ethnography*, *9*(2), 159–175.

Moeran, B., & Béji-Bécheur, A. (2021). Anthropology and the business school: An appraisal of past and future contributions. *Human Relations*, *74*(7), 933–954. doi:10.1177/0018726720978783

Moeran, B., & Garsten, C. (2015). Ethnography in/of the World of Work: Past, Present and Future. *Journal of Business Anthropology*, *4*(1), 146–169.

Morales Inga, S., & Tristán, O. M. (2018). Capturando la cultura: Tres aportes de la antropología a la selección de personal. *Palermo Business Review*, (18), 261–280.

Munizaga, B. J. (1988). La violencia doméstica y la sociedad. *Revista de Sociologia (Santiago)*, *0*(3), 35–43. doi:10.5354/0719-529X.1988.27565

Muñoz, R. (2011). *Formar en administración. Por una nueva fundamentación filosófica*. Siglo del Hombre. Fondo Editorial Universidad EAFIT.

Nader, L. (1972) *Up me anthropologist: perspectives gained from studying up*. Mimeo. https://files.eric.ed.gov/fulltext/ED065375.pdf

North, K., & Gita, K. (2014). *Knowledge Management. Value Creation through Organizational Learning*. Springer International Publishing.

Olive Negrete, J. C. (1981). *Antropología Mexicana*. Plaza y Valdés – Instituto Nacional de Antropología e Historia – Colegio Mexicano de Antropólogos.

Orlikowski, W. J. (2002). Knowing in practice: Enacting a collective capability in distributed organizing. *Organization Science*, *13*(3), 249–273. doi:10.1287/orsc.13.3.249.2776

Páramo, D. (2018). Antropología organizacional. *Revista científica Pensamiento y Gestión*, 1(45).

Pérez-Lizaur, M. comp. (2010) Empresa y Familia en México, una visión desde la antropología. Universidad Iberoamericana, México.

Radcliffe-Brown, A. (1952). *Structure and Function in Primitive Societv*. Oxford Univ. Press.

Rakowski, T., Kossakowski, R., & Siemienska, R. (2021). The multiple dimensions of technology in anthropology of organizations: An analytical framework. *Journal of Organizational Ethnography*, *10*(3), 297–311.

Ramírcz Carrillo, L. (1992) Estratificación, clase y parentesco: empresarios libaneses en el sureste de México. *Nueva Antropología*. https://www.redalyc.org/pdf/159/15904311.pdf

Richardson, F. (1955). Anthropology and Human Relations in Business and Industry. *Yearbook of Anthropology*. https://www.jstor.org/stable/3031158

Roberts, K., & Grabowski, M. (1996). Organizations, Technology and Structuring. En S. Clegg, C. Hardy & W. Nord, Handbook of Organization Studies (pp. 409-423). Sage.

Roca, J. (1998). *Antropologia Industrial y de la Empresa*. Ariel.

Roca i Girona, J. (2001) Antropólogos en la empresa? A propósito de la mal llamada cultura de la empresa. *Etnográfica*. http://ceas.iscte.pt/etnografica/docs/vol_05/N1/Vol_v_N1_69-100.pdf

Santibáñez, D. (1994) Una aproximación sistémico- cultural a la organización com unitaria. Memoria para optar al título profesional de Antropólogo social, Universidad de Chile, Santiago.

Sapienza, A., & Gupta, A. (2022). Organizational Anthropology: Bringing Cultural Insights to Business Studies. *Journal of Business Anthropology*, *11*(1), 1–9.

Scully, M. A. (2019). Organizational Anthropology: An Exploration of Its Potential Contributions to the Field of Human Resource Management. *Human Resource Management Review*, *29*(2), 131–143.

Smirnova, V. (2016). *Organizational culture*. Yurayt Publishing.

Turco, C. J. (2016). *The conversational firm: Rethinking bureaucracy in the age of social media*. Columbia University Press. doi:10.7312/turc17898

Urban, G., & Koh, K. (2013). *Ethnographic research on modern business corporation. Annual Review Anthropology* (Vol. 42). Estados Unidos., 10.11.

Van Maanen, J. (1987). *Tales of the field: On writing ethnography*. University of Chicago.

Villanueva, M., Serrano, C., & Vera, J. L. (1999). *Cien años de antropología física en México: inventario Bibliográfico*. Universidad Nacional Autónoma de México – Instituto de Investigaciones Antropológicas.

Warner, W. L. (1952). *Structure of American Life*. Edinburgh University Press.

Weeks, J. (2004). *Unpopular culture: The ritual of complaint in a British bank*. University of Chicago Press.

Yelvington, K., & Fisher, M. (2021). Anthropological Approaches to Organizational Culture: A Review and Integration. *Annual Review of Anthropology*, *50*(1), 399–415.

Chapter 6
Organizational Dynamics and Complexities in Healthcare Organizations

Maria D. Baez
https://orcid.org/0000-0002-5693-3825
Capitol Technology University, USA

Darrell Norman Burrell
https://orcid.org/0000-0002-4675-9544
Capitol Technology University, USA

Kevin Richardson
https://orcid.org/0009-0002-3212-8669
Capitol Technology University, USA

William Quisenberry
Purdue University Global, USA

Angela Hines
University of Arkansas, USA

Judith Mairs-Levy
A.T. Still University, USA

Laura Ann Jones
https://orcid.org/0000-0002-0299-370X
Capitol Technology University, USA

Marlena Daryousef
https://orcid.org/0000-0001-9513-501X
Colorado Technical University, USA

Amalisha Sabie Aridi
https://orcid.org/0000-0002-7869-5530
Capitol Technology University, USA

ABSTRACT

Research shows that 70-90% of mergers and acquisitions (M&As) fail due to culture clashes. The number of mergers and acquisitions in the healthcare industry has been increasing, driving the need for better change management practices. Hospital mergers and acquisitions are essential for financially struggling hospitals, especially rural hospitals. This chapter explores the value of management consulting interventions as tool to make mergers in healthcare more effective.

DOI: 10.4018/979-8-3693-1634-4.ch006

INTRODUCTION

Hospital mergers and acquisitions have been increasingly prevalent over the last decade and have accelerated since COVID-19. Between 2010 and 2018, 778 hospital mergers and 90% of metropolitan cities are considered highly concentrated according to the Herfindahl-Hirschman Index [HHI] (Schwartz et al., 2020). The benefits of hospital mergers and acquisitions are frequently debated. At the same time, most agree that hospital consolidation increases patient prices overall. In addition, it improves the quality of care and care coordination (Rangachari & Lashbrook, 2019; Schwartz et al., 2020). However, despite these uncertainties, hospital mergers and acquisitions are especially important for financially struggling hospitals. In the 2015-2019 American Hospital Association [AHA] (2021) annual survey, the critical driver for consolidation was due to financial distress or challenge. Additionally, more than one-third of these hospitals had declared bankruptcy, and consolidation saved 80% of these hospitals from bankruptcy (AHA, 2021). For these hospitals, consolidation allows them to preserve access to care.

Many of these hospitals that experience consolidation are rural hospitals. Between 2010 and 2021, 136 rural hospitals closed (AHA, 2022). Today, 673 hospitals have been identified as vulnerable to closure, and 355 are located in markets with high health disparities (AHA, 2022). Rural hospitals support their communities through economic activity by supplying jobs and fostering spending on healthcare services (AHA, 2022). The impact of these closures is detrimental to these communities. The closures are caused by poor financial performance, lack of Medicaid expansion, and the high percentage of insured and government programs (AHA, 2022). In addition to financial performance, rural hospitals face unique challenges, including workforce, regulatory, and coverage challenges (AHA, 2022). Due to these challenges, rural hospitals are often resourceful and innovative to combat these hardships to remain financially viable, including by undergoing mergers and acquisitions (AHA, 2022).

Rural hospitals have unique characteristics compared to non-rural hospitals. From a demographic perspective, rural hospitals serve poorer, sicker, and older populations than non-rural hospitals (Williams et al., 2020). Rural hospitals have lower volumes and profitability, face provider recruitment and staffing challenges, and offer fewer services than non-rural hospitals (Williams et al., 2020). In rural hospitals, change is often resisted by patients and stakeholders because of the patient population served and the economic activity rural hospitals provide their communities (Williams et al., 2020). Therefore, change within rural hospitals resulting from an acquisition can be challenging to overcome, given the unique characteristics and culture of rural hospitals (Rangachari & Lashbrook, 2019; Williams et al., 2020).

Background

The healthcare industry has changed dramatically over the years. The rise of hospital mergers and acquisitions is one of the most common changes. Hospitals merge or acquire other healthcare organizations to increase bargaining power, lower costs, and improve patient outcomes (Rangachari & Lashbrook, 2019). In recent years, the healthcare industry has seen an increase in hospital mergers and acquisitions (M&A), driven by rising healthcare costs, a changing regulatory landscape, and the need to achieve economies of scale (Rangachari & Lashbrook, 2019). However, while mergers and acquisitions can benefit healthcare organizations, such as increased efficiency and better patient care, they can also present significant challenges, such as cultural clashes and resistance to change (Rangachari & Lashbrook, 2019).

As a result, research on hospital mergers and acquisitions using organizational diagnostic and change management frameworks is required to understand better the impact of M&A on healthcare organizations

(Li & Zhang, 2020). Merging or acquiring a hospital, on the other hand, can be difficult and disruptive to the organization's operations and employees (Rangachari & Lashbrook, 2019). Several factors have contributed to the healthcare industry's trend toward consolidation, including changing reimbursement models, increased regulatory scrutiny, and the need to achieve economies of scale (Li & Zhang, 2020).

While hospital mergers and acquisitions can provide numerous benefits, such as increased access to care, increased efficiency, and improved patient outcomes, they can also present significant challenges, such as cultural clashes, power struggles, and resistance to change (Li & Zhang, 2020). For instance, the merger of Advocate Health Care and Aurora Health Care, two large healthcare systems in the Midwest, is one case study that highlights the importance of organizational diagnostic and change management in hospital M&A. With 27 hospitals and over 500 outpatient facilities, the merger, completed in 2018, created one of the largest healthcare systems in the United States (Rangachari & Lashbrook, 2019). The merger was intended to save money through economies of scale while improving care quality by sharing best practices and resources. However, the merger presented significant challenges, including cultural clashes between the two organizations and employee resistance to change (Rangachari & Lashbrook, 2019). To address these challenges, the organizations used an organizational diagnostic framework to assess the new organization's culture, structure, and processes and a change management framework to plan and implement organizational changes (Rangachari & Lashbrook, 2019). In addition, employees were involved in the change process, provided training and support, and established communication channels to address concerns and feedback (Li & Zhang, 2020).

Memorial Hermann Health System officials have announced that a proposed $14 billion merger between the Houston healthcare system and the Dallas-based Baylor Scott & White has been canceled in Texas (McAshan, 2019). Both healthcare giants released statements released on February 5, 2019, explaining the discontinuation, but Memorial Hermann officials declined to provide further details (McAshan, 2019). On October 1, 2018, the powerhouses announced plans to merge their 68 hospitals into one behemoth system that would increase the efficiency of healthcare delivery in Texas (McAshan, 2019). The two organizations promised to provide integrated, consumer-centric, cost-effective care for Texans as the state's most extensive nonprofit hospital system (McAshan, 2019).

Overall, these cases emphasize the importance of using organizational diagnostic, change management models, and frameworks in hospital mergers and acquisitions to address the challenges of integrating different cultures and processes and to ensure the merger or acquisition's success. Using these frameworks, healthcare organizations can better understand the impact of M&A on their organization and develop effective change management and patient care strategies. As a result, hospital mergers and acquisitions can provide significant benefits but also present significant challenges that necessitate careful organizational diagnostics and change management.

Problem Statement

Research shows that 70-90% of mergers and acquisitions (M&As) fail due to culture clashes (Rohan, 2019). The number of mergers and acquisitions in the healthcare industry has been increasing, driving the need for better change management practices (Schwartz et al., 2020). A large national hospital has recently purchased a small rural hospital. The integration of these two hospitals has been complex resulting in cultural conflicts, preventing the two organizations from becoming one cohesive organization following the acquisition. Failure of a successful integration can impact the organization's financial goals & outcomes and retention of employees, to name a few (Schwartz et al., 2020). However, rural hospitals face a greater risk of bankruptcy and closing down without the acquisition. To preserve access, organizations must integrate change management processes effectively (Baloh et al., 2017). Current literature focuses on single healthcare organizations' change or broad examples of specific change theory concepts. This paper hopes to fill this gap by summarizing and analyzing the findings of both types of research. Following this analysis, the paper will discuss recommendations and best practices for organizational change management from purchasing a small rural hospital from a larger national hospital.

Significance Statement

M&A has become popular in healthcare to achieve economies of scale, increase market share, and improve care. However, they face organizational complexity, change resistance, and patient care disruptions. Ninety-two hospital mergers and acquisitions were completed in 2020, up 12% from the previous year (Hut, 2022). Despite this, most M&A transactions fail (Deloitte, 2018), with some studies estimating failure rates as high as 70%. (McKinsey & Company, 2019). Healthcare organizations may lose money, staff morale, and patient wait times during M&As. (Rangachari & Lashbrook, 2019). Hospital mergers and acquisitions pose challenges and risks, so effective change management strategies are essential (Rangachari & Lashbrook, 2019).

This study uses Lewin's, Kotter's 8-Step Change Model, ADKAR, McKinsey's 7s Framework, and Roger's Innovation Adoption Curve to determine the best change management strategies for hospital mergers and acquisitions. The study will also examine Nudge's theory of behavioral change and Maurer's change resistance framework. Hospital mergers and acquisitions disrupt patient care, staff morale, and finances. This study will add to the literature on change management strategies, organizational diagnostic models, Roger's Innovation Adoption Curve, ADKAR Model, and Maurer's resistance to change framework for hospital mergers and acquisitions. Healthcare organizations, policymakers, and stakeholders involved in hospital M&A will benefit from its insights into change management and resistance mitigation strategies.

METHODS, THEORIES, AND LITERATURE REVIEW

This study examined healthcare organization dynamics and complexity to identify problems and solutions. Google Scholar, UNC Online Library, JSTOR, PubMed, CINAHL, Scopus, Web of Science, and ResearchGate found articles, journals, and books. Review data came from keyword searches, citation tracking, and manual book and journal searches. To improve understanding, the reevaluation includes a meta-analysis of the identified studies, including literature in the healthcare industry related to organizational change model policies, leadership, communication, collaboration, culture challenges, organizational culture, and technology. After merging all search results, duplicates and articles older than 20 years were removed. Titles and abstracts were used to screen the remaining publications, and the remaining full texts were evaluated for systematic review eligibility.

A Close Look at Common Change Management Contexts in Healthcare

We identified the six most commonly used change management contexts after reviewing the literature on studies of healthcare organizations that have used them are shown in Table 1, Healthcare Change

Management Schema. These frameworks have proven effective in assisting healthcare organizations in navigating change, improving patient outcomes, and increasing employee satisfaction. Understanding the strengths and weaknesses of each framework can help healthcare leaders choose the best model for their organization's specific needs. More in-depth particulars of each model will be provided in the other sections.

Table 1. Healthcare change management schema

Approach	Portray	Use Rationale
ADKAR Model	The ADKAR model is a popular change management framework in a variety of industries, including healthcare. It stands for Awareness, Desire, Knowledge, Ability, and Reinforcement and refers to a structured approach to managing change at the individual level.	Help the organization's leadership to understand and address the psychological and emotional barriers to change. The model can guide the implementation of new technology, improve patient safety, and address workforce shortages. Providing reinforcement and ongoing support can help to sustain changes over time and prevent backsliding.
Kaizen Method	The Kaizen method is a Japanese philosophy of continuous improvement that involves making small changes to processes and systems to achieve ongoing improvement. The word "Kaizen" translates to "change for the better" or "continuous improvement."	The Kaizen method is a systematic approach to improvement that involves identifying areas for improvement, analyzing the current state of the process, and making minor changes to improve the process. Even if it is widely used in the manufacturing industry, this approach has several implications for the healthcare industry, including improving patient outcomes, reducing costs, and improving staff morale.
Kotter's Model	Kotter's change management framework is an effective way to manage organizational change and overcome resistance. The eight steps outlined in the model can help organizations achieve their goals. By creating a sense of urgency, building a guiding coalition, and forming a strategic vision, organizations can enlist a volunteer army and remove barriers to action. Generating short-term wins and sustaining acceleration can help organizations institute change and achieve their goals.	Kotter's model has significant implications for the healthcare industry. In a constantly changing landscape, the ability to manage change effectively is essential to delivering high-quality patient care. The model can be used to create a culture of change within an organization, improving the ability to manage change and resist future changes. This, in turn, leads to improved patient care and staff satisfaction.
Lewin's Model	Lewin's model is a change management framework that helps organizations transition through different stages of change. The three stages are unfreezing, changing, and refreezing. Unfreezing helps break down the existing mindset and creates a need for change. Changing introduces new practices and behaviors to support the change. Refreezing solidifies the new practices and behaviors in the organization's culture.	In an environment that is constantly changing due to new regulations and technological advances, the ability to manage change effectively is essential to providing high-quality patient care. The Lewin model provides healthcare organizations with a structured approach to managing change, which can improve their ability to adapt to new practices and behaviors, improved patient outcomes and satisfaction among staff.
Maurer's Framework	The three levels of resistance identified by Maurer can help organizations to better understand and manage the different types of resistance employees may exhibit when faced with change. Emotional resistance may be based on fear and anxiety about the change, while intellectual resistance may stem from the belief that the change is unnecessary or will not work. Behavioral resistance may be characterized by employees actively resisting or sabotaging the change.	Maurer's approach to change is significant in healthcare organizations. It is important to identify the root causes of resistance and address them appropriately. This may involve providing support and training to employees to help them adjust to the changes, communicating the benefits of the change, and involving employees in the change process.
McKinsey's 7s Framework	The McKinsey 7S Framework is a management tool developed by McKinsey & Company to help organizations effectively manage change. The framework emphasizes the interconnectedness of seven vital internal elements that must be aligned to achieve success: strategy, structure, systems, staff, skills, style, and shared values. By examining these elements and ensuring they are aligned, organizations can improve their ability to achieve their goals and respond effectively to change.	Healthcare organizations are complex and dynamic, with many stakeholders and competing priorities. The 7S Framework is a tool that can help organizations better understand their internal workings and ensure they are aligned to achieve their goals. The Framework can be used to assess different areas of the organization, such as a quality improvement program or the implementation of a new healthcare information system. By using the 7S Framework to examine each of the seven elements and ensure they are aligned, healthcare organizations can improve patient care outcomes.
Nudge Theory	Nudge theory is a concept in behavioral economics that suggests that small, subtle changes to the environment or context in which people make decisions can influence their behavior positively, without restricting their freedom of choice. Nudge theory assumes that people are more likely to make decisions in their best interest if they are given gentle prompts or nudges in the right direction.	The healthcare industry can make use of the Nudge theory to improve patient outcomes in several ways. By making small changes to the patient's environment or context, healthcare providers can encourage healthier choices, better medication adherence, and reduced healthcare costs. It can help patients make better decisions for their health and well-being. Nudge theory is a powerful concept that can be used to improve patient outcomes and reduce healthcare costs by making small changes to the environment or context in which patients make decisions.

ADKAR Model

ADKAR is a change management approach utilized in healthcare organizations. A renowned provider of change management solutions, Prosci, created the ADKAR model as a framework for change management (Bowles & Myburgh, 2018; Gagnon et al., 2021). It is an acronym for awareness, desire, knowledge, ability, and reinforcement, representing the five building blocks required for successful change. It is also structured around the belief that organizational change cannot occur without personal change (Figure 1). Therefore, the model is based on the traits an individual must embody to successfully transition (Bowles & Myburgh, 2018; Varkey & Antonio, 2010).

The ADKAR model has significant implications in the healthcare industry for managing change and implementing new initiatives, such as introducing new technology, improving patient safety, or implementing new clinical practices. Understanding the ADKAR model's five building blocks allows healthcare organizations to identify potential barriers to change, develop strategies to overcome resistance, and ensure that individuals have the knowledge and skills to implement the change successfully.

Figure 1. ADKAR model

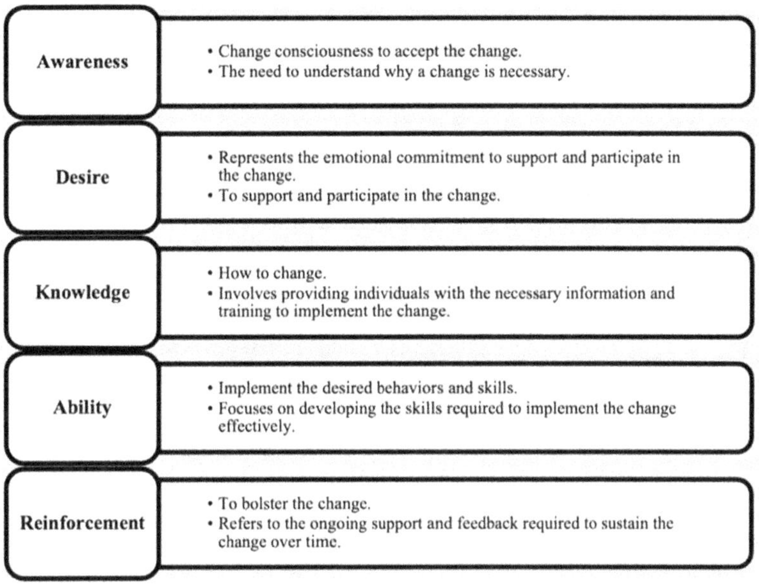

For instance, during the COVID-19 pandemic, a Texas hospital system used ADKAR and another tool to transition nurses from primary nursing to team nursing (Balluck et al., 2020). This model proved invaluable in transitioning nurses working alone to a team model. Similarly, ADKAR was used by a New York hospital system to transition its clinical staff to a new facility and care model (Hooper et al., 2019). They discovered that ADKAR was the best model for implementing this change, allowing the entire organization to change in tandem with the individuals (Wong et al., 2019).

Given the success of these organizations' use of ADKAR, this method may be more appropriate for changing clinical staff behaviors rather than operational or administrative processes. Similarly, researchers used the ADKAR model to implement a new electronic health record (EHR) system in a large healthcare organization in a study published in the Journal of Healthcare Information Management in 2021 (Wong et al., 2019). The researchers used the ADKAR model to identify and address potential resistance to change, provide targeted training and support to staff, and ensure the new EHR system was successfully implemented (Wong et al., 2019).

Kaizen Method

Kaizen means change for the good; Kai means "change," and Zen means "good." It is an iterative improvement that can be easily implemented (Morell-Santandreu et al., 2020). In application, kaizen is understood as continuous organizational improvement (Morell-Santandreu et al., 2020). According to Graban and Swartz (2018), it is often associated with "lean" efforts and is the theory underpinning Plan-Do-Study-Act [PDSA]. The five fundamental values of Kaizen can be observed in Figure 2.

Figure 2. Kaizen method

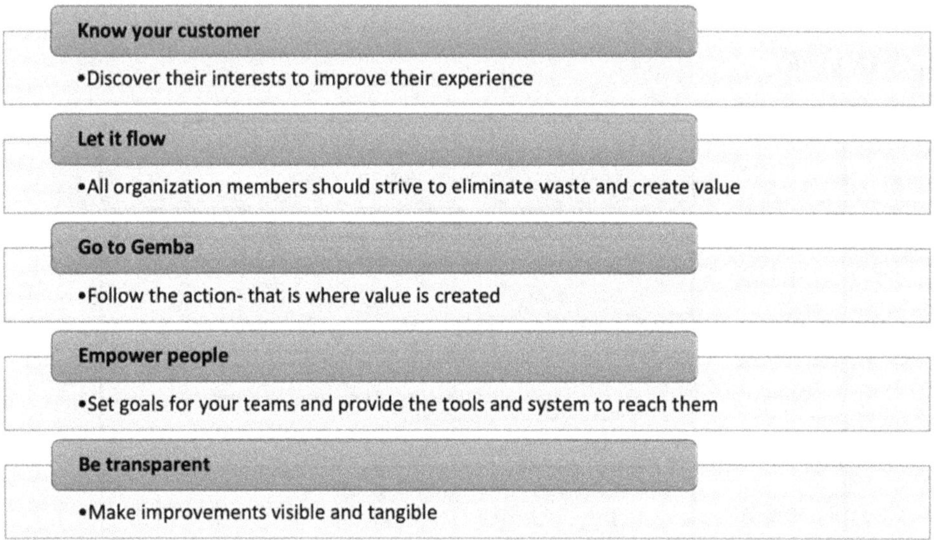

Designing a project using kaizen methodology is called a kaizen initiative. Often, healthcare projects are developed as a kaizen initiative to ensure continuous improvement. Using kaizen in healthcare is a way to promote both good changes for the organization and also for patients' benefit (Graban & Swartz, 2018). Several papers exploring the impact of kaizen initiatives in healthcare organizations have found them effective in reducing waste through time and cost reduction. Other research has also suggested that it can help support economic and social sustainability (Morell-Santandreu et al., 2020).

Research that measured the effectiveness of kaizen initiatives in healthcare settings found it helped address problems but did not adequately address the roots of complex issues or garner individual support. As a result, the authors recommended combining kaizen with other change management frameworks (Mazzocato et al., 2016). Another paper examining both quantitative and qualitative outcomes of two kaizen initiatives in a hospital found it had varied success rates. Specifically, they found that it only sometimes resulted in sustained success over time (Mazzocato et al., 2016).

Kotter's Model

The change management framework developed by Kotter is one of the theories of change management that is popular among healthcare organizations (Alkhaldi, 2019; Quan et al., 2019). The Kotter Model is a change management framework that is widely recognized and has been used extensively in healthcare organizations to manage complex organizational changes, and John P. Kotter developed it (Alkhaldi, 2019; Quan et al., 2019). Establishing a sense of urgency, creating a guiding coalition, developing a vision and strategy, communicating the change vision, empowering others to act on the picture, creating short-term wins, consolidating gains and producing more change, and anchoring new approaches in the organization's culture are the eight steps that are included in the Model and can be used to manage change successfully (Quan et al., 2019). According to one review of the relevant literature, more companies use the Kotter Model than other models (Alkhaldi, 2019; Harrison et al., 2021). Figure 2 presents the change management model developed by Kotter, which includes eight distinct steps (Harrison et al., 2021).

Figure 3. Kotter's eight steps model

According to Quan et al. (2019), creating a sense of urgency entails conducting market and competitive force research to identify current or potential crises. A solid guiding coalition requires a group with authority to lead the effort (Alkhaldi, 2019). Next, create a vision to guide the change effort, which includes coming up with an idea and accompanying strategies to make it a reality (Quan et al., 2019).

Finally, to instill new behaviors, communicate the vision, and enlist the help of a guiding coalition (Quan et al., 2019). Communicate the vision in all possible ways, including empowering others to act on it, removing barriers to change, and encouraging problem-solving innovation (Quan et al., 2019). Plan for and create short-term wins to recognize and reward employees contributing to progress. Change systems and policies incompatible with the vision to consolidate improvements and generate more change (Quan et al., 2019). Create succession plans to ensure leadership development by implementing new approaches (Harrison et al., 2021).

After initially publishing these steps, Kotter later identified phases in his model. Steps 1-3 establish a change-friendly environment, steps 4-6 enable and engage the organization, and steps 7-8 implement and sustain change (Baloh et al., 2017). Kotter's method is process-oriented and focuses on the change that a leader brings about. In healthcare, this is usually applied to the entire organization rather than individual projects (Gordon & Pollack, 2018). When Kotter's model was used in hospitals with team huddles, it worked when the preceding steps were followed. When the model had to be followed consistently, teams needed extra help to succeed. The researchers also discovered that Kotter's model worked best across multiple units (Baloh et al., 2017). Specific model steps are deemed more important than others, and the majority are modified to meet the organization's needs (Baloh et al., 2017; Harrison et al., 2021;).

Lewin's Model of Change

Kurt Lewin's model of change is widely accepted in psychology as a means for implementing change. Nevertheless, it is crucial to change an organization from its current state to its desired state (Hussain et al., 2018). Figure 4 describes the three stages of Lewin's approach (Haddad et al., 2019).

Figure 4. Lewin's model

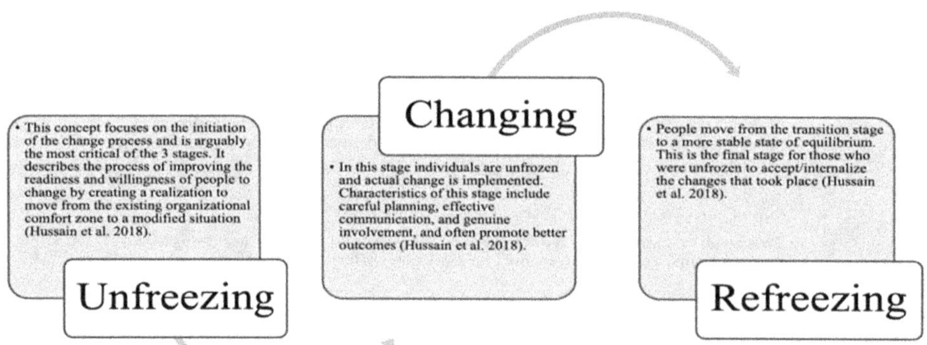

An article in the Canadian Journal of Nursing Informatics highlighted the challenges nurses face in the rapidly changing healthcare environment, specifically concerning implementing new medication barcoding technology. As with any new change in a healthcare organization, buy-in from nurses is essential to ensure a smooth transition of any informatics initiatives (Hussain et al., 2018). However, these changes can often be met with some degree of skepticism from nurses. The author argued that Lewis' Model is highly effective in helping guide the implementation of barcoding medication administration (BCMA) by supporting nurses through these transition periods (Hussain et al., 2018; Shirey, 2013). In addition, the model can help nurses identify strengths and resistances before implementing change (Shirey, 2013).

Maurer's Three Levels of Resistance to Change

Maurer's three levels of resistance framework is a model that helps organizational leaders see through the fog of the resistance that individuals inside the organization face and also provides appropriate ways to respond to resistance (Figure 5).

Figure 5. Maurer's resistance levels

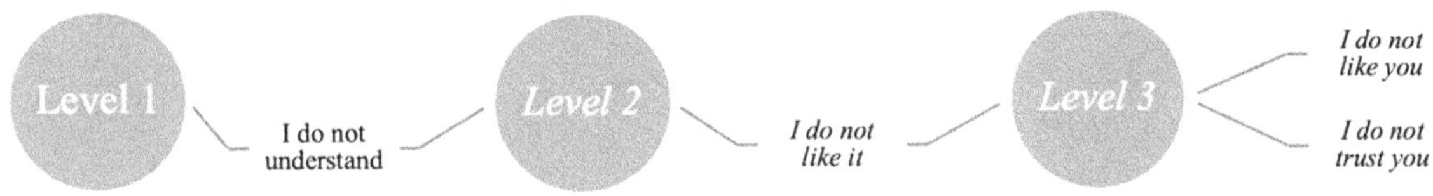

Level 1: "I do not understand." Employees are often quick to dismiss change. If they do not understand the change's reason, they assume it is poorly thought out and does not support it. Explaining and educating the employees about the change at a deeper level is essential. Careful selection of the order in which they are educated and explained is also essential. Having major influencers on board is crucial in supporting information sharing and educational efforts. Connecting it back to the dimensions, *I do not understand* it is a rational statement that warrants a rational response and a need for clarification as there is a lack of information (Reiling et al., 2022).

Level 2: "I do not like it." It is difficult to ascertain if employees do not understand or do not like the proposed change. Engaging directly with employees to distinguish between the two will be helpful. "I do not like it" provides a clear point of emotional resistance that requires a response that speaks to the emotions. Similarly, various models like the Kubles-Ross Change Model and Satir Model for Change directly also address emotional aspects of change (Reiling et al., 2022).

Level 3: "I do not like or trust you." This level is neither due to a lack of information (Level 1) nor an emotional reaction (Level 2). Instead, this level of resistance is due to relational dislike. Some examples can be the reputation of the acquiring company, experience with a type of customer, and distrust of the leadership. These areas must be addressed with honest responses that address relationship issues. A response that speaks to emotions or provides information may be a part of the response but alone cannot address the foundational relationship issue (Reiling et al., 2022).

McKinsey 7s Framework

According to a review analyzing McKinsey 7's framework, the 7s model is a strategic planning tool used to determine the current state of an org and compare it to its future needs, which is also called a gap analysis (Putri et al., 2021). This model aims to identify how seven elements of the organizations of interest can be aligned to optimize effectiveness (Figure 6). The model's creators argued that many factors influence organizational effectiveness, and the success of any organizational change depends on the interconnectedness of these factors (Putri et al., 2021). A healthcare study sought to identify the relationship between the organizational performance of a public hospital and its social (soft) elements. The researchers implemented the McKinsey 7s framework and determined its efficacy in meeting the researcher's needs. By surveying employees using questions structured around the seven elements of the McKinsey framework, researchers could assign performance *scores* to each element (Chmielewska et al., 2022). After completing their analysis, the study indicated that by inputting organizational performance into the 7s Framework using data, healthcare systems could more comprehensively diagnose organizational performance instead of solely relying on financial metrics (Chmielewska et al., 2022).

Figure 6. McKinsey 7's framework

Structure

- Represents how business units are organized with references to organizational structure. Relative to the other 6 elements, an organization's structure is more visible from the outside and easier to change (Jurevicius & Nami 2022).

Strategy

- A sound strategy is one that is clearly articulated, especially if the strategy emphasizes long-term outcomes. A sound strategy also places emphasis on vision, mission, and values (Jurevicius & Nami 2022).

Skills

- This element highlights the abilities that an organization's employees perform well. During organizational change, the question of what skills are really needed often arises (Jurevicius & Nami 2022).

Staff

- This aspect focuses on the type of employee needed and the number of employees needed to implement or adjust to change (Jurevicius & Nami 2022).

Style

- This factor focuses on the way the company is managed by top-level managers, how they interact, and what actions they take. In summation, it's the management style of company leadership (Jurevicius & Nami 2022).

System

- The processes and procedures of a company, which give an indication of the business's daily activities and how decisions are made. This aspect determines how business is done and should be the main focus during any org change (Jurevicius & Nami 2022).

Shared Values

- The core of the McKinsey model guide employee behavior and company actions and thus, are the foundation of every organization (Jurevicius & Nami 2022).

Nudge Theory

Nudge theory is a concept introduced by Richard Thaler and Cass Sunstein to highlight ideas around changing environmental and behavioral factors (Thaler & Sunstein, 2008). The theory is based on the idea that by shaping the environment, also known as choice architecture, one can influence the likelihood of one option being chosen over another. The critical mechanic for this *choice architecture* is that individuals still have freedom of choice and control of their decisions (Thaler & Sunstein, 2008). The Nudge Theory is a concept in behavioral economics that proposes that small environmental changes can influence people's behavior and decision-making. As shown in Figure 7, the Nudges can be classified into four quadrants providing information changing default option, changing environment providing incentives or disincentives based on their type of intervention, and can be implemented synchronously or asynchronously have several implications in the healthcare industry (Sant'Anna et al., 2021).

In healthcare, the Nudge Theory can be used to promote healthy behaviors and improve patient outcomes (Figure 7). For instance, hospitals can use "nudges" to encourage patients to take their medication as prescribed or to follow a specific diet. In addition, healthcare providers can influence patients' behavior and improve their adherence to treatment plans by using nudges, and various nudges can be used in healthcare (Sant'Anna et al., 2021).

Figure 7. Nudge theory
(Sant'Anna et al. 2021)

One kind of nudge is providing information, such as educating patients about the benefits of healthy behaviors or the risks of non-adherence to treatment. Another type of nudge is changing the default option, such as setting electronic health record defaults to encourage the generic prescribing of drugs instead of brand name drugs (Sant'Anna et al., 2021). A third type of nudge is changing the environment, such as making healthy food options visible and accessible in hospital cafeterias (Sant'Anna et al., 2021).

Furthermore, incentives or disincentives can encourage healthy behaviors or discourage unhealthy behaviors, such as providing rewards for meeting health goals or imposing penalties for non-adherence to treatment. Nudges can be implemented synchronously or asynchronously. Synchronous nudges are executed in real-time, such as reminders to take medication or providing feedback on physical activity levels. On the other hand, asynchronous nudges are implemented later, such as sending reminders to refill prescriptions or providing feedback on diet and exercise habits (Sant'Anna et al., 2021). Recent studies have shown the potential of the Nudge Theory in healthcare. For instance, nudges can promote healthy behaviors like physical activity, healthy eating, and smoking cessation. The authors recommend that healthcare providers use nudges and other behavioral interventions to maximize their impact (Sant'Anna et al., 2021). Another study by Thaler and Sunstein (2008) applied the Nudge Theory to healthcare decision-making. The authors propose that healthcare providers can use nudges to help patients make better decisions about their health, such as choosing a health insurance plan or a treatment option. By providing patients with information clearly and concisely, healthcare providers can nudge patients toward making informed decisions that align with their values and preferences (Thaler & Sunstein, 2008).

Resistance Dimension: Applications and Project Management Integration

Another category of research analyzed was related to resistance to change. Resistance to change is multi-dimensional and is often the reason for the failure of the planned change. Management often views resistance as employees willfully misbehaving. Still, a closer review has found that many concepts that complement and contrast each other are responsible for resistance to change (Mok & Wu, 2020). The nature of the human response to change is classified into active and passive resistance. *Active Resistance* takes the form of being critical, finding fault, ridiculing, appealing to fear, using facts selectively, blaming/accusing, sabotaging, intimidating/threatening, manipulating, blocking, undermining, starting rumors, and arguing (Mok & Wu, 2020). On the other hand, *Passive Resistance* includes conscious actions, such as agreeing verbally but not following through, failing to implement change, procrastinating, feigning ignorance, withholding information, and standing by and doing nothing (Mok & Wu, 2020).

Dimensions of Resistance to Change. Research using Likert scales has discovered that resistance has conferred spheres: a) *cognitive, affective, and behavioral-intentional; b) conscious/unconscious-deliberate/not deliberate; c) rational and irrational; d) overt/covert, visible/invisible* (Riolli & Savicki, 2006). Some scholars found evidence of *cognitive, affective, and behavioral-intentional* resistance when the change in process was communicated in two different manners to members of two different units faced with technological change (Riolli & Savicki, 2006). The unit that received clear communication and time with management to clarify their concerns was far less resistant than the unit which was given cursory attention by the management (Riolli & Savicki, 2006). Often misalignment within these dimensions leads to a condition of ambivalence. For example, an employee might think that restructuring is a good idea but may be anxious about the new responsibilities that it might bring (Piderit, 1999). Likewise, according to Piderit, 1999, *conscious/unconscious or deliberate/not deliberate* can be perceived in the staff since they might consciously resist change or not be aware that their response could be construed as resistant. Research proves that emotion and behavior often operate in unconscious or semiconscious ways (Brunton & Matheny, 2009).

On the other hand, change managers are trained to distinguish between *rational and irrational* reactions to change but often deem resistant employees to be irrational and judged as providing 'an unwarranted and detrimental response' (Ford et al., 2008). Expressing concern or gratitude to the management is rational behavior, but some forms of unconscious resistance can be perceived as irrational and maladaptive ways of coping with change (Bovey & Hede, 2001). Lastly, *overt and visible* resistance is apparent, and the identity of the resistor is known. Passive forms of resistance, such as employees ignoring a policy, are often invisible to others unless observers are remarkably perceptive. *Covert* resistance may be masked by *overt* compliance with some aspects of change, leading managers to believe that the change has been accepted (Prasad & Prasad, 2000). Overall, resistance to organizational change is a construct of many dimensions that may overlap. Not all of these are readily discernible to observers or acknowledged by those resisting. There is a need to create a model that encompasses all the dimensions of resistance to change and demonstrates the complex interplay between the dimensions.

Healthcare Integration Projects. Healthcare integration is often challenging and involves significant organizational transformation. For example, in a study of 12 healthcare organization transformations, five elements necessary for change were identified: (a) impetus to transform based on external pressure; (b) commitment to quality at the executive level; (c) engaging staff through improvement initiatives; (d) the alignment of goals through their resource allocation at all organizational levels; and (e) integration (Lukas et al., 2007). Similarly, a study in Ontario analyzed the division of the region's healthcare system into 14 local health integration networks.

As shown in Table 2, five significant outcomes emerged from the analysis, and those outcomes were laid out in accord with the organizational levels. First, the results from the study emphasize that traditional project management, as represented by the commonly accepted guides, does not align with the needs of healthcare integration projects. Second, an iterative approach was more beneficial due to the significant organizational change in working practices and cultures. Third, a decrease in front-end planning meant allowing for the work to start earlier in the project process and for adaptation in response to emergent change.

Table 2. Ontario case findings

Organizational Level		Outcome
1	System	Established project management processes only partly aligned with the needs of healthcare integration projects. Change management provided more benefits if used early in the project life cycle. Difficulties were experienced combining project management and change management because the states of each approach did not align.
2	Group	Benefits were seen in combining change management and project management in healthcare integration projects.
5	Individual	Practitioners took an intuitive and improvised approach to combine project management and change management.

Finally, study results indicated that managers improvised while conducting project and change management; this is valuable and effective in projects in the past where organizational change was required at the individual level (Leybourne, 2009).

Mergers and Acquisitions

In addition to analyzing various change management frameworks, resistance to change, and the combination of project and change management, this paper also examines high-impact studies on mergers and acquisitions (Kang et al., 2020). For example, authors of a study focusing on the strategic process of the M&A market used change management models to identify successful M&A integration: setting goals and aligning two different companies' cultural systems with those business goals (Kang et al., 2020). They recommend that employees must be involved with creating the organizational change – this can be encouraged through employee training and using that as a time to address and resolve any employee concerns. It is equally essential for managers at all levels of the organization to also take part in the M&A process to align on organizational change and initiate change (Kang et al., 2020). A successful M&A strategic plan has two main parts: the leader's right direction and change management. Table 3 shows solutions identified for company integration posts for M&A (Kang et al., 2020).

Table 3. Solutions for M&A integration posts

Target		Action
1	Leadership	Input on common goal setting identifies appropriate challenges to target and cultural learning between the two organizations.
2	Change Management Models	Direction on employee involvement in change through induction training and employee development aligned with the newly identified target goals.
3	Restructuring Operationally	Guidance on how employees report or move employees to new areas and teams based on skills, experiences, and challenges - to change how expenses match revenue and align new pay structure with new goals.

M&A typically requires complex change – formal change management processes and HR being involved in M&A planning from the beginning can help handle the complexities of integration. In an acquisition setting, intellectual capital is the primary driver for acquiring another organization. Thus, retaining key talent can be a primary goal for acquirers. As a result, the organization's development and human resources teams must work together effectively with minimal overlap. OD will work with the CEO and top leadership to strategically design change methods.

In contrast, HR will work with senior management to consult on people issues, leadership values, and behaviors throughout the process (Harrison et al., 2021). A disciplined approach to the change process is vital, and HR can be essential for this. HR is suggested to take the initiative in the following areas involving organizational change: retaining key talent, handling redundancies and other exits, supporting line managers, supporting individuals and teams, ensuring effective communications, re-engaging the 'survivors,' and combing action and learning (Harrison et al., 2021).

The acquisition of Hahnemann University Hospital by the American Academic Health System (AAHS) in 2018 is another case study that highlights the importance of organizational diagnostic and change management in hospital M&A (Armstrong & Eisenstein, 2020). The acquisition, intended to improve the financial stability of Hahnemann, a struggling hospital in Philadelphia, also presented significant challenges, such as the need to integrate different cultures and processes and address employee and patient concerns (Armstrong & Eisenstein, 2020). To address these issues, AAHS used an organizational diagnostic framework to assess Hahnemann's culture and processes and a change management framework to plan and implement organizational changes. This process included engaging employees and patients in the change process, providing training and support, and establishing communication channels to address concerns and feedback (Armstrong & Eisenstein, 2020).

A study focused on the administration of strategic agreements in public hospitals and the sustainability of M&A resulted in a guide to aid in successful hospital mergers and systems primarily involving guidance on strategic administration and objectives, staff management, and a new hospital complex structure. The resulting guide helps communicate between various stakeholders to improve overall engagement during a change (Cerezo-Espinosa de los Monteros et al., 2021). A combination of literature review and interviews of expert opinions helped create the guide that provides an overview of fifteen key factors for hospital M&A success (Table 4).

Table 4. Critical factors for hospital M&A success (Cerezo-Espinosa de los Monteros et al., 2021)

Factor	Motion
1	Establishing a new management structure
2	Developing a strategy for managing differences in culture and values
3	Involving healthcare workers and intermediate managers in decisions that affect them
4	A communication process to convey relevant information in a timely manner to employees
5	A common clinical strategy between the two hospitals
6	Information system appropriate for the merged institution
7	Improving quality with higher patient volumes
8	Integrating competing units
9	Merged education programs advantage
10	Emphasize benefits of integration
11	Align allocation of resources post-merger success
12	Referral capabilities for higher patient volume
13	Utilize geographic proximity
14	Reach increased operational efficiency
15	Sharing best practices across trusted partners

A goal of this study was to understand how best to implement standard work procedures in two merged hospitals, considering both clinical and non-clinical workflow to aid in successful and efficient restructuring post-M&A. Identified that increasing hospitals' cooperation, effectiveness, and employees' self-esteem is critical for improved quality and financial performance (Cerezo-Espinosa de los Monteros et al., 2021).

Rural Hospitals

Rural health centers in Kentucky implemented a proactive office encounter model to improve the delivery of their preventative care services, minimize gaps in care, and work towards reducing health disparities amongst the patient population. This study used Kotter's 8-step process for leading change to analyze how the Kentucky rural health center established the proactive office encounter model and the subsequent impacts (Carman et al., 2019).

The model created a climate for change within the smaller rural health center; the communication engaged and enabled the entire organization to participate. Additionally, the model implemented sustainable change by breaking down the informal hierarchy among employees to emphasize operational changes required to focus on preventative care (Carman et al., 2019).

Kotter's 8-step process for leading change provided a systematic guide for the health center to use as they established a change in focus from delivering chronic and emergent care to delivering preventive care. Using Kotter's model and applying all eight steps helped ensure that leaders were equipped with the ability to guide large-scale change, that all the employees involved in the change could understand the essential purpose of making this change, and that the care delivery change project is managed with the basis of that change resonating in the organization's culture (Carman et al., 2019).

Public health impact: the study showed that organizational change frameworks such as Kotter's model could be helpful in small-scale settings, although typically used in large-scale settings. In this case, it proved helpful for a federally qualified health center that does not have as many resources as larger health organizations. The change model enabled the Kentucky rural health center to implement the sustainable evidence-based intervention, which led to improved clinical workflow, patient outcomes, and population health (Carman et al., 2019).

RECOMMENDATIONS

Change in any organization is challenging, but merging two different types of hospitals is particularly challenging. The consulting team has determined best practices and approaches to improve organizational change by synthesizing the change management models discussed earlier in the paper and understanding the organization's unique challenges in acquiring a small rural hospital. Given this case's unique situation, best practices for organizational change management are listed below for a successful integration between the two hospitals (Table 5). The goal of implementing these best practices will prevent culture clashing by strongly emphasizing building culture and fostering transparency. Also, these best practices will support developing a robust and unified workforce to produce the business goals, objectives, and outcomes intended from the acquisition.

While many models and theories were discussed in the literature review, it is recommended to use Kotter's model during the implementation stage of integrating the two hospitals. First, Kotter's model is the most popular change management tool and is well utilized across health systems. Secondly, Kotter's model is easy to follow and, in some cases, more in-depth than existing models such as Lewin's. Finally, Kotter's model is the most appropriate for a large-scale change initiative. Some other models, such as the Kaizen model, are more appropriate for a specific project or a minor operational change. While the model does not include all factors, it gives an overview to guide organizations through change management.

Table 5. Best practices framework

	Practice	Intent
1	Communicate Early and Frequently (Step 4 of Kotter's)	At every step of change, employees should be communicated with ahead of time and frequently to promote a culture of transparency and community. Communication can involve the acquisition itself, the vision and proposed benefits, changes to employee compensation, and others fits.
2	Develop an M&A Task Force (Step 2 of Kotter's)	The organization should immediately establish a Task Force or Steering Committee that represents all areas of the new organization, including HR leaders, physicians, and other clinical leaders. The Task Force will discuss any major decisions and changes for the organization including retention, downsizing, and other operational changes according to the developed M&A strategy for the organization.
3	Prepare for Change by Conducting Thorough Due Diligence	HR should conduct assessments and surveys on culture, leadership, operations, and employee satisfaction with employees at both organizations. The organization will conduct other operational assessments on staffing & organizational structure, systems & technology, operations, and financials to account for all changes incurred during the acquisition. Due diligence will help prepare for change and inform any decisions around downsizing, retention, compensation, etc.
4	Prioritize Culture	The organization should establish a new or modified shared mission, vision, and core values that are in mutual alignment between the two organizations. The organization will conduct thorough culture assessments of the two organizations to understand gaps in alignment and inform change initiatives. The organization will foster a culture of transparency through over-communication.
5	Provide Resources	HR to provide resources around changes to employee employment agreements, compensation, benefits, policies and procedures. HR and management should provide robust employee training sessions on organizational changes led by HR, as well as operational changes, including systems & technology and policies & procedures led by management of departments.
6	Involve and Engage Employees at all Levels of the Organization (Step 5 of Kotter's)	A bottom-up approach will foster a stronger culture.
7	Establish Change Goals & Celebrate the Small Wins (Step 6 of Kotter's)	Leadership in collaboration with the Task Force should develop a strategic plan with clearly communicated change goals such as improved patient outcomes and access.

CONCLUSION

Given the current financial situation of healthcare organizations in the wake of the pandemic, the likelihood of insolvency and closure for rural hospitals is high. It is expected to get worse in the future. Even though rural hospitals are continually seeking out novel and original approaches to maintain their financial viability, the majority of the time, they resort to acquiring a larger hospital in order to maintain patient access. The integration of a small rural hospital and a large national hospital would frequently result in the emergence of cultural tensions. In order to provide best practices and recommendations for improving organizational change management, this case study examined various change management frameworks and concepts related to mergers and acquisitions and healthcare organizations. When comparing the different models for change management, it is suggested that Kotter's model be utilized as a starting point and guide to improving organizational change management. In addition, the best practices that have been established, such as making culture a priority and encouraging a culture of transparency, are critical factors that contribute to the success of change initiatives. Better business results will result from implementing these best practices and moving through Kotter's 8 steps in the correct order. At the same time, employee satisfaction will increase.

REFERENCES

Alkhaldi, H., Al-Sharafi, H., Al-Yafei, M. A., & Zaidan, M. (2019). The role of Kotter's 8-step model in lean management implementation in healthcare: A qualitative study. *Journal of Healthcare Leadership*, *11*, 87.

American Hospital Association. (2021, October 12). *New report: Partnerships, mergers, and acquisitions can help hospitals, and health systems maintain patient access to care*. AHA. https://www.aha.org/press-releases/2021-10-12-new-report-partnerships-mergers-and-acquisitions-can-help-hospitals-and

American Hospital Association. (2022, September). *Rural Hospital Closures Threaten Access*. AHA. https://www.aha.org/system/files/media/file/2022/09/rural-hospital-closures-threaten-access-report.pdf

Armstrong, E. R., & Eisenstein, L. G. (2020). The role of organizational development in the acquisition of Hahnemann University Hospital. *Journal of Organizational Change Management*, *33*(4), 468–476.

Balluck, J., Asturi, E., & Brockman, V. (2020). Use of the ADKAR® and CLARC ® change models to navigate staffing model changes during the COVID-19 pandemic. *Nurse leader*. https://pubmed.ncbi.nlm.nih.gov/32843885/

Baloh, J., Zhu, X., & Ward, M. M. (2017). Implementing team huddles in small rural hospitals: How does the Kotter model of change apply? *Journal of Nursing Management*, *26*(5), 571–578. doi:10.1111/jonm.12584 PMID:29250892

Bovey, W. H., & Hede, A. (2001b). Resistance to organizational change: The role of defence mechanisms. *Journal of Managerial Psychology*, *16*(7), 534–548. doi:10.1108/EUM0000000006166

Bowles, S., & Myburgh, C. (2018). Using the ADKAR change management model to drive hand hygiene compliance. *The Journal of Hospital Infection*, *99*(2), 231–235. PMID:30359649

Brunton, M., & Matheny, J. (2009). Divergent acceptance of change in a public health organization. *Journal of Organizational Change Management*, *22*(6), 600–619. doi:10.1108/09534810910997023

Carman, A. L., Vanderpool, R. C., Stradtman, L. R., & Edmiston, E. A. (2019). A change-management approach to closing care gaps in a federally qualified Health Center: A rural Kentucky case study. *Preventing Chronic Disease*, *16*, 180589. doi:10.5888/pcd16.180589 PMID:31400097

Cerezo-Espinosa de los Monteros, J., Castro-Torres, A., Gómez-Salgado, J., Fagundo-Rivera, J., Gómez-Salgado, C., & Coronado-Vázquez, V. (2021). Administration of Strategic Agreements in Public Hospitals: Considerations to Enhance the Quality and Sustainability of Mergers and Acquisitions. *International Journal of Environmental Research and Public Health*, *18*(8), 4051. doi:10.3390/ijerph18084051 PMID:33921426

Chmielewska, M., Stokwiszewski, J., Markowska, J., & Hermanowski, T. (2022, January 2). *Evaluating organizational performance of public hospitals using the McKinsey 7-S framework - BMC Health Services Research*. BioMed Central. doi:10.1186/s12913-021-07402-3

Deloitte. (2018). *The Future of Healthcare M&A*. Deloitte. https://www2.deloitte.com/content/dam/Deloitte/us/Documents/life-sciences-health-care/us-lshc-future-of-healthcare-mergers-and-acquisitions.pdf

Ford, J. D., Ford, L. W., & D'Amelio, A. (2008). Resistance to change: The rest of the story. *Academy of Management Review*, *33*(2), 362–377. doi:10.5465/amr.2008.31193235

Gordon, A., & Pollack, J. (2018). Managing Healthcare Integration: Adapting Project Management to the Needs of Organizational Change. *Project Management Journal*, *49*(5), 5–21. https://doi-org.libproxy.lib.unc.edu/10.1177/8756972818785321. doi:10.1177/8756972818785321

Graban, M., & Swartz, J. E. (2018). *Healthcare Kaizen: Engaging front-line staff in sustainable continuous improvements*. CRC Press. doi:10.1201/b12274

Haddad, Y. K., El-Darzi, E., Al-Tawil, Y. A., & Al-Najjar, Y. N. (2019). The application of Lewin's change management model to the implementation of a clinical pathway for joint replacement surgery. *Journal of Nursing Management*, *27*(7), 1419–1427.

Harrison, R., Fischer, S., Walpola, R. L., Chauhan, A., Babalola, T., Mears, S., & Le-Dao, H. (2021). Where do models for change management, improvement, and implementation meet? A systematic review of the applications of change management models in healthcare. *Journal of Healthcare Leadership*, *13*, 85–108. doi:10.2147/JHL.S289176 PMID:33737854

Hooper, V. D., Daniels, J., & Hanna, M. (2019). Using the ADKAR model to implement an electronic medical record system in a primary care clinic. *Journal of the American Association of Nurse Practitioners*, *31*(1), 24–30. PMID:30211782

Hussain, S. T., Lei, S., Akram, T., Haider, M. J., Hussain, S. H., & Ali, M. (2018). Lewin's change model: A critical review of the role of leadership and employee involvement in organizational change. *Journal of Innovation & Knowledge*, *3*(3), 123–127. doi:10.1016/j.jik.2016.07.002

Hut, N. (2022, November 7). *Healthcare M&A: A activity gained steam in Q4 2020.* HFMA. https://www.hfma.org/finance-and-business-strategy/strategic-partnerships-mergers-and-acquisitions/healthcare-m-a-deal-volume-gained-steam-in-q4-2020/

Kang, E., Nantharath, P., & Hwang, H.-J. (2020). The Strategic Process of Merger and Acquisition (M&A) Market Using Integrating Change Management. *Journal of Distribution Science*, *18*(6), 57–62. doi.org/10.15722/jds.18.6.202006.57

Leybourne, S. (2009). Project management and high-value superyacht projects: An improvisational and temporal perspective. *Project Management Journal*, *41*(1), 17–27. doi:10.1002/pmj.20140

Li, Z., & Zhang, J. (2020). The effects of hospital mergers and acquisitions on patient outcomes: A systematic review and meta-analysis. *Health Policy (Amsterdam)*, *124*(7), 747–755.

Lukas, C. V. D., Holmes, S. K., Cohen, A. B., Restuccia, J., Cramer, I. E., Schwartz, M., & Charns, M. P. (2007). Transformational change in Health Care Systems. *Health Care Management Review*, *32*(4), 309–320. doi:10.1097/01.HMR.0000296785.29718.5d PMID:18075440

Mazzocato, P., Stenfors-Hayes, T., von Thiele Schwarz, U., Hasson, H., & Nyström, M. E. (2016). Kaizen practice in Healthcare: A qualitative analysis of hospital employees' suggestions for improvement. *BMJ Open*, *6*(7), e012256. doi:10.1136/bmjopen-2016-012256 PMID:27473953

McAshan, B. R. (2019, August 16). *Memorial Hermann and Baylor Scott & White merger has been canceled.* TMC News. https://www.tmc.edu/news/2019/02/the-memorial-hermann-and-baylor-scott-white-merger-is-canceled/

McKinsey & Company. (2019). *Why M&A deals fail – and how to prevent it.* McKinsey. https://www.mckinsey.com/business-functions/strategy-and-corporate-finance/our-insights/why-m-and-a-deals-fail-and-how-to-prevent-it

Mok, W. Y., & Wu, V. (2020). Overcoming resistance to change: An ADKAR model approach. *Journal of Nursing Management*, *28*(2), 319–326. PMID:31789437

Morell-Santandreu, O., Santandreu-Mascarell, C., & García-Sabater, J. (2020). Sustainability and kaizen: Business model trends in healthcare. *Sustainability (Basel)*, *12*(24), 10622. doi:10.3390u122410622

Piderit, S. K. (1999). *Navigating relationships with coworkers: Understanding employees' attitudes toward an organizational change*. [Unpublished doctoral dissertation, University of Michigan, Ann Arbor, MI].

Prasad, P., & Prasad, A. (2000). Stretching the iron cage: The constitution and implications of routine workplace resistance. *Organization Science*, *11*(4), 387–403. doi:10.1287/orsc.11.4.387.14597

Prosci. (2018). *The PROSCI ADKAR® model.* Prosci Inc. https://www.prosci.com/methodology/adkar

Putri, A. D., Ghazali, A., & Ahluwalia, L. (2021). Analysis of company capability using 7s mckinsey framework to support corporate succession (case study: PT X Indonesia). *Manajemen Bisnis*, *11*(1), 44–53. doi:10.22219/mb.v11i1.17371

Quan, K. A., Lynch, M. A., Belden, J. L., Drake, C., & Kalus, R. (2019). Using Kotter's 8-step model for implementing electronic health record initiatives in ambulatory settings. *Applied Clinical Informatics*, *10*(6), 1006–1014.

Rangachari, P., & Lashbrook, A. (2019). Change management strategies during healthcare mergers and acquisitions: A systematic review. *Health Care Management Review*, *44*(3), 199–209.

Reiling, J., Maurer, R., Crowle, M., Giammalvo, P., & Craig, D. (2022, December 28). Maurer 3 levels of resistance & strategic project management. *The strategic project manager.* https://bethestrategicpm.com/the-maurer-3-levels-of-resistance-and-strategic-project-management/

Riolli, L., & Savicki, V. (2006). Impact of fairness, leadership, and coping on strain, burn-out and turnover in organizational change. *International Journal of Stress Management*, *13*(3), 351–377. doi:10.1037/1072-5245.13.3.351

Rohan, D. (2019, November 26). *7 steps to a successful HR M&A: A due diligence.* Bookboon. https://bookboon.com/blog/2017/06/7-steps-to-a-successful-hr-ma-due-diligence/

Sant'Anna, A., Vilhelmsson, A., & Wolf, A. (2021). Nudging healthcare professionals in clinical settings: A scoping review of the literature. *BMC Health Services Research*, *21*(1), 543. doi:10.118612913-021-06496-z PMID:34078358

Schwartz, K., Lopez, E., Rae, M., & Neuman, T. (2020, September 2). *What we know about provider consolidation.* Health Costs. https://www.kff.org/health-costs/issue-brief/what-we-know-about-provider-consolidation/

Shirey, M. R. (2013). Lewin's theory of planned change as a strategic resource. *The Journal of Nursing Administration, 43*(2), 69–72. doi:10.1097/NNA.0b013e31827f20a9 PMID:23343723

Thaler, R., & Sunstein, C. (2008). *Nudge: Improving decisions about health, wealth, and happiness.* Yale University Press.

Varkey, P., & Antonio, K. (2010). Change management for effective quality improvement: A Primer. *American Journal of Medical Quality*, *25*(4), 268–273. doi:10.1177/1062860610361625 PMID:20445133

Williams, D. Jr, Reiter, K. L., Pink, G. H., Holmes, G. M., & Song, P. H. (2020). Rural Hospital mergers increased between 2005 and 2016—What did those hospitals look like? *Inquiry*, *57*, 004695802093566. doi:10.1177/0046958020935666 PMID:32684072

Wong, Q., Lacombe, M., Keller, R., Joyce, T., & O'Malley, K. (2019). Leading change with ADKAR. *Nursing Management*, *50*(4), 28–35. doi:10.1097/01.NUMA.0000554341.70508.75 PMID:30921039

Chapter 7
Leadership Learning and Leadership Coaching in U.S. Governmental Cybersecurity Organizations and Departments

Amalisha Sabie Aridi
https://orcid.org/0000-0002-7869-5530
Capitol Technology University, USA

ABSTRACT

The cyberattack called SolarWinds carried out against the United States government has been characterized as a collective leadership failure. The United States Federal Government is confronted with the brutal reality of an understaffed or under-skilled cybersecurity workforce and a need for more competent leaders. The focus of federal organizations is increasingly shifting toward management and organizational efficiency. As a result, more and more of these companies are turning to executive coaching to strengthen the leadership abilities of government supervisors. Executive coaching has emerged as a prominent trend in recent years, becoming increasingly popular in pursuing organizational performance, business capacity, and leadership development. This study uses a qualitative research approach to explore the value and benefit of executive leadership coaching as a tool for developing technical managers.

INTRODUCTION

In the United States, the Cybersecurity and Infrastructure Security Agency (CISA) oversees the national effort to identify, manage, and eliminate risks to our cyber and physical infrastructure. The agency connects business and government stakeholders to each other and to information, analysis, and tools to help them create cyber, communications, and physical security and resilience, ensuring a safe and resilient infrastructure for the American people (Cybersecurity and Infrastructure Security Agency, 2023).

CISA collaborates to ensure cyber system security, resilience, and reliability. We collaborate with the private sector, academia, and government partners to cultivate a diverse cyber workforce, promote

DOI: 10.4018/979-8-3693-1634-4.ch007

safe technologies, and promote best practices (Cybersecurity and Infrastructure Security Agency, 2023). CISA shares information deploys detective and preventative technologies, publishes technical products and recommendations, and provides incident response and "hunt" skills to mitigate detected problems and a shifting threat landscape. CISA delivers critical infrastructure, SLTT governance, and capability-building services, information, and assistance to improve critical function cybersecurity risk management and raise the federal cybersecurity baseline (Cybersecurity and Infrastructure Security Agency, 2023).

CISA helps critical infrastructure stakeholders and partners strengthen national security and resilience. CISA consolidates and coordinates timely dissemination of cyber and physical threat information; provides incident-specific intelligence context and products to support decision making; and delivers CISA programs and services through 10 Regional hubs to support stakeholders as they prepare, respond, recover, and mitigate incidents (Cybersecurity and Infrastructure Security Agency, 2023).

CISA assesses risk to prioritize risk management. CISA creates risk management solutions to strengthen critical infrastructure and handle emerging and long-term hazards to National Critical Functions. Election Security and Resilience; Information and Communication Technologies Supply Chain Risk Management; Fifth Generation (5G) Mobile Networks; cybersecurity for Electromagnetic Pulse and Geomagnetic Disturbance, Positioning, Navigation, and Timing; and Pipeline Cybersecurity (Cybersecurity and Infrastructure Security Agency, 2023).

CISA creates creative and collaborative partnerships to help government and private sector stakeholders make informed and voluntary risk management decisions and investments. Multi-channel communication activities to establish public trust and understanding so stakeholders and the American people respond positively when called to act boost the Nation's readiness (Cybersecurity and Infrastructure Security Agency, 2023).

CISA enhances stakeholder risk mitigation capacity to protect vital infrastructure and public gatherings. CISA works with businesses, communities, and government at every level to strengthen the nation's vital infrastructure against cyber and physical threats as the physical and cyber worlds collide. CISA coordinates the national effort to manage physical risks to critical infrastructure, emphasizing cost-effective and easily implementable protective measures that mitigate a variety of threats, including those from targeted violence and domestic violent extremists, and collaborates across government and private sector stakeholders that own or operate the majority of critical infrastructure. Thus, having strong leaders in this organization and risk-management departments has never been more important (Cybersecurity and Infrastructure Security Agency, 2023).

The COVID-19 virus, civil instability, and mis- and disinformation operations plagued the nation in 2021. In December 2020, the Solar Winds supply chain hack showed how the virtual environment affects physical infrastructure. CISA deepened its public/private partnerships to increase operational engagement with external partners while the nation battled with these difficulties. The agency's response to cyber and physical incidents over the past year and new initiatives like CISA's Joint Cyber Defense Collaborative (JCDC) to unify cyber defense capabilities across multiple federal agencies, many state and local governments, and countless private sector entities showed this shift under new leadership and a new Administration (Cybersecurity and Infrastructure Security Agency, 2023).

There has never been a more important time for development of leaders that can enhance policy design and implementation, and bring digital, technological and innovation expertise into federal government agencies.

- Policy: Nearly every national priority depends on an accurate, thorough and contemporary understanding of how to use and leverage modern technology. Federal policies and programs that Americans depend on, including Medicare and our nation's defense, rely on digital services and information technology platforms. Looking ahead, any administration's cornerstone policy will inevitably rely on or be constrained by existing and new technologies such as artificial intelligence and machine learning. Building that policy without technologists at the table would be a mistake.

• Digital delivery: The federal government must increase its capacity to deliver services digitally to the public. Veterans should be able to access their benefits online and on mobile devices, the next-generation air traffic system must be delivered on time and within budget, and agency systems and data need to be secure from cyber threats. Unfortunately, time after time we have seen major federal information technology projects either fail or under-deliver with massive costs.

• Innovation: Some of the most important innovations in America have been led by federal institutions, including space exploration and the creation of the patent system. For the government to provide first-class services, it must test and adopt new practices, methodologies, and technologies, especially those proven to be effective in other sectors. The innovations of the next decades will dwarf those of the past decade through automation, artificial intelligence, bioengineering, quantum computing, the development of new materials, and much more. It will be critical to ensure that the federal government continues to drive policy that encourages the best aspects of innovation, manages the risks and strengthens the nation's leadership in technology (Cybersecurity and Infrastructure Security Agency, 2023).

There has never been a time when it was more important to have managers of cybersecurity who are also strong leaders. It is the responsibility of government officials to properly manage the millions of monies and resources that come from taxpayers (White, 2016). Leadership that is both effective and efficient, as well as solid decision-making abilities on the part of managers, are essential components in ensuring that these resources are used in an appropriate and efficient manner. The structure and function of government management in the modern government are both undergoing ongoing shifts (Goldsmith & Levensaler, 2016). These shifts provide some challenging high-stakes opportunities with regard to the influence and nature of leadership decision-making and leadership development (Goldring, 2015; White 2016).

The Merit Services Protection board has identified that most government agencies do not do an adequate job identifying and developing bad supervisors, with only 6 out of every 1,000 supervisors failing to pass their supervisory probationary period (Katz, 2018b). Katz (2018b) outlined that many government organizations are not effectively addressing supervisors with poor performance. The federal government has significant deficiencies with how managers are trained and developed (Katz, 2018b). Hence, organizational leaders must focus on fostering leadership development activities and strategically engaging themselves in leadership development programs to mitigate the harmful and destructive consequences and outcomes of the lack of effective leadership practices (Center for Leadership Studies, 2017; Ciporen, 2015; Gaddis & Foster, 2015).

PROBLEM STATEMENT

The cyberattack called SolarWinds carried out against the United States government has been characterized as a collective leadership failure. The United States Federal Government is confronted with the brutal reality of a cybersecurity workforce that is either understaffed or under-skilled, as well as a scarcity of competent leaders. The individual repercussions for employees of coping with bad management actions can lead to severe stress-related health concerns, which can be hazardous in and of itself (Miller-Jones, 2020).

According to a well-known survey by Gallup (2015), just thirty percent of workers in the United States are actively engaged in their jobs. Only 35 percent of managers are fully invested in the work they do. If leaders can improve their skills, they can reduce voluntary employee turnover by as much as 32 percent in their organizations (Center for Leadership Studies, 2017). Every organization does its best to improve poorly performing management through training (Gallup, 2015). The focus of federal organizations is increasingly shifting toward management and organizational efficiency, and as a result, more and more of these companies are turning to executive coaching to strengthen the leadership abilities of government supervisors (Censer, 2011; Katz, 2018a). Executive coaching has emerged as a prominent trend in recent years, and it is becoming increasingly popular in the pursuit of organizational performance, business capacity, and leadership development (Lebihan, 2011; McCarthy, 2011)

LITERATURE REVIEW

An examination of the literature exposes a wide-ranging comprehension of Killburg's (2000) executive coaching through six system factors (i.e., input, throughput, output, structure, process, and content), four psychological factors (i.e., conscience, idealized self, instinctual self, and rational self), four internal components of individual function (i.e., emotion, cognition, defense, and conflict), and three types of relationships (i.e., past, present, and focal). The studies in this literature review argue that executive coaching relates to mentoring, organizational culture, leadership development, and management development. These areas influence the outcomes related to efficiency, productivity, and engagement.

Kilburg (1996) identified six system factors (i.e., input, throughput, output, structure, process, and content), four psychological factors (i.e., conscience, idealized self, instinctual self, and rational self), four internal components of individual function (i.e., emotion, cognition, defense, and conflict), and three types of relationships (i.e., past, present, and focal) on which managers must do to be effective.

For most modern organizations, the insistent pace and pressure of business allow for continuous pressure to bear on employees, testing the physical and emotional resources of everyone. After Kilburg's (1996) study, theorists associated executive coaching with numerous constructs that are critical tenets of the conceptual model to include mentoring, organizational culture, leadership development, and management development (Rekalde et al., 2015).

Effects of Technology

In today's virtual work environment, the leadership does not always get opportunities to meet face-to-face with their teams; as a result, technological alternative strategies and methods are used to interrelate and network (Elkhouly et al., 2014). The changing landscape offered by groundbreaking technologies influences organizations' strategic planning (Elkhouly et al., 2014). Innovative technologies are successfully incorporated into organizational strategies and with impacts leading to successes (Elkhouly et al., 2014). Today's technology revolution is serving leaders throughout the world as new sources of power and governance and managers in the efforts to guide performance. Anderson (2017), in connection with the PEW Research Center, conducted research on technology usage gaps that exists between the generations. This research outlined the need for managers and organizations to have the ability to adapt their approaches to leverage technology effectively to improve processes. Short (2014) stated that employing technology will improve efficiency and effectiveness. According to Zveglich and Lacina (2014), employing technology can only enhance the advantageous features of coaching. These same technologies are supporting the capability of immediate feedback and assessment. Innovative technology saves time, an asset that increases as economies develop (Bishop et al., 2013).

To effectively develop better leaders, organizations need to leverage technological tools to enhance the leadership coaching and leadership development process. Teleconferencing, web conferencing, collaboration, and software video conferencing (Harris et al., 2015; Zveglich & Lacina, 2014) are the prominent IT tools to aid the monitoring rocess. According to Zveglich and Lacina (2014), using these tools effectively can aid in the leadership coaching, mentoring, and leadership development processes, ultimately leading to improved organizational effectiveness.

Executive Coaching

According to the United States Government Office of Personnel Management (OPM), specifically, Center for Leadership Studies (2017), coaching can enhance an organization's capability to be successful. Executive coaching is a form of leadership development that occurs because of a series of contracted one-to-one conversations with qualified coaches (deHaan et al. 2013). Positioned as an intercession regarding leadership development concerning the maximization of individuals' potentials, both personal and professional, executive coaching developed from a western cultural philosophy, (Nangalia & Nangalia, 2010). As of late, executive coaching emerged as a popular, integrated intervention, a significant developmental practice (Sperry, 2013) to achieve greater organizational effectiveness and leadership development (Mithiotis & Argirou, 2016). Brennand (2017) provides that even though coaching is among the tools that assist and develop the kinds of leaders needed for the 21st century, learning and development is often pushed to a lower precedence in times of fiscal constraint.

Executive coaching is a mixture of behavioral techniques and processes to support the coachee to attain a jointly identified set of goals to develop professional performance as well as personal satisfaction then subsequently to enhance the effectiveness of the coachee's organization within a formally described coaching agreement (Kilburg, 2000).

Research Design

The research implemented to be a qualitative in nature and had the aim of gaining an understanding of the lived experience of participants. At the same time, interpretations of executive coaching practices and themes emerge. The study employed a multi-various approach, and active participation was encouraged in the research process.

POPULATION AND SAMPLING (QUALITATIVE)

The general geographical segmentation of the targeted population involved experienced governmental supervisors. All participants had had executive coaching as an aspect of their leadership development activities in the greater Washington, D.C. region. They were recruited through government professional associations including, The Partnership for Public Service, National Federation of Federal Employees,

National Association of Hispanic Federal Executives, Blacks in Government, Federal Managers Association, Senior Executives Association (SEA), Young Government Leaders (YGL), Society of American Indian Government Employees (SAIGE), and Asian American Government Executives Network (AAGEN).

The population was restricted to participants fitting the above criteria. This selection constraint provided more currency and accuracy to the collected data because the emergence of coaching practices was recent in the U.S. Federal Government (Bartlett et al., 2014; Turner, 2010). Creswell (2013) stated that 10 participants are a sufficient sample to achieve possible phenomenological outcomes, as the phenomenological research was a purposive approach sought detailed and specific information through data. The actual number of participants in this study was 20.

RESULTS

Population and Demographics

The study included 20 participants who were supervisors in the federal government that had experienced executive coaching as an aspect of their own leadership development as a technical federal employee.

Table 1. Demographic information for interview participants

Category	Percent
Gender	
Male	60% (12 Men)
Female	40% (8 Women)
Age	
Age 20-30	10%
Age 31-40	40%
Age 41-50	30%
Age 51-60	20%
Years' Government Work Experience	
3-5 years	10%
6-10 years	30%
11-15 years	30%
16-20 years	40%
Years' Government Management Experience	
3-5 years	20%
6-10 years	30%
11-15 years	30%
16-20 years	20%
Ethnicity	
Caucasian	40% (8)
African American	30% (6)
Latino/Hispanic	10% (2)
Asian/Pacific Islander	20% (4)

RESEARCH FINDINGS

Interview Data Collection Questions

1. In what ways do you feel executive coaching impacted you as a leader?
2. What coaching tools and processes did you find most valuable, and why?
3. What do you see as the benefit, if any, of coaching as an aspect of a formal leadership development?

The three data collection questions, together generated a total of 22 themes, discussed in the following sections under each question topic in descending order of frequency of mention among the 20 participants.

QUESTIONS AND THEMES

Question Topic One: Ways in Which Executive Coaching Impacted Participants as Leaders

Theme One: Coaching "Improved Self-Awareness" (Stated by 20 Participants out of 20)

This theme is consistent with the claim of Kim (2014) that this outcome may result from mentoring and coaching. Self-awareness helps make leaders more able to take control over their own lives as well as to make more effective decisions as leaders of their organizations (Kim, 2014) So important is this quality—as recognized since the ancient Greeks inscribed "Know thyself" on the temple of Apollo—that if organizations "are to fit themselves for the real world," they must foster "ordinary heroes . . . leaders with a deep awareness of Self, who led with humility as well as courage" (Cowie, 2008). She adds, "When we know Self, we may be able to lead Self. And not until we can lead Self do, we earn the right to lead a team, lead an organization" (Cowie, 2008).

The prominence of this theme is consistent with Dean and Meyer's definition of the purpose of coaching as "to facilitate awareness and enhance interpersonal effectiveness" (Dean & Meyer, 2002, 7).

Theme Two: Coaching "Improved Emotional Intelligence" (stated by 19 participants, out of 20)

Emotional intelligence is a component of the intelligent leadership model (Keikha et al., 2017). In terms of Kilburg's (2000) categories, increased emotional intelligence is an output of the coaching process, having to do with conscience and the rational self, composed of emotion and cognition and affecting the present and future relationships. It is touched upon by many recent studies: Benavides (2008), Gavin (2018), Trevillion (2018), Roelofs (2019), and Bennett (2021).

Theme Three: Coaching "Improved [Participant's] Time and Priority Management as a Supervisor" (Stated by 15 Participants out of 20)

Improvements in time and priority management can be considered, in terms of Kilburg's categories, as outputs of the coaching process that involve the rational self, are composed of cognition, and affect present and focal relationships. In recent research, this theme is touched on by Trevillion (2018).

Interestingly, Nosheen (2013) cites improvements in time management skills as a benefit experienced by *mentors* as well as mentees in peer mentoring situations.

Theme Four: Coaching "Improved [Participant's] Communication Skills" (Stated by 15 Participants out of 20)

The prominence of this theme is consistent with the "interpersonal effectiveness" that coaching is intended to "enhance" (Dean & Meyer, 2002, p. 7). The patterns of communications among employees are an aspect of organizational culture (Plavin-Masterman, 2015) and reflect the employees' values (Isopeskul et al., 2016).

Theme Five: Coaching Provided "An Objective External Viewpoint" (Stated by 15 Participants out of 20)

In terms of Kilburg (2000)'s categories, an objective external viewpoint can be considered an input that has to do with the rational self, is composed of cognition, and affects present and focal relationships. Recent research that touches upon this theme includes the work of Benavides (2008) and Bennett (2021).

Theme Six: Coaching "Made [participant] a More Knowledgeable and Effective Supervisor" (Stated by 15 Participants out of 20)

In terms of Kilburg (2000)'s categories, a supervisor can be considered to become more knowledgeable and effective as an output of the coaching process that has to do with the rational and ideal selves, is composed of emotion and cognition, and affects present and focal relationships.

Question Topic Two: Coaching Tools and Processes Found Most Valuable

Theme Seven: "Relationship With Coach" (Mentioned by 20 Participants out of 20)

The importance of the coach's developing a rapport with the executive is stressed by Dean and Meyer as the first of the competencies a coach should possess (Dean & Meyer, 2002, p. 11). (Since Dean and Meyer's work, explicitly psychological techniques and skills have seen increased emphasis, especially cognitive-behavioral coaching [CBC], sometimes combined with other conceptual frameworks such as the GROW [goal, reality, options, will; Performance Consultants International, 2018] model [Lai & Palmer, 2019].)

Theme Eight: "Help [in] Interpret[ing] Behavioral Assessments" (Mentioned by 20 Participants out of 20)

This theme does not appear to be touched on by any other recent research. It is also stated somewhat ambiguously; the obvious interpretation is that the assessments are of the coachee's own behavior, but because these coachees are leaders, there is a possibility that the reference is to behavioral assessments of members of the coachee's team. Admittedly this interpretation is somewhat farfetched.

Theme Nine: "A Mechanism [for] Goal Setting and Planning" (Mentioned by 20 Participants out of 20)

In terms of Kalburgi's (2000) categories, this can be considered an input or an element of structure that involves primarily the rational self, consists of cognition, and affects present relationships. Recent research touching on this theme includes the studies by Gavin (2018) and Roelofs (2019).

Theme Ten: "Authentic Conversations" (Mentioned by 19 Participants out of 20)

The capacity for authentic conversations without fear of repercussions is essential to a trusting relationship between the coach and the coachee and is part of the thinking environment (Time to Think, 2020). In terms of Kilburg's (2000) categories, it can be considered a feature of structure that can involve all four psychological factors: conscience, idealized self, instinctual self, and rational self. It is composed of emotion and cognition, but it allows matters of conflict and defense to be raised. It affects present and focal relationships.

Theme Eleven: "Enthusiastic Support" (Mentioned by 19 Participants out of 20)

An emotionally supportive atmosphere is a goal of the thinking environment (Time to Think, 2020), where participants are instructed to compose their feedback to be five parts positives to each part challenging (Time to Think, 2020). Similarly, Gavin cites Crane (2002) to the effect that 80% (i.e., four parts) positive to 20% (i.e., one part) "filled with constructive ideas for improvements," a practice followed by Douglas Conant in his revitalization of Campbell's Soup (Gavin, 2018, p. 143). In terms of Kilburg's (2000) classes, it can be considered an input that engages the conscience and instinctual self for the benefit of the rational self, is composed of emotion and perhaps defense, and affects present and focal relationships. Another recent research touching upon this theme is that of Boysen et al. (2018).

Theme Twelve: "Help With Focus, Redirection, and Clarity" (Mentioned by 19 Participants out of 20)

This theme is essential for the change process that is the goal of all coaching. In terms of Kilburg's (2000) categories, this help can be considered an input that works with the rational self and the conscience, consists of processes of cognition and perhaps, to some extent, emotion, and affects present and possibly focal relationships. Recent research that touches upon this theme includes the work of Benavides (2008), Trevillion (2018), and Bennett (2021).

Theme 13: Coaching "Challenged [Participant's] Approaches and [Their] Own Thinking" (Mentioned by 19 Participants out of 20)

As stated by Kim (2014), mentors challenge mentees as well as guide and reassure them. For Boysen, Arya, and Page, "challenging thinking patterns" are one of the "foundations of the coaching process" (Boysen et al., 2021, p. 116). Without a challenge to thinking and behavior patterns, no one would have any motive to undertake the work of change at which all coaching aims, and without a challenge to erroneous thought patterns, coachees would have a strong motive to resist such change.

Theme 14: "Ask Questions" (Mentioned by 19 Participants out of 20)

It is not certain from this brief articulation of this theme whether it means that the coach asks questions (pointed or Socratic questions, or, as followers of Kline's ten components of a thinking environment call them, Incisive Questions [Time to Think, 2020]) of the coachee, which might be considered another case of Theme 13, or that the coachee feels free to ask questions of the coach, which would relate this theme to Theme 10. Perhaps both are meant. In terms of Kilburg's (2000) categories, the former case would be an input that involves all four psychological factors, consists of at least emotion and cognition and potentially all four internal components, and affects present and focal relationships. The latter case would be a component of structure and would involve primarily the rational self, consisting primarily of cognition and emotion, and affect present relationships. In either case, one way or another, this theme is touched upon by Benavides (2008), Boysen et al. (2018), Roelofs (2019), Bennett (2021), Boysen et al. (2021), and Johnston (2021) among recent research.

Theme 15: "Challenge Assumptions" (Mentioned by 18 Participants out of 20)

Again, as stated by Kim (2014) challenging mentees is one of the services mentors perform for them. It is difficult to ascertain where the boundary lies between this theme and Theme 13. What was stated about that theme applies here too.

Theme 16: "Provide Resources" (Mentioned by 18 Participants out of 20)

The brief statement of this theme covers a very broad range of possible meanings. "Resources" could mean anything from an offhand suggestion to a link on the World Wide Web to a full set of printed and audiovisual course materials, or even the coaches themselves. In terms of Kilburg's (2000) categorizations, this theme would appear to be an input, involving primarily the rational self and the components of cognition and emotion and affecting mostly present relationships. Because of the broad range of possible meanings, it was not possible to identify specific recent research that touches upon it.

Theme 17: "Provide Advice" (Mentioned by 18 Participants out of 20)

In terms of Kilburg's (2000) categories, this theme could be described as an input that engages primarily the rational self and possibly the conscience and ideal self, consisting primarily of cognition, and affecting present relationships. Among recent research, this theme is explicitly mentioned by Boysen et al. (2018), but it runs implicitly throughout the coaching literature.

Theme 18: "Objective Assessment and Feedback" (Mentioned by 18 Participants out of 20)

This theme is like Themes 13 and 15, but in terms of Kilburg's (2000) categorizations, this input may engage the instinctual self and incorporate emotion, defense, and conflict to a lesser extent than those, because this feedback is trusted to be objective rather than be presented as an attack on the coachee's thought patterns. It is explicitly touched on by Benavides (2008) and Roelofs (2019) among recent research.

Question Topic 3: Perceived Benefits of Coaching as an Aspect of a Formal Leadership Development Program

Theme 19: Coaching "Improved the Way That [Participant] Approached Being a Supervisor" (Mentioned by 20 Participants out of 20)

There is possible conceptual overlap of this theme with Theme 6; the exact boundaries are difficult to ascertain from the brief statements of the themes alone. Like that theme, this is, in terms of Kilburg's (2000) categorization, an output. It involves the ideal and rational selves and the conscience; it consists largely of cognition and emotion, and it affects present and possibly focal relationships. Recent research touching on this theme includes the work of Taconis (2018), Trevillion (2018), Roelofs (2019), and Boysen et al. (2021).

Theme 20: Coaching "Increase[d] Confidence" (Mentioned by 19 Participants out of 20)

As stated by Kim (2014), mentors build the confidence of mentees specifically by guiding them through the accomplishment of an intended purpose via the steps of intention, commitment, preparation, development, and accomplishment.

Other recent research that touches on this theme includes the work of Taconis (2018), Trevillion (2018), Roelofs (2019), and Brown et al. (2021). Moreover, the "self-efficacy" component of psychological capital (PsyCap) is literally glossed as "confidence" (Luthans et al., 2007, p. 542). Therefore, any study that does not explicitly mention "confidence" but relates PsyCap to coaching, such as that of Zuberbuhler et al. (2020), also touch on this theme.

Theme 21: Coaching [Helped] "Establish Better Career Development Goals" (Mentioned by 19 Participants out of 20)

Gavin (2018) mentions this theme explicitly. The relative lack of attention given to it may be because coaching is seen by coaches and employers (who pay for the coaching intervention) to improve the performance of the coachee in his or her present job; however, the large proportion of coachees who mentioned it here shows its importance to them. In terms of Kilburg's (2000) categories, this theme can be described as an output, having to do primarily with the rational self and composed primarily of cognition and emotion, and affecting present and possibly focal relationships.

Theme 22: Coaching "Improve[d] Comprehension of Strengths and Ways to Leverage Those Strengths" (Mentioned by 19 Participants out of 20)

This theme has, like several others, a rather broad statement; for example, it may refer to the coachee's own strengths or, in a leader, to the strengths of the coachee's team members. In terms of Kilburg's (2000) categories, this theme can be described as an output that involves primarily the rational self (and, to the extent that it refers to the coachee's own strengths, the conscience, and ideal self), consists primarily of cognition, and affects primarily present relationships. Recent research touching on it includes the work of Boysen et al. (2018) and Trevillion (2018).

Synthesis and Summary of Data

The three data collection questions, together generated a total of 22 themes, discussed in the following sections under each question topic in descending order of frequency of mention among the 20 participants.

CISA continues to drive fundamental cross agency organizational change to reduce the cybersecurity risk to the Federal Civilian Executive Branch (FCEB). By providing innovative technology capabilities, first-rate services, and real-time information, CISA helps federal agencies manage sophisticated cybersecurity risks. The need for cybersecurity managers that are effective leaders have never been more critical. Government leaders are responsible for successfully managing millions of taxpayer dollars and resources (White, 2016). Effective and efficient leadership and sound managerial decision-making skills are significant in ensuring these resources are used appropriately and efficiently. The nature of government management in the government today is continuously changing (Goldsmith & Levensaler, 2016). These changes represent some high-stakes challenges to the impact and nature of leadership decision-making (Goldring, 2015; White 2016). Social networks and media are creating a new level of accountability and transparency (Goldring 2015). Additionally, new technologies, human resource challenges, revenue scarcities, and political dynamics outline the complex nature of being an effective leader and managerial decision-maker in the federal government (White, 2016).

REFERENCES

Anderson, M. (2017). Key trends shaping technology in 2017. *Pew Research Center FACTANK*. https://www.pewresearch.org/fact-tank/2017/12/28/key-trends-shaping-technology-in-2017/

Bartlett, J. II, Boylan, R., & Hale, J. (2014). Executive coaching: An integrative literature review. *Journal of Human Resource and Sustainability Studies*, *2*(4), 188–195. doi:10.4236/jhrss.2014.24018

Benavides, L. (2008). *The relationship between executive coaching and organizational performance of female executives as a predictor for organizational success.* [Doctoral dissertation, University of San Francisco, CA]. https://repository.usfca.edu/diss/194

Bennett, K. (2021). Leaders' adaptive identity development in uncertain contexts: Implications for executive coaching. *International Journal of Evidence Based Coaching and Mentoring*, *19*(2), 54–69.

Bishop, T. F., Press, M. J., Mendelsohn, J. L., & Casalino, L. P. (2013). Electronic communication improves access, but barriers to its widespread adoption remain. *Health Affairs*, *32*(8), 1361–1367. https://proxy.cecybrary.com/login?url=https://search.proquest.com/docview/1428492209?accountid=144459. doi:10.1377/hlthaff.2012.1151 PMID:23918479

Boysen, S., Cherry, M., Amerie, W., & Takagawa, M. (2018). Organisational coaching outcomes: A comparison of a practitioner survey and key findings from the literature. *International Journal of Evidence Based Coaching and Mentoring*, *16*(1), 159–166.

Boysen, S. M., Arya, T., & Page, L. (2021). Creating a coaching culture in a non-profit. *International Journal of Evidence Based Coaching and Mentoring*, *19*(2), 115–132.

Brennand, C. (2017, February). *Unlocking a Federal Coaching Culture*. Association for Talent Development (ATD). https://www.td.org/Publications/Magazines/The-Public-Manager/Archives/2017/02/Unlocking-a-Federal-Coaching-Culture

Brown, R. P., Varghese, L., Sullivan, S., & Parsons, S. (2021). The impact of professional coaching on emerging leaders. *International Journal of Evidence Based Coaching and Mentoring*, *19*(2), 24–37.

Censer, M. (2011, October 30). Executive coaching contracts pick up speed. *The Washington Post*.

Center for Leadership Studies. (2017). *The Cost of Poor Leadership On Your Revenue And Culture*. GBS Corporate. https://www.gbscorporate.com/blog/the-cost-of-poor-leadership-on-your-revenue-and-culture

Ciporen, R. (2015). The emerging field of executive and organizational coaching: An overview. *New Directions for Adult and Continuing Education*, *2015*(148), 5–15. doi:10.1002/ace.20147

Cowie, K. (2008, May/June). The HR challenge: leadership development for ordinary heroes. *Ivey Business Journal*. https://iveybusinessjournal.com/publication/the-hr-challenge-leadership-development-for-ordinary-heroes/

Creswell, J. W. (2013). *Qualitative Inquiry and Research Design: Choosing Among Five Approaches*. Sage Publishing.

Dean, M. L., & Meyer, A. A. (2002). Executive coaching: In search of a model. *Journal of Leadership Education*, *1*(2), 3–17. doi:10.12806/V1/I2/RF1

Elkhouly, S., Ossman, M., Selim, M., & Zaghloul, M. (2014). Impact of E-leadership on leadership styles within the Egyptian government sector. *Competition Forum, 12*(1), 131-140. https://proxy.cecybrary.com/login?url=https://search.proquest.com/docview/1640568232?accountid=144459

Gaddis, B. H., & Foster, J. L. (2015). Meta-analysis of dark side personality characteristics and critical work behaviors among leaders across the globe: Findings and implications for leadership development and executive coaching. *Applied Psychology*, *64*(1), 25–54. doi:10.1111/apps.12017

Gallup. (2015). *The State of the American Manager.* The Gallup Organization. https://www.gallup.com/services/182138/state-american-manager.aspx

Gavin, C. S. (2018). The impact of leadership development using coaching. *Journal of Practical Consulting*, *6*(1), 137–147.

Goldring, C. C. (2015). A design for federal government leaders: Succession planning through knowledge management (Doctoral dissertation). *Available from ProQuest Dissertations & Theses Global*. (UMI No. 1688688202)

Goldsmith, A., & Levensaler, L. (2016, February). Build a great company culture with help from technology. *Harvard Business Review*. https://hbr.org/2016/02/build-a-great-company-culture-with-help-from-technology

Harris, B., Cheng, K. F., & Gorley, C. (2015). Benefits and barriers. *Journal of Workplace Learning*, *27*(3), 193–206. https://proxy.cecybrary.com/login?url=https://search.proquest.com/docview/1672560997?accountid=144459. doi:10.1108/JWL-07-2014-0053 PMID:26477117

Isopeskul, O., Shakina, M., & Georgieva, N. (2016). *Influence of stakeholders on organizational culture development*. PROXY. https://proxy.cecybrary.com/login?url=https://search.proquest.com/docview/1779263332?accountid=144459

Johnston, D. (2021). How do coaches and clients create and experience thinking environments? *International Journal of Evidence Based Coaching and Mentoring*, *S15*, 198–211.

Katz, E. (2018A, October 3). OPM Calls on Agencies to Implement Coaching Programs for Employees. *Government Executive*.

Katz, E. (2018B, January 10). Agencies Aren't Catching Bad Supervisors Early Enough. *Government Executive*.

Keikha, A., Hoveida, R., & Nour, M. Y. (2017). The development of an intelligent leadership model for state universities. *Foresight and STI Governance*, *11*(1), 66–74. doi:10.17323/2500-2597.2017.1.66.74.

Kilburg, R. R. (1996). Toward a conceptual understanding and definition of executive coaching. *Consulting Psychology Journal*, *48*(2), 134–144. doi:10.1037/1061-4087.48.2.134

Kilburg, R. R. (1996). Toward a conceptual understanding and definition of executive coaching. *Consulting Psychology Journal*, *48*(2), 134–144. https://scholar.google.com/scholar?hl=en&as_sdt=0%2C47&q=Kilburg%2C+R.+R.+%282000%29.+Executive+coaching%3A+Developing+managerial+wisdom+in+a+world+of+chaos.+Washington%2C+DC%3A+American+Psychological+Association.&btnG=. doi:10.1037/1061-4087.48.2.134

Kilburg, R. R. (2000). *Executive coaching: Developing managerial wisdom in a world of chaos*. American Psychological Association. doi:10.1037/10355-000

Kim, S. E. (2014). The mentor-protégé affinity on mentoring outcomes: The mediating effect of developmental networking. *International Review of Public Administration*, *19*(1), 91–106. doi:10.1080/12294659.2014.887368

Lai, Y.-L., & Palmer, S. (2019). Psychology in executive coaching: An integrated literature review. *Journal of Work-Applied Management*, *11*(2), 143–164. doi:10.1108/JWAM-06-2019-0017

Lebihan, R. (2011). Business schools tap coaching trend. *Australian Financial Review*, *14*, 27–28.

Luthans, F., Avolio, B. J., Avey, J. B., & Norman, S. M. (2007). Positive psychological capital: Measurement and relationship with performance and satisfaction. *Personnel Psychology*, *3*(60), 541–572. doi:10.1111/j.1744-6570.2007.00083.x

Miller-Jones, G. (2020, February 25). Ineffective Leadership and The Devastating Individual And Organizational Consequences. *Forbes*.

Mithiotis, A., & Argirou, N. (2016). Coaching: From challenge to opportunity. *Journal of Management Development*, *35*(4), 448–463. doi:10.1108/JMD-10-2014-0139

Nangalia, L., & Nangalia, A. (2010). The Coach in Asian Society: Impact of social hierarchy on the coaching relationship. *International Journal of Evidence Based Coaching and Mentoring*, *8*(1), 51–66.

Nosheen, R. N. (2013). Peer mentoring: Enhancing social cohesion in Pakistani Universities. *Higher Education, Skills and Work - Based Learning, 3*(2), 130-140. doi:10.1108/20423891311313162

Office of Personnel Management. (2017). *Center for leadership development*. OPM. https://leadership.opm.gov/index.aspx

Performance Consultants International. (2018). *GROW Model: GROWing people, performance, and purpose*. Coaching Performance. https://www.coachingperformance.com/wp-content/uploads/2018/10/GROW-Model-Guide.pdf

Plavin-Masterman, M. (2015). Are Walls Just Walls? Organizational culture emergence in a virtual firm. *Journal of Organizational Culture, Communications and Conflict, 19*(2), 43-68. https://proxy.cecybrary.com/login?url=https://search.proquest.com/docview/1750418352?accountid=144459

Rekalde, I., Landeta, J., & Albizu, E. (2015). Determining factors in the effectiveness of executive coaching as a management development tool. *Management Decision*, *53*(8), 1677–1697. https://proxy.cecybrary.com/login?url=https://search.proquest.com/docview/1718406443?accountid=144459. doi:10.1108/MD-12-2014-0666

Roelofs, B. (2019). How shadow coaching helps leaders to improve their performance on the job in real-time. *International Journal of Evidence Based Coaching and Mentoring*, *S13*, 49–62.

Short, T. W. (2014). Workplace mentoring: An old idea with new meaning (part 1). *Development and Learning in Organizations*, *28*(1), 8–11. doi:10.1108/DLO-09-2013-0077

Sperry, L. (2013). Executive coaching and leadership assessment: Past, present, and future. *Consulting Psychology Journal*, *65*(4), 284–288. doi:10.1037/a0035453

Taconis, M. (2018). How high potential coaching can add value – for participants and the organization. *International Journal of Evidence Based Coaching and Mentoring*, *S12*, 61–72.

Time to Think. (2020). *The ten components*. Time to Think. https://www.timetothink.com/thinking-environment/the-ten-components/

Trevillion, F. M. H. (2018). Executive coaching outcomes: An investigation into leadership development using five dyadic case studies illustrating the impact of executive coaching. *International Journal of Evidence Based Coaching and Mentoring*, *S12*, 21–40.

Turner, D. (2010). Qualitative interview design: A practical guide for novice investigators. *Qualitative Report*, *15*(3), 754–760.

White, H. D. (2016). Relevance theory and distributions of judgments in document retrieval. *Information Processing & Management*, *5*(53), 1080–1102.

Zuberbuhler, M. J. P., Salanova, M., & Martinez, I. M. (2020). Coaching-based Leadership Intervention Program: A controlled trial study. *Frontiers in Psychology*, *10*, 3066. doi:10.3389/fpsyg.2019.03066 PMID:32116873

Zveglich, L., & Lacina, R. (2014). *Powering up coaching by blending human factor with technology*. PROXY. https://proxy.cecybrary.com/login?url=https://search.proquest.com/docview/1552708249?accountid=144459

Chapter 8

Cybercrime and Cybersecurity Challenges in the Automotive Industry Utilizing Agent-Based Modeling (ABM)

Eugene Lewis
https://orcid.org/0000-0002-2956-0760
Capitol Technology University, USA

Darrell Norman Burrell
https://orcid.org/0000-0002-4675-9544
Marymount University, USA

Calvin Nobles
https://orcid.org/0000-0003-4002-1108
Illinois Institute of Technology, USA

Jennifer Ferreras-Perez
https://orcid.org/0009-0003-0972-1824
Marymount University, USA

Kevin Richardson
https://orcid.org/0009-0002-3212-8669
Capitol Technology University, USA

Angel J. Jones
https://orcid.org/0009-0007-9740-6611
University of Virginia, USA

Laura Ann Jones
https://orcid.org/0000-0002-0299-370X
Capitol Technology University, USA

ABSTRACT

Agent-based modeling (ABM) serves as a powerful and innovative tool to evaluate and address cybersecurity risks in the auto industry. With the increasing integration of advanced technologies in modern vehicles, the potential vulnerabilities and threats to cybersecurity have become a major concern. ABM allows cybersecurity experts to simulate complex interactions among autonomous agents representing various components of the automotive ecosystem, such as vehicles, manufacturers, suppliers, and hackers. ABM can effectively model real-world scenarios and assess how cyber threats propagate and spread throughout the system. It enables the identification of critical points of weakness and potential attack vectors, aiding in the development of proactive strategies to mitigate cybersecurity risks. Through iterative simulations and data-driven analysis, ABM empowers stakeholders in the auto industry to make informed decisions and implement robust security measures that safeguard against cyberattacks, ensuring the safety and trustworthiness of connected and autonomous vehicles.

DOI: 10.4018/979-8-3693-1634-4.ch008

INTRODUCTION

Cybersecurity is an ever-growing challenge for industries worldwide, and the automotive industry is no exception (Bocetta, 2022). With the increasing use of electronic systems in cars, the possibility of cyberattacks has also increased (Burkacky et al., 2021). Modern cars have numerous sensors, processors, and communication interfaces designed to work together seamlessly (Security Compass, 2019; Ritchell, 2021). Furthermore, the rise of connected cars and autonomous vehicles has increased the attack surface for hackers (Bocetta, 2022; Hamadneh & Esztergar-Kiss, 2022; Richell, 2021). These vehicles rely on wireless communication and are connected to the internet, which makes them vulnerable to cyber-attacks from anywhere in the world (Ritchell, 2021; Burkacky et al., 2021; Hamadneh & Esztergar-Kiss, 2022). However, this complexity also makes identifying vulnerabilities and protecting against cyber-attacks challenging (Lonzetta et al., 2018; Bocetta, 2022; Burkacky et al., 2021; Richell, 2021). Agent-based modeling (ABM) is a technique that can be used to simulate complex systems such as cybersecurity in the automotive industry (Bouard et al., 2013). Cybersecurity has become a critical concern in the modern world as technology advances rapidly (Security Compass, 2019). The rise of connected and autonomous vehicles has created new opportunities for hackers to exploit vulnerabilities and gain unauthorized access to systems (Lonzetta et al., 2018; Hamadneh & Esztergar-Kiss, 2022; Wan & Wang, 2022).

Agent-based modeling (ABM) has emerged as a valuable computational tool for addressing complex data and cybersecurity challenges faced by organizations collaborating with a variety of production vendors. In today's interconnected and data-driven business landscape, managing data and ensuring cybersecurity across multiple vendors can be highly intricate and critical. ABM provides a novel approach to simulate and analyze the interactions, dependencies, and vulnerabilities within the multi-vendor system, allowing stakeholders to gain deeper insights and develop effective strategies to safeguard data and bolster cybersecurity.

In a data-driven world where organizations engage with multiple production vendors, data management and cybersecurity have become pressing concerns. Ensuring data integrity, privacy, and security across a diverse vendor network is challenging, requiring advanced methodologies to analyze the complex interactions between vendors and the organization. ABM offers a powerful tool to simulate the behavior of individual agents, identify potential data vulnerabilities, and assess cybersecurity risks in a multi-vendor environment.

PROBLEM STATEMENT

Kingston (2023) postulates that automakers worldwide will commit an estimated $1.2 trillion to electrification globally through 2030 to build tens of millions of electric vehicles (EVs) (Hamadneh & Esztergar-Kiss, 2022; LCSCM, 2022; Wan & Wang, 2022). The number constitutes more than double the amount from two years ago. According to Blum (2022), 40% of attacks in the automobile industry derive from targeted back-end servers (LCSCM, 2022). The decrease in automakers worldwide to decrease emissions and petroleum use to improve green ecosystems to preserve natural resources is a continual innovation (Sripad, Kulandaivel, Pande, Sekar, & Viswanathan, 2017). Under the United States-Mexico-Canada Agreement (USMCA), the auto industry will have an annual production of 15 million vehicles per year beginning in 2022 (Hamadneh & Esztergar-Kiss, 2022; Kingston, 2023; Wan & Wang, 2022).

The automotive industry is highly competitive and plays an integral part in the growth and stability of the USMCA agreement (Kingston, 2023).

According to International Energy Agency (IEA), the organization projects that for the world to achieve net zero globally by 2050, six times more mineral inputs will be required by 2040 than today. This establishes a unique scholarly challenge in the cyber security space as automakers seek to establish a macro-level supply chain to improve ongoing chemical deposits affecting global warming and other critical gases within the environment (Mircea et al., 2016; Jankovic-Zugic et al., 2023; LCSCM, 2022). Additionally, an increased proprietary arises regarding the hacking and data security of intellectual property for the automakers. The problem statement is the growing challenge of cyber security attacks facing automakers seeking a competitive advantage in the auto industry. This paper will use qualitative interviews to explore the competency rate of electronic vehicle innovation and the security risks it poses (Mircea et al., 2016). The study will evaluate the information technology cyber security implications of shared data as electronic vehicles are solely computer-based, using code, electronic configurations, and digital algorithms to create greater efficiency (Mircea et al., 2016; Hamadneh & Esztergar-Kiss, 2022; Wan & Wang, 2022).

FINDING THE GAP IN THE RESEARCH

The rapid advancement of electronic vehicle (EV) distribution has continued to affect the implementation, delivery, production, and expansion auto industry (MacLennan, Marshall, Griffin, Purcell, Mcgwin, & Rue, 2008). Automakers face significant challenges as cyber-security breaches continue (Mircea et al., 2016). Many organizations contribute autonomous connectivity within vehicle system control units within the automaker community as a prime vulnerability area (Burkacky et al., 2021; Ahlsell et al., 2023). As electronic vehicles (EVs) become more technologically advanced by manipulating internal vehicle code and data functionality through computer usage, more challenges will arise (Bouard et al., 2013; Hamadneh & Esztergar-Kiss, 2022; Ahlsell et al., 2023). The revolution in automotive connectivity and the exponential growth into increased cybersecurity risks cause significant remodification and quality assurance variations (Burkacky et al., 2021; Blum, 2022; Ahlsell et al., 2023).

METHODOLOGY

The methodology for this research study is qualitative research approach of using focus groups. Qualitative research is an approach to understanding the lived experiences of individuals in the auto community, providing a glance into the automotive journey into cyberspace because of increased technology risks (Kingston, 2023; Creswell, 2014). Although the exploratory methodology is used in this study (Creswell, 2014). The qualitative research approach of using focus groups with subject matter experts offers several valuable benefits in collecting data, understanding trends, and uncovering best practices. By bringing together experts in a specific field, focus groups provide a platform for in-depth discussions and exchanges of ideas, which can yield rich and diverse perspectives. This collaborative environment allows researchers to explore complex issues comprehensively and gain a deeper understanding of the subject matter. Through open-ended questions and interactive discussions, focus groups facilitate the discovery of emerging trends, subtle nuances, and unanticipated insights that might be overlooked in other research methods. Moreover, subject matter experts can share their experiences and practical knowledge, enabling the identification of best practices that have proven successful in real-world scenarios. Overall, the qualitative approach with focus groups empowers researchers to explore multifaceted topics, capture nuanced data, and extract valuable insights to inform decision-making and drive innovation in the respective field. (Creswell, 2014).

The study investigates qualitative focus group data to understand the global risk of increased innovation and technology in the electronic vehicle automotive industry. This type of research provides researchers and scholars with interpretative data to discover patterns and themes that can change a growing problem in the industry. Statistics show that nearly 85% of attacks in 2021 were carried out remotely, outnumbering physical attacks from four to one (Blum, 2022). Blum (2022) further postulates that 54.1% of attacks were carried out by "Black Hat" (malicious) actors, which was an increase from the previous 49.3% in 2020. Moreover, statistics show keyless entry and critical fob attacks on 50% of all vehicle thefts as automobiles become more digital, utilizing electronic cloud technology for keyless entry and start functionality (Burkacky et al., 2021; Blum, 2022; Ahlsell et al., 2023). The study aims to explore further how cyber security may mitigate the automotive risks associated with data hacking, critical data anomalies, corruptive file transfer, and increased malware/firmware destroying valuable intellectual property to the automakers within the industry. The other goal is to explore the requisite knowledge attained by auto mechanics, auto software engineers, and quality assurance specialist who work with electronic vehicles (EVs) daily and who have first-hand knowledge of current cyber security challenges (Hamadneh & Esztergar-Kiss, 2022; Mircea et al., 2016; Wan & Wang, 2022).

The data collected in this investigative study utilized three (3) focus group discussions with four (4) individuals in each group. All of which each had cybersecurity certification. All twelve (12) work in the following automotive job areas within a plant or dealership:

(a) Systems Engineer (4)
(b) Auto Technician (6)
(c) Software Data Engineer (2)

Each participant has experience working with electronic vehicles for automakers nationwide over the last three (3) years. The study had 12 participants (10 males and two females). The participants comprised eight white males, one black male, and 3 Latino males. The two women were both of Latina descent. Eight participants had undergraduate degrees, two advanced-level master's degrees, and 2 received technical training education through the dealership or automaker

The qualitative interviews addressed the following problem statement questions:

1. What pressures are there for automakers as cyber-attacks continue to increase and pose significant mitigation risks to the auto technology industry?
2. How can cybersecurity analysts and automakers work together to mitigate system vulnerabilities and anomalies contributing to cyber auto security risk and outcomes in the industry?

CHALLENGES IN AUTOMOTIVE CYBERSECURITY

Cybersecurity challenges are increasing daily with the rise of new technologies and their integration into various industries (Bocetta, 2022). One of the most concerning developments in recent years has been the emergence of automotive hacking, which involves the exploitation of vulnerabilities in modern vehicles' software and hardware to gain unauthorized access or control (Bouard et al., 2013; Lonzetta et al., 2018; Security Compass, 2019; Burkacky et al., 2021; Hamadneh & Esztergar-Kiss, 2022). One of the critical challenges in automotive cybersecurity is the vast and diverse ecosystem of stakeholders involved in designing, manufacturing, and operating vehicles (Bocetta, 2022; Hamadneh & Esztergar-Kiss, 2022; Wan & Wang, 2022). ABM can help capture this complexity by modeling agents' behavior, such as automakers, suppliers, government regulators, and consumers. By modeling different types of agents (e.g., attackers, defenders, and users) and their interactions, researchers can identify vulnerabilities and develop strategies for mitigating risks (Security Compass, 2019; Burkacky et al., 2021). By incorporating the perspectives and incentives of these different agents, ABM can help identify potential conflicts and trade-offs in cybersecurity decision-making. Cybersecurity is a critical concern for the automotive industry. The key cybersecurity challenges consist of the following:

Table 1. Key cybersecurity challenges facing the automobile industry (Lonzetta et al., 2018)

	Constructs	Key Cybersecurity Challenges facing the Automobile Industry
1	Vulnerabilities in the software and hardware of vehicles	Many vehicles today have sophisticated software systems and sensors that make them vulnerable to cyber-attacks. Hackers can exploit these vulnerabilities to take control of the vehicle's systems, causing accidents or stealing personal data.
2	Lack of standardization and interoperability	The automotive industry needs standardized cybersecurity protocols and practices, making protecting vehicles and their components from cyber-attacks challenging.
3	Supply Chain Risks	Cybersecurity risks can also arise from the supply chain, where third-party vendors and suppliers may introduce vulnerabilities in-vehicle hardware and software components.
4	Human Error	Human error remains a significant cybersecurity risk in the automotive industry. Drivers and employees may inadvertently expose vehicles and systems to cyber-attacks by using weak passwords, sharing login credentials, or failing to install software updates.

A helpful tool for analyzing and mitigating cybersecurity risks. However, given the complexity and diversity of automotive systems, it is essential to continue developing new models and techniques for securing connected cars and autonomous vehicles (Bouard et al., 2013; Security Compass, 2019; Wan & Wang, 2022). Cybersecurity challenges have become increasingly prevalent in today's digital age, and the automotive industry is no exception (Bocetta, 2022; Burkacky et al., 2021; Hamadneh & Esztergar-Kiss, 2022). To address these challenges, the automotive industry must work together to establish common cybersecurity standards and protocols. This will require collaboration between manufacturers, suppliers, and other stakeholders to identify and address vulnerabilities, implement security controls, and monitor and respond to threats (Lonzetta et al., 2018). As vehicles become more connected and autonomous, they are vulnerable to cyber-attacks (Security Compass, 2019; Hamadneh & Esztergar-Kiss, 2022; Richell, 2021). Automotive hacking has emerged as a significant threat, with hackers potentially gaining control over a vehicle's systems, causing physical harm or property damage (Bouard et al., 2013; Burkacky et al., 2021; Nosibor, 2022). Cybersecurity challenges have become increasingly complex and pervasive in recent years as the number of connected devices and systems continues to grow (Mircea et al., 2016; Bocetta, 2022). Automotive cybersecurity is the increasing complexity of modern vehicles' software and hardware systems (Bouard et al., 2013). As more components are integrated into a vehicle's computer network, the attack surface for potential hackers grows exponentially. Furthermore, the diversity of technologies used in vehicles, such as GPS, Wi-Fi, and Bluetooth, presents a wide range of potential vulnerabilities that must be addressed (Bouard et al., 2013; Lonzetta et al., 2018; Yao, Ma, Hu, & Gu, 2022). This is particularly evident in the automotive industry, where the rise of connected and autonomous vehicles has led to a corresponding increase in the risk of automotive hacking (Bouard et al., 2013; Security Compass, 2019). Cybersecurity is keeping up with the constantly evolving threats. As new technologies are developed, hackers find new ways to exploit them (Bocetta, 2022). This is particularly true in the automotive industry, where vehicles are becoming increasingly connected and autonomous. The cyber-attack risk on cars has become a significant concern for automakers, governments, and consumers (Richell, 2021).

VULNERABILITIES IN SOFTWARE AND HARDWARE

The challenge in the automobile industry is the speed at which new vulnerabilities are discovered and exploited (Bouard et al., 2013; Lonzetta et al., 2018). Unlike traditional cyber-attacks, which may take days or weeks to execute, an automotive hack can occur in seconds, leaving little time for detection and response (Bocetta, 2022; Richell, 2021). This is particularly concerning given the potential safety risks of compromising a vehicle's control systems (Bouard et al., 2013). Agent-based modeling can help address automotive challenges by allowing researchers to simulate different scenarios and evaluate the effectiveness of various cybersecurity measures (Ahlsell et al., 2023). For example, by creating agents representing different types of hackers and vehicles, researchers can simulate attacks and assess how different security protocols, such as encryption and intrusion detection systems, impact the likelihood of a successful hack (Yao et al., 2022). Ultimately, the rise of automotive hacking highlights the urgent need for more robust cybersecurity measures in the automotive industry (Halahan & Chen, 2017; Ahlsell et al., 2023). By leveraging advanced modeling techniques such as agent-based modeling, researchers can better understand the complex dynamics of this emerging threat and develop more effective countermeasures to protect against it (Halahan & Chen, 2017; Nosibor, 2022). Cybersecurity challenges have become increasingly prevalent with the growing reliance on technology in various sectors of society, including the automotive industry (Mircea et al., 2016; Bocetta, 2022; Ahlsell et al., 2023). The rise of automotive hacking is a concern highlighted in recent years as vehicles become more connected and automated (Yao et al., 2022). Agent-based modeling (ABM) can be a helpful tool for exploring the potential impacts of such cyber security threats (Nosibor, 2022). One challenge in automotive hacking is the potential for malicious actors to access critical vehicle systems, such as the brakes or steering (Bouard et al., 2013). This could result in dangerous road situations for drivers, passengers, and others (Bouard et al., 2013; Yao et al., 2022). ABM can help explore the potential impacts of such attacks by simulating agents' behavior within a virtual environment. For example, researchers could model the behavior of a group of vehicles on a highway and then introduce a simulated cyber-attack that causes some vehicles to malfunction (Bouard et al., 2013; Yao et al., 2022). By observing the resulting behavior patterns among the other vehicles on the road, researchers can gain insights into the potential impact of a real-world attack (Yao et al., 2022).

LACK OF STANDARDIZATION AND INTEROPERABILITY

The lack of standardization and interoperability in cybersecurity in the automotive industry is a significant concern. As vehicles become increasingly connected and autonomous, robust cybersecurity measures are more critical than ever (Bocetta, 2022; Youd, 2022; Yao et al., 2022). One of the primary reasons for this lack of standardization is that the automotive industry needs to be more cohesive, with many different manufacturers, suppliers, and service providers operating independently (Bouard et al., 2013; Ahlsell et al., 2023). This has made it difficult to establish a common set of cybersecurity standards that all stakeholders can agree on and implement. The lack of standardization and interoperability in cybersecurity in the automotive industry is a significant challenge facing the sector today (Ahlsell et al., 2023). As vehicles become more connected and reliant on software, they become more vulnerable to cyber-attacks (Bouard et al., 2013; Youd, 2022; Richell, 2021). Unfortunately, the automotive industry has slowly adopted cybersecurity standards, leaving vehicles and drivers at risk (Ahlsell et al., 2023; Yao et al., 2022).

One of the main challenges is the need for more standardization in cybersecurity protocols and technologies used in different vehicles (Bouard et al., 2013). Each automaker has its own proprietary systems and protocols, making it difficult for third-party cybersecurity vendors to develop practical solutions that work across different vehicle models and brands (Bocetta, 2022; Ahlsell et al., 2023). This fragmentation can lead to vulnerabilities, as hackers can exploit the gaps between different systems (Lonzetta et al., 2018). Another challenge is the complexity of modern vehicles, which have dozens of interconnected systems and components that must all be secured (Bouard et al., 2013; Yao et al., 2022). This requires technical expertise and collaboration across multiple disciplines, including engineering, software development, and cybersecurity. Another area for improvement is the need for interoperability between different systems and components within a vehicle (Bouard et al., 2013). For example, the infotainment system, engine control unit, and other critical components may be developed by different vendors, making it challenging to ensure that they all work seamlessly together without introducing security risks (Bouard et al., 2013). To address these challenges, the automotive industry must prioritize standardization and interoperability in cybersecurity protocols and technologies (Halahan & Chen, 2017; Ahlsell et al., 2023). This can include developing industry-wide standards and guidelines for cybersecurity, such as the ISO 21434 standard for automotive cybersecurity (Ahlsell et al., 2023).

Additionally, automakers must collaborate more closely with third-party cybersecurity vendors to ensure their systems are compatible and effective across different vehicle models and brands (Ahlsell et al., 2023). Overall, the lack of standardization and interoperability in cybersecurity in the automotive industry is a critical issue that needs to be addressed to ensure the safety and security of connected and autonomous vehicles (Ahlsell et al., 2023; Yao et al., 2022). Furthermore, the lack of interoperability between different systems and components can create vulnerabilities that hackers can exploit (Lonzetta et al., 2018). For example, a flaw in one system could allow hackers to access other systems or even the entire vehicle (Ahlsell et al., 2023). In addition, the industry must invest in training and education to build cybersecurity expertise across all relevant disciplines. This will help ensure that all stakeholders understand the importance of cybersecurity and are equipped to identify and mitigate risks (Halahan &

Chen, 2017). Ultimately, the lack of standardization and interoperability in cybersecurity in the automotive industry is a complex challenge that will require a collaborative effort to overcome (Bouard et al., 2013). By working together to establish common standards and protocols and building expertise across all relevant disciplines, the industry can help protect vehicles and drivers from cyber threats (Ahlsell et al., 2023; Nosibor, 2022).

SUPPLY CHAIN RISKS

Supply chain risk factors in the automotive industry are increasingly becoming a connectivity issue, with vehicles relying on many electronic systems and software to operate efficiently (Halahan & Chen, 2017; IGSCP, 2022; LCSCP, 2022; Jankovic-Zugic et al., 2023). This connectivity presents significant opportunities for innovation and efficiency but also creates new risks that must be managed to ensure the safety and security of vehicles and their passengers (IGSCP, 2022; Jankovic-Zugic et al., 2023). Supply chain risks are a particular concern in the auto cybersecurity industry, as a single vulnerability in a component or system can have wide-ranging implications (IGSCP, 2022; Jankovic-Zugic et al., 2023; LCSCP, 2022). The auto cyber security industry is a crucial part of the global automotive sector, and it faces a range of supply chain risks that could impact the security and safety of vehicles (LCSCP, 2022; Jankovic-Zugic et al., 2023). Some of the key risks include:

Table 2. Supply chain risks and mitigating risks in the auto cyber security industry

	Supply Chain Risks	Mitigating Risks in the Auto Cyber Security Industry
1	Third-Party Supplier Risks	The auto cyber security industry relies on third-party suppliers for various components and services, including hardware, software, and cloud services. Any vulnerabilities or security flaws in these components or services could significantly risk the vehicle's overall security.
2	Cyber-Attacks	The auto cyber security industry relies on third-party suppliers for various components and services, including hardware, software, and cloud services. Any vulnerabilities or security flaws in these components or services could significantly risk the vehicle's overall security.
3	Intellectual Property Theft	The auto cyber security industry relies heavily on research and development to create innovative and effective security solutions. Intellectual property theft can result in a loss of competitive advantage, damage to reputation, and potentially compromised security systems.
4	Regulatory Compliance	The auto cyber security industry is subject to a range of regulatory requirements, including those related to data privacy and security. Failure to comply with these requirements can result in significant fines and damage to reputation.
5	Supply Chain Disruptions	Disruptions to the supply chain can occur due to various factors, including natural disasters, political instability, and trade disputes. These disruptions can impact the availability and cost of critical components and services, which can impact the security and safety of vehicles.

In monitoring cyber security vulnerabilities in the auto industry, leaders must evaluate compliance measurements to identify cyber threats (Bouard et al., 2013; Halahan & Chen, 2017; Lonzetta et al., 2018; IGSCP, 2022). The regulatory assessments of cyber threats in the automotive industry contribute to the supply chain risk as parts, and other materials are utilized through electronic digital formats (Bouard et al., 2013; IGSCP, 2022). To mitigate these risks, companies in the auto cyber security industry must implement robust supply chain risk management programs to ensure appropriate inventory distribution systems, which include regular assessments of third-party suppliers, monitoring of cyber threats, and compliance with regulatory requirements (Bouard et al., 2013; Halahan & Chen, 2017; Nosibor, 2022; IGSCP, 2022). Auto manufacturers should also have contingency plans in place to address potential disruptions to the supply chain.

Table 3. Demonstrates monitoring of cyber vulnerabilities in supply chains (Lonzetta et al., 2018; IGSCP, 2022)

	Monitoring of Cyber Vulnerabilities in Supply Chains	Compliance and regulatory assessments of cyber threats
1	Counterfeit components	Counterfeit electronic components are a significant risk in many industries, including the automotive industry. These components may be of inferior quality and may not meet the required specifications, which could lead to malfunctions or vulnerabilities in the vehicle's cybersecurity systems.
2	Malware and other cyber threats	Vehicles become more connected and vulnerable to cyber-attacks such as malware, ransomware, and denial-of-service attacks. These threats can be introduced into the supply chain through infected components or software and can cause significant damage to vehicles and their occupants.
3	Dependence on third-party suppliers	Automotive manufacturers often rely on third-party suppliers for critical components and systems, such as electronic control units (ECUs) and software. If one of these suppliers experiences a security breach or other disruption, it could have a cascading effect on the entire supply chain.
4	Lack of visibility	Automotive manufacturers may need more visibility into their supply chains, making identifying and managing risks difficult. This lack of visibility can be particularly challenging when identifying vulnerabilities in software or other digital components.
5	Regulatory compliance	As the auto cybersecurity industry evolves, many regulations and standards must be met. Failure to comply with these regulations could result in significant penalties and damage the manufacturer's reputation.

To manage these risks, automotive manufacturers must work closely with suppliers to meet cybersecurity and quality standards (Halahan & Chen, 2017; LCSCP, 2022). They should also implement rigorous testing and validation processes to ensure all components and systems function as expected. Finally, manufacturers should prioritize transparency and communication throughout the supply chain to quickly identify and address potential risks (IGSCP, 2022; LCSCP, 2022).

HUMAN ERROR

Human error can occur in the auto cyber industry as requirements increase. Attention to human error is essential as more vehicles are connected to the internet and equipped with advanced technologies. However, with this increased connectivity and complexity, the risk of human error has also grown. Human error can occur at various stages in the auto cyber industry, from design and development to testing, manufacturing, and maintenance.

Table 4. Human error within the cyber-auto industry

	Human Error	Examples within the Cyber-Auto Industry
1	Design and Development	Inadequate cybersecurity measures or poorly designed software can leave vehicles vulnerable to cyber-attacks. This can happen if designers and developers need more training or expertise in cybersecurity.
2	Testing	Software bugs or vulnerabilities may be noticed if testing needs to be more thorough. Testing may be rushed or incomplete if testers are overworked or need more resources.
3	Manufacturing	Errors during manufacturing can result in faulty hardware or software. This can happen if workers need to be adequately trained or production processes are well-controlled.
4	Maintenance	Cybersecurity risks can also arise during vehicle maintenance. For example, if mechanics need to have the necessary knowledge or tools to identify and fix cybersecurity issues, they may inadvertently introduce new vulnerabilities.

With the risk of human error in the auto cyber industry, it is vital to invest in training and education for all stakeholders, including designers, developers, testers, manufacturers, and maintenance personnel (Ahlsell et al., 2023). Human error is necessary as quality control processes must be considered to catch and correct errors before they can cause harm (Halahan & Chen, 2017). Additionally, regulatory bodies can help by establishing industry standards and vehicle cybersecurity requirements. The cyber auto industry, which deals with developing and maintaining software and systems in modern cars, is prone to human error like any other industry involving human work. One of the most significant risks associated with human error in the auto cyber industry is the potential for software bugs or vulnerabilities that cyber attackers can exploit (Halahan & Chen, 2017; Youd, 2022; Ahlsell et al., 2023).

These vulnerabilities can lead to serious safety issues, including accidents or theft of personal data from connected vehicles (Lonzetta et al., 2018; Yao et al., 2022). To mitigate the risk of human error, the auto cyber industry has implemented various best practices and standards for software development and testing, such as the Automotive SPICE framework and ISO 26262 functional safety standard (Lonzetta et al., 2018; Ahlsell et al., 2023). These standards provide guidelines for ensuring that software is developed and tested thoroughly and that potential vulnerabilities are identified and addressed before deployment (Halahan & Chen, 2017). Additionally, the auto cyber industry has also embraced the use of automation tools and artificial intelligence to improve the accuracy and efficiency of software development and testing (Halahan & Chen, 2017). These technologies can reduce the likelihood of human error and improve the overall quality of the software. Despite these efforts, human error can never be eliminated, and it remains a constant risk in the auto cyber industry. To manage this risk, ongoing training and education are critical for developers and other personnel developing and maintaining auto cyber systems (Youd, 2022). This can help to ensure that they are aware of best practices and potential risks and can take appropriate action to address them.

THEORETICAL FRAMEWORK EXPLAINED

Overview of Agent-Based Modeling

The theoretical framework for this study is agent-based modeling (ABM)(Yu & Bagheri, 2021). Agent-based modeling is a helpful tool in the automobile industry as it can be used to simulate and analyze the behavior of agents in complex systems (Ahlsell et al., 2023; Antelmi et al., 2023; Yu & Bagheri, 2021). In automotive cybersecurity, ABM can help identify potential attack scenarios and evaluate the effectiveness of countermeasures (Antelmi et al., 2023; Nikhil et al., 2023). For example, an ABM simulation could model the behavior of attackers and defenders in a network of connected vehicles and infrastructure (Yao et al., 2022). The simulation could also incorporate factors such as the type and severity of vulnerabilities, the skill level of attackers, and the effectiveness of security protocols (Antelmi et al., 2023). Agent-based modeling is a powerful tool that can be used to simulate complex systems and predict their behavior under different conditions (Antelmi et al., 2023; Nikhil et al., 2023). It involves creating agents representing individual entities within a system, such as vehicles or hackers, and defining rules for how they interact with each other and their environment (Antelmi et al., 2023; Yao et al., 2022). By modeling automotive hacking using an agent-based approach, we can better understand the dynamics of this emerging threat and develop more effective countermeasures to protect against it (Nikhil et al., 2023; Nosibor, 2022; Yu & Bagheri, 2021).

This approach involves creating a simulation model that represents the behavior of individual "agents" (e.g., vehicles, hackers, security systems) and then running the simulation to see how these agents interact and how the system behaves (Halahan & Chen, 2017; Nikhil et al., 2023). ABM can also help address the challenge of uncertainty in cybersecurity risk assessment (Antelmi et al., 2023; Yao et al., 2022). By analyzing the interactions between different agents in the automotive cybersecurity ecosystem, researchers can identify strategies to improve security and prevent cyber-attacks (Youd, 2022; DeAngelis & Diaz, 2019). Agent-based modeling is a powerful tool for simulating complex systems, and it can be applied to studying automotive cybersecurity challenges (Antelmi et al., 2023; Nikhil et al., 2023). In this context, an agent-based model can represent the various entities involved in the automotive cybersecurity ecosystem, including the vehicle, its various subsystems, software, sensors, network infrastructure, and potential attackers (Nikhil et al., 2023). The dynamic and constantly evolving nature of cyber threats make it difficult to predict and quantify the likelihood and impact of attacks (Yu & Bagheri, 2021; Nosibor, 2022). ABM can help capture this uncertainty by simulating various scenarios and evaluating the robustness of different cybersecurity strategies (Youd, 2022; DeAngelis & Diaz, 2019). The value of ABM is its ability to model complex systems with many interacting agents. In the case of automotive cybersecurity, this includes the behavior of hackers, the effectiveness of security measures, the response of car owners and manufacturers, and the role of regulators in enforcing security standards (Nikhil et al., 2023).

BENEFITS OF AGENT-BASED MODELING (ABM)

Application of ABM in Complex Organizational Data and Cybersecurity Problems ABM has demonstrated versatility in various fields, including economics, social sciences, and biology. In the context of organizational data and cybersecurity, ABM can provide several advantages:

Data Flow Analysis

ABM allows stakeholders to simulate data flow within the vendor network, identifying potential bottlenecks and areas of data congestion. Understanding data interactions among vendors facilitates data flow optimization.

Cybersecurity Risk Assessment

By incorporating cybersecurity-related behaviors of agents, ABM enables organizations to evaluate cybersecurity risks and vulnerabilities across the vendor network. This aids in the development of robust cybersecurity strategies.

Incident Response Planning

ABM can simulate data breaches or cyber-attacks to assess the organization's ability to respond effectively. This helps refine incident response plans and enhances overall cybersecurity preparedness.

Vendor Network Resilience

ABM can test the resilience of the vendor network against cyber threats and disruptions, allowing organizations to strengthen the network's ability to recover from adverse events.

Policy Validation

ABM allows organizations to assess the effectiveness of data management and cybersecurity policies before their implementation, minimizing potential risks.

Vendor Selection and Evaluation

ABM can evaluate the impact of different vendors on the organization's data management and cybersecurity goals, aiding in informed decision-making when selecting and assessing vendors.

Data Sharing Analysis

ABM simulations can identify opportunities for efficient data sharing between vendors and the organization while minimizing data privacy risks.

Simulations

One of the benefits of ABM is its ability to simulate the effects of different interventions and strategies on a system (Hill et al., 2017). For example, an ABM simulation of a cyberattack on a vehicle could help researchers and policymakers understand how different security measures affect the likelihood and severity of a successful attack. Another benefit of agent-based modeling (ABM) is understanding how different variables interact to produce specific outcomes (Yu & Bagheri, 2021). ABM involves modeling individual agents and their interactions with other agents and the environment. In cybersecurity, ABM can be used to model the behavior of hackers, defenders, and other actors in a cyberattack scenario. Overall, the rise of automotive hacking highlights the need for continued innovation and collaboration in cyber security (Halahan & Chen, 2017; DeAngelis & Diaz, 2019). ABM can be a valuable tool for exploring the potential impacts of cyber-attacks on vehicle systems and identifying effective strategies for mitigating such risks (Halahan & Chen, 2017; Richell, 2021). Cybersecurity is a crucial aspect of our modern society as we increasingly rely on technology for various activities (Bocetta, 2022; Youd, 2022). One of the emerging cybersecurity challenges is the rise of automotive hacking, which involves the exploitation of vulnerabilities in the software and hardware systems of modern vehicles (DeAngelis & Diaz, 2019; Yao et al., 2022). As more vehicles become connected to the internet and rely on complex software systems, the risk of cyberattacks increases (Youd, 2022; Yao et al., 2022). ABM simulations can identify opportunities for efficient data sharing between vendors and the organization while minimizing data privacy risks.

SECURITY MEASURES AND AGENT-BASED MODELING

Agent-based modeling is one approach that can be used to understand better and address these challenges (Bonabeau, 2002; DeAngelis & Diaz, 2019). Security measurements and diversification is other important indicator of ABM's flexibility. The model can simulate different types of attackers (e.g., insiders, outsiders, and state-sponsored actors) and their capabilities. The model can also simulate the responses of the car's security systems and the actions of the car's users (Bouard et al., 2013; Hill, Johansson, Dunkin, & Ingalls, 2017). Researchers can easily modify different parameters and inputs to simulate different scenarios and test the effectiveness of different security measures. This can be done without the need for expensive and time-consuming physical experiments. Using agent-based modeling gives industry manufacturers security measurements that prevent cyber security anomalies (Halahan & Chen, 2017; Yu & Bagheri, 2021). Academic researchers and industry experts can explore scenarios and test various security strategies to identify potential vulnerabilities and develop effective countermeasures. For example, they can simulate a cyber-attack on a connected vehicle network and evaluate how different security measures perform in response to the attack. Agent-based modeling is a technique that simulates agents' behavior within a system (Bonabeau, 2002; DeAngelis & Diaz, 2019). Agents can represent different components of a system, such as people, devices, or software programs (Bonabeau, 2002; Yu & Bagheri, 2021). By modeling the behavior of these agents, it is possible to identify potential vulnerabilities and develop strategies to mitigate them (Hill et al., 2017; Yu & Bagheri, 2021). The key benefits of agent-based modeling are its ability to simulate complex systems. Automotive systems are highly complex, with many interconnected components that can be difficult to analyze using traditional methods (Halahan & Chen, 2017; DeAngelis & Diaz, 2019). Agent-based modeling can be used to simulate the behavior of these components and identify potential vulnerabilities in the system (Bonabeau, 2002). An agent-based model could simulate a cyber-attack on a vehicle's braking system, considering factors such as the type of attack, the vulnerability of the braking system, and the response of the vehicle's software and hardware (Bouard et al., 2013). The model could then evaluate different cybersecurity strategies, such as using secure communication protocols, implementing intrusion detection systems, or increasing employee cybersecurity training.

AUTOMOTIVE HACKING

The rise of automotive hacking highlights the need for robust cybersecurity practices and protocols in the automotive industry (Bouard et al., 2013; Halahan & Chen, 2017). Agent-based modeling can be valuable for understanding and addressing the industry's complex cybersecurity challenges and developing effective strategies to protect vehicles and their occupants (Halahan & Chen, 2017; Ritchell, 2021). Addressing automotive hacking is the sheer complexity of the system (Danielis et al., 2023; Yao et al., 2022). Vehicles are now equipped with a wide range of sensors, processors, and communication channels, all of which must be secured to prevent unauthorized access and manipulation (Halahan & Chen, 2017; Yao et al., 2022). Moreover, the security of these systems must be maintained over the vehicle's lifetime, which can span many years and involve frequent software updates and hardware upgrades. Another challenge is the rapidly evolving nature of the threat landscape (Halahan & Chen, 2017; Nosibor, 2022). Hackers are constantly developing new methods and techniques for exploiting vulnerabilities in connected vehicles, and automakers must be prepared to adapt and respond to these threats in real time (Nosibor, 2022; Yao et al., 2022). In automotive hacking, agent-based modeling can be used to simulate the behavior of hackers and other malicious agents attempting to exploit vulnerabilities in the system (Bouard et al., 2013; Danielis et al., 2023). By analyzing the behavior of these agents, it is possible to identify weaknesses in the system and develop countermeasures to prevent attacks. Hackers can exploit vulnerabilities in electronic control units (ECUs) software and other connected systems to gain control of a vehicle's functions (Bouard et al., 2013). These attacks can be perilous, as hackers can manipulate steering, brakes, and other critical systems, leading to accidents and loss of life. ABM can be used to simulate different scenarios of automotive hacking attacks and the responses of the systems in place to prevent them. ABM can model the behavior of different agents, such as hackers, car owners, manufacturers, and regulators (Bouard et al., 2013; Yu & Bagheri, 2021; Danielis et al., 2023). By creating a virtual environment, researchers can test the effectiveness of different cybersecurity measures and identify potential vulnerabilities.

DATA COLLECTION

The data collected in this investigative study utilized three (3) focus group discussions with four (4) individuals in each group. All twelve (12) work in the following automotive job areas within a plant or dealership:

(d) Systems Engineer (4)
(e) Auto Technician (6)
(f) Software Data Engineer (2)

Each participant has experience working with electronic vehicles for automakers nationwide over the last three (3) years. The study had 12 participants (10 males and two females). The participants comprised eight white males, one black male, and 3 Latino males. The two women were both of Latina descent. Eight participants had undergraduate degrees, two advanced-level master's degrees, and 2 received technical training education through the dealership or automaker. All participants had at least one cybersecurity certification. The goal was to identify possible causes of data breaches from hackers stealing important proprietary data associated with electronic vehicles (Yao et al., 2022). Only two questions were asked to each participant during the investigation to understand the cyber security challenges facing automakers today.

Table 5. Focus group participants (job description, ethnicity, gender, education, years of service, and focus group session).

FOCUS GROUP PARTICIPANTS							
	Job Description	**Ethnicity**	**Gender Male or Female**	**Department**	**Education**	**Years of Service**	**Focus Group**
1	Systems Engineer	White	Male	Tech Data	Undergraduate	11	Group 1
2	Auto Technician	Latina	Female	Fabrication	Trade School	7	Group 1
3	Auto Technician	Black	Male	Production Control	Undergraduate	5	Group 1
4	Software Data Engineer	Latino	Male	Research & Development	Masters	8	Group 1
5	Systems Engineer	White	Male	Research & Development	Undergraduate	9	Group 2
6	Auto Technician	White	Male	Quality Assurance	Undergraduate	10	Group 2
7	Software Data Engineer	White	Male	Research & Development	Masters	4	Group 2
8	Systems Engineer	White	Male	Production Control	Undergraduate	9	Group 2
9	Auto Technician	Latino	Male	Quality Assurance	Trade School	7	Group 3
10	Auto Technician	Latina	Female	Logistics & Parts	Undergraduate	8	Group 3
11	Auto Technician	White	Male	Logistics & Parts	Undergraduate	10	Group 3
12	Systems Engineer	White	Male	Tech Data	Undergraduate	8	Group 3

FINDINGS

Focus Group Analysis

The qualitative interviews addressed the following problem statement questions:

1. What pressures are there for automakers as cyber-attacks continue to increase and pose significant mitigation risks to the auto technology industry?

The participants believed the following challenges from Table 1-4 were the most significant in mitigating cyber security risk.

Question One: Focus Group Participant Concurrence Assessment and Response

Table 1 Assessment.

Table 6. Key cybersecurity challenges facing the automobile industry. Participants' concurrence on cybersecurity challenges.

	Themes and Patterns	Key Cybersecurity Challenges facing the Automobile Industry	Participants' Concurrence on Cybersecurity Challenges
1	Vulnerabilities in the software and hardware of vehicles	Many vehicles today have sophisticated software systems and sensors that make them vulnerable to cyber-attacks. Hackers can exploit these vulnerabilities to take control of the vehicle's systems, causing accidents or stealing personal data.	Participants 1, 4, 5, 7, 8, and 12
2	Lack of standardization and interoperability	The automotive industry lacks standardized cybersecurity protocols and practices, making protecting vehicles and their components from cyber-attacks challenging.	Participants 2, 3, 6, 9, 10, and 11
3	Supply Chain Risks	Cybersecurity risks can also arise from the supply chain, where third-party vendors and suppliers may introduce vulnerabilities in-vehicle hardware and software components.	Participants 2, 3, 6, 9, 10, 11, and 12
4	Human Error	Human error remains a significant cybersecurity risk in the automotive industry. Drivers and employees may inadvertently expose vehicles and systems to cyber-attacks by using weak passwords, sharing login credentials, or failing to install software updates.	All Participants 1-12

Synopsis of Table 6 to Question One:

Some of the critical cyber security challenges in the automotive industry thematically include (1) vulnerabilities in the software and hardware of vehicles, (2) lack of standardization and interoperability, (3) supply chain risks, and (4) human error. The participants agreed that these themes and patterns significantly affect the cyber automotive industry. However, by consensus, human error is the greatest challenge. Vulnerabilities with software and hardware integration were a focal point for systems engineers and auto technicians. Although standardization and operability are still issues for electronic vehicle (EV) technology – Participants 1, 4, 5, 7, 8, and 12 have differing opinions. Based on specific phenomena, cyber security becomes the most significant risk when integration between software and hardware is not adequately assessed.

Table 2 Assessment.

Table 7. Supply chain risks and mitigating risks in the auto cyber security industry. Participants' concurrence on mitigating supply chain (SC) risk.

	Supply Chain Risks	**Mitigating Risks in the Auto Cyber Security Industry**	**Participants' Concurrence on Mitigating SC Risks**
1	Third-Party Supplier Risks	The auto cyber security industry relies on third-party suppliers for various components and services, including hardware, software, and cloud services. Any vulnerabilities or security flaws in these components or services could significantly risk the vehicle's overall security.	Participants 2, 3, 6, 9, 10, and 11 (All Auto Technicians)
2	Cyber-Attacks	The auto cyber security industry relies on third-party suppliers for various components and services, including hardware, software, and cloud services. Any vulnerabilities or security flaws in these components or services could significantly risk the vehicle's overall security.	Participants 1, 5, 8, and 12 (All Systems Engineer)
3	Intellectual Property Theft	The auto cyber security industry relies heavily on research and development to create innovative and effective security solutions. Intellectual property theft can result in a loss of competitive advantage, damage to reputation, and potentially compromised security systems.	Participants 1, 4, 5, 7, 8, and 12
4	Regulatory Compliance	The auto cyber security industry is subject to a range of regulatory requirements, including those related to data privacy and security. Failure to comply with these requirements can result in significant fines and damage to reputation.	Participants 1, 4, 5, 6, 7, 8
5	Supply Chain Disruptions	Disruptions to the supply chain can occur due to various factors, including natural disasters, political instability, and trade disputes. These disruptions can impact the availability and cost of critical components and services, which can impact the security and safety of vehicles.	Participants 2, 3, 6, 9, 10, 11, and 12

Synopsis of Table 7 to Question One:

During the focus group discussion, supply chain disruptions and data privacy in cyber security measurements were key thematic patterns in data breaches. The auto technicians expressed frustrations in distribution channels as lengthy lead items and parts become issues when working with quality assurance agents, especially when electronic technical collaboration is needed for connectivity. When using quality assurance measurements, technicians are required to follow a specific protocol. Unfortunately, when supply chain challenges arise from logistical discrepancies due to an inability to receive parts in time. For example, fabricated parts encompass technological and electrical wires to ensure electronic vehicles can read and display service on the computer display interface within the vehicle. Exposure to open-source code due to inner-connectivity ranges through Bluetooth or wireless communication creates critical component measurements diminishing the ability to secure data. Data breaches occur when the source code is not protected, creating a cyber security challenge for software administrators.

Table 3 Assessment.

Table 8. Demonstrates monitoring of cyber vulnerabilities in supply chains (IGSCP, 2022). Participants' concurrence to monitoring vulnerabilities.

	Monitoring of Cyber Vulnerabilities in Supply Chains	**Compliance and regulatory assessments of cyber threats**	**Participants' Concurrence to Monitoring Vulnerabilities**
1	Counterfeit components	Counterfeit electronic components are a significant risk in many industries, including the automotive industry. These components may be of inferior quality and may not meet the required specifications, which could lead to malfunctions or vulnerabilities in the vehicle's cybersecurity systems.	Participants 1, 4, 7, 8, 9, and 12
2	Malware and other cyber threats	Vehicles become more connected and vulnerable to cyber-attacks such as malware, ransomware, and denial-of-service attacks. These threats can be introduced into the supply chain through infected components or software and can cause significant damage to vehicles and their occupants.	All Participants agreed.
3	Dependence on third-party suppliers	Automotive manufacturers often rely on third-party suppliers for critical components and systems, such as electronic control units (ECUs) and software. If one of these suppliers experiences a security breach or other disruption, it could have a cascading effect on the entire supply chain.	Participants 2, 3, 6, 10, and 12
4	Lack of visibility	Automotive manufacturers may need more visibility into their supply chains, making identifying and managing risks difficult. This lack of visibility can be particularly challenging when identifying vulnerabilities in software or other digital components.	Participants 1-8, 10, and 12
5	Regulatory compliance	As the auto cybersecurity industry evolves, many regulations and standards must be met. Failure to comply with these regulations could result in significant penalties and damage the manufacturer's reputation.	Participants 2, 4, 6, 9, 10, and 11

Synopsis of Table 8 to Question One:

Participants were very concerned with the regulatory compliance issues and challenges during this session. All participants except for three individuals believed in "fear of making mistakes, almost being anal to the point to ensure competency without failure." All expressed that the job is rewarding. The compensation is beneficial. However, all experience tremendous pressure to perform as data vulnerabilities increase with each implementation of information technology migration to current operational systems. Another critical cause of data vulnerabilities with risk to hackers is increased pressure to meet production deadlines. Some individuals expressed reluctance to move faster for fear of syntax errors to code or providing open-source algorithms that create vulnerable spaces within the system, which cause data breaches. The data breaches often occur during system downloads when personnel leaves and Technology Analysts are upgrading or migrating the system to the following software application version. Hackers key in on finding the data anomaly in the code and a breach by distributing dangerous malware that enables data to be stolen. Some participants believed China and other countries are known for Data Hacking are responsible for these risks as they try to compete in a global economy where electronic vehicles (EVs) are the future. The issue and challenge are which automaker will get the most significant piece of the economic pie when consumers transition to electronic vehicles.

Table 4 Assessment.

Table 9. Human error within the cyber auto industry. Participants concurrence of examples within the cyber auto industry.

	Human Error	Examples within the Cyber-Auto Industry	Participants' Concurrence of Examples within the Cyber Auto Industry
1	Design and Development	Inadequate cybersecurity measures or poorly designed software can leave vehicles vulnerable to cyber-attacks. This can happen if designers and developers need more training or expertise in cybersecurity.	All participants agreed on 1-12.
2	Testing	Software bugs or vulnerabilities may be noticed if testing needs to be more thorough. Testing may be rushed or incomplete if testers are overworked or need more resources.	All participants agreed on 1-12.
3	Manufacturing	Errors during manufacturing can result in faulty hardware or software. This can happen if workers need to be adequately trained or production processes are well-controlled.	All the Auto Technicians agreed.
4	Maintenance	Cybersecurity risks can also arise during vehicle maintenance. For example, if mechanics need to have the necessary knowledge or tools to identify and fix cybersecurity issues, they may inadvertently introduce new vulnerabilities.	Participants 1, 2, 3, 7, 9, 10, and 12

Synopsis of Table 9 to Question One:

The concept of human error was an attractive focal point in the cyber-auto industry. During the focus group discussion, participants measured (1) design and development, (2) testing, (3) manufacturing, and (4) maintenance. The software engineers' most significant concern was design, development, and maintenance upgrades in the automotive internal operating system. Human error occurs when there are vulnerabilities. During were very concerned with the regulatory compliance issues and challenges. The data breaches often occur during system downloads when personnel leaves and technology analysts are upgrading or migrating the system to the next version of the software application. Hackers key in on finding the data anomaly in the code and a breach by distributing dangerous malware that enables data to be stolen. The human error becomes a primary issue when some key personnel forgets to access critical cards and leave computers without signing off the intranet operating system. These human errors with personnel not utilizing VPN access; instead of opening unsecured network sources.

2. How can cybersecurity analysts and automakers work together to mitigate system vulnerabilities and anomalies contributing to cyber auto security risk and outcomes in the industry?

Table 10. Mitigation of system vulnerabilities and anomalies contributing to cyber auto security risk and outcomes. Correlations between cyber security analysts and automakers.

Mitigation of System Vulnerabilities and Anomalies contributing to cyber auto security risk and outcomes	
Cybersecurity Analysts	**Automakers**
Develop a security infrastructure	Develop a security infrastructure measuring cost, quality, and delivery
Formulate agency-based modeling	Create agent-based modeling methodology and techniques that identify and store vulnerabilities.
Avoid system hacking through reset Algorithms and Data Storage with Key Codes and Passwords.	Develop internal software that depicts security anomalies and breaches when false data storage, key codes, and passwords are used.

Synopsis of Table 10 to Question Two:

All participants believed that to provide better quality assurance measurements Cybersecurity Professionals (Analysts, Software Engineers, Technicians, etc.) must work with Automakers to help leadership understand potential risks before development. Production mitigation risks occur when proper initiatives must be streamlined or forecasted before moving the product to the development phase. The contents of these developments must occur in the embryonic (introduction), implementation, development, and production phase of electronic vehicle mass production. Since the software has a higher risk of volatility to process improvements, 7 out of the 12 participants believed initial planning team (IPT) meetings to be essential in understanding the scope of software feeds to alleviate potential hacking into the mainframe of the software engineering process and also, establishing specific deliverables at each stage of development. However, all participants stated that the deliverables must be achievable. Often leadership enacts initiatives that need to be more forward-thinking with knowledge of how the requirement may be implemented (Danielis et al., 2023). Finally, setting reasonable milestones to incorporate (goal-setting initiatives) that impact the next stage of development (Danielis et al., 2023). While determining that the new process initiative will move forward once the present initiative is completed first. However, quality assurance measurements are paramount to the auto manufacturing process. Often deviations occur when leadership sets production quotas knowing that software integration electronic vehicles are impacted due to unexplained risks (Bouard et al., 2013; Ahlsell et al., 2023).

INSURANCE AND WARRANTY WITH ELECTRONIC VEHICLES

In The Cyber Security Space

The rise of electronic vehicles (EVs) has led to significant changes in the auto industry. Along with benefits such as reduced dependency on fossil fuels, improved fuel efficiency, and lower emissions (Sripad et al., 2017). However, there are challenges that EVs pose. One of those challenges is cybersecurity. As EVs become more connected and rely more on software and data, they become vulnerable to cyberattacks. This poses significant challenges for the insurance and warranty industries (Sripad et al., 2017). Insuring EVs is already complicated due to the unique nature of the technology. However, cyber threats introduce a new level of complexity. Insurance companies must consider the risk of cyberattacks and their potential consequences, including damage to the vehicle, data breaches, and even physical harm to drivers and passengers (Guo et al., 2021). The costs associated with these risks could be astronomical, and it is still being determined who would ultimately bear them (Balboni, Botsi, Francis, & Barata, 2020).

Moreover, warranty providers face a similar challenge. Parts and systems within EVs rely significantly on software and can be prone to cyber threats, which can trigger costly warranty claims. Therefore, warranty providers must be prepared to handle software-related claims and develop solutions to mitigate the risks of future claims.

Agent-based modeling in relationship to electronic vehicles is a powerful tool that can be used to simulate complex systems and analyze how different variables will affect the outcomes of insurance and warranties (Balboni et al., 2020). In the case of auto insurance and warranties, agent-based modeling can be used to understand how different policies and claims will affect the overall profitability of an insurance company. The process must define variables relevant to the modeled system within the cybersecurity insurance and warranty sector. These variables might include the type of vehicle being insured, the age and driving record of the individual driver, the location of the driver, and the type of insurance policy or warranty being offered (MacLennan et al., 2008). Once these variables are defined, an opportunity to create simulations using agent-based modeling is provided (Bonabeau, 2002). In this simulation, several "agents" represent different types of drivers with different characteristics (Hill et al., 2017). These agents interact with one another and with a simulated insurance company, making claims on their policies and engaging in other behaviors that impact the system (Bonabeau, 2002). As the simulation runs, the data is analyzed to understand how different policies and claims impact the insurance company's profitability. For example, certain types of policies may be more profitable in specific locations or for certain types of drivers, or certain types of claims are more expensive to process than others.

Using agent-based modeling to simulate the auto insurance and warranty system, individuals can gain valuable insights to help insurance companies optimize their policies and improve their profitability (Bonabeau, 2002). This approach represents an innovative and effective way to approach complex systems such as insurance and warranties and highlights the power of computational methods in modern data-driven decision-making. An auto warranty is a contract providing vehicle ownership protection against repair costs due to mechanical failure or breakdowns. However, with technology integration, modern cars now have sophisticated computer systems vulnerable to cyber-attacks. Cybersecurity threats can compromise the safety and performance of the vehicle and put the driver and passengers at risk. Thus, modern auto warranties now include coverage for cybersecurity-related issues. This coverage may provide protection against the cost of repairs, recovery of lost data or stolen identity, and other expenses related to cyber-attacks on your car. It is essential for vehicle owners to know the specifics of their warranty and whether cybersecurity is included in it to ensure they are adequately protected.

In conclusion, cybersecurity challenges remain a crucial concern for the future of electric vehicles. Insurers and warranty providers need to prepare for the risks associated with cyber threats and develop solutions to mitigate them. This will require collaboration among regulators, automakers, insurers, and warranty providers. Only then can we enjoy the benefits of technological breakthroughs without sacrificing our safety and security.

CONCLUSION

In conclusion, the rise of automotive hacking poses significant cybersecurity challenges for the automotive industry (Bouard et al., 2013; Ahlsell et al., 2023). Agent-based modeling is a promising approach to understanding and addressing these challenges. ABM can help capture the complexity and uncertainty of automotive cybersecurity and provide insights into potential attack scenarios and the effectiveness of countermeasures (Ahlsell et al., 2023). One of the main challenges in securing automobiles is the complexity of their electronic systems. Automotive hacking is a serious concern for the automotive industry and society (Bouard et al., 2013; Bouard et al., 2013; Danielis et al., 2023). Agent-based modeling provides a powerful tool for understanding and addressing this challenge, but it is only one part of a comprehensive approach to cybersecurity that must also include robust testing, continuous monitoring, and rapid response capabilities (Danielis et al., 2023).

One of the keys to the study's findings is understanding the role of the supply chains affecting cybersecurity risks. As auto manufacturers develop technology, technical manuals are often included with technical data used to manipulate software drivers (Bo, Xiaochen, & Yue, 2021). For example, if the technical manual display monitor provides data based on specific pressurized systems, the contents can be manipulated for personal use (Gkatsi, Vogt-Ardatjew, & Leferink, 2022). The Iron-Triangle Strategy Formation application to automakers attempting to resolve a growing challenge addresses three core planning strategies (Rathnakumara & Chandanie, 2022; Dieterich, Spath, & Ohlhausen, 2022):

Figure 1. The iron-triangle strategy formation
(Dieterich, Spath, & Ohlhausen, 2022).

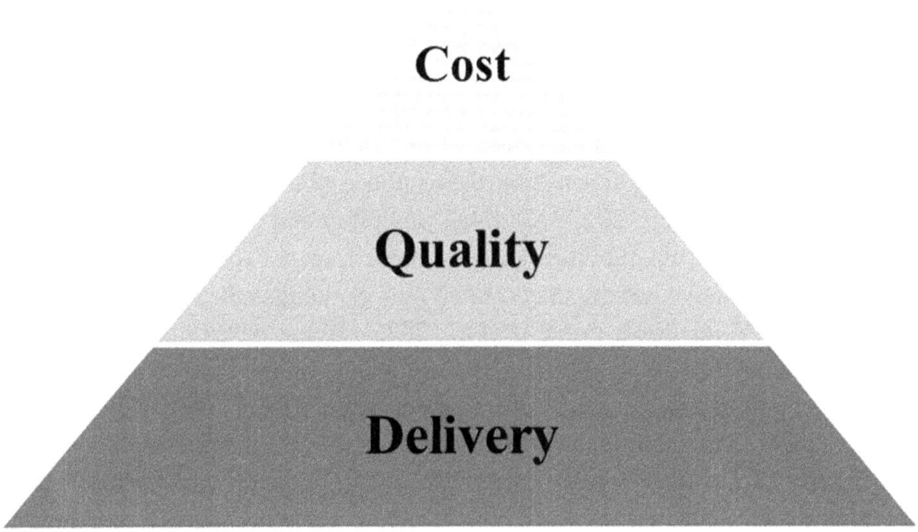

Table 11.

Strategy Factors	Strategy Formation and Description to Automakers needing to mitigate risk challenges of Electronic Vehicle (EV) Technology
Cost	Automakers must be willing to invest in the appropriate software applications to ensure data safety and security; Also, an emphasis on Data Administrators and Security Analysts to re-program and re-structure access points into the data privacy notification; Ensure limited individuals have access to secure data that could potentially cause rogue entities an access point for entry into the organization' software system.
Quality	Ensure Quality Assurance Representatives are supplied with the appropriate Quality Metrics (whether using Six Sigma, ISO 9000, ISO 9001, etc.) for improved service – through proper metric systems focused on deliverables and milestones at different phases of the auto development and production process.
Delivery	Provide production data to ensure the delivery of the software is not met with data anomalies or data redundancy in the code; proper use of technical manuals without providing consumers with unnecessary proprietary data to alleviate Data Hackers from determining entry data points within the automakers' mainframe and computer interface system.

The following areas require further exploration and investigation within the cyber automotive industry.

Table 12. Areas of exploration and cyber-automotive industry measurements

	Areas of Exploration	Cyber-Automotive Industry Measurements
1	Complexity	Modern vehicles are highly complex, with multiple interconnected systems and components. This complexity makes it challenging to identify and mitigate vulnerabilities.
2	Lack of Standards	There are currently no widely accepted standards for cybersecurity in the automotive industry. This lack of standards can make it challenging for manufacturers to ensure their vehicles are secure.
3	Human Factors	Many cybersecurity breaches are caused by human error, such as employees using weak passwords or failing to install software updates.
4	Rapidly evolving threats	The cybersecurity landscape is constantly evolving, with new threats emerging regularly. This requires manufacturers and policymakers to remain vigilant and adapt to new threats.

Furthermore, agent-based modeling is a powerful tool that can be used to simulate and test different scenarios of automotive hacking attacks and the response of the systems in place to prevent them (Ahlsell et al., 2023; Yu & Bagheri, 2021). With the flexibility and adaptability of ABM, researchers can quickly identify potential vulnerabilities and develop effective cybersecurity measures to protect against cyberattacks. Automotive hacking has created new challenges for cybersecurity experts (Bo et al., 2021; Bocetta, 2022; Youd, 2022; Danielis et al., 2023). Agent-based modeling is a valuable tool that can be used to simulate and analyze agents' behavior in complex systems such as those found in the automotive industry (Dieterich et al., 2022; Danielis et al., 2023). This technique makes it possible to identify potential vulnerabilities and develop mitigation strategies. Automotive cyber security requires stakeholder collaboration (Danielis et al., 2023). To effectively mitigate cyber security risks, manufacturers, government agencies, and other organizations must work together to identify and address vulnerabilities in-vehicle systems (Ahlsell et al., 2023; Youd, 2022; Gkatsi et al., 2022; Danielis et al., 2023). ABM can help explore the potential outcomes of different collaborative strategies, such as creating public-private partnerships or developing shared standards for cybersecurity practices (Danielis et al., 2023). The rise of automotive hacking presents significant cybersecurity challenges, but agent-based modeling can be a valuable tool for understanding and mitigating these risks (DeAngelis & Diaz, 2019; Youd, 2022; Gkatsi et al., 2022; Danielis et al., 2023). By modeling the behavior of different actors in a cyberattack scenario, ABM can help researchers and policymakers identify vulnerabilities and develop effective security strategies (Danielis et al., 2023).

REFERENCES

A. M. Cope, P., Campbell, J., Mohd, B. J., & Hayajneh, T. (2018). Security Vulnerabilities in Bluetooth Technology as Used in IoT. *Journal of Sensor and Actuator Networks, 7*(3) Lonzetta

Ahlsell, L., Jalal, D., Khajavi, S. H., Jonsson, P., & Holmström, J. (2023). Additive Manufacturing of Slow-Moving Automotive Spare Parts: A Supply Chain Cost Assessment. *Journal of Manufacturing and Materials Processing*, *7*(1), 8. doi:10.3390/jmmp7010008

Antelmi, A., Cordasco, G., D'Ambrosio, G., De Vinco, D., & Spagnuolo, C. (2023). Experimenting with Agent-Based Model Simulation Tools. *Applied Sciences (Basel, Switzerland)*, *13*(1), 13. doi:10.3390/app13010013

Balboni, P. E., Botsi, A., Francis, K., & Barata, M. T. (2020). *Designing Connected and Automated Vehicles around Legal and Ethical Concerns: Data Protection as a Corporate Social Responsibility.* SETN Workshops.

Blum, B. (24 Feb 2022). Cyberattacks on Cars increased by 225% in the last three years. *Innovation. Israel21c.* https://www.israel21c.org/cyberattacks-on-cars-increased-225-in-last-three-years/

Bo, L., Xiaochen, W., & Yue, F. (2021). Research on the functional safety of drive motor systems for the electric vehicle. *2021 International Conference on Artificial Intelligence and Electromechanical Automation (AIEA)*, (pp. 84–87). IEEE. 10.1109/AIEA53260.2021.00025

Bocetta, S. (14 Nov 2022). *The Risk of Cybersecurity Threats continues to grow for the Auto Industry.* GlobalSign by GMO. https://www.globalsign.com/en/blog/cybersecurity-threats-auto-industry

Bonabeau, E. (2002). Agent-based modeling: Methods and techniques for simulating human systems. *Proceedings of the National Academy of Sciences of the United States of America*, *99*(suppl_3), 7280–7287. doi:10.1073/pnas.082080899 PMID:12011407

Bouard, A., Burgkhardt, D., & Eckert, C. (2013). Middleware-based Security for Hyperconnected Applications in Future In-Car Networks. *ICST Transactions on Mobile Communications and Applications*, *1*(3), e7. doi:10.4108/mca.1.3.e7

Burkacky, O., Deichmann, J., Klein, B., Pototsky, K., & Gundbert, S. (March 2020). *Cybersecurity in automotive.* McKinsey & Company.

Danielis, R., Scorrano, M., Alessandro, M. P., & Blasuttigh, N. (2023). Simulating the Diffusion of Residential Rooftop Photovoltaic, Battery Storage Systems and Electric Cars in Italy. An Exploratory Study Combining a Discrete Choice and Agent-Based Modelling Approach. *Energies*, *16*(1), 557. doi:10.3390/en16010557

DeAngelis, D. L., & Diaz, S. G. (2019). Decision-Making in Agent-Based Modeling: A Current Review and Future Prospectus. *Frontiers in Ecology and Evolution*, *6*, 237. doi:10.3389/fevo.2018.00237

Dieterich, K. R., Spath, D., & Ohlhausen, P. (2022). The Collaborative Iron Triangle: A New Tool for Supporting a Project-Culture-Aware Management in Interorganizational R&D Projects. *Proceedings of the Design Society*, *2*, 141–150. doi:10.1017/pds.2022.15

Gkatsi, V., Vogt-Ardatjew, R., & Leferink, F. (2022). Evaluation of EM Vehicle Environment Measurement Methods for Risk-Based EMC Analysis. *2022 ESA Workshop on Aerospace EMC (Aerospace EMC)*, (pp. 1-6). IEEE. 10.23919/AerospaceEMC54301.2022.9828833

Guo, L., Yang, B., Ye, J., Velni, J. M., & Song, W. (2021). Attack-Resilient Lateral Stability Control for Four-Wheel-Driven EVs Considering Changed Driver Behavior Under Cyber Threats. *IEEE Transactions on Transportation Electrification*, *8*(1), 1362–1375. doi:10.1109/TTE.2021.3102134

Halahan, J., & Chen, W. (2017). Wireless Security Within New Model Vehicles. *Journal of Information Warfare*, *16*(3), 51–62. https://www.proquest.com/scholarly-journals/wireless-security-within-new-model-vehicles/docview/1968021066/se-2

Hamadneh, J., & Esztergar-Kiss, D. (2022). Evaluation of the impacts of autonomous vehicles on the mobility of user groups by using agent-based simulation. *Transport*, *37*(1), 1–16. doi:10.3846/transport.2022.16322

Hill, R. R., Johansson, B., Dunkin, A., & Ingalls, R. G. (2017). Agent-Based Modeling and Simulation. Encyclopedia of Machine Learning and Data Mining.

Jankovic-Zugic, A., Medic, N., Pavlovic, M., Todorovic, T., & Rakic, S. (2023). Servitization 4.0 as a Trigger for Sustainable Business: Evidence from Automotive Digital Supply Chain. *Sustainability (Basel)*, *15*(3), 2217. doi:10.3390u15032217

Kingston, B. (2023, February 28). *Building A North American Electric Vehicle Supply Chain*. brookings.edu. https://www.brookings.edu/articles/building-a-north-american-electric-vehicle-supply-chain/#:~:text=Automakers%20worldwide%20are%20committing%20an,from%20only%20one%20year%20ago

Latest challenges in supply chain management in the automotive industry (LCSCM). (2022). International Tax Review (ITR). https://www.proquest.com/scholarly-journals/latest-challenges-supply-chain-management/docview/2717541807/se-2

MacLennan, P. A., Marshall, T., Griffin, R., Purcell, M., Mcgwin, G. J., & Rue, L. W. (2008). Vehicle rollover risk and electronic stability control systems. *Injury Prevention*, *14*(3), 154–158. doi:10.1136/ip.2007.016576 PMID:18523106

Mircea, M., Croitorescu, V., & Oprean, M. (2016). Implementing New IT Security Solutions in Automotive Immobilizer Systems. *Applied Mechanics and Materials*, *822*, 354–359. . doi:10.4028/www.scientific.net/AMM.822.354

Nikhil, K. B., Fernandes, R., Rodrigues, A. P., Mahmud, M., Vijaya, P., Thippa, R. G., & Kaiser, M. S. (2023). TAKEN: A Traffic Knowledge-Based Navigation System for Connected and Autonomous Vehicles. *Sensors (Basel)*, *23*(2), 653. doi:10.339023020653 PMID:36679448

Nosibor, D. (5 July 2022). Automotive industry races against cybersecurity threats. *Security Magazine*. https://www.securitymagazine.com/articles/97932-automotive-industry-races-against-cybersecurity-threats

Rathnakumara, L., & Chandanie, H. (2022). Beyond the iron triangle: Accommodating sustainable construction in the new-normal conditions. *Proceedings of 10th World Construction Symposium 2022*. University of Moratowa. 10.31705/WCS.2022.14

Richell, R. (2021). The Rise of Cyber-Attacks in the Automotive Industry. *US Cyber security*. https://www.uscybersecurity.net/automotive-industry/

Security Compass. (2019). Cyber Security Challenges in the Automotive Industry. *Security Compass.* https://www.securitycompass.com/wp-content/uploads/cybersecurity-challenges-in-the-automotive-industry.pdf

Sripad, S., Kulandaivel, S., Pande, V., Sekar, V., & Viswanathan, V. (2017). Vulnerabilities of Electric Vehicle Battery Packs to Cyberattacks on Auxiliary Components. *ArXiv, abs/1711.04822*.

Wan, T., & Wang, Y. (2022). The Hazards of Electric Car Batteries and Their Recycling. *IOP Conference Series. Earth and Environmental Science*, *1011*(1), 012026. doi:10.1088/1755-1315/1011/1/012026

Yao, C., Ma, X., Hu, T., & Gu, X. (2022). A Game Theory Approach in Quality Classification and Secondary Use of Electric Vehicle Used Batteries. *Journal of Physics: Conference Series*, *2224*(1), 012138. doi:10.1088/1742-6596/2224/1/012138

Youd, F. (11 May 2022). Cybersecurity is a growing threat for the Automotive Industry. *just Auto*. https://www.just-auto.com/interview/cybersecurity-a-growing-threat-for-the-automotive-industry/

Yu, J. S., & Bagheri, N. (2021). Agent-Based Modeling. *Systems Medicine (New Rochelle, N.Y.)*.

Chapter 9
Exploring Violence Against Women as a Dire Social Justice Issue in Need of More Education, Priority, and Intervention

Grace McGrath
Marymount University, USA

ABSTRACT

This chapter explores "violence against women" as a social justice and public health issue. Violence against women is a form of discrimination and inequality that violates human rights. It is a gross violation of a person's right to life, liberty, and security, and is one of the most pervasive human rights issues in the United States. It disproportionately affects women of color, LGBTQ+ individuals, and other marginalized communities, often in more extreme and dangerous forms. It is a public health issue, as it can cause physical and psychological harm to victims and lead to long-term health problems, such as depression and anxiety. It can cause economic hardship for victims, as domestic violence and sexual assault often result in job loss, missed work days, and decreased productivity. Violence against women is a safety issue, as it can lead to increased fear and insecurity in public spaces, making it difficult for women to access services, work, and participate in public life. This chapter explores the topic through a review of current and emerging literature.

INTRODUCTION

Gender equity refers to fairness and justice in treating all genders. This includes the notion that all genders should have the same opportunities, rights, and resources, regardless of gender identity or expression. In the United States, gender equity is still far from being achieved. Gender stereotypes can contribute to gender inequity by limiting women's potential and their access to opportunities. This can be seen

DOI: 10.4018/979-8-3693-1634-4.ch009

through the pay gap and the lack of female representation in specific fields (Swim et al., 2017). Women are also paid less than men for equal work and are more likely to face gender-based discrimination in the workplace. Women in the United States are more likely to live in poverty than men and have less access to economic resources. This can lead to an overall lack of financial security and a decreased ability to access essential services, such as education and healthcare (Sisson, 2014).

Violence against women is a form of gender-based violence that disproportionately affects women and girls. It includes physical, sexual, and psychological abuse and economic and social coercion. According to the Centers for Disease Control and Prevention (CDC), one in three women will experience physical violence by an intimate partner in their lifetime. In addition, one in five women will experience sexual violence in their lifetime (CDC, 2023). These statistics underscore the need for more effective strategies to address the issue of violence against women.

Gender equity refers to the equitable treatment of men and women and the promotion of fairness in distributing power and resources. The United States has taken several steps to ensure gender equity, including the passage of the Equal Pay Act of 1963, Title IX of the Education Amendments of 1972, and the Family and Medical Leave Act of 1993 (U.S. Department of Labor, 2020). These laws have sought to address the wage gap between men and women, ensure equal access to education, and provide family and medical leave. Despite these efforts, gender inequity persists in the United States. A 2020 report from the Institute for Women's Policy Research found that women earned 82 cents for every dollar earned by men, and women of color earned even less (Institute for Women's Policy Research, 2020).

Additionally, women are still underrepresented in specific industries, such as STEM fields and positions of leadership. These inequities have led to several social and economic issues, including poverty and lack of access to resources. Violence against women is a pervasive issue in the United States and worldwide. It includes physical, sexual, and psychological violence (World Health Organization, 2019). According to the National Coalition Against Domestic Violence, 1 in 3 women in the United States have experienced physical violence from an intimate partner, and 1 in 5 women have experienced sexual violence (National Coalition Against Domestic Violence, 2020). Additionally, the U.S. Department of Justice reports that 1 in 4 college women have experienced some form of sexual violence (U.S. Department of Justice, 2019). This violence can occur in the home, while out in the world, and while going to school.

Underlying Causes of Gender Equity and Violence Against Women

The underlying causes of gender equity and violence against women are complex and multifaceted. One of the major causes of these issues is the persistence of gender stereotypes and gender roles in society. These gender roles are often reinforced through media, culture, and education, and they can limit opportunities for women and girls. Additionally, gender-based violence is often rooted in power imbalances between men and women and the notion that women and girls are not equal to men and boys. These beliefs can lead to the perpetration of violence against women, as well as other forms of gender-based discrimination.

Violence against women is a form of gender-based violence that occurs in both public and private spheres and is often an expression of power and dominance over women. This paper will discuss violence against women, its prevalence, and the various forms it takes. It will also explore the causes and consequences of violence against women and discuss the current strategies and initiatives taken to address this issue. The United Nations defines violence against women as "any act of gender-based violence that results in or is likely to result in physical, sexual, or psychological harm or suffering to women, including threats of such acts, coercion or arbitrary deprivation of liberty, whether occurring in public or private life" (U.N., 2016). This broad definition encompasses various actions, including physical, sexual, and psychological violence and economic and social control. The prevalence of violence against women is a global phenomenon that affects women of all ages, races, and socio-economic backgrounds. The World Health Organization (WHO) estimates that one in three women worldwide has experienced physical or sexual violence from an intimate partner or sexual violence by a non-partner at some point in their lives (WHO, 2019).

Additionally, the WHO estimates that up to 70% of women have experienced physical and/or sexual violence from an intimate partner in some countries (WHO, 2019). Forms of Violence Against Women Violence against women can take various forms, including physical, sexual, and psychological abuse. Physical abuse includes hitting, kicking, slapping, burning, choking, and using weapons. Sexual abuse includes rape, sexual assault, and forced marriage. Psychological abuse includes verbal abuse, intimidation, controlling behavior, and isolation.

Additionally, violence against women can take the form of economic abuse, using economic resources to control and restrict women's autonomy and freedom (U.N. Women, 2019). Causes of Violence Against Women numerous factors contribute to violence against women, including social, economic, and cultural factors. Social factors such as gender inequality, traditional gender roles, and gender stereotypes can perpetuate violence against women.

Problem Statement

Physical violence against women can lead to various physical injuries, including bruises, broken bones, and even death in extreme cases. In addition to the physical pain and suffering caused by violence, financial costs are associated with medical treatment and lost wages due to injury or death. According to a study conducted by the World Bank, the medical costs associated with treating physical injuries due to violence against women in the United States alone were estimated to be $4.1 billion in 2013 (Lane et al., 2018). In addition to the direct medical costs, indirect costs are associated with violence against women, such as lost productivity and increased healthcare utilization.

For example, a study conducted in India found that women who had experienced intimate partner violence were more likely to seek medical care, particularly reproductive health care, than women who had not experienced violence (Uthman et al., 2019). This suggests that violence against women can lead to increased healthcare costs for individuals and families and costs to society in the form of lost productivity. This study explores the complex nature of violence against women and looks for practical solutions from current and previous research.

Significance of the Paper

In addition to physical costs, violence against women also has psychological costs. The most common psychological consequence of violence against women is post-traumatic stress disorder (PTSD). PTSD can cause various symptoms, including intrusive thoughts, flashbacks, nightmares, and difficulty concentrating (McFarlane, 2011). These symptoms can lead to decreased quality of life, including poor academic performance, difficulty maintaining relationships, and social isolation (McFarlane, 2011). In addition to the psychological costs, there are also economic costs associated with PTSD. For example, a study by the National Institute of Mental Health found that the economic cost of PTSD treatment in the United States alone was estimated to be $3.3 billion in 2013 (Lane et al., 2018). This suggests that violence against women has physical, psychological, and economic costs. Economic Costs of Violence Against Women In addition to physical and psychological costs, violence against women also has economic costs. These costs include direct costs, such as medical expenses and lost wages due to injury or death, and indirect costs, such as lost productivity and increased healthcare utilization. For example, a study conducted in the United States found that women who had experienced intimate partner violence were more likely to miss work, resulting in an estimated loss of $1.8 billion in wages annually (Lane et al., 2018). In addition to direct and indirect costs, violence against women also has societal costs. These costs include costs associated with interventions to address violence against women, such as providing legal services, counseling, and shelter services. According to a United Nations Development Program report, the estimated global cost of providing such services was approximately $3.3 billion in 2017 (UNDP, 2017). This suggests that violence against women is a severe issue with high costs to individuals, families, communities, and society in ways with lasting impacts.

Theories From the Literature

Attachment Theory suggests that individuals who have experienced violence are more likely to have difficulty forming secure attachments with people in their lives (Sroufe, 1990).

Complex Trauma Theory suggests that individuals who experience or witness violence may develop psychological, behavioral, and physical problems (Van der Kolk, 2005).

Adverse Childhood Experiences Theory suggests that individuals who have experienced violence in childhood are more likely to suffer from psychological and physical problems in adulthood (Felitti et al., 1998).

Trauma Theory explains that trauma results from a person's inability to cope with the overwhelming emotions that arise from a traumatic experience (Kleim & Ehlers, 2008). According to this theory, the traumatic events experienced by women are stored in the body and can be triggered by reminders of the original experience. This can lead to re-experiencing the trauma and distress that may accompany physical and psychological symptoms (Kleim & Ehlers, 2008).

Biological/Neurobiological Theory explains that trauma affects the body's physiology and can cause changes in the brain that can lead to emotional and behavioral disturbances (McFarlane, 2011). It suggests that trauma can cause changes in the brain that can lead to a disruption in the functioning of the nervous system (McFarlane, 2011). This can lead to women experiencing symptoms such as depression, anxiety, and PTSD.

Social-Ecological Theory (Sameroff, 2010) suggests that individuals, families, and communities are all connected and influence each other, and that violence has ripple effects on each of these systems. It suggests that social conditions, such as poverty, racism, and discrimination, create environments in which violence is more likely to occur and that interventions should target each level of the social system to have the most impact on reducing violence. Social-Ecological Theory proposes that community education can be used to address violence against women by creating an environment that supports and encourages healthy relationships, as well as providing resources and education to help people better understand and address the issue (Sameroff, 2010)

The Theory of Gender and Power (TGP) proposes that gender roles in society are based on the power dynamics between men and women and that violence against women results from this power imbalance (Lombard, 2016). TGP proposes that community education can be used to address violence against women by helping to create a community in which both men and women are seen as equal, which would reduce the likelihood of violence occurring (Lombard, 2016).

Impact of Violence Against Women

In addition to the costs associated with violence against women, it is also essential to consider the impact of violence on the lives of victims and their families. Violence's physical, psychological, and economic costs can devastate individuals, families, and communities. For example, research has shown that violence against women can lead to various physical and psychological health problems, such as depression, anxiety, and post-traumatic stress disorder (PTSD) (Uthman et al., 2019). In addition, violence against women can lead to reduced quality of life, including poorer academic performance, difficulty maintaining relationships, and social isolation.

Violence against women disproportionately impacts women of color, as they are more likely to experience violence and face additional barriers to safety and justice (Matsumoto, 2020). African American women, in particular, experience higher levels of intimate partner violence than any other racial group in the U.S. (Lacy, 2017). Additionally, Native American and Alaska Native women are two and a half times more likely to be raped or assaulted than other races (U.S. Department of Justice, 2019). Furthermore, Latina and Asian American women are more likely to experience sexual violence than any other racial group (Lacy, 2017). Women of color also experience higher rates of economic insecurity and poverty, lack of access to health care, and inadequate education, leading to increased violence vulnerability (Matsumoto, 2020). The impact of violence and abuse on women of color is compounded by racial discrimination and oppression. Women of color often face greater mistrust and skepticism from law enforcement, making them hesitant to report violent crimes (Lacy, 2017).

Moreover, many of these women are unfamiliar with the legal system and lack access to legal resources (Matsumoto, 2020). Language barriers can also prevent women of color from seeking help or justice, as can stereotypes and cultural stigma (Lacy, 2017). Overall, violence against women significantly impacts women of color due to a greater risk of violence and fewer resources for dealing with it. Victims of color are more likely to experience abuse and less likely to receive appropriate assistance, leading to significant emotional, physical, and economic consequences.

Violence against women can be a form of violence that directly or indirectly impacts LGBTQ+ individuals. LGBTQ+ individuals, especially those who identify as transgender, are particularly at risk of experiencing violence due to their gender, sexual, or gender identity expression (Ristock, 2013). Research has found that transgender individuals are more likely to experience intimate partner violence, sexual violence, and stalking than cisgender individuals, as well as higher levels of physical and psychological abuse (Ristock, 2013). Additionally, transgender individuals may face increased vulnerability to violence due to their identity being challenged by those who do not respect or accept their gender expression or identity (Meschede et al., 2014). As such, violence against women can, directly and indirectly, impact LGBTQ+ individuals, making them more vulnerable to violence and abuse.

The generational impact of violence against women in the United States is widespread and devastating. Studies have shown that survivors of violence often pass on the psychological, physical, and emotional trauma of abuse to their children, which can lead to a cycle of violence across generations (Wong, 2016). Experiencing or witnessing violence in the home can lead to mental health problems and impair the development of a child's social and emotional skills (Langhinrichsen-Rohling, 2014). Children may also learn violent behavior from a parent who is an abuser, making them more likely to become either victims or perpetrators of violence later in life (Frye, 2017). In addition, the economic, physical, and mental health costs of violence against women are often passed on to their children, leading to an increased risk of poverty and associated adverse outcomes, such as poor educational attainment (Saunders & Browne, 2016).

Costs of Violence Against Women

Violence against women has a variety of physical, psychological, and economic costs, which can significantly impact individuals, families, and communities. These costs can be mitigated by providing interventions and services, such as legal services, counseling, and shelter services. However, to effectively address the issue of violence against women, it is essential to understand some strategies and initiatives developed to address violence against women. In recent years, the international community has taken steps to address this issue, such as adopting the United Nations Convention on the Elimination of All Forms of Discrimination Against Women (CEDAW) in 1979 (U.N. Women, 2019). Additionally, in 1994, the United Nations General Assembly established the International Day for the Elimination of Violence against Women, which is observed each year on November 25 (U.N. Women, 2019). At the national level, many countries have implemented laws, policies, and programs to address violence against women. For example, in the United States, the Violence Against Women Act (VAWA) was passed in 1994 and provided funding for programs that work to prevent and respond to violence against women (National Network to End Domestic Violence, 2019). Additionally, many countries have established specialized police units, crisis hotlines, and shelters to help victims of violence.

The Violence Against Women Act (VAWA) was passed in 1994 with bipartisan support and has been reauthorized four times with bipartisan support as well (The Violence, 2022, p. 2). However, now there are more questions about whether it may be reauthorized in the future with disagreement among parties about gun and transgender rights (The Violence, 2022, p. 2).

The act "creates and supports comprehensive, cost-effective responses to domestic violence, sexual assault, dating violence, and stalking" (Violence, 2022). The creation of the act needed to happen to address the severity of domestic violence, sexual assault, and stalking and was passed under the Violent Crime Control and Law Enforcement Act of 1994 (Legal, 2022). The passage of this bill was a big moment for advocates because many believed that states were failing to address the violence women were dealing with (Legal, 2022). It took four years to draft the bill because of disagreement on the part of the bill regarding civil rights that allowed victims to sue their attackers (Legal, 2022). People thought this would overwhelm the judicial system (Legal, 2022). The civil rights part of the legislation lasted for a while till it was struck down by the Supreme Court (Legal, 2022).

Even though that part of the act was lost, VAWA has still been very successful at improving services for victims and better educating those in power, like judges, about the violence of the impact like stalking does to women (Legal, 2022). For VAWA to be successful, the community must work together like police officers and victim advocates (Legal, 2022). Funds for this act are given out by the Office on Violence Against Women (OVW) (Legal, 2022). OVW was made just for this by the Department of Justice (Legal, 2022). OVW has given out $4 billion since 1994 to various states, tribal and local governments, and nonprofits trying to stop violence against women (Legal, 2022). President Biden was vital to getting this act passed as a Senator and called this the "proudest legislative accomplishment" of his career thus far (The Violence, 2022, p. 2).

Domestic violence was one of the key reasons this act was implemented. Before the act, "In 1980, the forceable rape crime rate, primarily against women, was 36.8 percent. By 1985, the rate increased to 37.1 percent. By 1990, the rate rose again to 41.2 percent" (DeMatteis, 2016, p. 267). Since domestic violence is still happening at a high rate, more supports are in place than before. On average, "nearly 20 people per minute are physically abused by an intimate partner in the United States. During one year, this equates to more than 10 million women and men" (NCADV, 2022).

The discourse around this policy created a new type of feminism. Carceral feminism is "activism aimed at increasing state enforcement against violence against women" (Whittier, 2016, p. 792). The goal of this type of feminism is "social justice as criminal justice" (Whittier, 2016, p, 792). Despite this new term creation, it is used by few people. That is because it is a critique term for the government allowing for women's liberation (Whittier, 2016, p. 792). Many supporters of VAWA would identify as intersectional feminists instead because it is more inclusive and solution-focused (Whittier, 2016, p. 793).

VAWA was reauthorized in 2000, 2005, 2013, and 2022. Furthermore, amendments have been made each time. These changes have been focused on safely being at the forefront. The most recent authorization has been strengthened in the following ways: "Reauthorizing all current VAWA grant programs until 2027...Expanding special criminal jurisdiction of Tribal courts...Increasing services and support for survivors from underserved and marginalized communities...Establishing a federal civil cause of action for individuals whose intimate visual images are disclosed without consent...Improving prevention and response to sexual violence...Strengthening the application of evidence-based practices by law enforcement in responding to gender-based violence...Improving the healthcare system's response... Updating the SMART Prevention Program and the CHOOSE Youth Program...Enacting the National Instant Criminal Background Check System (NICS) Denial Notification Act" (The United, 2022).

Trauma goes hand in hand with VAWA. That is why it is essential to do trauma-informed analyses, especially concerning vulnerable populations like undocumented immigrant women (Murshid & Bowen, 2018). Intimate partner violence (IPV) can hurt immigrant women in more brutal ways than women in general because there may not be as many resources for them, there is fear of being deported, and it may not be culturally acceptable to ask for help (Murshid & Bowen, 2018). IPV is scary to deal with as one person, but when children are involved, it can make seeking help much harder for an immigrant woman. That is why there is a push to see how VAWA's U-Visa policy could be improved by incorporating this thinking (Murshid & Bowen, 2018).

In line with that focus, there is also a renewed push to examine the experiences of immigrant women who self-petition under VAWA (Ingram et al., 2010). The law allows victims to self-petition for legal status, so immigration law does not make immigrant women feel they cannot leave a violent situation (Ingram et al., 2010). However, researchers have argued that going forward with other reauthorizations, "emotional, financial, and logistic barriers in applying" must be addressed to make this part of the law more effective (Ingram et al., 2010).

Assessment is vital to VAWA, and even though this act has created positive outcomes, there needs to be more research on how this affects violent crime (Boba & Lilley, 2009). According to Boba and Lilley (2009), data from 10,371 jurisdictions from 1996 to 2002 showed that "VAWA grants were associated with reductions in rape and assault." The researchers argue that more research like this should be done to show how effective VAWA has been so it can be known what programs are doing best and should be funded (Boba & Lilley, 2009).

Domestic violence and COVID-19 left great havoc on families and communities. According to Anurudran et al. (2020), "The United States National Domestic Violence Hotline...reported that many callers…indicated that their abusers are capitalizing on precautions related to COVID-19 to restrict their access to support networks further." The trauma from domestic violence increases over time as victims deal with mental health issues long after, which will only add to the public health burden already faced with COVID-19. Unemployment and its connection with domestic violence is also a meaningful conversation. Anderberg (2016) found that "female unemployment increases the risk of domestic abuse."

Mass shootings are a problem that plagues the United States, and they are in many ways connected to violence against women. Even with the Lautenberg Amendment, it is not enough to address this issue, and gun violence affects all of society, not just women (Issa, 2019, p. 673). It has been found that "gender-based crimes other than domestic violence, specifically stalking and sexual assault, are also indicative of a potential for future mass violence" (Issa, 2019, p. 673). That is why the researchers argue that misdemeanor crimes of stalking and sexual assault should be included in the Lautenberg Amendment (Issa, 2019, p. 673). This will benefit society and women in more ways than VAWA.

Domestic violence and sexual assault may seem clear-cut to those who do the work daily to support survivors, but it is less clear to the society surrounding them. Often the blame is on the woman and her actions. In many cases, there is no understanding of the relationship before the abuse. If a woman has children and does not leave when society sees fit, she is deemed a bad mother. It is not understood that many women stay because they have children and feel reliant on their abuser. This is seen especially with immigrant women who do not know help is available for them and their kids (Murshid & Bowen, 2018). VAWA has better educated many in power but less of the general public, thus creating this dichotomy.

There are many stakeholders in the VAWA discussion. Republicans had issues with VAWA, including transgender women; they thought it should focus more on biological females (The Violence, 2022, p. 2). Despite opinions like these, this type of law makes stakeholders from both sides want to work together; as Sen. Lisa Murkowski (R-Alaska) said, "No compromise is perfect, but what has been developed through this framework is a proposal that will help to prevent violence, to support our survivors [and] to hold perpetrators accountable," (The Violence, 2022, p. 2).

The National Domestic Violence Hotline is critical to VAWA being successful. They support the law, push for it to be reauthorized, and work with lawmakers to do so. VAWA is essential to them because it increases funding for their work, but also they have the resources to tell people who reach out to them how to benefit from VAWA. Without VAWA, their work would be more complex in helping victims get justice.

VAWA is crucial to women dealing with violence in the United States. It is not perfect, as discussed in this paper, but it is a start and supporting women when they need it most. It is also one of the few key things congressional stakeholders can agree on and work together to reauthorize. Societies' understanding of VAWA needs to continue to grow so women are treated with respect and dignity when leaving abusive situations. This is landmark legislation, and with it, the United States is a better place for women, albeit not what it could be, but a great start.

Best Practices for the Reduction of Violence Against Women

Several best practices can be implemented to reduce violence against women, such as adopting laws, policies, and programs that promote gender equality and empower women. These practices should address the root causes of violence against women, such as gender discrimination, unequal power dynamics, and unequal access to economic and social resources (U.N. Women, 2020). Laws and policies are an effective way to address the root causes of violence against women. For example, the U.N. has adopted the Convention on the Elimination of All Forms of Discrimination Against Women (CEDAW), a landmark international agreement that outlines a comprehensive set of rights and freedoms for women (U.N. Women, 2020). The CEDAW has been ratified by 189 countries and is considered the most comprehensive international agreement on eliminating discrimination against women (UN, 2020).

Additionally, countries should adopt laws that recognize and protect women's rights, including their right to freedom from violence (U.N. Women, 2020). These laws should be enforced, and perpetrators should be held accountable for their actions. In addition to laws and policies, it is crucial to implement educational and awareness programs that promote gender equality and raise awareness about the issue of violence against women. For example, programs that educate men and boys about gender equality and respectful relationships can effectively change attitudes and behaviors that contribute to violence against women (U.N. Women, 2020). Additionally, programs that focus on empowering women, such as providing access to economic and educational opportunities, can help reduce their vulnerability to violence (U.N. Women, 2020). It is also vital to ensure adequate resources available to victims of violence against women. This includes providing access to medical and psychological care, legal services, and shelter for those needing them (U.N. Women, 2020). Additionally, it is essential to create safe spaces for women to report violence and seek help, such as hotlines, crisis centers, and shelters (U.N. Women, 2020). These resources should be accessible and available to all women, regardless of their economic or social status.

Intervention Recommendations

In order to address gender equity and violence against women, it is essential to identify and implement solutions that focus on prevention, intervention, and policy change. Prevention Preventive efforts should address the root causes of violence and gender inequality, such as the cultural and social norms that perpetuate gender stereotypes and gender-based violence. Strategies could include providing education and awareness programs in schools and communities to teach about healthy relationships and gender equity and developing campaigns that challenge gender stereotypes and promote gender equality.

Partnering with community-based organizations that focus on supporting women in need (abuse recovery organizations). This way, funding continues to support their work, and women get help from the communities they live in.

Resources of the 24-hour women's helpline, including its online counseling service, were increased, women's shelters were available at all times, and counseling services were offered online and in person. Funding for counseling centers should be increased.

Streamlining processes to make applications for preliminary injunctions easier (police officers bring and pick up forms). There is close cooperation between health authorities, victim protection institutions, and the police in case of (suspected) infections, either of victims in shelters or of perpetrators barred from home.

The use of information campaigns (online, social media, print, TV) to raise awareness of the protection and support services that are available.

Victims of domestic violence should be provided with protection, accommodation, and care in crisis situations. This requires an increase in shelter locations and availabilities.

Introduce specialist services community centers from various disciplines, including social workers, psychologists, medical staff, legal professionals, and police, who will work under the same roof to provide appropriate support and protection to women and their children.

Introduce community counseling programs through web-based solutions, chat options, and group meetings of victims of domestic and gender-based violence.

Intervention strategies should focus on providing support to survivors of violence, as well as holding perpetrators of violence accountable. This could include providing access to resources such as counseling, legal services, and shelter and developing programs focusing on offender accountability and rehabilitation. Policy change is essential in addressing gender equity and violence against women. This could include passing laws protecting victims' rights, holding offenders accountable, and implementing policies focusing on gender equity in the workplace and education. Additionally, governments should focus on providing access to resources, such as healthcare and housing, that are critical for the well-being of survivors of violence. This is one of the main ways to create change because the government can create effective laws that will provide guidance where needed. Also, the government can be responsible for correcting false narratives around violence against women and not blaming the victim.

In order to implement strategies around violence against women to stop it from happening, in addition to what has been presented is to focus on funding and correcting the narrative around blaming the victim. Gender can be made very political, so in order to combat it becoming more polarizing, the facts and victims need to be heard. When you distance yourself from the affected group, it is hard to see why change matters, but when we make policy, government, and community-based organizations places where stories can be understood, change will happen with strategies talked about before.

Violence against women is a global issue that affects women of all ages, races, and socio-economic backgrounds. It takes many forms and is often an expression of power and dominance over women. The causes of violence against women are complex and multifaceted, and the consequences can have long-term impacts on individuals and societies. The international community has taken steps to address this issue, and many countries have implemented laws, policies, and programs to prevent and respond to violence against women. We must continue to take steps to address this issue and ensure that women can live free of violence.

Women in the United States experience a disproportionate rate of sexual assault, intimate partner violence, and stalking, as well as a significant gender wage gap and underrepresentation in leadership roles. However, there are a variety of potential solutions to address these issues, such as implementing and enforcing laws to protect women from gender-based violence and discrimination, increasing access to reproductive health care services and affordable child care, and increasing the representation of women in leadership roles. By addressing these issues, the United States can ensure that all women are treated fairly and equally.

REFERENCES

Anderberg, D., Rainer, H., Wadsworth, J., & Wilson, T. (2016, November). Violence: Theory and Evidence. *Economic Journal (London)*, *126*(597), 1947–1979. doi:10.1111/ecoj.12246

Anurudran, Y., Yared, L., Comrie, C., Harrison, K., & Burke, T. (2020). Domestic violence amid COVID-19. *International Journal of Gynaecology and Obstetrics: the Official Organ of the International Federation of Gynaecology and Obstetrics*, *150*(2), 255–256. doi:10.1002/ijgo.13247 PMID:32472696

Boba, & Lilley, D. (2009). Violence Against Women Act (VAWA) Funding: A Nationwide Assessment of Effects on Rape and Assault. *Violence Against Women, 15*(2), 168–185. https://doi.org/doi:10.1177/1077801208329146

Centers for Disease Control. (2023). *Fast Facts: Preventing Intimate Partner Violence*. CDC. https://www.cdc.gov/violenceprevention/intimatepartnerviolence/fastfact.html

DeMatteis. (2016). PROTECTING THE FREEDOM FOR WOMEN TO BE FREE FROM VIOLENCE: THE VIOLENCE AGAINST WOMEN ACT ENDURES. *Widener Law Review*, *22*(2), 267–270.

Department of Health and Human Services. (2020). Office on Women's Health. Retrieved from https://www.womenshealth.gov/about-us

U.S. Department of Justice. (2019). *Rape and sexual assault: Statistics*. USDOJ. https://www.justice.gov/ovw/rape-and-sexual-assault

U.S. Department of Labor. (2020). *Equal pay*. DoL. https://www.dol.gov/agencies/whd/equal-pay

World Health Organization. (2019). *Violence against women*. WHO. https://www.who.int/news-room/fact-sheets/detail/violence-against-women

Felitti, V. J., Anda, R. F., Nordenberg, D., Williamson, D. F., Spitz, A. M., Edwards, V., Koss, M. P., & Marks, J. S. (1998). Relationship of childhood abuse and household dysfunction to many of the leading causes of death in adults: The Adverse Childhood Experiences (ACE) Study. *American Journal of Preventive Medicine*, *14*(4), 245–258. doi:10.1016/S0749-3797(98)00017-8 PMID:9635069

Frye, A. (2017). Intergenerational transmission of violence: A review. *Trauma, Violence & Abuse*, *18*(5), 539–550. doi:10.1177/1524838016687564

Ingram, McClelland, D. J., Martin, J., Caballero, M. F., Mayorga, M. T., & Gillespie, K. (2010). Experiences of Immigrant Women Who Self-Petition Under the Violence Against Women Act. *Violence Against Women, 16*(8), 858–880. doi:10.1177/1077801210376889

Institute for Women's Policy Research. (2020). *The gender wage gap: 2019*. IWPR. https://iwpr.org/publications/gender-wage-gap-2019/

Issa. (2019). "A Profoundly Masculine Act": Mass Shootings, Violence Against Women, and the Amendment That Could Forge a Path Forward. *California Law Review, 107*(2), 673–. https://doi.org/doi:10.15779/Z382V2C98F

Kleim, B., & Ehlers, A. (2008). The trauma memory: Cognitive and behavioural perspectives. *Memory (Hove, England)*, *16*(2), 111–121.

Lacy, E. (2017). *Domestic violence in women of color.* NCADV. https://www.ncadv.org/blog/domestic-violence-in-women-of-color

Langhinrichsen-Rohling, J. (2014). Intergenerational transmission of family violence: From theory to prevention. *The American Journal of Family Therapy*, *42*(5), 391–406. doi:10.1080/01926187.2014.930491

Legal Momentum. (n.d.). *History of VAWA*. Legal Momentum. https://www.legalmomentum.org/history-vawa

Matsumoto, C. (2020). Domestic violence and women of color: What you need to know. *Love is Respect.* https://www.loveisrespect.org/content/domestic-violence-women-color/

McFarlane, A. (2011). Trauma and trauma-related disorders in women. In D. Levinson & M. Maercker (Eds.), *Trauma, post-traumatic stress and physical health* (pp. 91–109). Cambridge University Press.

Meschede, T., Seidel, T. D., & Schmitt, M. T. (2014). Understanding the connection between economic security and intimate partner violence for transgender individuals. *Journal of Marriage and Family, 76*(3), 573–588. doi:10.1111/jomf.12090

Murshid, N. S., & Bowen, E. A. (2018). A Trauma-Informed Analysis of the Violence Against Women Act's Provisions for Undocumented Immigrant Women. *Violence Against Women, 24*(13), 1540–1556. doi:10.1177/1077801217741991 PMID:29355086

National Coalition Against Domestic Violence. (2020). *Statistics*. NCADV. https://ncadv.org/statistics

National Network to End Domestic Violence. (2019). *VAWA: The Violence Against Women Act*. NNEDV. https://nnedv.org/content/vawa-violence-against-women-act/

NCADV: National Coalition Against Domestic Violence. (n.d.). *The Nation's Leading Grassroots Voice on Domestic Violence*. NCADV. https://ncadv.org/STATISTICS

Ristock, J. L. (2013). *Transgender abuse: Intimate partner violence and abuse in lesbian, gay, bisexual, transgender, and queer communities*. Routledge.

Sameroff, A. J. (2010). *The transactional model of development: How children and contexts shape each other*. American Psychological Association.

Saunders, D. G., & Browne, A. (2016). Intergenerational consequences of violence against women: A review of the literature. *Trauma, Violence & Abuse, 17*(3), 211–225. doi:10.1177/1524838014562517

Sisson, L. (2014). *Trends in poverty and economic insecurity among women in the United States*. Brookings. https://www.brookings.edu/research/trends-in-poverty-and-economic-insecurity-among-women-in-the-united-states/

Sroufe, L. A. (1990). An organizational perspective on the development of attachment. In M. Greenberg, D. Cicchetti, & E. M. Cummings (Eds.), *Attachment in the preschool years: Theory, research, and intervention* (pp. 209–235). University of Chicago Press.

Swim, J. K., Hyers, L. L., Cohen, L. L., & Ferguson, M. J. (2017). Everyday forms of sexism: Evidence for new measures and gender differences. Psychology of Women Quarterly, 407–425. doi:10.1177/0361684317691022

The United States Government. (2022, March 16). *Fact sheet: Reauthorization of the violence against women act (VAWA)*. The White House. https://www.whitehouse.gov/briefing-room/statements-releases/2022/03/16/fact-sheet-reauthorization-of-the-violence-against-women-act-vawa/

The Violence Against Women Act. (2022). *The Congressional Digest, 101*(2), 2-5.

United Nations. (U.N.). (2016). *Violence against women*. UN. https://www.un.org/en/sections/issues-depth/violence-against-women/

United Nations. (U.N.). (2019). *Violence against women and girls*. UN. https://www.unwomen.org/en/what-we-do/ending-violence-against-women/what-is-vaw

U.S. Department of Justice. (2019). *Rape and Sexual Assault: A Renewed Call to Action*. USDOJ. https://www.justice.gov/archives/opa/blog/rape-and-sexual-assault-renewed-call-action

U.S. Department of Justice. (2019). *Violence against women*. USDOJ. https://www.justice.gov/ovw/violence-women

Van der Kolk, B. A. (2005). Developmental trauma disorder: Towards a rational diagnosis for children with complex trauma histories. *Psychiatric Annals*, *35*(5), 401–408. doi:10.3928/00485713-20050501-06

Violence against women act. (n.d.). NNEDV. https://nnedv.org/content/violence-against-women-act/

Whittier. (2016). CARCERAL AND INTERSECTIONAL FEMINISM IN CONGRESS: The Violence Against Women Act, Discourse, and Policy. *Gender & Society*, *30*(5), 791–818. doi:10.1177/0891243216653381

Wong, M. (2016). Intergenerational transmission of violence and abuse. In M. B. Williams (Ed.), *Encyclopedia of domestic violence* (2nd ed., pp. 281–286). Routledge.

World Health Organization (WHO). (2020). *Violence against Women*. WHO. https://www.who.int/news-room/fact-sheets/detail/violence-against-women

Chapter 10
Laborera Risk Management Case Study of Artificial Intelligence for Human Resources

Marie L. Hall
Marymount University, USA

ABSTRACT

Laborera is a fictional company. The company is a cloud-based software vendor that specializes in human capital management applications. Laborera is entangled in a class action discrimination suit for its artificial intelligence tools that allegedly prescreen and disqualify applicants in protected categories. Porter's five forces model and McKinsey's strategic horizons offer a framework for strategic review. Deal and Kennedy and the Denison organizational culture model are used to strengthen Laborera's organizational culture. The Bridges transition model and the McKinsey 7-S model enable transition and thoughtful organizational change management. Laborera improves ethical decision making, including decision processes involving a human-machine team, using the fairness/justice approach, and the common good approach. This case study demonstrates theoretical applications of risk management for software companies desiring to leverage artificial intelligence within innovative software applications.

RISK MANAGEMENT CASE STUDY OF ARTIFICIAL INTELLIGENCE FOR HUMAN RESOURCES

Laborera, a fictional company, is a cloud-based software vendor specializing in human capital management and financial management applications. Entangled in a class action discrimination suit of $100 million, Laborera's artificial intelligence (AI) enabled software tools allegedly prescreen and disqualify applicants in protected categories. The unprecedented issue is whether Laborera, the AI developer rather than the employment agent, can be held liable for discrimination claims under Title VII of the Civil Rights Act of 1964 (Vogel, 2023). The jury has supported the plaintiff's claims, including African

DOI: 10.4018/979-8-3693-1634-4.ch010

Americans, Latina Americans, Arab American applicants, and current employees, that the AI-enabled screening process disqualified their resumes at a higher rate than Caucasian applicants. Regardless of the outcome, Laborera must act swiftly to resolve the underlying problem with its software products by engaging in a "risk-based review process throughout their product lifecycle to help mitigate any unintended consequences, as well as extensive legal reviews to help ensure compliance with regulations" (Gilbert, 2023, p. 1). Laborera has begun with a strategic review based on Porter's Five Forces Model and McKinsey's Strategic Horizons. Laborera will ensure that innovative technologies augment, rather than undermine, core values by leveraging Deal and Kennedy and The Denison Organizational Culture Model to strengthen their organizational culture. Redefining the strategy and aligning the culture will demand a transition and thoughtful corporate change management. Laborera should use the Bridges transition model and the McKinsey 7-S model to make the changes the business demands. Laborera will improve ethical decision-making involving a human-machine team using the Fairness/Justice approach and the Common Good Approach. This discrimination case has been a hard lesson on the improper ways to develop innovative processes that include machines in the otherwise human decision-making process.

PROBLEM STATEMENT

Laborera has failed to implement AI effectively, causing catastrophic financial harm to its financial operation and reputation, potentially an existential threat to the entire business. Laborera must ensure that no person is subject to a decision based solely on an AI application that relies on personal attributes of ethnicity, age, or gender as moderating variables. Simply put, that amounts to profiling, and it is wrong. However, leveraging equitable artificial intelligence to scale repeatable processes with greater speed and precision than humans promises economic benefits that can support the workforce and create the opportunity to free up resources for adding new software products. Laborera is clearly at a tipping point. Failing to leverage AI responsibly could ruin the business. Laborera needs a strategy, facilitated by culture, to transform its business processes using change management to improve the overall operating model of the company while driving ethical and responsible behaviors across business processes, whether those products use artificial intelligence.

LITERATURE REVIEW

Bernd Schmitt, a marketing expert from Columbia University, interviewed by Frieda Klotz (2016), explains that artificial intelligence may subsume many human resources functions that require analytical decision-making, and he implores companies to start planning now. Artificial intelligence systems are powerful prediction engines, according to Silverman (2020). At its roots, artificial intelligence is essentially applied statistics. Computers are applying statistics to data. Machines trained on biased training data (referring to historical correlations between race and opportunity) may statistically and systematically emulate human bias (Kennedy, 2021). Corporate leaders and boards must go beyond following current regulations and statutes and anticipate potential risks and consequences associated with how employers will use artificial intelligence systems; specifically, artificial intelligence technologies introduce risks to brand and reputation when used to worsen racial inequity (Silverman, 2020).

Mathematics of Discrimination

From a statistical perspective, data will demonstrate racial equality only when data elements that describe a person's race are no longer statistical predictors for differentiated outcomes related to employee selection, performance, or wealth (Kennedy, 2021). In the meantime, companies must be vigilant over machines trained using historical data, lest they replicate institutional and structural bias. Nevertheless, the long-anticipated rise of artificial intelligence to simplify complex business functions, including human resources functions, is upon us (Klotz, 2016). Rather than putting our heads in the sand, Kennedy (2021) proposes proactively and explicitly using statistics to uncover, investigate, change, eliminate, or improve the processes and procedures that structurally reinforce employee opportunities based on race. Kennedy (2021) explains that a wide-eyed approach to examining racial equity of policies and procedures using statistics, open communication, and a willingness to change can provide an equity framework for ensuring that artificial intelligence does not emulate structural causes of racism. Silverman (2020) argues that the very root of such risk management lies in examining whether AI application is 'consistent with all of our other beliefs, missions, and strategic objectives.'

Landmark court cases, such as Mobley v Workday, have substantiated claims that artificial intelligence screening tools discriminate against applicants because of race, gender, and ethnicity (Gilbert, 2023). Companies are becoming aware of their legal culpability for decision-making embedded in artificial intelligence capabilities that are becoming widely available for use in every part of the employment process, from recruiting, screening, and assessment to selection for future roles and disciplinary measures (Kerrigan et al., 2023). According to Kerrigan et al. (2023), emerging challenges with artificial intelligence are as far-reaching as sexual harassment of avatars in virtual workplaces called metaverses. In 2023, the Equal Employment Opportunity Commission (EEOC) is focused on protecting employment candidates from automated systems that "intentionally exclude or adversely impact protected groups" (O'Keefe & Libby, 2023, p. 1). In response, states like New Jersey and New York are making moves to regulate the use of artificial intelligence in employment decisions, and requiring companies to show their math, referring to "disparate impact analysis" required of companies to prove that these tools do not use variables associated with gender, race, or ethnicity to limit the opportunities of those populations that have endured institutional discrimination (O'Keefe & Morris, 2023, p. 1).

Strategy

In Porter's 2008 article, "The Five Competitive Forces That Shape Strategy," he explains that competitive advantage is about understanding the competition. Michael Porter's seminal work on Competitive Advantage introduced five forces that shape strategy among competitors, including barriers to entry, buying power, the threat of substitutes by alternative suppliers, and competitive rivalry (Porter, 1979).

McKinsey's Strategic Horizons is particularly well suited for examining the potential of disruptive technology such as artificial intelligence. The three horizons come from exploring the organizational and leadership approach observable across the S-Curves (slow, fast, and then slow) of good growth companies (McKenzie, 2009). The Strategic Horizons framework stresses the importance of company leadership to consider the next stage opportunities for growth without neglecting the present stage (White et al., 2000). The three horizons comprise extending and defending the core business in Horizon 1, building emerging business in Horizon 2, and creating viable options in Horizon 3 (White et al., 2000). While Laborera should plan these three horizons concurrently, they have different focus areas. Horizon 1 is about great execution to achieve results and maintain cash flow (White et al., 2000). Horizon 2 is top-line growth and positional advantage (White et al., 2000). And Horizon 3 is insight and foresight to achieve big payoffs and a high probability of success (While et al., 2000).

In the case of Laborera, they will benefit from looking across these three horizons simultaneously. Nevertheless, these strategic plans will not work absent a supportive culture. Laborera must foster a culture where fair and equitable treatment of each person is a core value and a design principle for software developed to enable recruiting and hiring.

Organizational Culture

The Deal and Kennedy Model (2002) synthesizes organizational cultures into four main types based on risk tolerance and speed of feedback. Those with the quickest feedback and highest risk tolerance are coined 'tough-guy, macho culture' (Deal et al., 2002). Those with fast feedback but low-risk tolerance have a 'work hard, play hard culture' compared to those with slow feedback and high-risk tolerance who have a 'bet your company culture' (Deal et al., 2002). Those low in both categories are deemed 'process culture' (Deal et al., 2002). These frames sum up company culture using the context of history, values, rituals, stories, heroes, and cultural networks (Deal et al., 2002).

The Denison Organizational Culture Model provides a validated survey tool for measuring involvement, consistency, adaptability, and mission that leaders use to analyze organizational culture as a driver for organizational effectiveness (Denison et al., 2006). Involvement measures employees' alignment and engagement (Denison et al., 2006). Consistency evaluates the values, systems, and processes to create leverage (Denison et al., 2006). Adaptability assesses response to the external environment (Denison et al., 2006). Moreover, mission evaluates whether everyone understands the company's goals and objectives (Denison et al., 2006). Together these measures provide insight into where to improve culture in ways that directly relate to market share, profitability, employee satisfaction, and customer satisfaction, ultimately enhancing the competitiveness of Laborera.

Change Management

Moving forward from the status quo, both strategically and culturally, will not simply require a change to recover from this lawsuit and move ahead successfully, but a transition. Bridges and Bridges (2017) Transition model is ideally suited for this Laborera and its stakeholders as they aspire to deal with the fear and uncertainty of leveraging artificial intelligence within human resources software applications and must build trust and confidence across stakeholders to survive as a company. The Bridges Transition model starts with the end, in the case of Laborera, the end of autonomous systems that allow for unfair discrimination by replicating historical patterns using artificial intelligence. An algorithm is simply a statistical model that cannot change itself. Laborera, the human workforce, and the clients who aspire to benefit from the benefits of speed, precision, and agility in recruiting must go through the stages of transition to divest our human resources systems and processes, automated or not, of bias and start something new.

The importance of organizational culture and the human experience of transition reveal that human interactions, referring to coordination, are more critical than an organizational structure for organizational effectiveness. The McKinsey 7-S model describes the importance of coordinating among the 7-Ss (Structure, Strategy, Systems, Style, Staff, Skills, and Subordinate Goals) for an organization to operate effectively (Waterman et al., 1980). Structure relates to how task allocation, whether by specialization, matrix, or another categorization, simplicity is the key in most successful organizations (Waterman et al., 1980). For Laborera, strategy refers to the actions Laborera plans to take to respond to emerging customer, legal, and competitor demands because of the discrimination lawsuit. Systems include all procedures to run the company (Waterman et al., 1980). Style refers to the company culture uncovered using the Deal and Kennedy Model (Waterman et al., 1980). Staff refers to combining carrots and sticks to develop, train, appease, enforce, and guide the workforce toward a shared vision (Waterman et al., 1980). Skills refer to the crucial attributes of workforce members, including a depth of understanding about creating artificial intelligence software and facilitating its responsible and ethical use (Waterman et al., 1980). The latter is a skill not often put upon the shoulders of software developers. Finally, Subordinate Goals refer to the company's higher-order goals, values, and aspirations (Waterman et al., 1980). Leveraging artificial intelligence for human resources processes may be similar in complexity to leveraging artificial intelligence in a hospital operating room. Smith et al. (2022) provide a practical example of pulling together all components of the McKinsey 7-S model to create a novel implementation of AI-enabled technology within the operating room, showing great promise for its application by Laborera within human resources decision-making work streams.

Ethical Decision-Making

An implicit cultural component is ethical decision-making for AI-enabled software design and development. Justice and fairness are similar but not interchangeable; justice refers to a generalizable standard of rightness, while fairness is the judgment of what is equitable in a specific situation (Velasquez, 1990). Justice is the measuring instrument, whereas fairness is the measurement. The Fairness/Justice Approach is a universal approach to decision-making that allows the decision-maker to reflect on whether an action is fair. But what about non-human decision-making agents, such as a machine learning algorithm that screens applications? Recall that artificial intelligence is a statistical model at its most basic element. While the software user is not absolved of the responsibility for candidate selection, Laborera is accountable for the design of artificial intelligence within its software. It is incumbent upon Laborera and its software developers to test the algorithm (the measuring instrument) to ensure that it may be used fairly and equitably. Mathematicians must be able to explain how the algorithm segments the selectees from non-selectees by identifying the moderating variables (ensuring they are not attributable to race, gender, or age) to ensure that the algorithm, acting as the measuring instrument, is fair.

The Common Good Approach is another universal approach to decision-making. Hussain (2018) defines the common good as "the facilities – whether material, cultural or institutional – that the members of a community provide to all the members to fulfill a relational obligation they all have to care for certain interests that they have in common." One of those established interests is at the root of Laborera's lawsuit: fair and equal opportunity for citizens seeking employment (Hussain, 2018). Consequently, Laborera has an undeniable role in designing software to support equitable hiring practices, creating an inextricable link between the value Laborera software provides to its customers and the good of the community.

Theories to Manage Risk

In summary, this literature review provides a framework for Laborera to create a competitive advantage through a strategy review using Porter's five forces and planning to achieve that strategy across the three horizons of growth. Laborera can apply the qualitative, Deal and Kennedy, and quantitative Denison Organizational model, to assess and align its culture to achieve the new strategy. The Bridges Theory of Transition provides an approach for leaving behind prior failed approaches to human resources software development to embark on the new. The tools provided by the McKinsey 7-S model will facilitate the systematic coordination across the company's 7-Ss (Structure, Strategy, Systems, Style, Staff, Skills, and Subordinate Goals) to build an effective organizational operating model. Laborera must recognize its expanded role from merely a software vendor to a responsible contributor for Laborera's customer's human resources decision-making processes. Because Laborera provides software that facilitates human-machine teaming in decision-making, Laborera is morally obliged to the AI-enabled machine role in those decision-making processes. Laborera can leverage principles from the Fairness/Justice and Common Good approaches to enhance those decision-making processes. Enterprise Risk Management (ERM) enables an organization to see itself by assessing its current situation, enumerating all the threats, defining actionable steps to accomplish goals, and creating actionable steps to counter threats. (Decker & Galer, 2013).

CURRENT SITUATION

Currently, Laborera is in crisis. Previously a highly regarded software company, the class action suit has done seemingly irreparable damage. Financially, the $100 million class action suit is the tip of the iceberg. Laborera faces additional financial risks in the form of lost revenue and loss of investor confidence. Investor relations have already plummeted, as exhibited by our plummeting stock price. Investors perceive our software as posing a moral hazard by discriminating against certain classes of applicants over others. Several of our critical financial backers have stepped back. The central question regards the responsibility of Laborera, as an AI developer, versus the purchaser of their technology, the employment agent, for liability of discrimination claims based upon Title VII of the Civil Rights Act of 1964.

The reputational damage is multifaceted. Externally, Laborera is already seeing a drop in software sales and diminishing investor confidence. From a human resources perspective, employee attrition has spiked, and morale is at an all-time low. Employment applications have already slowed, and our university recruiters are hearing that Laborera is falling out of favor with top students who view our practices as reckless. Some have even mocked Laborera calling the developers "Data Scientists without the Science." A fight broke out in one of our labs over it. And Laborera is vulnerable to additional IT risks. Managers are stressed out. Already caught on their heels by the error of discrimination against protected classes, managers worry that other statistical relationships underlying AI-enabled applications violate commonly understood employment laws.

It is no wonder some states, including New York and New Jersey, are implementing reactive legislation with more government control over software applications that enable human resources activities. As the regulatory environment becomes more complex, with new regulations and statutes, Laborera will have to design new policies and controls to comply; it will also be costly to address these new requirements. All that pressure, lack of clarity, and frustration turn the workplace into a pressure cooker of anxiety and unhappiness. Laborera must manage all the risks under this lawsuit, especially the financial, reputational, human resources, information technology, and regulatory risks outlined here. The following sections systematically address the issue and recommend solutions using the risk management theories and concepts outlined in the literature review.

ISSUES AND RESOLUTIONS

Considering the current situation, human resources issues are the top strategic challenge that Laborera faces. To achieve competitive advantage by building the best-in-class software, rebuilding and supporting the technical talent pipeline is critical for three of the five forces, the barrier to entry, threat of substitute, and alternative supplier forces. Financial issues are the second most important. Laborera must have an explicit strategy to rebuild the trust and confidence of its customer base for solid buying power, giving rise to favorable financial terms for the sale of its software. Thirdly, Laborera requires a viable strategy for packaging products that include software, services, and regulatory compliance to maximize its force related to competitive rivalry. We will facilitate collaborative leadership sessions with senior leaders to specify the initiatives and goals to enable this strategy.

Strategy

Laborera needs to start with the strategy. Enterprise Risk Management (ERM) begins with ensuring the strategic objectives and goals are well-understood outcomes (Decker & Galer, 2013). Laborera should develop an aggregated risk register that documents progress and risks across Software Development and AI, functional unit, and business unit initiatives. Start by outlining the critical issues facing Laborera. Financial risks stem from the class action lawsuit, fewer customers, fewer investors, and potentially new overhead costs due to regulation. Reputational risks include losing customers, investors losing faith, a diminished recruiting pipeline, and future employees distrustful of Laborera's operations and opportunities. Human resources risks include employee attrition, low morale, fights, anxiety, stress, and uncertainty. Information technology is vulnerable to known product flaws and yet-to-be-diagnosed software problems. Uncertainty surrounding emerging legislation and Laborera's ability to comply demands new processes, procedures, and controls. Laborera should review emerging risks and escalate any relevant risks to Laborera leadership. A disciplined risk management process will provide transparency to emerging risks and a clear strategy for risk mitigation.

Porter's Five Forces

Next, consider how each of Porter's five forces relates to Laborera, including barriers to entry, buying power, the threat of substitutes, alternative suppliers, and competitive rivalry (Porter, 1979). Ghicajanu (2021) provides a template for considering Porter's five forces for a furniture company. Using a similar procedure to Ghicajanu (2021), model these five forces to shape the strategy for a software company like Laborera specializing in human capital management applications.

Barriers to Entry

The first force, barriers to entry, refers to the ability of new companies to enter the competition and enable clients to identify top talent faster and with greater precision (Porter, 1979). Laborera must keep pace with or exceed other entrants' ability to leverage emerging technology like artificial intelligence to maintain an advantage over other companies hoping to break in. Laborera should gather and monitor competitive intelligence on the talent landscape, develop recruiting goals aligned with project demand and monitor its talent capability and capacity as a function of current and projected product demand.

Laborera should conduct personnel and workforce analytics to estimate the market for new skills for emerging multi-functional teams. Laborera should pay particular attention to staffing levels related to software developers, artificial intelligence data scientists, and legal labor categories. Laborera should identify any potential staffing risks in the aggregated risk register, monitor current and projected fill, and take action to strengthen its talent pipeline.

Buying Power

Regarding the second force, buying power, if this crisis reduces the pool of buyers, it will lower the cost of Laborera software (Porter, 1979). So it will be important that Laborera rebuilds buyer trust in software products that leverage artificial intelligence. Laborera should collect and analyze marketing data related to potential clients and the conversion rate for sales to monitor and forecast buyer interest. Further, it should monitor software revenue and per-unit price to develop leading indicators of changes in buyer sentiment. Laborera should identify potential risks to buyer sentiment and record those in the aggregated risk register, monitor current and projected software sales prices, and strengthen its brand trust and appeal with potential clients.

Threat of Substitutes

The third force, the threat of substitutes, suggests that Laborera should consider innovative ideas to differentiate its offerings that leverage artificial intelligence by wrapping customer support services into its offer to prove the value of software-plus services (Porter, 1979). Such services can enhance the responsible use of AI-enabled tools, distinguishing them from the competition. Laborera should collect competitive intelligence on other company offerings related to business process reengineering, compliance, and emerging statutory and regulatory requirements associated with using artificial intelligence to support human resources management activities. Laborera should analyze competitor offerings AI-Enabled Software plus Customer Support Services. In addition, Laborera should stay abreast of emerging statutory and regulatory requirements, evaluate the implementation requirements in detail, develop cost-effective implementation strategies, and include those costs in projected operating expenses. Laborera should continuously identify and review potential risks to its ability to differentiate its software offerings with services that enable the responsible and compliant use of AI. Laborera should monitor and forecast the associated costs for these services compared to its competition. Laborera should identify and monitor potential risks to its ability to differentiate product offerings in responsible AI services and compliance and fortify its compliance practice with the resources necessary for monitoring and engaging in legal and regulatory compliance.

Competitive Supply

The fourth force is related to the power of alternative suppliers (Porter, 1979). As a software company, Laborera's raw materials come from numerous suppliers. Still, the most limiting and competitive supply area that Laborera must consider will be developer talent, particularly for artificial intelligence. This area, already reflected within Barriers to Entry, requires double indemnity from Laborera. To shore up talent pipelines, Laborera should build relationships with top-tier schools and publish peer-reviewed academic papers to advertise its intellectual prowess. Laborera data scientists should participate in technical and ethical hack-a-thons to show off their technical prowess and social and moral responsibility. Participating in community competitions, events, conferences, and peer-reviewed publications will help build its reputation, relationships, and trust. Together these will strengthen its supply channels for top talent.

Competitive Rivalry

Finally, the fifth force is competitive rivalry. Software is a competitive and constantly evolving industry. To maintain an edge in the AI-enabled software competition, they can differentiate themselves through awareness and services surrounding compliance with emerging regulatory and statutory requirements for AI-enabled human resources software. Laborera should build and maintain a competitive market analysis related to compliance and regulation on human resources activities. Laborera should monitor to ensure that its offerings exceed those of competitors. Laborera should establish a compliance practice to monitor emerging requirements related to responsible and ethical applications of AI in human resources, as well as broad awareness of rules, regulations, and laws within the states and countries in which Laborera operates. The compliance practice should identify potential risks from current and emerging rivals, record those in the aggregated risk register, monitor current and projected costs associated with each applicable regulatory and statutory employment requirement by geographical area, and design mitigation strategies.

Together Porter's five forces for Laborera's strategy approach point to the importance of differentiative itself as a trustworthy brand among all its stakeholders. Having considered the forces at play, Laborera can contextualize them in alternative future planning horizons. Laborera should facilitate working groups with key stakeholders across business groups to identify Key Performance Indicators aligned with strategic objectives and incorporate those into Laborera's existing governance infrastructure.

McKinsey's Strategic Horizons

Laborera should simultaneously leverage McKinsey's Strategic Horizons to examine strategic solutions to the issues they face across three future Horizons (McKenzie, 2009). One could argue that their priority should be on Horizon 3, what's over the horizon, because the potential for artificial intelligence within human resources software poses litigious pitfalls that could pose existential threats to the company. McKinsey's strategic horizons framework will help leaders plan for multiple periods of growth simultaneously.

In the near term, Laborera needs to plan for the lawsuit, develop a crisis communication plan for customers and investors, and improve workforce internal communications and morale. Laborera's near-term focus must also address known product shortcomings. For the midterm, Laborera should build strategic plans to shore up recruiting pipelines, strengthen university relationships, build investor faith, and improve communication with and support the workforce. Laborer also needs to focus on developing a robust artificial intelligence assurance capability. In the longer term, Laborera needs to enhance processes and systems for anticipating and responding to emerging compliance requirements, building a bank of reputational credit, and ensuring the development of employee programs, training, and resources that enhance retention.

Culture

Culture describes the way people in the company relate to one another. Culture comprises three types of relationships: with our customers, our internal workforce, and organizational leaders and the employees they are responsible for (Beaudan et al., 2000). Because Laborera software includes AI, a non-human decision-making entity, Laborera will have to rethink the bounds of cultural influence. Unlike the relationship between Microsoft and its Office Products users, Laborera's AI-enabled software becomes an agent in its customers' recruiting and screening process. In addition to delighting its customers, Laborera must foster transparency and open communication about its AI-enabled software's strengths and weaknesses for human resources functions. Laborera must blend its culture with clients' cultures through formal partnership agreements with its consumers.

Laborera can shape such blended cultures by understanding shared drivers behind identifying top talent, encouraging AI developers to communicate directly with its customers engaged in the hiring process, reinforcing behaviors, and demanding software design that supports compliance with employment laws and regulations. Together, these leader actions recognize blended culture as a living entity (Beaudan et al., 2000). Further, if Laborera's client companies operate in other countries, this includes developing familiarity and attention to compliance in every country that Laborera works in (O'Toole, 2009). Laborera should require and implement teaming agreements with its customers to allow and reward organizational practices where employees for companies on both sides, within Laborera and its client companies, share information and contribute to the reengineering of human resources business processes that include Laborera's AI-enabled software as part of the customer's human resources decisions (O'Toole, 2009).

Laborera is clearly in a fast-paced software company under considerable pressure with a low tolerance for risk while entangled in a class action lawsuit. Laborera demonstrates characteristics of a "work hard, play hard" culture. The Deal and Kennedy Model offers a qualitative approach for assessing attributes such as individualism, cohesiveness, and performance to evaluate the consistency between which of the four cultures exist versus where it should be. Laborers can use the Denison Organizational Culture Model to provide quantitative insights that complement the qualitative Kennedy Model by identifying specific gaps in involvement, consistency, adaptability, and mission where leaders can tailor their approach to organizational effectiveness (Denison et al., 2006). For example, Laborera needs to create opportunities for its employees to engage in "fun" settings making connection a priority. Laborera should consider a variety of social gatherings, high-adventure outings for team-building, and shared learning experiences to increase competencies in new technology areas. These activities acknowledge and enhance Laborera's company culture using the context of history, values, rituals, stories, heroes, and cultural networks (Deal et al., 2002).

Change Management

We will use insights about cultural strengths and weaknesses to design approaches that mitigate the financial, reputational, human resources, information technology, and regulatory risks outlined above. We can accomplish this by facilitating working groups that examine each of the McKinsey 7-S areas, including Structure, Strategy, Systems, Style, Staff, Skills, and Subordinate Goals for more effective strategic operations (Waterman et al., 1980).

Bridges Transition

According to Bridge's Transition model, humans will go through three stages, the ending, the neutral zone, and the new beginning (Bridges & Bridges, 2017). The first stage, the end, will require Laborera to determine what should be left behind and what should be kept (Bridges & Bridges, 2017). Steven O Roberts, a Stanford Psychologist, identifies seven sources, including categories, factions, segregation, hierarchy, power, media, and passivism, that contribute to a system of race-based advantage (Roberts et al., 2020). The Bridge's Transition Model ending stage does not imply that Laborera should leave behind or abandon emerging AI-enabled technology but reckon with these sources of discrimination and leave those behind. During the second stage, the neutral zone, it will be essential to have clear leadership to ensure new processes and roles align with core values and objectives (Bridges & Bridges, 2017). Finally, the transition ends with new beginnings for Laborera, developing fresh, efficient, and fair software to enhance and facilitate employee identification, recruitment, and onboarding.

McKinsey 7-S

Laborera should focus mainly on style, staff, and skills as these are integral to Laborera's human resources challenges, internally among the current workforce and externally related to recruiting pipelines. Laborera should use a structured survey design process to capture the current state across each of the McKinsey 7-S areas by validating the survey objectives, defining the targeted audience, developing and refining the survey questions, obtaining appropriate approvals, and assessing the results for challenge areas. Laborera should use survey outputs to create impactful change management and communications deliverables tailored to the unique concerns of Laborera, its employees, and clients.

Combining Culture and Change

Leveraging AI-enabled technology in the operating rooms offered a phased template that Laborera can use as an analog for AI-enabled technology in candidate screening (Smith et al., 2022). Smith et al. (2022) identified 4 phases to transforming how the operating room runs when leveraging AI-enabled technology. Based on the challenge areas identified using the Denison and McKinsey 7-S tools, Laborer can model the following interventions for the novel implementation of artificial intelligence. The four phases include identifying the new skills required for the business process, defining the decision-making roles and controls, transitioning into the new business process, and launching the new approach using AI-enabled technology (Smith et al., 2022). Laborera will need to guide each of their customers down a similar transition path, providing not only the Laborera AI-enabled software but services to facilitate the adoption of new AI-enabled human resources processes. Laborera's multi-functional teams will resolve the underlying problem with its software products using a risk-based review process, including extensive legal compliance. The product lifecycle spans from software development and testing through introduction and implementation within the client environment.

Phase One: Build Multi-Disciplinary Teams

For Laborera, the necessary expertise in the future will move away from exclusively technical toward a multi-disciplinary team of software developers, data scientists with artificial intelligence expertise, lawyers with expertise in employment law, and customer experience managers (Smith et al., 2022). Laborera should use Creative Recombination to reorganize in-house talent and recombine them in creative new ways to simultaneously take a balanced approach to developing technical AI solutions and the human resources processes (Abrahamson, 2004). The benefits of this Creative Recombination are that it will be less expensive, preserve novel talent familiar with AI, involve less change given the current company chaos, and be less vulnerable to employee rejection (Abrahamson, 2004). Abrahamson explains that this is similar to rearranging the metaphorical Legos of the organization to achieve new joint technical and business capabilities.

Laborera's leadership must work hard to ensure its team of software developers, AI scientists, lawyers, and consumer counterparts have a healthy and emotionally safe environment built on trust and respect (Reid, 2013). Only then will people feel empowered to speak up to ensure both sides do their best to fulfill human resources business processes (Reid, 2013). Teaming provides the connective tissue between leadership values and human resources behaviors that enable the identification of top talent (O'Toole, 2009). Achieving cultural success hinges on trust (Reid, 2013). Organizational leaders drive culture and must listen to understand the state of the organization, share the mission and vision, and bring managers and employees along on the journey through training and meaningful feedback (Reid, 2013).

Phase Two: Define Decision-Making Roles and Controls

Before implementation, Laborera should meet with its clients to collaborate on a plan that defines the scope, risk, risk/mitigation strategies, impacted human resources functions, processes, and policies. Then pair a multi-disciplinary team from Laborera with the client to ensure a tight alignment of AI expertise and human resources know-how. Together the team will conduct a stakeholder impact analysis and develop a risk and implementation plan to be validated by appropriate leadership. Preplanning each implementation accelerates project coordination, identification of dependencies, and risk mitigation.

Phase Three: Leverage Agile Project Planning to Transition

As Laborera works with its clients to leverage AI-enabled tools, they must support agile project planning and execution, tailoring each transition phase toward AI-enabled processes to each client's unique talent demands (Smith et al., 2022). The difference between traditional and agile project planning efforts is the shift from project efficiency to stakeholder success (Serrador et al., 2015). The appropriate measure for Laborera's software should not be how efficiently the company can make AI-enabled software but how effectively its clients can leverage that software to responsibly and effectively identify top talent. Project teams that focus on stakeholder success are more satisfied with their deliverables, as are their clients, and their client's end users (Serrador et al., 2015).

Phase Four: Continuously Communicate New Processes and Progress

Consistent communication to get Human Resource partner buy-in and stakeholder engagement at the client company (Smith et al., 2022). Leaders must provide a persuasive and compelling narrative that resonates with employees' emotions and motivates them to engage in making the new business process work (Hill, 2009). There are three things that Laborera and its clients can do to leverage emotional intelligence to advance the ethical use of AI in human resources (Hill, 2009). Senior leaders should hold in-person forums about the transition ahead and encourage a safe and open exchange of ideas and concerns (Hill, 2009). Use that feedback to improve their message and frame the opportunity in ways that align with employee values and concerns (Hill, 2009). Then leaders should promote the refined vision and frequently seize opportunities to publicize successes to maintain momentum (Hill, 2009).

Maintain Momentum

Laborera and its clients must work together to accommodate institutional cultures and regulations to succeed (Smith et al., 2022). Even though planning helps change initiatives start well, fatigue frequently sets in, and change stalls (Beaudan, 2006). There are four things leaders can do to overcome institutional and cultural hurdles when momentum wains (Beaudan, 2006). Laborera's crisis is unprecedented, so they may need to adjust their goals metrics (Beaudan, 2006). Second, move a different pace after assessing how things are going by engaging with corporate governing bodies to get an objective perspective on compliance and management (Beaudan, 2006). Third, evaluate leaders and teams to ensure the mix of talents and personalities are working well together, and mix it up if needed so that everyone can do their best (Beaudan, 2006). Fourth, add a thrill to get out of the rut, using many techniques, including significant publicity, new rewards, a manufactured emergency, or a fun experience to change perspectives among leaders and teams (Beaudan, 2006). These improvements in style, staff, and skill coordination will improve processes and procedures to comply with emerging regulations while improving employee training, opportunities, morale, and mutual trust.

END STATE

Laborera will redefine its strategy to address the risks identified within the current situation and then measure, assess, and design interventions to align its culture with the new strategy, as illustrated in Table 1. With improved collaboration among the workforce and leadership, Laborera will identify and transform critical business processes in ways that enhance the overall operating model of the business and strengthen the strategic forces to create a competitive advantage. The reformed strategy and culture will enable Laborera to implement Artificial Intelligence within human resources software products fairly and equitably. Laborera AI-enabled software will responsibly and legally allow its customers to scale repeatable processes with greater speed and precision than manual processes delivering economic benefits while assuring equitable opportunities to all candidates for employment and building trust and confidence across Laborera's stakeholder ecosystem.

Table 1. Porter's five forces competitive advantage for Laborera

Five Forces	*Risk Area*	*Metrics*	*Interventions*
Barriers to entry	Software Developers	Competitive Intelligence on talent availability and recruiting goals aligned to projected product demand	Strengthen Talent Pipeline Multi-functional Teams Simplify Structure
Barriers to entry	AI Scientists	% Fill of AI Scientists v Product Demand	
Barriers to entry	HR Legal Expertise	% Fill of HR Legal Expertise v Compliance Demand	
Buying Power	Pool of Buyers	Moving Average Price of Laborera Software	Extensive Legal Reviews Comprehensive Communications Blend Laborera-Client Culture
Buying Power	Buyer Trust	Sentiment Level among Potential Clients	
Threat of Substitutes	Differentiated Offering	Competitive Intelligence on AI-Enabled Software plus Customer Support Services	Software plus Services Product Design
Competitive Supply	AI Talent / Data Scientists	Competitive Intelligence on talent availability and recruiting goals aligned to projected product demand	Strengthen Talent Pipeline
Competitive Rivalry	Compliance with emerging regulations and laws	Competitive Intelligence on Compliance and Automated Controls	Build Compliance Practice Conduct Extensive Legal Reviews

REFERENCES

Abrahamson, E. (2004). Managing Change in a World of Excessive Change: Counterbalancing Creative Destruction and Creative Recombination. *Ivey Business Journal*. https://iveybusinessjournal.com/publication/managing-change-in-a-world-of-excessive-change-counterbalancing-creative-destruction-and-creative-recombination/

Beaudan, E. (2006). Making Change Last: How to get beyond Change Fatigue. *Ivey Business Journal*. https://iveybusinessjournal.com/publication/making-change-last-how-to-get-beyond-change-fatigue/

Beaudan, E., & Smith, G. (2000). Corporate Culture: Asset or Liability. *Ivey Business Journal*. https://iveybusinessjournal.com/publication/corporate-culture-asset-or-liability/

Bridges, W., & Bridges, S. (2017). *Managing Transitions (25th Anniversary Edition): Making the Most of Change* (Special edition). Da Capo Lifelong Books.

Deal, T., & Kennedy, A. (2000). Corporate Cultures: The Rites and Rituals of Corporate Life. Revised ed. edition. Cambridge, Mass: Basic Books.

Decker, A., & Galer, D. (2013). *Enterprise Risk Management - Straight to the Point: An Implementation Guide Function by Function* (1st ed.). ERMSTTP, LLC.

Denison, D. R., Janovics, J., Young, J., & Cho, H. J. (2006). *Diagnosing Organizational Cultures: Validating a Model and Method*. Denison Consulting Group.

Ghicajanu, M. (2021). Competitive Analysis of the Business with the Michael Porter Model. *Annals of the University of Petrosani. Economics*, *21*(1), 169–178.

Gilbert, A. (2023). Workday AI Biased Against Black, Older Applicants, Suit Says. *Daily Labor Report*. https://news.bloomberglaw.com/daily-labor-report/workday-ai-biased-against-black-disabled-applicants-suit-says

Hill, D. (2009). *The Rhetoric and Reality of Successful Change Management. Ivey Business Journal*. https://iveybusinessjournal.com/publication/the-rhetoric-and-reality-of-successful-change-management/

Hussain, W. (2018). The Common Good. *Stanford Encyclopedia of Philosophy*. Stanford. https://www.academia.edu/35135973/The_Common_Good

Kennedy, E. J. (2021, Winter). Can Data Drive Racial Equity? *MIT Sloan Management Review*, *62*(2), 9–11.

Kerrigan, C. (2020). *AI, Machine Learning & Big Data Laws and Regulations*. Employment Law Risks and Artificial Intelligence, GLI. https://www.globallegalinsights.com/practice-areas/ai-machine-learning-and-big-data-laws-and-regulations/2-employment-law-risks-and-artificial-intelligence

Klotz, F. (2016, Fall). Are You Ready for Robot Colleagues? *MIT Sloan Management Review*, *58*(1).

McKinsey. (2009). *Enduring Ideas: The Three Horizons of Growth*. McKinsey. https://www.mckinsey.com/capabilities/strategy-and-corporate-finance/our-insights/enduring-ideas-the-three-horizons-of-growth#

O'Keefe, J., & Libby, C. (2023). *AI-Based Discrimination Top of the EEOC's Draft Enforcement Plan*. Law and the Workplace. https://www.lawandtheworkplace.com/2023/01/ai-based-discrimination-top-of-the-eeocs-draft-enforcement-plan/

O'Keefe, J., & Morris, H. (2023). *New Jersey and New York Introduce Bills to Regulate Sale and Use of 'Automated Employment Decision Tools*. Law and the Workplace. https://www.lawandtheworkplace.com/2023/02/new-jersey-and-new-york-introduce-bills-to-regulate-sale-and-use-of-automated-employment-decision-tools/

O'Toole, J. (2009). Connecting the Dots between Leadership, Ethics, and Corporate Culture. *Ivey Business Journal*. https://iveybusinessjournal.com/publication/connecting-the-dots-between-leadership-ethics-and-corporate-culture/

Porter, M. E. (1979, March-April). How Competitive Forces Shape Strategy. *Harvard Business Review*, 137–145. PMID:18271320

Porter, M. E. (2008). The Five Competitive Forces That Shape Strategy. *Harvard Business Review*. https://hbr.org/2008/01/the-five-competitive-forces-that-shape-strategy

Reid, J. (2013). Winning Workplace Cultures: An Imperative for Enabling Business Success. *Ivey Business Journal*. https://iveybusinessjournal.com/publication/winning-workplace-cultures-an-imperative-for-enabling-business-success/

Roberts, S., & Rizzo, M. (2020). "*The Psychology of American Racism.*" American Psychologist, In Press. 1. https://news.stanford.edu/2020/06/09/seven-factors-contributing-american-racism/ doi:0.31219/osf.io/w2h73

Serrador, P., & Pinto, J. K. (2015). Does agile work? – A quantitative analysis of agile project success. *International Journal of Project Management*, *33*(5), 1040–1051. doi:10.1016/j.ijproman.2015.01.006

Silverman, K. (2020, Fall). Why Your Board Needs a Plan for AI Oversight. *MIT Sloan Management Review*, *62*(1), 1–6.

Smith, T. G., Norasi, H., Herbst, K. M., Kendrick, M. L., Curry, T. B., Grantcharov, T. P., Palter, V. N., Hallbeck, M. S., & Cleary, S. P. (2022, December 1). Creating a Practical Transformational Change Management Model for Novel Artificial Intelligence–Enabled Technology Implementation in the Operating Room. *Mayo Clinic Proceedings. Innovations, Quality & Outcomes*, *6*(6), 584–596. doi:10.1016/j.mayocpiqo.2022.09.004 PMID:36324987

Velasquez, M., Andre, C., Shanks, T., & Meyer, M. J. (1990). Justice and Fairness. *Issues in Ethics*, *3*(2), 1–3.

Vogel, S. (2023). When AI Discriminates, Who's to Blame? *Talent Management*. https://www.reworked.co/talent-management/when-ai-discriminates-whos-to-blame/

Waterman, R. H. Jr, Peters, T. J., & Phillips, J. R. (1980, June 1). Structure is not organization. *Business Horizons*, *23*(3), 14–26. doi:10.1016/0007-6813(80)90027-0

White, D., Baghai, M., & Coley, S. (2000). *The alchemy of growth*. Perseus Books.

KEY TERMS AND DEFINITIONS

Artificial Intelligence: The ability of a digital computer to use a mathematical model to make inferences commonly associated with intelligent beings from data.

Inclusion and Diversity: A framework through which an organization should ensure through effort and policy that people with different characteristics all feel respected, accepted, supported, and valued in the work environment.

Discrimination: The unjust or prejudicial treatment of different categories of people, especially on ethnicity, age, sex, or disability.

Strategic Risk Management: Evaluating the likelihood of business decisions related to a company's plans to achieve its business objectives and choosing the ones that will enable the company to succeed.

Transition Management: A process of getting the best out of change and managing the conversion from one state to another.

Change Management: A structured process for planning and implementing new ways of operating.

Human Resources: The department and business activities associated with the hiring, administering, and training of personnel.

Responsible Artificial Intelligence: A multi-disciplinary effort to design and build AI systems with careful consideration of their fairness, accountability, and transparency.

Chapter 11
Exploring the Nature of Medical Device Privacy and Security Legal Regulations

Jennifer Ferreras-Perez
https://orcid.org/0009-0003-0972-1824
Marymount University, USA

Darrell Norman Burrell
https://orcid.org/0000-0002-4675-9544
Marymount University, USA

ABSTRACT

Medical devices, from wearable health trackers to pacemakers and telehealth visits, have become increasingly prevalent. Addressing concerns about data privacy and risk management is essential with the amount of personal data collected through these devices rising. While the Health Insurance Portability and Accountability Act (HIPAA) has long been considered the primary regulation for patient personal health information data, the Food and Drug Administration (FDA) and the Healthcare Supply Chain Association (HSCA) have enacted new guidelines that aim to hold medical device manufacturers accountable for data privacy and risk management. The chapter concludes that these legal regulations individually touch upon essential aspects of patient data privacy and medical device safety; however, their combined influence provides a more substantial base to hold medical de-vice manufacturers responsible for risk management and data protection.

INTRODUCTION

The rapid advancements in technology and medical devices, along with the increased interoperability of systems, services, and devices, have significantly improved patient care and lowered healthcare costs (Hein, 2022). Medical devices often save lives by performing critical functions that cannot be compromised without jeopardizing direct patient care. However, the growing number of cyber incidents is

DOI: 10.4018/979-8-3693-1634-4.ch011

directly proportional to the increased availability of consumer data generated by the adoption of medical devices and telemedicine (McKeon, 2021). In 2022, the amount of medical data collected from these devices was observed to have increased by 100% every three months, with the wearables market expected to reach a value of $195 billion by 2027 (Hein, 2022). Medical devices provide essential care, yet the continued cybersecurity threats that saturate the medical device industry raise concerns about the use of medical devices and patient data privacy. Research often focuses on the Health Insurance Portability and Accountability Act of 1996 (HIPAA) as the primary privacy regulation for patient personal health information data (Annas, 2003; Rights (OCR), 2008). However, the Food and Drug Administration (FDA) and Healthcare Supply Chain Association (HSCA) have enacted new guidelines to hold medical device manufacturers accountable for data privacy and risk management (Hein, 2022; McKeon, 2021). This research reviews the literature relevant to new regulations regarding medical devices and patient safety data privacy related to the manufacturer's responsibilities beyond HIPAA.

The healthcare industry has become increasingly reliant on digital systems and tools to enable the delivery of patient care (Reilly, 2019; Sweeney, 2020). The rapid adoption of digital technologies has exposed the healthcare sector to a growing array of cybersecurity threats and increased the risk of data breaches (Reilly, 2019; Sweeney, 2020). A key factor contributing to the prevalence of cybercrime within the healthcare sector is the proliferation of data (Reilly, 2019; Sweeney, 2020). Healthcare organizations generate and store vast amounts of sensitive patient data, including medical records, payment information, and other personal data (Reilly, 2019; Sweeney, 2020). As such, the healthcare industry has become a target for cybercriminals seeking to access and exploit this data (Reilly, 2019; Sweeney, 2020).

The development of connected medical devices has enabled the provision of medical care to a larger population with a greater degree of accuracy and efficiency (Ponemon Institute, 2018). In the past few years, connected medical devices have become increasingly vulnerable to security risks, particularly those related to cyber-attacks (Ponemon Institute, 2018). According to the 2018 Global State of Cybersecurity in Healthcare Organizations report from the (Ponemon Institute, the number of security incidents involving connected medical devices increased by more than 10 percent in the last four years (Ponemon Institute, 2018).

Connected medical devices are a rapidly growing technology in the healthcare sector, with a wide range of applications, including medical diagnostics, medical imaging, and medical monitoring Ponemon Institute, 2018). Using such devices has enabled healthcare providers to access and analyze patient data more quickly and accurately, improving patient outcomes Ponemon Institute, 2018). However, the interconnected nature of these devices also makes them vulnerable to cyber-attacks, which can compromise the security of patient data and the functioning of the medical devices themselves (Ponemon Institute, 2018).

According to the 2018 Global State of Cybersecurity in Healthcare Organizations report, the most common types of cyber-attacks on connected medical devices are malware, ransomware, phishing attempts, and unsecured access to medical devices (Ponemon Institute, 2018). Malware is malicious software designed to gain access to a system and steal data or cause damage to the device (Ponemon Institute, 2018). Ransomware encrypts a system's data and then demands payment to regain access. Phishing attempts involve using fraudulent emails or websites to access a person's personal information (Reilly, 2019; Sweeney, 2020). Unsecured access to medical devices can occur when a device is not secured correctly or when an unauthorized user can gain access to the device (Ponemon Institute, 2018).

In addition to the abovementioned threats, connected medical devices are also vulnerable to cyber-attacks from hackers, who can exploit vulnerabilities in the device's software or hardware (Ponemon Institute, 2018). For example, a hacker may gain access to a device by exploiting a vulnerability in its operating system or using a "man-in-the-middle" attack to access the device's data. Furthermore, unencrypted data transmission and data storage on unsecured networks can also make connected medical devices vulnerable to cyber-attacks (Ponemon Institute, 2018).

Problem Statement

The healthcare industry is under increasing pressure to ensure the privacy and security of patient data. In today's digital world, where medical records are increasingly digitalized, there is an ever-growing need to protect patient data from misuse and unauthorized access. From a legal and ethical perspective, the healthcare industry is responsible for safeguarding patient information and maintaining the confidentiality of patient records. Equally important is the need to ensure the accuracy and timeliness of data sharing and the security of data when it is stored, transmitted, or processed.

Data privacy and security are of utmost importance in the healthcare industry. Patient information is highly sensitive and confidential and must be protected from unauthorized access and misuse. In the United States, HIPAA (Health Insurance Portability and Accountability Act of 1996) provides a comprehensive set of privacy and security regulations for protecting patient data. HIPAA requires that healthcare providers, health plans, and vendors who create, maintain, or transmit protected health information (PHI) must implement several security measures, including physical, administrative, and technical safeguards, to ensure the security of PHI (HIPAA, 1996). Additionally, organizations must ensure that all patient data is accurate and up to date and is only shared with authorized personnel. This paper explores the nature of information security from cybercriminals through an exploration of current and emerging literature.

Method

A systematic literature search was conducted in the PubMed, MEDLINE, and Scopus databases, using the terms "medical device," "data privacy," "data security," "HIPAA," and "HSCA." The search was limited to English-language articles published between 2008 and 2018. The search yielded 130 relevant articles evaluated for relevance to the topic and problem statement.

LITERATURE REVIEW

Privacy and Data Privacy

In today's healthcare industry, connected medical devices are becoming increasingly popular. These devices offer healthcare providers a range of advantages and benefits, including improved patient outcomes, cost savings, and increased efficiency (Kapoor, 2019). However, with the increased use of connected medical devices comes an increased need for laws and legal requirements to ensure patient safety and protect healthcare organizations from potential risks (Kapoor, 2019).

Connected medical devices are defined as "any device, instrument, or system connected to a computer system, network, or other software used to monitor, measure, diagnose, or treat a patient's health condition" (Kapoor, 2019, p. 2). These devices allow healthcare providers to access real-time data, improving patient outcomes and reducing the need for manual interventions. Connected medical devices also provide healthcare providers with improved access to patient data, allowing them to make more informed decisions and improve the overall quality of care (Kapoor, 2019).

Privacy and data privacy are paramount concerns in the medical field, particularly concerning medical research and patient information. On one side, the need for medical research and data collection is essential for advancing medical procedures, treatments, and overall understanding of human health (Nass et al., 2009). On the other side, there is a growing necessity for the collection and use of Personal Health Information (PHI) and the regulatory measures needed to protect patient privacy (Nass et al., 2009). Both concepts hold significant value for society, as medical innovations, such as medical devices and telemedicine, improve access to diagnostics, therapies, and healthcare delivery. Moreover, redefining patient privacy gives individuals greater understanding and control over their PHI.

The rapid growth of technology and the healthcare industry has raised concerns about patients' personal information security. Medical data breaches have become increasingly prevalent, underscoring the importance of safeguarding PHI to maintain patient trust and comply with regulatory requirements (Nass et al., 2009). Various laws and regulations have been enacted to address privacy concerns and establish standards for protecting sensitive medical data.

The Health Insurance Portability and Accountability Act of 1996 (HIPAA) is a primary legal framework addressing medical data privacy. HIPAA's Privacy Rule establishes a minimum federal standard for protecting individually identifiable health information, including oral, written, and electronic forms of PHI (Rights (OCR), 2008). The legal rule lets individuals control how and when their PHI is disclosed, giving them a more active role in accessing and maintaining their medical records (Choi et al., 2006). Additionally, the Privacy Rule grants patients the right to amend their health information and obtain an account of when and why their PHI has been shared without their consent. This regulatory framework is centered on safeguarding individuals' PHI while allowing for the necessary exchange of health data to provide individual healthcare and ensure public health and safety (Annas, 2003; Rights (OCR), 2008).

Despite the protections afforded by HIPAA, the rapid advancement of technology and the increasing use of medical devices have raised new concerns about data privacy in healthcare. The expanding landscape of digital health tools and interconnected medical devices has introduced new vulnerabilities, making it essential to address these challenges proactively to ensure the privacy and security of patient data (Nass et al., 2009). This literature review will explore the current state of privacy and data privacy in medical devices, focusing on existing regulations and their implications for manufacturers and healthcare providers.

Health Insurance Portability and Accountability Act (HIPAA)

The Health Insurance Portability and Accountability Act (HIPAA) has long since been considered the primary regulatory reference for medical data privacy. Enacted in 1996, this federal law was created to improve the efficiency and effectiveness of the United States healthcare system, comprising two key sections. (Annas, 2003; Rights (OCR), 2008)The first, Health Care Access, Portability, and Renewability which is characterized as insurance reform, and the second, Administrative Simplification, which directed the Department of Health and Human Services (HHS) to develop national standards for the processing of electronic healthcare transactions requiring HIPAA covert entities to implement secure electronic access to health data and ad-here to HHS Privacy regulations. (Choi et al., 2006; Rights (OCR), 2008).

The HIPAA Privacy Rule involves personal health information in all forms, including oral, written, and electronic. According to the HHS National Institute of Health, the Privacy Rule's purpose is to "establish a minimum Federal standard for protecting the privacy of individually identifiable health information." (Rights (OCR), 2008) The Privacy Rule allows individuals to control how and when their PHI is disclosed, offering them a more active role in accessing and maintaining their medical records. (Choi et al., 2006) Furthermore, it provides the data owner the right to amend their health information and obtain a description of when and why their PHI has been shared if it happens without their consent. In other words, the HIPAA Privacy Rule's primary purpose is centered around the proper protection of individuals' PHI while allowing for the sharing of the health data required to provide individual health care and ensure the security of public health and safety without addressing the use of medical devices and the role manufacturer have in data safekeeping. (Annas, 2003; Rights (OCR), 2008)

Medical Devices

Medical devices are a crucial component of modern healthcare, providing essential support for diagnostics, treatment, and patient monitoring. For this study, medical devices will be defined by the Federal Food, Drug, and Cosmetic Act (FDCA) which states that a medical device is an instrument, machine, implant, or related article which includes any component or accessory intended for the use in the diagnosis, mitigation, cure, treatment, prevention of disease as intended to affect the structure or function of the body which could not otherwise be affected via chemical action. (Institute of Medicine et al., 2011) In other words, a medical device will be considered any electronic contraption that does not rely on chemical means to diagnose, mitigate, prevent, or provide therapy for the disease. These devices have seen significant growth in sophistication and complexity in recent decades, fueled by rapid technological advancements and an increased understanding of human physiology.

The benefits of medical devices are well-documented, with devices such as implantable cardiac defibrillators, insulin pumps, and prosthetic limbs transforming the lives of millions of people worldwide (Bashshur et al., 2017). However, the increasing reliance on technology and the proliferation of connected medical devices have also raised concerns about the potential risks associated with data security, privacy, and device safety.

Regulatory Framework for Medical Devices

The regulatory framework for medical devices aims to ensure the safety and effectiveness of these devices by setting standards and requirements for their design, manufacturing, marketing, and post-market surveillance. In the United States, the Food and Drug Administration (FDA) is the primary regulatory body responsible for overseeing medical devices, with regulations grouped into three classes based on the level of risk associated with the device: Class I (low risk), Class II (moderate risk), and Class III (high risk) (Institute of Medicine et al., 2011).

The European Union (E.U.) has a similar regulatory framework, with the European Medicines Agency (EMA) overseeing the regulation of medical devices across E.U. member states. The E.U. Medical Device Regulation (MDR) and In-vitro Diagnostic Medical Device Regulation (IVDR) came into force in 2017 and 2022, respectively, intending to improve patient safety, traceability, and transparency across the medical device lifecycle (European Commission, 2020).

Cybersecurity and Medical Devices

The increasing connectivity of medical devices and their integration into healthcare systems has led to growing concerns about the potential cybersecurity risks associated with these devices. Hacked or compromised devices can lead to severe consequences, including patient harm, unauthorized access to sensitive patient data, and disruption to healthcare services (Kruse et al., 2017).

Recognizing these risks, regulatory bodies such as the FDA and EMA have issued guidance on cybersecurity considerations for medical device manufacturers. The FDA's guidance on the management of cybersecurity in medical devices focuses on the pre-market and post-market phases of the device lifecycle, emphasizing the need for manufacturers to address cybersecurity risks during the design, development, and ongoing maintenance of their devices (U.S. Food and Drug Administration, 2018). Similarly, the EMA's guidance emphasizes the importance of risk management and the integration of cybersecurity considerations into developing and maintaining medical devices (European Medicines Agency, 2019).

Recent research has highlighted the need for a comprehensive approach to addressing cybersecurity risks in medical devices, incorporating collaboration between device manufacturers, healthcare providers, regulators, and other stakeholders (AAMI, 2020). Furthermore, experts have called for increased investments in cybersecurity research, education, and training to build a robust workforce capable of managing the growing complexity and scale of connected medical devices (Williams et al., 2019).

The U.S. Food and Drug Administration (FDA)

The regulations of medical devices originated in 1983 with rudimentary ideals that corresponded with the simplicity of the technological devices that were marketed at the time. By the 1970s, the original framework was no longer adequate or flexible enough for the new wave of devices which had increased in sophistication; Therefore, in 1976, congress introduced a new comprehensive system of regulations which, due to the continuous growth of technology, was then supplanted in 1990, once again amended in 1997 to the Federal Food, Drug, and Cosmetic Act (FDC) creating the grounds for the current U.S. Food and Drug Administration (FDA) medical device regulatory framework. (Institute of Medicine et al., 2011)

The FDA regulatory division classifies medical devices into three classes: class I - *low,* class II - *moderate, and class* III - *high-risk,* which determine the submission requirements for regulatory acceptance and compliance. (Institute of Medicine et al., 2011) The Pre-market Notification 510(k) clearance process is required for medical devices within categories I and II. This pre-market notification was established to allow new medical devices to be brought to market by demonstrating that they were substantially equivalent to already marketed devices, which were referred to as predicates. (Center for Devices and Radiological Health, 2020; Institute of Medicine et al., 2011)

Similarly, the Pre-market Approval (PMA) addresses the requirements for class III devices that pose a significant risk of illness and injury or are found drastically different to Class I and II predicate through the 510(k) process. The PMA procedure differs from other approval processes because it calls for clinical data to back up device claims. (Center for Devices and Radiological Health, 2020; Sutton, 2018)

The FDA expands medical device regulations to include medical device labeling and Medical Device Reporting (MDR) as part of general quality control. Medical device labeling instructs on using advertisement and promotional material, ensuring compliance with the Federal Food, Drug, and Cosmetic Act. (Institute of Medicine et al., 2011; Sutton, 2018) Adequate usage instructions must be provided on the label, with also requires accurate and free of misleading information. In addition to the labeling requirement, MDR is developed and submitted by device manufacturers or facility users to document adverse events connected to defective medical devices, such as critical injuries, malfunctions, or fatalities. (Sutton, 2018) Summarily, FDA's medical device regulations aim to improve the quality control and safety of medical device manufacturing by ensuring continuous monitoring and performance for the design, manufacturing, and implementation process.

The Health Supply Chain Association (HSCA)

The Healthcare Supply Chain Association (HSCA) is a trade association that represents healthcare group purchasing organizations (GPOs) throughout the United States. Its mission is to advocate for fair procurement practices and education to improve efficiency in buying and selling healthcare services. (McKeon, 2021) The HSCA's focus on medical device manufacturers, service providers, and healthcare delivery organizations stems from the desire to help protect patient health, safety, and privacy. (*Medical Device and Service Cybersecurity: Key Consideration for Manufacturers & Healthcare Delivery Organizations*, 2021)

As such, the HSCA has created a list of recommendations to address potential security risks to ensure continuous safekeeping proactively. Included in the general HSCA cybersecurity recommendations are the following:

- Designation of an information technology security officer
- Maintenance of anti-virus software and update of legacy devices
- Implementation of role-appropriate cyber training and assessments
- Regulatory compliance for the purchasing of medical devices
- Cybersecurity risks assessment
- Data encryption and data handling

In addition to the generalized recommendations, the HSCA released *'Recommendations for Medical Device Cybersecurity Terms and Conditions,'* which details potential purchasing contract terms and conditions that could aid in rapidly adopting stringent cybersecurity measures. (McKeon, 2021) This measure fortifies the security, privacy, and quality control postures by increasing the requirement with periodic phishing tests, proactive patching processes, proper network segmentation, firewall implementation, and the provision of an MDS2 from all medical device manufacturers. Devices(McKeon, 2021; *Medical Device and Service Cybersecurity: Key Consideration for Manufacturers & Healthcare Delivery Organizations*, 2021)

The manufacturer Disclosure Statement for Medical Device Security (MDS2) was Developed by the Healthcare Information and Management Systems Society (HIMSS) and the National Electrical Manufacturers Association (NEMA) and was most recently revised by NEMA. The Medical Imaging & Technology Alliance (MITA), the Manufacturer Disclosure Statement for Medical Device Security (*MDS2),* is used by manufacturers of medical devices as a voluntary standard to provide critical security-related information to healthcare delivery organizations. The MDS2 is intended to be used as part of the security procurement process because it defines the roles and responsibilities of manufacturers and healthcare delivery organizations in maintaining a connected device security posture. While not mandatory, device manufacturers often provide it upfront to ensure better visibility into the security and privacy profiles of the device advertised. (James, 2022)

CONCLUSION

The results from the literature outline that medical device manufacturers are facing increased scrutiny from the FDA and the HSCA and that new regulations and guidelines have been enacted to hold them accountable for data privacy and risk management. The articles reviewed in this study provided evidence of the challenges associated with ensuring data privacy and security in the medical device industry and the potential risks data breaches pose. The articles also highlighted the need for new regulations and guidelines to ensure the safety of patient data.

The HIPAA regulations aim to change how the public perceives privacy within the healthcare industry by educating patients about their privacy rights via the patient privacy rights notice. However, it does not address medical devices, device safety, and data privacy concerns. (*Medical Device and Service Cybersecurity: Key Consideration for Manufacturers & Healthcare Delivery Organizations*, 2021) To address these concerns, the FDA has developed a guide to assist the industry in identifying cybersecurity issues that manufacturers should consider when designing and developing medical devices and preparing pre-market submissions for those devices. Furthermore, the HSCA has created a list of recommendations for certifying suppliers of network-accessible medical devices, software, and services that complement and follow FDA guidelines. The HSCA aims to ensure that medical device manufacturers increase transparency by providing a manufacturer disclosure statement (MDS2). In conclusion, each of these regulations individually touches upon essential aspects of patient data privacy and medical device safety; However, their combined influence provides a more substantial base to hold medical device manufacturers responsible for risk management and data protection.

REFERENCES

AAMI. (2020). *Medical device cybersecurity: A guide for industry consensus standards and best practices*. Association for the Advancement of Medical Instrumentation. https://www.aami.org/docs/default-source/default-document-library/standards/medical-device-cybersecurity-guide-aami-tir97_a3-2020.pdf?sfvrsn=6

Annas, G. J. (2003). HIPAA Regulations—A New Era of Medical-Record Privacy? *The New England Journal of Medicine*, *348*(15), 1486–1490. doi:10.1056/NEJMlim035027 PMID:12686707

Bashshur, R. L., Howell, J. D., Krupinski, E. A., Harms, K. M., Bashshur, N., & Doarn, C. R. (2017). The empirical foundations of telemedicine interventions in primary care. *Telemedicine Journal and e-Health*, *23*(5), 342–375. doi:10.1089/tmj.2016.0045 PMID:27128779

Center for Devices and Radiological Health. (2020, September 4). *Overview of Device Regulation*. FDA. https://www.fda.gov/medical-devices/device-advice-comprehensive-regulatory-assistance/overview-device-regulation

Choi, Y. B., Capitan, K. E., Krause, J. S., & Streeper, M. M. (2006). Challenges Associated with Privacy in Health Care Industry: Implementation of HIPAA and the Security Rules. *Journal of Medical Systems*, *30*(1), 57–64. doi:10.100710916-006-7405-0 PMID:16548416

European Commission. (2020). *Medical Devices: Regulatory framework*. European Commission. https://ec.europa.eu/growth/sectors/medical-devices/regulatory-framework_en

European Medicines Agency. (2019). *EMA medical device guidance*. European Medicines Agency. https://www.ema.europa.eu/en/human-regulatory/overview/medical-devices

Health Insurance Portability and Accountability Act of 1996. (1996, August 20). ASPE. https://aspe.hhs.gov/reports/health-insurance-portability-accountability-act-1996

Hein, A. (2022, March 8). *Prioritizing Data Privacy and Cybersecurity in Medical Devices*. Clarkston Consulting. https://clarkstonconsulting.com/insights/cybersecurity-in-medical-device/

Institute of Medicine. Board on Population Health and Public Health Practice, & Committee on the Public Health Effectiveness of the FDA 510(k) Clearance Process. (2011). *Medical Devices and the Public's Health: The FDA 510(k) Clearance Process at 35 Years*. National Academies Press. https://ebookcentral.proquest.com/lib/marymountu/detail.action?docID=3378915

James, B. (2022, July 19). *The MDS2 Standard and Its Role in Medical Device Security*. Nova Leah. https://www.novaleah.com/understanding-mds2s-and-their-role-in-medical-device-cybersecurity/

Kapoor, S. (2019). An overview of connected medical devices. *Journal of Medical Devices*, *13*(1), 1–14. doi:10.1115/1.4043048

Kruse, C. S., Frederick, B., Jacobson, T., & Monticone, D. K. (2017). Cybersecurity in healthcare: A systematic review of modern threats and trends. *Technology and Health Care*, *25*(1), 1–10. doi:10.3233/THC-161263 PMID:27689562

McKeon, J. (2021, December 30). HSCA Releases Cybersecurity Guidelines for Medical Device Manufacturers. *HealthITSecurity*. https://healthitsecurity.com/news/hsca-releases-cybersecurity-guidelines-for-medical-device-manufacturers

Medical Device and Service Cybersecurity. (2021). *Key Consideration for Manufacturers & Healthcare Delivery Organizations*. Healthcare Supply Chain Association (HSCA). https://www.supplychainassociation.org/wp-content/uploads/2021/12/Cybersecurity-Key-Considerations-FINAL.pdf

Nass, S. J., Levit, L. A., & Gostin, L. O. (2009). *Beyond the HIPAA Privacy Rule: Enhancing Privacy, Improving Health Through Research*. National Academies Press., doi:10.17226/12458

Ponemon Institute. (2018). *2018 Global State of Cybersecurity in Healthcare Organizations*. Ponemon. https://www.ponemon.org/local/upload/file/2018_Global_State_of_Cybersecurity_in_Healthcare_Organizations.pdf

Reilly, M. (2019). Cybersecurity in healthcare: What can organizations do? *Forbes*. https://www.forbes.com/sites/michaelreilly/2019/02/04/cybersecurity-in-healthcare-what-can-organizations-do/#75f322bb7d7e

Sutton, B. (2018). *Overview of Regulatory Requirements: Medical Devices - Transcript*. FDA. https://www.fda.gov/training-and-continuing-education/cdrh-learn/overview-regulatory-requirements-medical-devices-transcript

Sweeney, J. (2020). *Cybersecurity for healthcare organizations: Strategies for protecting patient data*. UDEMY. https://blog.udemy.com/cybersecurity-for-healthcare-organizations/

Williams, P. A., Woodward, A. J., & Furdella, J. (2019). Building a robust health workforce to tackle the growing cybersecurity threats to healthcare. *International Journal of Medical Informatics, 124*, 81–84. doi:10.1016/j.ijmedinf.2019.01.012

Chapter 12
Examining Security Awareness Lapses and Critical Cyber Threats Against the Department of Defense Military Supply Chain Systems

S. Raschid Muller
https://orcid.org/0000-0002-1742-7575
University of Maryland Global Campus, USA

ABSTRACT

Cyber threats have become a major concern in today's world. As the United States Department of Defense (DoD) increasingly relies on the military supply chain systems to support the operations of their military forces, cyber threats have the potential to cause significant damage. These systems are responsible for the transportation, storage, and distribution of materials and equipment from the supplier to the end user, which includes both military personnel and civilian personnel. It is also responsible for the acquisition, maintenance, and disposal of materials and equipment. The purpose of this chapter is to examine the critical cyber threats posed to the DoD military supply chain systems and provide recommendations to address them.

INTRODUCTION

The military supply chain is integral to any military operation (D'Mello & Sharman, 2018). It is responsible for procuring, storing, and delivering supplies and equipment to the right place, at the right time, and in the right quantities (Bajwa, 2016). The military supply chain is complex, dynamic, and subject to numerous risks. Cyber threats to the military have become increasingly prominent over the past decade (Feng, 2019). Cyber-attacks can target any military area, from its communications networks and weapons systems to its personnel and critical infrastructure (US Department of Defense, 2017). Several

DOI: 10.4018/979-8-3693-1634-4.ch012

identified Nation states, criminal organizations, and terrorist groups are potential sources of cyber-attacks against military systems (Chu, 2019). In recent years, Russia and China identify as significant actors in cyber espionage against the United States (US Department of Defense, 2017). Criminal organizations are also a significant threat, with their activities ranging from the theft of sensitive data to the disruption of operations (Dudley, 2019). Several terrorist groups have engaged in cyber-attacks against the US to disrupt operations, causing panic and confusion (US Department of Defense, 2018).

The consequences of these threats can range from the disruption of operations and the loss of sensitive data to the destruction of critical infrastructure and the loss of life (US Department of Defense, 2017). Cyber-attacks seek access to sensitive information that could be used to gain an advantage on the battlefield (Chu, 2019). They can also disrupt operations and communications networks, potentially causing significant delays and disruption to military operations (US Department of Defense, 2017). In extreme cases, cyber-attacks can cause physical damage and destruction, such as the Stuxnet attack against Iranian nuclear facilities in 2010 (Langner, 2014).

In order to protect against these threats, the military must remain vigilant in its efforts to identify, prevent, and respond to cyber threats, which includes developing and implementing effective policies and procedures to protect against cyber-attacks and monitoring networks and systems for suspicious activity (US Department of Defense, 2017). The military must also train personnel on cybersecurity measures, such as secure password management and data storage (US Department of Defense, 2018). Additionally, the military must be prepared to respond to cyber threats by developing and maintaining an effective incident response plan (US Department of Defense, 2017). This paper provides an overview of the military supply chain, including the main elements and processes and the supply chain risks. It further discusses the role of logistics in military supply chains and the application of lean principles to the military supply chain. Finally, it examines the importance of supply chain security and resilience to the success of military operations.

Significance of the Study

The DoD's military supply chain systems are essential to the United States defense capabilities (Chu, 2019). The threat of disruption or compromise of these systems is a serious concern for the DoD. If these systems are compromised, critical supply chain operations could be disrupted, significantly disrupting the DoD's ability to operate. This could significantly impact national security and the United States' ability to respond to foreign and domestic threats. Therefore, understanding the critical cyber threats facing the DoD's military supply chain systems is essential to the DoD's ability to protect and defend the United States.

Methodology

In order to examine the critical cyber threats facing the DoD's military supply chain systems, a review of the literature was conducted. The literature review focused on scholarly articles, reports, and other sources that addressed the topic of critical cyber threats against the DoD's military supply chain systems. Key search terms included: cyber threats, cyber-defense, military supply chains, Department of Defense, hacking, information systems, software assurance, and nation-state actors. The databases and their hosts (shown in parentheses) included PEW Research, ABI Inform Complete (ProQuest), ResearchGate, Academia.edu, Business Source Premier (EBSCO), Google Scholar, ACM Digital Library, European

Reference Index for the Humanities and Social Sciences (ERIH), Baidu Scholar, and DOAJ (Directory of Open Access Journals).

General Problem Statement

Cyber awareness lapses assume leadership is lacking during cyber threats to the DoD supply chain (Sodhi et al., 2021; Muller, 2020). In 2020, Sunburst malware infected thousands of private networks. The US government agencies led some spectators to embrace frantic views of the event as the first step in the full-fledged cyber war. Sunburst intelligence operations will likely continue for a while, but it was not an act of war (Sodhi et al., 2021). The compromise of many federal and high-value private-sector networks yielded valuable information. This information provided access to more disruptive attacks, such as introducing deletion, disinformation, and suspicious alteration of data. While there is no public evidence of these attacks on targeted networks, all indications suggest this was a successful penetration of US government information systems (Sodhi et al., 2021).

People rely on software such as cloud computing behind an email service, a new fifth-generation (5G) telecommunications distribution, and the system that observes a distant oil rig. Software is an indispensable and widespread component of modern society (Herr et al., 2020). Unlike basic systems, the software is progressive. It depends on continual revisions from areas and updates to address security shortcomings and susceptibilities and to make practical improvements (Herr et al., 2020). Ongoing upkeep leaves software supply chains time-consuming, problematic, and continuous flexibility causing substantial risks for worldwide organizations (Herr et al., 2020).

Despite warnings from critical security community members and increased attention to supply-chain security, the software has primarily taken a backseat to hardware, especially 5G, in policy debates over supply-chain security (Seals, 2019). One of the top security challenges of mobile networks is software production within 5G networks. It fundamentally differs from prior wireless networks because they are mainly software-defined and virtualized (Seals, 2019). Historically known in hardware, network functions become virtual software capabilities in 5G, all organized via a flexible software control plane. Even the air interfaces in the radio access network are software-defined in 5G (Seals, 2019).

Specific Problem Statement

The research suggested that cyber threats are growing exponentially against targeted information systems. Unfortunately, cybersecurity awareness lapses when addressing cyber threats to the DoD supply chain supported by the same targeted systems. Cybersecurity is an issue consumers, executive management, and the board of directors take for granted, but INFOSEC analysts do not (Dempsey & Rosenquist, 2015; Muller & Burrell, 2022). INFOSEC analysts work daily to protect systems from attack and have been quite effective for many years (Muller & Lind, 2020). However, cyber threats are much more severe than ever and growing in frequency and severity. Everyone should consider cybersecurity, whether in an employee's personal or employer's professional life (Dempsey & Rosenquist, 2015).

What worked many years ago must be revised to protect companies in the present and future. First, what has changed are the technology platforms that are more colossal targets than ever, given the breadth of items controlled (Dempsey & Rosenquist, 2015). Second, the amount and value of the data produced and stored have grown advantageously for criminals. Third, the world's interconnectedness makes it easier for people to steal and disrupt (Dempsey & Rosenquist, 2015). Finally, perpetrators are more sophisticated, better organized, better funded, and more challenging to catch and bring to justice (Dempsey & Rosenquist, 2015). This research aims to report on security awareness lapses that leadership takes for granted when addressing cyber threats to the DoD supply chain. Additionally, this research aims to inform the supply chain community of the impacts of cybersecurity's lack of awareness on its overall effect on business continuity.

Definitions

Covered defense information. Covered defense information means all information that controls contact, usage, facsimile, conversion, execution, presentation, release, disclosure, or distribution (CUI Registry, 2017).

Critical cybersecurity threats. Critical cybersecurity threats are any malicious activity or attack that could compromise confidential data or disrupt a system or network (McKee, 2020).

Critical goods and materials. Critical goods and materials mean goods and raw materials currently defined under statute or regulation as necessary materials, technologies, or infrastructure (Biden, 2021).

Materiel distribution. Materiel distribution means an amount that results in a distribution to an unclassified or classified claim equal to or above 5% of such allowed claim (i.e., equipment, apparatus, and supplies used by an organization or institution; Leary, 2020).

MITRE ATT&CK. MITRE ATT&CK means Adversarial Tactics, Techniques, and Common Knowledge. This framework serves as a knowledge-base model for cyber adversary behavior and reflects several phases of an adversary's attack lifecycle (MITRE, 2021).

Supply chain. A supply chain includes a network of individuals, organizations, activities, resources, and technology used to create and sell products from manufacturing companies to delivery to consumers (Lutkevich, 2022).

Supply chain attack. A supply chain attack happens when someone infiltrates a company's system through an outside provider with access to the systems and data (Korolov, 2021).

Supply chain risk management. Supply chain risk management (SCRM) addresses the threats and weaknesses of commercially acquired information and communications technologies within and used by government information and weapon systems (MITRE, 2021).

LITERATURE REVIEW

Elements of Military Supply Chains

The main elements of a military supply chain are procurement, storage, and transportation (Feng, 2019). Procurement involves the acquisition of supplies and equipment from external sources. Storage includes the warehousing of supplies and equipment and the management of inventory (Feng, 2019). Transportation involves physically moving supplies and equipment from one location to another (Feng, 2019). These elements are interconnected and interdependent. For example, the availability of supplies is affected by transportation delays, while transportation capacity can be limited by storage capacity (Mavros, Heijman, & van der Vorst, 2018).

Several processes support the military supply chain. These include demand forecasting, procurement and contracting, inventory management, logistics support, and risk management (Smith, 2021).

- Demand forecasting involves the estimation of future demand for supplies and equipment.
- Procurement and contracting involve acquiring supplies and equipment from external sources.
- Inventory management involves the tracking and control of inventory levels.
- Logistics support involves managing the physical movement of supplies and equipment.
- Risk management involves identifying, assessing, and mitigating supply chain risks.

The military supply chain is subject to several risks. These include operational risks, such as transportation delays and inventory shortages (Newman, 2018). There are also financial risks, such as cost overruns and budget constraints (Newman, 2018). Finally, there are compliance risks, such as export control and environmental regulations. Supply chain risks can significantly impact the success of military operations (Newman, 2018). For example, an inventory shortage can delay the delivery of supplies, while a cost overrun can lead to budget constraints.

Logistics also plays an important role in military supply chains, which involves the planning, execution, and control of the physical movement of supplies and equipment (Feng, 2019). Logistics support includes the management of transportation, warehousing, inventory, and packaging (Feng, 2019). It also involves coordinating the various elements of the supply chain, such as procurement, storage, and transportation, and is essential for the efficient and effective operation of the military supply chain (Feng, 2019). Lastly, Kumar & Kumar (2020) stated that lean manufacturing principles also apply to the military supply chain, which focuses on eliminating waste, optimizing processes, reducing costs, and improving efficiency.

Cyber Attacks Against the U.S. Supply Chain

Most commercial, social, economic, governmental, and cultural activities occur in cyberspace and are susceptible to cyber-attacks (Li & Liu, 2021). Li and Liu surveyed and reviewed the proposed method's weaknesses and strengths of cyber security advances. Many private companies and government organizations worldwide are facing the problem of cyber-attacks and the danger of wireless communication technologies (Li & Liu, 2021). The world depends on electronic technology, and protecting data from cyber-attacks is challenging. The purpose of cyber-attacks is to harm companies financially (Li & Liu, 2021). However, in some other cases, cyber-attacks can have military or political purposes. Some of these damages are personal computer viruses, knowledge breaks, data distribution services (DDS), and other assault vectors. To this end, various organizations use various solutions to prevent damage caused by cyber-attacks (Li & Liu, 2021).

Global supply chains face many risks, however, few structured and systematic approaches exist to assess supply chain risks. Manuj and Mentzer (2011) investigated logistics, supply chain management, operations management, strategy, and international business to develop a global supply chain risk management (SCRM) model. In addition, cybersecurity is not simply a corporate concern but a supply chain issue (Manuj & Mentzer, 2011). This third report explored the US Department of Defense (DoD) supply chain responses to the recent Defense Federal Acquisition Regulations Supplement (DFARS) requirement. Findings showed that supply chain cybersecurity is critical, but the weakest link is small to medium-sized firms in the supply chain (Melnyk et al., 2018).

In today's environment, cybersecurity is imperative where innovation and responsiveness are critical performance requirements, and digital is becoming increasingly important (Melnyk et al., 2018). More often than not, cybersecurity is a corporate and information technology (IT) concern. Nevertheless,

Melnyk views the concern as narrow and limited. Another cybersecurity concern is supply chains that address all facets of a company's business. Appropriate cybersecurity levels involve the new DFARS requirement to ensure its safety (Melnyk et al., 2018) with some resistance. Melnyk et al. explored how members of the DoD supply chain respond to this requirement and cybersecurity. In this third article, the analysis and recommendations are critical to act upon within the DoD supply chain that operates with IT and intellectual property (IP; Melnyk et al., 2018).

Ghadge et al. (2012) examined supply chain risk management (SCRM) from universal systems by considering evolved typologies. Those researchers identified critical strategic changes in the field and outlined future requirements and research opportunities in SCRM (Ghadge et al., 2012). Earlier research findings from the systematic literature review (SLR) methodology strengthened the cross-validation against the results obtained from a related text mining activity (Ghadge et al., 2012). The SLR methodology provided a complete, impartial view of the advances of SCRM. As a result, significant research areas were multi-viewpoints, explanatory, and thematic data analysis (Ghadge et al., 2012). In addition, Ghadge et al.'s study indicated a growth of SCRM from the beginning to a longitudinal activity over the past decade. The holistic approach to SCRM was an essential missing link and closed the gap from earlier literature surveys. The outcome of the SLR provided vital insights into the present and future ventures of the SCRM field. The identified research gaps, insights, and future directions might encourage new research techniques to manage the risks in the worldwide supply chain environment (Ghadge et al., 2012).

The Chief Information Security Officer (CISO) is the official responsible for the organization's physical and cyber security position and has a complete view of the company's operational risks (Fruhlinger, 2021). However, any individual in the company can cause a supply chain attack when the organization's system infiltrates an outside provider with access to an organization's systems and data (Korolov, 2021). Such intentional or unintentional attacks change the surface of the typical business. As a result, additional suppliers and service providers influence sensitive data (Korolov, 2021).

Since 2021, the Biden-Harris Administration has navigated an unprecedented period in economic history (Sullivan & Deese, 2022). The COVID-19 pandemic uncovered specific weaknesses in the US domestic industrial base and significant supply chains. Those weaknesses resulted from years of under-investing, subcontracting, and offshoring over long-standing security, maintenance, and resistance. As a result, President Biden highlighted strengthening critical supply chains and rejuvenating the US industrial base (Sullivan & Deese, 2022). In February 2021, he signed Executive Order 14017 (EO), America's Supply Chains, which introduced an all-of-government review of the supply chains creating the US industrial base. This initial focus was on four critical products: (1) semiconductor devices and innovative packaging; (2) high-capacity batteries, including electric-vehicle batteries; (3) critical minerals and materials, including rare earth elements; and medications; (4) active pharmaceutical ingredients (APIs; Sullivan & Deese, 2022).

In June 2021, the Biden-Harris Administration reported a 100-day review of four critical products (Sullivan & Deese, 2022). The inspections identified ordinary susceptibilities and weaknesses across US supply chains. For example, many supply chains lacked US manufacturing capability, uneven incentives, and short-term private markets. In addition, an inadequate adoption occurred of industrial policies by partners, competitor nations, global sourcing, and limited international coordination (Sullivan & Deese, 2022).

DISCUSSION

Supply Chain Continuity and Disruptions

Supply chain continuity and disruptions are two cyber security events that could get easily overlooked (Nelson, 2020). Organizations should have a proactive plan for supply chain disruption caused by cybersecurity activities. Supply chains consist of internal and external business process interdependencies with crucial suppliers. As a result, business continuity planning and disaster recovery strategies considered the influence of cybersecurity threats and risks throughout the supply chain (Nelson, 2020). Discovery recovery strategies may mean the need for additional resources devoted to managing and monitoring supplier continuity risks from cyber security threats. As a result, businesses might be influenced and seen as tolerable risks for identified cyber security threats (Nelson, 2020). Those threats could drive investments in people, processes, tools, and systems to achieve business continuity internally and necessitate additional cybersecurity requirements for supply chain partners (Nelson, 2020).

Addressing Supply Chain Vulnerabilities

The US Department of Defense (2022) released a tactical plan to address supply chain weaknesses in the defense industrial base (DIB). Executive Order (EO) 14017, America's Supply Chains, directed Cabinet agencies to evaluate supply chains in sectors essential for America's economic and national security (US Department of Defense, 2022). Underscored are the historical strength and value of America's supply chains and fortified assets to build greater supply chain flexibility (US Department of Defense, 2022). In addition, the department focuses on strategic enablers that strengthen overall mission success and supply chain resilience, such as workforce, cyber posture, small business, and manufacturing capabilities (US Department of Defense, 2022).

Gaps in Supply Chains

Sodhi et al.'s (2011) findings characterize the diversity from the perspectives of operations and supply chain management scholars about three gaps:

1. A definition gap in how researchers define supply chain risk management (SCRM)
2. A process gap about inadequate coverage of response to risk incidents
3. A methodology gap in the inefficient use of empirical methods

Risk management is crucial in effectively operating supply chains in various uncertainties (Ho et al., 2015). Over the years, many researchers focused on SCRM by contributing to defining, operationalizing, and mitigating risks. Ho et al. reviewed and synthesized the extant literature on SCRM in the past decade. SCRM is a burgeoning area emerging from practitioners' and researchers' growing appreciation for supply chain risk (Sodhi et al., 2021).

However, there is a diverse perception of research in supply chain risk because Sodhi et al. (2021) have approached this area from different domains. The researchers' study of diversity from the perspectives of operations and supply chain management scholars allowed them to survey two focus groups (i.e., members of Supply Chain Thought Leaders and International SCRM groups) with open-ended questions (Sodhi et al., 2021). Finally, they surveyed operations and supply chain management researchers during the 2009 Institute for Operations Research and the Management Sciences (INFORMS) meeting in San Diego, California. Findings characterized the diversity of three gaps: (1) a definition gap in how researchers defined SCRM, (2) a process gap about inadequate coverage of response to risk incidents, and (3) a methodology gap of inefficient use of an empirical method (Sodhi et al., 2021). The DoD made sufficient progress on seven actions and outcomes recommended for improving supply chain management. Therefore, DoD removed this high-risk area. Congressional attention, DoD leadership commitment, and collaboration contributed to this successful outcome (see Figure 1).

Figure 1. DoD supply chain management

Note. Sodhi, M. S., Son, B.-G., & Tang, C. S. (2011). Researchers' perspectives on supply chain risk management. Production and Operations Management, 21(1), 1-13. https://doi.org/10.1111/j.1937-5956.2011.01251.x

Source: GAO analysis. | GAO-19-157SP

From 2014 to 2017, the DoD identified 18 actions and outcomes needed to implement its supply chain management and removed them from the High-Risk List. In the 2017 High-Risk Report, the DoD addressed 11 actions and met capacity and leadership action in materiel distribution. However, the DoD needed additional actions to implement the remaining seven measures and outcomes related to the monitoring criteria (see Figure 2).

Figure 2. Segments of GAO's Department Of Defense's supply chain management high-risk area
Note. Sodhi, M. S., Son, B.-G., & Tang, C. S. (2011). Researchers' perspectives on supply chain risk management. Production and Operations Management, 21(1), 1-13. https://doi.org/10.1111/j.1937-5956.2011.01251.x

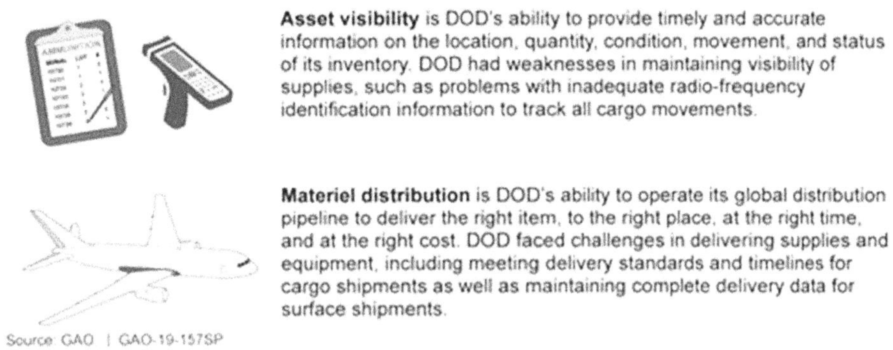

Asset Visibility

The DoD organizes approximately five million inventory items (i.e., spare parts), with a reported value of about $93 billion as of September 2017 (US Government Accountability Office, 2022). Therefore, to support the force's capabilities and ensure that the DoD does not spend resources not necessarily used with defense and national priorities. Supply chain management includes three segments—inventory management, asset visibility, and temporal distribution. The DoD supply chain management has been on the high-risk list for the past three decades (US Government Accountability Office, 2022).

Supply chain management includes three segments: inventory management, asset visibility, and temporal distribution (US Government Accountability Office, 2022). Since 1990, DoD Supply Chain Management has been on the high-risk list beginning with inventory management. Supply chain management was on the high-risk list due to inept and unproductive management practices that led to surplus inventory. In 2005, additional asset visibility and equipment distribution caused a high-risk list of weaknesses identified during operations in Iraq and Afghanistan. These backlogs of hundreds of pallets and containers at distribution points were part of significant weaknesses (US Government Accountability Office, 2022). In 2017, DoD removed inventory management from this area because it made vibrant improvements by reducing excess inventory by about $600 million, thus addressing high-risk criteria. These improvements resulted in demonstrable and sustained improvements (US Government Accountability Office, 2022).

Furthermore, DoD addressed the three remaining actions and outcomes outlined in 2017 to mitigate long-standing weaknesses in asset visibility. Senior-level officials managed asset visibility improvement efforts. The Asset Visibility Working Group issued the strategy, identified improvement opportunities, and monitored initiatives' implementation in 2014, 2015, and 2017 (see Figure 3).

Figure 3. Asset visibility
Note. Sodhi, M. S., Son, B.-G., & Tang, C. S. (2011). Researchers' perspectives on supply chain risk management. Production and Operations Management, 21(1), 1-13. https://doi.org/10.1111/j.1937-5956.2011.01251.x

Materiel Distribution

For the past five years, the DoD has met the criteria of commitment, capacity, and leadership commitment for materiel distribution (US Government Accountability Office, 2022). Further, DoD has fully addressed the four remaining actions and outcomes outlined in 2017 to mitigate or resolve long-standing weaknesses in material distribution (US Government Accountability Office, 2022). Consequently, the DoD has met the monitoring and demonstrated progress criteria for material distribution to remove this area from the High-Risk List, as shown in Figure 4 below.

Figure 4. Materiel distribution
Note. Sodhi, M. S., Son, B.-G., & Tang, C. S. (2011). Researchers' perspectives on supply chain risk management. Production and Operations Management, 21(1), 1-13. https://doi.org/10.1111/j.1937-5956.2011.01251.x

Types of Human Error

While the opportunities for human error are virtually infinite, two types of human error are (1) skill-based errors and (2) decision-based errors. The difference between these two depends on whether or not the person has the required knowledge to perform the correct action (Woods, 2019).

Skill-based errors. Everyone makes mistakes on the job, such as the supervisor and employees. The supervisor makes mistakes. The skill-based human error consists of slips, lapses, or mistakes when performing familiar tasks and activities (Woods, 2019). In these scenarios, the end-user knows the correct action but needs to follow that action due to a temporary lapse, mistake, or negligence. For example, these errors happen because of lack of sleep, not paying attention, distractions, or brief memory lapses (Woods, 2019).

Decision-based errors. Decision-based errors are when an employee makes a wrong decision (Woods, 2019). Many factors include the user needing more information about the specific circumstance or not even realizing that they decide through their inaction (Woods, 2019). Employers can reduce human error with practical security awareness training. Employees can learn how not being secure helps businesses drive particular behavior with intelligently-automated cyber security awareness training that employees might enjoy (Woods, 2019).

RECOMMENDATIONS

Based on the literature review, there are several potential strategies for mitigating the critical cyber threats facing the DoD's military supply chain systems. The DoD must consider several areas, including technology and data security protocols, monitoring and surveillance, and improved personnel training and education across the enterprise. Future recommendations consist of the federal government's following suggestions:

1. The government recognizes cybersecurity as a national and financial security concern within supply chains.
2. One of the recommendations is to shorten the process of accomplishing the new DFARS requirement.
3. The government should focus on immediate implementation and emphasize essential programmatic items in the supply chain.
4. The government should implement cybersecurity in DoD supply chains and develop a certification program focused on cybersecurity.
5. Significant contractors could develop a compelling business case for cybersecurity.
6. The DoD should help SMEs develop and use acceptable cybersecurity measures.
7. By rewarding proactive implementation, DoD should treat SME suppliers appropriately, whether early or late adopters.
8. For SME suppliers, focus on improving knowledge and awareness regarding cybersecurity.
9. DoD should understand that cybersecurity is now a cost to the business in today's cyber/digital market.
10. DoD should understand that cybersecurity is a corporate responsibility, not including subcontracting.
11. DoD should understand the need for supply chain cybersecurity. However, in response to increasing cyber risks in its supply chain and a new mandatory clause, the Defense Federal Acquisition Regulations Supplement (DFARS) failed to comply, resulting in the termination of its status as a DoD supplier.

Anecdotal evidence involving these defense suppliers indicated that the imposition of this requirement created numerous concerns. Some concerns were about what was needed for compliance. Other concerns were the costs and benefits of becoming compliant and the short-term problems. Some firms feared they were at a cost disadvantage regarding other suppliers who decided not to pursue compliance. These suppliers did not have to incur the costs faced by the suppliers seeking DFARS compliance.

Finally, there is concern over whether the DoD is serious enough to be willing to reduce its supplier base when there is trepidation regarding whether there are enough capable suppliers to serve DoD readiness and sustainment needs. Other recommendations were to improve resilience in supply chains and mitigate future disruptions across five broad categories. 1) Rebuild domestic production and innovation capabilities. 2) Support market developments that invest in workers, sustainability, and quality. 3) Leverage the Federal government's role as a purchaser and investor in critical goods. 4) Strengthen international trade rules and trade enforcement mechanisms. 5) Work with allies and partners to decrease weaknesses in worldwide supply chains.

Implications

The implications are a systematic approach undertaken for the literature review that provided future researchers and managers with an understanding of the SCRM field. In addition, the literature review offers essential clues on new research directions for SCRM by identifying gaps in current knowledge. The identified research insights, gaps, and future trends could encourage new research techniques to manage the risks in the globalized supply chain environment (Kertysova et al., 2018).

CONCLUSION

In conclusion, the DoD military supply chain systems are highly vulnerable to cyber-attacks due to their reliance on connected networks, systems, and databases. Cyber-attacks can disrupt the supply chain systems, leading to a loss of critical data and resources. As such, the DoD must take measures to protect its supply chain systems from these threats. This chapter has shown that organizations face internal and external multifaceted cyber risks in an increasingly complex cyber threat environment (Kertysova et al., 2018). Due to their potential to cause physical damage, operational disruptions, and reputational damage, cyber incidents are business risks. Malware and phishing constitute the most common threats companies across the United States encounter. Although the costs of a malware incident are relatively low compared to other kinds of attacks, its high rate of occurrence makes malware the costliest attack vector overall (Kertysova et al., 2018). Within the malware category, businesses in the United States should be particularly wary of emerging trends in ransomware attacks. Companies need to be proactive rather than reactive when dealing with cyber threats. In addition, it is essential to nurture a multidisciplinary approach toward cybersecurity that involves all key stakeholders. As this study has shown, public-private partnerships effectively deal with cyber threats.

REFERENCES

Administration for Strategic Preparedness and Response. (2022). *Strengthening the supply chain and industrial base*. U.S. Department of Health and Human Services. https://aspr.hhs.gov/MCM/IBx/2022Report/Pages/Strengthening-the-Supply-Chain-and-Industrial-Base.aspx

Bajwa, A. A., & Azim, M. (2016). Security of military supply chains: An analysis of threats, vulnerabilities and risk mitigation strategies. *International Journal of Physical Distribution & Logistics Management*, *46*(5), 537–558. doi:10.1108/IJPDLM-05-2015-0119

Bushwick, S. (2022). *Nearly $53 billion in Federal funding could revive the U.S. computer chip industry*. Scientific American. https://www.scientificamerican.com/article/nearly-53-billion-in-federal-funding-could-revive-the-u-s-computer-chip-industry/

Chu, M. (2019, June 4). *Five cyber threats the military must address*. CIO. https://www.cio.com/article/3359657/5-cyber-threats-the-military-must-address.html

D'Mello, S., & Sharma, M. (2018). Developments in military supply chains: A review. *International Journal of Physical Distribution & Logistics Management*, *48*(2), 113–138.

Dempsey, T., & Rosenquist, M. (2015). *Navigating the digital age: The definitive cybersecurity guide for directors and officers*. Caxton Business & Legal. https://www.nyse.com/publicdocs/Navigating_The_Digital_Age.pdf

Department of Energy. (2022). *DOE releases first-ever comprehensive strategy to secure America's clean energy supply chain*. DoE. https://www.energy.gov/articles/doe-releases-first-ever-comprehensive-strategy-secure-americas-clean-energy-supply-chain

Felice, W. F. (2022). 136 countries agree on a minimum global corporate tax, but Republicans say no. *Tampa Bay Times*. https://www.tampabay.com/opinion/2022/07/30/136-countries-agree-on-a-minimum-global-corporate-tax-but-republicans-say-no-column/

Feng, M. (2019). An overview of military logistics and supply chain management. *International Journal of Logistics Systems and Management*, *37*(1), 1–16. doi:10.1504/IJLSM.2019.103783

Ghadge, A., Dani, S., & Kalawsky, R. (2012). Supply chain risk management: Present and future scope. *International Journal of Logistics Management*, *23*(3), 313–339. doi:10.1108/09574091211289200

Herr, T., Loomis, W., Schroeder, E., Scott, S., Handler, S., & Zuo, T. (2020). *Broken trust: Lessons from Sunburst*. Atlantic Council. https://www.atlanticcouncil.org/in-depth-research-reports/report/broken-trust-lessons-from-sunburst/

Ho, W., Zheng, T., Yildiz, H., & Talluri, S. (2015). Supply chain risk management: A literature review. *International Journal of Production Research*, *53*(16), 5031–5069. doi:10.1080/00207543.2015.1030467

Kertysova, K., Frinking, E., van den Dool, K., Maričić, A., & Bhattacharyya, K. (2018). *Cybersecurity: Ensuring awareness and resilience of the private sector across Europe in the mounting cyber risks*. European Economic and Social Committee. The Hague Centre for Strategic Studies. https://www.eesc.europa.eu/sites/default/files/files/qe-01-18-515-en-n.pdf

Korolov, M. (2021). *Supply chain attacks show why you should be wary of third-party providers*. CSO United States. https://www.csoonline.com/article/3191947/supply-chain-attacks-show-why-you-should-be-wary-of-third-party-providers.html

Kumar, S., & Kumar, P. (2020). Performance improvement of military supply chain: A review. *Journal of Global Operations and Strategic Sourcing*, *13*(1), 124–147.

Leary, M. (2020). *Design for additive manufacturing*. Elsevier. doi:10.1016/B978-0-12-816721-2.00006-3

Li, Y., & Liu, Q. (2021). A comprehensive review study of cyber-attacks and cyber security: Emerging trends and recent developments. *Energy Reports*, *7*, 8176–8186. doi:10.1016/j.egyr.2021.08.126

Lutkevich, B. (2022). *Supply chain.* TechTarget. https://www.techtarget.com/whatis/definition/supply-chain#:~:text=A%20supply%20chain%20is%20the,delivery%20to%20the%20end%20user

Manuj, I., & Mentzer, J. T. (2011). Global supply chain risk management. *Journal of Business Logistics*, *29*(1), 133–155. doi:10.1002/j.2158-1592.2008.tb00072.x

McKee, S. (2020). *Critical cybersecurity threats to the supply chain.* SC Media. https://www.scmagazine.com/home/security-news/critical-cybersecurity-threats-to-the-supply-chain/

MITRE. (2021). *Supply chain risk management.* MITRE. https://www.mitre.org/publications/systems-engineering-guide/enterprise-engineering/systems-engineering-for-mission-assurance/supply-chain-risk--management

Muller, S. R. (2020). An Analysis and Discussion of the Defense Information Systems Agency's Level of Compliance and Integration of the US Congress' Title Viii National Defense Authorization Act FY 2015 Subtitle D-Federal Information Technology Acquisition Reform. *Annals of Computer Science and Information Systems, 24.*

Muller, S. R., & Burrell, D. N. (2022). Social Cybersecurity and Human Behavior. [IJHIoT]. *International Journal of Hyperconnectivity and the Internet of Things*, *6*(1), 1–13. doi:10.4018/IJHIoT.305228

Muller, S. R., & Lind, M. L. (2020). Factors in Information Assurance Professionals' Intentions to Adhere to Information Security Policies. [IJSSSP]. *International Journal of Systems and Software Security and Protection*, *11*(1), 17–32. doi:10.4018/IJSSSP.2020010102

Nelson, J. (2020). *How cybersecurity impacts business continuity planning and disaster recovery.* LMG Security. https://www.lmgsecurity.com/how-cybersecurity-impacts-business-continuity-planning-and-disaster-recovery/

Office of the U.S. Trade Representative. (2021). *U.S.-EU arrangements on global steel and aluminum excess capacity and carbon intensity.* USTR. https://ustr.gov/about-us/policy-offices/press-office/fact-sheets/2021/october/fact-sheet-us-eu-arrangements-global-steel-and-aluminum-excess-capacity-and-carbon-intensity

Seals, T. (2019). Software, supply-chain dangers top list of 5G cyber risks. *Threat Post.* https://threatpost.com/software-supply-chain-5g-cyber-risks/149135/

Shih, W. C. (2020). Global supply chains in a post-pandemic world. *Harvard Business Review.* https://hbr.org/2020/09/global-supply-chains-in-a-post-pandemic-world

Sodhi, M. S., Son, B. G., & Tang, C. S. (2021). Researchers' perspectives on supply chain risk management. *Production and Operations Management*, *21*(1), 1–13. doi:10.1111/j.1937-5956.2011.01251.x

Sullivan, J., & Deese, B. (2022). *Executive order on America's supply chains: A year of action and progress.* White House. https://www.whitehouse.gov/wp-content/uploads/2022/02/Capstone-Report-Biden.pdf

The White House. (2021). *Building resilient supply chains revitalizing American manufacturing and fostering broad-based growth: 100-day reviews under Executive Order 14017*. The White House. https://www.whitehouse.gov/wp-content/uploads/2021/06/100-day-supply-chain-review-report.pdf

U.S. Department of Agriculture. (2022). *Biden-Harris administration announces new actions to strengthen food supply chains, level the playing field for growers, and lower prices for American consumers*. The White House. USDoD. https://www.usda.gov/media/press-releases/2022/05/26/biden-harris-administration-announces-new-actions-strengthen-food

U.S. Department of Defense. (2017). *Department of Defense Cyber Strategy*. USDoD. https://media.defense.gov/2017/Aug/18/2001839282/-1/-1/1/DOD-CYBER-STRATEGY-2017.PDF

U.S. Department of Defense. (2022). *Defense department releases report on strengthening defense-critical supply chains*. USDoD. https://www.defense.gov/News/Releases/Release/Article/2944488/defense-department-releases-report-on-strengthening-defense-critical-supply-cha/

U.S. Department of the Treasury. (2022). *The impact of the American rescue plan after one year*. USDT. https://home.treasury.gov/news/press-releases/jy0645

U.S. Department of Transportation. (2022). *USDOT supply chains tracker shows historic levels of goods coming into U.S., continued challenges with congestion*. USDT. https://www.transportation.gov/briefing-room/usdot-supply-chain-tracker-shows-historic-levels-goods-coming-us-continued-challenges

U.S. Government Accountability Office. (2022). *DOD supply chain management*. GAO. https://www.gao.gov/highrisk/dod-supply-chain-management

U.S. House of Representatives. (2022). American Competes act includes major supply chain provisions spearheaded by Representatives Malinowski, Blunt Rochester, and Kinzinger. US HoR. https://malinowski.house.gov/media/press-releases/america-competes-act-includes-major-supply-chain-provisions-spearheaded

Woods, D. (2019). *The role of human error in successful cyber security breaches*. The Usecure team. https://blog.usecure.io/the-role-of-human-error-in-successful-cyber-security-breaches

Chapter 13
Harnessing the Power and Simplicity of Decision Trees to Detect IoT Malware

Marwan Omar
Illinois Institute of Technoilogy, USA

Rebet Jones
https://orcid.org/0009-0008-0487-1301
Capitol Technology University, USA

Darrell Norman Burrell
https://orcid.org/0000-0002-4675-9544
Marymount University, USA

Maurice Dawson
Illinois Institute of Technology, USA

Calvin Nobles
Illinois Institute of Technology, USA

Derek Mohammed
Saint Leo University, USA

Ali Kashif Bashir
Manchester Metropolitan University, UK

ABSTRACT

Due to its simple installation and connectivity, the internet of things (IoT) is susceptible to malware attacks. As IoT devices have become more prevalent, they have become the most tempting targets for malware. In this chapter, the authors propose a novel detection and analysis method that harnesses the power and simplicity of decision trees. The experiments are conducted using a real word dataset, MaleVis, which is a publicly available dataset. Based on the results, the authors show that this proposed approach outperforms existing state-of-the-art solutions in that it achieves 97.23% precision and 95.89% recall in terms of detection and classification. A specificity of 96.58%, F1-score of 96.40%, an accuracy of 96.43%, and an average processing time per malware classification of 789 ms.

DOI: 10.4018/979-8-3693-1634-4.ch013

INTRODUCTION

An intrusion refers to an effort made to compromise security objectives by infecting a system. Consequently, numerous tools and techniques have been devised to safeguard networks and systems against intrusions, including detection systems (Chiba, 2019; Irshad, 2020). As a result, intrusion detection encompasses techniques that classify data activity as either normal or intrusive (Omar, 2022; Irshad, 2019; Chaudry, 2020) in order to identify undesirable activities. An intrusion detection system (IDS) serves the purpose of identifying and preventing intruders from accessing a monitored network, both from external and internal sources. Typically, two methods of detection are employed for this purpose. For instance, misuse detection identifies intrusions by utilizing known attack signatures, while anomaly detection relies on deviations from a normal model (Guezzaz, 2021). Hybrid detection approaches combine both misuse detection and anomaly detection, aiming to enhance the detection rate and accuracy of IDS (Omar, 2023).

Although IDSs are efficient, they possess various limitations such as real-time detection, alarm generation, and data accuracy, which can result in suboptimal detection outcomes. Consequently, intrusion detection continues to be a significant and evolving field of research. The integration of machine learning (ML) methods has been explored to enhance intrusion detection and reinforce computer security. Several studies have examined the utilization of machine learning techniques to improve data quality and training, thereby enhancing the performance of intrusion detection (Fernandes, 2019; Kheraisat, 2019; Omar, 2021). Decision trees have been employed in numerous scenarios for classification purposes, with individual features being tested independently. Following each branch split, a single classification is assigned to it (Cavos, 2019; Jeong, 2016). Decision trees provide better representation of the training set and are capable of predicting values by incorporating instances beyond the training set. The decision tree constructed by the widely known algorithms ID3 and C4.5 is guaranteed to correspond to the provided data from these algorithms.

However, data is not always gathered in a structured manner, and unstructured data must undergo preprocessing before it can be analyzed. Additionally, selecting relevant features is a crucial step in reducing computational costs associated with modeling and enhancing the performance of predictive models (Masdarri, 2020; Alazzam, 2020).

This paper presents a proposed methodology that utilizes decision trees for network intrusion detection and decision-making accuracy. Feature engineering techniques were employed to improve the quality of the data. The study validates two significant contributions. Firstly, the quality of the data was enhanced by implementing the entropy decision method. Secondly, a classifier model was developed using decision tree algorithms to effectively detect network intrusions. For more comprehensive information, please refer to the subsequent section.

Significance of the Study

The study presented in this paper focuses on harnessing the power and simplicity of decision trees to detect IoT malware. The significance of this study lies in addressing the growing vulnerability of IoT devices to malware attacks. With the increasing prevalence of IoT devices and their autonomous operation, they have become attractive targets for malicious actors. Weak passwords, lack of security measures, insecure network connections, and outdated update procedures contribute to the vulnerabilities of IoT devices (Omar, 2022).

Current methods and analysis for understanding IoT malware using static approaches have proven to be ineffective. However, recent advancements in the field of deep learning have shown great potential in cybersecurity, leveraging their data mining, learning, and expression capabilities. By proposing a novel detection and analysis method based on decision trees, this study offers a promising approach to improve the detection and classification of IoT malware.

The experimental results using a real-world dataset, MaleVis, demonstrate the effectiveness of the proposed approach. Achieving 97.23% precision and 95.89% recall in terms of detection and classification, along with a specificity of 96.58%, F1-score of 96.40%, accuracy of 96.43%, and an average processing time per malware classification of 789 ms, the proposed approach outperforms existing state-of-the-art solutions.

The significance of this study can be summarized as follows:

1. Improved IoT Malware Detection: By harnessing the power of decision trees, the proposed approach offers a more effective method for detecting and classifying IoT malware. This is crucial in protecting IoT devices from potential security breaches and mitigating the risks associated with malware attacks.
2. Simplified Analysis: Decision trees provide a simple and interpretable framework for analyzing IoT malware. This allows malware analysts to spend less time analyzing malware and enables faster response and mitigation strategies.
3. Real-World Validation: The experiments conducted using a publicly available dataset, MaleVis, validate the effectiveness of the proposed approach in a real-world setting. This adds credibility to the study's findings and demonstrates its practical applicability.
4. Advancement in Cybersecurity: By leveraging machine learning techniques and focusing on IoT malware detection, this study contributes to the broader field of cybersecurity. It showcases the potential of decision trees as a viable approach in enhancing intrusion detection systems and strengthening the overall security of IoT ecosystems.

Problem Statement

The pursuit of researching IoT malware is an imperative and compelling endeavor in today's digital landscape. As the Internet of Things (IoT) permeates our daily lives, seamlessly connecting devices and systems, the threat of malicious actors exploiting this interconnectedness grows exponentially. The emergence of IoT malware poses multifaceted risks, ranging from privacy breaches and data theft to the disruption of critical infrastructure and even jeopardizing human lives. Understanding and combating this burgeoning menace necessitates comprehensive research efforts to decipher the intricacies of IoT vulnerabilities, develop robust security measures, and mitigate the potential consequences of large-scale attacks. By delving into the depths of IoT malware, researchers can illuminate the path towards a safer, more resilient IoT ecosystem, ensuring the protection of individuals, organizations, and societies as we navigate this transformative technological era (Omar, 2022, Omar 2021).

The proliferation of Internet of Things (IoT) devices has brought about increased vulnerability to malware attacks. The simplicity of installation and connectivity in IoT devices makes them attractive targets for malicious activities. Common security weaknesses in IoT devices, such as weak or guessable passwords, hard-coded passwords, lack of security measures, insecure network connections, and outdated update procedures, contribute to their susceptibility to malware attacks (Nobles, 2021, Omar, 2023).

To address this issue, effective detection and analysis methods for IoT malware are crucial. However, current methods that rely on static approaches have proven to be ineffective in understanding and combating IoT malware. The field of deep learning has shown significant advancements in recent years, providing powerful capabilities in data mining, learning, and expression, which have greatly benefited the field of cybersecurity. These advancements have the potential to reduce the time and effort required for malware analysis by security analysts (Hadi, 2018, Top, 2017).

In this study, we aim to propose a novel detection and analysis method that harnesses the power and simplicity of decision trees to tackle the problem of IoT malware detection. Decision trees are widely used in classification tasks, where each feature is tested individually, and a classification is assigned based on the branches and splits of the tree. They offer advantages in representing and predicting values, including those outside the training set, making them suitable for analyzing IoT malware (Khraisat, 2019).

The specific problem addressed in this study is the detection of IoT malware using decision tree-based classifiers. We seek to improve the effectiveness and efficiency of intrusion detection systems (IDS) by developing a decision tree model that can accurately differentiate between normal and intrusive activities in IoT networks. By leveraging decision tree algorithms and applying feature engineering techniques, we aim to enhance the quality of data used for analysis, leading to improved detection rates and reduced false positives (Amini, 2016, Aldweesh, 2020).

The proposed solution will be evaluated using a real-world dataset called MaleVis, which is publicly available and specifically designed for IoT malware detection. The performance of the proposed approach will be compared with existing state-of-the-art solutions to demonstrate its superiority in terms of detection and classification accuracy. Key performance metrics, such as precision, recall, specificity, F1-score, accuracy, and processing time per malware classification, will be analyzed to evaluate the effectiveness of the decision tree-based approach.

Overall, this study addresses the critical problem of IoT malware detection and aims to provide a robust and efficient solution using decision tree-based classifiers. By harnessing the power and simplicity of decision trees, we aim to improve the security of IoT devices and networks, mitigating the risks associated with malware attacks.

RELATED WORK

IoT security poses a significant concern due to the diverse nature of IoT systems and the inadequate security measures integrated into the devices themselves. The security challenges within the IoT domain are rooted in traditional security mechanisms, such as authentication, secure routing, encryption, key management protocols, authorization frameworks, intrusion detection systems (IDS), and other approaches. However, these conventional methods are insufficient to adequately safeguard IoT environments. Furthermore, the limited availability of energy and memory resources adds complexity to addressing security concerns. Given the distributed nature of IoT architectures, effective communication and data aggregation among sensors and devices are essential prior to connecting to the Internet through a smart gateway, utilizing protocols such as User Datagram Protocol (UDP), Transmission Control Protocol (TCP), Address Resolution Protocol (ARP), Internet Protocol version 6 (IPv6) Internet Control Message Protocol (ICMP), Internet Group Management Protocol (IGMP), or Reverse Address Resolution Protocol (RARP).

Intrusion detection serves as a defensive mechanism to monitor network traffic and identify vulnerabilities within the network infrastructure. It enables the detection and prevention of malicious activities (Omar, 2022).

Within the existing literature, numerous researchers have dedicated their efforts to enhancing intrusion detection systems to protect IoT environments. For instance, Misra et al. [24] and Kasinathan et al. (2022) have proposed novel security architectures for detecting Distributed Denial of Service (DDoS) attacks in IoT. In 2013, Raza et al. (2023) developed an IDS called SVELTE, which secured IoT using an integrated mini firewall and employed the Routing Protocol for Low-Power and Lossy Networks (RPL) as a routing protocol in IPv6 over Low-power Wireless Personal Area Network (6LoWPAN) networks. However, in 2015, Cervantes et al. (2022) benchmarked SVELTE and presented the Intrusion Detection of SiNkhole attacks on 6LoWPAN for InterneT of ThIngs (INTI) system, which aimed to detect sinkhole attacks on 6LoWPAN for IoT. Simulation results demonstrated that INTI exhibited a lower rate of false positives and negatives compared to SVELTE.

Furthermore, Sonar et al. (2021) proposed an intrusion detection approach to safeguard IoT against DDoS attacks. They explored the efficacy of deploying Machine Learning (ML) and Deep Learning (DL) algorithms in IDS to enhance IoT security. Hodo et al. introduced an Artificial Neural Network (ANN) IDS model for threat analysis classification in IoT networks, achieving an accuracy rate of over 99%. In 2017, Fadlullah et al. (2021) provided an overview of DL and ML techniques employed in intelligent network traffic analysis, focusing on their applications within IDS for IoT security. Simultaneously, Diro et al. (2021) developed a distributed attack DL detection scheme for IoT security, which demonstrated improved detection capabilities compared to centralized schemes, with accuracy increasing from 96% to over 99%.

Moreover, Prabavathy et al. (2022) proposed an IDS design based on cognitive fog computing for IoT environments. The design leveraged the OS-ELM algorithm implemented at distributed fog nodes, achieving 97.36% accuracy with a reduced false alarm rate of 0.37%. One year later, Verma et al. (2022) conducted a comparative analysis of various supervised ML algorithms to select a reliable classifier model for IoT security. They proposed an ensemble learning-based IDS model and demonstrated that the Gradient Boosting Machine (GBM) algorithm exhibited the highest sensitivity at 99.53%.

Over the last decade, some intrusion detection techniques have been adopted to achieve computer security objectives. The goal of intrusion detection research is to increase the effectiveness and capability of IDS through automatic responses. ML techniques are becoming more widely used in intrusion detection (Gu, 2019, Fang, 2020). As such, intrusion detection using ML is a classification project involving using labelled data to build classifiers that can determine the difference between normal and abnormal activity (Sommer, 2010). They allow an effective classifier to be trained and built using relevant data (Hassa, 2020, Sethi, 2020).

An anomaly-based intrusion detection system based on fuzzy SOM method was proposed by Karami et al., in 2018. A model for intrusion detection combining NB and DL technique was proposed by Tabash et al. in 2020. A genetic algorithm was used in the model for feature selection. The detection model proposed by Ghazali et al. for intrusive communication was published in 2015. These methods include Simple Cart, NB, BFTree, PART, and Ridor. For network intrusion detection, It achieved an accuracy of 89.24% using NSL-KDD dataset.

Using the random forest algorithm, Hadi et.al., proposed a model for selecting significant features in 2018. NSL-KDD was used to evaluate this model. According to this model are all within the CPI range. As a method to improve data quality, Gu et al. proposed ensemble SVM-based intrusion detection with

LMDRT transformations in 2019. Results show that the class performance on CICIDS2017 dataset is ACC 93.64%, DR 97.56%, and FAR 20.28%. A double PSO metaheuristic DL model was developed by Elmasry et al. in 2020 to detect network intrusions. ACC, DR, and FAR values are generated on the CICIDS2017 dataset. According to Prasard et al., a new IDS was proposed in 2019 that uses a probabilistic method in order to extract significant features from a subset of features (Tabash, 2020).

A state-of-the-art literature review demonstrates that the learning methods and the data quality are important factors determining the robustness of IDS (Ahmim, 2016, Guo, 2019, Jeyakumar,, 2015, Rostami, 2021, Ayo, 2020, Ghazali, 2015, Kevric, 2015).

Malware attacks can be detected and prevented using several methods. Systems for detecting and preventing incidents by intruders (IDPS) use several techniques. The data mining approach includes signature-based technologies, stateful protocol analyses, behavioral analyses and anomaly-based techniques. Different detection approaches are used in these technologies. Signature-based detection is an effective method for detecting already known threats but is not very effective when detecting previously unknown risks.

Similarly, they cannot be used to detect disguised threats when using evasion. On the other hand, anomaly-based screening can detect an invasion without requiring signatures. An unknown intrusion can instead be spotted by observing similar behaviour in other intrusions. Malware occurrences are identified through the concept of modelling normality associated with anomaly-based detection. Observing different activities and characteristics results in the creation of these sketches. It can uncover previously undiscovered threats because anomaly-based detection looks for abnormal patterns.

NOVEL NETWORK INTRUSION DETECTION APPROACH

This model consists of three main components, as illustrated in Figure 1: data quality, classifier construction, and network intrusion detection deployment. Here are the details of each component:

1. Data Quality Process: One of its primary responsibilities is the collection and preprocessing of data. The system follows a process that involves gathering and accumulating data from networks. After data collection, the collected network traffic undergoes preprocessing, which addresses data type incompatibilities and disregards them. Another step involves sanitizing the data and saving the results. The data is then further transformed, resulting in the final features of the network dataset. These features are selected using the entropy decision procedure.
2. Classifier Construction: This component begins after the completion of the first component. As the title suggests, the aim of the second component is to build a classifier model. The input for this phase is the transformed data obtained from the data quality process. The classifier construction has two main phases: model training and model validation. In the first phase, our proposed method involves training a decision tree classifier using three portions of the data. The model is then validated using the remaining data in the second phase.
3. Definition of Network Intrusion Detection Systems: To enhance the effectiveness of IDS, actual testing is necessary. This involves evaluating its ability to differentiate between normal and abnormal behaviors. Consequently, the accuracy of the IDS can be improved based on the classification results. Various approaches have been employed in prior research to detect and prevent intrusions. Researchers show great interest in intrusion detection and prevention as they strive to protect systems

from intrusion while adhering to network security regulations. This section provides a description of the different strategies utilized in previous research for intrusion detection and prevention.

3.2. Description of Proposed Solution: As mentioned earlier, our approach begins with the collection and transformation of data, followed by the selection of relevant features for analysis and detection. The creation of an accurate intrusion detection model requires high-quality data. Therefore, this step focuses on preparing the data for analysis and making informed decisions. To obtain a reliable training set, we perform feature extraction using the entropy decision on the original traffic within the network traffic. This step is crucial for improving the accuracy of our methodology. Additionally, it reduces training complexity by analyzing less data and aims to achieve a highly performant model in terms of accuracy, detection rate, and real-time detection. Before analyzing the network traffic, specific preprocessing techniques are applied to the collected data, followed by normalization. This process reduces the number of features in the collected network data.

To further enhance the accuracy of our approach, we implement proposed data quality techniques to transform the data. This enables the training and validation of an effective intrusion detection model using the decision tree algorithm to make timely decisions. Moreover, intrusion detection plays a critical role in cybersecurity, as it focuses on securing sensitive data stored in computer systems and networks. By preventing unauthorized access to the system, attackers are unable to obtain, corrupt, damage, or destroy this information. An intrusion detection system identifies security breaches in a computer network by monitoring network activity. Its purpose is to detect potential malware and mitigate its ability to cause harm. An intrusion prevention system (IPS) detects malware during operations and aims to prevent potential incidents. While the internet has brought about significant changes, it has also introduced numerous security vulnerabilities that must be addressed to maintain a secure environment.

Figure 1. Proposed network intrusion detection model

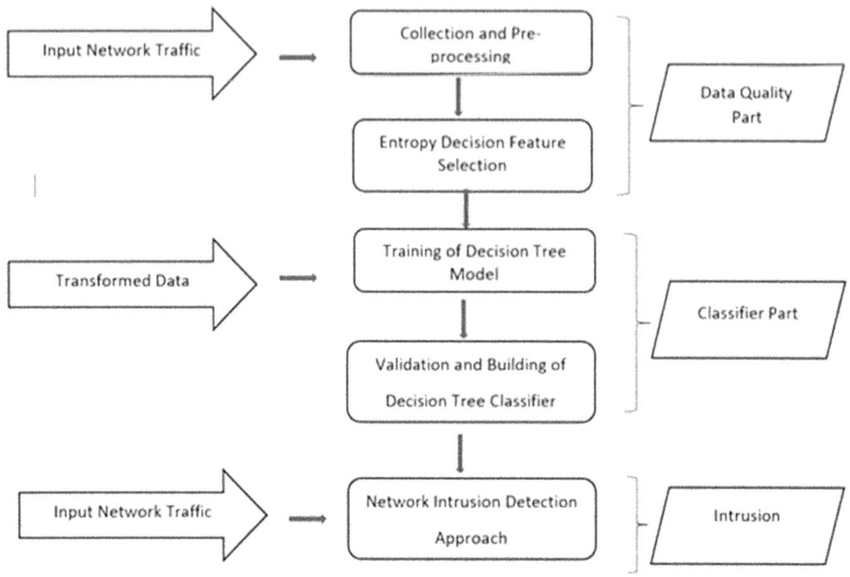

EXPERIMENTAL RESULTS AND DISCUSSION

Validating intrusion detection programs rely heavily on the evaluation of datasets. As a result, to evaluate an IDS using ML techniques, many available and appropriate datasets are available. We have chosen two types of datasets to evaluate and validate our approach, including NSL-KDD and CICIDS2017. The NSLKDD dataset is very practical because of its novelty and the sheer number of examples it contains. CICIDS2017 was created from a dataset created by Canadian Institute for Cyber Security. Presented here is an effective intrusion detection dataset that overcomes the limitations of the actual dataset.

Table 1. Hyperparameters deployed for model best performance

Hyperparameters	Values
Batch size	64
	Number of Epochs 25
Learning rate	1e-3
	Optimization Algorithm Adam
Loss function	Cross-entropy

Table 2. Shows the distribution of our Malevis dataset

Category	Type	Class	Samples	Total
Benign	-	Normal	1832	1832
Malware	Adware	Adposhel	494	2983
		Amonetize	497	
		BrowseFox	493	
		InstallCore	500	
		MultiPlug	499	
		Neoreklami	500	
	Trojan	Agent	470	4440
		Dinwod	499	
		Elex	500	
		HackKMS	499	
		Injector	495	
		Regrun	485	
		Snarasite	500	
		VBKrypt	496	
		Vilsel	496	
	Virus	Neshta	497	1997
		Sality	499	
		Expiro	501	
		VBA	500	
	Worm	Allaple	478	1974
		Autorun	496	
		Fasong	500	
		Hlux	500	
	Backdoor	Androm	500	1000
		Stantinko	500	

Figure 2. Shows the distribution of data samples across different classes of the dataset.

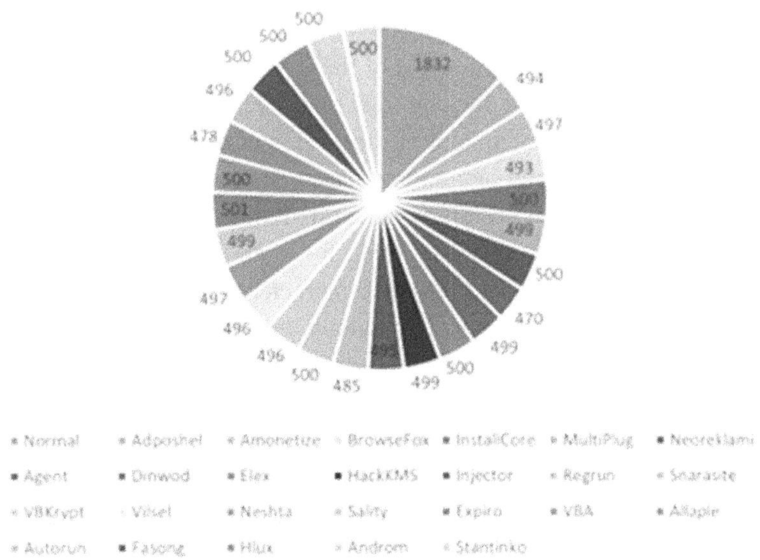

Table 3. Shows the performance of our decision tree based approach

Model	Spec (%)	F1-Score (%)	Acc (%)	Loss	APT per Malware Classification (ms)
ResNet18	94.14	96.39	95.03	0.181	146
Our approach	98.69	98.76	97.67	0.086	97
DenseNet161	97.97	94.67	96.66	0.156	480

In order to safeguard our systems and networks from attacks and intrusions on a daily basis, the implementation of intrusion detection and prevention systems (IDPS) is imperative. However, due to the limited availability of data, literature reviews serve as the primary means of collecting information in this domain. Consequently, this study engages in a comprehensive discussion of various techniques employed in IDPS, assessing their potential in mitigating attacks as well as their inherent limitations.

Within the existing literature, researchers have explored diverse approaches to detect abnormal behavior in systems, driven by the increasing significance of protecting systems from intrusions while preserving network security protocols. This study examines the mechanisms employed in prior research pertaining to intrusion detection and prevention, focusing on the development of a model for abuse detection using decision trees. By disintegrating drill information into simpler subsets through this structure, the model enhances its functionality. Simultaneously, a vector machine aids in generating anomaly detection hypotheses for each area. To further enhance the model's performance, information from identified malware is utilized to establish contours for standard behaviors.

IDPS methods offer several benefits in detecting system intrusions; however, they also present certain limitations. Signature-based detection alone cannot identify novel exposures, necessitating constant updates to the database. The maintenance of intrusion detection systems (IDS) is time-consuming, hindering the timely incorporation of new attack information. Anomaly-based detection systems, although effective, are susceptible to a significant rate of false alarms. Additionally, during the construction and training phases, monitoring of the system is usually inactive, rendering any activities during those periods illegitimate. The profile of typical behavior contours constantly requires updates due to the dynamic nature of user behavior. Furthermore, during the construction and training phases, the system is incapable of detecting anomalies. Consequently, the need for improvement within IDPS is essential to enhance the level of intrusion detection and prevention in light of these limitations.

In contrast, anomaly-based screening does not rely on predefined signatures to detect system intrusions. Instead, it identifies unknown incursions by observing comparable intrusion patterns. The concept of modeling normality is leveraged in anomaly-based detection strategies to identify instances of malware. In an intrusion detection system employing anomaly-based exposure, outlines representing the typical behavior of network users, applications, connections, and hosts are utilized. These outlines are developed over time, capturing various activities and characteristics. The advantage of anomaly-based detection lies in its ability to discover previously unknown threats.

Overall, the current research landscape acknowledges the importance of IDPS for securing information systems from potential malware and intrusion. Methods such as signature-based exposure and anomaly detection, utilizing classification and clustering techniques, have been employed. However, due to the continuous evolution of intrusion techniques by hackers, significant improvements are needed to augment the intrusion detection and prevention capabilities of IDPS. Anomaly-based detection, on the other hand, offers the advantage of detecting unknown threats without relying on signatures, thereby facilitating proactive detection in the face of emerging risks.

CONCLUSION AND FUTURE WORKS

In this study, we proposed a novel detection and analysis method for IoT malware using decision tree-based classifiers. By leveraging the power and simplicity of decision trees, we aimed to improve the effectiveness and efficiency of intrusion detection systems (IDS) in IoT networks. Through the analysis of a real-world dataset called MaleVis, we evaluated the performance of our approach and compared it with existing state-of-the-art solutions.

The results of our study demonstrate the effectiveness of decision tree-based classifiers in IoT malware detection. The proposed approach achieved high detection and classification accuracy, outperforming existing solutions in terms of precision, recall, specificity, F1-score, and overall accuracy. The utilization of decision trees, coupled with feature engineering techniques, led to improved detection rates and reduced false positives. The decision tree model successfully differentiated between normal and intrusive activities in IoT networks, providing a robust and efficient solution for malware detection.

Recommendations for Future Work

While this study has made significant progress in the field of IoT malware detection, there are several avenues for future research and improvement:

1. Dataset Expansion: The MaleVis dataset used in this study provided a valuable foundation for evaluating the proposed approach. However, expanding the dataset with a larger and more diverse set of malware samples would enhance the generalizability and robustness of the decision tree model. Including additional types of IoT devices and network configurations would better reflect real-world scenarios.
2. Ensemble Methods: Exploring the application of ensemble methods, such as random forests or gradient boosting, could further enhance the detection performance of IoT malware. Ensemble methods combine multiple decision trees to create a more accurate and robust classifier. Investigating the effectiveness of ensemble methods for IoT malware detection would be a worthwhile direction for future research.
3. Online Learning and Adaptive Models: IoT networks are dynamic in nature, and malware evolves over time. Developing online learning techniques and adaptive models that can continuously update and adapt to new malware variants would be valuable. This would enable the decision tree classifier to evolve and remain effective in detecting emerging threats in real-time.
4. Privacy-Preserving Techniques: As IoT devices often handle sensitive user data, privacy-preserving techniques should be integrated into the malware detection process. Exploring methods such as secure multiparty computation or federated learning can ensure that user data remains protected while still contributing to the improvement of the decision tree model's accuracy.
5. Integration with Network Security Frameworks: The proposed decision tree-based approach can be integrated with existing network security frameworks to provide a comprehensive and layered

defense against IoT malware. Investigating the interoperability and compatibility of the decision tree model with other security solutions would enhance the overall security posture of IoT networks.

In conclusion, this study has demonstrated the effectiveness of decision tree-based classifiers in IoT malware detection. The proposed approach shows promise in improving the security of IoT devices and networks. By expanding the dataset, exploring ensemble methods, incorporating online learning and adaptive models, employing privacy-preserving techniques, and integrating with existing network security frameworks, future research can further enhance the detection and mitigation of IoT malware, ultimately contributing to a safer and more secure IoT ecosystem.

REFERENCES

Ahmim, A., Maglaras, L., Ferrag, M. A., Derdour, M., & Janicke, H. (2019). *A novel hierarchical intrusion detection system based on decision tree and rules-based models,* (pp. 228–233). IEEE. https://ieeexplore.ieee.org/xpl/conhome/8790388/proceeding.

Alazzam, H., Sharieh, A., & Sabri, K. E. (2020). A feature selection algorithm for intrusion detection system based on Pigeon Inspired Optimizer. *Expert Systems with Applications*, *148*, 113249. doi:10.1016/j.eswa.2020.113249

Aldweesh, A., Derhab, A., & Ahmed, Z. E. (2020). Deep learning approaches for anomaly-based intrusion detection systems: A survey, taxonomy, and open issues. *Knowledge-Based Systems*, *189*, 105124. doi:10.1016/j.knosys.2019.105124

Amini, M., Rezaeenour, J., & Hadavandi, E. (2016). A neural network ensemble classifier for effective intrusion detection using fuzzy clustering and radial basis function networks. 3e International Journal on Artificial Intelligence Tools, 25(2). doi:10.1142/S0218213015500335

Ayo, F. E., Folorunso, S. O., Abayomi-Alli, A. A., Adekunle, A. O., Awotunde, J. B., & Awotunde, J. B. (2020). Network intrusion detection based on deep learning model optimized with rule-based hybrid feature selection. Information Security Journal: A Global Perspective, 29(6), 267–283. . doi:10.1080/19393555.2020.1767240

Burrell, D. N., Nobles, C., Cusak, A., Omar, M., & Gillesania, L. (2022). Cybercrime and the Nature of Insider Threat Complexities in Healthcare and Biotechnology Engineering Organizations. *Journal of Crime and Criminal Behavior*, *2*(2), 131–144. doi:10.47509/JCCB.2022.v02i02.04

Çavuşoğlu, Ü. (2019). U. Çavus¸o¨glu, "A new hybrid approach for intrusion detec-ˇ tion using machine learning methods,". *Applied Intelligence*, *49*(7), 2735–2761. doi:10.100710489-018-01408-x

Chaudhry, S. A., Farash, M. S., Kumar, N., & Alsharif, M. H. (2020). PFLUA-DIoT: A pairing free lightweight and unlinkable user access control scheme for distributed IoT environments. *IEEE Systems Journal*, *2020*, 3036425.

Chaudhry, S. A., Kim, I. L., Rho, S., Farash, M. S., & Shon, T. (2019). An improved anonymous authentication scheme for distributed mobile cloud computing services. *Cluster Computing*, *22*(S1, no. S1), 1595–1609. doi:10.100710586-017-1088-9

Chiba, Z., Abghour, N., Moussaid, K., El omri, A., & Rida, M. (2019). Intelligent approach to build a deep neural network based IDS for cloud environment using combination of machine learning algorithms. *Computers & Security*, *86*, 291–317. doi:10.1016/j.cose.2019.06.013

Fang, W., Tan, X., & Wilbur, D. (2020). Application of intrusion detection technology in network safety based on machine learning. *Safety Science*, *124*, 104604. doi:10.1016/j.ssci.2020.104604

Fernandes, G. Jr, Rodrigues, J. J. P. C., Carvalho, L. F., Al-Muhtadi, J. F., & Proença, M. L. Jr. (2019). A comprehensive survey on network anomaly detection. *Telecommunication Systems*, *70*(3), 447–489. doi:10.100711235-018-0475-8

Ghazali, A., Nuaimy, W., Al-Atabi, A., & Jamaludin, I. (2015). Comparison of classification models for Nsl-Kdd dataset for network anomaly detection. *Academic Journal of Science*, *4*(1), 199–206.

Gu, J., Wang, L., Wang, H., & Wang, S. (2019). A novel approach to intrusion detection using SVM ensemble with feature augmentation. *Computers & Security*, *86*, 53–62. doi:10.1016/j.cose.2019.05.022

Guezzaz, A., Asimi, A., Tbatou, Z., Asimi, Y., & Sadqi, Y. (2019). A global intrusion detection system using pcapsocks sniffer and multilayer perceptron classifier. *International Journal of Network Security*, *21*(3), 438–450.

Guezzaz, A., Asimi, Y., Azrour, M., & Asimi, A. (2021). Mathematical validation of proposed machine learning classifier for heterogeneous traffic and anomaly detection. *Big Data Mining and Analytics*, *4*(1), 18–24. doi:10.26599/BDMA.2020.9020019

Guo, C., Ping, Y., Liu, N., & Luo, S.-S. (2016). A two-level hybrid approach for intrusion detection. *Neurocomputing*, *214*, 391–400. doi:10.1016/j.neucom.2016.06.021

Hadi, A. (2018). Performance analysis of big data intrusion detection system over random forest algorithm. *International Journal of Applied Engineering Research: IJAER*, *13*(2), 1520–1527.

Hassan, M. M., Gumaei, A., Alsanad, A., Alrubaian, M., & Fortino, G. (2020). A hybrid deep learning model for efficient intrusion detection in big data environment. *Information Sciences*, *513*, 386–396. doi:10.1016/j.ins.2019.10.069

Irshad, A., Chaudhry, S. A., Alomari, O. A., Yahya, K., & Kumar, N. (2020). A novel pairing-free lightweight authentication protocol for mobile cloud computing framework. *IEEE Systems Journal*, *2020*, 2998721.

Irshad, A., Usman, M., Chaudhry, S. A., Naqvi, H., & Shafiq, M. (2020). A provably secure and efficient authenticated key agreement scheme for energy internet-based vehicle-to-grid technology framework. *IEEE Transactions on Industry Applications*, *56*(4), 4425–4435. doi:10.1109/TIA.2020.2966160

Jeyakumar, K., Revathi, T., & Karpagam, S. (2015). Intrusion detection using artificial neural networks with best set of features. *3e International Arab Journal of Information Technology, 12*(6A).

Ji, S.-Y., Jeong, B.-K., Choi, S., & Jeong, D. H. (2016). A multi-level intrusion detection method for abnormal network behaviors. *Journal of Network and Computer Applications*, *62*, 9–17. doi:10.1016/j.jnca.2015.12.004

Kevric, J., Jukic, S., & Subasi, A. (2017). An effective combining classifier approach using tree algorithms for network intrusion detection. *Neural Computing & Applications*, *28*(S1, no. S1), 1051–1058. doi:10.100700521-016-2418-1

Khraisat, A., Gondal, I., Vamplew, P., & Kamruzzaman, J. (2019). *Survey of intrusion detection systems: techniques, datasets and challenges* (Vol. 2). Cybersecurity.

Masdari, M., & Khezri, H. (2020). A survey and taxonomy of the fuzzy signature-based intrusion detection systems. *Applied Soft Computing*, *92*, 106301. doi:10.1016/j.asoc.2020.106301

Nobles, C. (2021). *Banking Cybersecurity Culture Influences on Phishing Susceptibility*. Temple University.

Omar, M. (2022a). Application of Machine Learning (ML) to Address Cybersecurity Threats. In Machine Learning for Cybersecurity: Innovative Deep Learning Solutions (pp. 1–11). Springer International Publishing Cham.

Omar, M. (2022b). Behavioral Analysis Principles. In *Defending Cyber Systems through Reverse Engineering of Criminal Malware* (pp. 19–36). Springer International Publishing Cham.

Omar, M. (2022d). Introduction to the Fascinating World of Malware Analysis. In *Defending Cyber Systems through Reverse Engineering of Criminal Malware* (pp. 1–7). Springer International Publishing Cham.

Omar, M. (2022e). *Machine Learning for Cybersecurity: Innovative Deep Learning Solutions. Springer Brief.* Springer. https://link.springer.com/book/978303115

Omar, M. (2022f). Malware Anomaly Detection Using Local Outlier Factor Technique. In Machine Learning for Cybersecurity: Innovative Deep Learning Solutions (pp. 37–48). Springer International Publishing Cham. doi:10.1007/978-3-031-15893-3_3

Omar, M. (2022g). Principles of Code-Level Analysis. In *Defending Cyber Systems through Reverse Engineering of Criminal Malware* (pp. 37–54). Springer International Publishing Cham.

Omar, M. (2022h). Static Analysis of Malware. In *Defending Cyber Systems through Reverse Engineering of Criminal Malware* (pp. 9–17). Springer International Publishing Cham.

Omar, M. (n.d.-a). *Defending Cyber Systems through Reverse Engineering of Criminal Malware Springer Brief.* Springer. https://link.springer.com/book/9783031116278

Omar, M., Gouveia, L. B., Al-Karaki, J., & Mohammed, D. (2022). ReverseEngineering Malware. In *Cybersecurity Capabilities in Developing Nations and Its Impact on Global Security* (pp. 194–217). IGI Global. doi:10.4018/978-1-7998-8693-8.ch010

Rostami, M., Berahmand, K., Nasiri, E., & Forouzandeh, S. (2021). Review of swarm intelligence-based feature selection methods. *Engineering Applications of Artificial Intelligence*, *100*, 104210. doi:10.1016/j.engappai.2021.104210

Sethi, K., Sai Rupesh, E., Kumar, R., Bera, P., & Venu Madhav, Y. (2020). A context-aware robust intrusion detection system: A reinforcement learning-based approach. *International Journal of Information Security*, *19*(6), 657–678. doi:10.100710207-019-00482-7

Sommer, A., & Paxson, V. (2010). Outside the closed world: on using machine learning for network intrusion detection. *Proceedings of the 2010 IEEE Symposium on Security and Privacy*, (pp. 305–316). IEEE. 10.1109/SP.2010.25

Tabash, M., Abd Allah, M., & Tawfik, B. (2020). Intrusion detection model using naive bayes and deep learning technique. *The International Arab Journal of Information Technology*, *17*(2), 215–224. doi:10.34028/iajit/17/2/9

Top^ırceanu, A., & Grosseck, G. (2017). Decision tree learning used for the classification of student archetypes in online courses. *Procedia Computer Science in Proceedings of the 21st International Conference on Knowledge Based and Intelligent Information and Engineering, 112*, 51–60. 10.1016/j.procs.2017.08.021

Chapter 14
The Business of Sports Marketing and the Growing Challenge of Name Image and Likeness (NIL) for Student Athletes

Eugene J. Lewis
https://orcid.org/0000-0002-2956-0760
Capitol Technology University, USA

ABSTRACT

The research focuses on sports marketing and the growing challenge of name, image, and likeness (NIL) activities for student athletes. Name, image, and likeness (NIL) is the common term for the ruling of the National Collegiate Athletic Association (NCAA) vs. Alston case centered around whether the NCAA could limit education-related payments to student-athletes. For many years, athletes argued that student-athletes should be paid due to college sports being non-amateur. Furthermore, coaches benefited from being paid high salaries based on student-athlete labor and exploitation at the price of an education. Several decades of backdoor payments to student-athletes and increased television revenues marketing deals to telecast high school and collegiate sports has opened the door for NIL activities to be introduced.

INTRODUCTION

Three quarters of National Collegiate Athletic Association (NCAA) athletes have interacted in some level of name, image, and likeness (NIL) activity since last July 2021, which helps facilitate NIL deals (Weber, 2020; Schultz, 2022). Football and men's basketball account for nearly 67% of NIL compensation, while male athletes lead NIL activities (62.7%) and receive 93% of donor compensation (Weber, 2020). Through 31 May 2021, the average NCAA Division 1 athlete had received $3,711 of money through NIL while some big-name players scored high-six figure deals (Weber, 2020; Gray & McEvoy, 2005; Luo

DOI: 10.4018/979-8-3693-1634-4.ch014

& Hamlin, 2022). The market of sports products and services have noticed the need to grow business as a new era of application (Ilioni, 2020). The NCAA's NIL policy allows students to be compensated for the use of their name, image, or likeness (Weber, 2020). Sports marketing as an independent field demonstrates an emerging demographic of increased individualization on new advanced marketing opportunities (Gray & McEvoy, 2005; Ilioni, 2020).

The inclusion of sports activities as a rule means athletes can receive endorsement deals and partnerships (Ilioni, 2020). Sports development and equity from outside organizations with distinct characteristics of creating funding source opportunities, starting brands, and individualization which present intangible service-driven investment in a competitive market (Gray & McEvoy, 2005; Masteralexis et al., 2005; Luo & Hamlin, 2022). The prospect of sports income in college before professional career starting provides a significant comprehensive promotional possibility for generating revenue (Ilioni, 2020). Student athletes can accept money from businesses in exchange for using them in products or advertisements and can also promote their brands or other companies in public appearances or through social media (Gray & McEvoy, 2005; Masteralexis et al., 2005). When eliminating football, the biggest NIL activity revenue driver in the market is basketball. However, women lead NIL activities by a slim margin. Major corporations are increasingly invested into NIL activities as a new place to spend marketing dollars (Gray & McEvoy, 2005; Masteralexis et al., 2005). When NIL activities began several major sponsors for major sports dropped out of sponsorship deals to sign collegiate athletes (Weber, 2020; Green, 2002). Corporations save more money by endorsing a collegiate athlete versus the high-profile professional athlete. The large corporations realize spending the traditional six-to-seven figure minimum to secure a professional athlete can be spent on five figures college athletes which constitutes a fraction of the cost (Gray & McEvoy, 2005; Masteralexis et al., 2005). Meanwhile, creating consumer brand engagement through an active local community (Weber, 2020).

Recruitment provides the economic context for larger growth opportunities as NIL contracts increase (Gray & McEvoy, 2005; Masteralexis et al., 2005). Currently, NIL sponsorship is coming from donors (currently 35%) through "collectives" (Weber, 2020; Green, 2002). Weber (2020) postulated more than 105 donor collectives are either formed or being put together, most of them linked to high-profile institutions for the purpose of NIL activities. Some practitioners believe the number will grow exponentially within the next 5-Years of NIL contracts (Weber, 2020; Hosick, 2022). Donor acquisition will be the leading source of NIL compensation effectively bringing "big business" to the forefront of college athletics. NIL policy is not a pay-for-play endeavor or a way to recruit. However, it provides students from less fortunate circumstances to benefit from their athletic abilities in their young adult years without penalty. For many years, the NCAA benefited from young adult labor offering an athletic scholarship as compensation for an education. But the continuous exploitation of collegiate athletes with long practice hours with limited hours for study has caused many to re-think the position of amateurism (Gray & McEvoy, 2005; Masteralexis et al., 2005).

The NCAA benefited from the social brand identification of collegiate athletes to their student bodies throughout all divisions causing the organization to be a multi-billion-dollar conglomerate. As collegiate athletes participate in NIL activities without jeopardizing their eligibility requirements. Other issues and challenges will exist pertaining to student earnings, athletic focus, and educational awareness. Institutions around the country have created their own rules to regulate these new opportunities to ensure students are still compliant with school code and state laws. Under the guidelines of NIL activities, student athletes have the right to publicity, advertising, and media to increase brand awareness as this ideal was not previously endorsed by the NCAA (Weber, 2020, Hosick, 2021). This study focuses on the sports marketing challenges surrounding the advent of NIL activities and the earning potential it creates.

PROBLEM STATEMENT

The problem statement consists of the growing challenge of regulating the following:

(1) The conflicting pressures of student-athletes and coaches' alignment with NIL activities and laws?
(2) The economic drivers and outcomes of corporate expectations of NIL activities?

SIGNIFICANCE OF THE STUDY

The significance of the study is that collegiate athletes earned an estimated $917 million in the first year of Name Image and Likeness (NIL) payments, which began in July 2021 (Weber, 2020; Hosick, 2021; Schafer, 2021). Sports data analytics provided statistical findings using technology viewing the athletic endorsement industry. The projected NIL market was forecasted to produce $1.14 billion in NCAA athletic compensation over the next 12 months (Weber, 2020; Hosick, 2021). See Table 1. Name, Image, and Likeness (NIL) Contracts in Overall Earnings (Weber, 2020).

Table 1. Name, image, and likeness (NIL) contracts in overall earnings (Weber, 2020).

Name, Image, and Likeness (NIL) Contracts in Overall Earnings Data provided thru Opendorse (2021)			
NIL Contracts by Year	**Date**	**Base Year Estimated Earnings**	**Forecasted Earnings**
1st Year of NIL Contracts	July 2021	$917 million	
2nd Year of NIL Contracts	July 2022		$1.14 billion

The overall earnings are of valuable importance as revenue streams increase creating greater significance to a growing challenge of equity and compensation (Schafer, 2021). The investigative research on this topic serves the current gap in research as the phenomenon related to NIL activities continues to be a sizzling topic in the sports world as numerous opportunities created for wealth and independence.

FINDING THE GAP IN THE RESEARCH

The gap in the research focuses on a growing singularity of NIL revenue streams as national advertisers are increasing their spending by 4x from Year 1 to Year 2 on NIL activities (Schultz, 2021; Shafer, 2021). The purpose of corporate sponsorship, collective groups, and other enterprises is to gain access to an extensive global reach amongst the youth movement (Green, 2002; Weber, 2020; Russo, 2022).

NIL contract holders are utilizing social media viewership to justify corporate spending on contracts related to specific sporting activities (Shafer, 2021; Weber, 2020). The leveraging of the NIL activity medium allows corporations to spend less and gain more as a result (Russo, 2022). Some of the top high school, collegiate, and professional athletes around the world are using NIL activities to build business enterprises across multi-streams of media, brands, and applications (Li, Zhang, Shelby, & Tzung-Cheng, 2022). The gap in the research signifies a growing development area as NIL activities will increase over the next 5 years (Russo, 2022; Weber, 2020). Scholars and practitioners believe sports marketing dollars will continue to be a growing concept within public and private industry (Russo, 2022). These studies indicate that student athletes generate substantial value for their schools and sport governing bodies, and that using NIL allows organizations to profit at the expense of the student-athlete (Li et al., 2022). Researchers conducting these studies focus on the sports revenue and the aggregate value of student-athlete identity.

METHODOLOGY

The methodology for this research study is exploratory design. The exploratory research discovers qualitative anomalies through a specific review of research collected. Exploratory research is one of the research methods conducted with an understanding of lived experiences as a phenomenon to be discovered. Although, exploratory methodology is being used in this study. The research provides a specific objective for two semi-structured questions to limit the data collection to one specific phenomena. The data in this case has a basic structure from the research design to collect information. It also initiates a formal inquiry amongst other researchers, scholars, and practitioners to provide supplement investigative research to contribute to future accumulated data to validate any previous prior theories, concepts, and hypothesis. The exploratory research methodology emphasizes content analysis in the sports marketing field of strategies developed from the literature. The aim is to utilize dispersed approaches and combine them into one comprehensive and relevant discussion based on current insights and cultural dynamics.

THEORETICAL FRAMEWORK EXPLAINED

The framework utilized in this study is the Product Life Cycle Theory in business. Although, sports marketing is a new concept within the marketing discipline (Li et al., 2022) The complexity of implementing sustainability initiatives is further exacerbated by an inquiry of business concepts outside of organizational boundaries and performance (Bianchi et al., 2022). The concept is growing exponentially. Product Life Cycle is the amount of time a product begins from its inception in the market until it eventually goes through a decline. Sports marketing has been in the introductory-growth phase for several years and has yet to mature as the industry is still growing amongst researchers, scholars, and academics. The Product Life Cycle consists of four stages: introduction, growth, maturity, and decline. See Figure 1.

Figure 1. Product life cycle

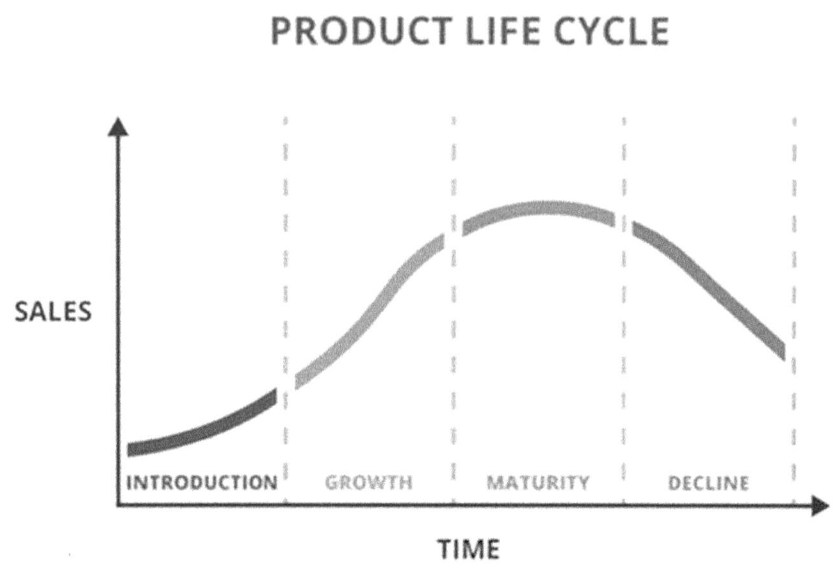

Although, the Product Life Cycle (PLC) is valuable to name, image, and likeness (NIL) activities it demonstrates how events can change over time. NIL value extends beyond the revenue for the institution and provide athletes with opportunities to generate revenue beyond performance. The power of social media is arguably more profound at the collegiate level where athletes generally do not have access to widespread media coverage or marketing brand value (Bianchi et al., 2022; Kunkel et al., 2021).

For this reason, investigation in the realm of social media to:

(1) Determine the NIL value that student-athletes possess on social media platforms
(2) Examine the role of the university brand in driving social media NIL value of student-athletes
(3) Advance a method to estimate the unique monetary value of athlete brands on social media independent of their performance value (Kunkel et al., 2021)

Theoretically, the research contributes to insight, deployment, and challenges since consumer interest and athletic integration has changed economies of scale. Student-athletes integration into the NIL strategy addresses all phases of the product life cycle (PLC) is a complex and demanding investigation that most organizations fail to convincingly overcome (Bianchi et al., 2022). The NIL rules and study suggests challenges of amateurism in the introductory phase of the product life cycle. This investigation represents one of the most valuable under researched forms of promotion and communication available to student athletes as maturity and growth stage of the product life cycle continues to increase (Kunkel et al., 2021). NIL activities suggest underlying challenges to the maturity stage as NCAA powerbrokers seek ways in which to invoke new rules and requirements to the current policy (Bianchi et al., 2022;

Kunkel et al., 2021). Satisfying such demands substantively add constraints to mature dominant phases of acquisition for existing structures that prioritize economic drivers over student-athlete responsibility (Bianchi et al., 2022). Internalizing and satisfying financial objectives can generate extra pressures on the NCAA power brokers and its leadership. The organization has growing fear of monetary power distribution to its student-athletes and what that might mean to the NCAA future of stakeholders, leadership, institutions, and coaches (Bianchi et al., 2022).

Currently, several coaches across the United States at well-renown institutions have complained about the new wave of economic freedom provided to collegiate athletes because of NIL contracts (Kunkel et al., 2021). In this study, the focus on the mediating role of organizational learning to disentangle the micro-foundations of institutional understanding of practice has furthered the conversation on NIL activities (Kunkel et al., 2021). The wealth generation in NCAA sports has quadrupled contributing to a billion-dollar industry that has always been provided to coaches through boosters from institutions and other mediums (Kunkel et al., 2021). With the influx of NIL activities, the economics have changed the landscape of sports no longer viewed as a "micro-economic benefit" to just NCAA leadership and coaches, but now provided through a "macro-economic" opportunity to male and female athletes around the country. Athletes are no longer at the mercy of institutions, NCAA power brokers, and leadership. The PLC theory reminds us that active stakeholders must assess the growth and maturity stage to continue to grow the economic bottom-line of collegiate sports. The NCAA stakeholders has a challenge in its partnership with student-athletes that have the economic talent to drive NIL activities. The NCAA cannot afford to shake the foundation of its material growth through student-athlete labor without partnership a decline could be imminent and affect the overall landscape of collegiate sports. The diversification of wealth creates a new power structure within sports supply and demand economics.

SPORTS MARKETING

The genesis of the term began in a 1978 issue of Advertising Age (Fullerton & Merz, 2008). The publication highlighted sports marketing as activities of consumers, industry product, and services who increasingly use sports as a viable promotional vehicle to increase profitability (Gray & McEvoy, 2005). Sports marketing has an array of concept variables important to a comprehensive idea: social media, mainstream media, branding, and product awareness as key performance concepts (KPCs). These KPCs include the marketing and advertising of sports through television, radio, and other media conglomerates creating revenue streams that encompass a new age of marketability. The reality of sports marketing is it continues to evolve.

The sports marketing value chain constitutes customer inputs, core processing, and outputs needed through economic development (income generation) and social involvement through the exchange process. Despite its acknowledged contributions to local, national, and global economies of scale; sports marketing is still relatively a new concept (Fullerton & Merz, 2008). Sports marketing activities are meant to satisfy sports consumers through direct marketing from the use of athletes, coaches, officials, spectators, listeners, readers, and collectors (Ilioni, 2020). Sports exude opportunity for universal attention, attraction, and promotion. The social identification involves association through sports group, institution, and community (Ilioni, 2020). Sports marketing development has two dimensions: (1) type of product and (2) level of sports integration (Fullerton & Merz, 2008).

In categorizing these two dimensions consumers need to understand that NIL activities as the product have many implications long-term to potential challenges. First, type of product addresses challenges consisting of monitoring the student-athletes ability to control wealth generation. Second, level of sports integration can be defined as a student-athlete from an underprivileged receives monetary compensation for his athletic ability will that athlete still be motivated to perform. The underlying principles for developing the framework are delineated through strategic product-based alignments as economies grow. The concept of sports marketing is ambiguous, and lacks applied strategic broadening, yet as a function of its environment provides action-based opportunities in industry.

NAME IMAGE AND LIKENESS (NIL) CONTRACTS

In October of 2019, the NCAA issued a press conference identifying its intent to enhance its rules regarding Name, Image, and Likeness (NIL) benefits (Kunkel et al., 2021; Wood, 2021). The concept of NIL represents student-athletes right of publicity mandated by the States its serves and the NCAA (Kunkel et al., 2021). Students all over the country have begun capitalizing on this policy by taking part in various NIL contracts (Dees, Cianfrone, & Andrew, 2021). The development of NIL is a direct result of questions surrounding amateurism versus professional activities. Researchers and scholars argue that student-athletes are not amateurs especially under the guise of multiple revenue streams created by institutions and NCAA leadership to maximize monetarily the athletic ability of its student athletes (Dees, Cianfrone, & Andrew, 2021; Wood, 2021). Sports like football and basketball due to its high revenue generating market provide funding to other athletic programs with its respective institutions. The opportunities provide interest through business engagements where the athlete is compensated for their name, image, or likeness. These activities include personal businesses, social media, promotional appearances, autographs, and camps. Companies have come from far and wide to start capitalizing on the popularity of student athletes. With the extreme popularity these athletes have on platforms like Instagram and TikTok, they can reach more people than ever, making it easy to convert their followers into earnings. Companies are reaching out to students, wanting to start partnerships, and paying them to post, show up to events and wear their merchandise. We have already seen athletes make thousands of dollars per semester from these endorsements. Bryce Young, a sophomore football star at the University of Alabama, has reportedly made over $1 million from NIL endorsements.

THE GROWING CHALLENGE OF NIL CONTRACTS

This is a state-by-state situation, and while the laws are largely the same, there are variations. The NIL policy promises to attract attention through social media. The social media plan requires partnership as a key to building a great strategy (Dees, Cianfrone, & Andrew, 2021; Wood, 2021). Student athletes do not have the time to build brands while having a steady course schedule. Therefore, an opportunity arises for sports marketing firms to provide services along with training for each respective athlete's sport (Hosick, 2021; Gray & McEvoy, 2005). The college athlete creates several opportunities for marketing firms seeking to gain an opportunity in the sports and entertainment market as the cost to advertise a student-athlete is significantly less than a professional athlete (Jara Pazmino & Pack, 2022). Moreover, marketing firms can provide a stream of income to the student athlete primarily focused on the brand image and recognition (Hosick, 2021). For each student athlete, establishing brand awareness is the key to performance. These marketers can supply great content, help athletes build intentional social media programs, and provide the tools necessary to improve and track data through metrics (Dees, Cianfrone, & Andrew, 2021).

Many states allow for a third party to connect businesses with athletes for NIL deals.

In states like Georgia, institutions can ask athletes to pool up to 75% of their NIL money to be shared with other athletes, but it is not a requirement (Gray & McEvoy, 2005; Hosick, 2021; Jara Pazmino & Pack, 2022). In Connecticut, athletes can use their school's logo if the school grants permission (Hosick, 2021; Jara Pazmino & Pack, 2022). Furthermore, NIL contracts in Louisiana are protected based on legal specifications that athletes NIL information is considered confidential. There are still a few states that have not bought into the NIL concept to attract student-athletes to their institutions.

These states that do not have NIL laws include:

(1) Indiana
(2) Kansas
(3) Minnesota
(4) New Hampshire
(5) North Dakota
(6) South Dakota

The states provided above do not have NIL laws for college athletes. In those cases, college athletes must adhere to the NCAA guidelines and interim policy (Hosick, 2021; Haws, 2022; Jara Pazmino & Pack, 2022). The NCAA suggests institution's role in the engagement of "pay-for-play" must adhere to the guidelines prohibiting violation of recruiting laws. NIL compliance is contingent on NCAA law and state regulations sanctioning athletic agreements for student-athletes (Hosick, 2021; Landry, & Baker, 2019). Recently, NCAA stakeholders requested institutions create committees responsible for investigating potential violations. The NCAA and conference leaders have "right of publicity" laws, which allow an individual to decide whether their name or image can be used for commercial gain (Haws, 2022; Jara Pazmino & Pack, 2022). There is no such federal law. Consistent activity is key to engaging and growing a social media audience to encourage sponsorship and endorsements of value (Haws, 2022; Jara Pazmino & Pack, 2022). In addition to adding followers, frequent posting ensures that branded posts won't dilute an athlete's social media footprint. It also provides athletes the cache to "prove" their engagement is real, rather than a one-post flash (Haws, 2022; Jara Pazmino & Pack, 2022). Social media posts are the top activity that athletes get paid for, followed by licensing rights, autographs, appearances, and running camps or lessons. The money is coming from brands, fans, and donors (Landry, & Baker, 2019). In many states, athletes aren't allowed to endorse liquor, tobacco, or sports betting. The new wave of NIL deals will only challenge the economic infrastructure of college sports (Haws, 2022).

FINDINGS AND RESULTS

Q1. The conflicting pressures of student-athletes and coaches' alignment with NIL activities and laws?

In answering our first research question, this study makes two main contributions to student-athlete and NIL activities. First, we explore how NIL activities are based on "Athlete Account Audience Size and Variations." See Table 2. NIL activities emphasize mediating roles of organizational learning through concepts involving interdisciplinary collaboration, communication, and constraints (Landry, & Baker, 2019). As various stakeholders can exert potentially conflicting pressures depending on their roles on the concept of balance. Some members within leadership, coaches, and staff are resistant to change. The external image based on the findings below show that even at the state level the concept of NIL activity is aligned with the implementation of its practices. The NIL activity structure demonstrate how facilitation or hindering student athletes' progression can potentially cause additional repercussions (Jara Pazmino & Pack, 2022). See Table 2. Overview of Athlete Account Audience Size and Variations (Kunkel et al., 2021).

Table 2. Overview of athlete account audience size and variations (Kunkel et al., 2021).

Overview of Athlete Account Audience Size and Variations (Kunkel et al., 2021)				
	Football		**Basketball**	
	Instagram	**Twitter**	**Instagram**	**Twitter**
Number of Athletes	7,591		1,139	
Number of Accounts	2,223 (29.3%)	3,880 (51.1%)	647 (56.8%)	757 (66.5%)
Number of Followers Max	299,569	542,951	494,929	599,994
Number of Followers M (SD)	6,142 (16,553)	3,458 (13,967)	12,422 (35,759)	6043 (24,878)
Number of Athletes with > 10,000 followers	273 (3.59%)	223 (2.93%)	143 (12.55%)	259 (22.73%)
Number of Athletes with > 50,000 followers	48 (0.63%)	20 (0.26%)	31 (2.72%)	46 (5.27%)
Number of Athletes with > 100,000 followers	12 (0.12%)	8 (0.11%)	16 (1.40%)	21 (1.84%)
Account Valuations				
Annual $ value CPM $4.77 Max	74,305	134,673	116,083	39,865
Annual $ value CPM $4.77 M(SD)	1,524 (4,107)	858 (3,466)	2,719 (7,352)	1,182 (3046)
Annual $ value CPM $10.14 Max	157,956	286,287	246,769	84,744
Annual $ value CPM $10.14 M(SD)	3,241 (8,731)	1,825 (7,368)	5780 (15,630)	2,512 (6,475)
Max = maximum; M = Mean; SD = standard deviation; Account valuations in USD$ and assume 52 sponsored posts per year at the specified CPM rate; The percentages listed refer to the proportion of athletes from within each sport.				

Currently, within the NCAA NIL policies there are no caps on student-athlete earning. The focus on NIL activity operations on extensive external pressures to clarify consumer reaction to economic distribution are through the laws enabling its growth utilizing social media. More than half of the US has passed an NIL law in 26 states. That number was six less than four months ago. In the table below, shows the findings based on lawmakers by state.

Figure 2. NIL laws by state (as of Mar 2021 and July 2021), the Drake Group

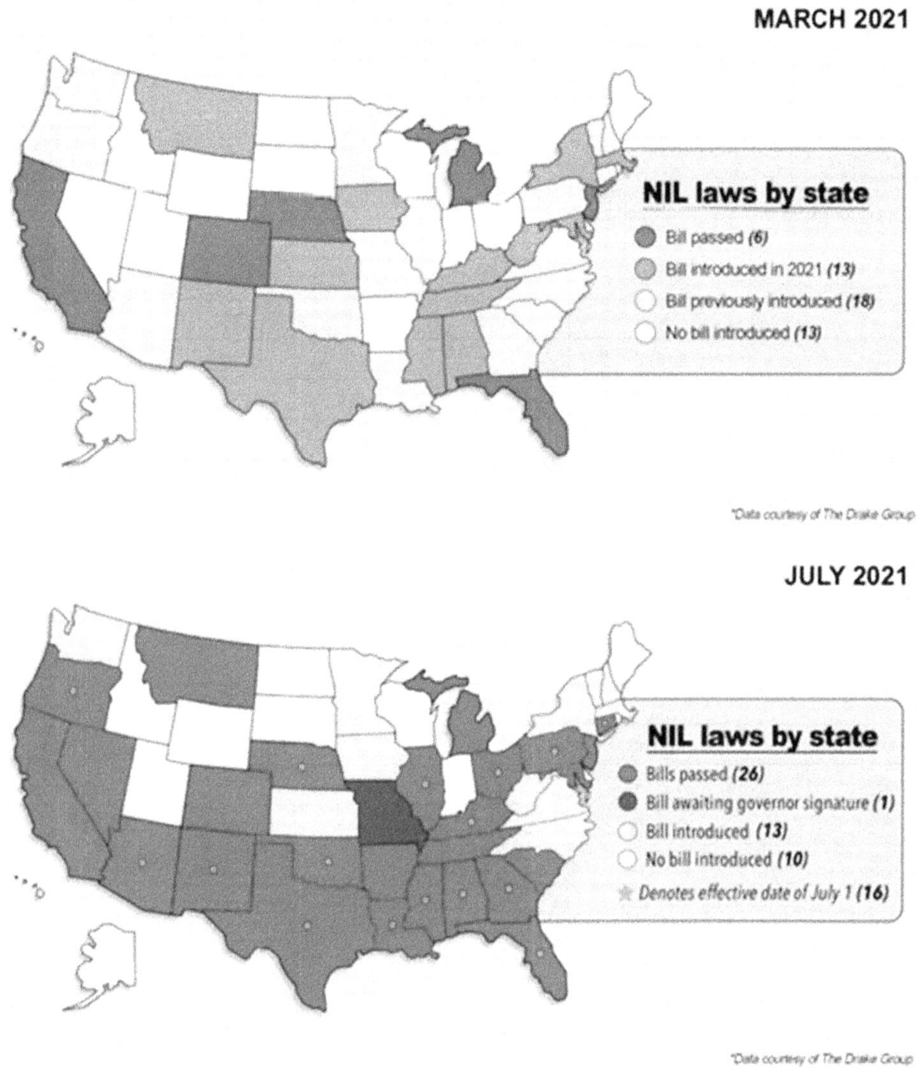

Q2. What are the economic drivers and outcomes of corporate expectations of NIL activities?

The present research findings indicate student-athletes social media presence and personality contribute to NIL value. According to Kunkel et al. (2021), NCAA rules change, and adoption of NIL activity will provide student athletes an opportunity to earn income. Consequently, hybrid engagements through social media activities will continue to rise because of potential account influencer capability (Landry, & Baker, 2019; Jara Pazmino & Pack, 2022). See Table 3. Overview of Athlete Account Audience Size and Variations (Kunkel et al., 2021).

Table 3. Overview of Instagram account audience, engagement, and value (Kunkel et al., 2021).

Overview of Instagram Account Audience, Engagement, and Value (Kunkel et al., 2021)						
	Top-Tier Male			Top-Tier Female		
Number of Accounts	450			332		
Sports Individual I Team	119 I 331			108 I 224		
Private I Public	166 I 284			202 I 130		
Verified	47			7		
	Max	**Mdn**	**M(SD)**	**Max**	**Mdn**	**M(SD)**
Posts	698	42	68	638	79	105
Followers	327,957	1,547	3,854	25,568	1,342	1,828
Following	2,779	810	880	4,103	937	985
Per-post likes	67,356	461	1,034	25,785	418	786
Per-Post likes / Followers Ratio	4,868	2,326	2,356	1.61	.2332	.2481
Per-Post Comments	726	15	22	1,169	14	26
Per-Post Comments / Followers Ratio	.0625	.0067	.0087	.0732	.0079	.0092
Account Valuations						
CPM $4.77 per post	1564	7	18	122	6	9
CPM $4.77 annual	81346	383	956	6,342	332	453
CPM $10.14 per post	3325	16	39	259	13	19
CPM $10.14 annual	172,925	815	956	13,481	707	453
Engagement	11,176	84	178	4768	74	140
Engagement annual	581,198	4,386	9,244	247,956	3,892	7,279
Hybrid	6,370	47	101	2,422	42	76
Hybrid Annual	331,272	2,451	5,271	125,955	2,184	3977
Max = maximum; M = Mean; SD = standard deviation; Account valuations in USD$; Number of accounts represents how many identified accounts by category (top-tier male and female athletes). Within each category, the (Kunkel et al., 2021) report how many accounts represent athletes who participate in individual vs team sports, have accounts set to private vs public and how many accounts have verified status. Account information includes maximum, median, and mean counts for posts made from an account, number of accounts that follow an account (followers), number of accounts an account follows (following), number of likes for a post, the ratio of likes to followers, number of comments for a post, and the ratio of comments to followers. Account valuations include maximum, median, and mean valuations on a per-post and annual basis for top-tier male and female athletes.						

The top 25 of the NIL 100 consists of the following high school and college athletes with current contracts more than the monetary value specified. Table 4. The NIL 100. Top 25 NIL Contract Value (Kunkel et al., 2021).

Table 4. The NIL 100; top 25 NIL contract value (Kunkel et al., 2021).

The NIL 100 Top 25 NIL Contract Value (Schultz, 2022)			
1	Bronny James	High School Basketball	$5.1 million
2	Mikey Williams	High School Basketball	$2.6 million
3	Bryce Young	Alabama Football	$1.8 million
4	Arch Manning	High School Football	$1.6 million
5	CJ Stroud	Ohio State Football	$1.1 million
6	Travis Hunter	High School Football	$870,000
7	Evan Stewart	High School Football	$801,000
8	Will Anderson	Alabama Football	$718,000
9	Spencer Rattler	South Carolina Football	$693,000
10	Amari Bailey	High School Basketball	$588,000
11	Aidan Hutchinson	Michigan Football	$557,000
12	Dior Johnson	High School Basketball	$522,000
13	Emoni Bates	Memphis Basketball	$506,000
14	JD Davison	Alabama Basketball	$445,000
15	Caleb Williams	Oklahoma/NCAA Transfer	$434,000
16	Braden Galloway	Clemson Football	$433,000
17	Chris Olave	Ohio State Football	$423,000
18	Dorian Thompson-Robinson	UCLA Basketball	$406,000
19	Kenny Pickett	Pitt Football	$401,000
20	Matt Corral	Ole Miss Football	$364,000
21	Jameson Williams	Alabama Football	$364,000
22	Jaxon Smith-Njigba	Ohio State Football	$357,000
23	Jared McCain	High School Basketball	$323,000
24	Kayvon Thibodeaux	Oregon Football	$319,000
25	Skyy Clark	High School Basketball	$313,000

To hear coaches tell it, NIL deals have either helped bring them the players they were looking for or it's just another level of competition to land the most elite athletes. Recall the sparring in May between Nick Saban, the coach of perennial national title contender Alabama, and rival Jimbo Fisher at Texas A&M — with Saban's side foray into criticism of HBCU standout Jackson State and its famous coach, Deion Sanders. Many athletes have become entrepreneurs, and some have agents. NIL also has allowed athletes to enter the transfer portal looking not only for a different team but also for a better shot at more cash from companies, brands or through the many collectives sprouting up everywhere since the July 2021 launch of the NIL era (Weber, 2020).

CONCLUSION

Male athletes lead the way in NIL activities — 62.7% vs. 37.3% for women, according to NIL platform (Weber, 2020; Hosick, 2021; Kunkel et al., 2022). Football players and men's basketball players received the highest percentage of deals when looking at the full slate of college sports (from data reported by Opendorse and other NIL platforms INFLCR and Athliance)(Landry, & Baker, 2019; Weber, 2020; Hosick, 2021; Jara Pazmino & Pack, 2022). A few women's sports tend to follow those two, especially basketball, volleyball, softball, and gymnastics. The money is largely concentrated in Division I athletics, though DII, DIII and NAIA players have been able to obtain deals (Landry, & Baker, 2019; Kunkel et al., 2022). The more niche the sport, the less likely it is to draw blockbuster deals; think tennis, field hockey, ice hockey and rowing (Schultz, 2022; Wood, 2021). But there are exceptions, as waterskiing and rifle see average deals of about $1,400 and $6,000, respectively (Weber, 2020; Jara Pazmino & Pack, 2022). The policy provides the following guidance to college athletes, recruits, their families, and member institutions:

- Individuals can engage in NIL activities that are consistent with the law of the state where the school is located. Colleges and universities may be a resource for state law questions.
- College athletes who attend a school in a state without an NIL law can engage in this type of activity without violating NCAA rules related to name, image, and likeness.
- Individuals can use a professional services provider for NIL activities.
- Student-athletes should report NIL activities consistent with state law or school and conference requirements to their school.

A key question is the relative performance of NIL activities amongst various sports marketing approaches in the accomplishment of business objectives (Hosick, 2021; Jara Pazmino & Pack, 2022). The performance measurements should consider the advantages and disadvantages of each approach concerning NIL activities (Landry, & Baker, 2019; Wood, 2021). There is some evidence which suggests sponsorship strategies may stimulate negative societal attitudes towards NIL activities and practices (Kunkel et al., 2022). The concepts can potentially identify conditions related to increased economic opportunities (Wood, 2021).

REFERENCES

Bianchi, G., Testa, F., Boiral, O., & Iraldo, F. (2022). Organizational Learning for Environmental Sustainability: Internalizing Life-Cycle Management. *Organization & Environment*, *35*(1), 103–129. doi:10.1177/1086026621998744

Çelik, Z. (2022). The Moderating Role of Influencer Attractiveness in the effect of Brand Love, Brand Trust, Brand Awareness, and Brand Image on Brand Loyalty. *Istanbul Ticaret Üniversitesi Sosyal Bilimler Dergisi*, *21*(43), 148–167. doi:10.46928/iticusbe.1050122

Dees, W., Cianfrone, B. A., & Andrew, D. P. (2021). Show Me the Money! A Review of Current Issues in the New NIL Era. *Journal of Applied Sport Management*. doi:10.7290/jasm13bamf

Fullerton, S., & Merz, R. (2008). The Four Domains of Sports Marketing: A Conceptual Framework. *Sport Marketing Quarterly*, *17*, 90–108.

Gray, D., & McEvoy, C. (2005). Sports marketing strategies and tactics. In B. Parkhouse (Ed.), *The Management of Sport: Its Foundation and Application*. McGraw-Hill, Inc.

Green, P. (2002, December 9). Sponsorship with no booths or logos. *Brandweek*, *43*(45), 16.

Haws, C. (2022). *The Death of Amateurism in the NCAA: How the NCAA Can Survive the New Economic Reality of College Sports*. Michigan Business & Entrepreneurial Law Review.

Hosick, M. B. (30 June 2021). *NCAA adopts interim name, image, and likeness policy*. Media Center. https://www.ncaa.org/news/2021/6/30/ncaa-adopts-interim-name-image-and-likeness-policy.aspx

Ilioni, C. (2020). Sports Marketing – A Necessity. *Annals of the University of Petrosani. Economics*, *20*(1), 63–70.

Jara Pazmino, E. S., & Pack, S. M. (2022). A Post-Pandemic Exploration of International Student-Athlete Personal Branding and Fan Interaction via Social Media. *The American Behavioral Scientist*.

Kunkel, T., Baker, B. J., Baker, T. A. III, & Doyle, J. P. (2021). There is no nil in NIL: Examining the social media value of student-athletes' names, images, and likeness. *Sport Management Review*, *24*(5), 839–861. doi:10.1080/14413523.2021.1880154

Landry, J. B., & Baker, T. A. (2019). *Change or Be Changed: A Proposal for the NCAA to Combat Corruption and Unfairness by Proactively Reforming Its Regulation of Athlete Publicity Rights*. Social Science Research Network.

Li, Y., Zhang, C., Shelby, L., & Huan, T.-C. (2022). Customers' self-image congruity and brand preference: A moderated mediation model of self-brand connection and self-motivation. *Journal of Product and Brand Management*, *31*(5), 798–807. doi:10.1108/JPBM-07-2020-2998

Luo, S., & Hamlin, R. (2022). A cross cultural comparison of brand love in consumer brand relationships: Is 'transmissive brand love' a potential platform for developing brand equity? *Journal of Brand Management*, *29*(5), 484–497. doi:10.105741262-022-00286-6

Masteralexis, L., Barr, C., & Humms, M. (Eds.). (2005). *Principle and practice of sports management*. Jones and Bartlett Publishers.

Russo, R. D. (13 Apr 2022). Saban: Current state of college football not 'sustainable.' *AP News*. https://apnews.com/article/college-football-sports-business-dabo-swinney-alabama-crimson-tide-8164758f34f295680c1668545549596e

Schafer, J. (1 July 2022). NIL: Here's how much athletes earned in the first year of new NCAA rules. *Yahoo Finance*. https://finance.yahoo.com/news/nil-heres-how-much-ncaa-athletes-earned

Schultz, N. (7 Jan 2022). On3 NIL 100: Ranking the Top 25 most valuable high school and college athletes. *On3.com*. https://www.on3.com/nil/news/on3-nil-100-ranking-top-25-most-valuable-high-school-college-athletes-bronny-james-arch-manning-bryce-young-travis-hunter/

Weber, S. (22 Apr 2020). NIL Draft. NFL Prospects with the Most Earning Potential on Social Media. *Opendorse. Endorsements & Sponsorships, NIL for Athletes*. https://opendorse.com/blog/nil-draft-nfl-prospects-with-the-most-earning-potential-on-social-media/

Wood, S. Y. (2021). *More Money, More Problems*. Texas A&M Journal of Property Law.

Chapter 15

Cybersecurity Risk:
The Business Significance of Ongoing Tracking

Sharon L. Burton
https://orcid.org/0000-0003-1653-9783
Capitol Technology University, USA

ABSTRACT

Technology as the single solution to risk is outdated and enables cybersecurity incidents. The no-involvement integrated focus on business and IT elements continues. Cyberattacks cost hundreds of billions of dollars. Consistent hacks and ransomware attacks help with the comprehension that cybersecurity risks should be managed in part under strategic management and organizational external business aspects, but apply risk tables and strategy evaluation processes. Organizations must focus more on managing risk. Project managers must be empowered with appropriate knowledge and skills, and receive consistent education as opposed to ineffective once-a-year education. Solutions must be crafted that include evolving cyberattacks. Offered is an agenda for project risk management to include cybersecurity. Described are positives that actions can provide to cybersecurity and basic project management. Intertwined are tools to use to assure effectiveness. The mission for this text is to catalyze research at the interface of cybersecurity, business, and technology.

INTRODUCTION

Actions are vital for risk project managers to gather data (Dalal et al., 2021) shared across organizations (specifically, the supply chain), and such data gathering should involve the business departments, not just information technology (Nobles, 2018) so that all understand the effects of risk events on business operations (Creazza et al., 2021). Continued are a no-involvement focus on business and IT elements in an integrated manner – an approach central to back the creation of an applicable and entirely strategic method to risk management. According to Lawton (2021), understanding and documenting risk has escalated due to the COVID-19 pandemic, environmental mandates, and supply chain disruptions; therefore,

DOI: 10.4018/979-8-3693-1634-4.ch015

organizations must review their systematic problems to reduce risk. Risks faced by contemporary organizations have multiplied in difficulty, fed by the quick stride of international influence through ubiquitous technology (Tucci, 2021). This text investigates and clarifies project risk data gathering, application, knowledge, and behavior in the cybersecurity environment and its effects. After the introduction, the reader will review the background, which includes information about risk and how it relates to cybersecurity. Next is the problem statement, significance of the research, methodology, research theories, and framework, the literature review, recommendations, conclusions, and solutions, and then the references.

BACKGROUND

Organizations must understand the capability of their risk project managers and leaders and ensure that these risk professionals understand shifting methods and needed tools (Yasuda et al., 2020). Risk project managers play a crucial role in identifying and managing potential project risks, which is critical to project success (Kerzner, 2019). However, it has been observed that risk project managers do not consistently apply data-gathering actions, which could result in incomplete or inaccurate risk assessments (Chapman & Ward, 2019; Tucci, 2019). This inconsistency could lead to inadequate risk management strategies and, ultimately, project failure (Muller & Turner, 2020). A possible explanation for the inconsistent application of data-gathering actions could be the lack of awareness or understanding of the importance of data gathering in risk management (Liu & Wang, 2021). In addition, the lack of standardization and formalized processes for risk management could also contribute to the inconsistent application of data-gathering actions (Pinto & Trailer, 2020). To address this issue, organizations can invest in training and development programs for risk project managers to increase their knowledge and skills in risk management, including data-gathering techniques (Hillson, 2022). The use of standardized risk management frameworks and tools could also provide a more structured approach to risk management and improve consistency in data-gathering actions (Abednego & Dwi Handayani, 2019). In conclusion, the inconsistent application of data-gathering actions by risk project managers could have significant consequences for project success. It is crucial for organizations to invest in training and development programs and standardize risk management processes to improve consistency in data-gathering actions.

First, let us review the question: what is risk project management, and who is responsible for it? Per Ahmed (2022), risk project management entails ascertaining possible risks, analyzing such risks, lessening risks, and averting forthcoming risks through monitoring. Significant risks identified by global leaders that affect the global stage are cyberattacks, data fraud, and theft; these long-term risk rest within the top 10 (World Economic Forum, 2020). Risk project managers are responsible for end-to-end project risk management (0'Connor, 2020). Specifically, project managers should review industry risk.

Risk is referenced and tracked as methodology industry risk; this risk references issues that can influence a certain business sector (Mehta, 2021). According to Mehta (2021), sequentially, industry risk can alter particular organizational sectors, positively and negatively. This risk is calculated as follows: risk equals threat x vulnerability. For analyzing global industry risk impact, two elements are utilized - cyclical and seasonal, plus competitive risk and growth (S&P Global Ratings, 2021). Cyclical (seasonal) risk is perceptive to organizational cycle highs and lows and is based on historical data (Kenton, 2020). Competitive risk and growth is a prospective analysis (S&P Global Ratings, 2021). These risks are viewed for very low and very high (Mehta, 2021; S&P Global Ratings, 2021). Another tracking of risk is cybersecurity risk. Cybersecurity risks must be tracked to ensure the safety of networks and data. The cyber risk formula, threat x vulnerability x information value, is a useful tool for assessing and managing risk (Wei & Xiao, 2019). Systematic tracking of threats, vulnerabilities, and data values allows for a comprehensive evaluation of the overall risk (Chen & Wang, 2021). Organizations should employ the cyber risk formula to help identify, manage, and mitigate cyber threats (Wang et al., 2023). Cyberattacks on organizations have a price tag of hundreds of billions of dollars (Schneider. 2022). IBM (2022) posited that the average price tag of data breaches in 2021 was $4.24 million dollars; the 2022 figure is expected to be $4.35 million. These costs and the consistent hacks and ransomware attacks help with grasping that cybersecurity risks should be managed partly under the strategic management and external business aspect of organizations but apply risk tables and strategy evaluation processes (Frigo et al., 2022). Cybersecurity has an overall strategy referencing technology, processes, and the human aspect (Cybsafe, 2022). Risk management relates to all three processes. Project managers must understand risk management and how to present and gather data during briefs, meetings, projects, and otherwise. Calculating and tracking cyber risk is viewed in terms of studying the named security threat, this security threat's extent of susceptibility, and the possibility of corruption (Cyber Risk Institute, 2020; United States Government Accountability Office [GAO] (2021). According to the GAO (2021), the federal government spends billions yearly on IT investments; however, existing is a void in well-ordered and effectual management regarding project planning, requirements gathering, and program managing and control. It is time that organizations focus more on grasping risk management, empowering the workforce [project managers] with appropriate knowledge (Hughes, 2021), developing resilient workforces by stopping ineffective once-a-year education (Burrell, 2020), reducing burn out (Nobles, 2022), and crafting solutions that can meet evolving threat sources such as cyberattacks (Tucci, 2021).

Biersteker et al. (2022) defined risk as an unknown event or situation that, when it befalls, has a positive or negative consequence on an overall project's aim. An exact NIST cybersecurity risk definition is "Cybersecurity risks relate to the loss of confidentiality, integrity, or availability of information, data, or information (or control) systems and reflect the potential adverse impacts to organizational operations (i.e., mission, functions, image, or reputation) and assets, individuals, other organizations, and the Nation" (National Institute of Standards and Technology [NIST], n.d., Cybersecurity Risk). "The effect of uncertainty on objectives," is the Office of Management and Budget [OMB] Circular A-11 (2019) definition of risk.

Typical cybersecurity risk issues are cyber criminals, developers of deficient and subnormal products and services, hacktivists, insider and service providers, nation-states, and inadequate configuration of cloud services such as Amazon S3 buckets. Amazon S3 is an object storage service; this service stores data as objects within bucket containers (Amazon Web Services, 2023). There can be up to 100 buckets per account. The composition of an object is a file, and as an option, all metadata describes that specific file (Amazon Web Services, 2023). Gather a visual understanding of S3 buckets from Figure 1.

Figure 1. Example of the Amazon S3
Adapted from Google image.

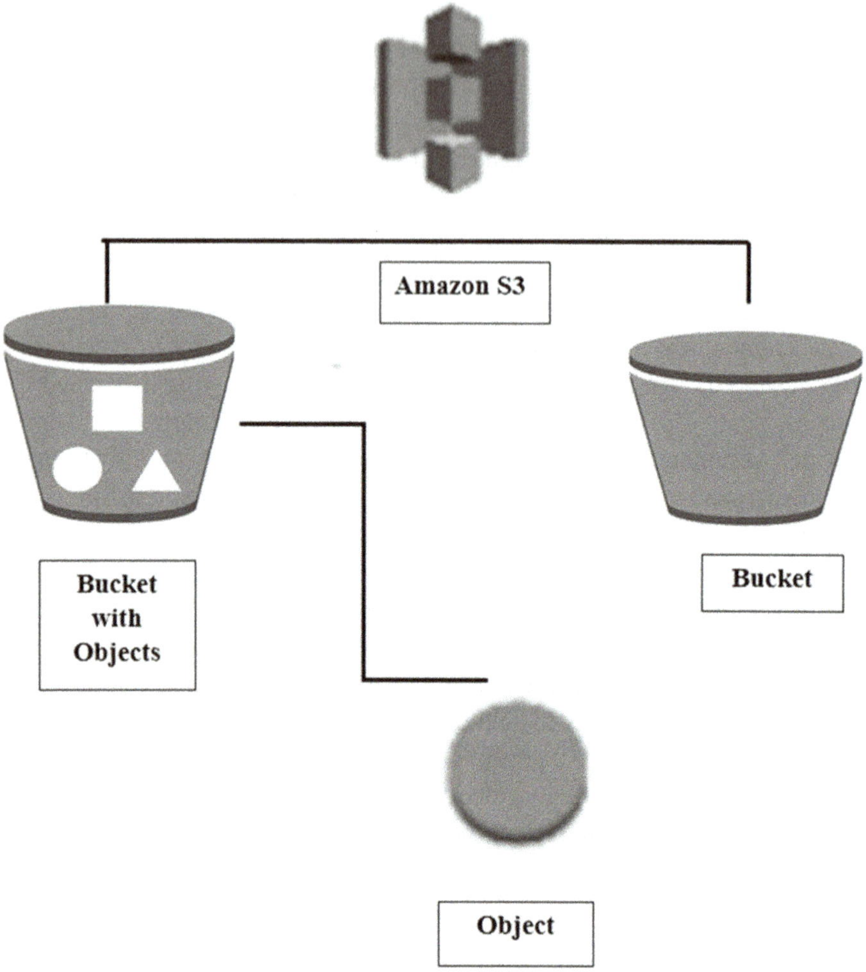

Cyberattacks and data breaches are performed for multiple motives and are immensely far-reaching (Nobles, 2018). Properly documenting as well as detecting risks is vital. Why? Appropriate documentation and detection affect the manner in that organizations capitalize on cybersecurity. Documenting risk is significant to cybersecurity (Peacock, 2022).

Specific to this text, a key point is the difference between cyber incidents, cyber threats, data breaches, and cyberattacks and how these points relate to project risk. Cyber incidents that could risk the privacy, discretion, honesty, or readiness of digital data or data systems can bring about grim outcomes (Patrick et al., 2022). Cyber threats, potential efficacious cyberattacks - data breaches, computer viruses, and Denial of Service (DoS) attacks, are malevolent actions that pursue to impair and pilfer data or interrupt digital life as a general rule (Patrick et al., 2022). Data breaches are incidents in which data is pilfered or extracted from a system without the system owners' knowledge or authorization (Mohammed, 2022). Cyberattacks include activist causes, denying service, disruption of critical infrastructure and vital services of the government or an organization, financial fraud, and information theft (Lin, 2022). Because the terms are used and may have been heard often but not understood, they are significant to know to comprehend the text.

Cybercriminals continue to grow their knowledge and remain creative. These offenders are persistent and unyielding in their explorations for the succeeding instruments, techniques, or vulnerabilities that will offer support to realize wanted purposes. Technology is expensive and must be updated. However, if left as an afterthought or hope of non-incidence, data breaches, and cyberattacks can be costly. Forgerock (2022), in the 2022 ForgeRock Consumer Identity Breach Report, reported that the 2022 retail sector of the United States averaged a single-cost data breach rise of nearly two-thirds at \$3.27 million. The city of Atlanta, GA, spent \$2.6M to salvage from a \$52,000 ransomware shock (Newman, 2018). Officials of Louisiana paid \$2.3 million answering cyberattacks across the state, over a year, on five incidents (Karlin, 2020; Ropek, 2019). The Washington, DC, Metropolitan Police department experienced a ransomware attack wherein 22 officers' profiles were published, and the hackers demanded \$4 million not to publish additional pilfered files (Collier, 2021).

As organizations and governments have embarked upon their digital transformation journeys, so have cybercriminals (Jones & Curry, 2021). These criminals are taking advantage of developments such as bring-your-own-device (BYOD), fifth-generation (5G) technology, Internet of Things (IoT), remote work, smart contracts (having encoded data and consisting of program code prone to susceptibilities), and cloud initiatives to permeate organizations, therefore considerably increasing their attack surface. Also, artificial intelligence (AI), machine learning (ml; Brandvoice, 2022), and augmented reality (AR; Waqas, 2022), all disruptive technologies (Ullah, 2018), are being exploited by cybercriminals to circulate malware and route pre-determined high-end targets (Brandvoice, 2022; Waqas, 2022). Per Hughes (2021), all such tools and assets pose a risk to the entire organization because cyber attackers can use these tools and support to present malicious software, withdraw delicate and complex data or commence many other nasty risks. The awareness that risk exists should propel organizations to be forward-thinking and recognize that risk management must not be narrowed to a lone department or completed on an extemporized foundation intimate of silos (Quinn et al., 2022).

Data shows that organizational failures continue to impede appropriate cybersecurity controls in critical infrastructure sectors (United States Government Accountability Office, 2020). The issue leaves the United States susceptible to attacks that have overwhelming and incapacitating consequences on security (Dawson et al., 2021). Furthermore, organizations and their leadership teams have shown intimidation of the digital biosphere and the risks from cyber threats (Jones & Curry, 2021). Moreover, as these technologies evolve, cybercriminals become increasingly cautious, surreptitious, elusive, and crafty (Brandvoice, 2022).

PROBLEM STATEMENT

The research team, Pandey et al. (2020), offered that there is no involvement focus on business and IT elements in an integrated way; this integrated approach is central to backing the creation of an applicable and entirely strategic method to risk management. The PricewaterhouseCoopers [PwC] (2022) Global Digital Trust Insights Survey, a survey regarding data trust, did not add technology-centered questions because more than technology alone is needed to streamline cybersecurity. The problem is that organizations are adopting security measures, specifically of the IT nature, but not gathering the business operations, details (Colicchia et al., 2019; Nobles, 2018). Adopting security measures, specifically of the IT nature but not gathering the business operations is not new; data showed that cyber risks were handled from a technical perspective in 2017 (Gaudenzi & Siciliano, 2017). Columbus (2020) denoted that in 2018 cybersecurity spending was at a Compound Annual Growth Rate (CAGR) of 12%; however, it is foretold to decrease to a CAGR of 7% up to 2023. Chief Information Security Officers and other C-suite leaders are recognizing risks must involve the business, not just IT (Columbus, 2020). The theory of cybersecurity supply chain risk management (CSCRM), a holistic approach to data gathering across the board, is expected to lead to better cyber resilience (Creazza et al., 2021). Overall, data shows the push to apply technology as a single solution. Cognizing project risk management is a common problem and is realized out of the void to gather data from business operations and the excessive number of identified cybersecurity incidents.

Correctly applying risk management benefits organizations that partake in the process (Amoah & Pretorius, 2020). TeamStage (2023) offered that 27% of organizations consistently apply risk management. Thirty-five percent of organizations intermittently apply risk management. On the other hand, data shows that some companies, no percentage given, do not see the need to undertake risk management systems (Amoah & Pretorius, 2020). As posited by TeamStage, 2013, just three percent of organizations do not apply risk management (TeamStage, 2023). The problem statement is that the project failure rate is up to 70%, with 27% of organizations dependably applying project risk project management.

SIGNIFICANCE OF THE RESEARCH

Risk management is vital because it allows organizations to have essential tools to sufficiently track, recognize, and handle potential risks (Quinn, 2022). This research offers project risk managers and other risk leaders information to advance competencies to work through product and service renewals, complexities, levels of uncertainties, and technical advancements. When a risk is acknowledged, it becomes ready to be studied for mitigation. Risk ownership is necessitated among organizations and should not be sectioned as organizational silos (Quinn et al., 2022).

The results of this study are anticipated to be explicitly used by small to medium-level organizations. However, they can be used by large organizations in cities within the United States for the purpose to develop risk management projects and other risk leaders. The results of this research are suggested as crucial to organizations pursuing to adopt behaviors of organizations that successfully register risks and have risk assessors and risk managers work together positively to mitigate risk (Andersson et al., 2020). Also, the results of this research could be valuable to risk project managers when reinforcing their organizational risk management frameworks as well as making available thought leadership regarding key considerations when updating existing and establishing new risk knowledge programs (Bahamid et al., 2022). Further, this research could be valuable to risk associations, vendors, and institutions that endorse and provide learning and development regarding risk management techniques (Jones, 2020). Moreover, this study may prove helpful to designers, supervisors, managers, and other key project leaders when assessing their existing and future projects, taking into consideration the risk management approaches conferred in the research (Bahamid et al., 2022).

METHODOLOGY

The literature review approach was used for this research. Bloomsburg University of Pennsylvania (2022) defines a literature review as a wide-ranging synopsis of preceding research. Because the literature review recognizes the research of preceding researchers, the literature review confirms for the reader that the current research has been well considered. The rationale for using the literature review was to distinguish the requisite for further research to justify this researcher's study. This methodology will support recognizing the connection of works in perspective of their contribution to the research subject-matter as well as other research (Bloomsburg University of Pennsylvania, 2022). An essential tool, the literature review, equipped this scholar to effectively navigate an increased information complexity (Bodolica & Spraggon, 2018).

This researcher performed this literature review up to and including papers published in 2023 utilizing an array of search terms that were prospective to return articles on risk project management and cyber security. Searches occurred between September 2022 and January 2023. Conducted were orderly searches of keywords that engendered listings of articles that were aptly germane for the examination. Terms sought were risk, cyber risk management, cyber risk, risk project management, and managed risk, as either the title or topic in the examination. Centered on the combination of the terms, this researcher sorted articles by establishing if the documents held information regarding risk project management. Sources used to locate the literature are academic fee-based databases and the Internet. Academic fee-based databases included as EBSCO Databases and Services (EBSCOhost Web, Business Searching Interface, and EBSCO Discovery Service), IEEE Xplore, Homeland Security Digital Library, ProQuest Dissertation Database, and ABI Inform Complete (ProQuest. The Internet search engine, Google Scholar, Google, was used to retrieve recent peer-reviewed literature.

RESEARCH THEORIES AND A FRAMEWORK

A methodical understanding of project risk management within the organizational sector offers an opening to enhance project risk management learning and development. As a result, project risk management theories give the theoretical relation amid two ideas to grow comprehension of the magnitude. Project risk management is challenging and driven by competencies (Podgórska & Pichlak, 2019). However, organizational leaders recognize the importance of risk project management for successful projects, integrating business and IT problem-solving (Wang & Yang, 2021). The ability to navigate project risks, as well as to participate in organizational debate on risk-related issues, project risk managers and other risk leaders need to cultivate risk competence.

The relevant theories guiding this research are the Risk Management theory and the Risk Colonization theory. These theories depict an accumulation of concepts, uncertainty, perception of responses to risk, strategies, and theories that strengthen and inform the research. The Risk Management Theory refers to the identification, analysis, assessment, decision-making, and risk treatment (Zhang et al., 2022). As a decision-making process, project risk management offers the benefit for the project risk manager to guide the documentation of risk and support the designated team to comprehend the documented risk and the plan of action, and the increased likelihood of a decreased miscarriage of stoppage (Priscila Ferreira de Araújo Lima et al., 2021). The Project Risk Management theory is vital to this research because it (a.) offers an augmented chance for recognizing and eluding risks, (b.) affords increased correct project forecasts, (c.) provides for amplified return on investment, and (d.) over time, due to successes, improves senior-level support for projects (Marle, 2020; Rane et al., 2021). A critique of project risk management is that risk managers and teams may not wholly comprehend risk concepts. Consequently, these leaders could apply inappropriate practices in planning and implementing project risk management. Next is the Risk Colonization theory.

The Risk Colonization Theory, proposed by Rothstein et al. (2006), references three points: (a) the requirement to reply to recently learned risks; (b.) the evolution of regulatory frameworks; and (c.) the usage of the determined risk tool, an organizing instrument, for governing in origination and innovation (Jones, 2020). The Rothstein et al. research team contended that the difficulties in improved accountability, coherence, and transparency regarding the guideline of societal risks could spawn institutional risks by exposing the impending constraints of the regulation (Rothstein et al., 2006). Their research initiated a difference concerning societal risks -threats to people of civilization and their environment (Van Weyenberge et al., 2016) and institutional risk, and perils to regulatory organizations to include the correctness and suitability of rules and systems of the regulation (Rothstein et al., 2006). The theory of risk colonization is essential to this researcher's study because outlining the points of regulation as risks aids as a valuable instrument for automatically managing the associated institutional threats (Rothstein et al., 2006).

A critique of Risk Colonization Theory is that when regulators utilize instituted risk evaluation guidelines, judicial reviews lean toward supporting regulatory agency choices (Baldwin, 2016). A point to review is that because of the theory of risk colonization, judicial reviews frequently discharge crucial disparagement of risk content assessments as being external to their means to review (Baldwin, 2016). With this said, a gap exists with organizations developing a launched risk assessment plan (Goetz et al., 2016); consequently, risk assessment guideline pronouncements could not be suitable for directing decision-making in a setting of risks and indecisions (Baldwin, 2016). Last is the cybersecurity framework.

Cybersecurity is critical for managing project risk. To ensure the safety and security of projects, organizations should use an industry cybersecurity framework such as NIST Cybersecurity Framework (NIST, 2019). NIST Cybersecurity Framework (CSF) provides a comprehensive set of standards, guidelines, and best practices to manage cybersecurity risks (NIST, 2020). It includes five core functions - Identify, Protect, Detect, Respond, and Recover (NIST, 2021). By implementing NIST CSF, organizations can minimize the risk of security breaches and ensure a successful project execution (NIST, 2023).

LITERATURE REVIEW

This literature review offers background learning on topic and gives discussion and analyses of published data involving cybersecurity and risk management – strategy and external. Information is offered as a systematized pattern that joins the summary and synthesis. This review ascertains the connection of publications in perspective of their contributions to the subject matter.

Understanding the Cyber Risk Profile

Understanding an organization's cyber risk profile is ascertaining the data deemed significant and worthwhile to insiders and outsiders, including information that could exact considerable disorder, interruption, and interference if inaccessible or corrupt. Addressed should be the most significant risks. The cyber risk profile is a joint approach for evaluating cybersecurity risk (Cyber Risk Institute, 2020). Let us review two tables, one and two, for some specific cybersecurity risk register categories and other categories that can be used to prepare risk registers when identifying risks (Tucci, 2021). While project managers track ransomware, phishing, data leakage, hacking, and insider threats, third party risk, and Nth risk are not consistently tracked. The data shows that cyber threats can arise from third-party compromises used to gain initial access (Insikt Group & Rapid 7 Group, 2019). Organizations are not always aware of their vulnerabilities due to Nth risk (Terdiman, 2021). Depending on the project, different types of categories may be listed. Review Table 1.

Table 1. Cybersecurity risk register categories

Types of Risk	Definitions
3rd Parties	Third party risk references distinct businesses or persons offering physical goods, software, or supplies or services. Examples of third parties include but not limited to contractors, consultants, software vendors, staffing agencies, and suppliers.
Nth	The Nth party is a fourth party (vendor for the third party) which could present risk to an organization, the same as a third party. The Nth party are notably tougher to track.
Ransomware	Ransomware is a type malware that warns to circulate the victim's personal data or continually block access to the data lest a ransom is paid. A simple ransomware might lock the system deprived of damaging files. Sophisticated malware uses a technique referenced crypto viral extortion.
Phishing	Phishing is the fraudulent action of remitting emails claiming to be from reputable organizations for the purpose to persuade persons to disclose personal data, such as PII-passwords, credit cards numbers, and biometrics.
Data Leakage	Data leakage is the unofficial transmission of information from within an organization to an external end point or recipient. The word can be used to describe data that is transferred electronically or physically.
Hacking	Hacking is a group of actions applied with the purpose to compromise digital services (i.e., computers, laptops, smartphones, tablets, to include entire networks). Most hacking is done for malicious purposes. Those who perform hacking are called hackers.
Insider Threats	The insider threat is a malevolent threat to any organization that occurs from individuals within the organization, such as the current workforce, former workers – contractors or business associates, who have inside data regarding the organization's security policies, procedures, information, and computer systems.

Table created by Dr. Sharon L. Burton

Assumptions may occur at all levels of the organization, so it is essential to determine internal and external stakeholders' expectations regarding risk communications. Both stakeholders are significant to the organization. Internal stakeholders are individuals whose concerns are associated with direct relationships and organizational performance (Wang, 2022). For example, a void of members of the internal workforce will lead to missing daily functions. Akin to internal stakeholders, external stakeholders must be kept informed. Risk leaders must ensure engagement with external stakeholders to affect problem-solving and generate positive community impact (Wang, 2022). Figure 2 depicts internal and external stakeholders who could engage in assumptions and have expectations.

Figure 2. Internal and external stakeholders
Figure created by Dr. Sharon L. Burton

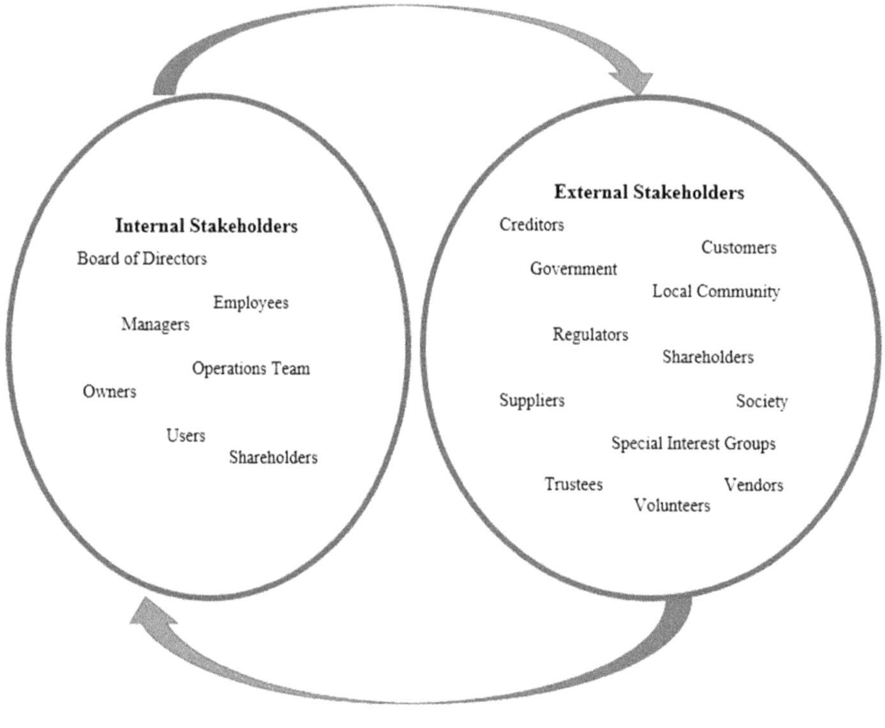

Table 2. Other risk register categories

Type of Risk	Definition
Brand/Reputational	Reputational risk references risk that is a menace to the profitability or sustainability of an organization or other entity that is caused by unfavorable public perception of the organization or its products or services.
Financial	Financial risk is risk that impacts the budget, in particularly overruns
Implementation	Implementation risk represents possible development or deployment failure
Legislative/Regulatory	Legislative/Regulatory risk is any change in the law and/or regulations that can effect real estate owners or occupants. Where might these changes take place? The local or the national level. Examples of legislative/regulatory risk: Zoning Changes, Building Codes, Access to Public Goods, Access to Public Utilities.
Operational	Operational risk references the risk of loss ensuing from unsuccessful or failed internal processes, people, systems, or external events that have the possibility to upset the flow of business operations. Losses could be financial - directly or indirectly.
Performance	Performance risk is risk that source outcomes that are conflicting with the specifications
Privacy	Privacy risk references risk that negatively impacts privacy such as personally identifiable information (PII) arising from peoples' individual data. Privacy risk could be the loss of organizational data such as intellectual capital, patents, banking data, and the like.
Resources	Resource risk refers to the chance that you may not be able to get all the necessary resources (human or equipment) required to complete a piece of work
Safety	Safety risk references the risk of bodily harm or property damage
Schedule	Schedule risk is risk regarding unplanned scheduling conflicts, like project delays, and the effect of the miscarriage
Strategic	Strategic risk is risk that references internal and external events that could make it problematic or even impractical to achieve organizational objectives and strategic goals. Such risks can have dire outcomes that effect organizations long term.
Supply Chain	Supply chain risk is the implementation of strategies to manage both exceptional risks along the supply chain grounded on incessant risk evaluation with the aim of lessening vulnerability and safeguarding continuity
Training	Training risk is risk involved if appropriate is not provided to the workforce. The void in training could lead to legal repercussions, diminished staff morale and amplified absence, and an increase in workplace accidents.

Table created by Dr. Sharon L. Burton

What does it mean to examine a risk profile? Examining pertains to sifting through the kind, and degree of threats met head-on by organizations, the chance of unfavorable effects, and the degree of disturbance and costs connected to every type of risk (Kaplan & Mikes, 2019).

For example, the proprietary and open-source software SolarWinds, now Log4j, proved capable of filtrating immense and monstrous risk to organizational systems with a waterfall consequence athwart supply chains. Without a correct record of software operating in the schemes, the cybersecurity workforce is visionless to the risk of being confronted and is vulnerable concerning ranking and arranging specific systems for decontamination or sorting due to priority (Hughes, 2021). Let us review an example, table three, for documenting risk.

Table 3. Cybersecurity risk documentation table

Date Risk Listed	**Risk Type** *Add types from tables 1& 2 in a dropdown.*	**Risk Context** *Reason for the risk*	**Risk Probability** *Add "High, Medium, Low" in a dropdown*	**Risk Significance** *Add "High, Medium, Low" in a dropdown*	**Risk Cost** *High Value Assets Add cost from specified stakeholder*	**Risk Response** *Add response for each risk*	**Risk Stakeholder** *Person responsible for key feedback*

Table created by Dr. Sharon L. Burton

Cybersecurity leaders and fusion participants must be able to distinguish data, which could lead to financial or reputational damage if it fell into the hands of cyber criminals or became available to the public. For example, think of the damage which could be caused if personally identifiable information (PII) such as biometric records, names, and social security numbers became publicly available or was hacked and sold on the black market. Humans, the essential links in cybersecurity, and significant actors of human-centric security (Nobles, 2018), must become recognized as organizations' most excellent vital line of defense (Hughes, 2021). The following subsections present information on effective risk strategies, situational and tactical risk strategies, risk and organizational brand, and effective crafting of risk tables.

Roles to Support the Identification of Risk

Identifying risk must include the business and technology sides of organizations. Even though this text specifically offers knowledge for risk project managers, there are other risk leaders. Risk leaders must remain astute regarding their organizational solutions and whether their associated technology is correct to combat emerging threats. Examples of risk leaders include but are not limited to Chief Risk Officer/Vice President, Director - Enterprise Risk Management, Director - Financial Risk Management, Director - IT Risk Management, Director - Insurance and Risk Management, Manager - Insurance Risk Management, Employee Benefits Manager, Claims Manager, Workers' Compensation Claims Manager, Business Continuity Manager, Business Resilience Manager, Safety Manager, Risk Enterprise-Wide Management Analyst, Financial Risk Management Analyst, Insurance Risk Management Analyst, and Claims Analyst; (the Risk Management Society [RIMS], 2022). Project risk managers, when determining risk, should understand the link to and be able to gain essential information from all contributors in the organization who focus on cyber security risk management and enterprise risk management. Relevant comprehension is that these key risk leaders should be duty-bound to utilize unswerving approaches to document, order, counter, and communicate risk solutions (Quinn, 2022).

Risk: Compliance, Technology, or Business Concern?

Although percentages are unknown, cybersecurity is considered a compliance concern wherein staff at all levels must follow security protocols and policies, and organizations must comply with legislation (Gurvirender & Sanjay, 2022); cybersecurity falls under a broader context. Protocols and policies are practical and have the effect of diminishing risks that could rigorously impair an organization. Protocols and policies are definite project management practices and techniques. They, too, are formal metrics to guide risk, quality, and the schedule, plus checklists to guide risk assessment, quality assurance, or task completion. Intensely managed projects could have definite protocols and policies regarding project management practices and techniques for all bodies of knowledge. Specific to this text is the subject risk. Rules-based risk management has not lessened the likelihood of a disaster, such as the 2021 Southern California Oil Spill (Haroun & Epstein, 2021); this is the same as rules-based risk management did not avert the failure of pecuniary institutions during the 2007–2008 credit crisis (Haggith, 2022; Rajan, 2020). The 2022 Global Digital Trust Insights Survey about data trust offers that the questions are not technology-centered because technology alone is not the solution to streamlined security (PricewaterhouseCoopers [PwC], 2022). Cybersecurity is a business concern (Nobles, 2018) wherein threats, attacks, and risks are enveloped.

Effective Risk Strategy

There are better risk management ideas than a one size fits all checklist. Project management course information offers that risk management is the custom of detecting, assessing, and averting or lessening risks to a project that is conceivable to influence desired outcomes (O'Connor, 2020). Risk must be learned, planned, and prioritized with a lucid comprehension of the needed objectives so all conceivable barriers can be identified that could influence the team's means to yield results. With this said, individuals' behaviors can represent significant risks (Burrell & Nobles, 2022). Thus, the creation of a cybersecurity culture can posture a significant input to augmenting cyber resilience, which necessitates the mixing of cybersecurity all through the organizational lifecycle safeguarding the organization, observing for an altering risk surface, advancing the capacity to focus on need updates for changing threats, and also guiding workforce behaviors in a positive direction (Huang & Pearlson, 2019).

Situational and Tactical Risk Strategies

Cybersecurity is referenced in terms such as a novel worldwide battlefield and cyber-Pearl Harbor (Schneider, 2022); the phrases scaffold how reliance on the world-wide-web enables risk susceptibilities that cyber attackers can ill-use. According to Nitzberg (1997), Information Security Engineer, the cyber battlefield, as a novel worldwide battlefield, is every scheme on the internet, intranets -corporate and governmental, schemes utilized in electronic commerce, and schemes utilized to offer services to society altogether. Alluding to the term cyber-Pearl Harbor, coined by Leon Panetta (2022), former Secretary of Defense in 2013, it warned of possible incidents which could overwhelm and distress the United States by striking businesses and organizational substructures, including the military. The two phrases are primary because they speak to risk in terms of situational awareness and tactical risk. Situational awareness references how humans distinguish and recognize rudiments and essentials of the work environment, grasp and project determined actions into the future, and analyze the reasoning avenue utilized (Fagerdal, 2022). Tactical risk references intended events, predicted events, unexpected events, and the chance to improve operational and organizational performance (Lammers et al., 2022; Handayani & Syahda, 2022).

Risk and the Reputational Brand

Managing projects' risk via well-thought-through risk tables helps protect the organizational brand reputation, an essential component of achievement for any organization. The financial costs suffered from data breaches, accompanied by other undesirable outcomes such as a damning reputation and possible perceived reduction of the organizational brand after a breach, can be high (Mohammed, 2022). Experiencing a data breach, Equifax's customers were subject to the pilferage of their personal information (DiPietro, 2017). This major hack distressed 143 million consumers (Johnson, 2017). Organizations' reputations have fundamental associations with their indispensable existing and present values, jointly with the ability to engender or extinguish their future values (Jones, 2020).

Another instance of a data breach is Capital One Bank's hack. An external person obtained an unapproved system entrance. Pilfered was PII (credit card customer data, 140,000 social security numbers, and 80,000 of the secured credit card customers associated bank account numbers) on card customers and people who previously applied for a credit card (Capital One, 2022; Dias et al., 2022). This hack hit Capital One's reputation for safely keeping customers' and potential customers' data. Capital One's chief operating officer (CEO) issued a public apology that was published on the internet.

Increasing knowledge of gathering risk requires documentation, and knowledge sharing will lead to augmented cognitive capabilities and situational awareness (Aggarwal et al., 2018; Veksler et al., 2018). Another example of how cybersecurity and risk connect is through cloud computing's, most notably, indivisibility, generated cybersecurity spillovers. Significant cybersecurity spillovers increase users' security protections; therefore, the spillovers safeguard users who may be void of adequate security (Verstraete & Zarsky, 2022). Breaches and hacks are cybersecurity risks that could emerge in cloud service environments and compromise cloud providers' hardware, networks, and software (Verstraete & Zarsky, 2022). This text is not about cloud storage, so this account and example stop here.

The Human Resources Aspect of Cyber Threats

Two aspects exist regarding cyber threats – the technical and human resource sides (Schneider, 2022). Cyberspace threats fall to trust, ties, connections, and relationships within the human resources arena. This human resource arena includes separate people, residents, fellow citizens, and populations who can, together, exert efforts to resolve challenges and concerns. Organizations and the interrelationship of social factors and individual's thoughts and behaviors impact workers' knacks, inspirations, and enthusiasms to be factored in information security (Gyllensten & Torner, 2021). Even though training exists, to include annual training in specific organizations, illuminations to ensure resilient and long-lasting positive responding human networks remain intricate and problematic. Answers could lay in the connection of rules having been fine-tuned to fit befittingly into work environments, encouraging organizational cultures, and specific accountability for workers' participatory and rule-compliant security conduct and action (Gyllensten & Torner, 2021).

The leadership must remember that cyber-enabled information operations aim for connections that encourage and shape trust amid individuals and groups. According to Ulrich et al., 2021, there could be differences between family-owned and non-family-owned organizations' methods of cyber risk defense. Ulrich et al. (2021) study findings revealed that family-owned organizations show increased cybersecurity risks yet miscarry to provide and capitalize effectively in cybersecurity compared to non-family businesses. The collective mistaken belief for small businesses, the inkling of security through insignificance, that small businesses are too insignificant to become a focus for cyber threats is inaccurate (Witts, 2022). Documentation shows that the lapse in organizational policies, procedures, and repetitive work could preserve individual positions within the family arrangement Ulrich et al. (2021). No matter the organization's size, there is a need to decipher needed organizational risk complexity. The idea is not to reduce system complexities because others are so doing or to restructure and simplify operations, processes, and procedures unthinkingly and inconsequentially, but to apply changes with awareness, mindfulness, and full consciousness of overall quality and effects (PricewaterhouseCoopers [PwC], 2022).

Witts (2022) states that the top five (5) major cyber security threats faced by small organizations are phishing attacks, malware attacks, ransomware, weak passwords, and insider threats. Edwards (2022) offers the top six (6) network security threats, a sub-set of cybersecurity. The numerous hacks and ransomware attacks reveal that there is needed risk avoidance work for family-owned as well as non-family-owned organizations. Organizations should focus on information and worker connections built upon positive trust to acculturate forward-thinking concurring workers and encourage in-group thinking and behaviors.

RECOMMENDATIONS, CONCLUSION, AND SOLUTIONS

To anticipate potential problems, organizations need proactive risk management. These indicators offer an advance warning about trends or events that can adversely affect the program's outcomes. Also, it is essential to have adequate risk management processes and procedures to abide by for disentangling conceivable risk events in projects (Amoah & Pretorius, 2020). Cutting-edge organizations realize that risk management cannot be restricted to a sole business unit or achieved on an unplanned footing on internal operational silos; risk ownership must be shared throughout the enterprise (Kim & Lee, 2019). Proactive risk management is a necessity to forestall latent and underlying concerns (The Joint Commission, 2022). Such documented markers provide prior warning concerning tendencies, movements, or occurrences that can distress the results of projects, as well as track sensitive risk with the help of indicators. Khaleq et al. (2021) posited that risk leaders must contemplate the limitations of the existing organizational know-how, fitness, or resources (funds, people, supplies). Stakeholder agreement and support must be gained. Customer satisfaction levels must be understood and incorporated. Also, external forces that could affect risk should be reviewed and documented (Khaleq et al., 2021). Despite available research, since 2005, organizations are still not consistently focusing on risk and are succumbing to data breaches.

According to Cardconnect (2022), data breaches are becoming more austere because of the first documented digital attack in 2005, wherein DSW Shoe Warehouse was hacked for 1.4 million credit card numbers. Research from the Ponemon Institute offers that a data breach's average cost has increased and surpassed past figures. The critical points extracted are as follows:

- 10% annually is the increase in the average total cost of a data breach increase
- Propelled by the COVID-19 pandemic, remote work, and digital transformation pushed the increased cost of data breaches
- Continued increases in data breaches in the field of healthcare (11 years sequentially)
- 44% of breaches entailed PII, the highest loss of records
- 20% of breaches represent the most common early attack vector
- $1.59 million (an average total cost) represents the most significant share of breach costs as lost business

(Todd, 2021)

Organizations need a top-down and bottom-up approach and proactive choices toward strengthening project risk documentation and analyses that lead to diminished data breaches and positive influence regarding data and system performance outcomes (Malsam, 2019). This research contends a close relationship between management ethics, trust, knowledge, and project risk management. Habituation, a cyberbehavior, must be consistently reviewed to lessen shrinking responses to replicated prompts or routinized behaviors. Such behaviors continue to be shown as disadvantageous to organizational security (Dalal et al., 2021). The influence of habituation becomes more convex as organizations progressively increase the number of informational cues workers receive day-to-day through modern know-how; this know-how is intended to intensify efficiency and effectiveness (Deloitte, 2018). Nobles (2018) states that most research regarding cybersecurity is fixated on progressing computer network systems because such researchers accept that information technology improvements and software development are the chief avenues to augment information security (Benson & Mcalaney, 2020). Mounting cybersecurity risks must be managed through the growth and advancement of system rationalization and malleable leadership skills (Burrell et al., 2021). Needed is an increased focus on project risk management knowledge. This focus can boost insightful and reasoning capabilities to include the discernment of environmental components, foundations, and happenings with deference to time or space, the command of such identification and comprehension, and the forecast of their imminent and forthcoming position.

REFERENCES

Abednego, M. R., & Dwi Handayani, N. (2019). The implementation of ERM framework in construction companies. *Journal of Engineering and Applied Sciences (Asian Research Publishing Network)*, *14*(2), 450–454.

Aggarwal, P., Frédéric, M., Gonzalez, M. C., & Dutt, V. (2018). Understanding cyber situational awareness in a cyber security game involving recommendation. *International Journal of Cyber Situational Awareness*, *3*(1), 11–38. doi:10.22619/IJCSA.2018.100118

Ahmed, I. (2022). Project risk management: 10 golden rules every project manager should follow. *Project Management.* https://project-management.com/project-risk-management-10-golden-rules-every-project-manager-should-follow/#:~:text=%20Project%20Risk%20Management%3A%2010%20Golden%20Rules%20Every,If%20you%20study%20failed%20projects%2C%20you...%20More%20

Amazon Web Services. (2023). What is Amazon S3? *AWS.* https://docs.aws.amazon.com/AmazonS3/latest/userguide/Welcome.html

Amoah, C., & Pretorius, L. (2020). Evaluation of the impact of risk management on project performance in small construction firms in South Africa: The case study of construction systems. *Journal of Engineering. Design and Technology*, *18*(3), 611–634. doi:10.1108/JEDT-06-2018-0098

Andersson, M. G., Elving, J., Nordkvist, E., Urdl, M., Engblom, L., Mader, A., Altmeyer, S., Kowalczyk, J., Lahrssen-Wiederholt, M., Tuominen, P., Joutsen, S., Suomi, J., Mikkelä, A., Hinkka, N., & Kirsi-Maarit Siekkinen, H. J. van der Fels-Klerx, van den Borne, B., & Beshir, A. (2020). Communication inside risk assessment and risk management (COMRISK): Final report. *EFSA Supporting Publications, 17*(7). doi:10.2903/sp.efsa.2020.EN-1891

Bahamid, R. A., Shu, I. D., Khoiry, M. A., Kassem, M. A., & Al-Sharafi, M. (2022). *The current risk management practices and knowledge in the construction industry buildings, 12*(7), 1016. doi:10.3390/buildings12071016

Benson, V., & Mcalaney, J. (2020). *Cyber Influence and Cognitive Threats*. Academic Press.

Biersteker, E., van Marrewijk, A., & Koppenjan, J. (2022). Identifying Subjective Perspectives on Managing Underground Risks at Schiphol Airport. *Project Management Journal*, *53*(2), 181–195. doi:10.1177/87569728221076092

Bloomsburg University of Pennsylvania. (2022). *Literature review*. Bloomsberg University. https://guides.library.bloomu.edu/litreview

Bodolica, V., & Spraggon, M. (2018). An end-to-end process of writing and publishing influential literature review articles: Do's and don'ts. *Management Decision*, *56*(11), 2472–2486. doi:10.1108/MD-03-2018-0253

Brandvoice, S. (2022, March 1). The top security threats of 2022. *Forbes*. https://www.forbes.com/sites/splunk/2022/03/01/the-top-security-threats-of-2022/?sh=6b1977512e5d

Burrell, D. N. (2020). Understanding the talent management intricacies of remote cybersecurity teams in covid-19 induced telework organizational ecosystems. Land *Forces. Academic Review*, *25*(3), 232–244. https://sciendo.com/article/10.2478/raft-2020-0028. doi:10.2478/raft-2020-0028

Burrell, D. N., Aridi, A. S., McLester, Q., Shufutinsky, A., Nobles, C., Dawson, M., & Muller, S. R. (2021). Exploring system thinking leadership approaches to the healthcare cybersecurity environment. [IJEACH]. *International Journal of Extreme Automation and Connectivity in Healthcare*, *3*(2), 20–32. doi:10.4018/IJEACH.2021070103

Burrell, D. N., & Nobles, C. (2022). Discovering the emergence of technical sociology in human capital systems and technology-driven organizations. [IJHCITP]. *International Journal of Human Capital and Information Technology Professionals*, *13*(1), 1–15. doi:10.4018/IJHCITP.300324

Capital One. (2022). *Information on the Capital One cyber incident*. Capitol One. https://www.capitalone.com/digital/facts2019/

Cardconnect. (2022). *The evolution of data breaches*. Connect Card. https://cardconnect.com/launchpointe/payment-trends/evolution-of-data-breaches

Chapman, C. B., & Ward, S. (2019). *How to manage project opportunity and risk: Why uncertainty management can be a much better approach than risk management*. Routledge.

Chen, Y., & Wang, Q. (2021). Cybersecurity risk management: A comprehensive approach. *IEEE Transactions on Software Engineering*, *47*(1), 1–14. doi:10.1109/TSE.2019.2940179

Colicchia, C., Creazza, A., & Menachof, D. A. (2019). Managing cyber and information risks in supply chains: Insights from an exploratory analysis. *Supply Chain Management*, *24*(2), 215–240. doi:10.1108/SCM-09-2017-0289

Collier, K. (2021, May 11). Hackers release personal info of 22 DC police officers. *NBC News.* https://www.nbcnews.com/tech/security/hackers-release-personal-info-22-dc-police-officers-rcna897

Columbus, L. (June 25, 2020). Why cybersecurity is really a business problem. *Forbes.* https://www.forbes.com/sites/louiscolumbus/2020/06/25/why-cybersecurity-is-really-a-business-problem/?sh=45b2b844436c

Cyber Risk Institute. (2020). *The Profile is the benchmark for cyber risk assessment.* CRI. https://cyber-riskinstitute.org/the-profile/

Cybsafe. (2022). What actually is "the human aspect of cyber security"? *CybSafe.* https://www.cybsafe.com/community/blog/what-is-human-aspect-of-cyber-security/

Dalal, R. S., Howard, D. J., Bennett, R. J., Posey, C., Zaccaro, S. J., & Brummel, B. J. (2022). Organizational science and cybersecurity: Abundant opportunities for research at the interface. *Journal of Business and Psychology*, *37*(1), 1–29. doi:10.100710869-021-09732-9 PMID:33564206

Dawson, M., Bacius, R., Gouveia, L. B., & Vassilakos, A. (2021). Understanding the challenge of cybersecurity in critical infrastructure sectors. *Land Forces Academy Review, Vol XXVI, Issue*, *1*(101), 69–75. doi:10.2478/raft-2021-0011

Deloitte. (2018). *Positive technology: Designing work environments for digital well-being*. Deloitte. https://www2.deloitte.com/us/en/insights/focus/ behavioral-economics/negative-impact-technology-business.html# endnote-sup-2

Dias, D., Borbinha, J., & Mendonça, P. (2022). Lessons from the Equifax and Capital One data breaches on social amplification of risk. *Review of Integrative Business and Economics Research*, *11*(4), 71–90. https://www.proquest.com/scholarly-journals/lessons-equifax-capital-one-data-breaches-on/docview/2681088996/se-2

DiPietro, B. (2017). Crisis of the week: Equifax hit with massive reputation breach. *The Wall Street Journal.* https://blogs.wsj.com/riskandcompliance/2017/09/19/crisis-of-the-week-equifax-hit-with-massive-reputation-breach/

Fagerdal, B., Lyng, H. B., Guise, V., Anderson, J. E., Thornam, P. L., & Wiig, S. (2022). Exploring the role of leaders in enabling adaptive capacity in hospital teams – a multiple case study. *BMC Health Services Research*, *22*(1), 1–17. doi:10.118612913-022-08296-5 PMID:35831857

Ferreira de Araújo Lima, P., Marcelino-Sadaba, S., & Verbano, C. (2021). Successful implementation of project risk management in small and medium enterprises: A cross-case analysis. [Project risk management in SMEs]. *International Journal of Managing Projects in Business*, *14*(4), 1023–1045. doi:10.1108/IJMPB-06-2020-0203

Forgerock. (2022). 2022 ForgeRock Consumer Identity Breach Report: Unauthorized access remains a top threat — It's time to render stolen passwords worthless for launching new attacks. *Forgerrock*. https://www.forgerock.com/resources/view/135321466/analyst-report/forgerock-identity-breach-report-2022.pdf

Fortinet. (2022). *What is an attack vector?* Fortinet. https://www.fortinet.com/resources/cyberglossary/attack-vector

Frigo, M., & Guccione, D. S. (2022). Strategic management of cybersecurity risks. *Strategic Finance, 103*(7), 23-25. https://www.proquest.com/scholarly-journals/strategic-management-cybersecurity-risks/docview/2614646599/se-2

Gaudenzi, B., & Siciliano, G. (2017). Just do it. Managing IT and cyber risks to protect the value creation. *Journal of Promotion Management, 23*(3), 1–14. doi:10.1080/10496491.2017.1294875

Goetz, M. R., Laeven, L., & Levine, R. (2016). Does the geographic expansion of banks reduce risk? *Journal of Financial Economics, 120*(2), 346–362. doi:10.1016/j.jfineco.2016.01.020

Gurvirender, T., & Sanjay, G. (2022). Editorial: Time to move away from compliance – cybersecurity in the context of needs and investments of organizations. *Organizational Cybersecurity Journal: Practice. Process and People, 2*(1), 1–2. doi:10.1108/OCJ-05-2022-018

Gyllensten, K., & Torner, M. (2021). The role of organizational and social factors for information security in a nuclear power industry. *Organizational Cybersecurity Journal: Practice, Process, and People, 1*(1), 1-20. https://www.emerald.com/insight/content/doi/10.1108/OCJ-04-2021-0012/full/pdf?title=the-role-of-organizational-and-social-factors-for-information-security-in-a-nuclear-power-industry

Haggith, D. (2022). *DollarCollapse.com: Alasdair Macleod: The real reason markets are breaking: Cycles are driven by credit*. Newstex., https://www.proquest.com/blogs-podcasts-websites/dollarcollapse-com-alasdair-macleod-real-reason/docview/2667244234/se-2

Handayani, W., & Syahda, E. R. (2022). Risk mitigation in supply chain management process: Procurement using house of risk method at PT. Pertamina EP asset 4. *Journal of Strategy and Business, 26*(1), 70–84. doi:10.20885/jsb.vol26.iss1.art5

Haroun, A., & Epstein, J. (2021, October 05). Southern California oil spill caused by a pipeline that split and was apparently dragged. *Business Insider.* https://www.proquest.com/newspapers/southern-california-oil-spill-caused-pipeline/docview/2579203564/se-2

Hillson, D. (2022). *Risk management for project managers: A practical approach*. Kogan Page Publishers.

Huang, K., & Pearlson, K. (2019). For what technology can't fix: building a model of organizational cybersecurity culture. *Proceedings of the 52nd Hawaii International Conference on System Sciences.* MIT Sloan School. https://web.mit.edu/smadnick/www/wp/2019-02.pdf

Hughes, C. (2021). The 7 CIS controls you should implement first. *CSO (Online)*. https://www.proquest.com/trade-journals/7-cis-controls-you-should-implement-first/docview/2612224339/se-2

IBM. (2022). *How much does a data breach cost in 2022?* IBM. https://www.ibm.com/security/data-breach

Insikt Group, & Rapid 7 Group. (2019). APT10 Targeted Norwegian MSP and US Companies in sustained campaign: Intrusions highlight ongoing exposure of third-party risk. *Recorded Future*. https://go.recordedfuture.com/hubfs/reports/cta-2019-0206.pdf

Johnson, R. (2017). Bank think Equifax breach threatens bank reputations, too. *American Banker*. https://www.americanbanker.com/opinion/equifax-breach-threatens-bank-reputations-too

Jones, L. A. (2020). *Reputation Risk and Potential Profitability: Best Practices to Predict and Mitigate Risk through Amalgamated Factors* (Order No. 28152966). Available from ProQuest Dissertations & Theses Global; ProQuest One Academic. (2466047018). https://www.proquest.com/dissertations-theses/reputation-risk-potential-profitability-best/docview/2466047018/se-2

Jones, S., & Curry, S. (2021). Strategically-thinking senior executives need to take a new view of the digital world - it is here to stay and is getting more scary. *Effective Executive, 24*(4), 30-36. https://www.proquest.com/scholarly-journals/strategically-thinking-senior-executives-need/docview/2622692144/se-2

Kaplan, R. S., & Mikes, A. (2019). Managing risks: A new framework. *Harvard Business Review*, *97*(2), 48–60.

Karlin, S. (2020). Louisiana has spent $2.3 M in recent cyberattack responses. *Governing*. https://www.governing.com/finance/louisiana-has-spent-2m-in-recent-cyberattack-responses.html

Kenton, W. (2020, March 26). Cyclical industry: What it is, characteristics, and examples. *Investopedia*. https://www.investopedia.com/terms/c/cyclical_industry.asp#:~:text=Technician%20(CMT).-,What%20Is%20a%20Cyclical%20Industry%3F,of%20economic%20downturn%20and%20contraction

Kerzner, H. (2019). *Project management: a systems approach to planning, scheduling, and controlling*. John Wiley & Sons.

Khaleq, S., Fletcher, K., & Du, C. (2021). Recognizing the value of enterprise risk management (ERM) through integration with strategy; acquisition; and planning, programming, budgeting and execution (ppbe). *Armed Forces Comptroller*, *66*(4), 38–44.

Kim, H., & Lee, S. (2019). An integrated approach to enterprise risk management: A systematic review of the literature and research directions. *Sustainability*, *11*(7), 1866. doi:10.3390u11071866

Lammers, T., Guertler, M., & Skirde, H. (2022). Can product modularization approaches help address challenges in technical project portfolio management? – laying the foundations for a methodology transfer. *International Journal of Information Systems and Project Management*, *10*(2), 26–42. doi:10.12821/ijispm100202

Lawton, G. (2021). What is risk management and why is it important? *TechTarget*. https://www.techtarget.com/searchcio/feature/9-common-risk-management-failures-and-how-to-avoid-them

Lin, T. C. W. (2022). Business warfare. Boston College. *Law School. Boston College Law Review. Boston College. Law School*, *63*(1), 1–64. https://www.proquest.com/scholarly-journals/business-warfare/docview/2637173474/se-2

Liu, Y., & Wang, Y. (2021). Research on the methods of enterprise risk management. *Journal of Physics: Conference Series*, *1776*(1), 012098. doi:10.1088/1742-6596/2037/1/012098

Malsam, W. (2019). Top down vs. bottom up management: What's the difference? *Project Manager.* https://www.projectmanager.com/blog/top-down-vs-bottom-up-management

Marle, F. (2020). an assistance to project risk management based on complex systems theory and agile project management. *Complexity*, *2020*, 1–20. Advance online publication. doi:10.1155/2020/3739129

Mehta, S. (2021). Industry risk. *Financial Edge*. https://www.fe.training/free-resources/credit/industry-risk

Mohammed, Z. (2022). Data breach recovery areas: An exploration of organization's recovery strategies for surviving data breaches. *Organizational Cybersecurity Journal: Practice. Process and People*, *2*(1), 41–59. doi:10.1108/OCJ-05-2021-0014

Muller, R., & Turner, R. (2020). The influence of project management standards, practices, and methodologies on project success. *Project Management Journal*, *51*(1), 18–33.

National Institute of Standards and Technology [NIST]. (2019). *NIST Cybersecurity Framework.* https://www.nist.gov/cyberframework

National Institute of Standards and Technology [NIST]. (2020). *Cybersecurity Framework Core.* https://www.nist.gov/cyberframework/core

National Institute of Standards and Technology [NIST]. (2021). *Cybersecurity Framework Functions.* https://www.nist.gov/cyberframework/functions

National Institute of Standards and Technology [NIST]. (2023). *Implementing the Cybersecurity Framework.* https://www.nist.gov/cyberframework/implementation

National Institute of Standards and Technology [NIST]. (n.d.). *Cybersecurity risk.* NIST. https://csrc.nist.gov/glossary/term/cybersecurity_risk

Newman, L. H. (April 23, 2018). Atlanta spent $2.6M to recover from a $52,000 ransomware scare. *Wired.* https://www.wired.com/story/atlanta-spent-26m-recover-from-ransomware-scare/

Nitzberg, S. (1997). The cyber battlefield -Is this the setting for the ultimate world war?Proceedings of the 20th National Information Systems Security Conference. *National Institute of Standards and Technology [NIST].* https://csrc.nist.gov/csrc/media/publications/conference-paper/1998/10/08/proceedings-of-the-21st-nissc-1998/documents/paperd10.pdf

Nobles, C. (2018). Botching human factors in cybersecurity in business organizations. Holistica –. *Journal of Business and Public Administration*, *9*(3), 71–88. doi:10.2478/hjbpa-2018-0024

Nobles, C. (2022). Stress, burnout, and security fatigue in cybersecurity: A human factors problem. HOLISTICA–. *Journal of Business and Public Administration*, *13*(1), 49–72. doi:10.2478/hjbpa-2022-0003

O'Connor, S. W. (2020). *The project risk management process | 5 tips for success.* Northeastern University. https://www.northeastern.edu/graduate/blog/project-risk-management/#:~:text=In%20project%20management%2C%20risk%20management,duration%20of%20a%20given%20project

Office of Management and Budget. (2019). *Preparation, Submission, And Execution Of The Budget.* (The White House, Washington, DC), OMB Circular No. A-11, December 18, 2019. https://www.whitehouse.gov/wpcontent/uploads/2018/06/a11.pdf

Özturan, P., & Grinstein, A. (2022). Can the marketing department benefit from socially responsible marketing activities? The role of legitimacy and customers' interest in social responsibility. *European Journal of Marketing*, *56*(2), 400–441. doi:10.1108/EJM-09-2020-0670

Pandey, S., Singh, R. K., Gunasekaran, A., & Kaushik, A. (2022). Cybersecurity risk in globalized supply chains: Conceptual framework. *Journal of Global Operations and Strategic Sourcing*, *13*(1), 103–128. doi:10.1108/JGOSS-05-2019-0042

Panetta, L. (2022). *Panetta warns of cyber Pearl Harbor*. Association of The United States Army. https://www.ausa.org/news/panetta-warns-cyber-pearl-harbor

Patrick, S. U., Timmermann, A., & Frank, V. (2022). Organizational aspects of cybersecurity in German family firms – do opportunities or risks predominate? *Organizational Cybersecurity Journal: Practice. Process and People*, *2*(1), 21–40. doi:10.1108/OCJ-03-2021-0010

Peacock, J. (2022). Risk register examples for cybersecurity leaders. *CyberSaint Security*. https://www.cybersaint.io/blog/risk-register-examples-for-cybersecurity

Pinto, J. K., & Trailer, J. W. (2020). *A guide to the project management body of knowledge (PMBOK guide)*. Project Management Institute.

Podgórska, M., & Pichlak, M. (2019). Analysis of project managers' leadership competencies: Project success relation: what are the competencies of polish project leaders? [Project managers' leadership competencies]. *International Journal of Managing Projects in Business*, *12*(4), 869–887. doi:10.1108/IJMPB-08-2018-0149

PricewaterhouseCoopers [PwC]. (2022). *2022 Global digital trust insights survey - The C-suite guide to simplifying for cyber readiness, today and tomorrow*. PWC. https://www.pwc.com/dti?WT.mc_id=CT3-PL300-DM1-TR1-LS2-ND30-PR5-CN_DTICyber-globaldti&gclid=CjwKCAjwrZOXBhACEiwA0EoRD3didnaMnMmSU0TwUUZekHAA8t-B0U4eTOBnZOZ1SzNBZ-QKux8g2BoCGcEQAvD_BwE&gclsrc=aw.ds

Quinn, S., Ivy, N., Barrett, M., Witte, G., & Gardner, R. K. (2022). *Prioritizing cybersecurity risk for enterprise risk management.* National Institute of Standards and Technology U. S. Department of Commerce. doi:10.6028/NIST.IR.8286B

Rajan, R. S. (2020, August 19). The impact of covid-19 on the financial system. *The Business Times*. https://www.proquest.com/newspapers/impact-covid-19-on-financial-system/docview/2435166197/se-2

Rane, S. B., Potdar, P. R., & Rane, S. (2021). Development of project risk management framework based on Industry 4.0 technologies. *Benchmarking*, *28*(5), 1451–1481. doi:10.1108/BIJ-03-2019-0123

Ropek, L. (2019, November 18). Ransomware again strikes Louisiana, forcing server shutdowns. *Government Technology.* https://www.govtech.com/security/ransomware-again-strikes-louisiana-forcing-server-shutdowns.html

Rothstein, H., Huber, M., & Gaskell, G. (2006). A theory of risk colonization: The spiraling regulatory logics or societal and institutional risks. *Economy and Society*, *35*(1), 91–112. doi:10.1080/03085140500465865

Schneider, J. (2022, January). A world without trust. *Foreign Affairs, 101*, 22–31. https://www.proquest.com/magazines/world-without-trust/docview/2616230643/se-2

S&P Global Ratings. (2021). *How we rate nonfinancial corporate entities.* S&P. https://www.spglobal.com/ratings/_division-assets/pdfs/041019_howweratenonfinancialcorporateentities.pdf

TeamStage. (2023). Project management statistics: trends and common mistakes in 2022. *TeamStage*. . https://teamstage.io/project-management-statistics/

Terdiman, D. (2021, May 24). The rise of Nth party risk: What you need to know. *Newsroom*. https://www.mastercard.com/news/perspectives/2021/the-rise-of-nth-party-risk/

The Joint Commission. (2022). Innovative combined proactive risk assessment identifies vulnerable points in healthcare processes. *The Joint Commission Journal on Quality and Patient Safety*. https://www.jointcommission.org/resources/news-and-multimedia/news/2022/06/innovative-combined-proactive-risk-assessment-identifies-vulnerable-points-in-healthcare-processes/#.Yu0isnbMJPY

the Risk Management Society [RIMS]. (2022). *Sample job descriptions: What is risk management?* Risk Management Society. https://www.rims.org/resources/sample-job-descriptions

Tucci, L. (2021). What is risk management and why is it important? *TechTarget*. https://media.techtarget.com/digitalguide/images/Misc/EA-Marketing/Eguides/What_is_Risk_Management_and_Why_is_it_Important.pdf

Ullah, F., Sepasgozar, S. M. E., & Wang, C. (2018). A systematic review of smart real estate technology: Drivers of, and barriers to, the use of digital disruptive technologies and online platforms. *Sustainability (Basel)*, *10*(9), 3142. doi:10.3390u10093142

Ulrich, P. S., Timmermann, A., & Frank, V. (2021). Organizational aspects of cybersecurity in German family firms – Do opportunities or risks predominate? *Organizational Cybersecurity Journal: Practice, Process, and People*, *2*(1), 21–40.

United States Government Accountability Office [GAO]. (2020). *Cybersecurity of federal networks and critical infrastructure: Opportunities for greater federal leadership*. GAO-21-68SP.

United States Government Accountability Office [GAO)]. (2021, April 16). *Information technology and cybersecurity significant attention is needed to address high-risk areas*. GAO. file:///C:/Users/Dr.%20Burton/Downloads/853207.pdf

Van Weyenberge, B., Deckers, X., Caspeele, R., & Merci, B. (2016). Development of a risk assessment method for life safety in case of fire in rail tunnels. *Fire Technology, 52*(5), 1465-1479. doi:http://dx.doi.org.proxy.cecybrary.com/10.1007/s10694-015-0469-y

Veksler, V. D., Buchler, N., LaFleur, C. G., Yu, M. S., Lebiere, C., & Gonzalez, C. (2020). Cognitive models in cybersecurity: Learning from expert analysts and predicting attacker behavior. *Frontiers in Psychology*, *11*, 1049. doi:10.3389/fpsyg.2020.01049 PMID:32612551

Verstraete, M., & Zarsky, T. (2022). Cybersecurity spillovers. *Brigham Young University Law Review*, *47*(3), 929–999. https://www.proquest.com/scholarly-journals/cybersecurity-spillovers/docview/2677676009/se-2

Wang, R. (2022). Organizational commitment in the nonprofit sector and the underlying impact of stakeholders and organizational support. *Voluntas*, *33*(3), 538–549. doi:10.100711266-021-00336-8 PMID:33686322

Wang, X., Li, J., Guo, X., & Zhang, Z. (2023). A risk management framework for cyber-physical systems. *IEEE Internet of Things Journal*, *10*(2), 1040–1051.

Waqas. (2022). Will immersive technology evolve or solve cybercrime? *INFOSEC*. https://resources.infosecinstitute.com/topic/will-immersive-technology-evolve-or-solve-cybercrime/

Wei, X., & Xiao, J. (2019). Threat intelligence: Cyber risk management. *International Journal of Information Management*, *44*, 99–107.

Witts, J. (2022). The top 5 biggest cyber security threats that small businesses face and how to stop them. *Expert Insights*. https://expertinsights.com/insights/the-top-5-biggest-cyber-security-threats-that-small-businesses-face-and-how-to-stop-them/

World Economic Forum. (2018). *These are the biggest risks the world faces*. WEF. https://www.weforum.org/agenda/2018/01/these-are-the-biggest-risks-the-world-faces-in-2018/

World Economic Forum. (2020). *The global risk report*. WEF. https://report-files.weforum.org/docs/WEF_Global_Risk_Report_2020.pdf

Yasuda, H., Kawamukai, H., & Nishimura, H. (2020). *Risk Analysis Based On Factors Of Failure In Small And Medium-Sized Company Projects*. 2020 9th International Congress on Advanced Applied Informatics (IIAI-AAI), Kitakyushu, Japan. 10.1109/IIAI-AAI50415.2020.00163

Zhang, S., Hou, W., Yin, J., & Lin, Z. (2022). A Review of research and practice on the theory and technology of reservoir dam risk assessment. *Sustainability (Basel)*, *14*(22), 14984. doi:10.3390u142214984

KEY TERMS AND DEFINITIONS

Cybercriminals: Cybercriminals are people or groups of people who utilize technology to exploit humans or technologies for malevolent purposes.

Cybersecurity: Cybersecurity is the use of diverse technologies, methods, and controls to safeguard systems, networks, programs, devices as well as information from cyberattacks.

Data Breach: A data breach references any incident wherein data is pilfered or removed from a system minus the realization or approval of the owner.

Risk: Risk is a position comprising contact to threat.

Risk Project Management: Risk project management involves learning conceivable risks, examining such risks, diminishing risks, and forestalling upcoming risks through consistent observation.

Sensitive Information: Sensitive information is that which necessitates safeguarding because such information's forfeiture, misapplication, alteration, or unlawful entree will harmfully impact organization or person.

Stakeholder: A stakeholder is a person or group with a vested concern in all decisions or actions of the given organization.

Chapter 16

Empowering Business Transformation:
The Positive Impact and Ethical Considerations of Generative AI in Software Product Management – A Systematic Literature Review

Nishant A. Parikh
https://orcid.org/0009-0000-0430-7825
Capitol Technology University, USA

ABSTRACT

Generative artificial intelligence (GAI) has made outstanding strides in recent years, with a good-sized impact on software product management. Drawing on pertinent articles from 2016 to 2023, this systematic literature evaluation reveals generative AI's potential applications, benefits, and constraints in this area. The study shows that technology can assist in idea generation, market research, customer insights, product requirements engineering, and product development. It can help reduce development time and costs through automatic code generation, customer feedback analysis, and more. However, the technology's accuracy, reliability, and ethical consideration persist. Ultimately, generative AI's practical application can significantly improve software product management activities, leading to more efficient use of resources, better product outcomes, and improved end-user experiences.

INTRODUCTION

Generative AI, residing at the cusp of the second and third wave of AI evolution as classified by DARPA (2023), is a testament to the transformative potential of AI. While the first wave comprised rule-based AI systems, and the second wave advanced to machine learning and deep learning applications, the third wave anticipates AI systems capable of contextual adaptation, akin to human understanding. Straddling

DOI: 10.4018/979-8-3693-1634-4.ch016

the second and third phases, generative AI leverages statistical learning to generate novel content such as text, images, or music, often utilizing deep learning frameworks such as Generative Adversarial Networks (GANs). As we progress into this intriguing realm, we unlock vast possibilities for technological transformation.

Generative AI refers to artificial intelligence that can create new content, such as images, text, or music, which did not exist before. It often involves learning from a large amount of input data and then generating something new that reflects the patterns or features observed in that data. In recent years, Artificial Intelligence Generated Content (AIGC) has not only intrigued the computer science community but also captivated societal interest with various products developed by major tech firms, including OpenAI's conversational AI system, ChatGPT, and their creative visual AI, DALL-E2. These models, underpinned by deep generative AI using neural networks, have made significant strides over the past decade (Cao et al., 2023). The most famous form of generative AI is the generative adversarial network (GAN), which consists of two neural networks competing to generate suitable content material. Other generative AI strategies include variational autoencoders (VAE) and transformers, including OpenAI's GPT-3, demonstrating unique competencies in producing human-like textual content (Radford et al., 2021).

Software product management is a crucial discipline that encompasses the activities and responsibilities involved in creating, delivering, and maintaining software products. Following the guidelines set by the International Software Product Management Association (ISPMA), software product managers are equipped with the knowledge and skills to effectively navigate the complex landscape of product strategy, planning, development, and management. By employing a holistic approach, software product management aims to align business objectives with customer needs, optimize product features, prioritize requirements, coordinate cross-functional teams, and oversee the entire product lifecycle. With its emphasis on user-centricity, value creation, and Agile methodologies, ISPMA provides a comprehensive framework that empowers software product managers to drive innovation, foster collaboration, and achieve sustainable success in today's dynamic software industry (ISPMA, 2023).

Software product management is a complicated and challenging discipline that includes various activities: market analysis, product analysis, product strategy, product planning, development, marketing, sales, support, and services. The achievement of software product management relies upon the software product manager's ability to understand the users' needs, market trends, and technological improvements. Generative artificial intelligence (GenAI) has emerged as a promising technology that may help software product managers enhance their decision-making and the quality of their products. This systematic literature evaluation aims to offer an overview of the current state of research on the applications of generative AI in software product management, focusing on the software product manager's activities.

The potential applications of generative AI in software product management are vast, and this article offers an in-depth evaluation of how these applications can transform the software product management field. The following sections will discuss the literature review and the benefits and potential limitations of incorporating generative AI in software product management.

Problem Statement

Generative AI is a revolutionary technology with the potential to modernize software product management by automating tasks, improving efficiency, and enhancing customer experience (Peng et al., 2023; Malik et al., 2022; Siggelkow & Terwiesch, 2023). Growing demand to modernize workflow across industries is expected to drive the demand for generative AI applications among industries. The global market for generative AI is expected to reach $109 billion by 2030 (Grandviewresearch, 2023). As per the McKinsey & Company (2022) report, 67% average share of respondents reported a revenue increase via AI adoption and 79% reported a cost decrease via AI adoption. The general problem is the need for software product managers to access new and innovative tools that can help them improve their decision-making and profitability and enhance the quality of their products. The specific problem is the lack of awareness of generative AI's potential in software product management. This study aims to bridge this knowledge gap, creating a more comprehensive understanding of how generative AI can be utilized in software product management along with the ethical considerations. It will empower product managers and business leaders to leverage this technology, potentially leading to the creation of superior products.

SIGNIFICANCE OF THE STUDY

The advent and rise of generative AI have dramatically transformed numerous industries, including software product management. Despite the increasing adoption of this technology, there is a lack of comprehensive studies that delve into the full extent of its application, impact, and ethical implications within the realm of product management. This gap is precisely what this study aims to fill.

The significance of this study lies in its potential to contribute a more holistic understanding of the role and value of generative AI in software product management. The findings from this research offer insights that are not only academically significant but also invaluable for business leaders, software product managers, and organizations in the tech industry.

According to Grand View Research, the global market for GenAI is expected to reach $109 billion by 2030 (Grandviewresearch, 2023). With GenAI increasingly becoming a significant part of business strategy and operations, understanding how to best utilize GenAI technologies is critical. This study provides qualitative findings that elucidate the practical benefits of generative AI in software product management, such as increased labor productivity, personalized customer experience, accelerated R&D, and the emergence of new business models. These insights are crucial for leaders who are at the helm of GenAI adoption in their organizations.

By discussing the ethical implications of generative AI, this research offers guidelines that ensure the technology's responsible use, a critical aspect that businesses need to consider in their AI strategies. This research also makes significant contributions to the broader discourse on GenAI and its impact on software product management, bridging the gap between academic research and practical application. By doing so, it expands the body of knowledge in applied research, ultimately paving the way for further exploration and development in the field.

The insights derived from this study can be utilized by businesses and software professionals to enhance their AI strategies, leading to improved organizational efficiency, better product outcomes, and superior customer experiences. Furthermore, these findings can stimulate discussion and policy formulation around the ethical use of AI, contributing to the responsible advancement of the technology.

In essence, this research, by exploring generative AI in software product management, will be of immense value for both academia and industry. Its implications are poised to drive innovation, enhance business processes, and inform ethical considerations in AI deployment.

LITERATURE REVIEW

This systematic literature review is based on a comprehensive analysis of existing studies related to the applications of generative AI in business and product management. The ISPMA (2023) framework is used to study applications in product management. The International Software Product Management Association (ISPMA) Product Management Framework is a well-known model designed specifically for managing software products. Paajoki (2020) identifies the ISPMA Product Management Framework as the best practice framework to adopt for any organization. The aim of this review is to identify and synthesize the current state of research, focusing on key application areas such as market research, product planning, product documentation, product requirements engineering, product development, user interface and user experience (UI/UX) design, customer insights, and Agile software development. The McKinsey 7-S Framework and Lewin's Change Model frame the review to evaluate how an organization can adopt this technology change, laying the foundation for product managers and business leaders to use the technology effectively and efficiently (Peters & Waterman, 1984; Lewin, 1947). Owen et al. (2013)'s Responsible Innovation framework and General Data Protection Regulation (GDPR, 2023) principles frame the discussion on ethics and privacy.

Relevant Studies in the Software Product Management

Idea Generation

Karim et al. (2022) researched the application of generative AI for idea generation, brainstorming, and producing research clues. Their work builds on prior research that developed a model for generating medical dialogues related to COVID-19. The authors utilized two GPT3-based models: GPT-NEO-125M and GPT-NEO-1.3B. The larger GPT-NEO-1.3B model consistently generated more coherent and interconnected ideas. Although their study focused on the medical domain, specifically COVID-19, Karim et al. suggest that the principles derived from their findings could be extended to other scientific or specialized disciplines. The findings show that the larger model generates more coherent text with linked ideas.

Market Research

Large Language Models (LLMs), such as GPT, are a type of AI created to understand and generate human-like language. Brand et al. (2023)'s research demonstrated that these models can be instrumental in understanding customer preferences. Brand et al. found that, when treated like a randomly selected customer, GPT exhibits responses that are realistic and consistent with values obtained from existing research. Although Brand et al. employ traditional market research paradigms to underscore the utility of GPT, LLMs may inspire new market research paradigms unrestricted by the constraints of human subject research. The authors also cautioned that LLMs are known to occasionally "hallucinate" and return incorrect information.

Customer Insights

Siggelkow and Terwiesch (2023) discussed the transformative potential of large language models such as OpenAI's ChatGPT and Google's Bard in enhancing customer experiences. Siggelkow and Terwiesch highlighted that these AI models can aid in recognizing customer needs by interpreting and integrating data, translating these needs into specific requests, and responding to customers with tailored solutions. Siggelkow and Terwiesch emphasized the importance of focusing on the customer, not just the technology, by addressing specific customer pain points and deploying AI to complement, not replace, a firm's unique capabilities.

Additionally, Siggelkow and Terwiesch (2023) underscored the value of the 'repeat' dimension in customer interactions, where firms learn from each interaction to improve future responses. Generative AI systems excel in this area, creating a positive feedback loop that enhances AI's understanding of the customer for more personalized and effective service. The authors warned against viewing AI as a substitute for human labor, suggesting instead that it should be seen as a tool to enhance a firm's capabilities in unique ways. Ultimately, while generative AI has the potential to revolutionize customer experiences, the authors emphasized the importance of strategic deployment to address customer needs and bolster a firm's distinctive value proposition.

Brynjolfsson et al. (2023) investigated the implementation of a generative AI conversational assistant across 5,179 customer support agents, finding that the AI tool notably increased worker productivity, enhanced customer sentiment, and decreased employee turnover rates. Particularly beneficial for newer and less-skilled workers, the AI tool substantially improved problem resolution and customer satisfaction but did not significantly assist the highest-skilled or more experienced workers. An analysis of the text from agent conversations suggested that AI recommendations guided less-skilled workers to communicate more similarly to high-skilled workers.

Product Requirements Engineering

Malik et al. (2022) focused on the critical process of Requirement Engineering (RE), which is integral to software development and involves defining, documenting, and maintaining software requirements. Malik et al. noted the significance of Software Requirement Specifications (SRS), key deliverables in the software development life cycle, and the problems arising from ambiguities and conflicts within these documents. To tackle this issue, Malik et al. proposed a two-phase process for automatic conflict detection in SRS documents that works directly with natural language requirements. The first phase involves transforming software requirements into numeric vectors using transformer-based sentence embeddings, with cosine similarity and ROC curves employed to identify potential conflicts. In the second phase, potential conflicts undergo analysis with general and software-specific Named Entity Recognition (NER), and an overlapping entity ratio is used to determine the final set of conflicts. The authors found an improvement in the F1-score for the OpenCoss and IBM-UAV datasets by 4% and 5%, respectively, underlining its effectiveness.

Agile Software Development

In Agile software development, generative AI can support various activities, such as sprint planning, backlog management, and estimation. For instance, Kim et al. (2021) proposed an AI-driven approach for estimating user story points in Agile projects, leveraging natural language processing techniques to analyze and estimate the effort required for user stories.

Fu and Tantithamthavorn (2022) introduced GPT2SP, an innovative Agile story point estimation approach, utilizing a GPT-2 pre-trained language model and Transformer-based architecture. The proposed method surpasses traditional techniques, such as Planning Poker, Analogy, and expert judgment, and Deep-SE, a deep learning-based approach. Through testing on over 23,000 issues spanning 16 open-source projects, GPT2SP exhibited superior accuracy, outperforming within-project estimates by 34%-57%, cross-project estimates by 39%-49%, and enhancing Deep-SE's performance by 6%-47%. A proof-of-concept tool was also developed to clarify the factors influencing the estimates. A practitioner survey highlighted the challenge of story point estimation. However, it also indicated that an AI-based approach with explanations, such as GPT2SP, was deemed more valuable and trustworthy.

Dam et al. (2019) introduced a framework that adapts and integrates various AI technologies to bolster Agile project management. Although areas in Agile project management are still challenging due to insufficient adequate support, their proposed analytics engine aims to provide decision support on multiple fronts. This includes descriptive analytics, a basic level of analytics that most existing Agile project management tools offer, primarily through data visualization via reports, dashboards, and scorecards.

Automated Code Generation

There have been several types of studies on code generation using generative AI techniques such as Transformer, but Peng et al. (2023) found that GitHub Copilot (which uses generative AI technology for code generation), an AI pair programmer providing context-based code suggestions, significantly boosts productivity. The study revealed that the group using Copilot completed tasks 55.8% faster, marking the first experiment of its kind to provide empirical evidence of the potential of AI tools to enhance human productivity. If extrapolated, a 55.8% productivity increase could lead to substantial economic cost savings and notably influence GDP growth.

Khan and Uddin (2022) examined the application of the Generative Pre-trained Transformer-3 (GPT-3) Codex in automating documentation generation in Software Engineering (SE). Codex demonstrates state-of-the-art performance, outperforming prior models by achieving an average BLEU (BiLingual Evaluation Understudy) score of 20.63 (11.2% improvement over earlier state-of-the-art techniques), even under basic settings. BLEU is a test which checks how good a computer program is at translating languages or generating text.

Park et al. (2023) discussed developing and evaluating the ALSI-Transformer, a transformer-based code comment generation model designed to improve source code comprehension in software development. In response to the increasing need for efficient code commenting as the scale of open-source software grows, the ALSI-Transformer uses a novel method of aggregating multimodal information through Gate Network.

UI/UX Design

The integration of AI technology is revolutionizing the Human-Computer Interaction (HCI) and User Experience (UX) landscapes, redefining user research, design, and evaluation methodologies (Xu, 2023). AI-based solutions enhance the UX quality, with increasing adoption prompted by heightened user awareness of technical innovation.

Houde et al. (2022) explored the objectives, obstacles, and operational practices of teams working on application modernization, as showcased by three projects. The authors discovered that user experience (UX) modernization is a complex, labor-intensive segment of the broader modernization process, involving numerous manual tasks performed by multiple team members, such as project managers, UX designers, and software engineers. Despite the crucial role of UX in these projects, this is often inadequately addressed compared to other tasks such as core code transformation into microservices. However, the authors recognized its potential as a promising avenue for implementing generative AI technologies. By identifying specific pain points in the UX modernization process, Houde et al. proposed using generative AI models as a possible solution. Houde et al. also envisioned a future scenario where these models could redefine the UX modernization workflow.

Relevant Studies in Ethics and Privacy

Brand et al. (2023) highlighted the problem of "hallucinations" and returning incorrect information with Large Language Models. It requires consistent human reviews to ensure the accuracy of the AI-generated output.

The rise in deep generative AI models has led to increasingly intricate models. However, their performance relies heavily on quality training data. Notably, these models often exhibit the 'black box' problem, limiting their interpretability and causing potential trust issues. Lastly, handling AI-generated content must address critical social concerns to ensure responsible and beneficial usage for society, emphasizing the importance of trustworthiness and responsibility in the field (Cao et al., 2023).

Generative AI presents legal risks, including potential infringement of intellectual property rights, including unresolved legal questions such as ownership and application of copyright, patent, and trademark laws to AI-generated content. Before leveraging the benefits of generative AI, businesses must understand these risks and devise strategies for self-protection. Essential measures include updating vendor and customer contracts with explicit disclosure about the use of generative AI and clauses safeguarding intellectual property rights. Furthermore, confidentiality provisions should be enhanced to prohibit confidential information in AI tool text prompts (Appel et al., 2023).

Dwivedi et al. (2023) discussed several key challenges that the rise of generative AI, such as ChatGPT, presents to the industry. Dwivedi et al. highlight serious ethical concerns, as these AI models lack the ability to understand or consider ethical and legal issues. This leads to potential misuse, including the production of deepfakes and disinformation. The inherent 'black box' nature of AI systems poses transparency and explainability issues. Biases can be replicated from the training data, unintentionally leading to misinformation. Legal issues abound, with few guidelines for AI development, unclear copyright boundaries, and dubious ownership of AI-generated content. The authors also foresee potential job losses and increased technology dependency following AI incorporation, stunting personal development and leaving organizations vulnerable if technology fails. Additionally, generative AI systems are limited to combining existing information, offering limited originality. The cultural and personal acceptance of AI could lead to a new form of digital divide. Lastly, the effective use of generative AI requires the ability to design efficient prompts, potentially necessitating widespread new skill training.

Relevant Studies in Business and Management

Korzynski et al. (2023) discussed the impact of generative AI on decision-making in business and management, suggesting that it may address certain limitations in human decision-making processes defined by the bounded rationality model. This model, proposed by Herbert Simon (Simon, 1987), highlights human cognitive limitations, imperfect information, and time constraints as factors affecting our ability to make rational decisions. The use of evolutionary algorithms and generative AI, accelerated by advancements in information technology, could enhance optimization theory and procedural rationality, particularly in customer service. Generative AI systems, such as ChatGPT, can provide structured, logical data to aid decision-makers in filtering and organizing options. The article also notes that demographic factors, such as age and gender, influence the adoption and usage of generative AI in decision-making. Younger users tend to be more technologically optimistic and open to using AI tools, while older users may rely more on their existing knowledge. Gender also plays a role, with men often being more inclined towards innovative technologies.

Korzynski et al. (2023) observed that generative AI, such as ChatGPT, is significantly transforming customer services, prompting a reevaluation of existing theories. With capabilities to interact with customers directly, AI could revolutionize service delivery and customer-organization relations. This has implications for relationship marketing theory, where AI can potentially bolster customer relationships through quick, personalized responses, leading to enhanced customer satisfaction and loyalty. Moreover, generative AI can enhance customer satisfaction and support the presumption concept by allowing consumers to play a more active role in their interactions with organizations. Lastly, in terms of customer experience management theory, generative AI offers new ways of delivering positive customer experiences and engagement. However, the relationship among generative AI services, customer engagement, loyalty, and the creation of new value for organizations requires further research.

REVIEW QUESTIONS

The research questions were categorized using Petticrew and Roberts' (2005) population, intervention, comparison, outcome, and context framework. The *population* is product managers & business leaders working in software organizations. *Intervention* is the Organization & Product Manager's role interfered with generative AI. The *outcome* is the applications and ethical considerations of generative AI in the field of Software Product Management. *Context* is software product companies. The study did not include a *comparison*. The following research questions (see Table 1) were the center of the qualitative study.

Table 1. Research questions and motivation

Research questions	Motivation
1. What are the applications of generative AI in software product management?	The research investigates the application of generative AI in software product management. It also aims to contribute to a deeper understanding of the role of generative AI in software product management and to identify potential areas for further research and development. The research results may assist software product managers wishing to leverage generative AI to improve their products and services.
2. What are the ethical challenges presented by Generative AI and what strategies can be employed to mitigate these issues?	Generative AI, with its potential to revolutionize business operations through increased automation, improved efficiency, and rapid decision-making, offers an array of benefits. Yet, as with any transformative technology, it brings with it a raft of ethical implications. These include concerns related to bias, transparency, data privacy, and potential misuse of AI-generated content, which, if left unaddressed, could potentially overshadow generative AI's benefits. This requires a comprehensive exploration of the holistic impact of generative AI on businesses, one that not only delves into its benefits but also grapples with the ethical difficulties arising from its use. By addressing this research question, we aim to shed light on the path businesses must navigate to successfully harness the potential of generative AI while remaining ethically compliant and responsible.

REVIEW METHODS

A literature review provided the data for this qualitative, descriptive study. Based on current and emerging studies on product management topics, we develop current applications of generative AI in software product management.

Data Source and Search Strategy

The search strategy involved querying significant databases, including IEEE Xplore, ACM Digital Library, EBSCOhost, and ProQuest Central. Google Scholar search engine was also used for the comprehensive research. Keywords such as "generative AI," "software product management," "Idea Generation," "Product Design," "Customer Insights," "project planning," "automated code generation," "UI/UX design," "Ethics," and "customer feedback analysis" were used in different combinations to identify relevant studies.

Study Selection

Each data source contains different inclusion and exclusion criteria. For example, Google Scholar does not have a full-text search or source type selection. It does not include popular magazines, newspapers, or internet articles. IEEE Xplore has full texts, conference proceedings, and IEEE-published standards. Likewise, each data source has different basic or advanced search selection criteria. Table 2 shows each data source's search criteria (inclusion and exclusion). The goal was to collect information for the years between 2016 and 2023, including all sources, full text, and English-language only.

Table 2. Database sources and inclusion/exclusion criteria

No.	Source	Search criteria (inclusion/exclusion)
1	Google Scholar	Inclusion: the years 2016–2023; any type
2	ACM Digital Library	Inclusion: The ACM Full-Text collection; the years 2016–2023
3	EBSCOhost	Inclusion: Full text; peer-reviewed, the years 2016–2023 Exclusion: Magazines, trade publications
4	IEEE Xplore	Inclusion: the years 2016–2023
5	ProQuest Central	Inclusion: Full text, peer-reviewed, the years 2016–2023 Exclusion: Source type: blogs, podcasts, & websites; trade journals, wire feeds, newspapers, magazines

Data Extraction and Data Synthesis

Applications of GenAI in Software Product Management

The ISPMA framework (Table 3) was used to synthesize the study. Based on the literature review, applications of generative AI in software product management were identified and aligned with ISPMA categories to better understand where generative AI can be used in the software product management framework.

Table 3. Applications of generative AI with ISPMA framework

Strategic Management	Product Strategy	Product Planning	Development	Marketing	Sales & Fulfillment	Delivery Service & Support
Corporate Strategy	Positioning & Product Definition	Customer Insight	Product Architecture and Management	Marketing Planning	Sales Planning	Service Planning and Preparation
Portfolio Management	Delivery Model & Service Strategy	Product Life Cycle Management	Development Environment Management	Value Communication	Customer Relationship Management	Service Execution
Innovation Management	Ecosystem Management	Roadmapping	Development Execution	Product Launches	Operational Sales	Technical Support
Resource Management	Sourcing	Release Planning	User Experience Design	Opportunity Management	Operational Fulfillment	Operations
Compliance Management	Pricing	Product Requirements Engineering	Detailed Requirements Engineering	Channel Preparation		
Market Analysis	Financial Management		Quality Management	Operational Marketing		
Product Analysis	Legal and IPR Management					

Continued on following page

Table 3. Continued

	Performance & Risk Management					

Note. The light blue cells show the applications of generative AI in the SPM category.

Although generative AI is a ground-breaking technology, it is still evolving. Its critical use case is a human-like content generation that can be applied to any use case requiring content writing (such as the product or technical documentation) or human-like conversations, such as automated customer support to provide customers with more logical and human-like responses along with the necessary information.

Market Analysis. Market analysis is a broad category of SPM, which involves market research, user research, competitive analysis, and many more sub-activities. It is still premature to apply GenAI to all activities. Technology can only help with the existing research-based knowledge. It cannot perform primary research by itself, such as carrying out customer interviews, but it may help analyze customer feedback and reduce Product Manager's time in feedback analysis. Karim et al. (2022) researched the application of generative AI for idea generation, brainstorming, and producing research clues. The research found that GenAI generates coherent and interconnected ideas based on the given knowledge base. Although the study was performed in the medical field, it can be applied to any discipline (Karim et al., 2022).

Positioning and Product Definition. This is another area GenAI can assist with as its primary use case is content writing. Based on the given market and product analysis knowledge, it can help create product definitions, including product naming, writing and suggesting product features, etc. Nguyen et al. (2021)'s research shows promising results in writing product descriptions for e-commerce products. However, it can be applied to any industry. Zhang et al. (2022) carried out similar research in product title generation.

Customer Insight and Support. Customer Insight is a critical use-case, as the GenAI technology helps in analyzing customer feedback and learning from that feedback, and in providing better and tailored future responses based on customer needs. GenAI technology has exploded the conversational bot market. According to Statista (2023), the size of the chatbot market is forecast to reach around 1.25 billion US dollars in 2025, a significant increase from the market size in 2016, which stood at 190.8 million US dollars. Brynjolfsson et al. (2023) demonstrated that the implementation of a generative AI conversational assistant enhanced productivity, customer sentiment, and reduced employee turnover in customer support, primarily aiding less experienced workers and boosting overall customer satisfaction.

Product Requirements Engineering and Detailed Requirements Engineering. These are the other use cases of GenAI that can help PMs write product documentation, including writing and estimative Agile stories (Kim et al., 2021, Fu and Tantithamthavorn, 2022). The incredible beauty of GenAI lies in Reinforcement Learning with Human Feedback (RLHF), which means that organizations or product managers can feed product-related data to the GenAI tool (such as OpenAI GPT API) for training purposes. The tool can help enhance product knowledge and detailed documentation, including writing Agile stories as the product owner. It can also be used as a product knowledge management system, where anyone from the organization or product team can obtain knowledge using the conversational AI tool.

PMs can also train the GenAI tool with competitors' information, including their products, attributes, pricing, website content, etc., information that can be leveraged to generate new ideas for positioning the product. Moreover, it can also be used to generate compelling product titles. Although Zhang et al. (2022) introduced a specific model to generate product titles in e-commerce, it can be used in any field.

User Experience Design. Generative AI is transforming User Experience (UX) design in notable ways, providing designers with innovative tools to enhance user engagement and satisfaction. Leveraging the power of machine-learning models such as GANs, generative AI can create numerous design variations, thereby aiding in rapid prototyping and experimentation. Furthermore, it allows for personalized experiences by tailoring interfaces based on user preferences and behaviors. It can also predict and address user needs by understanding and interpreting context, enabling more intuitive and responsive designs. Thus, generative AI paves the way for more user-centered, dynamic, and adaptive UX design (Xu, 2023; Houde et al., 2022).

Development Execution. It is another critical area where GenAI is becoming popular. Automatic code generation was a hot topic among researchers. Figure 1 below shows the maximum number of words used across all studies reviewed. There have been several GenAI models available to generate automatic code. GitHub is one of the most popular sites that provides a GenAI plugin to generate automatic code. Peng et al. (2023) found that the Copilot group completed tasks 55.8% faster.

In a six-week pilot study at Deloitte using 55 developers, most users rated the resulting code's accuracy at 65% or better, with most of the code coming from Codex. The Deloitte experiment found a 20%

Figure 1. Word cloud of the literature review

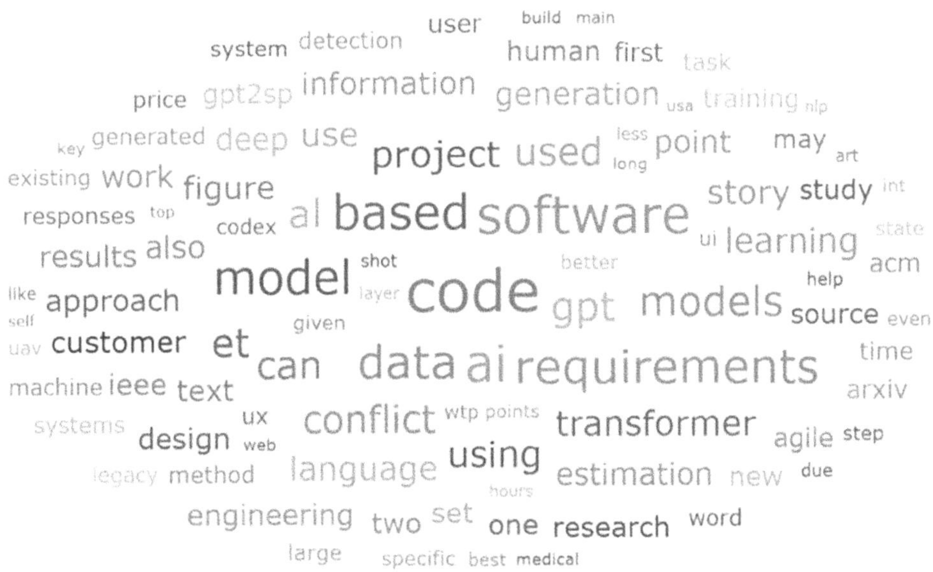

improvement in code development speed for relevant projects (Davenport & Mittal, 2022).

Change Management and Strategy Models in AI Implementation

When implementing generative AI, organizations can employ various change management and strategy models. The Lewin Change Model, for example, proposes a three-step process to change: unfreeze, change, and refreeze (Burnes, 2004). This model could be used in the context of introducing generative AI to an organization's existing operations.

Similarly, the McKinsey 7-S Framework emphasizes the importance of aligning seven key organizational elements: strategy, structure, systems, shared values, style, staff, and skills (Peters & Waterman, 1984). This framework could guide the strategic alignment of generative AI with the organization's overall objectives and culture.

Lewin's Change Model

Lewin's (1947) Change Model is a simple yet powerful model for understanding the process of change. The model suggests that change involves a three-stage process: unfreezing, changing (or transition), and refreezing. Here we apply this model to the implementation and acceptance of generative AI in an organization:

Unfreezing. In this stage, the organization recognizes the need for change. With respect to generative AI, the organization may identify opportunities for increased automation, improved efficiency, reduced manual effort, and improved decision-making (Brynjolfsson et al., 2023; Peng et al., 2023; Fu & Tantithamthavorn, 2022; Khan & Uddin, 2022; Park et al., 2023; Houde et al., 2022; Malik et al., 2022; Korzynski et al., 2023). The organization might also recognize potential limitations, such as concerns about the quality and accuracy of generated outputs, ethical considerations, and difficulties in integrating AI technologies into existing workflows and tools (Brand et al., 2023; Cao et al., 2023; Appel et al., 2023; Dwivedi et al., 2023).

Changing (Transition). This is the stage where the actual changes are implemented. In the context of generative AI, this could involve selecting and deploying AI systems, training staff to use them, and making necessary changes to workflows and processes. This stage would require addressing the challenges highlighted in the unfreezing stage. For instance, the organization would need to ensure the transparency and fairness of the AI systems, as well as their seamless integration with existing systems.

Refreezing. Once the changes are implemented and start to show benefits, the organization goes through a process of reinforcing and stabilizing the change. This could involve setting up procedures for monitoring and evaluating the performance of the generative AI systems, creating guidelines for ethical usage, and making any necessary adjustments to ensure the AI systems continue to deliver benefits while minimizing potential drawbacks.

Using Lewin's Change Model can help organizations understand the process of integrating generative AI, anticipate potential challenges, and devise strategies for successful implementation and ongoing improvement.

The McKinsey 7-S Framework

The McKinsey 7-S Framework is a management model consisting of seven interconnected key elements that are crucial for the success of any organization, and for a company to operate effectively, these elements must be aligned with each other. Here is how we could apply the 7-S framework to better understand the integration of generative AI in an organization:

Strategy. The organization should have a clear strategy related to how to leverage generative AI into an existing business model. This could involve automating repetitive tasks, speeding up decision-making processes, or improving workflows. The strategy should also consider potential challenges, such as ethical considerations and the quality and accuracy of outputs.

Structure. Incorporating generative AI would necessitate making changes to the organizational structure. Roles and responsibilities may need to be redefined to manage, monitor, and maintain the generative AI systems. For example, DevOps may have to adopt AIOps to manage GenAI applications.

Systems. Generative AI can be part of the systems that create, store, and process information. However, careful implementation is necessary to effectively integrate these AI technologies into existing workflows and tools.

Shared Values. The use of generative AI should align with the core values of the organization. For instance, if the organization values transparency and accountability, these values should be reflected in the way the AI is designed, trained, and used.

Skills. The organization must ensure that its staff has the necessary skills to work with generative AI systems. This could involve training existing staff or hiring new employees with AI expertise.

Style. The leadership style within the organization can affect how generative AI is implemented and used. For example, a participative leadership style might involve employees in the decision-making process regarding how and where to use generative AI.

Staff. The organization's staff will interact with the generative AI systems. The staff might need to review and ensure the accuracy of the AI-generated outputs. Staff perceptions about the benefits and limitations of generative AI will also affect the readiness with which the new technologies are adopted.

By considering each of these seven elements, an organization can ensure that generative AI is integrated effectively and used in a manner that aligns with its overall mission and values.

Ethical Implications of Generative AI

As generative AI becomes more prevalent, it is essential to consider its ethical implications. Issues such as bias in AI, data privacy, accountability, and the potential misuse of generated content are of concern (Brand et al., 2023; Cao et al., 2023; Appel et al., 2023; Dwivedi et al., 2023). Thus, it is imperative to develop robust ethical guidelines and regulatory measures to ensure the responsible use of generative AI.

Owen et al. (2013)'s Responsible Innovation Framework and General Data Protection Regulation (GDPR, 2023) principles frame the discussion on ethics and privacy.

Responsible Innovation Framework. The Responsible Innovation (RI) framework, also known as the AREA framework, was proposed by Owen et al. (2013) to ensure a balanced and ethical approach to the development and application of new technologies. It comprises four dimensions: anticipation, reflexivity, inclusion, and responsiveness.

Anticipation. Generative AI has the potential to transform software product management, offering increased automation, improved efficiency, and faster decision-making. By anticipating these benefits, developers and managers can design and implement GenAI strategies that maximize these advantages. However, anticipation must also account for potential issues, including concerns about the quality and accuracy of outputs, ethical considerations such as bias and transparency, and integration challenges. In this regard, potential legal risks, including potential infringement of intellectual property rights, must be carefully considered in advance. This proactive approach can ensure that safeguards are built into the system from the outset, reducing the risk of later issues.

Reflexivity. In developing and implementing GenAI, developers must be willing to engage in critical self-reflection. It is essential to scrutinize the decision-making processes surrounding GenAI use, continuously assessing the quality and accuracy of AI-generated outputs. Reflexivity will require human review of AI outputs to rectify any instances of "hallucination" or incorrect information. One should also take the issues related to the 'black box' problem, such as trust and interpretability, into account in this reflection.

Inclusion. Generative AI development should involve the input of a diverse range of stakeholders. This can help ensure that the AI system addresses a broad array of needs and concerns, including such ethical considerations as fairness and accountability and such practical issues as integration into existing workflows. Inclusion may also help address any potential legal concerns by involving legal experts who can advise on protecting intellectual property rights and handle any legal issues raised by AI-generated content.

Responsiveness. Responsiveness in the context of GenAI would mean being ready to adapt and respond to emerging issues once the technology is implemented. This could involve refining AI algorithms to improve output quality, amending procedures to better integrate AI into existing workflows, or adjusting practices to address ethical issues. On the legal side, responsiveness may involve staying up-to-date with changes in laws and regulations related to AI and intellectual property rights, and updating contracts and policies accordingly.

Applying the RI framework to GenAI can help ensure that this promising technology is used responsibly, with careful consideration given to potential benefits and challenges. It can also help ensure that its use respects ethical principles and legal requirements. This approach can help maximize the benefits of GenAI while minimizing potential risks and harms.

General Data Protection Regulation (GDPR). The GDPR was established to protect personal data and privacy rights of individuals within the European Union. It provides comprehensive guidelines and laws related to data collection, storage, and usage. With the rise of generative AI and the substantial data required to train these systems, GDPR's relevance becomes even more critical. One can apply the principles of GDPR to Generative AI, particularly in terms of its benefits and limitations.

The governing principles of the GDPR (2023) as defined in Article 5 are the following:

Lawfulness, fairness, and transparency (Article 5(1)a). GDPR requires that data processing be lawful, fair, and transparent to the data subject. Generative AI systems can enhance transparency by explaining their decision-making process and providing insight into how data is processed. However, the 'black box' nature of these models often makes this challenging, limiting transparency and potentially violating this principle.

Purpose limitation (Article 5(1)b). GDPR stipulates that data collected for specific purposes should not be used for others unless the data subject consents. This aligns with one of the critical ethical considerations in generative AI, ensuring that AI does not deviate from its intended purpose, which can be particularly problematic if it begins generating harmful or discriminatory content.

Data minimization (Article 5(1)c). This principle requires that only the minimum necessary data be collected and processed. Given that generative AI models often require vast amounts of data for training, this can pose a challenge. Businesses must balance the need for data with the requirement to protect individual privacy.

Accuracy (Article 5(1)d). The accuracy of generative AI models is essential in order to avoid the propagation of misinformation or harmful content. This principle aligns with GDPR's requirement for accurate data processing, emphasizing the need for valid and reliable training data.

Storage limitation (Article 5(1)e). GDPR requires that personal data should not be stored longer than necessary. For generative AI systems, this can be intricate, as retaining data for continuous learning and improvement may be essential. Businesses must develop strategies to anonymize or delete data once it is no longer needed.

Integrity and confidentiality (Article 5(1)f). Generative AI models, given their reliance on large datasets, must prioritize data security. GDPR mandates that personal data be processed in a way that ensures its security. This includes protecting it from unauthorized access, accidental loss, destruction, or damage.

Accountability (Article 5(2)). Lastly, GDPR requires that organizations take responsibility for all their data processing activities. In the context of generative AI, this could mean implementing audits and monitoring of AI systems to confirm proper functionality without causing harm or discrimination.

In conclusion, GDPR's principles provide a solid foundation for addressing some of the ethical and practical challenges posed by generative AI. Compliance with these principles can help businesses navigate the complex landscape of AI ethics, protecting individual rights while also leveraging the benefits of this revolutionary technology.

In additional to GDPR, the EU has another AI-specific regulation called the AI Act (The Artificial Intelligence Act, 2023). However, Hacker et al. (2023) argue that the current EU AI Act is ill-equipped to handle the rapid advances and impact of Large Generative AI Models (LGAIMs). Hacker et al. suggest that the current regulatory focus is misdirected, concentrating too much on the direct regulation of AI under the AI Act and neglecting important content moderation issues under the Digital Services Act (DSA). Hacker et al. advocate for more accurate terminology to capture the various actors in the evolving AI value chain, including developers who create and train the models. Hacker et al.caution against technology-specific regulations, which may become rapidly outdated, and suggest a more technology-neutral approach. Hacker et al.stress the urgent need for regulatory updates to maintain online discourse civility, create a level playing field for the development and deployment of new generation AI models, and keep pace with the rapid advancements in AI technologies such as GPT-4.

RESULTS

In software product management, generative AI has demonstrated potential across various applications, such as market analysis, positioning and product definition, customer insights and support, product requirements engineering, and development execution.

Studies show that large language models, such as GPT-3, can generate more coherent and interconnected ideas, create visually appealing and unique user interfaces, automatically estimate user story points, elaborate on natural language code, and analyze customer feedback (Karim et al., 2022; Kim et al., 2021). Additionally, generative AI can automate the process of requirement elicitation and analysis and software documentation, helping managers better understand and manage product requirements while reducing manual effort. Furthermore, generative AI has the potential to revolutionize market research by using large language models (Brand et al., 2023).

Overall, the applications of generative AI in software product management are vast and diverse, ranging from product discovery to delivery. By leveraging the capabilities of generative AI models, software product managers can automate tedious tasks, make data-driven decisions, and improve overall product quality. The integration of generative AI in software product management processes can potentially lead to better product outcomes, streamlined workflows, and more efficient use of resources across various stages of product development (Karim et al., 2022; Houde et al., 2022; Siggelkow & Terwiesch, 2023; Kim et al., 2021; Fu & Tantithamthavorn, 2022; Dam et al., 2019).

Table 4. Applications of generative AI in software product management

No.	Application	Summary
1	Market Research	Generative AI models such as GPT can be used in market research, acting as hypothetical customers to understand preferences. Models such as these could inspire new research paradigms unrestricted by human subject research (Brand et al., 2023). Generative AI can generate ideas and brainstorm in specialized disciplines, with larger models generating more coherent and interconnected ideas (Karim et al., 2022).
2	Positioning and Product Definition	GenAI, primarily used for content writing, can aid in product positioning and definition, including naming and feature suggestions, with demonstrated efficacy in writing e-commerce product descriptions and title generation across various industries (Nguyen et al., 2021; Zhang et al., 2022).
3	Customer Insights, Customer Support	Generative AI models such as ChatGPT and Google's Bard can enhance customer experiences by interpreting and integrating data, translating needs into requests, and responding with tailored solutions. Additionally, generative AI can create a positive feedback loop, enhancing an understanding of the customer for more personalized service (Siggelkow and Terwiesch, 2023).
4	Product Requirements Engineering	Generative AI can automate requirement elicitation and analysis, generating natural language requirement statements from structured data. Also, it can help detect conflicts in Software Requirement Specifications (SRS) documents (Malik et al., 2022). Generative AI can support sprint planning, backlog management, and estimation in Agile software development. AI models such as GPT-3 can automatically generate user stories based on provided input data, saving time, reducing human error, and improving the quality of user stories (Kim et al., 2021; Fu and Tantithamthavorn, 2022).
5	Development Execution	Generative AI can aid in automated code generation, enhancing productivity and efficiency. Tools such as GitHub Copilot have demonstrated a significant boost in productivity. Furthermore, generative AI can be used to automate documentation generation and improve the comprehension of source code in software development. Generative AI can create visually appealing and unique interfaces, streamlining the design process and enabling rapid prototyping. It can generate UI/UX designs based on user preferences and requirements, leading to more user-centric designs and improved product experiences (Peng et al., 2023; Khan and Uddin, 2022; Park et al., 2023; Houde et al., 2022).
6	Decision-making	Generative AI can enhance decision-making in business by addressing limitations of the bounded rationality model, with younger users and males typically more open to this technology's adoption (Korzynski et al., 2023).

Research Question One: What Are the Applications of Generative AI in Software Product Management?

Table 4 answers the first research question by summarizing the applications of generative AI in software product management.

Figure 2 illustrates the applications of generative AI in SPM.

Figure 2. Applications of generative AI in software product management

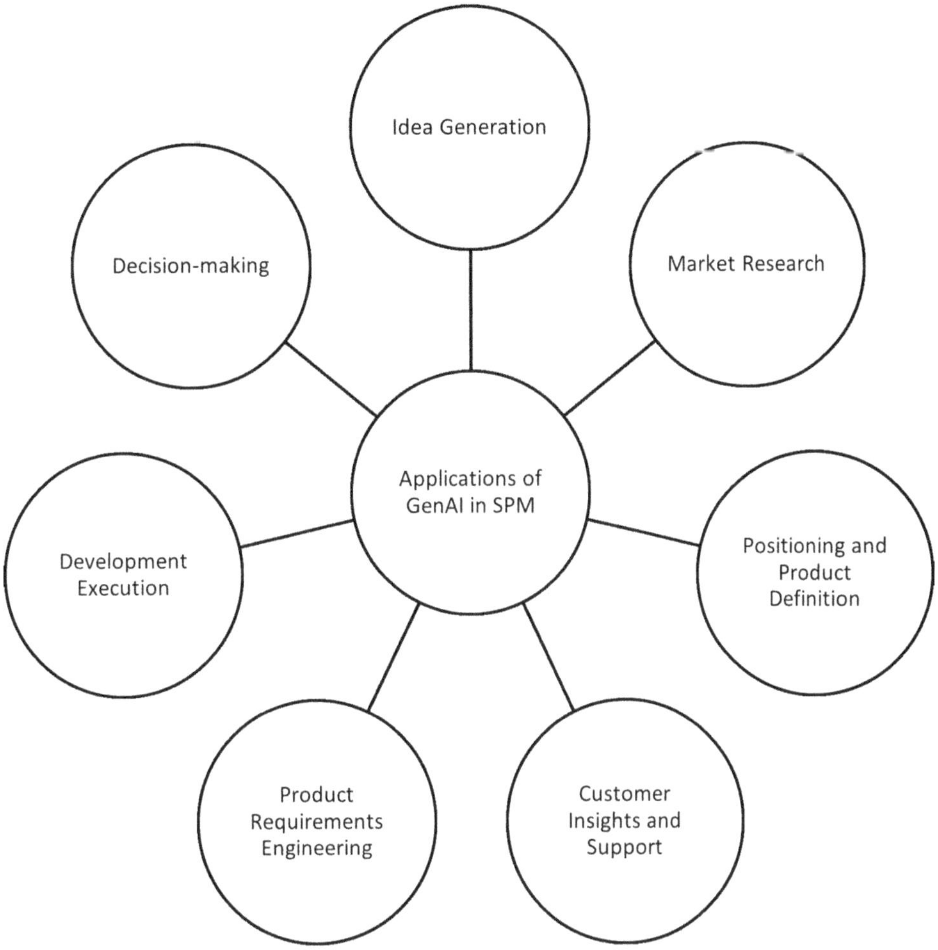

Research Question Two: What Are the Ethical Challenges Presented by Generative AI and What Strategies Can Be Employed to Mitigate These Issues?

Ethical Implications

The ethical implications of generative AI (GenAI) are diverse and consequential, underlining the need for rigorous guidelines and regulatory measures to ensure its responsible usage (Brand et al., 2023; Cao et al., 2023; Appel et al., 2023; Dwivedi et al., 2023).

Fairness. Bias is an inherent risk in GenAI. The AI system can inadvertently incorporate and propagate biases present in the data used for training, leading to skewed or prejudiced outputs (Brand et al.,

2023). Therefore, it is essential to ensure fairness and diverse training data to avoid potential harm or discrimination.

Data Privacy is another critical ethical consideration. As GenAI systems require extensive data for training, the likelihood of infringing on data privacy increases. Adhering to privacy regulations such as the GDPR (2023) is a step towards ensuring data privacy. GDPR's principles provide a comprehensive roadmap for data collection, storage, and usage (GDPR, 2023), guiding businesses in the ethical use of personal data for GenAI.

Accountability. Accountability in GenAI involves taking responsibility for the system's outputs. If an AI system generates harmful or inaccurate content, the onus is on the organization to rectify the situation and prevent recurrence (Cao et al., 2023).

Transparency. Potential misuse of GenAI-produced content is another pressing concern. There is the risk of fabricated or manipulated content being passed off as legitimate, which could have severe consequences on fields such as news and journalism, and on financial reports and legal documents (Appel et al., 2023). Rigorous verification mechanisms are necessary to prevent such misuse. The increase in deep generative AI models has led to increasingly intricate models. However, their performance relies heavily on quality training data. Notably, these models often exhibit the 'black box' problem, limiting their interpretability and causing potential trust issues (Cao et al., 2023).

Robustness. Brand et al. (2023) highlighted the problem of "hallucinations" and returning incorrect information with large language models. This requires consistent human reviews to ensure the accuracy of the AI-generated output.

Legal Risks. Generative AI presents legal risks, including potential infringement of intellectual property rights, including unresolved legal questions such as ownership and application of copyright, patent, and trademark laws to AI-generated content. Before leveraging the benefits of generative AI, businesses must understand these risks and devise strategies for self-protection. Essential measures include updating vendor and customer contracts with explicit disclosure about the use of generative AI and clauses safeguarding intellectual property rights. Furthermore, confidentiality provisions should be enhanced to prohibit confidential information in AI tool text prompts (Appel et al., 2023).

The Responsible Innovation (RI) framework, proposed by Owen et al. (2013), offers a comprehensive approach to addressing these ethical issues. The framework encourages anticipation, reflexivity, inclusion, and responsiveness to ensure the balanced development and application of GenAI. The GDPR and RI principles, when appropriately applied, can help mitigate these ethical challenges and guide the responsible use of GenAI.

However, regulatory challenges persist. Hacker et al. (2023) argued that the current EU AI Act fails to keep pace with the rapid advancements and impact of Large Generative AI Models (LGAIMs). The authors advocated for a more technology-neutral approach to regulation, highlighting the need to maintain online discourse civility, create a level playing field for new AI models, and keep up with rapid advancements in AI technologies.

In conclusion, while GenAI promises significant benefits, its ethical implications need careful consideration and proactive management. Using robust ethical guidelines, regulatory measures, and inclusive innovation practices will help maximize the advantages while minimizing potential risks and harms. Figure 3 illustrates ethical implications of generative AI.

Figure 3. Ethical implications of generative AI

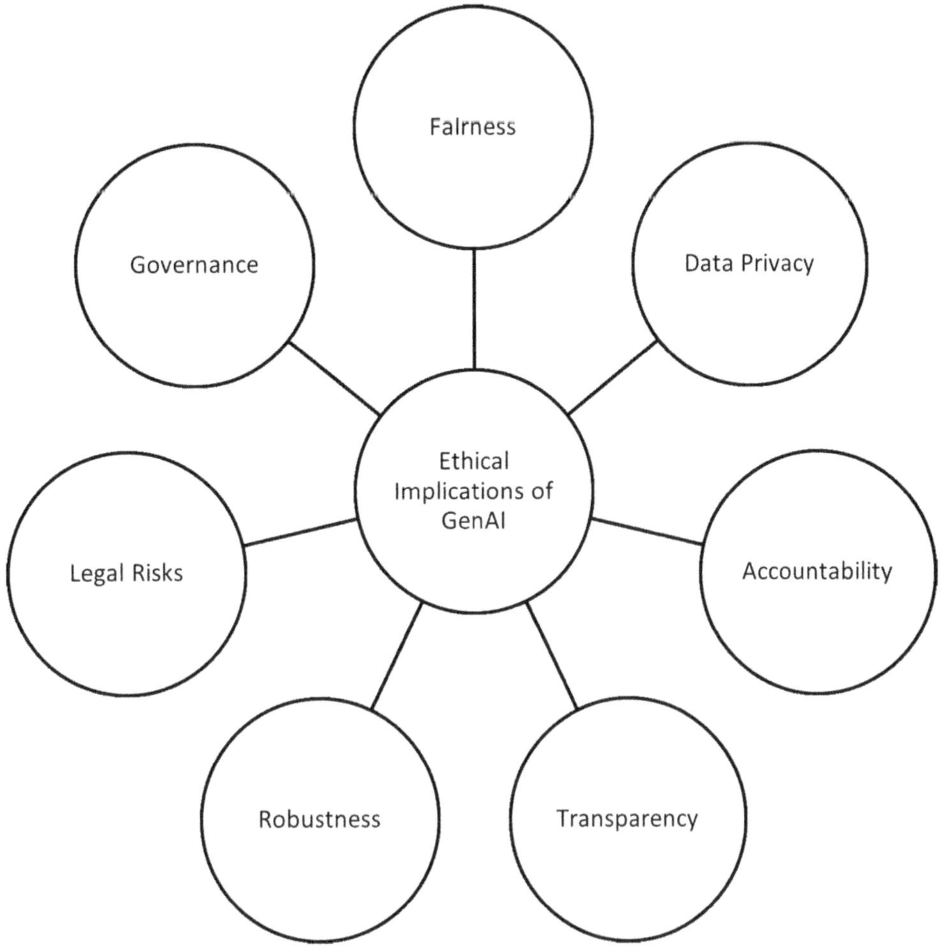

CONCLUSION

Generative AI offers promising advancements in business and software product management, helping to transform various aspects such as idea generation, market research, UI/UX design, Agile software development, requirement elicitation, product definition, product development, and customer support. Adopting generative AI technologies, huge language models such as GPT-3 can help software product managers automate time-consuming tasks, make data-driven decisions, and optimize overall product quality.

The role of generative AI in software product management is rapidly evolving, and product managers can use it from ideation to execution. As generative AI technologies evolve, software product managers and researchers must stay abreast of emerging trends and explore innovative ways to use these advancements in software product management effectively.

However, it is essential to acknowledge and address the potential limitations and challenges associated with implementing generative AI solutions in software product management. Bias, transparency, data privacy, accountability, ethical considerations, and integration difficulties should receive careful attention in practice and in future research. Product managers must still review content generated by generative AI to ensure its authenticity and accuracy.

Addressing these ethical concerns requires a proactive and reflexive approach as outlined by the Responsible Innovation Framework (Owen et al., 2013). Anticipating and responding to the challenges of generative AI requires inclusive and responsive strategies that involve diverse stakeholders and adapt to emerging issues. These principles, along with a thorough understanding of legal and regulatory standards, such as the GDPR (2023) and AI Act (2023), can help guide the development and implementation of generative AI technologies (Hacker et al., 2023).

In conclusion, generative AI holds transformative potential for businesses, yet its ethical implications call for comprehensive guidelines, regulatory measures, and a reflexive, anticipatory approach to its development and implementation. It is clear that the future of business will be increasingly intertwined with the responsible and ethical use of generative AI, requiring continuous dialogue, research, and review to ensure its benefits are fully realized while mitigating potential risks and harms.

FUTURE RESEARCH RECOMMENDATIONS

Based on the findings of this systematic literature review, several future research directions can be identified:

Develop more advanced generative AI models: An advanced GenAI model could better understand and cater to the specific needs of software product management processes, such as product strategy, product planning, and feature prioritization.

Integrate AI with Agile methodologies: Exploring how generative AI can be seamlessly integrated with existing Agile methodologies will be crucial for maximizing its potential benefits. It may involve adapting AI-generated user stories, project planning, and resource allocation strategies to align with Agile principles and practices.

Personalize AI assistance for software product managers: With the growing sophistication of generative AI models, it becomes possible to tailor these tools to the unique needs and preferences of individual product managers. Personalized AI assistants may be able to provide customized recommendations, insights, and support, enabling product managers to work more effectively and efficiently.

Lastly, evaluate the long-term impact of generative AI on software product management workflows, particularly in terms of efficiency, cost-effectiveness, and overall product quality.

The landscape of software product management is poised for significant transformation as generative AI technologies continue to evolve. By staying informed about the latest advances, embracing new applications, and addressing potential limitations and ethical concerns, software product managers can leverage the power of generative AI to drive innovation, efficiency, and success in their projects.

REFERENCES

Appel, G., Neelbauer, J., & Schweidel, D. A. (2023). *Generative AI has an intellectual property problem*. HBR. https://hbr.org/2023/04/generative-ai-has-an-intellectual-property-problem

BrandJ.IsraeliA.NgweD. (2023). Using gpt for market research. SSRN 4395751.

Brynjolfsson, E., Li, D., & Raymond, L. R. (2023). *Generative AI at Work (No. w31161)*. National Bureau of Economic Research. doi:10.3386/w31161

Cao, Y., Li, S., Liu, Y., Yan, Z., Dai, Y., Yu, P. S., & Sun, L. (2023). A comprehensive survey of AI-generated content (AIGC): A history of generative AI from GAN to chatGPT. arXiv preprint arXiv:2303.04226.

Dam, H. K., Tran, T., Grundy, J., Ghose, A., & Kamei, Y. (2019, May). Towards effective AI-powered agile project management. In *2019 IEEE/ACM, 41st international conference on software engineering: New ideas and emerging results* (ICSE-NIER) (pp. 41-44). IEEE. 10.1109/ICSE-NIER.2019.00019

Davenport, T. H., & Mittal, N. (2022, November 14). How generative AI is changing creative work. hbr. org: https://hbr.org/2022/11/how-generative-ai-is-changing-creative-work

Dwivedi, Y. K., Kshetri, N., Hughes, L., Slade, E. L., Jeyaraj, A., Kar, A. K., Baabdullah, A. M., Koohang, A., Raghavan, V., Ahuja, M., Albanna, H., Albashrawi, M. A., Al-Busaidi, A. S., Balakrishnan, J., Barlette, Y., Basu, S., Bose, I., Brooks, L., Buhalis, D., & Wright, R. (2023). "So what if ChatGPT wrote it?" Multidisciplinary perspectives on opportunities, challenges and implications of generative conversational AI for research, practice and policy. *International Journal of Information Management*, *71*, 102642. doi:10.1016/j.ijinfomgt.2023.102642

Fu, M., & Tantithamthavorn, C. (2022). Gpt2sp: A transformer-based agile story point estimation approach. *IEEE Transactions on Software Engineering*.

GDPR. (2023). *Principles relating to processing of personal data*. GDPR. https://gdpr-info.eu/art-5-gdpr/

Grandviewresearch. (2023, May). *Generative AI market size to reach $109.37 billion by 2030*. Grandview Research. https://www.grandviewresearch.com/press-release/global-generative-ai-market

Hacker, P., Engel, A., & Mauer, M. (2023). *Regulating ChatGPT and other large generative AI models*. arXiv preprint arXiv:2302.02337. doi:10.1145/3593013.3594067

Houde, S., Ross, S. I., Muller, M., Agarwal, M., Martinez, F., Richards, J., & Weisz, J. D. (2022, March). Opportunities for generative AI in UX modernization. In *Joint International Conference on Intelligent User Interfaces Workshops*: APEx-UI, HAI-GEN, HEALTHI, HUMANIZE, TExSS, SOCIALIZE.

ISPMA. (2023). *A comprehensive guide for effective software product management*. ISPMA. https://ispma.org/bok/

Karim, M. R., Antar, S. S., & Khan, M. A. (2022, December). Idea generation using transformer decoder models. In *Proceedings of the 2022 5th international conference on algorithms, computing and artificial Intelligence* (pp. 1-5). IEEE.

Khan, J. Y., & Uddin, G. (2022, October). Automatic code documentation generation using GPT-3. In *37th IEEE/ACM international conference on automated software engineering* (pp. 1-6). IEEE. 10.1145/3551349.3559548

Kim, H., Choi, B., & Cho, H. (2021). AI-driven user story points estimation based on natural language processing. *Journal of Systems and Software*, *171*, 110818.

Korzynski, P., Mazurek, G., Altmann, A., Ejdys, J., Kazlauskaite, R., Paliszkiewicz, J., & Ziemba, E. (2023). *Generative artificial intelligence as a new context for management theories: Analysis of ChatGPT*. Central European Management Journal.

Lewin, K. (1947). Frontiers in group dynamics: Concept, method and reality in social science; social equilibria and social change. *Human Relations*, *1*(1), 5–41. doi:10.1177/001872674700100103

Malik, G., Cevik, M., Parikh, D., & Basar, A. (2022). *Identifying the requirement conflicts in SRS documents using transformer-based sentence embeddings*. arXiv preprint arXiv:2206.13690.

McKinsey & Company. (2022, August). *McKinsey technology trends outlook 2022*. McKinsey. https://www.mckinsey.com/~/media/mckinsey/business%20functions/mckinsey%20digital/our%20insights/the%20top%20trends%20in%20tech%202022/McKinsey-Tech-Trends-Outlook-2022-Applied-AI.pdf

Nguyen, M. T., Nguyen, P. T., Nguyen, V. V., & Nguyen, Q. M. (2021, November). Generating product description with generative pre-trained transformer 2. In *2021 6th international conference on innovative technology in intelligent system and industrial applications (CITISIA)* (pp. 1-7). IEEE.

Owen, R., Stilgoe, J., Macnaghten, P., Gorman, M., Fisher, E., & Guston, D. (2013). A framework for responsible innovation. *Responsible innovation: Managing the responsible emergence of science and innovation in society*, 27-50.

Paajoki, A. (2020). *Best practices for and benefits from implementing ISPMA's SPM framework.*

Park, Y., Park, A., & Kim, C. (2023). ALSI-Transformer: Transformer-based code comment generation with aligned lexical and syntactic information. *IEEE Access: Practical Innovations, Open Solutions*, *11*, 39037–39047. doi:10.1109/ACCESS.2023.3268638

Peng, S., Kalliamvakou, E., Cihon, P., & Demirer, M. (2023). *The impact of AI on developer productivity: Evidence from github copilot.* arXiv preprint arXiv:2302.06590.

Peters, T. J., & Waterman, R. H. (1984). In search of excellence. *Nursing Administration Quarterly*, *8*(3), 85–86. doi:10.1097/00006216-198400830-00014

Radford, A., Narasimhan, K., Salimans, T., & Sutskever, I. (2021). Scaling laws for autoregressive generative modeling. arXiv preprint arXiv:2102.08602.

Siggelkow, N., & Terwiesch, C. (2023, April 4). Create winning customer experiences with generative AI. *Harvard Business Review*. https://www.hbr.org/2023/04/create-winning-customer-experiences-with-generative-ai

Simon, H. A. (1987). Making management decisions: The role of intuition and emotion. *The Academy of Management Perspectives*, *1*(1), 57–64. doi:10.5465/ame.1987.4275905

Statista. (2023, May 24). *Size of the chatbot market worldwide from 2021 to 2030.* Statista. https://www.statista.com/statistics/656596/worldwide-chatbot-market/

The Artificial Intelligence Act. (2023). *The Artificial Intelligence Act.* artificialintelligenceact.eu: https://artificialintelligenceact.eu/

Xu, W. (2023). *AI in HCI design and user experience.* arXiv preprint arXiv:2301.00987.

Zhang, M., Gang, Z., Yu, W., Huang, N., & Liu, W. (2022). MAA-PTG: Multimodal aspect-aware product title generation. *Journal of Intelligent Information Systems, 59*(1), 213–235. doi:10.100710844-022-00695-8

Chapter 17
A Review of EEG-Based Computer-Aided Detection of Brain Disorders Using a Different Strategy

Saranya Shanmugam
Vellore Institute of Technology, Chennai, India

Menaka Radhakrishnan
Vellore Institute of Technology, Chennai, India

ABSTRACT

The human brain plays a significant role in controlling the behavior of the human body with respect to sensory stimuli, external/internal motor stimuli, and so on. EEG signals are informative signals that contain knowledge about the condition of the brain. They are nonstationary and nonlinear in nature and so, it is hard to detect the subtle yet significant changes in the signals using just the human eye. This gives engineers the opportunity to apply numerous algorithms for the detection of such subtle yet significant changes in EEG signals. Various algorithms have been developed and are being used to extract the important features from EEG signals. It has been established through research that the nonlinear features of EEG mostly comprise the abrupt transitions and its chaotic and random behavior. In this chapter, the effect of EEG signals on diagnosing 6 brain disorders, namely, epilepsy, autism, Alzheimer's disease, Parkinson's disease, schizophrenia, and ischemic brain stroke, is discussed in detail.

1. INTRODUCTION

The brain governs all tasks performed by the human body and analyses information from the environment. The brain governs various activities as intelligence, emotion, creativity, and memory. The brain collectively processes the information from the senses to make the decision and store it for further analysis. The brain regulates our thoughts, memory, speech, and the operation of the organs in our body. The

DOI: 10.4018/979-8-3693-1634-4.ch017

brain and spinal cord are connected by the brainstem and parts of the Central Nervous System (CNS). The cerebral hemispheres are separated into lobes by fissures. There are four lobes in each hemisphere: frontal region, temporal region, parietal region, and occipital region. Each hemisphere lobe can be further categorized into areas that perform distinct duties. The interactions between the cerebral lobes and the right and left hemispheres are quite intricate. In the brain, There are two different types of cells in the brain: glia cells and neurons, which are nerve cells. Neurons have dendrites, a cell body, and an axon. Electrical and chemical impulses are used by nerve cells to deliver and receive information. An activated neuron will communicate its energy to all other neurons in its surroundings. Neurons communicate with one another by transmitting energy across a gap called a synapse. A neuron contains multiple fibers known as dendrites, taking up information from neighboring neurons. The information from dendrites and send to the cell body and it is decided for further processing. Brain disorders are caused by the impairment of the different brain regions. This chapter provides a comprehensive exploration of using EEG as a foundational signal for the automated diagnosis of various brain disorders, including epilepsy, autism, Alzheimer's disease, Parkinson's disease, schizophrenia, and ischemic brain stroke.

EEG signals are nonstationary, nonlinear, and non-Gaussian in nature. The acquisition of EEG signals is a non-invasive technique and is widely used for diagnosing brain disorders. Numerous conditions, such as brain tumors, problems associated with trauma, epilepsy, depression, and cerebrovascular lesions can be diagnosed using EEG signals. EEG traces are dissimilar for different responses of the brain. Generally, various signal processing techniques are applied to EEG signals to distinguish between abnormal and normal behaviour of the brain. These signals are produced by electrodes that are placed at various points on the scalp. EEG recordings are divided into two types: (i) monopolar (ii) bipolar. The voltage difference between an active electrode that is mounted on the scalp and a reference electrode that is mounted on the ear lobe gives us monopolar EEG recordings, whereas the voltage difference between two (active and reference) electrodes placed on the scalp alone gives us bipolar recordings. The position of electrodes placed on the scalp is always done according to the International 10-20 Standard for the placement of electrodes, i.e., Fp1, Fp2, F3, F4, T5, T6, F7, F8, Fz, Cz, Pz, O1, O2, T3, C3, C4, T4, P3, P4. Figure 1 depicts the Standard.

Figure 1. 10-20 international standard for the placement of the EEG electrodes.

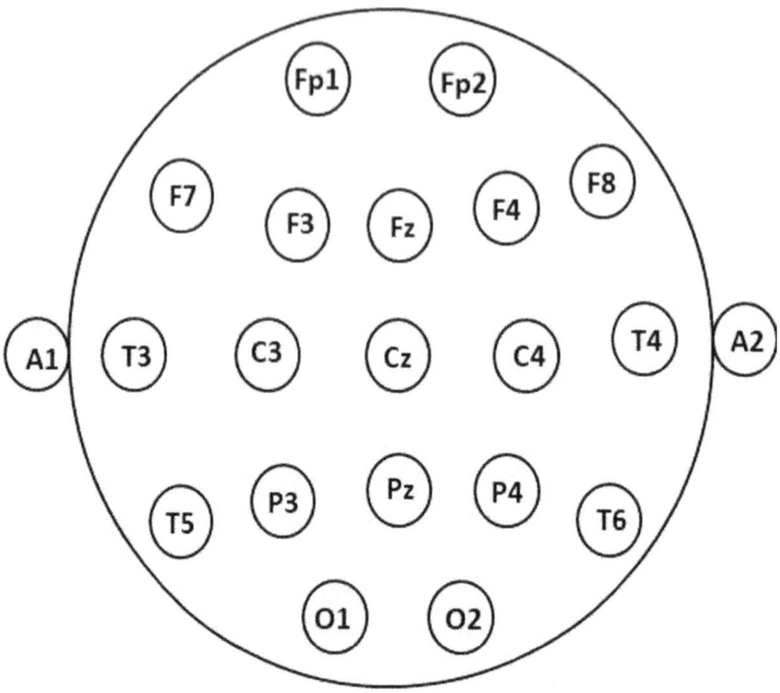

EEG signals can be categorized into five different rhythms or bands based on their frequencies: delta, theta, alpha, beta, and gamma. The delta band has a frequency range of 1-4 Hertz and is primarily associated with the depth of sleep, with higher delta rhythm indicating a deeper sleep. Additionally, an increase in delta waves is linked to an increase in internal working memory tasks such as concentration. The theta band, on the other hand, has a frequency range of 4-7 Hertz and is linked to cognitive workload and memory encoding and retrieval. The alpha band ranges from 7-12 Hertz and is prominent when subjects close their eyes and enter a peaceful state. These waves are used in biofeedback training to examine a person's calm state and are sometimes associated with attention and inhibition. The beta band has a frequency range of 12-30 Hertz and is observed during motor functions, with stronger beta wave frequencies indicating more movement in the body. There is evidence to suggest that the human brain may mimic limb movements observed in others, possibly synchronized by the beta band. Finally, the gamma band has a frequency greater than 30 Hertz, typically 40 Hertz, and serves as a carrier frequency to exchange data between different parts of the brain and reflect attentive focus. Gamma waves are also associated with rapid eye movements or micro-saccades.

2. PURPOSE OF THE STUDY

This diagnosis system can help radiologists, neurosurgeons, neurologists, and other clinical providers make better medical decisions.

3. PROBLEM STATEMENT

- Epilepsy is classified as a neurological disorder characterized by unexpected seizures, which can be detected through EEG performed through intracranial electrode placement or scalp electrode placement. With more than 50 million affected individuals worldwide, epilepsy is one of the most prevalent neurological disorders, with nearly 80% of cases occurring in low- and middle-income countries. The social stigma attached to the condition can cause emotional distress, but early diagnosis and appropriate treatment can help up to 70% of individuals avoid seizures.
- ASD is a complex neurodevelopmental disorder that involves both behavioral and neuropsychological deficits, with three main subtypes: Autistic Disorder, Asperger's Syndrome, and Pervasive Developmental Disorder. ASD affects around 1 in 100 children and can be treated with various approaches, including psychopathology, parent-child interactions, cognitive neuroscience, and applied behavioral analysis.
- AD is a neurodegenerative disease that affected an estimated 5.8 million Americans in 2020 and is projected to affect nearly 14 million by 2060. Symptoms can manifest after the age of 60, and early diagnosis is crucial because treatments can only slow down the progression of the disease.
- PD is another neurodegenerative disorder characterized by reduced dopamine levels and is more common in older individuals, with around 10 million people affected worldwide. While there is no cure, medication and surgical interventions can help alleviate symptoms.
- Schizophrenia (SZ) is a chronic brain disorder that affects thinking and behavior, with approximately 24 million affected individuals worldwide. Early diagnosis is critical, as untreated SZ can lead to cognitive and behavioral impairments. (Jahmunah et al, 2019).
- Ischemic Stroke (IS) occurs when blood flow to the brain is obstructed, making it one of the most common causes of death among adults worldwide. Approximately 87% of all strokes are ischemic, and CT scans are considered the standard tool for diagnosis. However, limited availability of CT scans in developing countries makes EEG signals a viable alternative for diagnosis.

4. SIGNIFICANT OF THE PROJECT

There are three objectives of this chapter

1. To explore different strategy to diagnose brain disorders
2. In search of relationship between EEG and Brain disorder diagnosis.
3. To think about a benefits of the early diagnosis of the brain disorders.

5. METHODOLOGY

The steps followed in the processing of EEG signals for the diagnosis of brain disorders are preprocessing, feature extraction, and classification. Figure 2 depicts the system for Brain disorder diagnosis.

Figure 2. Brain disorder diagnosis system

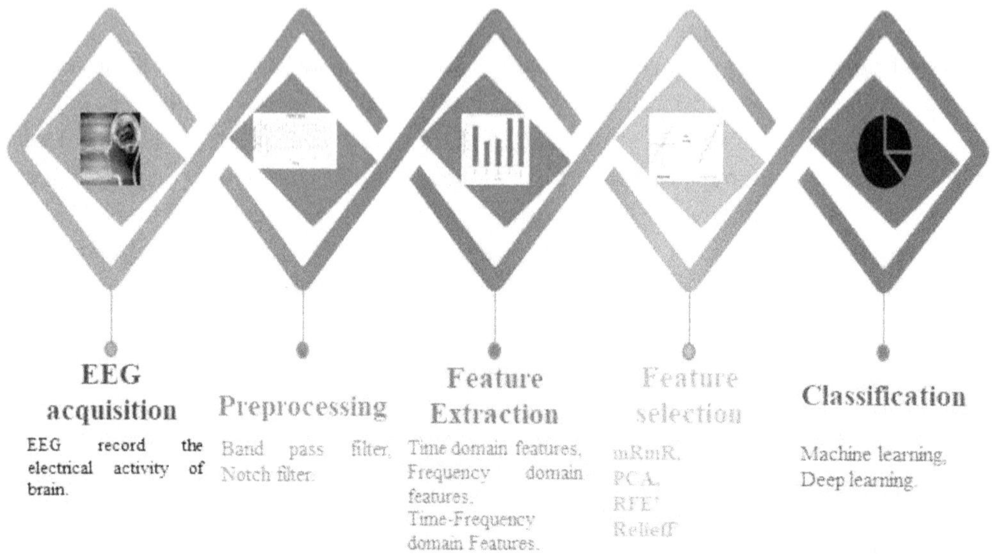

5.1 EEG and Epilepsy

Epilepsy is characterized by the occurrence of seizures due to abnormal brain activity. Epilepsy is mostly diagnosed using EEG signals. Several research studies have been conducted to develop machine learning and deep learning based approaches for epilepsy diagnosis using EEG signals. Brari and Belghith (2021) proposed a novel approach for extracting features from EEG signals, which is founded upon the determination of the Correlation Dimension. Their approach was subjected to rigorous experimental testing, which demonstrated its superior efficiency relative to existing works. Specifically, their method achieved near-perfect classification accuracy rates of 100% for almost all classification problems. Mandhouj et al. (2021) utilized the Short-Time Fourier Transform (STFT) and a Deep Convolutional Neural Network (DCNN) model for detecting and categorizing epilepsy seizures on the basis of EEG spectrogram images. They assessed the efficacy of their method using the publicly available EEG dataset of Bonn University, and achieved a remarkably high average accuracy rate of 98.22.%. Samee et al. (2022) introduced a novel method for precise and automated diagnosis of epileptic seizures from EEG signals, which combines Recurrent Neural Network (RNN) and Bi-directional Long Short-Term Memory (BiLSTMs) via fusion. Their model achieved impressive average accuracy rates of 98.90%, 98.50%, 98.20%, and 98.60% for sensitivity, precision, and specificity, respectively, thereby outperforming alternative learning models such as the RNN- Long Short-Term Memory(LSTM) and RNN-Gated Recurrent Units(GRU). These findings underscore the potential of machine learning-based techniques for accurately identifying and diagnosing epilepsy seizures using EEG signals.

Shoeibi et al. (2022) proposed approach involves the utilization of the Tunable-Q Wavelet Transform (TQWT) to decompose signals into multiple sub-bands, followed by the calculation of 13 different fuzzy entropies for feature extraction. An autoencoder is then employed for dimensionality reduction, and standard Adaptive Neuro-Fuzzy Inference System (ANFIS) and its variants with optimization algorithms are leveraged for classification. The method achieved remarkable results, with a binary classification accuracy of 99.74%, ternary classification accuracy of 99.46% on the Bonn dataset, and accuracy of 99.28% on the Freiburg dataset. Jiwani et al, (2022) proposed an automated system for seizure detection, which integrates Convolutional Neural Network (CNN) and LSTM models. This hybrid model extracts both spatial and temporal features from EEG signals, while requiring fewer trainable parameters and providing high accuracy, thus rendering it well-suited for real-time processing applications. The system achieved remarkable performance, with a maximum accuracy of 100% for distinguishing between healthy and seizure patients, as well as for sensitivity and specificity. Yousefi et al. (2022) proposed a multilayer perceptron neural network classifier for the diagnosis of epilepsy, which leverages the wavelet transform technique to process the data. The evaluation results revealed a moderate impact factor of the wavelet transform on the improvement of epilepsy data functions, and demonstrated that the utilization of the multilayer perceptron neural network resulted in a higher accuracy coefficient for expert assessments. Mir et al. (2023) proposed a deep learning model, named DCAE-ESD-Bi-LSTM, which adopts a Deep Convolutional Autoencoder—Bidirectional Long Short Memory approach for Epileptic Seizure Detection. The model demonstrated remarkable performance, achieving an accuracy rate of 99.8% on the CHB-MIT dataset and a classification accuracy of 99.7% on a dataset collected by the authors, thus indicating its robustness in both ideal and real-life scenarios.

Xin et al. (2022) employed an Attention Mechanism-based Wavelet Convolution Neural Network to decompose EEG signals into distinct frequency bands. Subsequently, the resulting bands were input into a Convolution Neural Network equipped with an attention mechanism to facilitate feature extraction and classification. Their algorithm demonstrated superior performance, attaining high classification accuracies of 98.89% and 99.70% on two separate databases. Li et al. (2023) put forth a feature extraction scheme that relies on Synchrosqueezing Short-Time Fourier Transform (SSTFT) and Graph regularized Non-negative Matrix Factorization (GNMF) for epileptic EEG detection. Their approach demonstrated remarkable performance, achieving a classification accuracy of at least 98.0% on short-term and long-term EEG recordings obtained from two public databases. These results attest to the effectiveness of the method in accurately identifying seizure events, thus highlighting the potential of leveraging advanced feature extraction techniques and deep learning models in the precise diagnosis of epileptic seizures using EEG data. Qiu et al. (2023) proposed a novel model called the Difference Attention ResNet-LSTM network (DARLNet), which combines a Residual Neural Network (ResNet) and a LSTM to capture spatial correlations and temporal dependencies, respectively. In addition, the DARLNet model incorporates a difference layer to extract additional information related to epileptic seizures and a channel attention module to focus on seizure-relevant information. The performance of the model was evaluated on the Bonn Electroencephalogram dataset, where it outperformed existing methods.

Amiri et al. (2023) proposed an automated method for identifying seizures using sparse Common Spatial Pattern (sCSP) and adaptive Short-time Fourier transform-based Synchrosqueezing Transform (adaptive FSST). The method uses sCSP to select optimal channels and discriminate seizure states and adaptive FSST to enhance the time-frequency representation of multi-component EEG signals. Their method achieved superior results to most of the best findings in the literature on the CHB-MIT epileptic EEG database. Qin et al. (2023) proposed a framework for recognizing EEG signals based on an improved version of the Variational Mode Decomposition (VMD) algorithm and deep forest. Their approach utilizes the improved VMD algorithm to decompose the original signal and construct a criterion for feature selection based on weighted minimum redundancy maximum relevance. The resulting features are then used to train a deep forest model to classify EEG signals. Liu et al. (2023) proposed a

Revised Tunable Q factor Wavelet Transform (RTQWT) as a more effective method to extract detailed features and improve the classification accuracy of EEG signals.

5.2 EEG and Autism

Autism is a neurodevelopmental disorder. It is derived from '*autos*' (Greek word), meaning 'an isolated self'. EEG is mainly used to understand the cognitive and behavioral challenges experienced by patients with disorders such as ASD. Measuring responses for sensory stimuli provide a 'potential biomarker of the disorder'. Sarmukadam et al. (2019) used EEGs to determine the sensory features of the neurological character of younger individuals who have autism. The brain creates some kind of trouble in children with ASD while they are expressing their emotions. Therefore, it is possible to use EEG signals to differentiate between various responses of sensory profile. The Principal Component Analysis(PCA) and time-frequency domain analysis of the EEG signals are used to identify an autistic patient and also help get better classification accuracy. Statistical features are extracted from the noiseless and clean EEG data. The necessary EEG channels, and its related features were chosen using feature selection based on correlation (Haputhanthri et al., 2019). There is an approach that was able to identify individuals with ASD based on the patterns of twelve functional connectivities (Sherkatghanad et al., 2020). An achievable 'rehabilitation tool' is used to help children with ASD wear smart glasses. These smart glasses with built-in cameras will obtain the images from the various directions. Deep Learning algorithms are used to process the obtained images and create meaningful and understandable images for children with ASD to better understand their surroundings (Khodatars et al., 2020). Pham et al. (2020) extract run-length-matrix-based features from EEG and autism classification is done by Probabilistic Neural Network classifier (Ten-fold cross-validation). Habeeb et al. (2019) obtained Dominance, valence, arousal and use Deep Neural Networks. Majumder et al. (2020) extract topological features using persistent homology and persistent entropy and use Support Vector Machine (SVM) with 10-fold stratified cross validation. Aslam and Altaf (2019) extract eight Power Spectral Densities (PSD), four Inter-Hemispheric Power Asymmetry Differences (IHPD), and four Scaled Inter-Hemispheric Power Asymmetry Ratios (SIHPR) for classification use Linear SVM classifier. Hadoush et al. (2019) calculate ellipse area, central tendency measure by using Empirical Mode Decomposition (EMD), Second-Order Difference Plot (SODP) and use PCA for feature reduction and classification is done by Artificial Neural Network(ANN) model with Levenberg-Marquardt Back-Propagation (LMBP) training function.

Radhakrishnan et al. (2021) conducted an evaluation of several deep learning architectures for detecting ASD and reported that ResNet50 yielded the highest accuracy of 81%. In addition, they analyzed the precision and recall metrics of the models. Grossi et al. (2021) employed a feature extraction software package to extract 12 and 36 features from the time-series of C3-C4 in two separate studies to identify the EEG signature of autism. Subsequently, they employed a hybrid system named Training with Input Selection and Testing (TWIST) and an ANN for the classification of EEG signals. The achieved classification accuracies were 100% for study 1 and 94.95% for study 2. Alturki et al. (2021) utilized Common Spatial Pattern (CSP) method along with entropy, energy, and band power to extract features from EEGs for the diagnosis of ASD. Four different classification techniques were employed, and it was found that the combination of CSP, (Local Binary Pattern) and K Nearesr Neighbour (KNN) yielded the best performance, with an average classification accuracy of approximately 98.46% and 98.62% for ASD diagnosis, respectively. The study also examined the impact of segment length, frequency band, and reduction number on the outcomes. Baygin et al. (2021) presented a novel approach for signal to image conversion for automatic detection of ASD from EEG signals. The method involves extracting features from EEG signals using 1D_LBP and generating spectrogram images using Short Time Fourier Transform (STFT). The generated images are then processed using a hybrid deep lightweight feature generator to extract the most discriminative features. These features are then fed into various shallow classifiers for ASD detection. The proposed approach achieved an accuracy of 96.44% using SVM classifier. The EEG signals are pre-processed and converted into spectrogram images using STFT. Machine learning and deep learning models are assessed separately, and the proposed deep learning model achieves superior accuracy (99.15%) compared to the machine learning model (95.25%) on a dataset containing EEG signals from individuals with ASD (Tawhid et al., 2021).

Ardakani et al. (2022) utilized a 2 Dimensional-(DCNN) to classify short signals of healthy individuals and those with ASD. The implementation of data augmentation methods led to an average accuracy of 88.29%, while 100% accuracy was achieved in detecting ASD subjects based on long EEG signals. Ari et al. (2022) proposed method aims to automate the detection of ASD using EEG recordings. The method combines the Douglas-Peucker algorithm, sparse coding-based feature mapping, and CNN. Melinda et al. (2023) study examines the impact of PSD on the EEG of children with autism by utilizing the Welch Periodogram method. The study also compares the PSD values of the EEG of children with autism to those of typically developing children. Portnova et al. (2023) primary focus is to analyze clinical electroencephalography analysis in typically developing children and children with autism, emphasizing the differences and similarities in EEG power spectral density, coherence, and peak alpha frequency between the two groups. The research suggests that the differences between ASD and Typical developing (TD) in the SensoriMotor Rhythm (SMR) index and instantaneous prevailing frequency diminish by the age of ten years, and new approaches are required to understand the underlying mechanisms of ASD. 73 EEG signals were gathered from patients, 41 of which were affected by ASD while 32 exhibited normal neural activity. Significant features were extracted from the EEG signals using Independent Component Analysis (ICA) and classification was performed using SVM. The results showed an accuracy of 90.41%. This approach can be beneficial in acquiring suitable sensory profiles for the early diagnosis and treatment of ASD (Subudhi et al., 2023). Nonlinear features were extracted from EEG signals obtained from 40 children diagnosed with ASD and 37 children with no neurodevelopmental disorder diagnosis. A total of 18 features were extracted from the EEG signals, and different SVM models were trained with different numbers of features. The SVM model with a polynomial kernel of degree 2 achieved the highest classification accuracy of 98.70% with a feature set of 20 (Oh et al., 2021). Chawla et al. (2023) proposed an automated method for diagnosing ASD from multichannel EEG signals using Flexible Analytic Wavelet Transform (FAWT) and multiscale permutation entropy features. The results indicate that CNN provides the highest accuracy, sensitivity, specificity, and area under the curve, with 99.19%, 99.34%, 99.21%, and 0.9997, respectively, for 10 s duration EEG segment. Their method shows promise for the accurate and early diagnosis of ASD using EEG signals.

5.3 EEG and Alzheimer's Disease

AD is a type of dementia. Generally, the symptoms are cognitive impairment and loss of memory thereby affecting occupational and social activities. It is a neurodegenerative disease. Tavares et al. (2019), discusses the extraction of the PSD in different wavebands of EEG signals. Initially, a t-test was applied to ascertain if they obtained features produce any important variation among the groups in question. Those features are merged to train a SVM model. Feature Selection yields the reduced, significant features that yield higher classification accuracy and discriminating power. Deep Neural Networks effectively operate even for a large number of datasets. Yu et al. (2019) proposed a Network-based Takagi-Sugeno-Kang (N–TSK) for the detection of AD, using the TSK fuzzy system with complex network theory. Network parameters are considered independent inputs, and a TSK model based on fuzzy-systems is established and additionally trained to detect AD from EEG signals. Besides, comparing the weighted and unweighted N–TSK performance results, the weighted N-TSK largely exceeds the unweighted N-TSK. The developed N–TSK model is used to detect neurological brain disorders from EEG signals with functional networks. They also particularly contribute to the identification as well as the diagnosis of AD. Ismail et al. (2019) utilized Fast Fourier Transform (FFT) and CNN for classification of AD. Özbek et al. (2021) aimed to differentiate individuals with Early-Onset Alzheimer's Disease (EOAD) from healthy controls by analyzing resting-state EEG alpha/theta power ratio. Spectral-power analysis on EEG data obtained using FFT and compared the delta, theta, alpha, and beta oscillations between the two groups. Their findings revealed that individuals with EOAD showed an increase in slow frequency bands and a decrease in fast frequency bands compared to healthy controls. The study also indicated that the best discriminating value between EOAD and young Healthy controls was the frontal alpha/theta power ratio, which had high sensitivity and specificity. Amini et al. (2021) conducted study to diagnose Alzheimer's disease utilizing EEG signals and employed the Time-Dependent Power Spectrum Descriptor (TD-PSD) method for feature extraction from the EEG signals and used a CNN to process the obtained data.

Şeker et al. (2021) aimed to investigate the utility of Permutation Entropy (PE) values for early diagnosis of AD. PE values were computed from various regions of the brain and analyzed their distribution to observe differences between individuals with Mild Cognitive Impairment (MCI)/AD and healthy controls (HC). They employed statistical analysis and a Multinomial Logistic Regression model to classify each participant individually based on their PE values. A primate brain pattern (PBP)-based model was utilized along with tunable q-factor wavelet transform to develop a multilevel feature extractor for classifying AD and healthy controls. The accuracy of the model was evaluated using KNN classifier with tenfold and leave-one-subject-out cross-validations, resulting in 100% and 92.01% accuracy, respectively, for AD vs. healthy classification (Dogan et al., 2022). Alessandrini et al. (2022) employed a RNN model for detecting abnormalities in EEG data and utilized a Robust Principal Component Analysis (RPCA) algorithm to improve the detection accuracy. The RPCA algorithm was employed to remove outliers from the EEG data. The study found that the RPCA algorithm was able to increase the detection accuracy by approximately 5% compared to the baseline PCA method. Puri et al. (2022) investigated the potential of Spectral Entropy (SE) and Kolmogorov Complexity (KC) feature sets for the automated detection of AD patients. The SVM classifier was utilized to evaluate the performance of these feature sets, and the results were promising with more than 95% accuracy achieved when both SE and KC feature sets were utilized. Fouladi et al. (2022) utilized the Time-Frequency Representation (TFR) to extract features from EEG signals. The extracted features were then classified using the Modified Convolutional Network and Convolutional Auto-Encoder Network. The study achieved an average classification accuracy of 92% and 89%, respectively. Azami et al. (2023) investigated the utility of entropy-based measures in different wake and sleep states, including a Slow-to-Fast-Activity Ratio (SFAR)-entropy, which measures the ratio of entropy of slow-to-fast activity, for discriminating dementia in AD from MCI and healthy controls. The results showed that SFAR-entropy measured during Rapid Eye Movement (REM) sleep was able to robustly discriminate AD dementia from MCI and healthy controls. Puri et al. (2023) utilized Low-Complexity Orthogonal Wavelet Filter Banks with vanishing moments (LCOWFBs-v) to decompose EEG signals into subbands and extracted two features, Higuchi's Fractal Dimension (HFD) and Katz's

Fractal Dimension (KFD), for classification of AD and MCI. The classification accuracy achieved was 98.5% and 98.6% using LCOWFBs-4 and LCOWFBs-6, respectively, with a cubic-support vector machine classifier and a 10-fold cross-validation technique. These findings demonstrate the potential of advanced analytical techniques, in conjunction with EEG recordings, to accurately classify AD and MCI from EEG signals.

5.4 EEG and Parkinson's Disease

PD is a long-term degenerative disease that influences one's control of emotions and movements due to the loss of dopamine that accompanies nerve cell damage. Major symptoms of Parkinson's are changes in writing and speech, muscle stiffness, instability in coordination and balance of the body, Bradykinesia (slowness of movements), and tremors in the limbs. Rehman et al. (2020) observed that classification models have major significant characteristics associated with gait regularity and age, step velocity and length, power spectral density and root mean square values. Digital-gait characteristics based on the signals separately provide 87.32% accuracy. To train the Six Partial Least Square-Discriminant Analysis (PLS-DA) models, classification performance of PLS-DA with PD are combinations of Participant Demographics (DEM) Data and Accelerometer derived Gait Characteristics (CHAR). The characteristics: SC(Signal Characteristics) + ST(Spatiotemporal)+ DEM are used. Tuncer et al. (2020) used the Singular Value Decomposition operator for extraction of the features from a constructed signal. The relief feature selection technique is used to choose fifty main distinctive features. Finally, classification is done by KNN with a 10-fold Cross Validation. Chawla et al. (2023) proposed a decision support system for automated diagnosis of PD, which employs a Flexible Analytic Wavelet Transform (FAWT) and entropy features. Their methodology comprises preprocessing the obtained EEG signals, breaking them down into five frequency sub-bands using the FAWT method, and calculating various entropy parameters from these sub-bands. Several classifiers, including support SVM, logistics, Random Forests (RF), Radial Basis Functions (RBF), and KNN, are utilized to identify suitable feature sets. Their approach yielded high accuracy, specificity, sensitivity, and area under the curve values in two datasets collected from Malaysia and the United States. Chu et al. (2021) utilized a CNN to detect early Parkinson's disease (PD) in patients by incorporating structured power spectral density with spatial distribution. They utilized a gradient-weighted class activation mapping visualization technique to determine the optimal frequency bands for identifying early PD. They proposed a new quantitative index called Spatial-mapping Relative Power (SRP) to identify individualized abnormalities in the spatial spectral characteristics of EEG in early PD. The CNN model achieved an accuracy of 99.87% ± 0.03%, and the characteristic frequency bands for identifying early PD were the high-delta (3.5–4.5 Hz) and low-alpha (7.5–11 Hz) frequency bands. The SRP values of these two characteristic bands in early PD patients were significantly higher than those in the control group, and the abnormalities were consistent at both group and individual levels.

Loh et al. (2021) put forth a model named Gabor Transformation and Deep Neural Network for Parkinson's Disease (GaborPDNet) for PD detection using EEG signals. The model employed a Gabor transform to convert EEG recordings into spectrograms. A 2 Dimensional-CNN was used for classification, which achieved high accuracy of 99.46% (±0.73) for 3-class classification (HC, PD patients with and without medication) using tenfold cross-validation. These findings underscore the potential of machine learning techniques in the automated diagnosis of PD through EEG signals, which can help in early detection and treatment of the disease. Khare et al. (2021) utilized Smoothed Pseudo-Wigner Ville Distribution (SPWVD) and CNN for PD detection. This method involves applying SPWVD to

EEG signals to obtain TFR, which is then processed by a CNN model called Parkinson's disease CNN (PDCNNet). The PDCNNet model was trained and evaluated on two public databases and was found to achieve high accuracy of 100% and 99.97% for dataset 1 and 2, respectively, in detecting PD. These findings demonstrate the potential of machine learning techniques to improve PD diagnosis using EEG signals. Lee et al. (2021) employed a Convolutional-Recurrent Neural Network (CRNN) that integrates both a CNN and a RNN that employs GRUs. The CRNN model attained a classification accuracy of 99.2%, precision of 98.9%, and recall of 99.4% in distinguishing PD patients from HC. Smrdel (2022) utilized the common spatial patterns (CSP) and Laplacian mask techniques to extract features from EEG signals, resulting in classification accuracies of 85% and 90%, respectively, for distinguishing between EEGs of individuals who were healthy controls and those who had Parkinson's disease. Aljalal et al. (2022) utilized the Discrete Wavelet Transform (DWT) to decompose EEG signals into sub-bands. They then extracted features from the wavelet packet-derived reconstructed signals using various entropy measures. Using the combination of DWT and Modified-Shannon Entropy (TShEn), they achieved high classification accuracy in detecting PD. Wang et al. (2022) utilized the energy of the frequency bands in EEG signals to create 2-dimensional images, which were subsequently classified using a Capsule Network (CapsNet). The CapsNet achieved an accuracy rate of 89.34% in classifying short-term EEG sections. Aljalal et al. (2022) explored the effectiveness of common spatial pattern, entropy, and machine learning methods for classifying extracted features from preprocessed EEG signals. The proposed methods were evaluated using two EEG datasets, and the results demonstrated high classification accuracy, sensitivity, and specificity for detecting off-medication PD, with values close to 99%. Pappalettera et al. (2022) obtained resting-state EEGs from PD patients and elderly subjects were analyzed. The study employed Approximate Entropy (ApEn) analysis to investigate EEGs in ten regions of interest. Results showed that PD patients had significantly higher ApEn values than elderly subjects, indicating that PD is associated with significant changes in brain complexity. Zhang et al. (2022) utilized a combination of time-frequency analysis and deep learning to classify four types of clinical sleep EEG data, including data from individuals with PD. The achieved accuracies for predicting PD were 99.92% in the 2-class classification task and 97.81% in the 3-class classification task. Oh et al. (2020) used thirteen-layer CNN for classification.

5.5 EEG and Schizophrenia

Schizophrenia is a chronic, lifelong disease that affects one's relationship with others. Patients will feel withdrawn from society and lost with reality. It could be treated by early diagnosis. EEG is specifically helpful to understand the cognitive as well as behavioral challenges experienced by schizophrenic patients. Oh et al. (2019) developed an 11-layer CNN model to automatically extract features from EEG signals and categorize them. Deviav et al. (2019) presented a free-viewing paradigm of EEG signals. Hassan et al. (2023) proposed a novel approach for schizophrenia detection that combines CNN and logistic regression. Their study achieved high accuracy rates of 90% and 98% for subject-based and non-subject-based testing, respectively; by using a combination of three channels, T4, T3, and Cz. Ruiz de Miras et al. (2023) used linear and non-linear measures extracted from EEG data to differentiate schizophrenia patients from healthy controls. Their method achieved high classification power in SVM with an AUC of 0.89. Khare et al. (2023) proposed SchizoNET, which achieved accuracy rates of 97.4%, 99.74%, and 96.35% on three different datasets using the Margenau-Hill time-frequency distribution-based CNN model. Kumar et al. (2023) used local descriptors, such as Histogram of Local Variance (HLV), and symmetrically weighted-local binary patterns (SLBP), to represent features of the EEG signals. These features were then subjected to a correlation-based feature selection algorithm and an AdaBoost classifier, achieving accuracy rates of 92.85% and 99.36% on two datasets. Agarwal and Singhal (2023) fused statistical features and Look-Ahead Pattern (LAP) features computed from sub-band components of the EEG signals, followed by the selection of significant features using Kruskal-Wallis test and the use of various machine learning classifiers. Their approach achieved accuracy rates of 98.62% and 99.24% in identifying SZ cases on two datasets using a boosted trees classifier. Lillo et al. (2022) used a random walk process and a CNN model to classify people into patients with schizophrenia and healthy subjects. Their approach obtained a 93% success rate in automating the classification of people with schizophrenia from 3 minutes of signal capture. Ko and Yang (2022) converted EEGs into images using time series image conversion algorithms and learned them with CNN models. They found that the Gramian Angular Field(GAF) algorithm showed significantly higher classification accuracy.

Sharma and Joshi (2022) proposed a hybrid deep-learning model called schizophrenia hybrid neural network (SzHNN), which combines CNN and LSTM to achieve the highest classification accuracy of 99.9% compared to other models. Aslan and Akin (2021) used the Continuous Wavelet Transform method to convert signals into 2D scalogram images, which were then trained with VGG16 to achieve high accuracy in classifying SZ patients and healthy individuals. The studies utilized different techniques to visualize the learning outcomes of their CNN networks, highlighting the relationship of frequency components between SZ and healthy individuals. Sobahi et al. (2022) describes a new signal to image mapping procedure and convolutional neural networks for efficient schizophrenia detection in EEG recordings. The procedure involves breaking down each channel of the input EEG recordings into EEG rhythms using wavelet transform and then using 1D Local Binary Pattern (LBP) to code the acquired rhythm signals. The coded beats are concatenated to form rows of the input picture, with the rows representing the channels of the input EEG signal and the columns representing the rhythms. Deep transfer learning is then used to classify SZ and healthy cases with a high accuracy score of 97.7%. Jindal et al. (2022) proposed an automated Multi SynchroSqueezing Transform (MSST)-based Bi-LSTM-deep CNN (Bi-CNN) model for SZ disease detection. The methodology involves 2D time-frequency representation of EEG activity using MSST, followed by feature extraction and classification of the decomposed EEG using the Bi-CNN model. The proposed methodology achieves an accuracy of 84.42% in SZ detection. Baygin et al. (2021) presented a model for automated accurate schizophrenia detection using Collatz pattern technique with EEG signals. The model comprises three stages, including a new feature generation function using Collatz Conjecture, Iterative Neighborhood Component Analysis (INCA) for selecting clinically significant features, and KNN classifier for automated SZ detection. The model is validated using two public schizophrenia databases and achieves a high classification accuracy of 99.47% and 93.58% for DB1 and DB2 datasets, respectively, with ten-fold cross-validation strategy. Akbari et al. (2021) focused on using the Phase Space Dynamic (PSD) of EEG signals to extract 15 graphical features for evaluating the chaotic behavior of PSD in healthy and schizophrenic subjects. They found that the KNN classifier with City-block distance achieved an average classification accuracy of 94.80%, sensitivity of 94.30%, and specificity of 95.20%. Krishnan et al. (2020) used Multivariate Empirical Mode Decomposition (MEMD) to decompose the EEG signal into Intrinsic Mode Functions (IMF) and computed five entropy measures from the IMF signal. They found that the Support Vector Machine based on Radial Basis Function (SVM-RBF) provided the highest accuracy and F1-score of 93%. Aydemir et al. (2022) introduced an automated method for detecting schizophrenia utilizing a Cyclic Group of Prime order Pattern (CGP17Pat). The model achieved an accuracy of 99.91% through 10-fold cross-validation and

84.33% using the Leave-One-Subject Out (LOSO) strategy. (Oh et al., 2019) used a deep CNN model to analyze EEG signals and achieved classification accuracies of 98.07% and 81.26% for non-subject based testing and subject based testing, respectively. Overall, these studies suggest that automated methods for detecting schizophrenia using EEG signals have the potential to provide accurate and reliable results.

5.6 EEG and Ischemic Stroke

IS is an important cause of fatal neural disorders amongst elders worldwide. Shreve et al. (2019) identified the subjects with large acute ischemic stroke based on their association with infarct volume, and their EEG was measured to detect stroke onset within hours. Gottlibe et al. (2020) utilized a portable EEG device to take short recordings and distinguish between a control group and stroke patients. EEG signals were collected during the acute phase of ischemic stroke, and the Revised Brain Symmetry Index (rsBSI) was used to describe the power spectrum symmetry between the right and left hemispheres. Wilkinson et al. (2020) investigated various ratios and indices such as Delta/Alpha Ratio (DAR), (Delta+ Theta)/(Alpha+Beta) Ratio (DTABR), pairwise-derived Brain Symmetry Index (pdBSI), and head movement using the on-board accelerometer and gyroscope. They found that DAR and DBATR increased in patients with increasing stroke severity, while pdBSI decreased in low frequencies and increased in high frequencies in patients who had a stroke. A classification tree was used to distinguish moderate to severe stroke patients from minor stroke and control groups with a sensitivity of 63%, specificity of 86%, and accuracy of 76%. Wang et al. (2022) studied the effect of different transcranial Direct Current Stimulation (tDCS) protocols on stroke and found that the alpha rhythm of EEG is modulated differently, with high alpha affected by clinical characteristics such as post-stroke time and motor deficits. Nurfirdausi et al. (2022) used a 32-channel EEG, CT scan, and NIHSS Scores to classify the severity of stroke. They extracted features such as DTABR, DAR, relative power ratio (RPR), and asymmetry using wavelet decomposition technique and classified the severity of stroke using a Feedforward Neural Network. The best performance was achieved with an epoch length of 60 seconds and 15 hidden layers, resulting in an accuracy of 89%. The study suggested that this EEG-based diagnostic system could be implemented in class C hospitals located in rural areas. Nurfirdausi et al. (2022) extract Shannon Entropy feature and utilize Decision tree for classification of stroke. Islam et al. (2022) used Welch periodogram estimation and Fast Fourier Transform to extract EEG band power and classified ischemic stroke using Adaptive Gradient Boosting models.

6. CONCLUSION

EEG signals are widely used for the diagnosis of brain disorders especially in the developing countries due to reduced availability of expensive machines like the fMRI (functional Magnetic Resonance Imaging). EEG signals can be utilized efficiently to learn about ailments and mental states pertaining to the brain. Generally, the inbuilt issues with the EEG signals are that they are highly nonlinear and non-stationary in nature, and that its optical interpretation is a dull process involving the scrutinisation of minute and random variations. To help biomedical researchers perform an enhanced analysis of methods to diagnose brain disorders using EEG signals, various articles were reviewed. Feature extraction and classification methods that are used for the diagnosis of 6 brain disorders namely Epilepsy, Autism Spectrum Disorder, Parkinson's disease, Alzheimer's disease, Schizophrenia and Ischemic Stroke were discussed in this review paper. Our key focus was on automating the diagnosis of brain disorders using EEG signals. In this review, we have compiled and corroborated the results of numerous brain disorder identification techniques that use EEG signals as the base for diagnosis. In addition to this, the challenges of the review are the improvement of the accuracy of EEG signals to identify the disorders in its early stages. The future direction of this review process is to develop a diagnostic system to perform a detection of the severity levels of each of those brain disorders and also to develop said system in a VLSI platform as a portable, handheld device.

REFERENCES

Agarwal, M., & Singhal, A. (2023). Fusion of pattern-based and statistical features for schizophrenia detection from EEG signals. *Medical Engineering & Physics*, *112*, 103949. doi:10.1016/j.medengphy.2023.103949 PMID:36842772

Akbari, H., Ghofrani, S., Zakalvand, P., & Tariq Sadiq, M. (2021). Schizophrenia recognition based on the phase space dynamic of EEG signals and graphical features. *Biomedical Signal Processing and Control*, *69*, 102917. doi:10.1016/j.bspc.2021.102917

Alessandrini, M., Biagetti, G., Crippa, P., Falaschetti, L., Luzzi, S., & Turchetti, C. (2022). EEG-based alzheimer's disease recognition using robust-PCA and LSTM recurrent neural network. *Sensors (Basel)*, *22*(10), 3696. doi:10.339022103696 PMID:35632105

Aljalal, M., Aldosari, S. A., AlSharabi, K., Abdurraqeeb, A. M., & Alturki, F. A. (2022). Parkinson's disease detection from resting-state EEG signals using common spatial pattern, entropy, and Machine Learning Techniques. *Diagnostics (Basel)*, *12*(5), 1033. doi:10.3390/diagnostics12051033 PMID:35626189

Aljalal, M., Aldosari, S. A., Molinas, M., AlSharabi, K., & Alturki, F. A. (2022). Detection of parkinson's disease from EEG signals using discrete wavelet transform, different entropy measures, and Machine Learning Techniques. *Scientific Reports*, *12*(1), 22547. Advance online publication. doi:10.103841598-022-26644-7 PMID:36581646

Alturki, F. A., Aljalal, M., Abdurraqeeb, A. M., Alsharabi, K., & Al-Shamma'a, A. A. (2021). Common spatial pattern technique with EEG signals for diagnosis of autism and epilepsy disorders. *IEEE Access : Practical Innovations, Open Solutions*, *9*, 24334–24349. doi:10.1109/ACCESS.2021.3056619

Amini, M., Pedram, M. M., Moradi, A. R., & Ouchani, M. (2021). Diagnosis of alzheimer's disease by time-dependent power spectrum descriptors and convolutional neural network using EEG Signal. *Computational and Mathematical Methods in Medicine*, *2021*, 1–17. doi:10.1155/2021/5511922 PMID:33981355

Amiri, M., Aghaeinia, H., & Amindavar, H. R. (2023). Automatic epileptic seizure detection in EEG signals using sparse common spatial pattern and adaptive short-time fourier transform-based synchrosqueezing transform. *Biomedical Signal Processing and Control*, *79*, 104022. doi:10.1016/j.bspc.2022.104022

Ardakani, H. A., Taghizadeh, M., & Shayegh, F. (2022). Diagnosis of autism disorder based on deep network trained by augmented EEG signals. *International Journal of Neural Systems*, *32*(11), 2250046. doi:10.1142/S0129065722500460 PMID:35997585

Ari, B., Sobahi, N., Alçin, Ö. F., Sengur, A., & Acharya, U. R. (2022). Accurate detection of autism using Douglas-Peucker algorithm, sparse coding based feature mapping and convolutional neural network techniques with EEG signals. *Computers in Biology and Medicine*, *143*, 105311. doi:10.1016/j.compbiomed.2022.105311 PMID:35158117

Aslam, A. R., & Altaf, M. A. (2019). An 8 channel patient specific neuromorphic processor for the early screening of autistic children through emotion detection. *2019 IEEE International Symposium on Circuits and Systems (ISCAS)*. 10.1109/ISCAS.2019.8702738

Aslan, Z., & Akin, M. (2021). A deep learning approach in automated detection of schizophrenia using SCALOGRAM images of EEG signals. *Physical and Engineering Sciences in Medicine*, *45*(1), 83–96. doi:10.100713246-021-01083-2 PMID:34822131

Aydemir, E., Dogan, S., Baygin, M., Ooi, C. P., Barua, P. D., Tuncer, T., & Acharya, U. R. (2022). CGP-17Pat: Automated schizophrenia detection based on a cyclic group of prime order patterns using EEG signals. *Health Care*, *10*(4), 643. doi:10.3390/healthcare10040643 PMID:35455821

Azami, H., Moguilner, S., Penagos, H., Sarkis, R. A., Arnold, S. E., Gomperts, S. N., & Lam, A. D. (2023). EEG entropy in REM sleep as a physiologic biomarker in early clinical stages of alzheimer's disease. *Journal of Alzheimer's Disease*, *91*(4), 1557–1572. doi:10.3233/JAD-221152 PMID:36641682

Baygin, M., Dogan, S., Tuncer, T., Datta Barua, P., Faust, O., Arunkumar, N., Abdulhay, E. W., Emma Palmer, E., & Rajendra Acharya, U. (2021). Automated ASD detection using hybrid deep lightweight features extracted from EEG signals. *Computers in Biology and Medicine*, *134*, 104548. doi:10.1016/j.compbiomed.2021.104548 PMID:34119923

Baygin, M., Yaman, O., Tuncer, T., Dogan, S., Barua, P. D., & Acharya, U. R. (2021). Automated accurate schizophrenia detection system using Collatz pattern technique with EEG signals. *Biomedical Signal Processing and Control*, *70*, 102936. doi:10.1016/j.bspc.2021.102936

Brari, Z., & Belghith, S. (2021). A novel machine learning approach for epilepsy diagnosis using EEG signals based on Correlation Dimension. *IFAC-PapersOnLine*, *54*(17), 7–11. doi:10.1016/j.ifacol.2021.11.018

Chawla, P., Rana, S. B., Kaur, H., & Singh, K. (2022). Computer-aided diagnosis of autism spectrum disorder from EEG signals using deep learning with FAWT and multiscale permutation entropy features. *Proceedings of the Institution of Mechanical Engineers. Part H, Journal of Engineering in Medicine*, *237*(2), 282–294. doi:10.1177/09544119221141751 PMID:36515392

Chawla, P., Rana, S. B., Kaur, H., Singh, K., Yuvaraj, R., & Murugappan, M. (2023). A decision support system for automated diagnosis of parkinson's disease from EEG using FAWT and entropy features. *Biomedical Signal Processing and Control*, *79*, 104116. doi:10.1016/j.bspc.2022.104116

Chu, C., Zhang, Z., Wang, J., Liu, S., Wang, F., Sun, Y., Han, X., Li, Z., Zhu, X., & Liu, C. (2021). Deep learning reveals personalized spatial spectral abnormalities of high delta and low alpha bands in EEG of patients with early parkinson's disease. *Journal of Neural Engineering*, *18*(6), 066036. doi:10.1088/1741-2552/ac40a0 PMID:34875634

Devia, C., Mayol-Troncoso, R., Parrini, J., Orellana, G., Ruiz, A., Maldonado, P. E., & Egana, J. I. (2019). EEG classification during scene free-viewing for schizophrenia detection. *IEEE Transactions on Neural Systems and Rehabilitation Engineering*, *27*(6), 1193–1199. doi:10.1109/TNSRE.2019.2913799 PMID:31034418

Dogan, S., Baygin, M., Tasci, B., Loh, H. W., Barua, P. D., Tuncer, T., Tan, R.-S., & Acharya, U. R. (2022). Primate brain pattern-based Automated Alzheimer's disease detection model using EEG signals. *Cognitive Neurodynamics*. Advance online publication. doi:10.100711571-022-09859-2 PMID:37265658

Fouladi, S., Safaei, A. A., Mammone, N., Ghaderi, F., & Ebadi, M. J. (2022). Efficient Deep Neural Networks for classification of alzheimer's disease and mild cognitive impairment from scalp EEG Recordings. *Cognitive Computation*, *14*(4), 1247–1268. doi:10.100712559-022-10033-3

Gottlibe, M., Rosen, O., Weller, B., Mahagney, A., Omar, N., Khuri, A., Srugo, I., & Genizi, J. (2020). Stroke identification using a portable EEG device – a pilot study. *Neurophysiologie Clinique*, *50*(1), 21–25. doi:10.1016/j.neucli.2019.12.004 PMID:32014371

Grossi, E., Valbusa, G., & Buscema, M. (2020). Detection of an autism EEG signature from only two EEG channels through features extraction and Advanced Machine Learning Analysis. *Clinical EEG and Neuroscience*, *52*(5), 330–337. doi:10.1177/1550059420982424 PMID:33349054

Habeeb, E., Ghazal, N., & Majzoub, S. (2019). Behavior analysis tool for autistic children using EEG signals. *2019 Advances in Science and Engineering Technology International Conferences (ASET)*. 10.1109/ICASET.2019.8714498

Hadoush, H., Alafeef, M., & Abdulhay, E. (2019). Automated identification for autism severity level: EEG analysis using empirical mode decomposition and second order difference plot. *Behavioural Brain Research*, *362*, 240–248. doi:10.1016/j.bbr.2019.01.018 PMID:30641159

Haputhanthri, D., Brihadiswaran, G., Gunathilaka, S., Meedeniya, D., Jayawardena, Y., Jayarathna, S., & Jaime, M. (2019). An EEG based channel optimized classification approach for autism spectrum disorder. *2019 Moratuwa Engineering Research Conference (MERCon)*. 10.1109/MERCon.2019.8818814

Hassan, F., Hussain, S. F., & Qaisar, S. M. (2023). Fusion of multivariate EEG signals for schizophrenia detection using CNN and Machine Learning Techniques. *Information Fusion*, *92*, 466–478. doi:10.1016/j.inffus.2022.12.019

Islam, M. S., Hussain, I., Rahman, M. M., Park, S. J., & Hossain, M. A. (2022). Explainable artificial intelligence model for stroke prediction using EEG Signal. *Sensors (Basel)*, *22*(24), 9859. doi:10.339022249859 PMID:36560227

Ismail, M., Hofmann, K., & El Ghany, M. A. (2019). Early diagnoses of alzheimer using EEG data and deep neural networks classification. *2019 IEEE Global Conference on Internet of Things (GCIoT)*. 10.1109/GCIoT47977.2019.9058417

Jahmunah, V., Lih Oh, S., Rajinikanth, V., Ciaccio, E. J., Hao Cheong, K., Arunkumar, N., & Acharya, U. R. (2019). Automated detection of schizophrenia using nonlinear signal processing methods. *Artificial Intelligence in Medicine*, *100*, 101698. doi:10.1016/j.artmed.2019.07.006 PMID:31607349

Jindal, K., Upadhyay, R., Padhy, P. K., & Longo, L. (2022). Bi-lstm-deep CNN for schizophrenia detection using MSST-spectral images of EEG signals. *Artificial Intelligence-Based Brain-Computer Interface*, 145–162. doi:10.1016/B978-0-323-91197-9.00011-4

Jiwani, N., Gupta, K., Sharif, M. H., Adhikari, N., & Afreen, N. (2022). A LSTM-CNN model for epileptic seizures detection using EEG signal. *2022 2nd International Conference on Emerging Smart Technologies and Applications (ESmarTA)*. 10.1109/eSmarTA56775.2022.9935403

Khare, S. K., Bajaj, V., & Acharya, U. R. (2021). PDCNNet: An Automatic Framework for the detection of parkinson's disease using EEG Signals. *IEEE Sensors Journal*, *21*(15), 17017–17024. doi:10.1109/JSEN.2021.3080135

Khare, S. K., Bajaj, V., & Acharya, U. R. (2023). Schizonet: A robust and accurate margenau–hill time-frequency distribution based deep neural network model for schizophrenia detection using EEG signals. *Physiological Measurement*, *44*(3), 035005. doi:10.1088/1361-6579/acbc06 PMID:36787641

Khodatars, M., Shoeibi, A., Sadeghi, D., Ghaasemi, N., Jafari, M., Moridian, P., Khadem, A., Alizadehsani, R., Zare, A., Kong, Y., Khosravi, A., Nahavandi, S., Hussain, S., Acharya, U. R., & Berk, M. (2021). Deep learning for neuroimaging-based diagnosis and rehabilitation of Autism Spectrum Disorder: A review. *Computers in Biology and Medicine*, *139*, 104949. doi:10.1016/j.compbiomed.2021.104949

Ko, D.-W., & Yang, J.-J. (2022). EEG-based schizophrenia diagnosis through time series image conversion and Deep Learning. *Electronics (Basel)*, *11*(14), 2265. doi:10.3390/electronics11142265

Krishnan, P. T., Joseph Raj, A. N., Balasubramanian, P., & Chen, Y. (2020). Schizophrenia detection using multivariateempirical mode decomposition and entropy measures from multichannel EEG signal. *Biocybernetics and Biomedical Engineering*, *40*(3), 1124–1139. doi:10.1016/j.bbe.2020.05.008

Kumar, T. S., Rajesh, K. N. V. P. S., Maheswari, S., Kanhangad, V., & Acharya, U. R. (2023). Automated schizophrenia detection using local descriptors with EEG signals. *Engineering Applications of Artificial Intelligence*, *117*, 105602. doi:10.1016/j.engappai.2022.105602

Lee, S., Hussein, R., Ward, R., Jane Wang, Z., & McKeown, M. J. (2021). A convolutional-recurrent neural network approach to resting-state EEG classification in parkinson's disease. *Journal of Neuroscience Methods*, *361*, 109282. doi:10.1016/j.jneumeth.2021.109282 PMID:34237382

Li, M., Chen, W., & Xia, M. (2023). GNMF-based quadratic feature extraction in SSTFT domain for epileptic EEG detection. *Biomedical Signal Processing and Control*, *80*, 104274. doi:10.1016/j.bspc.2022.104274

Lillo, E., Mora, M., & Lucero, B. (2022). Automated diagnosis of schizophrenia using EEG microstates and deep convolutional neural network. *Expert Systems with Applications*, *209*, 118236. doi:10.1016/j.eswa.2022.118236

Liu, Z., Zhu, B., Hu, M., Deng, Z., & Zhang, J. (2023). Revised tunable Q-factor wavelet transform for EEG-based epileptic seizure detection. *IEEE Transactions on Neural Systems and Rehabilitation Engineering*, *31*, 1707–1720. doi:10.1109/TNSRE.2023.3257306 PMID:37028382

Loh, H. W., Ooi, C. P., Palmer, E., Barua, P. D., Dogan, S., Tuncer, T., Baygin, M., & Acharya, U. R. (2021). GaborPDNet: Gabor Transformation and Deep Neural Network for parkinson's disease detection using EEG signals. *Electronics (Basel)*, *10*(14), 1740. doi:10.3390/electronics10141740

Majumder, S., Apicella, F., Muratori, F., & Das, K. (2020). Detecting autism spectrum disorder using topological data analysis. *ICASSP 2020 - 2020 IEEE International Conference on Acoustics, Speech and Signal Processing (ICASSP)*. 10.1109/ICASSP40776.2020.9054747

Mandhouj, B., Cherni, M. A., & Sayadi, M. (2021). An automated classification of EEG signals based on spectrogram and CNN for epilepsy diagnosis. *Analog Integrated Circuits and Signal Processing*, *108*(1), 101–110. doi:10.100710470-021-01805-2

Melinda, M., Enriko, I. K., Furqan, M., Irhamsyah, M., Yunidar, Y., & Basir, N. (2023). The effect of power spectral density on the electroencephalography of autistic children based on the welch periodogram method. *JURNAL INFOTEL*, *15*(1), 111–120. doi:10.20895/infotel.v15i1.874

Mir, W. A., Anjum, M., Izharuddin, I., & Shahab, S. (2023). Deep-EEG: An optimized and robust framework and method for EEG-based diagnosis of epileptic seizure. *Diagnostics (Basel)*, *13*(4), 773. doi:10.3390/diagnostics13040773 PMID:36832260

Nurfirdausi, A. F., Apsari, R. A., Wijaya, S. K., Prajitno, P., & Ibrahim, N. (2022). Wavelet decomposition and feedforward neural network for classification of acute ischemic stroke based on electroencephalography. *International Journal of Technology*, *13*(8), 1745. doi:10.14716/ijtech.v13i8.6132

Nurfirdausi, A. F., Wijaya, S. K., Prajitno, P., & Ibrahim, N. (2022). Classification of acute ischemic stroke EEG signal using entropy-based features, wavelet decomposition, and machine learning algorithms. *THE 6TH BIOMEDICAL ENGINEERING'S RECENT PROGRESS IN BIOMATERIALS, DRUGS DEVELOPMENT, AND MEDICAL DEVICES: Proceedings of the 6th International Symposium of Biomedical Engineering (ISBE) 2021*. 10.1063/5.0098733

Oh, S. L., Hagiwara, Y., Raghavendra, U., Yuvaraj, R., Arunkumar, N., Murugappan, M., & Acharya, U. R. (2018). A deep learning approach for parkinson's disease diagnosis from EEG signals. *Neural Computing & Applications*, *32*(15), 10927–10933. doi:10.100700521-018-3689-5

Oh, S. L., Jahmunah, V., Arunkumar, N., Abdulhay, E. W., Gururajan, R., Adib, N., Ciaccio, E. J., Cheong, K. H., & Acharya, U. R. (2021). A novel automated autism spectrum disorder detection system. *Complex & Intelligent Systems*, *7*(5), 2399–2413. doi:10.100740747-021-00408-8

Oh, S. L., Vicnesh, J., Ciaccio, E. J., Yuvaraj, R., & Acharya, U. R. (2019). Deep convolutional neural network model for automated diagnosis of schizophrenia using EEG signals. *Applied Sciences (Basel, Switzerland)*, *9*(14), 2870. doi:10.3390/app9142870

Özbek, Y., Fide, E., & Yener, G. G. (2021). Resting-state EEG Alpha/Theta power ratio discriminates early-onset alzheimer's disease from healthy controls. *Clinical Neurophysiology*, *132*(9), 2019–2031. doi:10.1016/j.clinph.2021.05.012 PMID:34284236

Pappalettera, C., Miraglia, F., Cotelli, M., Rossini, P. M., & Vecchio, F. (2022). Analysis of complexity in the EEG activity of parkinson's disease patients by means of approximate entropy. *GeroScience*, *44*(3), 1599–1607. doi:10.100711357-022-00552-0 PMID:35344121

Pham, T. H., Vicnesh, J., Wei, J. K., Oh, S. L., Arunkumar, N., Abdulhay, E. W., Ciaccio, E. J., & Acharya, U. R. (2020). Autism spectrum disorder diagnostic system using HOS bispectrum with EEG signals. *International Journal of Environmental Research and Public Health*, *17*(3), 971. doi:10.3390/ijerph17030971 PMID:32033231

Portnova, G. V., Nekrashevich, M. V., Morozova, M. V., Martynova, O. V., & Sharaev, M. G. (2023). New approaches to clinical electroencephalography analysis in typically developing children and children with autism. *Cognitive Systems Research*, *78*, 23–32. doi:10.1016/j.cogsys.2022.11.003

Puri, D., Nalbalwar, S., Nandgaonkar, A., & Wagh, A. (2021). EEG-based diagnosis of alzheimer's disease using Kolmogorov complexity. *Advances in Intelligent Systems and Computing*, 157–165. doi:10.1007/978-981-16-2008-9_15

Puri, D. V., Nalbalwar, S. L., Nandgaonkar, A. B., Gawande, J. P., & Wagh, A. (2023). Automatic detection of alzheimer's disease from EEG signals using low-complexity orthogonal wavelet filter banks. *Biomedical Signal Processing and Control*, *81*, 104439. doi:10.1016/j.bspc.2022.104439

Qin, X., Xu, D., Dong, X., Cui, X., & Zhang, S. (2023). EEG signal classification based on improved variational mode decomposition and Deep Forest. *Biomedical Signal Processing and Control*, *83*, 104644. doi:10.1016/j.bspc.2023.104644

Qiu, X., Yan, F., & Liu, H. (2023). A difference attention resnet-LSTM network for epileptic seizure detection using EEG signal. *Biomedical Signal Processing and Control*, *83*, 104652. doi:10.1016/j.bspc.2023.104652

Radhakrishnan, M., Ramamurthy, K., Choudhury, K. K., Won, D., & Manoharan, T. A. (2021). Performance analysis of deep learning models for detection of autism spectrum disorder from EEG signals. *TS. Traitement du Signal*, *38*(3), 853–863. doi:10.18280/ts.380332

Rehman, R. Z., Buckley, C., Mico-Amigo, M. E., Kirk, C., Dunne-Willows, M., Mazza, C., Shi, J. Q., Alcock, L., Rochester, L., & Del Din, S. (2020). Accelerometry-based digital gait characteristics for classification of parkinson's disease: What counts? *IEEE Open Journal of Engineering in Medicine and Biology*, *1*, 65–73. doi:10.1109/OJEMB.2020.2966295 PMID:35402938

Ruiz de Miras, J., Ibáñez-Molina, A. J., Soriano, M. F., & Iglesias-Parro, S. (2023). Schizophrenia classification using machine learning on resting state EEG signal. *Biomedical Signal Processing and Control*, *79*, 104233. doi:10.1016/j.bspc.2022.104233

Samee, N. A., Mahmoud, N. F., Aldhahri, E. A., Rafiq, A., Muthanna, M. S., & Ahmad, I. (2022). RNN and BiLSTM fusion for accurate automatic epileptic seizure diagnosis using EEG signals. *Life (Chicago, Ill.)*, *12*(12), 1946. doi:10.3390/life12121946 PMID:36556313

Sarmukadam, K., Sharpley, C. F., Bitsika, V., McMillan, M. M. E., & Agnew, L. L. (2019). A review of the use of EEG connectivity to measure the neurological characteristics of the sensory features in young people with autism. *Reviews in the Neurosciences*, *30*(5), 497–510. doi:10.1515/revneuro-2018-0070 PMID:30269108

Şeker, M., Özbek, Y., Yener, G., & Özerdem, M. S. (2021). Complexity of EEG Dynamics for early diagnosis of alzheimer's disease using permutation entropy Neuromarker. *Computer Methods and Programs in Biomedicine*, *206*, 106116. doi:10.1016/j.cmpb.2021.106116 PMID:33957376

Sharma, G., & Joshi, A. M. (2022). Szhnn: A novel and scalable deep convolution hybrid neural network framework for schizophrenia detection using multichannel EEG. *IEEE Transactions on Instrumentation and Measurement*, *71*, 1–9. doi:10.1109/TIM.2022.3212040

Sherkatghanad, Z., Akhondzadeh, M., Salari, S., Zomorodi-Moghadam, M., Abdar, M., Acharya, U. R., Khosrowabadi, R., & Salari, V. (2020). Automated detection of autism spectrum disorder using a convolutional neural network. *Frontiers in Neuroscience*, *13*, 1325. Advance online publication. doi:10.3389/fnins.2019.01325 PMID:32009868

Shoeibi, A., Ghassemi, N., Khodatars, M., Moridian, P., Alizadehsani, R., Zare, A., Khosravi, A., Subasi, A., Rajendra Acharya, U., & Gorriz, J. M. (2022). Detection of epileptic seizures on EEG signals using ANFIS classifier, autoencoders and fuzzy entropies. *Biomedical Signal Processing and Control*, *73*, 103417. doi:10.1016/j.bspc.2021.103417

Shreve, L., Kaur, A., Vo, C., Wu, J., Cassidy, J. M., Nguyen, A., Zhou, R. J., Tran, T. B., Yang, D. Z., Medizade, A. I., Chakravarthy, B., Hoonpongsimanont, W., Barton, E., Yu, W., Srinivasan, R., & Cramer, S. C. (2019). Electroencephalography measures are useful for identifying large acute ischemic stroke in the emergency department. *Journal of Stroke and Cerebrovascular Diseases*, *28*(8), 2280–2286. doi:10.1016/j.jstrokecerebrovasdis.2019.05.019 PMID:31174955

Smrdel, A. (2022). Use of common spatial patterns for early detection of parkinson's disease. *Scientific Reports*, *12*(1), 18793. Advance online publication. doi:10.103841598-022-23247-0 PMID:36335198

Sobahi, N., Ari, B., Cakar, H., Alcin, O. F., & Sengur, A. (2022). A new signal to image mapping procedure and convolutional neural networks for efficient schizophrenia detection in EEG Recordings. *IEEE Sensors Journal*, *22*(8), 7913–7919. doi:10.1109/JSEN.2022.3151465

Subudhi, A. K., Mohanty, M., Sahoo, S. K., Mohanty, S. K., & Mohanty, B. (2020). Automated delimitation and classification of autistic disorder using EEG signal. *Journal of the Institution of Electronics and Telecommunication Engineers*, *69*(2), 951–959. doi:10.1080/03772063.2020.1844076

Tavares, G., San-Martin, R., Ianof, J. N., Anghinah, R., & Fraga, F. J. (2019). Improvement in the automatic classification of alzheimer's disease using EEG after feature selection. *2019 IEEE International Conference on Systems, Man and Cybernetics (SMC)*. 10.1109/SMC.2019.8914006

Tawhid, M. N., Siuly, S., Wang, H., Whittaker, F., Wang, K., & Zhang, Y. (2021). A spectrogram image based intelligent technique for automatic detection of autism spectrum disorder from EEG. *PLoS One*, *16*(6), e0253094. Advance online publication. doi:10.1371/journal.pone.0253094 PMID:34170979

Tuncer, T., Dogan, S., & Acharya, U. R. (2020). Automated detection of parkinson's disease using minimum average maximum tree and singular value decomposition method with vowels. *Biocybernetics and Biomedical Engineering*, *40*(1), 211–220. doi:10.1016/j.bbe.2019.05.006

Wang, C., Chen, Y., Song, P., Yu, H., Du, J., Zhang, Y., & Sun, C. (2022). Varied response of EEG rhythm to different tDCS protocols and lesion hemispheres in stroke subjects with upper limb dysfunction. *Neural Plasticity*, *2022*, 1–9. doi:10.1155/2022/7790730 PMID:35941932

Wang, S., Wang, G., Pei, G., & Yan, T. (2022). An EEG-based approach for parkinson's disease diagnosis using Capsule Network. *2022 7th International Conference on Intelligent Computing and Signal Processing (ICSP)*. 10.1109/ICSP54964.2022.9778541

Wilkinson, C. M., Burrell, J. I., Kuziek, J. W., Thirunavukkarasu, S., Buck, B. H., & Mathewson, K. E. (2020). Predicting stroke severity with a 3-min recording from the muse portable EEG system for rapid diagnosis of stroke. *Scientific Reports*, *10*(1), 18465. Advance online publication. doi:10.103841598-020-75379-w PMID:33116187

Xin, Q., Hu, S., Liu, S., Zhao, L., & Zhang, Y.-D. (2022). An attention-based wavelet convolution neural network for epilepsy EEG classification. *IEEE Transactions on Neural Systems and Rehabilitation Engineering*, *30*, 957–966. doi:10.1109/TNSRE.2022.3166181 PMID:35404819

Yousefi, M. R., Golnejad, S., & Hosseini, M. M. (2022, April 9). *Comparison of EEG based epilepsy diagnosis using neural networks and wavelet transform*. arXiv.org. Retrieved March 28, 2023, from doi.org/. doi:10.48550/arXiv.2204.04488

Yu, H., Lei, X., Song, Z., Liu, C., & Wang, J. (2020). Supervised network-based fuzzy learning of EEG signals for alzheimer's disease identification. *IEEE Transactions on Fuzzy Systems*, *28*(1), 60–71. doi:10.1109/TFUZZ.2019.2903753

Zhang, R., Jia, J., & Zhang, R. (2022). EEG analysis of parkinson's disease using time–frequency analysis and deep learning. *Biomedical Signal Processing and Control*, *78*, 103883. doi:10.1016/j.bspc.2022.103883

KEY TERMS AND DEFINITIONS

Alzheimer's Disease (AD): A degenerative neurological condition called AD results in the death of brain cells and brain shrinkage.

Autism Spectrum Disorder(ASD): Developmental impairment known as ASD is brought on by variations in the brain. People with ASD may struggle with confined or repetitive activities or interests, as well as social communication and engagement.

Electroencephalography: (EEG): EEG is used to find irregularities in the electrical activity of the brain or in the brain's waves. The treatment involves applying electrodes to your scalp that are made up of tiny metal discs and thin wires. When your brain cells are active, the electrodes pick up very little electrical charges that are generated.

Epilepsy: A neurological condition known as epilepsy is characterised by aberrant brain activity that results in seizures or episodes of strange behaviour, sensations, and even loss of awareness.

Ischemic Brain Stroke: An ischemic stroke occurs when your brain's blood supply to certain regions is blocked by some sort of obstruction. Areas of the brain without blood flow cease to function and begin to perish. An ischemic stroke will result in permanent brain damage or possibly death if blood flow doesn't resume fast enough.

Parkinson's disease (PD): Parkinson's disease is a chronic condition that affects both the neurological system and the body parts that are under the control of the nervous system.

Schizophrenia: Schizophrenia is a severe mental illness where patients have aberrant perceptions of reality. Hallucinations, delusions, and very abnormal thought and behaviour are all possible symptoms of schizophrenia, which can make it difficult to carry out daily tasks and be devastating.

Chapter 18
Internal Control Review of Business Purchasing Card Programs

Teresa Manfreda-Foley
https://orcid.org/0009-0002-9136-9673
Marymount University, USA

ABSTRACT

This chapter examined the internal control procedures for an organization's purchasing card program. Utilizing the results of the company's most recent audit, it was found that inefficiencies existed in the company's internal control processes. The data provided also indicated that processes and procedures are not currently in place for the acceptable use of the company's credit card. This lack of policies and procedures led to the misappropriation of funds. Theoretical and practical implications were discussed in this chapter. This study reveals how a risk management plan can protect the institution and the employees.

INTRODUCTION

Purchasing credit cards (PCards) provides a cost effective and convenient means for employees to make purchases on behalf of the company. PCards are credit cards given to an employee so they can easily and quickly make purchases for the employer (Kurdziel, 2023). It allows employees to make purchases when needed and saves valuable time that could be spent waiting for a purchase order. They are also very convenient for employees who frequently travel. In addition to saving time by circumventing the procurement process, a well implemented PCard program can also offer savings and rebates.

Along with the convenience that a PCard program can bring to an organization, a level of risk comes with it. Multiple credit cards being used by various employees without appropriate oversight can open the door to unnecessary problems including fraud (Kurdziel, 2023). A financial risk management plan should be in place to protect the institution and all the users involved in the process. A well implemented plan allows the organization to enjoy the convenience that a PCard program allows while not having to worry about misuse of the program. In order to have a successfully run PCard program, policies and

DOI: 10.4018/979-8-3693-1634-4.ch018

procedures need to be put into place and the entire team that is involved in the process needs to be trained on those policies and procedures. The leadership team should support the plan and ensure that all staff members receive the proper training. The internal control process that will be presented in this research will benefit many stakeholders of an organization. Investors of a company will benefit because having sound internal controls in place minimizes risks. Employees would also benefit because they will now have policies and guidelines in place and the expectations of their roles will be clearly defined. The organization as whole will reduce its risks of experiencing a misuse of the PCard program.

CASE STUDY: OVERVIEW

The recent fiscal audit of Blue Oyster Bank (BOB) (fictitious name) identified misuse of the corporate credit card resulting in approximately $1.9M of losses over five years for expenses that are not directly tied to the company. The audit uncovered that 85% of BOB's Vice Presidents and Directors have been using the company's credit card for their personal use. The former CFO brought this issue to the CEO and COO's attention for two years prior to her resignation. It has also been noted that BOB does not have a policy in place regarding the usage of the company's credit card. In addition to a lack of policies and procedures, there is a deficiency in training and checks and balances. The following report will highlight the consequences of not fixing these issues, the impact of the issue on current employees, and a corrective action plan for moving forward.

CURRENT STATE OF BLUE OYSTER BANK AND THEIR EMPLOYEES

BOB can use this event as an opportunity to strengthen its risk management policies and just as importantly, check in with their employees. BOB faced a financial loss as a result of this occurrence. The organization can put controls in place to prevent such losses from occurring in the future. It is also important that they assess the impact of recent events on the staff. Ethical cases such as this one, can impact the work climate. In an ethical work climate, employees feel safe to do what they think is right even if it means speaking up about the wrongdoing of the company (ConnectedTrifecta, 2023). Financial losses impact the whole organization. Building a healthy work climate can be beneficial to all stakeholders. Other ethical decision-making theories that BOB should be aware of are the Fairness/Justice Approach and Virtue Approach.

The *Fairness of Justice Approach* demonstrates that equality is allocated among all groups (Young, 2013). If the parties involved in wrongdoing are not held accountable for their acts, that can leave other employees feeling that justice was not served. All employees should be held to the same standards. Employees should be issued a PCard based on their title and role within the company. If their position does not warrant the use of a card, they should not receive one. Likewise, if the use of the card is abused, those responsible should be held accountable. All employees should be held accountable at the same standards regardless of their title and position in the company. Those standards should be clearly laid out before the card is issued to any employee.

In the *Virtue Approach* we assume that there are certain ideals toward which we should strive, which provide for the full development of our humanity (Velasquez et. al, 2023). Virtue is related to what individuals and organizations desire to be when they become the best (Cameron, Bright and Caza, 2004).

An organization with a higher level of virtue is more successful. It can better cope with its problems (Durmuş & Ünal, 2017). There is a virtue ethics approach to Corporate Social Responsibility (CSR). CSR is a form of self-regulation that reflects a business's accountability and commitment to contributing to the well-being of communities and society through various environmental and social measures (Reckmann, 2023).

The virtue ethics approach to CSR starts with the premise idea that individual virtue is what counts, and that social responsibility is an outworking of individuals exercising the virtues in a corporate setting (McGhee, 2013). Virtue ethics-based CSR can encourage behaviors that can mitigate risk to the greatest extent (Chakrabarty & Bass, 2015). BOB needs to develop a culture of sound virtue and ethics to mitigate unethical individual and corporate behaviors.

NEED FOR CHANGE

An effective way for BOB to avoid financial losses in the future from the PCard program is to implement a risk management strategy and corrective action plan. Before doing so, it may be beneficial for management to understand the *Theory of Constraints* framework as it relates to BOB. The Theory of Constraints is a process improvement methodology developed by Dr. Eliyahu M. Goldratt. The theory emphasizes the importance of identifying the "system constraints" or bottleneck (Theory of Constraints Institute, 2021). A benefit of implementing the Theory of Constraints includes better control over operations and reduced conflict between team members (Theory of Constraints Institute, 2021). For BOB's situation, they must first identify any constraints that are causing inefficiencies or break downs in processes.

The end goal here is for BOB to reduce or eliminate misuse of the PCard by employees. The Theory of Constraints will help BOB identify the problem and thereby work to mitigate it for the future. There are five steps in the Theory of Constraints model:

1. Identify the constraint.
2. Exploit existing resources to improve upon the constraint.
3. Subordinate all other processes to support the constraint.
4. Elevate the constraint by bringing in more resources to support it.
5. Repeat the process to ensure continuous improvement in the process.

(Kuuse, 2021).

BOB has already begun this process through the findings of its recent audit which uncovered some of the deficiencies in the PCard program and process at the company. They are ready to build a corrective action plan.

CORRECTIVE ACTION PLAN

BOB should put a corrective action plan in place in order to avoid another loss in the future. To do so, it is important for the management team to understand the need for such controls. This plan will be a part of BOB's overall risk management strategy as well as its risk minimization plan. A risk management strategy is the process of identifying, analyzing, and treating risks (Spacey, 2017). Risk minimization is the process of reducing a risk exposure towards zero (Spacey, 2017).

The plan is outlined below:

1. Develop a written internal control procedure. Internal controls are designed to protect a company from fraud, abuse and inaccurate data recording and help the organization keep track of essential financial activities (Sani & Chaharmahalie, 2012). The procedure should include the following elements:
    a. Assign the CFO or another manager of the Finance team to be the administrator of the PCard program. The PCard administrator will be responsible for the issuance of the cards and the regular assessment of the program. Card issuance should only be to a limited number of employees and based on job title or role within the organization.
    b. Outline responsibilities of the Accounts Payable (AP) department: The AP department needs to ensure that all supporting documentation is in place before paying the monthly credit card. The AP department must get the signature of the PCard administrator to pay the final invoice. The PCard administrator also holds the responsibility to review the monthly purchases and backup to ensure that they comply with the policy and verify any deviations from the policy that exist. If they do, then disciplinary action must take place as set forth in the policy.
2. Before any cards are issued to employees, the employee must sign a statement that outlines the following:
    a. Allowable uses for the card, including spending limits. Consider lower spending limits- many banks that offer PCard programs allow the administrators to increase thresholds on an as-needed basis. This would be a temporary increase to allow a specific purchase to go through.
    b. Monthly requirements for paperwork from the cardholder (submission of itemized receipts, due dates, sign offs from supervisors, etc.). The cardholder is responsible for justifying their purchases and submitted the backup documentation for each purchase.
    c. Consequences for failure to follow procedures (disciplinary action including termination of employment). This standard needs to be understood and enforced in order to minimize the risk of misappropriated purchases.

BOB may consider using the *Nudge Theory* to urge employees to complete their training and comply with the new paperwork requirements. The Nudge Theory is the psychological approach that explains how we can subtly influence human behavior by offering small cues or "nudges" (Strick, 2023). Something as simple as email reminders stating that paperwork and training must be completed by a certain date or card privileges will be revoked.

3. Implement the *Plan-Do-Check-Adjust/Plan-Do-Check-Act (PDCA)* and make sure that regular internal and external audits take place. The scope of the audit will be to test a sample of PCard purchases that occurred during the year. The auditor will request backup to verify that the purchase was allowable, had the required internal approvals and that all supporting documentation was received.

PDCA is a model that is known for continual improvement that utilizes all four stages of planning, doing, checking, and acting or adjusting accordingly (Sydle, 2021). The internal audit forms an essential part of the 'Check' component of the cycle. (Mark1, 2019). For BOB to be successful in the long-term, they must aim for continuous improvement. This is where having the systems and checkpoints in place will help them be better placed to achieve its goals (Mark1, 2019).

The purpose of the corrective action plan is to help the company improve its processes and minimize risks. However, it is a change for BOB and with change can follow struggles with implementation. The *Bridges Transition Model* helps organizations individuals understand and more effectively manage and work through the personal and human side of change (William Bridges Associates, 2023).

There are three stages during change: Ending What Currently is, The Neutral Zone, and The New Beginning. This is an important concept for management to understand because for change to be successful, leaders need to support its employees through any transition to capitalize on opportunities for innovation and create organizational resilience (William Bridges Associates, 2023). BOB is embarking on some new beginnings that include a new leadership team and an enhanced risk management procedure. By recognizing the three stages of change, the Bridges Transition Model can help the entire team prepare for some new beginnings.

The recommended corrective action plan requires teamwork from all levels of the organization. It requires the cooperation and diligence of all employees that are involved in the PCard process. That includes, management, card users, and members of the finance department that are involved in the administration of the program and processing of payments to vendors. It can be compared to the *Canoe Theory.* The Canoe Theory compares an organization and its members to a canoe and its crew. Like canoes, businesses need every member to "paddle" together for greater success (Hibbard et al, 2007).

FUTURE OF BLUE OYSTER BANK

If BOB implements these steps, they have an opportunity to strengthen its risk management plan and continue to work on protecting not only the company's profits but the culture of the organization as well. BOB needs to keep in mind that past practices can impact the organization, but change is possible. The *Deal and Kennedy Cultural Model* tells states that history is a part of the corporate culture. A shared narrative of the past lays the foundation for corporate culture (MTCT, 2022). The model also identifies four distinct types of cultures that exist: Word hard/play hard, Tough guy/Macho, Bet Your Company, and Process (Seshagiri, 2020). This model can serve as a good starting point for leadership to understand the cultures that exist at BOB as they embark on guiding changes and introducing additional risk mitigation procedures.

BOB should keep in mind that the organizations corporate culture has been impacted by both positive and negative events from the past. However, as the model suggests, the organization needs to think of its corporate culture as an asset that needs to be managed. If BOB continues to assess its critical risk factors and strengthen its internal control system, they will continue to minimize risk and protect its assets. These assets include both people and profits. Control should not be seen as a burden on business but, rather, the means by which business opportunities are maximized and potential losses are reduced (Sani & Chaharmahalie, 2012).

The new leadership of BOB also will play an important role in laying the foundation for the company's future success. The leadership team should set an example of the behavior that is expected of all employees particularly as it pertains to following all policies and procedures. Businesses need to continuously strive to serve and promote a positive outcome for its stakeholders (Chang, 2021).

The *Value-Based Leadership Theory* states that ethical leaders that demonstrate an ethical voice will enhance the understanding of the next-level ethical role requirements thereby incorporating behavioral repertoires in an organizational setting (Chang, 2021). This leadership style and philosophy builds on the shared beliefs and assumptions of the leader and the team hence creating an experience of alignment and benefit from higher productivity (Falcone, 2022). The leadership team at BOB needs to demonstrate by example that they themselves will not take advantage of the new PCard program. They need to be diligent and cooperative with the staff that is responsible for following up with them when they request supporting documentation for purchases on the card. Value-based leadership can be an impactful tool to help guide teams to where we need them to be.

With a refreshed and strong leadership in place, BOB can also focus on a *Transformational Leadership* approach. Transformational Leadership is a leadership approach that causes change in individuals and social systems (Langston.edu, 2021). It can create valuable and positive change in the followers with the end goal of transforming followers into leaders (Langston.edu, 2021).

BOB leaders need to set an example to the organization of what behaviors are acceptable and lead by ethical values and examples. Be the leaders that inspire positive changes and show the team that you are invested in them as well. Transformational leaders help followers grow and develop into leaders by responding to individual followers' needs by empowering them and by aligning the objectives and goals of the individual followers, the leaders, the group, and the larger organization (Ugochukwu, 2023). This is the perfect time to "be the change" and add to the success of yourselves, your people, and the future of BOB.

REFERENCES

Akbolat, M., Durmuş, A. & Ünal, Ö. (2017). Örgütsel erdemliliğin personel güçlendirmeye etkisi ve otantik liderliğin aracı rolü [The effect of organizational virtuousness on employee empowerment and the mediating role of authentic leadership]. *İşletme Bilimi Dergisi, 5*(2), 71-87. doi:10.22139/jobs.322557

Cameron, K. S., Bright, D., & Caza, A. (2004). Exploring the relationships between organizational virtuousness and performance. *The American Behavioral Scientist, 47*(6), 766–790. doi:10.1177/0002764203260209

Chakrabarty, & Bass. (2015). *Comparing virtue, consequentialist, and deontological ethics-based corporate social responsibility: Mitigating microfinance risk institutional voids.* UT Miners. https://utminers.utep.edu/schakrabarty2/Chakrabarty_Bass_2015_JBE.pdf

Chang, S. M., Budhwar, P., & Crawshaw, J. (2021, April 6). *The emergence of value-based leadership behavior at the frontline of management: A role theory perspective and future research agenda.* Frontiers. https://www.frontiersin.org/articles/10.3389/fpsyg.2021.635106/full#refer1

E. M. (@socialworkplace) O., & (@socialworkplace), E. M. (2023, February 25). *How the ethical work climate of your organization can impact employee performance - connected trifecta.* Connected Trifecta - Where people, content and technology are a winning combination. https://connectedtrifecta.com/2021/10/how-the-ethical-work-climate-of-your-organization-can-impact-employee-performance/

Falcone, P. (2022, June 9). *Values-based leadership in action.* SHRM. https://www.shrm.org/resourcesandtools/hr-topics/employee-relations/pages/values-based-leadership-in-action.aspx

Hibbard, D. R., Hibbard, M. S., & Stockman, J. W. (2007). *The Canoe Theory: A Business Success Strategy for Leaders and Associates*. iUniverse.

Kaplan, J. (2022, August 16). *Play your pcards right: Internal controls over purchasing cards*. James Moore. https://www.jmco.com/articles/higher-education/pcard-internal-controls/

Kurdziel, K. (2022, August 16). *Play Your PCards Right: Internal Controls Over Purchasing Cards*. James Moore. https://www.jmco.com/articles/higher-education/pcard-internal-controls/

Kuuse, M. (2021, February 9). *How to use the Theory of Constraints? - mrpeasy*. Blog for Manufacturers and Distributors. https://manufacturing-software-blog.mrpeasy.com/theory-of-constraints/

Langston.edu. (2021). *Transformational Leadership*. Langston. https://www.langston.edu/sites/default/files/basic-content-files/TransformationalLeadership.pdf

Mark Business Systems. (2019, September 10). *The value of the internal audit in a good quality management system*. Mark Business Systems. https://mark1systems.com/the-value-of-the-internal-audit-in-a-good-quality-management-system/

McGhee, P. (2013). Virtue Ethics and CSR. In S. O. Idowu, N. Capaldi, L. Zu, & A. D. Gupta (Eds.), *Encyclopedia of Corporate Social Responsibility*. Springer., doi:10.1007/978-3-642-28036-8_616

MindTools. (2022). Deal and Kennedy's Cultural Model. *Mindtools*. https://www.mindtools.com/avnhbho/deal-and-kennedys-cultural-model

Reckmann, N. (2023, February 21). *What is Corporate Social Responsibility?* Business News Daily. https://www.businessnewsdaily.com/4679-corporate-social-responsibility.html

Sani, A. A., & Chaharmahalie, S. (2012). *Internal accounting controls*. ResearchGate. https://www.researchgate.net/profile/Alireza-Azimisani/publication/353298397_10119427240/links/60f1da2016f9f313008bbbc2/10119427240.pdf

Seshagiri, V. (2020). *Taking Calculated Risks: Deal and Kennedy's Risk and Feedback Model*. LinkedIn. https://www.linkedin.com/pulse/taking-calculated-risks-deal-kennedys-risk-feedback-model-seshagiri

Simplicable. (n.d.). *Risk minimization vs risk management*. Simplicable. https://simplicable.com/risk/risk-minimization-vs-risk-management

Strick, J. (2023, January 25). *Nudge theory: A really useful tool for workplace health and safety*. Health and Safety Software for Enterprises. https://www.ecoportal.com/blog/nudge-theory

Sydle, (2021). PDCA Cycle: *What Are the Stages and How Does It Work?* Sydle. https://www.sydle.com/blog/pdca-cycle-61ba2a15876cf6271d556be9/

Theory of Constraints Institute. (2021). *Theory of Constraints of Eliyahu M. Goldratt*. TOC Institute. https://www.tocinstitute.org/theory-of-constraints.html

Ugochukwu, C.b(2023, April 21). Transformational leadership theory: How to inspire and motivate. *Simply Psychology*. https://www.simplypsychology.org/what-is-transformational-leadership.html

University, S. C. (n.d.). *Thinking ethically*. Markkula Center for Applied Ethics. https://www.scu.edu/ethics/ethics-resources/ethical-decision-making/thinking-ethically/

Young, W. (2013). *Social Justice and fairness*. NAS. https://www.nas.org/blogs/article/social_justice_and_fairness

Chapter 19
The State of Cybersecurity Amidst Global Health Catastrophes:
Analyzing Instances of Threats in the Cyber Realm During the Onset of COVID-19

Andreas Vassilakos
https://orcid.org/0000-0002-6586-6126
Capitol Technology University, USA

Maurice Dawson
Illinois Institute of Technology, USA

Oteng Tabona
https://orcid.org/0000-0002-7334-2189
Botswana International University of Science and Technology, Botswana

Thabiso Maupong
https://orcid.org/0000-0002-0721-885X
Botswana International University of Science and Technology, Botswana

ABSTRACT

The effects of Coronavirus disease at a global level led the years 2020, 2021, and 2022. This global pandemic caused millions of organizations to shift to online workspaces to curb the rising numbers of contaminations. In doing this rapid change from physical to digital spaces, organizations were not adequately prepared for the aftermath. This included more sophisticated phishing attacks, directed scams, and taking advantage of poorly executed processes for the product supply chain. In this chapter, the authors will cover the events and the aftermath of security threats focusing on the onset of the pandemic.

DOI: 10.4018/979-8-3693-1634-4.ch019

INTRODUCTION

Since the first months of 2020, humanity has been facing a pandemic status due to the Coronavirus disease. The Coronavirus disease, or COVID-19, is an infectious disease caused by a novel coronavirus that causes respiratory-related symptoms and spreads through an infected person's droplets of saliva or discharge from the nose when they cough or sneeze (World Health Organization). The most potent weapon against the uncontrollable spread of the disease, along with the vaccination of vulnerable populations, has been the proposed social distancing. That has included keeping physical space between people at least six feet during interactions. Also, it has involved avoiding large crowds interactions and implementing teleworking, moving educational activities to online platforms, avoiding visiting loved ones in person, and canceling or postponing professional meetings and events (Johns Hopkins Medicine). People's reliance on digital mediums and the transition to predominantly electronic platforms has generated the ideal environment for threat agents to take advantage of the flaws of human factor security. It is well known that people are the weakest link in any system. During an already stressful state, it is easier for hackers to take advantage of the existing vulnerable nature of humans; an increased frequency of significant security events has been observed. Therefore, the researchers contribute to the cybersecurity efforts during the major security events of the COVID era by creating a case study analysis focusing on the first two years of the pandemic period.

SOCIAL ENGINEERING AND COVID-19

The implementation of social distancing helped control the pandemic and increased the risk of cybersecurity attacks that take advantage of the human element. The FBI's Internet Crime Complaint Center (IC3) is reported to have received 1,200 complaints related to COVID-19 scams (Abukari & Bankas, 2020). There has been an increase in the use of phishing campaigns, DOS attacks, fake news portals, and applications to deceive individuals and organizations by cyber actors (Abukari & Bankas, 2020). The number of cyber attacks affecting individuals has increased by approximately 41% compared to 4% of crimes against organizations (Buil-Gil et al., 2020). This is mainly because businesses closed temporarily during the lockdown, and individuals spent more time online.

The majority of the attacks were through socio-technical approaches via emails, websites, and mobile apps (Hijji & Alam, 2021). Various mobile applications were created to help disseminate corona updates. However, some applications were developed with malicious intent, such as CovidLock (Khan, Brohi, and Zaman, 2020). CovidLock locks out individuals and demands USD100 in bitcoins within 48 hours (Khan, Brohi, and Zaman, 2020). Also, an application called SMSTrojan was developed to exploit users during the pandemic (Khan, Brohi, and Zaman, 2020). A fake COVID-19 information app alleged to be from WHO was also created to steal browser cookies, passwords, browser history, and transaction information (GoldSparrow, 2020).

Nefarious agents have been taking advantage of techniques that incorporate the concepts of reciprocity, obligation, concession, scarcity, authority, consistency and commitment, liking, social proof, or any combination of these concepts (Hadnagy et al.). In the onset of the pandemic it was expected that future attacks that companies and civilians can potentially face would include websites that provide health practices for COVID-19, phone calls that suggest a family member is hospitalized, or text messages that include links leading to cures for an ill person. Information Technology is considered one of the 16 critical infrastructure sectors identified by the Department of Homeland Security (Cybersecurity and Infrastructure Security Agency). The Presidential Policy Directive 21 identifies the areas whose elements' security is a priority to avoid a massive catastrophic impact on security, national economic security, national public health or safety, and any combination of these (Cybersecurity and Infrastructure Security Agency).

SHIFT TOWARDS TELEWORKING

Due to the lockdown mandates imposed by most governments, organizations had to quickly adapt to the new norm. It was natural to observe a shift towards remote work, and the importance of technology in everyone's professional and personal lives had been magnified (Nabe, n.d.). Some organizations, in response to the Covid-19 pandemic, have adapted and incorporated "innovative organization of work through teleworking, if the job allows for working remotely" (Belzunegui-Eraso & Erro-Garcés, 2020). The shift to a remote workplace during the pandemic has proven to be a challenge as organizations need to enhance their knowledge on this mode of work, and specifically on how to "how to lead effectively and build highly functional virtual teams" (Contreras et al., 2020). With teleworking, organizations were able to mitigate any productivity hurdles during the global healthcare crisis and, but were creating challenges specific to their new work environment. Threat agents could easier target companies thanks to the increasing hybrid or fully remote work environment.

ATTACKS AGAINST EDUCATION

Educational institutions have had to reorient their business model towards remote learning for social distancing purposes during the pandemic. This shift increased the already vulnerable attack surface in the education sector. A report by the National Cyber Security Council (NCSC, 2020) indicates that there was about 69 percent of phishing attacks on schools in the UK in 2020, and 30 percent had been infected by malware (Security Risk Management, 2020). The reports further indicate that only 3 percent of the schools were aware of the breach once it occurred (Security Risk Management, 2020).

The use of online platforms and increased usage of own devices increased the entry point for hackers. The record-breaking number of cyber incidents was across all education institutions worldwide. The K-12 report in the USA states that there was an increase of 18 percent in publicly-disclosed cyber incidents in 2020 (Levin, 2021). The attacks equal more than two incidents per school day. The attacks ranged from less severe to more severe incidents, including school closures, financial losses, and data breaches directly linked to identity theft and credit card fraud. According to K-12 (Levin, 2021) report, 40 percent of cyber attacks were data breaches, 12% were ransomware, 5% were denial of service, 2% were phishing, and 45% were an emerging type of attack named class invasion. Class invasion attacks include unauthorized disruption of class through hate speech, shocking images, sounds, videos, and threats of violence.

Phishing emails have been on the rise. Emails were crafted formally related to the pandemic and could be opened in good faith. For instance, Indian schools reported that email scams and service impersonation against educational institutions were the most common types of attacks during the pandemic period (Barracuda Networks, 2020). Attackers used a Business Email Compromise (BEC) technique using well-known and reputable email providers such as Gmail. According to the Barracuda Networks report, there were over 1,000 cyber attacks in the education sector in India through spear-phishing during this period. Attackers leveraged urgent-looking subject lines such as "COVID-19 News Updates" and "COVID-19 School Meeting" to attract receivers' attention.

In the search for the COVID-19 vaccine, several universities involved in vaccine research were reported to have been attacked by foreign states (Corera, 2020). Toronto's York University was attacked by what is speculated to be ransomware after announcing a $25,000 COVID-19 research fund (IT World Canada, 2020). The attack affected about 15 systems, including Office 365, VPN, and Zoom (IT World Canada, 2020). The attack corrupted collaboration software and financial reports, restricted internet and network connectivity, and compromised the IT phone system (IT World Canada, 2020).

HEALTHCARE UNDER SIEGE

During the first months of lockdowns taking place in most countries worldwide, a surge in the instances of cybersecurity breaches was observed. Therefore, the researchers used data provided by the Office for Civil Rights of the U.S. Department of Health and Human Services to analyze reported healthcare breaches (U. S. Department of health & human services—Office for civil rights, n.d.). According to the data source, "As required by section 13402(e)(4) of the HITECH Act, the Secretary must post a list of breaches of unsecured protected health information affecting 500 or more individuals." The data source covers all reported breached cases that are under investigation by the Office for Civil Rights in the timeframe from 11/19/18 to 11/06/2020 (U. S. Department of health & human services—Office for civil rights, n.d.). It should be noted that the dataset might not accurately represent the actual picture due to the policy of affected parties required to disclose only breaches affecting more than 500 individuals.

After implementing data science methodologies, the researchers observed that the top three states with the most reported cases were Texas, New York, California, Florida, and Ohio, with 69, 53, 52, 35, and 31 number of cases accordingly (Figure 1).

Figure 1. Reported breaches by state
(Authors, 2023)

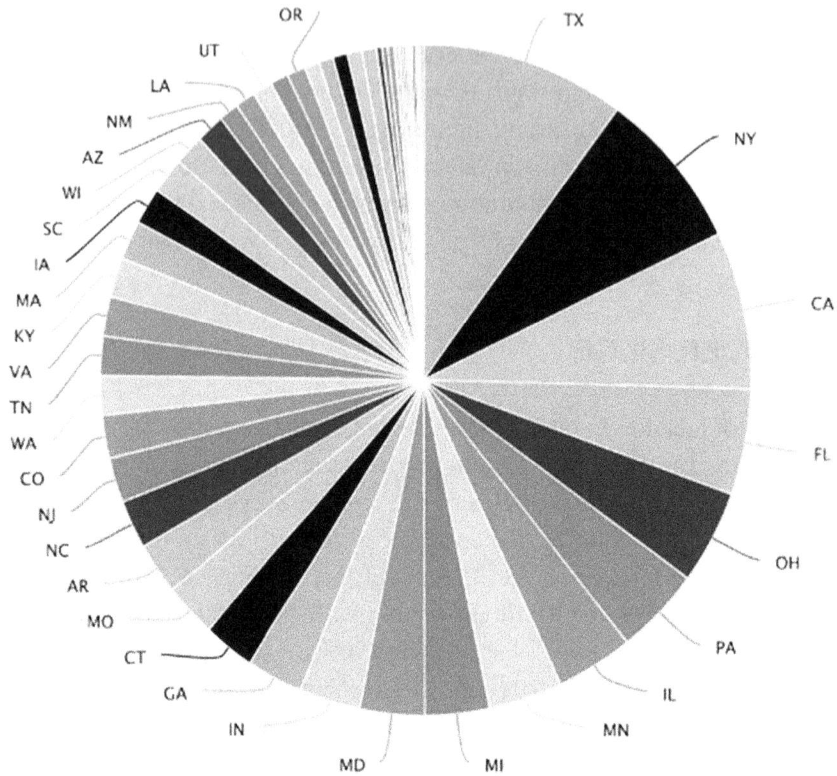

The data analysis showed that the top five observed locations of breached information were email, network server, paper/films, other, Electronic Medical Record, with 261, 197, 51, 39, and 25 number of cases accordingly (Figure 2).

Figure 2. Count of breaches by location of information
(Authors, 2023)

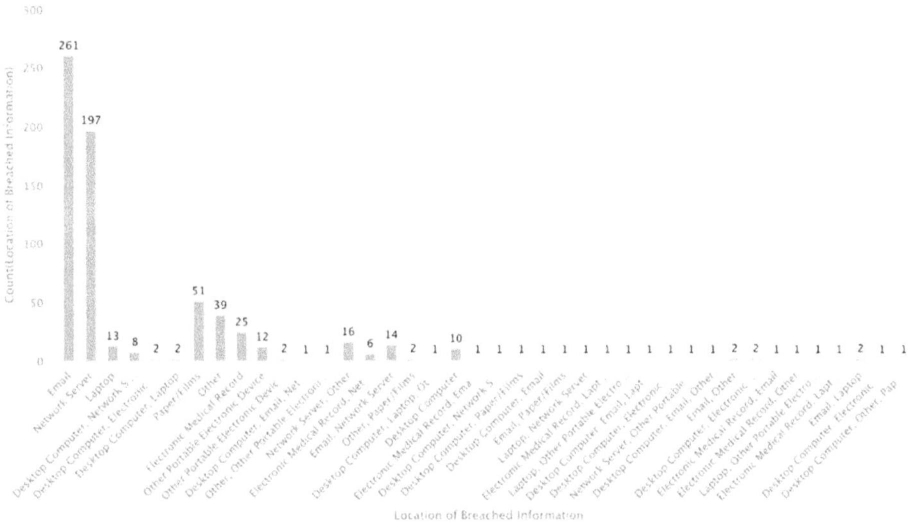

The researchers observed that the entity type reporting the highest number of breaches was Healthcare Providers, with a total of 557 cases (Figure 3). Business Associates and Health Plans followed with 73 and 55 cases, accordingly. Healthcare Clearing Houses reported 2 cases (Figure 3). Healthcare providers possess a massive amount of crucial information in the form of EHR, PHI, and e-PHI. The data contains sensitive information such as biometrics and records on patients' disabilities and conditions that can be used to cause damage, violate privacy, and promote nefarious agendas against those inflicted.

Figure 3. Count of entities breached by type
(Authors, 2023)

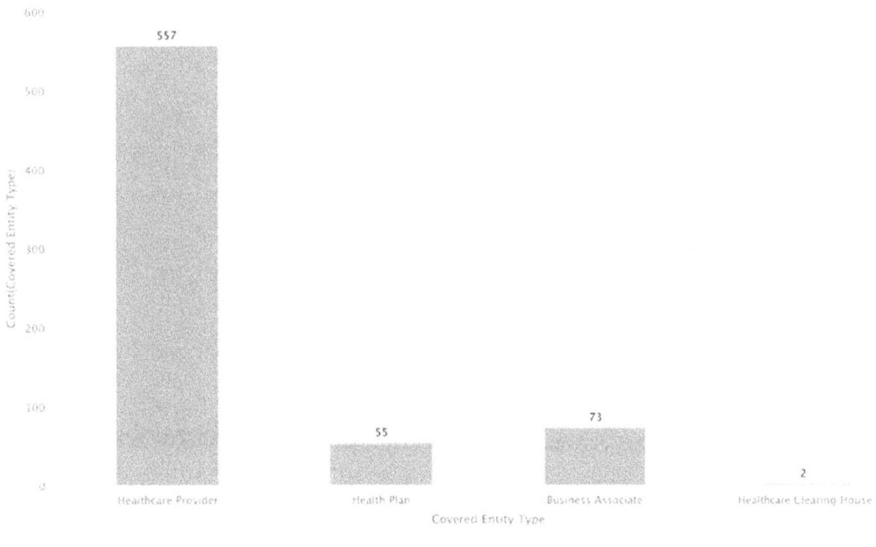

In the timeframe following 1/31/2020, which was the official public health emergency announcement by the Secretary of Health and Human Services (HHS) (White House, 2020), it is observed that the number of reported breaches increased. The researchers observed that the highest occurrence of reported healthcare breaches happened on 09/14/2020 after most states imposed lockdowns and most organizations and companies shifted predominantly to teleworking (Figure 4).

Figure 4. Reported breaches by date
(Authors, 2023)

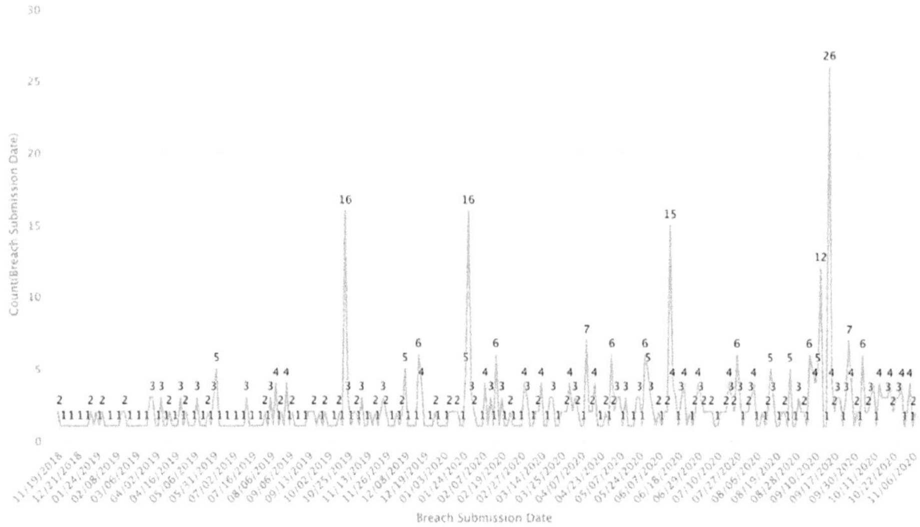

According to the number of reported cases, the five types of breaches in descending order are Hacking/IT Incident, Unauthorized Access/Disclosure, Theft, Loss, Improper Disposal with counts of 490 134, 38, 13, 12 accordingly (Figure 5). Hacking/IT incidents and Unauthorized Access/Disclosure were the two top types, which the researchers expected due to the surge of cyber attacks reported in news outlets.

Figure 5. Types of breaches
(Authors, 2023)

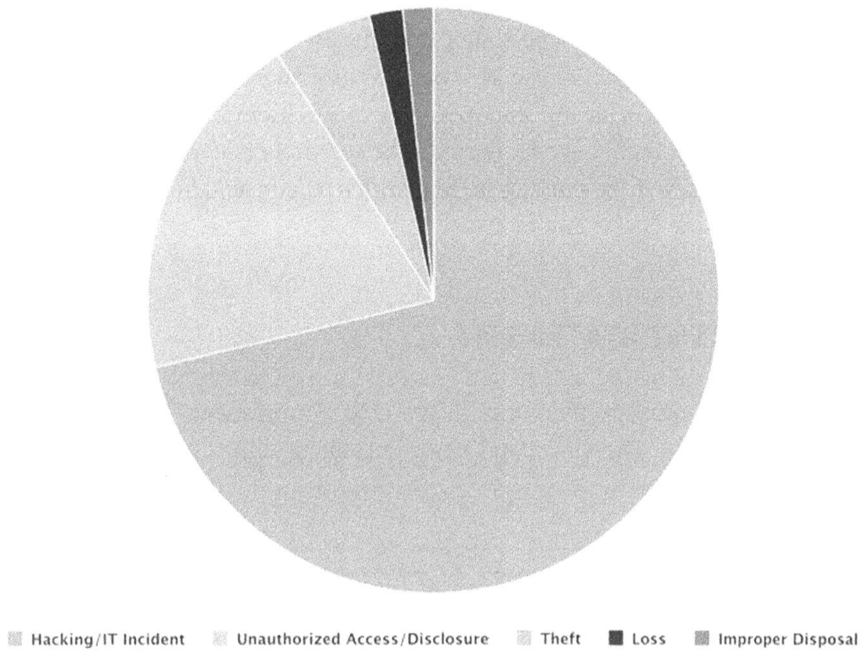

A patient in Germany was forced to be moved to a different hospital in early September due to a ransomware attack, which resulted in their death (NBC News, 2020). Many hospitals in New York, Nebraska, Ohio, Missouri, and Michigan have been targeted by ransomware in 2020 (CNN, 2020). Attacks like these have been increasingly being reported in news outlets since the COVID-19 global pandemic's offset.

As the data analysis proves, Cybersecurity incidents are becoming progressively more prevalent. During a global health crisis, the Healthcare sector is one of the priorities any country would have to protect its civilians' safety.

DDOS ATTACKS

Distributed Denial of Service (DDoS) attacks increased in frequency, intensity, and complexity during the COVID-19 pandemic (A10 Networks, 2020). DDoS attacks are reported to have increased by 12% within the second half of 2020 (Hope (2021), Khan (2021)). The increase of devices connected to the network (IoT), the shift to working remotely from home, online shopping, and improved connectivity contributed to the increase in the number of DDoS (Khan (2021), Hope (2021)). This is because hackers had more targets than ever before COVID-19. During COVID-19, we witnessed the most significant DDoS attack of 2.3Tbps toward Amazon Web Service (AWS) (Nicholson, 2020). The attack is a hopping increase of 70% from the previous significant attack in 2018 (Nicholson, 2020).

CONCLUSION

The unprecedented times humanity has been experiencing due to the catastrophic impact of the Coronavirus pandemic has proven to be also a period of opportunity for nefarious actors in the cyber realm. Cybersecurity attacks, either through the use of social engineering or more sophisticated vectors, have affected every sector. Combined with the imposed remote work environment, attacks against healthcare, education, and remote workers have increased. The researchers explored the impact of Covid on cybersecurity for the first years of the pandemic. In addition, the researchers conducted a data analysis of threats as they pertain to the healthcare industry.

CONFLICT OF INTEREST STATEMENT

The research item does not represent the views of the U.S. Government, Department of State, or any other U.S. Government agency. The views and work presented within this item strictly represent the authors' academic work.

REFERENCES

A10 Networks. (2020). *The State of DDoS Weapons (H2 2020)*. A10 Networks. https://www.a10networks.com/wp-content/uploads/A10-EB-The-State-of-DDoS-Weapons-Report.pdf

Abukari, A. M., & Bankas, E. K. (2020). Some cyber security hygienic protocols for teleworkers in COVID-19 pandemic period and beyond. *International Journal of Scientific and Engineering Research*, *11*(4), 1401–1407.

Belzunegui-Eraso, A., & Erro-Garcés, A. (2020). Teleworking in the context of the covid-19 crisis. *Sustainability (Basel)*, *12*(9), 3662. doi:10.3390u12093662

Buil-Gil, D., Miró-Llinares, F., Moneva, A., Kemp, S., & Díaz-Castaño, N. (2020). Cybercrime and shifts in opportunities during COVID-19: A preliminary analysis in the UK. *European Societies*, 1–13.

Contreras, F., Baykal, E., & Abid, G. (2020). E-leadership and teleworking in times of covid-19 and beyond: What we know and where do we go. *Frontiers in Psychology*, *11*, 590271. https://www.frontiersin.org/articles/10.3389/fpsyg.2020.590271. doi:10.3389/fpsyg.2020.590271 PMID:33362656

Corera, G. (2020, May 5). Coronavirus: Cyber-spies hunt Covid-19 research, US and UK warn. *BBC News*. https://www.bbc.com/news/technology-52551023

Cybersecurity and Infrastructure Security Agency. (n.d.). *Identifying Critical Infrastructure During COVID-19*. CISA. https://www.cisa.gov/identifying-critical-infrastructure-during-covid-19

GoldSparrow. (2020). *Oski Stealer*. Enigma Software. https://www.enigmasoftware.com/oskistealer-removal/.

Hadnagy, C., & Wozniak, S. (2018). *Social Engineering The Science of Human Hacking*. John Wiley & Sons, Incorporated. doi:10.1002/9781119433729

Hijji, M., & Alam, G. (2021). A Multivocal Literature Review on Growing Social Engineering Based Cyber-Attacks/Threats During the COVID-19 Pandemic: Challenges and Prospective Solutions. *IEEE Access : Practical Innovations, Open Solutions*, *9*, 7152–7169. doi:10.1109/ACCESS.2020.3048839 PMID:34786300

Hope, A. (2021, January 29). DDoS Attacks Increased Rapidly During the COVID-19 Pandemic as Hackers Exploited New Tools and Techniques. *CPO Magazine*. https://www.cpomagazine.com/cyber security/ddos-attacks-increased-rapidly-during-the-covid-19-pandemic-as-hackers-exploited-new-tools-and-techniques/

IT World Canada. (2020, May 6). York University cyber attack looks like ransomware, says security expert. *Financialpost*. https://financialpost.com/technology/tech-news/york-university-cyber-attack-looks-like-ransomware-says-security-expert

Johns Hopkins Medicine. (n.d.). *Coronavirus, Social Distancing and Self-Quarantine*. Johns Hopkins Medicine. https://www.hopkinsmedicine.org/health/conditions-and-diseases/coronavirus/coronavirus-social-distancing-and-self-quarantine

Khan, B. (2021, February 10). DDoS attacks intensify — Driven in part by COVID-19 and 5G. *Security magazine*. https://www.securitymagazine.com/articles/94570-ddos-attacks-intensify-driven-in-part-by-covid-19-and-5g

Khan, N. A., Brohi, S. N., & Zaman, N. (2020). *Ten deadly cyber security threats amid COVID-19 pandemic*.

Levin, D. A. (2021). *The State of K-12 Cybersecurity: 2020 Year in Review*. EdTech Strategies/K-12 Cybersecurity Resource Center and the K12 Security Information Exchange. Available online at: https://k12cybersecure.com/year-in-review/

Nabe, C. (n.d.). *Impact of covid-19 on cybersecurity*. Deloitte Switzerland. https://www2.deloitte.com/ch/en/pages/risk/articles/impact-covid-cybersecurity.html

Nicholson, P. (2020, December 8). AWS hit by Largest Reported DDoS Attack of 2.3 Tbps. *A10 Networks*. https://www.a10networks.com/blog/aws-hit-by-largest-reported-ddos-attack-of-2-3-tbps/

Security Risk Management, & Amstrong, I. (2020, October 9). *The perfect storm created by COVID-19: why the education sector needs to shift its cyber security focus*. Security Risk Management. https://www.srm-solutions.com/blog/the-perfect-storm-created-by-covid-19-why-the-education-sector-needs-to-shift-its-cyber-security-focus/

Whitman, M. E., & Mattford, H. J. (2019). *Management of information security*. Cengage Learning.

World Health Organization. (n.d.). *Coronavirus*. WHO. https://www.who.int/health-topics/coronavirus

Chapter 20
Reimagining Healthcare:
Medical Grade and Non-Medical Grade Wearables and New Cybersecurity Risks

Kim L. Brown-Jackson
https://orcid.org/0000-0001-9231-2076
Capitol Technology University, USA

ABSTRACT

Wearable biosensors are garnering substantial interest due to their potential to provide continuous, real-time health information via dynamic, noninvasive measurements of biochemical markers in biofluids, such as sweat, tears, oxygen levels, blood sugar levels, heart rate, and saliva, often through real-time Internet-connected health devices. Integrating biosensors into a system of internet-of-things (IoT) is essential for the progress of healthcare and medical monitoring as a function of a growing proactive instead of reactive patient-centered healthcare perspective. This use of technology also encompasses some information security risks. This chapter explores the nature of those risks and the utility of these monitoring tools.

INTRODUCTION

The wearable technology industry is growing rapidly, with an estimated market value of USD 460.25 billion by 2029 (Data Bridge, 2022). While wearables offer many benefits, they also present significant risks, including physical and virtual risks such as data security, interoperability, usability, and human factors. Organizations must take measures to protect wearables to ensure the safety of individuals and organizations. The path to digital health innovation has been one of incremental gains. The healthcare industry has long been touted as one that will be changed by digital technology. It is clear that we are at the start of this development from public policy, data management, privacy, and cybersecurity perspectives and empowering patients to be at the center of their own healthcare through access to self-management tools. A greater focus on preventative care will be the major theme of this transformation. This patient empowerment is possible thanks to new, digital technology like wearables, big data, or internet-of-things (IoT). Wearable sensors are becoming widespread in healthcare and biomedical monitoring systems to

DOI: 10.4018/979-8-3693-1634-4.ch020

respond adaptively to the health needs of aging populations, rising healthcare costs, and chronic diseases. This chapter explores and defines project risk, data collection, application, understanding, and behavior in the cybersecurity environment, as well as the impacts of these activities. Following the introduction, the reader will go over the background material, which will contain information about risk and how it pertains to cybersecurity. The issue statement is followed by the significance of the research, methodology, research theories and framework, literature review, suggestions, conclusions, and solutions, and references.

BACKGROUND

Biosensors and chemical sensors based on microelectromechanical systems (MEMS) technology have been developed to replace expensive and complex analytical devices in healthcare with compact and widely used sensors for healthcare applications. Integrating biosensors into a system of IoT is essential for the progress of healthcare and medical monitoring as a function of a growing proactive instead of reactive patient-centered healthcare perspective. Electrochemical sensors are beginning to be used in various analytical, medical diagnostic, and screening applications because of their high performance, portability, simplicity, and low cost. Many flexible, wearable and detachable sensors have been developed and commercialized to monitor relevant sports, healthcare, and medicine parameters.

Internet of Things (IoT), electronic devices that can be linked via internet networks, technology allows for the high visibility of wearable devices. Wearable devices are prevailing from healthcare to biomedical monitoring systems (Valentinuzzi, 2020). Wearables are novel mobile devices that continue to advance in acceptance mid consumers globally because of wearable multipurpose applications (Borowski-Beszta & Polasik, 2020). Another name for wearable devices is wearable technology, which is explained as innovative computing technologies that users and consumers wear (Jacobs et. al, 2019). Wearables used for healthcare allow constant measures regarding urgent biomarkers for medical analytics, physiological healthcare checking, and assessment (Rodgers et al., 2019; Valentinuzzi, 2020).

The concept of wearables is not new. The first actual wearables were created by Walter Huth, introduced in May of 1938, and required a battery pack (Valentinuzzi, 2020; Washington University School of Medicine, 2009) and an understanding has resulted in healthcare organizations with vulnerabilities within their systems (Burton, 2021). Today's wearable devices are significant because they are associated with individuals and IoT via straightforward contact with the body and clothing.

Today, wearables can be on the wrist, face, or within the body listed in Figure 1, Embedded Technology Locations. Also, the past decades rendered the incredible creation of electronics, biocompatible materials, and nanomaterials that brought about in the growth of implantable tools which allow analysis to gain opinion and forecast via small sensors and biomedical tools and momentously enhance the superiority and effectiveness of medical services.

Figure 1. Embedded technology locations
Source: Adapted by Dr. Kim L Brown

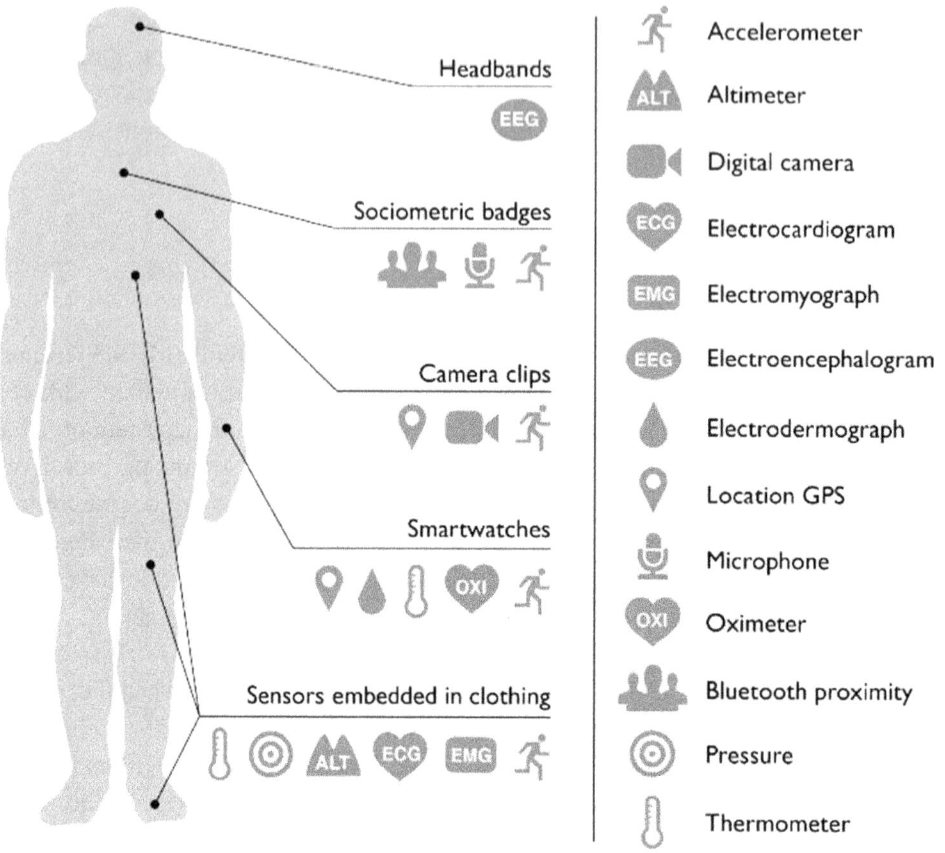

PROBLEM STATEMENT

Patients and users are concerned that in-person appointments and viewings will increase the likelihood of contracting Coronavirus Disease 2019 (COVID-19) (Shah, 2021; Fui, 2021). Yet, healthcare wearables and patients' and users' concerns are not that straightforward. Before fully embracing digitalization, healthcare cybersecurity experts should grasp digital security, since intended consumers would not be ready to utilize digital channels if cybersecurity cannot be ensured (Brown-Jackson, 2022). Federal law mandates that businesses (healthcare and banks) must be sure cybersecurity leaders at all levels comprehend information-security tools, technologies, and programs. A void of understanding has resulted in healthcare organizations with vulnerabilities within their systems (Burton, 2021).

SIGNIFICANCE OF THE RESEARCH

Wearable technology has the potential to improve public health readiness and health status monitoring. The relevance and interest in the quick deployment of wearable devices for contact tracing and early detection of COVID-19 to respond to the present epidemic is one such use case. Yet, cybersecurity and privacy policy issues must be considered throughout wearables research, development, implementation, usage, sharing, and storage. A salient point to consider are the pertinent legislation, regulations, and policies related to the use of wearables for COVID-19 applications, as well as the obstacles and suggestions connected with their usage.

Wearable technologies, both medical-grade and non-medical-grade, offer several benefits for health status monitoring and improving public health readiness. Medical-grade wearables, such as ECG moni tors, can provide accurate and reliable health data, leading to early detection of health conditions and better disease management (Zhang et al., 2020). Non-medical-grade wearables, such as fitness trackers, can provide insights into physical activity and sleep patterns, which can help individuals make informed decisions about their lifestyle and overall health (Kooiman et al., 2015; Yadav & Singh, 2021). Several studies suggest that technology wearables can save lives by detecting early signs of health issues and improving disease management. For instance, a study by Aziz et al. (2019) found that a wearable device that monitored heart rate variability could predict adverse cardiac events and potentially prevent sudden cardiac death. Another study by Liao et al. (2021) found that a wearable sensor could detect COVID-19 symptoms early and accurately, enabling prompt intervention and reducing the spread of the disease.

However, the use of technology wearables for healthcare applications requires careful consideration of regulatory and policy issues, including data privacy, security, and ownership (Wen et al., 2020). Additionally, there are concerns about the accuracy and reliability of wearables, as well as potential biases in data collection and analysis (Kooiman et al., 2015; Yadav & Singh, 2021). Therefore, it is essential to establish appropriate guidelines and standards for the development and use of technology wearables in healthcare.

While these operational contexts focus on COVID-19 applications of wearables, they can also be extrapolated more broadly to general infection detection. As such, many of the policies and regulations discussed here may be relevant for the use of wearables in response to infection for larger biodefense strategies. The use of artificial intelligence (AI) in the Petya malware attack highlights the increasing sophistication of cyber-attacks and the potential for AI to be used as a tool for malicious purposes. This incident raises concerns about the security of computer systems and the need for improved cybersecurity measures to prevent such attacks from happening in the future (Ruef, 2019).

The Petya malware attack is just one example of the growing threat of cyber attacks, which can have serious consequences for individuals, businesses, and governments alike. In response, there has been a push for greater investment in cybersecurity research and development, as well as increased collaboration between industry, government, and academic institutions (Sarker et al., 2021). Despite these efforts, the threat of cyber attacks continues to grow, as hackers become increasingly sophisticated and new technologies such as AI are developed and deployed. As such, there is an urgent need for ongoing research and innovation in the field of cybersecurity, to ensure that we are able to stay ahead of the evolving threat landscape (Khurana et al., 2020).

METHODOLOGY

This chapter is a content analysis of theoretical literature and a literature review. A literature review is a comprehensive and systematic analysis of existing research and scholarly articles related to a specific topic. It is an essential part of academic research, as it allows researchers to identify knowledge gaps, evaluate existing literature, and provide a theoretical framework for their own research (Levy & Ellis,

2021). Content analysis, on the other hand, is a research method that involves analyzing and interpreting communication messages to identify patterns and themes (Neuendorf, 2019).

The benefits of conducting a literature review and content analysis are numerous. Firstly, it enables researchers to identify existing knowledge gaps in a particular field and identify areas for further research (Tranfield, Denyer, & Smart, 2019). Secondly, it provides a foundation for the development of research questions and hypotheses (Greenhalgh & Peacock, 2019). Thirdly, it enables researchers to evaluate the quality and validity of existing research and identify any inconsistencies or contradictions in the literature (Hart, 2019).

Moreover, content analysis can provide researchers with a deeper understanding of how particular topics are discussed in the media or other communication channels (Neuendorf, 2019). It can also be used to identify trends and patterns in language use, which can be useful in analyzing social or cultural phenomena (Mullins, 2022).

In summary, the benefits of conducting a literature review and content analysis are many, including identifying knowledge gaps, developing research questions and hypotheses, evaluating the quality of existing research, and gaining a deeper understanding of how particular topics are discussed in the media. Therefore, they are essential tools for any academic research.

An orderly literature exploration ensued that concerned a methodical examination. More than 200 peer-reviewed documents were examined. The primary keywords and phrases included search healthcare technology wearables and COVID-19, healthcare technology wearables and cybersecurity, digital technology and healthcare wearables, wearables sensor technology, and digital healthcare. Secondary search words and phrases included medical grade wearable, non-medical grade wearables, organizational cybersecurity plans, mobile phone cybersecurity plans, wearable biosensors, biomedical monitoring, and regulatory guidance for wearables. The databases searched along with their hosts are as follows Medline, PubMed, Embase, Ebook, and First Research. Academic databases supported a level of surety regarding located data. These databases allowed the location of primary and secondary resources that permitted a level of verification with respect to the influence of the information found to include the information relevancy to the topic.

RESEARCH THEORIES AND FRAMEWORKS

Two theories are applied to this study; the Transformational Leadership Theory, and the Technology Acceptance Model (TAM). Theories and frameworks are essential components of research as they provide a systematic way of organizing and analyzing data and supporting the interpretation of results. The use of theories and frameworks helped this researcher to identify relevant literature, synthesize information, interpret results, and enhance the credibility of the research.

The Transformational Leadership Theory and the Technology Acceptance Model (TAM) provide a conceptual framework that used to guide the research process, supporting reviewing researchers to understand the interrelationships between different concepts (Makridakis, 2021; Schneider & Ingram, 2017). The theories supported the identification of relevant literature related to their research topic (Fridman et al., 2021; Hansen et al., 2017). Also, the theories laid a foundation for a systematic way of synthesizing information, and helping this researcher to identify patterns and relationships between different research points (Hancock, Curry, & Gulliford, 2018). The application of the given theories supported this researcher in interpreting the results of this qualitative research, providing a theoretical lens through which to understand the findings (Braun & Clarke, 2019). The theories helped to enhance the credibility of this study by providing a systematic and rigorous approach to research that is grounded in established theoretical principles (Huang & Zhang, 2022; Joshi & Mithas, 2017). Overall, the use of theories and frameworks is essential for conducting rigorous and meaningful research that contributes to the advancement of knowledge in a particular field.

Transformational Leadership Theory

Transformational leaders are those who inspire and motivate their followers to achieve their goals by focusing on a shared vision and fostering a sense of collaboration and empowerment (Bass & Riggio, 2020). In the context of healthcare wearables, transformational leadership can help healthcare providers and patients work together to improve patient outcomes. Transformational leadership theory, developed by James MacGregor Burns in 1978, argued that transformational leaders are able to inspire and motivate their followers by appealing to their values, beliefs, and aspirations. This theory emphasizes inspiring and motivating followers to achieve their highest potential and the organization's goals through the use of charisma, vision, and intellectual stimulation. It has been linked to the successful management of medical-grade and non-medical-grade wearables (Chen, 2018; Nguyen et al., 2019).

One benefit of transformational leadership is its ability to promote innovation and creativity. Leaders who employ this style encourage their team members to think critically and develop new ideas, which can be particularly helpful in the development and management of wearable technology. Additionally, transformational leaders prioritize communication and collaboration, which are essential components of successful wearables management (Bie et al., 2020; Kim et al., 2021). Furthermore, transformational leaders can create a culture of trust and respect, which can increase employee engagement and motivation. This can result in improved performance and productivity in managing wearables, including better maintenance of medical-grade wearables and more efficient handling of non-medical grade wearables (Klincová, 2017; Wang & Cheng, 2018).

A study by Abdollahi et al. (2021) found that transformational leadership positively affects healthcare professionals' attitudes and behaviors towards technology adoption, which includes the use of medical-grade wearables. In another study by Al-Dmour et al. (2020), transformational leadership was found to positively affect the adoption and implementation of digital healthcare technologies, which include wearables. Moreover, transformational leadership has been linked to improved patient outcomes in healthcare settings. For example, a study by Karami, et al., 2020 found that transformational leadership positively influenced patient safety culture in hospitals. In another study by Waheed et al. (2019), transformational leadership was found to positively affect patient satisfaction with healthcare services.

Ultimately, transformational leadership has significant benefits for managing both medical-grade and non-medical-grade wearables. It promotes innovation, collaboration, employee engagement, and improved patient outcomes. Future research could explore the specific strategies that transformational leaders can use to manage wearables effectively.

Critiques For Transformational Leadership Theory

Transformational leadership is not without its critiques. This leadership has been widely studied and has been recognized as an effective leadership style in various industries (Bass & Riggio, 2020; Leithwood et al., 2017). However, it also has its negative aspects, which need to be taken into account when considering its application to medical grade and non medical grade wearables. One criticism is that it can create a dependency on the leader, leading to a lack of initiative and creativity among followers (Liu et al., 2021).

In the context of medical-grade wearables, this could be problematic as healthcare professionals may become overly reliant on the technology and fail to exercise their own clinical judgment (Klein et al., 2019). A transformational leader who is too involved in the decision-making process of wearable technology may impede the user's ability to make their own choices. Additionally, the emphasis on individualized consideration in transformational leadership may not be applicable to all users of wearables. For instance, medical-grade wearables may require a more standardized approach to ensure accurate and reliable data collection (Brennan et al., 2020). Another criticism of transformational leadership is that it may not be suitable for all situations or contexts. Some researchers argue that transactional leadership may be more effective in certain settings, such as in emergency or high-stress situations (Van Dyne & Ang, 2018). This could be relevant for non-medical-grade wearables, which may be used in a variety of settings with different levels of stress or urgency. Additionally, there is concern that transformational leadership may be too focused on the leader's vision, potentially leading to a lack of consideration for other perspectives (Wang & Chen, 2017). In the context of wearables, this could be problematic if the leader's vision for the technology does not align with the needs or preferences of users. Thus, the application of transformational leadership in this context may not be effective.

Finally, transformational leadership may not be suitable for non-medical-grade wearables that are marketed to the general public. Research has shown that transformational leadership can lead to a focus on short-term gains rather than long-term sustainability (Avolio et al., 2018). This could result in wearables that prioritize immediate gratification over sustained health benefits. To sum up, while transformational leadership has its strengths, its negative aspects must also be considered when applying it to wearable technology. The appropriateness of this leadership style depends on the context in which the wearables are being used.

Technology Acceptance Model (TAM)

The Technology Acceptance Model (TAM) was developed by Fred Davis in 1989 to explain how individuals adopt and use technology based on their perceived usefulness and ease of use (Davis, 1989). The TAM has been widely used in the field of information systems and has been applied to various technologies, including wearable devices.

In the context of medical-grade and non-medical-grade wearable teams, the TAM can be used to understand how users perceive the usefulness and ease of use of these technologies (Liang et al., 2020). For example, if medical-grade wearable teams want to encourage the adoption of their devices, they can focus on emphasizing the usefulness of the devices for monitoring health and detecting potential issues early on, as well as making the devices easy to use for patients and healthcare providers. On the other hand, non-medical-grade wearable teams may focus on emphasizing the convenience and entertainment value of their devices to promote adoption by consumers.

The benefits of using the TAM include providing a framework for understanding user behavior and attitudes toward technology, identifying factors that influence technology adoption, and guiding the design and implementation of technology to improve user acceptance and adoption (Venkatesh et al., 2003). According to Alalwan, Dwivedi, and Rana (2019), the TAM provides a theoretical foundation for understanding the factors that influence technology adoption and usage. It also helps to identify the user's perceptions of the technology and their intention to use it. Moreover, the TAM guides the design and implementation of technology to improve user acceptance and adoption. Perceived usefulness refers to the extent to which an individual believes that using technology will enhance their performance and productivity. Perceived ease of use refers to the degree to which an individual believes that technology will be easy to learn and use. According to the TAM, these two factors have a direct impact on an individual's attitude toward using technology, which, in turn, influences their actual behavior (Brown-Jackson, 2017; Nikou & Economides, 2021). Overall, the Technology Acceptance Model provides a useful framework for understanding the complex factors that influence technology adoption and use. By understanding the factors that influence user behavior, organizations can design and implement technologies that are more likely to be adopted and accepted by their users.

Critiques For Technology Acceptance Model (TAM) Theory

The Technology Acceptance Model (TAM) has been criticized for its limited scope, lack of attention to contextual factors, and reliance on self-reported measures of technology use and adoption (Venkatesh et al, ng, 2019). One critique of TAM is its limited ability to capture the complex nature of technology use, as it only considers two factors (perceived usefulness and perceived ease of use) in determining users' acceptance of technology (Venkatesh et al., 201). The model also does not address the potential barriers to technology adoption, such as lack of training and support, which can hinder users' ability to use technology effectively (Karahanna, et al., 999; Wang, Zhang, & Liang, 2022). Two additional criticisms of the Technology Acceptance Model (TAM) are its failure to account for the dynamic nature of technology and the limited consideration of emotional and social factors in technology adoption.

First, the TAM has been criticized for its static approach to technology, which fails to account for the dynamic nature of technological innovation (Sun, Cao, & Fang, 2021). Technological advancements are constantly changing, and user perceptions and behaviors toward technology are influenced by these changes. Therefore, a static model such as the TAM may not be able to fully capture the complexity of technology adoption in the current dynamic environment.

Second, the TAM has also been criticized for its limited consideration of emotional and social factors that can influence technology adoption (Pavlou & Fygenson, 2019). Emotional factors such as enjoyment, satisfaction, and anxiety have been found to have a significant impact on technology adoption. Similarly, social factors such as peer influence and social norms also play a crucial role in shaping individuals' technology adoption decisions. However, the TAM does not account for these factors in its theoretical framework.

When it comes to medical-grade and non-medical-grade wearables, the TAM can still be applied as a framework for understanding users' attitudes and intentions toward using such devices. However, there may be additional factors at play, such as perceived risk and trust in the device's accuracy and reliability, particularly for medical-grade wearables (Chang, et al., 2020). One major problem with applying the TAM to wearables is that it was originally developed for understanding users' acceptance of desktop computing technology (Venkatesh & Davis, 2000), and may not fully capture the unique features and challenges of wearable devices. Additionally, there may be cultural and societal factors that influence users' attitudes and intentions that are not accounted for in the TAM (Venkatesh et al., 2019).

LITERATURE REVIEW

This literature review will explore wearable's positives and disadvantages, the influence of technology on healthcare wearables, technology wearables, cybersecurity risks, organizational leadership, and cybersecurity leadership. This review ascertains the connection of publications in perspective of their contributions to the subject matter. Covered are evolving technological examples like wearable devices and the IoT, which are able to boost the discovery rates of health risks to increase the overall quality of life. Wearables aid as instruments for finding and measuring physiological considerations for the purpose of ascertaining advancement, boundaries, and ranges of occasion for the creation of structures for monitoring health (Man et al., 2021; Olmedo-Aguirre et al., 2022

What are Wearables and Their Significance?

The integration of wearable technology in healthcare has gained momentum, thanks to its potential to provide new avenues for monitoring and managing health conditions. Wearables typically incorporate sensors that monitor vital signs such as heart rate, blood pressure, and oxygen levels, and advancements in technology have increased the potential for these devices to improve patient outcomes and support healthcare providers. Leaders in healthcare must understand the benefits of wearable technology and leverage them in their decision-making process to enhance patient care.

Continuous monitoring of patients is a key benefit of healthcare wearables. Wearable devices that track vital signs provide real-time feedback on the patient's health status, making it particularly useful for individuals with chronic conditions such as diabetes, hypertension, or heart disease. This real-time data enables patients and healthcare providers to identify potential issues before they become serious, allowing for timely intervention (Chou, Hsu, & Huang, 2019). In addition to continuous monitoring, healthcare wearables support the shift from reactive to proactive healthcare delivery. With continuous tracking of patient health data, healthcare providers can detect changes or trends in a patient's health status that may require intervention, resulting in improved patient outcomes and reduced healthcare costs associated with hospitalization or emergency care (Kilinc, 2019).

Furthermore, the use of wearables can facilitate patient engagement and empowerment. Patients who wear wearables are better informed about their health status, and this information can help them make informed decisions about their healthcare needs. Additionally, wearables can foster patient self-management and adherence to treatment plans (Klonoff, 2017; Sanches, 2021). However, the integration of wearables in healthcare requires effective leadership. Leaders must have a clear understanding of the technology and the potential benefits to patients and healthcare providers. They must also ensure that healthcare wearables comply with privacy regulations, protect sensitive patient data, and integrate with existing healthcare systems (Aminikhanghahi & Cook, 2018).

Leaders must also address issues related to the reliability and accuracy of wearable data. Wearables are not always 100% accurate, and healthcare providers must carefully evaluate the data provided by these devices to ensure that it is reliable and trustworthy (Hernandez et al., 2018). While non-medical grade wearables can provide useful information about physical activity, sleep, and other health-related metrics, they should not be used as a substitute for medical advice or treatment.

Leaders must provide training to healthcare providers on how to use the technology effectively and integrate the data into clinical decision-making processes (Kilinc, 2019). In conclusion, the use of wearable technology in healthcare has the potential to transform patient care and improve health outcomes.

Healthcare leaders must understand the benefits of healthcare wearables and effectively integrate them into clinical decision-making processes. By doing so, they can improve patient engagement, empower patients to manage their health, and support a proactive approach to healthcare delivery.

Pre-Internet and Wearables

Preceding the Internet, healthcare information was maintained in files in secure filing rooms. The patient's medical records were on paper. Diagnoses, laboratory reports, notes from medical visits, and medication instructions and guidelines were composed and preserved on documents for individual patients' health records. Records labeling included – the patient's surname, specified numbers of the patient's social security number, or a particular system code for charting and numbering records.

Lockheed created the electronic system entitled clinical information system. In the 1970s, the United States government brought about the use of electronic healthcare records, HER, with the Department of Veterans Affairs implementing a system (Deckro et al., 2021). Initial programming exertions fronted the creation of the Decentralized Hospital Computer Program (DHCP; Deckro et al., 2021). The 1990s had an impact on electronic records with the national deployment of DHCP, a graphic user interphase name CPRS used to interface with VISTA. DHCP was implemented nationwide by the Veterans Health Administration, and a Graphic User Interface referenced as CPRS was created and deployed for clinicians to engage with VistA (Deckro et al., 2021). Later health information began to be captured in wearable technology.

Medical Grade Wearables

According to Deamer (2019), the proliferation of smartphones, the miniaturization of sensors, and ease of integration have led to an increase in wearable products, some of which are now suitable for medical use. This has resulted in the rapid growth of the wearable technology market, which is projected to reach $32 billion by 2024, with an annual growth rate of 31% between 2018 and 2024. Medical wearables are at the forefront of two worlds: the medical device industry and the consumer wearables market. As Kang et al. (2022) note, the development of medical wearables is accelerating, and competition is increasing, prompting companies to ensure a high level of quality and medical-grade accuracy for the data produced by these devices.

Medical-grade wearables have been on the market for several years, with some of the earliest examples dating back to the early 2010s. For instance, the FDA cleared the Kardia Mobile ECG device in 2014, which was one of the first medical-grade wearables to receive clearance. Other examples include the BioSticker by BioIntelliSense, which received FDA clearance in 2019, and the Ava Fertility Tracker, which received FDA clearance in 2020 (Dishman, 2019; Kollmorgen, 2020).

A strong convergence exists between the consumer wearables and health/medical device markets. The latter devices are approved by the Food and Drug Administration (FDA) and subsequently to arduous examination. A salient point to know is that inclusive of the device is the digital system where the data is communicated. Healthcare experts are more inclined to depend on the data medical-grade devices transmit. Healthcare cybersecurity professionals should understand that consumer-grade devices are typically not Health Insurance Portability and Accountability Act (HIPAA) secure, and information may not be protected.

Cybersecurity and Wearable Technologies

Wearables continue to rise in popularity. The incessant need to monitor the heart and vital sign boundaries is propelling manufacturers to design and create wearable devices. The more data service persists to progress, wearables will necessitate the flair to access varying networks to help consumers remain connected to their medical and health information. In spite of all the positives, wearable devices have several disadvantages. These technologies could be susceptible to cyber threats and privacy concerns (Moon et al., 2019). Security trials exist like data loss (Rahman et al., 2021; Yu et al., 2015), malware infection, as well as unapproved retrieval of personal data (Cilliers, 2020). Numerous wearable technologies use a sensor, electrodes, and Bluetooth Low Energy (BLE) communication technology. This communication technology is able to be used to "assess nerve conduction, activation frequency, quantify and monitor electrical activity associated with muscle contractions and muscle response in injured tissue" (Vijayan et al., 2021). In other words, Bluetooth, a close-range wireless continuum, enables the linking of wearables to diverse mobile devices (Kolderup, 2021; McAfee, 2022).

According to McAfee (2022), the most fragile link regarding wearables is not the wearable but the mobile phone. Also, the technology can be affected by snooping and spying, analysis of the traffic, or the gathering of data from devices such as the personal identification number (PIN) code to access the phone (Cilliers, 2020; Vijayan et al., 2021). The data stolen by cyberhackers from wearables is used in multiple ways. One example of ill-gained information is knowing when a user is at home or away from home to possibly break into the home. Another example is to extract the data and give it to medical professionals to get prescriptions that can be sold on the black market (McAfee, 2020).

Critiques For Medical-Grade Wearables

According to the study by Cho et al. (2021), medical-grade wearables, such as smartwatches, fitness trackers, and personal electrocardiogram (ECG) monitors, are increasingly used by healthcare clinicians to monitor patient health and diagnose diseases in an effective and efficient way. Although these devices can help to revolutionize healthcare delivery, they also pose security and privacy risks due to their vulnerability to compromise and exploitation. While medical-grade wearables provide a great opportunity to streamline and improve patient care and become more prevalent these wearables pose significant security and privacy risks, and can also be easily hacked due to their lack of security and privacy protocols. According to the research by Soh et al. (2021), medical wearables can be vulnerable to compromise and exploitation, potentially leading to breaches of sensitive patient data. This chapter provides an overview of the security and privacy challenges facing medical-grade wearables and highlights ways in which these devices can be compromised.

The security of medical-grade wearables is a major concern for healthcare providers and patients alike. In today's digital world, medical information is readily available and can be accessed without proper authentication. For example, medical-grade wearables can be hacked by an attacker who is able to gain access to the device either physically or wirelessly (Blanford, 2020). For example, attackers can use Bluetooth, NFC, or other wireless networks to access the device and steal stored data or control it for malicious purposes (Lam, 2021). Additionally, attackers may use social engineering to manipulate the user into granting them access to the device or exploiting known vulnerabilities within the operating system or application (Kou & Tang, 2021).

In addition to security concerns, medical-grade wearables may also pose privacy risks to users. Some medical-grade wearables are designed to store personal health information (Elmandjra, 2020; Koushik et al., 2021). If a malicious attacker were to gain access to this data, they could use it for nefarious purposes, such as financial gain or blackmail. Furthermore, personal data shared by the user through medical-grade wearables may be vulnerable to being accessed and used by third parties without the user's knowledge or consent (Karweer et al., 2019). Although there is no one-size-fits-all solution to the security and privacy challenges posed by medical-grade wearables, there are a number of strategies that healthcare providers, app developers, device manufacturers, and other stakeholders can employ to enhance security and mitigate the risks posed by these devices. For example, two-factor authentication, encryption, and secure coding practices can all contribute to reducing the risk of exploitation (Cai et al., 2022). Additionally, healthcare providers and medical device manufacturers should be transparent with their users about the potential security and privacy risks associated with the device (Hainey et al., 2023). Providers should also ensure that they are compliant with any industry standards, such as the Health Insurance Portability and Accountability Act (HIPAA), and that they have strict procedures in place to ensure the secure sharing of data.

In conclusion, medical-grade wearables have the potential to revolutionize healthcare delivery by making healthcare more efficient and effective. However, due to their lack of security and privacy protocols, these devices are vulnerable to exploitation. To ensure the secure and responsible use of medical-grade wearables, healthcare providers and device manufacturers must prioritize security and privacy by implementing robust protocols, educating users on the potential risks, and complying with industry regulations.

Importance of Protecting Wearables

Wearables offer many benefits, including improved health outcomes, increased productivity, and enhanced quality of life. However, the data collected by wearables is often sensitive and can be used for nefarious purposes, such as identity theft, cyber espionage, and cyber warfare (Nguyen & Nguyen, 2020). Another study by Wynn et al. (2021) found that wearables have the conceivable effect of enhancing healthcare outcomes, however, healthcare organizations have to take precautions to safeguard these devices from cyberattacks in order to maintain patient safety and sensitive data protection. Additionally, wearables can be hacked, leading to compromised data and physical harm to the wearer. To ensure the safety of individuals and organizations, it is critical to protect wearables from these risks.

Risks Associated with Wearables

Several risks are associated with wearables, including physical and virtual risks. Physical risks include harm to the wearer if the wearable malfunctions, such as if a pacemaker is hacked, causing it to malfunction. Virtual risks include data security, interoperability, usability, and human factors. Data security is a significant concern, as wearables collect sensitive data such as personal health information, financial information, and geolocation data. If this data is compromised, it can lead to identity theft, financial fraud, and other cybercrimes. Interoperability refers to the ability of wearables to communicate with other devices and systems. If wearables are not interoperable, they may not be able to share data or communicate with other devices, leading to inefficiencies and potential errors. Usability refers to how easy the wearable is to use. If wearables are not user-friendly, they may not be used correctly, leading to errors or other issues. Human factors refer to how people interact with wearables. If wearables are not designed with human factors in mind, they may not be safe or effective.

Cost of Wearables for Users

As given by Gartner (2021), the Worldwide Wearable Devices user expenditure continued to increase between 2019 and 20122. Let us review the annual spending (i.e., 2019 was $ 46,194 million; 2020 was $ 68,985; 2021 was $81,499, and 2022 was $ 93,858; Gartner, 2021). Wearable technology's emergence as a popular trend in healthcare and fitness could have costs with a significant impact on users, thereby affecting their decisions about whether to purchase and use these devices. Medical-grade wearables (i.e., electrocardiogram (ECG) monitors, blood glucose monitors, and pulse oximeters) are typically designed to monitor vital signs and collect medical data, while non-medical-grade wearables (i.e., fitness trackers and smartwatches) are designed for personal health and fitness tracking. According to Roughan (2023), the wearable healthcare technology industry is expected to be valued over $30 billion by 2023. Moreover, wearables are predicted to expand at a compound annual growth rate of 14% through the year 2028 (Roughan, 2023). Revenue growth will be rapid.

The cost of medical-grade devices can be a barrier to their use, especially for people with lower incomes. However, the accuracy and reliability of medical-grade wearables make them a valuable tool for monitoring and managing medical conditions, which can improve overall health outcomes (Katz et al., 2020). Non-medical-grade wearables are generally more affordable than medical-grade wearables. The lower cost of these devices can make them more accessible to a wider range of people, but their accuracy and reliability may not be sufficient for medical purposes (Gauthier et al., 2021). The cost of wearables can also affect user behavior and adherence to device use. Research has shown that cost is a significant factor in determining whether people continue to use wearable devices over time (Oh et al., 2021). Higher-cost wearables may be more likely to be abandoned or used less frequently, especially if users do not see immediate or tangible benefits from their use.

In summary, the cost of medical-grade and non-medical-grade wearables can have a significant impact on users, affecting their decisions about whether to purchase and use these devices. While medical-grade wearables are generally more expensive, their accuracy and reliability make them valuable tools for managing medical conditions. Non-medical-grade wearables are generally more affordable but should not be used as a substitute for medical advice or treatment. Cost can also affect user behavior and adherence to device use, which should be taken into account when designing and promoting wearable technology.

Wearables for the Aging Populations

Data shows that modern technological developments and improvements suggest the likelihood of offering remote health care for aging populations. Wearables, such as smartwatches and fitness trackers, can be used to monitor vital signs, physical activity, and sleep quality, among other things. These devices can provide valuable data to healthcare providers, allowing for early detection of health problems and more personalized care (Yang & Silverman, 2021). According to this research team, the use of IoT technology in conjunction with wearables can allow for more comprehensive care of older adults. For example, sensors placed around the home can detect falls and alert caregivers or emergency services. IoT devices can also be used to remind older adults to take their medication or to monitor their adherence to a prescribed exercise regimen. Overall, wearables and IoT technology have the potential to greatly improve the quality of care for older adults. By providing continuous monitoring and personalized interventions, these technologies can help older adults maintain their independence and improve their overall health and well-being (Yang & Silverman, 2021).

Wearables have become increasingly popular among aging populations due to their potential benefits. Firstly, they can be used for remote monitoring of vital signs, such as heart rate and blood pressure, which can alert healthcare providers to potential health problems before they become serious (Lombardi et al., 2020). Secondly, they can encourage seniors to lead more active lifestyles and promote healthier behaviors, such as exercise and proper sleep (Kannisto et al., 2019). Finally, wearables can help seniors maintain independence by providing reminders for medication and other important tasks (Mehrotra et al., 2019).

However, there are also potential drawbacks to using wearables among aging populations. One concern is the potential for seniors to become overly reliant on technology, leading to a decreased ability to perform daily activities independently (Kannisto et al., 2019). Another concern is the possibility of wearables providing inaccurate or misleading information, leading to unnecessary interventions or missed diagnoses (Lombardi et al., 2020). Additionally, there are issues surrounding the privacy and security of personal health information (Mehrotra et al., 2019).

When it comes to medical-grade versus non-medical-grade wearables, it ultimately depends on the individual's specific health needs and condition. Medical-grade wearables are designed specifically for monitoring health and are subject to more rigorous testing and regulation (Chen et al., 2020). However, they are typically more expensive and may not be necessary for all individuals. Non-medical grade wearables, such as fitness trackers, can still provide useful information and encourage healthier behaviors, but may not be as accurate or reliable for medical purposes (Chen et al., 2020).

In brief, wearables offer numerous benefits for aging populations, including remote monitoring of vital signs and promoting healthy behaviors. However, there are also potential drawbacks, such as overreliance on technology and privacy concerns. When choosing between medical-grade and non-medical-grade wearables, it is important to consider individual health needs and preferences.

Wearables for the Non-Aging Populations

The development of wearable devices has revolutionized the healthcare industry by providing remote monitoring and management of non-aging populations. These devices are now being used to monitor vital signs, physical activity, and sleep patterns, providing clinicians with valuable information to make informed decisions about patient care. One such wearable that supports remote health monitoring is the smartwatch. According to research, smartwatches have shown the potential to detect early signs of health issues, such as irregular heartbeats, among non-aging populations (Lewallen et al., 2019). Several wearables are suitable for non-aging populations, including smartwatches, fitness trackers, and health monitoring devices. Fitness trackers are commonly used to monitor physical activity and provide feedback on exercise and diet routines (Chung et al., 2021). Health monitoring devices, such as blood pressure monitors and glucose monitors, are ideal for people with chronic conditions such as hypertension and diabetes.

The benefits of wearables for non-aging populations include improved health outcomes, increased patient engagement, and reduced healthcare costs. Wearables provide real-time data, enabling clinicians to detect health problems early and provide timely interventions, leading to better outcomes. Patients can also use wearables to track their progress, receive feedback on their health status, and take proactive steps toward managing their health. However, there are some drawbacks to wearable devices, including privacy concerns, data security, and accuracy issues. Wearables are often not regulated by healthcare authorities, which raises concerns about data privacy and security. There are also concerns about the accuracy of the data collected by wearables, which can lead to false alarms and unnecessary interventions.

Concisely, wearable devices have tremendous potential in supporting remote healthcare for non-aging populations. Smartwatches, fitness trackers, and health monitoring devices are among the best wearables for this population. The benefits of wearing wearables include improved health outcomes, increased patient engagement, and reduced healthcare costs. However, there are also concerns about privacy, data security, and accuracy issues that need to be addressed. Overall, wearable devices have the potential to transform the healthcare industry and improve the lives of non-aging populations.

Concerns About Privacy, Data Security, And Accuracy Issues That Need to be Addressed

Privacy, data security, and accuracy issues are major concerns surrounding the use of both medical and non-medical wearables. Alharthi and Alshehri (2022) note that wearables have become increasingly popular in recent years, providing users with various benefits, including the ability to track fitness goals, monitor health metrics, and improve overall wellness. However, these devices also pose significant risks to user privacy and data security, as they collect sensitive personal information that can be vulnerable to hacking and misuse (Alharthi & Alshehri, 2022). These devices collect a vast amount of personal information that can be exploited if it falls into the wrong hands.

Azimi et al., (2022) also discuss similar concerns highlighting the need for robust security measures and regulatory frameworks to ensure the safe and effective use of wearables. Regulations are needed to ensure data security and accuracy and to establish clear guidelines for how data is used and shared. This research team notes that while these devices offer many potential benefits, including improved disease management and early detection of health issues, they can also be inaccurate and unreliable, leading to false readings and misdiagnoses. In other words, the accuracy of the data collected by these devices can be questionable, leading to incorrect diagnoses and treatments (Azimi et al., 2022).

One of the earliest examples of medical wearables was the pacemaker, first introduced in the 1950s (Bunton, 2017). The history of wearables dates back several decades, with early examples including basic pedometers and heart rate monitors. However, it was not until the advent of modern technology that wearables became more advanced and widely adopted. Since then, medical wearables have evolved to include devices such as glucose monitors, heart rate monitors, and sleep trackers. Other current wearables include but are not limited to smartwatches, fitness trackers, and medical-grade devices used in clinical settings.

The benefits of wearables are numerous. Medical wearables can help patients monitor and manage chronic conditions, while non-medical wearables can motivate individuals to engage in healthy behaviors (Bakker et al., 2018; Gorman & Radford, 2021). However, there are also drawbacks, such as the potential for data breaches and the potential for inaccurate data to lead to incorrect diagnoses and treatments (Bäck et al., 2019; Miller et al., 2020). Ultimately, to address these concerns, it is important to establish clear regulations and guidelines for the use and sharing of data collected by wearables. Additionally, manufacturers should be held accountable for ensuring the accuracy and security of their devices (Sørensen et al., 2020). With proper safeguards in place, wearables can continue to provide significant benefits to both medical and non-medical users.

CONCLUSION AND RECOMMENDATIONS

Understanding solutions to protect wearables is very important to safety for individuals and organizations. Managing risks is paramount. If information conveyed through wearables is not appropriately protected, organizations could be subject to extravagant financial charges, legal proceedings, and harm to their standing or brand (Travelers Risk Control, 2022). Whenever there is modernization, there is associated risk. As with wearables, these risks can range from physical to virtual (i.e., cybersecurity, data security, interoperability, usability, and human factors). The wearable devices market is expected to be USD 460.25 billion by 2029 with consideration and influence by the deficiency of data security which will hinder the progress of the market in evolving markets (Data Bridge, 2022). A consideration is a regulatory landscape and analysis opportunities for formulating linked wearable technologies for market suitability (UL Solutions, 2022). As the wearables industry endures to grow and link with shifting networks, it must focus on emerging risks and safety concerns continuously. Many prominent cyber-attacks have directed the revelation of millions of personally identifiable information records (PII).

With the increased expansion in wearable technology transversely over a plethora of businesses, organizations with unforeseen options may not have previously thought of their market in the technology business and encounter new-fangled risks which require preparation and strategy. Keen awareness surrounding threats and adherence to approaches to aid and guard against these threats enables organizations to concentrate on the enhancement prospects that linked technologies to make them conceivable.

Organizational development (OD) is a method that evaluates the success of an organization throughout change by means of behavioral science from the viewpoint of people, clusters, or systems to encourage endurance and growth (Burrell, 2021; van den Brink, 2020). Based on the literature review there are several significant actions that healthcare organizations can take to change their organizational cultures to be more cybersecurity aware as they move to the more technology-driven approach, technology-driven wearables, driven by COVID-19. The following recommendations were developed:

1. Cybersecurity mindfulness training must deliver tailored awareness training with case studies regarding wearable technologies and risks.
2. Make mandatory cybersecurity and information security training required of all employees.
3. Educate about wearables glasses and their ability to remove lingering external risks that could be harmful to employee performance and safety. For example, smart glasses can eradicate accidents because of blind spots and notify staff of likely perils.
4. Create cybersecurity standards of conduct and cybersecurity protection requirements for all vendors and partners as a result of business relationships. Especially evaluate privacy policies and contracts to safeguard your organization against risk.
5. Institute cybersecurity continuity and resiliency responses and ensure training.
6. Employ encoded email or a document-sharing database to disseminate sensitive data.
7. Carefully guard login and access credentials to email and other services used in the transaction.
8. Teach log-in security and how to view email for safety.
9. Require the use of complex passwords
10. Ban sensitive business communications over unsecured Wi-Fi networks.
11. Invest in a cloud security platform. Shift information to cloud services.
12. Preserve updated firewalls and antivirus software. Keep both active and up-to-date.
13. Create document retention and destruction policies.

Recommendations for Healthcare Organizations

Healthcare organizations must take measures to protect wearables from these risks. To change their organizational cultures to be more cybersecurity aware, healthcare organizations should take the following actions:

- Develop a cybersecurity awareness program: Healthcare organizations should develop a cybersecurity awareness program that educates employees about the risks associated with wearables and how to protect against them.
- Conduct regular cybersecurity training: Healthcare organizations should conduct regular cybersecurity training to ensure that employees are up-to-date on the latest threats and best practices.
- Implement security measures: Healthcare organizations should implement security measures, such as firewalls, encryption, and access controls, to protect wearables from cyber threats.
- Conduct risk assessments: Healthcare organizations should conduct risk assessments to identify vulnerabilities in their wearables and develop strategies to mitigate those risks.
- Develop incident response plans: Healthcare organizations should develop incident response plans to respond to cyber incidents involving wearables.
- Involve stakeholders: Healthcare organizations should involve stakeholders, such as patients, providers, and regulators, in their cybersecurity efforts to ensure that all parties are aware of the risks and how to protect against them.
- Stay informed: Healthcare organizations should stay informed about the latest cybersecurity threats and trends to ensure that their wearables are protected against the latest risks.
- Hire cybersecurity experts: Healthcare organizations should hire cybersecurity experts to manage their wearables and ensure they are protected against cyber threats.

Wearables offer many benefits, but they also present significant risks, including physical and virtual risks such as data security, interoperability, usability, and human factors. Healthcare organizations must take measures.

FUTURE RESEARCH DIRECTIONS

Wearable biosensors have revolutionized the healthcare industry by providing real-time monitoring of various physiological parameters. The integration of these biosensors with the IoT has further enhanced their utility. However, this integration also poses information security risks that need to be addressed. As a result, it is recommended that both medical-grade and non-medical-grade wearable technology should include the effects of augmented reality to improve security and privacy.

According to a study conducted by Yao et al. (2021), augmented reality can be used to enhance the security and privacy of wearable biosensors. The study proposed an approach that uses augmented reality to visualize the data collected by the biosensors, thus enabling users to monitor their physiological parameters in real-time. The authors suggested that this approach could be useful for both medical-grade and non-medical-grade wearables.

- Implement privacy-enhancing technologies to protect patient data from unauthorized access and ensure data security. This can include encryption, data anonymization, and secure data transmission protocols. (Jha et al., 2021)

Similarly, another study conducted by Xu et al. (2020) recommended the use of augmented reality to enhance the user experience of wearable biosensors. The authors proposed a system that uses augmented reality to display the data collected by the biosensors, thus providing users with a more immersive and interactive experience.

- Incorporate AI algorithms to enhance the accuracy and reliability of wearable biosensors. For instance, AI can be used to detect early signs of medical conditions, improve real-time monitoring of vital signs, and predict health outcomes based on continuous monitoring data. (Jang et al., 2021)
- Develop AI-based decision support systems to help clinicians interpret data generated by wearable biosensors. These systems can identify abnormal patterns, generate alerts, and provide personalized treatment recommendations based on the patient's health status. (Zhong et al., 2021)
- Use explainable AI models that can provide clear and interpretable insights into the algorithms used for decision-making. This will help build trust in AI-powered wearable technology and increase adoption rates among patients and healthcare providers. (Wong et al., 2022)
- Conduct rigorous clinical trials to validate the safety, efficacy, and usability of AI-powered wearable biosensors. This will help identify potential limitations and challenges associated with the use of these devices in real-world clinical settings. (Sakellariou et al., 2022)
- Foster collaboration between stakeholders, including patients, clinicians, researchers, and industry partners, to promote the development and adoption of AI-powered wearable technology. This can help ensure that the technology meets the needs of all stakeholders and addresses critical healthcare challenges. (Althoff et al., 2021)

In conclusion, the integration of wearable biosensors with augmented reality has the potential to improve the security, privacy, and user experience of these devices. Future research should focus on developing practical implementations of these technologies to improve the effectiveness of wearable biosensors in healthcare and medical monitoring.

REFERENCES

Abdollahi, H., Lashkari, A. R., Sarbaz, M., Alizadeh, S., & Taghva, F. (2021). Examining the effect of transformational leadership on healthcare professionals' attitudes towards technology adoption: A structural equation modeling approach. *Health Informatics Journal*, *27*(2), 146–155.

Ake, A., & Arcand, M. (2020). The impact of mobile health monitoring on the evolution of patient-pharmacist relationships. *International Journal of Pharmaceutical and Healthcare Marketing*, *14*(1), 1–19. doi:10.1108/IJPHM-04-2019-0030

Al-Dmour, R. A., Al-Dmour, H. H., Tarhini, A., & Almajali, D. (2020). Investigating the effect of transformational leadership on the adoption of digital healthcare technology. *Technological Forecasting and Social Change*, *153*, 119946.

Alalwan, A. A., Dwivedi, Y. K., & Rana, N. P. (2019). Factors influencing adoption of mobile banking by Jordanian bank customers: Extending UTAUT2 with trust. *International Journal of Information Management*, *44*, 38–52. doi:10.1016/j.ijinfomgt.2018.09.017

Althoff, T., Saria, S., & Vayena, E. (2021). Wearables and the internet of things for health: Collaboration is key. *Nature Reviews. Materials*, *6*(6), 389–391.

Aminikhanghahi, S., & Cook, D. J. (2018). The promises and challenges of healthcare wearable devices. *Proceedings of the IEEE*, *106*(3), 353–366.

Andresen, H., Sasko, B., Patschan, D., Pagonas, N., & Ritter, O. (2021). Effective treatment of electrical storm by a wearable cardioverter defibrillator in a patient with severely impaired left ventricular function after myocardial infarction: A case report. *Journal of Medical Case Reports*, *15*(1), 1–7. doi:10.118613256-021-02833-2 PMID:33993888

Aroganam, G., Manivannan, N., & Harrison, D. (2019). Review on wearable technology sensors used in consumer sport applications. Sensors. *Sensors (Basel)*, *19*(9), 1983. Advance online publication. doi:10.339019091983 PMID:31035333

Avolio, B. J., Wang, D. G., & Li, M. (2018). Leadership: Recent developments and future directions. *Annual Review of Organizational Psychology and Organizational Behavior*, *5*, 133–156.

Avolio, B. J., & Yammarino, F. J. (2019). Introduction to, and overview of, transformational and charismatic leadership. In Transformational and Charismatic Leadership: The Road Ahead 10th Anniversary Edition (pp. 1-17). Emerald Publishing Limited.

Bäck, A., Cakici, B., & Sundermeier, J. (2019). Accuracy of wearable heart rate monitors. *Journal of Sports Science & Medicine*, *18*(3), 527–528.

Bakker, E. A., Lee, D. C., & Sui, X. (2018). Beyond the traditional: Using wearable technology to enhance self-report in exercise and nutrition research. *American Journal of Physiology. Endocrinology and Metabolism*, *315*(6), E846–E853.

Bass, B. M., & Riggio, R. E. (2020). *Transformational leadership*. Psychology Press.

Bie, M., Wang, Y., & Zou, X. (2020). Transformational leadership and employees' creativity: The mediating role of psychological safety and the moderating role of leader-member exchange. *Frontiers in Psychology*, *11*, 2032. doi:10.3389/fpsyg.2020.02032

Blanford, J. (2020). *The security risks of medical-grade wearables*. Forbes Magazine.

Borowski-Beszta, M., & Polasik, M. (2020). Wearable devices: New quality in sports and finance. *Journal of Physical Education and Sport*, *20*(2), 1077–1084. doi:10.7752/jpes.2020.s2150

Braun, V., & Clarke, V. (2019). Reflecting on reflexive thematic analysis. *Qualitative Research in Sport, Exercise and Health*, *11*(4), 589–597. doi:10.1080/2159676X.2019.1628806

Brennan, K., Lapinski, J., Durso, C., & Sheng, J. (2020). The role of wearables in healthcare transformation. *Journal of Law, Medicine & Ethics, 48*(sup1), 67-72. doi:10.1177/1073110520953441

Brown-Jackson, K. (2017). *Disrupting and retooling: A model for an effective community-based telehealth program (Order No. 28144638)*. ProQuest Central. (2440009177). https://www.proquest.com/dissertations-theses/disrupting-retooling-model-effective-community/docview/2440009177/se-2

Brown-Jackson, K. (2022). Grasping cybersecurity leadership as it relates to critical infrastructure protection. [IJSEUS]. *International Journal of Smart Education and Urban Society*, *13*(1), 1–14. doi:10.4018/IJSEUS.312233

Bunton, R. (2017). Wearable medical devices: Where are we now and what lies ahead? *Medical Device Technology*, *28*(2), 19–21.

Burns, J. M. (1978). *Leadership*. Harper & Row.

Burrell, D. N. (2021). *Cybersecurity leadership from a talent management organizational development lens* [Unpublished Exegesis]. Capitol Technology University.

Burton, S. L. (2021). Artificial intelligence (AI) and augmented reality (AR): Disambiguated in the telemedicine / telehealth sphere. *Buletin Scientific, 1*(51). https://www.armyacademy.ro/buletin/bul1_2021/Art_Burton.pdf

Burton, S. L. (2022). *Cybersecurity leadership from a telemedicine/telehealth knowledge and organizational development examination* [Doctoral dissertation, Capitol Technology University]. Capitol Technology University ProQuest Dissertations Publishing, 2022. 29066056.

Butt, M. A., Kazanskiy, N. L., & Khonina, S. N. (2022). Revolution in flexible wearable electronics for temperature and pressure monitoring—A review. *Electronics (Basel)*, *11*(5), 716. doi:10.3390/electronics11050716

Cai, W., Hsu, C., Zang, Y., & Chen, B. (2022). Security and privacy protection mechanisms for medical-grade wearables. *IEEE Transactions on Mobile Computing*, *21*(6), 1366–1380.

Chang, I.-C., Wang, K.-S., & Chiu, Y.-P. (2020). Examining the factors that affect users' intentions to continue to use medical wearables. *Health Information Science and Systems*, *8*(1), 1–10. doi:10.100713755-020-00117-7 PMID:31867102

Chen, X. (2018). How does transformational leadership affect employee innovation behavior in China? The mediating role of psychological capital. *Frontiers in Psychology*, *9*, 1112. doi:10.3389/fpsyg.2018.01112

Chen, Y., Wu, H., Wu, Y., & Wang, M. (2020). Medical-grade wearables and their applications in healthcare. *Sensors (Basel)*, *20*(3), 738. PMID:32013208

Cheung, M. L., Chau, K. Y., Sum Lam, M. H., Tse, G., Ho, K. Y., Flint, S. W., & Lee, K. Y. (2019). Examining consumers' adoption of wearable healthcare technology: The role of health attributes. *International Journal of Environmental Research and Public Health*, *16*(13), 2257. doi:10.3390/ijerph16132257 PMID:31247962

Cho, K., Lee, J., & Lee, K. (2021). Medical-grade wearables and remote diagnostics for healthcare. *Journal of Medical Systems*, *45*(4), 1–8. doi:10.100710916-021-01760-5

Chou, Y. H., Hsu, C. C., & Huang, W. C. (2019). Using wearable technology to improve patient outcomes. *Journal of Medical Systems*, *43*(5), 116. PMID:30905006

Chung, M. K., Lee, K. Y., Lee, S. H., Han, S. J., & Kim, S. R. (2021). Use of a fitness tracker for physical activity monitoring in patients with nonalcoholic fatty liver disease: Randomized controlled trial. *Journal of Medical Internet Research*, *23*(2), e24498.

Cilliers, L. (2020). Wearable devices in healthcare: Privacy and information security issues. *The HIM Journal*, *49*(2-3), 150–156. doi:10.1177/1833358319851684 PMID:31146589

Clowes, R. (2015). Thinking in the cloud: The cognitive incorporation of cloud-based technology. *Philosophy & Technology*, *28*(2), 261–296. doi:10.100713347-014-0153-z

Cojocaru, C., & Cojocaru, S. (2014). Sony vs. apple - iPod launching, a case study of leadership and innovation. *Manager,* (20), 115-125. https://www.proquest.com/scholarly-journals/sony-vs-apple-ipod-launching-case-study/docview/1684617694/se-2?accountid=167615

Condeco. (2022). The history of wearable technology. *Condeco.*. https://www.condecosoftware.com/blog/the-history-of-wearable-technology/#:~:text=1970s,of%20the%2070s%20and%2080s

Data Bridge Market Research. (2022). *What is the future market value for wearable device market?* Data Bridge Market Research. https://www.databridgemarketresearch.com/reports/global-wearable-devices-market

Davis, F. D. (1986). *A technology acceptance model for empirically testing new end-user information systems: Theory and results*. [Doctoral dissertation, Massachusetts Institute of Technology].

Davis, F. D. (1989). Perceived usefulness, perceived ease of use, and user acceptance of information technology. *Management Information Systems Quarterly*, *13*(3), 319–340. doi:10.2307/249008

Dawson, M. E., Jr. (2020). Cyber warfare threats and opportunities. *Universidade Fernando Pessoa*, Porto. http://hdl.handle.net/10284/9678

Deamer, L. (2019). Medical-grade devices vs. consumer wearables. Yole Développement. *Electronic Specifier*. https://www.electronicspecifier.com/products/wearables/medical-grade-devices-vs-consumer-wearables

Deckro, J., Phillips, T., Davis, A., Hehr, A., & Ochylski, S. (2021). Big data in the Veterans Health Administration: A nursing informatics perspective. *Journal of Nursing Scholarship*, *53*(3), 288–295. doi:10.1111/jnu.12631 PMID:33689232

Dishman, E. (2019, August 2). FDA clears BioIntelliSense's medical wearable for remote patient monitoring. *MedCity News*. https://medcitynews.com/2019/08/fda-clears-biointellisenses-medical-wearable-for-remote-patient-monitoring/

Dunn, J., Runge, R., & Snyder, M. (2018). Wearables and the medical revolution. *Personalized Medicine*, *15*(5), 429–448. https://www.futuremedicine.com/doi/10.2217/pme-2018-0044. doi:10.2217/pme-2018-0044 PMID:30259801

Elmandjra, M. (2020). *Wearables in healthcare – implications and opportunities*. Matrix Global Network.

Federal Bureau of Investigation (FBI). (2019). *What we investigate: The cyber threat*. FBI. https://www.fbi.gov/investigate/cyber

Fisher, R., Porod, C., & Peterson, S. (2021). Motivating employees and organizations to adopt a cybersecurity-focused culture. *Journal of Organizational Psychology*, *21*(1), 114–131. https://www.proquest.com/scholarly-journals/motivating-employees-organizationsadopt/docview/2512311256/se-2?accountid=167615

Fridman, I., Lucas, G., & Berson, J. (2021). Beyond the Pandemic: A Framework for Managing Multiple Crises. *Harvard Business Review*, *99*(2), 48–59.

Fui, L. W. (2021). 99 disruption of paediatric orthopaedic hospital services due to the COVID-19 pandemic in a region with minimal COVID-19 illness. *BMJ Paediatrics Open*, *5*, A28–A29. doi:10.1136/bmjpo-2021-RCPCH.57

Gartner. (2021, January 12). Gartner forecasts global spending on wearable devices to total $81.5 billion in 2021. *Gertner*. https://www.gartner.com/en/newsroom/press-releases/2021-01-11-gartner-forecasts-global-spending-on-wearable-devices-to-total-81-5-billion-in-2021

Gauthier, A. P., Kolla, G., Mayer, P., & Burtscher, M. (2021). Accuracy of consumer wearables for physical activity and sleep monitoring in daily living: A systematic review and meta-analysis. *Applied Sciences (Basel, Switzerland)*, *11*(5), 2075. doi:10.3390/app11052075

Gorman, E., & Radford, S. (2021). Fitbit as a tool for physical activity monitoring in the clinical setting: A systematic review. *Journal of Clinical Medicine*, *10*(3), 501. PMID:33535394

Greenhalgh, T., & Peacock, R. (2019). Effectiveness and efficiency of search methods in systematic reviews of complex evidence: Audit of primary sources. *BMJ (Clinical Research Ed.)*, *364*, l35. PMID:16230312

Greenleaf, R. K. (2019). *The servant as leader*. Paulist Press.

Guk, K., Han, G., Lim, J., Jeong, K., Kang, T., Lim, E. K., & Jung, J. (2019). Evolution of wearable devices with real-time disease monitoring for personalized healthcare. *Nanomaterials (Basel, Switzerland)*, *9*(6), 1–23. doi:10.3390/nano9060813 PMID:31146479

Hainey, T., Jones, K., McGregor, J., & McNeil, B. (2023). Enhancing security and privacy standards in medical-grade wearables. *Electronics & Communication Engineering Journal*, *35*(4), 217–239.

Hancock, J., Curry, E., & Gulliford, L. (2018). Reflexivity in qualitative research: A journey of learning. *Qualitative Report*, *23*(10), 2520–2534.

Hansen, D., Shneiderman, B., & Smith, M. A. (2017). *Analyzing social media networks with NodeXL: Insights from a connected world*. Morgan Kaufmann.

Hart, C. (2019). Doing a literature review: Releasing the social science research imagination. *Sage (Atlanta, Ga.)*.

Healthcare & Public Health Sector Coordinating Councils. (n.d.). *Health industry cybersecurity practices: Managing threats and protecting patients*. Department of Health and Human Services. https://www.phe.gov/Preparedness/planning/405d/Documents/HICP-Main-508.pdf

Heathcare Information Management Systems Society (HIMSS). (2021a). *Cybersecurity in healthcare*. HIMSS. https://www.himss.org/resources/cybersecurity-healthcare

Heathcare Information Management Systems Society (HIMSS). (2021b). *Future of healthcare report: Exploring healthcare stakeholders' expectations for the next chapter*. HIMSS. https://www.himss.org/resources/future-healthcare-report-exploring-healthcare-stakeholdersexpectations-next-chapter

Heifetz, R., & Linsky, M. (2002). *A survival guide for leaders*. HBR. https://hbr.org/2002/06/a-survival-guide-for-leaders

Hernandez, J., Shafique, S., & Ashraf, M. (2018). Challenges and opportunities of wearable healthcare technology: A review paper. *Journal of Engineering and Applied Sciences (Asian Research Publishing Network)*, *37*(2), 61–71.

Hofstede, G. (2019). *Culture and organizations*. Routledge.

Huang, L., & Zhang, Q. (2022). The role of theory in digital transformation research: A systematic literature review and future research directions. *Information & Management*, *59*(1), 103556. doi:10.1016/j.im.2021.103556

Hunter, J. C. (1998). *The servant: a simple story about the true essence of leadership*. Currency.

Jacobs, J. V., Hettinger, L. J., Huang, Y. H., Jeffries, S., Lesch, M. F., Simmons, L. A., Verma, S. K., & Willetts, J. L. (2019). Employee acceptance of wearable technology in the workplace. *Applied Ergonomics*, *78*(January), 148156. doi:10.1016/j.apergo.2019.03.003 PMID:31046946

Jang, H., Kim, D., Lee, J. Y., & Kim, J. (2021). Artificial intelligence in wearable biosensors: Current status and future prospects. *Biosensors & Bioelectronics*, *183*, 113193.

Joshi, K. D., & Mithas, S. (2017). Research note and review of the empirical ethical decision-making literature: Boundary conditions and extensions. *Information Systems Research*, *28*(1), 118–142.

Kang, H. S., & Exworthy, M. (2022, July 13). Wearing the future-wearables to empower users to take greater responsibility for their health and care: Scoping review. *JMIR mHealth and uHealth*, *10*(7), e35684. doi:10.2196/35684 PMID:35830222

Kannisto, K. A., Korhonen, J., Adams, C. E., Koivunen, M. H., & Vahlberg, T. (2019). Factors associated with perceptions of technology among older people with and without dementia. *Gerontechnology (Valkenswaard)*, *18*(2), 95–105.

Karweer, D., Walvekar, D., & Dangi, S. (2019). Adoption of medical-grade wearables in healthcare: Challenges and opportunities. *AIMS Medical Science*, *6*(1), 27–43.

Kaspersky. (2022). Top ten cybersecurity trends. *Kaspersky*. https://www.kaspersky.com/resource-center/preemptive-safety/cyber-security-trends

Katz, M. G., Ladapo, J. A., Redberg, R. F., & Turakhia, M. P. (2020). Medical-grade wearables and digital health technologies: What is their role in clinical cardiovascular disease management? *Journal of the American College of Cardiology*, *75*(23), 2975–2984. doi:10.1016/j.jacc.2020.04.053

Khurana, H., Ahmad, A., & Qureshi, M. A. (2020). AI-enabled cyber security: A comprehensive review. *IEEE Access : Practical Innovations, Open Solutions*, *8*, 109380–109403.

Kilinc, E. (2019). Healthcare Wearables for Disease Management: A Review of Current Technologies and Future Developments. *Journal of Medical Systems*, *43*(8), 259. PMID:31264009

Kim, H. J., Kim, M., & Kim, J. Y. (2021). Transformational leadership and employees' creative process engagement: Serial mediation of psychological safety and affective commitment. *Sustainability*, *13*(6), 3226. doi:10.3390u13063226

Klein, D., Bäumer, F., & Meister, S. (2019). Ethical considerations for digital health solutions in clinical applications: A scoping review. *BMC Medical Informatics and Decision Making*, *19*(1), 1–19. PMID:30616584

Klincová, M. (2017). The impact of transformational leadership on employee job satisfaction in healthcare. *Central European Business Review*, *6*(4), 41–50. doi:10.18267/j.cebr.179

Klonoff, D. C. (2017). Wearable technology and diabetes: New tools for diabetes self-management. *Journal of Diabetes Science and Technology*, *11*(4), 724–727. PMID:28299958

Kolderup, K. (2021, September 21). Bluetooth range and reliability: Myth vs fact. *IoT Now Magazine*. https://www.iot-now.com/2021/09/21/113171-bluetooth-range-and-reliability-myth-vs-fact/

Kollmorgen, S. (2020, August 11). Ava fertility tracker secures FDA clearance for over-the-counter use. *MobiHealthNews*. https://www.mobihealthnews.com/news/north-america/ava-fertility-tracker-secures-fda-clearance-over-counter-use

Kou, X., & Tang, Q. (2021). The introduction of medical-grade wearables: Security and privacy challenges. *International Journal of OT*, *20*(2), 131–143.

Koushik, S., Toit, T., Vrabel, K., Pérez-López, A., & Rigau, M. (2021). Security, privacy, and regulatory aspects of medical-grade wearables. *IEEE Journal of Biomedical and Health Informatics*, *25*(1), 230–241.

Lam, B. (2021). *How to protect your medical-grade wearables from being hacked*. Inveniosoft.

Landi, H. (2018). Heritage Valley Health System Hit with Petya Ransomware Attack. *Healthcare Informatics*, https://www.healthcare-informatics.com/news-item/cybersecurity/heritage-valley-health-system-hit-petya-ransomware-attack

Landi, H. (2018, January 29). PA health system, health IT vendor affected by global "Petya" ransomware attack. *Healthcare Innovation*. https://www.hcinnovationgroup.com/cybersecurity/article/13028840/pa-health-system-health-it-vendor-affected-by-global-petya-ransomware-attack

Leithwood, K., Harris, A., & Hopkins, D. (2017). Seven strong claims about successful school leadership revisited. *School Leadership & Management*, *37*(1-2), 5–22. doi:10.1080/13632434.2016.1224293

Levy, Y., & Ellis, T. J. (2021). *A guide to literature review writing: Why it is important and how to get started*. Emerald Publishing Limited.

Lewallen, J., Hanlon, J., Houts, P., & Engels, J. (2019). Detecting atrial fibrillation with a smartwatch: Results of the mRhythm study. *Heart Rhythm*, *16*(5), 766–767.

Liang, Y., Li, D., & Wang, Q. (2020). Technology acceptance model of medical wearable devices. A systematic review. *Journal of Healthcare Engineering*, *2020*, 1–10. doi:10.1155/2020/8822311

Liu, C., Zhu, J., Li, C., & Sun, Y. (2021). Effects of transformational leadership on followers' proactive behavior: A moderated mediation model. *Frontiers in Psychology*, *12*, 1–11.

Lombardi, C. M., Carbone, S., Sansoni, J., & Menditto, E. (2020). Advances in wearable technology and applications in healthcare: A review of the literature. *Diagnostics (Basel)*, *10*(9), 736.

Loonam, J., Eaves, S., Kumar, V., & Parry, G. (2018). Towards digital transformation: Lessons learned from traditional organizations. *Strategic Change*, *27*(2), 101–109. doi:10.1002/jsc.2185

Makridakis, S., Dimitriadis, S. I., & Kourentzes, N. (2021). Artificial intelligence in supply chain management: Theory, applications, and challenges. *International Journal of Production Research*, *59*(15), 4684–4706.

Man, L. C., Leung, W. K., & Chan, H. (2021). Driving healthcare wearable technology adoption for Generation Z consumers in Hong Kong. *Young Consumers*, *22*(1), 10–27. doi:10.1108/YC-04-2020-1123

Maygen, J. (2021. The history of the calculator watches. *Superwatches*. https://www.superwatches.com/the-history-of-calculator-watches/

McAfee. (2022, February 25). The wearable future is hackable. *McAfree.*. https://www.mcafee.com/blogs/privacy-identity-protection/hacking-wearable-devices/

McEwen, R. N. (2019). Flash, spirit, plex, stretch: A trans-disciplinary view of the media sensorium. *Canadian Journal of Communication*, *44*(4), 585–593. doi:10.22230/cjc.2019v44n4a3727

Mehrotra, S., Gupta, N., Rameez, M., & Alsharif, S. (2019). The role of wearable technology in elderly health monitoring. *Health Care*, *7*(3), 98. PMID:31430855

Meyer, J., & Heinze-Milne, S. (2020). The effectiveness of wearable activity trackers in increasing physical activity among older adults: A systematic review and meta-analysis. *Aging & Mental Health*, *24*(2), 151–160.

Miller, A. R., Tucker, C. A., & Lam, J. (2020). The accuracy of wearable fitness trackers in older adults. *Journal of Aging and Physical Activity*, *28*(4), 511–516.

Moon, N. W., Baker, P. M., & Goughnour, K. (2019). Designing wearable technologies for users with disabilities: Accessibility, usability, and connectivity factors. *Journal of Rehabilitation and Assistive Technologies Engineering*, *6*, 205566831986213. doi:10.1177/2055668319862137 PMID:35186318

Muller, S. R. (2021). A Perspective On the intersection of information security policies and I.A. awareness, factoring in end-user behavior. *Proceedings of the International Conference on Research in Management & Technovation*, (pp. 137–142). IEEE. 10.15439/2020KM1

Mullins, J. (2022). Content analysis. The International Encyclopedia of Communication Research Methods, 1-13.

Nelson, B. W., Low, C. A., Jacobson, N., Areán, P., & Torous, J. (2019). Brief report: Exploring the feasibility of feasibility studies in digital mental health. *Journal of Telemedicine and Telecare*, *25*(9), 550–554.

Neuendorf, K. A. (2019). *The content analysis guidebook*. Sage publications.

Nguyen, A., & Nguyen, D. T. (2020). Security and privacy in wearable technology. In *Internet of Things and Analytics for Agriculture* (pp. 289–316). Springer.

Nguyen, N. H., Tran, T. T., Vuong, T. T., Nguyen, T. H. T., Nguyen, T. T. H., & Vuong, Q. H. (2019). Factors affecting the adoption of wearable health technology among Vietnamese consumers. *BMC Public Health*, *19*(1), 1025. doi:10.118612889-019-7355-7 PMID:31366338

Nikou, S. A., & Economides, A. A. (2021). Mobile payment adoption: Investigating the roles of trust, social influence, and perceived usefulness. *Information & Management*, *58*(1), 103378. doi:10.1016/j.im.2020.103378

Northouse, P. G. (2016). *Leadership: Theory and practice*. Sage publications.

Oh, H. J., Lee, J. H., & Kim, J. H. (2021). Factors affecting continuous use of wearable devices in the health and fitness industry. *International Journal of Environmental Research and Public Health*, *18*(4), 1894. doi:10.3390/ijerph18041894 PMID:33669298

Oh, S., Kim, H. S., & Kim, Y. (2019). Feasibility of smartwatch use for social anxiety disorder: A randomized controlled trial. *Journal of Telemedicine and Telecare*, *25*(10), 628–635.

Oliveira, J. S., Rodrigues, A. F., Fernandes, J., & Neves, P. (2019). Experiential marketing: A literature review and research agenda. *Journal of Business Research*, *100*, 380–390. doi:10.1016/j.jbusres.2019.02.044

Olmedo-Aguirre, J., Reyes-Campos, J., Alor-Hernández, G., Machorro-Cano, I., Rodríguez-Mazahua, L., & Sánchez-Cervantes, J. L. (2022). Remote healthcare for elderly people using wearables: A Review. *Biosensors (Basel)*, *12*(2), 73. doi:10.3390/bios12020073 PMID:35200334

Oltsik, J. (2017). *The life and times of cybersecurity professionals*. ESG and ISSA: Research Report. https://www.esg-global.com/hubfs/issa/ESG-ISSA-Research-Report-LifeofCybersecurity-Professionals-Nov-. 2017.pdf?hsCtaTracking=a63e431c-d2ce-459d-8787-cc122a193baf%7Ce74f0327-0bbc-444a-b7a8-e2cd08d1999e Pando, A. (2019, May 2). Wearable health technologies and their impact on the health industry.*Forbes*. https://www.forbes.com/sites/forbestechcouncil/2019/05/02/wearable-health-technologies-and-their-impact-on-the-health-industry/?sh=1d8c30203af5

Passman, R. (2020). Atrial fibrillation detection using implantable cardiac monitors: Are we being too revealing? *American Heart Journal*, *219*, 137–139. doi:10.1016/j.ahj.2019.08.005 PMID:31862085

Pavlou, P. A., & Fygenson, M. (2019). Understanding and predicting electronic commerce adoption: An extension of the theory of planned behavior. *Management Information Systems Quarterly*, *23*(1), 115–143. doi:10.2307/25148720

Pierleoni, P., Belli, A., Palma, L., & Pellegrini, G. (2020). A survey on wearable sensor-based systems for health monitoring and prognosis. *Sensors (Basel)*, *20*(20), 5808. PMID:33066546

Rahman, M., Li, N., Athalye, A., & Liang, Z. (2021). *Synthetic-Injection Attacks: Stealing Data by Injecting Malicious Code into Common Libraries*. arXiv preprint arXiv:2108.00669.

Ramalingam, B., Nabarro, D., Oqubay, A., Carnall, D. R., & Wild, L. (2020). 5 principles to guide adaptive leadership. *Harvard Business Review*. https://hbr.org/2020/09/5-principles-to-guide-adaptive-leadership

Riaz, S., & Nawaz, S. (2022). Development of the attitude atonement scale for adults. *Journal of Behavioural Sciences*, *32*(1), 165. https://www.proquest.com/scholarly-journals/development-attitude-atonement-scale-adults/docview/2627931120/se-2?accountid=167615

Rodgers, M. M., Alon, G., Pai, V. M., & Conroy, R. S. (2019). Wearable technologies for active living and rehabilitation: Current research challenges and future opportunities. *Journal of Rehabilitation and Assistive Technologies Engineering*, *6*, 205566831983960. doi:10.1177/2055668319839607 PMID:31245033

Rothwell, J., Titcomb, J., & McGoogan, C. (2017, June 17). Peyta cyber-attack: Ransomware spreads across Europe with films in Ukraine, Britain, and Spain shut down. *The Daily Telegraph*. https://www.telegraph.co.uk/news/2017/06/27 Ukraine-hit-massive-cyber-attack1/

Roughan, G. (2023). Key wearable healthcare trends for 2023 and beyond. *Unleashed Inventory Management Software*. https://www.unleashedsoftware.com/blog/the-wearable-healthcare-trends-of-2021-and-beyond

Ruef, M. (2019). AI and cybersecurity: How artificial intelligence is making the online world safer. *IT Pro*. https://www.itpro.co.uk/security/34222/ai-and-cybersecurity-how-artificial-intelligence-is-making-the-online-world-safer

Sacred Heart University Library. (2020). *Organizing academic research papers: Limitations of the study*. Sacred Heart University Library. https://library.sacredheart.edu/c.php?g=29803&p=185934

Sakellariou, A., Shao, Y., & Gibson, O. J. (2022). Clinical trials of wearable biosensors: Challenges and opportunities. *NPJ Digital Medicine*, *5*(1), 1–10. PMID:35013539

Sanches, C., Moraes, R. C., Elias, P. C., & Ribeiro, M. Q. (2021). Wearables and their applications in the management of diabetes: Systematic review. *JMIR mHealth and uHealth*, *9*(6), e25066. doi:10.2196/25066

Sarker, R., Rayhan, F., Alam, M. S., & Uddin, M. Z. (2021). Cybersecurity Research and Development: A Critical Review. *International Journal of Network Security*, *23*(2), 203–217.

Sathyanarayana, A., Joty, S., & Fernandez-Luque, L. (2019). Research and applications of intelligent wearable devices in healthcare: A review. *BioMed Research International*, 2019.

Schneider, A. L., & Ingram, H. (2017). Deservingness and the politics of health care. *Journal of Health Politics, Policy and Law*, *42*(5), 835–862.

Shah, R., Wright, E., Tambakis, G., Holmes, J., Thompson, A., Connell, W., Lust, M., Niewiadomski, O., Kamm, M., Basnayake, C., & Ding, J. (2021). Telehealth model of care for outpatient inflammatory bowel disease care in the setting of the COVID-19 pandemic. *Internal Medicine Journal*, *51*(7), 1038–1042. Advance online publication. doi:10.1111/imj.15168 PMID:34278693

Shamir, B. (2019). Transformational leadership reconsidered: A critique of Burns. In *Transformational and Charismatic Leadership: The Road Ahead 10th Anniversary Edition* (pp. 19–47). Emerald Publishing Limited.

Sharma, A., Badea, M., Tiwari, S., & Marty, J. L. (2021, February 1). Wearable biosensors: An alternative and practical approach in healthcare and disease monitoring. *Molecules (Basel, Switzerland)*, *26*(3), 748. doi:10.3390/molecules26030748 PMID:33535493

Slanes, A. (2021). Academic research on the 2030 agenda: Challenges of a transdisciplinary field of study. *Global Policy*, *12*(3), 286–297. doi:10.1111/1758-5899.12912

Siu, L. H. (2020). Digitalization in practice: The fifth discipline advantage. *The Learning Organization*, *27*(1), 54–64. doi:10.1108/TLO-09-2019-0137

Smart Ring News. (2021). What are smart rings? How do they work? *Smart Ring News*. https://www.smartringnews.com/posts/what-are-smart-rings-how-do-they-work

Soh, J. H., Wu, Y., & Lee, Y. S. (2021). Privacy and security issues of medical-grade wearables. *Journal of Medical Systems*, *45*(5), 1–11. doi:10.100710916-021-01777-w

Sørensen, J. L., Skou Thomsen, A. S., & Schønning, V. (2020). Legal challenges of wearables in the workplace: Current state of the art and future challenges. *Journal of Occupational Health Psychology*, *25*(1), 91.

Statista. (2022). Forecast unit shipments of wrist-worn wearables worldwide from 2019 to 2024. *Statista*. https://www.statista.com/statistics/296565/wearables-worldwide-shipments/

StealthLabs. (2022). Number of cyber attacks in 2021 peaked all-time high. *StealthLabs*. https://www.stealthlabs.com/news/cyberattacks-increase-50-in-2021-peaking-all-time-high-of-925-weekly-attacks-per-organization/

Sun, H., Cao, J., & Fang, Y. (2021). Technology acceptance model: A systematic review and future research agenda. *Journal of Business Research*, *130*, 205–215. doi:10.1016/j.jbusres.2021.01.020

Thorp, E. O. (1998, October). The invention of the first wearable computer. In *Digest of Papers. Second International Symposium on Wearable Computers* (Cat. No. 98EX215), IEEE, 4-8. 10.1109/ISWC.1998.729523

Tranfield, D., Denyer, D., & Smart, P. (2019). Towards a methodology for developing evidence-informed management knowledge by means of systematic review. *British Journal of Management*, *30*(1), 6–20.

Travelers Risk Control. (2022). *How companies can help reduce risk from wearables*. TRC. https://www.travelers.com/resources/business-industries/technology/how-companies-can-help-reduce-risk-from-wearables

University of Louisville William F. Ekstrom Library. (2021). *Critical thinking and academic research: Assumptions*. University of Louisville. https://library.louisville.edu/ekstrom/criticalthinking/assumptions

Valentinuzzi, M. (2020, October). Hearing aid history: From ear trumpets to digital technology. *IEEE*. https://www.embs.org/pulse/articles/hearing-aid-history-from-ear-trumpets-to-digital-technology/

van den Brink, M. (2020). Reinventing the wheel over and over again: Organizational learning, memory and forgetting in doing diversity work. *Equality, Diversity and Inclusion*, *39*(4), 379–393. doi:10.1108/EDI-10-2019-0249

Van Dyne, L., & Ang, S. (2018). Leveraging diversity: Transformational leadership in diverse work groups. *Organizational Dynamics*, *47*(4), 229–238.

Varadarajan, P. R., & Yadav, M. S. (2002). Marketing strategy and the Internet: An organizing framework. *Journal of the Academy of Marketing Science*, *30*(4), 296–312. doi:10.1177/009207002236907

Vartanova, V. (2019 August 2). Smart wearables to unlock the next level of precision medicine. *MobiHealth News HIMSS Media*. https://www.mobihealthnews.com/news/north-america/smart-wearables-unlock-next-level-precision-medicine

Venkatesh, V., & Davis, F. D. (2000). A theoretical extension of the Technology Acceptance Model: Four longitudinal field studies. *Management Science*, *46*(2), 186–204. doi:10.1287/mnsc.46.2.186.11926

Venkatesh, V., Morris, M. G., Davis, G. B., & Davis, F. D. (2003). User acceptance of information technology: Toward a unified view. *Management Information Systems Quarterly*, *27*(3), 425–478. doi:10.2307/30036540

Venkatesh, V., Thong, J. Y. L., & Xu, X. (2019). Consumer acceptance and use of information technology: Extending the unified theory of acceptance and use of technology. *Management Information Systems Quarterly*, *43*(3), 689–712. doi:10.25300/MISQ/2019/13534

Vijayan, V., Connolly, J. P., Condell, J., McKelvey, N., & Gardiner, P. (2021). Review of wearable devices and data collection considerations for connected health. *Sensors (Basel)*, *21*(16), 5589. doi:10.339021165589 PMID:34451032

Waheed, A., Mohiuddin, S. G., Shah, M. A., & Butt, M. A. (2019). Impact of transformational leadership on patient satisfaction and safety outcomes: A survey of healthcare professionals in Pakistan. *Journal of Healthcare Leadership*, *11*, 19–31.

Wang, L., & Chen, Y. (2017). Transformational leadership, creativity, and organizational innovation: A multilevel study. *Leadership and Organization Development Journal*, *38*(3), 304–318.

Wang, Y., & Cheng, B. (2018). Transformational leadership and employee voice behavior: A Pygmalion mechanism. *Journal of Business Research*, *92*, 37–47. doi:10.1016/j.jbusres.2018.06.014

Wang, Y., Zhang, L., & Liang, Q. (2022). Examining the influence of technology support and training on technology acceptance and usage: A study of mobile healthcare applications. *International Journal of Medical Informatics*, *156*, 104704. doi:10.1016/j.ijmedinf.2022.104704

Washington University School of Medicine. (2009). Deafness in disguise. *Author.* http://beckerexhibits.wustl.edu/did/timeline/#:~:text=The%20first%20wearable%20vacuum%20tube,of%20the%20firm's%20own%20design

Wong, D. W., Goh, K. H., & Leung, K. S. (2022). Explainable artificial intelligence in healthcare: A review. *Journal of Medical Systems*, *46*(1), 1–10. PMID:36580140

Wynn, M. G., Wagner, D. L., Arora, S., & Payne, T. H. (2021). Wearable technology in healthcare: Facilitating better decision-making for individuals and organizations. *Journal of the American Medical Informatics Association : JAMIA*, *28*(6), 1376–1384.

Xu, X., Lu, Y., Chen, X., & Huang, X. (2020). A user experience-oriented design for wearable medical devices based on augmented reality. *IEEE Access : Practical Innovations, Open Solutions*, *8*, 196598–196609.

Yadav, U. N., & Singh, N. (2021). Wearables for health and wellness: Opportunities and challenges. *Journal of Ambient Intelligence and Humanized Computing*, *12*(3), 3087–3106. doi:10.100712652-020-02664-x

Yang, Y. T., & Silverman, S. (2021). Wearables and internet of things in older adults' care. In Handbook of Smart Homes, Health Care and Well-Being (pp. 301-314). Springer.

Yao, Y., Li, J., Yu, X., & Li, J. (2021). An augmented reality-based framework for secure and private wearable biosensors. *IEEE Access : Practical Innovations, Open Solutions*, *9*, 128741–128749.

Yu, Y., Han, F., Bao, Y., & Ou, J. (2015). A study on data loss compensation of WiFi-based wireless sensor networks for structural health monitoring. *IEEE Sensors Journal*, *16*(10), 3811–3818. doi:10.1109/JSEN.2015.2512846

Zhong, Q., Huang, C., & Zhu, X. (2021). Artificial intelligence-powered wearable devices for medical applications. *NPJ Digital Medicine*, *4*(1), 1–13. PMID:33398041

Chapter 21
Holistic Approaches to Workplace Health and Wellness:
Applying System Theory and Archetypes Consultancy to Governmental Institutions

Maria D. Baez
https://orcid.org/0000-0002-5693-3825
Capitol Technology University, USA

ABSTRACT

This study proposes a comprehensive consulting approach for the New York City Department of Health and Mental Hygiene (NYCDHMH) to improve workplace well-being. This study investigated how the COVID-19 pandemic affected workers' well-being and how to alleviate their fears. The paper proposes a management change strategy using archetypes and system theory. NYCDHMH has the resources to create and implement a workplace well-being program, thanks to the research. The data helped identify knowledge, resource, and procedure gaps that may impede progress. Archetypes revealed and clarified work environment perceptions and interactions of the organizational structure of the NYCDHMH. The organizational framework, operational methodologies, and protocols were assessed using system theory to identify potential shortcomings. The study will propose a butterfly effect-based learning institution to address organizational transformation communication, collaboration, and decision-making issues. Broad perspectives were provided to NYCDHMH to launch a successful employee well-being program.

SYSTEM THEORY AND ARCHETYPES CONSULTANCY ARE TRANSFORMING GOVERNMENTAL INSTITUTIONS

Globally speaking, the COVID-19 epidemic has significantly influenced organizations, including the New York City Department of Health and Mental Hygiene. The pandemic has made it clear how crucial it is to prioritize employees' health and well-being, and the department has upped its focus on doing so (DuBrin, 2019). One program the department has put in place to assist staff well-being throughout the

DOI: 10.4018/979-8-3693-1634-4.ch021

epidemic is providing mental health services and support. In a poll conducted by the American Psychological Association, 78% of participants said the pandemic had caused them significant stress (APA, 2020). As a result, the department has given staff access to online stress and anxiety management tools, virtual counseling services, and other mental health resources.

Along with providing resources for mental health, the department has launched several projects to enhance physical health and well-being. For instance, the division has promoted healthy eating and lifestyle practices by offering resources and supporting staff members who exercise and take breaks during the workday. These programs are a component of the department's overall focus, which has been a top priority for several years, on staff health and well-being. In addition, to promote employee well-being, the department developed a comprehensive mental health strategy in 2017 (NYC Department of Health and Mental Hygiene, 2017). The need to address the psychological, social, and emotional facets of employee well-being was acknowledged in the plan. It featured programs to support staff members' mental health, advertise healthy habits, and cultivate a welcoming and inclusive workplace atmosphere (Goleman, 2018).

The department strives to enhance organizational performance while promoting employees' general health and well-being by prioritizing employee health and well-being. Organizations can benefit significantly from employee well-being, including higher productivity, decreased absenteeism, and lower healthcare expenses (Harvard Business Review, 2019). However, organizations currently emphasize putting long-term preventive measures into place more than avoiding the effects above. For instance, creating an organization-wide mental health strategy, encouraging good, effective communication at work, and creating strategic mental health training plans for organizational leaders (Gray et al., 2019; Weir, 2013).

Implementing these programs helps employers keep their present staff members, attract and retain top talent, and keep them content and productive (Davolt, 2006; Singh, 2019). Around the world, workplaces have been significantly impacted by the COVID-19 pandemic issue, including the 2017-founded New York City Department of Health and Mental Hygiene (NYCDHMH). The pandemic has made it clear how crucial it is to pay attention to employee health and well-being for moral and practical reasons. The department has realized how crucial it is to establish ways to promote staff mental health and wellness during these challenging times. As a result, more studies and projects are now aimed at enhancing employee health and well-being. Neglecting the health and well-being of employees can have significant adverse effects on firms. According to studies, poor employee well-being has been linked to higher healthcare expenditures, decreased productivity, and increased absenteeism.

According to a poll by the American Psychological Association, 78% of participants said the COVID-19 pandemic has significantly increased their stress levels. This has led to increased mental health difficulties (APA, 2020). The New York City Department of Health and Mental Hygiene has developed an organizational mental health plan to address these problems. This strategy focuses on encouraging positive and productive workplace dialogue, offering assistance and support to workers struggling with mental health issues, and creating tactical training programs for organizational leaders. The department wants to enhance employees' overall health and well-being while also enhancing organizational performance by prioritizing employee mental health and well-being. The COVID-19 pandemic has highlighted how crucial it is for businesses to prioritize employee health and well-being. In response to this demand, the New York City Department of Health and Mental Hygiene has implemented several programs to help staff members' mental health and well-being. The department strives to enhance organizational performance while promoting employees' general health and well-being by prioritizing employee health and well-being.

The COVID-19 pandemic has made it clear how crucial it is to give employees' health and well-being a top priority. The New York City Department of Health and Mental Hygiene has responded by implementing many programs to help staff members' mental and physical health. The department aims to enhance organizational performance while promoting employees' general health and well-being by prioritizing their needs (New York City Department of Health and Mental Hygiene [NYCDHMH], 2017). In addition, NYCDHMH has opted to address the issue of the growing emphasis on health and well-being in the workplace.

Priority one is to learn how this government agency responds to the COVID-19 pandemic. Priority two is to add to the body of knowledge by participating in the solution. In addition to spending more than $300 billion annually on related medical care costs brought on by workplace tension, numerous studies have shown that failing to prioritize employees' health and well-being can reduce organizational productivity, increase absenteeism, and increase turnover rates (APA, 2020; NYCDHMH, 2017).

Problem Statement

The NYC Health Department recognizes the importance of promoting employee health and wellness to enhance productivity, minimize absenteeism, and foster a positive work environment. Despite the endeavors undertaken to enhance the health and well-being of employees within the workplace, a more all-encompassing strategy is necessary to tackle the diverse health requirements of the workforce effectively. Numerous studies (Baxter et al., 2019; Baicker et al., 2018) have elucidated the advantageous effects of workplace wellness programs on employees' health outcomes, job satisfaction levels, and healthcare expenditures. Implementing such programs necessitates an interdisciplinary approach considering employees' specific health needs and obstacles.

Moreover, the COVID-19 pandemic has exacerbated pre-existing health conditions and introduced novel ones, including mental health issues, social isolation, and occupational exhaustion, necessitating attention in the workplace (Kang et al., 2021; Hysong et al., 2021). The issues above require attention as they can potentially hinder the employees' job performance. Therefore, the New York City Health Department must develop a comprehensive and customized approach to promote health and wellness in the workplace, which considers employees' physical, mental, and social well-being. The proposed plan should encompass the involvement of employees, endorsement from leadership, and cooperation with health experts to effectively address the diverse health needs of the workforce and foster a conducive work environment.

Significance

This initiative aims to foster a comprehensive outlook on health and wellness within the workplace of the New York City Health & Mental Hygiene Department. This initiative aims to improve the well-being of employees, increase productivity and job satisfaction, and ultimately promote the organization's overall success. Implementing a holistic approach that promotes physical, mental, and emotional wellness within the workplace has substantial implications for employers and employees. The methodology above recognizes the interconnectedness of various aspects of health, encompassing bodily, psychological, and metaphysical well-being, thereby enabling individuals to optimize their holistic wellness. As a result, this may lead to a reduction in stress levels, an improvement in the balance between work and personal life, and an increase in job satisfaction. Implementing a thorough workplace health and wellness strategy can yield numerous benefits for organizations, including increased productivity, reduced rates of employee absenteeism, and lowered healthcare costs.

Furthermore, through the promotion of employee well-being, corporations have the potential to improve their overall reputation and attractiveness, as well as retain exceptional personnel. Several academic studies have highlighted the benefits of embracing a holistic approach to health and wellness in the workplace. For example, the Lancet Public Health research indicated that augmenting physical activity, nutrition, and mental health could lead to a 12% increase in employee productivity, as reported by NHS England in 2018. In addition, in 2018, Deloitte conducted a study that found that companies that prioritize the welfare of their staff witness a retention rate that is 44% higher and a productivity surge of 19%.

Organization Overview

The New York City Department of Health and Mental Hygiene (NYCDHMH) has been for over 200 years in the country is a leading government agency in the list as one of the largest public health entities in the world; it has an annual budget of $ 1.6 billion in the boroughs of The Bronx, Brooklyn, Manhattan, and Queens. Staten Island is the only borough not receiving funding from the department (City of New York [NYC], 2020). The primary mission of the New York City Department of Health and Mental Hygiene (NYCDHMH) is to protect and promote the health of the city's eight million residents in a variety of settings, including the degrees of restaurant inspection, licenses used by dogs, veterinary clinics, and the distribution of birth certificates to New Yorkers (NYC, 2020). This public body is also essential to epidemiological research, which is used in formulating decisions and guidelines about New York City residents' health and well-being. Beyond concerns about policies and programs, NYCDHMH has a social obligation that extends further. It is also active in solving health problems such as obesity, diabetes, heart disease, and HIV/AIDS. It is also an active agent in solving societal problems such as addiction to cigarettes and other substances, discrimination, racism, and the threat of bioterrorism (NYC, 2020).

Due to the rapid expansion of the structure over the previous year, the Office for the Prevention, Care, and Treatment of Alcohol and Drug Use (BADUPCT) lends its support to the initiatives of the New York City Department of Health and Mental Hygiene (NYCDMH) to request a proposal theme with administrative training, managerial training, and development of staff (NYC, 2020). Figure 1 shows the hierarchical organizational structure of The New York City Department of Health and Mental Hygiene. It is important to note that even though the NYCDHMH is a government office that has more than 6,000 employees at the level of the five boroughs, this proposal only covers personnel related to the Office of Prevention and Attention and Treatment of the Use of Alcohol and Drugs, whose staff currently amounts to a total of 100 people (NYC Health and Mental Hygiene [NYCHMH], 2023).

Figure 1. Hierarchical organizational structure of the New York City Department of Health and Mental Hygiene

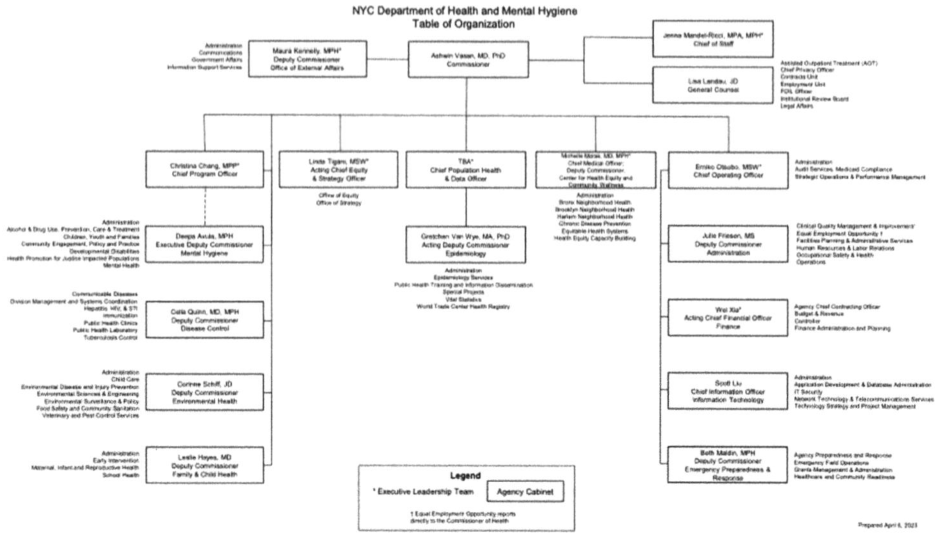

Lit Review to Providing Solutions Sought

Upon completing the process, the institution aims to enhance its leadership capacity to effectively handle change, expansion, and growth (Yukl, 2019; Brinkert, 2018; Caffarella, 2018). Additionally, the institution seeks to improve its management skills and competencies, foster teamwork and collaboration, and augment its organizational culture. All of these objectives are intended to be accomplished. Despite the initiation of specific programs by the upper management, the organization is still seeking means to enhance its structure and align it more effectively with its objectives (Cameron & Quinn, 2019; Kotter, 2018). The escalation in the count of recently promoted and newly appointed managers and supervisors with inadequate prior experience has led to a surge in the requirement for adequate managerial training concerning effective communication and operational frameworks (Brinkert, 2018).

The Critical Necessity for the Remodel. The New York City Department of Health and Mental Hygiene has implemented organizational and personnel changes in response to increased funding from the city to address the escalating problem of alcohol and drug abuse. Unfortunately, personnel changes have resulted in a decline in the overall standard of service. As a result, the management has broadened its focus on change management regarding the organizational culture (Burke, 2018). This includes diversity and inclusion, building and sustaining effective teams and enhancing leadership capacity to oversee the organization's growth and expansion. This action was taken to enhance the efficiency of change management.

Potential Effects. According to Gray et al. (2019) and Jones et al. (2019), recent studies conducted by retailers in the United States indicate that health improvements are significantly more significant among enterprises implementing health and wellness programs than those not. According to KFF et al. (2019), despite the restricted availability of data, the outcomes of these studies could influence the viewpoints and choices of decision-makers regarding the profitability of implementing such initiatives in the immediate and distant future. Organizations are increasingly adopting organizational structures that incorporate initiatives focused on their employees' mental and physical well-being to incentivize their workforce. As additional compensation, specific organizations provide complimentary counseling services to their staff members to encourage them to shed excess weight or quit smoking (Jones et al., 2019). The study's results indicate that innovative strategies, such as those mentioned, were developed based on insights from sociological and psychological sciences to facilitate modifying behavior resistant to change (Burke, 2018; KFF et al., 2019). As per the researchers who conducted the study, the results above should be utilized to advocate for personal well-being initiatives closely tied to a comprehensive reform vision. The perspective, as mentioned earlier, has the potential to facilitate future investments in initiatives aimed at enhancing organizational well-being and efficacy (Cutler et al., 2010).

According to a recent study by department store merchants in the United States, providing a workplace health plan for employees significantly impacts health improvement more than other enterprises that do not offer such plans. This event yields favorable outcomes for the organization, fostering collaboration among team members by establishing a workplace culture conducive to building trust. According to Madsen (2003), when employers offer resources and assistance to their employees to cultivate healthy habits and attain their objectives, it results in the sense of appreciation among the employees towards their employers.

The impact of employee availability on the initiation, execution, and maintenance of organizational wellness initiatives necessitates an assessment of their willingness to engage in a comprehensive health enhancement program. Madsen (2003) posits that an organization's ability to achieve and maintain a successful transition is contingent upon the dimensions of well-being demonstrated by individuals' resistance to change and the correlation between well-being and employee readiness for change. According to Smith (2005), if the individuals within the organization need more awareness regarding the importance of change, they possess the capacity to act as obstructive agents or advocates of change and resilient actors in future change initiatives.

Workplace health and wellness have recently gained significant attention as a critical concern. An increasing body of scholarly inquiry has been undertaken to examine the implications of this phenomenon for both individuals and enterprises. NYC Department of Health and Mental Hygiene acknowledges the significance of prioritizing health and wellness in the workplace. This literature review aims to provide a comprehensive overview of current research and discourse on the benefits of embracing a holistic perspective. Underscoring the importance of health and well-being within the workplace is an inescapable reality. The World Health Organization (WHO) has estimated that over 160 million individuals are diagnosed with work-related illnesses annually, and 7,600 individuals perish daily due to work-related injuries and diseases (WHO, 2018). Insufficient attention to personal health and well-being can result in adverse consequences for the individual and the organization. Poor health among individuals can lead to reduced productivity, higher absenteeism rates, and a diminished quality of life. Furthermore, the suboptimal health condition of an organization's workforce can adversely affect their productivity and morale, leading to an escalation in healthcare costs (Harvard Business Review, 2019).

Recent studies have indicated a significant correlation between the well-being and fitness of a company's employees and the organization's overall productivity. For example, according to a study published in the Harvard Business Review, companies that allocate resources toward employee health programs experience a significant return on investment. The study found that for every dollar invested, there is a 6:1 return on investment (Harvard Business Review, 2019). In addition, the International Labour Organization (ILO) conducted a study that revealed that workers who maintain good health exhibit higher productivity levels and take fewer sick leaves. This, in turn, leads to a substantial decrease in both medical care expenses and employee absenteeism (ILO, 2018).

Advantages of Taking a Holistic Approach. Adopting a holistic perspective that prioritizes the workforce's mental, emotional, and social well-being can yield numerous benefits for individuals and businesses. Assuming a more holistic perspective can lead to an elevation in an individual's sense of well-being, level of work involvement, and job satisfaction. According to Forbes (2019), a comprehensive perspective can result in enhanced productivity, reduced absenteeism, and diminished healthcare-related expenses for organizations.

Preserving personal health and overall wellness within the workplace is a significant consideration for both individuals and corporations. Recent studies have revealed a significant correlation between the well-being and fitness of a company's employees and the organization's overall effectiveness. Adopting a holistic perspective that prioritizes the workforce's mental, emotional, and social well-being can yield numerous benefits for individuals and businesses (Goleman, 2018). The results of this literary analysis provide substantiation for the emphasis that the New York City Health and Mental Hygiene Department has allocated towards promoting health and well-being within the professional setting. The recognition is grounded on the premise that the outcomes of this analysis furnish substantiation to endorse this emphasis.

METHODOLOGY

The present study employs a qualitative approach to investigate the viewpoints and encounters of all stakeholders in a department of a company of moderate size. The department under consideration comprises one hundred individuals, most of whom have recently recruited personnel, with the remaining members being longstanding employees. The department comprises a heterogeneous group of senior managers, mid-level managers, and supervisors in the management realm. The application of systems theory and archetypes functioned as a mechanism to apprehend the viewpoints of all constituents within the department, encompassing upper-level management, middle management, frontline supervisors, staff members, and clients. The comprehensive analysis, which incorporated all stakeholders, facilitated a thorough comprehension of the department and its obstacles in attaining its goals.

Systems Theory and Archetypes to Address Trend

The literature suggests two distinct feedback loops exist, namely reinforcement and balancing, as posited by Ramage and Shipp (2020) and Senge (2006). The system in question is exhibiting indications of reinforcement, as illustrated in Figure 2. The organization experienced a 68% increase in its overall structure during the previous year. In situations characterized by rapid development, it is commonly posited that reinforcing feedback diminishes the size of individual droplets, ultimately culminating in the formation of a larger jet (Ramage & Shipp, 2020; Senge, 2006).

Figure 2. Feedback loop with a reinforcement approach

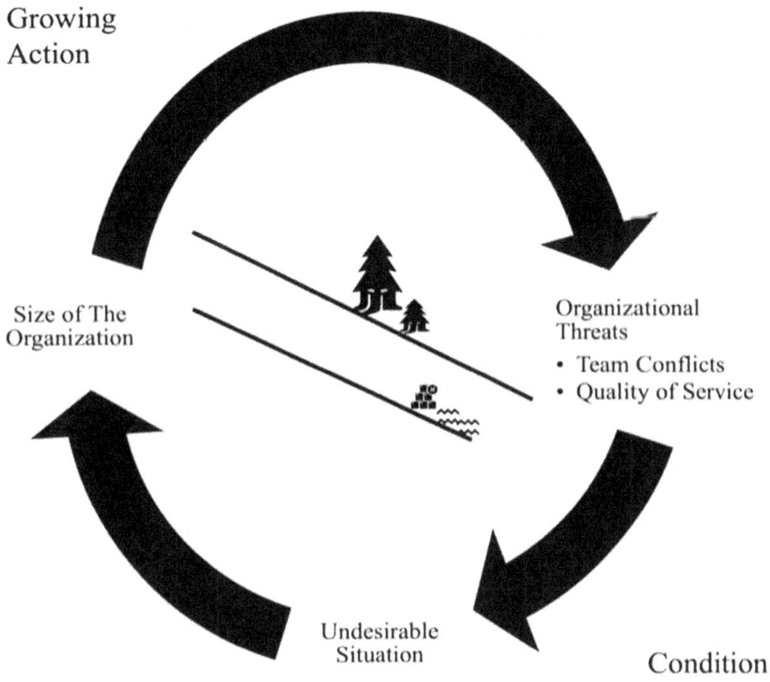

Assuming that recently appointed managers and supervisors have been either promoted from within the organization or recruited externally but have yet to receive adequate managerial training. Under such circumstances, behavioral manifestations could stem from a misalignment between the department's overarching goals and objectives and those of the broader organization. A comprehensive comprehension of the feedback loop process is imperative. The interaction of various sections within a system has led to the development of active internal forces. To comprehend the system's functioning holistically, it is imperative to identify the constituent factors that contribute to the problem. The amplification of each movement in a consistent direction leads to a reinforcement process that yields minor independent modifications. In the present scenario, wherein the organizational framework of the employees has expanded owing to the rise in funds and provision of services to the community, the efficient management of employee welfare is compromised. This phenomenon can be attributed to the expansion of the organizational workforce. Multilayer constructions comprising diminutive structures will only persist in undergoing undesired movements if external forces implement counteractive measures to rectify the issue.

The diagram depicted in Figure 3 illustrates a balancing feedback loop, which is an application of systems theory in the context of the growing emphasis on health and wellness in the workplace. The diagram outlines a strategy to achieve equilibrium and establish stability and resilience in the organizational cycle by balancing the process and providing structure. One potential solution for restoring balance to the process involves the addition of additional personnel. However, the implemented measures failed to yield the intended results due to the absence of a documented specification outlining the objectives to be pursued and inadequate communication regarding the nature of the work to be executed. If employees are not identified promptly, they may display unanticipated and detrimental conduct, including conscious or unconscious opposition to change. The manifestation of these behaviors can be attributed to the process of achieving balance. From a systemic perspective, the focus is primarily on long-term outcomes, irrespective of the presence or absence of a feedback loop. The archetype systems, including the limits to growth archetype, are constructed by assembling fundamental components, as highlighted by Ramage and Shipp (2020) and Senge (2006).

Figure 3. Balancing feedback loop

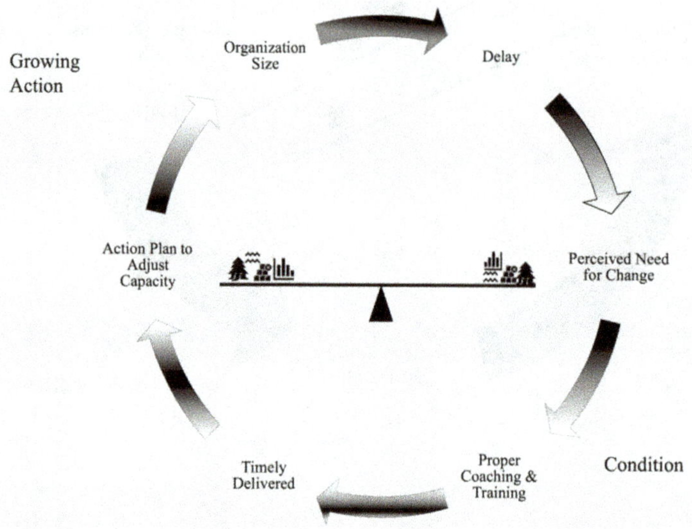

The proliferation of management and supervisory roles has led to a greater prevalence of the fortification process. Furthermore, it will disrupt the balance of the process, thereby affecting the system's efficiency. The principle of management being implemented in this scenario is depicted in Figure 4 and can be identified as the archetype of limits to growth. According to Senge (2006, p. 95), eliminating growth-limiting factors necessitates avoiding expansion. As an illustration, the growth strategy involved recruiting and appointing more personnel in managerial and supervisory positions to address the escalating demand for services (push growth). However, the departmental framework expanded without adequate focus on managerial training, constraining growth.

Figure 4. System overview through the limits to growth archetype

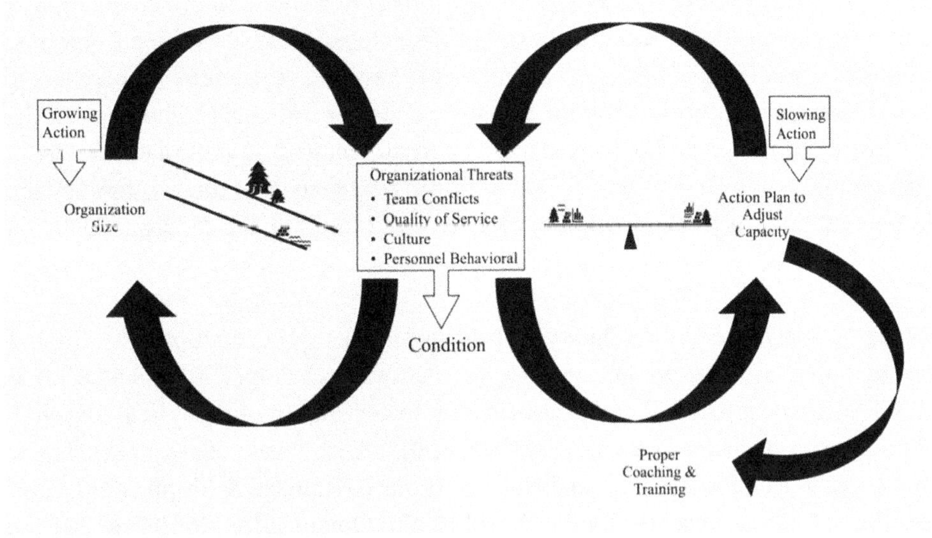

Adequate emphasis on employee training has the potential to impact the organizational culture and promote positive mental patterns. Failure to align with organizational objectives and loss of organizational identity may result in increased internal conflicts within group dynamics, as per Cameron and Diaz's (2018) findings. Each occurrence of growth restriction is distinct, and the approach to implementing the growth augmentation procedure varies from case to case.

Systems Theory Application on Employee Well-Being Programs in the Workplace

In light of the increasing recognition of the importance of health and wellness in the workplace, many enterprises have adopted systems theory as a conceptual model to tackle these complex concerns. The theory of systems highlights the interconnectedness of systems and the potential for modifications to one component of a system to generate reverberations that permeate the entire system. This methodology is appropriate for tackling the multifaceted physical and mental welfare of individuals engaged in occupational activities (Zulhasmi, 2021).

Recently, there has been increased awareness regarding the significance of employees' adherence to a healthy lifestyle during work hours (Ramage & Shipp, 2020; Zulhasmi et al., 2021). Numerous enterprises have realized that guaranteeing the well-being and contentment of their employees is imperative not solely from a philosophical and ethical stance but also from an economic perspective (Zulhasmi et al., 2021). Numerous studies have indicated that promoting health and wellness within the workplace can lead to heightened levels of productivity, enhanced employee engagement, and reduced healthcare costs (Zulhasmi et al., 2021). The application of systems theory can aid organizations in understanding the intricate interconnections between employee wellness and workplace conditions (Meadows, 2008; Ramage & Shipp, 2020; Senge, 2006). The application of systems theory can facilitate the achievement of this objective.

The conceptual framework of systems theory emphasizes the interrelatedness of all constituent elements that constitute a particular system (Meadows, 2008; Ramage & Shipp, 2020; Senge, 2006; Zulhasmi et al., 2021). The assertion posits that modifications implemented on only constituents of a specific system can impact all other constituents of the system and that the system in its entirety possesses a magnitude that surpasses the summation of the individual values of its constituents (Meadows, 2008; Ramage & Shipp, 2020; Senge, 2006). Applying systems theory in the context of workplace health and wellness can give organizations a holistic comprehension of how diverse facets of the work milieu and ethos can influence the general welfare of their workforce (Meadows, 2008; Ramage & Shipp, 2020; Senge, 2006). This information could be advantageous to promoting health and wellness in the workplace (Zulhasmi et al., 2021).

One instance of applying systems theory to practical issues in occupational health and wellbeing (HPW) is the creation of a *health-promoting workplace* (Ramage & Shipp, 2020; Senge, 2006; Zulhasmi et al., 2021). HPW are occupational environments that foster employees' physical, psychological, and social well-being through various activities and interventions (Zulhasmi et al., 2021). The work setting is commonly known as a conducive and salubrious workplace (Ramage & Shipp, 2020; Zulhasmi et al., 2021). As per the definition presented by the World Health Organization (WHO) in 2019, the HPW is distinguished by a joint endeavor between employees and supervisors to execute an ongoing enhancement procedure that is intended to preserve and augment the health, safety, and comprehensive welfare of workers, while simultaneously guaranteeing the durability of the workplace (Zulhasmi et al., 2021).

Developing an HPW program necessitates comprehensively applying systems thinking (Ramage & Shipp, 2020). For the technique to achieve success, it is imperative that it can recognize and tackle the interrelated elements that impact the welfare of the workforce (Meadows, 2008; Ramage & Shipp, 2020; Senge, 2006). According to Kramer et al. (2021), the components mentioned above encompass a range of factors that impact employee well-being, including the physical environment (e.g., lighting and air quality), job design (e.g., workload and autonomy), organizational culture (e.g., support for work-life balance and recognition of employee achievements), and social relationships (e.g., communication with colleagues and supervisor support). Businesses can create a conducive working environment that promotes their employees' emotional and physical well-being by implementing a comprehensive strategy that considers all relevant factors (Kramer et al., 2021; Ramage & Shipp, 2020; Senge, 2006; Zulhasmi et al., 2021).

The results of multiple research studies have determined that High-Performance Work Systems (HPWs) can bestow many advantages not solely upon the employees but also upon the organizations that hire them (Kramer et al., 2021). For example, the ILO (2019) research findings suggest that hiring HPW is associated with heightened productivity, decreased absenteeism, and reduced expenses related to medical treatment. In addition, the World Health Organization conducted a recent study that suggests implementing HPW is associated with increased job satisfaction levels and decreased job-related stress among employees (WHO, 2019).

According to the theoretical framework of systems theory, there is an inherent interconnectivity among all constituent elements, and systems comprise interdependent components that collaborate towards a shared objective (Meadows, 2008; Ramage & Shipp, 2020; Senge, 2006). In the workplace setting, it is crucial to acknowledge that employees' well-being and physical condition are not solely a matter of personal concern but rather a business matter that is impacted by various factors, including the physical environment, the work culture, and the management approaches (Kramer et al., 2021; Ramage & Shipp, 2020; Senge, 2006; Zulhasmi et al., 2021). Therefore, implementing a systems approach is deemed the most efficacious strategy for enterprises to effectively address the root causes of inadequate health and wellness among their workforce in the context of health and wellness management (Kramer et al., 2021; Ramage & Shipp, 2020; Senge, 2006; Zulhasmi et al., 2021).

The capacity of a system to adjust to alterations and uphold stability is facilitated by feedback loops, which are a fundamental constituent of systems theory (Meadows, 2008; Senge, 2006). Feedback loops facilitate the capacity to function. Incorporating feedback loops can function as a mechanism for overseeing staff members' physical and emotional welfare within the workplace health and wellness (Meadows, 2008; Ramage & Shipp, 2020; Senge, 2006). This also enables modifying organizational procedures and practices based on employee feedback (Meadows, 2008; Ramage & Shipp, 2020; Senge, 2006). For example, suppose employees express stress and an overwhelming workload. In that case, a business may utilize this feedback to modify task requirements, furnish supplementary resources or aid, or establish channels for stress alleviation (Meadows, 2008; Ramage & Shipp, 2020; Senge, 2006).

According to Ramage & Shipp (2020), emergent properties constitute a fundamental component of systems theory. The concept posits that properties emerge due to the interplay among a given system's diverse constituents. For example, the workplace health and wellness field may exhibit emergent qualities that encompass a variety of outcomes, such as the development of a communal atmosphere among staff members, heightened levels of job satisfaction, or increased productivity (Kramer et al., 2021; Ramage & Shipp; Zulhasmi et al., 2021). Organizations can foster a workplace culture that promotes their employees' physical and mental well-being by prioritizing the development of advantageous emergent traits (Senge, 2006; Zulhasmi et al., 2021).

Systems theory sheds light on the importance of boundaries and subsystems. Subsystems are discrete system elements with distinct properties and dynamics (Meadows, 2008; Ramage & Shipp, 2020; Senge, 2006). Boundaries refer to the physical division between subsystems (Senge, 2006). In the organizational context, the division may involve diverse departments or teams. As a result, organizations can customize their health and wellness initiatives to better align with the distinct demands of each subsystem, thereby acknowledging their unique requirements and dynamics and enabling the organizational environment to enhance their ability to cater to their entire demographic (Kramer et al., 2021; Meadows, 2008; Ramage & Shipp, 2020; Senge, 2006)

Applying systems theory in occupational health and wellbeing could lead to various tangible outcomes in reality (Senge, 2006; Zulhasmi et al., 2021). Utilizing methodologies derived from systems thinking, including causal loop diagrams and system maps, represents a viable approach for businesses to identify the key determinants that impact their employees' physical and mental health and well-being (Senge, 2006). The utilization of feedback loops can be utilized to monitor the effectiveness of health and wellness initiatives and subsequently modify them more suitably (Meadows, 2008; Ramage & Shipp, 2020; Senge, 2006). Adopting a systems approach toward health and wellness can enhance the overall efficacy of organizations by fostering a workplace culture that accords priority to their personnel's physical and mental well-being (Kramer et al., 2021; Meadows, 2008; Ramage & Shipp, 2020; Senge, 2006). This objective can be achieved through the systematic approach to addressing health and wellness, as Zaman et al. (2021) suggested.

According to Ramage and Shipp (2020) and Senge (2006) statements, applying systems theory can offer a beneficial structure for enterprises that aim to promote the health and fitness of their employees in the workplace. Appling system theory is essential because its implementation drives a comprehensive approach considering the interrelated factors that impact health (Meadows, 2008; Ramage & Shipp, 2020; Senge, 2006). As a result, organizations can establish a workplace setting that promotes their workforce's physical and mental welfare (Ramage & Shipp, 2020; Senge, 2006; Zulhasmi et al., 2021).

Empirical studies have demonstrated that Health and Productivity Wellness (HPW) programs provide diverse advantages to both employees and organizations (Kramer et al., 2021; Meadows, 2008; Ramage & Shipp, 2020; Senge, 2006; Zulhasmi et al., 2021). The benefits can be categorized into multiple groups (Ramage & Shipp, 2020; Senge, 2006). A significant association exists between companies prioritizing their employees' well-being and contentment and the probability of these companies experiencing favorable economic results (Kramer et al., 2021; Zulhasmi et al., 2021). The utilization of systems theory provides a comprehensive structure for effectively managing the complex challenges linked to sustaining and enhancing health and wellness in organizational settings (Ramage & Shipp, 2020; Senge, 2006; Zulhasmi et al., 2021). Organizations can foster a conducive environment for the health and well-being of their staff members by acknowledging the interrelatedness of systems, the importance of feedback loops, the emergence of features, and the delineation of boundaries (Kramer et al., 2021). Utilizing systems thinking tools in practical settings can facilitate identifying and resolving fundamental factors contributing to employees' suboptimal health and well-being outcomes (Ramage & Shipp, 2020; Senge, 2006). As a result, enhanced organizational performance and a more content and resilient workforce can be achieved (Zulhasmi et al., 2021).

Establishing a framework to develop the knowledge required to adapt to changes can be facilitated by applying systems theory and mental models, particularly in the context of a heightened emphasis on workplace health (Kramer et al., 2021; Senge, 2006). Developing organizational culture systematically enhances the leader's ability to manage changes effectively (Yukl, 2019). Senge (2006) posits that organizations may become entrapped by their organizational structure due to the diverse cognitive and social approaches of their personnel. The organization has the potential to facilitate the growth and advancement of individuals by providing support in enhancing personal mastery, management skills, capacity, and competencies through the provision of training and coaching (Ramage & Shipp, 2020; Senge, 2006; Yukl, 2019). The emergence of fresh individual conduct due to this process is expected to have a constructive impact on the overall organizational framework (Kramer et al., 2021; Zulhasmi et al., 2021). This occurrence can be likened to the butterfly effect, as previously noted in scholarly works (Gleick, 2008; Zaman et al., 2021).

Developing organizational culture systematically enhances the leader's ability to manage changes effectively (Kramer et al., 2021; Yukl, 2018; Zulhasmi et al., 2021). In order to enhance the significance of cooperation, collaboration, and organizational culture, it is advantageous to comprehend the cognitive frameworks that individuals utilize (Zaman et al., 2021; Zulhasmi et al., 2021). Moreover, leaders can identify and eradicate cognitive obstacles that impede the system's growth by promoting the cultivation of novel modes of cognition and cognitive frameworks (Ramage & Shipp, 2020; Yukl, 2019; Zulhasmi et al., 2021). The recognition that comprehending the impact of mental models is crucial for attaining enduring and uncomplicated resolutions can prompt leaders within organizations to engage in systematic thinking (Senge, 2006). Furthermore, individuals are more likely to comprehend that the consequences of a system are not solely derived from the summation of its constituent parts but also from the interrelationships among those components (Meadows, 2006; Zemke, 2001).

RECOMMENDATIONS

Establishing a Learning Organization

Establishing a learning organization characterized by an organizational culture that prioritizes the cultivation of self-leadership, alignment of members with the organizational vision, and collaborative teamwork toward shared objectives fosters a salubrious environment within the organization. Senge (2006) posits that an organization can be deemed a learning organization when each individual engages in independent learning. Upon achieving consensus among all members of the organization, it becomes feasible to establish an organizational learning system that fosters the promotion of health and well-being.

Promoting Personal Initiative and Leadership

The training and coaching sessions aim to promote self-leadership to address challenges related to establishing a coherent trajectory toward enhancing self-awareness, concentration, and compassion for every team member (Dawson, 2018). In addition, enhancing an individual's ability to explore and maintain emotional stability during stressful situations can cultivate improved and prosperous interconnections among team members.

Thinking as a Team

Facilitate enhancing engagement, well-being, and performance by acquiring a practical understanding of the application of system thinking and mental models in routine contexts. This will facilitate enhancing one's capacity to comprehend complex situations and effectively handle the interrelatedness among team members. In addition, by pursuing a collective organizational goal that transcends individual aspirations, individuals can enhance their ability to thrive and generate positive outcomes in a setting that fosters openness and constructive feedback.

Dismantling Hidden Fallacies

The butterfly effect is an essential factor when considering hidden pitfalls and the steps to address health and wellness concerns in the workplace. According to Gleick (2008), it is the effect and consequence of the actions, behaviors, and interactions of the elements in a system. Small changes in the system, whether anticipated or not, can lead to countless new events, such as blocking the ability of leadership to learn and develop. In some cases, entropy can lead to the disappearance of the organization if leaders do not act and implement strategies for change that value the significance and influence of the organization's development. Leadership at the individual and team levels in system dynamics is changeable and can be maintained over the long run.

The degree of organizational transformation is directly proportional to the leadership's thinking system and quality perspective. Paying attention to the outcomes of even minor organizational culture shifts resulting from staff training is essential. Leaders must make acceptable modifications to people training to avoid creating troublesome consequences. Cultivating a holistic vision within the context of the organizational culture is an essential step in creating a thinking system. To accomplish this objective, each member of the team or organization needs to be on board with the plan and think about a more comprehensive notion of the system's dynamics.

Revitalizing the Workplace

The presence of physically and mentally fit employees is positively correlated with increased productivity in the workplace. What strategies can be implemented to rejuvenate the workplace and enhance the well-being of employees? Increasing the scope of wellness programs can serve as a promising initiative. The significance of employee well-being in the workplace has led to a growing interest in motivational programs focused on wellness. The services above entail working in partnership with employers to identify their workforce's unique needs and challenges, devising customized wellness programs and initiatives, and evaluating the effectiveness of said interventions (Abebe, 2015). These initiatives aim to promote positive health practices among employees, reduce health risks and absenteeism, improve employee involvement and satisfaction, and ultimately enhance organizational performance (American Heart Association [AHA] 2019). In general, motivational programs aimed at promoting wellness in the workplace begin with a needs assessment to identify areas where employee well-being could be improved (Goetzel et al., 2014). Implementing workplace wellness programs involves collaborating with management to provide education and resources that promote a healthy organizational culture and enhance employee well-being.

Evaluating the effectiveness of wellness programs is crucial in determining their impact and making necessary adjustments. To ensure the effectiveness of wellness workplace consultation programs, the organization must cultivate a culture that prioritizes the welfare of its workforce and allocate adequate resources and investment toward these initiatives. Furthermore, it is recommended that employers engage their employees in creating and implementing wellness programs in the workplace to enhance employee involvement and responsibility. Moreover, it is recommended that the organization regularly communicate information about the benefits and resources provided by wellness programs to their employees to maximize employee engagement (Zulhasmi, 2021). To successfully implement wellness workplace consultation programs, organizations must prioritize employee well-being and allocate adequate resources toward these initiatives.

CONCLUSION

The paper expounded on the advantages of broadening wellness motivational programs to promote employee health and productivity. The utilization of such services may aid employees in mitigating stress levels, enhancing their mental and physical well-being, and augmenting their productivity. The study offered significant perspectives on utilizing system theory and archetype consultancy to enhance workplace health and wellness in governmental organizations. The data emphasize the significance of taking into account the complete workplace system and employing archetypes to comprehend the organizational culture and behaviors that influence the well-being of employees.

Applying system theory and archetypes consultancy offers a comprehensive framework for tackling health and wellness concerns in governmental organizations. The article highlights the necessity of adopting a comprehensive approach considering various factors. Additionally, it sheds light on governmental institutions' obstacles in encouraging workplace health and wellness. These challenges include bureaucratic hurdles, insufficient funding, and opposition to change. Finally, the challenges mentioned earlier can be effectively tackled by implementing systems thinking approach and utilizing archetypes. The present study offers significant perspectives for policymakers, organizational executives, and professionals who aim to enhance workplace health and wellness within governmental establishments. The methodology employed by the authors presents a potentially effective tactic for tackling workplace health and wellness concerns in a comprehensive and enduring manner, ultimately yielding advantages for both personnel and the entities they work for.

REFERENCES:

Abebe, N. (2015). The value of workplace wellness programs. *Employee Benefit Plan Review*, *70*(2), 7–9. https://tcsedsystem.idm.oclc.org/login?url=https://search-proquest-com.tcsedsystem.idm.oclc.org/docview/1703268946?accountid=34120

American Heart Association. (2019). *Workplace Health Solutions: Guidelines for a Holistic Approach.* AHA. https://www.heart.org/-/media/files/health-topics/workplace-health/workplace-health-solutions-guidelines-for-a-holistic-approach-ucm_497722.pdf

American Psychological Association. (2020). *Stress in America 2020: A National Mental Health Crisis.* APA. https://www.apa.org/news/press/releases/stress/2020/report

Baicker, K., Cutler, D., & Song, Z. (2010). Workplace wellness programs can generate savings. *Health Affairs*, *29*(2), 304–311. doi:10.1377/hlthaff.2009.0626 PMID:20075081

Brinkert, R. (2018). Authentic leadership: Clarifying the construct. *The Journal of Values Based Leadership*, *11*(1), 1–13.

Burke, W. W. (2018). *Organization change: Theory & practice* (5th ed.). SAGE.

Caffarella, R. S. (2018). *Planning programs for adult learners: A practical guide*. John Wiley & Sons.

Cameron, K. S., & Quinn, R. E. (2019). *Diagnosing and changing organizational culture: Based on the competing values framework*. John Wiley & Sons.

Cutler, D. M., Baicker, K., & Song, Z. (2010, February). *Workplace wellness programs can generate savings*. Harvard. https://scholar.harvard.edu/cutler/publications/workplace-wellness-programs-can-generate-savings

Davolt, S. (2006). Jobs that make you sane: Employees in the pink put employers in the green. *Employee Benefit News, pp. 1*, 1–1.

Dawson, J. F. (2018). Leadership development in the digital age. *Journal of Leadership Studies*, *12*(4), 34–45.

Deloitte. (2018). *Global Human Capital Trends: The Rise of the Social Enterprise*. Deloitte. https://www2.deloitte.com/global/en/pages/about-deloitte/articles/human-capital-trends.html

DuBrin, A. J. (2019). *Leadership: Research findings, practice, and skills*. Cengage Learning.

Forbes. (2019). The Business Case For Health And Wellbeing In The Workplace. *Forbes*. https://www.forbes.com/sites/nazbeheshti/2019/07/09/the-business-case-for-health-and-wellbeing-in-the-workplace/?sh=68a4568c39f1

Goetzel, R. Z., Henke, R. M., Tabrizi, M., Pelletier, K. R., Loeppke, R., Ballard, D. W., & Serxner, S. (2014). Do workplace health promotion (wellness) programs work? *Journal of Occupational and Environmental Medicine*, *56*(9), 927–934. doi:10.1097/JOM.0000000000000276 PMID:25153303

Goleman, D. (2018). The importance of emotional intelligence in leadership. International. *Journal of Management & Business Studies*, *8*(2), 67–72.

Gray, P., Senabe, S., Naicker, N., Kgalamono, S., Yassi, A., & Spiegel, J. M. (2019). Workplace-based organizational interventions promoting mental health and happiness among healthcare workers: A realist review. *International Journal of Environmental Research and Public Health*, *16*(22), 4396. doi:10.3390/ijerph16224396 PMID:31717906

Harvard Business Review. (2019). What is the Hard Return on Employee Wellness Programs? *Harvard Business Review.* https://hbr.org/2010/12/whats-the-hard-return-on-employee-wellness-programs

International Labor Organization. (2018). *Healthy Employees, Healthy Business: A Practical Guide to Workplace Health Promotion.* ILO. https://www.ilo.org/wcmsp5/groups/public/---ed_protect/---protrav/---safework/documents/publication/wcms_633408.pdf

Jones, D., Molitor, D., & Reif, J. (2019). What do workplace wellness programs do? Evidence from the Illinois workplace wellness study. *The Quarterly Journal of Economics*, *134*(4), 1747–1791. doi:10.1093/qje/qjz023 PMID:31564754

Kaiser Family Foundation. Song, Z., & Baicker, K. (2019, September 24). *Effect of a workplace wellness program on employee health and economic outcomes.* KFF. https://www.kff.org/health-costs/report/2018-employer-health-benefits-survey/

Kallio, J., Vildjiounaite, E., Kantorovitch, J., Kinnula, A., & Bordallo López, M. (2021). Unobtrusive Continuous Stress Detection in Knowledge Work—Statistical Analysis on User Acceptance. *Sustainability (Basel)*, *13*(4), 2003. doi:10.3390u13042003

Ko, C., Tang, S., & Shen, Y. (2021). Case Analysis and Thinking of Scheme Analysis Based on Mobile New Systems in Psychological Education. *Mobile Information Systems*, *2021*, 1–11. doi:10.1155/2021/1361071

Kotter, J. P. (2018). *Leading change*. Harvard Business Press.

Kramer, J., Kao, D., & Gorfinkel, L. (2021). Supporting Employee Mental Health and Well-being during COVID-19. *Harvard Business Review*. https://hbr.org/2021/02/supporting-employee-mental-health-and-well-being-during-covid-19

Madsen, S. R. (2003). Wellness in the workplace: Preparing employees for change. *Organization Development Journal*, *21*(1), 46. https://tcsedsystem.idm.oclc.org/login?url=https://search-proquest-com.tcsedsystem.idm.oclc.org/docview/198001436?accountid=34120

Meadows, D. H., & Wright, D. (2008). *Thinking in systems: A primer*. Chelsea Green Pub.

New York City Department of Health and Mental Hygiene. (2017). Mental Health Strategic Plan. NYCDHMH. https://www1.nyc.gov/assets/doh/downloads/pdf/about/mental-health-strategic-plan-2017.pdf

New York City Health and Mental Hygiene. (2023, April 6). *NYC Department of Health and Mental Hygiene Table of organization.* NYC Department of Health and Mental Hygiene. https://www.nyc.gov/assets/doh/downloads/pdf/public/dohmh-orgchart.pdf

NHS England. (2018). *Healthy Workforce: NHS Staff Health and Wellbeing Review.* NHS England. https://www.england.nhs.uk/wp-content/uploads/2018/07/healthy-workforce-nhs-staff-health-and-wellbeing-review.pdf

Ramage, M., & Shipp, K. (2020). Peter Senge. In Systems Thinkers (pp. 119–128). Springer London. doi:10.1007/978-1-4471-7475-2_12

Senge, P. M. (2006). *The fifth discipline: The art and practice of the learning organization.* Crown Business.

Singh, D. (2019). A literature review on employee retention with a focus on recent trends. *International Journal of Scientific Research in Science and Technology*, *6*(1), 425–431.

Smith, I. (2005). Achieving readiness for organizational change. *Library Management, 26*(6), 408–412. doi:http://dx.doi.org.tcsedsystem.idm.oclc.org/10.1108/01435120510623764

The City of New York. (2020). *About the NYC Department of Health and Mental Hygiene.* NYCDHMH. https://www1.nyc.gov/site/doh/about/about-doh.page

Weir, K. (2013). *Work, stress, and health.* American Psychological Association. http://www.apa.org/monitor/2013/09/stress-health.aspx

World Health Organization. (2018). *Global Estimates of Occupational Accidents and Work-related Illnesses 2017.* WHO. https://www.who.int/publications/i/item/global-estimates-of-occupational-accidents-and-work-related-illnesses-2017

Yukl, G. (2019). *Leadership in organizations.* Pearson Education.

Zaman, U., Raza, S. H., Abbasi, S., Aktan, M., & Farías, P. (2021). Sustainable or a butterfly effect in global tourism? Nexus of pandemic fatigue, covid-19-branded destination safety, travel stimulus incentives, and post-pandemic revenge travel. *Sustainability (Basel), 13*(22), 12834. doi:10.3390u132212834

Zemke, R. (2001). Systems thinking. *Training (New York, N.Y.), 38*(2), 40–46. https://tcsedsystem.idm.oclc.org/login?url=https://search-proquest-com.tcsedsystem.idm.oclc.org/docview/203391582?accountid=34120

Zulhasmi, R F., Zamralita, Z. and Saraswati, H, D, K. (2021). *The Influences of Psychological Capital and Job Resources Towards Work Engagement.* Atlantis Press. . doi:10.2991/assehr.k.210805.181

Chapter 22
Correcting Misappropriation in the Corporate Environment:
A Case Study

Andrea Renee McCready
https://orcid.org/0009-0007-0031-114X
Marymount University, USA

ABSTRACT

This case study describes the experience of an organization in crisis. An audit conducted by the company's board of directors revealed that directors have been charging personal expenses to their company charge cards. The company is losing an average of $375,000 per year to this practice. The former chief financial officer has resigned after two years of bringing this to the attention of the chief operating officer and the chief executive officer. Now the organization has new management in these three positions, but they need to find a strategy to manage the situation, which remains the same. The application of strategy models, organizational culture theories, ethical decision-making theories, and leadership theories are recommended as solutions to correct the unwanted behavior. Finally, the implementation of an accountable plan is recommended along with policy and procedure surrounding expenses.

INTRODUCTION

The direction and management of a company is a board of directors' legal responsibility under state law. Part of this duty encompasses effective oversight. Because a board delegates authority to the senior management of a company, there must be a continual flow of timely information between senior management and the board for true oversight to take place (Gregory, 2022). Audits are one effective tool at the disposal of a board to ensure the quality and accuracy of the information provided by management to the board. It also allows board members to hear a different perspective on the information given to the board, free from emphasis or bias.

Following one such audit conducted by the board of directors, a material source of risk has been identified. The company is losing $375,000 per year, on average, for the past 5 years to senior manage-

DOI: 10.4018/979-8-3693-1634-4.ch022

ment using corporate credit cards for personal purchases. The impetus for the board of directors' audit is unknown, however, the evidence points to poor financial performance by the company. An investigation into this issue revealed that, in addition to the overt financial losses suffered by the company, there has been a significant loss of human capital. The chief financial officer (CFO) resigned in frustration after 2 years of repeatedly bringing this issue to the attention of both the chief operating officer (COO) and the chief executive officer (CEO) to no avail.

The organization now has new officers in the CFO, COO, and CEO positions. What has not changed, however, are the policies, or more precisely, lack thereof that allowed this behavior in the first place. This report outlines a recommendation to mitigate the risks to the organization and to proffer a risk management strategy. Multiple models and theories are applied in part or in whole. Together they form an overall strategy for dealing with these issues.

PROBLEM STATEMENT

The problem of losing money and senior employees, while serious, is only part of the issue at hand. The fact that numerous officers felt it was acceptable to openly steal from the company points to a warped corporate culture coupled with a lack of policy and procedures. The issue is compounded by the fact that the management who must fix this problem are the same ones who are causing the problem. Resolution of this issue requires not only buy-in from senior management, but a complete reversal from past behavior.

A five-year loss of $1.87 MIL to theft is a sobering figure. It is clear from the loss of human capital that the current management of the company is ineffective, at best and a source of human resource risk at worst. These issues represent deficiencies that are a direct threat to the future viability of the company if not addressed.

LITERATURE REVIEW

Strategy Models

A review of literature of various strategy and leadership models provides a basis to plan the strategy for a much-needed course correction for this organization. An overall strategy is considered that will address the obvious problems and continually improve the organization beyond addressing the current crisis. Theories with a primarily internal locus were considered, as that is where this threat to the organization originates.

The Plan, Do, Check and Act (PDCA) is deceptively simple, but it effectively introduces the scientific method into the business. The PDCA cycle is used to walk through the process of introducing a solution, evaluating, adopting, abandoning, or running a proposed solution through the cycle again. The final step is to review the results. Users must determine what was wrong and what lessons should be learned from it (Panteli, et al., 2019). The cycle repeats as shown in Figure 1 Panteli et al., 2019).

Figure 1. From "Understanding healthcare quality strategies: a five-lens framework," by Panteli et al, 2019

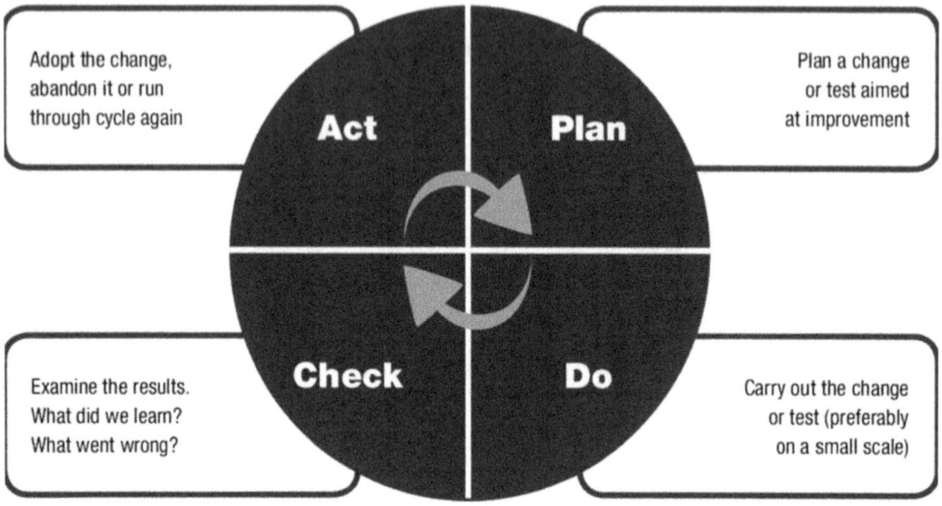

This tool provides a useful benchmark to determine the effectiveness of each solution proposed for this company. Using a tool such as the PDCA framework allows a critique of each change by asking the questions shown in figure 1. This is most effective when the changemakers are dispassionate and as unbiased as possible during the evaluation process.

Organizational Culture Theories

The Cultural Iceberg Model provides an apt metaphor for the issues experienced by the organization. Only a fraction of an organization's culture is visible. As with an iceberg, much of the iceberg is submerged and not visible to someone looking at it from the surface. What is visible in the organization is the unwanted behavior of what amounts to stealing from the company. What lies below the surface are the beliefs, values and thought patterns held in the people of the organization. The model is illustrated in Figure 2 Romford (2022).

Figure 2. From "Iceberg Model of Culture – Updated 2022 – A complete guide
By Romford, 2019

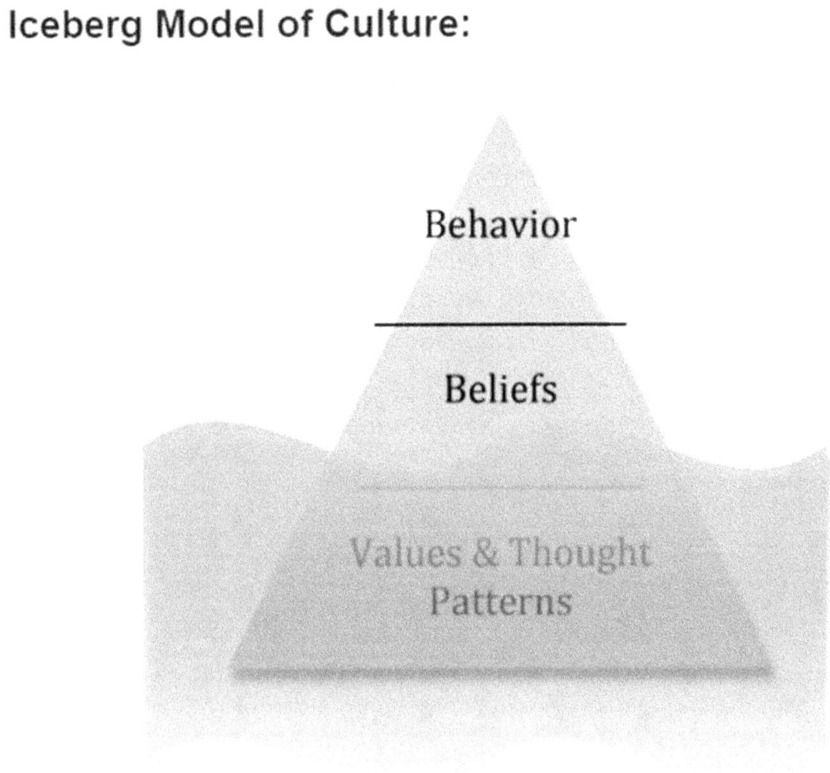

It is a worthwhile exercise to delve into why this behavior is occurring. Are the directors bad people with no moral compass? It is certainly possible, but it is not probable. There is a reason why this was allowed, and it behooves the board to ask questions to determine the reasons behind the behavior. It is in understanding the underlying reasons that one can see the solution and the way forward. Once the underlying ideology causing the issue is identified, one can begin to effect change within a culture.

The culture of this company is a source of risk as well as the primary problem. The toxic culture of this organization requires a shift if they are to effectively address the behavior of the directors and sustain change into the future. The Competing Values Framework identifies 4 types of cultures and allows the company to plot their current orientation within the 4 quadrants of Clan, Adhocracy, Hierarchy, and market. By plotting a second point, the desired culture, the figure illustrates an action plan for where an organization wishes to move within the framework (Opinno, 2020).

The relationship between culture and organizational effectiveness can be best understood when they are organized along two axes, as shown in Figure 3 The horizontal axis is focused on the internal on one end of the spectrum with an external focus on the opposite end. The vertical axis is more flexible at the top and as one moves toward the bottom increased control is applied. The quadrants show 4 distinct cultures and the primary concerns of each one (Opinno, 2020). This organization would benefit from movement into the hierarchical quadrant that is both more internally focused, more stable, and more controlled. The management of information as well as good communication up and down the chain of command will assist in the attainment of this goal.

Figure 3. From "Improving Organizational Culture with the Competing Values Framework," by Opinno, 2020

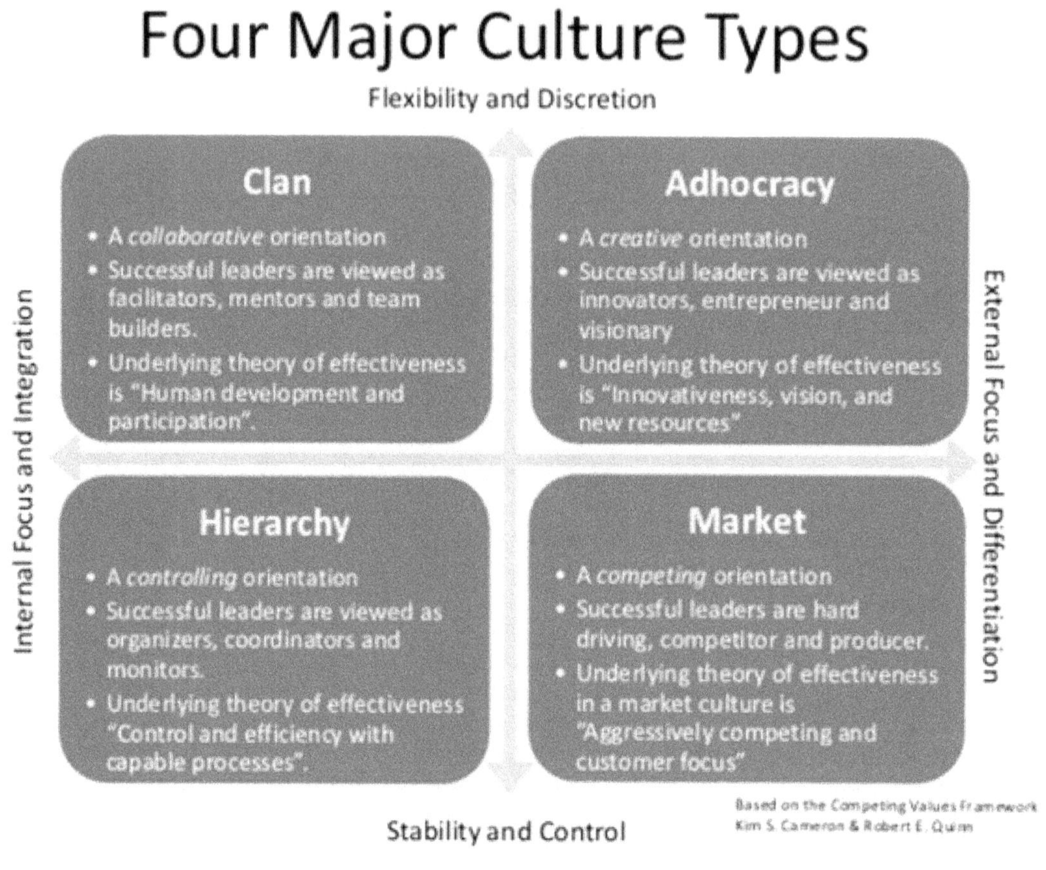

Change Management Theories

Lewin's Change Management Model is a simple three-step process for effecting change in an organization. The first step in the process is to unfreeze the existing situation. Once this unfreezing occurs, change or movement can happen. Finally, a refreezing occurs to ensure that the new behaviors stick. (Hussain et al., 2018). The application of Lewin's Change Management Model begins with an open and frank discussion with the directors. Since this behavior has been going on for many years, it is entrenched and harder to call into question. However, this step is necessary as a means to defrost the issue and bring the problems it is causing to light.

It would be wise to co-opt the directors into a discussion about how best to address this issue. Such a discussion will likely be eye-opening, and management stands to learn a great deal about how this came to be an issue and how to prevent it in the future. Most rational people would quickly adapt to the idea that the company losing $375,000 per year is a crisis. As stakeholders in the company, it is in the financial interest of the directors to become part of the solution. There is also a good chance they will lead the charge to correct it. The key is that they must see this as a problem they have the power to solve. Obtaining their buy-in is not essential, but it is desirable.

For those who are unable or unwilling to rally behind the proposed solution, there is a solution from the same mind who gave us the Five Stages of Grief, which are denial, anger, bargaining, depression, and acceptance (Chavan, et al., 2022). Kübler-Ross' Change Curve Model states that organizational change follows a similar pattern and creates similar emotions in employees. Strategies to mitigate resistance to change include communication and education, participation and involvement, support and facilitation, manipulation and co-option, negotiation and agreement, and finally, explicit and implicit coercion (Chavan, et al., 2022). This strategy list can be thought of as a continuum with the first in the list, communication and education, being the most desirable to the last, explicit and implicit coercion being the last resort and least desirable.

Ethical Decision-Making Theories

The Virtue Approach to ethics is a primary approach in normative ethics. Felgate defines this as the capacity to make skilled moral judgment according to a given context. A virtuous person is one who acts virtuously and has learned virtue as a skill. Virtue and skill are analogous in that they both require effort to develop (Felgate, 2020). A formal training program in ethics required by the company would be a solid foundation for change. True change must begin in the mind of the individual. If virtuousness is indeed a skill, then it can be taught and learned.

While virtue is focused on the decision maker, the Utilitarian Approach is more focused on the situation itself. Utilitarianism assesses the ethicality of the decision based on its social consequences (Dunn & Sainty, 2020). Does misappropriating funds away from the company serve the greater good? Probably not. Regardless of how each director justified the behavior of charging personal expenses to the company, it is doubtful they would feel the same way about it after pausing to consider the ethical problems created by their behavior. This rethinking can be facilitated through education.

Changing the corporate culture is not a process that happens quickly. Much like changing the course of a large ship, it takes time to turn around. Ethics training is an opportunity to instill corporate values in management. Integrity and personal responsibility are values that would serve the individual and the company as a whole. Once these values are instilled in the directors, they can be evangelists for these values and impart them to their staff. In time, culture can be shifted.

Leadership Theories

The Contingency Leadership Theory states that there is no one way for a leader to lead. The leader must adapt their leadership style to the situation at hand (Amoah-Mensah & Darkwa, 2018). One must also tailor the style to the group one is leading. For example, one would not lead a group of prisoners the same way one would lead a group of kindergarteners. This theory is very practical and useful in this situation. One will need a firm approach to lead the charge on this organizational change. One needs to command respect. The other side of that coin is that a leader must give respect to get it. The flexibility inherent in this theory makes it an effective choice for leading change within this organization. Choosing a leadership style can be equated to a bag of golf clubs. One must choose the best club for the shot one wishes to make given the distance and the conditions of the course. Similarly, leaders must be flexible and willing to pivot should it become apparent that a leadership style is not effective in a situation.

Servant Leadership Theory could potentially be a part of the Contingency Theory suggested. At first glance, the behavior of the directors seems to exude anything but leadership. It is quite the opposite of the servant leader. A servant leader is more concerned with the motivation to serve others and their needs than they are with serving their own self-interest. (Huning et al., 2020). This could be a training opportunity for the directors. A workshop on servant leadership could act as a Nudge toward the wanted behavior, which is for the directors to lead the change that they, themselves need to make. If the directors own this transformation process as the fruit of their ideas, it would be most effective.

Compliance Issues

Internal Revenue Service (IRS) provides guidelines for business expenses. Under an accountable plan, there must be a business purpose for the expense, substantiation, such as receipts, and any advances not used must be returned to the company. The Internal Revenue Code (IRC) allows a tax deduction for the business and the employees are reimbursed for their expenses tax-free. If an employee fails to substantiate expenses or the expenses have no business purpose, they become taxable income to the employee and are reported on the employee's Form W-2. Section 1.62-2 of the IRC explicitly outlines what is deductible as a business expense. Some common examples of legitimate business expenses are travel expenses, tools, supplies, and professional licenses (Roan, 2020).

Company credit cards are a convenient tool to empower employees to pay for business expenses and eliminate the need for advances. Cards do not, however, eliminate the need to report the business expenses to the company and to provide substantiation. In practice, this is often done monthly and coincides with the credit card billing cycle. The occasional personal expense can be documented and subtracted on the expense report. When an expense is partially business and partly personal is one potential scenario. This is not a problem as long as it is documented as a personal expense and paid for, ultimately, by the employee.

The importance of a sound accountable plan cannot be understated. It is easy for an organization to implement. The policy must be written, and it must require substantiation. Finally, it must be enforced at every level.

THE ORGANIZATION CURRENT STATE AND EFFECTS ON EMPLOYEES

This is an organization in crisis. The company is losing money at an alarming and unsustainable rate. Low employee morale is an issue, as evidenced by the departure of the top three officers in the company. From a compliance standpoint, the IRC is not being followed and expenses that are unsubstantiated should be treated as wages and reported on each employee's Form W-2 at the end of the year.

While the resignation of an employee who holds a large amount of institutional knowledge is costly, it is not the end of the world. However, it speaks volumes when there is high turnover among senior management, in particular. This creates unrest in the workforce and leads to speculation about what must be going on with the company. In the case of a publicly traded company, this can easily translate to falling stock prices. Even in a small business this can translate to employees who do not feel their efforts matter, so they don't bother to perform tasks as conscientiously as they once did.

When poor behavior is tolerated by management there is a tendency for turnover to accelerate. What remains are the underachieving employees who stick around because they have gotten the message that they will not be held accountable (Heibutzki, 2017). Another consideration is that when good employees leave, they may potentially take not only their talents, but institutional knowledge that can be appropriated by a shrewd competitor.

CHANGES NEEDED

A top-down policy change is in order to send the message that new policies and procedures are in place and will be strictly enforced. The implementation of an accountable plan that meets IRS guidelines is the top priority.

The culture of this company must change. A more accountable and controlled culture is the first step to shift this company's toxic culture. Directors and managers must be educated in ethics. Even a moral person may go along with the crowd if they are led to believe that a behavior is acceptable within a culture. For example, some directors may think that charging personal expenses to the company is not stealing at all. They may see it as part of their salary or a fringe benefit. A clear message needs to be sent that this behavior is both unacceptable and harmful to the company and it will no longer be allowed. However, when that message is to be received by those who run the company, it must be handled judiciously. A wrecking ball approach is likely to end badly for everyone involved. A velvet hammer approach is a much wiser alternative.

PLAN TO ADDRESS ISSUE

Adoption of an accountable plan for expense reporting is the first step to correct the behavior. This is done in lock step with new written policies that define business expenses and what is and is not appropriate. Progressive discipline for violations of the policy must be disseminated and unilaterally enforced. This is an excellent time to get buy-in from the directors who are causing the problem.

A mandatory meeting to discuss the issue with the full complement of management is imperative. The behavior needs to be brought out in the open and discussed. Explain why this is a problem and how the company is addressing it. Directors must see themselves as partners in the success of this initiative to right this wrong.

As a corrective measure and a training tool, each director's personal charges should be itemized for the current calendar year in a report by the CFO. For this measure to be most effective It should be handled discretely and respectfully. For example, it would be inappropriate for this report to be compiled by a junior staff member. To add emphasis, the highest-ranking officer in the company, in this case, the board president, should present this report to each director, either in a one-on-one meeting or in a letter, that the total amount of these items will need to be repaid to the company by a certain date. This is not about shaming the director. It should be approached collaboratively as an opportunity to correct an error. This provides the directors with amnesty and the opportunity to see the problem in writing. This will underscore the seriousness of the matter and set the tone for the future. If the director fails to repay the money, the amount will be added to their taxable wages on their Forms W2, and they will pay taxes on them at the end of the year.

DESIRED STATE

A shift to a more stable and controlled environment with a culture that embraces personal responsibility is the ideal for this organization. Employees are not unlike children in that they thrive in an environment where there is structure and clear rules and standards as well as consequences (Gulati, 2018). Implementation of new policies as outlined will not only save the company a substantial amount of money, but it will give employees a sense of security in knowing that the company is watching the bottom line. Everyone is expected to do their part, which promotes high morale. Once the proverbial bar is raised, it forces everyone into a choice. They can elevate themselves to meet the newly raised standard, or they can leave the organization. Either way, the company is better for it. It also provides a solid foundation for good stewardship of resources as a basis on which to build future success.

REFERENCES

Amoah-Mensah, A., & Darkwa, P. (2018). Leadership Styles of Owner-Managers and Employees' Performance: The Moderating Role of Age and Experience. *Romanian Economic Business Review, 13*(3), 47–73. http://proxymu.wrlc.org/login?url=https://www.proquest.com/scholarly-journals/leadership-styles-owner-managers-employees/docview/2224905922/se-2

ChavanS.BhattacharyaS. (2022). Study of employees' behavior during organizational change: effects of business theatre on Kübler-Ross model. Cardiometry, (22), 237-243. https://doi.org/ doi:10.18137/cardiometry.2022.22.237243

Dunn, P., & Sainty, B. (2020). Professionalism in accounting: A five-factor model of ethical decision-making. *Social Responsibility Journal, 16*(2), 255–269. doi:10.1108/SRJ-11-2017-0240

Felgate, Y. R. (2020). Human resource management moral competencies. *SA Journal of Human Resource Management*. https:// doi:10.4102/sajhrm.v18i0.1193

Gregory, H. (2022). *Board Oversight: Key Focus Areas for 2022*. Harvard Law School Forum on Corporate Governance. https://corpgov.law.harvard.edu/2022/01/05/board-oversight-key-focus-areas-for-2022/

Gulati, R. (2018). Structure That's Not Stifling. *Harvard Business Review*. https://hbr.org/2018/05/structure-thats-not-stifling

Heibutzki, R. (2017). The Effects of an Unproductive Workplace. *Career Trend*. https://careertrend.com/effects-unproductive-workplace-3931.html

Huning, T. M., Hurt, K. J., & Frieder, R. E. (2020). The effect of servant leadership, perceived organizational support, job satisfaction and job embeddedness on turnover intentions: An empirical investigation. [Servant leadership and work outcomes] *Evidence - Based HRM, 8*(2), 177-194. doi:10.1108/EBHRM-06-2019-0049

Hussain, S. (2018). Kurt Lewin's change model: A critical review of the role of leadership and employee involvement in organizational change. *Journal of Innovation & Knowledge*. https://reader.elsevier.com/reader/sd/pii/S2444569X16300087?token=313E0D5A13CB5CB8FB9AE2DC169DD21A61076E1A1F56D9AEDA9DC1E50D77A34E0A11EBA4128D5004AFCF4CB63EB95142&originRegion=us-east-1&originCreation=20230522000044

Opinno. (2020). Improving Organizational Culture with the Competing Values Framework. https://opinno.dev.opinnosites.com/project/improving-organizational-culture-competing-values-framework

Panteli, D. (2019). *Understanding healthcare quality strategies: a five-lens framework*. Research Gate. https://www.researchgate.net/publication/339386790_Understanding_healthcare_quality_strategies_a_five-lens_framework

Roan, D. (2020), Start or review an accountable plan. *Journal of Accountancy*. https://www.journalofaccountancy.com/issues/2020/feb/employee-expenses-accountable-plan.html

Romford, J. (2022, April 7). *Iceberg Model of Culture – Update 2022 – A Complete Guide*. Agility Portal. https://agilityportal.io/blog/iceberg-model-of-culture-updated-2022-a-complete-guide

Chapter 23

Brain Tumor Classification From Magnetic Resonance Imaging Using Deep Learning and Novel Data Augmentation

Naresh Tiwari
Capital Technology University, USA

Marwan Omar
Illinois Institute of Technoilogy, USA

Yazeed Ghadi
Al Ain University, UAE

ABSTRACT

The complex and time-consuming nature of magnetic resonance imaging (MRI) may make it difficult to autonomously diagnose tumors in the brain, possibly leading to erroneous detection and classification. Identifying brain tumors is a complex process due primarily to relying on multiple modules for a comprehensive evaluation. In response, advances in deep learning have paved the way for automated medical image analysis and diagnostics. Convolutional neural networks (CNNs) are crucial for visual learning and image classification. The current investigation presents a novel approach for data augmentation that is integrated with state-of-the-art models, namely Efficient-NetB0, VGG16, ResNet50, InceptionV3, and MobileNetV2, to accurately classify various types of brain tumors, including glioma, meningioma, and pituitary tumors. The algorithm was subjected to testing utilizing benchmark data from existing literature.

1. INTRODUCTION

A brain tumor is a pathological state that can be identified by the abnormal proliferation of cells within the cerebral tissues. As per the report by the World Health Organization (WHO), tumors are a substantial

DOI: 10.4018/979-8-3693-1634-4.ch023

cause of death worldwide(Khazaei et al., 2020),(GLOBOCAN, 2020). Brain tumors can be categorized into two distinct groups: benign and malignant. Benign tumors typically exhibit a sluggish growth rate, cannot infiltrate adjacent tissues or organs, and cause a minimal threat to overall health. As the reference (The PDQ Adult Treatment Editorial Board, 2002) states, the permanent abolition of benign tumors is typically achieved through surgical excision. On the contrary, malignant tumors can infiltrate adjacent tissues and organs, potentially leading to severe consequences if not promptly and efficiently managed (The NHS Inform website "Malignant brain tumour," 2023). The general categories of brain tumors comprise glioma, meningioma, and pituitary. Gliomas are tumors that develop in the glial cells surround ing and sustaining the neurons in the brain, whereas pituitary tumors grow in the pituitary gland (Johns Hopkins Medicine "Gliomas," 2023)(Mayo Clinic "Pituitary tumors," 2023). Meningioma is a tumor that develops in the meninges, which are the outermost layers of tissue surrounding the brain and spinal cord between the skull and the brain (Johns Hopkins Medicine "Meningioma," 2023). Meningioma is generally considered benign (non-cancerous), compared to glioma, which is malignant (cancerous), and pituitary tumors are recognized as benign. The manifestation of symptoms associated with a brain tumor is contingent upon its size and location. These symptoms may encompass headaches, alterations in auditory or visual perception, convulsions, unilateral weakness or numbness, and modifications in personality (MedicineNet "Brain Cancer," 2022). Furthermore, glioma can cause several symptoms, including but not limited to aphasia, visual disturbances or impairments, cognitive issues, and gait or balance disturbances (Johns Hopkins Medicine "Gliomas," 2023). Meningioma is known for causing subtle symptoms that gradually increase, such as changes in visual acuity and morning headaches (Johns Hopkins Medicine "Meningioma," 2023). Pituitary tumors compressing the optic nerve can result in headaches, blurred vision, and diplopia (Mayo Clinic "Pituitary tumors," 2023).

Hence, it is imperative to differentiate between these categories of tumors to facilitate clinical diagnosis and assessment of treatment efficacy. The proficiency of radiologists plays a pivotal role in the timely detection of brain malignancies. Magnetic resonance imaging (MRI) is a commonly employed modality for identifying and classifying various tumor types. However, it is subject to human interpretation and can pose difficulties in analyzing extensive datasets (Afshar et al. 2019). In diagnosing and treating brain tumors, it is common practice to defer biopsies until after definitive brain surgery, as per existing protocols (Rogers et al., 2015). Developing a comprehensive diagnostic tool for detecting and classifying tumors from magnetic resonance (MR) images is crucial in achieving precise diagnoses and mitigating the need for surgery and subjective assessments.

The healthcare industry has been significantly impacted by recent technological advancements, particularly in the areas of artificial intelligence (AI) and deep learning (DL) (Ahmad et al., 2022). These breakthroughs have revolutionized formerly ineffective healthcare sectors, including medical imaging, by providing essential resources. Various machine learning (ML) algorithms have enhanced medical imaging and healthcare, offering radiologists a new perspective. For instance, the authors of (Ahmad et al., 2021) provided efficient e-healthcare methods to address the multi-objective fuse detection problem. The study conducted a comparative analysis of four different algorithms: MK-NN, traditional K-NN, convolutional neural network (CNN), and backpropagation. The findings indicated that the enhanced K-NN method demonstrated superior resilience, precision, and efficiency in detecting fuse targets within e-healthcare applications. The investigation in (Bin Tufail et al., 2022) employed CNN architectures to categorize the initial phases of Alzheimer's disease (AD) using positron emission tomography. The architectures were employed in two-dimensional (2D) and three-dimensional (3D) domains. The 3D-CNN architecture outperformed rival models with precision levels of 89.21% on AD/NC (Normal Control),

71.70% on AD/MCI (Mild Cognitive Impairment), 62.25% on NC/MCI, and 59.73% on AD/NC/MCI classification tasks. To improve the model's performance, a random zoom-in/zoom-out approach was utilized for data augmentation. The findings corroborate the efficacy of employing DL models in the timely identification of Alzheimer's disease. The authors in (Bin Tufail et al., 2021) deployed 3D-CNN architectures to categorize diabetic retinopathy (DR) into binary and multiclass groups. They employed two distinct artificial data augmentation methods, specifically random weak Gaussian blurring and random shift, in conjunction with each other to enhance the spatial domain of the input images. The results indicate that the 3D-CNN structure outperformed the binary classification scenario when trained with augmentation techniques. However, in the multiclass scenario, the model that was trained without augmentation achieved the highest level of accuracy. The primary objective of this investigation (Mohi ud din dar et al., 2023) is to create a computer-aided system that can predict and classify AD at an early stage, utilizing neural networks on MRI datasets. The proposed framework employs a lightweight neural network called MobileNet, which accomplishes a 96.6% accuracy rate for multiclass AD stage classifications. The study by the authors revealed that the utilization of MobileNet in the context of disease detection yields better outcomes than pre-existing models.

Furthermore, this approach presents a unique methodology for detecting distinct phases of Alzheimer's disease. The primary aim of the inquiry (Haq et al. 2022) is to devise an algorithm that can effectively detect lung nodules in CT scan images to facilitate the prompt detection of cancer. The system utilizes many images to provide radiologists with additional information for analysis. The CNN algorithm's outcomes yielded an accuracy of 84.8%, a precision of 90.47%, and a specificity of 90.64%. These results are considered dependable in mitigating false positives. The research emphasized the necessity for a reliable instrument to aid radiologists in detecting nodules during their initial stages. In their study, the authors (Bin Tufail et al., 2021) employed PET and SPECT neuroimaging techniques in both the frequency and spatial domains to implement a 3D-CNN to extract features to facilitate multiclass classification of individuals belonging to the Alzheimer's disease (AD), Parkinson's disease (PD), and Normal Control (NC) groups.

CNNs are frequently utilized in medical image analysis and demonstrate proficiency in identifying and classifying various diseases due to the abovementioned factors. It can potentially classify brain tumors in MRI datasets. The MRI database has the potential to expand if different planes are utilized for the acquisition of MR images. Preprocessing is an important module, and the significance of preprocessing before feeding images into various networks to obtain classification results has been acknowledged (Kaplan et al., 2020). However, neural networks offer several advantages, such as the capacity to design characteristics and eliminate the need for preprocessing. The insufficiency of resources poses a significant challenge when utilizing the system for medical diagnostics or mobile platforms. If a clinical diagnostic procedure is deemed necessary for daily routine, it must possess overall beneficial properties.

The primary goals of our approach are:

Our study employs DL techniques and a CNNs to accurately classify glioma, meningioma, and pituitary tumors based on an MRI dataset.

- Medical imaging can frequently encounter issues such as noise, low contrast, and limited data, which can have a negative impact on the efficacy of DL algorithms utilized for tumor classification. Implementing novel data augmentation techniques has been proposed as a viable solution to address the challenges encountered in the DL model for brain tumor analysis.

- The present study employs novel data augmentation approaches to enhance the classification of brain tumors by utilizing transfer learning techniques, specifically with EfficientNetB0.
- The experimental results of our study demonstrate the usefulness of expanding a dataset by employing flipping, rotation, scaling, translation, and color adjustment techniques to improve accuracy.
- The study conducted a comparative analysis of the performance results of the presented framework with previous work.

This article comprises several distinct sections. Section 2 provides a comprehensive review of the relevant literature, whereas Section 3 delves into the dataset, proposed framework utilizing transfer learning, and optimization strategies. Section 4 presents the empirical results of the model. A discussion accompanies section 5, and the final section of the text provides the conclusion

1.1 Problem Statement

Accurate diagnosis and classification of brain tumors is crucial for determining appropriate treatment plans and

prognosis. However, analyzing brain tumor images can be a complex and time-consuming process for radiologists. Recently, deep learning has shown great promise for automating medical image analysis tasks. However, existing studies on brain tumor classification using deep learning have been limited by small datasets. This study aims to develop a more robust deep learning model for brain tumor classification by utilizing a novel data augmentation technique to effectively expand limited MRI datasets. The proposed model will be evaluated on its ability to correctly classify different types of brain tumors from MRI scans. The findings could help radiologists more efficiently and accurately diagnose and classify brain tumors, facilitating improved patient care and outcomes.

2. LITERATURE REVIEW

The categorizing of brain tumors into distinct classifications is a challenging task. The authors (McBee et al., 2018) discussed the potential clinical applications of DL in radiology and outlined the steps involved in a DL project in this field. While DL has demonstrated promising results in some radiology applications, it is not yet fully advanced enough to replace a radiologist's diagnostic work. However, there is potential for radiologists and DL algorithms to work together and improve diagnostic accuracy and efficiency. The ability of MRI to identify and categorize brain tumors has been the focus of numerous investigations that have employed diverse methodologies. A noteworthy study by Kaplan et al. [18] employed various feature extraction techniques, including LBP, nLBP, and αLBP, in their investigation. In addition, a diverse set of classification methods, such as KNN, ANN, RF, AIDE, and LDA, were applied to classify the brain tumors. Remarkably, their study achieved a significant success rate of 95.56% when nLBPd=1 and KNN were utilized as the classification method.

In a study by (Mohsen et al., 2018) the application of DNN (Deep Neural Network) for classifying brain tumors was investigated using a dataset of 66 MRI brain images. The authors employed feature extraction techniques to extract relevant image features, including discrete wavelet transformation and principal component analysis. Subsequently, a DNN-based classification system was tested, yielding promising results regarding tumor classification accuracy. (Rathi et al.,2022) employed a segmentation methodology utilizing kernel based probabilistic clustering algorithms on MRI brain images that were preprocessed with a median filter to remove noise. Subsequently, LDA was utilized to evaluate the key characteristics of the segmented data. Finally, DL techniques were applied to classify brain tumors based on the extracted features. Cheng et al. [22] developed a comprehensive dataset of brain tumors on the figshare platform, which has been widely employed in various studies for detecting brain malignancies. In a subsequent investigation, the authors (Cheng et al., 2015) tackled the challenging three-class problem of brain tumor detection. They utilized image dilation to magnify the tumor location and employed SVM for image classification. Features were extracted from the images using techniques such as intensity histogram, gray level co-occurrence matrix, and bag-of-words model. The proposed approach achieved a remarkable classification accuracy of 91.28%, underscoring its efficacy in accurately identifying brain tumors.

(Ismael and Abdel-Qader, 2018) proposed a classification framework that combined statistical features with neural network methods to diagnose brain cancer using MRI data. The authors employed 2D discrete wavelet transform and 2D Gabor filter techniques for feature extraction, along with feature selection, to enhance the accuracy of the backpropagation neural network classifier. Remarkably, the proposed framework achieved an impressive accuracy of 91.9% when tested on brain MRI data for cancer diagnosis. (Afshar et al., 2019) employed an approach in their study by utilizing a modified CNN framework called CapsNet to classify brain cancer from brain MR images. Remarkably, their proposed CapsNet-based approach achieved a notable success rate of 90.89%. (Pashaei et al., 2018) utilized CNN for feature extraction from brain images and then employed KELM for brain malignancy classification, achieving a high success rate of 93.68%. (Abiwinanda et al., 2019)conducted a study in which they employed five different CNNs architectures for brain tumor detection. Among these architectures, the two-layer convolution design achieved the best performance, with an accuracy rate of 84.19%. This finding suggests the effectiveness of this specific CNN architecture in accurately detecting brain tumors. (Phaye et al., 2018) utilized multiple CapsNet and improved the accuracy to 95.03% by replacing the standard convolution layer in CapsNet with a densely connected convolution layer. (Zhou et al., 2019) employed a combination of dense CNN and RNN for classification, achieving a remarkable accuracy of 92.13%.

These studies demonstrate the effectiveness of utilizing advanced DL techniques, such as Faster R-CNN and a combination of CNN and RNN, for accurate brain tumor classification using MRI data. (Avşar and Salçin, 2019) utilized DL techniques and developed a Faster R-CNN for brain tumor classification, achieving an impressive success rate of 91.66%. (Gumaei et al., 2019) proposed a hybrid feature extraction approach based on a RELM to enhance the accuracy of a classification method for brain tumor detection. They utilized RELM as a feature extractor to learn discriminative features from brain MRI data and then combined it with a classification algorithm for tumor classification. The proposed approach achieved a high success rate of 94.23% in accurately classifying brain tumors. (Anaraki et al., 2019) proposed a classification framework that combined CNN with a GA for brain tumor subtype classification, achieving an impressive accuracy of 94.2%. (Ghassemi et al., 2020) employed a deep-learning classification system for brain cancers using a GAN to generate discriminative features from brain MRI data. The GAN-based approach achieved a high classification success rate of 95.6%, showing the potential of generative models in improving brain cancer classification accuracy. (Swati et al., 2019) utilized popular deep neural network architectures, including AlexNet, VGG16, and VGG19, with fine-tuning techniques to classify brain tumors, resulting in an impressive accuracy of 94.82%. It highlights the effectiveness of these DL models in accurately classifying brain tumors from MRI data. (Noreen et al., 2021) employed fine-tuned DL models, including InceptionV3 and Xception, combined with various ML algorithms such as softmax, random forest, SVM, K-Nearest Neighbors, and ensemble techniques. Their highest achieved accuracy of 94.34% was obtained with an ensemble InceptionV3.

3. MATERIALS AND METHODS

This section presents a detailed description of the suggested data augmentation method employing CNNs for classifying brain tumors. The method comprises two main phases. In the first phase, input images undergo augmentation using novel techniques, including resizing the original images and labeling, which entails assigning class identifiers to augmented images. Subsequently, the dataset is divided into three subsets, training, validation and testing, as shown in Figure 3. In the second phase, the model is trained on the training data using the Adam optimizer (Kingma and Ba, 2015) (Robbins and Monro, 1951) categorical cross entropy and softmax. The model's performance is evaluated based on accuracy, precision, recall, and F1-score outcomes. The proposed method is visually depicted in Figure 1, providing a graphical representation of the overall approach.

Figure 1. Demonstrates the method to classify brain tumors using CNNs and the data augmentation technique

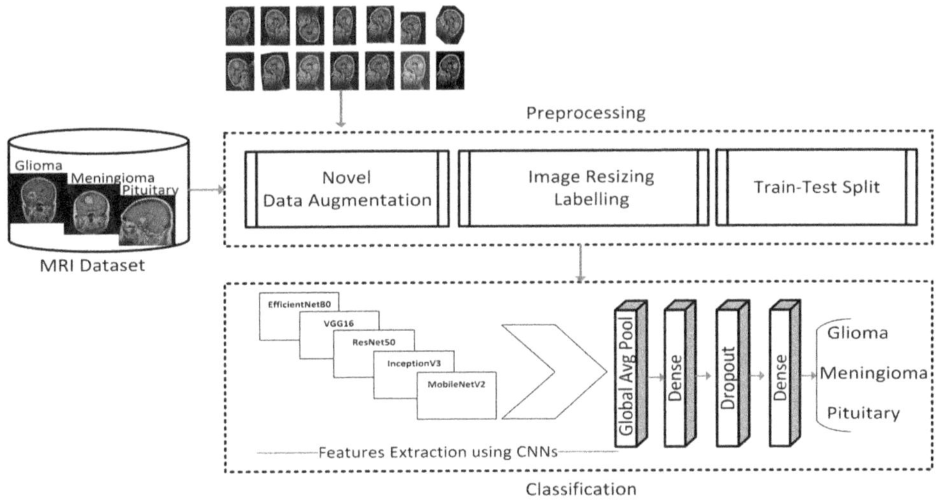

3.1. Dataset and Augmentation

The present study utilized a dataset from Nangfang Hospital and General Hospital Tianjin Medical University in China, comprising 3064 T1 weighted contrast-enhanced MR images. The pictures were assembled during the period spanning from 2005 to 2010 and subsequently made available for public viewing on the Internet in 2015. The Kaggle website offers a dataset in PNG format, which was later revised in 2017 (Cheng, 2017) [37, 38]. The study sample comprised 233 individuals who were diagnosed with three distinct types of tumors, namely glioma (1426 images), meningioma (708 images), and pituitary (930 images). The photographs were captured in three distinct planes, namely sagittal, axial, and coronal, with an initial resolution of 512 x 512 pixels. A graphical representation of the different tumor forms included in the dataset is provided in Figure 1.

Data augmentation is a valuable ML and computer vision strategy, aiming to expand the volume and variability of training data accessible for a model by generating diverse and augmented versions of the original dataset. The idea behind data augmentation is to artificially create new training examples by applying various transformations to the existing data. Data augmentation helps improve ML model's performance by making them more robust to variations in the input data. Utilizing this technique can mitigate overfitting, decreasing the possibility of the model excessively memorizing the training data. Figure 2 showcases illustrative examples of augmented images generated from a single source image by applying a novel combination of data augmentation techniques. The figures displayed in the image include the original image, examples of augmented images with horizontal and vertical flipping, random scaling, translation, and rotation applied independently to the x and y axes of the source image.

Additionally, it shows examples of augmented images with random sharpening, Gaussian blur, emboss effect, color multiplication, and linear contrast adjustment applied with varying probabilities and parameters (Alomar et al., 2023). These examples visually demonstrate the diverse and varied effects that can be achieved by applying the proposed data augmentation techniques, showcasing the potential for enhancing the variability and diversity of the augmented image dataset for training the model. The pseudocode (Algorithm 1), which outlines the data augmentation process, is provided below.

Algorithm 1: Pseudocode for Data Augmentation

```
Input:
- input_dir: Directory containing the original images
- output_dir: Directory to save the augmented images
- techniques: List of image augmentation techniques
Output:
- Augmented images saved in output_dir
1. Read the images from input_dir
2. Initialize an empty list to store the augmented images
3. Loop through each image in the input_dir:
a. Read the image
b. Apply the following augmentation techniques to the image:
- Flip horizontally with a probability of 0.5
- Flip vertically with a probability of 0.5
- Affine transformation with a scale range of 0.8 to 1.2 in x and y direction
- Affine transformation with a translation range of -0.1 to 0.1 in x and y di-
rection
- Affine transformation with a translation range of -0.2 to 0.2 in x and y di-
rection
- Affine transformation with a rotation range of -45 to 45 degrees
- Affine transformation with a rotation range of -90 to 90 degrees
- Affine transformation with a shear range of -16 to 16 degrees
- Sharpening with a alpha range of 0 to 1 and a lightness range of 0.75 to 1.5
- Gaussian blur with a sigma range of 0 to 0.5
- Embossing with an alpha range of 0 to 1 and a strength range of 0 to 0.5
```

```
- Color multiplication with a range of 1.4 to 1.6 and per_channel probability
of 0.2
- Linear contrast adjustment with a range of 0.5 to 2.0 and per_channel prob-
ability of 0.5
c. Save the augmented images in output_dir
```

Figure 2. Illustrates the images generated from a single original image using data augmentation techniques

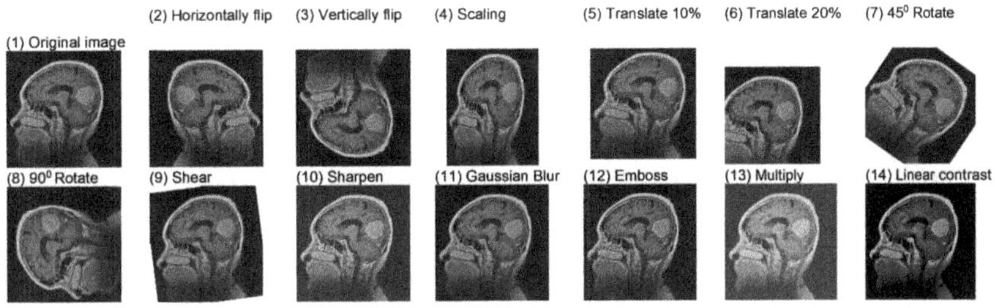

Figure 3. Visualization of original and augmented data with data distribution for training and testing the models

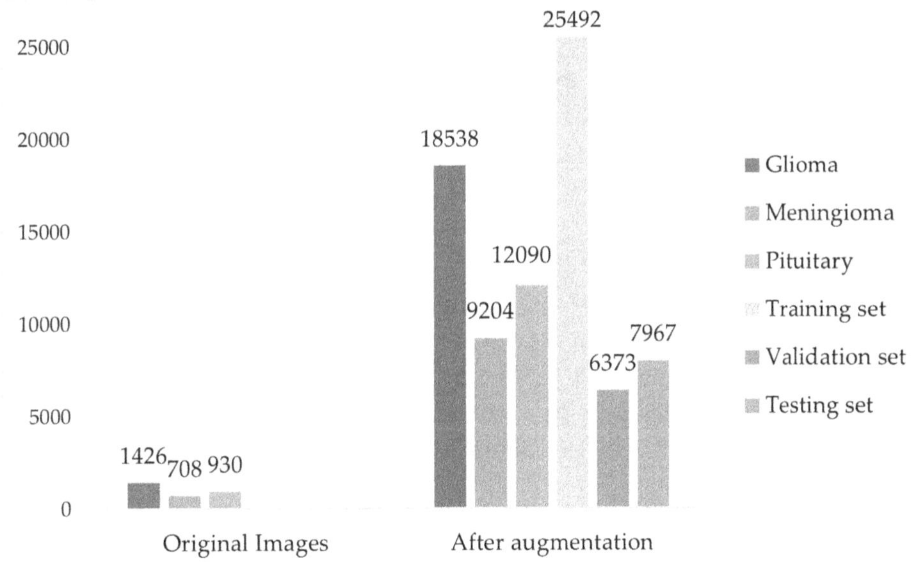

3.2. EfficientNetB0 Architecture

EfficientNetB0 (Tan and Le, 2019) is a CNN architecture that proposes achieving efficient model performance by leveraging a combination of width, depth, and resolution scaling. It uses a compound scaling method that scales the width (number of channels), depth (number of layers), and resolution (input image size) of the network simultaneously to find an optimal balance between accuracy and computational efficiency. EfficientNetB0 has several blocks, including a combination of convolutional, depth-wise convolutional, and fully connected layers. The number of parameters in EfficientNetB0 is approximately 5.3 million, making it a compact model compared to other popular CNN architectures. The EfficientNetB0 model incorporates multiple sizes of convolutional filters, such as 3x3, 5x5, and 1x1 pointwise filters. Furthermore, it utilizes bottleneck blocks integrating squeeze-and-excitation (SE) blocks to enhance its characteristic capacity. Overall, EfficientNetB0 is designed to be computationally efficient while maintaining competitive accuracy on benchmark datasets. Figure 4 shows the selected baseline EfficientNetB0 architecture.

Figure 4. Architectural representation of baseline EfficientNetB0 model

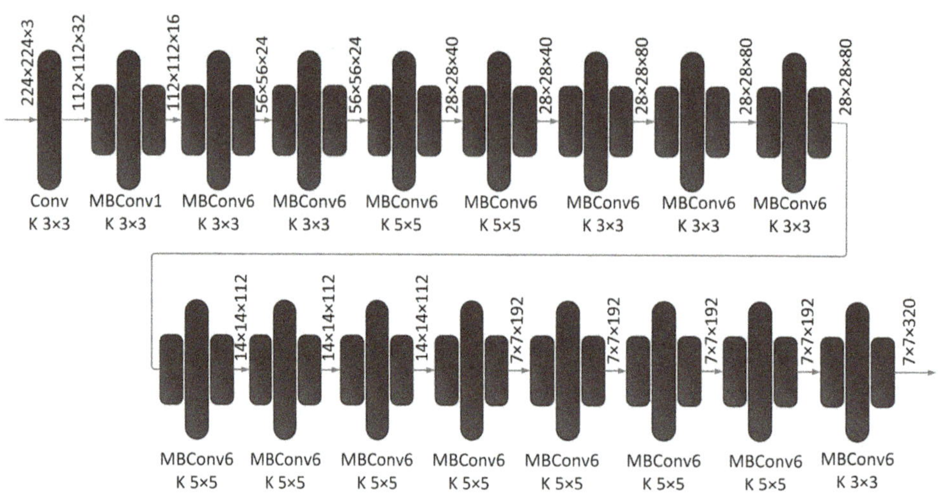

This study employed transfer learning techniques by utilizing the pre-trained models. In addition, the custom layers added included a global average pooling, dense with Rectified Linear Unit (ReLU) activation function, and a dropout layer for regularization. Finally, the dense output layer with softmax activation function was added for multi-classification, as shown in Figure 1. To prevent the base models from being further trained and potentially overwriting the pre-trained weights, we set all the layers of the models to be non-trainable, and only the custom layers were trained. Furthermore, we discussed the other CNNs models.

3.3. VGG16

Karen Simonyan and Zisserman (Simonyan and Zisserman, 2015) from the Visual Geometry Group at Oxford University introduced the VGG16 model in 2014. VGG16's architecture consists of a total of 16 layers, which include 13 convolutional layers and 3 fully linked layers. The convolutional layers used 3x3 filters with a stride size of 1 as they traversed the input data. The model used maximum pooling layers for down-sampling feature maps. These layers use a 2x2 pooling window and select the maximum value within each pooling window to conduct pooling operations. The pooling operation is carried out with a stride size of 2, which reduces the spatial dimensions. With 138 million parameters, VGG16 is extensively utilized for feature extraction within transfer learning.

3.4. ResNet50

As evidenced by extant literature (Szegedy et al., 2015), (Glorot and Bengio, 2010) deep neural networks have exhibited superior performance as their depth increases. As the network size increases, the problem of vanishing or exploding gradients becomes increasingly significant. The issue at hand was addressed by the developers of ResNet50 (He, Zhang, Ren, and Sun, 2016) through the implementation of a pioneering technique involving residual modules. Utilizing these modules facilitates the acquisition of residual mapping by the network, as opposed to the direct acquisition of the original mapping between inputs and outputs. This is accomplished by integrating abbreviated connections that circumvent specific layers and append the input to the output of the modules. The utilization of residual blocks alleviates the vanishing gradient issue while circumventing the degradation that arises with heightened network depth. The ResNet50 model is characterized by its architectural configuration, which integrates convolutional layers of different filter sizes (1x1, 3x3, and 1x1) into bottleneck blocks. Utilizing blocks, max pooling, and average pooling layers enables extracting pertinent features from input images.

3.5. InceptionV3

The InceptionV3 iteration exhibits a higher level of complexity than its antecedent, characterized by multiple layers arranged in a stacked configuration. The engineering of the models facilitates its ability to function with enhanced accuracy. Utilizing multiple kernel sizes at a comparable level presents a benefit as it leads to a wider network instead of a network with increased depth. The authors created a module by combining a max pooling layer at the same level, utilizing kernel sizes of 1×1, 3×3, and 5×5. The concatenation of output results is performed before forwarding to mitigate the model's computational demands, as the simultaneous addition of these layers would increase the computational resources required. To tackle this issue, the authors implemented a 1×1 convolutional layer after the max pooling layer, preceding the 3×3 and 5×5 layers. The use of 1×1 layers instead of 5×5 layers is implemented in this stratum to economize computational resources through the reduction of input channel quantity (Szegedy et al., 2016).

3.6. MobileNetV2

The architectural design prioritized providing services to mobile and embedded applications, aiming to balance precision and efficiency in computation and memory utilization. The model integrates distinct characteristics, namely inverted residual, linear bottlenecks, and width multiplier parameters, to achieve its intended outcome. The term "inverted residual" pertains to a series of convolutional layers that aim to increase the channel size of the input, execute convolutions utilizing a diminutive kernel, and subsequently project back to a decreased number of channels. The methodology optimizes the network's capability by reducing computational and memory demands. Conversely, linear bottlenecks employ a linear activation function instead of a non-linear variant, diminishing the requisite parameters. Finally, the width multiplier parameter facilitates the scaling of channel numbers in the network, thereby enabling additional customization and optimization (Sandler et al., 2018).

3.7. Optimization Techniques and Activation Functions

The utilization of Global Average Pooling (GAP) (Koffas, Picek, and Conti, 2022) is a beneficial technique for reducing the dimensionality of a feature map and extracting comprehensive information from the input. The subsequent equation can represent the mathematical function GAP *(x)*.

$$. GobalAvgPooling(x) = \frac{1}{k \times 1} \sum_{i=1}^{k} \sum_{j=1}^{l} x_{i,j} \tag{1}$$

The variable x denotes the feature map encompassing k channels and l spatial dimensions, namely height and width. The summation operation is denoted by the symbol $\sum$, with the indices i and j employed to iterate over the spatial dimensions of the feature map. The variable k also represents the number of channels in the feature map. The solution of this mathematical expression yields a vector comprising k values, wherein each value denotes the mean activation of the corresponding channel throughout all spatial positions within the feature map (Goodfellow, 2016).

The rectified linear activation unit (ReLU) (Nair and Hinton, 2010) has emerged as a prominent activation function in DL, owing to its simplicity and effectiveness compared to earlier activation functions such as sigmoid or tanh. The ReLU function is mathematically defined as

$$f(x) = \max(0, x) \tag{2}$$

Where x represents the input to the function, notably, both the ReLU function and its derivative are monotonic, exhibiting consistent behavior to the input values. Specifically, ReLU returns 0 for any negative input and returns the same input value for any positive input x. As a result, the output of ReLU ranges from 0 to infinity. ReLU is widely utilized as an activation function in neural networks, particularly in CNNs, and is often chosen as the default activation function. One of the key advantages of ReLU is its computational efficiency, as it involves simple element-wise operations that do not require heavy computational resources. ReLU introduces sparsity in the network, as it effectively deactivates neurons with negative inputs, leading to more efficient utilization of computational resources.

The swish activation function is a novel function that has been recently gained attention in DL and also used in efficient models. The Swish function is defined as follows:

$$F(x) = \frac{x}{1 + e^{-\beta x}} \tag{3}$$

Where β is a scaler parameter that can be learned during training, β→ ∞, the Swish function approaches the ReLU function, but it is still a smoother function. On the other hand, as β → 0, the Swish function approaches a linear function, which can be undesirable in some cases. The Swish function is similar in shape to the ReLU and LeakyReLU functions, and it has been shown to outperform these functions on several benchmark datasets. Additionally, it is a smoother function than ReLU and LeakyReLU, which can help to reduce the impact of noisy data on the training process.

In the models, the softmax function (Goodfellow, 2016) is employed as an activation function in the output layer to transform the input logits into a normalized probability distribution across the predicted output classes. The mathematical representation of the softmax function, denoted as σ, is given by the formula:

$$\sigma(\vec{x})_i = \frac{e^{x_i}}{\sum_{j=1}^{K} e^{x_j}} \tag{4}$$

Where represents the input logit for class *i*, denotes the standard exponential function of the input logits for class *i*, *K* represents the total number of classes, and represents the standard exponential function of the input logits for all classes *j*.

Figure 5. Illustration, the plots of ReLU, Swish, and Softmax activation functions with their respective equations

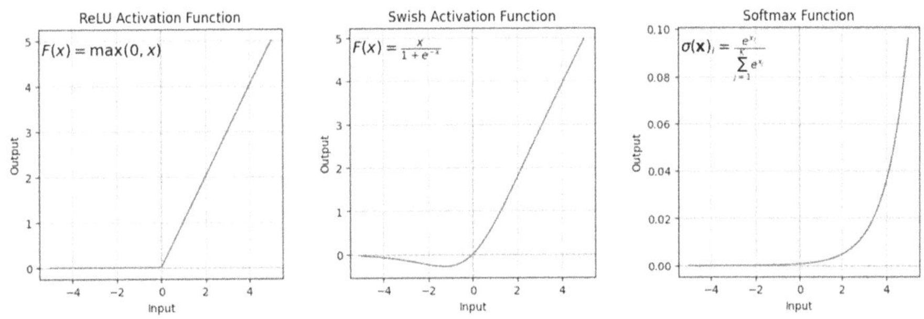

Dropout (The Brain Tumor Charity, 2022) is a regularization technique used in the suggested framework to prevent overfitting. It is a way to mitigate overfitting in neural networks by randomly setting a fraction of the weights to zero during training. The idea behind dropout is to prevent neurons from relying too heavily on the activations of other neurons during training, thus encouraging the network to learn more robust and generalized features. During each training iteration, a random fraction of neurons are "dropped out" by setting their weights to zero with a probability of keeping a neuron. It forces the remaining neurons to learn to represent the input data more independently, making the network less reliant on specific neurons and improving its ability to generalize to new data. Figure 6 illustrates the application of 50% random dropout in the network. Each neuron has a 50% chance of being deactivated during training, leading to some neurons being masked or disabled, promoting feature robustness and regularization.

Figure 6. A visualization of a dropout layer on the right side, with a dropout rate of 50%

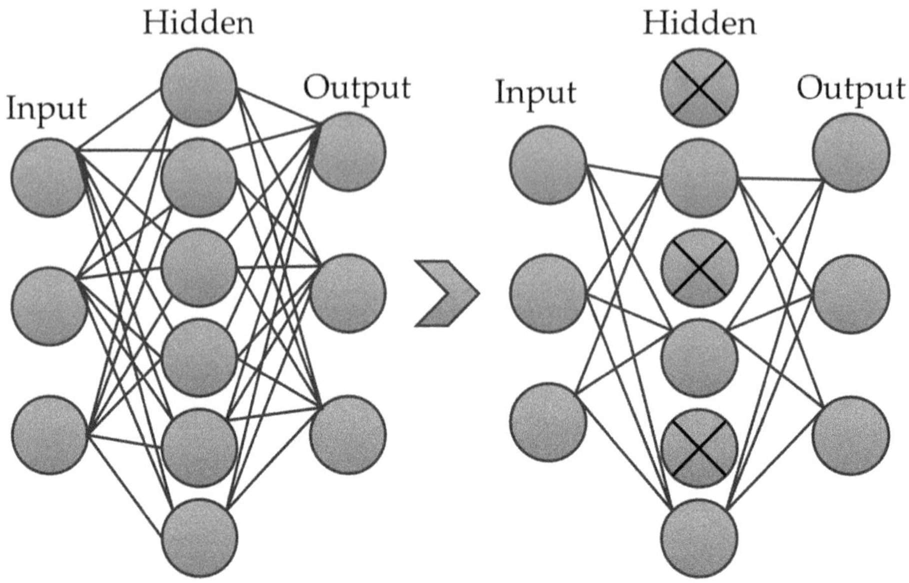

The categorical cross-entropy (CE) is a loss function used in the proposed framework for multiclass classification tasks. It can be defined mathematically as:

$$CE = -\sum_{i=1}^{i=N} y_i.\log(\hat{y}_i) \tag{5}$$

Where N represents the total number of classes in the task. In this equation, denotes the true label (ground truth) for class i, and represents the predicted probability for class i. The categorical cross-entropy loss measures the dissimilarity between the true labels and predicted probabilities. It computes the negative sum of the element-wise product of the true label vector and the natural logarithm of the predicted probability vector. The goal is to minimize this loss, which corresponds to maximizing the likelihood of the true labels given the predicted probabilities.

4. RESULTS AND DISCUSSION

The current study thoroughly investigates the classification of a dataset comprising 3064 MRI images depicting glioma, meningioma, and pituitary tumors. The state-of-the-art models are employed, and the dataset is augmented with novel data augmentation techniques to enhance classification accuracy. The dataset processed includes image resizing and partitioning into training, validation and testing sets, with random shuffling using a fixed random state value of 32 for consistency. Model training is performed for 30 epochs with a batch size of 8, utilizing a five-fold cross-validation approach and the Adam optimizer for optimization. Model performance is visually presented in Figure 7 for comprehensive analysis.

Figure 7. Visualizes the performance of the suggested EfficientNetB0 with proposed data augmentation methods, utilizing 5-fold cross-validation, and represents the mean accuracy and losses achieved by the model in classifying MRI images, thereby providing a concise and informative summary of the model's performance and contribution towards a better understanding of its capabilities for classifying diverse brain tumor types

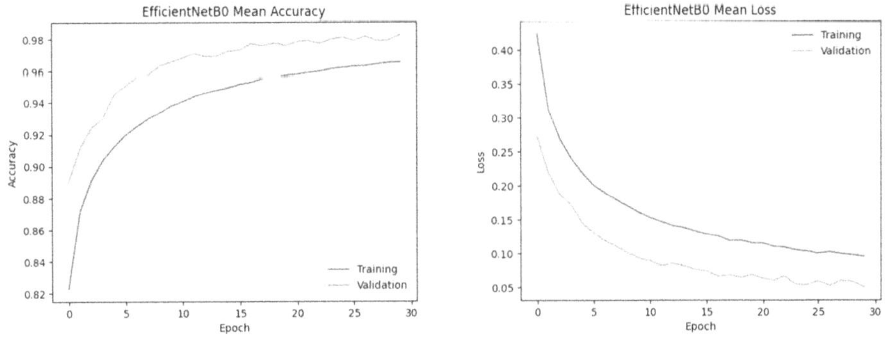

4.1. Hardware and Software Platform

The utilized platform leveraged established libraries such as TensorFlow, Keras, Pandas, Numpy, Matplotlib, and Sklearn to enhance and expedite the procedures of constructing models and processing data. The system was equipped with a high-performance NVIDIA GeForce GTX 1080 Ti graphics processing unit (GPU) for effective model training and optimization. The system has an Intel(R) Core(TM) i7-7800 central processing unit that operates at a clock speed of 3.5 GHz. Python 3.7 as the programming language is selected based on its extensive array of data processing, analysis, and visualization capabilities. The platform was equipped with a significant amount of Random Access Memory (RAM), 32 gigabytes, deemed necessary for efficient data management during the study.

4.2. Evaluation Matrices

The proposed system was evaluated using performance measures such as precision, recall, F1-score, and accuracy. Recall is a metric used to evaluate a model's ability to classify tumors accurately, which is calculated by dividing the number of true positives by the sum of true positives and false negatives. In contrast, the assessment of precision centers on the capacity of the model to prevent the misclassification of negative occurrences as positive ones. This ability is measured by computing the ratio of true positives to the sum of true positives and false positives. The F1-score is a mathematical representation of the harmonic mean between precision and recall. The computation involves the summation of precision and recall, dividing the resultant value by two and multiplying the quotient by two. The metric of accuracy is commonly employed to evaluate the efficacy of a model in precisely recognizing data. The calculation involves the division of the aggregate count of model predictions by the ratio of precise prognostications. Equations (6-9) depict the mathematical expressions for accuracy, recall, precision, and F1-score (Kuraparthi et al., 2021).

$$Recall = \frac{TP}{TP+FN} \tag{6}$$

$$Precision = \frac{TP}{TP+FP} \tag{7}$$

$$F1\text{-}Score = 2 \times \frac{Recall \times Precision}{Recall + Precision} \tag{8}$$

$$Accuracy = \frac{TP+TN}{TP+TN+FP+FN} \tag{9}$$

The outcomes of evaluating the recommended framework on the testing data are presented in Figure 8. The model's performance was meticulously assessed using average precision, recall, F1-score, and accuracy metrics. Impressively, the suggested framework in this study achieved an unprecedented peak accuracy rate of 98.32% by implementing the proposed data augmentation techniques. Furthermore, the model demonstrated remarkable precision, recall, and F1-score rates, showcasing its ability to classify tumors accurately. It is noteworthy to highlight that the models were trained using the default input sizes.

Figure 8. Represents the average precision, recall, F1-score, and accuracy evaluation metrics on the testing dataset obtained using state-of-the-art models

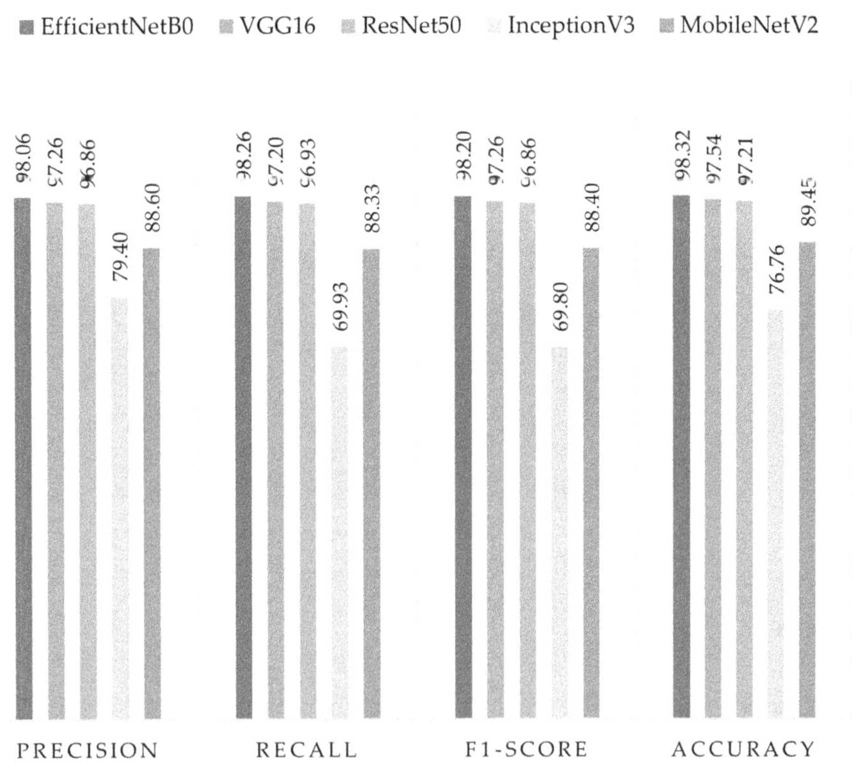

4.3. Confusion Matrix

The Confusion Matrix (Ting, 2017) is a tabular representation utilized for assessing the efficacy of a classification model. This study observed that the proposed network exhibited the satisfactory performance in multi-tumor classification when novel data augmentation techniques were employed. Furthermore, the network could identify each type of brain tumor accurately. The outcomes derived from the testing data are depicted in Figure 9. The strategic utilization of hyperparameters to optimize the learning process during neural network training is a well-established practice in the literature (Rasheed et al., 2023). In this study, the Adam optimizer was implemented. The adaptive learning rate of the Adam algorithm, which is based on estimates of gradient moments, facilitates faster convergence and can potentially enhance model performance. Furthermore, a five-fold cross-validation approach was utilized, randomly dividing the data into five subsets for training and evaluation. This robust approach facilitated a more accurate and reliable assessment of the model's performance on test data, considering potential data variability. The strategic amalgamation of these advanced methodologies and the implementation of innovative data augmentation techniques proved instrumental in achieving optimal outcomes during model training, resulting in heightened performance and robustness.

Figure 9. Presents the confusion matrices obtained from testing data with the suggested model EfficientNetB0. The figure depicts the prediction rates of the model, with panel (a) illustrating the average confusion matrix across 5-fold cross-validation and panel (b) displaying the combined results of each fold, resulting in an accuracy of 98.32%.

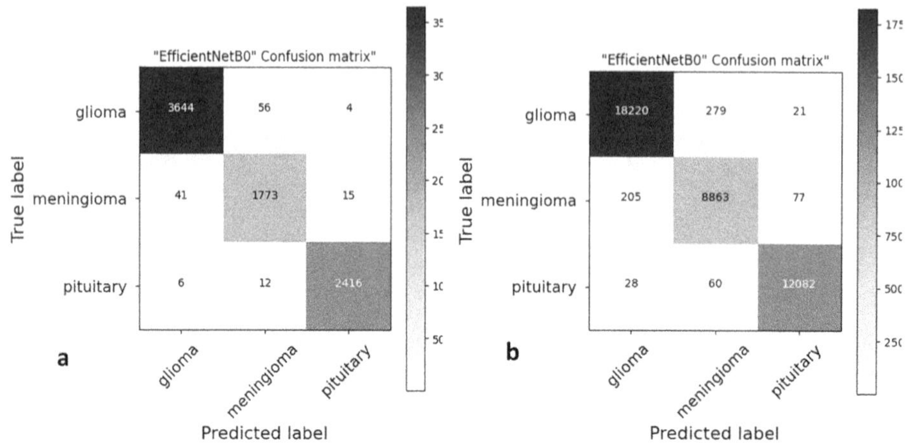

4.4. Discussion

The present study introduced innovative methods for data augmentation and recommended the utilization of an EfficientNetB0 model for the classification of primary brain tumor categories, including glioma, meningioma, and pituitary. Table 1 summarizes the outcomes derived from previous studies that have explored similar brain tumor types, although they deployed distinct methodologies. The proposed system's reliability is evidenced by the correctness of its prediction results, which surpass those of previous investigations with similar characteristics. The proposed framework employs a segment-free methodology. The loading of brain tumor images facilitates the acquisition of tumor classes, in contrast to alternative methodologies that necessitate supplementary manual procedures such as tumor feature extractions or localization. The study by (Afshar et al., 2019) demonstrated that coarse boundaries were employed as an auxiliary input to enhance the network's ability to generate improved classification results. The authors (Ismael and Abdel-Qader, 2018) performed feature extraction using a combination of DWT and the Gabor filter. These extracted features were subsequently utilized in a separate stage for classification. In reference (Pashaei, Sajedi, and Jazayeri, 2018) a CNN was utilized for feature extraction, which was subsequently classified by the Kernel Extreme Learning Machine (KELM). The researchers (Zhou et al., 2019) utilized DesnesNet to gather characteristics from axial slices, subsequently employed for classification.

On the other hand, reference (Avşar and Salçin, 2019) employed Recurrent CNN to extract features from MR images, which were then utilized to classify tumors. The feature was obtained by applying PCA-NGIST techniques and subsequently utilized for classification (Gumaei et al., 2019). The researchers (Anaraki, Ayati, and Kazemi, 2019) employed a genetic algorithm (GA) to optimize the CNN architecture for optimal classification accuracy. Nevertheless, the proposed framework attained a satisfactory classification rate even in the absence of the preceding stage, which would otherwise require an additional manual process for tumor localization before training. The researchers (Ghassemi, Shoeibi, and Rouhani, 2020) (Noreen et al., 2021) employed pre-training methodologies to address the issue, which yielded less accurate predictions than the suggested framework. In addition (Sadoon and Ali, 2021) applied a data augmentation approach that involved rotating images by 45 degrees, introducing salt and pepper noise, and performing mirror and up-down flipping from left to right. On the other hand, (Hossam H. Sultan and Nancy M. Salem, 2020) employed up-down flipping, left-right mirroring, salt noise addition, and rotation by 45 degrees for their data augmentation. (Badža and Barjaktarović, 2020) opted for a different strategy, which involved rotating images by 90 degrees and flipping them vertically. Despite their efforts, the accuracy obtained using these approaches was lower than that achieved using the novel data augmentation techniques proposed in our framework.

Table 1. Comparative analysis of proposed and previous framework

Authors	Methods	Average Precision	Average Recall	Average F1-Score	Accuracy
Afshar et al.	CapsNet	X	X	X	90.89
Ismael et al.	DWT-Gabor-NN	X	X	X	91.90
Pashaei et al.	CNN+KELM	94.6	58.43	93.00	93.68
Zhou et al.	LSTM+ DenseNet	X	X	X	94.20
Avşar et al.	R-CNN	97.00	X	95.00	91.66
Gumaei et al.	Hybrid PCA- NGIST+RELM	X	X	X	94.23
Anaraki et al.	CNN +GA	X	X	X	94.20
Ghassemi et al.	CNN based GAN	95.29	X	95.10	95.60
Swati et al.	VGG16 Fine-tune	89.17	X	91.50	94.65
Swati et al.	VGG19 Fine-tune	89.52	X	91.73	94.82
Swati et al.	AlexNet	84.56	X	86.83	89.95
Noreen et al.	InceptionV3 Ensemble	93.00	92.00	92.00	94.34
Sadoon et al.	CNN + Data augmentation	96.56	X	X	96.10
Sultan et al.	CNN + Data augmentation	96.06	94.43	X	96.13
Badza et al.	CNN + Data augmentation	97.15	97.82	97.47	97.28
Our approach	EfficientNetB0 + Data Augmentation	98.06	98.26	98.20	98.32

5. CONCLUSION

The present study introduced innovative data augmentation techniques in conjunction with the EfficientNetB0 CNN to precisely categorize numerous types of brain tumors, including glioma, meningioma, and pituitary tumors. Through a comparative analysis of the performance of EfficientNetB0 with data augmentation, our findings reveal that the proposed augmentation techniques with EfficientNetB0 demonstrate superior accuracy of 98.32%. It underscores the robust generalization capabilities of the model, making it a valuable tool in medicine for facilitating physicians in making prompt and accurate decisions related to brain tumor diagnoses. We hope to revolutionize medical imaging technology and enhance patient care by developing real-time brain tumor detection systems and 3D networks for other medical images.

REFERENCES

Abiwinanda, N., Hanif, M., Hesaputra, S. T., Handayani, A., & Mengko, T. R. (2019). Brain tumor classification using convolutional neural network. *IFMBE Proceedings*, *68*(1), 183–189. doi:10.1007/978-981-10-9035-6_33

Afshar, P., Plataniotis, K. N., & Mohammadi, A. (2019). Capsule Networks for Brain Tumor Classification Based on MRI Images and Coarse Tumor Boundaries. ICASSP, IEEE Int. Conf. Acoust. Speech Signal Process. IEEE. 10.1109/ICASSP.2019.8683759

Ahmad, I., Ullah, I., Khan, W. U., Ur Rehman, A., Adrees, M. S., Saleem, M. Q., Cheikhrouhou, O., Hamam, H., & Shafiq, M. (2021). Efficient Algorithms for E-Healthcare to Solve Multiobject Fuse Detection Problem. *Journal of Healthcare Engineering*, *2021*, 1–16. doi:10.1155/2021/9500304

Ahmad, S., Ullah, T., Ahmad, I., AL-Sharabi, A., Ullah, K., Khan, R. A., Rasheed, S., Ullah, I., Uddin, M. N., & Ali, M. S. (2022). A Novel Hybrid Deep Learning Model for Metastatic Cancer Detection. *Computational Intelligence and Neuroscience*, *2022*, 8141530. doi:10.1155/2022/8141530 PMID:35785076

Alomar, K., Aysel, H. I., & Cai, X. (2023). Data Augmentation in Classification and Segmentation: A Survey and New Strategies. *Journal of Imaging*, *9*(2), 46. doi:10.3390/jimaging9020046 PMID:36826965

Avşar, E., & Salçin, K. (2019). Detection and classification of brain tumours from MRI images using faster R-CNN. *Teh. Glas., 13*(4), 337–342. . doi:10.31803/tg-20190712095507

Badža, M. M., & Barjaktarović, M. C. (2020). Classification of Brain Tumors from MRI Images Using a Convolutional Neural Network. Appl. Sci., 10(6). doi:10.3390/app10061999

Bin Tufail, A. (2021). Diagnosis of Diabetic Retinopathy through Retinal Fundus Images and 3D Convolutional Neural Networks with Limited Number of Samples. *Wireless Communications and Mobile Computing*, *2021*, 1–15. doi:10.1155/2021/6013448

Bin Tufail, A. (2021). 3D convolutional neural networks-based multiclass classification of Alzheimer's and Parkinson's diseases using PET and SPECT neuroimaging modalities. *Brain Informatics*, *8*(1), 23. doi:10.118640708-021-00144-2 PMID:34725741

Bin Tufail, A. (2022). Early-Stage Alzheimer's Disease Categorization Using PET Neuroimaging Modality and Convolutional Neural Networks in the 2D and 3D Domains. *Sensors (Basel)*, *22*(12), 4609. doi:10.339022124609 PMID:35746389

Cheng, J. (2017). Figshare *brain tumor dataset*. [Data set].

Cheng, J., Huang, W., Cao, S., Yang, R., Yang, W., Yun, Z., Wang, Z., & Feng, Q. (2015, October). Enhanced Performance of Brain Tumor Classification via Tumor Region Augmentation and Partition. *PLoS One*, *10*(10), e0140381. doi:10.1371/journal.pone.0140381 PMID:26447861

Ghassemi, N., Shoeibi, A., & Rouhani, M. (2020). Deep neural network with generative adversarial networks pre-training for brain tumor classification based on MR images. *Biomedical Signal Processing and Control*, *57*, 101678. doi:10.1016/j.bspc.2019.101678

Gladis, S. P. V. P. (2015). Brain Tumor Detection and Classification Using Deep Learning Classifier on MRI Images. *Appl. Sci. Eng. Technol.*, *10*(2), 177–187. doi:10.19026/rjaset.10.2570

Glorot, X., & Bengio, Y. (2010). Understanding the difficulty of training deep feedforward neural networks. *Journal of Machine Learning Research*, *9*, 249–256.

Goodfellow, I. (2016). *Book: Deep Learning*. Prmu. [Online] www.deeplearningbook.org

Gumaei, A., Hassan, M. M., Hassan, M. R., Alelaiwi, A., & Fortino, G. (2019). A Hybrid Feature Extraction Method with Regularized Extreme Learning Machine for Brain Tumor Classification. *IEEE Access : Practical Innovations, Open Solutions*, *7*, 36266–36273. doi:10.1109/ACCESS.2019.2904145

Haq, I., Mazhar, T., Malik, M. A., Kamal, M. M., Ullah, I., Kim, T., Hamdi, M., & Hamam, H. (2022). Lung Nodules Localization and Report Analysis from Computerized Tomography (CT) Scan Using a Novel Machine Learning Approach. *Applied Sciences (Basel, Switzerland)*, *12*(24), 12614. doi:10.3390/app122412614

He, K., Zhang, X., Ren, S., & Sun, J. (2016). Deep residual learning for image recognition. In *Proceedings of the IEEE Computer Society Conference on Computer Vision and Pattern Recognition*. IEEE. 10.1109/CVPR.2016.90

Ismael, M. R., & Abdel-Qader, I. (2018). Brain Tumor Classification via Statistical Features and Back-Propagation Neural Network. *IEEE Int. Conf. Electro Inf. Technol*. IEEE. 10.1109/EIT.2018.8500308

Kabir Anaraki, A., Ayati, M., & Kazemi, F. (2019). Magnetic resonance imaging-based brain tumor grades classification and grading via convolutional neural networks and genetic algorithms. *Biocybernetics and Biomedical Engineering*, *39*(1), 63–74. doi:10.1016/j.bbe.2018.10.004

Kaplan, K., Kaya, Y., Kuncan, M., & Ertunç, H. M. (2015). Meningiomas: Knowledge base, treatment outcomes, and uncertainties. A RANO review. *Journal of Neurosurgery*, *122*(1), 4–23. doi:10.3171/2014.7.JNS131644 PMID:25343186

Khazaei, Z., Goodarzi, E., Borhaninejad, V., Iranmanesh, F., Mirshekarpour, H., Mirzaei, B., Naemi, H., Bechashk, S. M., Darvishi, I., Ershad Sarabi, R., & Naghibzadeh-Tahami, A. (2020). The association between incidence and mortality of brain cancer and human development index (HDI): An ecological study. *BMC Public Health*, *20*(1), 1–7. doi:10.118612889-020-09838-4 PMID:33183267

Kingma, D. P., & Ba, J. L. (2015). Adam: A method for stochastic optimization. *3rd International Conference on Learning Representations, ICLR 2015 - Conference Track Proceedings*. IEEE.

Koffas, S., Picek, S., & Conti, M. (2022). Dynamic Backdoors with Global Average Pooling. *Proceeding - IEEE Int. Conf. Artif. Intell. Circuits Syst.* IEEE. 10.1109/AICAS54282.2022.9869920

Kuraparthi, S., Reddy, M. K., Sujatha, C. N., Valiveti, H., Duggineni, C., Kollati, M., Kora, P., & Sravan, V. (2021). Brain tumor classification of MRI images using deep convolutional neural network. *TS. Traitement du Signal*, *38*(4), 1171–1179. doi:10.18280/ts.380428

McBee, M. P., Awan, O. A., Colucci, A. T., Ghobadi, C. W., Kadom, N., Kansagra, A. P., Tridandapani, S., & Auffermann, W. F. (2018). Deep Learning in Radiology. *Academic Radiology*, *25*(11), 1472–1480. doi:10.1016/j.acra.2018.02.018 PMID:29606338

Mohsen, H., El-Dahshan, E.-S. A., El-Horbaty, E.-S. M., & Salem, A.-B. M. (2018). Classification using deep learning neural networks for brain tumors. *Future Computing and Informatics Journal*, *3*(1), 68–71. doi:10.1016/j.fcij.2017.12.001

Nair, V., & Hinton, G. E. (2010). Rectified linear units improve Restricted Boltzmann machines. *ICML 2010 - Proceedings, 27th International Conference on Machine Learning*, (pp. 807–814). IEEE.

Noreen, N., Palaniappan, S., Qayyum, A., Ahmad, I., & Alassafi, M. O. (2021). Brain Tumor Classification Based on Fine-Tuned Models and the Ensemble Method. *Computers, Materials & Continua*, *67*(3), 3967–3982. doi:10.32604/cmc.2021.014158

Pashaei, A., Sajedi, H., & Jazayeri, N. (2018). Brain tumor classification via convolutional neural network and extreme learning machines. *2018 8th Int. Conf. Comput. Knowl. Eng. ICCKE 2018*. ICCKE. 10.1109/ICCKE.2018.8566571

PDQ Adult Treatment Editorial Board. (2002). Adult Central Nervous System Tumors Treatment (PDQ®): Patient Version. *PDQ Cancer Inf. Summ.* NCBI. https://www.ncbi.nlm.nih.gov/pubmed/26389458

PhayeS. S. R.SikkaA.DhallA.BathulaD. (2018). *Dense and Diverse Capsule Networks: Making the Capsules Learn Better*. arXiv. https://arxiv.org/abs/1805.04001

Rasheed, Z. (2023). Automated Classification of Brain Tumors from Magnetic Resonance Imaging Using Deep Learning. *Brain Sci., 13*. . doi:10.3390/brainsci13040602

Robbins, H., & Monro, S. (1951). A Stochastic Approximation Method. *Annals of Mathematical Statistics*, *22*(3), 400–407. doi:10.1214/aoms/1177729586

Sadoon, T. A., & Ali, M. H. (2021). Deep learning model for glioma, meningioma and pituitary classification. *Int. J. Adv. Appl. Sci.*, *10*(1), 88. doi:10.11591/ijaas.v10.i1.pp88-98

Sandler, M., Howard, A., Zhu, M., Zhmoginov, A., & Chen, L. C. (2018). MobileNetV2: Inverted Residuals and Linear Bottlenecks. Proc. *IEEE Comput. Soc. Conf. Comput. Vis. Pattern Recognit.,* (pp. 4510–4520). IEEE. 10.1109/CVPR.2018.00474

Simonyan, K., & Zisserman, A. (2015). Very Deep Convolutional Networks For Large-Scale Image Recognition. *Robots*. https://www.robots.ox.ac.uk/

Swati, Z. N. K., Zhao, Q., Kabir, M., Ali, F., Ali, Z., Ahmed, S., & Lu, J. (2019). Brain tumor classification for MR images using transfer learning and fine-tuning. *Computerized Medical Imaging and Graphics*, *75*, 34–46. doi:10.1016/j.compmedimag.2019.05.001 PMID:31150950

Szegedy, C. (2015). Going deeper with convolutions. *Proc. IEEE Comput. Soc. Conf. Comput. Vis. Pattern Recognit*. IEEE. 10.1109/CVPR.2015.7298594

Szegedy, C., Vanhoucke, V., Ioffe, S., Shlens, J., & Wojna, Z. (2016). Rethinking the Inception Architecture for Computer Vision. In *Proceedings of the IEEE Computer Society Conference on Computer Vision and Pattern Recognition,* (pp. 2818–2826). IEEE. 10.1109/CVPR.2016.308

Tan, M., & Le, Q. V. (2019). EfficientNet: Rethinking model scaling for convolutional neural networks. *36th Int. Conf. Mach. Learn.* ICML.

Ting, K. M. (2017). Confusion Matrix. *Encycl. Mach. Learn. Data Min*, (October), 260–260. doi:10.1007/978-1-4899-7687-1_50

Zhou, Y. (2019). Holistic brain tumor screening and classification based on densenet and recurrent neural network. Springer International Publishing. doi:10.1007/978-3-030-11723-8_21

Chapter 24
The Phygital Tomorrow:
Driving Culture Through Innovation – Employee Centricity and Digital Transformation

Cynthia A. Silvia
https://orcid.org/0000-0003-4934-603X
American Public University System, USA

Jennifer L. Koster
University of Cincinnati, USA

Aikyna Finch
https://orcid.org/0000-0002-0078-1973
American Public University, USA

ABSTRACT

This chapter discusses the future of the retail industry, driven by innovation, employee centricity, and digital transformation. The emerging trend of "phygital" marketing, blending physical and digital experiences for a seamless customer journey, is explored. Digitalization, digitization, and digital transformation are defined as methods for transforming the business model. Phygital marketing enhances customer engagement through interactive and immersive experiences. The impact of digitalization and innovation on various aspects of the business model is highlighted. The pandemic accelerated the shift towards phygital marketing, with social media and e-commerce playing a crucial role. By embracing phygital marketing, companies can engage with diverse customers and build lasting relationships.

DOI: 10.4018/979-8-3693-1634-4.ch024

INTRODUCTION

In recent years, the critical issues of diversity, equity, and inclusion have come to the forefront of national conversations in the United States, with many people advocating for and undertaking initiatives on these topics. According to a report by the Pew Research Center, "Racial and ethnic diversity varies greatly across the country, but the U.S. Census Bureau projects that, by 2050, more than half of the nation's population consists of a racial or ethnic minority" (Pew Research Center, 2015). Additionally, research by Deloitte (2017) suggests that retailers that make diversity and inclusion a priority in their hiring practices are more likely to have a competitive advantage and be more innovative. These factors, among others, make it increasingly important for individuals and organizations to understand and embrace diversity in all its forms.

The marketing world has become one area where diversity and inclusion are becoming increasingly important. With the rise of digital technology, companies can now reach a wider audience than ever, but this comes with the risk factor of needing to be more mindful of their customers' different cultures and beliefs. One trend that has emerged in recent years is "phygital" marketing, which involves blending physical and digital technology to create a seamless customer journey (Prior, P,2022). According to a report by Deloitte Digital, "Phygital creates a new set of expectations for consumers, who now demand a seamless and personalized experience across all touchpoints" (Deloitte Digital, 2019).

SIGNIFICANCE OF THE PAPER/STUDY STATEMENT

Phygital marketing can take many forms, from augmented reality experiences to pop-up shops offering exclusive in-store discounts to customers interacting with the brand online. The key is creating a unified experience that seamlessly integrates physical and digital touchpoints. One example of seamless integration is Nike's House of Innovation, which offers various immersive experiences, plays a key role in allowing consumers to interact with the brand in a new and immersive way. Immersive experiences include features like "Nike by You" customization stations and "Nike Expert Sessions," where customers can interact with the latest products and technologies from Nike experts (Nike, n.d.).

Today's consumers not only expect high-quality products and services but also seek memorable and personalized experiences, as noted with Nike. Marketing strategies now focus on creating meaningful interactions with customers at every online and offline touchpoint. According to Mikulić et al. (2019), phygital marketing results from merging online and offline worlds. This merging of online and offline worlds is "a harmonized experience that seamlessly blends the physical and digital worlds to offer a unified experience to the customer" (p. 5). For example, retailers can use digital technologies such as augmented reality (A.R.) and virtual reality (V.R.) to alter and enhance the in-store experience while simultaneously using data collected from online channels to personalize the experience for individual customers (Pantano & Viassone, 2015).

Phygital marketing, as highlighted by Mikulić et al. (2019), benefits businesses and offers several customer advantages. One of the key benefits is the seamless transition between online and offline channels, making the shopping experience more convenient and enjoyable. Customers can browse and research products online, then seamlessly move to an offline store to make a purchase, or vice versa (Mikulić et al., 2019). Additionally, phygital marketing can enhance customer engagement by providing interactive and immersive experiences that are impossible through traditional marketing channels

(Pantano & Viassone, 2015). Furthermore, phygital marketing offers customers a personalized and tailored shopping experience. Businesses can understand individual preferences, purchase histories, and behaviors by collecting and analyzing customer data from online channels.

Overall, phygital marketing has the potential to transform the way retailers engage with customers and create a seamless omnichannel experience. Innovative business models can enhance a company's competitive advantage and provide value for consumers by changing the company's strategy and value proposition (Kazmi & Jain, 2015). Companies should aim to deliver more excellent value while increasing profitability and revenue stream by changing the target market, the product or service offered to consumers, or the revenue model they follow. Changes to the operational model should focus on increased profitability and competitive advantage. A company could find suppliers that can provide a better contract, work with new partners, or get their products or services to customers quicker than competitors. Changes to the business model can affect the entire company and help them reach increased levels of success (Chesbrough, 2010).

Business Model Innovation

Business model innovation is often challenging. An innovative business model can be more impactful on the organization than product innovations. By analyzing the value proposition in operational strategies, a company can gain insights into essential changes to ensure the company's long-term success (Kazmi & Jain, 2015).

A company's strategic initiative involves providing exceptional service and delivering value to consumers. Part of a company's business model includes information about the target market, the needs of the customers, and how the company interacts with those customers and reaches them. An innovative business model enhances that company's strategy and finds new ways to deliver value to the consumer (Chesbrough, 2010).

Applicable Theories and Research

Phygital marketing refers to integrating physical and digital experiences in marketing efforts and has gained significant attention in recent years; however, the concepts are grounded in models that emerged much earlier. A review of the literature establishes the applicable theories and research findings relevant to phygital marketing:

Technology Acceptance Model (TAM): The TAM, developed by Fred Davis in 1986, posits that users' intention to use technology is influenced by perceived usefulness and ease of use. In the context of phygital marketing, this theory suggests that consumers are more likely to adopt and engage with phygital marketing efforts when they perceive them as valuable and easy to use. For example, a study by Nambisan and Zahra (2016) found that consumers are more likely to adopt phygital marketing strategies when they perceive them as helpful in enhancing their shopping experiences.

Social Presence Theory: Social presence theory, developed by Short, Williams, and Christie in 1976, proposes that communication technologies can create a sense of social presence, or the feeling of being together, even in mediated environments (Osei-Frimpong and McLean 2018). In phygital marketing, this theory suggests incorporating social elements, such as real-time interactions, social media integration, and user-generated content, into phygital marketing efforts can enhance consumers' sense of social presence, engagement, and purchase intention. For example, a study by Hajli (2015) found that incorporating social media features into advertising led to higher consumer engagement and purchase intention.

Experiential Marketing Theory: Experiential marketing theory, developed by Holbrook and Hirschman in 1982, emphasizes creating memorable and immersive consumer experiences. In the context of phygital marketing, this theory suggests that integrating physical and digital experiences can create unique and memorable experiences that can enhance consumers' emotional connections with brands, improve brand recall, and influence purchase behavior (Akman and Mishra, 2017). For example, a study by Akman and Mishra found that consumers who experienced a phygital shopping environment, where physical and digital elements were seamlessly integrated, reported higher levels of emotional engagement and purchase intention.

Multichannel Marketing Theory indicates that when brands provide an integrated and cohesive experience across different channels, the combined experience can positively impact customer satisfaction, loyalty, and purchase behaviors. Multichannel Marketing Theory: Verhoef, Kannan, and Iman explain this theory as one that emphasizes the importance of providing a consistent and seamless customer experience across multiple channels, including physical and digital touchpoints (2015). In phygital marketing, this theory can be applied to understand how integrating physical and digital channels can create a seamless and engaging customer journey (Verhoef, Kannan, & Inman, 2015).

Overall, the literature on phygital marketing suggests that incorporating theories and research findings from multiple disciplines, including marketing, consumer behavior, and technology acceptance, can provide valuable insights into understanding and leveraging the unique characteristics of phygital marketing efforts to create engaging and effective marketing strategies.

A New Innovative Business Model: Phygital Retail

A company's strategic initiative involves providing exceptional service and delivering value to consumers. An innovative business model enhances that company's strategy and finds new ways to deliver value to the consumer. A company's business model includes information about the targeted market, the needs of the customers, and how the company interacts with those customers and reaches out to them.

Innovative business models enhance a company's competitive advantage and provide value for the consumer by changing the company strategy and value proposition. The company should deliver increased value while increasing profitability and revenue stream. Companies can do this by changing their target market, the product or service they offer consumers or the revenue model they follow.

DEI and Phygital Retail: How are Employees Adapting?

Today's consumers expect more from brands than in the past, and the stakes are high for those retailers that do not take action on equity, diversity, and inclusion in the workplace. Today responses to racial inequities are unprecedented. People nationwide and more than 4200 towns and cities have staged protests, with 25 million participating (Buchanan, Bui &Patel, 2020; Pew Research Pole, 2020. According to a poll by McKinsey, 60% of African American Consumers reported discrimination while shopping in retail stores, while 50% reported discrimination while making purchases (Bennett et al., 2015). In 2019 women only held 26% of board seats in retailing and consumer companies, while ethnically diverse individuals held 16% of those seats, with 13% in executive positions (Business of Fashion, 2020).

Diversity is measured by who is represented in the workplace, whereas diversity and inclusion are measured by how personnel experience work. Phygital retailers must focus on maintaining a diverse and inclusive workforce, as one cannot exist without the other. The business case for increasing diversity, equity, and inclusion has several benefits, including solid financial performance. According to Burns, Elsworth, Field, and Harris (2021), diverse leadership and financial performance are strongly connected.

Often an innovative business model can be more impactful on the organization than product innovations. Changes to the operational model should focus on increased profitability and competitive advantage (Burns, Elsworth, Field, and Harris, 2021). A company could find suppliers that can provide a better contract, work with new partners, or get their products or services to customers quicker than competitors. Changes to the business model can affect the entire company and help them reach increased levels of success (Burns, T., Elsworth, D., Field, E., & Harris, T., 2021). Changes to the business model also help the company to be more aware of the changes that might affect the core business value. A company can conduct multiple tests to find an innovative strategy that best suits them. This innovative strategy is essential, especially if the company wants to offer new products or services and does not have data to support its decisions (Cheris, A., Coffman, J., Frasier, E., & Noether, A. 2021& Rai, T., & Dutkiewicz, C. (2022).

Diversity and inclusion will play a substantive role in creating a diverse and inclusive workforce. According to Aperian Global, winning the war on DEI takes top priority in finding and attracting the right talent. Edelman (2020) reports that as many as 40% of all millennials have turned down jobs because their potential employer was perceived to lack an inclusive mindset. More than 52% of people of color will not accept a position with a firm that refuses to speak out on racial inequality (Edelman,2020). A company that lacks a diverse mindset and fails to onboard diverse talent will lose relevance which is what phygital businesses are all about.

Advocating for Change

The needs and demands of consumers change frequently, and sometimes they no longer find value in a company's offerings. An innovative business model helps to keep up with the changing consumer needs. An innovative business model ensures the company provides in-demand products and services that generate new revenue. A company may innovate its business model to keep operations running smoothly. Innovating its business model helps to create a competitive advantage over other businesses that might better meet customer needs. Business model innovation is often challenging. By analyzing the value proposition in operational strategies, a company can gain insights into changes that are essential to ensure that the company has the chance of long-term success

Change in Mindset

Some business models have not led to success, while others have helped the company increase revenue. A prime example is the video game industry, which has undergone various business model innovations. When video games first came onto the market, video consoles were often expensive, meaning they only appealed to a smaller section of the target audience who could afford them. The development of manufacturing processes and technological advances eventually led to smaller consoles, expanding the target market and increasing revenue streams.

At one point, companies began selling consoles directly to the consumers, which helped to increase profits, and they no longer had to go through a third party to reach their target market. Further development occurred when developers created games for smartphones, creating a new innovative business model that offered a subscription fee for selling merchandise linked to the game.

The entertainment industry also experienced the impact of innovative business models. A perfect example of this is the on-demand movies and T.V. shows. When media became available to watch outside the movie cinema, customers could rent videos or DVDs from video stores. DVDs took up less shelf space and were easy for customers to transport and store. These DVDs were durable and thin enough that consumers could ship them through the personal post. Companies could reach consumers outside of their immediate geographical marketplace.

A third shift in the entertainment industry came when consumers wanted to buy Movies and T.V. shows without leaving their homes. This third shift was made possible through streaming services allowing consumers more choices than only selecting from the products in the company's stock. Streaming services allow companies to set up operations to fit the current customer's needs. Streaming services meant that the physical shelf space for selling DVDs was no longer an issue, and the operations of the business model changed dramatically.

The inability to adapt to customers' needs can lead to companies shutting down. An innovative business model that allows the company to adapt to the market can prove to be the primary driver behind a company staying in business over a long period. A key example would be cameras and videos. Initially, cameras and videos were large, bulky, difficult to transport, and expensive to own and operate. The main focus of cameras and videos was on the chemicals behind developing pictures from a camera film which required specialized knowledge and tools to complete the process. As a result, the consumers needed to change, and there was an increased desire to capture experiences in videos and films; this led to the digital camera, which is much easier to use and maintain, and transport. Companies that did not adapt to this new business model lost valuable business opportunities and competitive advantage, resulting in company closures. Soon their products became irrelevant and impacted the company's revenue streams. These companies lost the benefit of knowing their target market, resulting in new companies establishing a secure position by meeting the customer's emerging needs.

Digital Transformation

Digitalization and innovation apply to every business model, from supply chain to value proposition, marketing, and consumer acquisition. Digitalization is adopting digital technologies

Figure 1. Digitization steps

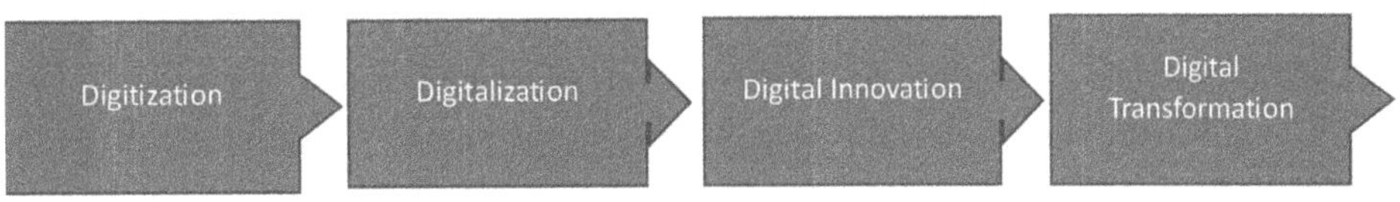

into every aspect of the business model. Digitalization uses digital data and technologies to create new ways to transform the business model. Digitalization is only possible with digitization. Digitization focuses on internalizing a process by combining digital data and technology to create new opportunities. Digital transformation is a combination of cultural change and digital technology. (Kimachia, 2022) Digital innovation creates new business models and processes that improve the organization's business model and processes by combining traditional business models and processes with new innovative ones to meet the needs of retailers in the future (Bloomberg Media Studios|IBM, 2020).

The Acceleration of DEI and the Phygital World

Retailers need to increase the acceleration of DEI efforts to improve underrepresentation in the phygital world of retail. Correcting this situation without improving underrepresentation in the phygital world takes years. A more inclusive, equitable, and diverse workforce creates a brand energy, motivating and inspiring strong advocacy across diverse populations. Creating a diverse, equitable, and inclusive phygital workforce harnesses many different perspectives and creates a culturally competent customer experience that turns shoppers into promoters, inspiring employees (Cheris, Coffman, Frasier, & Noether, 2021 and Rai & Dutkiewicz, 2022). Making DEI an inclusive part of phygital strategy assists in attracting a diverse group of candidates. Creating pathways for diverse talent to move up integrates strategically essential roles with their valuable experience. Inclusivity empowers organizational talent to thrive and perform to their fullest capacity. Mapping the customer base recalibrates the brand and marketing strategy by building a product assortment that caters to a diverse consumer population as brand ambassadors. Mapping the customer base improves the customer experience by applying it to a broader section of the population. Identifying opposition to DEI efforts in Phygital retail assists in proactively addressing any opposition by building awareness and anticipating concerns. According to Rai and Dutkiewicz (2022), 31.4% of employees report an increase in attention to DEI initiatives within their organizations over the past two years, while 44% feel that their organization has caused employees to feel isolated due to a lack of support for DEI initiatives.

The Phygital Tomorrow

The beginning of the pandemic sent retailers into a tailspin. Social media and E-commerce sent retailers scurrying to find a new form of retail to replace the old brick-and-mortar retailers. In a few short months, marketers began to mesh live streaming, videos, and social networking into a platform where influencers promote products on social media to encourage consumer interaction. With more than 160 million small to medium-sized retailers, Facebook allows these retailers to create single online stores on their social network (Davis, 2021). Social media platforms and disruptive models soon became the phygital retail of the future. By November, Instagram introduced Reels and Shop to support online retailers and short videos, allowing small retailers to set up online shops (Davis, 2021). At the time, Walmart allowed consumers to view and buy fashion items celebrity influencers wore. Most shoppers still prefer social interactions with brick-and-mortar brands; however, as time goes on, they are starting to adapt to the new Phygital retail of the future. Retailers are adopting these new marketing strategies to meet the needs of the new phygital consumer.

Diversity and inclusion are rising in importance in all aspects of society, including retailing and marketing. Retailers can now showcase their brands using interactive displays that allow consumers to flip through catalogs to see unique clothing styles and looks that mirror online shopping. Just walking by a coffee shop triggers a coupon to print on the consumer's cell. These digital overlays and augmented reality allow consumers to experience an entirely new form of retail. By embracing the principles of phygital marketing and creating experiences that seamlessly blend physical and digital touchpoints, companies can better engage with customers from diverse backgrounds and build long-lasting relationships that benefit both the brand and the consumer.

Retailers can now showcase their brands using interactive displays that allow consumers to flip through catalogs to see unique clothing styles and looks that mirror online shopping. These digital overlays and augmented reality allow consumers to experience an entirely new form of retail. Just walking by a coffee shop triggers a coupon to print on the consumer's cell. Phygital retail is positioned to take the best of digital and physical and mesh products with physical interactions allowing consumers to enjoy a new user experience.

Lessons Learned from the Pandemic

The pandemic has taught us that consumers value the interaction between physical products and personal interaction with sales associates in brick-and-mortar environments. Marketers must combine the best of all worlds in providing consumers with multi-layered shopping experiences that meet the customer's expectations while improving the user's experience. Welcome to the phygital future and beyond.

Phygital Retail: The New Innovative Retail

The new innovative retail landscape is a combination of blending the physical environment with the digital retail landscape in an effort to build a consistent customer journey across physical and digital touchpoints. This will take a diverse and inclusive workforce with the right talent to create this seamless journey. Diversity and inclusion are two critical cmponents necessary to creating a diverse and inclusve workforce. According to Aperian Global, winning the war on DEI will take top priority in finding and attracting the right talent. Edelman (2020) reports that as many as 40% of all millinnials have turned down jobs because their potential employer was perceived to lack an inclusive mindset. More than 52% of people of color will not accept a position with a firm that refuses to speak out on racial inequality (Edelman,2020). A company that lacks a diverse mindset and fails to onboard diverse talent will lose relevance which is what phygital businesses are all about.

Bridging the gaps between a brand's physical and digital marketplace can go in one of two ways. According to Hughes (2022) e-commerce will account for 24% of all retail sales by 2026. Where customers and employees choose to go, the retailers must follow if they choose to stay profitable. Designing a phygital strategy is no easy task and retailers must ensure that they invest in appropriate strategies to meet customers and employees needs (Hughes, 2022).

Today frontline retailers are facing serious staffing challenges since COVID with 32% of customers willing to leave a brand after having a bad experience (Hughes, 2022). Now connecting with employees and customers has never been more important. Retailers must build new experiences that work for them, the customers and the employees. Retailers should look to internal stakeholders as well as customers to help shape a phygital strategy that will add value to the organization's culture and at the same time keep up with technological advances (Hughes, 2022). Retailers must reduce repetitive tasks for associates while adding value to customer services.

DEI and Phygital Retail: How Are Employees and Consumers Adapting?

Today's consumers expect more from brands than in the past, and the stakes are high for those retailers that do not take action on equity, diversity, and inclusion in the workplace. People nationwide and more than 4200 towns and cities have staged protests, with 25 million participating (Buchanan, Bui &Patel, 2020; Pew Research Pole, 2020. Responses to racial inequities are unprecedented. According to a poll by McKinsey, 60% of African American Consumers reported discrimination while shopping in retail stores, while 50% reported discrimination while making purchases (Bennett et al., 2015. In 2019 women only held 26% of board seats in retailing and consumer companies, while ethnically diverse individuals held 16% of those seats, with 13% in executive positions (Business of Fashion, 2020).

Diversity is measured by who is represented in the workplace, whereas diversity and inclusion are measured by how personnel experience work. Phygital retailers must focus on maintaining a diverse and inclusive workforce, as one cannot exist without the other. The business case for increasing diversity, equity, and inclusion has several benefits, including solid financial performance. According to Burns, Elsworth, Field, and Harris (2021), diverse leadership and financial performance are strongly connected.

Research into the role(s) of diversity, equity, inclusion, and belonging (DEIB) in phygital marketing will continue to take place as phygital retail becomes the key focus of retail of the future. Companies will continue to integrate DEIB principles into their phygital marketing strategies to increase diverse representation in marketing content as it affects customer engagement and brand perception (Burns, T., Elsworth, D., Field, E., & Harris, T., 2021). Examining the representation of different cultures, beliefs, genders, races, and other diverse groups in phygital marketing campaigns will influence customer perceptions and behaviors of phygital retail.

Research nto the role of diversity, equity, inclusion, and belonging in phygitl marketing as digital transformation and phygitl mrketing will continue to provide vluble insights that will hlp organiztions thrive in the future (Burns, T., Elsworth, D., Field, E., & Harris, T., 2021). There will be many opportunities to research phygital marketing as it assumes a prominent position in the business community of tomorro.

Phygital Retail Data

Phygital marketing is, in part, by its very nature, digital; it carries inherent data security risks. As we move towards a phygital world, the focus on the ethical implications of phygital marketing and digital transformation needs to be explored. The ethical implications of phygital marketing strategies must be explored, including data privacy, security, transparency, and fairness issues. This could include investigating the ethical challenges associated with collecting, using, and analyzing customer data in phygital marketing and the need for ethical guidelines and practices to ensure responsible and sustainable use of digital technologies in marketing.

Today's customers are used to shopping in-store and online; however, the data behind these two experiences are often kept siloed. With a phygital strategy, it is crucial to connect the physical and digital data by elevating customer and employee experiences, increasing brand loyalty, and reducing attrition in the workforce (Hughes, 2022). Having a clear view of all warehouses, stores, and fulfillment center inventories, customers can choose to buy from the convenience of home or the sales floor, creating a consistent, personalized shopping experience that creates added value (Hughes, 2022). It is about allowing consumers to choose how they want to interact with the company's brand. An integrated stock management system allows flexibility in the fulfillment processes. Providing customers with a choice of delivery methods allows retailers to use a local store for fast delivery or opt for service by drones. Creating a memorable phygital experience is essential for retailers to stand out from competitors (Hughes, 2022).

With technology constantly evolving, we need to turn our attention to explore the impacrt of phygitl marketing on customer behavior. several areas would benefit from further exploration in phygital marketing, especially concerning the impact of phygital marketing on customer behavior would allow us to explore how customers perceive and respond to phygital marketing strategies, including using augmented reality (A.R.), virtual reality (V.R.), and other digital technologies in the in-store experience and online exerience. This would include examining customer preferences, attitudes, and behaviors towards phygital marketing and the impact on purchase decision-making, loyalty, and satisfaction.In previous years customers would shop their favorite retail stores and fill out a customer satisfaction survey. These analog touchpoints all but disappeaed during covid. Customer engagement is not a new phenomonon, however phygital marketing upgraded customer engagement to new levels as a result of technology impovements and the emergence of new marketing channels such as phygital marketng.

Phygital marketing uses all the traditional tools such as email, QR codes, and cookies to reshape the way a brand engages with consumers. During the pandemic consumers adapted to the buy online pick up in store routin also knownas BOPIS and the buy online return in store BORIS (Potharaju, 2021). The pandemic has forever changed he way companies and their employees communicate with their xcustomers. Some of this is the result of the dramaic shift to digital workplaces and telemedicine. The most dramaoic changes that took place were in retailing, however, these changes are not expected to reverse themselves (Kohli, Timelin, Fabius, & Veranen, 2020). According to McKinsey when consumers shifted to the adoption of online delivery options, these changes accellerated at the equivilent of ten years in eight short weeks (Kohli, Timelin, Fabius, & Veranen, 2020). Consumers soon found that the phygital landscape that bridged the gap between the physical and dgital provdes a cnvenient way to shop meeting their needs for safety and convenience (Kohli, Timelin, Fabius, & Veranen, 2020).

Another favorite way for consumers to connect to the favorite retailrs wer through the use of QR codes which were invented in 1994. They became popular in Asian markets and took hold here in the United States during the pandemic. Juniper Research suggests that 5.3 billion QR codes will be redeemed with the use of smartphones (Businesswire, 2018). Junniper also revealed that mobile loyalty card use will double to four billion cards by 2022. Chatbots and voice assistants were found to be major drivers of consumer loyalty (Businesswire, 2018).

CONCLUSION

Phygital marketing has the potential to revolutionize the way companies engage with customers and create seamless, high-quality experiences by blending physical and digital elements. The benefits of phygital marketing, such as increased convenience, personalization, and customer engagement, make it an incredibly compelling approach for companies looking to stay competitive in today's digital landscape.

A particularly critical aspect that companies must consider in their phygital marketing strategies is diversity, equity, inclusion, and belonging (DEIB). Recognizing and embracing the importance of DEIB in marketing, companies can develop a comprehensive understanding of how marketing efforts can play role in the impact of customers' diverse needs and expectations in the phygital era (Friska, 2022). In doing so, marketing campaigns create solid and lasting connections with consumers by effectively demonstrating appreciation by reflecting their customer base in their marketing campaigns.

Further, part of being innovative means being employee centric. Employee centricity plays a vital role in the success of digital transformation and phygital marketing initiatives. Companies should prioritize creating a culture of innovation, agility, and adaptability among employees, empowering them with the necessary skills and resources to drive digital transformation initiatives. Engaged and empowered employees can be powerful drivers of change and innovation within organizations, leading to a successful implementation of phygital marketing strategies and digital transformation initiatives.

For companies to thrive in the dynamic world of phygital marketing, they must prioritize innovation, DEIB, employee centricity, and digital transformation. By remaining current with the latest technological advancements, embracing diversity and inclusion, equity and belonging, and fostering a culture of innovation and agility, companies can effectively drive culture and create meaningful customer experiences in the era of digital transformation rather than remaining in the past, they will safely be part of the phygital tomorrow.

REFERENCES

Akman, I., & Mishra, A. (2017). Factors influencing consumer intention in social commerce adoption. *Information Technology & People (West Linn, Or.), 30*(2), 356-370. https://doi.org/ doi:10.1108/ITP-01-2016-0006

Asperian Global. (2021). *Eight Steps for Winning Over DEI Skeptics.* Asperian Global. https://www.aperianglobal.com/winning-over-dei-skeptics/

Bennett, A., Daddario, K., & Hill, R. (2015).Shopping While Nonwhite. Racial discrimination Among Minority Consumers. *Journal of Consumer Affairs, 49*(2), 328-55.

Bloomberg Media Studios, IBM. (2020). *How Smarter Businesses Transform in an Uncertain World.* Bloomberg Media Studios, IBM. https://www.ibm.com/downloads/cas/NJL6A0YO

Buchanan, B. & Patel, J. (2020). Black Lives may be the Largest movement in U.S. History. *New York Times.*

Budoian, I. (2021). *Digitalization: How to Use Digital Innovation to Grow Your Business.* Digital Leadership. https://digitalleadership.com/blog/use-digital-innovation-to-grow-your-business/#:~:text=The%20following%20three%20types%20of%20digital%20innovation%20create,3%20Building%20on%20traditional%20business%20models%20and%20processes

Burns, T., Elsworth, D., Field, E., & Harris, T. (2021). *The diversity imperative in retail.* McKinsey. https://www.mckinsey.com/industries/retail/our-insights/the-diversity-imperative-in-retail

Businesswire. (2018). *Juniper Research: Mobile QR Code Coupon Redemptions to Surge, Surpassing 5.3 Billion by 2022.* Businesswire. https://www.businesswire.com/news/home/20180103005014/en/Juniper-Research-Mobile-QR-Code-Coupon-Redemptions

Cheris, A., Coffman, J., Frasier, E., & Noether, A. (2021). *Diversity, Equity, and Inclusion in Retail: Breaking Down the Task Ahead.* Bain & Company. https://www.bain.com/insights/diversity-equity-and-inclusion-in-retail-breaking-down-the-task-ahead-infographic/

Davis, F. D. (1989). Perceived usefulness, perceived ease of use, and user acceptance of information technology. *Management Information Systems Quarterly, 13*(3), 319–340. doi:10.2307/249008

Davis, J. (2021). *The need for evolved phygital: Ramping up the experience*. Marketing Tech. https://www.marketingtechnews.net/news/2021/mar/15/the-need-for-evolved-phygital-ramping-up-the-experience/

Deloitte. (2017). *Diversity and Inclusion: The Reality Gap*. Dcloittc. https://www2.deloitte.com/content/dam/Deloitte/nl/Documents/human-capital/hc-diversity-inclusion-the-reality-gap.pdf

Deloitte Digital. (2019). *The Phygital Transformation: Blending Physical and Digital Experiences*. Deloitte. https://www2.deloitte.com/content/dam/Deloitte/fr/Documents/technologies/phygital-transformation-deloitte-digital.pdf

Edelman. (2020). *Trust Barometer Special Report: Brand Trust in 2020*. Edelman. https://www.edelman.com/research/brand-trust-2020

Friska, B. (2022). *Human Design for Your Powerful Marketing*. Human Design. https://humandesign.ai/blog/2022/12/22/human-design-for-your-powerful-marketing/

Hajli, N. (2015). Social commerce constructs and consumer's intention to buy. *International Journal of Information Management, 35*(2), 183–191. doi:10.1016/j.ijinfomgt.2014.12.005

Hughes, M. (2022). The Future of Retail is Phygital. *Forbes*. https://www.forbes.com/sites/mikehughes1/2022/10/31/the-future-of-retail-is-phygital/?sh=4fdfb3cc13b5

Indeed Editorial Team. (2023). *A guide to innovative business models (with examples)*. Indeed. https://uk.indeed.com/career-advice/career-development/innovative- business-models

Kimachia, K. (2022). *What Is Digitization vs Digitalization vs Digital Transformation?* Channel Insider. https://www.channelinsider.com/business-management/digitization-vs-digitalization/#:~:text=Digital%20transformation%20is%20the%20process%20of%20streamlining%20a,Digitalization%20is%20sometimes%20referred%20to%20as%20%E2%80%9Cdigital%20transformation.%E2%8

Kohli, S., Timelin, B., Fabius, V., & Veranen, S. M. (2020). *How COVID-19*. McKinsey & Company. https://www.mckinsey.com/~/media/McKinsey/Industries/Retail/Our%20Insights/How%20COVID%2019%20is%20changing%20consumer%20behavior%20now%20and%20forever/How-COVID-19-is-changing-consumer-behaviornow-and-forever.pdf

Potharaju, S. (2021). How Phygital Can Change The Way You Connect With Customers. *Forbes*. https://www.forbes.com/sites/forbesbusinesscouncil/2021/10/28/how-phygital-can-change-the-way-you-connect-with-customers/?sh=4ab9b7c74615

Chapter 25
Change Management and Cybersecurity in Healthcare:
Mitigating Human Factors and Risks

Sharon L. Burton
https://orcid.org/0000-0003-1653-9783
Capitol Technology University, USA

ABSTRACT

Two central problems in change management are the lack of attention to human factors (e.g., fatigue, human error, communication breakdowns, staffing issues, workload and stress, ergonomics, organizational factors, compliance and procedures, teamwork and collaboration, and inadequate training) and cybersecurity issues. Data shows that 62.7% of adverse effects affected patients, and healthcare professionals contributed 71.7% of the effects, with communication and protocol issues being related to the damage caused. A literature review and content analysis show the overall findings of prioritizing human factors engineering and cybersecurity concerns in their change management processes to mitigate risks and ensure patient safety. Overall, this research contributes to the fields of cybersecurity leadership and healthcare by raising awareness of the critical issues that must be addressed in change management and highlighting the need for healthcare organizations to prioritize human factors engineering and cybersecurity in their change management processes.

INTRODUCTION

Organizational development change management in healthcare is a critical process that involves the implementation of new technology and processes (i.e., electronic health records (EHRs) or clinical decision support systems (CDSSs) to enhance patient care and outcomes. Going forward in this publication, the term organizational development change management was referenced as change management. However, change management in healthcare also presents significant challenges in human factors engineering (i.e., fatigue, human error, communication breakdowns, staffing issues, workload and stress, design and ergonomics, organizational factors, compliance and procedures, teamwork and collaboration,

DOI: 10.4018/979-8-3693-1634-4.ch025

and inadequate training) and cybersecurity that must be addressed to avoid adverse outcomes (Ozair et al., 2020). Human factors engineering involves the interaction between individuals, technology, and the environment, while cybersecurity protects computer systems and networks from unauthorized access, theft, or damage (Halamka et al., 2021). Integrating new technology and processes can disrupt workflows, affect staff morale, and create new vulnerabilities in the system that cybercriminals could exploit. Studies have shown that most healthcare-related adverse events are caused by human factors engineering, such as burnout and work-related stress (Cohen, 2020), communication breakdowns, staffing issues, and inadequate training (Carayon et al., 2015). Approximately half of all respondents felt burnout, with nurses (56 percent) and other clinical personnel (54.1 percent) having the most significant levels (The Harvard Gazette, 2023). Medication mistakes that are examples of human factors engineering risks include administering medicine to the incorrect patient, giving a patient the wrong dosage of medication, giving a drug overdose, omitting a drug in error, and giving the drug at the wrong time. Another example is a void of training regarding electronic medical record systems (e.g., electronic medical records [EMRs], electronic health records [EHRs], and personal health records [PHRs].

Therefore, change management must consider the impact of new technology on staff members' workflows and communication, and ensure that staff receive adequate training and support to adapt to the changes (Burrell, 2021). Additionally, healthcare organizations are prime targets for cyberattacks due to the sensitive nature of the data and the increasing use of connected devices and networks. The healthcare industry experiences the highest data breach cost compared to other industries (Ponemon Institute, 2021). In 2020, more than 29 million health data were exposed, with hacking accounting for 67% of the breaches, the greatest of which was a ransomware assault on cloud service provider Blackbaud (Billauer, 2021). Thus, change management must consider the cybersecurity risks associated with new technology and processes and ensure that appropriate security measures and change processes are in place to protect against cyber threats. A robust systems approach and focus on change management requires shifting to a culture of change focused on human factors engineering, and cybersecurity.

The lack of attention given to human factors engineering and cybersecurity in change management in healthcare can result in adverse outcomes that can negatively impact patient care and compromise sensitive data. Therefore, healthcare organizations must prioritize human factors engineering and cybersecurity in their change management processes to mitigate risks and ensure patient safety. This paper has explored the connections between change management, human factors engineering, and cybersecurity in healthcare and the significant problems that must be addressed to ensure the successful implementation of new technology and processes.

BACKGROUND

In contemporary health service delivery, the capacity to adapt and embrace change is vital (Figueroa, 2019). Healthcare organizations should evaluate the expertise of their change management professionals and leaders and ensure they are well-versed in evolving methods, buy-in, and the necessary implementation plans for effective change management (Nilsen, 2020). The change management plan has to include the human factors engineering that could affect the change.

Healthcare professionals globally face the arduous task of enduring prolonged shifts filled with frequent interruptions, complex cases, and high-stress levels. Consequently, work-related stress and burnout have become pervasive issues within the industry, resulting in potential errors that jeopardize the well-being of both patients and healthcare providers. Factors such as workload demands, time pressure, task complexity, interruptions, and communication barriers all influence the cognitive and emotional load experienced by individuals. Consequently, these factors can have a cumulative effect on healthcare professionals, ultimately leading to diminished performance, compromised decision-making, and an increased likelihood of errors. Numerous issues pushed the need for change management understanding regarding human factors engineering and cybersecurity concerns.

Using data from 1984 and reviewing medical records of patients treated in New York hospitals, the Institute of Medicine projected that as many as 98,000 Americans lost their lives annually due to medical errors (Institute of Medicine, 2000; James, 2013). Further, the report concluded that the majority of errors are not attributed to incompetent healthcare professionals but rather to flawed systems and processes that cannot prevent errors. Additionally, the Institute of Medicine's findings underscore the significance of systemic deficiencies in healthcare settings, highlighting the need for comprehensive interventions targeting the improvement of organizational structures and processes. These insights emphasize the importance of focusing on systemic factors to mitigate medical errors and enhance patient safety rather than solely attributing blame to individual practitioners. This information regarding the prevalence of medical errors and the emphasis on systemic deficiencies aligns with the principles of change management and the recognition of human factors engineering in healthcare. Change management strategies are crucial in addressing the flawed systems and processes that contribute to medical errors, as they provide a structured approach to identifying, analyzing, and implementing necessary changes to improve patient safety. By acknowledging the role of systemic factors and focusing on organizational structures and processes, change management interventions can effectively target the root causes of errors and promote a culture of safety. Additionally, understanding human factors engineering, such as the limitations and vulnerabilities of healthcare professionals within complex healthcare systems, highlights the importance of creating supportive environments, providing appropriate training and resources (Burton, 2021), and implementing error-prevention strategies that account for human fallibility.

Another change management and human factors engineering issue was exemplified in the Veterans Association's backlog to schedule and offer help to veterans. According to Devine (2015), the Veterans Association faced a significant challenge in addressing a backlog of 611,000 healthcare cases, which unfortunately included the deaths of more than 307,000 veterans. Public knowledge became, as given by CNN Wire (2015), according to a report by the Office of Inspector General (OIG) of the Department of Veterans Affairs (VA); it was discovered that within the agency's healthcare enrollment system, approximately 800,000 records were stagnant. Among these records, it was identified that over 307,000 belonged to deceased veterans whose demise had occurred months or even years prior. Moreover, a substantial number of veterans registered in the Department of Veterans Affairs enrollment system had passed away before their applications for care had undergone processing. The information regarding the discovery of stagnant records and deceased veterans within the Department of Veterans Affairs (VA) healthcare enrollment system is significant to change management and human factors engineering within the context of healthcare. From a change management perspective, this information highlights the need for organizational change within the VA to address the inefficiencies and deficiencies in their healthcare enrollment system. Identifying such a large number of stagnant records and deceased veterans underscores the importance of implementing changes to improve the system's functionality, efficiency, and accuracy. Change management principles can guide the VA in implementing reforms, streamlining processes, and leveraging technology to prevent similar issues in the future. In terms of human factors engineering, this information emphasizes the potential consequences of flawed systems on patient safety and the well-being of veterans. The identification of deceased veterans whose applications for care were never processed raises concerns about the timely and effective delivery of healthcare services. Understanding human factors engineering helps to recognize the limitations and vulnerabilities of the system and the individuals operating within it. This insight prompts the need for interventions that focus not only on system improvements but also on supporting the well-being and workload management of healthcare professionals involved in the enrollment and care process.

Later, a revised estimation by Makary and Daniel (2016) now places the number of premature deaths caused by medical errors at 400,000. A conceivable rationalization for the inconsistent application of change management actions could be the need for more awareness or understanding of the importance of data gathering in change management. Such inconsistency could lead to inadequate change management strategic and cultural change, in due course, project failure (Muller & Turner, 2020). Igoe (2021) Igoe (2021) notes that healthcare change management data shows that ideas are produced; however, the ideas must consistently deliver on maximum impact.

METHODOLOGY

This research explores the benefits of conducting a literature review and content analysis in academic research. The literature review involved a systematic analysis of scholarly articles and research related to the advantages of these research methods (Levy & Ellis, 2021). Content analysis, on the other hand, involves analyzing communication messages to identify patterns and themes related to the benefits of these research methods (Neuendorf, 2019). Identified were relevant databases and sources, including seven academic databases like JSTOR, PubMed, Scopus, Web of Knowledge; Academic Search Complete; ProQuest; Eric; and publications related to the topic to conduct the research. After sorting 953 articles, and 155 journals examined, a combination of 200 journals, dissertations, and articles was selected for full analysis. The inclusion criteria for selecting resources were based on their relevance to the research topic and the quality of the research. The resources were systematically reviewed and categorized based on their research methods, research objectives, and findings. Content analysis was used to examine patterns and trends in language use to understand how specific subjects are communicated through various media or communication channels (Neuendorf, 2019). Through this analysis, the researcher identified patterns and trends in language use, which provided insights into social and cultural phenomena (Mullins, 2022). Some essential topics related to the issue emerge through content analysis of chosen articles. Relevant keywords and phrases emerged to help identify germane research terms and phrases such as change management, human factors engineering, cybersecurity issues, electronic health records, resistance to change, data breaches, organizational culture and readiness, and continuous learning. A literature review and content analysis helped identify key themes and trends; it provided a solid theoretical foundation for the research and supported the development of recommendations or interventions. The benefits of conducting a literature review and content analysis include a more comprehensive and informed understanding of a particular topic, which is essential in the research process. Integration of this information helps to build a conceptual model on Research Networks.

PROBLEM STATEMENT

Despite the growing use of new technology and procedures in the healthcare industry, change management frequently needs to address cybersecurity concerns and human factors engineering, which can have unfavorable effects that jeopardize patient care. Research by Carayon et al. (2015) indicated that the majority of healthcare-related adverse events are caused by human factors engineering. In contrast, the Ponemon Institute (2021) claims that the healthcare business has the highest average cost of a data breach compared to other industries. In order to reduce risks and guarantee patient safety, healthcare businesses urgently need to give human aspects and top cybersecurity priority in their change management procedures.

SIGNIFICANCE OF THE RESEARCH

Addressing the significance of human factors engineering and cybersecurity concerns in change management processes to mitigate risks and ensure patient safety is crucial because the data will enable healthcare organizations to focus on people, processes, technology, and structures associated with healthcare's quadruple (quad) aim, reducing costs; improving population health, patient experience, and team well-being—and productivity (Arnetz et al., 2020). This research offers change managers and other change leaders information to advance competencies to work through implementations for cultural change to affect communication, learning and development, measurements, and sustainability. When the need is recognized to shift to a change management culture, the understanding becomes ready to be studied for the associated elements and components to affect the change. Change to improve human factor concerns, cybersecurity issues and incorporate the quad four is needed among healthcare organizations to augment healthcare system performance (Arnetz et al., 2020). Business, as usual, should no longer be a focus (Ghandi, 2020).

The results of this research are anticipated to be unambiguously used by small to large -level healthcare organizations. The results of this research are suggested as crucial to organizations pursuing to adopt behaviors of healthcare organizations that successfully apply the cultural change and have leaders at all levels work together positively to affect zero harm (Thomas, 2020).

Also, the results of this research could be valuable to education and development professionals when preparing education regarding human factors engineering and cybersecurity for reinforcing organizational understanding (Burrell, 2019) and apply frameworks as well as making available thought leadership regarding key concerns when renewing current and creating new risk knowledge curriculums (Andronache, 2021). Further, this research could be valuable to communication professionals and vendors that prepare communication roadmaps (i.e., communication toolkits and plans) supporting change management to clarify goals and objectives. The communications documents offer guidance regarding what needs to be communicated, when it needs to be communicated, and how the communication should occur (Centers for Disease Control and Prevention, 2023). Moreover, this research may prove helpful to researchers, supervisors, managers, and other key program leaders when assessing their existing and future states, taking into consideration communication approaches conferred in the research

RESEARCH THEORIES AND FRAMEWORKS

One model and two frameworks guided this qualitative research. The technology acceptance model (TAM) has been widely used to explain the adoption and use of technology in various domains, including healthcare. The model's underlying reasoning was that, in the context of technology usage, the behavioral intention was affected by particular ideas about technology use rather than a general attitude toward behavioral intention (Marikyan & Papagiannidis, 2020). However, one of the main criticisms of TAM is its focus on individual-level perceptions of technology rather than the broader social and organizational context in which technology is implemented (Venkatesh et al., 2016). This limited scope can lead to overlooking the impact of external factors such as organizational culture, social norms, and power dynamics on technology acceptance and use. In summary, while the Technology Acceptance Model provides a valuable lens for understanding individual-level perceptions of technology, it may only partially capture the broader organizational context.

On the other hand, the change management framework provides a structured approach to planning and implementing organizational changes, including technology adoption. In healthcare, change is unavoidable (Barrow et al., 2022). Also, From the bedside to the boardroom, all healthcare practitioners have a role in enabling successful transformation. Further, applying best practices drawn from change theories may increase the likelihood of success and future practice improvement (Barrow et al., 2022). However, a potential negative of this change management framework is that it can be time-consuming and resource-intensive, requiring significant organizational buy-in and support. Additionally, it may need to fully account for the complex and dynamic nature of change in healthcare organizations, which can involve multiple stakeholders, competing priorities, and unpredictable outcomes (Hendy et al., 2012). While the Change Management Framework provides a structured approach to managing organizational change, it may need to fully account for the complexity of healthcare organizations and the unique challenges they face in implementing new technology and processes.

Supporting change management is the human factors engineering framework. Healthcare practitioners must address genuine human issues such as restricted attention spans, how fatigue affects performance, forgetfulness, and the capacity to concentrate on just one item at a time (USFHealth, 2023). Human factors engineering research uses information about human capabilities and limits to designing interactive systems involving people, equipment, and their surroundings in order to assure their efficacy, safety, and usability. This model purports that instead of attempting to remove human factors engineering (an impossible feat), the study of human factors engineering focuses on building systems that foresee potential failures. Understanding human factors engineering as they relate to healthcare is significant because, within healthcare, human factors engineering (and mistakes) may make or break a person's life. While the human factors engineering framework has its positives, critiques exist. The duties enacted by healthcare professionals and others, the technology they are required to utilize (Nobles, 2021, 2018), the work setting in which they operate, and the organizational rules that govern their activities may or may not be a suitable match for their strengths and limitations (Henriksen et al., 2008). This research team noted that once these system elements and providers' sensory, behavioral, and cognitive traits are not well-matched, unsatisfactory results in terms of effort exerted, quality of treatment, job satisfaction, and, probably most importantly, patient safety ensue.

LITERATURE REVIEW

This literature review aimed to gather relevant, current research on change management and cybersecurity in healthcare and mitigating human factors engineering and risks and to synthesize the research into a coherent overview of existing knowledge. This research provided a fundamental understanding of the subject. The study highlighted areas of past scholarship to avoid repetition and provide credit to other academics. Critiques of research are offered, too. Overall, the literature examination clarified and focused on the research topic.

Grasping Organizational Change Management

Before delving into the literature, let us review the question: What is change management, and who is responsible for it? Change Management is a systematic and planned approach to facilitating organizational change and enhancing an organization's overall effectiveness and performance (Igoe, 2021). Further, change management involves implementing interventions, strategies, and processes to support individuals, teams, and the organization in adapting to new ways of working, achieving desired outcomes, and responding to external environmental shifts. Change should include the change management process, staff engagement and communication, leadership and change agents, organizational culture and readiness, and continuous learning and evaluation (Fedynets, 2022).

The change management process in organizational development typically follows a structured framework to guide the stages of change. It often includes steps such as assessing the need for change, setting objectives, planning and implementing change interventions, evaluating outcomes, and sustaining the change over the long term (Waddell et al., 2019). The process recognizes the importance of involving stakeholders, communicating effectively, addressing resistance, and fostering employee engagement throughout the change journey.

Staff engagement is a critical element of successful change management in organizational development. Research emphasizes the significance of involving employees in decision-making, providing clear communication about the change, and creating opportunities for feedback and participation (Kotter, 2019; SHRM, 2023). Engaging staff throughout the change process fosters a sense of ownership, commitment, and motivation, thereby facilitating smoother transitions and higher chances of successful implementation.

Effective leadership plays a pivotal role in change management. Leaders are responsible for creating a shared vision, providing direction (Burton, 2021), and guiding employees through the change process (Phillips & Klein, 2023). Often identified from within the organization, change agents serve as catalysts for change, assisting in planning, implementing, and sustaining the change efforts. Their role involves promoting awareness, building coalitions, and supporting employees during the transition (Phillips & Klein, 2023).

Organizational culture and readiness significantly influence the success of change initiatives. A culture that values innovation, learning, and adaptability will likely embrace and support change (Cameron & Green, 2019). Assessing organizational readiness involves evaluating factors such as the organization's capacity for change, its history of change management, and the availability of resources (Abdurrohman & Kadiyono, 2020). Understanding the current culture and readiness level helps tailor change interventions and anticipate potential challenges.

Change management emphasizes the importance of continuous learning and evaluation. Learning involves capturing lessons from previous change efforts, sharing best practices, and promoting a culture of reflection and improvement (Michigan State University, 2023). Evaluation helps assess the impact of change initiatives, identify areas for improvement, and inform future change efforts. Utilizing appropriate metrics and feedback mechanisms enables organizations to monitor progress, adjust strategies, and ensure the change sustainability.

In conclusion, change management is a structured and intentional approach to driving organizational change, enhancing performance, and improving outcomes. It entails effectively managing the various components involved in change, including employee engagement, leadership, culture, and continuous learning. By understanding the process, involving stakeholders, and leveraging appropriate interventions, organizations can navigate the complexities of change and increase their capacity for successful adaptation.

Grasping Human Factors Engineering

Concerns about human factors engineering arose during World War II as a consequence of the work and experience of a number of professionals engaged in the research of then-current manned systems (Human Factors and Ergonomics Society [HFES], n. d.). Such studies were conducted regarding "system performance, problems encountered in information presentation, detection, and recognition, related action controls, workspace arrangement, and skills required "(HFES, n. d.). According to the Davidson (2013) of the University of Washington, John Karlin is considered the father of human factors engineering. He was an early researcher in behavioral science at Bell Labs.

Dr. Calvin Nobles (2021) defines human factors engineering as a scientific approach to enhancing system design to heighten human behavior and performance. According to Chapanis and Holstein (2022), human-factors engineering, also known as ergonomics or human engineering, is a discipline that uses physical and psychological knowledge to design objects and systems for human utilization. Human factors engineering refers to a body of knowledge, a method, and a career. Human factors engineering is crucial in every part of healthcare. Engineering is not a distinct goal or program but rather a method of thinking that should be included in the design of processes, roles, employment, and education and training.

The Connection Between Human Factors Engineering and Change Management

In addition, change management in healthcare must also consider human factors engineering as well as cybersecurity risks. The success of any change management process depends on the support and cooperation of stakeholders. Therefore, it is essential to consider the needs and preferences of all stakeholders when implementing new technology and processes. One of the main challenges with human factors engineering in change management is resistance to change. Healthcare professionals may resist new technology and processes due to fear of the unknown (Fette, 2019) or a lack of understanding of the benefits. Change management must address these concerns and provide adequate training and support to healthcare professionals to ensure they are comfortable with the new technology and processes (Burrell, 2021; Burton, 2022). Another challenge is communication. Effective communication is essential in change management to ensure all stakeholders know of the changes and their roles and responsibilities. Change management must ensure that all stakeholders receive clear and concise communication regarding the changes and their impact on patient care. Attention must remain on human factor engineering consistently.

The Lack of Attention Given to Human Factors Engineering: A Change Management Problem

Healthcare-related adverse events are a significant problem worldwide, and their occurrence can have severe consequences for patients, healthcare providers, and healthcare organizations (Carayon et al., 2015). Most adverse events [no percentage was given] are caused by human factors engineering such as communication breakdowns, staffing issues, and inadequate training (Carayon et al., 2015). An example of communication breakdowns, staffing issues, and possible inadequate training is when a healthcare worker in Valdosta, Georgia, caused a data breach at the South Georgia Medical Center. The employee downloaded unauthorized data to a thumb drive (Richards, 2022). The report offered that the ex-employee was charged with felony computer theft and criminal breach of computer privacy (Richards, 2022). It is essential to consider the impact of technology on staff members' workflows, all communication, and ensure that staff receives adequate training and support to mitigate these issues.

Impact of new technology on staff workflows. Implementing new technology can significantly impact staff members' workflows in healthcare organizations, leading to potential communication breakdowns and errors. According to Awan et al. (2021), implementing electronic health records (EHRs) can disrupt clinical workflows, leading to errors, reduced efficiency, and increased workload. To mitigate these issues, healthcare organizations must implement EHR systems that are user-friendly and meet staff's needs (Awan et al., 2021).

Training and support. Training and support are crucial to ensure that staff members can adapt to changes resulting from implementing new technology (Barnett et al., 2021). According to Yoo et al. (2019), healthcare providers require ongoing education and training to keep up with technological advancements, and organizations must provide adequate support and resources for staff to ensure successful implementation. This support can include dedicated IT support staff, ongoing training, and regular feedback and communication (Yoo et al., 2019).

Resistance to change. Resistance to change can be a significant barrier to successfully implementing new technology in healthcare organizations. According to Chen et al. (2020), healthcare providers may resist change due to concerns about job security, lack of involvement in decision-making, and lack of understanding of the benefits of new technology. To address these issues, healthcare organizations must involve staff members in the decision-making process and ensure that they understand the benefits of new technology and how it can improve patient care (Chen et al., 2020).

Impact on patient safety. The implementation of new technology can have a significant impact on patient safety in healthcare organizations. According to Tavares et al. (2019), the use of electronic medication administration records (eMARs) can significantly reduce medication errors in healthcare organizations. However, implementing eMARs requires staff to change their workflow and communication patterns, which can cause initial disruption and potentially impact patient safety. To mitigate these issues, healthcare organizations must ensure that staff receives adequate training and support to adapt to the new technology (Tavares et al., 2019).

The implementation of new technology in healthcare organizations can have significant benefits for patients and healthcare providers. However, according to Hefner et al. (2020), to ensure successful implementation, healthcare organizations must consider the impact of new technology on staff workflows and communication and ensure that staff receives adequate training and support to adapt to the changes. This support can include ongoing education and training, dedicated IT support staff, regular feedback and communication, and involving staff in decision-making. By addressing these issues, healthcare organizations can mitigate the human factors engineering contributing to adverse events and improve patient safety and quality of care.

Figure 1. Change management differentiation

<table>
<tr><th></th><th>Change Management Differentiation</th><th></th></tr>
<tr>
<td>Academy to Innovate HR (n.d.) https://www.aihr.com/blog/od-interventions/</td>
<td>
</td>
<td>• Intervention developed due to successful innovation implementation in organizational systems.
• Evaluate organizational structure's adaptability to change and effectiveness in function for effective assessment.
• Assess technology choices and workers' qualifications for effective implementation.</td>
</tr>
<tr>
<td>Horlick, A. (n.d.). https://shorturl.at/ntvBR</td>
<td>Organizational Development Change Management
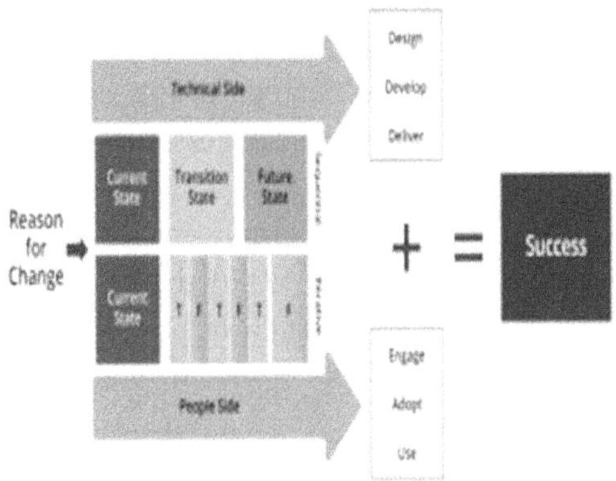
</td>
<td>• Maximize ROI by increasing employee adoption and usage of the project or initiative.</td>
</tr>
</table>

The Lack of Emphasis on Cybersecurity in Healthcare: A Change Management Problem

The healthcare industry has undergone significant changes in recent years with the increasing use of technology and digital transformation. This transformation has resulted in many benefits, including improved patient care, increased efficiency, and reduced costs (Brown-Jackson, 2017). However, transformation in healthcare has also brought about new challenges, including cybersecurity risks. Healthcare organizations are prime targets for cyberattacks due to the sensitive nature of their data and the increasing use of connected devices and networks. This text will discuss the major problem with change management in healthcare; the lack of emphasis on cybersecurity. It will also explore the importance of human factors in change management processes.

The problem with change management and cybersecurity in healthcare. Change management in healthcare is a complex process that involves various stakeholders, including clinicians, administrators, IT professionals, and patients. It aims to implement new technology, structures, and processes while minimizing disruption to patient care. However, many healthcare organizations need to consider the cybersecurity risks associated with these changes. According to a report by the Ponemon Institute (2021), the healthcare industry experiences the highest average cost of a data breach compared to other industries. This cost highlights the need for healthcare organizations to prioritize cybersecurity in their change management processes.

One of the crucial challenges with change management in healthcare is the need for more awareness and understanding of cybersecurity risks. Many healthcare professionals need to be trained in cybersecurity, and need to be made aware of the potential risks associated with new technology, structures, and processes. This knowledge void can result in a lack of appropriate security measures, leaving healthcare organizations vulnerable to cyber threats. Another challenge is the increasing use of connected devices and networks in healthcare. The Internet of Things (IoT) has brought about many benefits in healthcare, including remote monitoring and real-time data analysis. However, it has also created new cybersecurity risks, as these devices can be hacked or compromised. Change management in healthcare must consider the cybersecurity risks associated with IoT devices and ensure that appropriate security measures are in place.

The importance of cybersecurity in change management. Cybersecurity is a critical component of change management in healthcare. Healthcare organizations must consider the cybersecurity risks associated with new technology and processes and ensure appropriate security measures are in place. This process includes implementing firewalls, encryption, and access controls to protect sensitive data. One salient cybersecurity risk in healthcare is data breaches. Data breaches can compromise sensitive patient information, including personal health information (PHI) and financial information. Data breaches can also result in financial losses and reputational damage to healthcare organizations. Therefore, change management must ensure appropriate security measures to protect against data breaches. Another salient cybersecurity risk in healthcare is ransomware attacks. Ransomware attacks can encrypt critical data, preventing healthcare organizations from accessing it until a ransom is paid. Ransomware attacks can result in significant financial losses and disruption to patient care. Change management must ensure that healthcare organizations have adequate backup and recovery systems to mitigate the impact of ransomware attacks.

The Connection Between Human Factors Engineering and Cybersecurity

Human risks to cybersecurity necessitate human solutions, and human factors engineers are specialists in applying human performance and cognitive research to convoluted work contexts (Cunningham, 2021). Human factors engineering expertise and leadership education can lead to a more thorough security plan offering information to prepare to adapt to internal and external threats (Burton, 2021). Neglecting the human aspects of cybersecurity can lead to significant deficiencies in the ability to respond and react effectively to threats. Recognizing that cybercriminals hold a considerable influence over organizational cybersecurity preparations is crucial. These malicious actors primarily target organizational staff, exploiting their vulnerabilities to gain unauthorized access. Therefore, the understanding becomes evident that people are the initial and final line of defense in ensuring robust cybersecurity measures. The cornerstone of a successful cybersecurity strategy lies in engaging personnel throughout the entire process. Research emphasizes the importance of involving staff members in decision-making, providing clear and transparent communication about the changes being implemented, and creating opportunities for feedback and active participation (Kotter, 2019). By actively engaging staff members, organizations foster a sense of ownership, commitment, and motivation, ultimately facilitating smoother transitions and increasing the likelihood of successful implementation.

Within cybersecurity, effective communication among the individuals working within the system holds paramount importance. Such communication serves as the lifeblood ensuring all components' seamless operation. Robust communication channels enable prompt sharing of information, rapid detection of potential threats, and timely response to cyber incidents. Regular education and training sessions and awareness programs can further enhance the communication skills and cybersecurity knowledge of staff members, empowering them to safeguard organizational systems and data proactively.

Human factors engineering plays a critical role in establishing a comprehensive cybersecurity framework. This framework incorporates human-centered design principles, prioritizing individuals' capabilities, limitations, and behaviors within the cybersecurity ecosystem. By integrating human factors engineering throughout the entire cybersecurity system, from end-to-end, organizations can optimize human performance, minimize errors, and maximize overall system resilience.

While the advent of robotics and artificial intelligence (AI) has revolutionized various industries, it is crucial to recognize that these technologies cannot replace the human aspect of security. AI-powered systems may assist in automating specific cybersecurity tasks, such as anomaly detection and threat analysis, but they differ from substitute for human intelligence, intuition, and adaptability. Human cybersecurity professionals possess the ability to interpret complex contexts, make nuanced decisions, and exercise ethical judgment, qualities that are not easily replicated by machines. Therefore, a balanced approach that combines the strengths of both humans and technology is essential for comprehensive cybersecurity.

In short, neglecting the human aspects of cybersecurity can lead to significant deficiencies in responding effectively to threats. By recognizing the pivotal role of personnel and incorporating effective communication, active engagement, human factors engineering, and a balanced approach to technology, organizations can strengthen the cybersecurity posture. Investing in developing human capabilities, fostering a cybersecurity-aware culture, and continuously adapting to emerging threats will ultimately contribute to a more robust and resilient cybersecurity ecosystem (Burton, 2021).

RECOMMENDATIONS, CONCLUSION, AND SOLUTIONS

Understanding the factors contributing to work-related stress and burnout requires a comprehensive examination of the intricate interactions between healthcare professionals and their work environments.

To effectively address these challenges, healthcare organizations should implement proactive measures that promote early identification of workload-related issues. Implementing a change management strategy is paramount in establishing a systematic and sequential approach to recognizing challenges, effectuating modifications, and achieving successful execution. Also, integrating human factors engineering principles can enable the development of workload assessment tools and techniques that aid in determining an individual's maximum capacity. Such tools may involve objective measures, such as physiological indicators, cognitive performance assessments, and subjective self-report measures, including surveys and interviews. Key recommendations are as follows:

1. Effective implementation of workload assessment tools and techniques requires support and commitment from organizational leaders. Engaging leaders ensure the allocation of necessary resources, establishes a culture of prioritizing workload assessment, and facilitate the adoption of evidence-based practices throughout the healthcare organization.
2. Fostering a culture of open communication and psychological safety within healthcare teams is paramount. Creating an environment where healthcare professionals feel comfortable expressing their concerns is crucial. Encouraging open communication and psychological safety allows for the identifying early signs of stress and burnout. Healthcare teams should have mechanisms to facilitate dialogue, provide support, and promote overall well-being among staff members.
3. Implement interventions to optimize task allocation and improve workflow design: Healthcare organizations should explore interventions to optimize task allocation, minimize interruptions, and enhance workflow design. The interventions can involve redesigning processes, implementing technology solutions to streamline tasks, and creating guidelines for effective task delegation. By improving workflow efficiency, healthcare professionals can operate in a more conducive work environment, leading to improved well-being and enhanced patient safety.
4. Effectively addressing work-related stress and burnout necessitates overcoming a significant challenge: One of the primary challenges in addressing work-related stress and burnout is determining an individual's threshold for workload capacity. Human factors engineering principles can be pivotal in offering insights and interventions. Workload assessment tools incorporating objective measures (such as physiological indicators and cognitive performance assessments) and subjective self-report measures (including surveys and interviews) can help gauge workload capacity and identify potential risks of overload.

By incorporating a multidisciplinary approach, human factors engineering can provide a framework for understanding the complex interplay between individuals, technology, and organizational factors that influence performance and well-being in healthcare settings. By applying these recommendations, healthcare organizations can better understand and manage workload capacity, mitigate the risks of stress and burnout, and ultimately enhance the well-being of healthcare professionals while improving patient safety. Integrating human factors engineering principles into healthcare systems provides structured and evidence-based approach to addressing workload challenges and optimizing the work environment.

In conclusion, change management in healthcare is a critical process that must consider human factors engineering, and cybersecurity risks to ensure the successful implementation of new technology and processes (Holtz, 2021). The lack of attention given to these factors can result in adverse outcomes that can negatively impact patient care and compromise sensitive data. Healthcare organizations must prioritize human factors engineering and cybersecurity in their change management processes to mitigate risks and ensure patient safety. To address human factors engineering, healthcare organizations must consider the impact of new technology on staff workflows and communication, ensure that staff receives adequate training and support to adapt to the changes, and involve staff in the decision-making process (Burton, 2022). Communication is also essential in change management to ensure all stakeholders are aware of the changes and their impact on patient care. To address cybersecurity risks, healthcare organizations must consider the potential risks associated with new technology and processes, implement appropriate security measures such as firewalls, encryption, and access controls, and ensure that adequate backup and recovery systems are in place. Healthcare organizations must prioritize human factors engineering and cybersecurity in their change management processes to ensure patient safety and data protection. Overall, change management in healthcare requires a holistic approach that considers human factors engineering and cybersecurity risks to ensure the successful implementation of new technology and processes while minimizing disruption to patient care. By addressing these issues, healthcare organizations can improve patient safety and quality of care while also protecting sensitive data from cyber threats.

REFERENCES

Abdurrohman, M. F., & Kadiyono, A. L. (2019). Getting prepared: Employee readiness for changes. Referred Proceeding of the *1st International Conference on Finance, Economics, and Business (ICoFEB)*. EUDL. https://eudl.eu/pdf/10.4108/eai.12-11-2018.2288821

Andronache, A. (2021). Increasing security awarenesss through lenses of cybersecurity culture. *Journal of Information Systems & Operations Management, 15*(1).

Arnetz, B. B., Goetz, C. M., Arnetz, J. E., Sudan, S., vanSchagen, J., Piersma, K., & Reyelts, F. (2020). Enhancing healthcare efficiency to achieve the Quadruple Aim: An exploratory study. *BMC Research Notes, 13*(1), 362. doi:10.118613104-020-05199-8 PMID:32736639

Awan, O., El-Sayed, A. M., Alsudais, N., & Alabdulkarim, Y. (2021). Electronic Health Records (EHRs) implementation in Saudi Arabia: Benefits, challenges, and solutions. *Health Care, 9*(2), 140. PMID:33535608

Barnett, M. L., Ray, K. N., Souza, J., Mehrotra, A., & Friedberg, M. W. (2021). Trends in telemedicine use in a large commercially insured population, 2005-2017. *Journal of the American Medical Association, 323*(18), 1845–1847. doi:10.1001/jama.2020.23332 PMID:30480716

Barrow, J. M., Annamaraju, P., & Toney-Butler, T. J. (2022). Change management. *StatPearls Publishing LLC*. https://www.ncbi.nlm.nih.gov/books/NBK459380/

Billauer, B. P. (2021). Health held hostage: Hospitals under cyber-attack. *The American Council on Science and Health*. https://www.acsh.org/news/2021/06/23/health-held-hostage-hospitals-under-cyber-attack-15626

Brown-Jackson, K. L. (2019). *Disrupting and retooling: a model for an effective community-based telehealth program* (Order No. 28144638). Available from ProQuest Central; ProQuest Dissertations & Theses Global; ProQuest One Academic. https://www.proquest.com/dissertations-theses/disrupting-retooling-model-effective-community/docview/2440009177/se-2

Burrell, D. N. (2019). The impact of a top-down and bottom-up education and training approach on organizational performance. *Journal of Workplace Learning, 31*(3), 163–175.

Burrell, D. N. (2021). *Cybersecurity leadership from a talent management organizational development lens* [Unpublished Exegesis]. Capitol Technology University.

Burton, S. L. (2022). *Cybersecurity leadership from a Telemedicine/Telehealth knowledge and organizational development examination* (Order No. 29066056). Available from ProQuest Central; ProQuest Dissertations & Theses Global. (2662752457). https://www.proquest.com/dissertations-theses/cybersecurity-leadership-telemedicine-telehealth/docview/2662752457/se-2

Carayon, P., Wetterneck, T. B., Rivera-Rodriguez, A. J., Hundt, A. S., Hoonakker, P., Holden, R., & Gurses, A. P. (2015). Human factors systems approach to healthcare quality and patient safety. *Applied Ergonomics*, *45*(1), 14–25. doi:10.1016/j.apergo.2013.04.023 PMID:23845724

Centers for Disease Control and Prevention [CDC]. (2023). Communication planning: Adolescent and School Health. *Author.* https://www.cdc.gov/healthyyouth/fundedprograms/1807/communication_planning.htm

Chapanis, A., & Holstein, W. K. (2022). Human-factors engineering. *Encyclopedia Britannica.* https://www.britannica.com/topic/human-factors-engineering

Chen, H., Shekhar, R., & Easton, G. (2020). Overcoming resistance to healthcare innovation. *MIT Sloan Management Review*, *61*(1), 1–10.

Cohen, B. (2020, February 5). Workload, stress, and patient safety: how human factors can help. *Institute for Healthcare Improvement.* https://www.ihi.org/communities/blogs/-workload-stress-and-patient-safety-how-human-factors-can-help

Cunningham, M. (2021). Transforming the science of security with human factors. *Forcepoint.* https://www.forcepoint.com/blog/x-labs/transforming-science-security-human-factors

Davidson, A. (2013). John Karlin, father of human factors engineering. *University of Washington.* https://sites.uw.edu/adavid7/2013/02/10/john-karlin-father-of-human-factors-engineering/#:~:text=John%20Karlin%2C%20an%20early%20researcher,fascinating%20history%20of%20usability%20research

Devine, C. (2015, September 3). 307,000 veterans may have died awaiting Veterans Affairs healthcare, report says. *CNN Politics.* https://www.cnn.com/2015/09/02/politics/va-inspector-general-report/index.html

Fedynets, N. (2022). Change management mechanism in the organization in crisis conditions. *Acta Scientiarum Polonorum. Oeconomia*, *21*(3), 15–24. https://doi-org.captechu.idm.oclc.org/10.22630/ASPE.2022.21.3.10. doi:10.22630/ASPE.2022.21.3.10

Fette, J. (2019). Leading Transformational Change: Winning the Hearts and Minds. PM World. *Journal*, *8*(9), 1–8.

Figueroa, C. A., Harrison, R., Chauhan, A., & Meyer, L. (2019). Priorities and challenges for health leadership and workforce management globally: A rapid review. *BMC Health Services Research*, *19*(1), 239. doi:10.118612913-019-4080-7 PMID:31014349

Ghandi, T. K., Feeley, D., & Schummers, D. (2020). Zero harm in healthcare. *NEJM Catalyst Innovations in Care Delivery*, *1*(2), CAT.19.1137. Advance online publication. doi:10.1056/CAT.19.1137

Halamka, J., Blumenthal, D., & Samal, L. (2021). Healthcare and Cybersecurity: Bibliography and Selected Readings. *The New England Journal of Medicine*, *384*(10), 963–972. doi:10.1056/NEJMra2001465

Hefner, J. L., Sieck, C. J., & Walker, D. M. (2020). Considering the impact of healthcare information technology on workflow: An analysis of complexity, uncertainty, and communication in primary care. *International Journal of Medical Informatics*, *136*, 104079. doi:10.1016/j.ijmedinf.2020.104079

Hendy, J., Fulop, N., Reeves, B., Hutchings, A., & Collin, S. (2012). Implementing change in health systems: The role of sensemaking. *Journal of Health Organization and Management*, *26*(2), 215–233. PMID:22856177

Henriksen, K., Dayton, E., Keyes, M. A., Carayon, P., & Hughes, R. (2008). Patient safety and quality: An evidence-based handbook for nurses. In: Hughes RG, (ed) *Patient Safety and Quality: An Evidence-Based Handbook for Nurses*. Rockville (MD): Agency for Healthcare Research and Quality. https://www.ncbi.nlm.nih.gov/books/NBK2666/

Human Factors and Ergonomics Society [HFES]. (n. d.). *HFES history*. HFES. https://www.hfes.org/about-hfes/hfes-history#:~:text=Human%20factors%20concerns%20emerged%20during,the%20sea%2C%20and%20in%20space

Igoe, K. J. (2021). Change Management: Why It's So Important, and so challenging, in healthcare environments. *Harvard T. H. Chan School of Public Health*. https://www.hsph.harvard.edu/ecpe/change-management-why-its-so-important-and-so-challenging-in-health-care-environments/

Institute of Medicine. (2000). *To err is human: building a safer health system*. National Academy Press.

James, J. T. (2013). A new, evidence-based estimate of patient harms associated with hospital care. *Journal of Patient Safety*, *9*(3), 122–128. doi:10.1097/PTS.0b013e3182948a69 PMID:23860193

Kotter, J. (2014). *Accelerate: Building strategic agility for a faster-moving world*. Harvard Business Review Press.

Levy, Y., & Ellis, T. J. (2021). A systems approach to conduct an effective literature review in support of information systems research. Informing Science. *The International Journal of an Emerging Transdiscipline*, *24*, 185–212.

Makary, M., & Daniel, M. (2016). Medical error—The third leading cause of death in the US. *British Medical Journal*, *353*, i2139. doi:10.1136/bmj.i2139 PMID:27143499

Marikyan, D., & Papagiannidis, S. (2020). Theory review: Technology Acceptance Model (TAM). *TheoryHub*. https://open.ncl.ac.uk/theories/1/technology-acceptance-model/#:~:text=Davis%2C%201989).-,Theory,the%20successful%20implementation%20of%20technology.

Michigan State University. (2023). *Organizational change management: Definition & importance*. Michigan State University. https://www.michiganstateuniversityonline.com/resources/leadership/organizational-change-management/#:~:text=Managing%20a%20successful%20organizational%20change,production%20cycles%20and%20reducing%20costs

Muller, R., & Turner, R. (2020). The influence of project management standards, practices, and methodologies on project success. *Project Management Journal*, *51*(1), 18–33.

Mullins, J. (2022). Content analysis. The International Encyclopedia of Communication Research Methods, 1-13.

Neuendorf, K. A. (2019). *The content analysis guidebook*. Sage publications.

Nilsen, P., Seing, I., Ericsson, C., Birken, S. A., & Schildmeijer, K. (2020). Characteristics of successful changes in healthcare organizations: An interview study with physicians, registered nurses and assistant nurses. *BMC Health Services Research*, *20*(1), 147. doi:10.118612913-020-4999-8 PMID:32106847

Nobles, C. (2018). Botching human factors in cybersecurity in business organizations. *Holistica, 9*(3). https://sciendo.com/pdf/10.2478/hjbpa-2018-0024

Nobles, C. (2021). Exploring Senior Managers' Influencing of Human Factor to Reduce Human Errors in Cybersecurity. ProQuest. Capitol Technology University.

Ozair, F. F., Jamshed, N., Sharma, A., & Aggarwal, P. (2020). Ethical and social issues in healthcare technology implementation: A scoping review. *Journal of Medical Systems*, *44*(8), 1–14. doi:10.100710916-020-01629-5

Phillips, J., & Klein, J. D. (2023). Change management: From theory to practice. *TechTrends*, *67*(1), 189–197. doi:10.100711528-022-00775-0 PMID:36105238

Ponemon Institute. (2021). *2021 Cost of a data breach report: Global overview*. IBM. https://www.ibm.com/security/data-breach

Richards, T. (2022, January 14). Ex-hospital worker arrested in SGMC data breach. *Valdosta Daily Times*. https://www.valdostadailytimes.com/news/local_news/ex-hospital-worker-arrested-in-sgmc-data-breach/article_7ca92b22-a2e5-5541-b3b3-38472d3706b1.html

SHRM. (2023). *Managing organizational change*. SHRM. https://www.shrm.org/resourcesandtools/tools-and-samples/toolkits/pages/managingorganizationalchange.aspx

Tavares, J., Harrison, J., Williams, J., Gershon, R. R. M., & Kalman, M. (2019). Electronic medication administration records in long-term care: A systematic review. *Journal of the American Medical Directors Association*, *20*(2), 190–197.e3. doi:10.1016/j.jamda.2018.09.018

The Harvard Gazette. (2023). Doctors not the only ones feeling burned out. *The Harvard Gazette*. https://news.harvard.edu/gazette/story/2023/03/covid-burnout-hitting-all-levels-of-health-care-workforce/#:~:text=%E2%80%9CThey%20may%20be%20less%20likely,(54.1%20percent)%20reporting%20burnout

Thomas, E. J. (2020). The harms of promoting 'zero harm.'. *BMJ Quality & Safety*, *29*(1), 4–6. doi:10.1136/bmjqs-2019-009703 PMID:31597784

USFHealth. (2023). Human factors in healthcare. *USF Health Morsani College of Medicine*. https://www.usfhealthonline.com/resources/health-informatics/human-factors-in-healthcare/#:~:text=Rather%2C%20healthcare%20providers%20must%20consider,one%20thing%20at%20a%20time

Venkatesh, V., Thong, J. Y., & Xu, X. (2016). Unified theory of acceptance and use of technology: A synthesis and the road ahead. *Journal of the Association for Information Systems*, *17*(5), 328–376. doi:10.17705/1jais.00428

Waddell, D., Creed, A., Cummings, T. G., & Worley, C. G. (2019). *Organisational change: Development and transformation*. Cengage AU.

Wire, C. N. N. (2015, September 3). Report: 307,000 veterans may have died awaiting Veterans Affairs healthcare. *WTVR*. https://www.wtvr.com/2015/09/03/report-307000-veterans-may-have-died-awaiting-veterans-affairs-health-care

Yoo, S. J., Kim, S. S., Lee, K. H., & Hwang, H. (2019). Factors affecting healthcare service quality in the adoption of medical technologies. *BMC Health Services Research*, *19*(1), 987. doi:10.118612913-019-4795-5 PMID:31870361

KEY TERMS AND DEFINITIONS

Change Management: The process of planning, executing, and managing changes to an organization's processes, systems, policies, or structure is referred to as change management. It entails taking a methodical approach to moving an organization from its present state to a desired future state while minimizing disturbance and ensuring that the changes are appropriately integrated and embraced by the company's stakeholders.

Cybersecurity: Cybersecurity refers to the practice of protecting computers, servers, networks, electronic systems, and data from unauthorized access, damage, theft, disruption, or other forms of cyber threats. It involves a range of measures, technologies, policies, and practices designed to ensure the confidentiality, integrity, and availability of digital information and resources.

Data Breach: A data breach occurs when information is stolen or removed from a system without the owner's knowledge or authority.

Human Factors Engineering: The study of how people interact with systems, goods, and environments with the goal of enhancing performance, safety, and well-being is referred to as human factors engineering.

Risk Mitigation: Risk mitigation is a method for preparing for and mitigating the consequences of hazards that a firm may encounter. Risk mitigation, like risk reduction, takes actions to mitigate the negative consequences of risks and catastrophes on business continuity.

Technology Acceptance Model: The technology acceptance model (TAM) is a theory of information systems that describes how people learn to accept and utilize technology. According to the concept, two criteria influence whether a computer system is adopted by its prospective users: (1) perceived utility and (2) perceived ease of use.

Technology Adoption: The process of absorbing, integrating, and using new technology in society is referred to as technology adoption. The process is divided into many phases, which are commonly classified by the categories of individuals who utilize the technology.

Chapter 26

The Managerial Ethical and Operational Challenges of Hospital Cybersecurity

Darrell Norman Burrell
https://orcid.org/0000-0002-4675-9544
Marymount University, USA

Kim L. Brown-Jackson
https://orcid.org/0000-0001-9231-2076
Capitol Technology University, USA

Sharon L. Burton
https://orcid.org/0000-0003-1653-9783
Capitol Technology University, USA

Kevin Richardson
https://orcid.org/0009-0002-3212-8669
Capitol Technology University, USA

Calvin Nobles
https://orcid.org/0000-0003-4002-1108
Illinois Institute of Technology, USA

Jorja Wright
https://orcid.org/0000-0002-7028-995X
Capitol Technology University, USA

Delores Springs
https://orcid.org/0000-0003-0940-1225
Regent University, USA

S. Raschid Muller
https://orcid.org/0000-0002-1742-7575
Arizona State University, USA

Allison Huff
https://orcid.org/0000-0001-6102-8013
College of Medicine, University of Arizona, USA

Angel J. Jones
https://orcid.org/0009-0007-9740-6611
University of Virginia, USA

ABSTRACT

The COVID-19 pandemic has presented healthcare institutions with unprecedented challenges in maintaining robust cybersecurity practices to safeguard patient data and protect critical healthcare operations. This chapter explores the ethical, organizational cultural, and leadership complexities hospitals face in cybersecurity during and after the pandemic. Ethical considerations encompass patient privacy, informed consent, and the responsible use of emerging technologies. Organizational cultural challenges involve balancing patient care priorities with cybersecurity efforts, fostering a cybersecurity-aware culture, and mitigating insider threats. Drawing insights from real-world experiences and expert opinions, this chapter sheds light on the multifaceted nature of hospital cybersecurity challenges amidst a global crisis. This chapter explores the nature of these challenges through a management consultant hospital intervention in a hospital that has experienced a significant cybersecurity breach.

DOI: 10.4018/979-8-3693-1634-4.ch026

INTRODUCTION

The COVID-19 pandemic has intensified hospital cybersecurity's complexities, imposing unprecedented challenges on safeguarding patient data and ensuring uninterrupted healthcare operations (Wang & Alexander, 2021; Pranggono & Arabo, 2021). From rapidly shifting priorities and resource reallocation to the escalated threat landscape and expanding attack surfaces, hospitals confront a myriad of cybersecurity challenges (Wang & Alexander, 2021; Pranggono & Arabo, 2021). Moreover, this paper elucidates the imperative for continuous adaptation and collaborative measures to fortify cybersecurity resilience in the face of evolving threats (Wang & Alexander, 2021; Pranggono & Arabo, 2021).

Rapidly Shifting Priorities and Resource Reallocation

The exigencies of the pandemic have compelled hospitals to pivot their focus toward patient care and pandemic management, leading to potential resource reallocation from cybersecurity initiatives (Wang & Alexander, 2021; Pranggono & Arabo, 2021). Balancing immediate priorities while preserving cybersecurity readiness poses a delicate challenge to healthcare institutions.

Escalated Threat Landscape

The pandemic has spurred cybercriminal activities targeting hospitals (Wang & Alexander, 2021; Pranggono & Arabo, 2021). Phishing and social engineering attacks exploiting pandemic-related fears and misinformation have risen significantly. Furthermore, remote work vulnerabilities and telehealth platforms have become attractive targets for cyber adversaries seeking to infiltrate hospital systems.

Expanding Attack Surfaces

The proliferation of connected medical devices and the Internet of Things (IoT) in healthcare has expanded the attack surfaces. With the accelerated adoption of telemedicine services during the pandemic, hospitals face challenges in securing these novel digital channels and managing the associated risks (Wang & Alexander, 2021; Pranggono & Arabo, 2021).

Insider Threats and Human Error

Overwhelmed staff and the rapid shift to remote work have increased the likelihood of human error, inadvertently exposing sensitive data. Additionally, discontented employees may pose insider threats, making detecting and mitigating such risks imperative (Wang & Alexander, 2021; Pranggono & Arabo, 2021).

Post-COVID-19 Challenges

The anticipated post-COVID-19 era presents a unique set of challenges that warrant continued vigilance. Hospitals must address evolving threat landscapes and the potential persistence of ransomware attacks and nation-state cyber espionage targeting healthcare research and data (Wang & Alexander, 2021; Pranggono & Arabo, 2021).

Data Privacy and Compliance

Healthcare institutions must navigate heightened scrutiny regarding patient data privacy (Wang & Alexander, 2021; Pranggono & Arabo, 2021). Adherence to complex regulatory requirements, such as the Health Insurance Portability and Accountability Act (HIPAA) and General Data Protection Regulation (GDPR), poses a formidable challenge.

Resource Allocation and Budget Constraints

Economic ramifications from the pandemic may curtail cybersecurity budgets, necessitating reasonable allocation of resources amidst other pressing needs. Recruitment and retention of skilled cybersecurity professionals amid resource constraints remain a significant concern (Wang & Alexander, 2021; Pranggono & Arabo, 2021).

Strategies for Enhanced Resilience

Amid the complexities, hospitals can adopt proactive strategies to bolster cybersecurity resilience (Wang & Alexander, 2021; Pranggono & Arabo, 2021). This includes intensified cybersecurity awareness and training for staff, robust cybersecurity frameworks, collaboration, and information sharing among healthcare peers, and advocating for government support and incentives. With technological advancement, cybersecurity has become significant, and companies need to invest in this component (Wang & Alexander, 2021; Pranggono & Arabo, 2021). Developing cybersecurity is crucial as it protects the company from costly lawsuits while building customer trust since it assures protection against privacy infringement and data breaches. It is the importance of cybersecurity culture that this discussion seeks to work on the case of developing a risk management plan or risk management strategy to tackle a cybersecurity breach that was experienced in a company following the poorly designed cybersecurity culture (Wang & Alexander, 2021; Pranggono, & Arabo, 2021). In developing the risk management plan, the focus will be on identifying the ethical issues related to cybersecurity breaches, and the model utilized will be ethical decision-making. The risk management plan will be effectively established through several models, including the strategy, organizational culture, change management, and ethical or leadership decision-making models.

The increasing reliance on technology and the internet have led to a surge in cybersecurity risks, and organizations are often the primary targets of cyber-attacks (Wang & Alexander, 2021; Pranggono & Arabo, 2021). Cybersecurity breaches can compromise sensitive data, lead to financial losses, damage an organization's reputation, and even cause legal issues (Wang & Alexander, 2021; Pranggono & Arabo, 2021). Unfortunately, many organizations still lack the proper cybersecurity measures and culture to mitigate these risks effectively (Wang & Alexander, 2021; Pranggono & Arabo, 2021). This is the case for the organization in question, which recently experienced a cybersecurity breach that resulted in the loss of confidential customer information and, consequently, the loss of trust from its customers. The organization does not have a risk management plan or strategy in place to prevent similar incidents from occurring in the future.

Problem Statement

The organization faces multiple challenges as a result of the recent cybersecurity breach.

Lack of a risk management plan and strategy: The absence of a comprehensive risk management plan and strategy leaves the organization vulnerable to potential threats and unable to address cybersecurity issues proactively. This lack of preparedness significantly increases the likelihood of future breaches and hampers the organization's ability to respond effectively to incidents.

Poor cybersecurity culture: The organization's weak cybersecurity culture has led to inadequate security practices, insufficient employee training, and a lack of awareness regarding the importance of cybersecurity. This ineffective culture has contributed to the recent breach and threatens the organization's security and data protection.

Ethical issues arising from the breach: The cybersecurity breach has raised several ethical concerns, including the organization's responsibility to protect sensitive data, the potential violation of privacy rights, and the need to ensure transparency in addressing the breach. These ethical issues demand immediate attention and require the organization to adopt ethical decision-making models to guide its actions and rectify the situation.

Literature Review

A cybersecurity breach impacts the organization in several ways, one being the financial cost aspect (Quader & Janeja, 2021). The financial loss occurs in many forms, including the expense incurred on rebuilding the systems, lawsuits from affected customers, reduced revenue, and in other cases, ransom payment to hackers. The financial loss displays the company's failure to follow the duty-based ethical principle of avoiding doing harm. Ellis (2020) highlights that the duty-based theory works with the principle of people acting to prevent harm to individuals cared for. Duty-based theory refers to the ethics that guide people's behavior, and it highlights the need to act accordingly regardless of the good or bad consequences that may be produced.

With the increasing reliance on digital technologies and electronic health records, the healthcare sector has become an attractive target for cybercriminals seeking to exploit vulnerabilities and gain unauthorized access to sensitive patient information (Wang & Alexander, 2021; Pranggono & Arabo, 2021). A robust cybersecurity culture is essential to protect patients, preserve trust in the healthcare system, and prevent potentially catastrophic consequences from data breaches (Wang & Alexander, 2021; Pranggono & Arabo, 2021). Duty-Based Ethics provides a compelling framework to understand employees' responsibilities and obligations in upholding cybersecurity principles within hospital settings.

In today's rapidly evolving digital landscape, the healthcare industry faces unprecedented challenges in safeguarding sensitive patient data and maintaining the confidentiality, integrity, and availability of critical information systems (Wang & Alexander, 2021; Pranggono & Arabo, 2021). Hospitals must develop a robust cybersecurity culture encompassing all employees to address these challenges. By emphasizing the ethical duties of employees, this approach seeks to foster a collective commitment to cybersecurity best practices and risk mitigation, ultimately bolstering the overall cybersecurity posture of healthcare institutions (Wang & Alexander, 2021; Pranggono & Arabo, 2021).

Duty-Based Ethics Overview

Duty-Based Ethics, often associated with deontological moral theories, focuses on individuals' inherent moral duties and obligations, irrespective of the outcomes of their actions (Ellis, 2020). In cybersecurity, this ethical framework guides employees to act per their duty to protect patient data and information systems, regardless of external factors or potential consequences.

The Duty of Care

At the core of Duty-Based Ethics lies the principle of duty of care (Ellis, 2020). All hospital employees, irrespective of their roles or job functions, are morally obligated to exercise reasonable care in handling patient data and safeguarding hospital systems. This duty of care extends to data confidentiality, integrity, and availability, necessitating the adoption of security best practices and compliance with established protocols (Ellis, 2020).

The Duty to Report and Respond

Another vital aspect of Duty-Based Ethics in cybersecurity is reporting and responding promptly to potential threats or security incidents. Employees must be encouraged and empowered to report suspicious activities, data breaches, or security vulnerabilities without fear of retribution. Additionally, having an incident response plan ensures timely and effective measures to mitigate the impact of cybersecurity incidents.

The Duty to Educate

Creating a solid cybersecurity culture requires a commitment to continuous education and awareness. Employees must be informed about cybersecurity threats, attack vectors, and preventive measures. The duty to educate extends to reinforcing the importance of cybersecurity hygiene and compliance with established policies and guidelines.

The Duty of Accountability

Duty-Based Ethics emphasizes personal accountability for one's actions. Employees must recognize their responsibility to maintain a secure digital environment and protect patient data. This may involve regular cybersecurity training, signing confidentiality agreements, and adhering to professional codes of conduct.

The Duty to Collaborate

A robust cybersecurity culture thrives on collaboration among departments and employees (Ellis, 2020). Duty-Based Ethics encourages employees to work together, share information, and engage in cross-functional cooperation to enhance the overall security posture of the hospital.

McKinsey's Strategic Horizons Framework

The increasing frequency and sophistication of cyberattacks have underscored the pressing need for hospitals to cultivate a robust cybersecurity culture. McKinsey's Strategic Horizons framework offers a multi-dimensional strategy that empowers hospitals to develop a sustainable and proactive approach to cybersecurity, ensuring a resilient defense against potential breaches and mitigating the impact of past incidents.

Strategic Horizon One: Core Cybersecurity Practices Strengthening

Core Horizon (Horizon 1): Focuses on improving and sustaining the current business operations, including existing cybersecurity practices and policies (Baghai et al., 1999; Markopoulos et al., 2020). Strategic Horizon 1 entails enhancing core cybersecurity practices to address known vulnerabilities and weaknesses. Hospitals must undertake a comprehensive cybersecurity risk assessment to identify gaps in existing security measures. A cybersecurity audit should evaluate current policies, incident response plans, and security awareness training. Based on the findings, hospitals can prioritize areas for improvement and allocate necessary resources to bolster the foundation of their cybersecurity defense.

Strategic Horizon Two: Transformative Cybersecurity Initiatives

Adjacent Horizon (Horizon 2): Involves exploring and expanding into new, related areas of cybersecurity, such as adopting new technologies or partnering with external experts (Baghai et al., 1999; Markopoulos et al., 2020). Strategic Horizon 2 involves initiating transformative cybersecurity initiatives to tackle evolving cyber threats proactively. Hospitals should invest in state-of-the-art cybersecurity technologies, such as advanced threat detection systems, intrusion prevention, and encryption tools. Additionally, fostering a cybersecurity-centric organizational culture requires leadership commitment and workforce engagement. Implementing gamified cybersecurity training programs, rewards for vigilant reporting, and career development opportunities for cybersecurity professionals can inspire employees to embrace cybersecurity best practices actively.

Strategic Horizon Three: Disruptive Cybersecurity Innovation

Transformational Horizon (Horizon 3): Concentrates on creating breakthroughs and disruptive innovations in cybersecurity, which may involve significant changes to the business model or the development of new capabilities (Baghai et al., 1999; Markopoulos et al., 2020). Strategic Horizon 3 embraces disruptive innovation to stay ahead of the ever-changing threat landscape. Hospitals should explore emerging technologies like artificial intelligence and machine learning to predict and prevent cyberattacks. Collaborating with industry partners, academic institutions, and cybersecurity experts allows hospitals to access cutting-edge research and foster an environment of continuous learning and innovation.

Application to the Organization

The organization can assess its current, adjacent, and transformative cybersecurity and risk management opportunities by applying McKinsey's Strategic Horizons. This approach will enable the organization to identify and prioritize strategic initiatives that strengthen its cybersecurity posture and address potential threats.

Impact on Operations

By applying McKinsey's Strategic Horizons, the organization can identify new markets, technologies, and opportunities for innovation in cybersecurity and risk management (Govindarajan & Trimble, 2012). This approach will drive the organization to continuously improve its operations, adopt cutting-edge solutions, and stay ahead of emerging threats (Baghai et al., 1999; Markopoulos et al., 2020).

Organizational Culture Change

Implementing McKinsey's Strategic Horizons fosters a culture of innovation and risk-taking within the organization (Gupta et al., 2006). By encouraging employees to explore new ideas and challenge the status quo, the organization can create an environment that supports continuous learning, adaptation, and resilience in the face of evolving cybersecurity challenges. By aligning the organization's culture with its cybersecurity and risk management objectives, the organization can create an environment that supports and reinforces secure behaviors and practices (Alavi et al., 2018). This alignment will foster a culture of shared responsibility, vigilance, and continuous improvement, critical for maintaining a strong cybersecurity posture in an ever-evolving threat landscape.

John Kotter's Change Management Theory

In the ever-evolving healthcare landscape, hospitals face escalating challenges concerning data and cybersecurity. Adopting a proactive and resilient cybersecurity culture is imperative to protect patient information and maintain public trust. Hospitals are increasingly targeted by cyber threats, necessitating a shift in culture to prioritize data and cybersecurity. Kotter's Change Management Theory provides a structured approach to galvanizing organizations toward change. By instilling a shared perception of imminent threats and the need for action, this approach empowers hospitals to mobilize stakeholders and prioritize cybersecurity as a strategic imperative (Kotter, 2012). Kotter's Change Management Theory provides critical principles for creating a sense of urgency and explores its relevance in improving data and cybersecurity practices in hospital settings.

Establishing a Burning Platform

Creating a sense of urgency begins by identifying the pressing need for change (Kotter, 2012). Hospital leaders must communicate the severity of cybersecurity risks, illustrating the potential consequences of breaches on patient safety, regulatory compliance, and institutional reputation. Citing recent cyber incidents within the healthcare industry can help stakeholders grasp the immediate threat and recognize the necessity for transformation.

Engaging Key Stakeholders

Mobilizing support from critical stakeholders, including hospital leadership, department heads, and front-line staff, is pivotal in driving change (Kotter, 2012). Communicating the urgency of the cybersecurity issue should be a collaborative effort, fostering a shared understanding and commitment to the cause. Encouraging open dialogues and active participation from all levels of the organization can increase buy-in and ownership of the change process.

Creating a Sense of Crisis

Effectively conveying the gravity of the cybersecurity situation involves framing it as an ongoing crisis that requires immediate attention. Hospital leaders should regularly communicate data breaches, near misses, and potential vulnerabilities to underscore the urgency. Emphasizing the potential impact on patient care and organizational viability can evoke a strong emotional response, motivating individuals to take action.

Leveraging External Factors

Kotter's theory highlights the use of external data and trends to reinforce the urgency for change (Kotter, 2012). Hospitals can utilize benchmarking data, and industry reports showcasing cybersecurity weaknesses and the implications of inaction. Engaging with cybersecurity experts, governmental agencies, and industry associations can provide valuable insights and support in conveying the urgency to all stakeholders.

Demonstrating Short-term Wins

Creating early successes is crucial to sustaining momentum. Implementing quick and tangible improvements in data and cybersecurity, such as enhancing password policies, conducting vulnerability assessments, or implementing multi-factor authentication, can demonstrate the effectiveness of change efforts. Celebrating these small victories helps reinforce the sense of urgency and encourages continued engagement (Kotter, 2012). Impact on operations: Embracing Kotter's Change Management Theory can enhance the organization's adaptability, resilience, and overall performance, as employees become more adept at navigating change and responding to evolving cybersecurity threats (Appelbaum et al., 2012).

Kotter's Change Management Theory offers a systematic approach to instilling a sense of urgency within hospital organizations seeking to enhance data and cybersecurity practices. Hospitals can successfully drive cultural change by establishing a burning platform, engaging key stakeholders, creating a sense of crisis, leveraging external factors, demonstrating short-term wins, and emphasizing the immediacy of cybersecurity threats and the need for collective action positions hospitals to embrace a proactive and resilient cybersecurity culture, safeguarding sensitive patient data and maintaining trust in the healthcare system. By engaging employees in the change process and fostering a security-aware culture, Kotter's Change Management Theory can help the organization create an environment where employees take ownership of their cybersecurity responsibilities and actively participate in risk management efforts (Herold, 2014). This culture change will contribute to a more secure organization, better prepared to prevent and respond to cybersecurity breaches.

Ethical Decision Making Model: Rights Approach

A cybersecurity breach in a hospital poses significant ethical challenges, particularly when patient medical records and personal information are compromised. Hospitals can navigate the aftermath of a cybersecurity incident with an ethical and patient-centric approach by prioritizing the rights of affected individuals, respecting their privacy, and ensuring transparency in communication. Cybersecurity breaches in hospitals endanger patient data and raise profound ethical dilemmas. The Rights Approach, grounded in respecting individuals' rights and autonomy, provides a moral framework for addressing the aftermath of such breaches.

Prioritizing Patient Rights

The Rights Approach emphasizes the inherent rights of individuals, and in the context of a cybersecurity breach, hospitals must prioritize the rights of affected patients. This includes the right to privacy, confidentiality, and protection of personal information. Hospital administrators should ensure that patient welfare is at the forefront of decision-making processes and take all necessary steps to mitigate further harm (Beauchamp & Childress, 2001; Pellegrino, 1995; Miner & Petocz, 2003; Olsen, 2003)

Transparency in Communication

Maintaining open and transparent communication is crucial after a cybersecurity breach. Hospitals must promptly notify affected patients and relevant authorities about the breach, the extent of the compromised data, and the measures being taken to address the situation. Transparency fosters trust and allows patients to make informed decisions regarding their data and privacy (Beauchamp & Childress, 2001; Pellegrino, 1995; Miner & Petocz, 2003; Olsen, 2003)

Respecting Patient Autonomy

The Rights Approach underscores the importance of individual autonomy (Beauchamp & Childress, 2001; Pellegrino, 1995; Miner & Petocz, 2003; Olsen, 2003). In the context of a cybersecurity breach, hospitals should empower affected patients to exercise control over their data. Providing options for patients to review, correct, or delete their compromised information reflects respect for their autonomy and empowers them to take an active role in recovery.

Strengthening Cybersecurity Measures

An ethical response to a cybersecurity breach requires hospitals to reevaluate and strengthen their cybersecurity measures. The Rights Approach encourages hospitals to take preventive actions, such as conducting thorough security assessments, implementing encryption, and adopting multi-factor authentication, to safeguard patient data and uphold their rights.

Ensuring Accountability

The Rights Approach calls for holding responsible parties accountable for the breach. Hospitals should conduct thorough investigations to identify the incident's root cause and take appropriate actions against internal or external actors responsible for the breach. Accountability fosters a culture of responsibility and serves as a deterrent against future breaches.

Supporting Affected Individuals

In the aftermath of a cybersecurity breach, hospitals must prioritize supporting affected patients emotionally and practically. This involves providing resources for identity theft protection, counseling services for emotional distress, and clear avenues for patients to seek assistance dealing with potential consequences arising from the breach.

Application to the Organization

By applying the Rights Approach to ethical decision-making, the organization can ensure that the rights of individuals, including employees and stakeholders, are respected and protected during the decision-making process (Beauchamp & Childress, 2001). This approach will help the organization make ethical choices, particularly in cybersecurity and risk management, where individual rights such as privacy and autonomy are often at stake. The Rights Approach provides a guiding ethical framework for hospitals to respond to cybersecurity breaches where patient data and personal information are compromised. Hospitals can ethically navigate the aftermath of a breach by prioritizing patient rights, practicing transparency, respecting patient autonomy, strengthening cybersecurity measures, ensuring accountability, offering support to affected individuals, and upholding their commitment to patient care, trust, and confidentiality.

Impact on Operations

Adopting the Rights Approach can improve trust, transparency, and stakeholder satisfaction within the organization (Cavico & Mujtaba, 2010). By demonstrating a commitment to ethical decision-making and protecting individual rights, the organization can enhance its reputation and relationships with stakeholders, including customers, employees, and regulators.

Organizational Culture Change

By incorporating the Rights Approach into its decision-making processes, the organization can foster an ethical culture that values and respects the rights of all individuals (Paine, 1994). This culture change can improve employee morale, greater stakeholder trust, and a more ethical approach to managing cybersecurity risks and breaches.

Plan-Do-Check-Act (PDCA) Model

Cybersecurity attacks in hospitals, resulting in the theft of patient medical records and personal information, present critical challenges to patient privacy and organizational integrity. The rising frequency and sophistication of cybersecurity attacks demand a proactive and adaptable response from hospitals. The PDCA model, originating from quality management practices, provides a structured methodology to address vulnerabilities and strengthen cybersecurity defenses.

Plan

Identifying Vulnerabilities and Setting Objectives The first phase of the PDCA model involves planning and analysis (Taylor et al., 2014). Hospitals must conduct a comprehensive risk assessment to identify cybersecurity vulnerabilities and threats. By setting clear objectives and establishing cybersecurity policies and protocols, hospitals can create a framework to address potential breaches effectively.

Do

Implementing Cybersecurity Measures The "Do" phase entails implementing the planned cybersecurity measures. Hospitals should deploy security technologies, such as firewalls, intrusion detection systems, and encryption tools, to protect patient data. Training staff in cybersecurity best practices and fostering a security-conscious culture are essential components of this phase.

Check

The "Check" phase involves monitoring and evaluating the effectiveness of implemented cybersecurity measures (Taylor et al., 2014). Hospitals should regularly conduct security audits, penetration testing, and incident response drills to identify vulnerabilities and assess the preparedness of their cybersecurity defenses.

Act

Continuous Improvement and Incident Response In the "Act" phase, hospitals analyze the results from the "Check" phase and take appropriate actions to enhance cybersecurity resilience. Lessons learned from cybersecurity incidents should be incorporated into incident response plans, and necessary adjustments should be made to improve the overall cybersecurity posture of the hospital.

The Iterative Nature of the PDCA Model

The PDCA model is inherently iterative, emphasizing continuous improvement (Taylor et al., 2014). Hospitals should repeat the cycle regularly, incorporating feedback from incidents and emerging cyber threats. This iterative approach allows hospitals to adapt their cybersecurity strategies in response to evolving attack methods and vulnerabilities.

Collaboration and Information Sharing

Collaboration and information sharing are crucial in implementing the PDCA model for cybersecurity. Hospitals should partner with industry peers, cybersecurity organizations, and government agencies to exchange threat intelligence and best practices. By learning from others' experiences, hospitals can fortify their defenses against cyber threats.

The PDCA model provides a comprehensive and systematic framework for hospitals to address cybersecurity attacks and safeguard patient data. By planning, implementing, evaluating, and continuously improving cybersecurity measures, hospitals can establish a proactive and adaptive approach to mitigate the impact of cyber incidents. Embracing the iterative nature of the PDCA model, hospitals can strengthen their cybersecurity resilience and ensure the confidentiality, integrity, and availability of patient medical records and personal information.

INTERVENTION RECOMMENDATIONS

Comprehensive cybersecurity policy: Develop and implement a robust cybersecurity policy that outlines the organization's approach to securing its digital assets, including guidelines for access control, incident response, and disaster recovery. This policy should be reviewed and updated regularly to ensure that it remains effective in the face of evolving threats (Herold, 2014)

Employee conduct policy: Establish clear rules for employee behavior related to the handling of sensitive information, such as the use of strong passwords, encryption, and secure file-sharing practices. The policy should also address the consequences of non-compliance to ensure accountability.

Third-party vendor policy: Implement a policy that governs the organization's relationships with third-party vendors and partners, ensuring that they adhere to the same cybersecurity standards as the organization itself. This may include conducting regular security assessments and audits of vendors to verify compliance.

Training Programs

Cybersecurity awareness training: Implement regular training sessions to educate employees on the latest cybersecurity threats, best practices, and the organization's policies and procedures. This should include training on identifying and responding to phishing attacks, social engineering tactics, and other common threats(Albrechtsen & Hovdenkaar, 2009).

Role-specific training: Provide specialized training for employees with specific cybersecurity responsibilities, such as IT personnel, managers, and executives. This may include training on risk assessment, incident response, and compliance with relevant laws and regulations.

Continuous learning: Encourage employees to engage in ongoing professional development related to cybersecurity, such as attending conferences, webinars, or pursuing certifications. This can help keep the workforce up-to-date on the latest trends and best practices in the industry.

Intervention Strategies

Assess the current cybersecurity culture: Utilize Schein's model (Schein, 1985) to understand the existing organizational culture and its impact on cybersecurity. Analyze the artifacts, espoused beliefs and values, and basic underlying assumptions related to cybersecurity to identify areas where cultural improvements can be made.

Identify opportunities for improvement and potential risks: Apply McKinsey's Strategic Horizons (Baghai et al., 1999) to uncover areas where the organization can strengthen cybersecurity and risk management practices. Evaluate the core, adjacent, and transformational horizons for opportunities to enhance security measures, adopt new technologies, and improve risk management processes.

Develop a comprehensive risk management strategy: Formulate a plan that includes ethical considerations based on the Rights Approach (Beauchamp & Childress, 2001). Ensure that the strategy respects employees' and stakeholders' autonomy, privacy, and dignity while balancing the organization's need for effective security measures.

Creating urgency: Raise awareness of the importance of cybersecurity and the need for immediate action by sharing the potential consequences of a breach and the benefits of a proactive security posture.

Consolidating improvements: Continue to refine and implement changes to enhance cybersecurity further, addressing any obstacles or challenges that arise along the way.

Institutionalizing new approaches: Embed new cybersecurity practices and values into the organizational culture to ensure long-term success. Regularly review and update policies, procedures, and training programs to maintain security.

Clear and transparent commitment and communication from leadership: Encourage leaders to consistently communicate the importance of cybersecurity, share updates on initiatives, and provide feedback on employee performance (Bass & Riggio, 2006). This open communication helps build trust, aligns employees with the organization's goals, and reinforces the security-focused culture.

Continuous monitoring, assessment, and improvement of cybersecurity practices: Regularly evaluate the organization's security posture and techniques to identify vulnerabilities and areas for improvement (Ponemon Institute, 2020). Implement corrective actions as needed and continuously refine processes to defend against cyber threats.

Integration of ethical considerations into decision-making processes: Ensure that organizational decisions related to cybersecurity consider the rights and interests of employees, customers, and other stakeholders (Paine, 1994). By incorporating ethical considerations, the organization can build trust, foster transparency, and demonstrate its commitment to responsible business practices.

In conclusion, addressing the cybersecurity breach and its consequences within our organization is paramount. This paper has highlighted the critical issues stemming from the breach, including the lack of a risk management plan and strategy, poor cybersecurity culture, and ethical concerns. By drawing upon relevant strategy, organizational culture, change management, ethical decision-making, and leadership models, a comprehensive plan has been proposed to improve our organization's cybersecurity posture and risk management practices.

The plan focuses on assessing the current cybersecurity culture, identifying areas for improvement, developing a comprehensive risk management strategy, engaging senior leadership, and implementing a structured change management approach. By following these steps, our organization will be better equipped to prevent future breaches and create a secure environment where employees are engaged, motivated, and satisfied.

Ultimately, the successful execution of this plan will help our organization recover from the recent breach, foster a strong cybersecurity culture, and promote ethical decision-making across all levels. This proactive cybersecurity and risk management approach will ensure our organization's long-term success and resilience in an increasingly digital and interconnected world.

REFERENCES

Alavi, M., Leidner, D. E., & Kayworth, T. R. (2018). An empirical examination of the influence of organizational culture on knowledge management practices. *Journal of Management Information Systems, 22*(3), 191–224. doi:10.2753/MIS0742-1222220307

Albrechtsen, E., & Hovden, J. (2009). The information security digital divide between information security managers and users. *Computers & Security, 28*(6), 476–490. doi:10.1016/j.cose.2009.01.003

Appelbaum, S. H., Habashy, S., Malo, J. L., & Shafiq, H. (2012). Back to the future: Revisiting Kotter's 1996 change model. *Journal of Management Development, 31*(8), 764–782. doi:10.1108/02621711211253231

Baghai, M., Coley, S., & White, D. (1999). *The Alchemy of Growth: Practical Insights for Building the Enduring Enterprise*. Perseus Publishing.

Bass, B. M. (1985). *Leadership and performance beyond expectations*. Free Press.

Bass, B. M., & Riggio, R. E. (2006). *Transformational leadership* (2nd ed.). Psychology Press. doi:10.4324/9781410617095

Beauchamp, T. L., & Childress, J. F. (2001). *Principles of Biomedical Ethics* (5th ed.). Oxford University Press.

Cameron, K. S., & Quinn, R. E. (2006). *Diagnosing and changing organizational culture: Based on the competing values framework*. John Wiley & Sons.

Cavico, F. J., & Mujtaba, B. G. (2010). The state of business schools, corporate governance, and moral reasoning: An empirical study of business students. *Journal of Academic and Business Ethics, 3*, 1–22.

D'Arcy, J., Hovav, A., & Galletta, D. (2014). User awareness of security countermeasures and its impact on information systems misuse: A deterrence approach. *Information Systems Research, 20*(1), 79–98. doi:10.1287/isre.1070.0160

Ellis, P. (2020). Ethical concepts: Duty-based theories. *Journal of Kidney Care, 5*(1), 30–32. doi:10.12968/jokc.2020.5.1.30

Govindarajan, V., & Trimble, C. (2012). *Reverse innovation: Create far from home, win everywhere*. Harvard Business Review Press. doi:10.5437/08956308X5506003

Gupta, A. K., Smith, K. G., & Shalley, C. E. (2006). The interplay between exploration and exploitation. *Academy of Management Journal, 49*(4), 693–706. doi:10.5465/amj.2006.22083026

Herold, R. (2014). *Managing an Information Security and Privacy Awareness and Training Program*. CRC Press.

Judge, T. A., & Piccolo, R. F. (2004). Transformational and transactional leadership: A meta-analytic test of their relative validity. *The Journal of Applied Psychology, 89*(5), 755–768. doi:10.1037/0021-9010.89.5.755 PMID:15506858

Kotter, J. P. (2012). *Leading change*. Harvard Business School Press.

Markopoulos, E., Aggarwal, V., & Vanharanta, H. (2020). Democratization of intrapreneurship and corporate entrepreneurship within McKinsey's three horizons innovation space. In *Human Systems Engineering and Design II: Proceedings of the 2nd International Conference on Human Systems Engineering and Design (IHSED2019): Future Trends and Applications*, (pp. 1007–1017). Springer International Publishing. 10.1007/978-3-030-27928-8_150

Miner, M., & Petocz, A. (2003). Moral theory in ethical decision making: Problems, clarifications and recommendations from a psychological perspective. *Journal of Business Ethics*, *42*(1), 11–25. doi:10.1023/A:1021654015232

Moorthy, M. K., Seetharaman, A., Mohamed, Z. A., Gopalan, M., & San, L. H. (2015). The impact of information security events on the stock value of Malaysian firms: An event study approach. *Computers & Security*, *48*, 10–18.

Ng, B. Y., Kankanhalli, A., & Xu, Y. C. (2009). Studying users' computer security behavior: A health belief perspective. *Decision Support Systems*, *46*(4), 815–825. doi:10.1016/j.dss.2008.11.010

Olsen, D. P. (2003). Influence and coercion: Relational and rights-based ethical approaches to forced psychiatric treatment. *Journal of Psychiatric and Mental Health Nursing*, *10*(6), 705–712. doi:10.1046/j.1365-2850.2003.00659.x PMID:15005484

Paine, L. S. (1994). Managing for organizational integrity. *Harvard Business Review*, *72*(2), 106–117.

Pellegrino, E. D. (1995). Toward a virtue-based normative ethics for the health professions. *Kennedy Institute of Ethics Journal*, *5*(3), 253–277. doi:10.1353/ken.0.0044 PMID:10144959

Ponemon Institute. (2020). *Cost of a Data Breach Report*. Ponemon Institute. https://www.ibm.com/security/data-breach

Pranggono, B., & Arabo, A. (2021). COVID-19 pandemic cybersecurity issues. *Internet Technology Letters*, *4*(2), e247. doi:10.1002/itl2.247

Quader, F., & Janeja, V. P. (2021). Insights into organizational security readiness: Lessons learned from Cyber-attack case studies. *Journal of Cybersecurity and Privacy*, *1*(4), 638–659. doi:10.3390/jcp1040032

Romanosky, S. (2016). Examining the costs and causes of cyber incidents. *Journal of Cybersecurity*, *2*(2), 121–135. doi:10.1093/cybsec/tyw001

Schein, E. H. (1985). *Organizational Culture and Leadership* (1st ed.). Jossey-Bass.

Shaw, H., Duffy, K., & Taylor, N. (2009). Investigating the cyber security landscape in Ireland: An exploratory study. *Journal of Internet Services and Applications*, *6*(1), 1–17.

Taylor, M. J., McNicholas, C., Nicolay, C., Darzi, A., Bell, D., & Reed, J. E. (2014). Systematic review of the application of the plan-do-study-act method to improve quality in healthcare. *BMJ Quality & Safety*, *23*(4), 290–298. doi:10.1136/bmjqs-2013-001862 PMID:24025320

Wang, L., & Alexander, C. A. (2021). Cyber security during the COVID-19 pandemic. *AIMS Electronics and Electrical Engineering*, *5*(2), 146–157. doi:10.3934/electreng.2021008

Chapter 27
Cybercrime Risks and Solutions for Small and Medium-Sized Businesses (SMBs)

Calvin Nobles
https://orcid.org/0000-0003-4002-1108
Illinois Institute of Technology, USA

Kevin Richardson
https://orcid.org/0009-0002-3212-8669
Capitol Technology University, USA

Darrell Norman Burrell
https://orcid.org/0000-0002-4675-9544
Marymount University, USA

Angel J. Jones
https://orcid.org/0009-0007-9740-6611
University of Virginia, USA

Jennifer Ferreras-Perez
https://orcid.org/0009-0003-0972-1824
Marymount University, USA

ABSTRACT

The increasing prevalence of cybercrime poses significant challenges to small businesses, which often lack the resources and expertise to effectively manage their cybersecurity risk. This chapter investigates the potential of cybersecurity communities of practice (CoPs) as a viable solution to support small businesses in addressing these challenges and mitigating the risks associated with cybercrime. By participating in CoPs, small businesses can pool resources, share knowledge, and develop innovative strategies to tackle cybersecurity challenges. The collaborative nature of these communities enables small businesses to leverage collective knowledge and experiences, obtain unique insights from experts across diverse disciplines, and receive invaluable feedback from peers. In conclusion, the chapter argues that cybersecurity CoPs can play a vital role in enhancing the cybersecurity practices of small businesses, reducing cybercrime costs, and ultimately strengthening their overall cybersecurity risk management.

DOI: 10.4018/979-8-3693-1634-4.ch027

1. INTRODUCTION

The COVID-19 pandemic has dramatically shifted business operations to online platforms, with more transactions and businesses being conducted virtually than ever before. Increased cyber security risks and attacks for small businesses have accompanied this shift. As online purchases and business transactions increase, so does the risk of cyber security attacks (Kumar, 2020). According to Kratz (2020), the pandemic has made small businesses a prime target for cyber attacks due to their lack of resources and expertise in cyber security. Cybercriminals are taking advantage of the fact that many small business owners are unprepared for the increase in online activity, making them vulnerable to attacks such as phishing, malware, ransomware, and data breaches.

The rise in remote working has further exacerbated the increasing threat of cyber security attacks. Employees working remotely are more likely to be exposed to malicious software and cybersecurity threats (Kumar, 2020). In addition, the lack of physical security measures at remote workstations makes them vulnerable to attacks. Furthermore, using personal devices for work increases the risk of data breaches, as these devices are often less secure than the business's leading network.

Cybercrime has become a significant problem for small business owners today. Cybercrime is any crime committed using a computer or other digital device. As technology advances, so does the sophistication of cybercrime tactics, making it increasingly difficult for small business owners to protect themselves (Ncubukezi, Mwansa, & Rocaries, 2020). Organizations face increasing cybersecurity threats and risks, including small and medium-sized businesses. As cyber-attacks, data breaches, and ransomware attacks persist, organizations are feverishly working to harden networks, infrastructure, policies, and procedures; yet, small and medium-sized businesses (SMB) might not have the resources, expertise, or support to defend off cleverly planned cyber threats. Safeguarding consumers' sensitive data when conducting electronic commerce (e-commerce) transactions is an issue.

The U.S. Census Bureau reported that 45% of households refused to perform online operations due to data and privacy protection concerns (OECD, 2017). Cybercriminals are targeting (SMBs) because some entities lack cybersecurity resources and capabilities to prevent cyber incidents (Renaud & Weir, 2016). The Organization for Economic Cooperation and Development (OECD) (2017) reports that 94% of small businesses have internet capability, yet, most need to improve in leveraging the internet to its total capacity to include defending from malicious cyber activity. According to Renaud and Weir (2017), SMBs are subjected to data theft, disclosure, corruption, and data destruction, which often remain undisclosed to the public due to the trepidation of negative publicity and reputation damage.

In a 2015 survey regarding United Kingdom's SMBs, one in five entities failed to implement security measures, two out of five did not think cybersecurity attacks were imminent, and 11% of 3,000 SMB owners did not view small and medium-sized entities as potential cybersecurity targets (Renaud & Weir, 2016). The survey highlights SMB owners' need for more information security knowledge, which is too precarious in cybersecurity. Information and communications technology (ICT) enhances the quality of business (Bolek, Látečková, Romanová, & Korček, 2016); however, the integration of ICT by SMBs, such as the internet, mobile devices, websites, cloud computing, and social media enlarges the businesses' cyber attack surface. Increasing the cyber-attack surface requires SMBs to dedicate additional resources to protect against cyber threats in a resource-constraint situation. Cybersecurity CoPs are ideal platforms for disseminating information on industry-specific practices to SMBs.

Without a doubt, SMBs can capitalize on information sharing, open collaboration, and implementing best practices by using CoPs to overcome limited resources and expertise. Researchers define CoP as a collaborative group of stakeholders who share concerns and problems or are enthusiastic about a particular topic and aim to enhance knowledge and expertise in the specified area through continuous interaction (Gunawardena et al., 2009). According to Pattinson (2014), CoPs are teams of people adjoined by shared experiences and an affinity for a collaborative interest to build a joint enterprise. SMBs can form cybersecurity CoPs to exchange data on information security, best practices, cyber threat intelligence, and technologies via a collaborative capability such as a web-based collaboration platform to store and share information. By establishing CoPs, practitioners, researchers, technologists, information security professionals, and information technology leaders can address cybersecurity problems. SMBs vary in size, yet most leverage ICT for business transactions and processing sensitive data such as credit card information, customers' names, mailing addresses, email accounts, health information, and health insurance. Cybercriminals are targeting SMBs to exploit opportunities to exfiltrate sensitive data to sell on the black market. To offset the shortage of expertise, resources, and strategy, CoPs provide a platform to reinforce cybersecurity education and practices.

According to Forster-Holt (2013), small businesses employ 55 million workers, which accounts for 50 percent of the U.S. workforce; yet, defining what constitutes a small business needs to be explicitly defined. Eyal-Cohen (2012) asserts that small businesses energize the U.S. economy and establish the free enterprise spirit and competitive markets. A significant milestone for small businesses in the U.S. is the advancement from rural beginnings to thriving contributors, one of the world's most prosperous economies (Eyal-Cohen, 2012). According to Forster-Holt (2013), small businesses consist of one to 500 employees; however, Forster-Holt (2008) opined that defining SMB is challenging due to organizations developing quantitative and qualitative methodologies for what constitutes a business class. In the U.S., organizations with 250 or fewer employees equate to 99 percent of small companies (Forster-Holt, 2013). Terziovski (2010) asserts that SMBs are reactive, resource-limited, and need more strategies, suggesting that 63 percent of new SMBs fail within six years. Even though researchers have attempted to define SMB for regulatory and taxation purposes, the federal government uses a different criterion, further complicating efforts to reach an acceptable and standardized definition of a small business (Renner, 2001). For this paper, the definition of SMB is consequential because the salient objective pertains to leveraging cybersecurity CoPs to solidify information security strategies, best practices, and compliance through information sharing and collaboration.

2. PROBLEM STATEMENT

One of the most common types of cybercrime that small businesses face is phishing. Phishing attacks are "scams in which criminals send emails or texts pretending to be from a legitimate source to get the recipient to provide sensitive personal or business information" (Federal Trade Commission, 2020). According to the 2019 Verizon Data Breach Investigations Report, phishing accounted for 32% of all cyberattacks on small businesses, making it the most common attack vector (Verizon, 2019). In addition to phishing, small businesses also face a variety of other cyberattacks. These include malware (20%), malicious insiders (12%), and card skimming (9%) (Verizon, 2019). Malware is malicious code that can be used to access business systems. In contrast, malicious insiders are employees or contractors who use their access to corporate systems to commit cybercrimes (Verizon, 2019). Card skimming is an attack in which criminals use malicious software to steal credit card information from customers (Federal Trade Commission, 2020).

The consequences of cybercrime for small businesses can be severe. According to a study by the National Cyber Security Alliance (2018), 60% of small businesses that experience a cyberattack go out of business within six months. Furthermore, the costs associated with recovering from an attack can be significant, both in terms of lost revenue and the expense of hiring cybersecurity experts to help mitigate damage (National Cyber Security Alliance, 2018). This paper explores viable options for small businesses to address these cybercrime risks.

3. METHOD

The approach used was a narrative literature review. Narrative literature reviews are an effective way to analyze various sources and develop solutions to organizational problems. They provide an in-depth understanding of the literature and can offer practical solutions to real-world problems (Goodwin, 2004). The narrative literature review aims to comprehensively review the existing literature on a topic and identify patterns, trends, and gaps in the research (Dai & Wang, 2018). The narrative literature review is a qualitative approach that explores complex relationships between different variables and identifies unique solutions to organizational problems (Goodwin, 2004). Narrative literature reviews offer several advantages that make them practical approaches to finding solutions to organizational problems. First, narrative literature reviews can provide an in-depth understanding of a particular topic, allowing the researcher to explore the literature from various perspectives (Goodwin, 2004). Second, narrative literature reviews provide insights into the complexities of the research and can identify potential solutions to organizational problems (Dai & Wang, 2018). Finally, narrative literature reviews can provide a comprehensive overview of the existing literature and help identify gaps in the research (Goodwin, 2004).

4. INFORMATION SECURITY CONCERNS

Small businesses are particularly vulnerable to cybercrime due to their limited resources and often limited technical expertise (Walton, 2019). Small businesses generally have fewer resources to dedicate to cybersecurity, making them more vulnerable to cyberattacks. Additionally, small businesses may need more technical expertise to secure their systems properly. For example, many small businesses may need more resources or expertise to install or configure firewalls or other security measures to protect their systems from attack. Furthermore, many small businesses may be unaware of the risks posed by cybercrime and thus may not take the necessary steps to protect their systems (Lan et al., 2020).

In addition to limited resources and technical expertise, small businesses may be vulnerable to cybercrime due to their lack of awareness of cyber threats (Lan et al., 2020). Small businesses may be unaware of the risks posed by cybercrime and thus may not take the necessary steps to protect their systems. Furthermore, many small businesses may need more resources or expertise to implement security measures to protect their systems adequately. Additionally, many small businesses may need to be made aware of the various types of cyberattacks and the associated risks, making them more vulnerable to attack.

One particular area of risk is the use of third-party vendors, which can introduce various security issues if not appropriately managed. One of the most significant risks associated with third-party vendors is the potential for data breaches (Morency, 2014). Small businesses often rely on vendors to store and process sensitive customer information, such as credit card and Social Security numbers. If these vendors are not adequately secured, it can leave the small business open to a data breach which can be extremely costly in terms of both money and reputation (McKinsey & Company, 2017). Small businesses should ensure their vendors comply with the Payment Card Industry Data Security Standard (PCI DSS) and other relevant security standards to mitigate this risk. Additionally, they should ensure that any vendors they use have a comprehensive security policy and are regularly audited to ensure they follow best practices.

Another risk associated with third-party vendors is the potential for introducing malicious code or malware into a small business's network. If a vendor's system is compromised, cybercriminals can access the small business's network and potentially access sensitive data (McKinsey & Company, 2017). Small businesses should have a rigorous vendor risk assessment process to prevent this from happening.

Regardless of size, all organizations have a responsibility for governance, which pertains to protecting information security assets from malicious cyber activity (Bolek, Látečková, Romanová, & Korček, 2016). Cybercriminals primarily target large corporations because sizeable companies make lucrative targets; however, SMBs are progressively targeted by malicious actors because these businesses are ill-prepared for cyber-attacks and data breaches, thus, making SMBs more targetable vulnerable to malicious cyber-attacks. Nevertheless, SMBs experience a shortage of scalable and economical technological options (Osborn, 2015). Cyber threat vectors experienced by large corporations are often analogous to cyber threats observed by SMBs (Osborn, 2015); however, SMBs lack the resources and expertise to leverage comparable technological capabilities. The lack of scalable options results in large corporations resisting working with SMBs due to insufficient cybersecurity controls because they present significant cybersecurity risks. Large corporations are reluctant to leverage SMBs as third-party partners because most small companies lack cybersecurity infrastructure protection measures. It is general knowledge that most small businesses lack adequate information security expertise, which is problematic because SMBs can provide critical services to large entities.

Another imprudent miscalculation is that SMBs need to develop cybersecurity training programs. Cybersecurity education is necessary for all organizations, especially, for SMBs, given that cybersecurity education is a mandatory requirement for any information security strategy. In a survey, 66 percent of small business owners reported being responsible for leading the organization's cybersecurity efforts (NCSA, 2012); consequently, the owners need to be more task saturated to provide due diligence to cybersecurity operations. Another detrimental mistake made by SMBs is that anti-virus software and firewalls are adequate security controls (Sangani &Vijayakumar, 2012). A recent study highlighted that 83% of SMBs do not have a codified information security plan (NCSA, 2012), illustrating the lack of awareness regarding cybersecurity threats hampered by resource limitations resulting in significant risk-taking. Small and medium-sized firms are in dire need of cybersecurity awareness. Most SMBs lack the expertise to conduct training, especially those businesses with the owners as the sole employee, which is problematic. Large private and public organizations must maintain cybersecurity training programs directed by the Board of Directors for individual entities or comply with federally mandated regulations for federal agencies. Depending on the SMB, there is only a mandatory training requirement if the firm conducts business with a large entity that mandates cybersecurity training.

Researchers assert that malicious cyber activity, such as advanced persistent threats (APT), demands immediate attention (Brewer, 2014); however, SMBs' disinterest in cybersecurity education perpetuates negligence and potential targets for cybercriminals. Some SMBs are reluctant to believe that cybercriminals are targeting small firms. Governmental efforts such as the 2012 Small Business Study conducted by the National Cyber Security Alliance provide an in-depth analysis of cybersecurity and small businesses (NCSA, 2012). Recently, a U.S. Senate Cybersecurity Caucus member proposed the Small Business

Development Center (SBDC) Training Act, which will require 10 percent of the SBDC workforce to undergo training in cyber strategy counseling to aid SMBs (Watson, 2017). The effort will help SMBs identify the appropriate tools, cyber threats, skills, and practices to combat sophisticated attacks by enhancing security protocols to safeguard consumer data (Watson, 2017). Congressional leaders recognize the cybersecurity educational gap that SMBs are experiencing and are taking determined measures to increase cybersecurity training for SMBs.

Most reported cyber-attacks and data breaches in the media about large corporations. In 2016, 60 percent of cyber-incidents targeted small businesses with no defenses (Cook, 2017). A U.S. Congressman indicates that SMBs develop a false sense of security because most of the cyber incidents reported concern large corporations (Labossiere, 2016). The Congressman stressed the importance of hardening small business networks because most SMBs cannot recover from a cyber-attack (Labossiere, 2016). This is evident in SMBs not investing in cybersecurity defenses or developing an information security program, which could become challenging with the enforcement of the General Data Protection Regulation (GDPR) by the European Union. The GDPR applies to any organization conducting business transactions, processing, or collecting data on citizens of countries belonging to the European Union. The GDPR is relevant to illustrate that SMBs will be held to the same regulatory standards as large corporations to protect consumers' sensitive information starting in May 2018. Labossiere (2016) asserts that 83% of small firms still need a formal cybersecurity plan. Implementing information security practices protects benefit SMBs from data breaches and cyber-attacks and prevents malicious actors from accessing consumers' sensitive data. As the number of cyber-attacks continues to increase, SMBs face more significant cyber threats due to malicious actors seeking softer targets or inadequate infrastructure.

Cyber-attacks on SMBs could disrupt economic stability in the U.S. Small businesses account for 99 percent of all companies in the U.S. (Mayadunne & Park, 2016), where 79 percent of the owners are the sole employee (Kabir, 2019). Osborn (2014) reports that there are 4.9 million SMBs in the U.K., which accounts for 59 percent of the country's employment, highlighting the relevance of SMBs to the U.S. and U.K. national-level economies. In 2014, cyber incidents cost 400 billion dollars (Cook, 2017), and researchers forecast the cost of cyber incidents to escalate. Attacks on SMBs could disrupt national economies because of the number of employees hired by small and medium firms. Increasing cyber-attacks on SMBs is a national security concern and mandates support from the public sector, especially in cybersecurity education. Hypothetically, an advanced persistent threat that targets SMBs can inflict havoc and impede economic progress. Eighty percent of business owners must use adequate cybersecurity strategies and defenses to prevent cyber-attacks and data breaches (Cook, 2017). Governments, industry, and academia must quickly address this issue, knowing malicious cyber actors will continue targeting SMBs.

Another concerning issue in cybersecurity is the number of successful cyber-attacks and data breaches on third-party partners. Third-party partners such as lawyers, contractors, maintenance personnel, and accounting entities pose a significant threat to supported organizations (Germano, 2017). Companies outsource information security tasks to third-party vendors to leverage the expertise that might be outside the organization. Large corporations have an extensive network footprint with interminable access points, thus, making it challenging to mitigate known vulnerabilities and emerging threats (Germano, 2017). Similarly, SMBs have expanding networks that need to be improved. Third-party vendors need help to prevent data breaches due to systemic shortfalls in risk management, governance, and compliance (Buckley, Sanders, & Treliant, 2016). A 2016 study indicates that most institutions need more wherewithal to exercise leadership and oversight to determine the effectiveness of third-party partners in protecting critical and sensitive data (Buckley, Sanders, & Treliant, 2016). The uncertainty surrounding the cybersecurity practices of third-party vendors requires immediate attention, given that some SMBs rely on the same vendors to protect critical information.

Small and medium-sized companies need to work with organizations to develop scalable variants of technologies, processes, and support packages. For example, the Center for Internet Security (2017) provides a handbook outlining standard security controls and best practices for small companies that operate on a limited budget. Research indicates that institutions with the best information security processes continuously upgrade and modify business practices to combat evolving and emerging cybersecurity threats (CIS, 2017). Since 79 percent of U.S. small businesses do not have any employees (Kabir, 2019), these organizations could need help implementing and managing an effective information security program. It is a common practice for SMBs to contract their cybersecurity responsibilities to third-party entities. Even though SMBs leverage third-party vendors' expertise, a relevant concern is the increased cyber-attacks and data breaches aimed at third-party partners. Germano (2017) asserts that third-party partners need more advanced practices regarding legal, governance, risk, and technology implementation. There need to be more solutions to ensure third-party vendors adequately support SMBs.

A 2013 study conducted by a major consulting firm revealed that 69 percent of surveyed organizations could not account for all locations of stored data, and 74 percent of study participants failed to maintain adequate records of third-party partners with access to sensitive data (Buckley, Sanders, & Treliant, 2016). A subsequent study in 2015 highlights that large and small organizations need a codified and efficient process to evaluate and certify the information security practices of third-party partners (Buckley, Sanders, & Treliant, 2016). Based on the practices mentioned above, the efficacy of third-party partners to safeguard sensitive and critical information remains a challenge for businesses that outsource cybersecurity efforts. The security dilemma involving third-party partners represents a vital threat to U.S. economic progress. Advocacy and support from the U.S. government, industry, and academia are necessary to develop scalable technological solutions, information security practices, policies, and certification assessments to evaluate third-party partners. Additionally, third-party partners should be held accountable and active participants in collaborative forums to cultivate corrective solutions to existing security problems that affront SMBs.

Kluitenberg (2014) emphasizes that SMBs lack cybersecurity strategies and the appropriate security defenses because most fail to comprehend the essence of investing in cybersecurity. In fairness, cybersecurity resources, technologies, and talent are significant investments, even when scaled appropriately for SMBs. The current cybersecurity threat environment is incredibly dynamic, requiring SMBs to invest continuously in updated capabilities to combat emerging threats and vulnerabilities (Kluitenberg, 2014). A mounting concern with ICT (hardware and software) used by businesses is the growing number of technical defaults that malicious hackers exploit to access SMBs' networks and systems (Bolek et al., 2016). Unfortunately, SMBs are disadvantaged, especially firms without dedicated cybersecurity professionals, to maintain an active Patch Management Program, a requirement to reinforce software defaults. The cost of cybersecurity is not only a financial burden to all businesses; regardless of size, they have faced increased targeting of SMBs by criminals (Renauld &Weir, 2016), illustrating a growing threat, especially for small entities. Another salient concern is insufficient cybersecurity expertise at SMBs to fortify cybersecurity strategies and practices. Bolek et al. (2016) assert that organizations without cybersecurity personnel are challenged to align information security practices into the business strategy. A business strategy without information security objectives is ineffective, resulting in the inability to defend against nefarious cyber activities.

A shortage of cybersecurity professionals plagues the U.S. and the international community. One of the most troubling cybersecurity issues is the need for cybersecurity professionals and a discourse on what constitutes a qualified information security professional (Stefee, 2015). Researchers forecast that by 2020, the international community will be 1.5 million cybersecurity professionals (Furnell, Finch, & Fisher, 2017). SMBs are impacted by the need for cybersecurity professionals, including the ability to outsource third-party partners, given that academia, industry, and government are competing from the same talent pool. The current state of available cybersecurity talent contributes to unchallenged cybersecurity threats and vulnerabilities, as evidenced by the number of business attacks. As the complexity of cybersecurity operations continues to escalate, SMBs face heightened targeting attempts from nefarious cyber actors (Van Eeckhoutte, Král & Hradílek, 2019). There is yet to be an exact science to determine how to ensure SMBs are postured and protected from emerging and increasingly sophisticated cyberattacks or data breaches. Collective efforts between academia, industry, and government are necessary to ensure SMBs remain a strategic point of discourse.

5. THE COSTS OF CYBERCRIME FOR SMALL BUSINESSES

The cost of a cyber breach or cybercrime can be devastating, resulting in financial losses, reputational damage, and even criminal charges (Kotter & Worrell, 2020). The financial costs of a cyber breach or cybercrime can be staggering (Kotter & Worrell, 2020). These costs may include repairing or replacing damaged hardware or software, lost revenue due to business interruption, and costs associated with notifying customers of a breach (Kotter & Worrell, 2020). In addition, there may be legal costs associated with defending against cybercrime or data breach lawsuits (Kotter & Worrell, 2020). Finally, cybercrime and cyber breaches may also result in fines or penalties imposed by regulatory authorities (Kotter & Worrell, 2020).

In addition to financial costs, cyber breaches, and cybercrime can significantly impact a business's reputation (Dupont, 2020). Customers may hesitate to do business with a company that has been the victim of a cyber breach. The negative publicity resulting from a cyberattack can have a long-lasting impact (Dupont, 2020). As such, businesses must protect their reputation, such as regularly updating their security systems and staying current on the latest cyber threats (Kotter & Worrell, 2020).

Finally, small business owners may also face criminal liability during a cyber breach or cybercrime (Kotter & Worrell, 2020). Sometimes, the business owner may be liable for failing to take reasonable steps to protect their business from a cyberattack (Kotter & Worrell, 2020). In addition, business owners may be held liable for any losses or damages that result from a cybercrime (Kotter & Worrell, 2020). As such, small business owners need to protect their businesses from cyberattacks and cybercrime.

6. A COMMUNITY OF PRACTICE (COP)

The emergence of digital platforms and the use of technology has enabled small business owners to access resources and opportunities that were previously unavailable to them. However, this has also made them vulnerable to cybercrime and cybersecurity risks. To help protect small businesses from these threats, one option is for them to pool resources and use cybersecurity communities of practice (Smith, 2021).

Small businesses typically need more resources than larger companies possess regarding cybersecurity. Pooling resources gives small business owners access to the resources they would not have been able to obtain independently. This includes access to sophisticated tools, such as malware and virus protection software, and the expertise of cybersecurity professionals (Smith, 2021). These resources can help small businesses protect their data and systems from cyber criminals. Additionally, pooling resources can help small businesses reduce costs and increase efficiency. By sharing resources, such as software and hardware, small businesses can reduce their costs and increase their efficiency (Boroditsky, 2018)

Researchers define a CoP as a collaborative group of stakeholders with similar concerns, similar problems, and the fascination to share knowledge and expertise by collaborating regularly (Gunawardena et al., 2009; Pattinson, 2014). Communities of practice are based on three critical elements: what the group is about, mutual engagement, and the sharing of expertise and knowledge (Gunawardena et al., 2009). Practitioners and researchers assert that CoPs can serve as a vehicle to enhance technological learning and a vector to target innovations (Pattinson, 2014). CoPs are invaluable platforms to fill the existing cybersecurity knowledge and expertise gaps for SMBs. Research indicates that CoPs are regularly used by large organizations (Pattinson, 2014); nonetheless, SMBs can benefit from cybersecurity CoPs. The primary purpose of a CoP is for community practitioners to gain expertise through constant discourse with industry experts through shared experiences on best practices, technologies, and corrective actions (Wenger, 2011). Since many SMBs have limited resources, establishing cybersecurity CoPs is cost-effective for receiving information security training.

Through sponsorship and volunteering, cybersecurity champions can join the CoPs and provide information security training. Research by Iaquinto, Ison, and Faggian (2011) denotes that the external coordination of a CoP is more efficient than internal management due to the online or face-to-face community's administrative workload. Wenger (2010) asserts that sponsors and support staff are vital for assisting the CoPs with internal functions and providing the necessary resources to sustain the community. Iaquinto, Ison, and Faggian (2011) recommend a CoP Coordinator of CoPs (CCoC) to provide strategic guidance and oversight for the communities. Using the CCoC, the cybersecurity CoPs can first coordinate strategic-level training plans and agendas to address the more egregious information security problems (Pharo, 2014). The CCoC can provide expertise in synchronizing efforts to enhance the operational effectiveness of newly formed cybersecurity CoPs. Cybersecurity CoPs are new ventures and must adhere to a strict strategic plan, so sponsorship from public and private entities is imperative.

Some corporate executives appreciate CoPs, mainly embedded learning because information exchanges can provide details beyond the documented actualities (Harvey et al., 2013). Communities of practice have demonstrated the ability to expand beyond organizational boundaries into global entities (Wenger & Snyder, 2000). Corporations assess CoPs as invaluable resources to gain a competitive advantage; therefore, some businesses are creating CoPs rather than allowing communities to develop from spontaneity (Harvey et al., 2013). Just as corporations create CoPs, SMBs should advocate for cybersecurity CoPs on the principle of national security because small businesses are significant contributors to the national economy. The rapid integration of technology, diminishing training opportunities, and talent shortages (Jagasia, Baul, and Mallik, 2015), coupled with a dynamic threat environment, highlights the importance of CoPs in cybersecurity. As a result, cybersecurity CoPs intended to support SMBs can serve as a platform for developing scalable models that apply to small and medium businesses.

The Health Informatics of Australia (HISA) is an example of an organization leveraging a formal cybersecurity CoP to propagate discourse on emerging health information technology, fostering best practices, implementing governance and security controls, and enhancing information security leadership

(HISA, 2017). Empirical data on the effectiveness of cybersecurity CoPs remains scarce or unexplored by researchers and practitioners. Industry-specific studies are needed to determine the effectiveness of CoPs because each professional field has unique characteristics. Empirical findings from corporate CoPs indicate that organizations can benefit from sharing best practices, professional development, and discussing practice-specific problems (Wenger, 2010), fitting for SMBs. The concept and utilization of formal and informal CoPs are proven and capable entities for producing tacit knowledge, processes, and procedures in the corporate sector. The information technology industry lags behind other sectors in capitalizing on CoPs. Failure to create CoPs to educate and strengthen SMBs' cybersecurity strategy to mitigate emerging and persistent cyber threats could be a missed opportunity.

Communities of practice do not exist without weaknesses; Wenger (2010) identifies the following areas as challenging: comprehending the value of CoPs, determining the ownership of best practices, and communicating ongoing initiatives. Leaders in the CoPs should develop strategic objectives with a balanced scorecard and provide a monthly summary update to all interested internal and external stakeholders. The balance card is a mechanism for tracking the progress of specified objectives, and establishing strategic objectives will provide direction for the CoP. Community stakeholders must minimize the administrative burden on the practitioners so the members can focus on collaborating and exchanging information. For formal CoPs, the sponsors can hire support staff to perform the administrative responsibilities, allowing the community participants to concentrate on adding value to the knowledge and expertise transfer. For optimal performance, cybersecurity CoPs should have sponsors, especially from the government and industry, to ensure SMBs comply with regulations and recommended practices.

The practical benefits of CoPs outweigh the abovementioned limitations because SMBs need cybersecurity education and training. The flexibility of CoPs to convene face-to-face, online, or via email will comfortably accommodate SMBs. Another benefit of CoPs is that the community continues to evolve and transform; this self-perpetuation is driven by creating new data, practices, and relationships (Wenger, 2010). Given that information security is continuously evolving, cybersecurity CoPs that support SMBs will enable them to combat emerging threats through the communities' self-perpetuation mechanism.

The positive attributes of CoPs are the transfer of industry standards, the ability to solve practice-specific problems, increase professional proficiency, enhance strategy, and create new business efforts (Wenger, 2010). Without a doubt, through cybersecurity CoPs, SMBs can benefit from the attributes mentioned to implement information security strategies and practices to mitigate cybersecurity threats.

Cybersecurity communities of practice are collaborative teams of individuals dedicated to sharing information and resources related to cybersecurity. These communities provide a platform for small business owners to exchange ideas on cybersecurity topics and discuss best practices (Lambert, 2017). The communities also provide a space where small business owners can gain knowledge and expertise on cybersecurity topics. This can be invaluable for small business owners needing more resources or personnel to develop their cybersecurity strategies. Furthermore, these communities allow small business owners to network and collaborate with other professionals in the field. This can be beneficial for sharing resources and developing innovative solutions to cybersecurity challenges (Boroditsky, 2018).

7. FINAL CONCLUSION

The use of information technology (IT) and cybersecurity infrastructure is essential for small businesses to remain competitive in the current digital age. As technology advances, the complexity of IT and cybersecurity infrastructure increases, which makes it difficult for small businesses to stay up to date on the latest technologies and best practices (Shaffer, 2015). Managing IT and cybersecurity infrastructure can be daunting for small businesses, and having the right resources and expertise can be critical for their success. One approach that has been gaining traction for small businesses is using communities of practice (CoPs) to provide support and guidance in managing IT and cybersecurity infrastructure.

Undeniably, the increased targeting of SMBs by malicious cyber actors could affect the U.S. national economy because small businesses comprise a preponderance of companies and conduct a significant portion of economic transactions. Malicious cyber actors view SMBs as soft targets and seek to attack the underbelly of the U.S. economy by exploiting small and medium-sized companies, which are deemed less capable of protecting critical networks, systems, and consumers' sensitive data. Of concern to academia, government, and the industry is that many large companies rely on SMBs as third-party partners (Kissel and Moon, 2016). Invariably, cyber hackers seek to capitalize on the information security chasm due to SMBs lacking the resources and information security expertise to harden virtual networks and systems. Corporations have created CoPs across many industries to improve professional knowledge through knowledge management, primarily tacit knowledge. Communities of practice can provide a platform to disseminate critical cybersecurity information that SMBs can use to integrate best practices and processes and maintain partnerships to combat persistent and emerging cyber threats (Bolisani & Scarso, 2014). Government, industry, and academia stakeholders are exemplary partners to serve as community participants to train and educate SMBs, given the mutual concerns to mitigate advancing cyber threats to small and medium firms. Forming cybersecurity CoPs through the U.S. is a feasible solution to solidify the cybersecurity practices of SMBs. The dissemination of information security expertise from stakeholders to community affiliates could result in hardened cybersecurity practices to protect SMBs. The principal objective is to enable SMBs to protect critical systems and data from exploitation by using CoPs as an educational platform.

CoPs provide a platform for members to collaborate and work together to solve problems (Muller et al., 2019). By working together, members of the CoP can leverage their collective knowledge and experience to find creative solutions to complex problems. Additionally, CoPs often include experts from different backgrounds and disciplines, which can provide unique insights and perspectives on similar problems. This can be especially beneficial for small businesses that may not have access to the same resources as larger companies.

CoPs provide a supportive environment for members to ask questions and get feedback from their peers (Kersting et al., 2020). This can be especially beneficial for small businesses that may not have the same access to technical support as larger companies. Additionally, the feedback and advice of experienced members of the CoP can be invaluable in helping small businesses to make informed decisions about their IT and cybersecurity infrastructure.

In conclusion, small business owners can benefit from pooling resources and using cybersecurity communities of practice to protect them from cybercrime and cybersecurity risks. Pooling resources gives small business owners access to the resources they would not have been able to obtain on their own and can help reduce costs and increase efficiency. Cybersecurity communities of practice provide a platform for small business owners to exchange ideas and discuss best practices. Additionally, these communities provide a space where small business owners can gain knowledge and expertise on cybersecurity topics and network with other professionals in the field.

REFERENCES

Bolek, V., Látecková, A., Romanová, A., & Korcek, F. (2016). Factors Affecting Information Security Focused on SME and Agricultural Enterprises. *AGRIS On-Line Papers in Economics and Informatics*, *8*(4), 37–50. doi:10.7160/aol.2016.080404

Bolisani, E., & Scarso, E. (2014). The place of communities of practice in knowledge management studies: A critical review. *Journal of Knowledge Management*, *18*(2), 366–381. doi:10.1108/JKM-07-2013-0277

Boroditsky, M. (2018). The Benefits of Pooling Resources for Small Businesses. *Entrepreneur.* https://www.entrepreneur.com/article/293962

Brewer, R. (2014). Advanced persistent threats: Minimising the damage. *Network Security*, *2014*(4), 5–9. doi:10.1016/S1353-4858(14)70040-6

Center for Internet Security, (2017). *CIS Controls Implementation Guide for SMBs*. CIS.

Cook, K. D. (2017). *Effective Cyber Security Strategies for Small Businesses* [Doctoral dissertation, Walden University].

Dai, C., & Wang, X. (2018). A narrative literature review of organizational change management: Trends and challenges. *International Journal of Project Management*, *36*(3), 404–421.

Dupont, A. (2020). Cybersecurity and small businesses: The costs of not being prepared. *Journal of Small Business and Entrepreneurship*, *33*(5), 675–689.

Eyal-Cohen, M., (2012). *Down-sizing the little guy myth in legal definitions.*

Federal Trade Commission. (2020). *How to protect your business from cybercrime*. FTC. https://www.consumer.ftc.gov/articles/how-protect-your-business-cybercrime

Forster-Holt, N. (2009). What makes a business" small"? *Strategic Finance*, *90*(9), 20–22.

Forster-Holt, N. (2013). Entrepreneur as" End" repreneur: The Intention to Retire. *Small Business Institute Journal*, *9*(2), 29.

Furnell, S., Fischer, P., & Finch, A. (2017). Can't get the staff? The growing need for cyber-security skills. *Computer Fraud & Security*, *2017*(2), 5–10. doi:10.1016/S1361-3723(17)30013-1

Germano, J., & Center for Cybersecurity. (2017). *Third-party cyber risk and corporate social responsibility.* (White Paper) https://www.lawandsecurity.org/wp-content/uploads/2017/02/Germano.NYU_.ThirdPartyRiskWhitepaper.Feb2017.pdf

Goodwin, C. (2004). The use of narrative literature reviews in social research. *Qualitative Research*, *4*(3), 293–312.

Gunawardena, C. N., Hermans, M. B., Sanchez, D., Richmond, C., Bohley, M., & Tuttle, R. (2009). A theoretical framework for building online communities of practice with social networking tools. *Educational Media International*, *46*(1), 3–16. doi:10.1080/09523980802588626

Harvey, J. F., Cohendet, P., Simon, L., & Dubois, L. E. (2013). Another cog in the machine: Designing communities of practice in professional bureaucracies. *European Management Journal*, *31*(1), 27–40. doi:10.1016/j.emj.2012.07.008

Health Informatics for Australia (HISA). (2017). *What is the HISA Community of Practice?* HISA. https://www.hisa.org.au/cybersecurity/

Iaquinto, B., Ison, R., & Faggian, R. (2011). Creating communities of practice: Scoping purposeful design. *Journal of Knowledge Management*, *15*(1), 4–21. doi:10.1108/13673271111108666

Jagasia, J., Baul, U., & Mallik, D. (2015). A framework for communities of practice in learning organizations. *Business Perspectives and Research*, *3*(1), 1–20. doi:10.1177/2278533714551861

Kabir, M. R. (2019). *Comparison of Retirement Plan between Bangladesh & USA.*

Kersting, N., Sander, M., & Schumacher, S. (2020). Communities of practice and the sharing of tacit knowledge: A qualitative study. *International Journal of Knowledge Management*, *16*(1), 1–15.

Kissel, R., and Moon, H., (2016). *Small business information security: Fundamentals.* National Institute of Standards and Technology. doi:10.6028/NIST.IR.7621r1

Kluitenberg, H. (2014). Security risk management in it small and medium enterprises. In *Proc. 20th Twente Student Conf. I.T.* IEEE.

Kotter, K., & Worrell, K. (2020). Cybercrime and the costs to small business owners. *Journal of Applied Security Research*, *15*(2), 115–127.

Kratz, L. (2020). Cyber security risks to small businesses during the COVID-19 pandemic. *Small Business Trends.* https://smallbiztrends.com/2020/04/cyber-security-risks-to-small-business-during-covid-19.html

Kumar, A. (2020). COVID-19: Cyber security risks and measures for small businesses. *The Economic Times.* https://economictimes.indiatimes.com/small-biz/startups/newsbuzz/covid-19-cyber-security-risks-and-measures-for-small-businesses/articleshow/76271477.cms?from=mdr

Labossiere, D. L. (2016). *A matrix for small business owners to better protect their network* [Doctoral dissertation, Utica College].

Lambert, J. (2017). *Cybersecurity Communities of Practice: What They Are and How They Help.* Secure World Expo. https://www.secureworldexpo.com/cyber-security-strategy/cybersecurity-communities-of-practice-what-they-are-and-how-they-help

Lan, T. D., Gagnon, S., & Nguyen, P. (2020). Factors Contributing to Small Business Vulnerability to Cyberattacks. *International Journal of Cybersecurity and Digital Forensics*, *6*(2), 139–154. doi:10.4018/IJCDF.2020010105

Mayadunne, S., & Park, S. (2016). An economic model to evaluate information security investment of risk-taking small and medium enterprises. *International Journal of Production Economics*, *182*, 519–530. doi:10.1016/j.ijpe.2016.09.018

McKinsey & Company. (2017). *Cybersecurity for small and medium-sized businesses: A guide for executives*. McKinsey. https://www.mckinsey.com/~/media/McKinsey/Business%20Functions/Risk/Our%20Insights/Cybersecurity%20for%20small%20and%20medium%20sized%20businesses/Cybersecurity-for-small-and-medium-sized-businesses_Full%20report_A4.ashx

Morency, K. (2014). Cybersecurity finally takes center stage in the U.S. *J. High Tech. L.*, *15*, 192.

Muller, M., Park, J., & Kyei, G. (2019). The effectiveness of communities of practice in knowledge management: A systematic review. *International Journal of Information Management*, *46*, 49–64.

National Cyber Security Alliance. (2018). The impact of cybercrime on small businesses. *Stay Safe Online*. https://www.staysafeonline.org/ncsam/resources/impact-of-cybercrime-on-small-businesses/

National Cyber Security Alliance (NCSA). (2012). National Small Business Study. *Stay Safe Online*. https://staysafeonline.org/wp-content/uploads/2017/09/2012-NCSA-Symantec-Small-Business-Study.pdf

Ncubukezi, T., Mwansa, L., & Rocaries, F. (2020, December). A review of the current cyber hygiene in small and medium-sized businesses. In *2020 15th International Conference for Internet Technology and Secured Transactions (ICITST)* (pp. 1-6). IEEE. 10.23919/ICITST51030.2020.9351339

OECD. (2017). Bridging policy silos to boost trust online. *The OECD Observer. Organisation for Economic Co-Operation and Development*. doi:10.1787/42b03ed1-en

Osborn, E., (2014). *Business versus technology: Sources of the perceived lack of cyber security in SMBs*.

Pattinson, S., & Preece, D. (2014). Communities of practice, knowledge acquisition, and innovation: A case study of science-based SMBs. *Journal of Knowledge Management*, *18*(1), 107–120. doi:10.1108/JKM-05-2013-0168

Pharo, E., Davison, A., McGregor, H., Warr, K., & Brown, P. (2014). Using communities of practice to enhance interdisciplinary teaching: Lessons from four Australian institutions. *Higher Education Research & Development*, *33*(2), 341–354. doi:10.1080/07294360.2013.832168

Renaud, K., & Weir, G. R. (2016). August. Cybersecurity and the Unbearability of Uncertainty. In *Cybersecurity and Cyberforensics Conference (CCC)*, (pp. 137–143). IEEE. 10.1109/CCC.2016.29

Renner, S. (2001). August. A community of interest approach to data interoperability. In Federal database colloquium (Vol. 1, p. 2).

Sangani, N. K., & Vijayakumar, B. (2012). Cyber security scenarios and control for small and medium enterprises. *Informações Econômicas*, *16*(2), 58.

Shaffer, A. (2015). *Communities of Interest: Collaborating on Technology Challenges*. DEFENSE ACQUISITION UNIV FT BELVOIR VA.

Smith, A. (2021). What is a community of practice? *Techopedia*. https://www.techopedia.com/definition/33941/community-of-practice-cop

Terziovski, M. (2010). Innovation practice and its performance implications in small and medium enterprises (SMBs) in the manufacturing sector: A resource-based view. *Strategic Management Journal*, *31*(8), 892–902.

Van Eeckhoutte, E., Král, M., & Hradílek, T. (2019). Cyber Security of Small and Medium-Sized Enterprises: A Systematic Literature Review. *International Journal of Cybersecurity and Digital Forensics*, *5*(3), 154–184. doi:10.4018/IJCDF.2019070109

Verizon. (2019). *2019 Verizon Data Breach Investigations Report*. Verizon. https://enterprise.verizon.com/resources/reports/2019-data-breach-investigations-report.pdf

Walton, A. (2019). Cybersecurity for Small Businesses: What Are the Risks and How Can They Be Mitigated? *Small Business Trends*. https://smallbiztrends.com/2019/03/cybersecurity-for-small-business.html

Watson, R. (2017). Law aims to heighten cybersecurity: Proposed Cyber Training Act would certify SBDC employees nationwide to help small businesses fight online threats. *Grand Rapids Business Journal*, *35*, 3–4.

Wenger, E., (2010). Communities of practice and social learning systems: the career of a concept. *Social learning systems and communities of practice, 3*, 179–198.

Wenger, E. (2011). *Communities of practice: A brief introduction.*

Wenger, E. C., & Snyder, W. M. (2000). Communities of practice: The organizational frontier. *Harvard Business Review*, *78*(1), 139–146.

Chapter 28
Towards Investigation of the Perceived Leadership Effect on Supply Chain Cyber Security:
Building a Qualitative Study in Botswana

Andreas Vassilakos
https://orcid.org/0000-0002-6586-6126
Capitol Technology University, USA

ABSTRACT

Humanity is currently experiencing an influx of threats against the global supply chain. Many of them have resulted in catastrophic outcomes. It has never been more critical for organizations and governments to tackle this vital issue. Developing nations amid digital transformation efforts are especially vulnerable. In this chapter, the researcher lays the foundation for a phenomenological qualitative study in Botswana. The author briefly provides background on supply chain cybersecurity and Industry 4.0. The methodology of an ongoing study in Botswana is presented, including its purpose, research design, data-gathering procedures, and protocol. The significance of the study, as well as limitations and delimitations, are described. The research questions aim to paint a holistic picture of the examined topic. The author includes some notable responses to offer a glance through the eyes of the participants on the investigated phenomenon. The researcher aims to continue with the analysis within a subsequent academic item.

INTRODUCTION

In 2020, an Advanced Persistent Threat (APT) attack was observed targeting numerous high-importance parties resulting in ongoing compromises of both government and non-governmental network infrastructure (Cybersecurity & Infrastructure Security Agency, 2021). The nefarious agents were likely of Russian origin. A task force was composed of the combined forces of the Federal Bureau of Investigation (FBI),

DOI: 10.4018/979-8-3693-1634-4.ch028

Cybersecurity and Infrastructure Security Agency (CISA), Office of the Director of National Intelligence (ODNI), and National Security Agency (NSA) (Cybersecurity & Infrastructure Security Agency, 2021).

It provided an approximate number of 18,000 customers of SolarWinds' Orion item. The affected customers were from both the public and private sectors; several U.S. Government agencies were affected by this attack (Cybersecurity & Infrastructure Security Agency, 2021). The global supply chain is becoming a progressively more frequent target of nefarious actors. Numerous tools are used by threat agents, including malware, APT, and manipulating computer hardware. Such attacks can become a hurdle to the economic growth and technological evolution of developing nations. Several researchers have reported the gap in literature surrounding the topic. Ghadge et al. state that "the limited set of papers available for this study suggests that little academic attention has addressed this field compared to other topics/technologies interfacing with supply chain management." Khan and Estay emphasize the need to generate case studies to enhance the understanding of cybersecurity threats related to the Supply Chain. Cheung et al. identified the lack of sufficient studies focused on cybersecurity in logistics and supply chain management, as many items have focused on the importance of logistics activities in supply chains but overlooked the importance of cybersecurity. The lack of literature is alarming when the financial implications of cyber attacks are more than $400 billion globally, as calculated in a study conducted by the Center for Strategic and International Studies (CSIS) and McAfee.

SUPPLY CHAIN BACKGROUND

In the past couple of years, Supply Chain has been a frequently contemplated topic, especially in the context of its unfortunate current state due to the COVID19 pandemic. According to IBM (n.d.), "Supply chain management is the handling of the entire production flow of a good or service — starting from the raw components to delivering the final product to the consumer." Essentially it covers the whole lifecycle that begins with the resources needed to produce a product and ends with the final product used by customers.

According to Handfield (2021), SCM relies on two fundamental ideas. First, all products that reach the end-users represent the combined effort of many participating organizations; these organizations are considered a supply chain (Handfield, 2021). Second, even though supply chains have existed for an extensive period, most companies were focused only on their internal operations and ignored the bigger picture, which resulted in the ineffective operation of supply chains (Handfield, 2021).

Within supply chains, organizations are connected thanks to physical and information flows (Handfield, 2021). Physical flows include the "transformation, movement, and storage of goods and materials" (Handfield, 2021). Information flows are responsible for the coordination between organizations that create a supply chain for their future plans but also manage their everyday flow of materials within the supply chain (Handfield, 2021).

Supply Chain Management (SCM), in its traditional state, comprises five elements: planning, sourcing, manufacturing, delivery and logistics, and returning (IBM, n.d.). The Planning component is responsible for managing all essential resources to satisfy the market needs for a product or a service (IBM, n.d.). The Sourcing component handles the selection of suppliers that provide the goods and services needed to create a final product or service (IBM, n.d.). The Manufacturing component is responsible for organizing activities required to "accept raw materials, manufacture the product, test for quality, package for shipping and schedule for delivery" (IBM, n.d.). The Delivery and Logistics element is responsible for activities that include coordinating customer orders, scheduling deliveries, load dispatching, customer invoicing, and payment receiving (IBM, n.d.). Finally, the Returning component helps develop a network that handles returns of defective, excess, or unwanted products (IBM, n.d.).

The efficient application of SCM practices is of immense importance for the smooth operation of our society. The utilization of supply chain management systems in an effective manner ensures cost, waste, and time minimization within the production cycle (IBM, n.d.). According to IBM (n.d.), a few examples where effective SCM increases the value to the supply chain cycle include identifying potential problems, optimizing price dynamically, and improving the allocation of "available to promise" inventory.

INDUSTRY 4.0

Our lives have drastically improved in the past couple of centuries thanks to the significant innovation resulting from the three industrial revolutions initiated in the 1800s (SAP, 2022). Every subsequent wave of the industrial revolution introduced a new technology, which started with the first wave and the invention of the steam engine, continued with the second one and the incorporation of the assembly line, and then the third one introduced computation as part of manufacturing (SAP, 2022). All three initial waves of the industrial revolution provided fodder for disruption in the ways that manufacturing functions and work is done, which had an immense impact on humanity and our lives (SAP, 2022). Industry 4.0 comes with "high levels of automation and unparalleled data exchange levels with unknown security risks" (Dawson, 2021), which creates new challenges for cybersecurity professionals.

Industry 4.0 is responsible for the implementation of the Industrial Internet of Things (IIoT) and cyber-physical systems to "monitor and control physical things like machinery, robots, and vehicles" (SAP, 2022). Cyber-physical systems are smart systems that integrate algorithms to contribute to the operations of IIoT (SAP, 2022). Essentially Industry 4.0 moved the supply chain into a "smart" era, which touched manufacturing, factories, warehousing, and logistics in general (SAP, 2022). According to Dawson et al. (2021), the "manufacturing sector is moving to Industry 4.0, and this will bring about entirely new challenges that are introduced due to the complex hyperconnectivity and increased size of the threat landscape".

Industry 4.0 relies on nine technological elements: big data and AI analytics, horizontal and vertical integration, cloud computing, augmented reality, additive manufacturing, 3D printing, autonomous robots, simulation or digital twins, and cybersecurity (SAP, 2022). In the supply chain context, Industrial 4.0 has brought unprecedented change. According to Alicke et al. (2016), "Supply Chain 4.0 - the application of the Internet of Things, the use of advanced robotics, and the application of advanced analytics of big data in supply chain management: place sensors in everything, create networks everywhere, automate anything, and analyze everything to improve performance and customer satisfaction significantly". The supply chain, in general, is getting progressively more reliant on secure technology, which brings cybersecurity to the forefront and encourages the integration of good supply chain risk management practices.

SUPPLY CHAIN RISK MANAGEMENT

In the context of contemporary international business, it is increasingly vital for organizations to mitigate any threats against their supply chains. Due to the enhanced complexity of supply chains, the emergence of risks related to finance, regulations, and law create a landscape where risk management should be a focal point (Deloitte, 2022). According to a Deloitte Touche Tohmatsu Limited survey (Deloitte, 2022), "85 percent of surveyed global supply chains had experienced at least one disruption in the past 12 months".

Organizations participating in a supply chain can achieve the mitigation of this risk by employing a five-step process as recommended by Deloitte (2022). First, an organization has to become familiarized with a potential supplier. Second, the organization must ensure that they receive the items they initially requested. Then, they must ensure they pay only for items they have received (Deloitte, 2022). Consequently, the organization must ensure effective prevention or resolution of potential disputes. Finally, the organization must be aware of and prepared to safeguard against risks in the sales process (Deloitte, 2022). Organizations should be incredibly attentive to their supply chain risk management efforts, as the threats in the cyber realm have dramatically increased in recent years, and nefarious actors can attempt attacks against any part of a supply chain to promote their agendas.

SUPPLY CHAIN CYBERSECURITY

Supply chain attacks are described as the " type of cyberattack that targets a trusted third-party vendor who offers services or software vital to the supply chain" (Crowdstrike, 2021). One can identify some illuminating statistics within CrowdStrike's Global Security Attitude Survey (Crowdstrike, 2021). Among the surveyed organizations, 84% agree that "software supply chain attacks could become one of the biggest cyber threats" targeting similar organizations in the next three years, 36% in the last 12 months "vetted all new and existing suppliers for security purposes", 45% "experienced at least one software supply chain attack in the last 12 months" which increased from a 32% in 2018, and 59% of affected organizations that were breached for the first time from a supply chain attack were not ready due to lack of response strategy (Crowdstrike, 2021).

Because organizations increase the defense measures and increasingly harden their infrastructure, nefarious actors have moved towards supply chain attacks that incorporate creative ways that allow them not to be easily detected and instead target third parties associated with an organization (Crowdstrike, 2021). Therefore, it is observed that supply chain attacks have increased by 430% over the past years (Crowdstrike, 2021).

Supply chain attacks can happen to any company whose infrastructure relies on third-party vendors (Proofpoint, 2022). Supply chain attacks often occur when attackers compromise products of trusted vendors, which aim to patch previous vulnerabilities (Fortinet, 2022). The three main categories of supply chain attacks are physical supply chain threats, software supply chain threats, digital supply chain threats, and business email compromise (Proofpoint, 2022).

Physical supply chain threats are possible when foreign components are introduced into the manufacturing of circuit boards that allow threat actors to monitor data associated with the hosting hardware (Proofpoint, 2022). Software supply chain threats are possible when third-party vendors install software with unknown vulnerabilities and subsequently introduce a backdoor for nefarious agents to monitor and control the organization's systems (Proofpoint, 2022). Digital supply chain threats happen when third-party libraries that software developers use at an organization are injected with malicious code, which introduces vulnerabilities to the finished product (Proofpoint, 2022). A business email compromise is associated with attack attempts targeting financial employees with the intent to either compromise a company's account and email or trick the victim into sending money and information to the malicious party (Proofpoint, 2022).

After an organization has been targeted by a supply chain attack and falls victim to it, domains including corporate revenue, brand reputation, and vendor relationships can be affected negatively on an extreme scale (Proofpoint, 2022). Many supply chain attacks take advantage of vulnerabilities in third-party dependencies, especially software packages. Common vulnerabilities and exposures (CVEs) are bought and sold on the dark web, and the market has exploded in growth.

In the past years, we have experienced a significant number of supply chain attacks in the cyber realm. The impact of many of these cases is still noticeable in the cybersecurity industry. In 2021, Alex Birshan, a security researcher, managed to infiltrate Microsoft, Uber, Apple, and Tesla by escalating vulnerabilities related to application dependencies pertaining to services to end-users (Fortinet, 2022). As part of his security research, he managed to transmit fake data packets to high-profile users in a non-nefarious way (Fortinet, 2022).

In 2021 the Mimecast attack resulted from a successful security certificate compromise that allowed threat actors to authenticate Mimecast's services on Microsoft 365 Exchange Web Services (Fortinet, 2022). Few users were affected, as 10% of Mimecast's customers use applications that rely on the breached certificate (Fortinet, 2022). One of the most notorious attacks in recent years, the SolarWinds attack in 2020, resulted from a backdoor injection into the Orion IT update tool (Fortinet, 2022). The attack affected over 18,000 customers and organizations (Fortinet, 2022). In 2018, ASUS was targeted by an attack that took advantage of an update feature and impacted the systems of 500,000 users (Fortinet, 2022).

ATTACK VECTORS DURING COVID-19

Since 2019, humanity has been experiencing a global health catastrophe due to COVID-19 (coronavirus disease), an infectious disease resulting from the SARS-CoV-2 virus (World Health Organization, 2022). The emergency state has escalated due to the increased attack occurrences in the cyber realm. It is a fact that nefarious actors thrive during times of uncertainty.

The most critical threats for 2020 and 2021 were ransomware, malware, cryptojacking, e-mail threats, data threats, availability and integrity threats, disinformation/misinformation, and non-malicious threats. The top five most targeted sectors (See Figure 1.) were governments, digital service providers, the general public, healthcare, and finance (ENISA, 2021).

Figure 1. Timeline of observed incidents related to prime threats per sector
Source: Enisa, 2021

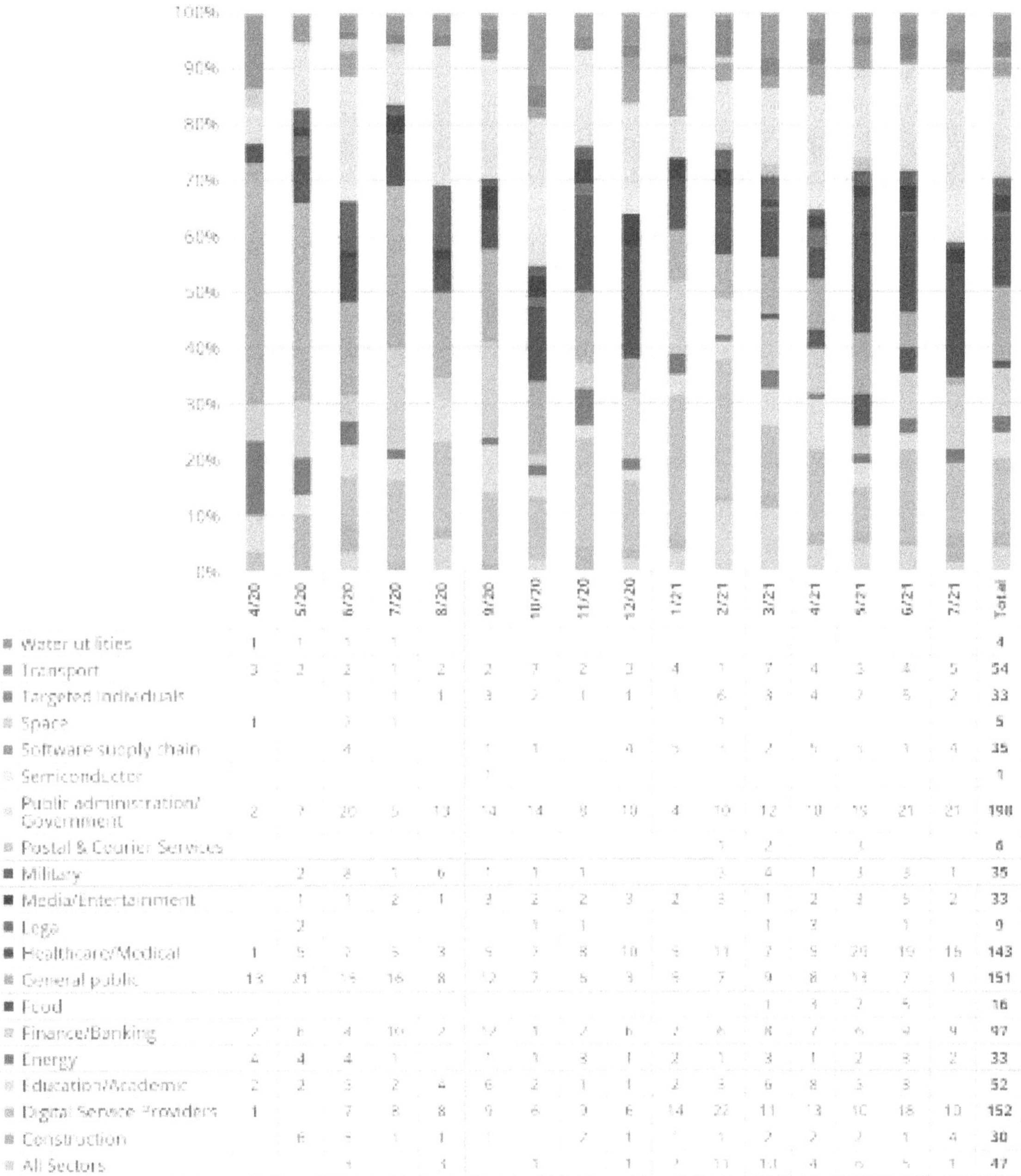

Non-malicious threats are usually the result of human error or system misconfiguration (ENISA, 2021). This type of threat is often overlooked but increased in importance during the COVID-19 pandemic due to the emergency move to remote work and remote learning along with the accelerated adoption of cloud infrastructure. The changing computing infrastructure landscape resulted in a larger attack surface with higher value targets in the cloud (Accenture, 2021).

BOTSWANA BACKGROUND

For this study, the country of focus is Botswana. It is a country located in the southern African region, north of South Africa. The country's economy relies on mineral extraction and diamond mining, and tourism is a growing sector due to the nation's natural habitat and conservation efforts (Central Intelligence Agency, 2022). The telecommunication market is "one of the most liberalized in the region" (Central Intelligence Agency, 2022).

According to a study by Symantec (2016), Botswana is one of the most attacked targets in the African continent (See Figure 2.), ranking eighth with a 3% percentage within Africa and an incident count of 37,880.

Figure 2. Top ten source African countries for attacks in 2016
Source: Symantec, 2016

COUNTRY	RANK	PERCENTAGE WITHIN AFRICA	INCIDENT COUNT
South Africa	1	25%	314,880
Egypt	2	12%	149,685
Kenya	3	9%	108,765
Nigeria	4	7%	89,100
Mauritius	5	6%	73,134
Algeria	6	6%	60,381
Seychelles	7	4%	45,661
Botswana	8	3%	37,880
Morocco	9	3%	34,464
Tunisia	10	3%	32,187

METHODOLOGY

Purpose

This study aimed to investigate the perceived effect of leadership in combating cybersecurity threats against the logistics of developing nations with a focus on the African region. Botswana was the country of focus. An emphasis was given to the supply chain subfield of logistics. Also, the researcher tried to capture the essence of the experience in a holistic manner as the interviewed cybersecurity professionals in the location of interest described.

Research Design

The researcher utilized qualitative phenomenology as the methodology of this study.

Data Gathering

Data from both the pilot study and research participants was collected similarly. At the beginning of the interview, the participants were requested to provide demographic information (race, gender, educational background, professional experience, city and country, and professional title. All participants were asked the same central question and 13 sub-questions supporting the main one. The purpose of these questions was to allow the participants to discuss how they felt about the investigated phenomenon.

Research Population

The population of this study was limited to participants associated with the cybersecurity, logistics, and supply chain management fields within the country of Botswana. The participants had to identify as one of either three categories:

Category 1: Subject matter experts in cybersecurity, Information Technology, logistics, supply chain Management, or any appropriate field.

Category 2: Academics with a research focus on cybersecurity, Information Technology, logistics, supply chain management, or any appropriate field.

Category 3: Government leaders or officials in positions related to cybersecurity, Information Technology, logistics, or any appropriate sectors.

All participants had to hold at least a Bachelor's degree, preferably in a field related to the nature of the study; this included computer science, information technology, information systems, business administration, supply chain management, and any fields deemed relevant after careful examination. The years of experience and possession of relevant professional certifications were taken into consideration when the educational background was deemed insufficient. After willing participants were identified, a demographic survey was conducted to assess if they did fit any of the criteria described above. All participants were 18 years old or older.

All participants filled out the demographic survey prior to signing their consent form. The demographic survey was used to collect data on the participants' gender, age, extended home region, country of residence, highest degree or level of education that they have attained, years of work experience they possess, current job title, and an option to include any professional certifications they might hold.

The sample size consisted of fifteen individuals satisfying the criteria described above (See Table 1.). There were no benefits for participants participating in the study, no compensation was provided, and their participation was strictly voluntary. All participants were recruited using the LinkedIn social media and professional network platform.

Table 1. Qualitative research population demographics

Participant (N#)	Gender	Age	Highest Degree/Level of Education	Years of Work Experience	Current Job Title
1	Male	30-45	Ph.D. or higher	10	Academic
2	Male	30-45	Master's Degree	6	Digital Forensics Analyst
3	Male	18-30	Bachelor's Degree	3	Graduate Student
4	Male	30-45	Ph.D. or higher	7	Academic
5	Male	30-45	Bachelor's Degree	6	IT Security Specialist
6	Male	18-30	Bachelor's Degree	5	Business Process Analyst
7	Male	18-30	Bachelor's Degree	5	Systems Engineer
8	Female	30-45	Bachelor's Degree	5	IT Officer
9	Male	18-30	Bachelor's Degree	2	Software Developer
10	Female	18-30	Bachelor's Degree	2	Cyber Security Analyst
11	Male	30-45	Master's Degree	15	Information Technology Manager
12	Female	30-45	Master's Degree	11	Information Technology Manager
13	Male	30-45	Bachelor's Degree	21	Head of Information and Communications Technology Department
14	Male	45+	Master's Degree	25	Managing Director
15	Female	18-30	Bachelor's Degree	6	Cyber Incident Response Team (CIRT) Analyst
16	Male	30-45	Master's Degree	15	Academic

Source: Author, 2023

Significance

With supply chain attacks progressively being an immense problem for organizations, research on how to combat these threats is necessary. While researching academic journals and publications, the researcher identified a knowledge gap in leadership's effect on the cybersecurity stance of supply chain and logistics organizations or, in general, the supply chain and logistics as a target. The gap is increasingly crucial in the context of developing nations. The researcher intended to contribute to scholarly published items that can enhance organizations' efforts to combat nefarious actors in the realm of supply chain and logistics focused on the selected countries of the African continent.

This study's implication for positive social change included the potential to improve organizations' cybersecurity stance regardless of their type and, in advance, all that might be affected by potential breaches related to the supply chain and logistics fields. The focus on the selected countries of the African region intends to combat a potential factor hindering further development.

Protocol

In order to ensure that interviewers capture the exact data they want, good interviewers will use one of three approaches: a structured interview, a semi-structured interview, or an unstructured interview. Each of these is approached differently, and each is designed with a specific goal in mind (Terrell, 2016). For this study, the researcher aimed to implement the structured interview approach. The goal of using the structured interview approach, where the researcher asks specific questions, is to prevent the person being interviewed from straying much in their answers (Terrell, 2016). Using the structured interview approach allows the researcher to develop clear, focused questions aimed at collecting data in the area of interest (Terrell, 2016). All questions asked during this research had to be standardized, asked in the same order with no changes in the manner they are asked so that the researcher ensures validity (Terrell, 2016).

The author additionally selected the structured interview approach to overcome research challenges associated with the global pandemic humanity was experiencing at the time of the data collection. The author also aimed to overcome the challenges that would emerge due to inconsistent IT infrastructure, network access, and electrical grid the participants have access to in the examined location. In the case either the IT infrastructure, network access, or electrical grid would fail or would not allow for a smooth interview experience, the participants were provided with the option to provide their answers in a written form and share them through email. Originally the researcher intended to visit the country of interest and interview all individuals in person, but the global pandemic did not allow this plan to be fulfilled. The combined use of Zoom and email correspondence made the data collection possible.

Research Questions

After diving into the relevant literature and following consultations with subject matter experts, the researcher developed the following questionnaire to investigate the research question. The questions were dynamic in nature. The questions were finalized after further literature was examined and the pilot study phase was conducted.

Central Question: How do cybersecurity professionals describe the effects of leadership on the cybersecurity posture of organizations in regards to threats against logistics with an emphasis on supply chain?

Sub-question 1: How would you describe cybersecurity as an organizational resource?

Sub-question 2.1: How do you perceive the increasing cybersecurity threats at a local scale?

Sub-question 2.2: How do you perceive the increasing cybersecurity threats at a global scale?

Sub-question 3: What role do you feel management and leadership plays in effective cybersecurity? If you feel it doesn't play a role, please explain why. If it doesn't play a role, what would be the issue?

Sub-question 4: Who do you feel is responsible in an organizational setting for the increasing rate of observed cybersecurity threats?

Sub-question 5: How important do you feel is the protection of supply chain and logistics?

Sub-question 6: What measures would you say could improve cybersecurity in supply chain and logistics?

Sub-question 7: In what ways do you collaborate with your organization's supply chain / logistics team?

Sub-question 8: How would you describe the stance of your organization's management and leadership on the importance of securing against threats on the supply chain and logistics?

Sub-question 9: Who's responsible for logistics and specifically supply chain accountability in your organization?

Sub-question 10: Would you feel that the reliability of the internet has an effect on the security of supply chain? If yes, in what way?

Sub-question 11: Would you feel that the reliability of the electrical grid has an effect on the security of supply chain? If yes, in what way?

Sub-question 12: Would you feel that the reliability of infrastructure in general has an effect on the security of supply chain? If yes, in what way?

Sub-question 13: Is there a government regulation or policy that serves as your guideline? What is the government regulation or policy that you follow?

LIMITATIONS AND DELIMITATIONS

The limitations of this study were the following:

Limitation 1: The study was restricted to the country of Botswana.

Limitation 2: The small size of the research sample limits the generalization of the data outcomes.

Limitation 3: The data gathering was limited to the means allowed by the current global circumstances and access to IT, electricity, and network connectivity.

Delimitations for this study include that due to a large number of eligible participants in the study population, the research sample will be focused only on members located within Botswana. It should be noted that the research questions were modified as further literature was identified during the composition of the research items prior to the phenomenological study being conducted (Terrell, 2016)

RESEARCH DATA ACCESS, PROTECTION, USAGE, AND CONFIDENTIALITY

The only persons with access to the data were the principal researcher and his dissertation chair. Data was collected using Zoom's recording functionality. In the cases where the participants would have preferred a different video conference platform (e.g., Google Meet or Microsoft Teams), the researcher was willing to comply, so maximum flexibility was provided and offered to follow any such preferences. Only the researcher accessed all recorded sessions. All data was planned to be retained for at least five years in case the researcher deems additional analysis necessary.

All data collected during this study were collected with the intent to be analyzed and used for the corresponding author's doctoral dissertation and possibly sent out to conferences, presentations, and other publications, as applicable strictly to him.

Participants were assigned a participant ID before entry into the Zoom room. Their names and any other Personally Identifiable Information (PII) were not included in the data analysis and will not be included anywhere in the results of the study.

CONSENT AND ETHICS

Consent was obtained using a consent form sent to every participant prior to scheduling the conducted interviews. Participants had to sign the consent item before taking part in the study. There were no vulnerable participants in this study. There were no potential risks associated with participating. The corresponding author received research, ethics, compliance, and safety training by the Collaborative

Institutional Training Initiative (CITI Program) in January of 2021 and holds a valid certificate through February 2026.

RESULTS AND DISCUSSION

This study aimed to explore the lived experiences of professionals in Botswana. For the purpose of this study, since the author investigates a phenomenon, a qualitative study was deemed appropriate. The data collection and analysis were conducted using methods commonly incorporated in phenomenological studies. The findings presented here are a result of the deep perspective shared by people experiencing the researched phenomenon in their everyday personal and work lives.

Notable Answers

Some of the notable answers by the research participants according to each question are as follows. The notable answers provide further context and paint the holistic image of the examined topic.

Central Question

N4: "With regard to Botswana, I think it's a new area that people are looking into. Currently, we don't have policies for that"…"Generally, you won't find people with that experience. People are mostly ignorant when it comes to cybersecurity."

N16: "Well, I would start by saying that my experience here in Africa is that most organizations don't really get the support that I think they need especially from government in that line. And even though companies that are totally independent and try to raise money and be effective in this area, they don't necessarily get the support that they need. So I would say in Africa, and especially in developing countries here in Southern Africa, there's a lot of room that needs improvement, especially when it comes to government participation and also funding, when it comes to such organizations that are involved in such."

Sub-question 1: How would you describe cybersecurity as an organizational resource?

N5: "Here in Botswana, as a developing country, we are lagging behind"…"our leadership here in these developing countries, they don't understand what, really, cyber security is. They don't really understand. We are trying so hard. Our IT leaders they are trying by all means to catch up with the imagined threats, to understand what is really cybersecurity."

N7: "I think I would describe cyber security as like a key asset any organization should have. Looking at how things are changing with the recent pandemic, it has sort of fast forwarded the world into digitalization. And as we move into digitalization, I believe it is important for organizations to have cyber security implemented in their organizations."

N14: "Undervalued. Severely undervalued. Evidence to base it, look at organizational structures, how many cyber security individuals and roles exist within organizations. It's only now that you're start seeing departments that focus on it, but I think it's definitely undervalued."

Sub-question 2.1: How do you perceive the increasing cybersecurity threats at a local scale?

N4: "In terms of cybersecurity here, I think it's very hard to notice or to know the extent of cybersecurity, because in most cases, things don't get reported, and you wouldn't know even a way to get the statistics. There are no statistics that we can find in terms of cybersecurity. In most cases, people will have been hacked, but they wouldn't realize that they've been hacked or their systems have been compromised. I think maybe this is due to the fact that people are ignorant, and people also think that they are law-abiding, so they are not a target. That's how it is. In terms of reporting, it's very hard to know. With regard to the threat landscape here, there is limited information."

N7: "At the local scale I would say cyber security is more of a myth, more of uncharted waters. A lot of people don't actually understand it locally. So it's very key for organizations to teach employees and for people who are around really to learn about cyber security because it doesn't just affect organizations. Even individuals need to know how to protect themselves online, especially when it comes to free wifi connections at the mall, people need to understand what things like VPNs are, what firewalls do. So locally I'd say we have a long way to go. We have to learn every day because every day cyber security in the cyber-verse changes. So we have to keep up with the pace."

N9: "I feel we as Botswana, we are not up to par with the latest frameworks and technologies and we haven't developed risk measures that will be able to tackle those threats"…" we are still trying to catch up at a very slow rate."

N10: "So the thing with our country, it's a third world country. Cyber security hasn't really affected it that much and the country itself is not really emphasizing it. Things started changing for our country during the COVID pandemic. That's when we started taking cyber security and the cyber world seriously"…"We still have a long way to go as Botswana. We have a lot of errors, we have a lot of weak links. So locally in our country, cyber security is not as serious and it's really weak."

Sub-question 2.2: How do you perceive the increasing cybersecurity threats at a global scale?

N10: "From studies that I've been reading looks like everything now it's more serious, because even our own country, we are benchmarking our cyber security strategies from countries in a global landscape."

N16: "Every day there's a new threat. Every day there's something new, different from yesterday."

Sub-question 3: What role do you feel management and leadership plays in effective cybersecurity? If you feel it doesn't play a role, please explain why. If it doesn't play a role, what would be the issue?

N11: "Leadership SHOULD be the overseeing patrons of cybersecurity because they have a more conceptual view of the business activities hence they should also map those activities to risks associated with them. Data loss is still one of the main business risks so as management approves for more hiring and more devices they should have a mindset of sitting down with IT to understand the risks that may come with that."

N11: "Often times Leadership and Management perceive cybersecurity as an isolated IT function that they wash their hands off and just wait for reports, which can come in with bad news. They need to allow for any cybersecurity strategy to be drawn from the onset with them around the same table with IT."

N4: "Looking at the current landscape here, they don't play a role, which they should. For example, we have an IT director. When they start talking about cybersecurity, they all think about the physical security, but in terms of education, they don't do the education part. It's very critical for them to be playing that role in terms of protecting ... even including education. If, right now, today, you show them a security loophole on their system, what do they do?"…" They don't try to understand, and they don't follow any particular standards."

Sub-question 4: Who do you feel is responsible in an organizational setting for the increasing rate of observed cybersecurity threats?

N11: "Everyone from bottom-up, but surely IT and Management should be the main patrons of cybersecurity."

N5: "In this instance, it's us. Because… our IT security managers are trying to catch up. They've just being put there because they have more than 10 years or 15 years of experience with IT infrastructures. So, they're trying to catch up. We are the foot soldiers on the ground who are supposed to feed them with the real thing."

N9: "I would say untrained employees".." Those that are not tech savvy, that are not made aware of certain threats."

Sub-question 5: How important do you feel is the protection of supply chain and logistics?

N4: "It's critical. Looking at the fact that we are becoming more digital, and especially the IoT concept, we are buying those devices from different countries, so they need to be checked before they go into a country."

N7: "I would say it is very paramount to protect the supply chain and logistics of any organization. Take me, for example. I work in a hospital. So if we do not protect the supply chain and logistics, it could mean dire consequences for the organization. It's very key to make sure that this field is secure as much as possible to protect the organization and to protect the organization's resources, not just what they're procuring, but the people actually working in that department or that field as well."

Sub-question 6: What measures would you say could improve cybersecurity in supply chain and logistics?

N11: "Have a clearly written strategy; often companies say they are cybersecurity aware as they go about doing supply chain and logistics activities but if you ask for a copy of their latest risk management document (which should include cybersecurity) then finger pointing starts and no one wants to own to it."

N4: "I think the first one would be policy implementation. There needs to be a policy against that, and then after the policy being developed, we need to have the processes towards that. Maybe, for example, it's a device or software. What processes should you go through? Then we do the implementation of those processes. There needs to be that policy, processes, and then people need to be trained to actually facilitate that."

N6: "I think regular audits. I think companies that are getting services from this third parties should have access to those companies audit findings. If it's possible have their own audit being performed and have it written return down in a service level agreement that this is what we expect from you in a cybersecurity type of way."

N10: "For us in our country, I think the main idea or issue that can improve cyber security either in the supply chain or generally is to just start learning about it more."

N12: "For starters, I think education, like teaching people about the cyber security threats, how to protect themselves. If maybe they feel they are threatened somehow, what they can do and what they shouldn't do. First of all, that should be the first step, education, because knowledge is power."

Sub-question 7: In what ways do you collaborate with your organization's supply chain / logistics team?

N12: "We work together to achieve transparency and to promote ethical standards, and also to encourage our employees or our supply chain department to adapt change. Because with cyber, you have to always make sure that you upgrade or you tighten your security all the time."

Sub-question 8: How would you describe the stance of your organization's management and leadership on the importance of securing against threats on the supply chain and logistics?

N4: "Honestly, if I'm to talk to the management and propose this, I don't think it would be something that would be taken seriously…Nothing will happen, no effect at the moment, no effect."

N10: "Now it's one of the most important things to them because COVID has forced a lot of people to change how they've been working. Previously, it wasn't really a top priority. Now it's important to have cyber security and protection against threats in all the departments in the organization. So I think now it has changed and it has its top priority to the management."

N14: "I think it's still goes back to not a high enough priority and it's very basic so the stance is not very established. I think if I was to think about it, all of the different companies and entities that we interface with, I don't think any of them have a specific focus on protection of cybersecurity or protection of assets from cybersecurity threats specifically around logistics and supply chain. The logistics and supply chain sector in itself in Botswana is primarily made out of very low level organizations, not technologically advanced."

Sub-question 9: Who's responsible for logistics and specifically supply chain accountability in your organization?

N15: "So this would be all the key parties I've talked about. You'd have your procurement who even start drafting the contract itself, sorry, the tender itself. And then you'd have your legal guys and then you'd have your IT and security. Of course they'd be overseen by a management committee, maybe with finance here and other guys, but those are your major three that take part."

Sub-question 10: Would you feel that the reliability of the internet has an effect on the security of supply chain? If yes, in what way?

N5: "Yeah. It has affected mostly, because technology is not quite used here in this country. People prefer manual systems, so they struggle a lot. Some, they end up avoiding to purchase some things online, due to the fear that they can be scammed, or technophobia. Yeah, they're afraid of new changes."

N10: "So pre-COVID the answer would have been no, because 90% of the things that happen in organizations in Botswana are not related to anything in the internet. They were all manual. It was all paper, so it was impossible to say there would be any cyber security threats to it then, because everything was done manually. Post-COVID now, because people had to work from home and organizations had to start relying on the internet, the answer would be yes. It's a new thing to us now to rely on the internet and all."

Sub-question 11: Would you feel that the reliability of the electrical grid has an effect on the security of supply chain? If yes, in what way?

N5: "Yeah. The reliability of electricity in this country is bad, because not all organizations have backup generators, but we can just go on a blackout for eight hours, from early morning, around 8:00 AM, up until 7:00 PM. Yeah, but some organizations, they rely on some backup, they have backup generators. Botswana is a developing country. It is a small country that doesn't have much resources. So, the absence of electricity, of course, it will affect."

Sub-question 12: Would you feel that the reliability of infrastructure in general has an effect on the security of supply chain? If yes, in what way?

N14: "Yes, absolutely. Absolutely. So, the rest, yeah, so everything from road infrastructure to water infrastructure, to sanitization, to the general working and living environments, has a direct impact on logistics and supply chain and the movements of goods locally, nationally, regionally, right? If you have poor infrastructure, your goods cost more to move around, they also take a lot longer, that has a negative impact on any sector."

Sub-question 13: Is there a government regulation or policy that serves as your guideline? What is the government regulation or policy that you follow?

N7: "Right now I would say there's not really a government regulation policy as it pertains to cyber security. Cyber security is uncharted waters in this country. So even the top people in government need to be educated about cyber security. They need to be shown the importance of actually learning and investing more into cyber security, especially today. So apparently organizations just function as they see fit. We copy organizations from overseas. We do read online, but as a nation, we don't really have a solid policy that actually speaks to cyber security."

N12: "Not quite. We come up with our own regulations and policies that we have to follow, not necessarily that they come from government."

FUTURE RESEARCH DIRECTIONS

The researcher structured the research questions so that they could investigate the focused phenomenon. The foundation has been established, and future research is necessary. The intention for the next steps is to analyze the collected data appropriately as phenomenological studies dictate it.

The researcher aim to continue the research activities in the southern African region and utilize the study in Botswana as a template. After more studies are completed within countries of the southern African region, the author aims to conduct a comparative analysis. This way, they can identify potential patterns and what the differences are between the researched countries.

Ultimately, the author aims to develop a framework that developing nations in the African continent can implement for the protection of their supply chain and logistics through appropriate leadership and technological practices.

CONCLUSION

With the alarming increase in supply chain cyber-attacks, further efforts must be made to secure against such threats. In the context of developing nations, supply chain attacks have the potential to disrupt efforts toward digital transformation and economic prosperity. In this paper, the researcher outlined an ongoing qualitative study to investigate the perceived leadership effect on supply chain cyber security in Botswana. The author presented the foundation of the study but also allowed for a glimpse of the living phenomenon through the eyes of the research population. The steps towards the completion of the study are planned to be completed within a subsequent publication. The researcher aims to fill in the literature gap on the explored topic and proceed with additional research as described within the "future research directions" section.

CONFLICT OF INTEREST STATEMENT

The research item does not represent the views of the U.S. Government, Department of State, or any other U.S. Government agency. The views and work presented within this item strictly represent the author's academic work.

REFERENCES

Accenture. (2021). *Threats Unmasked Cyber Threat Intelligence Report* (No. 2). Accenture. https://www.accenture.com/_acnmedia/PDF-173/Accenture-Cyber-Threat-Intelligence-Report-Vol-2.pdf#zoom=40

Alicke, K., Rachor, J., & Seyfert, A. (2016, October 27). *Supply Chain 4.0 – the next-generation digital supply chain | McKinsey*. McKinsey & Company. https://www.mckinsey.com/business-functions/operations/our-insights/supply-chain-40--the-next-generation-digital-supply-chain

Boyens, J. M., Paulsen, C., Moorthy, R., & Bartol, N. (2015). *Supply Chain Risk Management Practices for Federal Information Systems and Organizations (NIST SP 800-161; p. NIST SP 800-161)*. National Institute of Standards and Technology. doi:10.6028/NIST.SP.800-161

Central Intelligence Agency. (2022). Botswana. In *The World Factbook*. Central Intelligence Agency. https://www.cia.gov/the-world-factbook/countries/botswana/

Cheung, K.-F., Bell, M. G. H., & Bhattacharjya, J. (2021). Cybersecurity in logistics and supply chain management: An overview and future research directions. *Transportation Research Part E, Logistics and Transportation Review*, *146*, 102217. doi:10.1016/j.tre.2020.102217

Creswell, J. W., & Creswell, J. D. (2018). *Research design: Qualitative, quantitative, and mixed methods approaches* (5th ed.). SAGE.

Cybersecurity & Infrastructure Security Agency. (2021). *Joint Statement by the Federal Bureau of Investigation (FBI), the Cybersecurity and Infrastructure Security Agency (CISA), the Office of the Director of National Intelligence (ODNI), and the National Security Agency (NSA)*. CISA. https://www.cisa.gov/news/2021/01/05/joint-statement-federal-bureau-investigation-fbi-cybersecurity-and-infrastructure

Dawson, M. (2021). Cybersecurity Impacts for Artificial Intelligence use within Industry 4.0. *Science Bulletin*, *26*(1), 24–31. doi:10.2478/bsaft-2021-0003

Dawson, M., Bacius, R., Gouveia, L. B., & Vassilakos, A. (2021). Understanding the Challenge of Cybersecurity in Critical Infrastructure Sectors. *Land Forces Academy Review*, *26*(1), 69–75. doi:10.2478/raft-2021-0011

Deloitte. (n.d.). *Risk management in the supply chain*. Deloitte. https://www2.deloitte.com/us/en/pages/risk/articles/risk-management-in-supply-chain.html

ENISA. (2021). *Enisa threat landscape 2021*. European Union Agency For Cybersecurity. https://www.cde.ual.es/wp-content/uploads/2021/11/TPAE21293ENN.en_.pdf

Ferreira, A., & Cruz-Correia, R. (2021). Covid-19 and cybersecurity: Finally, an opportunity to disrupt? *JMIRx Med*, *2*(2), e21069. doi:10.2196/21069 PMID:34032816

Fortinet. (2022). *Supply chain attacks: Examples and countermeasures*. Fortinet. https://www.fortinet.com/resources/cyberglossary/supply-chain-attacks

Ghadge, A., Weiß, M., Caldwell, N. D., & Wilding, R. (2019). Managing cyber risk in supply chains: A review and research agenda. *Supply Chain Management*, *25*(2), 223–240. doi:10.1108/SCM-10-2018-0357

Handfield, R. (2021, August 19). What is supply chain management (Scm)? *Supply Chain Resource Cooperative*. https://scm.ncsu.edu/scm-articles/article/what-is-supply-chain-management-scm

IBM. (n.d.). *What is supply chain management?* IBM. https://www.ibm.com/topics/supply-chain-management

Khan, O., & Estay, D. A. S. (2015). Supply Chain Cyber-Resilience: Creating an Agenda for Future Research. *Technology Innovation Management Review*, 8. doi:10.22215/timreview/885

McAfee Center for Strategic and International Studies. (2014). *Net losses: Estimating the global cost of cyber-crime.* CSIS. https://csis-website-prod.s3.amazonaws.com/s3fs-public/legacy_files/files/attachments/140609_rp_economic_impact_cybercrime_report.pdf

Proofpoint. (2022). *What is a supply chain attack? - Definition, examples & more | proofpoint us*. Proofpoint. https://www.proofpoint.com/us/threat-reference/supply-chain-attack

Qualitative data analysis software. (n.d.). nvivo. https://www.qsrinternational.com/nvivo-qualitative-data-analysis-software/home

SAP. (2022). *What is industry 4.0?* SAP. https://www.sap.com/insights/what-is-industry-4-0.html

Symantec. (2016). *Cyber Security Trends and Government Responses in Africa*. Symantec.

Terrell, S. R. (2016). Writing a proposal for your dissertation: Guidelines and examples. *The Guilford Press*.

World Health Organization. (2022). *Coronavirus disease (COVID-19)*. WHO. https://www.who.int/health-topics/coronavirus

Compilation of References

Caglayan, A., Horsanali, M. O., Kocadurdu, K., Ismailoglu, E., & Guneyli, S. (2022). Deep learning model-assisted detection of kidney stones on computed tomography. *International Braz J Urol*, *48*(5), 830–839. doi:10.15901677-5538.ibju.2022.0132 PMID:35838509

Chaiyarit, S., & Thongboonkerd, V. (2020). Mitochondrial dysfunction and kidney stone disease. *Frontiers in Physiology*, *11*, 566506. doi:10.3389/fphys.2020.566506 PMID:33192563

Cui, Y., Sun, Z., Ma, S., Liu, W., Wang, X., Zhang, X., & Wang, X. (2021). Automatic detection and scoring of kidney stones on noncontrast C.T. images using STONE nephrolithometry: Combined deep learning and thresholding methods. *Molecular Imaging & Biology*, *23*(3), 436–445. doi:10.100711307-020-01554-0 PMID:33108801

De Perrot, T., Hofmeister, J., Burgermeister, S., Martin, S. P., Feutry, G., Klein, J., & Montet, X. (2019). Differentiating kidney stones from phleboliths in unenhanced low-dose computed tomography using radiomics and machine learning. *European Radiology*, *29*(9), 4776–4782. doi:10.100700330-019-6004-7 PMID:30747299

Elton, D. C., Turkbey, E. B., Pickhardt, P. J., & Summers, R. M. (2022). A deep learning system for automated kidney stone detection and volumetric segmentation on noncontrast C.T. scans. *Medical Physics*, *49*(4), 2545–2554. doi:10.1002/mp.15518 PMID:35156216

Fitri, L. A., Haryanto, F., Arimura, H., YunHao, C., Ninomiya, K., Nakano, R., Haekal, M., Warty, Y., & Fauzi, U. (2020). Automated classification of urinary stones based on microcomputed tomography images using convolutional neural network. *Physica Medica*, *78*, 201–208. doi:10.1016/j.ejmp.2020.09.007 PMID:33039971

Flores-Araiza, D., ... (2022). Interpretable deep learning classifier by detection of prototypical parts on kidney stones images. arXiv preprint arXiv:2206.00252.

Gharaibeh, M., Alzu'bi, D., Abdullah, M., Hmeidi, I., Al Nasar, M. R., Abualigah, L., & Gandomi, A. H. (2022). Radiology imaging scans for early diagnosis of kidney tumors: A review of data analytics-based machine learning and deep learning approaches. *Big Data and Cognitive Computing*, *6*(1), 29. doi:10.3390/bdcc6010029

Große Hokamp, N., Lennartz, S., Salem, J., Pinto dos Santos, D., Heidenreich, A., Maintz, D., & Haneder, S. (2020). Dose independent characterization of renal stones by means of dual energy computed tomography and machine learning: An ex-vivo study. *European Radiology*, *30*(3), 1397–1404. doi:10.100700330-019-06455-7 PMID:31773296

Haq, I., Ullah, N., Mazhar, T., Malik, M. A., & Bano, I. (2022). A Novel Brain Tumor Detection and Coloring Technique from 2D M.R.I. Images. *Applied Sciences (Basel, Switzerland)*, *12*(11), 5744. doi:10.3390/app12115744

Abdelrahman, A., & Viriri, S. (2022). Kidney Tumor Semantic Segmentation Using Deep Learning: A Survey of State-of-the-Art. *Journal of Imaging*, *8*(3), 55. doi:10.3390/jimaging8030055 PMID:35324610

Haq, I., Mazhar, T., Malik, M. A., Kamal, M. M., Ullah, I., Kim, T., Hamdi, M., & Hamam, H. (2022). Lung Nodules Localization and Report Analysis from Computerized Tomography (C.T.) Scan Using a Novel Machine Learning Approach. *Applied Sciences (Basel, Switzerland)*, *12*(24), 12614. doi:10.3390/app122412614

Hou, X., et al. (2019). Cascaded semantic segmentation for kidney and tumor.

Howles, S. A., & Thakker, R. V. (2020). Genetics of kidney stone disease. *Nature Reviews. Urology*, *17*(7), 407–421. doi:10.103841585-020-0332-x PMID:32533118

Iftikhar, H., Khan, M., Khan, Z., Khan, F., Alshanbari, H. M., & Ahmad, Z. (2023). A Comparative Analysis of Machine Learning Models: A Case Study in Predicting Chronic Kidney Disease. *Sustainability (Basel)*, *15*(3), 2754. doi:10.3390u15032754

Isensee, F., & Maier-Hein, K. H. (2019). An attempt at beating the 3D U-Net. arXiv preprint arXiv:1908.02182. doi:10.24926/548719.001

Jendeberg, J., Thunberg, P., & Lidén, M. (2021). Differentiation of distal ureteral stones and pelvic phleboliths using a convolutional neural network. *Urolithiasis*, *49*(1), 41–49. doi:10.100700240-020-01180-z PMID:32107579

Jeong, J., Chang, K., Lee, J., & Choi, J. (2022). A warning system for urolithiasis via retrograde intrarenal surgery using machine learning: An experimental study. *BMC Urology*, *22*(1), 80. doi:10.118612894-022-01032-5 PMID:35668401

Khamparia, A., & Pandey, B. (2020). A novel integrated principal component analysis and support vector machines-based diagnostic system for detection of chronic kidney disease. *International Journal of Data Analysis Techniques and Strategies*, *12*(2), 99–113. doi:10.1504/IJDATS.2020.106641

E. M. (@socialworkplace) O., & (@socialworkplace), E. M. (2023, February 25). *How the ethical work climate of your organization can impact employee performance - connected trifecta.* Connected Trifecta - Where people, content and technology are a winning combination. https://connectedtrifecta.com/2021/10/how-the-ethical-work-climate-of-your-organization-can-impact-employee-performance/

Längkvist, M., Jendeberg, J., Thunberg, P., Loutfi, A., & Lidén, M. (2018). Computer aided detection of ureteral stones in thin slice computed tomography volumes using Convolutional Neural Networks. *Computers in Biology and Medicine*, *97*, 153–160. doi:10.1016/j.compbiomed.2018.04.021 PMID:29730498

Linehan, W. M. (2012). Genetic basis of kidney cancer: Role of genomics for the development of disease-based therapeutics. *Genome Research*, *22*(11), 2089–2100. doi:10.1101/gr.131110.111 PMID:23038766

Aminsharifi, A., Irani, D., Pooyesh, S., Parvin, H., Dehghani, S., Yousofi, K., Fazel, E., & Zibaie, F. (2017). Artificial neural network system to predict the postoperative outcome of percutaneous nephrolithotomy. *Journal of Endourology*, *31*(5), 461–467. doi:10.1089/end.2016.0791 PMID:28287830

Ma, F., Sun, T., Liu, L., & Jing, H. (2020). Detection and diagnosis of chronic kidney disease using deep learning-based heterogeneous modified artificial neural network. *Future Generation Computer Systems*, *111*, 17–26. doi:10.1016/j.future.2020.04.036

Mazhar, T., & … . (2023). The role of machine learning and deep learning approaches for the detection of skin cancer. *Health Care*, *12*(3), 269. PMID:36766989

Mazhar, T., Nasir, Q., Haq, I., Kamal, M. M., Ullah, I., Kim, T., Mohamed, H. G., & Alwadai, N. (2022). A Novel Expert System for the Diagnosis and Treatment of Heart Disease. *Electronics (Basel)*, *11*(23), 3989. doi:10.3390/electronics11233989

Mu, G., et al. (2019). Segmentation of kidney tumor by multi-resolution vb-nets.

Ochoa-Ruiz, G., ... (2022). On the in vivo recognition of kidney stones using machine learning. arXiv preprint arXiv:2201.08865.

Parakh, A., Lee, H., Lee, J. H., Eisner, B. H., Sahani, D. V., & Do, S. (2019). Urinary stone detection on C.T. images using deep convolutional neural networks: Evaluation of model performance and generalization. *Radiology. Artificial Intelligence*, *1*(4), e180066. doi:10.1148/ryai.2019180066 PMID:33937795

Phyu, T. N. (2009). Survey of classification techniques in data mining. In *Proceedings of the international multiconference of engineers and computer scientists*.

Poore, W., & .... (2020). Obesity and its impact on kidney stone formation. *Reviews in Urology*, *22*(1), 17. PMID:32523467

Rizzo, A., Racca, M., Dall'Armellina, S., Rescigno, P., Banna, G. L., Albano, D., Dondi, F., Bertagna, F., Annunziata, S., & Treglia, G. (2023). The Emerging Role of PET/CT with PSMA-Targeting Radiopharmaceuticals in Clear Cell Renal Cancer: An Updated Systematic Review. *Cancers (Basel)*, *15*(2), 355. doi:10.3390/cancers15020355 PMID:36672305

Salazar, L. H. A., Leithardt, V. R. Q., Parreira, W. D., da Rocha Fernandes, A. M., Barbosa, J. L. V., & Correia, S. D. (2022). Application of machine learning techniques to predict a patient's no-show in the healthcare sector. *Future Internet*, *14*(1), 3. doi:10.3390/fi14010003

Ang, A. J., Sharma, A. A., & Sharma, A. (2020). Nephrolithiasis: Approach to diagnosis and management. *Indian Journal of Pediatrics*, *87*(9), 716–725. doi:10.100712098-020-03424-7 PMID:32794099

Salazar, L. H., & .... (2020). Using different models of machine learning to predict attendance at medical appointments. *Journal of Information Systems Engineering & Management*, *5*(4), em0122. doi:10.29333/jisem/8430

Schena, F. P., Anelli, V. W., Trotta, J., Di Noia, T., Manno, C., Tripepi, G., D'Arrigo, G., Chesnaye, N. C., Russo, M. L., Stangou, M., Papagianni, A., Zoccali, C., Tesar, V., Coppo, R., Tesar, V., Maixnerova, D., Lundberg, S., Gesualdo, L., Emma, F., ... Cangemi, C. (2021). Development and testing of an artificial intelligence tool for predicting end-stage kidney disease in patients with immunoglobulin A nephropathy. *Kidney International*, *99*(5), 1179–1188. doi:10.1016/j.kint.2020.07.046 PMID:32889014

Shabaniyan, T., Parsaei, H., Aminsharifi, A., Movahedi, M. M., Jahromi, A. T., Pouyesh, S., & Parvin, H. (2019). An artificial intelligence-based clinical decision support system for large kidney stone treatment. *Australasian Physical & Engineering Sciences in Medicine*, *42*(3), 771–779. doi:10.100713246-019-00780-3 PMID:31332724

Siener, R. (2021). Nutrition and kidney stone disease. *Nutrients*, *13*(6), 1917. doi:10.3390/nu13061917 PMID:34204863

Singh, N. P., Bapi, R. S., & Vinod, P. (2018). Machine learning models to predict the progression from early to late stages of papillary renal cell carcinoma. *Computers in Biology and Medicine*, *100*, 92–99. doi:10.1016/j.compbiomed.2018.06.030 PMID:29990647

Terry, R. S., Whelan, P. S., & Lipkin, M. E. (2020). New devices for kidney stone management. *Current Opinion in Urology*, *30*(2), 144–148. doi:10.1097/MOU.0000000000000710 PMID:31895890

Thongprayoon, C., Krambeck, A. E., & Rule, A. D. (2020). Determining the true burden of kidney stone disease. *Nature Reviews. Nephrology*, *16*(12), 736–746. doi:10.103841581-020-0320-7 PMID:32753740

Uribarri, J. (2020). Chronic kidney disease and kidney stones. *Current Opinion in Nephrology and Hypertension*, *29*(2), 237–242. doi:10.1097/MNH.0000000000000582 PMID:31972597

Wang, Z., Zhang, Y., Zhang, J., Deng, Q., & Liang, H. (2021). Recent advances on the mechanisms of kidney stone formation. *International Journal of Molecular Medicine*, *48*(2), 1–10. doi:10.3892/ijmm.2021.4982 PMID:34132361

Yang, S. W., Hyon, Y. K., Na, H. S., Jin, L., Lee, J. G., Park, J. M., Lee, J. Y., Shin, J. H., Lim, J. S., Na, Y. G., Jeon, K., Ha, T., Kim, J., & Song, K. H. (2020). Machine learning prediction of stone-free success in patients with urinary stone after treatment of shock wave lithotripsy. *BMC Urology*, *20*(1), 1–8. doi:10.118612894-020-00662-x PMID:32620102

Awad, A. I., & Hassaballah, M. (2016). *Image feature detectors and descriptors. Studies in Computational Intelligence*. Springer International Publishing. doi:10.1007/978-3-319-28854-3

Yildirim, K., Bozdag, P. G., Talo, M., Yildirim, O., Karabatak, M., & Acharya, U. R. (2021). Deep learning model for automated kidney stone detection using coronal C.T. images. *Computers in Biology and Medicine*, *135*, 104569. doi:10.1016/j.compbiomed.2021.104569 PMID:34157470

Zhang, H. (2018). Chronic kidney disease survival prediction with artificial neural networks. In *2018 IEEE International Conference on Bioinformatics and Biomedicine (BIBM)* (pp. 1639-1642). 10.1109/BIBM.2018.8621294

Zhao, C. (2023). Development of a Convolutional Neural Network for Automated Detection of Kidney Stones on Computed Tomography Images. *Journal of Digital Imaging*, •••, 1–9.

Zheng, S. (2020). Kidney stone detection on CT images using deep learning with convolutional neural network. *Journal of Medical Imaging and Health Informatics*, *10*(10), 2195–2201.

Bell, J. (2022). What is machine learning? Machine Learning and the City: Applications in Architecture and Urban Design, 207-216.

Bennett, C. C. (2018). Artificial intelligence for diabetes case management: the intersection of physical and mental health. arXiv preprint arXiv:1810.03044.

Berry, M. W., Mohamed, A., & Yap, B. W. (2019). *Supervised and unsupervised learning for data science*. Springer.

Black, K. M., Law, H., Aldoukhi, A., Deng, J., & Ghani, K. R. (2020). Deep learning computer vision algorithm for detecting kidney stone composition. *BJU International*, *125*(6), 920–924. doi:10.1111/bju.15035 PMID:32045113

Brisbane, W., Bailey, M. R., & Sorensen, M. D. (2016). An overview of kidney stone imaging techniques. *Nature Reviews. Urology*, *13*(11), 654–662. doi:10.1038/nrurol.2016.154 PMID:27578040

A. M. Cope, P., Campbell, J., Mohd, B. J., & Hayajneh, T. (2018). Security Vulnerabilities in Bluetooth Technology as Used in IoT. *Journal of Sensor and Actuator Networks, 7*(3) LonzettaA10 Networks. (2020). *The State of DDoS Weapons (H2 2020).* A10 Networks. https://www.a10networks.com/wp-content/uploads/A10-EB-The-State-of-DDoS-Weapons-Report.pdf

AAMI. (2020). *Medical device cybersecurity: A guide for industry consensus standards and best practices*. Association for the Advancement of Medical Instrumentation. https://www.aami.org/docs/default-source/default-document-library/standards/medical-device-cybersecurity-guide-aami-tir97_a3-2020.pdf?sfvrsn=6

Abate, A. F., Bisogni, C., Cascone, L., Castiglione, A., Costabile, G., & Mercuri, I. (2020). Social robot interactions for social engineering: Opportunities and open issues. *2020 IEEE Intl Conf on Dependable, Autonomic and Secure Computing, Intl Conf on Pervasive Intelligence and Computing, Intl Conf on Cloud and Big Data Computing, Intl Conf on Cyber Science and Technology Congress (DASC/PiCom/CBDCom/CyberSciTech).* IEEE. 10.1109/DASC-PICom-CBDCom-CyberSciTech49142.2020.00097

Abdollahi, H., Lashkari, A. R., Sarbaz, M., Alizadeh, S., & Taghva, F. (2021). Examining the effect of transformational leadership on healthcare professionals' attitudes towards technology adoption: A structural equation modeling approach. *Health Informatics Journal*, *27*(2), 146–155.

Abdullahi, R., & Mansor, N. (2018). Fraud prevention initiatives in the Nigerian public sector: Understanding the relationship of fraud incidences and the elements of fraud triangle theory. *Journal of Financial Crime*, *25*(2), 527–544. doi:10.1108/JFC-02-2015-0008

Abdurrohman, M. F., & Kadiyono, A. L. (2019). Getting prepared: Employee readiness for changes. Referred Proceeding of the *1st International Conference on Finance, Economics, and Business (ICoFEB)*. EUDL. https://eudl.eu/pdf/10.4108/eai.12-11-2018.2288821

Abebe, N. (2015). The value of workplace wellness programs. *Employee Benefit Plan Review*, *70*(2), 7–9. https://tcsedsystem.idm.oclc.org/login?url=https://search-proquest-com.tcsedsystem.idm.oclc.org/docview/1703268946?accountid=34120

Abednego, M. R., & Dwi Handayani, N. (2019). The implementation of ERM framework in construction companies. *Journal of Engineering and Applied Sciences (Asian Research Publishing Network)*, *14*(2), 450–454.

Abiwinanda, N., Hanif, M., Hesaputra, S. T., Handayani, A., & Mengko, T. R. (2019). Brain tumor classification using convolutional neural network. *IFMBE Proceedings*, *68*(1), 183–189. doi:10.1007/978-981-10-9035-6_33

Abrahamson, E. (2004). Managing Change in a World of Excessive Change: Counterbalancing Creative Destruction and Creative Recombination. *Ivey Business Journal*. https://iveybusinessjournal.com/publication/managing-change-in-a-world-of-excessive-change-counterbalancing-creative-destruction-and-creative-recombination/

Abukari, A. M., & Bankas, E. K. (2020). Some cyber security hygienic protocols for teleworkers in COVID-19 pandemic period and beyond. *International Journal of Scientific and Engineering Research*, *11*(4), 1401–1407.

Abulencia, J. (2021). The cost of cybercrime in the US healthcare sector. *Computer Fraud & Security*, *2021*(11), 8–13. doi:10.1016/S1361-3723(21)00117-2

Accenture. (2021). *Threats Unmasked Cyber Threat Intelligence Report* (No. 2). Accenture. https://www.accenture.com/_acnmedia/PDF-173/Accenture-Cyber-Threat-Intelligence-Report-Vol-2.pdf#zoom=40

Adelmeyer, M., & Teuteberg, F. (2018). Cloud Computing Adoption in Critical Infrastructures-Status Quo and Elements of a Research Agenda. *Proceedings of the Multikonferenz Wirtschaftsinformatik*, *2018*, 1345–1356.

Administration for Strategic Preparedness and Response. (2022). *Strengthening the supply chain and industrial base*. U.S. Department of Health and Human Services. https://aspr.hhs.gov/MCM/IBx/2022Report/Pages/Strengthening-the-Supply-Chain-and-Industrial-Base.aspx

Afesorgbor, S. K., van Bergeijk, P., & Demena, B. A. (2021). *Does COVID-19 threaten globalization?* International Institute of Social Studies (ISS). ISS working papers. General series No. 683

Afshar, P., Plataniotis, K. N., & Mohammadi, A. (2019). Capsule Networks for Brain Tumor Classification Based on MRI Images and Coarse Tumor Boundaries. ICASSP, IEEE Int. Conf. Acoust. Speech Signal Process. IEEE. 10.1109/ICASSP.2019.8683759

Agarwal, M., & Singhal, A. (2023). Fusion of pattern-based and statistical features for schizophrenia detection from EEG signals. *Medical Engineering & Physics*, *112*, 103949. doi:10.1016/j.medengphy.2023.103949 PMID:36842772

Aggarwal, P., Frédéric, M., Gonzalez, M. C., & Dutt, V. (2018). Understanding cyber situational awareness in a cyber security game involving recommendation. *International Journal of Cyber Situational Awareness*, *3*(1), 11–38. doi:10.22619/IJCSA.2018.100118

Ahlsell, L., Jalal, D., Khajavi, S. H., Jonsson, P., & Holmström, J. (2023). Additive Manufacturing of Slow-Moving Automotive Spare Parts: A Supply Chain Cost Assessment. *Journal of Manufacturing and Materials Processing*, *7*(1), 8. doi:10.3390/jmmp7010008

Ahmad, I., Ullah, I., Khan, W. U., Ur Rehman, A., Adrees, M. S., Saleem, M. Q., Cheikhrouhou, O., Hamam, H., & Shafiq, M. (2021). Efficient Algorithms for E-Healthcare to Solve Multiobject Fuse Detection Problem. *Journal of Healthcare Engineering*, *2021*, 1–16. doi:10.1155/2021/9500304

Ahmad, S., Ullah, T., Ahmad, I., AL-Sharabi, A., Ullah, K., Khan, R. A., Rasheed, S., Ullah, I., Uddin, M. N., & Ali, M. S. (2022). A Novel Hybrid Deep Learning Model for Metastatic Cancer Detection. *Computational Intelligence and Neuroscience*, *2022*, 8141530. doi:10.1155/2022/8141530 PMID:35785076

Ahmed, I. (2022). Project risk management: 10 golden rules every project manager should follow. *Project Management.* https://project-management.com/project-risk-management-10-golden-rules-every-project-manager-should-follow/#:~:text=%20Project%20Risk%20Management%3A%2010%20Golden%20Rules%20Every,If%20you%20study%20failed%20projects%2C%20you...%20More%20

Ahmim, A., Maglaras, L., Ferrag, M. A., Derdour, M., & Janicke, H. (2019). *A novel hierarchical intrusion detection system based on decision tree and rules-based models,* (pp. 228–233). IEEE. https://ieeexplore.ieee.org/xpl/conhome/8790388/proceeding.

Akbari, H., Ghofrani, S., Zakalvand, P., & Tariq Sadiq, M. (2021). Schizophrenia recognition based on the phase space dynamic of EEG signals and graphical features. *Biomedical Signal Processing and Control*, *69*, 102917. doi:10.1016/j.bspc.2021.102917

Akbolat, M., Durmuş, A. & Ünal, Ö. (2017). Örgütsel erdemliliğin personel güçlendirmeye etkisi ve otantik liderliğin aracı rolü [The effect of organizational virtuousness on employee empowerment and the mediating role of authentic leadership]. *İşletme Bilimi Dergisi, 5*(2), 71-87. doi:10.22139/jobs.322557

Ake, A., & Arcand, M. (2020). The impact of mobile health monitoring on the evolution of patient-pharmacist relationships. *International Journal of Pharmaceutical and Healthcare Marketing*, *14*(1), 1–19. doi:10.1108/IJPHM-04-2019-0030

Akman, I., & Mishra, A. (2017). Factors influencing consumer intention in social commerce adoption. *Information Technology & People (West Linn, Or.), 30*(2), 356-370. https://doi.org/ doi:10.1108/ITP-01-2016-0006

Alalwan, A. A., Dwivedi, Y. K., & Rana, N. P. (2019). Factors influencing adoption of mobile banking by Jordanian bank customers: Extending UTAUT2 with trust. *International Journal of Information Management*, *44*, 38–52. doi:10.1016/j.ijinfomgt.2018.09.017

Alavi, M., Leidner, D. E., & Kayworth, T. R. (2018). An empirical examination of the influence of organizational culture on knowledge management practices. *Journal of Management Information Systems*, *22*(3), 191–224. doi:10.2753/MIS0742-1222220307

Alazzam, H., Sharieh, A., & Sabri, K. E. (2020). A feature selection algorithm for intrusion detection system based on Pigeon Inspired Optimizer. *Expert Systems with Applications*, *148*, 113249. doi:10.1016/j.eswa.2020.113249

Albrechtsen, E., & Hovden, J. (2009). The information security digital divide between information security managers and users. *Computers & Security*, *28*(6), 476–490. doi:10.1016/j.cose.2009.01.003

Al-Dmour, R. A., Al-Dmour, H. H., Tarhini, A., & Almajali, D. (2020). Investigating the effect of transformational leadership on the adoption of digital healthcare technology. *Technological Forecasting and Social Change*, *153*, 119946.

Aldweesh, A., Derhab, A., & Ahmed, Z. E. (2020). Deep learning approaches for anomaly-based intrusion detection systems: A survey, taxonomy, and open issues. *Knowledge-Based Systems*, *189*, 105124. doi:10.1016/j.knosys.2019.105124

Alessandrini, M., Biagetti, G., Crippa, P., Falaschetti, L., Luzzi, S., & Turchetti, C. (2022). EEG-based alzheimer's disease recognition using robust-PCA and LSTM recurrent neural network. *Sensors (Basel)*, *22*(10), 3696. doi:10.339022103696 PMID:35632105

Algarni, A., Xu, Y., Chan, T., & Tian, G. (2013). *Toward understanding social engineering.*

Alicke, K., Rachor, J., & Seyfert, A. (2016, October 27). *Supply Chain 4.0 – the next-generation digital supply chain | McKinsey*. McKinsey & Company. https://www.mckinsey.com/business-functions/operations/our-insights/supply-chain-40--the-next-generation-digital-supply-chain

Ali, M. H., Jaber, M. M., Abd, S. K., Rehman, A., Awan, M. J., Damaševičius, R., & Bahaj, S. A. (2022). Threat Analysis and Distributed Denial of Service (DDoS) Attack Recognition in the Internet of Things (IoT). *Electronics (Basel)*, *11*(3), 494. doi:10.3390/electronics11030494

Aljalal, M., Aldosari, S. A., AlSharabi, K., Abdurraqeeb, A. M., & Alturki, F. A. (2022). Parkinson's disease detection from resting-state EEG signals using common spatial pattern, entropy, and Machine Learning Techniques. *Diagnostics (Basel)*, *12*(5), 1033. doi:10.3390/diagnostics12051033 PMID:35626189

Aljalal, M., Aldosari, S. A., Molinas, M., AlSharabi, K., & Alturki, F. A. (2022). Detection of parkinson's disease from EEG signals using discrete wavelet transform, different entropy measures, and Machine Learning Techniques. *Scientific Reports*, *12*(1), 22547. Advance online publication. doi:10.103841598-022-26644-7 PMID:36581646

Alkhaldi, H., Al-Sharafi, H., Al-Yafei, M. A., & Zaidan, M. (2019). The role of Kotter's 8-step model in lean management implementation in healthcare: A qualitative study. *Journal of Healthcare Leadership*, *11*, 87.

Alomar, K., Aysel, H. I., & Cai, X. (2023). Data Augmentation in Classification and Segmentation: A Survey and New Strategies. *Journal of Imaging*, *9*(2), 46. doi:10.3390/jimaging9020046 PMID:36826965

Althoff, T., Saria, S., & Vayena, E. (2021). Wearables and the internet of things for health: Collaboration is key. *Nature Reviews. Materials*, *6*(6), 389–391.

Alturki, F. A., Aljalal, M., Abdurraqeeb, A. M., Alsharabi, K., & Al-Shamma'a, A. A. (2021). Common spatial pattern technique with EEG signals for diagnosis of autism and epilepsy disorders. *IEEE Access : Practical Innovations, Open Solutions*, *9*, 24334–24349. doi:10.1109/ACCESS.2021.3056619

Alvesson, M., & Berg, P. O. (1992). *Corporate culture and organizational symbolism: An overview*. Walter de Gruyter. doi:10.1515/9783110136074

Amazon Web Services. (2023). What is Amazon S3? *AWS*. https://docs.aws.amazon.com/AmazonS3/latest/userguide/Welcome.html

American Heart Association. (2019). *Workplace Health Solutions: Guidelines for a Holistic Approach.* AHA. https://www.heart.org/-/media/files/health-topics/workplace-health/workplace-health-solutions-guidelines-for-a-holistic-approach-ucm_497722.pdf

American Hospital Association. (2021, October 12). *New report: Partnerships, mergers, and acquisitions can help hospitals, and health systems maintain patient access to care.* AHA. https://www.aha.org/press-releases/2021-10-12-new-report-partnerships-mergers-and-acquisitions-can-help-hospitals-and

American Hospital Association. (2022, September). *Rural Hospital Closures Threaten Access.* AHA. https://www.aha.org/system/files/media/file/2022/09/rural-hospital-closures-threaten-access-report.pdf

American Psychological Association. (2020). *Stress in America 2020: A National Mental Health Crisis*. APA. https://www.apa.org/news/press/releases/stress/2020/report

Amini, M., Rezaeenour, J., & Hadavandi, E. (2016). A neural network ensemble classifier for effective intrusion detection using fuzzy clustering and radial basis function networks. 3e International Journal on Artificial Intelligence Tools, 25(2). doi:10.1142/S0218213015500335

Aminikhanghahi, S., & Cook, D. J. (2018). The promises and challenges of healthcare wearable devices. *Proceedings of the IEEE*, *106*(3), 353–366.

Amini, M., Pedram, M. M., Moradi, A. R., & Ouchani, M. (2021). Diagnosis of alzheimer's disease by time-dependent power spectrum descriptors and convolutional neural network using EEG Signal. *Computational and Mathematical Methods in Medicine*, *2021*, 1–17. doi:10.1155/2021/5511922 PMID:33981355

Amiri, M., Aghaeinia, H., & Amindavar, H. R. (2023). Automatic epileptic seizure detection in EEG signals using sparse common spatial pattern and adaptive short-time fourier transform-based synchrosqueezing transform. *Biomedical Signal Processing and Control*, *79*, 104022. doi:10.1016/j.bspc.2022.104022

Amoah, C., & Pretorius, L. (2020). Evaluation of the impact of risk management on project performance in small construction firms in South Africa: The case study of construction systems. *Journal of Engineering. Design and Technology*, *18*(3), 611–634. doi:10.1108/JEDT-06-2018-0098

Amoah-Mensah, A., & Darkwa, P. (2018). Leadership Styles of Owner-Managers and Employees' Performance: The Moderating Role of Age and Experience. *Romanian Economic Business Review*, *13*(3), 47–73. http://proxymu.wrlc.org/login?url=https://www.proquest.com/scholarly-journals/leadership-styles-owner-managers-employees/docview/2224905922/se-2

Anderberg, D., Rainer, H., Wadsworth, J., & Wilson, T. (2016, November). Violence: Theory and Evidence. *Economic Journal (London)*, *126*(597), 1947–1979. doi:10.1111/ecoj.12246

Anderson, M. (2017). Key trends shaping technology in 2017. *Pew Research Center FACTANK*. https://www.pewresearch.org/fact-tank/2017/12/28/key-trends-shaping-technology-in-2017/

Andersson, M. G., Elving, J., Nordkvist, E., Urdl, M., Engblom, L., Mader, A., Altmeyer, S., Kowalczyk, J., Lahrssen-Wiederholt, M., Tuominen, P., Joutsen, S., Suomi, J., Mikkelä, A., Hinkka, N., & Kirsi-Maarit Siekkinen, H. J. van der Fels-Klerx, van den Borne, B., & Beshir, A. (2020). Communication inside risk assessment and risk management (COMRISK): Final report. *EFSA Supporting Publications, 17*(7). doi:10.2903/sp.efsa.2020.EN-1891

Andresen, H., Sasko, B., Patschan, D., Pagonas, N., & Ritter, O. (2021). Effective treatment of electrical storm by a wearable cardioverter defibrillator in a patient with severely impaired left ventricular function after myocardial infarction: A case report. *Journal of Medical Case Reports*, *15*(1), 1–7. doi:10.118613256-021-02833-2 PMID:33993888

Andronache, A. (2021). Increasing security awarenesss through lenses of cybersecurity culture. *Journal of Information Systems & Operations Management*, *15*(1).

Ani, U. P., He, H., & Tiwari, A. (2017). Review of cybersecurity issues in industrial critical infrastructure: Manufacturing in perspective. *Journal of Cyber Security Technology*, *1*(1), 32–74. doi:10.1080/23742917.2016.1252211

Annas, G. J. (2003). HIPAA Regulations—A New Era of Medical-Record Privacy? *The New England Journal of Medicine*, *348*(15), 1486–1490. doi:10.1056/NEJMlim035027 PMID:12686707

Anteby, M. (2013). *Manufacturing morals: The values of silence in business school education*. University of Chicago Press. doi:10.7208/chicago/9780226092508.001.0001

Antelmi, A., Cordasco, G., D'Ambrosio, G., De Vinco, D., & Spagnuolo, C. (2023). Experimenting with Agent-Based Model Simulation Tools. *Applied Sciences (Basel, Switzerland)*, *13*(1), 13. doi:10.3390/app13010013

Anurudran, Y., Yared, L., Comrie, C., Harrison, K., & Burke, T. (2020). Domestic violence amid COVID-19. *International Journal of Gynaecology and Obstetrics: the Official Organ of the International Federation of Gynaecology and Obstetrics*, *150*(2), 255–256. doi:10.1002/ijgo.13247 PMID:32472696

Appel, G., Neelbauer, J., & Schweidel, D. A. (2023). *Generative AI has an intellectual property problem*. HBR. https://hbr.org/2023/04/generative-ai-has-an-intellectual-property-problem

Appelbaum, S. H., Habashy, S., Malo, J. L., & Shafiq, H. (2012). Back to the future: Revisiting Kotter's 1996 change model. *Journal of Management Development*, *31*(8), 764–782. doi:10.1108/02621711211253231

Ardakani, H. A., Taghizadeh, M., & Shayegh, F. (2022). Diagnosis of autism disorder based on deep network trained by augmented EEG signals. *International Journal of Neural Systems*, *32*(11), 2250046. doi:10.1142/S0129065722500460 PMID:35997585

Ari, B., Sobahi, N., Alçin, Ö. F., Sengur, A., & Acharya, U. R. (2022). Accurate detection of autism using Douglas-Peucker algorithm, sparse coding based feature mapping and convolutional neural network techniques with EEG signals. *Computers in Biology and Medicine*, *143*, 105311. doi:10.1016/j.compbiomed.2022.105311 PMID:35158117

Armani, A. B., Petrini, M., & Santos, A. C. (2020). What are the attributes of sustainable leadership? *Revista Brasileira de Gestão de Negócios*, *22*(4), 820–835. doi:10.7819/rbgn.v22i4.4086

Armstrong, E. R., & Eisenstein, L. G. (2020). The role of organizational development in the acquisition of Hahnemann University Hospital. *Journal of Organizational Change Management*, *33*(4), 468–476.

Arnetz, B. B., Goetz, C. M., Arnetz, J. E., Sudan, S., vanSchagen, J., Piersma, K., & Reyelts, F. (2020). Enhancing healthcare efficiency to achieve the Quadruple Aim: An exploratory study. *BMC Research Notes*, *13*(1), 362. doi:10.118613104-020-05199-8 PMID:32736639

Aroganam, G., Manivannan, N., & Harrison, D. (2019). Review on wearable technology sensors used in consumer sport applications. Sensors. *Sensors (Basel)*, *19*(9), 1983. Advance online publication. doi:10.339019091983 PMID:31035333

Aslam, A. R., & Altaf, M. A. (2019). An 8 channel patient specific neuromorphic processor for the early screening of autistic children through emotion detection. *2019 IEEE International Symposium on Circuits and Systems (ISCAS)*. 10.1109/ISCAS.2019.8702738

Aslan, Z., & Akin, M. (2021). A deep learning approach in automated detection of schizophrenia using SCALOGRAM images of EEG signals. *Physical and Engineering Sciences in Medicine*, *45*(1), 83–96. doi:10.100713246-021-01083-2 PMID:34822131

Asperian Global. (2021). *Eight Steps for Winning Over DEI Skeptics*. Asperian Global. https://www.aperianglobal.com/winning-over-dei-skeptics/

Avolio, B. J., & Yammarino, F. J. (2019). Introduction to, and overview of, transformational and charismatic leadership. In Transformational and Charismatic Leadership: The Road Ahead 10th Anniversary Edition (pp. 1-17). Emerald Publishing Limited.

Avolio, B. J., Wang, D. G., & Li, M. (2018). Leadership: Recent developments and future directions. *Annual Review of Organizational Psychology and Organizational Behavior*, *5*, 133–156.

Avşar, E., & Salçin, K. (2019). Detection and classification of brain tumours from MRI images using faster R-CNN. *Teh. Glas.*, *13*(4), 337–342. . doi:10.31803/tg-20190712095507

Awan, O., El-Sayed, A. M., Alsudais, N., & Alabdulkarim, Y. (2021). Electronic Health Records (EHRs) implementation in Saudi Arabia: Benefits, challenges, and solutions. *Health Care*, *9*(2), 140. PMID:33535608

Aydemir, E., Dogan, S., Baygin, M., Ooi, C. P., Barua, P. D., Tuncer, T., & Acharya, U. R. (2022). CGP17Pat: Automated schizophrenia detection based on a cyclic group of prime order patterns using EEG signals. *Health Care*, *10*(4), 643. doi:10.3390/healthcare10040643 PMID:35455821

Ayo, F. E., Folorunso, S. O., Abayomi-Alli, A. A., Adekunle, A. O., Awotunde, J. B., & Awotunde, J. B. (2020). Network intrusion detection based on deep learning model optimized with rule-based hybrid feature selection. Information Security Journal. A Global Perspective, 29(6), 267–283. . doi:10.1080/19393555.2020.1767240

Azami, H., Moguilner, S., Penagos, H., Sarkis, R. A., Arnold, S. E., Gomperts, S. N., & Lam, A. D. (2023). EEG entropy in REM sleep as a physiologic biomarker in early clinical stages of alzheimer's disease. *Journal of Alzheimer's Disease*, *91*(4), 1557–1572. doi:10.3233/JAD-221152 PMID:36641682

Baba, M. (2012). Anthropology and Business: Influence and Interests. *Journal of Business Anthropology*, *1*(1), 20–71. doi:10.22439/jba.v1i1.3546

Bäck, A., Cakici, B., & Sundermeier, J. (2019). Accuracy of wearable heart rate monitors. *Journal of Sports Science & Medicine*, *18*(3), 527–528.

Badža, M. M., & Barjaktarović, M. C. (2020). Classification of Brain Tumors from MRI Images Using a Convolutional Neural Network. Appl. Sci., 10(6). doi:10.3390/app10061999

Baer, D. (2014). Here's why companies are desparate to hire anthrologists. *Business Insider.* https://www.businessinsider.com/heres-why-companies-aredesperatetohireanthropologists-2014-3

Baesens, B., Van Vlasselaer, V., & Verbeke, W. (2015). *Fraud Analytics Using Descriptive, Predictive, and Social Network Techniques: A Guide to Data Science for Fraud Detection (Wiley and SAS Business Series)* (1st ed.). Wiley. doi:10.1002/9781119146841

Baghai, M., Coley, S., & White, D. (1999). *The Alchemy of Growth: Practical Insights for Building the Enduring Enterprise*. Perseus Publishing.

Bahamid, R. A., Shu, I. D., Khoiry, M. A., Kassem, M. A., & Al-Sharafi, M. (2022). *The current risk management practices and knowledge in the construction industry buildings, 12*(7), 1016. doi:10.3390/buildings12071016

Baicker, K., Cutler, D., & Song, Z. (2010). Workplace wellness programs can generate savings. *Health Affairs*, *29*(2), 304–311. doi:10.1377/hlthaff.2009.0626 PMID:20075081

Bajwa, A. A., & Azim, M. (2016). Security of military supply chains: An analysis of threats, vulnerabilities and risk mitigation strategies. *International Journal of Physical Distribution & Logistics Management*, *46*(5), 537–558. doi:10.1108/IJPDLM-05-2015-0119

Baker, S. E., & Dutton, E. (2021). Sociology and anthropology of organizations: Overlapping histories, converging futures. *Annual Review of Sociology*, *47*, 17–36. doi:10.1146/annurev-soc-080220-024059

Bakker, E. A., Lee, D. C., & Sui, X. (2018). Beyond the traditional: Using wearable technology to enhance self-report in exercise and nutrition research. *American Journal of Physiology. Endocrinology and Metabolism*, *315*(6), E846–E853.

Balboni, P. E., Botsi, A., Francis, K., & Barata, M. T. (2020). *Designing Connected and Automated Vehicles around Legal and Ethical Concerns: Data Protection as a Corporate Social Responsibility*. SETN Workshops.

Balluck, J., Asturi, E., & Brockman, V. (2020). Use of the ADKAR® and CLARC ® change models to navigate staffing model changes during the COVID-19 pandemic. *Nurse leader*. https://pubmed.ncbi.nlm.nih.gov/32843885/

Baloh, J., Zhu, X., & Ward, M. M. (2017). Implementing team huddles in small rural hospitals: How does the Kotter model of change apply? *Journal of Nursing Management*, *26*(5), 571–578. doi:10.1111/jonm.12584 PMID:29250892

Bardhan, R., Byrd, T., & Boyd, J. (2022). *Workforce Management during the Time of COVID-19—Lessons Learned and Future Measures*. COVID. doi:10.3390/covid3010001

Barfield, T. (Ed.). (2000). *Diccionario de Antropología*. Siglo XXI Editores.

Barley, S. R. (1986). Technology as an occasion for structuring: Evidence from observations of CT scanners and the social order of radiology departments. *Administrative Science Quarterly*, *31*(1), 78–108. doi:10.2307/2392767 PMID:10281188

Barnett, M. L., Ray, K. N., Souza, J., Mehrotra, A., & Friedberg, M. W. (2021). Trends in telemedicine use in a large commercially insured population, 2005-2017. *Journal of the American Medical Association*, *323*(18), 1845–1847. doi:10.1001/jama.2020.23332 PMID:30480716

Barrow, J. M., Annamaraju, P., & Toney-Butler, T. J. (2022). Change management. *StatPearls Publishing LLC*. https://www.ncbi.nlm.nih.gov/books/NBK459380/

Barsh, J. (2008). Innovative management: A conversation with Gary Hamel and Lowell Bryan. (cover story). *The McKinsey Quarterly*, *1*, 24.

Bartlett, J. II, Boylan, R., & Hale, J. (2014). Executive coaching: An integrative literature review. *Journal of Human Resource and Sustainability Studies*, *2*(4), 188–195. doi:10.4236/jhrss.2014.24018

Basaldúa, M. (2005). Los empresarios de la compañía industrial cerillera de san Juan del Rio: Antropología de la industria cerillera. [Tesis de doctorado, Universidad Iberoamericana. México].

Bashshur, R. L., Howell, J. D., Krupinski, E. A., Harms, K. M., Bashshur, N., & Doarn, C. R. (2017). The empirical foundations of telemedicine interventions in primary care. *Telemedicine Journal and e-Health*, *23*(5), 342–375. doi:10.1089/tmj.2016.0045 PMID:27128779

Bass, B. M. (1985). *Leadership and performance beyond expectations*. Free Press.

Bass, B. M., & Riggio, R. E. (2020). *Transformational leadership*. Psychology Press.

Bate, S. P. (1997). Whatever happened to organizational anthropology? A review of the field of organizational ethnography and anthropological studies. *Human Relations*, *50*(9), 1147–1175. doi:10.1177/001872679705000905

Baumgartner, R. J., & Ebner, D. (2010). Corporate sustainability strategies: Sustainability profiles and maturity levels. *Sustainable Development (Bradford)*, *18*(2), 76–89. doi:10.1002d.447

Baygin, M., Dogan, S., Tuncer, T., Datta Barua, P., Faust, O., Arunkumar, N., Abdulhay, E. W., Emma Palmer, E., & Rajendra Acharya, U. (2021). Automated ASD detection using hybrid deep lightweight features extracted from EEG signals. *Computers in Biology and Medicine*, *134*, 104548. doi:10.1016/j.compbiomed.2021.104548 PMID:34119923

Baygin, M., Yaman, O., Tuncer, T., Dogan, S., Barua, P. D., & Acharya, U. R. (2021). Automated accurate schizophrenia detection system using Collatz pattern technique with EEG signals. *Biomedical Signal Processing and Control*, *70*, 102936. doi:10.1016/j.bspc.2021.102936

Beauchamp, T. L., & Childress, J. F. (2001). *Principles of Biomedical Ethics* (5th ed.). Oxford University Press.

Beaudan, E. (2006). Making Change Last: How to get beyond Change Fatigue. *Ivey Business Journal*. https://iveybusinessjournal.com/publication/making-change-last-how-to-get-beyond-change-fatigue/

Beaudan, E., & Smith, G. (2000). Corporate Culture: Asset or Liability. *Ivey Business Journal*. https://iveybusinessjournal.com/publication/corporate-culture-asset-or-liability/

Bechky, B. A. (2003). Sharing meaning across occupational communities: The transformation of understanding on a production floor. *Organization Science*, *14*(3), 312–330. doi:10.1287/orsc.14.3.312.15162

Beck, N., Brüderl, J., & Woywode, M. (2008). Momentum or deceleration? Theoretical and methodological reflections on the analysis of organizational change. *Academy of Management Journal*, *51*(3), 413–435. doi:10.5465/amj.2008.32625943

Beerannavar, C. R. (2020). The role of corporations in achieving ecological sustainability: Evaluating the environmental performance of corporations. In *Interdisciplinary Approaches to Public Policy and Sustainability* (pp. 228–247). IGI Global. https://www.igi-global.com/book/interdisciplinary-approaches-public-policy-sustainability/227626 doi:10.4018/978-1-7998-0315-7.ch011

Beinhocker, E. D. (2006). The adaptable corporation. *The McKinsey Quarterly*, *2*, 76.

Bélanger, A. et LeBlanc, M-N. (2011). *Socio-anthropologie de la culture populaire. Séminaire de Doctorat en sociologie. SOC 9004-40.* Montréal: Université du Québec à Montréal (UQÀM). [inédito].

Belzunegui-Eraso, A., & Erro-Garcés, A. (2020). Teleworking in the context of the covid-19 crisis. *Sustainability (Basel)*, *12*(9), 3662. doi:10.3390u12093662

Benavides, L. (2008). *The relationship between executive coaching and organizational performance of female executives as a predictor for organizational success.* [Doctoral dissertation, University of San Francisco, CA]. https://repository.usfca.edu/diss/194

Bennett, A., Daddario, K., & Hill, R. (2015).Shopping While Nonwhite. Racial discrimination Among Minority Consumers. *Journal of Consumer Affairs, 49*(2), 328-55.

Bennett, K. (2021). Leaders' adaptive identity development in uncertain contexts: Implications for executive coaching. *International Journal of Evidence Based Coaching and Mentoring*, *19*(2), 54–69.

Benson, V., & Mcalaney, J. (2020). *Cyber Influence and Cognitive Threats*. Academic Press.

Berg, P. O., & Faucheux, C. (1982). *The Symbolic Management of Company Cultures*. Unpublished book manuscript, INSEAD, Fontainebleau.

Bermúdez, H. L. (2017). Sociology and Anthropology in administrator training. In Forum Doctoral (pp. 27-27).

Beshears, J., Gillingham, K., Groom, B., & Jotzo, F. (2019). The Benefits and Challenges of Sustainability Leadership. *Sustainability*, *11*(11), 3168. doi:10.3390u11113130

Bevan, R. (2015). *The Changemaking Checklists: A Toolkit for Planning, Leading, and Sustaining Change*. ChangeStart Press.

Bianchi, G., Testa, F., Boiral, O., & Iraldo, F. (2022). Organizational Learning for Environmental Sustainability: Internalizing Life-Cycle Management. *Organization & Environment*, *35*(1), 103–129. doi:10.1177/1086026621998744

Bie, M., Wang, Y., & Zou, X. (2020). Transformational leadership and employees' creativity: The mediating role of psychological safety and the moderating role of leader-member exchange. *Frontiers in Psychology*, *11*, 2032. doi:10.3389/fpsyg.2020.02032

Biersteker, E., van Marrewijk, A., & Koppenjan, J. (2022). Identifying Subjective Perspectives on Managing Underground Risks at Schiphol Airport. *Project Management Journal*, *53*(2), 181–195. doi:10.1177/87569728221076092

Billauer, B. P. (2021). Health held hostage: Hospitals under cyber-attack. *The American Council on Science and Health*. https://www.acsh.org/news/2021/06/23/health-held-hostage-hospitals-under-cyber-attack-15626

Bin Tufail, A. (2021). 3D convolutional neural networks-based multiclass classification of Alzheimer's and Parkinson's diseases using PET and SPECT neuroimaging modalities. *Brain Informatics*, *8*(1), 23. doi:10.118640708-021-00144-2 PMID:34725741

Bin Tufail, A. (2021). Diagnosis of Diabetic Retinopathy through Retinal Fundus Images and 3D Convolutional Neural Networks with Limited Number of Samples. *Wireless Communications and Mobile Computing*, *2021*, 1–15. doi:10.1155/2021/6013448

Bin Tufail, A. (2022). Early-Stage Alzheimer's Disease Categorization Using PET Neuroimaging Modality and Convolutional Neural Networks in the 2D and 3D Domains. *Sensors (Basel)*, *22*(12), 4609. doi:10.339022124609 PMID:35746389

Bishop, T. F., Press, M. J., Mendelsohn, J. L., & Casalino, L. P. (2013). Electronic communication improves access, but barriers to its widespread adoption remain. *Health Affairs*, *32*(8), 1361–1367. https://proxy.cecybrary.com/login?url=https://search.proquest.com/docview/1428492209?accountid=144459. doi:10.1377/hlthaff.2012.1151 PMID:23918479

Blanford, J. (2020). *The security risks of medical-grade wearables*. Forbes Magazine.

Bloomberg Media Studios, IBM. (2020). *How Smarter Businesses Transform in an Uncertain World*. Bloomberg Media Studios, IBM. https://www.ibm.com/downloads/cas/NJL6A0YO

Bloomsburg University of Pennsylvania. (2022). *Literature review*. Bloomsberg University. https://guides.library.bloomu.edu/litreview

Blum, B. (24 Feb 2022). Cyberattacks on Cars increased by 225% in the last three years. *Innovation. Israel21c*. https://www.israel21c.org/cyberattacks-on-cars-increased-225-in-last-three-years/

Boba, & Lilley, D. (2009). Violence Against Women Act (VAWA) Funding: A Nationwide Assessment of Effects on Rape and Assault. *Violence Against Women, 15*(2), 168–185. https://doi.org/ doi:10.1177/1077801208329146

Bocetta, S. (14 Nov 2022). *The Risk of Cybersecurity Threats continues to grow for the Auto Industry*. GlobalSign by GMO. https://www.globalsign.com/en/blog/cybersecurity-threats-auto-industry

Bodolica, V., & Spraggon, M. (2018). An end-to-end process of writing and publishing influential literature review articles: Do's and don'ts. *Management Decision*, *56*(11), 2472–2486. doi:10.1108/MD-03-2018-0253

Bogue, R. (2019). Strong prospects for robots in retail. *The Industrial Robot*, *46*(3), 326–331. doi:10.1108/IR-01-2019-0023

Bo, L., Xiaochen, W., & Yue, F. (2021). Research on the functional safety of drive motor systems for the electric vehicle. *2021 International Conference on Artificial Intelligence and Electromechanical Automation (AIEA)*, (pp. 84–87). IEEE. 10.1109/AIEA53260.2021.00025

Bolek, V., Látecková, A., Romanová, A., & Korcek, F. (2016). Factors Affecting Information Security Focused on SME and Agricultural Enterprises. *AGRIS On-Line Papers in Economics and Informatics*, *8*(4), 37–50. doi:10.7160/aol.2016.080404

Bolisani, E., & Scarso, E. (2014). The place of communities of practice in knowledge management studies: A critical review. *Journal of Knowledge Management*, *18*(2), 366–381. doi:10.1108/JKM-07-2013-0277

Bolton, M. (2022). A system leverage points approach to governance for sustainable development. *Sustainability Science*, *17*(6), 2427–2457. doi:10.100711625-022-01188-x

Bonabeau, E. (2002). Agent-based modeling: Methods and techniques for simulating human systems. *Proceedings of the National Academy of Sciences of the United States of America*, *99*(suppl_3), 7280–7287. doi:10.1073/pnas.082080899 PMID:12011407

Borgolte, K., & Feamster, N. (2020). *Understanding the Performance Costs and Benefits of Privacy-focused Browser Extensions. Proceedings of The Web Conference 2020*. Association for Computing Machinery. https://doi-org.proxymu.wrlc.org/10.1145/3366423.3380292

Boroditsky, M. (2018). The Benefits of Pooling Resources for Small Businesses. *Entrepreneur.* https://www.entrepreneur.com/article/293962

Borowski-Beszta, M., & Polasik, M. (2020). Wearable devices: New quality in sports and finance. *Journal of Physical Education and Sport*, *20*(2), 1077–1084. doi:10.7752/jpes.2020.s2150

Borowski, I., & Pahl-Wostl, C. (2008). Where can social learning be improved in international river basin management in Europe? *European Environment*, *18*(4), 216–227. doi:10.1002/eet.479

Bouard, A., Burgkhardt, D., & Eckert, C. (2013). Middleware-based Security for Hyperconnected Applications in Future In-Car Networks. *ICST Transactions on Mobile Communications and Applications*, *1*(3), e7. doi:10.4108/mca.1.3.e7

Bovey, W. H., & Hede, A. (2001b). Resistance to organizational change: The role of defence mechanisms. *Journal of Managerial Psychology*, *16*(7), 534–548. doi:10.1108/EUM0000000006166

Bowles, S., & Myburgh, C. (2018). Using the ADKAR change management model to drive hand hygiene compliance. *The Journal of Hospital Infection*, *99*(2), 231–235. PMID:30359649

Boyens, J. M., Paulsen, C., Moorthy, R., & Bartol, N. (2015). *Supply Chain Risk Management Practices for Federal Information Systems and Organizations (NIST SP 800-161; p. NIST SP 800-161).* National Institute of Standards and Technology. doi:10.6028/NIST.SP.800-161

Boysen, S. M., Arya, T., & Page, L. (2021). Creating a coaching culture in a non-profit. *International Journal of Evidence Based Coaching and Mentoring*, *19*(2), 115–132.

Boysen, S., Cherry, M., Amerie, W., & Takagawa, M. (2018). Organisational coaching outcomes: A comparison of a practitioner survey and key findings from the literature. *International Journal of Evidence Based Coaching and Mentoring*, *16*(1), 159–166.

BrandJ.IsraeliA.NgweD. (2023). Using gpt for market research. SSRN 4395751.

Brand, U., & Wissen, M. (2020). Homo economicus as a dangerous fetish: A plea for the social-ecological transformation of the economy. *Environmental Politics*, *29*(5), 836–855.

Brandvoice, S. (2022, March 1). The top security threats of 2022. *Forbes.* https://www.forbes.com/sites/splunk/2022/03/01/the-top-security-threats-of-2022/?sh=6b1977512e5d

Brari, Z., & Belghith, S. (2021). A novel machine learning approach for epilepsy diagnosis using EEG signals based on Correlation Dimension. *IFAC-PapersOnLine*, *54*(17), 7–11. doi:10.1016/j.ifacol.2021.11.018

Braun, V., & Clarke, V. (2019). Reflecting on reflexive thematic analysis. *Qualitative Research in Sport, Exercise and Health*, *11*(4), 589–597. doi:10.1080/2159676X.2019.1628806

Brennan, K., Lapinski, J., Durso, C., & Sheng, J. (2020). The role of wearables in healthcare transformation. *Journal of Law, Medicine & Ethics, 48*(sup1), 67-72. doi:10.1177/1073110520953441

Brennand, C. (2017, February). *Unlocking a Federal Coaching Culture.* Association for Talent Development (ATD). https://www.td.org/Publications/Magazines/The-Public-Manager/Archives/2017/02/Unlocking-a-Federal-Coaching-Culture

Brewer, R. (2014). Advanced persistent threats: Minimising the damage. *Network Security, 2014*(4), 5–9. doi:10.1016/S1353-4858(14)70040-6

Bridges, W., & Bridges, S. (2017). *Managing Transitions (25th Anniversary Edition): Making the Most of Change* (Special edition). Da Capo Lifelong Books.

Brinkert, R. (2018). Authentic leadership: Clarifying the construct. *The Journal of Values Based Leadership, 11*(1), 1–13.

Brown-Jackson, K. (2017). *Disrupting and retooling: A model for an effective community-based telehealth program (Order No. 28144638).* ProQuest Central. (2440009177). https://www.proquest.com/dissertations-theses/disrupting-retooling-model-effective-community/docview/2440009177/se-2

Brown-Jackson, K. L. (2019). *Disrupting and retooling: a model for an effective community-based telehealth program* (Order No. 28144638). Available from ProQuest Central; ProQuest Dissertations & Theses Global; ProQuest One Academic. https://www.proquest.com/dissertations-theses/disrupting-retooling-model-effective-community/docview/2440009177/se-2

Brown-Jackson, K. (2022). Grasping cybersecurity leadership as it relates to critical infrastructure protection. [IJSEUS]. *International Journal of Smart Education and Urban Society, 13*(1), 1–14. doi:10.4018/IJSEUS.312233

Brown, R. P., Varghese, L., Sullivan, S., & Parsons, S. (2021). The impact of professional coaching on emerging leaders. *International Journal of Evidence Based Coaching and Mentoring, 19*(2), 24–37.

Brunton, M., & Matheny, J. (2009). Divergent acceptance of change in a public health organization. *Journal of Organizational Change Management, 22*(6), 600–619. doi:10.1108/09534810910997023

Brynjolfsson, E., Li, D., & Raymond, L. R. (2023). *Generative AI at Work (No. w31161).* National Bureau of Economic Research. doi:10.3386/w31161

Buchanan, B. & Patel, J. (2020). Black Lives may be the Largest movement in U.S. History. *New York Times.*

Buchanan, D., Fitzgerald, L., Ketley, D., Gollop, R., Jones, J. L., Lamont, S. S., Neath, A., & Whitby, E. (2005). No going back: A review of the literature on sustaining organizational change. *International Journal of Management Reviews, 7*(3), 189–205. doi:10.1111/j.1468-2370.2005.00111.x

Budoian, I. (2021). *Digitalization: How to Use Digital Innovation to Grow Your Business.* Digital Leadership. https://digitalleadership.com/blog/use-digital-innovation-to-grow-your-business/#:~:text=The%20following%20three%20types%20of%20digital%20innovation%20create,3%20Building%20on%20traditional%20business%20models%20and%20processes

Buhl, A., Schmidt-Keilich, M., Muster, V., Blazejewski, S., Schrader, U., Harrach, C., Schäfer, M., & Süßbauer, E. (2019). Design thinking for sustainability: Why and how design thinking can foster sustainability-oriented innovation development. *Journal of Cleaner Production, 231*, 1248–1257. doi:10.1016/j.jclepro.2019.05.259

Buil-Gil, D., Miró-Llinares, F., Moneva, A., Kemp, S., & Díaz-Castaño, N. (2020). Cybercrime and shifts in opportunities during COVID-19: A preliminary analysis in the UK. *European Societies*, 1–13.

Bulakh, V. (2017). *Online fraud economy: Characterization and defense* (M. Gupta, Ed.). Indiana University.

Bunton, R. (2017). Wearable medical devices: Where are we now and what lies ahead? *Medical Device Technology*, *28*(2), 19–21.

Burkacky, O., Deichmann, J., Klein, B., Pototsky, K., & Gundbert, S. (March 2020). *Cybersecurity in automotive*. McKinsey & Company.

Burke, A., van Stel, A., & Thurik, R. (2010). Blue Ocean vs. Five Forces. *Harvard Business Review*. https://hbr.org/2010/05/blue-ocean-vs-five-forces

Burke, W. W. (2018). *Organization change: Theory & practice* (5th ed.). SAGE.

Burns, T., Elsworth, D., Field, E., & Harris, T. (2021). *The diversity imperative in retail*. McKinsey. https://www.mckinsey.com/industries/retail/our-insights/the-diversity-imperative-in-retail

Burns, J. M. (1978). *Leadership*. Harper & Row.

Burrell, D. N., Nobles, C., Cusak, A., & Omar, M. (2022). Cybercrime and the Nature of Insider Threat Complexities in Healthcare and Biotechnology Engineering Organizations. *Journal of Crime and Criminal Behavior.*

Burrell, D. N. (2019). The impact of a top-down and bottom-up education and training approach on organizational performance. *Journal of Workplace Learning*, *31*(3), 163–175.

Burrell, D. N. (2020). Understanding the talent management intricacies of remote cybersecurity teams in covid-19 induced telework organizational ecosystems. Land *Forces. Academic Review*, *25*(3), 232–244. https://sciendo.com/article/10.2478/raft-2020-0028. doi:10.2478/raft-2020-0028

Burrell, D. N. (2021). *Cybersecurity leadership from a talent management organizational development lens* [Unpublished Exegesis]. Capitol Technology University.

Burrell, D. N., Aridi, A. S., McLester, Q., Shufutinsky, A., Nobles, C., Dawson, M., & Muller, S. R. (2021). Exploring system thinking leadership approaches to the healthcare cybersecurity environment. [IJEACH]. *International Journal of Extreme Automation and Connectivity in Healthcare*, *3*(2), 20–32. doi:10.4018/IJEACH.2021070103

Burrell, D. N., & Nobles, C. (2022). Discovering the emergence of technical sociology in human capital systems and technology-driven organizations. [IJHCITP]. *International Journal of Human Capital and Information Technology Professionals*, *13*(1), 1–15. doi:10.4018/IJHCITP.300324

Burrell, D. N., Nobles, C., Cusak, A., Omar, M., & Gillesania, L. (2022). Cybercrime and the Nature of Insider Threat Complexities in Healthcare and Biotechnology Engineering Organizations. *Journal of Crime and Criminal Behavior*, *2*(2), 131–144. doi:10.47509/JCCB.2022.v02i02.04

Burton, S. L. (2021). Artificial intelligence (AI) and augmented reality (AR): Disambiguated in the telemedicine / telehealth sphere. *Buletin Scientific, 1*(51). https://www.armyacademy.ro/buletin/bul1_2021/Art_Burton.pdf

Burton, S. L. (2022). *Cybersecurity leadership from a Telemedicine/Telehealth knowledge and organizational development examination* (Order No. 29066056). Available from ProQuest Central; ProQuest Dissertations & Theses Global. (2662752457). https://www.proquest.com/dissertations-theses/cybersecurity-leadership-telemedicine-telehealth/docview/2662752457/se-2

Burton, S. L. (2022). *Cybersecurity leadership from a telemedicine/telehealth knowledge and organizational development examination* [Doctoral dissertation, Capitol Technology University]. Capitol Technology University ProQuest Dissertations Publishing, 2022. 29066056.

Bushwick, S. (2022). *Nearly $53 billion in Federal funding could revive the U.S. computer chip industry*. Scientific American. https://www.scientificamerican.com/article/nearly-53-billion-in-federal-funding-could-revive-the-u-s-computer-chip-industry/

Businesswire. (2018). *Juniper Research: Mobile QR Code Coupon Redemptions to Surge, Surpassing 5.3 Billion by 2022*. Businesswire. https://www.businesswire.com/news/home/20180103005014/en/Juniper-Research-Mobile-QR-Code-Coupon-Redemptions

Butt, M. A., Kazanskiy, N. L., & Khonina, S. N. (2022). Revolution in flexible wearable electronics for temperature and pressure monitoring—A review. *Electronics (Basel)*, *11*(5), 716. doi:10.3390/electronics11050716

Caffarella, R. S. (2018). *Planning programs for adult learners: A practical guide*. John Wiley & Sons.

Cai, Y., Yee, G. O. M., Gu, Y. X., & Lung, C.-H. (2020). Threats to Online Advertising and Countermeasures: A Technical Survey. *Digital Threats: Research and Practice*. https://doi-org.proxymu.wrlc.org/10.1145/3374136

Cai, W., Hsu, C., Zang, Y., & Chen, B. (2022). Security and privacy protection mechanisms for medical-grade wearables. *IEEE Transactions on Mobile Computing*, *21*(6), 1366–1380.

Cameron, K. S., Bright, D., & Caza, A. (2004). Exploring the relationships between organizational virtuousness and performance. *The American Behavioral Scientist*, *47*(6), 766–790. doi:10.1177/0002764203260209

Cameron, K. S., & Quinn, R. E. (2019). *Diagnosing and changing organizational culture: Based on the competing values framework*. John Wiley & Sons.

Cao, Y., Li, S., Liu, Y., Yan, Z., Dai, Y., Yu, P. S., & Sun, L. (2023). A comprehensive survey of AI-generated content (AIGC): A history of generative AI from GAN to chatGPT. arXiv preprint arXiv:2303.04226.

Capital One. (2022). *Information on the Capital One cyber incident*. Capitol One. https://www.capitalone.com/digital/facts2019/

Carayon, P., Wetterneck, T. B., Rivera-Rodriguez, A. J., Hundt, A. S., Hoonakker, P., Holden, R., & Gurses, A. P. (2015). Human factors systems approach to healthcare quality and patient safety. *Applied Ergonomics*, *45*(1), 14–25. doi:10.1016/j.apergo.2013.04.023 PMID:23845724

Cardconnect. (2022). *The evolution of data breaches*. Connect Card. https://cardconnect.com/launchpointe/payment-trends/evolution-of-data-breaches

Carman, A. L., Vanderpool, R. C., Stradtman, L. R., & Edmiston, E. A. (2019). A change-management approach to closing care gaps in a federally qualified Health Center: A rural Kentucky case study. *Preventing Chronic Disease*, *16*, 180589. doi:10.5888/pcd16.180589 PMID:31400097

Carnavalet, X.D., & Mannan, M. (2019). Privacy and Security Risks of "Not-a-Virus" Bundled Adware: The Wajam Case. *ArXiv, abs/1905.05224.*

Caudill, W. (1958). Some Uses of Anthropology: Theoretical and Applied. *American Anthropologist New Series, 60*(4), 762-764.

Caulkins, D. D., & Ann, J. (2013). *Companion to Organizational Anthropology*. Blackwell Publishing.

Caulkins, D., & Jordan, A. T. (Eds.). (2013). *A Companion to Organizational Anthropology*. Wiley-Blackwell.

Cavico, F. J., & Mujtaba, B. G. (2010). The state of business schools, corporate governance, and moral reasoning: An empirical study of business students. *Journal of Academic and Business Ethics*, *3*, 1–22.

Çavuşoğlu, Ü. (2019). U. Çavus¸o ¨ glu, "A new hybrid approach for intrusion detec- ˘ tion using machine learning methods,". *Applied Intelligence*, *49*(7), 2735–2761. doi:10.100710489-018-01408-x

Çelik, Z. (2022). The Moderating Role of Influencer Attractiveness in the effect of Brand Love, Brand Trust, Brand Awareness, and Brand Image on Brand Loyalty. *Istanbul Ticaret Üniversitesi Sosyal Bilimler Dergisi*, *21*(43), 148–167. doi:10.46928/iticusbe.1050122

Cely-López, C. L., & Gómez-Niño, O. (2016). An anthropological perspective of organizations from sociocultural characterization, management, and social accounting. The case of a tertiary education institution. *Cuadernos de Contabilidad*, *17*(43).

Censer, M. (2011, October 30). Executive coaching contracts pick up speed. *The Washington Post.*

Center for Devices and Radiological Health. (2020, September 4). *Overview of Device Regulation*. FDA. https://www.fda.gov/medical-devices/device-advice-comprehensive-regulatory-assistance/overview-device-regulation

Center for Internet Security, (2017). *CIS Controls Implementation Guide for SMBs*. CIS.

Center for Leadership Studies. (2017). *The Cost of Poor Leadership On Your Revenue And Culture*. GBS Corporate. https://www.gbscorporate.com/blog/the-cost-of-poor-leadership-on-your-revenue-and-culture

Centers for Disease Control and Prevention [CDC]. (2023). Communication planning: Adolescent and School Health. *Author.* https://www.cdc.gov/healthyyouth/fundedprograms/1807/communication_planning.htm

Centers for Disease Control. (2023). *Fast Facts: Preventing Intimate Partner Violence*. CDC. https://www.cdc.gov/violenceprevention/intimatepartnerviolence/fastfact.html

Central Intelligence Agency. (2022). Botswana. In *The World Factbook*. Central Intelligence Agency. https://www.cia.gov/the-world-factbook/countries/botswana/

Cerezo-Espinosa de los Monteros, J., Castro-Torres, A., Gómez-Salgado, J., Fagundo-Rivera, J., Gómez-Salgado, C., & Coronado-Vázquez, V. (2021). Administration of Strategic Agreements in Public Hospitals: Considerations to Enhance the Quality and Sustainability of Mergers and Acquisitions. *International Journal of Environmental Research and Public Health*, *18*(8), 4051. doi:10.3390/ijerph18084051 PMID:33921426

Cerutti, M. (2003) Los estudios empresariales en América Latina ¿el debate interminable? *Boletín de Historia Económica*. https://www.audhe.org.uy/Boletin_Audhe/Boletin_2/Boletin_02_Cerutti.pdf

Chakrabarty, & Bass. (2015). *Comparing virtue, consequentialist, and deontological ethics-based corporate social responsibility: Mitigating microfinance risk institutional voids.* UT Miners. https://utminers.utep.edu/schakrabarty2/Chakrabarty_Bass_2015_JBE.pdf

Chang, S. M., Budhwar, P., & Crawshaw, J. (2021, April 6). *The emergence of value-based leadership behavior at the frontline of management: A role theory perspective and future research agenda*. Frontiers. https://www.frontiersin.org/articles/10.3389/fpsyg.2021.635106/full#refer1

Chang, I.-C., Wang, K.-S., & Chiu, Y.-P. (2020). Examining the factors that affect users' intentions to continue to use medical wearables. *Health Information Science and Systems*, *8*(1), 1–10. doi:10.100713755-020-00117-7 PMID:31867102

Chanlat, J. (1994). Hacia una antropología de la organización. En Gestión y política pública, 317-364, México.

Chanlat, J. F. (2019). Antropología de las organizaciones. *Revista del Centro de Estudios de Sociología del Trabajo*, (11), 17–39.

Chapanis, A., & Holstein, W. K. (2022). Human-factors engineering. *Encyclopedia Britannica*. https://www.britannica.com/topic/human-factors-engineering

Chapman, C. B., & Ward, S. (2019). *How to manage project opportunity and risk: Why uncertainty management can be a much better approach than risk management.* Routledge.

Chaudhry, S. A., Farash, M. S., Kumar, N., & Alsharif, M. H. (2020). PFLUA-DIoT: A pairing free lightweight and unlinkable user access control scheme for distributed IoT environments. *IEEE Systems Journal*, *2020*, 3036425.

Chaudhry, S. A., Kim, I. L., Rho, S., Farash, M. S., & Shon, T. (2019). An improved anonymous authentication scheme for distributed mobile cloud computing services. *Cluster Computing*, *22*(S1, no. S1), 1595–1609. doi:10.100710586-017-1088-9

ChavanS.BhattacharyaS. (2022). Study of employees' behavior during organizational change: effects of business theatre on Kübler-Ross model. Cardiometry, (22), 237-243. https://doi.org/ doi:10.18137/cardiometry.2022.22.237243

Chawla, P., Rana, S. B., Kaur, H., & Singh, K. (2022). Computer-aided diagnosis of autism spectrum disorder from EEG signals using deep learning with FAWT and multiscale permutation entropy features. *Proceedings of the Institution of Mechanical Engineers. Part H, Journal of Engineering in Medicine*, *237*(2), 282–294. doi:10.1177/09544119221141751 PMID:36515392

Chawla, P., Rana, S. B., Kaur, H., Singh, K., Yuvaraj, R., & Murugappan, M. (2023). A decision support system for automated diagnosis of parkinson's disease from EEG using FAWT and entropy features. *Biomedical Signal Processing and Control*, *79*, 104116. doi:10.1016/j.bspc.2022.104116

Cheng, J. (2017). Figshare *brain tumor dataset.* [Data set].

Cheng, J., Huang, W., Cao, S., Yang, R., Yang, W., Yun, Z., Wang, Z., & Feng, Q. (2015, October). Enhanced Performance of Brain Tumor Classification via Tumor Region Augmentation and Partition. *PLoS One*, *10*(10), e0140381. doi:10.1371/journal.pone.0140381 PMID:26447861

Chen, H., Shekhar, R., & Easton, G. (2020). Overcoming resistance to healthcare innovation. *MIT Sloan Management Review*, *61*(1), 1–10.

Chen, L., Chen, J., & Xia, C. (2022). Social network behavior and public opinion manipulation. *Journal of Information Security and Applications*, *64*, 103060. doi:10.1016/j.jisa.2021.103060

Chen, X. (2018). How does transformational leadership affect employee innovation behavior in China? The mediating role of psychological capital. *Frontiers in Psychology*, *9*, 1112. doi:10.3389/fpsyg.2018.01112

Chen, Y., & Wang, Q. (2021). Cybersecurity risk management: A comprehensive approach. *IEEE Transactions on Software Engineering*, *47*(1), 1–14. doi:10.1109/TSE.2019.2940179

Chen, Y., Wu, H., Wu, Y., & Wang, M. (2020). Medical-grade wearables and their applications in healthcare. *Sensors (Basel)*, *20*(3), 738. PMID:32013208

Cheris, A., Coffman, J., Frasier, E., & Noether, A. (2021). *Diversity, Equity, and Inclusion in Retail: Breaking Down the Task Ahead.* Bain & Company. https://www.bain.com/insights/diversity-equity-and-inclusion-in-retail-breaking-down-the-task-ahead-infographic/

Cherrier, H., & Türe, M. (2022). Blame work and the scapegoating mechanism in market status-quo. *Journal of Business Research*, *144*, 1207–1217. doi:10.1016/j.jbusres.2022.02.061

Cheung, K.-F., Bell, M. G. H., & Bhattacharjya, J. (2021). Cybersecurity in logistics and supply chain management: An overview and future research directions. *Transportation Research Part E, Logistics and Transportation Review*, *146*, 102217. doi:10.1016/j.tre.2020.102217

Cheung, M. L., Chau, K. Y., Sum Lam, M. H., Tse, G., Ho, K. Y., Flint, S. W., & Lee, K. Y. (2019). Examining consumers' adoption of wearable healthcare technology: The role of health attributes. *International Journal of Environmental Research and Public Health*, *16*(13), 2257. doi:10.3390/ijerph16132257 PMID:31247962

Chiba, Z., Abghour, N., Moussaid, K., El omri, A., & Rida, M. (2019). Intelligent approach to build a deep neural network based IDS for cloud environment using combination of machine learning algorithms. *Computers & Security*, *86*, 291–317. doi:10.1016/j.cose.2019.06.013

Chmielewska, M., Stokwiszewski, J., Markowska, J., & Hermanowski, T. (2022, January 2). *Evaluating organizational performance of public hospitals using the McKinsey 7-S framework - BMC Health Services Research*. BioMed Central. doi:10.1186/s12913-021-07402-3

Choi, Y. B., Capitan, K. E., Krause, J. S., & Streeper, M. M. (2006). Challenges Associated with Privacy in Health Care Industry: Implementation of HIPAA and the Security Rules. *Journal of Medical Systems*, *30*(1), 57–64. doi:10.100710916-006-7405-0 PMID:16548416

Cho, K., Lee, J., & Lee, K. (2021). Medical-grade wearables and remote diagnostics for healthcare. *Journal of Medical Systems*, *45*(4), 1–8. doi:10.100710916-021-01760-5

Chou, Y. H., Hsu, C. C., & Huang, W. C. (2019). Using wearable technology to improve patient outcomes. *Journal of Medical Systems*, *43*(5), 116. PMID:30905006

Christensen, C. M., Marx, M., & Stevenson, H. H. (2006). The tools of cooperation and change. *Harvard Business Review*, *84*(10), 73–80. PMID:17040041

Chu, M. (2019, June 4). *Five cyber threats the military must address*. CIO. https://www.cio.com/article/3359657/5-cyber-threats-the-military-must-address.html

Chu, C., Zhang, Z., Wang, J., Liu, S., Wang, F., Sun, Y., Han, X., Li, Z., Zhu, X., & Liu, C. (2021). Deep learning reveals personalized spatial spectral abnormalities of high delta and low alpha bands in EEG of patients with early parkinson's disease. *Journal of Neural Engineering*, *18*(6), 066036. doi:10.1088/1741-2552/ac40a0 PMID:34875634

Chung, M. K., Lee, K. Y., Lee, S. H., Han, S. J., & Kim, S. R. (2021). Use of a fitness tracker for physical activity monitoring in patients with nonalcoholic fatty liver disease: Randomized controlled trial. *Journal of Medical Internet Research*, *23*(2), e24498.

Cilliers, L. (2020). Wearable devices in healthcare: Privacy and information security issues. *The HIM Journal*, *49*(2-3), 150–156. doi:10.1177/1833358319851684 PMID:31146589

Ciporen, R. (2015). The emerging field of executive and organizational coaching: An overview. *New Directions for Adult and Continuing Education*, *2015*(148), 5–15. doi:10.1002/ace.20147

CISOMAG. (2020, January 10). 10 IoT Security Incidents That Make You Feel Less Secure. *Cyber Security Magazine*. https://cisomag.com/10-iot-security-incidents-that-make-you-feel-less-secure/

Clifton, D., & Amran, A. (2011). The stakeholder approach: A sustainability perspective. *Journal of Business Ethics*, *98*(1), 121–136. doi:10.100710551-010-0538-6

Clowes, R. (2015). Thinking in the cloud: The cognitive incorporation of cloud-based technology. *Philosophy & Technology*, *28*(2), 261–296. doi:10.100713347-014-0153-z

Cohen, B. (2020, February 5). Workload, stress, and patient safety: how human factors can help. *Institute for Healthcare Improvement.* https://www.ihi.org/communities/blogs/-workload-stress-and-patient-safety-how-human-factors-can-help

Cojocaru, C., & Cojocaru, S. (2014). Sony vs. apple - iPod launching, a case study of leadership and innovation. *Manager,* (20), 115-125. https://www.proquest.com/scholarly-journals/sony-vs-apple-ipod-launching-case-study/docview/1684617694/se-2?accountid=167615

Colicchia, C., Creazza, A., & Menachof, D. A. (2019). Managing cyber and information risks in supply chains: Insights from an exploratory analysis. *Supply Chain Management*, *24*(2), 215–240. doi:10.1108/SCM-09-2017-0289

Collier, K. (2021, May 11). Hackers release personal info of 22 DC police officers. *NBC News.* https://www.nbcnews.com/tech/security/hackers-release-personal-info-22-dc-police-officers-rcna897

Columbus, L. (June 25, 2020). Why cybersecurity is really a business problem. *Forbes*. https://www.forbes.com/sites/louiscolumbus/2020/06/25/why-cybersecurity-is-really-a-business-problem/?sh=45b2b844436c

Compin, F. (2016). Do financial criminals commit perfect crimes? *Journal of Financial Crime*, *23*(3), 624–636. doi:10.1108/JFC-03-2015-0018

Condeco. (2022). The history of wearable technology. *Condeco.*. https://www.condecosoftware.com/blog/the-history-of-wearable-technology/#:~:text=1970s,of%20the%2070s%20and%2080s

Contreras, F., Baykal, E., & Abid, G. (2020). E-leadership and teleworking in times of covid-19 and beyond: What we know and where do we go. *Frontiers in Psychology*, *11*, 590271. https://www.frontiersin.org/articles/10.3389/fpsyg.2020.590271. doi:10.3389/fpsyg.2020.590271 PMID:33362656

Cook, K. D. (2017). *Effective Cyber Security Strategies for Small Businesses* [Doctoral dissertation, Walden University].

Corera, G. (2020, May 5). Coronavirus: Cyber-spies hunt Covid-19 research, US and UK warn. *BBC News*. https://www.bbc.com/news/technology-52551023

Correia, M. S. (2019). Sustainability: An Overview of the Triple Bottom Line and Sustainability Implementation. [IJoSE]. *International Journal of Strategic Engineering*, *2*(1), 29–38. https://www.igi-global.com/article/sustainability/219322. doi:10.4018/IJoSE.2019010103

Corsín Jiménez, A. (2007). *The Anthropology of Organizations*. Ashgate Publishing Limited.

Cowie, K. (2008, May/June). The HR challenge: leadership development for ordinary heroes. *Ivey Business Journal.* https://iveybusinessjournal.com/publication/the-hr-challenge-leadership-development-for-ordinary-heroes/

Creswell, J. W. (2013). *Qualitative Inquiry and Research Design: Choosing Among Five Approaches*. Sage Publishing.

Creswell, J. W., & Creswell, J. D. (2018). *Research design: Qualitative, quantitative, and mixed methods approaches* (5th ed.). SAGE.

Cunningham, M. (2021). Transforming the science of security with human factors. *Forcepoint*. https://www.forcepoint.com/blog/x-labs/transforming-science-security-human-factors

Cutler, D. M., Baicker, K., & Song, Z. (2010, February). *Workplace wellness programs can generate savings*. Harvard. https://scholar.harvard.edu/cutler/publications/workplace-wellness-programs-can-generate-savings

Cyber Risk Institute. (2020). *The Profile is the benchmark for cyber risk assessment.* CRI. https://cyberriskinstitute.org/the-profile/

Cybersecurity & Infrastructure Security Agency. (2021). *Joint Statement by the Federal Bureau of Investigation (FBI), the Cybersecurity and Infrastructure Security Agency (CISA), the Office of the Director of National Intelligence (ODNI), and the National Security Agency (NSA).* CISA. https://www.cisa.gov/news/2021/01/05/joint-statement-federal-bureau-investigation-fbi-cybersecurity-and-infrastructure

Cybersecurity and Infrastructure Security Agency. (n.d.). *Identifying Critical Infrastructure During COVID-19.* CISA. https://www.cisa.gov/identifying-critical-infrastructure-during-covid-19

Cybersecurity is Patient Safety. (2022). US Senate Intelligence Committee. https://www.warner.senate.gov/public/_cache/files/f/5/f5020e27-d20f-49d1-b8f0-bac298f5da0b/0320658680B8F1D29C9A94895044DA31.cips-report.pdf

Cybsafe. (2022). What actually is "the human aspect of cyber security"? *CybSafe*. https://www.cybsafe.com/community/blog/what-is-human-aspect-of-cyber-security/

Czarniawska, B. (2012). Organization theory meets anthropology: A story of an encounter. *Journal of Business Anthropology*, *1*(1), 118–140. doi:10.22439/jba.v1i1.3549

D'Arcy, J., Hovav, A., & Galletta, D. (2014). User awareness of security countermeasures and its impact on information systems misuse: A deterrence approach. *Information Systems Research*, *20*(1), 79–98. doi:10.1287/isre.1070.0160

D'Mello, S., & Sharma, M. (2018). Developments in military supply chains: A review. *International Journal of Physical Distribution & Logistics Management*, *48*(2), 113–138.

Dai, C., & Wang, X. (2018). A narrative literature review of organizational change management: Trends and challenges. *International Journal of Project Management*, *36*(3), 404–421.

Dalal, R. S., Howard, D. J., Bennett, R. J., Posey, C., Zaccaro, S. J., & Brummel, B. J. (2022). Organizational science and cybersecurity: Abundant opportunities for research at the interface. *Journal of Business and Psychology*, *37*(1), 1–29. doi:10.100710869-021-09732-9 PMID:33564206

Dam, H. K., Tran, T., Grundy, J., Ghose, A., & Kamei, Y. (2019, May). Towards effective AI-powered agile project management. In *2019 IEEE/ACM, 41st international conference on software engineering: New ideas and emerging results* (ICSE-NIER) (pp. 41-44). IEEE. 10.1109/ICSE-NIER.2019.00019

Danielis, R., Scorrano, M., Alessandro, M. P., & Blasuttigh, N. (2023). Simulating the Diffusion of Residential Rooftop Photovoltaic, Battery Storage Systems and Electric Cars in Italy. An Exploratory Study Combining a Discrete Choice and Agent-Based Modelling Approach. *Energies*, *16*(1), 557. doi:10.3390/en16010557

Daramola, O. E., Abu, J. M., Daramola, L. O., & Akande, T. M. (2019). Medical Identity Fraud in Health Insurance Schemes: Creating Awareness in Nigeria. *Asian Journal of Case Reports in Medicine and Health*, *2*(1), 1–6.

Data Bridge Market Research. (2022). *What is the future market value for wearable device market?* Data Bridge Market Research. https://www.databridgemarketresearch.com/reports/global-wearable-devices-market

Davenport, T. H., & Mittal, N. (2022, November 14). How generative AI is changing creative work. hbr.org: https://hbr.org/2022/11/how-generative-ai-is-changing-creative-work

Davidson, A. (2013). John Karlin, father of human factors engineering. *University of Washington.* https://sites.uw.edu/adavid7/2013/02/10/john-karlin-father-of-human-factors-engineering/#:~:text=John%20Karlin%2C%20an%20early%20researcher,fascinating%20history%20of%20usability%20research

Davis, F. D. (1986). *A technology acceptance model for empirically testing new end-user information systems: Theory and results*. [Doctoral dissertation, Massachusetts Institute of Technology].

Davis, J. (2019a, January 31). Phishing hack breaches PHI of 23,000 Colorado patients for 3 months. *Health IT Security*. https://healthitsecurity.com/news/phishing-hack-breaches-phi-of- 23000-colorado-patients-for-3-months

Davis, J. (2021). *The need for evolved phygital: Ramping up the experience*. Marketing Tech. https://www.marketing-technews.net/news/2021/mar/15/the-need-for-evolved-phygital-ramping-up-the-experience/

Davis, F. D. (1989). Perceived usefulness, perceived ease of use, and user acceptance of information technology. *Management Information Systems Quarterly*, *13*(3), 319–340. doi:10.2307/249008

Davolt, S. (2006). Jobs that make you sane: Employees in the pink put employers in the green. *Employee Benefit News, pp. 1*, 1–1.

Dawson, M. E., Jr. (2020). Cyber warfare threats and opportunities. *Universidade Fernando Pessoa*, Porto. http://hdl.handle.net/10284/9678

Dawson, J. F. (2018). Leadership development in the digital age. *Journal of Leadership Studies*, *12*(4), 34–45.

Dawson, M. (2021). Cybersecurity Impacts for Artificial Intelligence use within Industry 4.0. *Science Bulletin*, *26*(1), 24–31. doi:10.2478/bsaft-2021-0003

Dawson, M., Bacius, R., Gouveia, L. B., & Vassilakos, A. (2021). Understanding the challenge of cybersecurity in critical infrastructure sectors. *Land Forces Academy Review, Vol XXVI, Issue*, *1*(101), 69–75. doi:10.2478/raft-2021-0011

Deal, T., & Kennedy, A. (2000). Corporate Cultures: The Rites and Rituals of Corporate Life. Revised ed. edition. Cambridge, Mass: Basic Books.

Deamer, L. (2019). Medical-grade devices vs. consumer wearables. Yole Développement. *Electronic Specifier*. https://www.electronicspecifier.com/products/wearables/medical-grade-devices-vs-consumer-wearables

DeAngelis, D. L., & Diaz, S. G. (2019). Decision-Making in Agent-Based Modeling: A Current Review and Future Prospectus. *Frontiers in Ecology and Evolution*, *6*, 237. doi:10.3389/fevo.2018.00237

Dean, M. L., & Meyer, A. A. (2002). Executive coaching: In search of a model. *Journal of Leadership Education*, *1*(2), 3–17. doi:10.12806/V1/I2/RF1

Decker, A., & Galer, D. (2013). *Enterprise Risk Management - Straight to the Point: An Implementation Guide Function by Function* (1st ed.). ERMSTTP, LLC.

Deckro, J., Phillips, T., Davis, A., Hehr, A., & Ochylski, S. (2021). Big data in the Veterans Health Administration: A nursing informatics perspective. *Journal of Nursing Scholarship*, *53*(3), 288–295. doi:10.1111/jnu.12631 PMID:33689232

Dees, W., Cianfrone, B. A., & Andrew, D. P. (2021). Show Me the Money! A Review of Current Issues in the New NIL Era. *Journal of Applied Sport Management*. doi:10.7290/jasm13bamf

Del Val, M. P., & Fuentes, C. M. (2003). Resistance to change: A literature review and empirical study. *Management Decision*.

Deloitte Digital. (2019). *The Phygital Transformation: Blending Physical and Digital Experiences*. Deloitte. https://www2.deloitte.com/content/dam/Deloitte/fr/Documents/technologies/phygital-transformation-deloitte-digital.pdf

Deloitte. (2017). *Diversity and Inclusion: The Reality Gap*. Deloitte. https://www2.deloitte.com/content/dam/Deloitte/nl/Documents/human-capital/hc-diversity-inclusion-the-reality-gap.pdf

Deloitte. (2018). *Global Human Capital Trends: The Rise of the Social Enterprise*. Deloitte. https://www2.deloitte.com/global/en/pages/about-deloitte/articles/human-capital-trends.html

Deloitte. (2018). *Positive technology: Designing work environments for digital well-being*. Deloitte. https://www2.deloitte.com/us/en/insights/focus/ behavioral-economics/negative-impact-technology-business.html# endnote-sup-2

Deloitte. (2018). *The Future of Healthcare M&A*. Deloitte. https://www2.deloitte.com/content/dam/Deloitte/us/Documents/life-sciences-health-care/us-lshc-future-of-healthcare-mergers-and-acquisitions.pdf

Deloitte. (n.d.). *Risk management in the supply chain*. Deloitte. https://www2.deloitte.com/us/en/pages/risk/articles/risk-management-in-supply-chain.html

DeMatteis. (2016). PROTECTING THE FREEDOM FOR WOMEN TO BE FREE FROM VIOLENCE: THE VIOLENCE AGAINST WOMEN ACT ENDURES. *Widener Law Review*, *22*(2), 267–270.

Dempsey, T., & Rosenquist, M. (2015). *Navigating the digital age: The definitive cybersecurity guide for directors and officers*. Caxton Business & Legal. https://www.nyse.com/publicdocs/Navigating_The_Digital_Age.pdf

Denison, D. R., Janovics, J., Young, J., & Cho, H. J. (2006). *Diagnosing Organizational Cultures: Validating a Model and Method*. Denison Consulting Group.

Department of Energy. (2022). *DOE releases first-ever comprehensive strategy to secure America's clean energy supply chain*. DoE. https://www.energy.gov/articles/doe-releases-first-ever-comprehensive-strategy-secure-americas-clean-energy-supply-chain

Department of Health and Human Services. (2020). Office on Women's Health. Retrieved from https://www.womenshealth.gov/about-us

Devia, C., Mayol-Troncoso, R., Parrini, J., Orellana, G., Ruiz, A., Maldonado, P. E., & Egana, J. I. (2019). EEG classification during scene free-viewing for schizophrenia detection. *IEEE Transactions on Neural Systems and Rehabilitation Engineering*, *27*(6), 1193–1199. doi:10.1109/TNSRE.2019.2913799 PMID:31034418

Devine, C. (2015, September 3). 307,000 veterans may have died awaiting Veterans Affairs healthcare, report says. *CNN Politics*. https://www.cnn.com/2015/09/02/politics/va-inspector-general-report/index.html

Dias, D., Borbinha, J., & Mendonça, P. (2022). Lessons from the Equifax and Capital One data breaches on social amplification of risk. *Review of Integrative Business and Economics Research*, *11*(4), 71–90. https://www.proquest.com/scholarly-journals/lessons-equifax-capital-one-data-breaches-on/docview/2681088996/se-2

Dieterich, K. R., Spath, D., & Ohlhausen, P. (2022). The Collaborative Iron Triangle: A New Tool for Supporting a Project-Culture-Aware Management in Interorganizational R&D Projects. *Proceedings of the Design Society*, *2*, 141–150. doi:10.1017/pds.2022.15

DiPietro, B. (2017). Crisis of the week: Equifax hit with massive reputation breach. *The Wall Street Journal*. https://blogs.wsj.com/riskandcompliance/2017/09/19/crisis-of-the-week-equifax-hit-with-massive-reputation-breach/

Dishman, E. (2019, August 2). FDA clears BioIntelliSense's medical wearable for remote patient monitoring. *MedCity News*. https://medcitynews.com/2019/08/fda-clears-biointellisenses-medical-wearable-for-remote-patient-monitoring/

Dogan, S., Baygin, M., Tasci, B., Loh, H. W., Barua, P. D., Tuncer, T., Tan, R.-S., & Acharya, U. R. (2022). Primate brain pattern-based Automated Alzheimer's disease detection model using EEG signals. *Cognitive Neurodynamics*. Advance online publication. doi:10.100711571-022-09859-2 PMID:37265658

Domínguez Folgueras, M. (2019). ¿Cuánto vale el trabajo doméstico en España? *Observatorio Social de La Caixa*. https://bit.ly/2Rmnhyg

Donner, H., & Steep, M. (2021). Monetizing the IoT Revolution. *Sustainability (Basel)*, *13*(4), 2195. doi:10.3390u13042195

DuBrin, A. J. (2019). *Leadership: Research findings, practice, and skills*. Cengage Learning.

Duca, I., & Gherghina, R. (2018). CSR Initiatives: An opportunity for the business environment. In *Ethics and Decision-Making for Sustainable Business Practices* (pp. 187-202). IGI Global. https://www.igi-global.com/book/corporate-social-responsibility/197763

Dunn, J., Runge, R., & Snyder, M. (2018). Wearables and the medical revolution. *Personalized Medicine*, *15*(5), 429–448. https://www.futuremedicine.com/doi/10.2217/pme-2018-0044. doi:10.2217/pme-2018-0044 PMID:30259801

Dunn, P., & Sainty, B. (2020). Professionalism in accounting: A five-factor model of ethical decision-making. *Social Responsibility Journal*, *16*(2), 255–269. doi:10.1108/SRJ-11-2017-0240

Dupont, A. (2020). Cybersecurity and small businesses: The costs of not being prepared. *Journal of Small Business and Entrepreneurship*, *33*(5), 675–689.

Durrance, B. (1997). The evolutionary vision of Dee Hock: From chaos to chaords. *Training and Development-Alexandria-American Society for Training and Development*, *51*(4), 24–31.

Dwivedi, Y. K., Kshetri, N., Hughes, L., Slade, E. L., Jeyaraj, A., Kar, A. K., Baabdullah, A. M., Koohang, A., Raghavan, V., Ahuja, M., Albanna, H., Albashrawi, M. A., Al-Busaidi, A. S., Balakrishnan, J., Barlette, Y., Basu, S., Bose, I., Brooks, L., Buhalis, D., & Wright, R. (2023). "So what if ChatGPT wrote it?" Multidisciplinary perspectives on opportunities, challenges and implications of generative conversational AI for research, practice and policy. *International Journal of Information Management*, *71*, 102642. doi:10.1016/j.ijinfomgt.2023.102642

Ebrahimi, M., Surdeanu, M., Samtani, S., & Chen, H. (2018). Detecting Cyber Threats in Non-English Dark Net Markets: A Cross-Lingual Transfer Learning Approach. *2018 IEEE International Conference on Intelligence and Security Informatics (ISI)*, 85–90. Federal Trade Commission. https://www.consumer.ftc.gov/articles/pdf-0009-taking-charge.pdf

Edelman. (2020). *Trust Barometer Special Report: Brand Trust in 2020.* Edelman. https://www.edelman.com/research/brand-trust-2020

Elkhouly, S., Ossman, M., Selim, M., & Zaghloul, M. (2014). Impact of E-leadership on leadership styles within the Egyptian government sector. *Competition Forum, 12*(1), 131-140. https://proxy.cecybrary.com/login?url=https://search.proquest.com/docview/1640568232?accountid=144459

Ellis, P. (2020). Ethical concepts: Duty-based theories. *Journal of Kidney Care*, *5*(1), 30–32. doi:10.12968/jokc.2020.5.1.30

Elmandjra, M. (2020). *Wearables in healthcare – implications and opportunities*. Matrix Global Network.

ENISA. (2021). *Enisa threat landscape 2021*. European Union Agency For Cybersecurity. https://www.cde.ual.es/wp-content/uploads/2021/11/TPAE21293ENN.en_.pdf

Epstein, M. J., & Buhovac, A. R. (2008). *Making sustainability work: Best practices in managing and measuring corporate social, environmental, and economic impacts*. Greenleaf.

Esteva Fabregat, C. (1955). *Carácter social y familia obrera en México*. [Tesis de Maestría en etnología, presentada en la Escuela de Antropología e Historia de México].

Esteva Frabegat, C. (1984). *[1973]. Antropología industrial*. Anthropos.

European Commission. (2020). *Medical Devices: Regulatory framework*. European Commission. https://ec.europa.eu/growth/sectors/medical-devices/regulatory-framework_en

European Medicines Agency. (2019). *EMA medical device guidance*. European Medicines Agency. https://www.ema.europa.eu/en/human-regulatory/overview/medical-devices

Eyal-Cohen, M., (2012). *Down sizing the little guy myth in legal definitions.*

Fagerdal, B., Lyng, H. B., Guise, V., Anderson, J. E., Thornam, P. L., & Wiig, S. (2022). Exploring the role of leaders in enabling adaptive capacity in hospital teams – a multiple case study. *BMC Health Services Research*, *22*(1), 1–17. doi:10.118612913-022-08296-5 PMID:35831857

Falcone, P. (2022, June 9). *Values-based leadership in action*. SHRM. https://www.shrm.org/resourcesandtools/hr-topics/employee-relations/pages/values-based-leadership-in-action.aspx

Fang, W., Tan, X., & Wilbur, D. (2020). Application of intrusion detection technology in network safety based on machine learning. *Safety Science*, *124*, 104604. doi:10.1016/j.ssci.2020.104604

Federal Bureau of Investigation (FBI). (2019). *What we investigate: The cyber threat*. FBI. https://www.fbi.gov/investigate/cyber

Federal Trade Commission. (2020). *How to protect your business from cybercrime*. FTC. https://www.consumer.ftc.gov/articles/how-protect-your-business-cybercrime

Fedynets, N. (2022). Change management mechanism in the organization in crisis conditions. *Acta Scientiarum Polonorum. Oeconomia*, *21*(3), 15–24. https://doi-org.captechu.idm.oclc.org/10.22630/ASPE.2022.21.3.10. doi:10.22630/ASPE.2022.21.3.10

Felgate, Y. R. (2020). Human resource management moral competencies. *SA Journal of Human Resource Management*. https:// doi:10.4102/sajhrm.v18i0.1193

Felice, W. F. (2022). 136 countries agree on a minimum global corporate tax, but Republicans say no. *Tampa Bay Times*. https://www.tampabay.com/opinion/2022/07/30/136-countries-agree-on-a-minimum-global-corporate-tax-but-republicans-say-no-column/

Felitti, V. J., Anda, R. F., Nordenberg, D., Williamson, D. F., Spitz, A. M., Edwards, V., Koss, M. P., & Marks, J. S. (1998). Relationship of childhood abuse and household dysfunction to many of the leading causes of death in adults: The Adverse Childhood Experiences (ACE) Study. *American Journal of Preventive Medicine*, *14*(4), 245–258. doi:10.1016/S0749-3797(98)00017-8 PMID:9635069

Feng, M. (2019). An overview of military logistics and supply chain management. *International Journal of Logistics Systems and Management*, *37*(1), 1–16. doi:10.1504/IJLSM.2019.103783

Fernandes, G. Jr, Rodrigues, J. J. P. C., Carvalho, L. F., Al-Muhtadi, J. F., & Proença, M. L. Jr. (2019). A comprehensive survey on network anomaly detection. *Telecommunication Systems*, *70*(3), 447–489. doi:10.100711235-018-0475-8

Ferreira de Araújo Lima, P., Marcelino-Sadaba, S., & Verbano, C. (2021). Successful implementation of project risk management in small and medium enterprises: A cross-case analysis. [Project risk management in SMEs]. *International Journal of Managing Projects in Business*, *14*(4), 1023–1045. doi:10.1108/IJMPB-06-2020-0203

Ferreira, A., & Cruz-Correia, R. (2021). Covid-19 and cybersecurity: Finally, an opportunity to disrupt? *JMIRx Med*, *2*(2), e21069. doi:10.2196/21069 PMID:34032816

Fette, J. (2019). Leading Transformational Change: Winning the Hearts and Minds. PM World. *Journal*, *8*(9), 1–8.

Figueroa, C. A., Harrison, R., Chauhan, A., & Meyer, L. (2019). Priorities and challenges for health leadership and workforce management globally: A rapid review. *BMC Health Services Research*, *19*(1), 239. doi:10.118612913-019-4080-7 PMID:31014349

Fisher, M. (2012a). *Wall Street Women*. Duke University Press, Durham, North Carolina. Fisher, M. (2012b), Toward a feminist para-ethnography on gender equality policy making in business. *Collaborative Anthropologies*, *5*. doi:10.1353/cla.2012.0009

Fisher, R., Porod, C., & Peterson, S. (2021). Motivating employees and organizations to adopt a cybersecurity-focused culture. *Journal of Organizational Psychology*, *21*(1), 114–131. https://www.proquest.com/scholarly-journals/motivating-employees-organizationsadopt/docview/2512311256/se-2?accountid=167615

Forbes. (2019). The Business Case For Health And Wellbeing In The Workplace. *Forbes*. https://www.forbes.com/sites/nazbeheshti/2019/07/09/the-business-case-for-health-and-wellbeing-in-the-workplace/?sh=68a4568c39f1

Ford, J. D., Ford, L. W., & D'Amelio, A. (2008). Resistance to change: The rest of the story. *Academy of Management Review*, *33*(2), 362–377. doi:10.5465/amr.2008.31193235

Forgerock. (2022). 2022 ForgeRock Consumer Identity Breach Report: Unauthorized access remains a top threat — It's time to render stolen passwords worthless for launching new attacks. *Forgerrock*. https://www.forgerock.com/resources/view/135321466/analyst-report/forgerock-identity-breach-report-2022.pdf

Forster-Holt, N. (2009). What makes a business" small"? *Strategic Finance*, *90*(9), 20–22.

Forster-Holt, N. (2013). Entrepreneur as" End" repreneur: The Intention to Retire. *Small Business Institute Journal*, *9*(2), 29.

Fortinet. (2022). *Supply chain attacks: Examples and countermeasures*. Fortinet. https://www.fortinet.com/resources/cyberglossary/supply-chain-attacks

Fortinet. (2022). *What is an attack vector?* Fortinet. https://www.fortinet.com/resources/cyberglossary/attack-vector

Fotaki, M., Altman, Y., & Koning, J. (2020). Spirituality, symbolism, and storytelling in twentyfirst-century organizations: Understanding and addressing the crisis of imagination. *Organization Studies*, *41*(1), 7–30. doi:10.1177/0170840619875782

Fouladi, S., Safaei, A. A., Mammone, N., Ghaderi, F., & Ebadi, M. J. (2022). Efficient Deep Neural Networks for classification of alzheimer's disease and mild cognitive impairment from scalp EEG Recordings. *Cognitive Computation*, *14*(4), 1247–1268. doi:10.100712559-022-10033-3

Franken, A., Edwards, C., & Lambert, R. (2009). Executing strategic change: Understanding the critical management elements that lead to success. *California Management Review*, *51*(3), 49–73. doi:10.2307/41166493

Fridman, I., Lucas, G., & Berson, J. (2021). Beyond the Pandemic: A Framework for Managing Multiple Crises. *Harvard Business Review*, *99*(2), 48–59.

Frigo, M., & Guccione, D. S. (2022). Strategic management of cybersecurity risks. *Strategic Finance, 103*(7), 23-25. https://www.proquest.com/scholarly-journals/strategic-management-cybersecurity-risks/docview/2614646599/se-2

Friska, B. (2022). *Human Design for Your Powerful Marketing*. Human Design. https://humandesign.ai/blog/2022/12/22/human-design-for-your-powerful-marketing/

Frye, A. (2017). Intergenerational transmission of violence: A review. *Trauma, Violence & Abuse*, *18*(5), 539–550. doi:10.1177/1524838016687564

Fui, L. W. (2021). 99 disruption of paediatric orthopaedic hospital services due to the COVID-19 pandemic in a region with minimal COVID-19 illness. *BMJ Paediatrics Open*, *5*, A28–A29. doi:10.1136/bmjpo-2021-RCPCH.57

Fullerton, S., & Merz, R. (2008). The Four Domains of Sports Marketing: A Conceptual Framework. *Sport Marketing Quarterly*, *17*, 90–108.

Fu, M., & Tantithamthavorn, C. (2022). Gpt2sp: A transformer-based agile story point estimation approach. *IEEE Transactions on Software Engineering*.

Fumagalli, A. (2019). Fordism and Taylorism: Two Parallel Historical Trajectories or Two Sides of the Same Coin? *Journal of Economic Issues*, *53*(2), 411–418.

Furlan, S., & Bajec, M. (2008). Holistic approach to fraud management in health insurance. *Journal of Information and Organizational Sciences*, *32*(2), 99–114.

Furnell, S., Fischer, P., & Finch, A. (2017). Can't get the staff? The growing need for cyber-security skills. *Computer Fraud & Security*, *2017*(2), 5–10. doi:10.1016/S1361-3723(17)30013-1

Gaddis, B. H., & Foster, J. L. (2015). Meta-analysis of dark side personality characteristics and critical work behaviors among leaders across the globe: Findings and implications for leadership development and executive coaching. *Applied Psychology*, *64*(1), 25–54. doi:10.1111/apps.12017

Gallup. (2015). *The State of the American Manager.* The Gallup Organization. https://www.gallup.com/services/182138/state-american-manager.aspx

Gao, J., Li, L., Kong, P., Bissyandé, T. F., & Klein, J. (2019). Should You Consider Adware as Malware in Your Study? *2019 IEEE 26th International Conference on Software Analysis, Evolution and Reengineering (SANER)* (pp. 604-608). IEEE.

García Canclini, N. (1982). *Las Culturas Populares en el capitalismo*. Nueva Imagen.

García Mora, C., & Krotz, E. (1988). *La antropología en México: panorama histórico* (Vol. 9). Instituto Nacional de Antropología e Historia.

Garrison, G., Wakefield, R. L., & Kim, S. (2015). The effects of IT capabilities and delivery model on cloud computing success and firm performance for cloud supported processes and operations. *International Journal of Information Management*, *35*(4), 377–393. doi:10.1016/j.ijinfomgt.2015.03.001

Garsten, C., & Nyqvist, A. (2022). Anthropological perspectives on the study of organizations: Historical trends and future directions. *Current Anthropology*, *63*(1), 1–17.

Garsten, Ch., & Anette, N. (2013). *Organizational Anthropology: Doing Ethnography in and Among Complex Organizations*. Pluto Press.

Gartner. (2021, January 12). Gartner forecasts global spending on wearable devices to total $81.5 billion in 2021. *Gertner.* https://www.gartner.com/en/newsroom/press-releases/2021-01-11-gartner-forecasts-global-spending-on-wearable-devices-to-total-81-5-billion-in-2021

Garvare, R., & Johansson, P. (2010). Management for sustainability–A stakeholder theory. *Total Quality Management & Business Excellence*, *21*(7), 737–744. doi:10.1080/14783363.2010.483095

Gaudenzi, B., & Siciliano, G. (2017). Just do it. Managing IT and cyber risks to protect the value creation. *Journal of Promotion Management*, *23*(3), 1–14. doi:10.1080/10496491.2017.1294875

Gauthier, A. P., Kolla, G., Mayer, P., & Burtscher, M. (2021). Accuracy of consumer wearables for physical activity and sleep monitoring in daily living: A systematic review and meta-analysis. *Applied Sciences (Basel, Switzerland)*, *11*(5), 2075. doi:10.3390/app11052075

Gavin, C. S. (2018). The impact of leadership development using coaching. *Journal of Practical Consulting*, *6*(1), 137–147.

GDPR. (2023). *Principles relating to processing of personal data*. GDPR. https://gdpr-info.eu/art-5-gdpr/

Genes, R. (2016). Code cyber: Preventing breaches at hospitals and health care practices. *Journal of Health Care Compliance*, *18*(3), 13–18.

Germano, J., & Center for Cybersecurity. (2017). *Third-party cyber risk and corporate social responsibility.* (White Paper) https://www.lawandsecurity.org/wp-content/uploads/2017/02/Germano.NYU_.ThirdPartyRiskWhitepaper.Feb2017.pdf

Ghadge, A., Dani, S., & Kalawsky, R. (2012). Supply chain risk management: Present and future scope. *International Journal of Logistics Management*, *23*(3), 313–339. doi:10.1108/09574091211289200

Ghadge, A., Weiß, M., Caldwell, N. D., & Wilding, R. (2019). Managing cyber risk in supply chains: A review and research agenda. *Supply Chain Management*, *25*(2), 223–240. doi:10.1108/SCM-10-2018-0357

Ghandi, T. K., Feeley, D., & Schummers, D. (2020). Zero harm in healthcare. *NEJM Catalyst Innovations in Care Delivery*, *1*(2), CAT.19.1137. Advance online publication. doi:10.1056/CAT.19.1137

Ghassemi, N., Shoeibi, A., & Rouhani, M. (2020). Deep neural network with generative adversarial networks pre-training for brain tumor classification based on MR images. *Biomedical Signal Processing and Control*, *57*, 101678. doi:10.1016/j.bspc.2019.101678

Ghazali, A., Nuaimy, W., Al-Atabi, A., & Jamaludin, I. (2015). Comparison of classification models for Nsl-Kdd dataset for network anomaly detection. *Academic Journal of Science*, *4*(1), 199–206.

Ghicajanu, M. (2021). Competitive Analysis of the Business with the Michael Porter Model. *Annals of the University of Petrosani. Economics*, *21*(1), 169–178.

Gibbs, D. (2009). Sustainability entrepreneurs, ecopreneurs and the development of a sustainable economy. *Greener Management International,* (55).

Gilbert, A. (2023). Workday AI Biased Against Black, Older Applicants, Suit Says. *Daily Labor Report.* https://news.bloomberglaw.com/daily-labor-report/workday-ai-biased-against-black-disabled-applicants-suit-says

Ginter, A. (2016). *SCADA Security - What's broken and how to fix it.* Abterra Technologies, Inc.

Giovannini, S., Zeppetella, G., & Lazzarotti, V. (2019). Sustainable development and corporate financial performance: Evidence from the panel data. *Management Decision*, *57*(4), 990–1009.

Gkatsi, V., Vogt-Ardatjew, R., & Leferink, F. (2022). Evaluation of EM Vehicle Environment Measurement Methods for Risk-Based EMC Analysis. *2022 ESA Workshop on Aerospace EMC (Aerospace EMC)*, (pp. 1-6). IEEE. 10.23919/AerospaceEMC54301.2022.9828833

Gladis, S. P. V. P. (2015). Brain Tumor Detection and Classification Using Deep Learning Classifier on MRI Images. *Appl. Sci. Eng. Technol.*, *10*(2), 177–187. doi:10.19026/rjaset.10.2570

Glas, B. (2021). *A08:2021 – Software and Data Integrity Failures.* A08 Software and Data Integrity Failures - OWASP Top 10:2021. https://owasp.org/Top10/A08_2021-Software_and_Data_Integrity_Failures/

Glorot, X., & Bengio, Y. (2010). Understanding the difficulty of training deep feedforward neural networks. *Journal of Machine Learning Research*, *9*, 249–256.

Gluckman, M. (1940). *Analysis of a Social Situation in Zululand.* Manchester University.

Goetzel, R. Z., Henke, R. M., Tabrizi, M., Pelletier, K. R., Loeppke, R., Ballard, D. W., & Serxner, S. (2014). Do workplace health promotion (wellness) programs work? *Journal of Occupational and Environmental Medicine*, *56*(9), 927–934. doi:10.1097/JOM.0000000000000276 PMID:25153303

Goetz, M. R., Laeven, L., & Levine, R. (2016). Does the geographic expansion of banks reduce risk? *Journal of Financial Economics*, *120*(2), 346–362. doi:10.1016/j.jfineco.2016.01.020

Goldring, C. C. (2015). A design for federal government leaders: Succession planning through knowledge management (Doctoral dissertation). *Available from ProQuest Dissertations & Theses Global*. (UMI No. 1688688202)

Goldsmith, A., & Levensaler, L. (2016, February). Build a great company culture with help from technology. *Harvard Business Review*. https://hbr.org/2016/02/build-a-great-company-culture-with-help-from-technology

GoldSparrow. (2020). *Oski Stealer*. Enigma Software. https://www.enigmasoftware.com/oskistealer-removal/.

Goleman, D. (2018). The importance of emotional intelligence in leadership. International. *Journal of Management & Business Studies*, *8*(2), 67–72.

Gonnet, J. (2012). Cultura, organizaciones y antropología. Una revisión crítica. Avá. *Revista de Antropología* (21), 151-170. https://www.redalyc.org/articulo.oa?id=16903026800

Gonzàlez Gamio, A. (2003). *Manuel Gamio: una lucha sin final*. Universidad Nacional Autónoma de México.

Goodfellow, I. (2016). *Book: Deep Learning*. Prmu. [Online] www.deeplearningbook.org

Goodwin, C. (2004). The use of narrative literature reviews in social research. *Qualitative Research*, *4*(3), 293–312.

Gordon, A., & Pollack, J. (2018). Managing Healthcare Integration: Adapting Project Management to the Needs of Organizational Change. *Project Management Journal*, *49*(5), 5–21. https://doi-org.libproxy.lib.unc.edu/10.1177/8756972818785321. doi:10.1177/8756972818785321

Gorman, E., & Radford, S. (2021). Fitbit as a tool for physical activity monitoring in the clinical setting: A systematic review. *Journal of Clinical Medicine*, *10*(3), 501. PMID:33535394

Gottlibe, M., Rosen, O., Weller, B., Mahagney, A., Omar, N., Khuri, A., Srugo, I., & Genizi, J. (2020). Stroke identification using a portable EEG device – a pilot study. *Neurophysiologie Clinique*, *50*(1), 21–25. doi:10.1016/j.neucli.2019.12.004 PMID:32014371

Govindarajan, V., & Trimble, C. (2012). *Reverse innovation: Create far from home, win everywhere*. Harvard Business Review Press. doi:10.5437/08956308X5506003

Graban, M., & Swartz, J. E. (2018). *Healthcare Kaizen: Engaging front-line staff in sustainable continuous improvements*. CRC Press. doi:10.1201/b12274

Grandviewresearch. (2023, May). *Generative AI market size to reach $109.37 billion by 2030*. Grandview Research. https://www.grandviewresearch.com/press-release/global-generative-ai-market

Grant, M. J., & Booth, A. (2009). A typology of reviews: An analysis of 14 review types and associated methodologies. *Health Information and Libraries Journal*, *26*(2), 91–108. doi:10.1111/j.1471-1842.2009.00848.x PMID:19490148

Gravano, A. (1992). Antropología Práctica, muestra y posibilidades de la Antropología Organizacional. Publicar en Antropología y Ciencias Sociales, Buenos Aires.

Gravano, A. (1995). La imaginación antropológica; interpelaciones a la otredad construida y al método antropológico. *Publicar en Antropología y Ciencias Sociales.*, *5*, 71–91.

Gray, D., & McEvoy, C. (2005). Sports marketing strategies and tactics. In B. Parkhouse (Ed.), *The Management of Sport: Its Foundation and Application*. McGraw-Hill, Inc.

Gray, P., Senabe, S., Naicker, N., Kgalamono, S., Yassi, A., & Spiegel, J. M. (2019). Workplace-based organizational interventions promoting mental health and happiness among healthcare workers: A realist review. *International Journal of Environmental Research and Public Health*, *16*(22), 4396. doi:10.3390/ijerph16224396 PMID:31717906

Greenhalgh, T., & Peacock, R. (2019). Effectiveness and efficiency of search methods in systematic reviews of complex evidence: Audit of primary sources. *BMJ (Clinical Research Ed.)*, *364*, 135. PMID:16230312

Greenleaf, R. K. (2019). *The servant as leader*. Paulist Press.

Green, P. (2002, December 9). Sponsorship with no booths or logos. *Brandweek*, *43*(45), 16.

Gregory, H. (2022). *Board Oversight: Key Focus Areas for 2022*. Harvard Law School Forum on Corporate Governance. https://corpgov.law.harvard.edu/2022/01/05/board-oversight-key-focus-areas-for-2022/

Grinde, J., & Khare, A. (2008). The ant, the grasshopper or Schrödinger's cat: An exploration of concepts of sustainability. *Journal of Environmental Assessment Policy and Management*, *10*(2), 115–141. doi:10.1142/S1464333208003007

Grossi, E., Valbusa, G., & Buscema, M. (2020). Detection of an autism EEG signature from only two EEG channels through features extraction and Advanced Machine Learning Analysis. *Clinical EEG and Neuroscience*, *52*(5), 330–337. doi:10.1177/1550059420982424 PMID:33349054

Guerra, S., & Fletcher, G. (2021). Overview of Approaches to the Use and Licensing of COTS Digital Devices in Safety Critical Industries. *12th Nuclear Plant Instrumentation, Control and Human-Machine Interface Technologies (NPIC&HMIT 2021)*.

Guezzaz, A., Asimi, A., Tbatou, Z., Asimi, Y., & Sadqi, Y. (2019). A global intrusion detection system using pcapsocks sniffer and multilayer perceptron classifier. *International Journal of Network Security*, *21*(3), 438–450.

Guezzaz, A., Asimi, Y., Azrour, M., & Asimi, A. (2021). Mathematical validation of proposed machine learning classifier for heterogeneous traffic and anomaly detection. *Big Data Mining and Analytics*, *4*(1), 18–24. doi:10.26599/BDMA.2020.9020019

Gu, J., Wang, L., Wang, H., & Wang, S. (2019). A novel approach to intrusion detection using SVM ensemble with feature augmentation. *Computers & Security*, *86*, 53–62. doi:10.1016/j.cose.2019.05.022

Guk, K., Han, G., Lim, J., Jeong, K., Kang, T., Lim, E. K., & Jung, J. (2019). Evolution of wearable devices with real-time disease monitoring for personalized healthcare. *Nanomaterials (Basel, Switzerland)*, *9*(6), 1–23. doi:10.3390/nano9060813 PMID:31146479

Gulati, R. (2018). Structure That's Not Stifling. *Harvard Business Review*. https://hbr.org/2018/05/structure-thats-not-stifling

Gumaei, A., Hassan, M. M., Hassan, M. R., Alelaiwi, A., & Fortino, G. (2019). A Hybrid Feature Extraction Method with Regularized Extreme Learning Machine for Brain Tumor Classification. *IEEE Access : Practical Innovations, Open Solutions*, *7*, 36266–36273. doi:10.1109/ACCESS.2019.2904145

Gunawardena, C. N., Hermans, M. B., Sanchez, D., Richmond, C., Bohley, M., & Tuttle, R. (2009). A theoretical framework for building online communities of practice with social networking tools. *Educational Media International*, *46*(1), 3–16. doi:10.1080/09523980802588626

Guo, C., Ping, Y., Liu, N., & Luo, S.-S. (2016). A two-level hybrid approach for intrusion detection. *Neurocomputing*, *214*, 391–400. doi:10.1016/j.neucom.2016.06.021

Guo, L., Yang, B., Ye, J., Velni, J. M., & Song, W. (2021). Attack-Resilient Lateral Stability Control for Four-Wheel-Driven EVs Considering Changed Driver Behavior Under Cyber Threats. *IEEE Transactions on Transportation Electrification*, *8*(1), 1362–1375. doi:10.1109/TTE.2021.3102134

Gupta, A. K., Smith, K. G., & Shalley, C. E. (2006). The interplay between exploration and exploitation. *Academy of Management Journal*, *49*(4), 693–706. doi:10.5465/amj.2006.22083026

Gurvirender, T., & Sanjay, G. (2022). Editorial: Time to move away from compliance – cybersecurity in the context of needs and investments of organizations. *Organizational Cybersecurity Journal: Practice. Process and People*, *2*(1), 1–2. doi:10.1108/OCJ-05-2022-018

Gyllensten, K., & Torner, M. (2021). The role of organizational and social factors for information security in a nuclear power industry. *Organizational Cybersecurity Journal: Practice, Process, and People, 1*(1), 1-20. https://www.emerald.com/insight/content/doi/10.1108/OCJ-04-2021-0012/full/pdf?title=the-role-of-organizational-and-social-factors-for-information-security-in-a-nuclear-power-industry

Habeeb, E., Ghazal, N., & Majzoub, S. (2019). Behavior analysis tool for autistic children using EEG signals. *2019 Advances in Science and Engineering Technology International Conferences (ASET)*. 10.1109/ICASET.2019.8714498

Hacker, P., Engel, A., & Mauer, M. (2023). *Regulating ChatGPT and other large generative AI models*. arXiv preprint arXiv:2302.02337. doi:10.1145/3593013.3594067

Haddad, Y. K., El-Darzi, E., Al-Tawil, Y. A., & Al-Najjar, Y. N. (2019). The application of Lewin's change management model to the implementation of a clinical pathway for joint replacement surgery. *Journal of Nursing Management*, *27*(7), 1419–1427.

Hadi, A. (2018). Performance analysis of big data intrusion detection system over random forest algorithm. *International Journal of Applied Engineering Research: IJAER*, *13*(2), 1520–1527.

Hadnagy, C., & Wozniak, S. (2018). *Social Engineering The Science of Human Hacking*. John Wiley & Sons, Incorporated. doi:10.1002/9781119433729

Hadoush, H., Alafeef, M., & Abdulhay, E. (2019). Automated identification for autism severity level: EEG analysis using empirical mode decomposition and second order difference plot. *Behavioural Brain Research*, *362*, 240–248. doi:10.1016/j.bbr.2019.01.018 PMID:30641159

Haenlein, M., & Kaplan, A. (2021). Artificial intelligence and robotics: Shaking up the business world and society at large. *Journal of Business Research*, *124*, 405–407. doi:10.1016/j.jbusres.2020.10.042

Haggith, D. (2022). *DollarCollapse.com: Alasdair Macleod: The real reason markets are breaking: Cycles are driven by credit*. Newstex., https://www.proquest.com/blogs-podcasts-websites/dollarcollapse-com-alasdair-macleod-real-reason/docview/2667244234/se-2

Hainey, T., Jones, K., McGregor, J., & McNeil, B. (2023). Enhancing security and privacy standards in medical-grade wearables. *Electronics & Communication Engineering Journal*, *35*(4), 217–239.

Hajli, N. (2015). Social commerce constructs and consumer's intention to buy. *International Journal of Information Management*, *35*(2), 183–191. doi:10.1016/j.ijinfomgt.2014.12.005

Halahan, J., & Chen, W. (2017). Wireless Security Within New Model Vehicles. *Journal of Information Warfare*, *16*(3), 51–62. https://www.proquest.com/scholarly-journals/wireless-security-within-new-model-vehicles/docview/1968021066/se-2

Halamka, J., Blumenthal, D., & Samal, L. (2021). Healthcare and Cybersecurity: Bibliography and Selected Readings. *The New England Journal of Medicine*, *384*(10), 963–972. doi:10.1056/NEJMra2001465

Hamadneh, J., & Esztergar-Kiss, D. (2022). Evaluation of the impacts of autonomous vehicles on the mobility of user groups by using agent-based simulation. *Transport*, *37*(1), 1–16. doi:10.3846/transport.2022.16322

Hammersley, M., & Atkinson, P. (2007). *Ethnography*. Routledge.

Hancock, J., Curry, E., & Gulliford, L. (2018). Reflexivity in qualitative research: A journey of learning. *Qualitative Report*, *23*(10), 2520–2534.

Handayani, W., & Syahda, E. R. (2022). Risk mitigation in supply chain management process: Procurement using house of risk method at PT. Pertamina EP asset 4. *Journal of Strategy and Business*, *26*(1), 70–84. doi:10.20885/jsb.vol26.iss1.art5

Handfield, R. (2021, August 19). What is supply chain management (Scm)? *Supply Chain Resource Cooperative*. https://scm.ncsu.edu/scm-articles/article/what-is-supply-chain-management-scm

Hansen, D., Shneiderman, B., & Smith, M. A. (2017). *Analyzing social media networks with NodeXL: Insights from a connected world*. Morgan Kaufmann.

Hansen, L. H., Møller, P., & Scholderer, J. (2019). Corporate responsibility and sustainability: An introduction. *International Journal of Management Reviews*, *21*(4), 1034–1052.

Haputhanthri, D., Brihadiswaran, G., Gunathilaka, S., Meedeniya, D., Jayawardena, Y., Jayarathna, S., & Jaime, M. (2019). An EEG based channel optimized classification approach for autism spectrum disorder. *2019 Moratuwa Engineering Research Conference (MERCon)*. 10.1109/MERCon.2019.8818814

Harit, A., Ezzati, A., & Elharti, R. (2017, March). Internet of things security: challenges and perspectives. In *Proceedings of the Second International Conference on Internet of things, Data and Cloud Computing*, (pp. 1-8). ACM. 10.1145/3018896.3056784

Haroun, A., & Epstein, J. (2021, October 05). Southern California oil spill caused by a pipeline that split and was apparently dragged. *Business Insider*. https://www.proquest.com/newspapers/southern-california-oil-spill-caused-pipeline/docview/2579203564/se-2

Harris, B., Cheng, K. F., & Gorley, C. (2015). Benefits and barriers. *Journal of Workplace Learning*, *27*(3), 193–206. https://proxy.cecybrary.com/login?url=https://search.proquest.com/docview/1672560997?accountid=144459. doi:10.1108/JWL-07-2014-0053 PMID:26477117

Harrison, R., Fischer, S., Walpola, R. L., Chauhan, A., Babalola, T., Mears, S., & Le-Dao, H. (2021). Where do models for change management, improvement, and implementation meet? A systematic review of the applications of change management models in healthcare. *Journal of Healthcare Leadership*, *13*, 85–108. doi:10.2147/JHL.S289176 PMID:33737854

Hart, C. (2019). Doing a literature review: Releasing the social science research imagination. *Sage (Atlanta, Ga.)*.

Harvard Business Review. (2019). What is the Hard Return on Employee Wellness Programs? *Harvard Business Review*. https://hbr.org/2010/12/whats-the-hard-return-on-employee-wellness-programs

Harvey, D. (2004). *La condición de la posmodernidad*. Amorrortu editores.

Harvey, J. F., Cohendet, P., Simon, L., & Dubois, L. E. (2013). Another cog in the machine: Designing communities of practice in professional bureaucracies. *European Management Journal*, *31*(1), 27–40. doi:10.1016/j.emj.2012.07.008

Harwell, D. (2023, April 15). The military loved Discord for Gen Z recruiting. Then the leaks began. *The Washington Post*. https://www.washingtonpost.com/technology/2023/04/15/discord-military-recruitment-pentagon-document-leaks/

Hassan, F., Hussain, S. F., & Qaisar, S. M. (2023). Fusion of multivariate EEG signals for schizophrenia detection using CNN and Machine Learning Techniques. *Information Fusion*, *92*, 466–478. doi:10.1016/j.inffus.2022.12.019

Hassan, M. M., Gumaei, A., Alsanad, A., Alrubaian, M., & Fortino, G. (2020). A hybrid deep learning model for efficient intrusion detection in big data environment. *Information Sciences*, *513*, 386–396. doi:10.1016/j.ins.2019.10.069

Hawkins, T. G., & Gravier, M. J. (2019). Integrating COTS technology in defense systems: A knowledge-based framework for improved performance. *European Journal of Innovation Management*, *22*(3), 493–523. doi:10.1108/EJIM-08-2018-0177

Haws, C. (2022). *The Death of Amateurism in the NCAA: How the NCAA Can Survive the New Economic Reality of College Sports*. Michigan Business & Entrepreneurial Law Review.

Health Informatics for Australia (HISA). (2017). *What is the HISA Community of Practice?* HISA. https://www.hisa.org.au/cybersecurity/

Health Insurance Portability and Accountability Act of 1996. (1996, August 20). ASPE. https://aspe.hhs.gov/reports/health-insurance-portability-accountability-act-1996

Healthcare & Public Health Sector Coordinating Councils. (n.d.). *Health industry cybersecurity practices: Managing threats and protecting patients*. Department of Health and Human Services. https://www.phe.gov/Preparedness/planning/405d/Documents/HICP-Main-508.pdf

Heathcare Information Management Systems Society (HIMSS). (2021a). *Cybersecurity in healthcare*. HIMSS. https://www.himss.org/resources/cybersecurity-healthcare

Heathcare Information Management Systems Society (HIMSS). (2021b). *Future of healthcare report: Exploring healthcare stakeholders' expectations for the next chapter*. HIMSS. https://www.himss.org/resources/future-healthcare-report-exploring-healthcare-stakeholdersexpectations-next-chapter

Heckscher, C. M. (2018). Anthropology and Organizational Development: An Ethnographic Approach to Organizational Change. *Journal of Business Anthropology*, *7*(1), 117–134.

Hefner, J. L., Sieck, C. J., & Walker, D. M. (2020). Considering the impact of healthcare information technology on workflow: An analysis of complexity, uncertainty, and communication in primary care. *International Journal of Medical Informatics*, *136*, 104079. doi:10.1016/j.ijmedinf.2020.104079

Heibutzki, R. (2017). The Effects of an Unproductive Workplace. *Career Trend*. https://careertrend.com/effects-unproductive-workplace-3931.html

Heifetz, R., & Linsky, M. (2002). *A survival guide for leaders*. HBR. https://hbr.org/2002/06/a-survival-guide-for-leaders

Hein, A. (2022, March 8). *Prioritizing Data Privacy and Cybersecurity in Medical Devices*. Clarkston Consulting. https://clarkstonconsulting.com/insights/cybersecurity-in-medical-device/

He, K., Zhang, X., Ren, S., & Sun, J. (2016). Deep residual learning for image recognition. In *Proceedings of the IEEE Computer Society Conference on Computer Vision and Pattern Recognition*. IEEE. 10.1109/CVPR.2016.90

Henderson, E., Schaper, M. T., & Robins, A. (2018). Measuring value created through sustainability initiatives. *Sustainability*, *10*(2), 590.

Hendy, J., Fulop, N., Reeves, B., Hutchings, A., & Collin, S. (2012). Implementing change in health systems: The role of sensemaking. *Journal of Health Organization and Management*, *26*(2), 215–233. PMID:22856177

Henriksen, K., Dayton, E., Keyes, M. A., Carayon, P., & Hughes, R. (2008). Patient safety and quality: An evidence-based handbook for nurses. In: Hughes RG, (ed) *Patient Safety and Quality: An Evidence-Based Handbook for Nurses.* Rockville (MD): Agency for Healthcare Research and Quality. https://www.ncbi.nlm.nih.gov/books/NBK2666/

Hernández, V. (2013) Genealogía de una elite rural: elucidación antropológica de una práctica de poder. *Mundo Agrario, 13*(26). https://www.redalyc.org/pdf/845/84527468004.pdf

Hernandez, J., Shafique, S., & Ashraf, M. (2018). Challenges and opportunities of wearable healthcare technology: A review paper. *Journal of Engineering and Applied Sciences (Asian Research Publishing Network), 37*(2), 61–71.

Herold, D. M., Fedor, D. B., Caldwell, S., & Liu, Y. (2008). The effects of transformational and change leadership on employees' commitment to a change: A multilevel study. *The Journal of Applied Psychology, 93*(2), 346–357. doi:10.1037/0021-9010.93.2.346 PMID:18361637

Herold, R. (2014). *Managing an Information Security and Privacy Awareness and Training Program.* CRC Press.

Herr, T., Loomis, W., Schroeder, E., Scott, S., Handler, S., & Zuo, T. (2020). *Broken trust: Lessons from Sunburst.* Atlantic Council. https://www.atlanticcouncil.org/in-depth-research-reports/report/broken-trust-lessons-from-sunburst/

Hibbard, D. R., Hibbard, M. S., & Stockman, J. W. (2007). *The Canoe Theory: A Business Success Strategy for Leaders and Associates.* iUniverse.

Hibbard, D., Hibbard, M., & Stockman, J. (2006). The Canoe Theory: A Business Success Strategy for Leaders and Associates (0 ed.). iUniverse, Inc.

Hijji, M., & Alam, G. (2021). A multivocal literature review on growing social engineering based cyber-attacks/Threats during the COVID-19 pandemic: Challenges and prospective solutions. *IEEE Access : Practical Innovations, Open Solutions, 9*, 7152–7169. doi:10.1109/ACCESS.2020.3048839 PMID:34786300

Hill, D. (2009). *The Rhetoric and Reality of Successful Change Management. Ivey Business Journal.* https://iveybusinessjournal.com/publication/the-rhetoric-and-reality-of-successful-change-management/

Hill, R. R., Johansson, B., Dunkin, A., & Ingalls, R. G. (2017). Agent-Based Modeling and Simulation. Encyclopedia of Machine Learning and Data Mining.

Hillson, D. (2022). *Risk management for project managers: A practical approach.* Kogan Page Publishers.

Hock, D. (2000). The art of chaordic leadership. *Leader to Leader, 15*(Winter), 20–26.

Hofstede, G. (2019). *Culture and organizations.* Routledge.

Holzberg, C., & Maureen, G. (1981). *Anthropology and Industry reappraisal and new directions. Ann. Review of Anthropology* (Vol. 10). Estados Unidos. doi:10.1146/annurev.an.10.100181.001533

Hooper, V. D., Daniels, J., & Hanna, M. (2019). Using the ADKAR model to implement an electronic medical record system in a primary care clinic. *Journal of the American Association of Nurse Practitioners, 31*(1), 24–30. PMID:30211782

Hope, A. (2021, January 29). DDoS Attacks Increased Rapidly During the COVID-19 Pandemic as Hackers Exploited New Tools and Techniques. *CPO Magazine.* https://www.cpomagazine.com/cyber-security/ddos-attacks-increased-rapidly-during-the-covid-19-pandemic-as-hackers-exploited-new-tools-and-techniques/

Horst, H., Miller, D., & Sinanan, J. (2021). Anthropological perspectives on organizational hierarchy: A review and synthesis. *Current Opinion in Psychology, 42*, 7–12. doi:10.1016/j.copsyc.2021.03.011

Hosick, M. B. (30 June 2021). *NCAA adopts interim name, image, and likeness policy*. Media Center. https://www.ncaa.org/news/2021/6/30/ncaa-adopts-interim-name-image-and-likeness-policy.aspx

Houde, S., Ross, S. I., Muller, M., Agarwal, M., Martinez, F., Richards, J., & Weisz, J. D. (2022, March). Opportunities for generative AI in UX modernization. In *Joint International Conference on Intelligent User Interfaces Workshops*: APEx-UI, HAI-GEN, HEALTHI, HUMANIZE, TExSS, SOCIALIZE.

Ho, W., Zheng, T., Yildiz, H., & Talluri, S. (2015). Supply chain risk management: A literature review. *International Journal of Production Research*, *53*(16), 5031–5069. doi:10.1080/00207543.2015.1030467

Huang, K., & Pearlson, K. (2019). For what technology can't fix: building a model of organizational cybersecurity culture. *Proceedings of the 52nd Hawaii International Conference on System Sciences*. MIT Sloan School. https://web.mit.edu/smadnick/www/wp/2019-02.pdf

Huang, L., & Zhang, Q. (2022). The role of theory in digital transformation research: A systematic literature review and future research directions. *Information & Management*, *59*(1), 103556. doi:10.1016/j.im.2021.103556

Hughes, C. (2021). The 7 CIS controls you should implement first. *CSO (Online)*. https://www.proquest.com/trade-journals/7-cis-controls-you-should-implement-first/docview/2612224339/se-2

Hughes, M. (2022). The Future of Retail is Phygital. *Forbes*. https://www.forbes.com/sites/mikehughes1/2022/10/31/the-future-of-retail-is-phygital/?sh=4fdfb3cc13b5

Human Factors and Ergonomics Society [HFES]. (n. d.). *HFES history*. HFES. https://www.hfes.org/about-hfes/hfes-history#:~:text=Human%20factors%20concerns%20emerged%20during,the%20sea%2C%20and%20in%20space

Humphreys, J., & Boje, D. (2013). Organizational leadership for sustainability: Achieving a triple bottom line. *Business Strategy and the Environment*, *22*(1), 7–17.

Huning, T. M., Hurt, K. J., & Frieder, R. E. (2020). The effect of servant leadership, perceived organizational support, job satisfaction and job embeddedness on turnover intentions: An empirical investigation. [Servant leadership and work outcomes] *Evidence - Based HRM*, *8*(2), 177-194. doi:10.1108/EBHRM-06-2019-0049

Hunter, J. C. (1998). *The servant: a simple story about the true essence of leadership*. Currency.

Hussain, S. (2018). Kurt Lewin's change model: A critical review of the role of leadership and employee involvement in organizational change. *Journal of Innovation & Knowledge*. https://reader.elsevier.com/reader/sd/pii/S2444569X163-00087?token=313E0D5A13CB5CB8FB9AE2DC169DD21A61076E1A1F56D9AEDA9DC1E50D77A34E0A11EBA4128D5004AFCF4CB63EB95142&originRegion=us-east-1&originCreation=20230522000044

Hussain, W. (2018). The Common Good. *Stanford Encyclopedia of Philosophy*. Stanford. https://www.academia.edu/35135973/The_Common_Good

Hussain, S. T., Lei, S., Akram, T., Haider, M. J., Hussain, S. H., & Ali, M. (2018). Lewin's change model: A critical review of the role of leadership and employee involvement in organizational change. *Journal of Innovation & Knowledge*, *3*(3), 123–127. doi:10.1016/j.jik.2016.07.002

Hut, N. (2022, November 7). *Healthcare M&A: A activity gained steam in Q4 2020*. HFMA. https://www.hfma.org/finance-and-business-strategy/strategic-partnerships-mergers-and-acquisitions/healthcare-m-a-deal-volume-gained-steam-in-q4-2020/

Iaquinto, B., Ison, R., & Faggian, R. (2011). Creating communities of practice: Scoping purposeful design. *Journal of Knowledge Management*, *15*(1), 4–21. doi:10.1108/13673271111108666

IBM. (2022). *How much does a data breach cost in 2022?* IBM. https://www.ibm.com/security/data-breach

IBM. (n.d.). *What is supply chain management?* IBM. https://www.ibm.com/topics/supply-chain-management

Igoe, K. J. (2021). Change Management: Why It's So Important, and so challenging, in healthcare environments. *Harvard T. H. Chan School of Public Health*. https://www.hsph.harvard.edu/ecpe/change-management-why-its-so-important-and-so-challenging-in-health-care-environments/

Ilioni, C. (2020). Sports Marketing – A Necessity. *Annals of the University of Petrosani. Economics*, *20*(1), 63–70.

Indeed Editorial Team. (2023). *A guide to innovative business models (with examples)*. Indeed. https://uk.indeed.com/career-advice/career-development/innovative- business-models

Ingram, McClelland, D. J., Martin, J., Caballero, M. F., Mayorga, M. T., & Gillespie, K. (2010). Experiences of Immigrant Women Who Self-Petition Under the Violence Against Women Act. *Violence Against Women, 16*(8), 858–880. doi:10.1177/1077801210376889

Insikt Group, & Rapid 7 Group. (2019). APT10 Targeted Norwegian MSP and US Companies in sustained campaign: Intrusions highlight ongoing exposure of third-party risk. *Recorded Future*. https://go.recordedfuture.com/hubfs/reports/cta-2019-0206.pdf

Institute for Women's Policy Research. (2020). *The gender wage gap: 2019*. IWPR. https://iwpr.org/publications/gender-wage-gap-2019/

Institute of Medicine. (2000). *To err is human: building a safer health system*. National Academy Press.

Institute of Medicine. Board on Population Health and Public Health Practice, & Committee on the Public Health Effectiveness of the FDA 510(k) Clearance Process. (2011). *Medical Devices and the Public's Health: The FDA 510(k) Clearance Process at 35 Years*. National Academies Press. https://ebookcentral.proquest.com/lib/marymountu/detail.action?docID=3378915

International Labor Organization. (2018). *Healthy Employees, Healthy Business: A Practical Guide to Workplace Health Promotion*. ILO. https://www.ilo.org/wcmsp5/groups/public/---ed_protect/---protrav/---safework/documents/publication/wcms_633408.pdf

Irshad, A., Chaudhry, S. A., Alomari, O. A., Yahya, K., & Kumar, N. (2020). A novel pairing-free lightweight authentication protocol for mobile cloud computing framework. *IEEE Systems Journal*, *2020*, 2998721.

Irshad, A., Usman, M., Chaudhry, S. A., Naqvi, H., & Shafiq, M. (2020). A provably secure and efficient authenticated key agreement scheme for energy internet-based vehicle-to-grid technology framework. *IEEE Transactions on Industry Applications*, *56*(4), 4425–4435. doi:10.1109/TIA.2020.2966160

Islam, M. S., Hussain, I., Rahman, M. M., Park, S. J., & Hossain, M. A. (2022). Explainable artificial intelligence model for stroke prediction using EEG Signal. *Sensors (Basel)*, *22*(24), 9859. doi:10.339022249859 PMID:36560227

Ismael, M. R., & Abdel-Qader, I. (2018). Brain Tumor Classification via Statistical Features and Back-Propagation Neural Network. *IEEE Int. Conf. Electro Inf. Technol.* IEEE. 10.1109/EIT.2018.8500308

Ismail, M., Hofmann, K., & El Ghany, M. A. (2019). Early diagnoses of alzheimer using EEG data and deep neural networks classification. *2019 IEEE Global Conference on Internet of Things (GCIoT)*. 10.1109/GCIoT47977.2019.9058417

Isopeskul, O., Shakina, M., & Georgieva, N. (2016). *Influence of stakeholders on organizational culture development*. PROXY. https://proxy.cecybrary.com/login?url=https://search.proquest.com/docview/1779263332?accountid=144459

ISPMA. (2023). *A comprehensive guide for effective software product management*. ISPMA. https://ispma.org/bok/

Issa. (2019). "A Profoundly Masculine Act": Mass Shootings, Violence Against Women, and the Amendment That Could Forge a Path Forward. *California Law Review, 107*(2), 673–. https://doi.org/ doi:10.15779/Z382V2C98F

IT World Canada. (2020, May 6). York University cyber attack looks like ransomware, says security expert. *Financialpost.* https://financialpost.com/technology/tech-news/york-university-cyber-attack-looks-like-ransomware-says-security-expert

Jacobs, J. V., Hettinger, L. J., Huang, Y. H., Jeffries, S., Lesch, M. F., Simmons, L. A., Verma, S. K., & Willetts, J. L. (2019). Employee acceptance of wearable technology in the workplace. *Applied Ergonomics, 78*(January), 148156. doi:10.1016/j.apergo.2019.03.003 PMID:31046946

Jagasia, J., Baul, U., & Mallik, D. (2015). A framework for communities of practice in learning organizations. *Business Perspectives and Research, 3*(1), 1–20. doi:10.1177/2278533714551861

Jahmunah, V., Lih Oh, S., Rajinikanth, V., Ciaccio, E. J., Hao Cheong, K., Arunkumar, N., & Acharya, U. R. (2019). Automated detection of schizophrenia using nonlinear signal processing methods. *Artificial Intelligence in Medicine, 100*, 101698. doi:10.1016/j.artmed.2019.07.006 PMID:31607349

James, B. (2022, July 19). *The MDS2 Standard and Its Role in Medical Device Security.* Nova Leah. https://www.nova-leah.com/understanding-mds2s-and-their-role-in-medical-device-cybersecurity/

James, J. T. (2013). A new, evidence-based estimate of patient harms associated with hospital care. *Journal of Patient Safety, 9*(3), 122–128. doi:10.1097/PTS.0b013e3182948a69 PMID:23860193

Janaszek, M. (2018). State of package.json dependencies. *Medium.* https://medium.com/warsawjs/ state-of-package-json-dependencies-de99828b6c3f.

Jang, H., Kim, D., Lee, J. Y., & Kim, J. (2021). Artificial intelligence in wearable biosensors: Current status and future prospects. *Biosensors & Bioelectronics, 183*, 113193.

Jankovic-Zugic, A., Medic, N., Pavlovic, M., Todorovic, T., & Rakic, S. (2023). Servitization 4.0 as a Trigger for Sustainable Business: Evidence from Automotive Digital Supply Chain. *Sustainability (Basel), 15*(3), 2217. doi:10.3390u15032217

Jara Pazmino, E. S., & Pack, S. M. (2022). A Post-Pandemic Exploration of International Student-Athlete Personal Branding and Fan Interaction via Social Media. *The American Behavioral Scientist.*

Jaumier, S. (2020). Why does the study of alternative organizations (so badly) need anthropology? In R. Mir & A.-L. Fayard (Eds.), *The Routledge Companion to Anthropology and Business* (pp. 414–432). Routledge. DO. doi:10.4324/9781003052456-22

Jepsen, A. L., & Eskerod, P. (2009). Stakeholder analysis in projects: Challenges in using current guidelines in the real world. *International Journal of Project Management, 27*(4), 335–343. doi:10.1016/j.ijproman.2008.04.002

Jeyakumar, K., Revathi, T., & Karpagam, S. (2015). Intrusion detection using artificial neural networks with best set of features. *3e International Arab Journal of Information Technology, 12*(6A).

Jiang, R. (2022). Exploring Employees' Computer Fraud Behaviors using the Fraud Triangle Theory. *Pacific Asia Journal of the Association for Information Systems, 14*(4), 4.

Jindal, K., Upadhyay, R., Padhy, P. K., & Longo, L. (2022). Bi-lstm-deep CNN for schizophrenia detection using MSST-spectral images of EEG signals. *Artificial Intelligence-Based Brain-Computer Interface*, 145–162. doi:10.1016/B978-0-323-91197-9.00011-4

Ji, S.-Y., Jeong, B.-K., Choi, S., & Jeong, D. H. (2016). A multi-level intrusion detection method for abnormal network behaviors. *Journal of Network and Computer Applications, 62*, 9–17. doi:10.1016/j.jnca.2015.12.004

Jiwani, N., Gupta, K., Sharif, M. H., Adhikari, N., & Afreen, N. (2022). A LSTM-CNN model for epileptic seizures detection using EEG signal. *2022 2nd International Conference on Emerging Smart Technologies and Applications (ESmarTA)*. 10.1109/eSmarTA56775.2022.9935403

Johns Hopkins Medicine. (n.d.). *Coronavirus, Social Distancing and Self-Quarantine*. Johns Hopkins Medicine. https://www.hopkinsmedicine.org/health/conditions-and-diseases/coronavirus/coronavirus-social-distancing-and-self-quarantine

Johnson, R. (2017). Bank think Equifax breach threatens bank reputations, too. *American Banker.* https://www.americanbanker.com/opinion/equifax-breach-threatens-bank-reputations-too

Johnson, C. E. (2020). *Meeting the Ethical Challenges of Leadership: Casting Light or Shadow* (7th ed.). SAGE Publications, Inc.

Johnston, D. (2021). How do coaches and clients create and experience thinking environments? *International Journal of Evidence Based Coaching and Mentoring*, *S15*, 198–211.

Jones, L. A. (2020). *Reputation Risk and Potential Profitability: Best Practices to Predict and Mitigate Risk through Amalgamated Factors* (Order No. 28152966). Available from ProQuest Dissertations & Theses Global; ProQuest One Academic. (2466047018). https://www.proquest.com/dissertations-theses/reputation-risk-potential-profitability-best/docview/2466047018/se-2

Jones, S., & Curry, S. (2021). Strategically-thinking senior executives need to take a new view of the digital world - it is here to stay and is getting more scary. *Effective Executive, 24*(4), 30-36. https://www.proquest.com/scholarly-journals/strategically-thinking-senior-executives-need/docview/2622692144/se-2

Jones, D., Molitor, D., & Reif, J. (2019). What do workplace wellness programs do? Evidence from the Illinois workplace wellness study. *The Quarterly Journal of Economics*, *134*(4), 1747–1791. doi:10.1093/qje/qjz023 PMID:31564754

Jones, J., Aguirre, D., & Calderone, M. (2004). 10 principles of change management. *Strategy & Business*, 35.

Jordan, A. (2013). *Bussines Anthropology*. Waveland Press, Inc.

Joshi, K. D., & Mithas, S. (2017). Research note and review of the empirical ethical decision-making literature: Boundary conditions and extensions. *Information Systems Research*, *28*(1), 118–142.

Judge, T. A., & Piccolo, R. F. (2004). Transformational and transactional leadership: A meta-analytic test of their relative validity. *The Journal of Applied Psychology*, *89*(5), 755–768. doi:10.1037/0021-9010.89.5.755 PMID:15506858

Kabir Anaraki, A., Ayati, M., & Kazemi, F. (2019). Magnetic resonance imaging-based brain tumor grades classification and grading via convolutional neural networks and genetic algorithms. *Biocybernetics and Biomedical Engineering*, *39*(1), 63–74. doi:10.1016/j.bbe.2018.10.004

Kabir, M. R. (2019). *Comparison of Retirement Plan between Bangladesh & USA*.

Kaiser Family Foundation. Song, Z., & Baicker, K. (2019, September 24). *Effect of a workplace wellness program on employee health and economic outcomes*. KFF. https://www.kff.org/health-costs/report/2018-employer-health-benefits-survey/

Kallio, J., Vildjiounaite, E., Kantorovitch, J., Kinnula, A., & Bordallo López, M. (2021). Unobtrusive Continuous Stress Detection in Knowledge Work—Statistical Analysis on User Acceptance. *Sustainability (Basel)*, *13*(4), 2003. doi:10.3390u13042003

Kanade, D.M. (2018). Internet of Things Security: Challenges and Opportunities. *International Journal for Research in Applied Science and Engineering Technology*.

Kang, E., Nantharath, P., & Hwang, H.-J. (2020). The Strategic Process of Merger and Acquisition (M&A) Market Using Integrating Change Management. *Journal of Distribution Science*, *18*(6), 57–62. doi.org/10.15722/jds.18.6.202006.57

Kang, H. S., & Exworthy, M. (2022, July 13). Wearing the future-wearables to empower users to take greater responsibility for their health and care: Scoping review. *JMIR mHealth and uHealth*, *10*(7), e35684. doi:10.2196/35684 PMID:35830222

Kannisto, K. A., Korhonen, J., Adams, C. E., Koivunen, M. H., & Vahlberg, T. (2019). Factors associated with perceptions of technology among older people with and without dementia. *Gerontechnology (Valkenswaard)*, *18*(2), 95–105.

Kaplan, J. (2022, August 16). *Play your pcards right: Internal controls over purchasing cards*. James Moore. https://www.jmco.com/articles/higher-education/pcard-internal-controls/

Kaplan, K., Kaya, Y., Kuncan, M., & Ertunç, H. M. (2015). Meningiomas: Knowledge base, treatment outcomes, and uncertainties. A RANO review. *Journal of Neurosurgery*, *122*(1), 4–23. doi:10.3171/2014.7.JNS131644 PMID:25343186

Kaplan, R. S., & Mikes, A. (2019). Managing risks: A new framework. *Harvard Business Review*, *97*(2), 48–60.

Kapoor, S. (2019). An overview of connected medical devices. *Journal of Medical Devices*, *13*(1), 1–14. doi:10.1115/1.4043048

Karim, M. R., Antar, S. S., & Khan, M. A. (2022, December). Idea generation using transformer decoder models. In *Proceedings of the 2022 5th international conference on algorithms, computing and artificial Intelligence* (pp. 1-5). IEEE.

Karlin, S. (2020). Louisiana has spent $2.3 M in recent cyberattack responses. *Governing*. https://www.governing.com/finance/louisiana-has-spent-2m-in-recent-cyberattack-responses.html

Karweer, D., Walvekar, D., & Dangi, S. (2019). Adoption of medical-grade wearables in healthcare: Challenges and opportunities. *AIMS Medical Science*, *6*(1), 27–43.

Kaspersky. (2022). Top ten cybersecurity trends. *Kaspersky*. https://www.kaspersky.com/resource-center/preemptive-safety/cyber-security-trends

Katz, E. (2018A, October 3). OPM Calls on Agencies to Implement Coaching Programs for Employees. *Government Executive*.

Katz, E. (2018B, January 10). Agencies Aren't Catching Bad Supervisors Early Enough. *Government Executive*.

Katz, B. (2018). *Connecting care for patients: Interdisciplinary care transition and collaboration*. Jones & Bartlett Learning.

Katz, M. G., Ladapo, J. A., Redberg, R. F., & Turakhia, M. P. (2020). Medical-grade wearables and digital health technologies: What is their role in clinical cardiovascular disease management? *Journal of the American College of Cardiology*, *75*(23), 2975–2984. doi:10.1016/j.jacc.2020.04.053

Kayan, H., Nunes, M., Rana, O. F., Burnap, P., & Perera, C. (2022). Cybersecurity of Industrial Cyber-Physical Systems: A Review. *ACM Computing Surveys*, *54*(11s), 1–35. doi:10.1145/3510410

Keikha, A., Hoveida, R., & Nour, M. Y. (2017). The development of an intelligent leadership model for state universities. *Foresight and STI Governance*, *11*(1), 66–74. doi:10.17323/2500-2597.2017.1.66.74.

Kennedy, J. P. (2017). Functional redundancy as a response to employee theft within small businesses. *Security Journal; London*, *30*(1), 162–183.

Kennedy, E. J. (2021, Winter). Can Data Drive Racial Equity? *MIT Sloan Management Review*, *62*(2), 9–11.

Kenton, W. (2020, March 26). Cyclical industry: What it is, characteristics, and examples. *Investopedia*. https://www.investopedia.com/terms/c/cyclical_industry.asp#:~:text=Technician%20(CMT).-,What%20Is%20a%20Cyclical%20Industry%3F,of%20economic%20downturn%20and%20contraction

Kerrigan, C. (2020). *AI, Machine Learning & Big Data Laws and Regulations*. Employment Law Risks and Artificial Intelligence, GLI. https://www.globallegalinsights.com/practice-areas/ai-machine-learning-and-big-data-laws-and-regulations/2-employment-law-risks-and-artificial-intelligence

Kersting, N., Sander, M., & Schumacher, S. (2020). Communities of practice and the sharing of tacit knowledge: A qualitative study. *International Journal of Knowledge Management*, *16*(1), 1–15.

Kertysova, K., Frinking, E., van den Dool, K., Maričić, A., & Bhattacharyya, K. (2018). *Cybersecurity: Ensuring awareness and resilience of the private sector across Europe in the mounting cyber risks*. European Economic and Social Committee. The Hague Centre for Strategic Studies. https://www.eesc.europa.eu/sites/default/files/files/qe-01-18-515-en-n.pdf

Kerzner, H. (2019). *Project management: a systems approach to planning, scheduling, and controlling*. John Wiley & Sons.

Kevric, J., Jukic, S., & Subasi, A. (2017). An effective combining classifier approach using tree algorithms for network intrusion detection. *Neural Computing & Applications*, *28*(S1, no. S1), 1051–1058. doi:10.100700521-016-2418-1

Khaleq, S., Fletcher, K., & Du, C. (2021). Recognizing the value of enterprise risk management (ERM) through integration with strategy; acquisition; and planning, programming, budgeting and execution (ppbe). *Armed Forces Comptroller*, *66*(4), 38–44.

Khan, B. (2021, February 10). DDoS attacks intensify — Driven in part by COVID-19 and 5G. *Security magazine*. https://www.securitymagazine.com/articles/94570-ddos-attacks-intensify-driven-in-part-by-covid-19-and-5g

Khan, J. Y., & Uddin, G. (2022, October). Automatic code documentation generation using GPT-3. In *37th IEEE/ACM international conference on automated software engineering* (pp. 1-6). IEEE. 10.1145/3551349.3559548

Khan, N. A., Brohi, S. N., & Zaman, N. (2020). *Ten deadly cyber security threats amid COVID-19 pandemic*.

Khan, O., & Estay, D. A. S. (2015). Supply Chain Cyber-Resilience: Creating an Agenda for Future Research. *Technology Innovation Management Review*, 8. doi:10.22215/timreview/885

Khare, S. K., Bajaj, V., & Acharya, U. R. (2021). PDCNNet: An Automatic Framework for the detection of parkinson's disease using EEG Signals. *IEEE Sensors Journal*, *21*(15), 17017–17024. doi:10.1109/JSEN.2021.3080135

Khare, S. K., Bajaj, V., & Acharya, U. R. (2023). Schizonet: A robust and accurate margenau–hill time-frequency distribution based deep neural network model for schizophrenia detection using EEG signals. *Physiological Measurement*, *44*(3), 035005. doi:10.1088/1361-6579/acbc06 PMID:36787641

Khazaei, Z., Goodarzi, E., Borhaninejad, V., Iranmanesh, F., Mirshekarpour, H., Mirzaei, B., Naemi, H., Bechashk, S. M., Darvishi, I., Ershad Sarabi, R., & Naghibzadeh-Tahami, A. (2020). The association between incidence and mortality of brain cancer and human development index (HDI): An ecological study. *BMC Public Health*, *20*(1), 1–7. doi:10.118612889-020-09838-4 PMID:33183267

Khodatars, M., Shoeibi, A., Sadeghi, D., Ghaasemi, N., Jafari, M., Moridian, P., Khadem, A., Alizadehsani, R., Zare, A., Kong, Y., Khosravi, A., Nahavandi, S., Hussain, S., Acharya, U. R., & Berk, M. (2021). Deep learning for neuroimaging-based diagnosis and rehabilitation of Autism Spectrum Disorder: A review. *Computers in Biology and Medicine*, *139*, 104949. doi:10.1016/j.compbiomed.2021.104949

Khraisat, A., Gondal, I., Vamplew, P., & Kamruzzaman, J. (2019). *Survey of intrusion detection systems: techniques, datasets and challenges* (Vol. 2). Cybersecurity.

Khurana, H., Ahmad, A., & Qureshi, M. A. (2020). AI-enabled cyber security: A comprehensive review. *IEEE Access : Practical Innovations, Open Solutions*, *8*, 109380–109403.

Kilburg, R. R. (1996). Toward a conceptual understanding and definition of executive coaching. *Consulting Psychology Journal*, *48*(2), 134–144. doi:10.1037/1061-4087.48.2.134

Kilburg, R. R. (2000). *Executive coaching: Developing managerial wisdom in a world of chaos*. American Psychological Association. doi:10.1037/10355-000

Kilinc, E. (2019). Healthcare Wearables for Disease Management: A Review of Current Technologies and Future Developments. *Journal of Medical Systems*, *43*(8), 259. PMID:31264009

Kimachia, K. (2022). *What Is Digitization vs Digitalization vs Digital Transformation?* Channel Insider. https://www.channelinsider.com/business-management/digitization-vs-digitalization/#:~:text=Digital%20transformation%20is%20the%20process%20of%20streamlining%20a,Digitalization%20is%20sometimes%20referred%20to%20as%20%E2%80%9Cdigital%20transformation.%E2%8

Kim, H. J., Kim, M., & Kim, J. Y. (2021). Transformational leadership and employees' creative process engagement: Serial mediation of psychological safety and affective commitment. *Sustainability*, *13*(6), 3226. doi:10.3390u13063226

Kim, H., Choi, B., & Cho, H. (2021). AI-driven user story points estimation based on natural language processing. *Journal of Systems and Software*, *171*, 110818.

Kim, H., & Lee, S. (2019). An integrated approach to enterprise risk management: A systematic review of the literature and research directions. *Sustainability*, *11*(7), 1866. doi:10.3390u11071866

Kim, S. E. (2014). The mentor-protégé affinity on mentoring outcomes: The mediating effect of developmental networking. *International Review of Public Administration*, *19*(1), 91–106. doi:10.1080/12294659.2014.887368

King, M. C. (2008). What sustainability should mean. *Challenge*, *51*(2), 27–39. doi:10.2753/0577-5132510204

Kingma, D. P., & Ba, J. L. (2015). Adam: A method for stochastic optimization. *3rd International Conference on Learning Representations, ICLR 2015 - Conference Track Proceedings*. IEEE.

Kingston, B. (2023, February 28). *Building A North American Electric Vehicle Supply Chain*. brookings.edu. https://www.brookings.edu/articles/building-a-north-american-electric-vehicle-supply-chain/#:~:text=Automakers%20worldwide%20are%20committing%20an,from%20only%20one%20year%20ago

Kissel, R., and Moon, H., (2016). *Small business information security: Fundamentals*. National Institute of Standards and Technology. doi:10.6028/NIST.IR.7621r1

Kleim, B., & Ehlers, A. (2008). The trauma memory: Cognitive and behavioural perspectives. *Memory (Hove, England)*, *16*(2), 111–121.

Klein, D., Bäumer, F., & Meister, S. (2019). Ethical considerations for digital health solutions in clinical applications: A scoping review. *BMC Medical Informatics and Decision Making*, *19*(1), 1–19. PMID:30616584

Klincová, M. (2017). The impact of transformational leadership on employee job satisfaction in healthcare. *Central European Business Review*, *6*(4), 41–50. doi:10.18267/j.cebr.179

Klonoff, D. C. (2017). Wearable technology and diabetes: New tools for diabetes self-management. *Journal of Diabetes Science and Technology*, *11*(4), 724–727. PMID:28299958

Klotz, F. (2016, Fall). Are You Ready for Robot Colleagues? *MIT Sloan Management Review*, *58*(1).

Kluitenberg, H. (2014). Security risk management in it small and medium enterprises. In *Proc. 20th Twente Student Conf. I.T.* IEEE.

Ko, C., Tang, S., & Shen, Y. (2021). Case Analysis and Thinking of Scheme Analysis Based on Mobile New Systems in Psychological Education. *Mobile Information Systems*, *2021*, 1–11. doi:10.1155/2021/1361071

Ko, D.-W., & Yang, J.-J. (2022). EEG-based schizophrenia diagnosis through time series image conversion and Deep Learning. *Electronics (Basel)*, *11*(14), 2265. doi:10.3390/electronics11142265

Koffas, S., Picek, S., & Conti, M. (2022). Dynamic Backdoors with Global Average Pooling. *Proceeding - IEEE Int. Conf. Artif. Intell. Circuits Syst.* IEEE. 10.1109/AICAS54282.2022.9869920

Kohli, S., Timelin, B., Fabius, V., & Veranen, S. M. (2020). *How COVID-19.* McKinsey & Company. https://www.mckinsey.com/~/media/McKinsey/Industries/Retail/Our%20Insights/How%20COVID%2019%20is%20changing%20consumer%20behavior%20now%20and%20forever/How-COVID-19-is-changing-consumer-behaviornow-and-forever.pdf

Kolderup, K. (2021, September 21). Bluetooth range and reliability: Myth vs fact. *IoT Now Magazine*. https://www.iot-now.com/2021/09/21/113171-bluetooth-range-and-reliability-myth-vs-fact/

Kollmorgen, S. (2020, August 11). Ava fertility tracker secures FDA clearance for over-the-counter use. *MobiHealth-News*. https://www.mobihealthnews.com/news/north-america/ava-fertility-tracker-secures-fda-clearance-over-counter-use

Koontz, T. M., & Thomas, C. W. (2006). What do we know and need to know about the environmental outcomes of collaborative management? *Public Administration Review*, *66*(s1), 111–121. doi:10.1111/j.1540-6210.2006.00671.x

Korgaonkar, P., Becerra, E. P., Mangleburg, T., & Bilgihan, A. (2021). Retail employee theft: When retail security alone is not enough. *Psychology and Marketing*, *38*(5), 721–734. doi:10.1002/mar.21460

Korolov, M. (2021). *Supply chain attacks show why you should be wary of third-party providers*. CSO United States. https://www.csoonline.com/article/3191947/supply-chain-attacks-show-why-you-should-be-wary-of-third-party-providers.html

Korzynski, P., Mazurek, G., Altmann, A., Ejdys, J., Kazlauskaite, R., Paliszkiewicz, J., & Ziemba, E. (2023). *Generative artificial intelligence as a new context for management theories: Analysis of ChatGPT*. Central European Management Journal.

Kostadinov, D. (2021, June 7). *Machine learning for social engineering*. Infosec Resources. https://resources.infosecinstitute.com/topic/machine-learning-for-social-engineering/

Kostera, M. (2018). *Anthropological Approach to Organizations: Understanding and Managing the Human Dimension*. Palgrave Macmillan.

Kotler, P., & Lee, N. (2016). *Corporate social responsibility: Doing the most good for your company and your cause*. John Wiley & Sons.

Kottak, C. P. (2011). *Antropología cultural*. McGrawHill.

Kotter, J. (2014). *Accelerate: Building strategic agility for a faster-moving world*. Harvard Business Review Press.

Kotter, J. P. (2018). *Leading change*. Harvard Business Press.

Kotter, K., & Worrell, K. (2020). Cybercrime and the costs to small business owners. *Journal of Applied Security Research*, *15*(2), 115–127.

Kotukh, Y. V., Kislov, D., Yarovoi, T., Kotsiuba, R. O., & Bondarenko, O. H. (2021). *Cybercrime and subculture of cybercriminals*. Linguistics and Culture Review. doi:10.21744/lingcure.v5nS4.1769

Koushik, S., Toit, T., Vrabel, K., Pérez-López, A., & Rigau, M. (2021). Security, privacy, and regulatory aspects of medical-grade wearables. *IEEE Journal of Biomedical and Health Informatics*, *25*(1), 230–241.

Kou, X., & Tang, Q. (2021). The introduction of medical-grade wearables: Security and privacy challenges. *International Journal of OT*, *20*(2), 131–143.

Krambia-Kapardis, M., & Zopiatis, A. (2021). *Contemporary Organization Theory: A Critical Review of the Field.* Palgrave Macmillan.

Kramer, J., Kao, D., & Gorfinkel, L. (2021). Supporting Employee Mental Health and Well-being during COVID-19. *Harvard Business Review*. https://hbr.org/2021/02/supporting-employee-mental-health-and-well-being-during-covid-19

Kratz, L. (2020). Cyber security risks to small businesses during the COVID-19 pandemic. *Small Business Trends*. https://smallbiztrends.com/2020/04/cyber-security-risks-to-small-business-during-covid-19.html

Krishnan, P. T., Joseph Raj, A. N., Balasubramanian, P., & Chen, Y. (2020). Schizophrenia detection using multivariateempirical mode decomposition and entropy measures from multichannel EEG signal. *Biocybernetics and Biomedical Engineering*, *40*(3), 1124–1139. doi:10.1016/j.bbe.2020.05.008

Krotz, E. (1993). Antropología y antropólogos en México: elementos de balance para construir perspectivas: (pp. 361-380). En: Balance de la Antropología en América Latina y el Caribe Universidad Nacional Autónoma de México. México.

Kruse, C. S., Frederick, B., Jacobson, T., & Monticone, D. K. (2017). Cybersecurity in healthcare: A systematic review of modern threats and trends. *Technology and Health Care*, *25*(1), 1–10. doi:10.3233/THC-161263 PMID:27689562

Kumar, A. (2020). COVID-19: Cyber security risks and measures for small businesses. *The Economic Times*. https://economictimes.indiatimes.com/small-biz/startups/newsbuzz/covid-19-cyber-security-risks-and-measures-for-small-businesses/articleshow/76271477.cms?from=mdr

Kumar, S., Kant, S., & Amburgey, T. L. (2007). Public agencies and collaborative management approaches: Examining resistance among administrative professionals. *Administration & Society*, *39*(5), 569–611. doi:10.1177/0095399707303635

Kumar, S., & Kumar, P. (2020). Performance improvement of military supply chain: A review. *Journal of Global Operations and Strategic Sourcing*, *13*(1), 124–147.

Kumar, T. S., Rajesh, K. N. V. P. S., Maheswari, S., Kanhangad, V., & Acharya, U. R. (2023). Automated schizophrenia detection using local descriptors with EEG signals. *Engineering Applications of Artificial Intelligence*, *117*, 105602. doi:10.1016/j.engappai.2022.105602

Kunda, G. (1986). *Engineering culture: Control and commitment in a high-tech corporation.* Temple University Press.

Kunkel, T., Baker, B. J., Baker, T. A. III, & Doyle, J. P. (2021). There is no nil in NIL: Examining the social media value of student-athletes' names, images, and likeness. *Sport Management Review*, *24*(5), 839–861. doi:10.1080/14413523.2021.1880154

Kuraparthi, S., Reddy, M. K., Sujatha, C. N., Valiveti, H., Duggineni, C., Kollati, M., Kora, P., & Sravan, V. (2021). Brain tumor classification of MRI images using deep convolutional neural network. *TS. Traitement du Signal*, *38*(4), 1171–1179. doi:10.18280/ts.380428

Kurdziel, K. (2022, August 16). *Play Your PCards Right: Internal Controls Over Purchasing Cards.* James Moore. https://www.jmco.com/articles/higher-education/pcard-internal-controls/

Kuuse, M. (2021, February 9). *How to use the Theory of Constraints? - mrpeasy.* Blog for Manufacturers and Distributors. https://manufacturing-software-blog.mrpeasy.com/theory-of-constraints/

Labong, R. C. (2019). Identity Theft Protection Strategies: A Literature Review. *Journal of Academic Research*, *4*(2), 1–12.

Labossiere, D. L. (2016). *A matrix for small business owners to better protect their network* [Doctoral dissertation, Utica College].

Lacy, E. (2017). *Domestic violence in women of color.* NCADV. https://www.ncadv.org/blog/domestic-violence-in-women-of-color

Lai, Y.-L., & Palmer, S. (2019). Psychology in executive coaching: An integrated literature review. *Journal of Work-Applied Management*, *11*(2), 143–164. doi:10.1108/JWAM-06-2019-0017

Lam, B. (2021). *How to protect your medical-grade wearables from being hacked.* Inveniosoft.

Lambert, J. (2017). *Cybersecurity Communities of Practice: What They Are and How They Help.* Secure World Expo. https://www.secureworldexpo.com/cyber-security-strategy/cybersecurity-communities-of-practice-what-they-are-and-how-they-help

Lammers, T., Guertler, M., & Skirde, H. (2022). Can product modularization approaches help address challenges in technical project portfolio management? – laying the foundations for a methodology transfer. *International Journal of Information Systems and Project Management*, *10*(2), 26–42. doi:10.12821/ijispm100202

Landi, H. (2018). Heritage Valley Health System Hit with Petya Ransomware Attack. *Healthcare Informatics*, https://www.healthcare-informatics.com/news-item/cybersecurity/heritage-valley-health-system-hit-petya-ransomware-attack

Landi, H. (2018, January 29). PA health system, health IT vendor affected by global "Petya" ransomware attack. *Healthcare Innovation.* https://www.hcinnovationgroup.com/cybersecurity/article/13028840/pa-health-system-health-it-vendor-affected-by-global-petya-ransomware-attack

Landry, J. B., & Baker, T. A. (2019). *Change or Be Changed: A Proposal for the NCAA to Combat Corruption and Unfairness by Proactively Reforming Its Regulation of Athlete Publicity Rights.* Social Science Research Network.

Langhinrichsen-Rohling, J. (2014). Intergenerational transmission of family violence: From theory to prevention. *The American Journal of Family Therapy*, *42*(5), 391–406. doi:10.1080/01926187.2014.930491

Langston.edu. (2021). *Transformational Leadership.* Langston. https://www.langston.edu/sites/default/files/basic-content-files/TransformationalLeadership.pdf

Lan, T. D., Gagnon, S., & Nguyen, P. (2020). Factors Contributing to Small Business Vulnerability to Cyberattacks. *International Journal of Cybersecurity and Digital Forensics*, *6*(2), 139–154. doi:10.4018/IJCDF.2020010105

Lashaw, A. (2020). The Complexities of Being a Practicing Anthropologist in Organizations: An Analysis of the Ethics of the AAA and EPIC Codes of Ethics. *Journal of Business Anthropology*, *9*(2), 200–220.

Latest challenges in supply chain management in the automotive industry (LCSCM). (2022). International Tax Review (ITR). https://www.proquest.com/scholarly-journals/latest-challenges-supply-chain-management/docview/2717541807/se-2

Lawton, G. (2021). What is risk management and why is it important? *TechTarget.* https://www.techtarget.com/searchcio/feature/9-common-risk-management-failures-and-how-to-avoid-them

Leary, M. (2020). *Design for additive manufacturing.* Elsevier. doi:10.1016/B978-0-12-816721-2.00006-3

Lebeau, S. (2017). *Minnesota Business.* https://www.minnesotabusiness.com/anthropology-business

Lebihan, R. (2011). Business schools tap coaching trend. *Australian Financial Review*, *14*, 27–28.

Lee, S., Hussein, R., Ward, R., Jane Wang, Z., & McKeown, M. J. (2021). A convolutional-recurrent neural network approach to resting-state EEG classification in parkinson's disease. *Journal of Neuroscience Methods*, *361*, 109282. doi:10.1016/j.jneumeth.2021.109282 PMID:34237382

Legal Momentum. (n.d.). *History of VAWA*. Legal Momentum. https://www.legalmomentum.org/history-vawa

Leithwood, K., Harris, A., & Hopkins, D. (2017). Seven strong claims about successful school leadership revisited. *School Leadership & Management*, *37*(1-2), 5–22. doi:10.1080/13632434.2016.1224293

Levin, D. A. (2021). *The State of K-12 Cybersecurity: 2020 Year in Review*. EdTech Strategies/K-12 Cybersecurity Resource Center and the K12 Security Information Exchange. Available online at: https://k12cybersecure.com/year-in-review/

Levy, Y., & Ellis, T. J. (2021). *A guide to literature review writing: Why it is important and how to get started*. Emerald Publishing Limited.

Levy, Y., & Ellis, T. J. (2021). A systems approach to conduct an effective literature review in support of information systems research. Informing Science. *The International Journal of an Emerging Transdiscipline*, *24*, 185–212.

Lewallen, J., Hanlon, J., Houts, P., & Engels, J. (2019). Detecting atrial fibrillation with a smartwatch: Results of the mRhythm study. *Heart Rhythm*, *16*(5), 766–767.

Lewin, K. (1947). Frontiers in group dynamics: Concept, method and reality in social science; social equilibria and social change. *Human Relations*, *1*(1), 5–41. doi:10.1177/001872674700100103

Leybourne, S. (2009). Project management and high-value superyacht projects: An improvisational and temporal perspective. *Project Management Journal*, *41*(1), 17–27. doi:10.1002/pmj.20140

Liang, X., Li, D., & Wang, Q. (2020). Technology acceptance model of medical wearable devices: A systematic review. *Journal of Healthcare Engineering*, *2020*, 1–10. doi:10.1155/2020/8822311

Lillo, E., Mora, M., & Lucero, B. (2022). Automated diagnosis of schizophrenia using EEG microstates and deep convolutional neural network. *Expert Systems with Applications*, *209*, 118236. doi:10.1016/j.eswa.2022.118236

Li, M., Chen, W., & Xia, M. (2023). GNMF-based quadratic feature extraction in SSTFT domain for epileptic EEG detection. *Biomedical Signal Processing and Control*, *80*, 104274. doi:10.1016/j.bspc.2022.104274

Limberg, H., & Rodriguez, L. (Eds.). (2020). *Handbook of Organizational Anthropology*. Routledge.

Lin, T. C. W. (2022). Business warfare. Boston College. *Law School. Boston College Law Review. Boston College. Law School*, *63*(1), 1–64. https://www.proquest.com/scholarly-journals/business-warfare/docview/2637173474/se-2

Liu, C., Zhu, J., Li, C., & Sun, Y. (2021). Effects of transformational leadership on followers' proactive behavior: A moderated mediation model. *Frontiers in Psychology*, *12*, 1–11.

Liu, Y., Lin, F. Y., Ahmad-Post, Z., Ebrahimi, M., Zhang, N., Hu, J. L., Xin, J., Li, W., & Chen, H. (2020). Identifying, Collecting, and Monitoring Personally Identifiable Information: From the Dark Web to the Surface Web. *2020 IEEE International Conference on Intelligence and Security Informatics (ISI)*, (pp. 1–6). IEEE. 10.1109/ISI49825.2020.9280540

Liu, Y., & Wang, Y. (2021). Research on the methods of enterprise risk management. *Journal of Physics: Conference Series*, *1776*(1), 012098. doi:10.1088/1742-6596/2037/1/012098

Liu, Z., Zhu, B., Hu, M., Deng, Z., & Zhang, J. (2023). Revised tunable Q-factor wavelet transform for EEG-based epileptic seizure detection. *IEEE Transactions on Neural Systems and Rehabilitation Engineering*, *31*, 1707–1720. doi:10.1109/TNSRE.2023.3257306 PMID:37028382

Li, Y., & Liu, Q. (2021). A comprehensive review study of cyber attacks and cyber security: Emerging trends and recent developments. *Energy Reports*, *7*, 8176–8186. doi:10.1016/j.egyr.2021.08.126

Li, Y., Zhang, C., Shelby, L., & Huan, T.-C. (2022). Customers' self-image congruity and brand preference: A moderated mediation model of self-brand connection and self-motivation. *Journal of Product and Brand Management*, *31*(5), 798–807. doi:10.1108/JPBM-07-2020-2998

Li, Z., & Zhang, J. (2020). The effects of hospital mergers and acquisitions on patient outcomes: A systematic review and meta-analysis. *Health Policy (Amsterdam)*, *124*(7), 747–755.

Llobera, J. (1975). *(Comp.): La antropología como ciencia*. Anagrama.

Loh, H. W., Ooi, C. P., Palmer, E., Barua, P. D., Dogan, S., Tuncer, T., Baygin, M., & Acharya, U. R. (2021). GaborPDNet: Gabor Transformation and Deep Neural Network for parkinson's disease detection using EEG signals. *Electronics (Basel)*, *10*(14), 1740. doi:10.3390/electronics10141740

Lokanan, M. E. (2018). Informing the fraud triangle: Insights from differential association theory. *Journal of Theoretical Accounting Research*, *14*(1), 55–98.

Lombardi, C. M., Carbone, S., Sansoni, J., & Menditto, E. (2020). Advances in wearable technology and applications in healthcare: A review of the literature. *Diagnostics (Basel)*, *10*(9), 736.

Lomnitz, L. (1975). Anthropology of scientific research at UNAM. In *Science and Development* (Vol. 6). CONACYT.

Loonam, J., Eaves, S., Kumar, V., & Parry, G. (2018). Towards digital transformation: Lessons learned from traditional organizations. *Strategic Change*, *27*(2), 101–109. doi:10.1002/jsc.2185

Lourau, R. (1979). *El análisis institucional*. Amorrortu.

Lucey, J. (2008). Why is the failure rate for organization change so high? *Management Services: Journal of the Institute of Practitioners in Work Study. Organization and Methods*, *52*(4), 10–19.

Lukas, C. V. D., Holmes, S. K., Cohen, A. B., Restuccia, J., Cramer, I. E., Schwartz, M., & Charns, M. P. (2007). Transformational change in Health Care Systems. *Health Care Management Review*, *32*(4), 309–320. doi:10.1097/01.HMR.0000296785.29718.5d PMID:18075440

Luo, S., & Hamlin, R. (2022). A cross cultural comparison of brand love in consumer brand relationships: Is 'transmissive brand love' a potential platform for developing brand equity? *Journal of Brand Management*, *29*(5), 484–497. doi:10.105741262-022-00286-6

Lüscher, L. S., & Lewis, M. W. (2008). Organizational change and managerial sensemaking: Working through paradox. *Academy of Management Journal*, *51*(2), 221–240. doi:10.5465/amj.2008.31767217

Luthans, F., Avolio, B. J., Avey, J. B., & Norman, S. M. (2007). Positive psychological capital: Measurement and relationship with performance and satisfaction. *Personnel Psychology*, *3*(60), 541–572. doi:10.1111/j.1744-6570.2007.00083.x

Lutkevich, B. (2022). *Supply chain*. TechTarget. https://www.techtarget.com/whatis/definition/supply-chain#:~:text=A%20supply%20chain%20is%20the,delivery%20to%20the%20end%20user

Lynn, C. K. (2002). Private eyes are watching you: Consumer online privacy protection-lessons from home and abroad. *Texas International Law Journal*, *37*(2), 387–420.

MacLennan, P. A., Marshall, T., Griffin, R., Purcell, M., Mcgwin, G. J., & Rue, L. W. (2008). Vehicle rollover risk and electronic stability control systems. *Injury Prevention*, *14*(3), 154–158. doi:10.1136/ip.2007.016576 PMID:18523106

Madsen, S. R. (2003). Wellness in the workplace: Preparing employees for change. *Organization Development Journal*, *21*(1), 46. https://tcsedsystem.idm.oclc.org/login?url=https://search-proquest-com.tcsedsystem.idm.oclc.org/docview/198001436?accountid=34120

Maestre Alfonso, J. (1983). *Introducción a la Antropología social*. Akla.

Maglaras, L. A., Kim, K. H., Janickc, H., Ferrag, M. A., Rallis, S., Fragkou, P., Maglaras, A., & Cruz, T. J. (2018). Cyber security of critical infrastructures. *Ict Express*, *4*(1), 42–45. doi:10.1016/j.icte.2018.02.001

Majumder, S., Apicella, F., Muratori, F., & Das, K. (2020). Detecting autism spectrum disorder using topological data analysis. *ICASSP 2020 - 2020 IEEE International Conference on Acoustics, Speech and Signal Processing (ICASSP)*. 10.1109/ICASSP40776.2020.9054747

Makary, M., & Daniel, M. (2016). Medical error—The third leading cause of death in the US. *British Medical Journal*, *353*, i2139. doi:10.1136/bmj.i2139 PMID:27143499

Makipere, K., & Yip, G. (2008). Sustainable leadership. *Business Strategy Review*, *19*(1), 64–67. doi:10.1111/j.1467-8616.2008.00521.x

Makridakis, S., Dimitriadis, S. I., & Kourentzes, N. (2021). Artificial intelligence in supply chain management: Theory, applications, and challenges. *International Journal of Production Research*, *59*(15), 4684–4706.

Malik, G., Cevik, M., Parikh, D., & Basar, A. (2022). *Identifying the requirement conflicts in SRS documents using transformer-based sentence embeddings*. arXiv preprint arXiv:2206.13690.

Malinowski, B. (1944). *A scientific theory of culture and other essays*. University of North Carolina Press.

Malsam, W. (2019). Top down vs. bottom up management: What's the difference? *Project Manager*. https://www.projectmanager.com/blog/top-down-vs-bottom-up-management

Mancini, M. (2014). Medical identity theft in the emergency department: Awareness is crucial. *The Western Journal of Emergency Medicine*, *15*(7), 899–901. doi:10.5811/westjem.2014.8.22438 PMID:25493150

Mandhouj, B., Cherni, M. A., & Sayadi, M. (2021). An automated classification of EEG signals based on spectrogram and CNN for epilepsy diagnosis. *Analog Integrated Circuits and Signal Processing*, *108*(1), 101–110. doi:10.100710470-021-01805-2

Mangala, D., & Kumari, P. (2015). Corporate fraud prevention and detection: Revisiting the literature. *Journal of Commerce and Accounting Research.*, *4*(1), 52–62. doi:10.21863/jcar/2015.4.1.006

Man, L. C., Leung, W. K., & Chan, H. (2021). Driving healthcare wearable technology adoption for Generation Z consumers in Hong Kong. *Young Consumers*, *22*(1), 10–27. doi:10.1108/YC-04-2020-1123

Manuj, I., & Mentzer, J. T. (2011). Global supply chain risk management. *Journal of Business Logistics*, *29*(1), 133–155. doi:10.1002/j.2158-1592.2008.tb00072.x

Marcus, G. E. (2021). Anthropological engagements with organizational travel. *Anthropological Theory*, *21*(2-3), 332–346. doi:10.1177/1463499620977503

Marikyan, D., & Papagiannidis, S. (2020). Theory review: Technology Acceptance Model (TAM). *TheoryHub*. https://open.ncl.ac.uk/theories/1/technology-acceptance-model/#:~:text=Davis%2C%201989).-,Theory,the%20successful%20implementation%20of%20technology.

Mark Business Systems. (2019, September 10). *The value of the internal audit in a good quality management system*. Mark Business Systems. https://mark1systems.com/the-value-of-the-internal-audit-in-a-good-quality-management-system/

Markopoulos, E., Aggarwal, V., & Vanharanta, H. (2020). Democratization of intrapreneurship and corporate entrepreneurship within McKinsey's three horizons innovation space. In *Human Systems Engineering and Design II: Proceedings of the 2nd International Conference on Human Systems Engineering and Design (IHSED2019): Future Trends and Applications*, (pp. 1007–1017). Springer International Publishing. 10.1007/978-3-030-27928-8_150

Marle, F. (2020). an assistance to project risk management based on complex systems theory and agile project management. *Complexity*, *2020*, 1–20. Advance online publication. doi:10.1155/2020/3739129

Marzal, M. M. (1996). *Historia de la anthropologìa. Volume I. Anthropologìa indìgena*. Ediciones Abya-Yala.

Masdari, M., & Khezri, H. (2020). A survey and taxonomy of the fuzzy signature-based intrusion detection systems. *Applied Soft Computing*, *92*, 106301. doi:10.1016/j.asoc.2020.106301

Masteralexis, L., Barr, C., & Humms, M. (Eds.). (2005). *Principle and practice of sports management*. Jones and Bartlett Publishers.

Matos Moctezuma, E. (1987). Román Piña Chan y la Escuela Nacional de Antropología e Historia: (pp. 81-90). En: Homenaje a Román Piña Chan Universidad Nacional Autónoma de México – Instituto de Investigaciones Antropológicas. México.

Matsumoto, C. (2020). Domestic violence and women of color: What you need to know. *Love is Respect*. https://www.loveisrespect.org/content/domestic-violence-women-color/

Matyokurehwa, K., Rudhumbu, N., Gombiro, C., & Chipfumbu-Kangara, C. (2022). Enhanced social engineering framework mitigating against social engineering attacks in higher education. *Security and Privacy*, *5*(5), e237. doi:10.1002py2.237

Mayadunne, S., & Park, S. (2016). An economic model to evaluate information security investment of risk-taking small and medium enterprises. *International Journal of Production Economics*, *182*, 519–530. doi:10.1016/j.ijpe.2016.09.018

Maygen, J. (2021. The history of the calculator watches. *Superwatches*. https://www.superwatches.com/the-history-of-calculator-watches/

Mazzocato, P., Stenfors-Hayes, T., von Thiele Schwarz, U., Hasson, H., & Nyström, M. E. (2016). Kaizen practice in Healthcare: A qualitative analysis of hospital employees' suggestions for improvement. *BMJ Open*, *6*(7), e012256. doi:10.1136/bmjopen-2016-012256 PMID:27473953

McAfee Center for Strategic and International Studies. (2014). *Net losses: Estimating the global cost of cyber-crime*. CSIS. https://csis-website-prod.s3.amazonaws.com/s3fs-public/legacy_files/files/attachments/140609_rp_economic_impact_cybercrime_report.pdf

McAfee. (2022, February 25). The wearable future is hackable. *McAfree.*. https://www.mcafee.com/blogs/privacy-identity-protection/hacking-wearable-devices/

McAshan, B. R. (2019, August 16). *Memorial Hermann and Baylor Scott & White merger has been canceled*. TMC News. https://www.tmc.edu/news/2019/02/the-memorial-hermann-and-baylor-scott-white-merger-is-canceled/

McBee, M. P., Awan, O. A., Colucci, A. T., Ghobadi, C. W., Kadom, N., Kansagra, A. P., Tridandapani, S., & Auffermann, W. F. (2018). Deep Learning in Radiology. *Academic Radiology*, *25*(11), 1472–1480. doi:10.1016/j.acra.2018.02.018 PMID:29606338

McEwen, R. N. (2019). Flash, spirit, plex, stretch: A trans-disciplinary view of the media sensorium. *Canadian Journal of Communication*, *44*(4), 585–593. doi:10.22230/cjc.2019v44n4a3727

McFarlane, A. (2011). Trauma and trauma-related disorders in women. In D. Levinson & M. Maercker (Eds.), *Trauma, post-traumatic stress and physical health* (pp. 91–109). Cambridge University Press.

McGhee, P. (2013). Virtue Ethics and CSR. In S. O. Idowu, N. Capaldi, L. Zu, & A. D. Gupta (Eds.), *Encyclopedia of Corporate Social Responsibility*. Springer., doi:10.1007/978-3-642-28036-8_616

McGuire, M. (2006). Collaborative public management: Assessing what we know and how we know it. *Public Administration Review*, *66*(s1), 33–43. doi:10.1111/j.1540-6210.2006.00664.x

McKee, S. (2020). *Critical cybersecurity threats to the supply chain.* SC Media. https://www.scmagazine.com/home/security-news/critical-cybersecurity-threats-to-the-supply-chain/

McKeon, J. (2021, December 30). HSCA Releases Cybersecurity Guidelines for Medical Device Manufacturers. *HealthITSecurity*. https://healthitsecurity.com/news/hsca-releases-cybersecurity-guidelines-for-medical-device-manufacturers

McKinsey & Company. (2017). *Cybersecurity for small and medium-sized businesses: A guide for executives*. McKinsey. https://www.mckinsey.com/~/media/McKinsey/Business%20Functions/Risk/Our%20Insights/Cybersecurity%20for%20small%20and%20medium%20sized%20businesses/Cybersecurity-for-small-and-medium-sized-businesses_Full%20report_A4.ashx

McKinsey & Company. (2019). *Why M&A deals fail – and how to prevent it.* McKinsey. https://www.mckinsey.com/business-functions/strategy-and-corporate-finance/our-insights/why-m-and-a-deals-fail-and-how-to-prevent-it

McKinsey & Company. (2022, August). *McKinsey technology trends outlook 2022*. McKinsey. https://www.mckinsey.com/~/media/mckinsey/business%20functions/mckinsey%20digital/our%20insights/the%20top%20trends%20in%20tech%202022/McKinsey-Tech-Trends-Outlook-2022-Applied-AI.pdf

McKinsey. (2009). *Enduring Ideas: The Three Horizons of Growth.* McKinsey. https://www.mckinsey.com/capabilities/strategy-and-corporate-finance/our-insights/enduring-ideas-the-three-horizons-of-growth#

Meadows, D. H., & Wright, D. (2008). *Thinking in systems: A primer*. Chelsea Green Pub.

Medical Device and Service Cybersecurity. (2021). *Key Consideration for Manufacturers & Healthcare Delivery Organizations.* Healthcare Supply Chain Association (HSCA). https://www.supplychainassociation.org/wp-content/uploads/2021/12/Cybersecurity-Key-Considerations-FINAL.pdf

Mehrotra, S., Gupta, N., Rameez, M., & Alsharif, S. (2019). The role of wearable technology in elderly health monitoring. *Health Care*, *7*(3), 98. PMID:31430855

Mehta, S. (2021). Industry risk. *Financial Edge*. https://www.fe.training/free-resources/credit/industry-risk

Melinda, M., Enriko, I. K., Furqan, M., Irhamsyah, M., Yunidar, Y., & Basir, N. (2023). The effect of power spectral density on the electroencephalography of autistic children based on the welch periodogram method. *JURNAL INFOTEL*, *15*(1), 111–120. doi:10.20895/infotel.v15i1.874

Méndez, P. F., Clement, F., Palau-Salvador, G., Diaz-Delgado, R., & Villamayor-Tomas, S. (2022). Understanding the governance of sustainability pathways: Hydraulic megaprojects, social–ecological traps, and power in networks of action situations. *Sustainability Science*, 1–19. doi:10.100711625-022-01258-0

Mendoza, A. R. (2021). Disruptions in global value chains due to COVID-19: Stylized facts and policy lessons. *The Philippine Review of Economics*, *58*(1&2), 214–240. doi:10.37907/9ERP1202JD

Menéndez, E. (1996). *Fundamentals of economics*.

Menéndez, E. (2006). Participación social en salud: las representaciones y las prácticas. In E. Menéndez (Ed.), *Spinelli, H.: Participación social ¿para qué?* (pp. 81–115). Lugar Editorial.

Meschede, T., Seidel, T. D., & Schmitt, M. T. (2014). Understanding the connection between economic security and intimate partner violence for transgender individuals. *Journal of Marriage and Family*, *76*(3), 573–588. doi:10.1111/jomf.12090

Metzgar, E., & Orr, S. (2020). Anthropology and organizational culture: An analysis of cultural change and resistance. *International Journal of Business and Social Science*, *11*(6).

Metzger, M. J. (2018). *2018 Global Corporate Sustainability Report*. EY. https://www.ey.com/Publication/vwLUAssets/ey-global-corporate-sustainability-report-2018/$FILE/ey-global-corporate-sustainability-report-2018.pdf

Meyer, J., & Heinze-Milne, S. (2020). The effectiveness of wearable activity trackers in increasing physical activity among older adults: A systematic review and meta-analysis. *Aging & Mental Health*, *24*(2), 151–160.

Michigan State University. (2023). *Organizational change management: Definition & importance*. Michigan State University. https://www.michiganstateuniversityonline.com/resources/leadership/organizational-change-management/#:~:text=Managing%20a%20successful%20organizational%20change,production%20cycles%20and%20reducing%20costs

Miller, C. (n.d.). *The legitimate vulnerability market: the secretive world of 0-day exploit sales.*

Miller, A. R., Tucker, C. A., & Lam, J. (2020). The accuracy of wearable fitness trackers in older adults. *Journal of Aging and Physical Activity*, *28*(4), 511–516.

Miller-Jones, G. (2020, February 25). Ineffective Leadership and The Devastating Individual And Organizational Consequences. *Forbes.*

Mills, W. (1961). *La imaginación sociológica*. Fondo de Cultura Económica.

MindTools. (2022). Deal and Kennedy's Cultural Model. *Mindtools.* https://www.mindtools.com/avnhbho/deal-and-kennedys-cultural-model

Miner, M., & Petocz, A. (2003). Moral theory in ethical decision making: Problems, clarifications and recommendations from a psychological perspective. *Journal of Business Ethics*, *42*(1), 11–25. doi:10.1023/A:1021654015232

Mircea, M., Croitorescu, V., & Oprean, M. (2016). Implementing New IT Security Solutions in Automotive Immobilizer Systems. *Applied Mechanics and Materials*, *822*, 354–359. . doi:10.4028/www.scientific.net/AMM.822.354

Mirchandani, D., & Ikerd, J. (2008). Building and maintaining sustainable organizations. *Organizational Management Journal*, *5*(1), 40–51. doi:10.1057/omj.2008.6

Mir, R., & Fayard, A.-L. (2021). Anthropology and organizational studies: A symbiotic connection. In R. Mir & A.-L. Fayard (Eds.), *The Routledge Companion to Anthropology and Business* (pp. 1–13). Routledge.

Mir, W. A., Anjum, M., Izharuddin, I., & Shahab, S. (2023). Deep-EEG: An optimized and robust framework and method for EEG-based diagnosis of epileptic seizure. *Diagnostics (Basel)*, *13*(4), 773. doi:10.3390/diagnostics13040773 PMID:36832260

Mithiotis, A., & Argirou, N. (2016). Coaching: From challenge to opportunity. *Journal of Management Development*, *35*(4), 448–463. doi:10.1108/JMD-10-2014-0139

MITRE. (2021). *Supply chain risk management*. MITRE. https://www.mitre.org/publications/systems-engineering-guide/enterprise-engineering/systems-engineering-for-mission-assurance/supply-chain-risk--management

Moeran, B. (2020). Lloyd Warner and the Emergence of Organizational Anthropology. *Journal of Organizational Ethnography*, *9*(2), 159–175.

Moeran, B., & Béji-Bécheur, A. (2021). Anthropology and the business school: An appraisal of past and future contributions. *Human Relations*, *74*(7), 933–954. doi:10.1177/0018726720978783

Moeran, B., & Garsten, C. (2015). Ethnography in/of the World of Work: Past, Present and Future. *Journal of Business Anthropology*, *4*(1), 146–169.

Mohammed, Z. (2022). Data breach recovery areas: An exploration of organization's recovery strategies for surviving data breaches. *Organizational Cybersecurity Journal: Practice. Process and People*, *2*(1), 41–59. doi:10.1108/OCJ-05-2021-0014

Mohan, G. C., & Kumar, D. (2020). Identity theft: A small step towards big financial crimes. *Journal of Financial Crime*, *27*(3), 897–910. doi:10.1108/JFC-01-2020-0014

Mohsen, H., El-Dahshan, E.-S. A., El-Horbaty, E.-S. M., & Salem, A.-B. M. (2018). Classification using deep learning neural networks for brain tumors. *Future Computing and Informatics Journal*, *3*(1), 68–71. doi:10.1016/j.fcij.2017.12.001

Mok, W. Y., & Wu, V. (2020). Overcoming resistance to change: An ADKAR model approach. *Journal of Nursing Management*, *28*(2), 319–326. PMID:31789437

Moon, N. W., Baker, P. M., & Goughnour, K. (2019). Designing wearable technologies for users with disabilities: Accessibility, usability, and connectivity factors. *Journal of Rehabilitation and Assistive Technologies Engineering*, *6*, 205566831986213. doi:10.1177/2055668319862137 PMID:35186318

Moorthy, M. K., Seetharaman, A., Mohamed, Z. A., Gopalan, M., & San, L. H. (2015). The impact of information security events on the stock value of Malaysian firms: An event study approach. *Computers & Security*, *48*, 10–18.

Morales Inga, S., & Tristán, O. M. (2018). Capturando la cultura: Tres aportes de la antropología a la selección de personal. *Palermo Business Review*, (18), 261–280.

Morell-Santandreu, O., Santandreu-Mascarell, C., & García-Sabater, J. (2020). Sustainability and kaizen: Business model trends in healthcare. *Sustainability (Basel)*, *12*(24), 10622. doi:10.3390u122410622

Morency, K. (2014). Cybersecurity finally takes center stage in the U.S. *J. High Tech. L.*, *15*, 192.

Mugariri, P., Abdullah, H., García-Torres, M., Parameshchari, B. D., & Abdul Sattar, K. N. (2022). Promoting information privacy protection awareness for Internet of Things (IoT). *Mobile Information Systems*, *2022*, 1–11. Advance online publication. doi:10.1155/2022/4247651

Muhtar, S., Sutaryo, M., & Sriyanto, S. (2018). Corruption in Indonesian local government: Study on triangle fraud theory. *International Journal of Business and Society*, *19*, 536–552.

Mui, G., & Mailley, J. (2015). A tale of two triangles: Comparing the fraud triangle with criminology's crime triangle. *Accounting Research Journal*, *28*(1), 45–58. doi:10.1108/ARJ-10-2014-0092

Muller, S. R. (2020). An Analysis and Discussion of the Defense Information Systems Agency's Level of Compliance and Integration of the US Congress' Title Viii National Defense Authorization Act FY 2015 Subtitle D-Federal Information Technology Acquisition Reform. *Annals of Computer Science and Information Systems, 24*.

Muller, S. R. (2021). A Perspective On the intersection of information security policies and I.A. awareness, factoring in end-user behavior. *Proceedings of the International Conference on Research in Management & Technovation*, (pp. 137–142). IEEE. 10.15439/2020KM1

Muller, M., Park, J., & Kyei, G. (2019). The effectiveness of communities of practice in knowledge management: A systematic review. *International Journal of Information Management*, *46*, 49–64.

Muller, R., & Turner, R. (2020). The influence of project management standards, practices, and methodologies on project success. *Project Management Journal*, *51*(1), 18–33.

Muller, S. R., & Burrell, D. N. (2022). Social Cybersecurity and Human Behavior. [IJHIoT]. *International Journal of Hyperconnectivity and the Internet of Things*, *6*(1), 1–13. doi:10.4018/IJHIoT.305228

Muller, S. R., & Lind, M. L. (2020). Factors in Information Assurance Professionals' Intentions to Adhere to Information Security Policies. [IJSSSP]. *International Journal of Systems and Software Security and Protection*, *11*(1), 17–32. doi:10.4018/IJSSSP.2020010102

Mullet, V., Sondi, P., & Ramat, É. (2021). A Review of Cybersecurity Guidelines for Manufacturing Factories in Industry 4.0. *IEEE Access : Practical Innovations, Open Solutions*, *9*, 23235–23263. doi:10.1109/ACCESS.2021.3056650

Mullins, J. (2022). Content analysis. The International Encyclopedia of Communication Research Methods, 1-13.

Munizaga, B. J. (1988). La violencia doméstica y la sociedad. *Revista de Sociologia (Santiago)*, *0*(3), 35–43. doi:10.5354/0719-529X.1988.27565

Muñoz, R. (2011). *Formar en administración. Por una nueva fundamentación filosófica*. Siglo del Hombre. Fondo Editorial Universidad EAFIT.

Murphy, J., Gretzel, U., & Pesonen, J. (2019). Marketing robot services in hospitality and tourism: The role of anthropomorphism. *Journal of Travel & Tourism Marketing*, *36*(7), 784–795. doi:10.1080/10548408.2019.1571983

Murphy, P. R., & Free, C. (2016). Broadening the fraud triangle: Instrumental climate and fraud. *Behavioral Research in Accounting*, *28*(1), 41–56. doi:10.2308/bria-51083

Murshid, N. S., & Bowen, E. A. (2018). A Trauma-Informed Analysis of the Violence Against Women Act's Provisions for Undocumented Immigrant Women. *Violence Against Women*, *24*(13), 1540–1556. doi:10.1177/1077801217741991 PMID:29355086

Murtaza, H., Rahman, M. M., & Jalil, M. A. (2020). Corporate Sustainability: An Overview. *Corporate Social Responsibility and Environmental Management*, *27*(1), 64–73.

Nabe, C. (n.d.). *Impact of covid-19 on cybersecurity*. Deloitte Switzerland. https://www2.deloitte.com/ch/en/pages/risk/articles/impact-covid-cybersecurity.html

Nader, L. (1972) *Up me anthropologist: perspectives gained from studying up*. Mimeo. https://files.eric.ed.gov/fulltext/ED065375.pdf

Nair, V., & Hinton, G. E. (2010). Rectified linear units improve Restricted Boltzmann machines. *ICML 2010 - Proceedings, 27th International Conference on Machine Learning*, (pp. 807–814). IEEE.

Nangalia, L., & Nangalia, A. (2010). The Coach in Asian Society: Impact of social hierarchy on the coaching relationship. *International Journal of Evidence Based Coaching and Mentoring*, *8*(1), 51–66.

Nass, S. J., Levit, L. A., & Gostin, L. O. (2009). *Beyond the HIPAA Privacy Rule: Enhancing Privacy, Improving Health Through Research*. National Academies Press., doi:10.17226/12458

National Coalition Against Domestic Violence. (2020). *Statistics*. NCADV. https://ncadv.org/statistics

National Cyber Security Alliance (NCSA). (2012). National Small Business Study. *Stay Safe Online*. https://staysafeonline.org/wp-content/uploads/2017/09/2012-NCSA-Symantec-Small-Business-Study.pdf

National Cyber Security Alliance. (2018). The impact of cybercrime on small businesses. *Stay Safe Online*. https://www.staysafeonline.org/ncsam/resources/impact-of-cybercrime-on-small-businesses/

National Institute of Standards and Technology [NIST]. (2019). *NIST Cybersecurity Framework*. https://www.nist.gov/cyberframework

National Institute of Standards and Technology [NIST]. (2020). *Cybersecurity Framework Core*. https://www.nist.gov/cyberframework/core

National Institute of Standards and Technology [NIST]. (2021). *Cybersecurity Framework Functions*. https://www.nist.gov/cyberframework/functions

National Institute of Standards and Technology [NIST]. (2023). *Implementing the Cybersecurity Framework*. https://www.nist.gov/cyberframework/implementation

National Institute of Standards and Technology [NIST]. (n.d.). *Cybersecurity risk*. NIST. https://csrc.nist.gov/glossary/term/cybersecurity_risk

National Network to End Domestic Violence. (2019). *VAWA: The Violence Against Women Act*. NNEDV. https://nnedv.org/content/vawa-violence-against-women-act/

NCADV: National Coalition Against Domestic Violence. (n.d.). *The Nation's Leading Grassroots Voice on Domestic Violence*. NCADV. https://ncadv.org/STATISTICS

Ncubukezi, T., Mwansa, L., & Rocaries, F. (2020, December). A review of the current cyber hygiene in small and medium-sized businesses. In *2020 15th International Conference for Internet Technology and Secured Transactions (ICITST)* (pp. 1-6). IEEE. 10.23919/ICITST51030.2020.9351339

Nelson, J. (2020). *How cybersecurity impacts business continuity planning and disaster recovery*. LMG Security. https://www.lmgsecurity.com/how-cybersecurity-impacts-business-continuity-planning-and-disaster-recovery/

Nelson, B. W., Low, C. A., Jacobson, N., Areán, P., & Torous, J. (2019). Brief report: Exploring the feasibility of feasibility studies in digital mental health. *Journal of Telemedicine and Telecare*, *25*(9), 550–554.

Neuendorf, K. A. (2019). *The content analysis guidebook*. Sage publications.

New York City Department of Health and Mental Hygiene. (2017). Mental Health Strategic Plan. NYCDHMH. https://www1.nyc.gov/assets/doh/downloads/pdf/about/mental-health-strategic-plan-2017.pdf

New York City Health and Mental Hygiene. (2023, April 6). *NYC Department of Health and Mental Hygiene Table of organization*. NYC Department of Health and Mental Hygiene. https://www.nyc.gov/assets/doh/downloads/pdf/public/dohmh-orgchart.pdf

Newman, L. H. (April 23, 2018). Atlanta spent $2.6M to recover from a $52,000 ransomware scare. *Wired*. https://www.wired.com/story/atlanta-spent-26m-recover-from-ransomware-scare/

Ng, B. Y., Kankanhalli, A., & Xu, Y. C. (2009). Studying users' computer security behavior: A health belief perspective. *Decision Support Systems*, *46*(4), 815–825. doi:10.1016/j.dss.2008.11.010

Nguyen, M. T., Nguyen, P. T., Nguyen, V. V., & Nguyen, Q. M. (2021, November). Generating product description with generative pre-trained transformer 2. In *2021 6th international conference on innovative technology in intelligent system and industrial applications (CITISIA)* (pp. 1-7). IEEE.

Nguyen, A., & Nguyen, D. T. (2020). Security and privacy in wearable technology. In *Internet of Things and Analytics for Agriculture* (pp. 289–316). Springer.

Nguyen, N. H., Tran, T. T., Vuong, T. T., Nguyen, T. H. T., Nguyen, T. T. H., & Vuong, Q. H. (2019). Factors affecting the adoption of wearable health technology among Vietnamese consumers. *BMC Public Health, 19*(1), 1025. doi:10.118612889-019-7355-7 PMID:31366338

NHS England. (2018). *Healthy Workforce: NHS Staff Health and Wellbeing Review*. NHS England. https://www.england.nhs.uk/wp-content/uploads/2018/07/healthy-workforce-nhs-staff-health-and-wellbeing-review.pdf

Nicholson, P. (2020, December 8). AWS hit by Largest Reported DDoS Attack of 2.3 Tbps. *A10 Networks*. https://www.a10networks.com/blog/aws-hit-by-largest-reported-ddos-attack-of-2-3-tbps/

Nikhil, K. B., Fernandes, R., Rodrigues, A. P., Mahmud, M., Vijaya, P., Thippa, R. G., & Kaiser, M. S. (2023). TAKEN: A Traffic Knowledge-Based Navigation System for Connected and Autonomous Vehicles. *Sensors (Basel), 23*(2), 653. doi:10.339023020653 PMID:36679448

Nikou, S. A., & Economides, A. A. (2021). Mobile payment adoption: Investigating the roles of trust, social influence, and perceived usefulness. *Information & Management, 58*(1), 103378. doi:10.1016/j.im.2020.103378

Nilsen, P., Seing, I., Ericsson, C., Birken, S. A., & Schildmeijer, K. (2020). Characteristics of successful changes in healthcare organizations: An interview study with physicians, registered nurses and assistant nurses. *BMC Health Services Research, 20*(1), 147. doi:10.118612913-020-4999-8 PMID:32106847

Nirenberg, J., & Romine, P. (2000). The crafting of leadership: Values, moral assumptions and organizational change. *OD Practitioner, 32*(2), 4–17.

Nitzberg, S. (1997). The cyber battlefield -Is this the setting for the ultimate world war?Proceedings of the 20th National Information Systems Security Conference. *National Institute of Standards and Technology [NIST]*. https://csrc.nist.gov/csrc/media/publications/conference-paper/1998/10/08/proceedings-of-the-21st-nissc-1998/documents/paperd10.pdf

Nobles, C. (2018). Botching human factors in cybersecurity in business organizations. *Holistica, 9*(3). https://sciendo.com/pdf/10.2478/hjbpa-2018-0024

Nobles, C. (2021). Exploring Senior Managers' Influencing of Human Factor to Reduce Human Errors in Cybersecurity. ProQuest. Capitol Technology University.

Nobles, C. (2018). Botching human factors in cybersecurity in business organizations. Holistica –. *Journal of Business and Public Administration, 9*(3), 71–88. doi:10.2478/hjbpa-2018-0024

Nobles, C. (2021). *Banking Cybersecurity Culture Influences on Phishing Susceptibility*. Temple University.

Nobles, C. (2022). Stress, burnout, and security fatigue in cybersecurity: A human factors problem. HOLISTICA–. *Journal of Business and Public Administration, 13*(1), 49–72. doi:10.2478/hjbpa-2022-0003

Nohria, N., & Beer, M. (2000). Cracking the Code of Change. *Harvard Business Review*. https://hbr.org/2000/05/cracking-the-code-of-change

Noreen, N., Palaniappan, S., Qayyum, A., Ahmad, I., & Alassafi, M. O. (2021). Brain Tumor Classification Based on Fine-Tuned Models and the Ensemble Method. *Computers, Materials & Continua, 67*(3), 3967–3982. doi:10.32604/cmc.2021.014158

North, K., & Gita, K. (2014). *Knowledge Management. Value Creation through Organizational Learning*. Springer International Publishing.

Northouse, P. G. (2016). *Leadership: Theory and practice*. Sage publications.

Nosheen, R. N. (2013). Peer mentoring: Enhancing social cohesion in Pakistani Universities. *Higher Education, Skills and Work - Based Learning, 3*(2), 130-140. doi:10.1108/20423891311313162

Nosibor, D. (5 July 2022). Automotive industry races against cybersecurity threats. *Security Magazine*. https://www.securitymagazine.com/articles/97932-automotive-industry-races-against-cybersecurity-threats

Ntounis, N., & Gounaris, S. (2018). Employee engagement in corporate sustainability: The roles of sustainability leadership and corporate social responsibility. *Business Strategy and the Environment*, *27*(1), 86–99.

Nurfirdausi, A. F., Wijaya, S. K., Prajitno, P., & Ibrahim, N. (2022). Classification of acute ischemic stroke EEG signal using entropy-based features, wavelet decomposition, and machine learning algorithms. *THE 6TH BIOMEDICAL ENGINEERING'S RECENT PROGRESS IN BIOMATERIALS, DRUGS DEVELOPMENT, AND MEDICAL DEVICES: Proceedings of the 6th International Symposium of Biomedical Engineering (ISBE) 2021*. 10.1063/5.0098733

Nurfirdausi, A. F., Apsari, R. A., Wijaya, S. K., Prajitno, P., & Ibrahim, N. (2022). Wavelet decomposition and feedforward neural network for classification of acute ischemic stroke based on electroencephalography. *International Journal of Technology*, *13*(8), 1745. doi:10.14716/ijtech.v13i8.6132

O'Connor, S. W. (2020). *The project risk management process | 5 tips for success*. Northeastern University. https://www.northeastern.edu/graduate/blog/project-risk-management/#:~:text=In%20project%20management%2C%20risk%20management,duration%20of%20a%20given%20project

O'Keefe, J., & Libby, C. (2023). *AI-Based Discrimination Top of the EEOC's Draft Enforcement Plan*. Law and the Workplace. https://www.lawandtheworkplace.com/2023/01/ai-based-discrimination-top-of-the-eeocs-draft-enforcement-plan/

O'Keefe, J., & Morris, H. (2023). *New Jersey and New York Introduce Bills to Regulate Sale and Use of 'Automated Employment Decision Tools*. Law and the Workplace. https://www.lawandtheworkplace.com/2023/02/new-jersey-and-new-york-introduce-bills-to-regulate-sale-and-use-of-automated-employment-decision-tools/

O'Rourke, D. (2015). Corporate sustainability engagement with external stakeholders: A strategic guide. *Business Strategy and the Environment*, *24*(1), 12–20.

O'Toole, J. (2009). Connecting the Dots between Leadership, Ethics, and Corporate Culture. *Ivey Business Journal*. https://iveybusinessjournal.com/publication/connecting-the-dots-between-leadership-ethics-and-corporate-culture/

OECD. (2017). Bridging policy silos to boost trust online. *The OECD Observer. Organisation for Economic Co-Operation and Development*. doi:10.1787/42b03ed1-en

Office of Information Security. (2023, March 9). *Data Exfiltration Trends in Healthcare*. Data Exfiltration Trends in Healthcare. https://www.hhs.gov/sites/default/files/data-exfiltration-in-healthcare-tlpclear.pdf

Office of Management and Budget. (2019). *Preparation, Submission, And Execution Of The Budget*. (The White House, Washington, DC), OMB Circular No. A-11, December 18, 2019. https://www.whitehouse.gov/wpcontent/uploads/2018/06/a11.pdf

Office of Personnel Management. (2017). *Center for leadership development*. OPM. https://leadership.opm.gov/index.aspx

Office of the U.S. Trade Representative. (2021). *U.S.-EU arrangements on global steel and aluminum excess capacity and carbon intensity*. USTR. https://ustr.gov/about-us/policy-offices/press-office/fact-sheets/2021/october/fact-sheet-us-eu-arrangements-global-steel-and-aluminum-excess-capacity-and-carbon-intensity

Oh, H. J., Lee, J. H., & Kim, J. H. (2021). Factors affecting continuous use of wearable devices in the health and fitness industry. *International Journal of Environmental Research and Public Health, 18*(4), 1894. doi:10.3390/ijerph18041894 PMID:33669298

Ohm, M., Plate, H., Sykosch, A., & Meier, M. (2020). Backstabber's Knife Collection: A Review of Open Source Software Supply Chain Attacks. *Lecture Notes in Computer Science, 12223*, 23–43. doi:10.1007/978-3-030-52683-2_2

Oh, S. L., Hagiwara, Y., Raghavendra, U., Yuvaraj, R., Arunkumar, N., Murugappan, M., & Acharya, U. R. (2018). A deep learning approach for parkinson's disease diagnosis from EEG signals. *Neural Computing & Applications, 32*(15), 10927–10933. doi:10.100700521-018-3689-5

Oh, S. L., Jahmunah, V., Arunkumar, N., Abdulhay, E. W., Gururajan, R., Adib, N., Ciaccio, E. J., Cheong, K. H., & Acharya, U. R. (2021). A novel automated autism spectrum disorder detection system. *Complex & Intelligent Systems, 7*(5), 2399–2413. doi:10.100740747-021-00408-8

Oh, S. L., Vicnesh, J., Ciaccio, E. J., Yuvaraj, R., & Acharya, U. R. (2019). Deep convolutional neural network model for automated diagnosis of schizophrenia using EEG signals. *Applied Sciences (Basel, Switzerland), 9*(14), 2870. doi:10.3390/app9142870

Oh, S., Kim, H. S., & Kim, Y. (2019). Feasibility of smartwatch use for social anxiety disorder: A randomized controlled trial. *Journal of Telemedicine and Telecare, 25*(10), 628–635.

Olive Negrete, J. C. (1981). *Antropología Mexicana*. Plaza y Valdés – Instituto Nacional de Antropología e Historia – Colegio Mexicano de Antropólogos.

Oliveira, J. S., Rodrigues, A. F., Fernandes, J., & Neves, P. (2019). Experiential marketing: A literature review and research agenda. *Journal of Business Research, 100*, 380–390. doi:10.1016/j.jbusres.2019.02.044

Olmedo-Aguirre, J., Reyes-Campos, J., Alor-Hernández, G., Machorro-Cano, I., Rodríguez-Mazahua, L., & Sánchez-Cervantes, J. L. (2022). Remote healthcare for elderly people using wearables: A Review. *Biosensors (Basel), 12*(2), 73. doi:10.3390/bios12020073 PMID:35200334

Olsen, D. P. (2003). Influence and coercion: Relational and rights-based ethical approaches to forced psychiatric treatment. *Journal of Psychiatric and Mental Health Nursing, 10*(6), 705–712. doi:10.1046/j.1365-2850.2003.00659.x PMID:15005484

Oltsik, J. (2017). *The life and times of cybersecurity professionals*. ESG and ISSA: Research Report. https://www.esg-global.com/hubfs/issa/ESG-ISSA-Research-Report-LifeofCybersecurity-Professionals-Nov-. 2017. pdf?hsCtaTracking=a63e431c-d2ce-459d-8787-cc122a193baf%7Ce74f0327-0bbc-444a-b7a8-e2cd08d1999e Pando, A. (2019, May 2). Wearable health technologies and their impact on the health industry. *Forbes*. https://www.forbes.com/sites/forbestechcouncil/2019/05/02/wearable-health-technologies-and-their-impact-on-the-health-industry/?sh=1d8c30203af5

Omair, B., & Alturki, A. (2020). A Systematic Literature Review of Fraud Detection Metrics in Business Processes. *IEEE Access : Practical Innovations, Open Solutions, 8*, 26893–26903. doi:10.1109/ACCESS.2020.2971604

Omar, M. (2022a). Application of Machine Learning (ML) to Address Cybersecurity Threats. In Machine Learning for Cybersecurity: Innovative Deep Learning Solutions (pp. 1–11). Springer International Publishing Cham.

Omar, M. (2022e). *Machine Learning for Cybersecurity: Innovative Deep Learning Solutions. Springer Brief*. Springer. https://link.springer.com/book/978303115

Omar, M. (2022f). Malware Anomaly Detection Using Local Outlier Factor Technique. In Machine Learning for Cybersecurity: Innovative Deep Learning Solutions (pp. 37–48). Springer International Publishing Cham. doi:10.1007/978-3-031-15893-3_3

Omar, M. (n.d.-a). *Defending Cyber Systems through Reverse Engineering of Criminal Malware Springer Brief.* Springer. https://link.springer.com/book/9783031116278

Omar, M. (2022b). Behavioral Analysis Principles. In *Defending Cyber Systems through Reverse Engineering of Criminal Malware* (pp. 19–36). Springer International Publishing Cham.

Omar, M. (2022d). Introduction to the Fascinating World of Malware Analysis. In *Defending Cyber Systems through Reverse Engineering of Criminal Malware* (pp. 1–7). Springer International Publishing Cham.

Omar, M. (2022g). Principles of Code-Level Analysis. In *Defending Cyber Systems through Reverse Engineering of Criminal Malware* (pp. 37–54). Springer International Publishing Cham.

Omar, M. (2022h). Static Analysis of Malware. In *Defending Cyber Systems through Reverse Engineering of Criminal Malware* (pp. 9–17). Springer International Publishing Cham.

Omar, M., Gouveia, L. B., Al-Karaki, J., & Mohammed, D. (2022). ReverseEngineering Malware. In *Cybersecurity Capabilities in Developing Nations and Its Impact on Global Security* (pp. 194–217). IGI Global. doi:10.4018/978-1-7998-8693-8.ch010

Omitola, T., & Wills, G. (2018). Towards mapping the security challenges of the Internet of Things (IoT) supply chain. *Procedia Computer Science, 126,* 441-450. doi:10.1016/j.procs.2018.07.278

Opinno. (2020). Improving Organizational Culture with the Competing Values Framework. https://opinno.dev.opinnosites.com/project/improving-organizational-culture-competing-values-framework

Orlikowski, W. J. (2002). Knowing in practice: Enacting a collective capability in distributed organizing. *Organization Science, 13*(3), 249–273. doi:10.1287/orsc.13.3.249.2776

Osborn, E., (2014). *Business versus technology: Sources of the perceived lack of cyber security in SMBs.*

Owen, R., Stilgoe, J., Macnaghten, P., Gorman, M., Fisher, E., & Guston, D. (2013). A framework for responsible innovation. *Responsible innovation: Managing the responsible emergence of science and innovation in society*, 27-50.

Ozair, F. F., Jamshed, N., Sharma, A., & Aggarwal, P. (2020). Ethical and social issues in healthcare technology implementation: A scoping review. *Journal of Medical Systems, 44*(8), 1–14. doi:10.100710916-020-01629-5

Özbek, Y., Fide, E., & Yener, G. G. (2021). Resting-state EEG Alpha/Theta power ratio discriminates early-onset alzheimer's disease from healthy controls. *Clinical Neurophysiology, 132*(9), 2019–2031. doi:10.1016/j.clinph.2021.05.012 PMID:34284236

Özturan, P., & Grinstein, A. (2022). Can the marketing department benefit from socially responsible marketing activities? The role of legitimacy and customers' interest in social responsibility. *European Journal of Marketing, 56*(2), 400–441. doi:10.1108/EJM-09-2020-0670

Paajoki, A. (2020). *Best practices for and benefits from implementing ISPMA's SPM framework.*

Page, S. (2010). Integrative leadership for collaborative governance: Civic engagement in Seattle. *The Leadership Quarterly, 21*(2), 246–263. doi:10.1016/j.leaqua.2010.01.005

Paine, L. S. (1994). Managing for organizational integrity. *Harvard Business Review, 72*(2), 106–117.

Pal, O., Srivastava, V., & Alam, B. (2017). Cyber security risks and challenges in supply chain. *International Journal of Advanced Research in Computer Science*, *8*(5), 662–666. doi:10.26483/ijarcs.v8i5.3385

Pandey, S., Singh, R. K., Gunasekaran, A., & Kaushik, A. (2022). Cybersecurity risk in globalized supply chains: Conceptual framework. *Journal of Global Operations and Strategic Sourcing*, *13*(1), 103–128. doi:10.1108/JGOSS-05-2019-0042

Panetta, L. (2022). *Panetta warns of cyber Pearl Harbor*. Association of The United States Army. https://www.ausa.org/news/panetta-warns-cyber-pearl-harbor

Panteli, D. (2019). *Understanding healthcare quality strategies: a five-lens framework*. Research Gate. https://www.researchgate.net/publication/339386790_Understanding_healthcare_quality_strategies_a_five-lens_framework

Pappalettera, C., Miraglia, F., Cotelli, M., Rossini, P. M., & Vecchio, F. (2022). Analysis of complexity in the EEG activity of parkinson's disease patients by means of approximate entropy. *GeroScience*, *44*(3), 1599–1607. doi:10.100711357-022-00552-0 PMID:35344121

Páramo, D. (2018). Antropología organizacional. *Revista científica Pensamiento y Gestión*, 1(45).

Parker, G., Van Alstyne, M., & Choudary, S. (2016). *Platform revolution:How networked markets are transforming the economy and how to make them work for you*. Norton & Company, Inc.

Park, Y., Park, A., & Kim, C. (2023). ALSI-Transformer: Transformer-based code comment generation with aligned lexical and syntactic information. *IEEE Access: Practical Innovations, Open Solutions*, *11*, 39037–39047. doi:10.1109/ACCESS.2023.3268638

Paschal, U., Nwankwo, W., Masajuwa, F. U., Imoisi, S., & Chinedu, P. U. (2021). Cybercrime detection and prevention efforts in the last decade: An overview of the possibilities of machine learning models. https://doi.org/ doi:10.48047/rigeo.11.07.92

Pashaei, A., Sajedi, H., & Jazayeri, N. (2018). Brain tumor classification via convolutional neural network and extreme learning machines. *2018 8th Int. Conf. Comput. Knowl. Eng. ICCKE 2018*. ICCKE. 10.1109/ICCKE.2018.8566571

Passman, R. (2020). Atrial fibrillation detection using implantable cardiac monitors: Are we being too revealing? *American Heart Journal*, *219*, 137–139. doi:10.1016/j.ahj.2019.08.005 PMID:31862085

Patrick, S. U., Timmermann, A., & Frank, V. (2022). Organizational aspects of cybersecurity in German family firms – do opportunities or risks predominate? *Organizational Cybersecurity Journal: Practice. Process and People*, *2*(1), 21–40. doi:10.1108/OCJ-03-2021-0010

Pattinson, S., & Preece, D. (2014). Communities of practice, knowledge acquisition, and innovation: A case study of science-based SMBs. *Journal of Knowledge Management*, *18*(1), 107–120. doi:10.1108/JKM-05-2013-0168

Pavlou, P. A., & Fygenson, M. (2019). Understanding and predicting electronic commerce adoption: An extension of the theory of planned behavior. *Management Information Systems Quarterly*, *23*(1), 115–143. doi:10.2307/25148720

PDQ Adult Treatment Editorial Board. (2002). Adult Central Nervous System Tumors Treatment (PDQ®): Patient Version. *PDQ Cancer Inf. Summ.* NCBI. https://www.ncbi.nlm.nih.gov/pubmed/26389458

Peacock, J. (2022). Risk register examples for cybersecurity leaders. *CyberSaint Security*. https://www.cybersaint.io/blog/risk-register-examples-for-cybersecurity

Pellegrino, E. D. (1995). Toward a virtue-based normative ethics for the health professions. *Kennedy Institute of Ethics Journal*, *5*(3), 253–277. doi:10.1353/ken.0.0044 PMID:10144959

Peng, S., Kalliamvakou, E., Cihon, P., & Demirer, M. (2023). *The impact of AI on developer productivity: Evidence from github copilot.* arXiv preprint arXiv:2302.06590.

Pérez-Lizaur, M. comp. (2010) Empresa y Familia en México, una visión desde la antropología. Universidad Iberoamericana, México.

Performance Consultants International. (2018). *GROW Model: GROWing people, performance, and purpose.* Coaching Performance. https://www.coachingperformance.com/wp-content/uploads/2018/10/GROW-Model-Guide.pdf

Perrini, F., & Tencati, A. (2006). Sustainability and stakeholder management: The need for new corporate performance evaluation and reporting systems. *Business Strategy and the Environment, 15*(5), 296–308. doi:10.1002/bse.538

Peters, T. J., & Waterman, R. H. (1984). In search of excellence. *Nursing Administration Quarterly, 8*(3), 85–86. doi:10.1097/00006216-198400830-00014

Petropoulos, G. (2022, February 2). *The dark side of artificial intelligence: Manipulation of human behaviour.* Bruegel. https://www.bruegel.org/blog-post/dark-side-artificial-intelligence-manipulation-human-behaviour

Pham, T.-H., Vicnesh, J., Wei, J. K., Oh, S. L., Arunkumar, N., Abdulhay, E. W., Ciaccio, E. J., & Acharya, U. R. (2020). Autism spectrum disorder diagnostic system using HOS bispectrum with EEG signals. *International Journal of Environmental Research and Public Health, 17*(3), 971. doi:10.3390/ijerph17030971 PMID:32033231

Pharo, E., Davison, A., McGregor, H., Warr, K., & Brown, P. (2014). Using communities of practice to enhance interdisciplinary teaching: Lessons from four Australian institutions. *Higher Education Research & Development, 33*(2), 341–354. doi:10.1080/07294360.2013.832168

PhayeS. S. R.SikkaA.DhallA.BathulaD. (2018). *Dense and Diverse Capsule Networks: Making the Capsules Learn Better.* arXiv. https://arxiv.org/abs/1805.04001

Phillips, J., & Klein, J. D. (2023). Change management: From theory to practice. *TechTrends, 67*(1), 189–197. doi:10.100711528-022-00775-0 PMID:36105238

Piderit, S. K. (1999). *Navigating relationships with coworkers: Understanding employees' attitudes toward an organizational change.* [Unpublished doctoral dissertation, University of Michigan, Ann Arbor, MI].

Pierleoni, P., Belli, A., Palma, L., & Pellegrini, G. (2020). A survey on wearable sensor-based systems for health monitoring and prognosis. *Sensors (Basel), 20*(20), 5808. PMID:33066546

Pinto, J. K., & Trailer, J. W. (2020). *A guide to the project management body of knowledge (PMBOK guide).* Project Management Institute.

Plavin-Masterman, M. (2015). Are Walls Just Walls? Organizational culture emergence in a virtual firm. *Journal of Organizational Culture, Communications and Conflict, 19*(2), 43-68. https://proxy.cecybrary.com/login?url=https://search.proquest.com/docview/1750418352?accountid=144459

Podgórska, M., & Pichlak, M. (2019). Analysis of project managers' leadership competencies: Project success relation: what are the competencies of polish project leaders? [Project managers' leadership competencies]. *International Journal of Managing Projects in Business, 12*(4), 869–887. doi:10.1108/IJMPB-08-2018-0149

Ponemon Institute. (2018). *2018 Global State of Cybersecurity in Healthcare Organizations.* Ponemon. https://www.ponemon.org/local/upload/file/2018_Global_State_of_Cybersecurity_in_Healthcare_Organizations.pdf

Ponemon Institute. (2020). *Cost of a Data Breach Report.* Ponemon Institute. https://www.ibm.com/security/data-breach

Ponemon Institute. (2021). *2021 Cost of a data breach report: Global overview*. IBM. https://www.ibm.com/security/data-breach

Ponemon Institute. (2022). *Cost of a Data Breach*. Ponemon Institute. https://www.ibm.com/downloads/cas/3R8N1DZJ

Pool, J. K., Akhlaghpour, S., Fatehi, F., & Burton-Jones, A. (2019). *Causes and Impacts of Personal Health Information (PHI) Breaches: A Scoping Review and Thematic Analysis*. AISEL. https://aisel.aisnet.org/pacis2019/71/

Porter, M. E. (2001). Strategy and the Internet. *Harvard Business Review*. https://hbr.org/2001/03/strategy-and-the-internet

Porter, M. E. (2008). The Five Competitive Forces That Shape Strategy. *Harvard Business Review*. https://hbr.org/2008/01/the-five-competitive-forces-that-shape-strategy

Porter, M. E. (1979, March-April). How Competitive Forces Shape Strategy. *Harvard Business Review*, 137–145. PMID:18271320

Porter, M., & Kramer, M. (2006). Strategy and society: The link between competitive advantage and corporate social responsibility. *Harvard Business Review*, *84*(12), 78–92. PMID:17183795

Portnova, G. V., Nekrashevich, M. V., Morozova, M. V., Martynova, O. V., & Sharaev, M. G. (2023). New approaches to clinical electroencephalography analysis in typically developing children and children with autism. *Cognitive Systems Research*, *78*, 23–32. doi:10.1016/j.cogsys.2022.11.003

Potharaju, S. (2021). How Phygital Can Change The Way You Connect With Customers. *Forbes*. https://www.forbes.com/sites/forbesbusinesscouncil/2021/10/28/how-phygital-can-change-the-way-you-connect-with-customers/?sh=4ab9b7c74615

Pranggono, B., & Arabo, A. (2021). COVID-19 pandemic cybersecurity issues. *Internet Technology Letters*, *4*(2), e247. doi:10.1002/itl2.247

Prasad, P., & Prasad, A. (2000). Stretching the iron cage: The constitution and implications of routine workplace resistance. *Organization Science*, *11*(4), 387–403. doi:10.1287/orsc.11.4.387.14597

PricewaterhouseCoopers [PwC]. (2022). *2022 Global digital trust insights survey - The C-suite guide to simplifying for cyber readiness, today and tomorrow*. PWC. https://www.pwc.com/dti?WT.mc_id=CT3-PL300-DM1-TR1-LS2-ND30-PR5-CN_DTICyber-globaldti&gclid=CjwKCAjwrZOXBhACEiwA0EoRD3didnaMnMmSU0TwUUZekHAA8t-B0U4eTOBnZOZ1SzNBZ-QKux8g2BoCGcEQAvD_BwE&gclsrc=aw.ds

Proofpoint. (2022). *What is a supply chain attack? - Definition, examples & more | proofpoint us*. Proofpoint. https://www.proofpoint.com/us/threat-reference/supply-chain-attack

Prosci. (2018). *The PROSCI ADKAR® model*. Prosci Inc. https://www.prosci.com/methodology/adkar

Puri, D., Nalbalwar, S., Nandgaonkar, A., & Wagh, A. (2021). EEG-based diagnosis of alzheimer's disease using Kolmogorov complexity. *Advances in Intelligent Systems and Computing*, 157–165. doi:10.1007/978-981-16-2008-9_15

Puri, D. V., Nalbalwar, S. L., Nandgaonkar, A. B., Gawande, J. P., & Wagh, A. (2023). Automatic detection of alzheimer's disease from EEG signals using low-complexity orthogonal wavelet filter banks. *Biomedical Signal Processing and Control*, *81*, 104439. doi:10.1016/j.bspc.2022.104439

Putri, A. D., Ghazali, A., & Ahluwalia, L. (2021). Analysis of company capability using 7s mckinsey framework to support corporate succession (case study: PT X Indonesia). *Manajemen Bisnis*, *11*(1), 44–53. doi:10.22219/mb.v11i1.17371

Qin, X., Xu, D., Dong, X., Cui, X., & Zhang, S. (2023). EEG signal classification based on improved variational mode decomposition and Deep Forest. *Biomedical Signal Processing and Control*, *83*, 104644. doi:10.1016/j.bspc.2023.104644

Qiu, X., Yan, F., & Liu, H. (2023). A difference attention resnet-LSTM network for epileptic seizure detection using EEG signal. *Biomedical Signal Processing and Control*, *83*, 104652. doi:10.1016/j.bspc.2023.104652

Quader, F., & Janeja, V. P. (2021). Insights into organizational security readiness: Lessons learned from Cyber-attack case studies. *Journal of Cybersecurity and Privacy*, *1*(4), 638–659. doi:10.3390/jcp1040032

Qualitative data analysis software. (n.d.). nvivo. https://www.qsrinternational.com/nvivo-qualitative-data-analysis-software/home

Quan, K. A., Lynch, M. A., Belden, J. L., Drake, C., & Kalus, R. (2019). Using Kotter's 8-step model for implementing electronic health record initiatives in ambulatory settings. *Applied Clinical Informatics*, *10*(6), 1006–1014.

Quinn, S., Ivy, N., Barrett, M., Witte, G., & Gardner, R. K. (2022). *Prioritizing cybersecurity risk for enterprise risk management*. National Institute of Standards and Technology U. S. Department of Commerce. doi:10.6028/NIST.IR.8286B

Quinn, R. E., Hildebrandt, H. W., Rogers, P. S., & Thompson, M. P. (1991). A Competing Values Framework for Analyzing Presentational Communication in Management Contexts. *Journal of Business Communication*, *28*(3), 213–232. doi:10.1177/002194369102800303

Radcliffe-Brown, A. (1952). *Structure and Function in Primitive Society*. Oxford Univ. Press.

Radford, A., Narasimhan, K., Salimans, T., & Sutskever, I. (2021). Scaling laws for autoregressive generative modeling. arXiv preprint arXiv:2102.08602.

Radhakrishnan, M., Ramamurthy, K., Choudhury, K. K., Won, D., & Manoharan, T. A. (2021). Performance analysis of deep learning models for detection of autism spectrum disorder from EEG signals. *TS. Traitement du Signal*, *38*(3), 853–863. doi:10.18280/ts.380332

Rahman, M., Li, N., Athalye, A., & Liang, Z. (2021). *Synthetic-Injection Attacks: Stealing Data by Injecting Malicious Code into Common Libraries*. arXiv preprint arXiv:2108.00669.

Rajan, R. S. (2020, August 19). The impact of covid-19 on the financial system. *The Business Times*. https://www.proquest.com/newspapers/impact-covid-19-on-financial-system/docview/2435166197/se-2

Rakowski, T., Kossakowski, R., & Siemienska, R. (2021). The multiple dimensions of technology in anthropology of organizations: An analytical framework. *Journal of Organizational Ethnography*, *10*(3), 297–311.

Ramage, M., & Shipp, K. (2020). Peter Senge. In Systems Thinkers (pp. 119–128). Springer London. doi:10.1007/978-1-4471-7475-2_12

Ramalingam, B., Nabarro, D., Oqubay, A., Carnall, D. R., & Wild, L. (2020). 5 principles to guide adaptive leadership. *Harvard Business Review*. https://hbr.org/2020/09/5-principles-to-guide-adaptive-leadership

Ramírez Carrillo, L. (1992) Estratificación, clase y parentesco: empresarios libaneses en el sureste de México. *Nueva Antropología*. https://www.redalyc.org/pdf/159/15904311.pdf

Rane, S. B., Potdar, P. R., & Rane, S. (2021). Development of project risk management framework based on Industry 4.0 technologies. *Benchmarking*, *28*(5), 1451–1481. doi:10.1108/BIJ-03-2019-0123

Rangachari, P., & Lashbrook, A. (2019). Change management strategies during healthcare mergers and acquisitions: A systematic review. *Health Care Management Review*, *44*(3), 199–209.

Rasheed, Z. (2023). Automated Classification of Brain Tumors from Magnetic Resonance Imaging Using Deep Learning. *Brain Sci.*, *13*. . doi:10.3390/brainsci13040602

Rathnakumara, L., & Chandanie, H. (2022). Beyond the iron triangle: Accommodating sustainable construction in the new-normal conditions. *Proceedings of 10th World Construction Symposium 2022*. University of Moratowa. 10.31705/WCS.2022.14

Reckmann, N. (2023, February 21). *What is Corporate Social Responsibility?* Business News Daily. https://www.businessnewsdaily.com/4679-corporate-social-responsibility.html

Rehman, R. Z., Buckley, C., Mico-Amigo, M. E., Kirk, C., Dunne-Willows, M., Mazza, C., Shi, J. Q., Alcock, L., Rochester, L., & Del Din, S. (2020). Accelerometry-based digital gait characteristics for classification of parkinson's disease: What counts? *IEEE Open Journal of Engineering in Medicine and Biology*, *1*, 65–73. doi:10.1109/OJEMB.2020.2966295 PMID:35402938

Reid, J. (2013). Winning Workplace Cultures: An Imperative for Enabling Business Success. *Ivey Business Journal*. https://iveybusinessjournal.com/publication/winning-workplace-cultures-an-imperative-for-enabling-business-success/

Reiling, J., Maurer, R., Crowle, M., Giammalvo, P., & Craig, D. (2022, December 28). Maurer 3 levels of resistance & strategic project management. *The strategic project manager.* https://bethestrategicpm.com/the-maurer-3-levels-of-resistance-and-strategic-project-management/

Reilly, M. (2019). Cybersecurity in healthcare: What can organizations do? *Forbes*. https://www.forbes.com/sites/michaelreilly/2019/02/04/cybersecurity-in-healthcare-what-can-organizations-do/#75f322bb7d7e

Rekalde, I., Landeta, J., & Albizu, E. (2015). Determining factors in the effectiveness of executive coaching as a management development tool. *Management Decision*, *53*(8), 1677–1697. https://proxy.cecybrary.com/login?url=https://search.proquest.com/docview/1718406443?accountid=144459. doi:10.1108/MD-12-2014-0666

Renaud, K., & Weir, G. R. (2016). August. Cybersecurity and the Unbearability of Uncertainty. In *Cybersecurity and Cyberforensics Conference (CCC),* (pp. 137–143). IEEE. 10.1109/CCC.2016.29

Renner, S. (2001). August. A community of interest approach to data interoperability. In Federal database colloquium (Vol. 1, p. 2).

Riaz, S., & Nawaz, S. (2022). Development of the attitude atonement scale for adults. *Journal of Behavioural Sciences*, *32*(1), 165. https://www.proquest.com/scholarly-journals/development-attitude-atonement-scale-adults/docview/2627931120/se-2?accountid=167615

Richards, T. (2022, January 14). Ex-hospital worker arrested in SGMC data breach. *Valdosta Daily Times*. https://www.valdostadailytimes.com/news/local_news/ex-hospital-worker-arrested-in-sgmc-data-breach/article_7ca92b22-a2e5-5541-b3b3-38472d3706b1.html

Richardson, F. (1955). Anthropology and Human Relations in Business and Industry. *Yearbook of Anthropology*. https://www.jstor.org/stable/3031158

Richell, R. (2021). The Rise of Cyber-Attacks in the Automotive Industry. *US Cyber security.* https://www.uscybersecurity.net/automotive-industry/

Riolli, L., & Savicki, V. (2006). Impact of fairness, leadership, and coping on strain, burn-out and turnover in organizational change. *International Journal of Stress Management*, *13*(3), 351–377. doi:10.1037/1072-5245.13.3.351

Ristock, J. L. (2013). *Transgender abuse: Intimate partner violence and abuse in lesbian, gay, bisexual, transgender, and queer communities*. Routledge.

Roan, D. (2020), Start or review an accountable plan. *Journal of Accountancy*. https://www.journalofaccountancy.com/issues/2020/feb/employee-expenses-accountable-plan.html

Robbins, H., & Monro, S. (1951). A Stochastic Approximation Method. *Annals of Mathematical Statistics, 22*(3), 400–407. doi:10.1214/aoms/1177729586

Roberts, K., & Grabowski, M. (1996). Organizations, Technology and Structuring. En S. Clegg, C. Hardy & W. Nord, Handbook of Organization Studies (pp. 409-423). Sage.

Roberts, S., & Rizzo, M. (2020). "*The Psychology of American Racism.*" American Psychologist, In Press. 1. https://news.stanford.edu/2020/06/09/seven-factors-contributing-american-racism/ doi:0.31219/osf.io/w2h73

Robins, A., & Schaper, M. T. (2017). *The sustainability advantage: Seven business case benefits of a triple bottom line.* Sage Publications.

Roca i Girona, J. (2001) Antropólogos en la empresa? A propósito de la mal llamada cultura de la empresa. *Etnográfica.* http://ceas.iscte.pt/etnografica/docs/vol_05/N1/Vol_v_N1_69-100.pdf

Roca, J. (1998). *Antropologia Industrial y de la Empresa.* Ariel.

Rodgers, M. M., Alon, G., Pai, V. M., & Conroy, R. S. (2019). Wearable technologies for active living and rehabilitation: Current research challenges and future opportunities. *Journal of Rehabilitation and Assistive Technologies Engineering, 6*, 205566831983960. doi:10.1177/2055668319839607 PMID:31245033

Roelofs, B. (2019). How shadow coaching helps leaders to improve their performance on the job in real-time. *International Journal of Evidence Based Coaching and Mentoring, S13*, 49–62.

Rohan, D. (2019, November 26). *7 steps to a successful HR M&A: A due diligence.* Bookboon. https://bookboon.com/blog/2017/06/7-steps-to-a-successful-hr-ma-due-diligence/

Romanosky, S. (2016). Examining the costs and causes of cyber incidents. *Journal of Cybersecurity, 2*(2), 121–135. doi:10.1093/cybsec/tyw001

Romford, J. (2022, April 7). *Iceberg Model of Culture – Update 2022 – A Complete Guide.* Agility Portal. https://agilityportal.io/blog/iceberg-model-of-culture-updated-2022-a-complete-guide

Ropek, L. (2019, November 18). Ransomware again strikes Louisiana, forcing server shutdowns. *Government Technology.* https://www.govtech.com/security/ransomware-again-strikes-louisiana-forcing-server-shutdowns.html

Rostami, M., Berahmand, K., Nasiri, E., & Forouzandeh, S. (2021). Review of swarm intelligence-based feature selection methods. *Engineering Applications of Artificial Intelligence, 100*, 104210. doi:10.1016/j.engappai.2021.104210

Rothstein, H., Huber, M., & Gaskell, G. (2006). A theory of risk colonization: The spiraling regulatory logics or societal and institutional risks. *Economy and Society, 35*(1), 91–112. doi:10.1080/03085140500465865

Rothwell, J., Titcomb, J., & McGoogan, C. (2017, June 17). Peyta cyber-attack: Ransomware spreads across Europe with films in Ukraine, Britain, and Spain shut down. *The Daily Telegraph.* https://www.telegraph.co.uk/news/2017/06/27 Ukraine-hit-massive-cyber-attack1/

Roughan, G. (2023). Key wearable healthcare trends for 2023 and beyond. *Unleashed Inventory Management Software.* https://www.unleashedsoftware.com/blog/the-wearable-healthcare-trends-of-2021-and-beyond

Ruef, M. (2019). AI and cybersecurity: How artificial intelligence is making the online world safer. *IT Pro.* https://www.itpro.co.uk/security/34222/ai-and-cybersecurity-how-artificial-intelligence-is-making-the-online-world-safer

Ruiz de Miras, J., Ibáñez-Molina, A. J., Soriano, M. F., & Iglesias-Parro, S. (2023). Schizophrenia classification using machine learning on resting state EEG signal. *Biomedical Signal Processing and Control, 79*, 104233. doi:10.1016/j.bspc.2022.104233

Russo, R. D. (13 Apr 2022). Saban: Current state of college football not 'sustainable.' *AP News*. https://apnews.com/article/college-football-sports-business-dabo-swinney-alabama-crimson-tide-8164758f34f295680c1668545549596e

S&P Global Ratings. (2021). *How we rate nonfinancial corporate entities.* S&P. https://www.spglobal.com/ratings/_division-assets/pdfs/041019_howweratenonfinancialcorporateentities.pdf

Sacred Heart University Library. (2020). *Organizing academic research papers: Limitations of the study*. Sacred Heart University Library. https://library.sacredheart.edu/c.php?g=29803&p=185934

Sadoon, T. A., & Ali, M. H. (2021). Deep learning model for glioma, meningioma and pituitary classification. *Int. J. Adv. Appl. Sci.*, *10*(1), 88. doi:10.11591/ijaas.v10.i1.pp88-98

Sakellariou, A., Shao, Y., & Gibson, O. J. (2022). Clinical trials of wearable biosensors: Challenges and opportunities. *NPJ Digital Medicine*, *5*(1), 1–10. PMID:35013539

Samee, N. A., Mahmoud, N. F., Aldhahri, E. A., Rafiq, A., Muthanna, M. S., & Ahmad, I. (2022). RNN and BiLSTM fusion for accurate automatic epileptic seizure diagnosis using EEG signals. *Life (Chicago, Ill.)*, *12*(12), 1946. doi:10.3390/life12121946 PMID:36556313

Sameroff, A. J. (2010). *The transactional model of development: How children and contexts shape each other*. American Psychological Association.

Sanches, C., Moraes, R. C., Elias, P. C., & Ribeiro, M. Q. (2021). Wearables and their applications in the management of diabetes: Systematic review. *JMIR mHealth and uHealth*, *9*(6), e25066. doi:10.2196/25066

Sandler, M., Howard, A., Zhu, M., Zhmoginov, A., & Chen, L. C. (2018). MobileNetV2: Inverted Residuals and Linear Bottlenecks. Proc. *IEEE Comput. Soc. Conf. Comput. Vis. Pattern Recognit.*, (pp. 4510–4520). IEEE. 10.1109/CVPR.2018.00474

Sangani, N. K., & Vijayakumar, B. (2012). Cyber security scenarios and control for small and medium enterprises. *Informações Econômicas*, *16*(2), 58.

Sani, A. A., & Chaharmahalie, S. (2012). *Internal accounting controls.* ResearchGate. https://www.researchgate.net/profile/Alireza-Azimisani/publication/353298397_10119427240/links/60f1da2016f9f313008bbbc2/10119427240.pdf

Sant'Anna, A., Vilhelmsson, A., & Wolf, A. (2021). Nudging healthcare professionals in clinical settings: A scoping review of the literature. *BMC Health Services Research*, *21*(1), 543. doi:10.118612913-021-06496-z PMID:34078358

Santibáñez, D. (1994) Una aproximación sistémico- cultural a la organización com unitaria. Memoria para optar al título profesional de Antropólogo social, Universidad de Chile, Santiago.

SAP. (2022). *What is industry 4.0?* SAP. https://www.sap.com/insights/what-is-industry-4-0.html

Sapienza, A., & Gupta, A. (2022). Organizational Anthropology: Bringing Cultural Insights to Business Studies. *Journal of Business Anthropology*, *11*(1), 1–9.

Sarker, R., Rayhan, F., Alam, M. S., & Uddin, M. Z. (2021). Cybersecurity Research and Development: A Critical Review. *International Journal of Network Security*, *23*(2), 203–217.

Sarmukadam, K., Sharpley, C. F., Bitsika, V., McMillan, M. M. E., & Agnew, L. L. (2019). A review of the use of EEG connectivity to measure the neurological characteristics of the sensory features in young people with autism. *Reviews in the Neurosciences*, *30*(5), 497–510. doi:10.1515/revneuro-2018-0070 PMID:30269108

Sarumi, J.A., & Okunoye, A. (2021). A Review of Potential Threats in Supply Chain Cyber Security. *Advances in Multidisciplinary and scientific Research Journal Publication.*

Sathyanarayana, A., Joty, S., & Fernandez-Luque, L. (2019). Research and applications of intelligent wearable devices in healthcare: A review. *BioMed Research International*, 2019.

Saunders, D. G., & Browne, A. (2016). Intergenerational consequences of violence against women: A review of the literature. *Trauma, Violence & Abuse*, *17*(3), 211–225. doi:10.1177/1524838014562517

Schafer, J. (1 July 2022). NIL: Here's how much athletes earned in the first year of new NCAA rules. *Yahoo Finance*. https://finance.yahoo.com/news/nil-heres-how-much-ncaa-athletes-earned

Schein, E. H. (1985). *Organizational Culture and Leadership* (1st ed.). Jossey-Bass.

Schneider, A. L., & Ingram, H. (2017). Deservingness and the politics of health care. *Journal of Health Politics, Policy and Law*, *42*(5), 835–862.

Schneider, J. (2022, January). A world without trust. *Foreign Affairs*, *101*, 22–31. https://www.proquest.com/magazines/world-without-trust/docview/2616230643/se-2

Schultz, N. (7 Jan 2022). On3 NIL 100: Ranking the Top 25 most valuable high school and college athletes. *On3.com*. https://www.on3.com/nil/news/on3-nil-100-ranking-top-25-most-valuable-high-school-college-athletes-bronny-james-arch-manning-bryce-young-travis-hunter/

Schwartz, K., Lopez, E., Rae, M., & Neuman, T. (2020, September 2). *What we know about provider consolidation.* Health Costs. https://www.kff.org/health-costs/issue-brief/what-we-know-about-provider-consolidation/

Schwartz, Y. (2017). *Recovering corporate patriotism*. National Affairs. https://www.nationalaffairs.com/publications/detail/recovering-corporate-patriotism

Schwarz, J. M., & Sattler, H. (2019). Corporate sustainability and stock returns in the U.S. stock market. Sustainability Accounting. *Management and Policy Journal*, *10*(1), 111–144.

Scully, M. A. (2019). Organizational Anthropology: An Exploration of Its Potential Contributions to the Field of Human Resource Management. *Human Resource Management Review*, *29*(2), 131–143.

Seals, T. (2019). Software, supply-chain dangers top list of 5G cyber risks. *Threat Post*. https://threatpost.com/software-supply-chain-5g-cyber-risks/149135/

Security Compass. (2019). Cyber Security Challenges in the Automotive Industry. *Security Compass*. https://www.securitycompass.com/wp-content/uploads/cybersecurity-challenges-in-the-automotive-industry.pdf

Security Risk Management, & Amstrong, I. (2020, October 9). *The perfect storm created by COVID-19: why the education sector needs to shift its cyber security focus*. Security Risk Management. https://www.srm-solutions.com/blog/the-perfect-storm-created-by-covid-19-why-the-education-sector-needs-to-shift-its-cyber-security-focus/

Sehgal, P., Kumar, B., Sharma, M., Salameh, A. A., Kumar, S., & Asha, P. (2022). Role of IOT in Transformation of Marketing: A Quantitative Study of Opportunities and Challenges. *Webology, 19*(1).

Şeker, M., Özbek, Y., Yener, G., & Özerdem, M. S. (2021). Complexity of EEG Dynamics for early diagnosis of alzheimer's disease using permutation entropy Neuromarker. *Computer Methods and Programs in Biomedicine*, *206*, 106116. doi:10.1016/j.cmpb.2021.106116 PMID:33957376

Senge, P. M. (2006). *The fifth discipline: The art and practice of the learning organization*. Crown Business.

Senge, P., Smith, B., Kruschwitz, N., Laur, J., & Schley, S. (2009). The necessary revolution. *Leader to Leader*, *51*(51), 24–28. doi:10.1002/ltl.314

Serrador, P., & Pinto, J. K. (2015). Does agile work? – A quantitative analysis of agile project success. *International Journal of Project Management*, *33*(5), 1040–1051. doi:10.1016/j.ijproman.2015.01.006

Seshagiri, V. (2020). *Taking Calculated Risks: Deal and Kennedy's Risk and Feedback Model*. LinkedIn. https://www.linkedin.com/pulse/taking-calculated-risks-deal-kennedys-risk-feedback-model-seshagiri

Sethi, K., Sai Rupesh, E., Kumar, R., Bera, P., & Venu Madhav, Y. (2020). A context-aware robust intrusion detection system: A reinforcement learning-based approach. *International Journal of Information Security*, *19*(6), 657–678. doi:10.100710207-019-00482-7

Shaffer, A. (2015). *Communities of Interest: Collaborating on Technology Challenges*. DEFENSE ACQUISITION UNIV FT BELVOIR VA.

Shah, R., Wright, E., Tambakis, G., Holmes, J., Thompson, A., Connell, W., Lust, M., Niewiadomski, O., Kamm, M., Basnayake, C., & Ding, J. (2021). Telehealth model of care for outpatient inflammatory bowel disease care in the setting of the COVID-19 pandemic. *Internal Medicine Journal*, *51*(7), 1038–1042. Advance online publication. doi:10.1111/imj.15168 PMID:34278693

Shamir, B. (2019). Transformational leadership reconsidered: A critique of Burns. In *Transformational and Charismatic Leadership: The Road Ahead 10th Anniversary Edition* (pp. 19–47). Emerald Publishing Limited.

Sharma, A., Badea, M., Tiwari, S., & Marty, J. L. (2021, February 1). Wearable biosensors: An alternative and practical approach in healthcare and disease monitoring. *Molecules (Basel, Switzerland)*, *26*(3), 748. doi:10.3390/molecules26030748 PMID:33535493

Sharma, G., & Joshi, A. M. (2022). Szhnn: A novel and scalable deep convolution hybrid neural network framework for schizophrenia detection using multichannel EEG. *IEEE Transactions on Instrumentation and Measurement*, *71*, 1–9. doi:10.1109/TIM.2022.3212040

Shaw, H., Duffy, K., & Taylor, N. (2009). Investigating the cyber security landscape in Ireland: An exploratory study. *Journal of Internet Services and Applications*, *6*(1), 1–17.

Sherkatghanad, Z., Akhondzadeh, M., Salari, S., Zomorodi-Moghadam, M., Abdar, M., Acharya, U. R., Khosrowabadi, R., & Salari, V. (2020). Automated detection of autism spectrum disorder using a convolutional neural network. *Frontiers in Neuroscience*, *13*, 1325. Advance online publication. doi:10.3389/fnins.2019.01325 PMID:32009868

Shih, W. C. (2020). Global supply chains in a post-pandemic world. *Harvard Business Review*. https://hbr.org/2020/09/global-supply-chains-in-a-post-pandemic-world

Shirey, M. R. (2013). Lewin's theory of planned change as a strategic resource. *The Journal of Nursing Administration*, *43*(2), 69–72. doi:10.1097/NNA.0b013e31827f20a9 PMID:23343723

Shoeibi, A., Ghassemi, N., Khodatars, M., Moridian, P., Alizadehsani, R., Zare, A., Khosravi, A., Subasi, A., Rajendra Acharya, U., & Gorriz, J. M. (2022). Detection of epileptic seizures on EEG signals using ANFIS classifier, autoencoders and fuzzy entropies. *Biomedical Signal Processing and Control*, *73*, 103417. doi:10.1016/j.bspc.2021.103417

Short, T. W. (2014). Workplace mentoring: An old idea with new meaning (part 1). *Development and Learning in Organizations*, *28*(1), 8–11. doi:10.1108/DLO-09-2013-0077

Shreve, L., Kaur, A., Vo, C., Wu, J., Cassidy, J. M., Nguyen, A., Zhou, R. J., Tran, T. B., Yang, D. Z., Medizade, A. I., Chakravarthy, B., Hoonpongsimanont, W., Barton, E., Yu, W., Srinivasan, R., & Cramer, S. C. (2019). Electroencephalography measures are useful for identifying large acute ischemic stroke in the emergency department. *Journal of Stroke and Cerebrovascular Diseases*, *28*(8), 2280–2286. doi:10.1016/j.jstrokecerebrovasdis.2019.05.019 PMID:31174955

SHRM. (2023). *Managing organizational change*. SHRM. https://www.shrm.org/resourcesandtools/tools-and-samples/toolkits/pages/managingorganizationalchange.aspx

Sianes, A. (2021). Academic research on the 2030 agenda: Challenges of a transdisciplinary field of study. *Global Policy*, *12*(3), 286–297. doi:10.1111/1758-5899.12912

Siggelkow, N., & Terwiesch, C. (2023, April 4). Create winning customer experiences with generative AI. *Harvard Business Review*. https://www.hbr.org/2023/04/create-winning-customer-experiences-with-generative-ai

Silverman, K. (2020, Fall). Why Your Board Needs a Plan for AI Oversight. *MIT Sloan Management Review*, *62*(1), 1–6.

Simon, H. A. (1987). Making management decisions: The role of intuition and emotion. *The Academy of Management Perspectives*, *1*(1), 57–64. doi:10.5465/ame.1987.4275905

Simonyan, K., & Zisserman, A. (2015). Very Deep Convolutional Networks For Large-Scale Image Recognition. *Robots*. https://www.robots.ox.ac.uk/

Simplicable. (n.d.). *Risk minimization vs risk management*. Simplicable. https://simplicable.com/risk/risk-minimization-vs-risk-management

Singh, D. (2019). A literature review on employee retention with a focus on recent trends. *International Journal of Scientific Research in Science and Technology*, *6*(1), 425–431.

Sisson, L. (2014). *Trends in poverty and economic insecurity among women in the United States*. Brookings. https://www.brookings.edu/research/trends-in-poverty-and-economic-insecurity-among-women-in-the-united-states/

Siu, L. H. (2020). Digitalization in practice: The fifth discipline advantage. *The Learning Organization*, *27*(1), 54–64. doi:10.1108/TLO-09-2019-0137

Sloan, P. (2009). Redefining stakeholder engagement: From control to collaboration. *Journal of Corporate Citizenship*, *36*(36), 25–40. doi:10.9774/GLEAF.4700.2009.wi.00005

Smart Ring News. (2021). What are smart rings? How do they work? *Smart Ring News*. https://www.smartringnews.com/posts/what-are-smart-rings-how-do-they-work

Smirnova, V. (2016). *Organizational culture*. Yurayt Publishing.

Smith, A. (2021). What is a community of practice? *Techopedia*. https://www.techopedia.com/definition/33941/community-of-practice-cop

Smith, I. (2005). Achieving readiness for organizational change. *Library Management, 26*(6), 408–412. doi:http://dx.doi.org.tcsedsystem.idm.oclc.org/10.1108/01435120510623764

Smith, T. G., Norasi, H., Herbst, K. M., Kendrick, M. L., Curry, T. B., Grantcharov, T. P., Palter, V. N., Hallbeck, M. S., & Cleary, S. P. (2022, December 1). Creating a Practical Transformational Change Management Model for Novel Artificial Intelligence–Enabled Technology Implementation in the Operating Room. *Mayo Clinic Proceedings. Innovations, Quality & Outcomes*, *6*(6), 584–596. doi:10.1016/j.mayocpiqo.2022.09.004 PMID:36324987

Smrdel, A. (2022). Use of common spatial patterns for early detection of parkinson's disease. *Scientific Reports*, *12*(1), 18793. Advance online publication. doi:10.103841598-022-23247-0 PMID:36335198

Snyder, H. (2019). Literature review as a research methodology: An overview and guidelines. *Journal of Business Research, 104*, 333–339. doi:10.1016/j.jbusres.2019.07.039

Sobahi, N., Ari, B., Cakar, H., Alcin, O. F., & Sengur, A. (2022). A new signal to image mapping procedure and convolutional neural networks for efficient schizophrenia detection in EEG Recordings. *IEEE Sensors Journal*, *22*(8), 7913–7919. doi:10.1109/JSEN.2022.3151465

Sodhi, M. S., Son, B. G., & Tang, C. S. (2021). Researchers' perspectives on supply chain risk management. *Production and Operations Management*, *21*(1), 1–13. doi:10.1111/j.1937-5956.2011.01251.x

Soh, J. H., Wu, Y., & Lee, Y. S. (2021). Privacy and security issues of medical-grade wearables. *Journal of Medical Systems*, *45*(5), 1–11. doi:10.100710916-021-01777-w

Sommer, A., & Paxson, V. (2010). Outside the closed world: on using machine learning for network intrusion detection. *Proceedings of the 2010 IEEE Symposium on Security and Privacy*, (pp. 305–316). IEEE. 10.1109/SP.2010.25

Song, C. S., & Kim, Y. K. (2022). The role of the human-robot interaction in consumers' acceptance of humanoid retail service robots. *Journal of Business Research*, *146*, 489–503. doi:10.1016/j.jbusres.2022.03.087

Sørensen, J. L., Skou Thomsen, A. S., & Schønning, V. (2020). Legal challenges of wearables in the workplace: Current state of the art and future challenges. *Journal of Occupational Health Psychology*, *25*(1), 91.

Sperry, L. (2013). Executive coaching and leadership assessment: Past, present, and future. *Consulting Psychology Journal*, *65*(4), 284–288. doi:10.1037/a0035453

Sripad, S., Kulandaivel, S., Pande, V., Sekar, V., & Viswanathan, V. (2017). Vulnerabilities of Electric Vehicle Battery Packs to Cyberattacks on Auxiliary Components. *ArXiv, abs/1711.04822.*

Sroufe, L. A. (1990). An organizational perspective on the development of attachment. In M. Greenberg, D. Cicchetti, & E. M. Cummings (Eds.), *Attachment in the preschool years: Theory, research, and intervention* (pp. 209–235). University of Chicago Press.

Statista. (2022). Forecast unit shipments of wrist-worn wearables worldwide from 2019 to 2024. *Statista.* https://www.statista.com/statistics/296565/wearables-worldwide-shipments/

Statista. (2023, May 24). *Size of the chatbot market worldwide from 2021 to 2030.* Statista. https://www.statista.com/statistics/656596/worldwide-chatbot-market/

StealthLabs. (2022). Number of cyber attacks in 2021 peaked all-time high. *StealthLabs.* https://www.stealthlabs.com/news/cyberattacks-increase-50-in-2021-peaking-all-time-high-of-925-weekly-attacks-per-organization/

Stebbins, M. W., & Shani, A. B. (2009). Clinical inquiry and reflective design in a secrecy-based organization. *The Journal of Applied Behavioral Science*, *45*(1), 59–89. doi:10.1177/0021886308327235

Sternstein, J. (2017). Healthcare security ailments and treatments the world needs to know. *ISSA Journal*, *15*(9), 25–30.

Strick, J. (2023, January 25). *Nudge theory: A really useful tool for workplace health and safety.* Health and Safety Software for Enterprises. https://www.ecoportal.com/blog/nudge-theory

Subudhi, A. K., Mohanty, M., Sahoo, S. K., Mohanty, S. K., & Mohanty, B. (2020). Automated delimitation and classification of autistic disorder using EEG signal. *Journal of the Institution of Electronics and Telecommunication Engineers*, *69*(2), 951–959. doi:10.1080/03772063.2020.1844076

Sullivan, J., & Deese, B. (2022). *Executive order on America's supply chains: A year of action and progress.* White House. https://www.whitehouse.gov/wp-content/uploads/2022/02/Capstone-Report-Biden.pdf

Sun, H., Cao, J., & Fang, Y. (2021). Technology acceptance model: A systematic review and future research agenda. *Journal of Business Research*, *130*, 205–215. doi:10.1016/j.jbusres.2021.01.020

Sutton, B. (2018). *Overview of Regulatory Requirements: Medical Devices - Transcript*. FDA. https://www.fda.gov/training-and-continuing-education/cdrh-learn/overview-regulatory-requirements-medical-devices-transcript

Swati, Z. N. K., Zhao, Q., Kabir, M., Ali, F., Ali, Z., Ahmed, S., & Lu, J. (2019). Brain tumor classification for MR images using transfer learning and fine-tuning. *Computerized Medical Imaging and Graphics*, *75*, 34–46. doi:10.1016/j.compmedimag.2019.05.001 PMID:31150950

Sweeney, J. (2020). *Cybersecurity for healthcare organizations: Strategies for protecting patient data*. UDEMY. https://blog.udemy.com/cybersecurity-for-healthcare-organizations/

Swim, J. K., Hyers, L. L., Cohen, L. L., & Ferguson, M. J. (2017). Everyday forms of sexism: Evidence for new measures and gender differences. Psychology of Women Quarterly, 407–425. doi:10.1177/0361684317691022

Sydle, (2021). PDCA Cycle: *What Are the Stages and How Does It Work?* Sydle. https://www.sydle.com/blog/pdca-cycle-61ba2a15876cf6271d556be9/

Symantec. (2016). *Cyber Security Trends and Government Responses in Africa*. Symantec.

Szczepkowski, D., & Szczepkowski, P. (2021). *Adware as one form of disinformation*. Studia Administracji i Bezpieczeństwa. doi:10.5604/01.3001.0015.6253

Szegedy, C. (2015). Going deeper with convolutions. *Proc. IEEE Comput. Soc. Conf. Comput. Vis. Pattern Recognit.* IEEE. 10.1109/CVPR.2015.7298594

Szegedy, C., Vanhoucke, V., Ioffe, S., Shlens, J., & Wojna, Z. (2016). Rethinking the Inception Architecture for Computer Vision. In *Proceedings of the IEEE Computer Society Conference on Computer Vision and Pattern Recognition,* (pp. 2818–2826). IEEE. 10.1109/CVPR.2016.308

Tabash, M., Abd Allah, M., & Tawfik, B. (2020). Intrusion detection model using naive bayes and deep learning technique. *The International Arab Journal of Information Technology*, *17*(2), 215–224. doi:10.34028/iajit/17/2/9

Taconis, M. (2018). How high potential coaching can add value – for participants and the organization. *International Journal of Evidence Based Coaching and Mentoring*, *S12*, 61–72.

Tan, M., & Le, Q. V. (2019). EfficientNet: Rethinking model scaling for convolutional neural networks. *36th Int. Conf. Mach. Learn.* ICML.

Tavares, G., San-Martin, R., Ianof, J. N., Anghinah, R., & Fraga, F. J. (2019). Improvement in the automatic classification of alzheimer's disease using EEG after feature selection. *2019 IEEE International Conference on Systems, Man and Cybernetics (SMC)*. 10.1109/SMC.2019.8914006

Tavares, J., Harrison, J., Williams, J., Gershon, R. R. M., & Kalman, M. (2019). Electronic medication administration records in long-term care: A systematic review. *Journal of the American Medical Directors Association*, *20*(2), 190–197.e3. doi:10.1016/j.jamda.2018.09.018

Tawhid, M. N., Siuly, S., Wang, H., Whittaker, F., Wang, K., & Zhang, Y. (2021). A spectrogram image based intelligent technique for automatic detection of autism spectrum disorder from EEG. *PLoS One*, *16*(6), e0253094. Advance online publication. doi:10.1371/journal.pone.0253094 PMID:34170979

Taylor, M. J., McNicholas, C., Nicolay, C., Darzi, A., Bell, D., & Reed, J. E. (2014). Systematic review of the application of the plan-do-study-act method to improve quality in healthcare. *BMJ Quality & Safety*, *23*(4), 290–298. doi:10.1136/bmjqs-2013-001862 PMID:24025320

TeamStage. (2023). Project management statistics: trends and common mistakes in 2022. *TeamStage*. . https://teamstage.io/project-management-statistics/

Tenuta, P. (2010). The measurement of sustainability. *Review of Business Research*, *10*(2), 163–171.

Terdiman, D. (2021, May 24). The rise of Nth party risk: What you need to know. *Newsroom*. https://www.mastercard.com/news/perspectives/2021/the-rise-of-nth-party-risk/

Terrell, S. R. (2016). Writing a proposal for your dissertation: Guidelines and examples. *The Guilford Press*.

Terziovski, M. (2010). Innovation practice and its performance implications in small and medium enterprises (SMBs) in the manufacturing sector: A resource-based view. *Strategic Management Journal*, *31*(8), 892–902.

Thalen, M. (2021, June 24). Exclusive: Hacker reveals smart meters are spilling secrets about the Texas snowstorm. *The Daily Dot*. https://www.dailydot.com/debug/hacker-smart-meter-texas-snowstorm/

Thaler, R., & Sunstein, C. (2008). *Nudge: Improving decisions about health, wealth, and happiness*. Yale University Press.

The Artificial Intelligence Act. (2023). *The Artificial Intelligence Act*. artificialintelligenceact.eu: https://artificialintelligenceact.eu/

The City of New York. (2020). *About the NYC Department of Health and Mental Hygiene*. NYCDHMH. https://www1.nyc.gov/site/doh/about/about-doh.page

The Harvard Gazette. (2023). Doctors not the only ones feeling burned out. *The Harvard Gazette*. https://news.harvard.edu/gazette/story/2023/03/covid-burnout-hitting-all-levels-of-health-care-workforce/#:~:text=%E2%80%9CThey%20may%20be%20less%20likely,(54.1%20percent)%20reporting%20burnout

The Joint Commission. (2022). Innovative combined proactive risk assessment identifies vulnerable points in healthcare processes. *The Joint Commission Journal on Quality and Patient Safety*. https://www.jointcommission.org/resources/news-and-multimedia/news/2022/06/innovative-combined-proactive-risk-assessment-identifies-vulnerable-points-in-healthcare-processes/#.Yu0isnbMJPY

the Risk Management Society [RIMS]. (2022). *Sample job descriptions: What is risk management?* Risk Management Society. https://www.rims.org/resources/sample-job-descriptions

The Three Strikes and You're Out Law. (n.d.). LAO. https://lao.ca.gov/analysis_1995/3strikes.html

The United States Government. (2022, March 16). *Fact sheet: Reauthorization of the violence against women act (VAWA)*. The White House. https://www.whitehouse.gov/briefing-room/statements-releases/2022/03/16/fact-sheet-reauthorization-of-the-violence-against-women-act-vawa/

The Violence Against Women Act. (2022). *The Congressional Digest, 101*(2), 2-5.

The White House. (2021). *Building resilient supply chains revitalizing American manufacturing and fostering broad-based growth: 100-day reviews under Executive Order 14017*. The White House. https://www.whitehouse.gov/wp-content/uploads/2021/06/100-day-supply-chain-review-report.pdf

Theory of Constraints Institute. (2021). *Theory of Constraints of Eliyahu M. Goldratt*. TOC Institute. https://www.tocinstitute.org/theory-of-constraints.html

Thomas, E. J. (2020). The harms of promoting 'zero harm.'. *BMJ Quality & Safety*, *29*(1), 4–6. doi:10.1136/bmjqs-2019-009703 PMID:31597784

Thorp, E. O. (1998, October). The invention of the first wearable computer. In *Digest of Papers. Second International Symposium on Wearable Computers* (Cat. No. 98EX215), IEEE, 4-8. 10.1109/ISWC.1998.729523

Time to Think. (2020). *The ten components.* Time to Think. https://www.timetothink.com/thinking-environment/the-ten-components/

Ting, K. M. (2017). Confusion Matrix. *Encycl. Mach. Learn. Data Min,* (October), 260–260. doi:10.1007/978-1-4899-7687-1_50

Title 18 U.S. Code § 798 - Disclosure of classified information (2012, January 3). U.S Government Publishing Office. https://www.govinfo.gov/app/details/USCODE-2011-title18/USCODE-2011-title18-partI-chap37-sec798&collectionCode=USCODE

Top^ırceanu, A., & Grosseck, G. (2017). Decision tree learning used for the classification of student archetypes in online courses. *Procedia Computer Science in Proceedings of the 21st International Conference on Knowledge Based and Intelligent Information and Engineering, 112*, 51–60. 10.1016/j.procs.2017.08.021

Tranfield, D., Denyer, D., & Smart, P. (2019). Towards a methodology for developing evidence-informed management knowledge by means of systematic review. *British Journal of Management*, *30*(1), 6–20.

Travelers Risk Control. (2022). *How companies can help reduce risk from wearables.* TRC. https://www.travelers.com/resources/business-industries/technology/how-companies-can-help-reduce-risk-from-wearables

Trevillion, F. M. H. (2018). Executive coaching outcomes: An investigation into leadership development using five dyadic case studies illustrating the impact of executive coaching. *International Journal of Evidence Based Coaching and Mentoring*, *S12*, 21–40.

Tucci, L. (2021). What is risk management and why is it important? *TechTarget*. https://media.techtarget.com/digitalguide/images/Misc/EA-Marketing/Eguides/What_is_Risk_Management_and_Why_is_it_Important.pdf

Tuncer, T., Dogan, S., & Acharya, U. R. (2020). Automated detection of parkinson's disease using minimum average maximum tree and singular value decomposition method with vowels. *Biocybernetics and Biomedical Engineering*, *40*(1), 211–220. doi:10.1016/j.bbe.2019.05.006

Turco, C. J. (2016). *The conversational firm: Rethinking bureaucracy in the age of social media*. Columbia University Press. doi:10.7312/turc17898

Turner, D. (2010). Qualitative interview design: A practical guide for novice investigators. *Qualitative Report*, *15*(3), 754–760.

U.S. Department of Agriculture. (2022). *Biden-Harris administration announces new actions to strengthen food supply chains, level the playing field for growers, and lower prices for American consumers.* The White House. USDoD. https://www.usda.gov/media/press-releases/2022/05/26/biden-harris-administration-announces-new-actions-strengthen-food

U.S. Department of Defense. (2017). *Department of Defense Cyber Strategy.* USDoD. https://media.defense.gov/2017/Aug/18/2001839282/-1/-1/1/DOD-CYBER-STRATEGY-2017.PDF

U.S. Department of Defense. (2022). *Defense department releases report on strengthening defense-critical supply chains.* USDoD. https://www.defense.gov/News/Releases/Release/Article/2944488/defense-department-releases-report-on-strengthening-defense-critical-supply-cha/

U.S. Department of Justice. (2019). *Rape and Sexual Assault: A Renewed Call to Action.* USDOJ. https://www.justice.gov/archives/opa/blog/rape-and-sexual-assault-renewed-call-action

U.S. Department of Justice. (2019). *Rape and sexual assault: Statistics*. USDOJ. https://www.justice.gov/ovw/rape-and-sexual-assault

U.S. Department of Justice. (2019). *Violence against women*. USDOJ. https://www.justice.gov/ovw/violence-women

U.S. Department of Labor. (2020). *Equal pay*. DoL. https://www.dol.gov/agencies/whd/equal-pay

U.S. Department of the Treasury. (2022). *The impact of the American rescue plan after one year*. USDT. https://home.treasury.gov/news/press-releases/jy0645

U.S. Department of Transportation. (2022). *USDOT supply chains tracker shows historic levels of goods coming into U.S., continued challenges with congestion*. USDT. https://www.transportation.gov/briefing-room/usdot-supply-chain-tracker-shows-historic-levels-goods-coming-us-continued-challenges

U.S. Government Accountability Office. (2022). *DOD supply chain management*. GAO. https://www.gao.gov/highrisk/dod-supply-chain-management

U.S. Government Accounting Office. (2013). GAO's 2013 high-risk update Medicare and Medicaid (*GAO Publication No. GAO-13-433T*). USGAO.

U.S. House of Representatives. (2022). American Competes act includes major supply chain provisions spearheaded by Representatives Malinowski, Blunt Rochester, and Kinzinger. US HoR. https://malinowski.house.gov/media/press-releases/america-competes-act-includes-major-supply-chain-provisions-spearheaded

Ugochukwu, C.b(2023, April 21). Transformational leadership theory: How to inspire and motivate. *Simply Psychology*. https://www.simplypsychology.org/what-is-transformational-leadership.html

Ullah, F., Sepasgozar, S. M. E., & Wang, C. (2018). A systematic review of smart real estate technology: Drivers of, and barriers to, the use of digital disruptive technologies and online platforms. *Sustainability (Basel)*, *10*(9), 3142. doi:10.3390u10093142

Ulrich, P. S., Timmermann, A., & Frank, V. (2021). Organizational aspects of cybersecurity in German family firms – Do opportunities or risks predominate? *Organizational Cybersecurity Journal: Practice, Process, and People*, *2*(1), 21–40.

United Nations. (U.N.). (2016). *Violence against women*. UN. https://www.un.org/en/sections/issues-depth/violence-against-women/

United Nations. (U.N.). (2019). *Violence against women and girls*. UN. https://www.unwomen.org/en/what-we-do/ending-violence-against-women/what-is-vaw

United States Government Accountability Office [GAO)]. (2021, April 16). *Information technology and cybersecurity significant attention is needed to address high-risk areas*. GAO. file:///C:/Users/Dr.%20Burton/Downloads/853207.pdf

United States Government Accountability Office [GAO]. (2020). *Cybersecurity of federal networks and critical infrastructure: Opportunities for greater federal leadership*. GAO-21-68SP.

University of Louisville William F. Ekstrom Library. (2021). *Critical thinking and academic research: Assumptions*. University of Louisville. https://library.louisville.edu/ekstrom/criticalthinking/assumptions

University, S. C. (n.d.). *Thinking ethically*. Markkula Center for Applied Ethics. https://www.scu.edu/ethics/ethics-resources/ethical-decision-making/thinking-ethically/

Urban, G., & Koh, K. (2013). *Ethnographic research on modern business corporation. Annual Review Anthropology* (Vol. 42). Estados Unidos., 10.11.

Urciuoli, L., Männistö, T., Hintsa, J., & Khan, T. (2013). Supply Chain Cyber Security – Potential Threats. *Information & Security: An International Journal*, *29*, 51–68.

USFHealth. (2023). Human factors in healthcare. *USF Health Morsani College of Medicine*. https://www.usfhealthonline.com/resources/health-informatics/human-factors-in-healthcare/#:~:text=Rather%2C%20healthcare%20providers%20must%20consider,one%20thing%20at%20a%20time

Vadrevu, P., & Perdisci, R. (2019). What You See is NOT What You Get: Discovering and Tracking Social Engineering Attack Campaigns. In *Proceedings of the Internet Measurement Conference (IMC '19)* (pp.308-321). Association for Computing Machinery. https://doi-org.proxymu.wrlc.org/10.1145/3355369.3355600

Valentinuzzi, M. (2020, October). Hearing aid history: From ear trumpets to digital technology. *IEEE*. https://www.embs.org/pulse/articles/hearing-aid-history-from-ear-trumpets-to-digital-technology/

Van Alstyne, Parker, & Choudary. (2016). Pipelines, Platforms, and the New Rules of Strategy. *Harvard Business Review*, *94*(4), 54–62.

van den Brink, M. (2020). Reinventing the wheel over and over again: Organizational learning, memory and forgetting in doing diversity work. *Equality, Diversity and Inclusion*, *39*(4), 379–393. doi:10.1108/EDI-10-2019-0249

Van der Kolk, B. A. (2005). Developmental trauma disorder: Towards a rational diagnosis for children with complex trauma histories. *Psychiatric Annals*, *35*(5), 401–408. doi:10.3928/00485713-20050501-06

Van Dyne, L., & Ang, S. (2018). Leveraging diversity: Transformational leadership in diverse work groups. *Organizational Dynamics*, *47*(4), 229–238.

Van Eeckhoutte, E., Král, M., & Hradílek, T. (2019). Cyber Security of Small and Medium-Sized Enterprises: A Systematic Literature Review. *International Journal of Cybersecurity and Digital Forensics*, *5*(3), 154–184. doi:10.4018/IJCDF.2019070109

Van Maanen, J. (1987). *Tales of the field: On writing ethnography*. University of Chicago.

Van Weyenberge, B., Deckers, X., Caspeele, R., & Merci, B. (2016). Development of a risk assessment method for life safety in case of fire in rail tunnels. *Fire Technology*, *52*(5), 1465-1479. doi:http://dx.doi.org.proxy.cecybrary.com/10.1007/s10694-015-0469-y

Varadarajan, P. R., & Yadav, M. S. (2002). Marketing strategy and the Internet: An organizing framework. *Journal of the Academy of Marketing Science*, *30*(4), 296–312. doi:10.1177/009207002236907

Vareschi, R. D., & Picoto, W. N. (2021). The critical factors for cloud computing adoption during SARS-CoV-2 pandemic. [OJAKM]. *Online Journal of Applied Knowledge Management*, *9*(2), 46–64. doi:10.36965/OJAKM.2021.9(2)46-64

Varkey, P., & Antonio, K. (2010). Change management for effective quality improvement: A Primer. *American Journal of Medical Quality*, *25*(4), 268–273. doi:10.1177/1062860610361625 PMID:20445133

Vartanova, V. (2019 August 2). Smart wearables to unlock the next level of precision medicine. *MobiHealth News HIMSS Media*. https://www.mobihealthnews.com/news/north-america/smart-wearables-unlock-next-level-precision-medicine

Veksler, V. D., Buchler, N., LaFleur, C. G., Yu, M. S., Lebiere, C., & Gonzalez, C. (2020). Cognitive models in cybersecurity: Learning from expert analysts and predicting attacker behavior. *Frontiers in Psychology*, *11*, 1049. doi:10.3389/fpsyg.2020.01049 PMID:32612551

Velasquez, M., Andre, C., Shanks, T., & Meyer, M. J. (1990). Justice and Fairness. *Issues in Ethics*, *3*(2), 1–3.

Venkatesh, V., & Davis, F. D. (2000). A theoretical extension of the Technology Acceptance Model: Four longitudinal field studies. *Management Science*, *46*(2), 186–204. doi:10.1287/mnsc.46.2.186.11926

Venkatesh, V., Morris, M. G., Davis, G. B., & Davis, F. D. (2003). User acceptance of information technology: Toward a unified view. *Management Information Systems Quarterly*, *27*(3), 425–478. doi:10.2307/30036540

Venkatesh, V., Thong, J. Y. L., & Xu, X. (2019). Consumer acceptance and use of information technology: Extending the unified theory of acceptance and use of technology. *Management Information Systems Quarterly*, *43*(3), 689–712. doi:10.25300/MISQ/2019/13534

Venkatesh, V., Thong, J. Y., & Xu, X. (2016). Unified theory of acceptance and use of technology: A synthesis and the road ahead. *Journal of the Association for Information Systems*, *17*(5), 328–376. doi:10.17705/1jais.00428

Verizon. (2019). *2019 Verizon Data Breach Investigations Report*. Verizon. https://enterprise.verizon.com/resources/reports/2019-data-breach-investigations-report.pdf

Verizon. (2022). *Data Breach Investigations Report*. Verizon. https://www.verizon.com/business/resources/T449/reports/dbir/2022-data-breach-investigations-report-dbir.pdf

Verstraete, M., & Zarsky, T. (2022). Cybersecurity spillovers. *Brigham Young University Law Review*, *47*(3), 929–999. https://www.proquest.com/scholarly-journals/cybersecurity-spillovers/docview/2677676009/se-2

Vijayan, V., Connolly, J. P., Condell, J., McKelvey, N., & Gardiner, P. (2021). Review of wearable devices and data collection considerations for connected health. *Sensors (Basel)*, *21*(16), 5589. doi:10.339021165589 PMID:34451032

Villanueva, M., Serrano, C., & Vera, J. L. (1999). *Cien años de antropología física en México: inventario Bibliográfico*. Universidad Nacional Autónoma de México – Instituto de Investigaciones Antropológicas.

Violence against women act . (n.d.). NNEDV. https://nnedv.org/content/violence-against-women-act/

Vogel, S. (2023). When AI Discriminates, Who's to Blame? *Talent Management*. https://www.reworked.co/talent-management/when-ai-discriminates-whos-to-blame/

Waddell, D., Creed, A., Cummings, T. G., & Worley, C. G. (2019). *Organisational change: Development and transformation*. Cengage AU.

Waheed, A., Mohiuddin, S. G., Shah, M. A., & Butt, M. A. (2019). Impact of transformational leadership on patient satisfaction and safety outcomes: A survey of healthcare professionals in Pakistan. *Journal of Healthcare Leadership*, *11*, 19–31.

Walton, A. (2019). Cybersecurity for Small Businesses: What Are the Risks and How Can They Be Mitigated? *Small Business Trends*. https://smallbiztrends.com/2019/03/cybersecurity-for-small-business.html

Wang, S., Wang, G., Pei, G., & Yan, T. (2022). An EEG-based approach for parkinson's disease diagnosis using Capsule Network. *2022 7th International Conference on Intelligent Computing and Signal Processing (ICSP)*. 10.1109/ICSP54964.2022.9778541

Wang, C., Chen, Y., Song, P., Yu, H., Du, J., Zhang, Y., & Sun, C. (2022). Varied response of EEG rhythm to different tDCS protocols and lesion hemispheres in stroke subjects with upper limb dysfunction. *Neural Plasticity*, *2022*, 1–9. doi:10.1155/2022/7790730 PMID:35941932

Wang, J., Gupta, M., & Rao, H. R. (2015). Insider threats in a financial institution: Analysis of attack-proneness of information systems applications. *Management Information Systems Quarterly*, *39*(1), 91–112. doi:10.25300/MISQ/2015/39.1.05

Wang, L., & Alexander, C. A. (2021). Cyber security during the COVID-19 pandemic. *AIMS Electronics and Electrical Engineering*, *5*(2), 146–157. doi:10.3934/electreng.2021008

Wang, L., & Chen, Y. (2017). Transformational leadership, creativity, and organizational innovation: A multilevel study. *Leadership and Organization Development Journal*, *38*(3), 304–318.

Wang, R. (2022). Organizational commitment in the nonprofit sector and the underlying impact of stakeholders and organizational support. *Voluntas*, *33*(3), 538–549. doi:10.100711266-021-00336-8 PMID:33686322

Wang, X., Li, J., Guo, X., & Zhang, Z. (2023). A risk management framework for cyber-physical systems. *IEEE Internet of Things Journal*, *10*(2), 1040–1051.

Wang, Y., & Cheng, B. (2018). Transformational leadership and employee voice behavior: A Pygmalion mechanism. *Journal of Business Research*, *92*, 37–47. doi:10.1016/j.jbusres.2018.06.014

Wang, Y., Zhang, L., & Liang, Q. (2022). Examining the influence of technology support and training on technology acceptance and usage: A study of mobile healthcare applications. *International Journal of Medical Informatics*, *156*, 104704. doi:10.1016/j.ijmedinf.2022.104704

Wang, Z., Zhu, H., & Sun, L. (2021). Social engineering in cybersecurity: Effect mechanisms, human vulnerabilities and attack methods. *IEEE Access : Practical Innovations, Open Solutions*, *9*, 11895–11910. doi:10.1109/ACCESS.2021.3051633

Wan, T., & Wang, Y. (2022). The Hazards of Electric Car Batteries and Their Recycling. *IOP Conference Series. Earth and Environmental Science*, *1011*(1), 012026. doi:10.1088/1755-1315/1011/1/012026

Waqas. (2022). Will immersive technology evolve or solve cybercrime? *INFOSEC*. https://resources.infosecinstitute.com/topic/will-immersive-technology-evolve-or-solve-cybercrime/

Warner, W. L. (1952). *Structure of American Life*. Edinburgh University Press.

Washington University School of Medicine. (2009). Deafness in disguise. *Author.* http://beckerexhibits.wustl.edu/did/timeline/#:~:text=The%20first%20wearable%20vacuum%20tube,of%20the%20firm's%20own%20design

Waterman, R. H. Jr, Peters, T. J., & Phillips, J. R. (1980, June 1). Structure is not organization. *Business Horizons*, *23*(3), 14–26. doi:10.1016/0007-6813(80)90027-0

Watson, R. (2017). Law aims to heighten cybersecurity: Proposed Cyber Training Act would certify SBDC employees nationwide to help small businesses fight online threats. *Grand Rapids Business Journal*, *35*, 3–4.

Weber, S. (22 Apr 2020). NIL Draft: NFL Prospects with the Most Earning Potential on Social Media. *Opendorse. Endorsements & Sponsorships, NIL for Athletes.* https://opendorse.com/blog/nil-draft-nfl-prospects-with-the-most-earning-potential-on-social-media/

Weeks, J. (2004). *Unpopular culture: The ritual of complaint in a British bank.* University of Chicago Press.

Weir, K. (2013). *Work, stress, and health.* American Psychological Association. http://www.apa.org/monitor/2013/09/stress-health.aspx

Wei, X., & Xiao, J. (2019). Threat intelligence: Cyber risk management. *International Journal of Information Management*, *44*, 99–107.

Wenger, E. (2011). *Communities of practice: A brief introduction.*

Wenger, E., (2010). Communities of practice and social learning systems: the career of a concept. *Social learning systems and communities of practice, 3*, 179–198.

Wenger, E. C., & Snyder, W. M. (2000). Communities of practice: The organizational frontier. *Harvard Business Review*, *78*(1), 139–146.

White, D., Baghai, M., & Coley, S. (2000). *The alchemy of growth*. Perseus Books.

White, H. D. (2016). Relevance theory and distributions of judgments in document retrieval. *Information Processing & Management*, *5*(53), 1080–1102.

Whitman, M. E., & Mattford, H. J. (2019). *Management of information security*. Cengage Learning.

Whittier. (2016). CARCERAL AND INTERSECTIONAL FEMINISM IN CONGRESS: The Violence Against Women Act, Discourse, and Policy. *Gender & Society, 30*(5), 791–818. doi:10.1177/0891243216653381

Wilhelm, W. K. (2004). The fraud management lifecycle theory: A holistic approach to fraud management. *Journal of Economic Crime Management*, *2*(2), 1–38.

Wilkinson, C. M., Burrell, J. I., Kuziek, J. W., Thirunavukkarasu, S., Buck, B. H., & Mathewson, K. E. (2020). Predicting stroke severity with a 3-min recording from the muse portable EEG system for rapid diagnosis of stroke. *Scientific Reports*, *10*(1), 18465. Advance online publication. doi:10.103841598-020-75379-w PMID:33116187

Williams, P. A., Woodward, A. J., & Furdella, J. (2019). Building a robust health workforce to tackle the growing cybersecurity threats to healthcare. *International Journal of Medical Informatics, 124*, 81–84. doi:10.1016/j.ijmedinf.2019.01.012

Williams, D. Jr, Reiter, K. L., Pink, G. H., Holmes, G. M., & Song, P. H. (2020). Rural Hospital mergers increased between 2005 and 2016—What did those hospitals look like? *Inquiry*, *57*, 004695802093566. doi:10.1177/0046958020935666 PMID:32684072

Winder, D. (2021, February 14). Cybercrime Joker Retires With A Reported $2.1 Billion In Bitcoin. *Forbes Magazine*. https://www.forbes.com/sites/daveywinder/2021/02/14/cybercrime-joker-retires-becomes-a-bitcoin-billionaire/

Wire, C. N. N. (2015, September 3). Report: 307,000 veterans may have died awaiting Veterans Affairs healthcare. *WTVR*. https://www.wtvr.com/2015/09/03/report-307000-veterans-may-have-died-awaiting-veterans-affairs-health-care

Witts, J. (2022). The top 5 biggest cyber security threats that small businesses face and how to stop them. *Expert Insights*. https://expertinsights.com/insights/the-top-5-biggest-cyber-security-threats-that-small-businesses-face-and-how-to-stop-them/

Wong, D. W., Goh, K. H., & Leung, K. S. (2022). Explainable artificial intelligence in healthcare: A review. *Journal of Medical Systems*, *46*(1), 1–10. PMID:36580140

Wong, M. (2016). Intergenerational transmission of violence and abuse. In M. B. Williams (Ed.), *Encyclopedia of domestic violence* (2nd ed., pp. 281–286). Routledge.

Wong, Q., Lacombe, M., Keller, R., Joyce, T., & O'Malley, K. (2019). Leading change with ADKAR. *Nursing Management*, *50*(4), 28–35. doi:10.1097/01.NUMA.0000554341.70508.75 PMID:30921039

Woods, D. (2019). *The role of human error in successful cyber security breaches*. The Usecure team. https://blog.usecure.io/the-role-of-human-error-in-successful-cyber-security-breaches

Wood, S. Y. (2021). *More Money, More Problems*. Texas A&M Journal of Property Law.

World Economic Forum. (2018). *These are the biggest risks the world faces*. WEF. https://www.weforum.org/agenda/2018/01/these-are-the-biggest-risks-the-world-faces-in-2018/

World Economic Forum. (2020). *The global risk report*. WEF. https://report-files.weforum.org/docs/WEF_Global_Risk_Report_2020.pdf

World Health Organization (WHO). (2020). *Violence against Women*. WHO. https://www.who.int/news-room/fact-sheets/detail/violence-against-women

World Health Organization. (2018). *Global Estimates of Occupational Accidents and Work-related Illnesses 2017*. WHO. https://www.who.int/publications/i/item/global-estimates-of-occupational-accidents-and-work-related-illnesses-2017

World Health Organization. (2019). *Violence against women*. WHO. https://www.who.int/news-room/fact-sheets/detail/violence-against-women

World Health Organization. (2022). *Coronavirus disease (COVID-19)*. WHO. https://www.who.int/health-topics/coronavirus

World Health Organization. (n.d.). *Coronavirus*. WHO. https://www.who.int/health-topics/coronavirus

Wynn, M. G., Wagner, D. L., Arora, S., & Payne, T. H. (2021). Wearable technology in healthcare: Facilitating better decision-making for individuals and organizations. *Journal of the American Medical Informatics Association : JAMIA*, *28*(6), 1376–1384.

Xin, Q., Hu, S., Liu, S., Zhao, L., & Zhang, Y.-D. (2022). An attention-based wavelet convolution neural network for epilepsy EEG classification. *IEEE Transactions on Neural Systems and Rehabilitation Engineering*, *30*, 957–966. doi:10.1109/TNSRE.2022.3166181 PMID:35404819

Xu, W. (2023). *AI in HCI design and user experience*. arXiv preprint arXiv:2301.00987.

Xu, X., Lu, Y., Chen, X., & Huang, X. (2020). A user experience-oriented design for wearable medical devices based on augmented reality. *IEEE Access : Practical Innovations, Open Solutions*, *8*, 196598–196609.

Yadav, U. N., & Singh, N. (2021). Wearables for health and wellness: Opportunities and challenges. *Journal of Ambient Intelligence and Humanized Computing*, *12*(3), 3087–3106. doi:10.100712652-020-02664-x

Yang, Y. T., & Silverman, S. (2021). Wearables and internet of things in older adults' care. In Handbook of Smart Homes, Health Care and Well-Being (pp. 301-314). Springer.

Yao, C., Ma, X., Hu, T., & Gu, X. (2022). A Game Theory Approach in Quality Classification and Secondary Use of Electric Vehicle Used Batteries. *Journal of Physics: Conference Series*, *2224*(1), 012138. doi:10.1088/1742-6596/2224/1/012138

Yao, Y., Li, J., Yu, X., & Li, J. (2021). An augmented reality-based framework for secure and private wearable biosensors. *IEEE Access : Practical Innovations, Open Solutions*, *9*, 128741–128749.

Yasuda, H., Kawamukai, H., & Nishimura, H. (2020). *Risk Analysis Based On Factors Of Failure In Small And Medium-Sized Company Projects*. 2020 9th International Congress on Advanced Applied Informatics (IIAI-AAI), Kitakyushu, Japan. 10.1109/IIAI-AAI50415.2020.00163

Yeboah-Ofori, A., Ismail, U. M., Swidurski, T., & Opoku-Boateng, F. (2021). Cyberattack ontology: A knowledge representation for cyber supply chain security. *2021 International Conference on Computing, Computational Modelling and Applications (ICCMA)*. IEEE. 10.1109/ICCMA53594.2021.00019

Yelvington, K., & Fisher, M. (2021). Anthropological Approaches to Organizational Culture: A Review and Integration. *Annual Review of Anthropology*, *50*(1), 399–415.

Yoo, S. J., Kim, S. S., Lee, K. H., & Hwang, H. (2019). Factors affecting healthcare service quality in the adoption of medical technologies. *BMC Health Services Research*, *19*(1), 987. doi:10.118612913-019-4795-5 PMID:31870361

Youd, F. (11 May 2022). Cybersecurity is a growing threat for the Automotive Industry. *Just Auto*. https://www.just-auto.com/interview/cybersecurity-a-growing-threat-for-the-automotive-industry/

Young, W. (2013). *Social Justice and fairness*. NAS. https://www.nas.org/blogs/article/social_justice_and_fairness

Yousefi, M. R., Golnejad, S., & Hosseini, M. M. (2022, April 9). *Comparison of EEG based epilepsy diagnosis using neural networks and wavelet transform*. arXiv.org. Retrieved March 28, 2023, from doi.org/. doi:10.48550/arXiv.2204.04488

Yu, H., Lei, X., Song, Z., Liu, C., & Wang, J. (2020). Supervised network-based fuzzy learning of EEG signals for alzheimer's disease identification. *IEEE Transactions on Fuzzy Systems*, *28*(1), 60–71. doi:10.1109/TFUZZ.2019.2903753

Yu, J. S., & Bagheri, N. (2021). Agent-Based Modeling. *Systems Medicine (New Rochelle, N.Y.)*.

Yukl, G. (2019). *Leadership in organizations*. Pearson Education.

Yu, Y., Han, F., Bao, Y., & Ou, J. (2015). A study on data loss compensation of WiFi-based wireless sensor networks for structural health monitoring. *IEEE Sensors Journal*, *16*(10), 3811–3818. doi:10.1109/JSEN.2015.2512846

Zainuddin, N., Deraman, N., Loh, V. V., & Hafsah, A. (2022). A systematic review on flexibility enablers in logistics survivability. *Quantum Journal of Social Sciences and Humanities, 3*(6), 116-131. https://www.qjssh.com/index.php/qjssh/article/view/200

Zaman, U., Raza, S. H., Abbasi, S., Aktan, M., & Farías, P. (2021). Sustainable or a butterfly effect in global tourism? Nexus of pandemic fatigue, covid-19-branded destination safety, travel stimulus incentives, and post-pandemic revenge travel. *Sustainability (Basel)*, *13*(22), 12834. doi:10.3390u132212834

Zemke, R. (2001). Systems thinking. *Training (New York, N.Y.)*, *38*(2), 40–46. https://tcsedsystem.idm.oclc.org/login?url=https://search-proquest-com.tcsedsystem.idm.oclc.org/docview/203391582?accountid=34120

Zhang, M., Gang, Z., Yu, W., Huang, N., & Liu, W. (2022). MAA-PTG: Multimodal aspect-aware product title generation. *Journal of Intelligent Information Systems*, *59*(1), 213–235. doi:10.100710844-022-00695-8

Zhang, R., Jia, J., & Zhang, R. (2022). EEG analysis of parkinson's disease using time–frequency analysis and deep learning. *Biomedical Signal Processing and Control*, *78*, 103883. doi:10.1016/j.bspc.2022.103883

Zhang, S., Hou, W., Yin, J., & Lin, Z. (2022). A Review of research and practice on the theory and technology of reservoir dam risk assessment. *Sustainability (Basel)*, *14*(22), 14984. doi:10.3390u142214984

Zhong, Q., Huang, C., & Zhu, X. (2021). Artificial intelligence-powered wearable devices for medical applications. *NPJ Digital Medicine*, *4*(1), 1–13. PMID:33398041

Zhou, Y. (2019). Holistic brain tumor screening and classification based on densenet and recurrent neural network. Springer International Publishing. doi:10.1007/978-3-030-11723-8_21

Zimbardo, P. G. (2004). A situationist perspective on the psychology of evil: Understanding how good people are transformed into perpetrators. In A. G. Miller (Ed.), The social psychology of good and evil, (pp (Vol. 498, pp. 21–50). The Guilford Press.

Zuberbuhler, M. J. P., Salanova, M., & Martinez, I. M. (2020). Coaching-based Leadership Intervention Program: A controlled trial study. *Frontiers in Psychology*, *10*, 3066. doi:10.3389/fpsyg.2019.03066 PMID:32116873

Zulhasmi, R F., Zamralita, Z. and Saraswati, H, D, K. (2021). *The Influences of Psychological Capital and Job Resources Towards Work Engagement*. Atlantis Press. . doi:10.2991/assehr.k.210805.181

Zveglich, L., & Lacina, R. (2014). *Powering up coaching by blending human factor with technology*. PROXY. https://proxy.cecybrary.com/login?url=https://search.proquest.com/docview/1552708249?accountid=144459

About the Contributors

Darrell Norman Burrell is visiting scholar at the Samuel DeWitt Proctor Institute for Leadership, Equity, and Justice at Rutgers University. Dr. Burrell has two doctorate degrees and five graduate degrees. Dr. Burrell received his first doctoral degree in Health Education from A.T. Still University in 2010. In 2021, Dr. Burrell completed his 2nd doctorate, a Doctor of Philosophy (Ph.D.) in Cybersecurity Leadership and Organizational Behavior at Capitol Technology University, Laurel, MD. Dr. Burrell completed a Master of Arts in Interfaith Action at Claremont Lincoln University as a Global Peacemaker Fellow in 2016. He has an EdS (Education Specialist Post Master's Terminal Degree) in Higher Education Administration from The George Washington. He has two graduate degrees, one in Human Resources Management/Development and another in Organizational Management from National Louis University. Dr. Burrell has a graduate degree in Sales and Marketing Management from Prescott College. He has over 20 years of management, teaching, and training experience in academia, government, and private industry.

***

María D. Báez is an organizational leadership psychologist, consultant, and coach. She is the founder-CEO of MBaez Consulting Llc, an organization specializing in organizational diagnostic and change management. She also provides leadership development and growth training, such as mindful leadership applied to diversity, inclusion, equity, ethics, organizational readiness, and emotional intelligence. She has a Bachelor of Industrial Engineering, a Master of Operations Management, and a second Master of Business Administration with a concentration in Human Resources. Her first book, written in English and Spanish, What is happening to me? What do I do? It has changed the lives of many girls around the world. After facing a difficult transition with language, gender, and racial discrimination, she overcame the challenges to become an expert in corporate human resources, immigration policies/practices/procedures, and organizational leadership psychology. Some of her work and certifications include the Mindful Leader Talk Podcast, Certified Workplace Mindfulness Facilitator, Mindfulness-Based Stress Reduction, New York City and New York State M/WBE, Certified Success Principles Trainer, Strategic Intervention Trainer, and Visiting Scholar at the Rutgers Center for Minority Serving Institutions, the visiting scholars' program of the Samuel DeWitt Proctor Institute for Leadership, Equity, and Justice. Maria's diverse background should be of great value to organizations that realize that business, technology, and education have client engagements and operations that are highly global, international, and culturally diverse.

Ali Bashir is an expert in networks and cybersecurity, author of over 350 research articles, solved several research and industrial problems, and build products/solutions.

Kim L. Brown-Jackson holds a Doctorate of Business Administration (DBA) in Quality Systems Management with specialization in Health Systems, a Master's in Biomedical Sciences in Pathology and Molecular Oncology with additional course work in Ph.D. in same areas, an Associates in Biotechnology and Forensic Science, an executive professional certificate in MBA, and Bachelor's in Biological Sciences with a cluster minor in Business Administration. She holds numerous professional certifications. Dr. Brown-Jackson has over 25 years of experience as a practitioner, academician, quality healthcare leader and performance and learning strategist guiding business process improvement through biomedical services, public health, advanced drug development, telemedicine/ telehealth initiatives, and leadership development. Specializes in regulatory compliant industries (biologics, medical device, pharmaceutical, financial, and aviation safety). She has taught at the collegiate, government, and corporate levels. She has contributed to over 6 book chapters, over 30 peer-reviewed journals, and delivered numerous presentations at conferences and on panels.

Sharon L. Burton works as a dissertation chair, faculty member, facilitator, author, speaker, and consultant. She has over 100 academic publications to her name and has spoken at over 30 professional conferences. In addition, she has prior experience leading, transforming, driving results, and supporting agile solutions. She is a value generator from problem to solution. Strong collaborator and relationship builder capable of communicating and deciphering technical communication to non-technical audiences and senior leadership while also providing technical resources with business process knowledge. Management of cross-functional, virtual, and on-site teams is required. Dr. Burton has previously held the positions of Chief Learning & Compliance Officer-Administrator Representative, Board of Trustees; Chief Learning Officer, Senior Project Manager, and Senior Change Management Officer. She has also served on a cyber-security board. She is a mentor and coach, as well as a learner advocate. The following degrees are held: A Ph.D. in Cybersecurity Leadership, a DBA in Quality Systems Management (Business Process Improvement), and two MBA degrees in Human Resources Management and Management. She has a number of certifications. Dr. Burton is available to speak at conferences, forums, and other initiatives.

Marlena Daryousef holds an MBA and Doctor of Management degree from Colorado Technical University with over ten years of business development and consulting across multiple business verticals. Marlena has a proven track record of helping both startups and established businesses improve their business optimization, stakeholder engagement, quality and risk management processes, and problem-solving.

Maurice Dawson is an Assistant Professor of Information Technology and Management within the College of Computing at Illinois Institute of Technology. Additionally, he serves as Director and Distinguished Member of the IIT Center for Cyber Security and Forensics Education (C2SAFE) and responsible for working with the faculty who are members of this center. He has a Doctor of Computer Science from Colorado Technical University and a Doctor of Philosophy in Cyber Security from the Intelligent Systems Research Centre at London Metropolitan University. Additionally, he is the co-editor of Developing Next-Generation Countermeasures for Homeland Security Threat Prevention, and New Threats and Countermeasures in Digital Crime and Cyber Terrorism, published by IGI Global in

2017, and 2015 respectively. Dawson has received a Fulbright Scholar Grant to the School of Electrical Engineering and Computer Science at South Ural State University in Russia in 2015 for Business Intelligence and more recently an award to the College of Computer & Information Science of Prince Sultan University in Saudi Arabia for cyber security for the period of 2017-2018.

Michelle Espinoza earned her MBA from the University of Arizona. Her research presently centers on detecting and preventing fraud in platform-based businesses.

Jennifer Ferreras-Perez is a Doctor of Science in Cybersecurity student at Marymount University. She holds a Bachelor's degree in Forensic Pharmacology and two Master's degrees in Cybersecurity and IT. Her research focuses on the human factors of cybersecurity, particularly on how human cognitive limitations can impact cyber hygiene. Apart from her dissertation research, Jennifer has conducted studies on the benefits of implementing password managers in small and medium-sized enterprises, the impact of diversity in cybersecurity, and AI security risks in healthcare. Jennifer's academic journey began with her undergraduate studies in Forensic Pharmacology, which sparked her interest in the intersection of science and technology. She later pursued a career in cybersecurity and earned two master's degrees in the field. Her current research on human factors in cybersecurity is motivated by a desire to understand how individuals can be better equipped to protect themselves and their organizations from cyber threats. Jennifer's work has the potential to contribute significantly to the field of cybersecurity and promote safer digital practices for all.

Aikyna Finch is a Podcaster, Social Media Coach, and TEDx Speaker. She coaches in Empowerment, Life, and Social Media at the individual and group levels from her company, Finch and Associates LLC. She is the host of the Dr. Finch Experience® Podcast broadcasted by her company, Changing Minds Online™. She speaks and livestreams on Motivation, Education, and Social Media. In 2018, she founded the Social Power Summit, an event with a Live and Virtual component for Women in STEM and People of Color in Social Media to have a platform where they can shine. In 2020, she started her tech coaching brand called Technically Intuitive®. It began as a column she wrote on The Coach Guardian, and from there, this brand now includes training on social media. In November 2022, she became a TEDX DeerPark Speaker with her presentation on "The Benefits of AI on Social Media." Currently, she is a DEIB Facilitator and a board member for three organizations. Dr. Finch is an Educator. She received a Doctorate of Management, an MBA in Technology Management, and an Executive MBA from Colorado Technical University. She has an MS in Management in Marketing and an MS in Information Systems in IT Project Management from Strayer University, and a BS in Aeronautical Technology in Industrial Electronics from the School of Engineering of Tennessee State University. She is a former Campus and Faculty Dean who established enrollment records. She has published and presented on topics related to youth and adult education, social media, and job search.

Marie L. Hall is currently a Strategy and Management Consulting executive at Accenture Federal Services. She has extensive operations research and systems analysis experience optimally allocating and forecasting manpower, designing, and directing war games for the Chairman of the Joint Chiefs Strategic Seminars, as Chief Data Scientist at the Defense Intelligence Agency, and as the Director of Programs, Budget and Acquisition for the Joint Artificial Intelligence Center. She has served on the faculty at West Point, in both the Department of Mathematical Sciences and as the Chief of the Institutional Research and Analysis Branch. She has also served a combat tour on the NATO Training Mission Afghanistan / Combined Security Transition Command – Afghanistan. She graduated from West Point with a Bachelor of Science in Mechanical Engineering, and holds two Master's in Engineering Management, and Operations Analysis. She currently lives in Arlington, Virginia and is enrolled in the Doctorate of Business Administration (DBA) at Marymount University.

María Fernanda Higuera-Cota is a research professor.

Allison Huff is an assistant professor in UArizona's Department of Family & Community Medicine. Dr. Huff focuses on technology to address complex disorders, particularly focusing on how technology impacts SDOH. Previously, she was a behavioral health clinician working with individuals with serious mental illnesses and substance use disorders. Dr. Huff is PI and Co-I on several NSF, HRSA, and industry sponsored grants and leads clinical trials and research programs. She also is a mentor for several underserved pre-professional health and pre-med students each summer and through the academic year. Dr. Huff's Doctor of Health Education is from A.T. Still University, her Master of Education in Instructional Technology is from University of Oklahoma, and her Bachelor's in Psychology is from University of West Florida.

Angel J. Jones began his 24-year cybersecurity career as a service member with the U.S. Department of Homeland Security, Coast Guard, investigating cybercrime. His expertise has made him the go-to subject matter expert for complex cybersecurity and cyber investigation matters. Dr. Jones' experience includes serving as the Chief Information Security Officer for several global firms and senior executive roles in the federal government, proactively protecting organizations from adversarial dynamic cyber threats. Dr. Jones is an adjunct professor at the University of Virginia and an advisory board member for the Boston University Center for Cybercrime Investigation and Cybersecurity. Further, Dr. Jones holds several industry certifications, including the Certified Information Systems Security Professional (CISSP), Certified Information Security Manager (CISM), Certified Information Systems Auditor (CISA), Certified Chief Information Security Officer (CCISO), Certified in Risk and Information Systems Control (CRISC), Certified Data Privacy Solutions Engineer (CDPSE), Certified Information Privacy Manager (CIPM), Certified Ethical Hacker (CEH), EnCase Certified Examiner (EnCE), Digital Forensics Certified Practitioner (DFCP), AWS Certified Solutions Architect – Professional, AWS Certified Security - Specialty and Project Management Professional (PMP).

Laura Jones has designed and implemented risk management programs from concept to global execution for organizations across multiple industries, primarily in information security, organizational governance, risk management, compliance, human factors, and quality systems management. With a broad range of experiences and niche skills, she integrates quality assurance principles and systems-thinking approaches with leading practices to optimize business processes and gain insights into critical aspects of human factors aligned to organizational sustainability. She has received several industry-level awards for establishing best-in-class programs. She is regarded as a strategist and practitioner in the risk management sector.

Rebet Jones - Contributing Author| **María Fernanda Higuera-Cota** is an IT leader and PHD student at Cap Tech University.

Jennifer Koster spent the first part of her professional life in the business sector before earning her Master's degree and PhD and following her passion for teaching in 2011. She teaches primarily English and literature courses but also Appalachian Studies and Introduction to Business. Jennifer is a certified Professional Coach as well. In her spare time, Jennifer values spending time with her family above all else. She is also actively engaged with the Citizens Foster Care Review Boards throughout her home state of Kentucky.

Eugene J. Lewis is a leading Marketer and Information Systems Specialist in all areas of Marketing, Management, and Information Systems. Dr. Lewis is a leading expert in technical core competencies in marketing as well as Diversity & Inclusion (Organizational Dynamics). Currently, Dr. Lewis serves in the Aviation & Defense Industry working in the Cargo CH-47 Helicopters Foreign Military Sales Program Office for the US Army. Previously, he served as the Assistant Professor of Marketing at Oakwood University as a full-time and part-time instructor in Marketing, Management (Leadership), and Computer Information Systems. Moreover, lecturing students in areas such as: advertising management, consumer behavior, global marketing, marketing management, organizational dynamics, project management, sales management, and project management, logistics and supply chain management integrating marketing methodologies. Dr. Lewis is a highly sought-after practitioner as his education and experience provide a real-world example of the integration within the marketing management and technology field. As an International Program Manager, he gives several briefings to dignitaries and foreign leadership around the world in areas of logistics and supply chain management. Much of his employment experience consists of incorporating new innovative concepts to provide consumers with the requisite knowledge necessary to understand the value of emotional (EQ) and business intelligence (BI) with incorporating technology. Dr. Lewis enjoys giving back to the community spending much of his free time assisting young people in underprivileged areas instructing them in the sweet science. Dr. Lewis has been a Boxing Coach and Instructor for over 13 years. He is a registered Coach with United States Boxing Association for the Southeastern Region. Dr. Lewis believes in the efficacy of developing young people. He is originally from Seattle, Washington. His family still resides in the Pacific Northwest. He enjoys every opportunity available to travel, write poetry, play his guitar, and meet inspiring people.

Teresa Manfreda-Foley is an experienced accounting and business management professional with over 25 years' experience in many industries including construction, manufacturing, retail, higher education, and non-profit organizations. Driven by a quest for learning and a deep sense of integrity, she takes immense pride in analyzing situations and providing viable and financially sound options for successful outcomes. Teresa has been with Brookdale Community College since 2013 and has held various management positions throughout her tenure. In 2019 she became the Vice President, Finance & Operations/CFO. Her goals are aligned with the strategic plan for the Institution's future while maintaining the financial health of the College and realigning the organization for optimization. She serves on the President's Cabinet and Executive Leadership Council and the Information Technology Governance Steering Committee. She holds a BS in business administration/accounting concentration from Monmouth University, and an MBA in accounting from Southern New Hampshire University. She is currently pursuing her Doctorate in Business Administration from Marymount University.

Thabiso Maupong is a Senior Lecturer in Computer Science and Information Systems department.

Andrea McCready is an enrolled agent with over twenty years of experience and the owner of a tax and accounting practice in Hannibal, MO. She is also a registered representative with Prudential Advisors. She is currently a doctoral student at Marymount University in the College of Business, Intelligence, Leadership and Technology. Prior degrees include an MBA from William Woods University and a BSBA with a concentration in accounting from Columbia College. McCready is a member of Rotary International and proudly serves in both her local club and at the district level.

Grace McGrath is a class of 2020 graduate of the University at Albany. They were a Business Major and Education Minor. Throughout their three undergrad years, they learned so much through various internships, jobs, and outside community engagement. After college, they accepted a position at the Office of the Commissioner of Higher Education in Helena, Montana, as an AmeriCorps VISTA. Now, they currently work at Marymount University as a Graduate Admissions Coordinator. They also attend graduate school at Marymount University, pursuing their master's degree in Forensic and Legal Psychology. In their downtime, they do freelance copywriting and volunteer work. After getting their master's degree, they want to pursue being a federal higher education policy advisor focused on victims' advocacy.

Horace C. Mingo, MSc. is a Professional with 20+ years of experience in Information Technology as a Business Analyst, Enterprise Solutions Architect, Software Engineer, and IT Manager. He specializes in cybersecurity, agile projects, software development, IT governance, and project management. Mr. Mingo is a second-year doctoral student at Marymount University. His current research interests are focused on building secure organizational ecosystems for the next generation of industrial controls, supply chains, and infrastructures targeted by malicious entities. He has an AAS in Electromechanical Technology from Excelsior University, a BA in Management & Organizational Development from Spring Arbor University, an MBA in Strategic Management from Davenport University, and a MSc in Information Systems from Lawrence Technological University.

Derek Mohammed holds the academic rank of full Professor in Computer Science, in the College of Computing, Artificial Intelligence, Robotics and Data Science at Saint Leo University. Dr. Mohammed is the founding Director of the Center for Cybersecurity Education at Saint Leo University. Dr. Mohammed has over twenty five years of professional and academic experience in the information systems field. Dr. Mohammed holds several industry certifications, which include CISSP, CISA, CISM, and PMP. Dr. Mohammed is a reviewer for the Journal of Information Security: A Global Perspective. His research interest includes Cybersecurity, Network Security, and Compliance.

S. Raschid Muller is a Cybersecurity Executive with 20 years of experience working in the federal government. Academically, he serves as a Professor at the University of Maryland Global Campus where he teaches undergraduate courses within the School of Cybersecurity and Information Technology. At the graduate level, he teaches graduate courses at Arizona State University, the University of the Cumberlands, and chairs doctoral committees at Capitol Technology University . Dr. Muller previously served as the DISA Information Operation Faculty Chair from 2017-2019 at National Defense University and continues to serve as a guest lecturer. Dr. Muller is a 2020 Brookings Institute - LEGIS Fellow and 2021 U.C. Berkeley ELA Fellow in the Goldman School of Public Policy. In 2020 he served on the House Committee for Homeland Security on Capitol Hill. He has been assigned to the Subcommittee on Cybersecurity, Infrastructure Protection, and Innovation (CIPI) where his portfolio included;

Cybersecurity and Infrastructure Security Agency (CISA) oversight, drafting and introducing cyber legislation, election security, and cyber acquisitions.

Calvin Nobles is a Cybersecurity Professional and Human Factors Engineer with more than 25 years of experience. He is a Department Chair and Associate Professor at the Illinois Institute of Technology. He retired from the Navy and worked in the Financial and Services Industry for several years. He authored a book on the integration of technologically advanced aircraft in general aviation. He serves on the Cybersecurity Advisory Board at Stillman College and the Intelligence and National Security Alliance Cyber Council. He is a Cybersecurity Fellow at Harvard University.

Marwan Omar serves as a full time faculty member of computer science and IT at Nawroz university, Duhok, Iraq. Omar is recognized for his information security expertise and knowledge and holds a security + certification from Comptia. Research interests are: cyber security, mobile security, open source software, and cloud computing.

Nishant A. Parikh is a dynamic professional with a diverse academic background and extensive experience in computer science and product management. Graduating with a Bachelor's degree in Computer Science from Gujarat University in 2005 and an MBA from Webster University in 2020, Nishant combines technical expertise with business acumen. Currently serving as the Director in Product Management at Mastercard, he drives strategic direction and spearheads the development of innovative software solutions. Passionate about the field, Nishant has immersed himself in research at Capitol Technology University since 2022, exploring the challenges, trends, and solutions in product management. As an avid writer, he shares his insights, addressing the multifaceted issues faced by product managers. Nishant's visionary leadership, industry knowledge, and commitment to innovation make him a driving force in shaping the future of software product management.

William Quisenberry resides in Lexington, KY, and has a diverse background that includes studying and practicing within the field of business administration, coordinating implementation projects for Fortune 500 clients, managing and overseeing vendors/suppliers, operations management, project management, marketing, research analysis, consulting, and teaching at the collegiate level. Dr. Quisenberry has collaborated and worked on projects with a variety of major organizations in the marketplace that include: Lexmark International, Halliburton, Branch Banking and Trust, The U.S. Department of Veterans Affairs, Wal-Mart, The U.S. Army Corps of Engineers, Accenture, IBM, Best Buy, Lockheed Martin, John Hancock Financial, and the World Trade Center Association. Dr. Quisenberry holds a Bachelor of Business Administration (BBA) degree in Finance, a BBA in Marketing, as well as a Master of Business Administration degree from Sullivan University's Graduate School of Business, and a Post-Graduate Certification in Forensic Accounting from Davenport University. He also possesses a Doctor of Business Administration (DBA) degree with a specialization in Leadership from Walden University.

Menaka R. from Vellore Institute of Technology, Chennai has more than 25 years of experience in teaching. She has worked on DST funded projects, possess a rich hands-on experience in medical image and signal processing and an active IEEE member. She has nearly 50 publications in peer reviewed international journals and conferences. She is the Director and Professor, Centre for cyber physical systems in VIT Chennai. She has overall 33 years of work experience in Industry, Academic and Research areas.

Her previous researches include development for CAD approaches for Stroke, Brain tumor, Parkinson's disease, autism etc.

Emad Rahim is an award-winning author, educator, entrepreneur, Fulbright Scholar and TEDx Speaker. He currently serves as the Kotouc Endowed Chair for the Project Management Center of Excellence at Bellevue University, Associate Professor at the College of Science and Technology, and Adjunct Faculty at Cornell University. He formerly served as the University Dean of Business at Colorado Tech and Director of Venture Connect at Morrisville State College, and Entrepreneur-in-Residence at Oklahoma State University, Visiting Scholar at Rutgers University and Syracuse University.

Kevin Richardson occupies the role of Associate Professor of Business & Technology at Edward Waters University. His professional journey is marked by notable achievements, as he is a recognized Certified Diversity Professional and a Certified Trainer. With an impressive academic background, Dr. Richardson boasts two doctoral degrees and three graduate degrees. In 2016, he successfully attained his inaugural doctorate degree specializing in Operations and Quality Management Systems from The National Graduate School located in Washington, DC. Subsequently, in 2021, Dr. Richardson secured a distinguished Philosophy of Doctorate (Ph.D.) in Technology Management of Information Systems from Capitol Technology University situated in Laurel, MD. He also holds a Master of Science in Natural Resources Economics and Corporate Sustainability from Virginia Tech University in Blacksburg, VA. Dr. Richardson's academic pursuits extend to a Master's degree in Information Systems Engineering Management from Harrisburg Science & Technology University in Harrisburg, PA. He further diversified his knowledge with a third master's degree in Counseling Psychology obtained from Springfield College in Charleston, SC. Possessing a wealth of experience spanning over 25 years, Dr. Richardson has contributed significantly to the realms of management, teaching, and training across academia, government, and private industries. His tenure as an educator encompasses various institutions including Edward Waters University, Bethune Cookman University, Allen University, The National Graduate School of Quality Management, and Morris College.

Amalish Sabie-Aridi is a Professor & Doctorate Committee Chair. Extensive Expertise in Higher education teaching, Students' academic mentoring & Curriculum & program design. Agile Executive leader & manager with proven experience in managing operations and teams, improving processes and procedures, and improving overall efficiency and productivity. Strong interpersonal skills with the ability to relate effectively with diverse individuals at all levels of an organization as well as key internal and external clients through management and effective communication both written and orally; able to build rapport quickly while providing high levels of service that exceed expectations within strict deadlines with the ability to adapt to a rapidly changing environment. Skilled in implementing and executing operational plans and strategies; experienced in developing and training staff, Executive Coaching & Organization, and leadership development. Solid ability to successfully analyze organizational needs and develop solutions for enhancing performance and profitability on a global scale Author & Researcher with an impressive record of peer-reviewed journals and literature share. High-Profile expertise and calibers in Organization Behavior, Strategic Leadership, Strategic Management& Corporate Economics, Project Management/Product Management/Diversity & Inclusion Specialist/Qualitative & Quantitative methodologies expertise. Global & International attendance & Outreach with a respectable record of Awards: Global Goodwill Ambassador. Honor Ambassador of Overseas Alliance for Creativity.

Saranya Shanmugam from Vellore Institute of Technology in Chennai, is actively engaged in cutting-edge research on biosignal processing. Her area of interest include biomedical image and signal processing.

Delores Springs served in healthcare, human services, and nonprofit leadership for over twenty years. Dr. Springs' compassion and drive for perfection are her strongest attributes. She specializes in designing competence building strategies and solutions in nonprofit, healthcare, government, academic, for-profit, and human service-oriented sectors. Dr. Springs has a doctorate in Strategic Leadership with a concentration in Strategic Foresight, a master's degree in Human Services and Executive leadership, and a bachelor's degree in Psychology. Along with her educational background, she holds specializations in Healthcare Organization Operations, Building Foundations in Global Health, and in other areas that include Lean Six Sigma, Diversity & Inclusion, Project Management, and other certifications in business and leadership.

Oteng Tabona graduated with an MEng. in Computer Engineering in 2012 from Cardiff University in the UK and PhD. in Big Data and Digital Forensics in 2017 from the University of South Wales in the UK. He worked as a Lecturer in Computer Science and Information System at Botswana International University of Science and Technology (BIUST) from 2018 – 2022. In August 2022 – May 2023, Dr. Tabona joined Higher Colleges of Technology Abu Dhabi campus, lecturing in cybersecurity. Currently he is a senior lecturer in cyber security at the University of the West of England (UWE) in Bristol. His research interest includes Big Data Forensics, and IoT Forensics and Security.

Omar Vargas-González is Professor and Head of Systems and Computing Department at Tecnologico Nacional de Mexico Campus Ciudad Guzman, professor at Telematic Engineering at Centro Universitario del Sur Universidad de Guadalajara with a master degree in Computer Systems. Has been trained in Innovation and Multidisciplinary Entrepreneurship at Arizona State University (2018) and a Generation of Ecosystems of Innovation, Entrepreneurship and Sustainability for Jalisco course by Harvard University T.H. Chan School of Health. At present conduct research on diverse fields such as Entrepreneurship, Economy, Statistics, Mathematics and Information and Computer Sciences. Has colaborated in the publication of over 20 scientific articles and conducted diverse Innovation and Technological Development projects

José Vargas-Hernandez is a research professor.

Andreas Vassilakos is a critical infrastructure doctoral candidate at Capitol Technology University. He holds two graduate degrees; a Master of Cyber Forensics and Security and a Master of Business Administration. His research interests are in cyber warfare, supply chain cybersecurity, critical infrastructure, and IT leadership and management.

Jorja Wright is a logistics manager for the Dept. of the Army. She focuses on maintaining optimal inventory stock posture, cultivating effective organizational processes, and fostering sustainable employee relationships. She received her doctorate degree in Executive Leadership from University of Charleston-West Virginia. She earned her MBA from the Nathan M. Bisk College of Business at Florida Institute of Technology, concentrating in healthcare management. Finally, she has a bachelor's degree in biology and a minor in chemistry from University of Alabama-Huntsville. During her graduate school tenure, Dr. Wright has published over 20 various peer-reviewed articles and conference proceedings on leadership and cybersecurity, to healthcare management and logistics. Dr. Wright is an innovative and talented professional with a diverse educational background focused on implementing policies that improve agile strategies, organizational sustainability and promoting scholarship within the business discipline.

Index

A

B

C

D

E

F

G

H

I

S

T

U

V

W

www.ingramcontent.com/pod-product-compliance
Lightning Source LLC
LaVergne TN
LVHW080404011026
849161LV00009B/2346
9798369316344